Lecture Notes in Computer Science 13177

More information about this subseries at https://link.springer.com/bookseries/7410

Goichiro Hanaoka · Junji Shikata ·
Yohei Watanabe (Eds.)

Public-Key Cryptography – PKC 2022

25th IACR International Conference on Practice and Theory of Public-Key Cryptography
Virtual Event, March 8–11, 2022
Proceedings, Part I

Springer

Editors
Goichiro Hanaoka
National Institute of Advanced Industrial Science and Technology (AIST)
Tokyo, Japan

Junji Shikata
Yokohama National University
Yokohama, Japan

Yohei Watanabe
The University of Electro-Communications
Tokyo, Japan

ISSN 0302-9743 ISSN 1611-3349 (electronic)
Lecture Notes in Computer Science
ISBN 978-3-030-97120-5 ISBN 978-3-030-97121-2 (eBook)
https://doi.org/10.1007/978-3-030-97121-2

LNCS Sublibrary: SL4 – Security and Cryptology

This Springer imprint is published by the registered company Springer Nature Switzerland AG
The registered company address is: Gewerbestrasse 11, 6330 Cham, Switzerland

Preface

The 25th IACR International Conference on Practice and Theory of Public-Key Cryptography (PKC 2022) was held virtually during March 8–11, 2022. (Initially, the conference was scheduled to be held in Yokohama, Japan, but unfortunately, due to the prolonged global outbreak of COVID-19, it was finally decided to hold the conference virtually.) This conference is organized annually by the International Association of Cryptologic Research (IACR), and is the main IACR-sponsored conference with an explicit focus on public-key cryptography. The proceedings are comprised of two volumes and include the 39 papers that were selected by the Program Committee. (Initially, 40 papers were accepted, but one of them was later withdrawn by the authors.)

A total of 137 submissions were received for consideration for this year's program. Submissions were assigned to at least three reviewers, while submissions by Program Committee members received at least five reviews. The review period was divided into two stage. The first stage was reserved for individual reviewing and lasted four weeks. It was followed by the second stage, which lasted about five weeks, in which the Program Committee members engaged in discussion. On a number of occasions, authors were contacted regarding reviewer questions and provided clarifications. One of the papers was conditionally accepted and received a final additional round of reviewing. The reviewing and paper selection process was a difficult task and I am deeply grateful to the members of the Program Committee for their hard and thorough work. Additionally, my deep gratitude is extended to the 145 external reviewers who assisted the Program Committee. PKC 2022 was the first PKC to use HotCRP in the peer review process. I would like to express my sincere thanks to Kevin McCurley for his support in using HotCRP.

Two invited talks were given at PKC 2022. The first invited talk, entitled "The First 25 Years of the PKC Annual Conference", was delivered by Yuliang Zheng, who is the chair of the PKC steering committee. Since PKC 2022 was the 25th PKC, this invited talk was a review of the history of the past quarter century. The second invited talk, entitled "The Beginning of the End: The First NIST PQC Standards", was delivered by Dustin Moody. In this invited talk, he presented the latest status of NIST Post-Quantum Cryptography Standardization. I would like to express my deepest gratitude to both invited speakers for accepting the invitation and contributing to the program this year as well as all the authors who submitted their work. I would like to also thank co-editors of these two volumes, Junji Shikata and Yohei Watanabe, who served as general co-chairs this year. I would also like to express my appreciation to the PKC 2022 local organizing committee members (Keita Emura, Ryuya Hayashi, Takahiro Matsuda, Takayuki Nagane, Yusuke Naito, Kazumasa Shinagawa, Jacob Schuldt, Naoto Yanai, and Kazuki Yoneyama) for their dedication and cooperation. Finally, I am deeply grateful to our industry sponsors, listed on the conference's website, who provided generous financial support.

March 2022 Goichiro Hanaoka

Organization

General Chair

Junji Shikata	Yokohama National University, Japan
Yohei Watanabe	University of Electro-Communications, Japan

Program Committee Chair

Goichiro Hanaoka	AIST, Japan

Steering Committee

Masayuki Abe	NTT, Japan
Jung Hee Cheon	Seoul National University, South Korea
Yvo Desmedt	University of Texas at Dallas, USA
Juan Garay	Texas A&M University, USA
Goichiro Hanaoka	AIST, Japan
Aggelos Kiayias	University of Edinburgh, UK
Tanja Lange	Eindhoven University of Technology, Netherlands
David Pointcheval	ENS, France
Moti Yung	Google and Columbia University, USA
Yuliang Zheng (Chair)	University of Alabama at Birmingham, USA

Program Committee

Prabhanjan Ananth	University of California, Santa Barbara, USA
Daniel Apon	NIST, USA
Christian Badertscher	IOHK, Switzerland
Manuel Barbosa	University of Porto and INESC TEC, Portugal
Carsten Baum	Aarhus University, Denmark
Jonathan Bootle	IBM Research Zurich, Switzerland
Chris Brzuska	Aalto University, Finland
Liqun Chen	University of Surrey, UK
Ilaria Chillotti	ZAMA, France
Craig Costello	Microsoft Research, USA
Geoffroy Couteau	Paris Diderot University, France
Bernardo David	IT University of Copenhagen, Denmark
Nico Döttling	CISPA, Germany

Thomas Espitau	NTT, Japan
Sebastian Faust	TU Darmstadt, Germany
Dario Fiore	IMDEA Software Institute, Spain
Pierre-Alain Fouque	ENS, France
Pierrick Gaudry	CNRS, Nancy, France
Junqing Gong	East China Normal University, China
Rishab Goyal	MIT, USA
Goichiro Hanaoka	AIST, Japan
Shuichi Katsumata	AIST, Japan
Elena Kirshanova	Immanuel Kant Baltic Federal University, Russia, and Ruhr-Universität Bochum, Germany
Fuyuki Kitagawa	NTT, Japan
Ilan Komargodski	Hebrew University of Jerusalem, Israel, and NTT Research, USA
Tanja Lange	Technische Universiteit Eindhoven, The Netherlands
Changmin Lee	KIAS, South Korea
Benoit Libert	CNRS and ENS de Lyon, France
Feng-Hao Liu	Florida Atlantic University, USA
Giulio Malavolta	Max Planck Institute for Security and Privacy, Germany
Alexander May	Ruhr-Universität Bochum, Germany
Jiaxin Pan	NTNU, Norway
Alice Pellet-Mary	CNRS and University of Bordeaux, France
Christophe Petit	Université libre de Bruxelles, Belgium
Bertram Poettering	IBM Research Zurich, Switzerland
Jacob Schuldt	AIST, Japan
Luisa Siniscalchi	Aarhus University, Denmark
Yongsoo Song	Seoul National University, South Korea
Akshayaram Srinivasan	Tata Institute of Fundamental Research, India
Igors Stepanovs	ETH Zürich, Switzerland
Atsushi Takayasu	University of Tokyo, Japan
Qiang Tang	University of Sydney, Australia
Serge Vaudenay	EPFL, Switzerland
Benjamin Wesolowski	Institut de Mathématiques de Bordeaux, France
David Wu	University of Texas at Austin, USA
Keita Xagawa	NTT, Japan
Bo-Yin Yang	Academia Sinica, Taiwan
Yu Yu	Shanghai Jiao Tong University, China
Mark Zhandry	Princeton University and NTT Research, USA

Additional Reviewers

Nuttapong Attrapadung
Subhadeep Banik
Razvan Barbulescu
James Bartusek
Andrea Basso
Balthazar Bauer
Daniel J. Bernstein
Pedro Branco
Yanlin Chen
Arka Rai Choudhuri
Sherman S. M. Chow
Daniel Collins
Sandro Coretti
Maria Corte-Real Santos
Ben Curtis
Jan Czajkowski
Poulami Das
Thomas Decru
Rafael Del Pino
Amit Deo
Jelle Don
Jesko Dujmovic
Julien Duman
Reo Eriguchi
Andreas Erwig
Daniel Escudero
Andre Esser
Hanwen Feng
Matthias Fitzi
Cody Freitag
Hiroki Furue
Rachit Garg
Romain Gay
Nicholas Genise
Lorenzo Gentile
Satrajit Ghosh
Aarushi Goel
Aditya Gulati
Keisuke Hara
Dominik Hartmann
Keitaro Hashimoto
Kathrin Hoevelmanns
Loïs Hughenin-Dumittan
Yasuhiko Ikematsu
Ilia Iliashenko
Ryoma Ito
Joseph Jaeger
Aayush Jain
Sam Jaques
Yao Jiang
Fatih Kaleoglu
Harish Karthikeyan
Hamidreza Khoshakhlagh
Jiseung Kim
Duhyeong Kim
Susumu Kiyoshima
Dimitris Kolonelos
Yashvanth Kondi
Anders Konring
David Kretzler
Mikhail Kudinov
Sabrina Kunzweiler
Péter Kutas
Qiqi Lai
Changmin Lee
Jiangtao Li
Yanan Li
Xiao Liang
Mingyu Liang
Jacob Lichtinger
Damien Ligier
Xiangyu Liu
Jiahui Liu
Zhen Liu
Patrick Longa
George Lu
Yuan Lu
Ji Luo
Lin Lyu
Monosij Maitra
Takahiro Matsuda
Pierre Meyer
Carl Miller
Niklas Miller
Hart Montgomery
Pedro Moreno-Sánchez

Fabrice Mouhartem
Alexander Munch-Hansen
Michael Naehrig
Ryo Nishimaki
Anca Nitulescu
Semyon Novoselov
Julian Nowakowski
Kazuma Ohara
Jean-Baptiste Orfila
Maximilian Orlt
Pascal Paillier
Lorenz Panny
Alain Passelègue
Ray Perlner
Thomas Peters
Sihang Pu
Chen Qian
Tian Qiu
Willy Quach
Anais Querol
Divya Ravi
Michael Reichle
Siavash Riahi
Angela Robinson
Yusuke Sakai
Shingo Sato
Lars Schlieper
Yu-Ching Shen
Sina Shiehian
Tjerand Silde
Daniel Slamanig
Daniel Smith-Tone
Yongha Son
Fang Song
Nick Spooner
Shifeng Sun
Abdullah Talayhan
Bénédikt Tran
Ida Tucker
Bogdan Ursu
Prashant Vasudevan
Michael Walter
Yuyu Wang
Han Wang
Zhedong Wang
Florian Weber
Charlotte Weitkaemper
Yunhua Wen
Stella Wohning
David Wu
Shota Yamada
Takashi Yamakawa
Yusuke Yoshida
Greg Zaverucha
Runzhi Zeng
Xiao Zhang
Yongjun Zhao

Contents – Part I

Cryptographic Protocols

Tools

SNARKs and NIZKs

Contents – Part II

Cryptanalysis

Multitarget Decryption Failure Attacks and Their Application to Saber and Kyber

Jan-Pieter D'Anvers(✉) and Senne Batsleer

imec-COSIC, KU Leuven, Kasteelpark Arenberg 10, Bus 2452,
3001 Leuven-Heverlee, Belgium
janpieter.danvers@esat.kuleuven.be

Abstract. Many lattice-based encryption schemes are subject to a very small probability of decryption failures. It has been shown that an adversary can efficiently recover the secret key using a number of ciphertexts that cause such a decryption failure. In PKC 2019, D'Anvers et al. introduced 'failure boosting', a technique to speed up the search for decryption failures. In this work we first improve the state-of-the-art multitarget failure boosting attacks. We then improve the cost calculation of failure boosting and extend the applicability of these calculations to permit cost calculations of real-world schemes. Using our newly developed methodologies we determine the multitarget decryption failure attack cost for all parameter sets of Saber and Kyber, showing among others that the quantum security of Saber can theoretically be reduced from 172 bits to 145 bits in specific circumstances. We then discuss the applicability of decryption failure attacks in real-world scenarios, showing that an attack might not be practical to execute.

Keywords: Post-Quantum Cryptography · Lattice-based cryptography · Decryption failure attacks · Failure boosting

1 Introduction

Lattice-based cryptography is known for its versatility, bringing forth among others encryption schemes [4,23], digital signatures [24,26] and fully homomorphic encryption [16] and identity based encryption [17]. Moreover, lattice-based cryptographic schemes are among the most promising candidates for post-quantum cryptography, i.e. cryptography that is secure even in the presence of quantum computers.

In 2016, the United States National Institute of Standards and Technology (NIST) announced a standardization process with the goal of standardizing one or more post-quantum encryption and digital signature schemes [1]. July 2020 saw the start of the third round of this process, with 3 out of 4 finalists for public key encryption being lattice-based (and 2 out of the 5 alternate 'backup' schemes).

G. Hanaoka et al. (Eds.): PKC 2022, LNCS 13177, pp. 3–33, 2022.
https://doi.org/10.1007/978-3-030-97121-2_1

To improve efficiency, many lattice-based encryption schemes are not perfectly correct, which means that even after a correct execution of the protocol, it is possible that the decryption fails to retrieve the correct message or key. Such an event is called a decryption failure, and the ciphertext that caused the failure is referred to as a failing ciphertext. Three of the lattice-based NIST candidates are subject to such decryption failures: Saber [10], Kyber [8] and FrodoKEM [25].

While the probabilities of these decryption failures are chosen sufficiently small to avoid any impact on performance, they have been used to stage attacks against these schemes. Decryption failure attacks can be roughly divided into two categories: chosen-ciphertext attacks and valid-ciphertext attacks. The first type was introduced by Jaulmes and Joux [21] and can efficiently recover the secret key if it is reused, by crafting specific ciphertexts that fail based on properties of the secret key. However, this attack type can be prevented by using a chosen-ciphertext transformation such as the Fujisaki-Okamoto transformation.

The second type of decryption failure attacks remains a threat even in the presence of chosen-ciphertext security measures. The idea behind this type of attack is to input a large number of correctly generated ciphertexts in search for failing ciphertexts. The authors of Kyber [8] noted that it is possible to do a Grover search for ciphertexts with higher than average failure probability. D'Anvers et al. [12] showed how to retrieve the secret key based on correctly generated but failing ciphertexts, and introduced 'failure boosting', a framework to speed up the search for failing ciphertexts. This was later extended in [11] to 'directional failure boosting', which introduced a method that further speeds up the failing ciphertext search when one or more failing ciphertext have already been found. The latter work studied a simplified lattice-based scheme and focussed on attacking a single target showing that the cost of a decryption failure attack is dominated by the cost of finding the first failure. Moreover, they introduced a simple multitarget attack specifically designed for scenarios where a maximum number of decapsulations can be performed per target. Around the same time, Guo et al. proposed specific decryption failure attacks on ss-ntru-pke [18] and LAC [19].

As opposed to attacks focusing on decryption failures, Bindel and Schanck [7] showed that correctly generated ciphertexts also provide a small amount of information about the secret. While the errors in individual message bits were assumed to happen independently in many NIST submission documents, D'Anvers et al. [13] showed that these errors are in fact correlated, showing an underestimation of the decryption failure probability for schemes that use error correction and thus an overestimation of the security of these schemes. Dachman-Soled et al. [9] developed a tool to include 'hints' into a LWE hard problem and showed that it can be used to retrieve the secret key using failing ciphertexts.

Our Contributions: We first improve the state-of-the-art multitarget decryption failure attack using a levelled approach in Sect. 4, leading to a more efficient attack especially for schemes with low failure probability. Secondly, we enhance the techniques to estimate the cost of decryption failure attacks, and extend them to include practical schemes such as Saber and Kyber: Sect. 5 points out three inaccuracies in the directional failure boosting calculation for the simplified scheme of [11], which are discussed and remedied. Section 6 shows that this traditional approach of calculating the directional failure boosting cost is not directly applicable to practical schemes such as Kyber and Saber due to compression of the ciphertexts and introduces new methods that adapt the traditional directional failure boosting approach to these real-world schemes. Thirdly, Sect. 7 introduces two additional constraints an attacker might face when mounting a decryption failure attack, which have not been taken into account in previous failure boosting attacks. As a result, in Sect. 8 we discuss the impact of decryption failure attacks on Kyber and Saber.

2 Preliminaries

2.1 Notation

Denote with $\mathbb{Z}_q$ the ring of integers modulo q, represented in $(-q/2, q/2]$. Let R_q be the ring $\mathbb{Z}_q[X]/(X^N + 1)$, with N a power of two, and let $R^{l_1 \times l_2}$ be the ring of $l_1 \times l_2$ matrices over R_q. We denote matrices with bold upper case (e.g. $\mathbf{A}$) and vectors and polynomials with bold lower case (e.g. $\mathbf{b}$).

Denote with $\lfloor \cdot \rfloor$ flooring to the nearest lower integer, with $\lfloor \cdot \rceil$ rounding to the nearest integer where ties are rounded upwards, and with $\lfloor \cdot \rceil_{q \to p}$ dividing by p/q followed by rounding, i.e. $\lfloor x \rceil_{q \to p} = \lfloor p/q \cdot x \rceil$. Let $|\cdot|$ denote taking the absolute value. These notations are extended to vectors, matrices and polynomials element wise. The l_2 norm of a polynomial or vector of integers $\mathbf{x}$ is defined as $||\mathbf{x}||_2 = \sqrt{\sum_i \mathbf{x}_i^2}$ and for a vector of polynomials $\mathbf{y}$ as $||\mathbf{y}||_2 = \sqrt{\sum_i ||\mathbf{y}_i||_2^2}$.

Let $x \leftarrow \chi$ mean sampling x according to a probability distribution χ, and let $\mathbf{X} \leftarrow \chi(R^{l_1 \times l_2})$ denote sampling $\mathbf{X} \in R^{l_1 \times l_2}$ with polynomial coefficients according to the distribution χ. When the values are sampled pseudorandomly based on a seed r, this is denoted as $\mathbf{X} \leftarrow \chi(R^{l_1 \times l_2}; r)$. The uniform distribution is denoted $\mathcal{U}$.

We write $P[E]$ to denote the probability of an event E. To simplify notation we denote with $P[a]$ the probability of sampling an element a from a certain distribution χ when this distribution is clear from the context, i.e. $P[x = a \mid x \leftarrow \chi]$. Analogous, we denote with $\mathbb{E}[a]$ the expected value of an element a as sampled from its distribution χ when this distribution is clear from the context.

2.2 Cryptographic Definitions

We define a Public Key Encryption scheme (PKE) as a triplet of functions (`KeyGen`, `Encrypt`, `Decrypt`), where the key generation `KeyGen` generates a public key pk and secret key sk, where the encryption `Encrypt` take a public key pk and a message m from the message space $\mathcal{M}$ to generate a ciphertext ct, and where the decryption `Decrypt` retrieves the message m with high probability from the ciphertext ct using the secret key sk. A PKE is δ-correct if:

$$\mathbb{E}\left[P[\texttt{Decrypt}(\texttt{Encrypt}(m, pk), sk) \neq m]\right] \leq \delta.$$

Similarly, we define a Key Encapsulation Mechanism (KEM) as the functions (`KeyGen`, `Encaps`, `Decaps`), where `KeyGen` generates a public key pk and secret key sk, where `Encaps` generates a key k from keyspace $\mathcal{K}$ and a ciphertext ct given a public key pk, and where `Decaps` outputs a key k' or $\perp$ when given a ciphertext ct and corresponding secret key sk. We say that a KEM is δ-correct if:

$$\mathbb{E}\left[P[\texttt{Decaps}(ct, sk) \neq k : (ct, k) \leftarrow \texttt{Encaps}(pk)]\right] \leq \delta.$$

The Module Learning with Errors (Mod-LWE) is a hard mathematical problem introduced by Langlois and Stehlé [22], as a generalization of the Learning with Errors (LWE) [26] and Ring Learning with Errors (Ring-LWE) [24] problems. Given integers N, q and l, the ring $R_q = \mathbb{Z}[X]/(X^N + 1)$, a distribution with limited variance χ and a secret element $\mathbf{s} \in R_q^l$, samples from the Mod-LWE distribution $\mathcal{L}_{R,N,q,l,\chi,\mathbf{s}}$ are generated as:

$$(\mathbf{a}, \mathbf{b} := \mathbf{a}^T\mathbf{s} + \mathbf{e}) \tag{1}$$

$$\text{where: } \mathbf{a} \leftarrow \mathcal{U}(R_q^l); \mathbf{e} \leftarrow \chi(R_q) \tag{2}$$

We will specifically focus on the case where N is a power of two. The decision Mod-LWE problem is then, given k samples, to determine whether they were generated as Mod-LWE samples from $\mathcal{L}_{R,N,q,l,\chi,\mathbf{s}}$ or from the uniform distribution $\mathcal{U}(R_q^l \times R_q)$. The search Mod-LWE problem consists of recovering the secret $\mathbf{s}$ from k Mod-LWE samples. LWE is a specific instance where $R_q = \mathbb{Z}_q$ and Ring-LWE the specific instance where $l = 1$.

Learning with Rounding (LWR), as introduced by Banerjee et al. [5], is a similar problem where the error $\mathbf{e}$ is replaced with a deterministic error obtained by rounding. Analogous to the LWE problem, variants of LWR include Ring-LWR and Mod-LWR. Given two moduli q and p, where $q > p$, sampling from the Mod-LWR distribution can be described as:

$$(\mathbf{a}, \mathbf{b} := \lfloor \mathbf{a}^T\mathbf{s} \rceil_{q\rightarrow p}) \tag{3}$$

$$\text{where: } \mathbf{a} \leftarrow \mathcal{U}(R_q^l) \tag{4}$$

In this paper we will specifically consider the case where $p|q$. The Mod-LWR decisional and search problem are defined similar to their respective Mod-LWE versions, where in the decisional problem an adversary has to distinguish between sampling from a Mod-LWR or uniform distribution, and where in the search problem an adversary is tasked to retrieve the secret $\mathbf{s}$ from k Mod-LWR samples.

2.3 Lattice-Based Encryption

A generic PKE based on the Mod-LWE or Mod-LWR assumption is given in Algorithm 1 to 3, where q, p_1, p_2 and t are scheme dependent integers, where χ_s and χ_e are scheme specific probability distributions with small variance, where $r \in \mathcal{R} = \{0, 1\}^{256}$ and where the message space $\mathcal{M}$ consists of polynomials in R_q with coefficients $\{0, 1\}$.

Algorithm 1: `PKE.KeyGen()`

$\mathbf{A} \leftarrow \mathcal{U}(R_q^{l\times l})$
$\mathbf{s}, \mathbf{e} \leftarrow \chi_s(R_q^{l\times 1}) \times \chi_e(R_q^{l\times 1})$
$\mathbf{b} := \lfloor \mathbf{A}\mathbf{s} + \mathbf{e} \rceil_{q\to p_1}$
return $(pk = (\mathbf{b}, \mathbf{A}), sk = \mathbf{s})$

Algorithm 2: `PKE.Enc`$(pk = (\mathbf{b}, \mathbf{A}), \mathbf{m} \in \mathcal{M}; r)$

$\mathbf{s}', \mathbf{e}' \leftarrow \chi_s(R_q^{l\times 1}; r) \times \chi_e(R_q^{l\times 1}; r)$
$\mathbf{e}'' \leftarrow \chi_e(R_q; r)$
$\mathbf{b}' := \lfloor \mathbf{A}^T\mathbf{s}' + \mathbf{e}' \rceil_{q\to p_2}$
$\mathbf{b}_q := \lfloor \mathbf{b} \rceil_{p_1\to q}$
$\mathbf{v}' := \lfloor \mathbf{b}_q^T\mathbf{s}' + \mathbf{e}'' + \lfloor q/2 \rfloor \cdot \mathbf{m} \rceil_{q\to t}$
return $ct = (\mathbf{v}', \mathbf{b}')$

Algorithm 3: `PKE.Dec`$(sk = \mathbf{s}, ct = (\mathbf{v}', \mathbf{b}'))$

$\mathbf{b}'_q := \lfloor \mathbf{b}' \rceil_{p_2\to q}$
$\mathbf{v}'_q := \lfloor \mathbf{v}' \rceil_{t\to q}$
$\mathbf{m}' := \lfloor \lfloor 2/q \rfloor (\mathbf{v}'_q - \mathbf{b}'^T_q \mathbf{s}) \rceil$
return $\mathbf{m}'$

This generic protocol can be used to describe Saber, Kyber and the scheme studied in [11], which was designed to simplify the study of failure boosting and will be referred to as Katana. The parameters of these schemes are given in Table 1. For Saber and Kyber we consider the round 3 submissions as described in [6] and [27] respectively, which are the most recent versions at the time of writing.

For Kyber, the distributions χ_s and χ_e are centered binomial distributions with limited variance. There is no public key compression (i.e. $q = p_1$) but there is ciphertext compression (i.e. $q > p_2 > t$). Saber[1] similarly uses a centered binomial distribution for χ_s, but its distribution χ_e always returns zero. Saber does both public key and ciphertext compression (e.g. $q > p_1 = p_2 > t$). Katana is an idealized scheme with Gaussian distributions for χ_s and χ_e and without compression of the public key or ciphertext (i.e. $q = p_1 = p_2 = t$).

Table 1. Parameters of Katana, Saber and Kyber. The security is based on the estimates of Albrecht et al. [2,3]

	L	N	q	$\sigma(\mathbf{s}_i)$	$\sigma(\mathbf{e}_i + \mathbf{u}_i)$	$P[F]$	Classical	Quantum
Katana [11]	3	256	8192	2.00	2.00	2^{-119}	2^{195}	2^{177}
Saber [6]	3	256	8192	1.41	2.29	2^{-136}	2^{189}	2^{172}
Kyber768 [27]	3	256	3329	1.00	1.00/1.38†	2^{-164}	2^{181}	2^{164}

† Standard deviation of the error term in the public key and ciphertext respectively

[1] Saber has slightly different rounding methods, but this does not impact our study as the failure condition remains the same.

2.4 Chosen-Ciphertext Security

To protect against chosen-ciphertext attacks, designers typically convert their passively secure PKE to an actively secure KEM using a generic transformation such as a post-quantum variant [20,28] of the Fujisaki-Okamoto [14,15] transformation. The obtained KEM then has a similar key generation, while the encapsulation and decapsulation are constructed as described in Algorithms 4 and 5 respectively. The idea behind this transformation is that the input ciphertext is checked using a re-encryption of the message, and the ciphertext is rejected if the input ciphertext is not valid. As a result of this procedure, an adversary does not learn anything from inputting invalid ciphertexts. However, in case of a valid ciphertext that leads to a decryption failure, the re-encryption still fails and we will assume that an attacker is able to recognize such event.

Algorithm 4: $\texttt{KEM.Encaps}(pk)$

$m \leftarrow \mathcal{U}(\{0,1\}^{256})$
$(\overline{K}, r) := \mathcal{G}(pk, m)$
$ct := \texttt{PKE.Enc}(pk, m, r)$
$K := \mathcal{H}(\overline{K}, r)$
return (ct, K)

Algorithm 5: $\texttt{KEM.Decaps}(sk, pk, ct, K)$

$m' := \texttt{PKE.Dec}(sk, ct)$
$(\overline{K}, r') := \mathcal{G}(pk, m')$
$ct' := \texttt{PKE.Enc}(pk, m'; r')$
if $ct = ct'$ **then**
  return $K := \mathcal{H}(\overline{K}, r')$
else
  return $K := \perp$

2.5 Decryption Failures

A decryption failure is an event where one fails to recover message or key, which can even happen after following the correct protocol. The occurrence of decryption failures depends on the secret terms $\mathbf{s}, \mathbf{s}', \mathbf{e}, \mathbf{e}', \mathbf{e}''$ in combination with the rounding errors $\mathbf{u}, \mathbf{u}', \mathbf{u}''$, which are defined as:

$$\mathbf{u} := \mathbf{b}_q - (\mathbf{A}\mathbf{s} + \mathbf{e}) \tag{5}$$

$$\mathbf{u}' := \mathbf{b}'_q - (\mathbf{A}^T\mathbf{s}' + \mathbf{e}') \tag{6}$$

$$\mathbf{u}'' := \mathbf{v}'_q - (\mathbf{b}_q^T\mathbf{s}' + \mathbf{e}'' + \mathbf{m}) \tag{7}$$

Expanding the value of the received message m', we get:

$$\mathbf{m}' = \lfloor \lfloor 2/q \rfloor (\mathbf{v}'_q - \mathbf{b}'^T_q \mathbf{s}) \rceil \tag{8}$$

$$= \mathbf{m} + \lfloor \lfloor 2/q \rfloor ((\mathbf{e} + \mathbf{u})^T\mathbf{s}' - \mathbf{s}^T(\mathbf{e}' + \mathbf{u}') + (\mathbf{e}'' + \mathbf{u}'')) \rceil \tag{9}$$

and a decryption failure occurs if any coefficient of this error term exceeds the threshold $q_t = q/4$, which can be formalized as follows:

$$||(\mathbf{e} + \mathbf{u})^T\mathbf{s}' - \mathbf{s}^T(\mathbf{e}' + \mathbf{u}') + (\mathbf{e}'' + \mathbf{u}'')||_\infty > q_t$$

Failure Vectors: Following [12] we define the failure vectors $\mathcal{S}$, $\mathcal{C}$, $\mathcal{G}$ as:

$$\mathcal{S} = \begin{pmatrix} -\mathbf{s} \\ \mathbf{e}+\mathbf{u} \end{pmatrix} \quad \mathcal{C} = \begin{pmatrix} \mathbf{e}'+\mathbf{u}' \\ \mathbf{s}' \end{pmatrix} \quad \mathcal{G} = \mathbf{e}''+\mathbf{u}'' \tag{10}$$

which simplifies the failure condition to:

$$||\mathcal{S}^T\mathcal{C}+\mathcal{G}||_\infty > q_t$$

Geometric Notation: To streamline notation, we will use the geometric notation as introduced in [11]. The vector $\overline{\mathcal{S}} \in \mathbb{Z}_q^{lN\times 1}$ is an integer vector representation of $\mathcal{S}$, obtained by arranging all coefficients of the polynomials of $\mathcal{S}$ in a vector. Additionally, the rotation of a vector of polynomials $\mathcal{C}$ is defined as:

$$\mathcal{C}^{(r)} := X^r \cdot \mathcal{C}(X^{-1}) \mod X^N+1. \tag{11}$$

Using this notation, the ith coefficient of $\mathcal{S}^T\mathcal{C}$ can be calculated as $\overline{\mathcal{S}}^T\overline{\mathcal{C}^{(i)}}$. An illustration of these concepts is given in Example 1. For more information about this representation we refer to [11].

Example 1. [11] For a secret $\mathcal{S}$ and a ciphertext $\mathcal{C}$ in $\mathbb{Z}_q^{2\times 1}[X]/(X^3+1)$:

$$\mathcal{S} = \begin{bmatrix} \mathcal{S}_{0,0}+\mathcal{S}_{0,1}X+\mathcal{S}_{0,2}X^2 \\ \mathcal{S}_{1,0}+\mathcal{S}_{1,1}X+\mathcal{S}_{1,2}X^2 \end{bmatrix}, \quad \mathcal{C} = \begin{bmatrix} \mathcal{C}_{0,0}+\mathcal{C}_{0,1}X+\mathcal{C}_{0,2}X^2 \\ \mathcal{C}_{1,0}+\mathcal{C}_{1,1}X+\mathcal{C}_{1,2}X^2 \end{bmatrix}$$

we get the following vectors:

$$\overline{\mathcal{S}} = \begin{bmatrix} \mathcal{S}_{0,0} \\ \mathcal{S}_{0,1} \\ \mathcal{S}_{0,2} \\ \mathcal{S}_{1,0} \\ \mathcal{S}_{1,1} \\ \mathcal{S}_{1,2} \end{bmatrix}, \quad \overline{\mathcal{C}^{(0)}} = \begin{bmatrix} \mathcal{C}_{0,0} \\ -\mathcal{C}_{0,2} \\ -\mathcal{C}_{0,1} \\ \mathcal{C}_{1,0} \\ -\mathcal{C}_{1,2} \\ -\mathcal{C}_{1,1} \end{bmatrix} \quad \overline{\mathcal{C}^{(1)}} = \begin{bmatrix} \mathcal{C}_{0,1} \\ \mathcal{C}_{0,0} \\ -\mathcal{C}_{0,2} \\ \mathcal{C}_{1,1} \\ \mathcal{C}_{1,0} \\ -\mathcal{C}_{1,2} \end{bmatrix} \quad \overline{\mathcal{C}^{(3)}} = \begin{bmatrix} -\mathcal{C}_{0,0} \\ \mathcal{C}_{0,2} \\ \mathcal{C}_{0,1} \\ -\mathcal{C}_{1,0} \\ \mathcal{C}_{1,2} \\ \mathcal{C}_{1,1} \end{bmatrix} \ldots$$

Definitions: We will denote with F a decryption failure, and with S a successful decryption. F_i will denote an error at the ith coefficient of $\mathcal{S}^T\mathcal{C}+\mathcal{G}$, which happens when the absolute value of this coefficient is bigger than q_t. Similarly S_i will denote a successful decryption of the ith coefficient. Using the geometric notation we can say that an error F_i occurs if:

$$\left|\overline{\mathcal{S}}^T\overline{\mathcal{C}^{(i)}}+\mathcal{G}_i\right| > q_t$$

We will use the shorthand $P_F[ct]$ to denote the failure probability $P[F|ct]$ for a certain ciphertext ct, which can be formalized as:

$$P_F[ct] = \sum_{\forall \mathcal{S}} P[\mathcal{S}] \cdot P[F|ct,\mathcal{S}]$$

Sometimes, we will group ciphertexts in classes, where a class cl bundles all ciphertexts with certain properties, e.g. $cl = \{\forall ct : ||\mathcal{C}||_2 = c, \mathcal{G} = g\}$. In this case

$P_F[cl]$ denotes the weighted average of the failure probabilities of all ciphertexts in the class cl, which can be formalized as:

$$P_F[cl] = \sum_{\forall ct: ct \in cl} P[ct] \cdot P[F|ct]$$

3 Failure Boosting Attacks

By exploiting decryption failures, an attacker can mount an attack that retrieves the secret key. The crux of such an attack is that failing ciphertexts give information that can be used to reconstruct the secret key as described in [11,12] and [9]. In this paper we will focus on the process to obtain these failing ciphertexts as efficiently as possible.

We specifically target schemes that are IND-CCA secured, which implies that non-valid ciphertexts are rejected by the decapsulation regardless of the occurrence of a decryption failure and thus that they can not give any information. As such the attack surface is limited to submitting valid ciphertexts and observing whether a failure occurs.

Failure boosting [12] is a technique to increase the failure probability of valid ciphertexts submitted for decapsulation. It is a two step process consisting of a precomputation step and a query step. We will discuss the cost of a failure boosting attack using two metrics: work $\mathcal{W}$ and queries $\mathcal{Q}$. Work describes the cost of precomputation, where $1\mathcal{W}$ is defined as the cost of generating one ciphertext, while $\mathcal{Q}$ describes the total number of decapsulation queries performed.

Precomputation: During precomputation, the adversary performs an offline search for weak ciphertexts, i.e. valid ciphertexts with a high failure probability. This is accomplished by randomly generating ciphertexts until a ciphertext with failure probability above a certain threshold f_t is found. The probability of finding such a ciphertext can be expressed as follows:

$$\alpha(f_t) = \sum_{\forall ct: P_F[ct] > f_t} P[ct]. \tag{12}$$

Finding a weak failure will take on average $\alpha(f_t)^{-1}$ work, but this can be sped up quadratically using a quantum computer to $\sqrt{\alpha(f_t)^{-1}}$ work.

Querying: Once a weak ciphertext is found, it is submitted for decapsulation and the adversary observes whether it triggers a decryption failure. A failure happens with probability $\beta(f_t)$ for a given threshold f_t, which can be calculated as follows:

$$\beta(f_t) = \frac{\sum_{\forall ct: P_F[ct] > f_t} P[ct] \cdot P_F[ct]}{\sum_{\forall ct: P_F[ct] > f_t} P[ct]} = \frac{\sum_{\forall ct: P_F[ct] > f_t} P[ct] \cdot P_F[ct]}{\alpha(f_t)}. \tag{13}$$

The query step can not be sped up using quantum computers as an adversary has typically no quantum access to the decapsulation oracle. An adversary needs on average $\beta(f_t)^{-1}$ queries to obtain one decryption failure.

Attack Cost: For a given threshold f_t, finding a decryption failure costs on average $\alpha(f_t)^{-1}\beta(f_t)^{-1}$ work and $\beta(f_t)^{-1}$ queries, which can be reduced to $\sqrt{\alpha(f_t)^{-1}\beta(f_t)^{-1}}$ work when Grover search is used during precomputation.

3.1 Directional Failure Boosting

Directional failure boosting [11] improves failure boosting and can be used when at least one other failure has been found. It specifically uses information of previously found failing ciphertexts to improve the search for new failures. In [11], this is done by calculating $\mathcal{E}$, an estimate of the direction of the secret $\overline{\mathcal{S}}$, and taking this into account in the failure estimation $P_F[ct, \mathcal{E}]$.

Directional failure boosting dramatically reduces the cost of finding additional failures after the first failure has been found. As a result, in a single target attack the work and number of queries is dominated by finding the first failure and thus the cost of a single target attack can be approximated as the cost of finding the first failure. An in depth discussion of directional failure boosting can be found in [11].

3.2 Estimation of Efficiency

The cost of (directional) failure boosting is described by Eq. 12 and 13, which requires to sum over all possible ciphertexts. This is clearly infeasible, but can be simplified by making an approximate failure model and grouping ciphertexts with similar failure probability. Two such models were presented in the literature: Gaussian approximation and geometric approximation.

Gaussian Approximation [12]*:* The Gaussian approximation considers the coefficients of $\mathcal{S}^T\mathcal{C}$ to follow a Gaussian distribution with zero mean and variance depending on $\mathcal{C}$. This assumption can be used to accurately estimate failure boosting efficiency, but does not work for directional failure boosting estimations. The calculation method as presented in [12] takes both $\mathcal{C}$ and $\mathcal{G}$ into account in the weak ciphertext selection. For more information about the exact calculation methodology we refer the reader to [12].

Geometric Approximation [11]*:* The geometric approximation assumes that the angle ϕ between $\overline{\mathcal{S}}^T\overline{\mathcal{C}^{(i)}}$ behaves as a uniformly random angle in dimension $2Nl$. This approximation corresponds to the assumption that χ_s and χ_e are continuous Gaussian distributions with zero mean. Using the geometric approximation, the condition on an error at the ith coefficient can be rewritten from:

$$\left|\overline{\mathcal{S}}^T\overline{\mathcal{C}^{(i)}} + \mathcal{G}_i\right| > q_t \tag{14}$$

to:

$$|\ ||\mathcal{S}||_2 \cdot ||\mathcal{C}||_2 \cdot \cos(\phi) + \mathcal{G}_i| > q_t \tag{15}$$

In directional failure boosting, the vectors $\overline{\mathcal{S}}$ and $\overline{\mathcal{C}^{(i)}}$ are first expanded in a part parallel and a part orthogonal to the estimate of the secret $\mathcal{E}$:

$$\left|\overline{\mathcal{S}}_{\perp}^{T}\overline{\mathcal{C}^{(i)}}_{\perp} + \overline{\mathcal{S}}_{||}^{T}\overline{\mathcal{C}^{(i)}}_{||} + \mathcal{G}_i\right| > q_t \tag{16}$$

which can be further expanded to:

$$\left|\begin{matrix} ||\mathcal{S}||_2 \cdot ||\mathcal{C}||_2 \cdot \cos(\theta_{SE}) \cdot \cos(\theta_{C^iE}) + \\ ||\mathcal{S}||_2 \cdot ||\mathcal{C}||_2 \cdot \sin(\theta_{SE}) \cdot \sin(\theta_{C^iE}) \cdot \cos(\psi) + \mathcal{G}_i \end{matrix}\right| > q_t \tag{17}$$

with ψ a uniformly random angle in dimension $2Nl - 1$. In D'Anvers et al. [11], the $\mathcal{G}$ term was neglected in the calculations. A more detailed explanation of this technique can be found in [11].

Attack Cost Estimation: Using the above approximations, one can bundle ciphertexts with similar failure probability in classes cl to reduce the cost of calculating $\alpha(f_t)$ and $\beta(f_t)$. The values of $\alpha(f_t)$ and $\beta(f_t)$ can be calculated using the formulas below, with the difference that $P[cl]$ is the probability of a randomly generated ciphertext belongs to the specific class cl, and $P_F[cl]$ the failure probability of ciphertexts in that class.

$$\alpha(f_t) \approx \sum_{\forall cl: P_F[cl] > f_t} P[cl] \tag{18}$$

$$\beta(f_t) \approx \frac{\sum_{\forall cl: P_F[cl] > f_t} P[cl] \cdot P_F[cl]}{\alpha(f_t)} \tag{19}$$

For example, under the geometric approximation, one bundles all ciphertexts with similar $||\mathcal{C}||_2$ for failure boosting. Directional failure boosting in the geometric approximation defines classes based on $||\mathcal{C}||_2$ and the closest angle $\mathrm{maxcos_i}(\theta_{\mathrm{C^{(i)}E}})$ between the rotations of the ciphertext and the estimate of the secret $\mathcal{E}$.

4 Multitarget Attacks

One of the main constraints in a practical attack is the number of queries that can be performed. For example, NIST [1] set a maximum of $q_{limit} = 2^{64}$ decapsulation queries per target that can be performed during an attack. One possibility to circumvent such limitation is to consider multiple targets, with the goal of breaking one of these targets.

Such a multitarget attack queries a certain number of targets $T^{(0)}$, where each target has an individual query limit. The goal is to retrieve the secret key for at least one of these targets. We assume that multitarget protection is in place, so that ciphertexts are only valid for one given public key and thus target. Such multitarget protection is easily obtained by incorporating (a hash of) the public key in the ciphertext generation, which is the case for Saber and Kyber.

4.1 Naive Multitarget

A naive variant of the multitarget attack was introduced in [11], which proceeded as follows: First, find the first failure by performing at most $q_{limit}/2$ per target, which in total implies a maximum of $T^{(0)} \cdot q_{limit}/2$ queries. Then, focus on the target that caused the failure and continue with a single target attack on this target with query limit $q_{limit}/2$.

First note that due to multitarget protection, each generated weak ciphertext is linked to a specific public key and can only be used for that target. Moreover, one can assume that given only the public key the adversary has no efficient way to retrieve information about the secret key $\mathcal{S}$ without solving the Mod-LWE/LWR problem. This implies that he has no efficient way to distinguish between targets with higher or lower failure probability and thus that generating a weak ciphertext and querying it has exactly the same failure probability at each target.

Assuming that successful queries do not contribute any information about the targets, the failure probability at each target stays the same until a decryption failure has been found. Therefore, we can say that finding one failure at $T^{(0)}$ targets with a maximum of $q_{limit}/2$ queries per target has the same cost as finding one failure at one target with a maximum of $T^{(0)} \cdot q_{limit}/2$ queries, so that the cost of finding the first failure in the naive multitarget attack can be described with:

$$\sqrt{\alpha_0^{-1}\beta_0^{-1}} \text{ work, and } \beta_0^{-1} \text{ queries,} \tag{20}$$

under the condition that:

$$\beta_0^{-1} < T^{(0)} \cdot q_{limit}/2, \tag{21}$$

where α_i and β_i denote the optimal values for $\alpha(f_t)$ and $\beta(f_t)$ for the ith failure, which can be determined by selecting the value of f_t that optimally reduces the work while fulfilling the query limit constraint.

To estimate the cost of finding the follow-up failures, we can use the approximation from [11], which states that in a single target attack the attack cost is dominated by finding the first failure. In this case, the first failure of the single target attack is the second overall failure so that the cost of finding the follow up failures can be calculated as:

$$\sqrt{\alpha_1^{-1}\beta_1^{-1}} \text{ work, and } \beta_1^{-1} \text{ queries,} \tag{22}$$

under the condition that:

$$\beta_1^{-1} < q_{limit}/2, \tag{23}$$

One can easily see that the total number of queries per target is always under q_{limit} in this scenario.

4.2 Levelled Multitarget

When the cost of finding the second failure is the dominant factor, this naive multitarget attack can be improved using a levelled approach. Notice that the naive multitarget attack essentially reduces the cost of the attack by relaxing the query limit constraint for finding the first failure. To reduce the cost of finding the second failure, we can similarly focus on multiple targets to relax the query constraint. However, this requires the attacker to find multiple failing ciphertexts in the first step of the attack.

More specifically, in the first phase, the attacker aims at obtaining $T^{(1)}$ targets using under $q_{limit}/3$ queries per target (which is a total of $T^{(0)} \cdot q_{limit}/3$ queries). This has a cost of:

$$T^{(1)} \sqrt{\alpha_0^{-1} \beta_0^{-1}} \text{ work and } T^{(1)} \beta_0^{-1} \text{ queries.} \tag{24}$$

Under the condition that:

$$T^{(1)} \beta_0^{-1} < T^{(0)} \cdot q_{limit}/3. \tag{25}$$

The attacker can then use $T^{(1)} \cdot q_{limit}/3$ queries to find the next failure, which has a cost of:

$$\sqrt{\alpha_1^{-1} \beta_1^{-1}} \text{ work and } \beta_1^{-1} \text{ queries.} \tag{26}$$

Under the condition that:

$$\beta_1^{-1} < T^{(1)} \cdot q_{limit}/3. \tag{27}$$

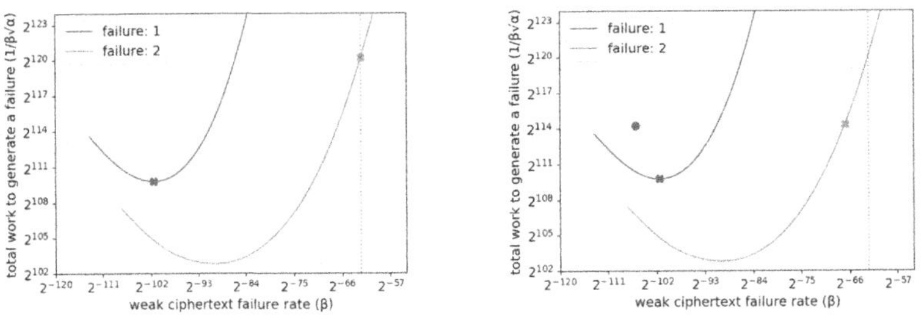

(a) Naive multitarget[11] (b) Levelled multitarget

Fig. 1. Example of multitarget attacks on Katana, with 2^{64} targets and maximum 2^{64} queries. The cost of finding one failure is indicated with x. The cost of finding $T^{(1)}$ failures using failure boosting in the first phase is given by the blue dot, and the corresponding number of queries can be found as β^{-1} where β is the x-axis value of this point. In the naive multitarget attack the cost is dominated by finding the second failure in under 2^{64} queries. In the levelled approach the cost of the two phases is equalized.

Table 2. Comparison of the naive and levelled multitarget attack. Note that α and β values are not the same between both methods as the difference in query limits leads to a different optimal f_t.

	Naive multitarget [11]		Levelled multitarget [ours]	
	work	queries	work	queries
first failure	$\sqrt{\alpha_0^{-1}\beta_0^{-1}}$	$T^{(0)} \cdot q_{limit}/2$	$T^{(1)}\sqrt{\alpha_0^{-1}\beta_0^{-1}}$	$T^{(0)} \cdot q_{limit}/(3T^{(1)})^{\dagger}$
second failure	$\sqrt{\alpha_1^{-1}\beta_1^{-1}}$	$q_{limit}/2$	$\sqrt{\alpha_1^{-1}\beta_1^{-1}}$	$T^{(1)} \cdot q_{limit}/3$
follow up failures	negligible	–	$\sqrt{\alpha_2^{-1}\beta_2^{-1}}$	$q_{limit}/3$

† per failure, total query limit is $T^{(0)} \cdot q_{limit}$

Once a second failure is found for a given target, the attack continues with a single target attack on that target using at most $q_{limit}/3$ queries. An overview of this levelled multitarget approach is given in Table 2. Note that the query limit per phase is chosen so that the total number of queries at each target over all failures is always under q_{limit}. Figure 1 gives a graphical comparison of the naive and multitarget attack on Katana.

In principle it is possible to extend this approach to more levels: if the third failure would be more expensive than the previous two failures one can target $T^{(2)}$ targets to reduce the cost of finding the third failure. However, we did not find a situation in which this was applicable, as finding the third failure is typically much cheaper than finding previous failures.

5 Better Failure Boosting Estimation

The calculation of the work necessary to perform a multitarget attack is not straightforward. Especially the cost of directional failure boosting is expensive to determine and requires multiple approximations to be able to practically compute. D'Anvers et al. [11] introduced crude approximations to reduce the computational cost of this calculation.

Apart from the geometric approximation, as explained in Subsect. 3.2, they did not consider $\mathcal{G}$, simplified the distribution of $||\mathcal{S}||_2$ into its average and used a simplified formula for the calculation of θ_{SE}. Additionally, there is a weak key effect in multitarget attacks which has not been addressed before[2].

These simplifications are justifiable in the single target attack, where the cost of the second failure is significantly lower than the cost of the first failure. However, in multitarget attacks, where the second failure cost might be dominant, it is important to have an accurate estimation of the cost to find this failure. We will first detail the weak key effect, then we will improve the estimation of $\cos(\theta_{SE})$ and finally we will consider the distribution of $||\mathcal{S}||_2$ and $\mathcal{G}$. We will clearly compare our improvements with the state-of-the-art. In this section we

[2] Guo et al. [18] have used the terminology ('weak keys') in their attack, but this refers to public keys that are vulnerable against specific types of ciphertexts.

focus on the case where $\chi_s = \chi_e$ and schemes without rounding, while in Sect. 6 we will extend the estimation techniques for more general schemes, including the NIST finalists Kyber and Saber.

5.1 Weak Keys

Some targets might have secret keys that are more prone to decryption failures, which we will call weak keys. It does not seem possible to efficiently identify targets with weak keys from their public key. However, in a multitarget attack, weak key targets are more prone to produce a failing ciphertext. This means that in the second phase of the attack, when looking for the second failure of a certain target, this target will have higher failure probability compared to a single target attack.

In particular, the norm of the secret $||\mathcal{S}||_2$ determines the failure probability of a given target. We will show that the a posteriori distribution of $||\mathcal{S}||_2$, given a multitarget attack where in the first phase $T^{(0)}$ targets are considered, and with failure boosting threshold f_t can be approximated using:

$$P[||\mathcal{S}||_2] \cdot \frac{T^{(0)} P\left[F \mid ||\mathcal{S}||_2, f_t\right]}{P\left[F \mid ||\mathcal{S}||_2, f_t\right] + (T^{(0)} - 1) \cdot P\left[F \mid f_t\right]} \tag{28}$$

To derive this formula, we first introduce the notation $F(t, q)$ to describe the event where the overall first failure occurs at target t on the qth query. Similarly, we define $S(t, q)$ as a success at target t on the qth query. $F(t, \cdot)$ signifies the event where the first failure occurs at target t, regardless of at which query this happens. Without loss of generality we denote the target where the first failure occurs as target $t = 0$, which implies that $||\mathcal{S}||_2$ denotes the norm of $\mathcal{S}$ for the 0th target. To simplify the derivation, we will assume that the ith query is performed at all targets at the same time, after which they are all checked for decryption failures. We can then write:

$$P[||\mathcal{S}||_2 \mid F(0, \cdot), f_t] \tag{29}$$

$$= P[||\mathcal{S}||_2 \mid f_t] \cdot \frac{P[F(0, \cdot) \mid ||\mathcal{S}||_2, f_t]}{P[F(0, \cdot) \mid f_t]} \tag{30}$$

$$\approx T^{(0)} \cdot P[||\mathcal{S}||_2] \cdot P[F(0, \cdot) \mid ||\mathcal{S}||_2, f_t] \tag{31}$$

where the latter step uses the fact that a failure occurs with equal probability at all $T^{(0)}$ targets without extra information about the norms $||\mathcal{S}||_2$ of the targets.

The term $P[F(0, \cdot) \mid ||\mathcal{S}||_2, f_t]$ can then be extended by explicitly writing it out as a sum over the probabilities of failures at each query round:

$$P[F(0, \cdot) \mid ||\mathcal{S}||_2, f_t] \tag{32}$$

$$= \sum_{q=0}^{\infty} P\left[\begin{array}{c} F(t, q), S(i, j) \\ \forall i \in \{0, \ldots, T^{(0)} - 1\}, j \in \{0, \ldots, q\} : (i, j) \neq (t, q) \end{array} \middle| \; ||\mathcal{S}||_2, f_t\right] \tag{33}$$

$$= \sum_{q=0}^{\infty} P\left[\begin{array}{c} F(0, q), S(0, j) \\ \forall j \in \{0 \ldots, q - 1\} \end{array} \middle| \; ||\mathcal{S}||_2, f_t\right] \cdot P\left[\begin{array}{c} S(1, j) \\ \forall j \in \{0 \ldots, q\} \end{array} \middle| \; f_t\right]^{T^{(0)} - 1} \tag{34}$$

The failure probability of a target is reduced slightly when successful ciphertexts are found. However, this effect is small, as the information embedded in successful ciphertexts is limited. We therefore assume that the failure probability of ciphertexts does not change when finding successful ciphertexts. This allows us to simplify the expression as:

$$\approx \sum_{q=0}^{\infty} P\left[F \mid ||\mathcal{S}||_2, f_t\right] \cdot P\left[S \mid ||\mathcal{S}||_2, f_t\right]^q \cdot P\left[S \mid f_t\right]^{(T^{(0)}-1)(q+1)}$$

$$\approx P\left[F \mid ||\mathcal{S}||_2, f_t\right] \cdot P\left[S \mid f_t\right]^{(T^{(0)}-1)} \sum_{q=0}^{\infty} \left(P\left[S \mid ||\mathcal{S}||_2, f_t\right] \cdot P\left[S \mid f_t\right]^{(T^{(0)}-1)}\right)^q \tag{35}$$

$$\approx \frac{P\left[F \mid ||\mathcal{S}||_2, f_t\right] \cdot P\left[S \mid f_t\right]^{(T^{(0)}-1)}}{1 - P\left[S \mid ||\mathcal{S}||_2, f_t\right] \cdot P\left[S \mid f_t\right]^{(T^{(0)}-1)}}$$

$$\approx \frac{P\left[F \mid ||\mathcal{S}||_2, f_t\right]}{P\left[F \mid ||\mathcal{S}||_2, f_t\right] + (T^{(0)} - 1) \cdot P\left[F \mid f_t\right]} \tag{36}$$

where Eq. 35 is an infinite geometric sum, and Eq. 36 takes a Taylor approximation where only the highest order terms are kept. We will discuss the effect of weak keys in the next section, after its effects on θ_{SE} have been addressed.

5.2 Calculating θ_{SE}

The angle θ_{SE} can be estimated using the simplified failure equation. Assuming a failure occurred at the ith location we know:

$$\overline{\mathcal{S}}^T \overline{\mathcal{C}^{(i)}} > q_t, \tag{37}$$

which can be rewritten as:

$$\cos(\theta_{SE}) > \frac{q_t}{||\mathcal{S}||_2 ||\mathcal{C}||_2}. \tag{38}$$

The fact that uniform angles in high dimensions strongly tend to orthogonality can be used to approximate this to:

$$\cos(\theta_{SE}) = \frac{q_t}{||\mathcal{S}||_2 ||\mathcal{C}||_2}. \tag{39}$$

As such, we can estimate the expected value of $\cos(\theta_{SE})$ by assuming independence between $\mathbb{E}\left[||\mathcal{S}||_2\right]$ and $\mathbb{E}\left[||\mathcal{C}||_2\right]$ as:

$$\mathbb{E}\left[\cos(\theta_{SE})\right] = \frac{q_t}{\mathbb{E}\left[||\mathcal{S}||_2\right] \mathbb{E}\left[||\mathcal{C}||_2\right]}. \tag{40}$$

In [11], the values of $\mathbb{E}\left[||\mathcal{S}||_2\right]$ and $\mathbb{E}\left[||\mathcal{C}||_2\right]$ were estimated over the original a priori distribution. However, failure boosting increases the expected norm of $||\mathcal{C}||_2$ and the weak key effect increases the expected norm of $\mathbb{E}\left[||\mathcal{S}||_2\right]$. Both effects will decrease $\mathbb{E}[\cos(\theta_{SE})]$ and therefore diminish the efficiency of directional failure boosting.

We take these effects into account by considering the a posteriori distributions as follows:

$$\mathbb{E}[||\mathcal{C}||_2] = \sum_{||\mathcal{C}||_2} ||\mathcal{C}||_2 \cdot P[||\mathcal{C}||_2 \mid f_t] \tag{41}$$

$$\mathbb{E}[||\mathcal{S}||_2] = \sum_{||\mathcal{S}||_2} ||\mathcal{S}||_2 \cdot P[||\mathcal{S}||_2 \mid F(0,\cdot), f_t] \tag{42}$$

Note that our expression of $\mathbb{E}[\cos(\theta_{SE})]$ is now significantly better than in previous works, but still not exact for the following reasons: First, $\mathbb{E}[||\mathcal{C}||_2]$ will be slightly higher than calculated above as failures happen with higher probability for higher values of $||\mathcal{C}||_2$. However, this effect is limited as failure boosting pushes $||\mathcal{C}||_2$ to high values where the tails decrease rapidly. Therefore the values of $||\mathcal{C}||_2$ will be strongly focussed around the cut-off value. Secondly, the independence assumption used to obtain Eq. 40 is not exact. Nevertheless, the approximation is good enough for our purposes.

Comparison to State-of-the-art: Figure 2a shows the effect of including the weak key effect and improving the $\cos(\theta_{SE})$ estimation. On one hand, one can see that the weak key reduces the failure probability, which is the leftmost point on the curve, from 2^{-115} to 2^{-107}. On the other hand, the increase in $\mathbb{E}[||\mathcal{S}||_2]$ and $\mathbb{E}[||\mathcal{C}||_2]$ and subsequent reduction of $\mathbb{E}[\cos(\theta_{SE})]$ reduces the effectiveness of directional failure boosting, an effect that becomes more pronounced with higher precomputation.

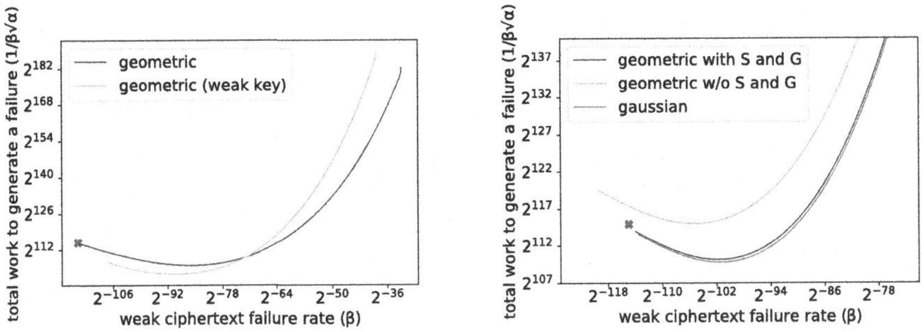

(a) Weak key effect on directional failure boosting cost (second failure) of Katana. The orange curve is estimated using $\beta=2^{-101}, T^{(0)}=2^{64}$.

(b) Effect of inclusion of $||\mathcal{S}||_2$ and $\mathcal{G}$ in the failure boosting calculation (first failure) of Katana.

Fig. 2. Effect of inclusion of weak keys and $||\mathcal{S}||_2$ and $\mathcal{G}$ on Katana. The red cross indicates the failure probability of Katana (or equally the cost of finding a failure when random guessing). (Color figure online)

5.3 Inclusion of $\mathcal{S}$ and $\mathcal{G}$

In [11], the distributions of $||\mathcal{S}||_2$ and $\mathcal{G}$ were simplified to their mean to speed up calculations. However, the side-effect of this is an underestimation of the failure probability and the attack efficiency. In our calculations, we take into account the distribution of both $||\mathcal{S}||_2$ and $\mathcal{G}$.

Failure Boosting: Failure boosting calculations under the geometric approximation can be calculated by making classes based on $||\mathcal{C}||_2$ and using Eqs. 18 and 19 to determine $\alpha(f_t)$ and $\beta(f_t)$.

Including $\mathcal{S}$ and $\mathcal{G}$ does not change the ciphertext probability $P[cl]$, but does impact the failure probability $P_F[cl]$ needed to calculate $\alpha(f_t)$ and $\beta(f_t)$. A more exact expression of this failure probability that takes into account $||\mathcal{S}||_2$ and $\mathcal{G}$ can be derived as follows:

$$P_F[cl] = P_F[||\mathcal{C}||_2] \tag{43}$$

$$= \sum_{||\mathcal{S}||_2} P[||\mathcal{S}||_2] \cdot P[F \mid ||\mathcal{C}||_2, ||\mathcal{S}||_2] \tag{44}$$

$$= \sum_{||\mathcal{S}||_2} P[||\mathcal{S}||_2] \cdot \left(1 - \prod_{i=0}^{N-1} (1 - P[F_i \mid ||\mathcal{C}||_2, ||\mathcal{S}||_2])\right) \tag{45}$$

$$= \sum_{||\mathcal{S}||_2} P[||\mathcal{S}||_2] \cdot \left(1 - \prod_{i=0}^{N-1} \left(1 - \sum_{\mathcal{G}_i} P[\mathcal{G}_i] \cdot P[F_i \mid ||\mathcal{C}||_2, ||\mathcal{S}||_2, \mathcal{G}_i]\right)\right) \tag{46}$$

where $P[F_i \mid ||\mathcal{C}||_2, ||\mathcal{S}||_2, \mathcal{G}_i]$ can be calculated following the geometric approximation of Eq. 15 as:

$$P[F_i \mid ||\mathcal{S}||_2, ||\mathcal{C}||_2, \mathcal{G}_i] = \begin{array}{c} P[\cos(\phi) > \frac{q_t - \mathcal{G}_i}{||\mathcal{S}||_2 \cdot ||\mathcal{C}||_2} \mid ||\mathcal{C}||_2, ||\mathcal{S}||_2, \mathcal{G}_i] \\ +P[\cos(\phi) < \frac{-q_t - \mathcal{G}_i}{||\mathcal{S}||_2 \cdot ||\mathcal{C}||_2} \mid ||\mathcal{C}||_2, ||\mathcal{S}||_2, \mathcal{G}_i] \end{array}, \tag{47}$$

and where ϕ can be modelled as a uniformly random angle in dimension $2Nl$.

Directional Failure Boosting: The procedure for directional failure boosting is more complicated, as one should make a list over all values of $||\mathcal{C}||_2$ and $\mathrm{maxcos_i}(\theta_{\mathrm{C^{(i)}E}})$. As before, the calculation of $P[cl]$ is the same as in [11], but the calculation of $P_F[cl]$ additionally should take into account $||\mathcal{S}||_2$ and $\mathcal{G}$.

Without loss of generality we will assume that the highest value of $\cos(\theta_{C^{(i)}E})$ occurs at $i = 0$, so that $\mathrm{maxcos_i}(\theta_{\mathrm{C^{(i)}E}}) = \cos(\theta_{\mathrm{C^{(0)}E}})$. Similar to the derivation of Eq. 46, the failure probability can then be calculated as:

$$P_F[cl] = P_F[||\mathcal{C}||_2, \theta_{C^{(0)}E}] \tag{48}$$
$$= \sum_{||\mathcal{S}||_2} P[||\mathcal{S}||_2] \cdot P[F \mid ||\mathcal{C}||_2, \theta_{C^{(0)}E}, ||\mathcal{S}||_2] \tag{49}$$
$$= \sum_{||\mathcal{S}||_2} P[||\mathcal{S}||_2] \cdot \left(1 - \prod_{i=0}^{N-1} (1 - P[F_i \mid ||\mathcal{C}||_2, \theta_{C^{(0)}E}, ||\mathcal{S}||_2])\right) \tag{50}$$
$$\approx \sum_{||\mathcal{S}||_2} P[||\mathcal{S}||_2] \cdot \left(1 - \left(\begin{array}{l}(1 - P[F_0 \mid ||\mathcal{C}||_2, \theta_{C^{(0)}E}, ||\mathcal{S}||_2]) \cdot \\ \prod_{i=1}^{N-1} (1 - P[F_i \mid ||\mathcal{C}||_2, \cos(\theta_{C^{(i)}E}) \leq \cos(\theta_{C^{(0)}E}), ||\mathcal{S}||_2])\end{array}\right)\right) \tag{51}$$
$$\approx \sum_{||\mathcal{S}||_2} P[||\mathcal{S}||_2] \cdot \tag{52}$$
$$\left(1 - \left(\begin{array}{l}\left(1 - \sum_{\mathcal{G}_0} P[\mathcal{G}_0] \cdot P[F_0 \mid ||\mathcal{C}||_2, \theta_{C^{(0)}E}, ||\mathcal{S}||_2, \mathcal{G}_0]\right) \cdot \\ \prod_{i=1}^{N-1} \left(1 - \sum_{\mathcal{G}_i} P[\mathcal{G}_i] \cdot P[F_i \mid ||\mathcal{C}||_2, \cos(\theta_{C^{(i)}E}) \leq \cos(\theta_{C^{(0)}E}), ||\mathcal{S}||_2, \mathcal{G}_i]\right)\end{array}\right)\right)$$

$P[F_i \mid ||\mathcal{C}||_2, \theta_{C^{(i)}E}, ||\mathcal{S}||_2, \mathcal{G}_i]$ can be estimated using the geometric assumption and Eq. 17 as:

$$P\left[\cos(\psi) > \frac{q_t - \mathcal{G}_i - ||\mathcal{S}||_2 \cdot ||\mathcal{C}||_2 \cdot \cos(\theta_{SE}) \cdot \cos(\theta_{C^{(i)}E})}{||\mathcal{S}||_2 \cdot ||\mathcal{C}||_2 \cdot \sin(\theta_{SE}) \cdot \sin(\theta_{C^{(i)}E})} \mid ||\mathcal{S}||_2, ||\mathcal{C}||_2, \mathcal{G}_i, \cos(\theta_{C^{(i)}E})\right]$$
$$+P\left[\cos(\psi) < \frac{-q_t - \mathcal{G}_i - ||\mathcal{S}||_2 \cdot ||\mathcal{C}||_2 \cdot \cos(\theta_{SE}) \cdot \cos(\theta_{C^{(i)}E})}{||\mathcal{S}||_2 \cdot ||\mathcal{C}||_2 \cdot \sin(\theta_{SE}) \cdot \sin(\theta_{C^{(i)}E})} \mid ||\mathcal{S}||_2, ||\mathcal{C}||_2, \mathcal{G}_i, \cos(\theta_{C^{(i)}E})\right]$$

with ψ a uniformly random angle in dimension $2Nl - 1$.

The value $P[F_i \mid ||\mathcal{C}||_2, \cos(\theta_{C^{(i)}E}) \leq \cos(\theta_{C^{(0)}E}), ||\mathcal{S}||_2, \mathcal{G}_i]$ can be calculated by taking a weighted average over all $\theta_{C^{(i)}E}$ values for which $\cos(\theta_{C^{(i)}E}) \leq \cos(\theta_{C^{(0)}E})$ as:

$$P[F_i \mid ||\mathcal{C}||_2, \cos(\theta_{C^{(i)}E}) \leq \cos(\theta_{C^{(0)}E}), ||\mathcal{S}||_2, \mathcal{G}_i] \tag{53}$$
$$= \sum_{\forall \theta_{C^{(i)}E} : \cos(\theta_{C^{(i)}E}) \leq \cos(\theta_{C^{(0)}E})} P[\theta_{C^{(i)}E}] \cdot P[F_i \mid ||\mathcal{C}||_2, \theta_{C^{(i)}E}, ||\mathcal{S}||_2, \mathcal{G}_i] \tag{54}$$

Approximate Distributions. Note that both the failure boosting and directional failure boosting methods require to loop over all possible values of $||\mathcal{C}||_2, \theta_{C^0 E}, ||\mathcal{S}||_2, \mathcal{G}_i$, which is a costly process. To reduce calculation time, these distributions are approximated using a subset of points in the distribution. We use 200 points to approximate $||\mathcal{C}||_2$ and $\theta_{C^{(i)}E}$, 100 points to approximate $||\mathcal{S}||_2$ and a maximum of 40 points to approximate $\mathcal{G}_i$.

Comparison to state-of-the-art: From Fig. 2b, we see that the method that does not take into account $||\mathcal{S}||_2$ and $\mathcal{G}$ does indeed underestimate the failure probability. This effect will become larger for realistic schemes such as Saber and Kyber, who have a larger variance of the distribution of $\mathcal{G}$. Our new methodology that takes $||\mathcal{S}||_2$ and $\mathcal{G}$ into account does match with the reference calculation using the Gaussian approximation, which further confirms our method. Note that this figure presents failure boosting (for the first failure), and that the Gaussian approximation can not be used for directional failure boosting.

6 Dealing with Uneven Distributions

The cost estimation as described above can not directly be used for calculation of practical schemes that use rounding, such as Kyber or Saber, or more generally schemes that have uneven distributions for the coefficients of $\mathcal{S}$ and $\mathcal{C}$. The main reasons are twofold: first, when the distributions of $\mathbf{s}$ and $\mathbf{e}$ do not have the same variance, values of $||\mathbf{e}'+\mathbf{u}'||_2$ and $||\mathbf{s}'||_2$ have different impact on the overall failure probability. Therefore, using $||\mathcal{C}||_2$ as a predictor of the failure probability, as used in the traditional calculation of direction failure boosting [11], does not give accurate results. Secondly, when rounding occurs, the distributions of $\mathbf{e}$ and $\mathbf{e}'$ are typically not centered and thus the assumption of them following a uniform distribution is not valid.

Note that the Gaussian approximation which is used for the failure boosting (first failure) does not have these problems. Unfortunately it does not seem possible to port the Gaussian assumption to directional failure boosting due to the skew introduced in the distribution of $\mathcal{S}^T\mathcal{C}$ when directional failure boosting is applied.

The problems described above have a significant effect on the accuracy of the failure boosting estimation (blue) as can be seen from Fig. 3. First, one can see that performing no precomputation (i.e. the leftmost point on the curve, which corresponds to the failure probability before failure boosting) does not correspond to the actual failure probability by a large margin. As an additional check we plotted the Gaussian estimation (green) for finding the first failure, which clearly further shows the discrepancy between both estimations. Looking ahead, we also plotted the geometric-uneven estimate (orange) which will be developed in this section.

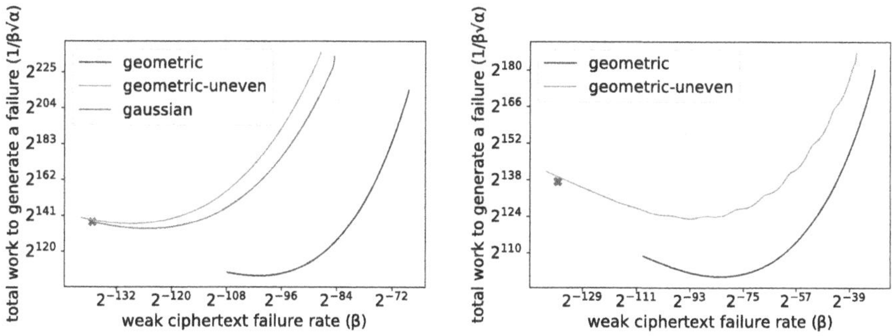

(a) Failure boosting (first failure)

(b) Directional failure boosting (second failure)

Fig. 3. Comparison of estimated cost of (directional) failure boosting for Saber. Geometric refers to the method of Sect. 5, while geometric-uneven indicates the improved method of Sect. 6 Red cross indicates failure probability (when no precomputation is performed). Gaussian estimation is given for failure boosting as a reference. (Color figure online)

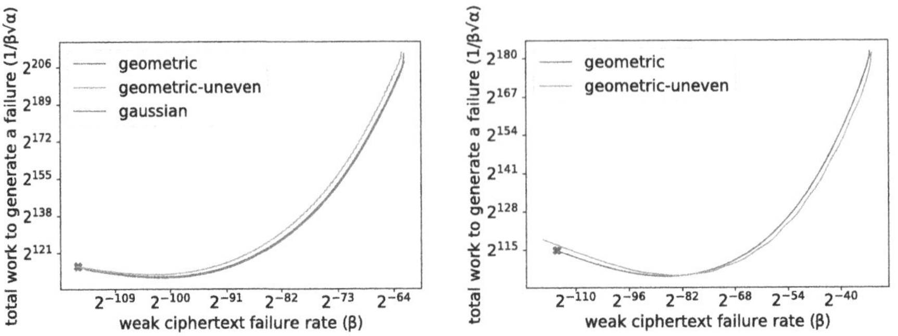

(a) Failure boosting (first failure)

(b) Directional failure boosting (second failure)

Fig. 4. Comparison of estimated cost of (directional) failure boosting for Katana. Geometric refers to the method of Sect. 5, while geometric-uneven indicates the improved method of Sect. 6 Red cross indicates failure probability (when no precomputation is performed). Gaussian estimation is given for failure boosting as a reference. (Color figure online)

6.1 Uneven Distributions

When the variance of the coefficients of $\mathbf{s}$ and $\mathbf{e}+\mathbf{u}$ differs, the impact of $||\mathbf{e}'+\mathbf{u}'||_2$ and $||\mathbf{s}'||_2$ varies and they should be considered separately instead of combined in the term $||\mathcal{C}||_2$. For sake of brevity, we will use the following abbreviations:

$$\begin{aligned} \mathcal{C}_0 &= \mathbf{e}' + \mathbf{u}' \quad & \mathcal{S}_0 &= -\mathbf{s} \\ \mathcal{C}_1 &= \mathbf{s}' & \mathcal{S}_1 &= \mathbf{e} + \mathbf{u} \end{aligned} \tag{55}$$

Uneven Failure Boosting: Instead of grouping ciphertexts based on $||\mathcal{C}||_2$, ciphertexts will be grouped in classes based on $||\mathcal{C}_0||_2$ and $||\mathcal{C}_1||_2$. The probability of a class $P[cl]$ can be easily calculated as $P[||\mathcal{C}_0||_2] \cdot P[||\mathcal{C}_1||_2]$, where the distribution of the norms can be calculated exhaustively. The failure probability $P_F[cl]$ becomes more involved to calculate.

Similar to the approach of Subsect. 5.3, we first include the effect of $\mathcal{S}$ and $\mathcal{G}$, with the difference that we split $||\mathcal{S}||_2$ into $||\mathcal{S}_0||_2$ and $||\mathcal{S}_1||_2$ which leads to:

$$P_F[cl] = P_F[||\mathcal{C}_0||_2, ||\mathcal{C}_1||_2] = \tag{56}$$

$$\sum_{||\mathcal{S}_0||_2} \sum_{||\mathcal{S}_1||_2} \left(\begin{array}{l} P[||\mathcal{S}_0||_2] \cdot P[||\mathcal{S}_1||_2] \cdot \\ \left(1 - \left(1 - \sum_{\mathcal{G}_i} P[\mathcal{G}_i] \cdot P[F_i \mid ||\mathcal{C}_0||_2, ||\mathcal{C}_1||_2, ||\mathcal{S}_0||_2, ||\mathcal{S}_1||_2, \mathcal{G}_i]\right)^N\right) \end{array} \right)$$

To find an expression for $P[F_i \mid ||\mathcal{C}_0||_2, ||\mathcal{C}_1||_2, ||\mathcal{S}_0||_2, ||\mathcal{S}_1||_2, \mathcal{G}_i]$ we go back to the failure term which we rewrite as:

$$\mathcal{S}^T \mathcal{C} + \mathcal{G}_i \tag{57}$$

$$= \mathcal{S}_0^T \cdot \mathcal{C}_0 + \mathcal{S}_1^T \cdot \mathcal{C}_1 + \mathcal{G}_i \tag{58}$$

$$= ||\mathcal{S}_0||_2 \cdot ||\mathcal{C}_0||_2 \cdot \cos(\phi_0) + ||\mathcal{S}_1||_2 \cdot ||\mathcal{C}_1||_2 \cdot \cos(\phi_1) + \mathcal{G}_i \tag{59}$$

Under the geometric assumption, the distribution of ϕ_0 and ϕ_1 can be approximated as angles from the uniform angle distribution in dimension lN. This allows us to calculate the error probability at the ith location for given values of $cond_1 := (||\mathcal{S}_0||_2, ||\mathcal{S}_1||_2, ||\mathcal{C}_0||_2, ||\mathcal{C}_1||_2, \mathcal{G}_i)$ as:

$$
\begin{aligned}
&P[F \mid cond_1] && (60)\\
&= P[|\, ||\mathcal{S}_0||_2 \cdot ||\mathcal{C}_0||_2 \cdot \cos(\phi_0) + ||\mathcal{S}_1||_2 \cdot ||\mathcal{C}_1||_2 \cdot \cos(\phi_1) + \mathcal{G}_i| > q_t \mid cond_1] && (61)\\
&= \sum_{\phi_0} P[\phi_0] \begin{pmatrix} P[\cos(\phi_1) > \frac{q_t - \mathcal{G}_i - ||\mathcal{S}_0||_2 \cdot ||\mathcal{C}_0||_2 \cdot \cos(\phi_0)}{||\mathcal{S}_1||_2 \cdot ||\mathcal{C}_1||_2} \mid cond_1] + \\ P[\cos(\phi_1) < \frac{-q_t - \mathcal{G}_i - ||\mathcal{S}_0||_2 \cdot ||\mathcal{C}_0||_2 \cdot \cos(\phi_0)}{||\mathcal{S}_1||_2 \cdot ||\mathcal{C}_1||_2} \mid cond_1] \end{pmatrix} && (62)
\end{aligned}
$$

Uneven Directional Failure Boosting: Directional failure boosting not only considers $||\mathcal{C}_0||_2$ and $||\mathcal{C}_1||_2$, but also the angle between the ciphertext and the estimate $\mathcal{E}$. Similar to splitting $||\mathcal{C}||_2$ these angles and the estimate $\mathcal{E}$ also should be split. We will denote with $\mathcal{E}_0$ the estimation of the direction of the secret $\mathcal{S}_0$ and with $\mathcal{E}_1$ the estimation of the direction of the secret $\mathcal{S}_1$. The angles $\theta_{C_0^i E_0}$ and $\theta_{C_0^i E_0}$ denote the angle between $\overline{\mathcal{C}^{(i)}}_0$ and $\mathcal{E}_0$ and between $\overline{\mathcal{C}^{(i)}}_1$ and $\mathcal{E}_1$ respectively.

Ciphertext are then combined in classes based on both the norms and the angles. Ideally one would take the maximal angle out of the lN available angles similar to [11]:

$$cl := \left(||\mathcal{C}_0||_2, ||\mathcal{C}_1||_2, \max_i \cos(\theta_{C_0^i E_0}), \max_i \cos(\theta_{C_1^i E_1}) \right).$$

However, for computational efficiency we only consider failures F_0 at the zeroth coefficient, so that the classes are defined by:

$$cl := \left(||\mathcal{C}_0||_2, ||\mathcal{C}_1||_2, \theta_{C_0^0 E_0}, \theta_{C_1^0 E_1} \right).$$

The failure probability is under the same approximation equal to:

$$P_F[cl] \approx P[F_0|cl]$$

For the calculation of $\alpha(f_t)$ and $\beta(f_t)$, the class probability $P[cl]$ can be simplified using independence between the class properties as: $P[||\mathcal{C}_0||_2] \cdot P[||\mathcal{C}_1||_2] \cdot P[\theta_{C_0^0 E_0}] \cdot P[\theta_{C_1^0 E_1}]$. For the failure probability $P_F[cl]$ we first include the influence of $||\mathcal{S}_0||_2$, $||\mathcal{S}_1||_2$ and $\mathcal{G}_0$ as:

$$
\begin{aligned}
&P_F[cl] \approx P[F_0 \mid cl] && (63)\\
&= \sum_{||\mathcal{S}_0||_2} \sum_{||\mathcal{S}_1||_2} \sum_{\mathcal{G}_0} \begin{pmatrix} P[||\mathcal{S}_0||_2] \cdot P[||\mathcal{S}_1||_2] \cdot P[\mathcal{G}_0] \cdot \\ P[F_0 \mid ||\mathcal{C}_0||_2, ||\mathcal{C}_1||_2, ||\mathcal{S}_0||_2, ||\mathcal{S}_1||_2, \mathcal{G}_0, \theta_{C_0^0 E_0}, \theta_{C_1^0 E_1}] \end{pmatrix},
\end{aligned}
$$

and further denoting $cond_2 := \left(||\mathcal{C}_0||_2, ||\mathcal{C}_1||_2, ||\mathcal{S}_0||_2, ||\mathcal{S}_1||_2, \mathcal{G}_0, \theta_{C_0^0 E_0}, \theta_{C_1^0 E_1} \right)$, this becomes:

$$= \sum_{||\mathcal{S}_0||_2} \sum_{||\mathcal{S}_1||_2} \sum_{\mathcal{G}_0} P[||\mathcal{S}_0||_2] \cdot P[||\mathcal{S}_1||_2] \cdot P[\mathcal{G}_0] \cdot P[F_0 \mid cond_2]. \qquad (64)$$

To find an expression for the error probability $P[F_0 \mid cond_2]$, we rewrite the failure term as follows:

$$\overline{\mathcal{S}}^T \overline{\mathcal{C}^{(0)}} + \mathcal{G}_0 \quad (65)$$
$$= \overline{\mathcal{S}}_0^T \overline{\mathcal{C}^{(0)}}_0 + \overline{\mathcal{S}}_1^T \overline{\mathcal{C}^{(0)}}_1 + \mathcal{G}_0 \quad (66)$$
$$= \overline{\mathcal{S}}_{0,\parallel}^T \overline{\mathcal{C}^{(0)}}_{0,\parallel} + \overline{\mathcal{S}}_{0,\perp}^T \overline{\mathcal{C}^{(0)}}_{0,\perp} + \overline{\mathcal{S}}_{1,\parallel}^T \overline{\mathcal{C}^{(0)}}_{1,\parallel} + \overline{\mathcal{S}}_{1,\perp}^T \overline{\mathcal{C}^{(0)}}_{1,\perp} + \mathcal{G}_0 \quad (67)$$
$$= ||\mathcal{S}_0||_2 ||\mathcal{C}_0||_2 \cos(\theta_{S_0 E_0}) \cos(\theta_{C_0^0 E_0}) + ||\mathcal{S}_0||_2 ||\mathcal{C}_0||_2 \sin(\theta_{S_0 E_0}) \sin(\theta_{C_0^0 E_0}) \cos(\psi_0)$$
$$+ ||\mathcal{S}_1||_2 ||\mathcal{C}_1||_2 \cos(\theta_{S_1 E_1}) \cos(\theta_{C_1^0 E_1}) + ||\mathcal{S}_1||_2 ||\mathcal{C}_1||_2 \sin(\theta_{S_1 E_1}) \sin(\theta_{C_1^0 E_1}) \cos(\psi_1)$$
$$+ \mathcal{G}_0, \quad (68)$$

with $\theta_{S_0 E_0}$ and $\theta_{S_1 E_1}$ the angles between $\mathcal{S}_0$ and $\mathcal{E}_0$, and $\mathcal{S}_1$ and $\mathcal{E}_1$ respectively. Following the geometric approximation, ψ_0 and ψ_1 are uniformly random angles in dimension $Nl - 1$. The failure probability can then be calculated as:

$$P[F_0 \mid cond_2] = \quad (69)$$
$$\sum_{\psi_0} P[\psi_0] \begin{pmatrix} P[\cos(\psi_1) > \frac{q_t - \mathcal{G}_0 - w}{||\mathcal{S}_1||_2 ||\mathcal{C}_1||_2 \sin(\theta_{S_1 E_1}) \sin(\theta_{C_1^0 E_1})} \mid cond_2, \psi_0] \\ +P[\cos(\psi_1) < \frac{-q_t - \mathcal{G}_0 - w}{||\mathcal{S}_1||_2 ||\mathcal{C}_1||_2 \sin(\theta_{S_1 E_1}) \sin(\theta_{C_1^0 E_1})} \mid cond_2, \psi_0] \end{pmatrix},$$

where:

$$w = \begin{pmatrix} ||\mathcal{S}_1||_2 ||\mathcal{C}_1||_2 \cos(\theta_{S_1 E_1}) \cos(\theta_{C_1^0 E_1}) \\ +||\mathcal{S}_0||_2 ||\mathcal{C}_0||_2 \cos(\theta_{S_0 E_0}) \cos(\theta_{C_0^0 E_0}) \\ +||\mathcal{S}_0||_2 ||\mathcal{C}_0||_2 \sin(\theta_{S_0 E_0}) \sin(\theta_{C_0^0 E_0}) \cos(\psi_0) \end{pmatrix}. \quad (70)$$

6.2 Meet-in-the-middle Speedup

While the uneven directional failure boosting method is much more precise for schemes with uneven distributions than the original method of [11], it is computationally very demanding. The prescribed calculation in Subsect. 6.1 sums over the distributions of $\mathcal{C}_0$, $\mathcal{C}_1$, $\mathcal{S}_0$, $\mathcal{S}_1$, $\mathcal{G}_0$, $\theta_{C_0^0 E_0}$, $\theta_{C_1^0 E_1}$ and ψ_0. Even when these distributions are approximated, the trade-off between computational cost and accuracy remains unsatisfactory. In this section we will introduce a meet-in-the-middle approach to reduce the computational cost of this method.

From Eq. 68, we can see that the failure equation can be written as:

$$x_0 \cos(\psi_0) + x_1 \cos(\psi_1) + z + \mathcal{G}_0 \quad (71)$$

where:

$$x_0 = ||\mathcal{C}_0||_2 \cdot ||\mathcal{S}_0||_2 \cdot \sin(\theta_{C_0^0 E_0}) \cdot \sin(\theta_{SE_0}) \quad (72)$$
$$x_1 = ||\mathcal{C}_1||_2 \cdot ||\mathcal{S}_1||_2 \cdot \sin(\theta_{C_1^0 E_1}) \cdot \sin(\theta_{SE_1}) \quad (73)$$
$$z = \begin{pmatrix} ||\mathcal{C}_0||_2 \cdot ||\mathcal{S}_0||_2 \cdot \cos(\theta_{C_0^0 E_0}) \cdot \cos(\theta_{SE_0}) + \\ ||\mathcal{C}_1||_2 \cdot ||\mathcal{S}_1||_2 \cdot \cos(\theta_{C_1^0 E_1}) \cdot \cos(\theta_{SE_1}) \end{pmatrix} \quad (74)$$

The work can then be split into a precomputation, where the failure probability given x_0, x_1 and z is calculated (i.e. $P_F[x_0, x_1, z]$), and the directional failure boosting calculation itself, which can now use the precomputed values of $P_F[x_0, x_1, z]$ to reduce calculations. During precomputation $P_F[x_0, x_1, z]$ is calculated for a wide range of x_0, x_1 and z values as:

$$P_F[x_0, x_1, z] \approx P[F_0 \mid x_0, x_1, z] \tag{75}$$

$$= P[|x_0 \cos(\phi_0) + x_1 \cos(\phi_1) + z + \mathcal{G}_0| > q_t \mid x_0, x_1, z] \tag{76}$$

$$= \sum_{\mathcal{G}_0} \sum_{\phi_0} P[\mathcal{G}_0] \cdot P[\phi_0] \cdot P[|x_0 \cos(\phi_0) + x_1 \cos(\phi_1) + z + \mathcal{G}_0| > q_t \mid x_0, x_1, z] \tag{77}$$

$$= \sum_{\mathcal{G}_0} \sum_{\phi_0} P[\mathcal{G}_0] \cdot P[\phi_0] \cdot \begin{pmatrix} P[\cos(\phi_1) > \frac{q_t - z - \mathcal{G}_0 - x_0 \cos(\phi_0)}{x_1} \mid x_0, x_1, z] + \\ P[\cos(\phi_1) < \frac{-q_t - z - \mathcal{G}_0 - x_0 \cos(\phi_0)}{x_1} \mid x_0, x_1, z] \end{pmatrix} \tag{78}$$

Using the precomputation, the directional failure boosting calculation of $P_F[ct]$ can then be simplified as:

$$P_F[ct] \approx P[F_0 | ct] \tag{79}$$

$$= \sum_{||\mathcal{S}_0||_2} \sum_{||\mathcal{S}_1||_2} P[||\mathcal{S}_0||_2] \cdot P[||\mathcal{S}_1||_2] \cdot P[F_0 | ct, ||\mathcal{S}_0||_2, ||\mathcal{S}_1||_2] \tag{80}$$

$$= \sum_{||\mathcal{S}_0||_2} \sum_{||\mathcal{S}_1||_2} \left(\begin{array}{l} P[||\mathcal{S}_0||_2] \cdot P[||\mathcal{S}_1||_2] \cdot \\ P \left[F_0 \left| \begin{array}{l} x_0 = ||\mathcal{C}_0||_2 \cdot ||\mathcal{S}_0||_2 \cdot \sin(\theta_{C_0^0 E_0}) \cdot \sin(\theta_{SE_0}), \\ x_1 = ||\mathcal{C}_1||_2 \cdot ||\mathcal{S}_1||_2 \cdot \sin(\theta_{C_1^0 E_1}) \cdot \sin(\theta_{SE_1}), \\ z = \begin{pmatrix} ||\mathcal{C}_0||_2 \cdot ||\mathcal{S}_0||_2 \cdot \cos(\theta_{C_0^0 E_0}) \cdot \cos(\theta_{SE_0}) + \\ ||\mathcal{C}_1||_2 \cdot ||\mathcal{S}_1||_2 \cdot \cos(\theta_{C_1^0 E_1}) \cdot \cos(\theta_{SE_1}) \end{pmatrix} \end{array} \right. \right] \end{array} \right) \tag{81}$$

with the values of $P[F_0 \mid x_0, x_1, z]$ as calculated in the precomputation.

The precomputation loops over a grid of (x_0, x_1, z) values, and for each gridpoint sums over the distribution of $\mathcal{G}_0$ and ϕ_0. In total, the precomputation thus only loops 5 distributions. The (x_0, x_1, z) grid is calculated over 100 values for each of the elements, and intermediate values of $P[F_0 \mid x_0, x_1, z]$ are linearly interpolated.

The directional failure boosting loops over the distributions of $\mathcal{C}_0$, $\mathcal{C}_1$, $\mathcal{S}_0$, $\mathcal{S}_1$, $\theta_{C_0^0 E_0}$, $\theta_{C_1^0 E_1}$, which is a total of 6 distributions. This can be compared to the loop over 8 distributions in the direct method that does not use meet-in-the-middle calculations. As a result, our meet-in-the-middle approach makes it possible to practically calculate the cost of directional failure boosting for practical schemes such as Saber and Kyber.

6.3 Removing the Bias

One of the assumptions that is explicitly used for the geometric estimation of (directional) failure boosting is that the angles ψ_0 and ψ_1 are distributed uniformly random. This corresponds to the idealized scenario where the secret is drawn from a continuous Gaussian distribution, but it is well approximated by binomial distribution, which is typically used in practical designs. In case of rounding, there is typically a bias in the distribution due to a non-zero mean, as a result of which there will be a 'sense of direction' in $\mathcal{C}_0$ and $\mathcal{S}_1$.

To remove this 'sense of direction' we subtract the mean of the distribution of the coefficients of $\mathcal{C}_0$ and $\mathcal{S}_1$:

$$\mathcal{C}'_0 = \mathcal{C}_0 - \mu_{\chi_e+\chi_s} \tag{82}$$
$$\mathcal{S}'_1 = \mathcal{S}_1 - \mu_{\chi_e+\chi_s}, \tag{83}$$

This subtraction needs to be compensated to keep a correct failure equation, which can be done as follows:

$$\mathcal{S}_0^T \mathcal{C}_0 + \mathcal{S}_1^T \mathcal{C}_1 + \mathcal{G} \tag{84}$$
$$= \mathcal{S}_0^T \mathcal{C}'_0 + \mathcal{S}_1'^T \mathcal{C}_1 + (\mathcal{G} + \mu_{\chi_e+\chi_s} \cdot \mathcal{S}_0 + \mu_{\chi_e+\chi_s} \mathcal{C}_1) \tag{85}$$

And thus by selecting:

$$\mathcal{G}' = \mathcal{G} + \mu_{\chi_e+\chi_s} \cdot \mathcal{S}_0 + \mu_{\chi_e+\chi_s} + \mathcal{C}_1, \tag{86}$$

we can use the failure term $\mathcal{S}_0^T \mathcal{C}'_0 + \mathcal{S}_1'^T \mathcal{C}_1 + \mathcal{G}'$, which has exactly the same failure probability. However, this term will give slightly lower efficiency of failure boosting, as an adversary only considers $\mathcal{C}_0$ and $\mathcal{C}_1$, and not $\mathcal{G}$, to determine the weakness of ciphertexts. To apply this adjustment to previous techniques one just has to use the $\mathcal{C}'_0$, $\mathcal{S}'_1$ and $\mathcal{G}'$ instead of $\mathcal{C}_0$, $\mathcal{S}_1$ and $\mathcal{G}$.

6.4 Discussion

Figure 3 and Fig. 4 give an indication of the accuracy of our newly developed geometric-uneven methods. First, one can see that both in the case of Saber and Katana, the attack cost when performing no precomputation (the leftmost point on the curves) is approximately the failure probability. This is expected behaviour, but it is not the case for Saber in the geometric calculations following Sect. 5. This is a first indication that the geometric-uneven method is more accurate than the standard geometric method in this case.

Secondly, one can see that the geometric-uneven curve is relatively close to the Gaussian curve in the failure boosting (first failure) case. For Saber the geometric-uneven approximation gives a significantly more accurate result compared to the geometric approximation. Overall, the geometric-uneven estimation gives an overestimation of the attack cost, which is logical in view of the assumptions and approximations made in its derivation (e.g. only considering F_0 and making the distributions symmetric). On the other hand, for Katana the geometric approach is more accurate than the geometric-uneven approach, which makes sense as the scheme has $\chi_s = \chi_e$ and does not perform rounding.

One can therefore conclude that the geometric approach is best suited for symmetric non-rounding schemes like Katana, while the geometric-uneven approach is considerably better than the geometric approach for practical schemes such as Saber and Kyber.

7 Attack Constraints

In previous derivations, as in literature [11,12], it is assumed that there is an unlimited number of possible ciphertexts. However, for schemes that use the FO transformation, ciphertexts are generated deterministicaly from a message $m \in \mathcal{M}$, and as such there are only $|\mathcal{M}|$ ciphertexts for each public key. When an attacker performs strong failure boosting, this maximum number of ciphertexts $|\mathcal{M}|$ might be a limit to the number of weak ciphertexts an adversary can generate, which in turn could limit or even obstruct an attack.

In a failure boosting attack an adversary first searches for weak ciphertexts, which occur with a probability $\alpha(f_t)$. This means that there are on average $|\mathcal{M}| \cdot \alpha(f_t)$ weak ciphertexts that can be found at each target, and thus $|\mathcal{M}| \cdot \alpha(f_t) \cdot T_1$ in total for T_1 targets. It is expected that an attacker needs $\beta(f_t)^{-1}$ of these weak ciphertexts to find one decryption failure and thus an adversary that wants to collect T_2 failures would need $\beta(f_t)^{-1} \cdot T_2$ weak ciphertexts. In short, there are on average $|\mathcal{M}| \cdot \alpha(f_t) \cdot T_1$ weak ciphertexts available, and an adversary would need on average $\beta(f_t)^{-1} \cdot T_2$ of them to proceed to the next phase of the attack.

From the above we can conclude that if $\beta(f_t)^{-1} \cdot T_2 > |\mathcal{M}| \cdot \alpha(f_t) \cdot T_1$, it is probable that the attacker will not find sufficient unique ciphertexts to obtain T_2 decryption failures. Even in the case where $\beta(f_t)^{-1} \cdot T_2 \approx |\mathcal{M}| \cdot \alpha(f_t) \cdot T_1$, the attack will become less efficient as the adversary will with high probability generate non-unique weak ciphertexts, which requires him to restart the precomputation. For $\beta(f_t)^{-1} \cdot T_2 < |\mathcal{M}| \cdot \alpha(f_t) \cdot T_1$, these effects can be expected to be negligible, as there will be enough weak ciphertexts to avoid duplication. To take this observation into account one can add an additional constraint in the attack calculations using the following restriction on f_t: $\beta(f_t)^{-1} \cdot \alpha(f_t)^{-1} < |\mathcal{M}| \cdot T_1/T_2$.

Another possible obstacle for an attacker is the maximum depth D_{max} of the quantum computer used for the precomputation. Such depth limit reduces the Grover search success probability if $\sqrt{\alpha(f_t)^{-1}} \gg D_{max}$. This can be compensated for by splitting the search space in p partitions and performing a Grover search of depth D_{max} in each partition. Asymptotically one would need $\alpha(f_t)^{-1}/D_{max}^2$ partitions to find a weak ciphertext with probability close to 1.

Thus, when $\sqrt{\alpha(f_t)^{-1}} \leq D_{max}$, the maximum depth does not restrict the Grover search and the cost to find a weak ciphertext is $\sqrt{\alpha(f_t)^{-1}}$, but when $\sqrt{\alpha(f_t)^{-1}} > D_{max}$, the cost is $D_{max} \cdot \alpha(f_t)^{-1}/D_{max}^2 = \alpha(f_t)^{-1}/D_{max}$.

8 Results

We calculated the multitarget attack cost using the geometric-uneven approach for all parameter sets of Saber, Kyber and uSaber with a query limit of 2^{64} per target. In Table 3, we first give the attack cost for 2^{40} and 2^{64} targets following the procedure described until Sect. 6, where $|\mathcal{M}| = \infty$ and $D_{max} = \infty$.

We then recalculate the results for 2^{64} targets with the following restrictions: in a first instance $|\mathcal{M}| = 2^{256}$, which is the case for the current designs of these schemes, and a second instance $|\mathcal{M}|$ is taken equal to the equivalent AES strength, i.e. 2^{128} schemes that are in NIST category 1, 2^{192} for schemes in NIST category 3 and 2^{256} for schemes in NIST category 5. The maximum depth is in both cases set to $D_{max} = 2^{96}$, which is the worst case scenario put forward by NIST [1]. A graphical overview of the attack for all parameter sets of Saber and Kyber is given in the eprint version of this paper, where the full line represents $D_{max} = \infty$ and where the dotted line represents $D_{max} = 2^{96}$.

An interested reader can generate their own numbers and figures for specific constraints using the python source code, which is made available at https://github.com/KULeuven-COSIC/PQCRYPTO-decryption-failures.

8.1 Impact on Saber and Kyber

Before discussing the security impact of our attack on the targeted schemes, we want to go into some considerations considering the attack model. The failure boosting attack cost is expressed in terms of precomputational work $\mathcal{W}$ and queries $\mathcal{Q}$: $1\mathcal{W}$ refers to the cost of 1 offline encapsulation and the quantum speedup is assumed to be quadratic, ignoring subexponential costs; $1\mathcal{Q}$ describes the cost of 1 decapsulation, which is performed as classical computations.

In a real-life scenario, one needs to take into account the fact that $1\mathcal{Q}$ involves performing a decapsulation query online on the targets hardware, which might be a critical constraint in mounting a practical attack. For Saber, in an ideal scenario our attack requires at least 2^{98} queries and thus encapsulations performed on the attacked hardware for an attack that costs $2^{168}\mathcal{W}$. For the attack reported in Table 3, the query cost is 2^{126} queries.

Moreover, in the offline precomputation step one has to take into account the cost of performing the encapsulation ($1\mathcal{W}$). The Grover search is additionally constraint when considering a depth d for executing one encapsulation, leading to a cost of $\alpha(f_t)^{-1} \cdot d/D_{max}\mathcal{W}$ when $\sqrt{\alpha(f_t)^{-1}} > D_{max}/d$ where the cost of one encapsulation is still counted as $1\mathcal{W}$.

Our analysis shows that the category 3 instance of Saber is theoretically vulnerable for a decryption failure attack. A decryption failure attack on Saber would cost $2^{145}\mathcal{W}$ and $2^{126}\mathcal{Q}$ in the specific setting where $q_{limit} = 2^{64}$ and $T^{(0)} = 2^{64}$, which can be compared to the claimed 2^{172} coreSVP security. However, practical execution of the attack would not be straightforward due to the constraints outlined above. The other parameter sets of Saber and Kyber are not vulnerable to the decryption failure attack we developed, in case of Kyber1024 and FireSaber this is due to the constraints on the number of ciphertexts due to $|\mathcal{M}|$. The uSaber parameter sets are not vulnerable to the decryption failure attacks we developed, even without additional constraints.

8.2 Increasing the Attack Cost

One option to increase the attack cost could be to reduce $|\mathcal{M}|$. Such a design change does not incur an efficiency cost but is limited by the security of the overall scheme as a too low value for $|\mathcal{M}|$ could impact the security under traditional attacks. The effect of a reduction of $|\mathcal{M}|$ to 2^{128} and 2^{192} for schemes of

Table 3. Cost of failure boosting attacks on various schemes. Security values are given $\log_2$. Empty cells indicate an attack is not possible in under $2^{256}\mathcal{W}$.

	Quantum sec.	$P[F]$	Single target	$T^{(0)} = 2^{40}$ $(\mathcal{W}/\mathcal{Q})$ $\lvert\mathcal{M}\rvert = \infty$, $D_{max} = \infty$		$T^{(0)} = 2^{64}$ $(\mathcal{W}/\mathcal{Q})$ $\lvert\mathcal{M}\rvert = \infty$, $D_{max} = \infty$		$T^{(0)} = 2^{64}$ $(\mathcal{W}/\mathcal{Q})$ $\lvert\mathcal{M}\rvert = 2^{256}$, $D_{max} = 2^{96}$		$T^{(0)} = 2^{64}$ $(\mathcal{W}/\mathcal{Q})$ $\lvert\mathcal{M}\rvert = \text{AES}^{\dagger}$, $D_{max} = 2^{96}$	
				Naive	Levelled	Naive	Levelled	Naive	Levelled	Naive	Levelled
LightSaber	107	2^{-120}	–	117/102	117/102	116/108	116/108	116/108	116/108	–	124/115
Saber [6]	172	2^{-136}	–	157/102	**157**/102	148/125	**141**/126	**148**/126	**141**/126	–	**144**/126
FireSaber	236	2^{-165}	–	–	–	–	**216**/126	–	–	–	–
Kyber512	107	2^{-139}	–	138/102	138/102	131/118	131/118	131/118	131/118	–	–
Kyber768 [27]	165	2^{-164}	–	208/102	208/102	187/112	175/126	–	186/126	–	–
Kyber1024	232	2^{-174}	–	–	–	–	**228**/126	–	–	–	–
uLightSaber	101	2^{-184}	–	–	–	–	–	–	–	–	–
uSaber [6]	165	2^{-167}	–	–	–	–	–	–	–	–	–
uFireSaber	232	2^{-154}	–	–	–	–	–	–	–	–	–
Saber - $2t$	172	2^{-156}	–	213/102	213/102	180/126	**170**/126	–	174/126	–	–
Saber - $4t$	172	2^{-165}	–	247/102	247/102	196/126	187/126	–	215/126	–	–

† $\lvert\mathcal{M}\rvert$ taken equal to the number of messages in the corresponding AES instance i.e. 2^{128} schemes that are in NIST category 1, 2^{192} for schemes in NIST category 3 and 2^{256} for schemes in NIST category 5.

category 1 and 3 respectively is detailed in the last column of Table 3. Note that this change will especially restrain the efficiency of finding follow up failures, as the term $|\mathcal{M}| \cdot T_1/T_2$ is typically much higher for finding the first failure due to a high value of the number of targets T_1. Therefore, a reduction in $|\mathcal{M}|$ is also a good precaution for future advances in decryption failure attacks as will be discussed in Subsect. 8.3.

Looking at the error term $(\mathbf{e}+\mathbf{u})^T\mathbf{s}' - \mathbf{s}^T(\mathbf{e}'+\mathbf{u}')+(\mathbf{e}''+\mathbf{u}'')$, the compression error $\mathbf{u}''$ can be a significant factor in decryption failures in schemes with strong compression of $\mathbf{v}'$ (i.e. large q/t). In this case the attack cost can be increased by increasing t. This comes at a modest cost in ciphertext size, but generally has no impact on the security of the scheme under non-decryption failure attacks. For Saber, increasing t to $2t$ would make the attack more expensive than solving the Mod-LWR problem while increasing the ciphertext size with only 256 bits. The impact of such a change for Saber is given in the last rows of Table 3.

If increasing t is not sufficient, one needs to adapt the distributions of χ_s and χ_e, which would impact both security as design and thus would require a more in-depth analysis.

8.3 Possible Future Advances

In this subsection we go into detail on possible future advances in failure boosting and its cost estimations.

Failure Boosting The cost calculation of failure boosting takes into account both $\mathcal{C}$ and $\mathcal{G}$ and makes two assumptions. The first being that errors at different coefficients of the message are independent, which has been shown by D'Anvers et al. [13] to be a valid assumption for schemes without error correction. The second being the Gaussian assumption as discussed in Subsect. 3.2. As a result, the attack cost calculation of failure boosting is nearly optimal in the failure boosting framework.

Directional Failure Boosting The directional failure boosting calculation uses more assumptions and approximations that make the estimate less accurate. Specifically, the attack relies on two assumptions: The geometric-uneven assumption states that the distributions of $\mathcal{S}_0$, $\mathcal{C}_0$, $\mathcal{S}_1$ and $\mathcal{C}_1$ are multivariate Gaussian distributed with zero mean and equal variance for each coefficient. This is a fairly good approximation for binomial distributions with large variance, but is less accurate for small variance binomial distributions or uniform distributions as is the case in Kyber and Saber. The second assumption is the independency assumption that is also used in the failure boosting calculation and is valid for schemes without error correction.

Furthermore, the directional failure boosting calculation in this work considers a slightly suboptimal attack as some terms are not taken into account in the weak ciphertext selection criterion: First, the attack does not take into account $\mathcal{G}$ in the weak key selection (but it does for the failure probability calculation). Secondly, it removes the bias of $\mathcal{S}_0$ and $\mathcal{C}_1$ due to rounding, and adds it to the term $\mathcal{G}$ as explained in Subsect. 6.3. Therefore, the above approximations correspond to executable attacks, but the attack is slightly suboptimal as a better weak ciphertext selection criterion (e.g. taking $\mathcal{G}$ into account) would lead to a more efficient attack.

Finally, the directional failure boosting calculation makes two significant approximations: First, in the geometric-uneven directional failure boosting approach, only the error probability of the first bit of the message is considered. This would lead to an underestimation of the failure probability and thus an overestimation of the attack cost. Secondly, the distributions of the different variables are approximated using a limited number of points.

The previous assumptions and approximations are necessary to allow efficient calculation of the attack cost. However, they could result in a less optimal attack and a less accurate cost estimation for directional failure boosting. During the development of our cost estimation methods in Sects. 5 and 6 we showed that our calculation methods are still reasonably accurate using three checks:

First we checked the failure probability when no precalculation is performed, which should correspond to the failure probability of the scheme. As shown in the paper, this is always approximately the case for our cost estimation methods (but not in case of Saber or Kyber in the geometric case, which led us to argue that this method is not appropriate for Saber or Kyber).

Secondly, we checked our geometric and geometric-uneven methods in the failure boosting case using the more accurate Gaussian approximation, where we could see that our newly developed methods give approximately the same result. Note that this comparison is not possible in the directional failure boosting case.

Thirdly, we verified the geometric-uneven method using the geometric method in case of Katana. As the latter method makes less approximations and as its assumptions are valid for Katana, this comparison can be used to verify some of the new assumptions (i.e. removing the bias in Subsect. 6.3 and only considering errors at the first coefficient in Subsect. 6.1) made in the geometric-uneven method compared to the geometric method.

Table 4. Cost ($\log_2$) of obtaining the first and second failure in our multitarget attack and cost of obtaining only the first failure if the second failure would be free. $q_{limit} = 2^{64}$ and $T^{(0)} = 2^{64}$. Text is made bold for dominating factor in the attack cost. When performing a levelled multitarget attack where $T^{(1)} \neq 1$, the search for the second failure is considered dominant.

	Full attack		First failure
	$\mathcal{W}_0/\mathcal{Q}_0$	$\mathcal{W}_1/\mathcal{Q}_1$	$\mathcal{W}_0/\mathcal{Q}_0$
LightSaber	**116/108**	104/62	116/108
Saber	140/126	**140/68**	133/125
FireSaber	215/126	**215/68**	188/128
Kyber512	**131/118**	129/62	131/118
Kyber768	174/126	**175/69**	161/128
Kyber1024	228/126	**219/71**	191/128

Conclusion For schemes where the attack cost is dominated by finding the first failure, the calculated cost will be close to the optimal decryption failure attack cost (unless a radical new attack is discovered that outperforms failure boosting). For schemes with an attack cost dominated by directional failure boosting, the estimation will be less accurate. In a worst case attack scenario (from the designers perspective) one could assume the directional failure boosting cost to be reduced even more, leading to an attack that is essentially dominated by finding the first failure. Note that this is a very conservative approach and does not correspond to an existing attack scenario. An overview of the dominant attack costs can be found in Table 4.

References

1. Submission requirements and evaluation criteria for the post-quantum cryptography standardization process (2016). https://csrc.nist.gov/CSRC/media/Projects/Post-Quantum-Cryptography/documents/call-for-proposals-final-dec-2016.pdf
2. Albrecht, M.R., et al.: Estimate all the LWE, NTRU schemes!. In: SCN 18, LNCS (2018)
3. Albrecht, M.R., Player, R., Scott, S.: On the concrete hardness of learning with errors. J. Math. Cryptol. **9**(3), 169–203 (2015)
4. Bai, S., Galbraith, S.D.: An improved compression technique for signatures based on learning with errors. In: Benaloh, J. (eds.) Topics in Cryptology. LNCS, vol. 8366. Springer, Cham (2014). https://doi.org/10.1007/978-3-319-04852-9_2
5. Banerjee, A., Peikert, C., Rosen, A.: Pseudorandom functions and lattices. In: Pointcheval, D., Johansson, T. (eds.) LNCS, vol. 7237, pp. 719–737. Springer, Heidelberg (2012). https://doi.org/10.1007/978-3-642-29011-4_42
6. Basso, A., et al.: SABER. Technical report, national institute of standards and technology (2020). https://csrc.nist.gov/projects/post-quantum-cryptography/round-3-submissions
7. Bindel, N., Schanck, J.M.: Decryption failure is more likely after success. In: Ding, J., Tillich, J.P. (eds.) Post-Quantum Cryptography. PQCrypto 2020. LNCS, vol. 12100. Springer, Cham (2020). https://doi.org/10.1007/978-3-030-44223-1_12
8. Bos, J., et al.: CRYSTALS - Kyber: a CCA-secure module-lattice-based KEM. IACR ePrint, 634 (2020)
9. Dachman-Soled, D., Ducas, L., Gong, H., Rossi, M.: LWE with side information: attacks and concrete security estimation. In: CRYPTO 2020, Part II, LNCS (2020)
10. D'Anvers, J.P., Karmakar, A., Sinha Roy, S., Vercauteren, F.: Saber: module-LWR based key exchange, CPA-Secure encryption and CCA-Secure KEM. In: Joux, A., Nitaj, A., Rachidi, T. (eds.) Progress in Cryptology. LNCS, vol. 10831. Springer, Cham (2018). https://doi.org/10.1007/978-3-319-89339-6_16
11. D'Anvers, J.P., Rossi, M., Virdia, F.: (One) Failure is not an option: bootstrapping the search for failures in lattice-based encryption schemes. In: Canteaut, A., Ishai, Y. (eds.) Advances in Cryptology. LNCS, vol. 12107. Springer, Cham. https://doi.org/10.1007/978-3-030-45727-3_1
12. D'Anvers, J.-P., Vercauteren, F., Verbauwhede, I.: On the impact of decryption failures on the security of LWE/LWR based schemes. Cryptology ePrint Archive, Report 2018/1089 (2018). https://eprint.iacr.org/2018/1089

13. D'Anvers, J.-P., Vercauteren, F., Verbauwhede, I.: The impact of error dependencies on ring/mod-LWE/LWR based schemes. In: Post-Quantum Cryptography - 10th International Conference, PQCrypto 2019 (2019)
14. Dent, A.W.: A Designer's guide to KEMs. In: Paterson, K.G. (eds.) Cryptography and Coding. Cryptography and Coding 2003. LNCS, vol. 2898. Springer, Heidelberg (2003). https://doi.org/10.1007/978-3-540-40974-8_12
15. Fujisaki, E., Okamoto, T.: Secure integration of asymmetric and symmetric encryption schemes. J. Cryptol. (1) (2013)
16. Gentry, C., Boneh, D.: A fully homomorphic encryption scheme. Stanford University Stanford (2009)
17. Gentry, C., Peikert, C., Vaikuntanathan, V.: Trapdoors for hard lattices and new cryptographic constructions. In: STOC 2008. ACM (2008)
18. Guo, Q., Johansson, T., Nilsson, A.: A generic attack on lattice-based schemes using decryption errors with application to ss-ntru-pke. Cryptology ePrint Archive, Report 2019/043 (2019). https://eprint.iacr.org/2019/043
19. Guo, Q., Johansson, T., Yang, J.: A novel CCA attack using decryption errors against LAC. In: Galbraith, S., Moriai, S. (eds.) Advances in Cryptology. LNCS, vol. 11921. Springer, Cham (2019). https://doi.org/10.1007/978-3-030-34578-5_4
20. Hofheinz, D., Hovelmanns, K., Kiltz, E.: A modular analysis of the Fujisaki-Okamoto transformation. In: Kalai, Y., Reyzin, L. (eds.) Theory of Cryptography. TCC 2017. LNCS, vol. 10677. Springer, Cham (2017). https://doi.org/10.1007/978-3-319-70500-2_12
21. Jaulmes, É., Joux, A.: A chosen-ciphertext attack against NTRU. In: Bellare, M. (ed.) CRYPTO 2000. LNCS, vol. 1880, pp. 20–35. Springer, Heidelberg (2000). https://doi.org/10.1007/3-540-44598-6_2
22. Langlois, A., Stehle, D.: Worst-case to average-case reductions for module lattices. Des. Codes Cryptogr. **75**, 565–599 (2015). https://doi.org/10.1007/s10623-014-9938-4
23. Lyubashevsky, V.: Fiat-shamir with aborts: applications to lattice and factoring-based signatures. In: ASIACRYPT (2009)
24. Lyubashevsky, V., Peikert, C., Regev, O.: On Ideal Lattices and Learning with Errors over Rings. In: Gilbert, H. (ed.) EUROCRYPT 2010. LNCS, vol. 6110, pp. 1–23. Springer, Heidelberg (2010). https://doi.org/10.1007/978-3-642-13190-5_1
25. Naehrig, M., et al.: Technical report, NIST (2017)
26. Regev, O.: On lattices, learning with errors, random linear codes, and cryptography. ACM, In: STOC (2005)
27. Schwabe, P., et al.: CRYSTALS-KYBER. technical report, national institute of standards and technology (2020). https://csrc.nist.gov/projects/post-quantum-cryptography/round-3-submissions
28. Targhi, E.E., Unruh, D.: Post-quantum security of the Fujisaki-Okamoto and OAEP transforms. In: Hirt, M., Smith, A. (eds.) Theory of Cryptography. TCC 2016. LNCS, vol. 9986. Springer, Heidelberg (2016). https://doi.org/10.1007/978-3-662-53644-5_8

Post-quantum Security of Plain OAEP Transform

Ehsan Ebrahimi(✉)

Department of Computer Science, University of Luxembourg, Esch-sur-Alzette, Luxembourg
ehsan.ebrahimi@uni.lu

Abstract. In this paper, we show that OAEP transform is indistinguishable under chosen ciphertext attack in the quantum random oracle model if the underlying trapdoor permutation is quantum partial-domain one-way. The existing post-quantum security of OAEP (TCC 2016-B [14]) requires a modification to the OAEP transform using an extra hash function. We prove the security of the OAEP transform without any modification and this answers an open question in one of the finalists of NIST competition, NTRU submission [6], affirmatively.

Keywords: Post-quantum Security · OAEP · Quantum Random Oracle Model

1 Introduction

The rapid progress on quantum computing and the existence of quantum algorithms like Shor's algorithm [12] has sparked the necessity of replacing old cryptography with post-quantum cryptography. Toward this goal, the National Institute of Standards and Technology (NIST) has initiated a competition for post-quantum cryptography. In this paper we address an open question in one of the finalists of NIST competition, NTRU submission [6]. The security of (unmodified) Optimal Asymmetric Encryption Padding (OAEP) in the quantum random oracle model has been mentioned as an interesting open question in [6][1]. The existing post-quantum security proof of OAEP [14] requires a modification to OAEP transform. (See details below.)

The random oracle model [1] is a powerful model in which the security of a cryptographic scheme is proven assuming the existence of a truly random function that is accessible by all parties including the adversary. But in real world applications, the random oracle will be replaced with a cryptographic hash function and the code of this function is public and known to the adversary. Following [4], we use the quantum random oracle model in which the adversary can make queries to the random oracle in superposition (that is, given a superposition of inputs, he can get a superposition of output values). This is necessary since a

[1] In the Subsect. 2.4.5 (titled: An IND-CCA2 PKE using Q-OAEP) of the version dated September 2020.

G. Hanaoka et al. (Eds.): PKC 2022, LNCS 13177, pp. 34–51, 2022.
https://doi.org/10.1007/978-3-030-97121-2_2

quantum adversary attacking a scheme based on a real hash function is necessarily able to evaluate that function in superposition. Hence the random oracle model must reflect that ability if one requests post-quantum security.

Bellare and Rogaway [2] proposed OAEP transform, for converting a trapdoor permutation into a public-key encryption scheme using two random oracles. It was believed that the OAEP-cryptosystem is provable secure in the random oracle model based on one-wayness of trapdoor permutation, but Shoup [13] showed it is an unjustified belief. Later, Fujisaki et al. [9] proved IND-CCA security of the OAEP-cryptosystem based on a stronger assumption, namely, partial-domain one-wayness of the underlying permutation.

Is OAEP transform secure in the standard model? A recent work to study this question [5] shows that a full instantiation of RSA-OAEP is only possible for two variants of RSA-OAEP (called 't-clear' and 's-clear'). Also, we emphasize that the positive results in [5] hold against a classical adversary and one needs to investigate the possibility of such instantiation in the post-quantum setting. For instance, the partial instantiations are based on algebraic properties of the RSA assumption that trivially does not hold in the post-quantum setting. Or the full instantiation of t-clear RSA-OAEP is based on non-standard assumptions (called 'XOR-type' assumptions) for which an intuitive justifications has been only given in light of the multiplicative structure of RSA, and etc. Even though the post-quantum instantiation of the random oracles in OAEP is a relevant research question, it is not in the scope of this paper and we leave a further investigation as an open question. Here, we investigate the security of OAEP transform in the quantum random oracle model.

Post-quantum security of OAEP transform has been studied in [14]. The authors modified OAEP transform (called it Q-OAEP) using an extra hash function that is length-preserving and show that Q-OAEP is IND-CCA secure in the quantum random oracle model. The extra hash function in Q-OAEP is used to extract the preimage of a random oracle queries in the security proof. In this work, we show that this extra hash function is unnecessary. We use Zhandry's compressed oracle technique [17] to prove IND-qCCA security of OAEP transform (without any modification) in the quantum random oracle model. IND-qCCA notion introduced in [3] is an adaptation of IND-CCA in which the adversary is allowed to make quantum decryption queries, but, the challenge query is restricted to be classical. Since security in the sense of IND-qCCA implies IND-CCA security, our result answers an open question in one of the finalists of NIST competition, NTRU [6], affirmatively.

Note that in the IND-qCCA notion, the adversary's challenge queries are restricted to be classical. Proposing a quantum IND-CCA notion that grants the adversary the possibility of submitting quantum challenge queries is a challenging task with some partial successes [7,10]. We postpone verifying the security of OAEP transform in the sense of definitions in [7,10] until a definite definition is given.

Organization. In Sect. 2, we present some basics of quantum information and computation, security definitions needed in the paper and an introduction for the

Compressed Standard Oracle that has been introduced in [17] which we use in the paper. In Sect. 3, we present the OAEP scheme and show that it is IND-qCCA secure in the quantum random oracle model.

2 Preliminaries

Notations. Let MSP shows the message space. The notation $x \xleftarrow{\$} X$ means that x is chosen uniformly at random from the set X. For a natural number n, $[n]$ means the set $\{1, \cdots, n\}$. $\Pr[P : G]$ is the probability that the predicate P holds true where free variables in P are assigned according to the program in G. The function $\mathsf{negl(n)}$ is any non-negative function that is smaller than the inverse of any non-negative polynomial $p(n)$ for sufficiently large n. That is, $\lim_{n\to\infty} \mathsf{negl(n)} p(n) = 0$ for any polynomial $p(n)$. For a function f, f_x denotes the evaluation of f on the input x, that is $f(x)$. For a bit-string x of size more-than-equal k, $[x]_k$ are the k least significant bits of x and $[x]^k$ are the k most significant bits of x. For two bits b and b', $[b = b']$ is 1 if $b = b'$ and it is 0 otherwise.

2.1 Quantum Computing

We present basics of quantum computing in this subsection. The interested reader can refer to [11] for more information. For two vectors $|\Psi\rangle = (\psi_1, \psi_2, \cdots, \psi_n)$ and $|\Phi\rangle = (\phi_1, \phi_2, \cdots, \phi_n)$ in $\mathbb{C}^n$, the inner product is defined as $\langle \Psi, \Phi\rangle = \sum_i \psi_i^* \phi_i$ where ψ_i^* is the complex conjugate of ψ_i. Norm of $|\Phi\rangle$ is defined as $\| \, |\Phi\rangle \, \| = \sqrt{\langle \Phi, \Phi\rangle}$. The n-dimensional Hilbert space $\mathcal{H}$ is the complex vector space $\mathbb{C}^n$ with the inner product defined above. A quantum system is a Hilbert space $\mathcal{H}$ and a quantum state $|\psi\rangle$ is a vector $|\psi\rangle$ in $\mathcal{H}$ with norm 1. A unitary operation over $\mathcal{H}$ is a transformation $\mathbb{U}$ such that $\mathbb{U}\mathbb{U}^\dagger = \mathbb{U}^\dagger\mathbb{U} = \mathbb{I}$ where $\mathbb{U}^\dagger$ is the Hermitian transpose of $\mathbb{U}$ and $\mathbb{I}$ is the identity operator over $\mathcal{H}$. Norm of an operator $\mathbb{U}$ is $\|\mathbb{U}\| = \max_{|\psi\rangle} \|\mathbb{U}\,|\psi\rangle\|$. The computational basis for $\mathcal{H}$ consists of $\log n$ vectors $|b_i\rangle$ of length $\log n$ with 1 in the position i and 0 elsewhere. With this basis, the Hadamard unitary is defined as

$$\mathbb{H} : |b\rangle \to \frac{1}{\sqrt{2}}(|\bar{b}\rangle + (-1)^b \, |b\rangle),$$

for $b \in \{0,1\}$ where $\bar{b} = 1 - b$. The controlled-swap unitary is defined as

$$|b\rangle \, |\psi_0\rangle \, |\psi_1\rangle \to |b\rangle \, |\psi_b\rangle \, |\psi_{\bar{b}}\rangle,$$

for $b \in \{0,1\}$. The controlled-unitary $\mathbb{U}$ ($c\mathbb{U}$) is define as:

$$c\mathbb{U}|b\rangle \, |\Psi\rangle \to \begin{cases} |b\rangle\mathbb{U}\,|\Psi\rangle & \text{if } b = 1 \\ |b\rangle \, |\Psi\rangle & \text{if } b = 0 \end{cases}.$$

The bit-flip unitary $\mathbb{X}$ maps $|b\rangle$ to $|\bar{b}\rangle$ for $b \in \{0,1\}$. An orthogonal projection $\mathbb{P}$ over $\mathcal{H}$ is a linear transformation such that $\mathbb{P}^2 = \mathbb{P} = \mathbb{P}^\dagger$. A measurement on a

Hilbert space is defined with a family of projectors that are pairwise orthogonal. An example of measurement is the computational basis measurement in which any projection is defined by a basis vector. The output of computational measurement on a state $|\Psi\rangle$ is i with probability $\|\langle b_i, \Psi\rangle\|^2$ and the post measurement state is $|b_i\rangle$. For a general measurement $\{\mathbb{P}_i\}_i$, the output of this measurement on a state $|\Psi\rangle$ is i with probability $\|\mathbb{P}_i |\Psi\rangle\|^2$ and the post measurement state is $\frac{\mathbb{P}_i|\Psi\rangle}{\|\mathbb{P}_i|\Psi\rangle\|}$.

For two operators $\mathbb{U}_1$ and $\mathbb{U}_2$, the commutator is $[\mathbb{U}_1, \mathbb{U}_2] = \mathbb{U}_1\mathbb{U}_2 - \mathbb{U}_2\mathbb{U}_1$. For two quantum systems $\mathcal{H}_1$ and $\mathcal{H}_2$, the composition of them is defined by the tensor product and it is $\mathcal{H}_1 \otimes \mathcal{H}_2$. For two unitary $\mathbb{U}_1$ and $\mathbb{U}_2$ defined over $\mathcal{H}_1$ and $\mathcal{H}_2$ respectively, $(\mathbb{U}_1 \otimes \mathbb{U}_2)(\mathcal{H}_1 \otimes \mathcal{H}_2) = \mathbb{U}_1(\mathcal{H}_1) \otimes \mathbb{U}_2(\mathcal{H}_2)$. In this paper, QFT over an n-qubits system is $\mathbb{H}^{\otimes n}$.

If a system is in the state $|\Psi_i\rangle$ with the probability p_i, we interpret this with a quantum ensemble $E = \{(|\Psi_i\rangle, p_i)\}_i$. Different outputs of a quantum algorithm can be represented as a quantum ensemble. The density operator corresponding with the ensemble E is $\rho = \sum_i p_i|\Psi_i\rangle\langle\Psi_i|$ where $|\Psi_i\rangle\langle\Psi_i|$ is the operator acting as $|\Psi_i\rangle\langle\Psi_i| : |\Phi\rangle \to \langle\Psi_i, \Phi\rangle|\Psi_i\rangle$. The trace distance of two density operators ρ_1, ρ_2 is defined as $\mathrm{TD}(\rho_1, \rho_2) := \frac{1}{2}\operatorname{tr}|\rho_1 - \rho_2|$ where tr is the trace of a square matrix (the sum of entries on the main diagonal) and $|\rho_1 - \rho_2| := \sqrt{(\rho_1 - \rho_2)^\dagger(\rho_1 - \rho_2)}$. Note that the trace distance of two pure states $|\Psi\rangle, |\Phi\rangle$ is defined as $\mathrm{TD}(|\Psi\rangle\langle\Psi|, |\Phi\rangle\langle\Phi|)$.

Any classical function $f : X \to Y$ can be implemented as a unitary operator $\mathbb{U}_f$ in a quantum computer where $\mathbb{U}_f : |x, y\rangle \to |x, y \oplus f(x)\rangle$ and it is clear that $\mathbb{U}_f^\dagger = \mathbb{U}_f$. A quantum adversary has standard oracle access to a classical function f if it can query the unitary $\mathbb{U}_f$.

2.2 Definitions

Here, we define a public-key encryption scheme, the IND-qCCA security notion and the quantum partial-domain one-wayness.

Definition 1. *A public-key encryption scheme $\mathcal{E}$ consists of three polynomial-time (in the security parameter n) algorithms, $\mathcal{E} = (\mathrm{Gen}, \mathrm{Enc}, \mathrm{Dec})$, such that:*

1. Gen, *the key generation algorithm, is a probabilistic algorithm which on input 1^n outputs a pair of keys, $(pk, sk) \leftarrow \mathrm{Gen}(1^n)$, called the public key and the secret key for the encryption scheme, respectively.*
2. Enc, *the encryption algorithm, is a probabilistic algorithm which takes as input a public key pk and a message $m \in \mathsf{MSP}$ and outputs a ciphertext $c \leftarrow \mathrm{Enc}_{pk}(m)$. The message space, MSP, may depend on pk.*
3. Dec, *the decryption algorithm, is a deterministic algorithm that takes as input a secret key sk and a ciphertext c and returns the message $m := \mathrm{Dec}_{sk}(c)$. It is required that the decryption algorithm returns the original message, i.e., $\mathrm{Dec}_{sk}(\mathrm{Enc}_{pk}(m)) = m$, for every $(pk, sk) \leftarrow \mathrm{Gen}(1^n)$ and every $m \in \mathsf{MSP}$. The algorithm* Dec *returns $\perp$ if ciphertext c is not decryptable.*

In the following, we define the IND-qCCA security notion [3] in the quantum random oracle model. The IND-qCCA security notion for a public-key encryption scheme allows the adversary to make quantum decryption queries but the challenge query is classical. We define $\mathbb{U}_{\mathrm{Dec}}$ as:

$$\mathbb{U}_{\mathrm{Dec}}\,|c,y\rangle \to \begin{cases} |c, y\oplus \perp\rangle & \text{if } c^* \text{ is defined } \wedge\ c = c^* \\ |c, y\oplus \mathrm{Dec}_{sk}(c)\rangle & \text{otherwise} \end{cases},$$

where c^* is the challenge ciphertext and $\perp$ is a value outside of the output space. We say that a quantum algorithm $\mathcal{A}$ has quantum access to the random oracle H if $\mathcal{A}$ can submit queries in superposition and the oracle H answers to these queries by applying a unitary transformation that maps $|x,\ y\rangle$ to $|x,\ y\oplus H(x)\rangle$.

Definition 2 (IND-qCCA in the quantum random oracle model). *A public-key encryption scheme $\mathcal{E}$ = (Gen, Enc, Dec) is IND-qCCA secure if for any* ***quantum*** *polynomial-time adversary $\mathcal{A}$*

$$\Pr\left[b = 1 : b \leftarrow \mathsf{Exp}^{qCCA,qRO}_{\mathcal{A},\mathcal{E}}(n)\right] \le 1/2 + \mathit{negl}(n),$$

where $\mathsf{Exp}^{qCCA,qRO}_{\mathcal{A},\mathcal{E}}(n)$ game is define as:
$\mathsf{Exp}^{qCCA,qRO}_{\mathcal{A},\mathcal{E}}(n)$ game:

Key Gen: *The challenger runs* Gen(1^n) *to obtain a pair of keys (pk, sk) and chooses random oracles.*

Query: *The adversary $\mathcal{A}$ given the public key pk, the* ***quantum*** *oracle access to $\mathbb{U}_{\mathrm{Dec}}$ and the* ***quantum*** *access to the random oracles, chooses two* ***classical*** *messages m_0, m_1 of the same length and sends them to the challenger. The challenger chooses a random bit b and responds with $c^* \leftarrow \mathrm{Enc}_{pk}(m_b)$.*

Guess: *The adversary $\mathcal{A}$ continues to query the decryption oracle and the random oracles. Finally, the adversary $\mathcal{A}$ produces a bit b'. The output of the game is $[b = b']$.*

Definition 3 (Quantum partial-domain one-way function). *We say a permutation $f : \{0,1\}^{n+k_1} \times \{0,1\}^{k_0} \to \{0,1\}^m$ is quantum partial-domain one-way if for any polynomial-time quantum adversary A,*

$$\Pr\left[\tilde{s} = s : s \xleftarrow{\$} \{0,1\}^{n+k_1},\ t \xleftarrow{\$} \{0,1\}^{k_0},\ \tilde{s} \leftarrow A(f(s,t))\right] \le \mathit{negl}(n).$$

2.3 Compressed Standard Oracle

In this section, we briefly present the Compressed Standard Oracle (CStO) that has been introduced in [17]. The interested reader can refer to [8,17] for more details.

In the standard quantum random oracle model, a function $H : \{0,1\}^m \to \{0,1\}^n$ is chosen uniformly at random from the set of all functions (lets call it

Ω_H) and superposition queries will be answered by the unitary $\mathbb{U}_H$ that maps $|x,\ y\rangle$ to $|x,\ y \oplus H(x)\rangle$. Another perspective to consider this is that the oracle puts the superposition of all functions on his private register[2] and a query is implemented as

$$\mathsf{StO} : |x,\ y\rangle \sum_H \frac{1}{\sqrt{|\Omega_H|}} |H\rangle \rightarrow \sum_H \frac{1}{\sqrt{|\Omega_H|}} |x,\ y \oplus H(x)\rangle |H\rangle.$$

Note that if the oracle measures its internal state in the computational basis, this corresponds to choosing H uniformly at random from Ω_H and answer with $\mathbb{U}_H$. So these two oracles are perfectly indistinguishable. Now if we apply QFT to the output register before and after applying StO, we will get the Phase oracle that operates as follows:

$$\mathsf{PhO} : |x, y\rangle \sum_H \frac{1}{\sqrt{|\Omega_H|}} |H\rangle \rightarrow \sum_H \frac{1}{\sqrt{|\Omega_H|}} (-1)^{y \cdot H(x)} |x, y\rangle |H\rangle.$$

Let $\mathfrak{D}$ represent the truth table of the function H and $P_{x,y}$ represent the truth table of the point function that is y on the input x and it is zero elsewhere. With this notation we can write the query above as follows:

$$\mathsf{PhO} : |x,\ y\rangle \sum_{\mathfrak{D}} \frac{1}{\sqrt{|\Omega_H|}} |\mathfrak{D}\rangle \rightarrow \sum_{\mathfrak{D}} \frac{1}{\sqrt{|\Omega_H|}} (-1)^{P_{x,y} \cdot \mathfrak{D}} |x, y\rangle |\mathfrak{D}\rangle.$$

Now if the oracle applies QFT to the oracle register after applying PhO, it will get:

$$\mathsf{QFT}_{\mathfrak{D}}\mathsf{PhO} : |x,\ y\rangle \sum_{\mathfrak{D}} \frac{1}{\sqrt{|\Omega_H|}} |\mathfrak{D}\rangle \rightarrow |x, y\rangle |P_{x,y}\rangle.$$

Note that $\mathsf{QFT}_{\mathfrak{D}}$ only effects the oracle state and it is undetectable to the adversary. At this stage, the oracle will symmetrically store the inputs/outputs of the adversary's queries in its private register. Informally, if the oracle is able to move the entry that is not zero in the database $P_{x,y}$ to the beginning of its private register and remove all the zero slots (without the adversary's detection), the private register of the oracle can contain a polynomial number of registers[3].

$$\mathsf{RmoV}_{\mathfrak{D}}\mathsf{MoV}_{\mathfrak{D}}\mathsf{QFT}_{\mathfrak{D}}\mathsf{PhO} : \sum_{x,y} \alpha_{x,y} |x, y\rangle \sum_{\mathfrak{D}} \frac{1}{\sqrt{|\Omega_H|}} |\mathfrak{D}\rangle \rightarrow \sum_{x,y} \alpha_{x,y} |x, y\rangle |x, y\rangle.$$

Following the perspective above, Zhandry [17] developed the CStO that its private register can be implemented efficiently, symmetrically stores the inputs/outputs of the adversary's queries in its private register and it is perfectly indistinguishable from the standard oracle (StO).

Lemma 1 (Lemma 4 in [17]). CStO *and* StO *are perfectly indistinguishable.*

---

[2] This requires an exponential number of registers that is not efficient.

[3] This informal 'move' and 'remove' operations are detectable to the adversary and they are given only to build the intuition behind CStO.

For the rest, we import the representation of CStO from [8]. Let $\mathfrak{D} = \otimes_{x \in X} \mathfrak{D}_x$ be the oracle register. The state space of $\mathfrak{D}_x$ is generated with vectors $|y\rangle$ for $y \in Y \cup \{\bot\}$. Let $F_{\mathfrak{D}_x}$ be a unitary acting on $\mathfrak{D}_x$ that maps $|\bot\rangle$ to $\mathsf{QFT}\,|0\rangle$ and vice versa. And for any vector orthogonal to $|\bot\rangle$ and $\mathsf{QFT}\,|0\rangle$, F is identity. We define CStO to be the following unitary acting on the input register, the output register and the $\mathfrak{D}$ register.

$$\mathsf{CStO} = \sum_x |x\rangle\langle x| \otimes F_{\mathfrak{D}_x} CNOT_{Y\mathfrak{D}_x} F_{\mathfrak{D}_x},$$

where $CNOT_{Y\mathfrak{D}_x} |y, y_x\rangle = |y \oplus y_x, y_x\rangle$ for $y, y_x \in Y$ and it is identity on $|y, \bot\rangle$. The initial state of $\mathfrak{D}$ register is $\otimes_{x \in X} |\bot\rangle$.

We call a query to CStO 'dummy' if its output register is set to the uniform superposition. Note that for such a query $CNOT_{Y\mathfrak{D}_x}$ is identity and therefore CStO is identity.

In the following, we present preliminaries for Theorem 3.1 in [8] that will be used in the security proof in Sect. 3. For a fixed relation $R \subset X \times Y$, Γ_R is the maximum number of y's that fulfill the relation R where the maximum is taken over all $x \in X$:

$$\Gamma_R = \max_{x \in X} |\{y \in Y | (x, y) \in R\}|.$$

We define a projector $\Pi^x_{\mathfrak{D}_x}$ that checks if the register $\mathfrak{D}_x$ contains a value $y \neq \bot$ such that $(x, y) \in R$:

$$\Pi^x_{\mathfrak{D}_x} := \sum_{y \ s.t. \ (x,y) \in R} |y\rangle\langle y|_{\mathfrak{D}_x}.$$

Let $\bar{\Pi}^x_{\mathfrak{D}_x} = \mathbb{I}_{\mathfrak{D}_x} - \Pi^x_{\mathfrak{D}_x}$. We define the measurement $\mathbb{M}$ to be the set of projectors $\{\Sigma^x\}_{x \in X \cup \{\emptyset\}}$ where

$$\Sigma^x := \bigotimes_{x' < x} \bar{\Pi}^{x'}_{\mathfrak{D}_{x'}} \otimes \Pi^x_{\mathfrak{D}_x} \text{ for } x \in X \text{ and } \Sigma^\emptyset := \mathbb{I} - \sum_x \Sigma^x. \quad (1)$$

Informally, the measurement $\mathbb{M}$ checks for the smallest x for which $\mathfrak{D}_x$ contains a value $y \neq \bot$ such that $(x, y) \in R$. If no register $\mathfrak{D}_x$ contains a value $y \neq \bot$ such that $(x, y) \in R$, the outcome of $\mathbb{M}$ is $\emptyset$. We define a purified measurement $\mathbb{M}_{\mathfrak{D}P}$ corresponding to $\mathbb{M}$ that XORs the outcome of the measurement to an ancillary register:

$$\mathbb{M}_{\mathfrak{D}P} |\phi, z\rangle_{\mathfrak{D}P} \rightarrow \sum_{x \in X \cup \{\emptyset\}} \Sigma^x |\phi\rangle_{\mathfrak{D}} |z \oplus x\rangle_P.$$

The following lemma states that CStO and $\mathbb{M}_{\mathfrak{D}P}$ almost commute if Γ_R is small proportional to the size of Y.

Lemma 2 (Theorem 3.1 in [8]). *For any relation R and Γ_R defined above, the commutator $[\mathsf{CStO}, \mathbb{M}_{\mathfrak{D}P}]$ is bounded as follows:*

$$\|[\mathsf{CStO}, \mathbb{M}_{\mathfrak{D}P}]\| \leq 8 \cdot 2^{-n/2} \sqrt{2\Gamma_R}.$$

It has been shown that a quantum adversary needs an exponential number of quantum queries to a random oracle to find a collision [16]. As an immediate corollary, a random injective function is indistinguishable from a random oracle for a quantum polynomial-time adversary. We use this corollary in the security proof of OAEP.

Lemma 3 (From [16]). *Any quantum adversary making q queries to a random oracle $H : \{0,1\}^m \to \{0,1\}^n$ outputs a collision for H with probability at most $C(q+1)^3/2^n$ where C is a universal constant.*

In addition to the lemmas above, we use the 'gentle-measurement lemma' [15] in the proof. Informally, it states that if an output of a measurement is almost certain for a quantum state, the measurement does not disturb the state much.

Lemma 4 (gentle-measurement lemma). *Let $\mathbb{M} = \{\mathbb{P}_i\}_i$ is a measurement. For any state $|\Psi\rangle$, if there exists an i such that $\|\mathbb{P}_i |\Psi\rangle\|^2 \geq 1 - \epsilon$, then $\mathrm{TD}(|\Psi\rangle, \mathbb{M}|\Psi\rangle) \leq \sqrt{\epsilon} + \epsilon$.*

3 Security of OAEP

In this section, we define OAEP transformation and prove that it is IND-qCCA secure in the quantum random oracle model if the underlying trapdoor permutation is quantum partial-domain one-way. (Since IND-qCCA security trivially implies IND-CCA security, our result shows that OAEP transform is IND-CCA in the quantum random oracle model if the underlying trapdoor permutation is quantum partial-domain one-way.)

Definition 4 (OAEP). *Let $G : \{0,1\}^{k_0} \to \{0,1\}^{n+k_1}$, $H : \{0,1\}^{n+k_1} \to \{0,1\}^{k_0}$ be random oracles. The encryption scheme $OAEP = (\mathrm{Gen}, \mathrm{Enc}, \mathrm{Dec})$ is defined as:*

1. Gen*: Specifies an instance of the injective function f and its inverse f^{-1}. Therefore, the public key and secret key are f and f^{-1} respectively.*
2. Enc*: Given a message $m \in \{0,1\}^n$, the encryption algorithm computes*

$$s := m\|0^{k_1} \oplus G(r) \quad and \quad t := r \oplus H(s),$$

where $r \xleftarrow{\$} \{0,1\}^{k_0}$, and outputs the ciphertext $c := f(s,t)$[4]*.*
3. Dec*: Given a ciphertext c, the decryption algorithm does the following: Compute $f^{-1}(c) = (s,t)$ and then,*
   (a) query the random oracle H on input s, query the random oracle G on input $t \oplus H(s)$ and compute $M := s \oplus G(t \oplus H(s))$. In addition it submits two dummy queries to the random oracle G[5]*.*

[4] Q-OAEP in [14] outputs the ciphertext $c := (f(s,t), H'(s,t))$ for a fresh random oracle H'.

[5] Note that these dummy queries are required to make the number of queries submitted to G equal in the Games 1 and 2 in the security proof.

(b) if the k_1 least significant bits of M are zero then return the n most significant bits of M, otherwise return $\perp$.

Note that k_0 and k_1 depend on the security parameter n.

We prove the security of OAEP for the parameters $k_0 - n = O(n)$ (this is needed to show that Games 1 and 2 are indistinguishable) and $n + k_1 \geq k_0$ (because we need to replace the random oracle G with a random injective function in Game 1).

Here we sketch the main ideas to prove the IND-qCCA security of OAEP in the quantum random oracle. We start with the IND-qCCA game in QROM in which the adversary wins if he guesses the challenge bit b correctly. By introducing some (indistinguishable) intermediate games we reach the last game in which the adversary's success probability is 1/2. In the last game, the adversary is not allowed to query the randomness r^* that is used to obtain the challenge ciphertext c^*. (Since queries are quantum, this is prevented by measuring the input register of the queries to G by the projective measurement $\mathbb{M}_{r^*} = \{\mathbb{P}_1 = |r^*\rangle\langle r^*|, \mathbb{P}_0 = \mathbb{I} - \mathbb{P}_1\}$ and aborting if the outcome is 1.) Therefore, $G(r^*)$ is a random value for the adversary and $m_b||0^{k_1} \oplus G(r^*)$ hides the challenge bit b information-theoretically.

Note that at some steps of the proof, the indistinguishability of two games (specifically two last games in the proof) needs to be reduced to the partial-domain one-wayness of the underlying permutation. A reduction adversary to break the partial-domain one-wayness of the underlying permutation needs to answer the decryption queries without knowing f^{-1}. In this step, the reduction adversary uses the databases of the compressed standard oracles corresponding to the random oracles H, G for decryption. (On the input c it searches over the inputs/outputs of the random oracle queries in the databases of H, G that satisfies $c = f(s, r \oplus H_s)$ and $[G_r \oplus s]_{k_1} = 0^{k_1}$ and outputs $[G_r \oplus s]^n$.) However, it is not straightforward to show that this new decryption algorithm is indistinguishable from the decryption algorithm of the OAEP scheme. This is because a decryption algorithm that uses the databases to decrypt may cause detectable effects on the databases. In other words, the extraction of data from the databases may be detectable to the adversary. Here we use Lemma 2 to show that the oracle can extract information from the databases without an adversary's detection. We show this indistinguishability by modifying the decryption algorithm of the OAEP scheme step by step to reach the decryption algorithm that only uses the databases.

Theorem 1. *If the underlying permutation is quantum partial-domain one-way, then the OAEP scheme is IND-qCCA secure in the quantum random oracle model.*

Proof. Let Ω_H and Ω_G be the set of all function $G : \{0,1\}^{k_0} \rightarrow \{0,1\}^{n+k_1}$ and $H : \{0,1\}^{n+k_1} \rightarrow \{0,1\}^{k_0}$, respectively. Let S_G shows the set of all injective functions from $\{0,1\}^{k_0}$ to $\{0,1\}^{n+k_1}$. Let A be a polynomial-time quantum adversary that attacks the OAEP-cryptosystem in the sense of IND-qCCA in the quantum random oracle model and makes at most q_H and q_G queries to the random oracles H and G respectively and q_{dec} decryption queries.

Game 0: This is IND-qCCA game in qROM, $\mathsf{Exp}^{qCCA,qRO}_{\mathcal{A},\mathcal{OAEP}}(n)$.

Game 0:

$$\begin{array}{l}\textbf{let } (pk, sk) \leftarrow \text{Gen}(1^n),\ r^* \xleftarrow{\$} \{0,1\}^{k_0},\ b \xleftarrow{\$} \{0,1\},\ H \xleftarrow{\$} \Omega_H, G \xleftarrow{\$} \Omega_G \\ \textbf{let } m_0, m_1 \leftarrow A^{H,G,\mathbb{U}_{\text{Dec}}}(pk) \\ \textbf{let } s^* := m_b||0^{k_1} \oplus G(r^*),\ t^* := r^* \oplus H(s^*),\ c^* := f(s^*, t^*) \\ \textbf{let } b' \leftarrow A^{H,G,\mathbb{U}_{\text{Dec}}}(c^*) \\ \textbf{return } [b = b']\end{array}$$

Game 1: In this game, we consider H is being implemented as the compressed standard oracles CStO_H and G is replaced with a random injective function.

Game 1:

$$\begin{array}{l}\textbf{let } (pk, sk) \leftarrow \text{Gen}(1^n),\ r^* \xleftarrow{\$} \{0,1\}^{k_0},\ b \xleftarrow{\$} \{0,1\},\ G \xleftarrow{\$} S_G \\ \textbf{let } m_0, m_1 \leftarrow A^{\mathsf{CStO}_H,G,\mathbb{U}_{\text{Dec}}}(pk) \\ \textbf{let } s^* := m_b||0^{k_1} \oplus G(r^*),\ t^* := r^* \oplus H(s^*),\ c^* := f(s^*, t^*) \\ \textbf{let } b' \leftarrow A^{\mathsf{CStO}_H,G,\mathbb{U}_{\text{Dec}}}(c^*) \\ \textbf{return } [b = b']\end{array}$$

Since CStO_H and the standard oracles StO_H are perfectly indistinguishable by Lemma 1, this change does not effect the adversary's success probability. And changing the random oracle G to a random injective function is distinguishable by a probability at most $C(q_G+3q_{dec}+2)^3/2^{n+k_1}$ by Lemma 3. (Each decryption query makes three random oracle queries to G, so the total number of queries to G is at most $q_G + 3q_{dec}$ plus 1 for the challenge query.)

Game 2: In this game we change $\mathbb{U}_{\text{Dec}}$ oracle to $\mathbb{U}_{\text{Dec}^{(1)}}$ described below. Let $\mathfrak{D}_H$ denotes the database of CStO_H. We define the relation R^H_c to be the set of all (s, H_s) such that $[G(H_s \oplus [f^{-1}(c)]_{k_0}) \oplus s]_{k_1} = 0^{k_1}$. Given the relation R^H_c, the projectors Σ^s_c for $s \in \{0,1\}^{n+k_1}$ and $\Sigma^{\emptyset}_c$ are defined similar to Eq. (1). Now the measurement $\mathbb{M}^H = \{\Sigma^s_c\}_{s\in\{0,1\}^{n+k_1}\cup\{\emptyset\}}$ checks if there exists a pair in $\mathfrak{D}_H$ satisfying the relation R^H_c or not. If there is more than one pair satisfying the relation R^H_c, the smallest s will be the output of $\mathbb{M}^H$. If there is no such a pair the output of $\mathbb{M}^H$ is $\emptyset$. Let $\mathbb{M}^c_{\mathfrak{D}_H,P_H}$ be the following purified measurement corresponding to $\mathbb{M}^H$:

$$\mathbb{M}^c_{\mathfrak{D}_H,P_H} |\phi, z\rangle_{\mathfrak{D}_H P_H} \to \sum_{s\in\{0,1\}^{n+k_1}\cup\{\emptyset\}} \Sigma^s_c |\phi\rangle_{\mathfrak{D}_H} |z \oplus s\rangle_{P_H}.$$

We define the unitary $\mathbb{M}_{\mathfrak{D}_H,P_H}$ that operates on the ciphertext, $\mathfrak{D}_H$ and P_H registers as:

$$\mathbb{M}_{\mathfrak{D}_H,P_H} |c\rangle |\phi, z\rangle_{\mathfrak{D}_H P} \to |c\rangle \otimes \mathbb{M}^c_{\mathfrak{D}_H,P_H} |\phi, z\rangle_{\mathfrak{D}_H P_H}.$$

Note that $\mathbb{M}_{\mathfrak{D}_H,P_H}$ is an involution, that is, $\mathbb{M}_{\mathfrak{D}_H,P_H}\mathbb{M}_{\mathfrak{D}_H,P_H} = \mathbb{I}$. For each decryption query, $\mathbb{U}_{\mathrm{Dec}^{(1)}}$ first applies the $\mathbb{M}_{\mathfrak{D}_H,P_H}$ unitary with the P_H register initiated with 0. Then it executes $\mathbb{U}_{\mathrm{Dec}}$ without submitting the two dummy queries to the random oracle G. We denote this slightly modified decryption algorithm by $\mathbb{U}'_{\mathrm{Dec}}$. (We omit these dummy queries since $\mathbb{M}_{\mathfrak{D}_H,P_H}$ makes two queries to G in each decryption query.) Finally it applies the $\mathbb{M}_{\mathfrak{D}_H,P_H}$ again.

$$\mathbb{U}_{\mathrm{Dec}^{(1)}} = \mathbb{M}_{\mathfrak{D}_H,P_H}\ \mathbb{U}'_{\mathrm{Dec}}\ \mathbb{M}_{\mathfrak{D}_H,P_H}.$$

Game 2:

> **let** $(pk, sk) \leftarrow \mathrm{Gen}(1^n)$, $r^* \xleftarrow{\$} \{0,1\}^{k_0}$, $b \xleftarrow{\$} \{0,1\}$, $G \xleftarrow{\$} S_G$
> **let** $m_0, m_1 \leftarrow A^{\mathsf{CStO}_H, G, \mathbb{U}_{\mathrm{Dec}^{(1)}}}(pk)$
> **let** $s^* := m_b||0^{k_1} \oplus G(r^*)$, $t^* := r^* \oplus H(s^*)$, $c^* := f(s^*, t^*)$
> **let** $b' \leftarrow A^{\mathsf{CStO}_H, G, \mathbb{U}_{\mathrm{Dec}^{(1)}}}(c^*)$
> **return** $[b = b']$

We prove $\mathbb{M}_{\mathfrak{D}_H,P_H}$ and $\mathbb{U}'_{\mathrm{Dec}}$ almost commute to show the indistinguishability of these two games. Note that $\mathbb{M}_{\mathfrak{D}_H,P_H}$ only interfaces with $\mathbb{U}'_{\mathrm{Dec}}$ when $\mathbb{U}'_{\mathrm{Dec}}$ makes a query to the random oracle H. In other words, the reason that $\mathbb{M}_{\mathfrak{D}_H,P_H}$ does not commute with $\mathbb{U}'_{\mathrm{Dec}}$ is that $\mathbb{U}'_{\mathrm{Dec}}$ makes a random oracle query to H in each decryption query. By Lemma 2, if we commute $\mathbb{M}^{c}_{\mathfrak{D}_H,P_H}$ and $\mathbb{U}_{\mathrm{Dec}}$, this will be distinguishable to the adversary with a probability at most $8 \cdot 2^{-\frac{k_0}{2}}\sqrt{2\Gamma_{R^c_H}}$. Since G is an injective function $\Gamma_{R^c_H} = 2^n$. Therefore the distinguishing advantage of the adversary is at most $2^{\frac{n-k_0}{2}+\frac{7}{2}}$ that is negligible because $k_0 - n = O(n)$. The overall advantage of the adversary in distinguishing these two games is at most $q_{dec}2^{\frac{n-k_0}{2}+\frac{7}{2}}$.

Game 3: In this game we replace the random injective function with a compressed standard oracle CStO_G. (First we replace the random injective function with a random oracle and then we change it to a compressed standard oracle. We do these two changes in one game in favor of reducing the total number of games in the proof.)

Game 3:

> **let** $(pk, sk) \leftarrow \mathrm{Gen}(1^n)$, $r^* \xleftarrow{\$} \{0,1\}^{k_0}$, $b \xleftarrow{\$} \{0,1\}$,
> **let** $m_0, m_1 \leftarrow A^{\mathsf{CStO}_H, \mathsf{CStO}_G, \mathbb{U}_{\mathrm{Dec}^{(1)}}}(pk)$
> **let** $s^* := m_b||0^{k_1} \oplus G(r^*)$, $t^* := r^* \oplus H(s^*)$, $c^* := f(s^*, t^*)$
> **let** $b' \leftarrow A^{\mathsf{CStO}_H, \mathsf{CStO}_G, \mathbb{U}_{\mathrm{Dec}^{(1)}}}(c^*)$
> **return** $[b = b']$

Replacing the random injective function with a random oracle G is distinguishable with a probability at most $C(q_G+3q_{dec}+1)^3/2^{n+k_1}$ by Lemma 3. Then, a random oracle G is perfectly indistinguishable from a CStO_G by Lemma 1.

Game 4: In this game we change $\mathbb{U}_{\mathrm{Dec}^{(1)}}$ oracle to $\mathbb{U}_{\mathrm{Dec}^{(2)}}$ described below. Let $\mathfrak{D}_G$ denotes the database of CStO_G. We define the relation R_c^G to be the set of all (r, G_r) such that $[[f^{-1}(c)]^{n+k_1} \oplus G_r]_{k_1} = 0^{k_1}$. Given the relation R_c^G, the projectors Σ_c^r for $r \in \{0,1\}^{k_0}$ and $\Sigma_c^{\emptyset}$ are defined similar to Eq. (1). Now the measurement $\mathbb{M}^G = \{\Sigma_c^r\}_{r\in\{0,1\}^{k_0}\cup\{\emptyset\}}$ checks if there exists a pair in $\mathfrak{D}_G$ satisfying the relation R_c^G or not. If there are more than one pair satisfying the relation R_c^G, the smallest r will be the output of $\mathbb{M}^G$. If there is no such a pair the output of $\mathbb{M}^G$ is $\emptyset$. Let $\mathbb{M}^c_{\mathfrak{D}_G,P_G}$ be the following purified measurement corresponding to $\mathbb{M}^G$:

$$\mathbb{M}^c_{\mathfrak{D}_G,P_G} |\phi, z\rangle_{\mathfrak{D}_G P_G} \to \sum_{r\in\{0,1\}^{k_0}\cup\{\emptyset\}} \Sigma_c^r |\phi\rangle_{\mathfrak{D}_G} |z \oplus r\rangle_{P_G}.$$

We define the unitary $\mathbb{M}_{\mathfrak{D}_G,P_G}$ that operates on the ciphertext, $\mathfrak{D}_G$ and P_G registers as:

$$\mathbb{M}_{\mathfrak{D}_G,P_G} |c\rangle |\phi, z\rangle_{\mathfrak{D}_G,P_G} \to |c\rangle \otimes \mathbb{M}^c_{\mathfrak{D}_G,P_G} |\phi, z\rangle_{\mathfrak{D}_G P_G}.$$

Note that $\mathbb{M}_{\mathfrak{D}_G,P_G}$ is an involution. For each decryption query, $\mathbb{U}_{\mathrm{Dec}^{(2)}}$ first applies the $\mathbb{M}_{\mathfrak{D}_H,P_H}$ unitary with the P_H register initiated with 0. Then it applies the $\mathbb{M}_{\mathfrak{D}_G,P_G}$ unitary with the P_G register initiated with 0. Then it executes $\mathbb{U}'_{\mathrm{Dec}}$. And finally it applies $\mathbb{M}_{\mathfrak{D}_G,P_G}$ and $\mathbb{M}_{\mathfrak{D}_H,P_H}$ again.

$$\mathbb{U}_{\mathrm{Dec}^{(2)}} = \mathbb{M}_{\mathfrak{D}_H,P_H}\, \mathbb{M}_{\mathfrak{D}_G,P_G}\, \mathbb{U}'_{\mathrm{Dec}}\, \mathbb{M}_{\mathfrak{D}_G,P_G}\, \mathbb{M}_{\mathfrak{D}_H,P_H}.$$

Game 4:

let $(pk, sk) \leftarrow \mathrm{Gen}(1^n)$, $r^* \xleftarrow{\$} \{0,1\}^{k_0}$, $b \xleftarrow{\$} \{0,1\}$
let $m_0, m_1 \leftarrow A^{\mathsf{CStO}_H,\mathsf{CStO}_G,\mathbb{U}_{\mathrm{Dec}^{(2)}}}(pk)$
let $s^* := m_b||0^{k_1} \oplus G(r^*)$, $t^* := r^* \oplus H(s^*)$, $c^* := f(s^*, t^*)$
let $b' \leftarrow A^{\mathsf{CStO}_H,\mathsf{CStO}_G,\mathbb{U}_{\mathrm{Dec}^{(2)}}}(c^*)$
return $[b = b']$

In order to show the indistinguishability of two games, we show that $\mathbb{U}'_{\mathrm{Dec}}$ and $\mathbb{M}_{\mathfrak{D}_G,P_G}$ almost commutes (then $\mathbb{M}_{\mathfrak{D}_G,P_G}$ will cancel out with its second application and we will get $\mathbb{U}_{\mathrm{Dec}^{(1)}}$). Note that $\mathbb{U}'_{\mathrm{Dec}}$ does not commute with $\mathbb{M}_{\mathfrak{D}_G,P_G}$ because it makes a random oracle query to G in each decryption query. In other words, $\mathbb{U}'_{\mathrm{Dec}}$ would commute with $\mathbb{M}_{\mathfrak{D}_G,P_G}$ if $\mathbb{U}'_{\mathrm{Dec}}$ had not made a random oracle query to G. By Lemma 2, if we commute $\mathbb{M}^c_{\mathfrak{D}_G,P_G}$ and $\mathbb{U}_{\mathrm{Dec}}$, this will be distinguishable to the adversary with a probability at most $8 \cdot 2^{-\frac{n+k_1}{2}} \sqrt{2\Gamma_{R^c_G}}$. Since $\Gamma_{R^c_G} = 2^n$, the overall distinguishing advantage of the adversary is at most $q_{dec} 2^{-\frac{k_1}{2}+\frac{7}{2}}$.

Game 5: In this game we change $\mathbb{U}_{\text{Dec}^{(2)}}$ oracle to $\mathbb{U}_{\text{Dec}^{(3)}}$ described below. For each decryption query, $\mathbb{U}_{\text{Dec}^{(3)}}$ first applies $\mathbb{M}_{\mathfrak{D}_H,P_H}$ and then $\mathbb{M}_{\mathfrak{D}_G,P_G}$ with the P_H and P_G registers initiated with 0. Then, if c^* is defined and $c = c^*$ it XORs $\perp$ to the output register. Otherwise, if the P_H register contains $\emptyset$ or the P_G register contains $\emptyset$ it XORs $\perp$ to the output register and make a dummy query to the random oracles G, H. If the P_H and P_G registers do not contain $\emptyset$, it executes $\mathbb{U}'_{\text{Dec}}$:

$$|c,y\rangle\,|z_1\rangle_{P_H}\,|z_2\rangle_{P_G} \to \begin{cases} |c, y\oplus \perp\rangle\,|z_1\rangle\,|z_2\rangle & \text{if } c^* \text{ is defined } \wedge\ c = c^* \\ |c, y\oplus \perp\rangle\,|z_1\rangle\,|z_2\rangle & \text{if } z_1 = \emptyset \vee z_2 = \emptyset \\ |c, y \oplus \text{Dec}_{f^{-1}}(c)\rangle\,|z_1\rangle\,|z_2\rangle & \text{if } z_1 \neq \emptyset\ \wedge\ z_2 \neq \emptyset \end{cases}.$$

Finally, it applies the unitary $\mathbb{M}_{\mathfrak{D}_G,P_G}$ and $\mathbb{M}_{\mathfrak{D}_H,P_H}$.

Game 5:

> **let** $(pk, sk) \leftarrow \text{Gen}(1^n)$, $r^* \xleftarrow{\$} \{0,1\}^{k_0}$, $b \xleftarrow{\$} \{0,1\}$
> **let** $m_0, m_1 \leftarrow A^{\text{CStO}_H, \text{CStO}_G, \mathbb{U}_{\text{Dec}^{(3)}}}(pk)$
> **let** $s^* := m_b||0^{k_1} \oplus G(r^*)$, $t^* := r^* \oplus H(s^*)$, $c^* := f(s^*, t^*)$
> **let** $b' \leftarrow A^{\text{CStO}_H, \text{CStO}_G, \mathbb{U}_{\text{Dec}^{(3)}}}(c^*)$
> **return** $[b = b']$

We show that $\mathbb{U}_{\text{Dec}^{(2)}}$ and $\mathbb{U}_{\text{Dec}^{(3)}}$ algorithms are indistinguishable. Below, we recall a bit modified version of the decryption algorithm $\mathbb{U}_{\text{Dec}^{(2)}}$:

$$|c,y\rangle\,|z_1\rangle_{P_H}\,|z_2\rangle_{P_G} \to \begin{cases} |c, y\oplus \perp\rangle\,|z_1\rangle\,|z_2\rangle & \text{if } c^* \text{ is defined } \wedge\ c = c^* \\ |c, y \oplus \text{Dec}_{f^{-1}}(c)\rangle\,|z_1\rangle\,|z_2\rangle & \text{if } z_1 = \emptyset \vee z_2 = \emptyset \\ |c, y \oplus \text{Dec}_{f^{-1}}(c)\rangle\,|z_1\rangle\,|z_2\rangle & \text{if } z_1 \neq \emptyset\ \wedge\ z_2 \neq \emptyset \end{cases}.$$

Note that if for any ciphertext c for which $z_1 = \emptyset$ or $z_2 = \emptyset$, $\text{Dec}_{f^{-1}}$ (on input c) returns $\perp$ then the algorithms $\mathbb{U}_{\text{Dec}^{(2)}}$ and $\mathbb{U}_{\text{Dec}^{(3)}}$ return the same output in all three cases. In the claim below, we show that if $z_1 = \emptyset$ or $z_2 = \emptyset$, $\text{Dec}_{f^{-1}}(c)$ returns $\perp$ with an overwhelming probability. The high-level argument to prove this claim is that the adversary is not able to output a valid ciphertex (we call a ciphertext c valid if $\text{Dec}_{f^{-1}}(c) \neq \perp$) with an overwhelming probability unless it executes the encryption oracle, that is, unless it executes the random oracle queries. (Note that the ciphertex space is $\{0,1\}^{n+k_0+k_1}$ and the total number of the valid ciphertexts is 2^{n+k_0}. So a random ciphertext is a valid ciphertext with a probability at most $1/2^{k_1}$.) Then we show that if an adversary can distinguish these two games with a non-negligible probability, then a reduction adversary can output a valid ciphertext c for which $z_1 = \emptyset$ or $z_2 = \emptyset$ with a non-negligible probability and this is a contradiction to the claim shown below.

Claim. A ciphertext c for which $z_1 = \emptyset$ or $z_2 = \emptyset$ is a valid ciphertext with a probability at most $1/2^{k_1}$.

Proof. Let c is a ciphertext for which $z_1 = \emptyset$ and let $f^{-1}(c) = (s', t')$. Note that since $z_1 = \emptyset$, there is no pair (s, H_s) in $\mathfrak{D}_H$ that satisfies $[s \oplus G(H_s \oplus t')]_{k_1} = 0^{k_1}$. This means that either $[s' \oplus G(H_{s'} \oplus t')]_{k_1} \neq 0^{k_1}$ or the adversary has not queried the input s' to H. Clearly if $[s' \oplus G(H_{s'} \oplus t')]_{k_1} \neq 0^{k_1}$, $\mathrm{Dec}_{f^{-1}}(c) = \perp$ and c is an invalid ciphertext. And if s' has not been queried to H, $H_{s'}$ is a random value from the adversary's point of view. Therefore, $[s' \oplus G(t' \oplus H_{s'})]_{k_1} = 0^{k_1}$ holds with a probability at most $1/2^{k_1}$. That is, c is a valid ciphertext with a probability at most $1/2^{k_1}$.

Let c is a ciphertext for which $z_2 = \emptyset$ and let $f^{-1}(c) = (s', t')$. Note that since $z_2 = \emptyset$, there is no pair (r, G_r) in $\mathfrak{D}_G$ that satisfies $[s' \oplus G_r]_{k_1} = 0^{k_1}$. This means that either $[s' \oplus G(t' \oplus H_{s'})]_{k_1} \neq 0^{k_1}$ or the adversary has not queried the input $t' \oplus H_{s'}$ to G. If $[s' \oplus G_r]_{k_1} \neq 0^{k_1}$, $\mathrm{Dec}_{f^{-1}}(c) = \perp$ and c is an invalid ciphertext. If $t' \oplus H_{s'}$ has not been queried to G, since G is a random oracle, the probability that $[s' \oplus G(t' \oplus H_{s'})]_{k_1} = 0^{k_1}$ is at most $1/2^{k_1}$. That is, c is a valid ciphertext with a probability at most $1/2^{k_1}$. □

Now let $\mathcal{A}$ is an adversary that distinguishes these two games with a non-negligible advantage. That is, at least one of the $\mathcal{A}$'s decryption queries is of the form

$$\sum_{c_i \text{ for which } z_1=\emptyset \text{ or } z_2=\emptyset,\ j} \alpha_{i,j} |c_i\rangle |y_j\rangle + |\Psi\rangle,$$

where for any i $\mathrm{Dec}_{f^{-1}}(c_i) \neq \perp$ and $\sum_{i,j} \|\alpha_{i,j}\|^2$ is non-negligible. (Note that if there is no such a query, one can exclude the ciphertexts c_i for which $\mathrm{Dec}_{f^{-1}}(c_i) \neq \perp$ and $z_1 = \emptyset$ or $z_2 = \emptyset$ from the query using an appropriate projective measurement without the adversary's detection (by Lemma 4) in each decryption query and therefore two games will be indistinguishable.)

Now a reduction adversary $\mathcal{B}$ runs $\mathcal{A}$ and measures one of its decryption queries at random. It is clear that $\mathcal{B}$ is able to output a valid ciphertex c for which $z_1 = \emptyset$ or $z_2 = \emptyset$ with a non-negligible probability. And this is a contradiction to the claim above.

Game 6: The decryption algorithm $\mathbb{U}_{\mathrm{Dec}^{(3)}}$ in Game 5 searches over databases $\mathfrak{D}_H, \mathfrak{D}_G$ to find pairs $(s, H_s), (r, G_r)$ such that $[G(H_s \oplus [f^{-1}(c)]_{k_0}) \oplus s]_{k_1} = 0^{k_1}$ and $[[f^{-1}(c)]^{n+k_1} \oplus G_r]_{k_1} = 0^{k_1}$ respectively. Instead of using f^{-1}, we can simply search for pairs $(s, H_s), (r, G_r)$ that satisfy $c = f(s, r \oplus H_s)$ and $[G_r \oplus s]_{k_1} = 0^{k_1}$. In this game, we change $\mathbb{U}_{\mathrm{Dec}^{(3)}}$ a new decryption oracle $\mathbb{U}_{\mathrm{Dec}^{(4)}}$ that searches the databases $\mathfrak{D}_H$ and $\mathfrak{D}_G$ to decrypt. Let Search be a function that on input $(c, \mathfrak{D}_H, \mathfrak{D}_G)$ searches for the pairs (s, H_s) in $\mathfrak{D}_H$ and (r, G_r) in $\mathfrak{D}_G$ such that $c = f(s, r \oplus H_s)$ and $[G_r \oplus s]_{k_1} = 0^{k_1}$. If it finds such pairs, it returns $(1, [G_r \oplus s]^n)$, otherwise it returns $(0, \perp)$.

Let $Q_{b'}Q_m$ be quantum registers of size $(n+1)$ that are initiated with zero. The unitary $\mathbb{U}_{\mathrm{Dec}^{(4)}}$ first applies the unitary $\mathbb{U}_{\mathsf{Search}}$ where its output is stored in $Q_{b'}Q_m$ registers. Then it does as the following:

$$|c, y\rangle\,|b', m\rangle_{Q_{b'}Q_m} \to \begin{cases} |c, y \oplus \perp\rangle\,|b', m\rangle & \text{if } c^* \text{ is defined } \wedge\ c = c^* \\ |c, y \oplus \perp\rangle\,|b', m\rangle & \text{if } b' = 0 \\ |c, y \oplus m\rangle\,|b', m\rangle & \text{if } b' = 1 \end{cases},$$

it submits two dummy queries to the random oracle G in all cases, and it submits a dummy query to the random oracles G, H when $b' = 0$ and when $b' = 1$. Finally, it applies $\mathbb{U}_{\mathsf{Search}}$ to undo $Q_{b'}Q_m$ registers to zero.

Game 6:

> **let** $(pk, sk) \leftarrow \mathrm{Gen}(1^n)$, $r^* \xleftarrow{\$} \{0,1\}^{k_0}$, $b \xleftarrow{\$} \{0,1\}$
> **let** $m_0, m_1 \leftarrow A^{\mathsf{CStO}_H, \mathsf{CStO}_G, \mathbb{U}_{\mathrm{Dec}(4)}}(pk)$
> **let** $s^* := m_b || 0^{k_1} \oplus G(r^*)$, $t^* := r^* \oplus H(s^*)$, $c^* := f(s^*, t^*)$
> **let** $b' \leftarrow A^{\mathsf{CStO}_H, \mathsf{CStO}_G, \mathbb{U}_{\mathrm{Dec}(4)}}(c^*)$
> **return** $[b = b']$

We show that $\mathbb{U}_{\mathrm{Dec}(3)}$ and $\mathbb{U}_{\mathrm{Dec}(4)}$ are indistinguishable.

1. When c^* is defined and $c = c^*$, both algorithms XOR $\perp$ to the output register and make two random oracle queries to G.
2. When $b' = 0$, it is clear that either z_1 is $\emptyset$ or z_2 is $\emptyset$. Both algorithms XOR $\perp$ to the output register and make three random oracle queries to G and one random oracle query to H.
3. When $b' = 1$, it is clear that $z_1 \neq \emptyset$ and $z_2 \neq \emptyset$. So both algorithms XOR $[G_r \oplus s]^n$ to the output register and make three random oracle queries to G and one random oracle query to H.

Game 7: This is identical to Game 6, except it measures all the queries to CStO_G with the projective measurements $\mathbb{M}_{r^*}$. If there is an 1-output measurement, it aborts and returns a random bit.

Game 7:

> **let** $(pk, sk) \leftarrow \mathrm{Gen}(1^n)$, $r^* \xleftarrow{\$} \{0,1\}^{k_0}$, $b \xleftarrow{\$} \{0,1\}$
> $\mathbb{M}_{r^*} = \{\mathbb{P}_1 = |r^*\rangle\langle r^*|, \mathbb{P}_0 = \mathbb{I} - \mathbb{P}_1\}$,
> **run until** *there is an 1-output measurement with* $\mathbb{M}_{r^*}$
> | **let** $m_0, m_1 \leftarrow A^{\mathsf{CStO}_H, \mathsf{CStO}_G, \mathbb{U}_{\mathrm{Dec}(4)}}(pk)$
> | **let** $s^* := m_b || 0^{k_1} \oplus G(r^*)$, $t^* := r^* \oplus H(s^*)$, $c^* := f(s^*, t^*)$
> | **let** $b' \leftarrow A^{\mathsf{CStO}_H, \mathsf{CStO}_G, \mathbb{U}_{\mathrm{Dec}(4)}}(c^*)$
> **return** $[b = b']$

Let q_{G1} be the total number of queries submitted to G before the challenge query. Let q_{G2} be the total number of queries submitted to G after the challenge query. $(q_{G1} + q_{G2} = q_G + 3q_{dec}.)$ If there is no query to CStO_G with a non-negligible weight on the state $|r^*\rangle$, we can use Lemma 4 (gentle-measurement lemma) to show that these two games are indistinguishable. In more details, let ρ_i is the state of the i-th query (for $i \in [q_G + 3q_{dec}]$) and let $\mathbb{M}_{r^*}(\rho_i)$ returns 1 with the probability ϵ_i. By the gentle-measurement lemma, the trace distance between

$\mathbb{M}_{r^*}(\rho_i)$ and ρ_i is at most $\sqrt{\epsilon_i}+\epsilon_i$. So overall, these two games are distinguishable with the advantage of at most $2(q_G + 3q_{dec})\sqrt{\max_i\{\epsilon_i\}}$. Therefore, if $\max_i\{\epsilon_i\}$ is negligible, two games are indistinguishable.

Since r^* is a random value that has not been used before the challenge query $\mathbb{M}_{r^*}(\rho_i)$ returns 1 with a probability at most $1/2^{k_0}$ for any $i \in [q_{G1}]$. So the measurements before the challenge query are distinguishable with a probability at most $2q_{G1}\sqrt{2^{-k_0}}$ that is negligible.

It is left to show that the measurements after the challenge query are indistinguishable. Proof by contrary, let assume $\mathcal{A}$ makes a query to CStO_G after the challenge query with a non-negligible weight on $|r^*\rangle$. From $\mathcal{A}$, we can construct an adversary $\mathcal{B}$ that breaks the quantum partial-domain one-wayness of f. In more details, $\mathcal{B}$ on input $c^*\big(:= f(s^*,t^*)$ for uniformly random $s^*,t^*\big)$, chooses a random element i from $[q_{G2}]$ and a random bit b, runs the adversary $\mathcal{A}$, answers the random oracle queries and decryption queries using two compressed oracles CStO_H, CStO_G and finally it measures the input register of the i-th query to CStO_G and the database $\mathfrak{D}_H$ with the computational basis measurement, returns an output and aborts. In the following we describe $\mathcal{B}$ in more details.

Simulation of Random Oracle Queries. For H-queries, the adversary $\mathcal{B}$ uses CStO_H. For G-queries, $\mathcal{B}$ does as follows. Let G' be a random oracle with the same domain and co-domain as G. Let Find be an operator that on inputs $r, c^*, \mathfrak{D}_H$, checks if there exists a pair (s, H_s) in $\mathfrak{D}_H$ such that $c^* = f(s, r \oplus H_s)$. If there exists such a pair it returns $(1, s)$. Otherwise, it returns $(0, 0^{n+k_1})$. Note that since f is a permutation, the Find unitary either returns $(0, 0^{n+k_1})$ or returns $(1, s^*)$. For each query, $\mathcal{B}$ first applies Find operator with an ancillary register $Q_{b'}Q_s$ of $(1 + n + k_1)$ qubits initiated with zero. Then, if the query is conducted before the challenge query or the $Q_{b'}$ is set to 0, it forwards the query to $\mathsf{CStO}_{G'}$, otherwise, it XORs $m_b||0^{k_1} \oplus s^*$ to the output register:

$$G : |r, y\rangle\, |\mathfrak{D}_H\rangle \rightarrow \begin{cases} |r, y \oplus G'(r)\rangle & \text{if } m_b \text{ is not defined} \\ |r, y \oplus G'(r)\rangle & \text{if } \mathsf{Find}(r, c^*, \mathfrak{D}_H) = (0, 0^{n+k_1}) \\ |r, y \oplus (m_b||0^{k_1} \oplus s^*)\rangle & \text{if } \mathsf{Find}(r, c^*, \mathfrak{D}_H) = (1, s^*) \end{cases}.$$

And finally it applies the Find operator again. Since f is a permutation, there exists only one r such that $c^* = f(s^*, r \oplus H_{s^*})$ and that is r^*. For any $r \neq r^*$ the oracle G and the random oracle G' are the same, therefore, the simulation of G-queries will be indistinguishable from the random oracle G' unless the adversary submits a post-challenge query with a non-negligible weight on the state $|r^*\rangle$ and $\mathsf{Find}(r^*, c^*, \mathfrak{D}_H) = (1, s^*)$. (And if this happens, it breaks the quantum partial-domain one-wayness of f explained below.)

The Challenge Query. Upon receiving m_0 and m_1 from $\mathcal{A}$, the adversary $\mathcal{B}$ returns c^* as the challenge ciphertext. (Note that the way we simulate G-queries $G(r^*) := m_b||0^{k_1} \oplus s^*$ and $c^* = f(s^*, r^* \oplus H_{S^*})$ that is a perfect simulation of the challenge query.)

Simulation of Decryption Queries. $\mathcal{B}$ uses the oracle $\mathbb{U}_{\text{Dec}^{(4)}}$ on inputs $\mathfrak{D}_H$ and $\mathfrak{D}_{G'}$ for the decryption queries. Note that G and G' only differ on the input r^* for which $c^* = f(s^*, r^* \oplus H_{s^*})$. Since $\mathbb{U}_{\text{Dec}^{(4)}}$ on input c^* does not use its database and returns $\perp$, the simulation of the decryption queries is perfect.

Output of $\mathcal{B}$. The adversary $\mathcal{B}$ measures the $(q_{G1} + i)$-th random oracle query to CStO_G with $\mathbb{M}_{r^*}$ and the database $\mathfrak{D}_H$ with the computational basis measurement. Since there exists a query with a non-negligible weight on the state $|r^*\rangle$, the adversary $\mathcal{B}$ can obtain r^* with a non-negligible probability. Then, the adversary searches over the database $\mathfrak{D}_H$ to find a pair (s^*, H_{s^*}) such that $c^* = f(s^*, r^* \oplus H_{s^*})$. If it finds such a pair, it returns s^* as the partial inverse of f on c^* and aborts. Otherwise, it returns $s^* = G'(r^*) \oplus m_b||0^{k_1}$ as the partial inverse of f on the input c^*. (Note that when there is no pair (s^*, H_{s^*}) in $\mathfrak{D}_H$ such that $c^* = f(s^*, r^* \oplus H_{s^*})$, that is $\mathsf{Find}(r^*, c^*, \mathfrak{D}_H) = (0, 0^{n+k_1})$, the G-queries are answered with the random oracle G'. Therefore, the equation $c^* = f(x, r^* \oplus H(x))$ holds for $x = G'(r^*) \oplus m_b||0^{k_1}$.) Since f is quantum partial-domain one-way, Games 6 and 7 are indistinguishable.

Now, it is clear that Game 7 returns 1 with the probability 1/2 because if one of the measurements returns 1, the output of the game is a random bit. If none of the measurements return 1, $G(r^*)$ remains an uniformly random value for $\mathcal{A}$ and consequently $m_b||0^{k_1} \oplus G(r^*)$ is an uniformly random value for $\mathcal{A}$. So the probability that $\mathcal{A}$ guesses b is 1/2. Finally, since each two consecutive games are indistinguishable, the probability that $\mathcal{A}$ guesses b in Game 0 is $1/2 + \mathsf{negl(n)}$ and this finishes the proof of the theorem. □

Acknowledgment. We would like to thank anonymous reviewers for their useful comments and suggestions.

References

1. Bellare, M., Rogaway, P.: Random oracles are practical: a paradigm for designing efficient protocols. In: Denning, D.E., Pyle, R., Ganesan, R., Sandhu, R. S., Ashby, V.: (eds.), CCS '93, Proceedings of the 1st ACM Conference on Computer and Communications Security, Fairfax, Virginia, USA, pp. 62–73. ACM (1993)
2. Bellare, M., Rogaway, P.: Optimal asymmetric encryption. In: Santis, A.D., (ed.) Proceedings of the Advances in Cryptology - EUROCRYPT '94, Workshop on the Theory and Application of Cryptographic Techniques, LNCS, vol. 950, pp. 92–111. Springer, Cham (1994). https://doi.org/10.1007/BFb0053428
3. Boneh, D., Zhandry, M.: Secure signatures and chosen ciphertext security in a quantum computing world. In: Canetti, R., Garay, J. A., (eds.) Proceedings of the Advances in Cryptology - CRYPTO 2013–33rd Annual Cryptology Conference, LNCS, vol. 8043, pp. 361–379. Springer (2013). https://doi.org/10.1007/978-3-642-40084-1_21
4. Boneh, D., Dagdelen, O., Fischlin, M., Lehmann, A., Schaffner, C., Zhandry, M.: Random oracles in a quantum world. In: Lee, D.H., Wang, X. (eds.) Advances in Cryptology. LNCS, vol. 7073. Springer (2011). https://doi.org/10.1007/978-3-642-25385-0_3

5. Cao, N., O'Neill, A., Zaheri, M.: Toward RSA-OAEP without random oracles. In: Kiayias, A., Kohlweiss, M., Wallden, P., Zikas, V. (eds.) Public-Key Cryptography. LNCS, vol. 12110. Springer, Cham (2020). https://doi.org/10.1007/978-3-030-45374-9_10
6. Chen, C.: Ntru (2020). https://ntru.org
7. Chevalier, C., Ebrahimi, E., Vu, Q. H.: On the security notions for encryption in a quantum world. IACR Cryptol. ePrint Arch., 237 (2020)
8. Don, J., Fehr, S., Majenz, C., Schaffner, C.: Online-extractability in the quantum random-oracle model. Cryptology ePrint Archive, pp. 280 (2021). https://eprint.iacr.org/2021/280
9. Fujisaki, E., Okamoto, T., Pointcheval, D., Stern, J.: RSA-OAEP is secure under the RSA assumption. J. Cryptol. **17**(2), 81–104 (2004)
10. Gagliardoni, T., Krämer, J., Struck, P.: Quantum indistinguishability for public key encryption. IACR Cryptol. ePrint Arch., 266 (2020)
11. Nielsen, M.A., Chuang, I.L.: Quantum computation and quantum information (10th Anniversary edition). Cambridge University Press (2016)
12. Shor, P.W.: Polynomial-time algorithms for prime factorization and discrete logarithms on a quantum computer. SIAM J. Comput. **26**(5), 1484–1509 (1997)
13. Shoup, V.: OAEP reconsidered. In: Kilian, J., (ed.) Proceedings of the Advances in Cryptology - CRYPTO 2001, 21st Annual International Cryptology Conference, LNCS, Santa Barbara, California, USA, vol. 2139, pp. 239–259. Springer (2021)
14. Targhi, E.E., Unruh, D.: Post-quantum security of the Fujisaki-Okamoto and OAEP transforms. In: Hirt, M., Smith, A. (eds.) Theory of Cryptography. TCC 2016. LNCS, vol. 9986. Springer (2016). https://doi.org/10.1007/978-3-662-53644-5_8
15. Winter, A.J.: Coding theorem and strong converse for quantum channels. IEEE Trans. Inf. Theory, **45**(7), 2481–2485 (1999)
16. Zhandry, M.: A note on the quantum collision and set equality problems. Quantum Inf. Comput. **15**(7and8), 557–567 (2015)
17. Zhandry, M.: How to record quantum queries, and applications to quantum indifferentiability. In: Boldyreva, A., Micciancio, D. (eds.) Advances in Cryptology. LNCS, vol. 11693. Springer, Cham (2019). https://doi.org/10.1007/978-3-030-26951-7_9

On the Security of OSIDH

Pierrick Dartois[1,2(✉)] and Luca De Feo[2]

[1] Corps des Mines, Paris, France
pierrick.dartois@mines-paristech.fr
[2] IBM Research Europe, Zürich, Switzerland
pkc22@defeo.lu

Abstract. The Oriented Supersingular Isogeny Diffie–Hellman is a post-quantum key exchange scheme recently introduced by Colò and Kohel. It is based on the group action of an ideal class group of a quadratic imaginary order on a subset of supersingular elliptic curves, and in this sense it can be viewed as a generalization of the popular isogeny based key exchange CSIDH. From an algorithmic standpoint, however, OSIDH is quite different from CSIDH. In a sense, OSIDH uses class groups which are more structured than in CSIDH, creating a potential weakness that was already recognized by Colò and Kohel. To circumvent the weakness, they proposed an ingenious way to realize a key exchange by exchanging partial information on how the class group acts in the neighborhood of the public curves, and conjectured that this additional information would not impact security.

In this work we revisit the security of OSIDH by presenting a new attack, building upon previous work of Onuki. Our attack has exponential complexity, but it practically breaks Colò and Kohel's parameters unlike Onuki's attack. We also discuss countermeasures to our attack, and analyze their impact on OSIDH, both from an efficiency and a functionality point of view.

Keywords: Post-quantum cryptography · Isogenies · Cryptographic group actions

1 Introduction

Cryptographic group actions have recently attracted much interest owing to their supposed quantum-resistance and to their versatility. Brassard and Yung [9] initiated the study of group actions in cryptography, but it was Couveignes [15] and Rostovtsev and Stolbunov [36] who independently exhibited the first post-quantum key exchange based on a group action. The invention of CSIDH[1] [11], the first efficient post-quantum group action, spurred a wave of interest on the topic. Among the many applications of CSIDH, we may cite the signature scheme CSI-FiSh [6], threshold [19] and ring [5] signatures, oblivious transfer [20,30],

[1] The "Commutative Supersingular Diffie–Hellman", pronounced *sea-side*.

G. Hanaoka et al. (Eds.): PKC 2022, LNCS 13177, pp. 52–81, 2022.
https://doi.org/10.1007/978-3-030-97121-2_3

oblivious PRFs [7] and hash proof systems [2]. As of today, all known post-quantum group actions are obtained from isogenies of elliptic curves, either ordinary or supersingular, and are all understood as instances of the celebrated theory of *complex multiplication*.

Drawing inspiration from CSIDH, Colò and Kohel recently proposed a generalization they called OSIDH, for "Oriented Supersingular Diffie–Hellman" [14]. Like CSIDH, OSIDH is based on the action of the class group of a quadratic imaginary order on a set of supersingular curves. But while CSIDH's group action is fully determined by the Frobenius endomorphism, OSIDH's action is determined by an arbitrary endomorphism which they call an *orientation*. Besides the added technicalities involved in working with orientations, to complete a key exchange in OSIDH Alice and Bob need to exchange significantly more information than in CSIDH. Colò and Kohel conjectured nevertheless that this additional information does not adversely affect the security of the cryptosystem.

In this work, we present a new classical attack that casts doubts on the viability of OSIDH. Albeit exponential in complexity, we give evidence that it breaks in practice the parameters that Colò and Kohel suggested would match the security of CSIDH-512.[2] The only exponential step in our attack is an SVP computation in a lattice that depends exclusively on the system parameters. The attack can be countered by increasing the dimension of the lattice and the other parameters accordingly, however we argue that this patch is of dubious interest for post-quantum cryptography: besides making OSIDH prohibitively expensive, it makes it at best as secure as lattice based schemes, without the efficiency, the versatility and the security reductions that go with them.

A more advanced countermeasure is to stretch parameters to a point where, according to standard heuristics, no short enough vectors exist in the lattice. This countermeasure is less costly, yet we argue that it does not completely rescue OSIDH. Indeed, our attack shows that OSIDH fails at satisfying the standard axioms of a cryptographic group action, and thus powerful schemes such as CSI-FiSh [6] cannot be securely built on it. This pretty much confines OSIDH to the role of a key exchange of mostly theoretical interest, for the time being.

On the positive side, we argue that, because OSIDH is not properly speaking a cryptographic group action, Kuperberg's quantum algorithm does not appear to apply to it. It is conceivable, then, that the best quantum algorithm against OSIDH would have exponential, rather than subexponential, complexity.

1.1 Overview

The theory of complex multiplication establishes a link between the abelian extensions of quadratic imaginary number fields and elliptic curves. If $\mathcal{O}$ is an order in a quadratic imaginary number field, an elliptic curve is said to have complex multiplication (CM) by $\mathcal{O}$ when its endomorphism ring is isomorphic

---

[2] CSIDH-512 was originally claimed to match the NIST-1 security level. Recent works have questioned the quantum security of CSIDH [8,33], but to this day CSIDH-512's classical security claim still holds unchanged.

to $\mathcal{O}$. For example, ordinary curves over finite fields always have CM by some quadratic order.

An isogeny $\varphi : E \to E'$ between two curves with CM by the same order $\mathcal{O}$ is called *horizontal* [27]. The same way it identifies elements of $\mathcal{O}$ to endomorphisms, CM identifies (invertible) ideals of $\mathcal{O}$ to isogenies. Invertible fractional ideals of $\mathcal{O}$ form an abelian group, and their identification with isogenies defines a group action on the set of elliptic curves with CM by $\mathcal{O}$ by

$$\mathfrak{a} \cdot E := E',$$

where $\varphi_{\mathfrak{a}} : E \to E'$ is the isogeny associated to $\mathfrak{a} \subset \mathcal{O}$. By this definition, principal ideals of $\mathcal{O}$ act trivially, and the fundamental theorem of CM states that the ideal class group $\mathrm{Cl}(\mathcal{O})$—the quotient of the invertible by the principle ideals—acts faithfully and transitively on the set of elliptic curves with CM by $\mathcal{O}$. See [16,38,44] for more details.

The correspondence with isogenies lets us evaluate the action of $\mathrm{Cl}(\mathcal{O})$ effectively. A prime q that splits in $\mathcal{O}$ factors as a product $(q) = \mathfrak{q}\bar{\mathfrak{q}}$ of prime ideals of norm q. These are the only two ideals of norm q in $\mathcal{O}$, and to each corresponds an isogeny of degree q. As long as we can compute the two horizontal isogenies of degree q starting from E, we can thus evaluate the action of $\mathfrak{q}$ and $\bar{\mathfrak{q}}$. Which isogeny corresponds to which ideal can be determined by looking at how the Frobenius endomorphism of E acts on the kernels of the isogenies.

This is the idea at the heart of Couveignes' [15] and Rostovtsev and Stolbunov's [36] key exchange schemes: On the one hand the group action can be evaluated efficiently; on the other hand it is assumed to be hard, given two curves E, E' with CM by $\mathcal{O}$, to find the element $\mathfrak{a} \in \mathrm{Cl}(\mathcal{O})$ such that $\mathfrak{a} \cdot E = E'$, or, equivalently, a horizontal isogeny $\varphi : E \to E'$.

However, computing isogenies has complexity polynomial in the degree, and thus only for a small fraction of all ideals we can efficiently evaluate the CM action. We can work around this limitation by fixing a list of ideals of small norm $\mathfrak{q}_1, \mathfrak{q}_2, \dots, \mathfrak{q}_t$, and representing elements of $\mathrm{Cl}(\mathcal{O})$ as linear combinations of these generators:

$$\mathfrak{a} = \prod_{i=1}^{t} \mathfrak{q}_i^{e_i}.$$

Provided enough generators, any element $\mathfrak{a}$ can be represented by an exponent vector $(e_1, \dots, e_t)$ of small norm, and the CM action can thus be evaluated using only $\sum_{i=1}^{t} |e_i|$ efficient isogeny computations.

Although any element of $\mathrm{Cl}(\mathcal{O})$ may be represented in this factored form, it is not necessarily the case that such representation can be easily computed for any input.

In [2], this is called a Restricted Effective Group Action (REGA), as opposed to Effective Group Actions (EGA) where the action of any group element can be efficiently evaluated. It is believed that REGAs are less powerful than EGAs, as some protocols are only known for the latter [19], and many others are much less efficient when instantiated from the former [2,5,6,18].

Given a set of generators $\mathfrak{q}_1, \dots \mathfrak{q}_t$, it is natural to introduce the *relation lattice*

$$L = \left\{ (e_1, \dots, e_t) \;\middle|\; \prod_{j=1}^{t} [\mathfrak{q}_i]^{e_i} = [1] \text{ in } \mathrm{Cl}(\mathcal{O}) \right\}. \tag{1}$$

Then, by definition $\mathrm{Cl}(\mathcal{O}) \simeq \mathbb{Z}^t/L$, *i.e.* two exponent vectors represent the same element of $\mathrm{Cl}(\mathcal{O})$ if and only if they differ by an element of L. If L can be computed, then any exponent vector $\mathbf{e}$ can be transformed in an equivalent vector $\mathbf{e}' = \mathbf{e} - \mathbf{c}$ of small norm by finding a close vector $\mathbf{c} \in L$ to $\mathbf{e}$. This is the idea behind CSI-FiSh [6], and a general technique to transform any REGA into an EGA, assuming these computations can be done efficiently.

OSIDH. Supersingular curves have endomorphism rings isomorphic to maximal orders in a quaternion algebra, but these contain infinitely many quadratic imaginary orders, which make it possible to define a CM group action on subsets of supersingular curve. For example, when $p \equiv 3$ [8] and $p > 3$, the endomorphism ring of any supersingular curve defined over a prime field $\mathbb{F}_p$ contains a subring isomorphic to $\mathcal{O} := \mathbb{Z}[\sqrt{-p}]$. This is, in fact, the subring of $\mathbb{F}_p$-rational endomorphisms of the curve. CSIDH [11] uses precisely this case to define a supersingular analogue of Couveignes and Rostovtsev–Stolbunov. The identification of the Frobenius endomorphism with $\sqrt{-p}$ makes it possible to compute the CM action exactly like in the ordinary case; moreover, the shift to supersingular curves enables a range of optimizations that make CSIDH vastly more practical.

OSIDH seeks to replicate the ideas of CSIDH, but using a different quadratic order $\mathcal{O} \hookrightarrow \mathrm{End}(E)$. To do so, it needs to construct a quadratic order $\mathcal{O}$ with exponentially large class group, and compute a curve in the associated CM orbit. This is done by starting from a maximal quadratic order with small class group, *e.g.* $\mathbb{Z}[i]$, for which it is easy to find an associated supersingular curve E_0. Then, a chain $E_0 \to E_1 \to \cdots \to E_n$ of *descending* (*i.e.* not horizontal) isogenies of degree ℓ is taken, to which is associated a chain of increasingly small orders $\mathcal{O}_i := \mathbb{Z} + \ell^i\mathcal{O}$. Colò and Kohel call the inclusion $\mathcal{O}_i \hookrightarrow \mathrm{End}(E_i)$ an $\mathcal{O}_i$*-orientation* of E_i, and, since $\mathcal{O}_{i+1} \subset \mathcal{O}_i$, the whole chain $E_0 \to \cdots \to E_n$ is $\mathcal{O}_n$-oriented. At each descending step the size of the class group $\mathrm{Cl}(\mathcal{O}_i)$ is multiplied roughly by ℓ (see [16, Theorem 7.24]), and it is proved that $\mathrm{Cl}(\mathcal{O}_n)$ acts faithfully and transitively on the set of (primitively) $\mathcal{O}_n$-oriented curves (see Theorem 1).

The action of $\mathrm{Cl}(\mathcal{O}_n)$ on descending chains $E_0 \to \cdots \to E_n$ can be computed efficiently using the same techniques as above (with a set of generating prime ideals). However Colò and Kohel remark that the inverse problem, that of computing the element $\mathfrak{a} \in \mathrm{Cl}(\mathcal{O}_n)$ mapping a chain to another, is not hard, unlike in CSIDH. Ideally, one would like to only publish the final element of the chain E_n, and act with $\mathrm{Cl}(\mathcal{O}_n)$ on it. However in doing so the information on the orientation is lost, and thus the action of $\mathrm{Cl}(\mathcal{O}_n)$ cannot be computed.

Colò and Kohel suggest, instead, to publish E_n along with the information on how a list of generators $\mathfrak{q}_1, \dots, \mathfrak{q}_t \in \mathrm{Cl}(\mathcal{O}_n)$ acts on E_n up to a bounded distance.

Namely, they publish E_n along with *horizontal chains* $\mathfrak{q}_i^e \cdot E_n$ for all $1 \le i \le t$ and $-r \le e \le r$ for some pre-determined bound r. From this information, the action of exponentially many elements of $\mathrm{Cl}(\mathcal{O}_n)$ on E_n can be evaluated efficiently. Remarkably, the analogous information in CSIDH is publicly available, so it may be believed that publishing $\mathfrak{q}_i^e \cdot E_n$ in OSIDH does not harm security.

Our Contribution. We show that the additional information conveyed by the horizontal isogeny chains in OSIDH can be leveraged to recover the descending chain $E_0 \to \cdots \to E_n$, and thus the secret.

Our attack builds upon the work of Onuki [32], who showed that being able to evaluate a single endomorphism of $\mathcal{O}_n$ on points of E_n is enough to recover the descending chain. For this, it is necessary to express the endomorphism as a cycle $E_n \to \cdots \to E_n$ of small degree isogenies, equivalently as a product $\prod_i \mathfrak{q}_i^{e_i}$. To find such an isogeny cycle, Onuki resorts to an expensive meet-in-the-middle procedure, which seems difficult to put into practice.

We observe that finding a product $\prod_i \mathfrak{q}_i^{e_i}$ corresponding to a cycle amounts to finding a vector in the relation lattice L defined in Eq. (1). A basis for L can be computed from the description of $\mathcal{O}_n$, without involving any elliptic curve computations, and in polynomial time, thanks to the special structure of $\mathcal{O}_n$. To obtain an effectively computable isogeny cycle, the vector in L must be short, so that we can use the published horizontal chains. Such a short vector, if it exists, can be found by an SVP computation: this is the only step in our attack which has exponential complexity, namely in the number t of public generators. After the short vector is found, all subsequent steps in Onuki's attack take polynomial time.

In practice, following CSIDH, Colò and Kohel suggested $t = 74$ for an instantiation of OSIDH deemed to be as secure as CSIDH-512. This falls well short of the dimension needed to thwart SVP attacks, and indeed in our experiments we were able to construct the lattice and find a short vector in less than one hour on an ordinary laptop.

A simple countermeasure is to increase the number of primes t and $\#\mathrm{Cl}(\mathcal{O}_n)$ accordingly, until the relation lattice becomes large enough to stop SVP computations, however this appears to be extremely expensive. A cheaper countermeasure would be to keep t relatively small, but increase the size of $\mathrm{Cl}(\mathcal{O}_n)$ so that no short enough vectors are expected to exist in L. We argue that, no matter what solution is chosen, one desirable property of CM group actions is lost: CSI-FiSh was made possible by the computation of the relation lattice of CSIDH-512; furthermore, each CSI-FiSh signature solves a CVP problem in dimension $t = 74$. Neither of these is possible with OSIDH after we apply one of the patches above. It seems, indeed, that the security of OSIDH is fundamentally in conflict with the possibility of evaluating the CM group action for any possible input, and thus that it cannot be used as a foundation for protocols based on EGAs or even REGAs.

Plan. In the next section we present the mathematical foundations of OSIDH, then in Sect. 3 we present the protocol itself. In Sect. 4 we present our attack, and in Sect. 5 the countermeasures against it, and their consequences, both positive and negative, for OSIDH.

2 Oriented Supersingular Elliptic Curves

We start by briefly recalling the mathematical framework of OSIDH, presented in detail by Colò–Kohel [14] and Onuki [32].

2.1 Oriented Elliptic Curves and Isogenies

Let K be a quadratic imaginary field and E an elliptic curve defined over a finite field. A *K-orientation* of E is an embedding $\iota : K \hookrightarrow \mathrm{End}(E) \otimes \mathbb{Q}$. If $\mathcal{O}$ is an order of K, we say that (E, ι) is an *$\mathcal{O}$-orientation* if $\iota(\mathcal{O}) \subseteq \mathrm{End}(E)$. An $\mathcal{O}$-orientation is *primitive* if $\mathcal{O}$ is maximal for this inclusion, or in other words, if $\iota(\mathcal{O}) = \mathrm{End}(E) \cap \iota(K)$.

Example 1. The elliptic curve $E : y^2 = x^3 + x$ defined over $\mathbb{F}_p$ ($p \equiv 3$ [4]) has a $\mathbb{Q}(i)$-orientation, mapping $i = \sqrt{-1}$ to the endomorphism

$$\phi : (x, y) \in E \longmapsto (-x, ay) \in E,$$

with $a \in \mathbb{F}_{p^2}$ such that $a^2 = -1$. This is a primitive $\mathbb{Z}[i]$-orientation.

When E is ordinary, $\mathrm{End}(E) \otimes \mathbb{Q}$ is itself a quadratic imaginary field, hence, there is only one K-orientation (up to complex conjugation). The case of supersingular elliptic curves is more interesting: $\mathrm{End}(E) \otimes \mathbb{Q}$ is a quaternion algebra and we can embed infinitely many quadratic fields inside, so there are infinitely many orientations of E.

Let (E, ι_E) and (F, ι_F) be two K-oriented elliptic curves. An isogeny $\varphi : E \longrightarrow F$ is *K-oriented* if $\varphi_*(\iota_E) = \iota_F$, where $\varphi_*(\iota_E)$ is the K-orientation of F defined as follows:

$$\forall \alpha \in K, \quad \varphi_*(\iota)(\alpha) = \frac{1}{\deg(\varphi)} \varphi \iota(\alpha) \widehat{\varphi}.$$

A K-oriented isogeny $\lambda : (E, \iota_E) \longrightarrow (F, \iota_F)$ is a (K-oriented) *isomorphism* if it has an inverse isogeny $F \longrightarrow E$ that is also K-oriented $(F, \iota_F) \longrightarrow (E, \iota_E)$.

Let $\varphi : (E, \iota_E) \longrightarrow (F, \iota_F)$ be a K-oriented isogeny, $\mathcal{O} := \iota_E^{-1}(\mathrm{End}(E))$ and $\mathcal{O}' := \iota_F^{-1}(\mathrm{End}(F))$, so that ι_E is a primitive $\mathcal{O}$-orientation and ι_F is a primitive $\mathcal{O}'$-orientation. We say that φ is *horizontal*, *ascending* or *descending*, respectively when $\mathcal{O} = \mathcal{O}'$, $\mathcal{O} \subsetneq \mathcal{O}'$ or $\mathcal{O} \supsetneq \mathcal{O}'$. There is no reason for this to be verified in general, except when φ has prime degree. In that case, the index relating $\mathcal{O}$ and $\mathcal{O}'$ also divides $\deg(\varphi)$ [27, Chapter 4, Proposition 21]. Finally, an isomorphism is always horizontal.

2.2 Class Group Action

Let K be a quadratic imaginary field and $\mathcal{O}$ be an order of K. Let p be a prime number. We consider the set $\mathrm{SS}_{\mathcal{O}}^{pr}(p)$ of isomorphism classes of primitively $\mathcal{O}$-oriented supersingular elliptic curves defined over $\overline{\mathbb{F}}_p$.

Proposition 1. *[32, Proposition 3.2] $SS_{\mathcal{O}}^{pr}(p)$ is not empty if and only if p does not split in K and is prime to the conductor of $\mathcal{O}$.*

In the following, we shall assume that $\mathrm{SS}_{\mathcal{O}}^{pr}(p)$ is not empty. We define a group action of $\mathrm{Cl}(\mathcal{O})$ on $\mathrm{SS}_{\mathcal{O}}^{pr}(p)$. Let $\mathfrak{a} \subseteq \mathcal{O}$ be an ideal of norm prime to p and (E, ι) be a primitively $\mathcal{O}$-oriented supersingular elliptic curve defined over $\mathbb{F}_{p^2}$. We define the $\mathfrak{a}$-*torsion subgroup* by

$$E[\mathfrak{a}] := \bigcap_{\alpha \in \mathfrak{a}} \ker(\iota(\alpha)).$$

By [39, Proposition III.4.12], there exists a separable isogeny $\varphi_{\mathfrak{a}} : E \longrightarrow F$ of kernel $E[\mathfrak{a}]$. If $\mathfrak{a}$ is an invertible $\mathcal{O}$-ideal (*i.e.* one whose norm is prime to the conductor of $\mathcal{O}$), then $\varphi_{\mathfrak{a}}$ is a horizontal isogeny by [32, Proposition 3.5]. In that case, we write

$$\mathfrak{a} \cdot (E, \iota) := (F, (\varphi_{\mathfrak{a}})_*(\iota)).$$

A separable isogeny being determined by its kernel up to isomorphism [39, Proposition III.4.11], we easily get that the isomorphism class of $\mathfrak{a} \cdot (E, \iota)$ only depends on $\mathfrak{a}$ and the isomorphism class of (E, ι).

Furthermore, if $\mathfrak{b}$ is another invertible $\mathcal{O}$-ideal of norm prime to p and if $\varphi_{\mathfrak{b}} : F \longrightarrow G$ has kernel $F[\mathfrak{b}]$, then $\ker(\varphi_{\mathfrak{b}} \circ \varphi_{\mathfrak{a}}) = E[\mathfrak{a}\mathfrak{b}]$, by [44, Proposition 3.12] or [31, Proposition 7.28]. Hence, if we set

$$\mathfrak{a}^{-1} \cdot (E, \iota) := \overline{\mathfrak{a}} \cdot (E, \iota),$$

we define an action of the group of fractional $\mathcal{O}$-ideals prime to p on $\mathrm{SS}_{\mathcal{O}}^{pr}(p)$. Since the action of principal ideals is trivial, we get an action of the ideal class group

$$\mathrm{Cl}(\mathcal{O}) \times \mathrm{SS}_{\mathcal{O}}^{pr}(p) \longrightarrow \mathrm{SS}_{\mathcal{O}}^{pr}(p).$$

This action is faithful [32, Theorem 3.4], but not transitive.

Example 2. The orientation of Example 1 and its composition with the complex conjugation are two non-isomorphic $\mathbb{Z}[i]$-orientations. But the ideal class group $\mathrm{Cl}(\mathbb{Z}[i])$ is trivial, so the orbits contain only one element. Hence, the group action of $\mathrm{Cl}(\mathbb{Z}[i])$ on $\mathrm{SS}_{\mathbb{Z}[i]}^{pr}(p)$ cannot be transitive.

This example illustrates the general case (see [32, Proposition 3.3]): there are always two orbits related by complex conjugation (or equivalently by the action of the p-th Frobenius isogeny). In [32, § 3.2], Onuki constructs one of these orbits "canonically", as the image of $\mathrm{Ell}(\mathcal{O})$, the set of isomorphism classes of elliptic curves defined over $\mathbb{C}$ with complex multiplication by $\mathcal{O}$ by a reduction modulo p map: $\rho_{\mathcal{O}} : \mathrm{Ell}(\mathcal{O}) \longrightarrow \mathrm{SS}_{\mathcal{O}}^{pr}(p)$ (that he defines properly). Onuki also proves that:

Theorem 1. *[32, Theorem 3.4] The group* $Cl(\mathcal{O})$ *acts faithfully and transitively on* $\rho_{\mathcal{O}}(Ell(\mathcal{O}))$.

Since $\mathrm{Cl}(\mathcal{O})$ also acts freely and transitively on $\mathrm{Ell}(\mathcal{O})$ (see [38, Proposition II.1.2]) it follows that $\rho_{\mathcal{O}}$ is injective. In the following we shall restrict our attention to the ideal class group action on the orbit $\rho_{\mathcal{O}}(\mathrm{Ell}(\mathcal{O}))$.

2.3 Oriented Supersingular Isogeny Graphs

Let $\mathrm{Ell}(K)$ be the union of $\mathrm{Ell}(\mathcal{O})$ for every order $\mathcal{O}$ of K with conductor prime to p and $\mathrm{SS}_K(p)$ be the set of K-oriented supersingular elliptic curves up to K-oriented isomorphism. Then, we have an injective map

$$\rho : \mathrm{Ell}(K) \longrightarrow \mathrm{SS}_K(p)$$

naturally induced by the maps $\rho_{\mathcal{O}} : \mathrm{Ell}(\mathcal{O}) \longrightarrow \mathrm{SS}^{pr}_{\mathcal{O}}(p)$ for all orders $\mathcal{O}$ of K with conductor prime to p.

We say that two K-oriented isogenies are *K-equivalent* if they are equal up to multiplication on the right and on the left by K-oriented isomorphisms. Let $\ell \neq p$ be a prime number. The *K-oriented supersingular ℓ-isogeny graph* $G_\ell(K,p)$ is the graph whose set of vertices is $\rho(\mathrm{Ell}(K))$ and whose edges are K-oriented ℓ-isogenies up to K-equivalence.

By the injectivity of ρ, this graph is isomorphic to the ℓ-isogeny graph of elliptic curves over $\mathbb{C}$ with complex multiplication by an order of K. It follows that $G_\ell(K,p)$ is infinite (unlike the supersingular ℓ-isogeny graph over $\overline{\mathbb{F}}_p$) and that every ℓ-isogeny from a vertex of $G_\ell(K,p)$ has codomain in $G_\ell(K,p)$.

In addition, as Kohel proved [27, Chapter 4, Proposition 23], the connected components of $G_\ell(K,p)$ have a volcano structure (see Fig. 1). From each vertex on the crater, there are $1 + \left(\frac{\Delta_K}{\ell}\right)$ horizontal and $1/[\mathcal{O}^\times : (\mathbb{Z}+\ell\mathcal{O})^\times]\left(\ell - \left(\frac{\Delta_K}{\ell}\right)\right)$ descending ℓ-isogenies up to K-equivalence. From each vertex outside of the crater, there are ℓ descending and one ascending ℓ-isogeny up to K-equivalence.

Unlike the supersingular ℓ-isogeny graph, $G_\ell(K,p)$ is infinite because vertices carry additional information: the K-orientation. Hence, the graph $G_\ell(K,p)$ refolds when we forget orientations and consider j-invariants only (see Fig. 1). Equivalently, the forgetful map $\rho(\mathrm{Ell}(K)) \longrightarrow \mathrm{SS}(p)$ is not injective ($\mathrm{SS}(p)$ being the set of supersingular elliptic curves over $\overline{\mathbb{F}}_p$, up to isomorphism). This is inconvenient because in OSIDH, K-oriented elliptic curves are represented by their j-invariants only in order to use modular polynomials. Luckily, we have:

Theorem 2. *[14, Proposition 13] When restricted to the union of* $Ell(\mathcal{O})$ *with* $|disc(\mathcal{O})| < p$, *the forgetful map becomes injective.*

2.4 Effective Computation of the Ideal Class Group Action

Let ℓ be a small prime ($\neq p$). For all $i \in \mathbb{N}$, let $\mathcal{O}_i := \mathbb{Z} + \ell^i \mathcal{O}_K$. OSIDH is based on the ideal class group action of $\mathrm{Cl}(\mathcal{O}_n)$ on the canonical orbit $\rho(\mathrm{Ell}(\mathcal{O}_n))$ for $n \in \mathbb{N}$ big enough. By Theorem 1, this is a cryptographic group action.

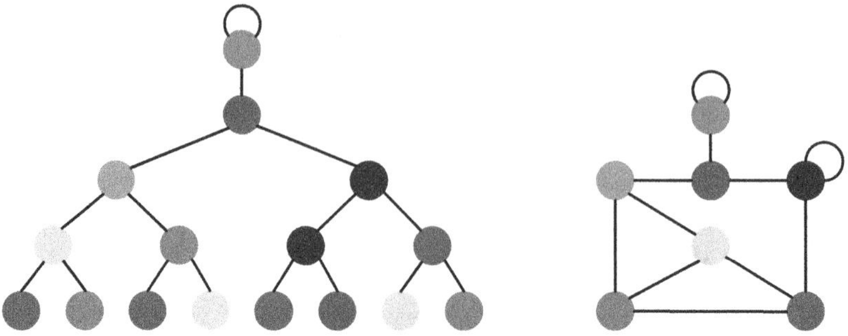

Fig. 1. On the left: Representation of a connected component (with volcano structure) of $G_2(\mathbb{Q}(i), 79)$, the $\mathbb{Q}(i)$-oriented supersingular 2-isogeny graph over $\mathbb{F}_{79^2}$ up to depth 4. **On the right:** Supersingular 2-isogeny graph over $\mathbb{F}_{79^2}$ (left graph refolded). **NB:** Elliptic curves with the same color have the same j-invariant.

Unfortunately, there is no known algorithm to compute the group action on $\rho(\mathrm{Ell}(\mathcal{O}_n))$ directly. Colò and Kohel's trick is to work in the K-oriented supersingular ℓ-isogeny graph. Instead of considering a vertex $(E_n, \iota_n) \in \rho(\mathrm{Ell}(\mathcal{O}_n))$ alone, we consider the *descending chain* of K-oriented ℓ-isogenies in the graph:

$$(E_0, \iota_0) \longrightarrow \cdots \longrightarrow (E_n, \iota_n),$$

with $(E_i, \iota_i) \in \rho(\mathrm{Ell}(\mathcal{O}_i))$ for all $i \in [\![1\ ;\ n]\!]$.

Let $\mathfrak{q} \subseteq \mathcal{O}_K$ be an ideal of norm prime to ℓ and p. Then, we have a commutative diagram of K-oriented isogenies:

$$\begin{array}{ccccccccc}
(E_0, \iota_0) & \longrightarrow & (E_1, \iota_1) & \longrightarrow & \cdots & \longrightarrow & (E_{n-1}, \iota_{n-1}) & \longrightarrow & (E_n, \iota_n) \\
\downarrow & & \downarrow & & & & \downarrow & & \downarrow \\
(F_0, \iota'_0) & \longrightarrow & (F_1, \iota'_1) & \longrightarrow & \cdots & \longrightarrow & (F_{n-1}, \iota_{n-1}) & \longrightarrow & (F_n, \iota'_n),
\end{array}$$

where $(F_i, \iota'_i) := (\mathfrak{q} \cap \mathcal{O}_i) \cdot (E_i, \iota_i)$, for all $i \in [\![0\ ;\ n]\!]$, the down arrows are the isogenies associated to the $\mathfrak{q} \cap \mathcal{O}_i$ and the arrows between the (F_i, ι'_i) are ℓ-isogenies. Such a diagram is called an *ℓ-ladder of degree* $q := N(\mathfrak{q})$ and the chain at the bottom $(F_i, \iota'_i)_{0 \leq i \leq n}$ is also denoted by $\mathfrak{q} \cdot (E_i, \iota_i)_{0 \leq i \leq n}$.

When the norm q is a small prime number, the descending ℓ-isogeny chain $(F_i, \iota'_i)_{0 \leq i \leq n}$ can be easily computed, assuming $(E_i, \iota_i)_{0 \leq i \leq n}$ is known. The ending element is the result of the group action by $\mathfrak{q} \cap \mathcal{O}_n$ we wanted to compute in the first place: $(F_n, \iota'_n) := (\mathfrak{q} \cap \mathcal{O}_n) \cdot (E_n, \iota_n)$. Assuming that $p > q\ell^{2n}|\mathrm{disc}(K)|$, we can perform this computation with j-invariants only and omit the orientations (this is a consequence of Theorem 2, see [32, Theorem 6.2]).

Assume that $j(F_i)$ is known. Then, $j(F_{i+1})$ is solution of the modular equations:

$$\begin{cases} \Phi_\ell(j(F_i), x) = 0 \\ \Phi_q(j(E_{i+1}), x) = 0 \end{cases} \iff \gcd(\Phi_\ell(j(F_i), x), \Phi_q(j(E_{i+1}), x)) = 0. \qquad (\star_i)$$

For i big enough, Eq. ($\star_i$) admits only one solution [32, Theorem 6.2], so we can easily go down the chain of F_i.

To compute the first values of $j(F_i)$ we cannot use Eq. ($\star_i$) because there are multiple solutions (both $j(F_i) = j(\mathfrak{q} \cdot E_i)$ and $j(\overline{\mathfrak{q}} \cdot E_i)$ are solutions). Hence, we explicitly compute the torsion subgroups $E_i[\mathfrak{q} \cap \mathcal{O}_i]$ and use Vélu's formulas [43]. Colò and Kohel chose K so that $\mathrm{Cl}(\mathcal{O}_K)$ is trivial ($K = \mathbb{Q}(i)$ or $\mathbb{Q}(\sqrt{-3})$ in practice), so that $j(F_0) = j(E_0)$ and we save the first computation.

With this algorithm, we can compute the ideal class group action, as visualized in Fig. 2.

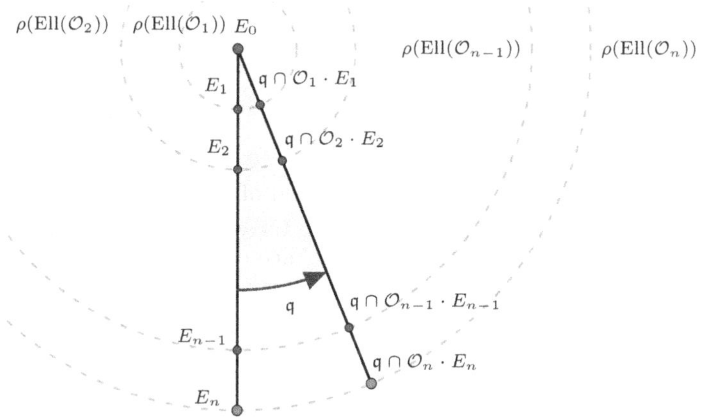

Fig. 2. Action of the prime ideal $\mathfrak{q}$ on the descending ℓ-isogeny chain.

3 Oriented Supersingular Isogeny Diffie–Hellman

The material of this section mostly replicates Colò and Kohel [14]. Nonetheless, in Sect. 3.3 we give a more detailed account of the attack on their straw man key exchange [14, § 5.1], and we improve it using lattice reduction.

3.1 The OSIDH Setup

As explained in Sect. 2.4, we choose a quadratic imaginary number field K such that $\mathrm{Cl}(\mathcal{O}_K)$ is trivial ($K = \mathbb{Q}(i)$ or $K = \mathbb{Q}(\sqrt{-3})$), ℓ a small prime and p a large prime that does not split in K (cf. Proposition 1). Let $\mathcal{O}_i := \mathbb{Z} + \ell^i \mathcal{O}_K$ for all $i \in \mathbb{N}^*$ and $n \in \mathbb{N}^*$ large enough. OSIDH uses the group action of $\mathrm{Cl}(\mathcal{O}_n)$ on the orbit $\rho(\mathrm{Ell}(\mathcal{O}_n))$.

According to the terminology of [2], this is a restricted cryptographic group action (REGA), because we can use the algorithm of Sect. 2.4 with (prime) ideals of small norm only. Hence, we choose a set of generators: let $q_1, \ldots, q_t$ be small distinct primes, distinct from ℓ, and all splitting in K, and let $\mathfrak{q}_j$ be prime $\mathcal{O}_K$-ideals lying above q_j for all $j \in [\![1\ ;\ t]\!]$. We assume that the $\mathfrak{q}_j \cap \mathcal{O}_n$ genrate $\mathrm{Cl}(\mathcal{O}_n)$.

3.2 A Straw Man Key Exchange Scheme

With the setup of the previous section, let $(E_i, \iota_i)_{0\le i\le n}$ be a public descending ℓ-isogeny chain (represented as a list of j-invariants) such that E_0 is primitively $\mathcal{O}_K$-oriented.

Alice and Bob separately choose secret exponents $e_1, \ldots, e_t$ and $f_1, \ldots, f_t$ lying in the integer range $[\![-r\ ;\ r]\!]$ (where r is a small positive integer) and respectively compute the action of

$$\mathfrak{a} := \prod_{j=1}^{t} \mathfrak{q}_j^{e_j} \qquad \text{and} \qquad \mathfrak{b} := \prod_{j=1}^{t} \mathfrak{q}_j^{f_j}$$

on $(E_i, \iota_i)_{0\le i\le n}$ step by step, using the method of Sect. 2.4.

Then, Alice sends $\mathfrak{a} \cdot (E_i, \iota_i)_{0\le i\le n}$ to Bob (as a list of j-invariants) and Bob sends $\mathfrak{b} \cdot (E_i, \iota_i)_{0\le i\le n}$ to Alice. In the end, Alice computes $\mathfrak{a} \cdot (\mathfrak{b} \cdot (E_i, \iota_i)_{0\le i\le n})$ and Bob computes $\mathfrak{b} \cdot (\mathfrak{a} \cdot (E_i, \iota_i)_{0\le i\le n})$, so that both parties share the chain

$$\mathfrak{a} \cdot (\mathfrak{b} \cdot (E_i, \iota_i)_{0\le i\le n}) = \mathfrak{b} \cdot (\mathfrak{a} \cdot (E_i, \iota_i)_{0\le i\le n}) = \mathfrak{ab} \cdot (E_i, \iota_i)_{0\le i\le n}.$$

We shall now see that this protocol is insecure: given knowledge of the chain $(E_i, \iota_i)_{0\le i\le n}$ and of, say, $\mathfrak{a} \cdot (E_i, \iota_i)_{0\le i\le n}$, an attacker can recover the secret ideal class $[\mathfrak{a}]$.

3.3 Inverting the Class Group Action on Descending Chains

Given two chains $(E_i, \iota_i)_{0\le i\le n}$ and $(F_i, \iota_i')_{0\le i\le n} := \mathfrak{a} \cdot (E_i, \iota_i)_{0\le i\le n}$ with a secret ideal class $[\mathfrak{a}] \in \mathrm{Cl}(\mathcal{O}_n)$, we explain how to recover $[\mathfrak{a}]$. As Colò and Kohel indicate [14, § 5.1], there are two methods to do that. The first one exploits the chains to recover the full endomorphism rings $\mathrm{End}(E_n)$ and $\mathrm{End}(F_n)$ [22,45], then computes a connecting ideal between those quaternion orders [28], and finally finds an equivalent ideal in $\mathcal{O}_n$. The second method, which we are now going to illustrate, only uses the ideal class group action.

For $i \in [\![0\ ;\ n-1]\!]$, suppose that we know an ideal of $\mathfrak{a}_i = \prod_{j=1}^{t} \mathfrak{q}_j^{e_{i,j}}$ of $\mathcal{O}_K$, such that

$$\mathfrak{a}_i \cdot (E_k, \iota_k)_{0\le k\le i} = (F_k, \iota_k')_{0\le k\le i}.$$

Then $[\mathfrak{a} \cap \mathcal{O}_i] = [\mathfrak{a}_i \cap \mathcal{O}_i]$ in $\mathrm{Cl}(\mathcal{O}_i)$ and $\mathfrak{a}_i \cap \mathcal{O}_i$ is determined up to multiplication by principal ideals of $\mathcal{O}_i$, *i.e.* by elements of $\mathcal{O}_i$. We look for an ideal $\mathfrak{a}_{i+1} = \prod_{j=1}^{t} \mathfrak{q}_j^{e_{i+1,j}}$ of $\mathcal{O}_K$ such that

$$\mathfrak{a}_{i+1} \cdot (E_k, \iota_k)_{0\le k\le i+1} = (F_k, \iota_k')_{0\le k\le i+1}.$$

Then, $[\mathfrak{a}_{i+1} \cap \mathcal{O}_i] = [\mathfrak{a} \cap \mathcal{O}_i] = [\mathfrak{a}_i \cap \mathcal{O}_i]$ is in $\mathrm{Cl}(\mathcal{O}_i)$, *i.e.* $\mathfrak{a}_{i+1} \cap \mathcal{O}_i \equiv \mathfrak{a}_i \cap \mathcal{O}_i \bmod P(\mathcal{O}_i)$. Hence, to determine $\mathfrak{a}_{i+1}$, one only has to find an ideal $\mathfrak{b}_i = \prod_{j=1}^{t} \mathfrak{q}_j^{d_j}$ such that $\mathfrak{b}_i \cap \mathcal{O}_i$ is principal and

$$[(\mathfrak{a}_i \cdot \mathfrak{b}_i) \cap \mathcal{O}_{i+1}] \cdot E_{i+1} = F_{i+1}. \qquad (\star)$$

Then, we can set $\mathfrak{a}_{i+1} := \mathfrak{a}_i \cdot \mathfrak{b}_i$, so that $e_{i+1,j} := e_{i,j} + d_j$ for all $j \in [\![1\ ;\ t]\!]$. Both $\mathfrak{a}_{i+1} \cap \mathcal{O}_{i+1}$ and $\mathfrak{b}_i \cap \mathcal{O}_{i+1}$ are determined up to principal ideals of $\mathcal{O}_{i+1}$, thus $[\mathfrak{b}_i \cap \mathcal{O}_{i+1}]$ is in the kernel of the surjective group homomorphism

$$[\mathfrak{c}] \in \mathrm{Cl}(\mathcal{O}_{i+1}) \twoheadrightarrow [\mathfrak{c}\mathcal{O}_i] \in \mathrm{Cl}(\mathcal{O}_i),$$

whose order is ℓ for $i \geq 1$ and $\frac{1}{[\mathcal{O}_K^\times : \mathcal{O}_1^\times]}\left(\ell - \left(\frac{\Delta_K}{\ell}\right)\right)$ for $i = 0$ (by [16, Theorem 7.24]), so we only have to test a few values for $\mathfrak{b}_i$ until Eq. $(\star)$ is satisfied.

However, we have to make sure that all the values of $\mathfrak{b}_i$ to be tested can be expressed in terms of the $\mathfrak{q}_j$, and that the exponents $e_{i+1,j}$ of $\mathfrak{a}_i \cdot \mathfrak{b}_i$ are short enough to make the computation of $[(\mathfrak{a}_i \cdot \mathfrak{b}_i) \cap \mathcal{O}_{i+1}] \cdot E_{i+1}$ practical.

Expressing $\ker(\mathrm{Cl}(\mathcal{O}_{i+1}) \twoheadrightarrow \mathrm{Cl}(\mathcal{O}_i))$ in terms of the $\mathfrak{q}_j$. We need to investigate the structure of the ideal class groups, which turns out to be very simple.

Lemma 1. *One of the following results hold:*

(i) *For all $n \geq 1$, $\mathrm{Cl}(\mathcal{O}_n)$ is cyclic.*
(ii) *For all $n \geq 2$, $\mathrm{Cl}(\mathcal{O}_n) \simeq (\mathbb{Z}/\ell\mathbb{Z}) \times (\mathbb{Z}/h_{n-1}\mathbb{Z})$ with*

$$h_{n-1} := \#\mathrm{Cl}(\mathcal{O}_{n-1}) = \frac{\ell^{n-2}}{[\mathcal{O}_K^\times : \mathcal{O}_1^\times]}\left(\ell - \left(\frac{\Delta_K}{\ell}\right)\right),$$

where $\Delta_K := \mathrm{disc}(K)$.

The last case only happens when $\ell = 2$ or when $\ell \geq 3$ ramifies in K (this condition is necessary but not sufficient).

Proof. See the extended version of this work [17].

The result above leads to a straightforward way to express $\ker(\mathrm{Cl}(\mathcal{O}_{i+1}) \twoheadrightarrow \mathrm{Cl}(\mathcal{O}_i))$. The strategy is first to use Algorithm 1 to compute a basis of $\mathrm{Cl}(\mathcal{O}_n)$ *i.e.* a generator or a pair of generators without non trivial relations. Then, we use Algorithm 2 to express the kernels for $i \in [\![0\ ;\ n-1]\!]$. Both algorithms use discrete algorithm computations which are not costly (polynomial in n) with Pohlig-Hellman's algorithm [35], since the ideal class groups are smooth.

Reducing the Exponents of $\mathfrak{a}_i \cdot \mathfrak{b}_i$. Once $\mathfrak{b}_i$ is expressed in terms of the $\mathfrak{q}_j$, *i.e.* when the exponents d_j are known, we still have to make sure that the exponents $e_{i+1,j} = e_{i,j} + d_j$ of $\mathfrak{a}_i \cdot \mathfrak{b}_i$ are small. We define the *relation lattice*

$$L_{i+1} := \left\{ (e_1, \dots, e_t) \in \mathbb{Z}^t \,\middle|\, \prod_{j=1}^{t} [\mathfrak{q}_j \cap \mathcal{O}_{i+1}]^{e_j} = [1] \quad \text{in } \mathrm{Cl}(\mathcal{O}_{i+1}) \right\},$$

Algorithm 1: Computing a basis of $\mathrm{Cl}(\mathcal{O}_n)$.

Data: $\mathfrak{q}_1, \cdots, \mathfrak{q}_j$, n.
Result: A basis of $\mathrm{Cl}(\mathcal{O}_n)$.

Compute the order d_j of $[\mathfrak{q}_j] \in \mathrm{Cl}(\mathcal{O}_n)$ for all $j \in [\![1\ ;\ t]\!]$;
$m \leftarrow \mathrm{lcm}_{1\leq j\leq t} d_j$;
Find a product of the $[\mathfrak{q}_j]$, $[\mathfrak{g}]$ of order m in $\mathrm{Cl}(\mathcal{O}_n)$;
if $m = \#Cl(\mathcal{O}_n)$ **then**
    Return $\mathfrak{g}$;
else
    Find $[\mathfrak{q}_j] \notin \langle[\mathfrak{g}]\rangle$ (try to compute the discrete logarithm until it fails);
    Compute the discrete logarithm k of $[\mathfrak{q}_j]^\ell$ to base $[\mathfrak{g}]$; // $[\mathfrak{q}_j]^\ell \in \langle[\mathfrak{g}]\rangle$
    $k' \leftarrow k/\ell$; // $\ell \mid k$ since $[\mathfrak{q}_j]^\ell$'s order divides m/ℓ
    $[\mathfrak{h}] \leftarrow [\mathfrak{q}_j][\mathfrak{g}]^{-k'}$;
    Return $([\mathfrak{g}], [\mathfrak{h}])$;
end

Algorithm 2: Expressing $\ker(\mathrm{Cl}(\mathcal{O}_{i+1}) \twoheadrightarrow \mathrm{Cl}(\mathcal{O}_i))$ in terms of the $\mathfrak{q}_j$.

Data: $\mathfrak{q}_1, \cdots, \mathfrak{q}_j$, a basis of $\mathrm{Cl}(\mathcal{O}_n)$, $i \in [\![0\ ;\ n-1]\!]$.
Result: A generator of $\ker(\mathrm{Cl}(\mathcal{O}_{i+1}) \twoheadrightarrow \mathrm{Cl}(\mathcal{O}_i))$ in terms of the $\mathfrak{q}_j$.

if *$\#Cl(\mathcal{O}_n)$ is cyclic* **then**
    $[\mathfrak{g}] \leftarrow$ entry generator of $\mathrm{Cl}(\mathcal{O}_n)$;
    $h_i \leftarrow \#\mathrm{Cl}(\mathcal{O}_i)$;
    Return $[\mathfrak{g} \cap \mathcal{O}_{i+1}]^{h_i}$;
else
    if $i \geq 3$ **then**
        $([\mathfrak{g}], [\mathfrak{h}]) \leftarrow$ entry basis of $\mathrm{Cl}(\mathcal{O}_n)$;
        $h_{i-1} \leftarrow \#\mathrm{Cl}(\mathcal{O}_i)/\ell$;
        Return $[\mathfrak{g} \cap \mathcal{O}_{i+1}]^{h_{i-1}}$;
    else
        Describe the kernel exhaustively;
    end
end

then two vectors $\mathbf{e}_{i+1} := (e_{i+1,j})_{1\leq j\leq t}$ define the same element of $\mathrm{Cl}(\mathcal{O}_{i+1})$ if and only if they differ by an element of L_{i+1}. Thus we may compute L_{i+1} and then find an element $\mathbf{c} \in L_{i+1}$ close to $\mathbf{e}_{i+1}$, so to replace $\mathbf{e}_{i+1}$ by $\mathbf{e}'_{i+1} := \mathbf{e}_i - \mathbf{c}$.

We explain how to compute a basis of L_{i+1} when $\mathrm{Cl}(\mathcal{O}_{i+1})$ is cyclic. To do so, we start by computing a generator $[\mathfrak{g}]$ of $\mathrm{Cl}(\mathcal{O}_{i+1})$ using Algorithm 1. Then, we compute the discrete logarithms x_j of the $[\mathfrak{q}_j]$ to base $[\mathfrak{g}]$, which is easily done since $\mathrm{Cl}(\mathcal{O}_{i+1})$ has smooth order. Define the row vector $\mathbf{x} := (x_1, \ldots, x_t)$, and let $h_{i+1} = \#\mathrm{Cl}(\mathcal{O}_{i+1})$, then

$$L_{i+1} := \left\{ \mathbf{e} \in \mathbb{Z}^t \;\middle|\; \forall k \in [\![1\ ;\ r]\!], \quad \mathbf{x}\cdot\mathbf{e} \equiv 0\ [h_{i+1}] \right\},$$

where $\mathbf{x} \cdot \mathbf{e}$ denotes the dot product. The dual of this lattice is

$$L_{i+1}^* := \mathbb{Z}^t + \mathbb{Z}\frac{1}{h_{i+1}}\mathbf{x}^T,$$

so we easily find a basis C of L_{i+1}^* by computing the Hermite Normal Form of the matrix $(h_{i+1}I_t|\mathbf{x}^T)$, using [13, Algorithm 2.4.4]. Then, $B := (C^T)^{-1}$ is a basis of L_{i+1}.

When $\mathrm{Cl}(\mathcal{O}_{i+1})$ is not cyclic, we proceed similarly. We find a basis $([\mathfrak{g}], [\mathfrak{h}])$ using Algorithm 1, we compute the discrete logarithm (x_j, y_j) of the $[\mathfrak{q}_j]$ to this base, using Sutherland's Algorithm [40, Algorithm 2]. L_{i+1} is now defined by two equations $\mathbf{x} \cdot \mathbf{e} \equiv 0\ [h_i]$ and $\mathbf{y} \cdot \mathbf{e} \equiv 0\ [\ell]$, with $\mathbf{x} := (x_1, \ldots, x_t)$, $\mathbf{y} := (y_1, \ldots, y_t)$ and $h_i := \#\mathrm{Cl}(\mathcal{O}_i)$. The basis C of L_{i+1}^* is the Hermite Normal Form of the matrix $(h_i\ell I_t|\ell\mathbf{x}^T|h_i\mathbf{y}^T)$, and finally $B := (C^T)^{-1}$ is a basis of L_{i+1}.

All these operations are polynomial in $i \leq n$ and t. To find a vector $\mathbf{c} \in L_{i+1}$, close to $\mathbf{e}_{i+1}$ we can use Babai's nearest plane algorithm [3] running in time $O(t^6)$. Theoretically, the distance $\|\mathbf{c} - \mathbf{e}_{i+1}\|$ (in norm ℓ_2) will be exponential but in practice, for $t \sim 10^2$, this distance will be reasonably low, making this attack practical.

For bigger values of t, one has to find a balance between the time complexity of the CVP algorithm and the distance $\|\mathbf{c} - \mathbf{e}_{i+1}\|$, closely related to the time complexity of the operation $[\mathfrak{a}_i \cdot \mathfrak{b}] \cdot E_{i+1}$. This could be done with Espitau and Kirchner's algorithm [23], leading to a subexponential attack of time complexity $L_t[1/2, c] = \exp((c+o(1))\sqrt{t\log(t)})$, with $c \simeq 0.229$ (see Appendix A). To reach a security level of 128 bits would require to take $t \geq 3 \cdot 10^4$, which is unrealistic.

3.4 The OSIDH Key Exchange

To obtain a secure key exchange, one must avoid publishing the full chains $\mathfrak{a} \cdot (E_i, \iota_i)_{0 \leq i \leq n}$ and $\mathfrak{b} \cdot (E_i, \iota_i)_{0 \leq i \leq n}$. Ideally, Alice and Bob would only exchange the final elements $E_{A,n} := [\mathfrak{a}] \cdot E_n$ and $E_{B,n} := [\mathfrak{b}] \cdot E_n$. However, this is not enough information for one party to evaluate the group action on the other party's public curve. Colò and Kohel proposed that the parties exchange the horizontal chains

$$[\mathfrak{q}_j]^{-r} \cdot E_{A,n} \to \cdots \to E_{A,n} \to \cdots \to [\mathfrak{q}_j]^r \cdot E_{A,n}$$

$$\text{and} \quad [\mathfrak{q}_j]^{-r} \cdot E_{B,n} \to \cdots \to E_{B,n} \to \cdots \to [\mathfrak{q}_j]^r \cdot E_{B,n}$$

for all $j \in [\![1\ ;\ t]\!]$, instead. This is sufficient to compute $[\mathfrak{a}] \cdot E_{B,n}$ and $[\mathfrak{b}] \cdot E_{A,n}$, provided the exponents occurring in $\mathfrak{a}$ and $\mathfrak{b}$ are chosen in $[\![-r\ ;\ r]\!]$. See [14, § 5.2] for details (Fig. 3).

Colò and Kohel conjecture that this additional information cannot be leveraged to find the secrets, then, in [14, § 6], suggest a concrete set of parameters inspired by CSIDH-512. Concretely, they take $K = \mathbb{Q}(i)$, $\ell = 2$, and $n = 256$, to obtain a class group of size $\approx 2^{256}$, ensuring 2^{128} security against meet-in-the-middle attacks. Then, like in CSIDH, they set $r = 5$ and $t = 74$, so that $(2r+1)^t \approx 2^{256}$, which ensures that the secret key space covers nearly all of $\mathrm{Cl}(\mathcal{O}_n)$.

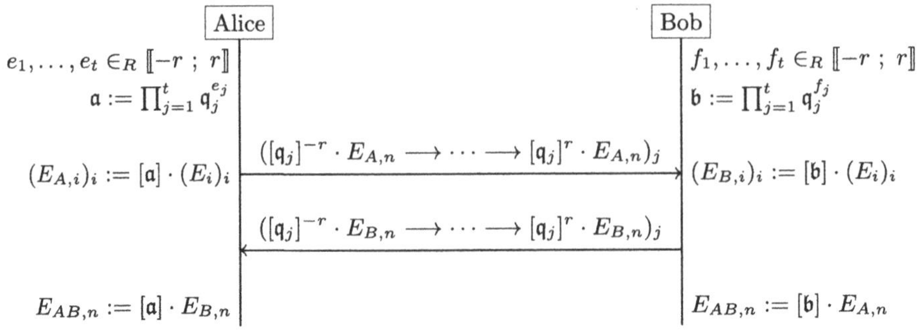

Fig. 3. The OSIDH protocol as presented in [14, § 5.2].

4 Our Attack on OSIDH

As explained in Sect. 3.3, the knowledge of the descending ℓ-isogeny chains $(E_i, \iota_i)_{0 \leq i \leq n}$ and $(F_i, \iota'_i)_{0 \leq i \leq n} := [\mathfrak{a}] \cdot (E_i, \iota'_i)_{0 \leq i \leq n}$ is sufficient to recover the secret ideal class $[\mathfrak{a}] \in \mathrm{Cl}(\mathcal{O}_n)$. In this section, we prove that the knowledge of the $\mathfrak{q}_j$-action horizontal chains

$$[\mathfrak{q}_j]^{-r} \cdot F_n \to \cdots \to F_n \to \cdots \to [\mathfrak{q}_j]^r \cdot F_n$$

for all $j \in [\![1 \; ; \; t]\!]$ may give away enough information to recover $(F_i, \iota'_i)_{0 \leq i \leq n}$, depending on the choice of parameters n, t and r.

4.1 Onuki's Idea

In [32, § 6.3], Onuki claims that the knowledge of a K-oriented endomorphism $\iota'_n(\beta)$ with $\beta \in \mathcal{O}_n \setminus \mathcal{O}_{n+1}$ is sufficient to recover the whole chain $(F_i, \iota'_i)_{0 \leq i \leq n}$.

We explain how such an endomorphism $\iota'_n(\beta)$ helps recover F_{n-1}, adapting the ideas of Petit's attack on SIDH [34] (in particular § 4.3). The same method can then be applied recursively to recover the whole chain. Let θ be a generator of $\mathcal{O}_K$. Then $\ell^n\theta$ generates $\mathcal{O}_n$ and we can write $\beta := a + b\ell^n\theta$ with $a, b \in \mathbb{Z}$ and $\ell \nmid b$ (since $\beta \notin \mathcal{O}_{n+1}$). Since $\iota'_n(a) = [a]$, we can infer $\iota'_n(b\ell^n\theta)$ from $\iota'_n(\beta)$.

Lemma 2. *We have* $\ker(\iota'_n(b\ell^n\theta)) \cap F_n[\ell] = \ker(\widehat{\varphi}_{n-1})$, *where* $\varphi_{n-1} : F_{n-1} \longrightarrow F_n$ *is the last K-oriented isogeny of the chain* $(F_i, \iota'_i)_{0 \leq i \leq n}$.

Proof. Let $G := \ker(\iota'_n(b\ell^n\theta)) \cap F_n[\ell]$. We have

$$\iota'_n(b\ell^n\theta) = [\ell]\iota'_n(b\ell^{n-1}\theta) = \varphi_{n-1}\iota'_{n-1}(b\ell^{n-1}\theta)\widehat{\varphi}_{n-1}$$

and $b\ell^{n-1}\theta \in \mathcal{O}_{n-1}$, so that $\iota'_{n-1}(b\ell^{n-1}\theta) \in \mathrm{End}(F_{n-1})$, and consequently, $\ker(\widehat{\varphi}_{n-1}) \subseteq \ker(\iota'_n(b\ell^n\theta))$. Since $\deg(\varphi_{n-1}) = \ell$, we have also $\ker(\widehat{\varphi}_{n-1}) \subseteq F_n[\ell]$ so that $\ker(\widehat{\varphi}_{n-1}) \subseteq G$. So G is either cyclic of order ℓ and equal to $\ker(\widehat{\varphi}_{n-1})$ or of order ℓ^2 and equal to the entire ℓ-torsion subgroup $F_n[\ell]$. If the latter holds, $\iota'_n(b\ell^n\theta)$ factors through $[\ell]$ by [39, Corollary III.4.11] and $b\ell^{n-1}\theta \in \mathcal{O}_n$, so $\ell | b$. A contradiction. Hence, $G = \ker(\widehat{\varphi}_{n-1})$.

By the lemma, if we evaluate $\iota_n'(b\ell^n\theta)$ on $F_n[\ell]$, we can recover $\ker(\widehat{\varphi}_{n-1})$ and compute $\widehat{\varphi}_{n-1}$ with Vélu's formulas [43] to recover F_{n-1}. Using modular equations to push the chains using the algorithm of Sect. 2.4, we can also compute

$$[\mathfrak{q}_j]^{-r} \cdot F_{n-1} \to \cdots \to F_{n-1} \to \cdots \to [\mathfrak{q}_j]^r \cdot F_{n-1}$$

for all $j \in [\![1 \; ; \; t]\!]$, with the knowledge of F_{n-1} and

$$[\mathfrak{q}_j]^{-r} \cdot F_n \to \cdots \to F_n \to \cdots \to [\mathfrak{q}_j]^r \cdot F_n.$$

Hence, we can apply our method recursively to recover the whole chain $(F_i)_{0 \le i \le n}$.

Now, the problem is to find a K-oriented endomorphism $\iota_n'(\beta)$ with $\beta \in \mathcal{O}_n \setminus \mathcal{O}_{n+1}$. Onuki suggests to find β such that $\beta\mathcal{O}_n = I \cdot J$, where $I := \prod_{j=1}^t (\mathfrak{q}_j \cap \mathcal{O}_n)^{e_j}$ with $e_1, \cdots, e_t \in [\![-r \; ; \; r]\!]$ and J is an $\mathcal{O}_n$-ideal of norm as small as possible. Then $\iota_n'(\beta)$ will be a composite of the isogenies $F_n \longrightarrow [I] \cdot F_n$ with kernel $F_n[I]$ and $[I] \cdot F_n \longrightarrow [IJ] \cdot F_n = F_n$, with kernel $[I] \cdot F_n[J]$. The first isogeny can be computed with the knowledge of the $\mathfrak{q}_j$-action chains

$$[\mathfrak{q}_j]^{-r} \cdot F_n \to \cdots \to F_n \to \cdots \to [\mathfrak{q}_j]^r \cdot F_n$$

for all $j \in [\![1 \; ; \; t]\!]$ (applying the method of [14, § 5.2]). Onuki suggests a meet-in-the middle exhaustive search strategy to compute the second isogeny. However, there is no guarantee that we find a K-oriented isogeny with this method (which is essential for the attack to work). Besides, Onuki's attack is very costly. It not only requires the computation of the second isogeny (in $\Omega(\sqrt{N(J)})$ operations) but it also requires, before that, an exhaustive search for $\beta \in \mathcal{O}_n \setminus \mathcal{O}_{n+1}$ with a big factor $I = \prod_{j=1}^t (\mathfrak{q}_j \cap \mathcal{O}_n)^{e_j}$ and a small factor J. The time complexity of such an attack is $\Omega(\ell^{2n/3}/(r+1)^{t/3})$ (see Appendix B). Hence, it would require more than 2^{100} operations with Colò and Kohel's parameters ($n = 256$, $t = 74$, $\ell = 2$ and $r = 5$). In [32, §6.3], Onuki underestimated the complexity as he neglected the exhaustive search for β, which led him to recommend $n \ge 10^3$.

In the following, we present another method based on a lattice reduction to find $\iota_n'(\beta)$ that breaks Colò and Kohel's parameters.

4.2 Finding Endomorphisms via Relations

Let us assume that

$$\beta\mathcal{O}_n = \prod_{j=1}^t (\mathfrak{q}_j \cap \mathcal{O}_n)^{e_j},$$

with $e_1, \ldots, e_t \in [\![-2r \; ; \; 2r]\!]$ and write $e_j := e_j' + e_j''$ with $e_j', e_j'' \in [\![-r \; ; \; r]\!]$ for all $j \in [\![1 \; ; \; t]\!]$. Then, with the knowledge of the $\mathfrak{q}_j$-action horizontal chains

$$[\mathfrak{q}_j]^{-r} \cdot F_n \to \cdots \to F_n \to \cdots \to [\mathfrak{q}_j]^r \cdot F_n$$

for all $j \in [\![1\ ;\ t]\!]$, we can compute the isogenies

$$\varphi : F_n \longrightarrow \prod_{j=1}^{t} [\mathfrak{q}_j]^{e'_j} \cdot F_n \quad \text{and} \quad \psi : F_n \longrightarrow \prod_{j=1}^{t} [\mathfrak{q}_j]^{-e''_j} \cdot F_n = \prod_{j=1}^{t} [\mathfrak{q}_j]^{e'_j} \cdot F_n,$$

and finally compute $\iota'_n(\beta) = \widehat{\psi} \circ \varphi$.

Hence, to find a suitable β and compute $\iota'_n(\beta)$, it suffices to find a non-zero vector of ∞-norm $\leq 2r$ in the relation lattice of the $\mathfrak{q}_j$ in $\mathcal{O}_n$

$$L_n := \left\{ (e_1, \ldots, e_t) \in \mathbb{Z}^t \,\middle|\, \prod_{j=1}^{t} [\mathfrak{q}_j \cap \mathcal{O}_n]^{e_j} = [1] \quad \text{in } \mathrm{Cl}(\mathcal{O}_n) \right\}.$$

As explained in Sect. 3.3, L_n can be computed in polynomial time in n and t. But can we find short enough vectors in L_n? Assuming that L_n behaves as a random lattice, the following results answer this question with an estimate of the first minimum for the ∞-norm $\lambda_1^{(\infty)}(L_n)$.

Lemma 3 (Aono, Espitau and Nguyen [46, Theorem 11]**)**

(i) *The set $\mathcal{I}_{N,d}$ for full-rank sublattices of $\mathbb{Z}^d$ with covolume N is finite.*
(ii) *Let Λ be a random variable following the uniform distribution on $\mathcal{I}_{N,d}$. Then, for all $\varepsilon > 0$, there exists $d_0, N_0 \in \mathbb{N}^*$ such that for all $d \geq d_0$ and $N \geq N_0$*

$$\mathbb{P}\left[\left| \lambda_1^{(\infty)}(\Lambda) - \frac{N^{\frac{1}{d}}}{2} \right| \leq \frac{\log\log(d)}{d} \frac{N^{\frac{1}{d}}}{2} \right] \geq 1 - \varepsilon.$$

Proof. **(i)** $\mathcal{I}_{N,d}$ is in bijection with the matrices of $M_d(\mathbb{Z})$ in Hermite Normal Form with discriminant $\pm N$. (i) follows.

(ii) This result has already been proved in [46, Theorem 11] for the norm ℓ_2. The reasoning would be exactly the same here. We only have to replace the Gaussian Heuristic function $h(d) = 1/\mathrm{Vol}(B_2(0,1))^{1/d}$ by the constant $1/\mathrm{Vol}(B_\infty(0,1))^{1/d} = 1/2$ in the inequality.

Lemma 4. *$Covol(L_n) = \#Cl(\mathcal{O}_n)$.*

Proof. We have an exact sequence

$$\{0\} \longrightarrow L_n \longrightarrow \mathbb{Z}^t \longrightarrow \mathrm{Cl}(\mathcal{O}_n) \longrightarrow \{0\},$$

where the first map is the natural inclusion $L_n \subseteq \mathbb{Z}^t$ and the second one is

$$(e_1, \ldots, e_t) \in \mathbb{Z}^t \longmapsto \prod_{j=1}^{t} [\mathfrak{q}_j]^{e_j} \in \mathrm{Cl}(\mathcal{O}_n).$$

It is surjective because the $[\mathfrak{q}_j]$ generate $\mathrm{Cl}(\mathcal{O}_n)$. As a consequence, $\mathrm{Cl}(\mathcal{O}_n) \simeq \mathbb{Z}^t/L_n$, so that $\mathrm{Covol}(L_n) = \#(\mathbb{Z}^t/L_n) = \#\mathrm{Cl}(\mathcal{O}_n)$.

Colò and Kohel recommend to define a secret key space

$$\left\{ \prod_{j=1}^{t} [\mathfrak{q}_j]^{e_j} \;\middle|\; (e_1, \ldots, e_t) \in [\![-r \; ; \; r]\!]^t \right\}$$

large enough to (heuristically) cover all of $\mathrm{Cl}(\mathcal{O}_n)$ without many redundancies to make it computationally hard to find short cycles in the key space that break OSIDH, as explained earlier. This leads to $\mathrm{Covol}(L_n) = \#\mathrm{Cl}(\mathcal{O}_n) \simeq (2r+1)^t$. Assuming that L_n behaves as a random lattice in $\mathcal{I}_{\#\mathrm{Cl}(\mathcal{O}_n),t}$, we have

$$\lambda_1^{(\infty)}(L_n) \leq \left(1 + \frac{\log\log(t)}{t}\right) \frac{(\#\mathrm{Cl}(\mathcal{O}_n))^{\frac{1}{t}}}{2} \simeq \left(1 + \frac{\log\log(t)}{t}\right)\left(r + \frac{1}{2}\right) \leq 2r$$

for t big enough. Hence, we expect L_n to contain short enough vectors, thus enabling our attack, at least in theory.

Complexity Analysis. All operations in our attack are polynomial in n and t on a classical computer, except the search for a nontrivial vector $\mathbf{e} \in L_n \setminus \{0\}$ such that $\|\mathbf{e}\|_\infty \leq 2r$, which takes exponential time in t. The most direct way to find $\mathbf{e}$ is to solve the shortest vector problem (SVP) in ∞-norm, and the best known algorithm for this is due to Aggarwal and Mukhopadhyay [1], and runs in heuristic time $2^{0.62t+o(t)}$. We have no theoretical guarantee that shortest vectors in ℓ_2 norm are shortest vectors in ∞-norm but there is a margin between $\lambda_1^{(\infty)}(L_n)$ and $2r$, so SVP algorithms in ℓ_2 norm are relevant here. The best SVP algorithm in ℓ_2 norm is due to Becker, Ducas, Gama and Laarhoven [4] and runs in time $(3/2)^{t/2+o(t)} \simeq 2^{0.292t+o(t)}$.

Neglecting polynomial terms and factors, we may assume that our attack runs in $2^{0.292t+o(t)}$. Thus, to reach 128 bits of classical security, we would have at the very least to take $t \approx 400$. As for other parameters, the setup of OSIDH requires $n \simeq t\log(2r+1)/\log(\ell)$ (since $\ell^n \simeq \#\mathrm{Cl}(\mathcal{O}_n) \simeq (2r+1)^t$), however we are going to argue that this bound is not sufficient for security.

4.3 Extending the Attack by Exhaustive Search

As we saw, our attack is possible only when $\lambda_1^{(\infty)}(L_n) \leq 2r$ and this inequality always holds when the key space covers $\mathrm{Cl}(\mathcal{O}_n)$. When the key space is significantly smaller than $\mathrm{Cl}(\mathcal{O}_n)$, *i.e.* when $\#\mathrm{Cl}(\mathcal{O}_n) \gg (2r+1)^t$, Lemma 3 ensures that $\lambda_1^{(\infty)}(L_n) \simeq (\#\mathrm{Cl}(\mathcal{O}_n))^{1/t}/2 > 2r$. Nevertheless, we can extend the attack to address this case.

Let us assume that we found a short vector $\mathbf{e} \in L_n$ with norm $\|\mathbf{e}\|_\infty > 2r$. Then, we may write $\mathbf{e} := \mathbf{e}' + \mathbf{e}'' + \mathbf{d}$ with $\mathbf{e}', \mathbf{e}'', \mathbf{d} \in \mathbb{Z}^t$ such that $\|\mathbf{e}'\|_\infty = \|\mathbf{e}''\|_\infty = r$ and $\mathbf{d}$ has ∞-norm as small as possible. As previously, we can compute the K-oriented isogenies

$$\varphi : F_n \longrightarrow F' := \prod_{j=1}^{t} [\mathfrak{q}_j]^{e'_j} \cdot F_n \quad \text{and} \quad \psi : F_n \longrightarrow F'' := \prod_{j=1}^{t} [\mathfrak{q}_j]^{-e''_j} \cdot F_n.$$

with kernel $F_n[\prod_{j=1}^t [\mathfrak{q}_j]^{e'_j}]$ and $F_n[\prod_{j=1}^t [\mathfrak{q}_j]^{-e''_j}]$ respectively. In order to compute the endomorphism of F_n associated to $\mathbf{e}$ (whose kernel is $F_n[\prod_{j=1}^t \mathfrak{q}_j^{e_j}]$), it remains to compute the isogeny $F' \longrightarrow F''$ associated to $\mathbf{d}$ (whose kernel is $F'[\prod_{j=1}^t \mathfrak{q}_j^{d_j}]$). Following Onuki's idea, we compute this isogeny by a meet-in-the-middle style search. Let us write $\mathbf{d} := \mathbf{d}' + \mathbf{d}''$ with $d'_j := \lfloor d_j/2 \rfloor$ and $d''_j := d_j - d'_j$ for all $j \in [\![1 \; ; \; t]\!]$. We compute K-oriented isogenies

$$\phi : F' \longrightarrow \prod_{j=1}^t [\mathfrak{q}_j]^{d'_j} \cdot F' \quad \text{and} \quad \phi' : F'' \longrightarrow \prod_{j=1}^t [\mathfrak{q}_j]^{-d''_j} \cdot F'' = \prod_{j=1}^t [\mathfrak{q}_j]^{d'_j} \cdot F'$$

of kernel $F'[\prod_{j=1}^t [\mathfrak{q}_j]^{d'_j}]$ and $F''[\prod_{j=1}^t [\mathfrak{q}_j]^{-d''_j}]$ respectively, by exhaustively testing all isogenies of degree $\prod_{j=1}^t q_j^{|d'_j|}$ and $\prod_{j=1}^t q_j^{|d''_j|}$ respectively, until the codomains of ϕ and ϕ' match. In that case, the desired endomorphism will be the composite $\widehat{\psi} \circ \widehat{\phi'} \circ \phi \circ \varphi$. Note that, as in Onuki's attack, we have no theoretical guarantee that such an isogeny will actually be K-oriented (which is necessary to perform the attack). However, assuming the attack succeeds, we can estimate its complexity.

Proposition 2. *Under the heuristic assumption that L_n behaves like a random lattice among lattices of covolume $\#\mathrm{Cl}(\mathcal{O}_n)$ and that the shortest vector of L_n can be found in negligible time, our attack performs in time*

$$\Omega\left((q_1+1)^{\frac{1}{4}\ell^{n/t}-r}\right),$$

where $q_1 := N(\mathfrak{q}_1)$ is assumed to be the smallest prime among the $q_j := N(\mathfrak{q}_j)$ for $j \in [\![1 \; ; \; t]\!]$.

Proof. The dominant step in our attack is clearly the meet-in-the-middle search, and its time complexity is (up to polynomial factors)

$$\Omega\left(\prod_{j=1}^t (q_j+1)^{|d'_j|} + \prod_{j=1}^t (q_j+1)^{|d''_j|}\right).$$

Indeed, we search among all composites of chains of q_j-isogenies of length $|d'_j|$ and $|d''_j|$ for $j \in [\![1 \; ; \; t]\!]$. Besides, by [39, Corollary III.4.11], we know that the number of isogenies of prime degree q is $q+1$. The number of isogenies to test, and the time complexity of our exhaustive search follows. By assumption, $\mathbf{d}'$ and $\mathbf{d}''$ cut $\mathbf{d}$ in half and $\mathbf{e} = \mathbf{e}' + \mathbf{e}'' + \mathbf{d}$, so that

$$\|\mathbf{e}\|_\infty \leq \|\mathbf{e}'\|_\infty + \|\mathbf{e}''\|_\infty + \|\mathbf{d}\|_\infty = 2r + \|\mathbf{d}\|_\infty$$

and $\|\mathbf{d}\|_\infty \geq \|\mathbf{e}\|_\infty - 2r \geq \lambda_1^{(\infty)}(L) - 2r$. But by Lemma 3, we have

$$\lambda_1^{(\infty)}(L) \geq \left(1 - \frac{\log\log(t)}{t}\right) \frac{(\#\mathrm{Cl}(\mathcal{O}_n))^{\frac{1}{t}}}{2} \underset{t\to+\infty}{\sim} \frac{\ell^{\frac{n}{t}}}{2}.$$

The result follows.

In conclusion, to ensure an asymptotic security level of λ bits, we would need

$$(q_1+1)^{\frac{1}{4}\ell^{n/t}-r} \geq 2^{\lambda} \iff n \geq \frac{t}{\log(\ell)} \log\left(4r + \frac{4\lambda\log(2)}{\log(q_1+1)}\right).$$

Note that initially, Colò and Kohel proposed $n \simeq t\log(2r+1)/\log(\ell)$, so this bound is more restrictive.

4.4 Implementation of Our Attack

Tests on Toy Parameters. We implemented the OSIDH protocol and our attack in `Sagemath` [42] for toy parameters: $\ell = 2$, $r = 3$, $t = 10$, $n = 28$ and $K = \mathbb{Q}(i)$. The source code can be found on `Github`[3]. The attack is divided into three steps:

Step 1: Our lattice based chain recovery of both Alice's and Bob's chains.
Step 2: A recovery of Alice's ideal class using the algorithm presented in Sect. 3.2.
Step 3: The shared secret chain computation by acting with Alice's ideal class on Bob's chain.

Time performance results were obtained from a sample of 60 executions on a Mac Book Pro mid-2015 equipped with an Intel Core i7-4870HQ clocked at 2.5 GHz. They are presented in the following table:

	Protocol	Chain attack (half of step 1)	Step 2	Step 3	Complete attack
Average (in s)	84.83	135.44	98.19	6.97	376.05
Standard deviation (in s)	5.61	7.15	13.06	1.61	18.29
Margin of error (95 %) on the average (in s)	1.46	1.90	3.40	0.42	4.76

For the modular polynomials that were used in our implementation, we give credit to Sutherland's online database[4] computed with the algorithms of [10].

Attacking Real Parameters. For 128 bits of classical security, Colò and Kohel suggest $\ell = 2$, $r = 5$, $t = 74$, $n = 256$ and $K = \mathbb{Q}(i)$. Our implementation of the full attack cannot handle such parameters, however our attempt at implementing the OSIDH protocol itself cannot handle them either. In fact, we are not aware of any implementation of OSIDH using the parameters originally suggested in [14, § 6].

[3] See https://github.com/Pierrick-Dartois/OSIDH.
[4] See https://math.mit.edu/~drew/ClassicalModPolys.html.

Ironically, the practical bottleneck in the attack is not the exponential time lattice reduction step, but rather the class group action computation, which is essentially shared with OSIDH itself, and which runs in polynomial time (see Lemma 5). The culprit are the extremely large modular polynomials that the implementation needs to handle, requiring several GB of storage.

On the contrary, the lattice reduction step in the attack can easily handle the real parameters, and much more. Indeed, we were able to compute the relation lattice L_n for the originally proposed parameters in 64 min. Most of this time was spent computing the (polynomial time) discrete logarithms, while the lattice reduction step, performed via `fpylll`'s implementation of BKZ [37,41] with block size $k = 4$, found a vector $\mathbf{e} \in L_n$ of ∞-norm $\|\mathbf{e}\|_\infty = 9 < 2r$ in less than 0.5 s.

In conclusion, we believe that our lattice based attack could be very efficient in practice for the originally proposed parameters, as well as larger ones, provided one is able to efficiently implement OSIDH itself.

5 Countermeasures

Because our attack has exponential complexity, it is still possible to safely instantiate OSIDH by increasing parameters. We analyze here the available options.

5.1 Increase t, and Everything Else

The simplest countermeasure is to increase the number t of prime ideals $\mathfrak{q}_j$, which governs the dimension of the relation lattice, to the point where solving SVP becomes infeasible. As we saw in Sect. 4.2 if we use the Becker–Ducas–Gama–Laarhoven algorithm [4] to solve SVP in norm ℓ_2, we need at least $t \approx 400$ to achieve 128 bits of classical security. However, the size of $\mathrm{Cl}(\mathcal{O}_n)$, and thus the prime p, shall be increased accordingly to satisfy $\#\mathrm{Cl}(\mathcal{O}_n) \approx (2r+1)^t$. Otherwise, we could consider only the $t' < t$ first $\mathfrak{q}_j$ (where t' is such that $\#\mathrm{Cl}(\mathcal{O}_n) \approx (2r+1)^{t'}$) and still perform our attack with a smaller relation lattice of dimension t'. We may partly compensate this increase of t by decreasing r; we may in fact even restrict to just three values ($r = 1$) for the secret exponents, *e.g.* $e_j \in \{-1, 0, 1\}$. With $t \approx 400$, $\ell = 2$ and $r = 1$, this would lead to $n \approx 630$.

This increase is significant compared to $n = 256, t = 74$ as suggested by Colò and Kohel, or even $n = 1428, t = 100$ as suggested by Onuki [14, § 6.3], and we expect them to severely affect performance, as the following analysis indicates.

Lemma 5. *Let $(E_i)_{0 \le i \le n}$ be a descending ℓ-isogeny chain such that E_0 is $\mathcal{O}_K$-oriented and $\mathfrak{a} := \prod_{j=1}^{t} \mathfrak{q}_j^{e_j}$ with $e_1, \ldots, e_t$ sampled in $[\![-r\ ;\ r]\!]$. Then, the computation of $\mathfrak{a} \cdot (E_i)_{0 \le i \le n}$ requires $O(nt^3 \log^2(t) + n^2)$ operations over $\mathbb{F}_{p^2}$ on average, with the constant inside O depending on r and ℓ.*

Proof. See the extended version of this work [17].

A possibly even worse consequence of this countermeasure is that it tightly binds the security of OSIDH to a lattice assumption. Qualitatively, security would look much worse than that of any lattice based scheme, since it appears to be impossible to prove any kind of security reduction of OSIDH to a standard lattice problem. Quantitatively, it seems hard to justify the practical interest of such a slow scheme, when lattice based schemes are several orders of magnitude faster.

5.2 Increase $\#\mathrm{Cl}(\mathcal{O}_n)$, Keep the Same Key Space

Alternatively, we may ensure that $\#\mathrm{Cl}(\mathcal{O}_n) \simeq \ell^n$ is much larger than $(2r+1)^t$, so that the key space

$$\left\{ \prod_{j=1}^{t} [\mathfrak{q}_j]^{e_j} \mid (e_1, \dots, e_t) \in [\![-r\ ;\ r]\!]^t \right\}$$

is far from covering all of $\mathrm{Cl}(\mathcal{O}_n)$, and thus $\lambda_1^{(\infty)}(L_n) > 2r$. The analysis in Sect. 4.3 suggests taking

$$n \geq \frac{t}{\log(\ell)} \log\left(4r + \frac{4\lambda \log(2)}{\log(q_1+1)}\right)$$

for a security level of λ bits.

We can adapt Colò and Kohel's choice of parameters ($K = \mathbb{Q}(i), \ell = 2, r = 5, t = 74$) by taking $n = 575$ instead of $n = 256$ to attain $\lambda = 128$ bits of security. The increase for n, and thus for p, is roughly comparable to the previous countermeasure; however, by keeping the same value for t, we do not need to introduce larger modular polynomials, and can thus hope for a significantly faster result.

Onuki's choice of parameters in [32, §6.3] ($n = 1428$, $t = 100$, $\ell = 2$, $r = 3$ and $K = \mathbb{Q}(i)$) also follows this countermeasure but such an increase in n is not necessary and results form a cost underestimation of his attack, as we explained in Sect. 4.1.

5.3 OSIDH and Cryptographic Group Actions

Besides affecting efficiency, both countermeasures also have adverse effects on the possibility of using the OSIDH group action in contexts other than key exchange. Brassard and Yung [9], then Couveignes [15], then Alamati, De Feo, Montgomery and Patranabis [2] established the axiomatic foundations of cryptographic group actions. The latter call Effective Group Action (EGA) a group action $(G, X, \cdot)$ where, among other axioms, the value $g \cdot x$ can be efficiently computed for any $g \in G$ and any $x \in X$. They also observe that CSIDH does not naturally satisfy this axiom, and thus define a better abstraction named Restricted Effective Group Actions (REGA), where $g \cdot x$ can be efficiently evaluated for any x, but only for a few g taken from a fixed list.

OSIDH satisfies neither the axioms of EGAs, nor of REGAs. Indeed, the class group action of OSIDH can only be computed with the help of the horizontal chains, however these are "single use": after computing $G_n := \left(\prod_j \mathfrak{q}_j^{e_j}\right) \cdot F_n$ there is no way to compute the horizontal chains for G_n without knowing the secret descending chain $(F_i)_{0 \leq i \leq n}$, and thus of evaluating a new action on G_n. Colò and Kohel did not claim anything else than a key exchange, and for that the limitations of OSIDH are not an issue. However it is natural to ask whether the same primitives that are known from the CSIDH group action can be built from the OSIDH action. This is where the countermeasures to our attack become an obstacle.

An important step for CSIDH was the computation of the class group structure of CSIDH-512, paved the way for the CSI-FiSh signature scheme [6]. Thanks to this intensive computational effort, it became possible to compute a reduced basis for the relation lattice of CSIDH-512, which is used to evaluate the action of arbitrary exponent vectors, much in the same way as we did in Sect. 13, thus effectively making CSIDH-512 into an EGA. The class group structure of OSIDH is much easier to compute than in CSIDH, and thus one may have hoped that the analogue of CSI-FiSh would be easy to define. However it is clear that we cannot ask the OSIDH relation lattice to be, at the same time, easy and hard to reduce: easy for a CSI-FiSh style CVP computation, and hard to prevent our attack. Thus, it would seem that neither CSI-FiSh, nor any of the applications derived from it [2,5,19], can be replicated in the OSIDH context.

Remark 1. There seems to be a small positive upside, though, to OSIDH not being a cryptographic group action in the usual sense: the best generic attacks against (R)EGA, both classical and quantum, do not seem to apply to OSIDH!

Indeed, the best classical attack against (R)EGAs is a Pollard Rho-style random walk algorithm [24,25], which necessitates to compute long random walks by chaining many group actions. This is not possible for OSIDH, for which we argued the group action can only be evaluated a limited number of times. The next best algorithm would be a meet-in-the-middle search, which has the same time complexity, but worse space complexity.

Possibly more remarkably, the best quantum algorithm against (R)EGAs is Kuperberg's subexponential algorithm for the hidden shift problem [29]. This algorithm repeatedly calls a quantum oracle that evaluates the group action in superposition for all possible group elements. If we apply the countermeasure of Sect. 5.2, then the OSIDH group action can only be evaluated on a negligibly small subset of the whole class group. It has already been remarked that Kuperberg algorithm doesn't appear to work when the oracle is only used to evaluate the action for a small fraction of the group elements [12], and thus wouldn't apply to this variant of OSIDH. The next best quantum against OSIDH would be, again, a meet-in-the-middle strategy, possibly applying some Grover-style accelerations [26], which has exponential complexity, putting OSIDH in a much better place than CSIDH regarding quantum security.

6 Conclusion

We presented a new classical attack against OSIDH that practically breaks the parameters proposed for 128 bits security. The attack has exponential complexity, and can thus be countered by increasing parameters. However the increased parameters heavily impact the performance of a scheme which is already very slow, and they also severely limit the number of other cryptographic primitives one may hope to derive from the OSIDH group action.

It must be stressed that there is, as of today, no reduction of the security of OSIDH to a well studied isogeny problem, and thus the security of the countermeasures we propose remains somewhat dubious. More scrutiny of the security assumptions supporting OSIDH would be beneficial.

Interestingly, we remarked that one of the countermeasures we propose appears to defeat not only our attack, but also Kuperberg's quantum attack. It would be interesting to investigate the quantum security of OSIDH more in depth.

None of the countermeasures we propose is particularly efficient, and OSIDH itself is challenging to implement. A detailed study of performance optimizations applicable to OSIDH, and of potential efficiency-minded variants, would be very welcome.

A Time Complexity of the Chain Attack of Sect. 3.3

We refer to Sect. 3.3 for the notations. As explained in Sect. 3.3, the dominant step in the attack is to find a close vector to $\mathbf{e}_{i+1}$ in L_{i+1} and compute the action of $[\mathfrak{a}_i \cdot \mathfrak{b}_i]$ on E_{i+1}. This operation has to be repeated at most $\simeq \ell$ times for all $i \in [\![0\ ;\ n-1]\!]$, so at most $n\ell$ times.

If we find $\mathbf{c} \in L_{i+1}$ close to $\mathbf{e}_{i+1}$ and set $\mathbf{e}'_{i+1} := \mathbf{e}_{i+1} - \mathbf{c}$, so that $[\mathfrak{a}_i \cdot \mathfrak{b}_i] = \prod_{j=1}^{t} [\mathfrak{q}_j]^{e'_{i+1,j}}$ in $\mathrm{Cl}(\mathcal{O}_{i+1})$, then the time complexity of the operation $[\mathfrak{a}_i \cdot \mathfrak{b}_i] \cdot E_{i+1}$ is

$$\Theta\left((i+1)\sum_{j=1}^{t} P(q_j, n)|e'_{i+1,j}|\right),$$

where P is a polynomial. Hence, the complexity is $\Theta(\|\mathbf{e}'_{i+1}\|_1)$ up to a polynomial factor (in n, t and the q_j). Since $\|\mathbf{e}'_{i+1}\|_2 \leq \|\mathbf{e}'_{i+1}\|_1 \leq \sqrt{t}\|\mathbf{e}'_{i+1}\|_2$, the complexity becomes $\Theta(\|\mathbf{e}'_{i+1}\|_2)$ up to a polynomial factor.

Theorem 3 *[23, Theorem 3.3]. Let $\Lambda \subseteq \mathbb{Z}^d$ be a lattice of rank d, $B := (\mathbf{b}_1, \ldots, \mathbf{b}_d)$, a basis of Λ, a target $\mathbf{x} \in \mathbb{R}^d$ and $k \in \mathbb{N}^*$ such that $d > 2k$. Under some heuristic assumptions, there exists an algorithm finding $\mathbf{c} \in \Lambda$ such that*

$$\|\mathbf{x} - \mathbf{c}\|_2 = \Theta\left(GH(k)^{\frac{d}{2k}}\, Covol(\Lambda)^{\frac{1}{d}}\right),$$

where GH is the Gaussian heuristic function: $GH(k) := \Gamma(k/2+1)^{1/k}/\sqrt{\pi}$. *This algorithm runs in time*

$$(T_{CVP}(k) + T_{SVP}(k))P\left(k, d, \log \|\mathbf{x}\|_2, \log \max_{1\leq i\leq d} \|\mathbf{b}_i\|_2\right),$$

where $T_{CVP}(k)$ *and* $T_{SVP}(k)$ *are the time complexities of oracles for CVP and SVP in dimension* k *for the norm* ℓ_2 *respectively and* P *is a polynomial.*

The best known algorithms for CVP and SVP are due to [21] and [4] respectively. They run in time $T_{CVP}(k) = 2^{c_1 k+o(k)}$ and $T_{SVP}(k) = \left(\frac{3}{2}\right)^{k/2+o(k)} = 2^{c_2 k+o(k)}$ respectively, with $c_1 \approx 0.264$ and $c_2 \approx 0.292$. The time complexity of the attack follows

$$T := 2^{c_2 k+o(k)} + \frac{1}{\sqrt{\pi}^{\frac{1}{k}}}\Gamma\left(\frac{k}{2}+1\right)^{\frac{t}{2k^2}} \ell^{\frac{n}{t}}$$

up to polynomial factors, where we used the fact that $\mathrm{Covol}(L_n) = \#\mathrm{Cl}(\mathcal{O}_n) \simeq \ell^n$ and neglected $T_{CVP}(k)$ compared to $T_{SVP}(k)$. Using the Stirling equivalent $\Gamma(k/2+1) \sim \sqrt{\pi k}(k/2e)^{k/2}$ as $k \to +\infty$ and setting $k := \lfloor \kappa\sqrt{t\log_2(t)}\rfloor$, with $\kappa := 1/\sqrt{8c_2}$ in order to optimize the complexity, we get

$$T = 2^{(\sqrt{c_2/8}+o(1))\sqrt{t\log_2(t)}} = \exp((c+o(1))\sqrt{t\log(t)}),$$

with $c := \sqrt{c_2/8\log(2)} \simeq 0.229$, assuming that ℓ and n are constant and $t \to +\infty$.

B Complexity Analysis of Onuki's Attack Presented in Sect. 4.1

We use the notations of Sect. 4.1 explaining Onuki's attack which consists in computing a K-oriented endomorphism $\iota'_n(\beta) \in \mathrm{End}(F_n)$ for $\beta \in \mathcal{O}_n \setminus \mathcal{O}_{n+1}$. We look for β such that $\beta\mathcal{O}_n = I \cdot J$, with a big factor $I := \prod_{j=1}^t (\mathfrak{q}_j \cap \mathcal{O}_n)^{e_j}$, where $e_1, \cdots, e_t \in [\![-r\ ;\ r]\!]$, and a small factor J. Then $\iota'_n(\beta)$ will be computed as the composite of the isogeny associated to I and the isonegy associated to J. The first one is easy to compute with the knowledge of the action of powers of $\mathfrak{q}_j$ on F_n. The second one can be computed by a meet-in-the-middle strategy in $\Omega(\sqrt{N(J)})$ operations (as explained in Sect. 4.3).

We proceed as follows to select a suitable β. Let θ be a generator of $\mathcal{O}_K$, so that $\ell^n\theta$ generates $\mathcal{O}_n$. We sample $\beta := a + b\ell^n\theta$ with a and b sampled uniformly at random in $[\![-m\ ;\ m]\!]$ and $[\![-m\ ;\ m]\!] \setminus \ell\mathbb{Z}$ respectively, for m big enough. We stop the sampling when $N(\beta)$ has a big enough divisor $Q := \prod_{j=1}^t q_j^{e'_j}$ with $e'_1, \cdots, e'_t \in [\![0\ ;\ r]\!]$, let's say $Q \geq x$, where the threshold x is to be chosen. We make the heuristic assumption that $N(\beta)$ has the same arithmetic properties as a uniform variable in $[\![N_{min}\ ;\ N_{max}]\!]$. Under this assumption, we have the following result:

Lemma 6. *The average time complexity of Onuki's attack [32, §6.3] is:*

$$C(x) \geq \frac{x}{(r+1)^t} + \frac{\kappa\sqrt{N_{max}}}{\sqrt{x}(r+1)^t},$$

where $\kappa := \frac{1}{2\sqrt{q_1}}\left(1 - \frac{1}{q_1}\right)$ *and* x *is the threshold for the value of the norm of the ideal* $J = \prod_{j=1}^t \mathfrak{q}_j^{e_j}$ *dividing* β*. The optimal value for the threshold is* $x_m := (\kappa/2)^{2/3} N_{max}^{1/2}(r+1)^{t/3}$ *and the optimal average time complexity is:*

$$C(x_m) = \Omega\left(\frac{\sqrt{N_{max}}}{(r+1)^{\frac{t}{3}}}\right) = \Omega\left(\frac{\ell^{\frac{2n}{3}}}{(r+1)^{\frac{t}{3}}}\right),$$

since $N_{max} \geq N_{min} \geq \ell^{2n}$.

Proof. Under the heuristic assumption we made, we can assume that $N := N(\beta)$ is a uniform random variable in the range $[\![N_{min}\ ;\ N_{max}]\!]$. We define the random variable:

$$Q := Q(N) = \prod_{j=1}^{t} q_j^{\min(r, v_{q_j}(N))}.$$

The cost of the exhaustive search for a suitable β is then:

$$C_1(x) = \frac{1}{\mathbb{P}(Q(N) \geq x)} = \frac{N_{max} - N_{min}}{\#S(x)},$$

with:

$$\begin{aligned} S(x) &:= \left\{ y \in [\![N_{min}\ ;\ N_{max}]\!] \,\middle|\, \prod_{j=1}^{t} q_j^{\min(r, v_{q_j}(y))} \geq x \right\} \\ &= \bigcup_{\substack{(e_1,\cdots,e_t)\in[\![0\ ;\ r]\!]^t \\ x \leq \prod_{j=1}^t q_j^{e_j} \leq N_{max}}} \left\{ k \prod_{j=1}^{t} q_j^{e_j} \,\middle|\, k \in \left[\!\!\left[\left\lceil \frac{N_{min}}{\prod_{j=1}^t q_j^{e_j}} \right\rceil\ ;\ \left\lfloor \frac{N_{max}}{\prod_{j=1}^t q_j^{e_j}} \right\rfloor \right]\!\!\right] \right\} \end{aligned}$$

so that:

$$\begin{aligned} \#S(x) &\leq \sum_{\substack{(e_1,\cdots,e_t)\in[\![0\ ;\ r]\!]^t \\ x \leq \prod_{j=1}^t q_j^{e_j} \leq N_{max}}} \left(\left\lfloor \frac{N_{max}}{\prod_{j=1}^t q_j^{e_j}} \right\rfloor - \left\lceil \frac{N_{min}}{\prod_{j=1}^t q_j^{e_j}} \right\rceil \right) \\ &\leq \sum_{\substack{(e_1,\cdots,e_t)\in[\![0\ ;\ r]\!]^t \\ x \leq \prod_{j=1}^t q_j^{e_j} \leq N_{max}}} \frac{N_{max} - N_{min}}{\prod_{j=1}^t q_j^{e_j}} \\ &\leq \frac{N_{max} - N_{min}}{x} \# \left\{ (e_1, \cdots, e_t) \in [\![0\ ;\ r]\!]^t \,\middle|\, x \leq \prod_{j=1}^{t} q_j^{e_j} \leq N_{max} \right\} \\ &\leq (N_{max} - N_{min}) \frac{(r+1)^t}{x}. \end{aligned} \tag{1}$$

It follows that the search for β costs:

$$C_1(x) \geq \frac{x}{(r+1)^t}. \tag{2}$$

The average cost of the meet-in-the-middle procedure to find the isogeny associated to J is:

$$C_2(x) \geq \mathbb{E}\left[\sqrt{\frac{N}{Q(N)}} \mid Q(N) \geq x\right] \geq \sqrt{A}\mathbb{P}(N \geq AQ(N)|Q(N) \geq x),$$

where we used Markov's inequality with $A > 0$ to be chosen. Hence:

$$C_2(x) \geq \sqrt{A}\frac{\mathbb{P}(\{N \geq AQ(N)\} \cap \{Q(N) \geq x\})}{\mathbb{P}(Q(N) \geq x)} = \frac{\sqrt{A}\#T(A)}{\#S(x)}, \tag{3}$$

with:

$$T(A) := \left\{ k\prod_{j=1}^t q_j^{e_j} \,\middle|\, N_{max} \geq \prod_{j=1}^t q_j^{e_j} \geq x \right.$$
$$\left. \text{and} \quad k \in [\![\max\left(\lceil A \rceil, \left\lceil \frac{N_{min}}{\prod_{j=1}^t q_j^{e_j}} \right\rceil\right) \; ; \; \left\lfloor \frac{N_{max}}{\prod_{j=1}^t q_j^{e_j}} \right\rfloor]\!] \right\}.$$

We take $A := N_{max}/(q_1 x)$, so that for all $e_1, \cdots, e_t \in [\![0 \; ; \; r]\!]$ such that $N_{max} \geq \prod_{j=1}^t q_j^{e_j} \geq x$, we have:

$$\frac{N_{min}}{\prod_{j=1}^t q_j^{e_j}} \leq \frac{N_{min}}{x} < \frac{N_{max}}{q_1 x} = A,$$

since $N_{max}/N_{min} \simeq m^2 \gg q_1$. Without loss of generality, we can assume that x is a product of the q_j. Hence:

$$\#T(A) \geq \left\lfloor \frac{N_{max}}{x} \right\rfloor - A \geq \frac{N_{max}}{x} - \frac{N_{max}}{q_1 x} - 1 = \frac{N_{max}}{2x}\left(1 - \frac{1}{q_1}\right),$$

under the fair assumption that $x \leq N_{max}/2(1-1/q_1)$. This inequality combined with Eq. (1) and Eq. (3) leads to:

$$C_2(x) \geq \frac{(N_{max})^{\frac{3}{2}}(1-1/q_1)}{2\sqrt{q_1 x}(r+1)^t(N_{max}-N_{min})} \geq \frac{\sqrt{N_{max}}}{2\sqrt{q_1 x}(r+1)^t}\left(1 - \frac{1}{q_1}\right). \tag{4}$$

Combining Eq. (2) and Eq. (4), we find that Onuki's attack has average complexity:

$$C(x) \geq C_1(x) + C_2(x) \geq \frac{x}{(r+1)^t} + \frac{\kappa\sqrt{N_{max}}}{\sqrt{x}(r+1)^t},$$

with $\kappa := \frac{1}{2\sqrt{q_1}}\left(1 - \frac{1}{q_1}\right)$. The optimal value for x is obtained by differenciating of the function defined over $\mathbb{R}_+^*$:

$$x \longmapsto \frac{x}{(r+1)^t} + \frac{\kappa\sqrt{N_{max}}}{\sqrt{x}(r+1)^t}.$$

References

1. Aggarwal, D., Mukhopadhyay, P.: Improved algorithms for the shortest vector problem and the closest vector problem in the infinity norm (2018)
2. Alamati, N., De Feo, L., Montgomery, H., Patranabis, S.: Cryptographic group actions and applications. In: Moriai, S., Wang, H. (eds.) ASIACRYPT 2020. LNCS, vol. 12492, pp. 411–439. Springer, Cham (2020). https://doi.org/10.1007/978-3-030-64834-3_14
3. Babai, L.: On Lovász' lattice reduction and the nearest lattice point problem (shortened version). In: STACS (1985)
4. Becker, A., Ducas, L., Gama, N., Laarhoven, T.: New directions in nearest neighbor searching with applications to lattice sieving. In: Krauthgamer, R. (ed.) 27th SODA, pp. 10–24. ACM-SIAM, January 2016. https://doi.org/10.1137/1.9781611974331.ch2
5. Beullens, W., Katsumata, S., Pintore, F.: Calamari and Falafl: logarithmic (linkable) ring signatures from isogenies and lattices. In: Moriai, S., Wang, H. (eds.) ASIACRYPT 2020. LNCS, vol. 12492, pp. 464–492. Springer, Cham (2020). https://doi.org/10.1007/978-3-030-64834-3_16
6. Beullens, W., Kleinjung, T., Vercauteren, F.: CSI-FiSh: efficient isogeny based signatures through class group computations. In: Galbraith, S.D., Moriai, S. (eds.) ASIACRYPT 2019. LNCS, vol. 11921, pp. 227–247. Springer, Cham (2019). https://doi.org/10.1007/978-3-030-34578-5_9
7. Boneh, D., Kogan, D., Woo, K.: Oblivious pseudorandom functions from isogenies. In: Moriai, S., Wang, H. (eds.) ASIACRYPT 2020. LNCS, vol. 12492, pp. 520–550. Springer, Cham (2020). https://doi.org/10.1007/978-3-030-64834-3_18
8. Bonnetain, X., Schrottenloher, A.: Quantum security analysis of CSIDH. In: Canteaut, A., Ishai, Y. (eds.) EUROCRYPT 2020. LNCS, vol. 12106, pp. 493–522. Springer, Cham (2020). https://doi.org/10.1007/978-3-030-45724-2_17
9. Brassard, G., Yung, M.: One-way group actions. In: Menezes, A.J., Vanstone, S.A. (eds.) CRYPTO 1990. LNCS, vol. 537, pp. 94–107. Springer, Heidelberg (1991). https://doi.org/10.1007/3-540-38424-3_7
10. Bröker, R., Lauter, K., Sutherland, A.V.: Modular polynomials via isogeny volcanoes. Math. Comput. **81**(278), 1201–1231 (2011)
11. Castryck, W., Lange, T., Martindale, C., Panny, L., Renes, J.: CSIDH: an efficient post-quantum commutative group action. In: Peyrin, T., Galbraith, S. (eds.) ASIACRYPT 2018. LNCS, vol. 11274, pp. 395–427. Springer, Cham (2018). https://doi.org/10.1007/978-3-030-03332-3_15
12. Chavez-Saab, J., Chi-Dominguez, J.J., Jaques, S., Rodriguez-Henriquez, F.: The SQALE of CSIDH: square-root Vélu quantum-resistant isogeny action with low exponents. Cryptology ePrint Archive, Report 2020/1520 (2020). https://eprint.iacr.org/2020/1520
13. Cohen, H.: A Course in Computational Algebraic Number Theory. Springer, Heidelberg (1993). https://doi.org/10.1007/978-3-662-02945-9
14. Colò, L., Kohel, D.: Orienting supersingular isogeny graphs. J. Math. Cryptol. **14**(1), 414–437 (2020). https://doi.org/10.1515/jmc-2019-0034
15. Couveignes, J.M.: Hard homogeneous spaces. Cryptology ePrint Archive, Report 2006/291 (2006). https://eprint.iacr.org/2006/291
16. Cox, D.A.: Primes of the form $x^2 + ny^2$. Wiley (2013)
17. Dartois, P., De Feo, L.: On the security of OSIDH. Cryptology ePrint Archive, Report 2021/1681 (2021). https://ia.cr/2021/1681

18. De Feo, L., Galbraith, S.D.: SeaSign: compact isogeny signatures from class group actions. In: Ishai, Y., Rijmen, V. (eds.) EUROCRYPT 2019. LNCS, vol. 11478, pp. 759–789. Springer, Cham (2019). https://doi.org/10.1007/978-3-030-17659-4_26
19. De Feo, L., Meyer, M.: Threshold schemes from isogeny assumptions. In: Kiayias, A., Kohlweiss, M., Wallden, P., Zikas, V. (eds.) PKC 2020. LNCS, vol. 12111, pp. 187–212. Springer, Cham (2020). https://doi.org/10.1007/978-3-030-45388-6_7
20. de Saint Guilhem, C.D., Orsini, E., Petit, C., Smart, N.P.: Semi-commutative masking: a framework for isogeny-based protocols, with an application to fully secure two-round isogeny-based OT. In: Krenn, S., Shulman, H., Vaudenay, S. (eds.) CANS 2020. LNCS, vol. 12579, pp. 235–258. Springer, Cham (2020). https://doi.org/10.1007/978-3-030-65411-5_12
21. Ducas, L., Laarhoven, T., van Woerden, W.P.J.: The randomized slicer for CVPP: sharper, faster, smaller, batchier. In: Kiayias, A., Kohlweiss, M., Wallden, P., Zikas, V. (eds.) PKC 2020. LNCS, vol. 12111, pp. 3–36. Springer, Cham (2020). https://doi.org/10.1007/978-3-030-45388-6_1
22. Eisenträger, K., Hallgren, S., Lauter, K., Morrison, T., Petit, C.: Supersingular isogeny graphs and endomorphism rings: reductions and solutions. In: Nielsen, J.B., Rijmen, V. (eds.) EUROCRYPT 2018. LNCS, vol. 10822, pp. 329–368. Springer, Cham (2018). https://doi.org/10.1007/978-3-319-78372-7_11
23. Espitau, T., Kirchner, P.: The nearest-colattice algorithm: Time-approximation tradeoff for approx-CVP. Open Book Ser. **4**, 251–266 (2020). https://doi.org/10.2140/obs.2020.4.251
24. Galbraith, S.D., Hess, F., Smart, N.P.: Extending the GHS Weil descent attack. In: Knudsen, L.R. (ed.) EUROCRYPT 2002. LNCS, vol. 2332, pp. 29–44. Springer, Heidelberg (2002). https://doi.org/10.1007/3-540-46035-7_3
25. Galbraith, S.D., Stolbunov, A.: Improved algorithm for the isogeny problem for ordinary elliptic curves. Appl. Algebra Eng. Commun. Comput. **24**(2), 107–131 (2013). https://doi.org/10.1007/s00200-013-0185-0
26. Jaques, S., Schrottenloher, A.: Low-gate quantum golden collision finding. Cryptology ePrint Archive, Report 2020/424 (2020). https://eprint.iacr.org/2020/424
27. Kohel, D.: Endomorphism rings of elliptic curves over finite fields (1996). http://iml.univ-mrs.fr/~kohel/pub/thesis.pdf
28. Kohel, D.R., Lauter, K., Petit, C., Tignol, J.P.: On the quaternion-isogeny path problem. LMS J. Comput. Math. **17**(A), 418–432 (2014)
29. Kuperberg, G.: A subexponential-time quantum algorithm for the dihedral hidden subgroup problem. SIAM J. Comput. **35**(1), 170–188 (2005)
30. Lai, Y.F., Galbraith, S.D., de Saint Guilhem, C.: Compact, efficient and UC-secure isogeny-based oblivious transfer. Cryptology ePrint Archive, Report 2020/1012 (2020). https://eprint.iacr.org/2020/1012
31. Milne, J.S.: Complex multiplication (2020). https://www.jmilne.org/math/CourseNotes/cm.html
32. Onuki, H.: On oriented supersingular elliptic curves (2020). https://arxiv.org/abs/2002.09894
33. Peikert, C.: He gives C-sieves on the CSIDH. In: Canteaut, A., Ishai, Y. (eds.) EUROCRYPT 2020. LNCS, vol. 12106, pp. 463–492. Springer, Cham (2020). https://doi.org/10.1007/978-3-030-45724-2_16
34. Petit, C.: Faster algorithms for isogeny problems using torsion point images. In: Takagi, T., Peyrin, T. (eds.) ASIACRYPT 2017. LNCS, vol. 10625, pp. 330–353. Springer, Cham (2017). https://doi.org/10.1007/978-3-319-70697-9_12

35. Pohlig, S.E., Hellman, M.E.: An improved algorithm for computing logarithms over GF(p) and its cryptographic significance. IEEE Trans. Inf. Theor. IT **24**(1), 106–110 (1978)
36. Rostovtsev, A., Stolbunov, A.: Public-key cryptosystem based on isogenies. Cryptology ePrint Archive, Report 2006/145 (2006). https://eprint.iacr.org/2006/145
37. Schnorr, C.P.: A hierarchy of polynomial time lattice basis reduction algorithms. Theor. Comput. Sci. **53**, 201–224 (1987)
38. Silverman, J.H.: Advanced Topics in The Arithmetic of Elliptic Curves. Springer, New York (1994). https://doi.org/10.1007/978-1-4612-0851-8
39. Silverman, J.H.: Integral points on elliptic curves. In: The Arithmetic of Elliptic Curves. GTM, vol. 106, pp. 269–307. Springer, New York (2009). https://doi.org/10.1007/978-0-387-09494-6_9
40. Sutherland, A.V.: Structure computation and discrete logarithms in finite abelian p-groups. Math. Comput. **80**(273), 477–500 (2010)
41. The FPLLL development team: FPyLLL, a Python wraper for the fplll lattice reduction library, Version: 0.5.6 (2021). https://github.com/fplll/fpylll
42. The Sage Developers: SageMath, the Sage Mathematics Software System (Version 9.2) (2021). https://www.sagemath.org
43. Vélu, J.: Isogénies entre courbes elliptiques. Comptes-rendus de l'Académie des Sciences **273**, 238–241 (1971). https://gallica.bnf.fr
44. Waterhouse, W.C.: Abelian varieties over finite fields. Annales scientifiques de l'École Normale Supérieure **2**(4), 521–560 (1969). http://eudml.org/doc/81852
45. Wesolowski, B.: The supersingular isogeny path and endomorphism ring problems are equivalent. Cryptology ePrint Archive, Report 2021/919 (2021). https://ia.cr/2021/919
46. Yoshinori Aono, T.E., Nguyen, P.Q.: Random lattices: theory and practice. https://espitau.github.io/bin/random_lattice.pdf

Time-Memory Tradeoffs for Large-Weight Syndrome Decoding in Ternary Codes

Pierre Karpman[1(✉)] and Charlotte Lefevre[2(✉)]

[1] Institute of Engineering, University of Grenoble Alpes, CNRS, Grenoble INP, LJK, Grenoble 38000, France
pierre.karpman@univ-grenoble-alpes.fr

[2] Radboud University, Nijmegen, The Netherlands
charlotte.lefevre@ru.nl

Abstract. We propose new algorithms for solving a class of large-weight syndrome decoding problems in random ternary codes. This is the main generic problem underlying the security of the recent Wave signature scheme (Debris-Alazard *et al.* 2019), and it has so far received limited attention. At SAC 2019 Bricout *et al.* proposed a reduction to a binary subset sum problem requiring many solutions, and used it to obtain the fastest known algorithm. However —as is often the case in the coding theory literature— its memory cost is proportional to its time cost, which makes it unattractive in most applications.

In this work we propose a range of memory-efficient algorithms for this problem, which describe a near-continuous time-memory tradeoff curve. Those are obtained by using the same reduction as Bricout *et al.* and carefully instantiating the derived subset sum problem with exhaustive-search algorithms from the literature, in particular dissection (Dinur *et al.* 2012) and dissection in tree (Dinur 2019). We also spend significant effort adapting those algorithms to decrease their *granularity*, thereby allowing them to be smoothly used in a syndrome decoding context when not *all* the solutions to the subset sum problem are required. For a proposed parameter set for Wave, one of our best instantiations is estimated to cost 2^{177} bit operations and requiring $2^{88.5}$ bits of storage, while we estimate this to be 2^{152} and 2^{144} for the best algorithm from Bricout *et al.*.

1 Introduction

At ASIACRYPT 2019, Debris-Alazard *et al.* proposed a new (conjecturally post-quantum secure) code-based signature scheme called Wave [4]. Some of the more unusual and notable features of this scheme are that it is based on *ternary* linear codes, *i.e.* codes whose alphabet is $\mathbb{F}_3$, and that its security relies in part on the generic hardness of some *large-weight* syndrome decoding problems. Most of the existing cryptography and coding-theory literature does not quite address either of those aspects as it tends to focus on binary codes (where low- and large-weight problems are symmetric) and, in the few existing adaptations to q-ary codes, on low-weight problems [2,10,12,13,16].

G. Hanaoka et al. (Eds.): PKC 2022, LNCS 13177, pp. 82–111, 2022.
https://doi.org/10.1007/978-3-030-97121-2_4

Shortly following the introduction of Wave, Bricout *et al.* introduced new dedicated algorithms for solving the specific large-weight ternary syndrome decoding instances underlying Wave's security [1]. Their approach consists in exploiting the fact that a large-weight syndrome may be found by: 1) finding a *full*-weight syndrome for a smaller derived sub-problem and; 2) extending this smaller solution to one for the original problem, hoping that it satisfies the weight constraint. While this overall strategy is quite typical of the family of *information-set decoding* algorithms, the fact that the first step searches for *full*-weight syndromes over $\mathbb{F}_3$ leads to a clean reduction to a {0,1}-subset sum problem. Furthermore, since the success probability of the second step is typically small, one in fact needs to repeat the first one many times; the best results are then obtained when many solutions for the latter can be obtained at a low (ideally constant) amortised cost. Bricout *et al.* consider several algorithms for solving the subset sum problem and obtain their best results by using Wagner's k-tree algorithm [17] with an adaptation of the so-called representation technique. For parameter sizes relevant to Wave's security, their best algorithm has an asymptotic time cost of $\mathcal{O}(2^{0.0176n})$, where n is the length of the code. However, the memory cost of this algorithm is also $\mathcal{O}(2^{0.0176n})$; while this is a common behaviour of the "fastest" algorithms from the cryptography and coding theory literature, this is an unattractive feature for "real-life" implementations as (beyond a certain point) memory is much more expensive than time in existing hardware, and certainly not on par as analyses focusing on optimising time cost alone somewhat implicitly assume.

Our Contribution. In this paper, we perform a detailed study of time-memory tradeoffs for the large-weight ternary syndrome decoding problem, in the regime relevant to Wave's security. We use the same reduction to {0,1}-subset sum as Bricout *et al.*, and the tradeoffs are obtained by acting on one parameter used in the reduction and, more importantly, by carefully instantiating the resolution of the subset sum problem with memory-efficient algorithms. For this task we rely on the dissection [6] and dissection in tree [5] frameworks. One main hurdle in efficiently applying both frameworks to the syndrome decoding setting is that they are designed to *exhaustively* solve general-birthday (or subset sum-like) problems, which they do at a low (possibly constant) amortised cost. The reduction by Bricout *et al.* only requires comparatively few solutions, and providing more than necessary inevitably leads to a sub-optimal instantiation. We thus spend a significant effort in adapting both frameworks to lower the *granularity* at which they return solutions (*i.e.* the minimum number of solution that can be returned with constant amortised cost), so that only the right amount is computed. This eventually leads to attractive time-memory tradeoffs which significantly outperform the results of Bricout *et al.* when taking the cost of memory into account. We however make no attempt at accurately modeling the cost of memory *access* which we assume to be constant and only compute for our algorithms the cost of memory *storage*. A summary of our results is shown in Table 1 in the asymptotic regime where we include the product of time and memory costs as a primitive tool of comparison between different tradeoffs.

Table 1. Asymptotic exponents (in base 2) of some algorithms for solving a ternary syndrome decoding problem for a random code of length n, dimension $0.676n$, and syndrome weight $0.948366n$.

Time	Memory	Time × Memory	Tradeoff	Algorithm
$0.0176n$	$0.0176n$	$0.0352n$	$T = M$	k-Tree + representations [1]
$0.02014n$	$0.01007n$	$0.03021n$	$T = M^2$	4,4-Dissection (Sect. 5)
$0.02256n$	$0.007521n$	$0.03008n$	$T = M^3$	2,11-Dissection (Sect. 5)
$0.02335n$	$0.005838n$	$0.02919n$	$T = M^4$	3,11-Dissection (Sect. 5)

Structure of the Paper. We recall some definitions and state our problem in Sect. 2. We then present the framework of Bricout *et al.* in a detailed and self-contained way in Sect. 3, while also emphasising the role played by the granularity. Section 4 recalls some classical frameworks for the generalised birthday problem and applies them (sometimes with some tweaks) to syndrome decoding, and Sect. 5 does the same with the more recent dissection-in-tree framework. Finally Sect. 6 presents numerical results applied to the most recent parameter set for Wave.

2 Preliminaries

2.1 Notation and Definitions

Except specified otherwise, we assume to be in a *ternary* setting, *i.e.* with all structures defined over $\mathbb{F}_3$.

Vectors (resp. matrices) names are written in a bold font and in lower (resp. upper) case, for instance $\boldsymbol{x}$ (resp. $\boldsymbol{M}$); vectors are *row* vectors. The ith coordinate of a vector $\boldsymbol{x}$ is written $\boldsymbol{x}_i$, and indices start from 1. The (Hamming) weight $\mathrm{wt}(\boldsymbol{x})$ of an n-dimensional vector $\boldsymbol{x}$ is the size of its support, *i.e.* $\#\{i \in [\![1,n]\!] \mid \boldsymbol{x}_i \neq 0\}$, where $[\![1,n]\!] = \{1, 2, \ldots, n\}$.

A (ternary) *linear code* of *length* n and *dimension* k is a k-dimensional linear subspace of $\mathbb{F}_3^n$; any code with such parameters is said to be an $[n,k]$ linear code. A *parity-check matrix* of an $[n,k]$ (ternary) linear code $\mathcal{C}$ is any full-rank matrix $\boldsymbol{H} \in \mathbb{F}_3^{(n-k)\times n}$ s.t. $\boldsymbol{x} \in \mathcal{C} \Leftrightarrow \boldsymbol{x}\boldsymbol{H}^T = \boldsymbol{0}$, where $\boldsymbol{0} \in \mathbb{F}_3^{n-k}$ is the null vector.

We use $x := y$ (resp $x =: y$) to define x as being equal to y (resp. y as being equal to x), and $x \twoheadleftarrow \mathcal{S}$ means that x has been drawn uniformly at random from the finite set $\mathcal{S}$; except specified otherwise, this drawing is supposed to be independent from any other.

We say that an algorithm $\mathcal{A}$ returning S distinct (and *a priori* independent) outputs in time $\mathcal{O}(ST)$ runs in *amortised time* $\mathcal{O}(T)$. Also, in order to simplify notation, we often drop the "$\mathcal{O}(\cdot)$" when discussing the cost of algorithms. Finally, except specified otherwise, the logarithm function log is in base 2.

2.2 The Large-Weight Ternary Syndrome Decoding Problem

We now define the *ternary syndrome decoding problem* (or "SDP" for short), which is the main problem studied in this paper. We specialise the definition to the ternary case, *i.e.* with all underlying structures with coefficients in $\mathbb{F}_3$, but generalizations to other fields are straightforward.

Problem 1 (Ternary syndrome decoding problem). Let $\boldsymbol{H} \in \mathbb{F}_3^{(n-k)\times n}$ be a parity-check matrix for an $[n, k]$ ternary linear code, $w \in [\![1, n]\!]$, $\boldsymbol{s} \in \mathbb{F}_3^{n-k}$. The *ternary syndrome decoding problem* with inputs $\boldsymbol{H}$, $\boldsymbol{s}$, w asks to find $\boldsymbol{e} \in \mathbb{F}_3^n$ s.t.:

1. $\boldsymbol{e}\boldsymbol{H}^T = \boldsymbol{s}$;
2. $\mathrm{wt}(\boldsymbol{e}) = w$.

We may refer to $\boldsymbol{s}$ as the target *syndrome*, and to $\boldsymbol{e}$ as an *error*.

A natural variant of this problem, which we however do not consider here, is to constraint the weight of $\boldsymbol{e}$ not to a single value w but only requiring that it be included in some interval.

In all of this work we only consider instances of Problem 1 with the following additional restrictions:

1. We consider uniformly random linear codes:
$$\boldsymbol{H} \twoheadleftarrow \left\{\boldsymbol{M} \in \mathbb{F}_3^{(n-k)\times n} \mid \mathrm{rank}(\boldsymbol{M}) = n - k\right\}.$$
2. We consider uniformly random syndromes: $\boldsymbol{s} \twoheadleftarrow \mathbb{F}_3^{n-k}$.
3. The code parameters n and k and the target weight w are proportional, with the same ratios as in the "updated" parameters for the Wave signature scheme given by Bricout *et al.* [1], *viz.* $k = 0.676n$, $w = 0.948366n$. In the following we refer to this setting as the *Wave regime* which, since $w \approx 0.95n$ is a particular instance of a *large-weight* regime.

Remark 2. The Wave regime as defined above corresponds to a setting for which no efficient (in particular no polynomial-time) algorithm for solving the problem is known, yet one expects a random instance to have a number of solution exponential in the length n of the code. We refer to [4, §3] for more details on the topic and on parameter selection for Wave in general.

3 A Framework for Solving the Ternary Syndrome Decoding Problem

At SAC 2019 [1], Bricout *et al.* formalised a high-level framework to solve (hard) instances of the ternary syndrome decoding problem They name this framework "PGE+SS", standing for *partial Gaussian elimination + subset sum*, and its structure closely follows the one used by similar *information set decoding* (or ISD) algorithms used in the (more usual) binary setting. Since our work fully adheres to this framework we wish to give here a self-contained description of its main ideas and analysis, and refer to [1] for more details.

3.1 The PGE+SS Framework

Let $\boldsymbol{H} \in \mathbb{F}_3^{(n-k)\times n}$, $\boldsymbol{s}$, w define an instance of Problem 1; the PGE+SS framework fixes two additional parameters $l \in [\![0, n-k]\!]$ and $p \in [\![0, \min(w, k+l)]\!]$. One then does the following:

1. *Partial information set selection.* Pick $\boldsymbol{P} \in \mathbb{F}_3^{n\times n}$ uniformly at random among the permutation matrices that are s.t. the $n-k-l$ first columns of $\boldsymbol{HP}$ are linearly independent.
2. *Partial Gaussian elimination.* Compute the reduced row-echelon form of $\boldsymbol{HP}$, stopping after the first $n-k-l$ rows have been processed. This returns an invertible matrix $\boldsymbol{S} \in \mathrm{GL}(n-k, 3)$ s.t.:
$$\boldsymbol{SHP} =: \begin{pmatrix} \boldsymbol{I}_{n-k-l} & \boldsymbol{H}_1 \\ 0 & \boldsymbol{H}_2 \end{pmatrix},$$
with $\boldsymbol{H}_1 \in \mathbb{F}_3^{(n-k-l)\times(k+l)}$, $\boldsymbol{H}_2 \in \mathbb{F}_3^{l\times(k+l)}$, and further let $\boldsymbol{s}' = \begin{pmatrix}\boldsymbol{s}_1' & \boldsymbol{s}_2'\end{pmatrix} := \boldsymbol{sS}^T$, with $\boldsymbol{s}_1' \in \mathbb{F}_3^{n-k-l}$, $\boldsymbol{s}_2' \in \mathbb{F}_3^{l}$.
Remark then that if $\boldsymbol{e}'$ is a solution to the syndrome decoding problem instance defined by $\boldsymbol{SHP}$, $\boldsymbol{s}'$ and w then $\boldsymbol{e}'\boldsymbol{P}^T$ is a solution to the initial instance, as from $\boldsymbol{e}'\boldsymbol{P}^T\boldsymbol{H}^T\boldsymbol{S}^T = \boldsymbol{s}'$ one has $(\boldsymbol{e}'\boldsymbol{P}^T)\boldsymbol{H}^T = \boldsymbol{s}$.
3. *Subset sum problem resolution.* Solve the syndrome decoding problem instance defined by $\boldsymbol{H}_2$, $\boldsymbol{s}_2'$ and weight p and return S distinct solutions $\{\boldsymbol{e}_2' \in \mathbb{F}_3^{k+l}\}$, where S is a parameter to be determined later. For large-weight ternary syndrome decoding and well-chosen parameters l and p, this in fact reduces to a {0,1}-subset sum problem (see Sects. 3.2 and 4.1 and [1, §2] for details).
4. *Probabilistic reconstruction.* For every solution $\boldsymbol{e}_2'$ returned at step 3 compute the unique vector $\boldsymbol{e}_1' := \boldsymbol{s}_1' - \boldsymbol{e}_2'\boldsymbol{H}_1^T$ s.t. $\begin{pmatrix}\boldsymbol{e}_1' & \boldsymbol{e}_2'\end{pmatrix}\boldsymbol{P}^T\boldsymbol{H}^T\boldsymbol{S}^T = \begin{pmatrix}\boldsymbol{s}_1' & \boldsymbol{s}_2'\end{pmatrix}$, and if $\mathrm{wt}(\boldsymbol{e}_1') = w - p$ return $\begin{pmatrix}\boldsymbol{e}_1' & \boldsymbol{e}_2'\end{pmatrix}\boldsymbol{P}^T$ as a solution to the initial problem. If none of the solutions satisfied the weight constraint the algorithm fails.

Remark 3. Prange's algorithm [14] corresponds to the setting $l = 0$. In that case the subset sum problem from step 3 becomes trivial since the zero-dimensional $\boldsymbol{s}_2'$ imposes no constraint. Yet for the same number of returned solutions S and for most target weights w the success probability of step 4 is in this case typically smaller than for $l > 0$.

We now analyse some aspects of the PGE+SS framework, but only in the regime relevant to us, *i.e.* when the target weight w is close to n (but lower than the Gilbert-Varshamov bound). In particular we only consider the case where $p = k + l$, that is where the solutions for the smaller syndrome decoding sub-problem at step 3 are required to be full-weight. This has two consequences: 1) except for very large values of l, this maximises the probability that a solution to the sub-problem extends to a solution to the initial problem in step 4; 2) since there are exactly two non-zero elements in $\mathbb{F}_3$, this sub-problem can be solved by using an algorithm for the (quite common) {0,1}-subset sum problem.

3.2 Required Number of Solution for the Subset-Sum Problem

With the above constraint on the PGE+SS parameterization, the number S of returned solution to the sub-problem required for the algorithm to succeed with constant probability becomes only a function of n, l, k and w (or in fact only n and l inasmuch as k and w depend on n in the Wave regime): assuming independence of the solutions, it precisely needs to be proportional to the inverse probability that $\boldsymbol{e}'$ as computed in step 4 has the right weight; we compute this probability in Proposition 4, and often denote S_l its inverse in the remainder of this paper.

Proposition 4. *Let $\boldsymbol{H}$, $\boldsymbol{s}$, w define a random instance of Problem 1 in the Wave regime, and $\boldsymbol{H}_1$, $\boldsymbol{H}_2$, $\boldsymbol{s}'_1$, $\boldsymbol{s}'_2$ be as in Sect. 3.1. Then assuming that the syndrome decoding sub-problem defined by $\boldsymbol{H}_2$, $\boldsymbol{s}'_2$, $k+l$ has many solutions, and if $\boldsymbol{e}'_2$ is picked uniformly at random among them, one has:*

$$\Pr[wt(\boldsymbol{e}'_1) = w - k - l] \approx \frac{\binom{n-k-l}{w-k-l}2^{w-k-l}}{3^{n-k-l}}, \tag{1}$$

where $\boldsymbol{e}'_1 \in \mathbb{F}_3^{n-k-l}$ is equal to $\boldsymbol{s}'_1 - \boldsymbol{e}'_2\boldsymbol{H}_1^T$.

Proof. Let $\boldsymbol{P}$ be as in Sect. 3.1 and $\mathcal{S}$ denote the set of solutions to the main decoding problem; we have that $\text{wt}(\boldsymbol{e}'_1) = w - k - l$ iff. $(\boldsymbol{e}'_1\ \boldsymbol{e}'_2)\,\boldsymbol{P}^T \in \mathcal{S}$. Thus $\Pr[\text{wt}(\boldsymbol{e}'_1) = w - k - l] = \Pr[\exists\, \boldsymbol{e} \in \mathcal{S}, \boldsymbol{e} = (*\ \boldsymbol{e}'_2)\,\boldsymbol{P}^T]$, *i.e.* the probability that there is a solution with the right structure.[1]

To compute this probability, we first assume that the elements of $\mathcal{S}$ are uniformly distributed among the $2^w\binom{n}{w}$ weight-w vectors of $\mathbb{F}_3^n$. Also, since the Wave regime is such that w is far away from the Gilbert-Varshamov bounds we approximate the expected size of $\mathcal{S}$ by $\mathbb{S} := 2^w\binom{n}{w}/3^{n-k}$. Similarly, the expected number of solution to the sub-problem is approximated by $\mathbb{S}_2 := 2^{k+l}/3^l$.

Now for $\boldsymbol{e} \in \mathcal{S}$ to have the right structure, two conditions must be satisfied: 1) it must have the right support, which happens with probability $\binom{n-k-l}{w-k-l}/\binom{n}{w}$; 2) it must be equal to $\boldsymbol{e}'_2$ on the right part, which happens with probability $\mathbb{S}_2^{-1}$ conditioned on having the right support (since by construction this part then constitutes a solution to the sub-problem). Finally, equating the probability with

[1] Note that since $\boldsymbol{e}'_1$ is fully determined by $\boldsymbol{e}'_2$ there can be at most one such solution.

the (approximated) expectancy, we get $\Pr[\mathrm{wt}(e'_1) = w - k - l] = \mathbb{S} \times \mathbb{S}_2^{-1} \times \binom{n-k-l}{w-k-l}/\binom{n}{w}$. □

In practice we sometimes rely in our cost computations on the same simpler asymptotic estimate for Eq. (1) as [3, Lemma 1.2].

Remark 5. In the Wave regime, $S_l < 2^{k+l}/3^l$, the number of solutions to the sub-problem, so by properly choosing S at step 3 one can ensure that the algorithm succeeds w.h.p..

3.3 Parameterization of the Subset-Sum Problem

The choice for the (unique) parameter l of the PGE+SS framework has a considerable influence on the final cost of solving the problem. Some of the consequences are quite obvious: if l is small, then the decoding sub-problem is easy to solve, but the required number of solution S_l is huge; similarly, if l is large one requires much fewer solutions but solving the sub-problem becomes much harder. A slightly less naïve observation is that although at first sight one is asking in step 3. to solve a problem similar to the original (*viz.* a syndrome decoding problem), the fact that *many* solutions are required (and not just one) opens the way to specific optimisations; in particular one may aim at finding theses solutions at a low (ideally constant) *amortised cost*, so that the total time cost be proportional to S_l. To reach this goal one has at its disposal a full range of powerful algorithms for the subset sum problem. Yet those algorithms are not without some limitations, and their (efficient) usage is often not straightforward. We now mention two of those limitations at a high level, and explore their consequences systematically in Sects. 4 and 5.

- The algorithms we consider have an intrinsic non-trivial *granularity* at which they return solutions. This is the smallest number of solutions that an algorithm may return at its nominal (usually constant) amortised cost, see Definition 6. In our case one incurs some loss in using an algorithm if its granularity is larger than the number of required solutions S_l.
- They also all have a large memory cost, sometimes equal to their granularity.

Definition 6 (Granularity of an Algorithm). *Let $\mathcal{A}$ be an algorithm that returns S outputs and runs in amortised time $\mathcal{O}(T)$. We define its* granularity *as the least positive integer $S' \leq S$ s.t. there exists a tweaked algorithm $\mathcal{A}'$ for the same problem that returns S' outputs in amortised time $\mathcal{O}(T)$.*

The above can be summarised as the following rough estimation for the cost of a PGE+SS instantiation in our case: a subset sum algorithm that returns S solutions in amortised constant time and with memory cost M and granularity S' can be used to solve the decoding problem with memory cost M,[2] and time cost $\max(S_l, S')$.

[2] If $S_l > M$, one would in practice interleave steps 3. and 4 so as to avoid storing all S_l solutions at the same time.

4 Fundamental Algorithms for the Generalised Birthday Problem

4.1 Subset Sum as a Generalised Birthday Problem

In this section we present and compare two families of algorithms that solve the generalised birthday problem (whose definition we recall in Problem 7, in the specific case of $\mathbb{F}_3^n$): the k-tree algorithm and its variants [17] and the dissection framework [6]. Both can be seen as a way to generalise the meet-in-the-middle algorithm.

Problem 7 (Generalised birthday problem or r-list problem). Let $L_1, \ldots, L_r$ be r lists of vectors uniformly sampled from $\mathbb{F}_3^n$ and $\boldsymbol{s} \in \mathbb{F}_3^n$ be a *target*, the *generalised birthday problem* asks to find $(\boldsymbol{x}_1, \ldots, \boldsymbol{x}_r) \in L_1 \times \cdots \times L_r$ s.t. $\sum_{i=1}^{r} \boldsymbol{x}_i = \boldsymbol{s}$.

An algorithm solving Problem 7 can be used in the PGE+SS framework to solve the subset sum problem arising from the sub decoding problem in the full-weight regime.

Let us hereafter denote by $\boldsymbol{H} \in \mathbb{F}_3^{l\times(k+l)}$ and $\boldsymbol{s} \in \mathbb{F}_3^l$ the matrix $\boldsymbol{H}_2$ and vector $\boldsymbol{s}_2'$ from Sect. 3.1 respectively. Then finding a full-weight vector $\boldsymbol{e}$ s.t. $\boldsymbol{e}\boldsymbol{H}^T = \boldsymbol{s}$ can be done by: 1) building r lists $L_i = \{\boldsymbol{x}\boldsymbol{H}^T : \boldsymbol{x} \in \mathcal{W}_i\}$, where the elements of the sets $\mathcal{W}_i$ have full weight on a set of indices $\mathcal{I}_i$ and weight zero on its complementary and $\mathcal{I}_1, \ldots, \mathcal{I}_r$ forms a partition of $[\![0, k+l]\!]$; 2) solving a generalised-birthday problem with input $L_1, \ldots, L_r$ and $\boldsymbol{s}$.

This is a classical approach in general, and it was successfully applied to ternary syndrome decoding by Bricout *et al.*, who consider a number of variants of the k-tree algorithm [1]. We recall their results and start exploring some related time-memory tradeoffs next.

4.2 Application of the k-Tree Algorithm to Syndrome Decoding

From now on assume that $r =: 2^a$ is a power of two. Recall that the basic k-tree algorithm [17] works as follows: at the first step, subtract the target $\boldsymbol{s}$ to every element of L_r, then for each pair of lists (L_{2i-1}, L_{2i}), $i \in [\![1, 2^{a-1}]\!]$, compute the merged list $L_i' := L_{2i-1} \bowtie_w L_{2i} := \{\boldsymbol{x}_u + \boldsymbol{x}_v : (\boldsymbol{x}_u, \boldsymbol{x}_v) \in L_{2i-1} \times L_{2i}, \boldsymbol{x}_u =_w -\boldsymbol{x}_v\}$, where w is a parameter and $\boldsymbol{x} =_w \boldsymbol{y}$ means that $\boldsymbol{x}$ and $\boldsymbol{y}$ are equal on their last w coordinates. This process is then repeated on the lists $L_1', \ldots, L_{2^{a-1}}'$ with the equality constraint being imposed on the w' coordinates before the last w ones, etc.; after a iterations in total, and provided that $w + w'' + \cdots = l = \dim(\boldsymbol{s})$, all the elements of the last list (if non empty) are solutions to the problem.

In a classical and typical parameterization of the k-tree algorithm, one takes $w = w' = \cdots$ and lists of initial size equal to the "entropy" of a size-w constraint; in our case this is 3^w. This ensures that on average the size of all lists (except possibly the last one) remains equal to 3^w at every level of the tree and this also gives the memory cost of the algorithm (up to a factor 2^a if the lists cannot be generated on-the-fly). Then the two typical choices for w are $l/(a+1)$ and l/a;

in the former case the expected size of the root list is 1, while it is $3^w = 3^{l/a}$ in the latter. This last parameterization is of particular interest in our context since it gives an algorithm with time and memory cost $\mathcal{O}(2^a 3^{l/a})$ that on average returns $3^{l/a}$ solutions. The amortised cost per solution is then $\mathcal{O}(2^a)$, or $\mathcal{O}(1)$ as a is in fact often a constant, and the granularity is $3^{l/a}$.

As we have just described it, the k-tree algorithm only returns in the root lists solutions which are highly structured which, put another way, means that it highly decimates the number of possible solutions to be found among the initial lists. Yet if more than $3^{l/a}$ solutions are needed, two (non-exclusive) options exist: 1) restart the algorithm from new lists (if possible); 2) jointly change the merging condition for two pairs of lists at the same level, so that one merges elements s.t. $\boldsymbol{x}_u =_w -\boldsymbol{x}_v + \boldsymbol{t}$ and the other elements s.t. $\boldsymbol{x}_u =_w -\boldsymbol{x}_v - \boldsymbol{t}$; this is easily implementable by simply adding (resp. subtracting) the right w coordinates of $\boldsymbol{t}$ to one of the two lists for each pair. This second option in fact lets one now exhaustively search for all the possible solutions, something we will discuss again in Sect. 4.3. We illustrate this and the general process of a typical k-tree instantiation in Fig. 1 for $a = 3$.

Remark 8. We defined here the k-tree algorithm with as input a number of lists which is a power of two. It is possible to adapt the algorithm to a relaxed setting without this constraint, but there is no added gain[3] in doing it.

Bricout *et al.* use the k-tree algorithm within the PGE+SS framework to solve hard instances of the ternary syndrome decoding problem [1]. In a basic application, the only additional constraint to what has already been described above is that for a fixed l parameter, the depth of the tree must be s.t. it is possible to build lists of size $3^{l/a}$ at its leaves. When elements of those initial lists are of the form $\{\boldsymbol{x}\boldsymbol{H}^T : \boldsymbol{x} \in \mathcal{W}_i\}$, this list population constraint can be expressed as:

$$3^{l/a} \leq 2^{(k+l)/2^a}. \tag{2}$$

This simply expresses the fact that there are 2^a lists of full-weight vectors to build at the leaves of the tree and one must then split the support of the domain $\mathbb{F}_3^{k+l}$ into that many equally-sized disjoint sets.

For a fixed l parameter, the memory (and the granularity) of this application of the k-tree algorithm is minimised by simply selecting the largest a for which this constraint is satisfied.

Smoothed k-Tree Algorithm. Smoothing the k-tree algorithm is a technique that allows to slightly relax constraint (2) by adding one more level to the tree than what it dictates. This corresponds to the *extended k-tree algorithm* of Minder and Sinclair [11, Theorem 3.1], and it was adapted to the ternary case under this name by Bricout *et al.* [1].

In a nutshell the idea is the following: if one cannot build initial lists that are large enough, the constraint size w from the level 1 lists to level 2 is lowered

[3] In the next part, the gain is formally defined in Definition 10.

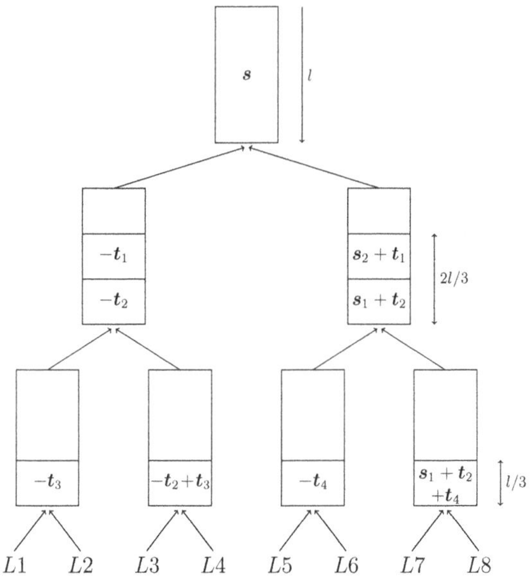

Fig. 1. Illustration of the k-tree algorithm with $M = 3^{l/3}$. For only one iteration of the tree, the targets $\boldsymbol{t}_i$ are all set to $\mathbf{0}$. For more than one iteration, the targets $\boldsymbol{t}_i$ must be set to non-zero values, and every distinct tuple of $\boldsymbol{t}_i$'s provides disjoint solutions.

so as to increase the size of the latter; then this increased (expected) list size is preserved all the way up to the root of the tree. Schematically this translates into a sequence of constraints sizes $w < w' = w'' = \cdots$ which sum to l; the memory cost is then equal to $3^{w'}$, which is more than if one had had constraints of identical sizes, *i.e.* one has to "pay" for the dissatisfaction of Eq. (2) with memory. Nonetheless, in the case of the SDP, adding one more level to the tree to apply the smoothing technique is always more beneficial, even if this is done at a less favourable time/memory ratio. We summarise the consequences of smoothing as Proposition 9, which restates [1, Prop. 4].

Proposition 9. *Let l, k, n be as above and $a > 3$ be a constant. If $3^{l/(a-1)} \leq 2^{(k+l)/2^{a-1}}$, then one can use a smoothed k-tree algorithm with a levels to obtain 2^m solutions to the generalised birthday problem in amortised constant time and memory cost 2^m, where:*

$$m = \frac{1}{a-2}\left(l\log(3) - \frac{k+l}{2^{a-1}}\right).$$

Proof. We only prove this informally without showing optimality nor checking initial conditions, our main goal here being to illustrate the inner workings of smoothing.

Let $\varsigma := l\log(3)$ normalise in base 2 the size of the dimension-l ternary constraint that one wishes to solve and $\tau := (k+l)/2^a$ be the logarithm of the maximum size of 2^a lists of full-weight vectors partitioning the domain. We wish to find initial and subsequent constraints w and $w' = w'' = \cdots$ s.t.: 1) $w' = 2\tau - w$; 2) $w + (a-1)w' = \varsigma$. The first condition expresses the fact that the constraint of size w ensures that the first level lists merge into lists of expected size $2^{w'}$; the structure of the k-tree algorithm together with the second condition then ensure the fact that the root list contains $2^{w'}$ solutions to the problem, and since $w < w'$ that the algorithm runs in amortised constant time and with memory $2^m := 2^{w'}$.

To find the stated value of m, one simply substitutes $2\tau - w$ for w' into $w + (a-1)w' = \varsigma$ and solves the latter for w, *i.e.*:

$$\begin{aligned} & w + (a-1)(2\tau - w) = \varsigma \\ \Leftrightarrow\ & (a-1)2\tau - (a-2)w = \varsigma \\ \Leftrightarrow\ & w = ((a-1)2\tau - \varsigma)/(a-2) \end{aligned}$$

Using again $w' = 2\tau - w$ one then gets:

$$\begin{aligned} & w' = [2(a-2)\tau - ((a-1)2\tau - \varsigma)]/(a-2) \\ \Leftrightarrow\ & w' = (\varsigma - 2\tau)/(a-2) = (l\log(3) - (k+l)/2^{a-1})/(a-2). \end{aligned}$$

□

Using Representations. Bricout *et al.* obtained their best result in the Wave regime by applying the so-called representation technique [8] to their ternary k-tree algorithm, slightly beating their instantiations that used smoothing. We do not detail this approach since we do not consider it in our work, and refer to [1] for details. When optimised for time, this uses a tree with $a = 7$ levels and parameter $l = 0.060835n$ and solves the decoding problem in asymptotic time and memory $\mathcal{O}(2^{0.0176n})$.

Time-Memory Tradeoffs from the k-Tree Algorithm. Recall that within the PGE+SS framework, solving the sub decoding problem for parameter l in amortised constant time with granularity and memory cost S' allows to solve the initial problem with memory cost S' and time cost $\max(S_l, S')$. Since the (smoothed) k-tree algorithm may in principle be used for any l one then naturally obtains a time-memory tradeoff by varying this parameter and using the best variant of the k-tree algorithm to solve the derived sub-problem. Choosing this variant is a rather straightforward consequence of what has been presented above and we give pseudocode for this parameter selection in the full version [9] for both "standard" and smoothed k-tree algorithms We show the resulting time-memory tradeoff curves in Fig. 2, where we also include the best attack of Bricout *et al.* as a point of comparison. One may notice there the natural discontinuity exhibited by the standard k-tree algorithm and the fact that the smoothed variant is indeed always superior. The near monotonicity of the curves is consequence of the fact that the granularity of the k-tree algorithm is low and thence does not limit the performance of the algorithm, except for the relatively large l parameters used to draw the bottom right part of the graph.

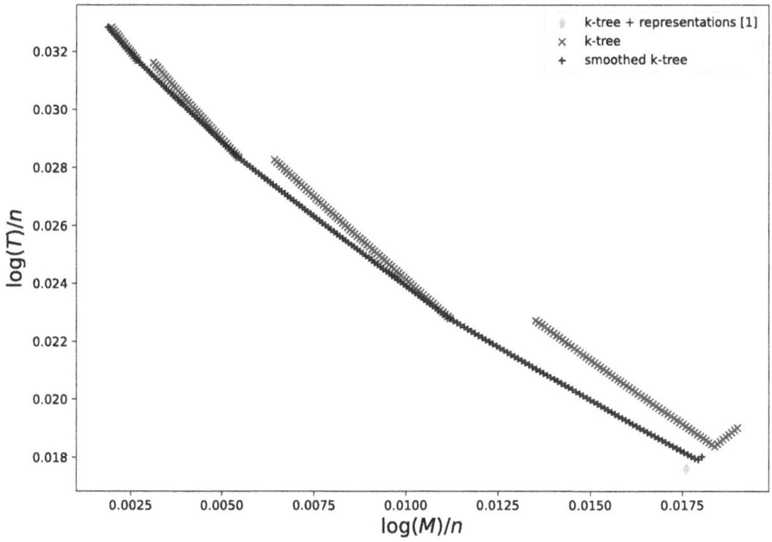

Fig. 2. Time-Memory tradeoffs from the (smoothed) k-tree algorithm.

4.3 Solving Generalised Birthday Problems with Dissection

The *dissection* framework was introduced by Dinur *et al.* at CRYPTO 2012 to solve "composite" problems in a memory-efficient way [6]. The main initial motivation was provided by the generic key recovery attack of iterated block ciphers, but the framework adapts easily to an r-list problem and was already used in this context by Esser *et al.* and Dinur [5,7], who also study it in some non-exhaustive regimes. Dissection generalises the meet-in-the-middle algorithm in a different way than the k-tree algorithm (with both techniques also being refinements of [15]). Its main originality is that instead of merging lists along a (typically) balanced binary tree, it uses a recursive asymmetric decomposition; the solutions of the smaller sub-problem resulting from this decomposition are stored in memory and combined with solutions for the larger problem that are generated on-the-fly. Altogether, this asymmetric decomposition and the structure of the algorithm make dissection a memory-friendly family of algorithms.

An important notion to quantitatively analyse dissection algorithms (and algorithms for the r-list problem in general) is the *gain* [6], which we state in Problem 10 in our specific ternary case. In there, and in all of the following, we let by definition the size of the r initial lists of Problem 7 be equal to 3^m, and often treat m as a parameter.

Definition 10. *Let $\mathcal{A}$ be an algorithm that solves Problem 7 with r lists in $\mathbb{F}_3$ in time $\mathcal{O}(3^{mT})$ and memory $\mathcal{O}(3^{mM})$ with $m \in \mathbb{R}$. Then its gain is defined as $\mathit{gain}(\mathcal{A}) := r - (T + M)$.*

This should be understood as a gain *over* the time-memory tradeoff offered by the meet-in-the-middle algorithm, which always has gain 0. Any positive gain then gives a better tradeoff than the latter. Hereafter we use $\mathfrak{gain}(r)$ to denote the gain of an r-dissection that solves an r-list problem (or sometimes simply g, when r is clear from the context).

We now illustrate the dissection framework with two examples.

Example 11 (4-Dissection). The 4-dissection is simply the exhaustive variant of the k-tree algorithm with two levels as described in Sect. 4.2, and it was in fact well-known before the general formulation of the dissection framework. Unlike instantiations with a larger number of lists, it also uses a symmetric decomposition. Starting from four lists $L_{1,\ldots,4}$ of size 3^m and with a target $\boldsymbol{s}$ of dimension $l := 2m$, one introduces an intermediate target $\boldsymbol{t}$ of dimension m. Then for each value of $\boldsymbol{t}$, one applies the k-tree algorithm to $L_1 + \boldsymbol{t} := \{\boldsymbol{x} + (0\ \boldsymbol{t}) : \boldsymbol{x} \in L_1\}$, L_2, $L_3 - \boldsymbol{t}$, $L_4 - \boldsymbol{s}$, obtaining as a result a list of solutions with a unique structure (*viz.* $\boldsymbol{x}_{1,\ldots,4}$ s.t. $\boldsymbol{x}_1 + \boldsymbol{x}_2 =_m -\boldsymbol{t}$, $\boldsymbol{x}_3 + \boldsymbol{x}_4 =_m \boldsymbol{s} + \boldsymbol{t}$), and enumerating all values for $\boldsymbol{t}$ yields all the solutions to be found within $L_{1,\ldots,4}$. The memory cost and the granularity is 3^m and the time cost 3^{2m}, also equal to the expected number of returned solutions. The product of the time and memory cost is then 3^{3m}, which is a factor 3^m less than what one would get from meet-in-the-middle algorithms, hence the gain is equal to 1.

Example 12 (7-Dissection). The 7-dissection is the first instantiation of the framework with gain 2. It groups its 7 input lists into a group of three (resp. four) lists, for which a meet-in-the-middle algorithm (resp. 4-dissection) will be used. Let again 3^m be the size of the initial lists, and $\boldsymbol{t}_1$ and $\boldsymbol{t}_2$ be as in Fig. 3, which also illustrates the structure of the algorithm; to solve a 7-list problem for a target $\boldsymbol{s}$ of size $3m$ one does the following for all values of $\boldsymbol{t}_1$ and $\boldsymbol{t}_2$:

1. Exhaustively search for all solutions to a 3-list problem for the $2m$ target $(\boldsymbol{s}_2 - \boldsymbol{t}_2\ \boldsymbol{s}_1 - \boldsymbol{t}_1)$, using a meet-in-the-middle algorithm with memory (resp. time) cost $\mathcal{O}(3^m)$ (resp. $\mathcal{O}(3^{2m})$), and store all solutions in a list L'.
2. Exhaustively search for all solutions to a 4-list problem for the $2m$ target $(\boldsymbol{t}_2\ \boldsymbol{t}_1)$, using 4-dissection with memory and granularity (resp. time) cost $\mathcal{O}(3^m)$ (resp. $\mathcal{O}(3^{2m})$), and for every returned solution $\boldsymbol{x} = (*\ \boldsymbol{t}_2\ \boldsymbol{t}_1)$ check on-the-fly if there is $\boldsymbol{x}' \in L'$ s.t. they sum to $\boldsymbol{s}$.

The total memory cost is $\mathcal{O}(3^m)$, the time cost and number of returned solutions is $\mathcal{O}(3^{4m})$, and the granularity is given by the size of the intermediate target $(\boldsymbol{t}_2\ \boldsymbol{t}_1)$ for the 4-dissection and thence 3^{2m}.

In general an r-dissection of gain g is built from an $(r - g - 1)$-dissection and a meet-in-the-middle algorithm with $g + 1$ lists. This leads to a *magic sequence* (M_n) of gains [6], where M_g is the least r s.t. there is an r-dissection with gain g. Dinur *et al.* showed that $M_g = \frac{(g+1)(g+2)}{2} + 1 \approx g^2/2$, leading to the following approximation:

$$\mathfrak{gain}(r) \approx \sqrt{2r} \tag{3}$$

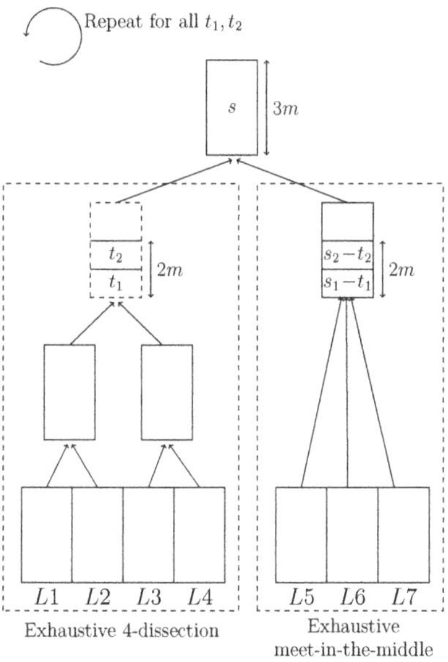

Fig. 3. 7-Dissection with initial lists of size 3^m and a target $\boldsymbol{s}$ of size $3m$. A list drawn with dashed lines is not stored in memory and processed on-the-fly.

One may also characterise an r-dissection with gain g from the fact that it returns all the $3^{m(r-g-1)}$ solutions to an r-list problem with target size $(g+1)m$ in amortised constant time and with memory cost $\mathcal{O}(3^m)$. Since in this case the intermediate target $\boldsymbol{t}$ used in the recursion is of size gm, it also follows that in this regime the granularity of the dissection is at most $3^{m(r-g-1)}/3^{gm} = 3^{m(r-2g-1)}$. Remark that it is also straightforward to exhaustively solve for target sizes smaller than $(g+1)m$ by running many times a dissection with dummy targets of the latter size.

The above description concerns dissection with a memory cost equal to the size of the initial lists, but the framework can be easily extended to use more memory [6]. For any integer $\mu > 1$, one increases the number μ_r of lists in the meet-in-the-middle step and returns a list L' of partial solutions of size $3^{\mu m}$ while also allowing the recursive dissection to have memory cost $3^{\mu m}$. Denoting $\boldsymbol{gain}(r, \mu)$ the gain of such an r-dissection with memory parameter μ, one has the relation $\mu_r = \boldsymbol{gain}(r, \mu) + \mu$. A convenient consequence of generalising dissection in this way is that in some sense an r-dissection with $\mu = 1$ and $m = n$ is equivalent to an rN-dissection with $\mu = N$ and $m = n/N$, where $N \geq 1$ is an arbitrary integer. In our context where we have considerable freedom in the choice for the initial number of lists, this remark simplifies the search for good parameterization of the dissection to solve the problem at hand. Indeed, considering one r-dissection with r large and allowing μ to vary is enough to reasonably represent all tradeoffs offered by the dissection framework, as we do in Fig. 4. In the following description we however let $\mu = 1$ unless mentioned otherwise.

4.4 Application of the Dissection Framework to Syndrome Decoding

Since the dissection framework can be used to solve an r-list problem, it readily applies to the full-weight sub decoding problem encountered in the PGE+SS framework, in exactly the same way as the k-tree algorithm does. In principle this provides a range of memory-efficient tradeoffs to solve the (full) decoding problem, yet the main hurdle in a straightforward application of dissection to this context is that its granularity is quite coarse; in particular it is coarser than the one of the k-tree algorithm. In this section we slightly adapt the dissection to decrease its granularity and make it more easily applicable to the PGE+SS framework. We then compare the results with instantiations based on the (smoothed) k-tree algorithm in the next Sect. 4.5.

Let n, l, r, m be as above; a straightforward adaptation of Eq. (2) to the use of dissection is:

$$3^m \leq 2^{(k+l)/r}. \tag{4}$$

By design, an r-dissection with gain g returns solutions to an r-list problem with target size (at most) $(g+1)m$ in amortised constant time. If used within the PGE+SS framework, one thus ideally requires that $l \leq (g+1)m$. When the size l of the sub-problem increases, and since g increases monotonically with r one may require to increase r at some point in order to remain in the same regime. Yet since S_l *decreases* with l while the granularity of the dissection increases with r, this eventually results in unattractive instantiations of the PGE+SS framework where more solutions to the sub-problem are returned than needed. Essentially this quick analysis hints at the fact that the dissection framework is mostly useful in the low-memory regime implied by small values of l.

Improving the Granularity of the Dissection. Recall that at a high level, the granularity of an r-dissection with gain g in the amortised constant time regime is equal to $3^{m(r-2g-1)}$.

One may first remark that since such a dissection recursively decomposes into an $(r-1-g)$-dissection and a meet-in-the-middle algorithm on $g+1$ lists, and since the solutions returned by the former are processed on-the-fly, one may possibly reduce the granularity by asking the former to return fewer solutions (*i.e.* not to be exhaustive in its resolution of the recursive sub-problem). However this will only decrease the granularity if the lowered cost of this non-exhaustive dissection does not become smaller than the one of the meet-in-the-middle, which otherwise would dominate the running time. Yet if this condition is not met one may replace this meet-in-the-middle algorithm by a $(g+1)$-dissection to do the exact same work at a lower cost,[4] as already considered by Dinur [5]. We illustrate this in Example 13 and generalise the process in Proposition 14.

Example 13 (11-Dissection with Lowered Granularity). An 11-dissection has gain 3 and is composed of a 7-dissection and a meet-in-the-middle algorithm. In the amortised constant time regime the 7-dissection has granularity at most 3^{2m} but the meet-in-the-middle with 4 lists and memory 3^m has time cost 3^{3m}, so the granularity of the 11-dissection for a target of size $4m$ is given by the latter and equal to 3^{3m}. Even though this is already smaller than what one would obtain by asking the 7-dissection to exhaustively return the 3^{4m} solutions to its sub-problem of size $3m$, it is possible to do better: since a 4-dissection has gain 1, using one instead of a meet-in-the-middle algorithm lets one building the list L' in time 3^{2m}, thus lowering the overall granularity to 3^{2m}.

Proposition 14. *The granularity of an r-dissection with gain g, initial lists size* 3^m *and target size at most* $m(g+1)$ *is* $3^{m(g-\mathtt{gain}(g+1))}$.

Proof. It is enough to prove the statement for target sizes exactly $m(g+1)$, since lower sizes can then be accommodated for by considering one or more larger dummy targets.

We prove this by induction on the gain g.

The base case $g = 1$ corresponds to a 4-, 5- or 6-dissection. We have already seen in Example 11 that the granularity of the 4-dissection is 3^m. The 5- and 6-dissection just add one or two additional lists to a 4-dissection and thus cannot have a lower granularity.

We now assume that the property holds for any dissection of gain $g - 1 \geq 1$, and will prove it for any dissection of gain g. Consider an r-dissection of gain g; by construction it is built from an $(r-g-1)$-dissection of gain $g-1$ and (with our tweak) an exhaustive $(g+1)$-dissection. The time cost of the $(g+1)$-dissection is $\mathcal{O}(3^{m(g-\mathtt{gain}(g+1))})$ while it returns 3^m intermediate solutions, and by induction the granularity of the $(r-g-1)$-dissection is $3^{m(g-1-\mathtt{gain}(g))}$. Since $1+\mathtt{gain}(g) \geq \mathtt{gain}(g+1)$, the latter dissection is more fine-grained than the former; it is then possible to ask the $(r-g-1)$-dissection to return only $3^{m(g-\mathtt{gain}(g+1))}$ solutions with a target size of mg in amortised constant time. The remaining target size required to merge the solutions of the two sub dissections into solutions of the main one being m, one expects to find $3^{m(g-\mathtt{gain}(g+1))}$ of them and so the r-dissection is able to provide that many solutions in amortised constant time.

□

Despite the improvement provided by Proposition 14, the granularity of the dissection remains too high in our context for many values of l, as shown in Example 15.

[4] Remark that there would be no point in doing this in an exhaustive dissection since in that case the cost of the (exhaustive) $(r-1-g)$-dissection is always higher than the one of the meet-in-the-middle.

Example 15. Let $l = 0.04n$, one has $S_l \approx 3^{0.0148n}$. Solving the derived r-list problem using dissection in the amortised constant time regime and with minimum memory gives the constraint $m = l/(g+1)$ and the granularity is thus $3^{m(g-\mathit{gain}(g+1))} = 3^{l(g-\mathit{gain}(g+1))/(g+1)}$; this latter quantity is lower-bounded by $3^{0.02n}$ for any g and therefore no suitable dissection has a granularity less than S_l. This fact is illustrated in Fig. 4 where no instantiation reaches the grey line representing a time cost of S_l.

We conclude by proposing another tweak to the dissection framework to further reduce its granularity. Recall that we let $\mu = 1$ for simplicity, but the process generalises to other values in the same way as the original dissection. Let us again consider an r-dissection of gain g with initial lists of size 3^m and denote by 3^s the desired number of solution. Assume that $s < m(g - \mathit{gain}(g+1))$, so that the granularity guaranteed by Proposition 14 is too high. The idea here is to reduce the dominating time cost of the exhaustive $(g+1)$-dissection by asking for fewer solutions, which mechanically means that the number of solutions that need to be returned by the $(r-g-1)$-dissection has to be increased. In some sense this consists in balancing the cost of the two sub-problems in the (typically highly asymmetric) dissection, and thus making it somewhat closer to a k-tree algorithm. A possible explanation as to why this eventually leads to better results is that when only a very small fraction of the total number of solutions is required, more symmetric algorithms (one of whose drawbacks is that they highly decimate the solution space) tend to perform better. More formally one asks for 3^{s+c} solutions in the $(r-g-1)$-dissection and 3^{m-c} in the $(g+1)$-dissection for some $c \in \mathbb{R}$, and the overall time cost is minimised under the equality constraint:

$$s + c = m(g - \mathit{gain}(g+1)) - c,$$

which gives:

$$c = \frac{m(g - \mathit{gain}(g+1)) - s}{2}$$

One must also satisfy the "granularity constraint" given by the $(r-g-1)$-dissection, *viz.*:

$$s + c \geq m(g - 1 - \mathit{gain}(g)).$$

There are then two possibilities:

$$\begin{cases} s \geq m(g - \mathit{gain}(g+1)) & : \mathit{gain}(g+1) = \mathit{gain}(g) + 1 \\ s \geq m(g - 2 - \mathit{gain}(g+1)) & : \mathit{gain}(g+1) = \mathit{gain}(g) \end{cases}$$

As it was initially assumed that $s < m(g - \mathit{gain}(g+1))$, this technique is thus only useful if $\mathit{gain}(g+1) = \mathit{gain}(g)$. In that case and under the above conditions, one can check that the granularity constraint of the $(g+1)$-dissection is satisfied and so the overall time cost is given by $\mathcal{O}(3^{s+c}) = \mathcal{O}(3^{(m(g-\mathit{gain}(g+1))+s)/2})$. This is simply the middle point (in the exponent) between the granularity of the original dissection and the number of required solutions. Here the solutions are not obtained in amortised constant time any more, but one does not "waste" any in the sense that only the desired number is returned.

In Fig. 4, the time-memory tradeoffs obtained by using this modified dissection are drawn in black.

Finally one may somewhat further extend the above by using a u-dissection instead of a $(g+1)$-dissection for some parameter u, further balancing the cost of the two sub dissections. This does not provide an added gain from the above but allows a finer control of the time/memory ratio.

Results. We illustrate the time-memory tradeoffs offered by the dissection to solve the ternary syndrome decoding problem in the Wave regime in Fig. 4. For simplicity, this graph illustrates the tradeoffs obtained using only a fixed (sub-optimal) value of $l = 0.04n$; the best tradeoffs, all using $l < 0.034n$, are shown in Fig. 5 in the next Sect. 4.5. The figure was obtained by using the parameter selection algorithms given in the full version [9] and implemented in https://github.com/charlotte-lefevre/TM_tradeoffs_SDP. All the results come from a single 400-dissection which, as remarked previously, allows to implicitly consider many dissections with fewer initial lists by simply varying μ. We do not consider r-dissections with $r > 400$, since it would only improve the tradeoffs $T \approx M^m$ with $m > 20$. The figure reads as follows: each line represents a different value for μ in ascending order from left to right, and each point on a line represents a different value for m, the $\log_3$ of initial lists size. The additional tradeoffs obtained with the last proposed tweak to improve its granularity are singled out as black crosses, and provide here the best results.

Finally a notable aspect of the results shown in Fig. 4 (which also applies to Fig. 5) is that there is very little interest in increasing the memory allocated to the dissection beyond a certain point.

4.5 Comparison of the k-Tree and Dissection Frameworks

The k-tree and dissection frameworks may both be used to solve the same r-list problems. In this short section we wish to compare these two options and show in which regimes they respectively perform better. We again let by definition 3^m be the initial lists size.

We start with an example, comparing a 16-dissection with a 16-tree algorithm. The 16-dissection of gain $g = 4$ is split into an 11-dissection and a 5-dissection, with a total recursion depth equal to 5; the maximal target size for which this dissection may provide solutions in amortised constant time is thus equal to $5m = (g+1)m$. The 16-tree algorithm has a total number of levels equal to 4, and the maximal target size for which it may provide solutions in amortised constant time is $4m$. Now considering a full-weight sub syndrome decoding problem of target size l, setting m to $l/5$ (resp. $l/4$) minimises the memory cost and granularity of the 16-dissection (resp. 16-tree algorithm) while allowing to find solutions in amortised constant time. In this case the dissection's granularity is

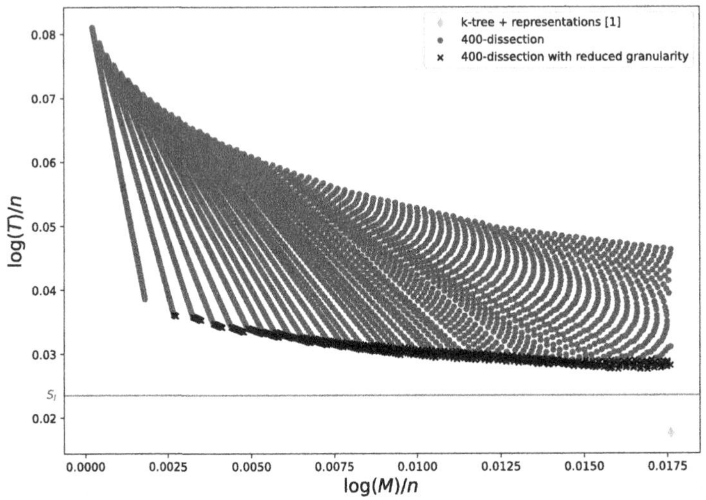

Fig. 4. Time-memory tradeoffs offered by the use of a 400-dissection within the PGE+SS framework with $l = 0.04n$. The grey line represents the desired number of solution S_l for this particular l.

$3^{3l/5}$ while the one of the k-tree is $3^{l/4}$. It is thus mostly beneficial to use the more memory-efficient 16-dissection over a 16-tree algorithm when $S_l \geq 3^{3l/5}$, which asymptotically holds for $l \lessapprox 0.028n$, while the granularity of the 16-tree itself will not be a limiting factor until the much larger value of $l \approx 0.051n$; since S_l is decreasing with increasing l in this range, it means that a 16-tree is able to reach a lower time cost than a 16-dissection, but with a comparably higher memory cost.

More generally, we may compare a 2^a-tree with a 2^a-dissection: from Eq. (3) the gain of the dissection is approximately $2^{(a+1)/2}$, and it follows from Proposition 14 that its granularity is approximately $3^{m2^{a/2}}$, which is to be compared with the much lower 3^m for the k-tree algorithm. The maximum target size for which the dissection may provide solutions in amortised constant time is then $\approx m2^{(a+1)/2}$, much larger than the k-tree algorithm at am. One may then again remark that the dissection is much more memory-efficient than the k-tree algorithm as it allows to return exponentially-more solutions in amortised constant time with the same memory usage, but that its efficient usage may be limited by an exponentially-larger granularity.

We conclude this comparison by plotting in Fig. 5 the best time-memory tradeoffs we obtained by applying the dissection & k-tree frameworks to ternary syndrome decoding in the Wave regime. In consistency with the above analysis, dissection performs significantly better than the k-tree algorithm in the low-memory regime where the total memory cost $M \lessapprox 3^{0.0073n}$; there is also little interest in using memory larger than $\approx 3^{0.0025n}$ since doing so only very moderately decreases the time cost. All of those points correspond to small values for the l parameter for which the dissection granularity matches the large number of required solutions. In the large-memory regime the dissection looses its interest and it becomes significantly outperformed by the k-tree algorithm whose fine granularity is not limiting until much larger values of l.

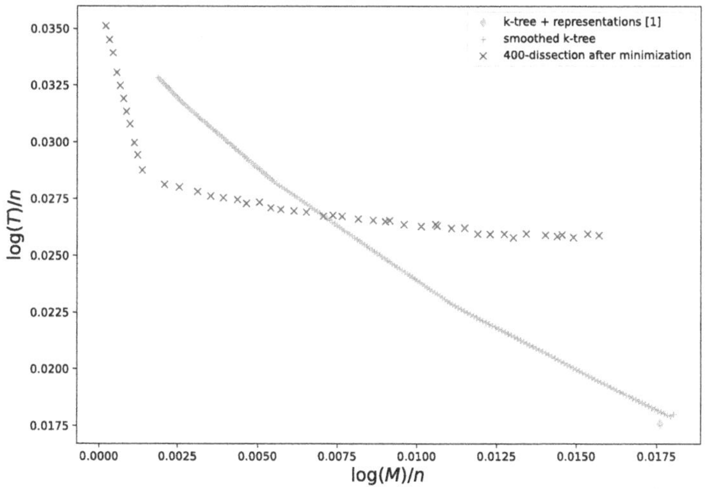

Fig. 5. Time-memory tradeoffs for the ternary syndrome decoding problem in the Wave regime from the k-tree & dissection frameworks. The results for the dissection are the best tradeoffs obtained from a 400-dissection after minimisation with l, μ and m.

5 Dissection in Tree for Syndrome Decoding

We now present the "hybrid" *Multiple-Layer List Sum Algorithms* (which we will call "dissection in tree" for short) introduced by Dinur as a framework to solve generic generalised birthday problems [5], and apply it to ternary syndrome decoding. Similarly to the algorithms of the previous section, fully exploiting the framework in our particular case requires careful parameter selection and some modifications in particular to improve the granularity.

5.1 The Main Algorithm of Dissection in Tree

The idea behind dissection in tree is in fact quite straightforward: it consists in replacing the binary tree structure underlying the k-tree algorithm with an n-ary one and using (typically exhaustive) n-dissection to implement the merging of lists at each level. Similarly as in the k-tree framework, the merging is usually done w.r.t. targets whose sizes ensure that the expected list size is maintained constant through the tree, except possibly at the root level.

We first illustrate this in our case with a tree of three levels of 4-dissection, which we denote as a *3,4-dissection*; Fig. 6 shows the structure of the resulting tree. This instance provides some of the best tradeoffs we were able to obtain for syndrome decoding in the Wave regime.

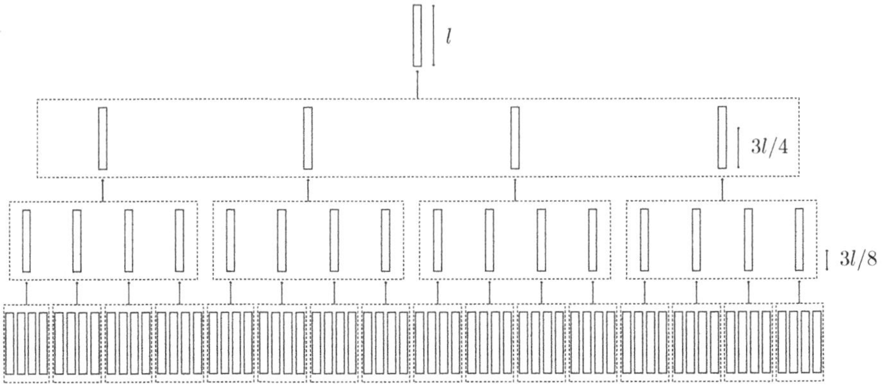

Fig. 6. Illustration of 4-dissection with three levels and $M = 3^{l/8}$.

Since in this case the number of leaves is equal to $4^3 = 64$, and again letting 3^m denote by definition the cardinal of the lists, an immediate adaptation of the constraint from Eq. (2) gives here:

$$3^m \leq 2^{\frac{k+l}{64}} \tag{5}$$

To keep a constant expected size for the lists of the first two levels, the target size is set to $3m$. At the last level, the remaining target size is equal to $l - 6m$, where l again denotes the total target size. The expected number of returned solutions S for a thusly parameterised 3,4-dissection is then given by:

$$S = \frac{3^{4m}}{3^{l-6m}} = \frac{3^{10m}}{3^l}$$

Since the time cost of an exhaustive 4-dissection is $\mathcal{O}(3^{2m})$, one obtains the following constraint for the solutions to be returned in amortised constant time:

$$\frac{3^{10m}}{3^l} \geq 3^{2m} \;\therefore\; m \geq \frac{l}{8},$$

and one would typically use the minimal admissible value $m = \frac{l}{8}$.

Comparison with a 64-Tree. It is quite relevant to compare the performance of 3,4-dissection and a k-tree instance with 6 levels, since both instantiations have a similar structure and use the same number of lists. When applied to syndrome decoding and even without specific adaptation, the 3,4-dissection performs systematically better: as shown above, it is able to provide solutions to the sub decoding problem for a target of size l in amortised constant time with memory cost $\mathcal{O}(3^{l/8})$, while the 64-tree requires a memory of size $\mathcal{O}(3^{l/6})$ to achieve the same. Informally one effect at play here is that using a dissection allows to find solutions that are less structured compared to a k-tree algorithm, and one thus does not require to increase the memory as much as the latter does to compensate for a high decimation of the solution space. One beneficial effect of a lower memory consumption is then that it leads to a wider range of target sizes: the constraint from Eq. (5) is "easier" to satisfy than Eq. (2), thus allowing for lower time cost for identical memory costs. There is however one downside to using dissection in tree: the granularity of $3^{l/4} = 3^{2m} = 3^{2(l/8)}$ of the 3,4-dissection is coarser than the $3^{l/6}$ of the 64-tree, which can be explained from the use of inherently coarser dissections to perform the merging. While this never makes 3,4-dissection "worse" than a 64-tree, it does prevent exploiting its full potential.

We summarise this comparison in Fig. 7, which plots the best time-memory tradeoffs obtained from raw 3,4-dissection and 64-tree and various values of l (shown in false colour). Two regimes are clearly observable for the 3,4-dissection whose coarse granularity makes it returning too many solutions for somewhat large values of l.

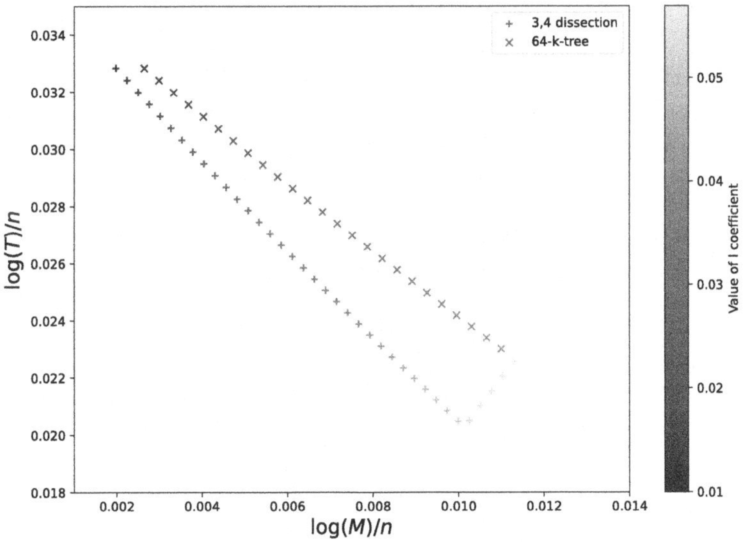

Fig. 7. Best time-memory tradeoff for the syndrome decoding problem in the Wave regime using raw 3,4-dissection and 64-tree.

The analysis of a general raw h, r-dissection tree is a straightforward extension of the above example for the 3,4-dissection.

Letting again 3^m be by definition the initial list size, enforcing equally-sized lists gives target sizes of $m(r-1)$ at every level of the tree but the last, where it is $l-m(r-1)(h-1)$. Then if we let $g = \boldsymbol{gain}(r)$, the cost of one dissection is equal to $\mathcal{O}(3^{m(r-1-g)})$ and returning solutions in amortised constant time translates into the following:

$$\frac{3^{mr}}{3^{l-m(r-1)(h-1)}} \geq 3^{m(r-1-g)} \quad \therefore \quad m \geq \frac{l}{(r-1)(h-1)+1+g}, \tag{6}$$

or simply $m = l/((r-1)(h-1)+1+g)$ when minimising the memory.

Finally, the straightforward generalisation of Eq. (5) is given by:

$$3^m \leq 2^{\frac{k+l}{rh}} \tag{7}$$

We provide the full algorithm for this parameter selection in the full version [9], and an implementation at https://github.com/charlotte-lefevre/TM_tradeoffs_SDP.

5.2 Improvements for Syndrome Decoding

We now present (and ultimately combine) two improvements to the dissection in tree: the first aims at reducing its granularity while the second is a straightforward adaptation of the smoothing technique. The price to pay for both are exponentially larger memory costs and thus less favourable tradeoffs.

Improving the Granularity of the Dissection in Tree. In a raw dissection tree, the dissections performed at every level are exhaustive. To decrease the overall granularity, one idea would then be to consider non-exhaustive dissections so that fewer solutions are eventually returned. This however also requires to decrease the target sizes at every level to compensate, and thus also to increase the initial list sizes if one wishes to return solutions in amortised constant time.

Let α be a new parameter s.t. the r-dissection now enumerates only $3^{m(r-\alpha)}$ candidates from the product of the r input lists. Enforcing equally-sized lists gives target sizes of $m(r-1-\alpha)$ at every level of the tree but the last, where it is $l-m(h-1)(r-1-\alpha)$. The expected number of returned solutions is then equal to:

$$S = \frac{3^{m(r-\alpha)}}{3^{l-m(h-1)(r-1-\alpha)}} \tag{8}$$

Each dissection now costs $\mathcal{O}(3^{m(r-g-1-\alpha)})$ (provided that this is not lower than their granularity), and returning solutions in amortised constant time translates into the following:

$$\frac{3^{m(r-\alpha)}}{3^{l-m\times(h-1)(r-1-\alpha)}} \geq 3^{m(r-g-1-\alpha)}$$

$$\therefore \; m \geq \frac{l}{(h-1)(r-1)+1+g-\alpha(h-1)} \tag{9}$$

The memory increase for positive values of α is then visible by comparing Eq. (6) and Eq. (9).

It remains to determine the optimal α, which in the amortised constant time regime is constrained by two phenomena:

1. The number of returned solutions must not be greater than necessary, *i.e.* $S \leq S_l$. Letting $s = \log_3(S_l)$ and injecting the minimal value for m given by Eq. (9) into Eq. (8) gives (after a tedious computation):
$$[l - (h-1)s] \times \alpha \geq [l(r-g-1) - s(g+1+(h-1)(r-1))] \tag{10}$$
2. The required number of solution at every level must not be lower than the granularity of the dissection. From Proposition 14 this gives:
$$r - g - 1 - \alpha > g - \mathit{gain}(g+1) \tag{11}$$

One would then pick the smallest value of α satisfying both constraints to minimise the overall memory cost. We provide the full algorithm for this parameter selection in the full version [9], and an implementation at https://github.com/charlotte-lefevre/TM_tradeoffs_SDP.

Smoothing the Dissection Tree. Since the dissection tree features a population constraint similar to the k-tree algorithm, we may adapt to it the smoothing technique from Proposition 9. This leads to the following:

Proposition 16. *Let l, r, h be fixed, $g := \mathit{gain}(r)$. If $3^l > 2^{(k+l)/(r^{h-1})}$ and $3^{l/(g+1+(r-1)(h-2))} < 2^{(k+l)/(r^{h-1})}$, then one can use a smoothed tree with h levels of r-dissections to obtain $2^{m(r-g-1)}$ solutions to the generalised birthday problem with r lists in amortised constant time, where:*
$$m = \frac{1}{(h-2)(r-1)+g}\left(l \log_2(3) - \frac{k+l}{r^{h-1}}\right).$$

The proof is similar to the one of Proposition 9 and given in the full version [9], along with the parameter selection algorithm.

Combination of the Improvements. There are settings where both previous improvements may be jointly necessary. This can be done by using a two-step process: the bottom level of the tree is used to satisfy a constraint of size t, which becomes a parameter, in a possibly non-exhaustive way as controlled by a parameter β. As in a smoothed tree, the goal is to produce intermediate lists of size 3^m (where m is another parameter), starting from ones of size $3^{\tilde{m}}$, $\tilde{m} := \log_3(2^{\frac{k+l}{r^h}})$. Then the $h-1$ remaining levels are required to satisfy a target of size $l-t$ with input lists of size 3^m, in a possibly non-exhaustive way as controlled by a parameter α.

Parameters leading to valid instances in amortised constant time must then satisfy the following constraints:

1. The expected list size is larger than 3^m after the first level:

$$\frac{3^{\tilde{m}\times(r-\beta)}}{3^t} \geq 3^m \ \therefore\ \beta \leq r - \frac{m+t}{\tilde{m}}$$

2. The parameter α is constrained by Eqs. (10) and (11).
3. The parameter β is constrained by Eq. (11).
4. The cost is dominated by the upper part of the tree:

$$3^{\tilde{m}\times(c-\beta)} \leq 3^{m(c-\alpha)} \ \therefore\ \beta \geq c - \frac{m}{\tilde{m}}(c-\alpha),$$

where $c := r - g - 1$.

When searching for valid parameterizations, it is best to first select the value for t and to take it as large as possible as this minimises the memory cost. This makes sense, intuitively, since in that case the tree is as close as possible to a balanced (non-smoothed) one.

The full parameter selection algorithm is given in the full version [9] and an implementation is provided at https://github.com/charlotte-lefevre/TM_tradeoffs_SDP. The impact of the granularity improvements, also combined with smoothing, are illustrated for the 3,4-dissection in Fig. 8. Thanks to these improvements, the 3,4-dissection is now applicable to larger memory regimes but at the cost of less favourable tradeoffs (clearly observable from the changes of the slopes).

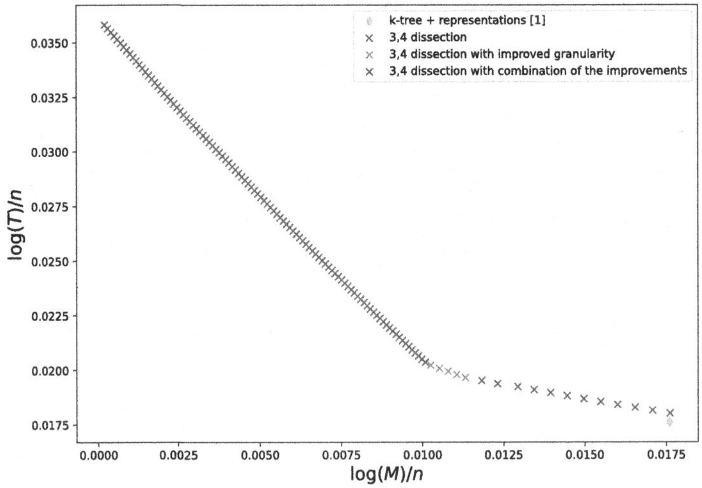

Fig. 8. Best time-memory tradeoff for the syndrome decoding problem in the Wave regime using 3,4-dissection. From $M \approx 2^{0.01n}$, the granularity of the 3,4-dissection becomes too coarse, so that non-exhaustive dissections are henceforth considered. Then at $M \approx 2^{0.0112n}$, Eq. (7) is no more satisfied, leading thus to the use of the smoothing technique

5.3 Experimental Results

As a proof of concept, we implemented the 3,4-dissection algorithm using Sage. The main aim here is to check that the practical number of iterations of the *Subset sum step* before finding a solution to the SDP coincides with the theoretical prediction. This implementation is not fully optimised and relies on a general-purpose finite-field linear algebra software packaged within Sage. This restricts its usage to relatively small parameters and we only considered instances up to $n = 875$, which in the Wave regime translates to $k = 591$, $l = 48$. With this instantiation, one iteration of the *Subset sum step* combined with the *Probabilistic reconstruction step* takes on average 800 s on a (virtualised) i386 processor.[5] With 10 runs of the full algorithm, 5.7 iterations of the *Subset sum step* were necessary on average before finding a solution, which is somewhat consistent with the theoretically expected 2.9, especially given the small number of runs. Moreover, with the instantiation $n = 560, k = 379, l = 34$, the average number of iterations with 110 runs is 12.05, which comes very close to the 12.3 expected number of iterations.

The code of this proof-of-concept implementation is available at https://github.com/charlotte-lefevre/TM_tradeoffs_SDP.

6 Application to Wave

We summarise our best time-memory tradeoffs for solving the syndrome decoding problem in the Wave regime in Fig. 9. We do this in two settings: in Fig. 9b we use asymptotic estimates similar to the ones used in the previous sections, while Fig. 9a is an estimate in bit complexity for concrete proposed security parameters. The plots were all drawn using the parameter selection algorithms presented in the full version [9], and the code is available at https://github.com/charlotte-lefevre/TM_tradeoffs_SDP.

From these figures it is notable that dissection in tree always outperforms k-tree instantiations (except in the regime where time and memory are about equal) and almost always outperforms dissection (it is about equivalent in the very low memory regime). For instance, the bit complexity estimate for the 3,4-dissection at $M \approx 2^{90}$ is about 2^{25} times less than using a smoothed k-tree algorithm with the same amount of memory. For low-memory regimes, the best instances use layered dissections with 2 levels, while from $M \approx 2^{0.009n}$, the best tradeoffs are obtained with $4,4$ or $3,4$-dissections.

[5] The computer used for the tests has an Apple M1 processor, but Sage uses Apple's Intel emulator.

Table 2. Bit cost estimates for various tradeoffs for solving the generic syndrome decoding problem, $n = 7236$, $k = 4892$, $w = 6862$.

Time	Memory	Target tradeoff	Algorithm
2^{152}	2^{144}	$T = M$	k-Tree + representations [1]
2^{162}	2^{130}	$T = M^{5/4}$	3,4-Dissection
2^{177}	$2^{88.5}$	$T = M^2$	3,4-Dissection
2^{194}	$2^{64.8}$	$T = M^3$	2,11-Dissection
2^{213}	$2^{42.6}$	$T = M^5$	2,16-Dissection
2^{247}	$2^{24.6}$	$T = M^{10}$	2,29-Dissection

The bit costs of Fig. 9a correspond to Wave's "new" parameters $n = 7236$, $k = 4892$, $w = 6862$ [1], and were computed using the following assumptions or simplifications:

- Elements of $\mathbb{F}_3$ are stored on 2 bits, and elementary operations in $\mathbb{F}_3^n$ cost $2n$ bit operations.
- Polynomial factors of the algorithms are taken into account.
- Polynomial factors in the estimate for S_l are taken into account.
- Computing $L_1 \bowtie_w L_2$ for some lists L_1, L_2 of elements of $\mathbb{F}_3^n$ and some w costs $2n(\#L_1 + \#L_2)$ as long as the size of the result is not larger than one of the input lists.

The last simplification implies a constant cost for memory access, which is an unrealistic underestimation for most of the considered memory sizes. The provided costs should thus not be interpreted as precise estimates but rather as intermediate points between asymptotic computations and a full and accurate modelling of an attack, which is out of the scope of this paper.

Finally, we list some of the most notable tradeoffs for concrete parameters in Table 2.

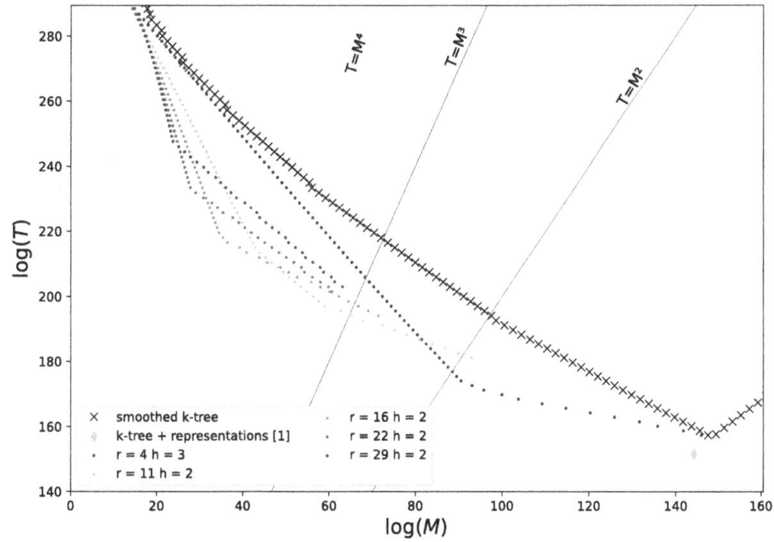

(a) Bit cost for fixed parameters.

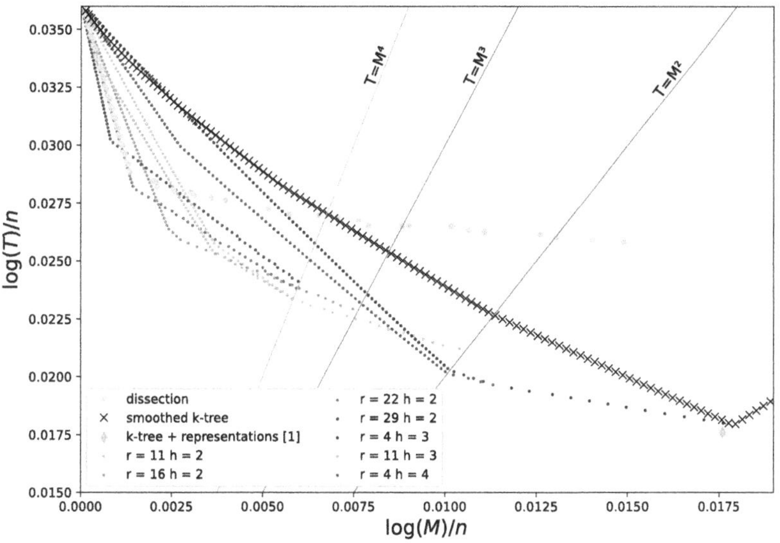

(b) Asymptotic cost.

Fig. 9. Summary of obtained time-memory tradeoffs. For the dissection in tree, r denotes the dissection used and h the number of levels.

Acknowledgements. The first author was partially supported by the French National Research Agency in the framework of the *Investissements d'avenir* programme (ANR-15-IDEX-02). The second author is in part supported by the Netherlands Organisation for Scientific Research (NWO) under grant OCENW.KLEIN.435. Part of this work was done when the second author was with Université Grenoble Alpes, and was partially supported by the LabEx PERSYVAL-Lab (ANR-11-LABX-0025-01) in the framework of the *Investissement d'avenir* programme. Finally we wish to thank the reviewers for all their comments.

References

1. Bricout, R., Chailloux, A., Debris-Alazard, T., Lequesne, M.: Ternary syndrome decoding with large weight. In: Paterson, K.G., Stebila, D. (eds.) SAC 2019. LNCS, vol. 11959, pp. 437–466. Springer, Cham (2020). https://doi.org/10.1007/978-3-030-38471-5_18
2. Coffey, J.T., Goodman, R.M.: The complexity of information set decoding. IEEE Trans. Inf. Theory **36**(5), 1031–1037 (1990)
3. Debris-Alazard, T.: Cryptographie fondée sur les codes: nouvelles approches pour constructions et preuves; contribution en cryptanalyse. (Code-based Cryptography: New Approaches for Design and Proof; Contribution to Cryptanalysis). PhD thesis, Pierre and Marie Curie University, Paris (2019)
4. Debris-Alazard, T., Sendrier, N., Tillich, J.-P.: Wave: a new family of trapdoor one-way preimage sampleable functions based on codes. In: Galbraith, S.D., Moriai, S. (eds.) ASIACRYPT 2019. LNCS, vol. 11921, pp. 21–51. Springer, Cham (2019). https://doi.org/10.1007/978-3-030-34578-5_2
5. Dinur, I.: An algorithmic framework for the generalized birthday problem. Des. Codes Cryptogr. **87**(8), 1897–1926 (2018). https://doi.org/10.1007/s10623-018-00594-6
6. Dinur, I., Dunkelman, O., Keller, N., Shamir, A.: Efficient dissection of composite problems, with applications to cryptanalysis, knapsacks, and combinatorial search problems. In: Safavi-Naini, R., Canetti, R. (eds.) CRYPTO 2012. LNCS, vol. 7417, pp. 719–740. Springer, Heidelberg (2012). https://doi.org/10.1007/978-3-642-32009-5_42
7. Esser, A., Heuer, F., Kübler, R., May, A., Sohler, C.: Dissection-BKW. In: Shacham, H., Boldyreva, A. (eds.) CRYPTO 2018. LNCS, vol. 10992, pp. 638–666. Springer, Cham (2018). https://doi.org/10.1007/978-3-319-96881-0_22
8. Howgrave-Graham, N., Joux, A.: New generic algorithms for hard knapsacks. In: Gilbert, H. (ed.) EUROCRYPT 2010. LNCS, vol. 6110, pp. 235–256. Springer, Heidelberg (2010). https://doi.org/10.1007/978-3-642-13190-5_12
9. Karpman, P., Lefevre, C.: Time-memory tradeoffs for large-weight syndrome decoding in ternary codes. IACR Cryptol. ePrint Arch. Full version, to appear (2022)
10. Meurer, A.: A coding-theoretic approach to cryptanalysis. PhD thesis, Ruhr University Bochum (2013)
11. Minder, L., Sinclair, A.: The extended k-tree algorithm. J. Cryptol. **25**(2), 349–382 (2012)
12. Niebuhr, R., Cayrel, P.-L., Bulygin, S., Buchmann, J. On lower bounds for information set decoding over $\mathbb{F}_q$. In: SCC 2010, vol. 10, pp. 143–157 (2010)

13. Peters, C.: Information-set decoding for linear codes over Fq. In: Sendrier, N. (ed.) PQCrypto 2010. LNCS, vol. 6061, pp. 81–94. Springer, Heidelberg (2010). https://doi.org/10.1007/978-3-642-12929-2_7
14. Prange, E.: The use of information sets in decoding cyclic codes. IRE Trans. Inf. Theory **8**(5), 5–9 (1962)
15. Schroeppel, R., Shamir, A.: A $T = \mathcal{O}(2^{n/2})$, $S = \mathcal{O}(2^{n/4})$ algorithm for certain NP-complete problems. SIAM J. Comput. **10**(3), 456–464 (1981)
16. Torres, R.C.: Asymptotic analysis of ISD algorithms for the q-ary case. In: Proceedings of the Tenth International Workshop on Coding and Cryptography WCC 2017 (2017)
17. Wagner, D.: A generalized birthday problem. In: Yung, M. (ed.) CRYPTO 2002. LNCS, vol. 2442, pp. 288–304. Springer, Heidelberg (2002). https://doi.org/10.1007/3-540-45708-9_19

Syndrome Decoding Estimator

Andre Esser(✉) and Emanuele Bellini(✉)

Cryptography Research Center, Technology Innovation Institute, Abu Dhabi, UAE
{andre.esser,emanuele.bellini}@tii.ae

Abstract. The selection of secure parameter sets requires an estimation of the attack cost to break the respective cryptographic scheme instantiated under these parameters. The current NIST standardization process for post-quantum schemes makes this an urgent task, especially considering the announcement to select final candidates by the end of 2021. For code-based schemes, recent estimates seemed to contradict the claimed security of most proposals, leading to a certain doubt about the correctness of those estimates. Furthermore, none of the available estimates include most recent algorithmic improvements on decoding linear codes, which are based on information set decoding (ISD) in combination with nearest neighbor search. In this work we observe that *all* major ISD improvements are build on nearest neighbor search, explicitly or implicitly. This allows us to derive a framework from which we obtain *practical* variants of all relevant ISD algorithms including the most recent improvements. We derive formulas for the practical attack costs and make those online available in an easy to use estimator tool written in python and C. Eventually, we provide classical and quantum estimates for the bit security of all parameter sets of current code-based NIST proposals.

Keywords: ISD · syndrome decoding · nearest neighbor · estimator · code-based

1 Introduction

The current NIST standardization process for post quantum schemes is announced to finally select proposals to be standardized around the end of 2021. After this initial selection it is still a long procedure until the final standards for the chosen schemes will be obtained. One major challenge will be the selection of secure parameter sets for standardization, which match the respective security levels given by NIST. To determine and evaluate parameter sets a precise estimation of the attack cost of the best known attacks on the schemes or the corresponding primitives is necessary.

Before such estimates can be derived efficiently, the best practical attacks must be identified. Code based schemes usually rely on the hardness of the syndrome decoding problem, which given a random matrix $H \in \mathbb{F}_2^{(n-k)\times n}$, a syndrome $\mathbf{s} \in \mathbb{F}_2^{n-k}$ and an integer ω asks to find an error vector $\mathbf{e} \in \mathbb{F}_2^n$ with exactly ω coordinates equal to one that satisfies $H\mathbf{e} = \mathbf{s}$. The best known algorithms

G. Hanaoka et al. (Eds.): PKC 2022, LNCS 13177, pp. 112–141, 2022.
https://doi.org/10.1007/978-3-030-97121-2_5

to solve this problem all belong to a class of algorithms known as information set decoding (ISD), initially discovered by Prange in 1962 [29]. Since then there have been numerous works building on the same initial idea [4,8,11,16,23,24,31]. Usually, these works study the problem for $\omega = cn$, where c is constant. For this choice they improve the asymptotic runtime exponent. However, all code based NIST PQC submissions rely on sublinear error weight, i.e. $\omega = o(n)$. In this setting the advantage of improved algorithms of the ISD class over Prange's initial approach has been shown to asymptotically vanish, i.e., they only affect second order terms [32]. Since usually these improvements come along with a polynomial overhead, it is per se not clear which algorithms actually yield practical improvements.

Estimators for concrete hardness approximation of the syndrome decoding problem have previously been studied in [17,28] and more recently in [3]. So far these works consider only a subset of the mentioned improvements, not including the most recent variants, which are usually based on nearest neighbor search techniques [8,24]. The omission of these improvements in [3] might be due to the use of practically costly, but theoretically close to optimal routines to instantiate the nearest neighbor search in the original works of [8,24]. The BIKE submission gives a similar reasoning for disregarding these works in the security analysis based on polynomial overhead [1]. Contrary, we show that by substituting the used routines by more practical nearest neighbor search techniques these variants yield complexity improvements with regard to the cryptographic setting. Furthermore we uncover relations between all significant algorithmic improvements of the ISD class. More precisely, we show that all major ISD improvements use nearest neighbor search techniques, explicitly or implicitly. Using this relation we derive an algorithmic framework, which allows us to obtain variants of all advanced ISD techniques, including the improvements made by May-Meurer-Thomae (MMT) [23], Becker-Joux-May-Meurer (BJMM) [4], May-Ozerov [24] and Both-May [8]. Finally the framework allows us to analyze the complexity of all algorithms in a unified and practical model giving a fair comparison and concrete hardness estimations.

Related Work. In [28] Peters gives a concrete analysis of Stern's algorithm for decoding codes over $\mathbb{F}_q$ including the case of $q = 2$. Peters focuses especially on optimized strategies for the initial Gaussian elimination part of ISD algorithms, adopting techniques introduced in [7,9]. While including some of these improvements in our estimates, we refrain from exhaustively optimizing this step. This allows us to keep the analysis and formulas comprehensible. Also note that for more recent ISD algorithms the complexity of the Gaussian elimination procedure does not dominate.

In [17] the authors present a non-asymptotic analysis of the MMT and BJMM algorithm, providing estimates for some selected parameter sets. Unfortunately no source code is provided to easily obtain estimates for parameter sets of more recent schemes. Also the analysis omits some practical details, as for instance the necessity for balanced weight distributions in successful runs of the algorithms. Also a heuristic approach to determine the number of iterations of the algorithms is used, whereas we use an exact computation.

The most recent study of concrete costs of ISD algorithms was performed in [3]. Here the bit complexity estimates for the algorithmic cost of performing the MMT algorithm on nearly all proposed parameter sets are significantly lower than claimed by the submissions. Accordingly, this work raised some discussions (in the NIST PQC forum [33,34]) about whether the currently proposed parameter sets of code based schemes actually match their security levels and if so where to obtain more reliable estimates. We found that the analysis of [3] is slightly flawed for both advanced ISD algorithms that are considered, namely the BJMM and the MMT algorithm. We give a more detailed description of that flaw in the full version of this paper [12]. Besides that flaw the authors also use techniques that might affect the success probability of the algorithms, but are not mentioned in the latter analysis (as for instance a trimming of lists that exceed certain sizes). However, the analysis of the other ISD variants given in [3] seems to be correct.

In [8] Both and May describe an ISD improvement entirely based on nearest neighbor search. They also consider nearest neighbor algorithms other than May-Ozerov, which was motivated by the non-fulfillment of necessary prerequisites. However, their analysis is purely asymptotical and focuses entirely on the constant error regime.

Our Contribution. The contribution of this work is twofold. First we uncover relations between major ISD improvements, showing that all of them are build on nearest neighbor search. In the case of the BJMM and MMT algorithms, this view allows us to detect and finally correct deficiencies in the way the nearest neighbor search is performed. Our fix results in two new variants of the BJMM algorithm, which practically (and probably also asymptotically) outperform the original BJMM algorithm. Our work therefore contributes substantially to a better understanding of ISD algorithms.

Moreover, as another contribution, we give a unified framework based on nearest neighbor search, which allows to obtain variants of all major ISD improvements. By an easy exchange of the used nearest neighbor routines we obtain *practical* variants of the improvements by May-Ozerov and Both-May, which were previously disregarded in the context of concrete hardness estimations.

By an analysis of our framework for different instantiations we obtain formulas for the concrete complexity to solve the syndrome decoding problem. We implemented these estimates for all variants considered in this work (and more[1]) and provide the source code in form of an easy to use estimator program (mostly) written in *python*.[2] This allows for an effortless recomputation of our

[1] The focus of this work lies on advanced algorithms, but our estimator also provides the estimates for asymptotically inferior procedures.

[2] The estimator can be downloaded at https://github.com/Crypto-TII/syndrome_decoding_estimator.

results, estimation of the security levels for newly proposed parameter sets as well as custom modifications if required.

Finally we give the classical estimates for all proposed parameter sets of code-based schemes being part of the third round of the NIST PQC call, namely Classic McEliece [10], BIKE [1] and HQC [25]. Here we consider different memory access cost models and memory limitations. We find that essentially all parameter sets of the three schemes match their claimed security levels, with a slight outlier in form of the McEliece category three parameter set. Also we provide quantum estimates under the NIST metric of a `maxdepth` constraint, which limits the depth of the quantum circuit. We find that under this constraint even a very optimistic analysis of the quantum version of Prange's ISD algorithm [5] lets all proposed parameter sets match their claimed quantum security level.

The rest of the paper is organized as follows. In Sect. 2 we give basic definitions and present the practical nearest neighbor algorithms used in our analyses. In Sect. 3 we outline the nearest neighbor relations between known ISD variants. A reader only interested in concrete hardness estimations may skip this section. Subsequently, in Sect. 4 we present and analyze the framework and its instantiations to obtain formulas for practical cost estimations. Finally in Sect. 5 we present our hardness estimates for the classical and quantum security of McEliece, BIKE and HQC.

2 Preliminaries

We denote vectors as bold lower case letters and matrices with capital letters. We let I_n be the $n \times n$ identity matrix. For an integer $i \in \mathbb{N}$ we define $[i] := \{1, 2, \ldots, i\}$. Let $\mathbf{v} = (v_1, v_2, \ldots v_n)$ be a vector and $S \subseteq [n]$ then we denote by $\mathbf{v}_S$ the projection of $\mathbf{v}$ onto its coordinates indexed by S. For $\mathbf{w} \in \mathbb{F}_2^n$ we define $\mathrm{wt}(\mathbf{w}) := |\{i \in [n] \mid w_i = 1\}|$ to be the Hamming weight of $\mathbf{w}$. Furthermore we let $\mathcal{B}_p^n := \{\mathbf{w} \in \mathbb{F}_2^n \mid \mathrm{wt}(\mathbf{w}) = p\}$ be the set of all binary vectors of length n and Hamming weight p.

Coding Theory. A binary linear code $\mathcal{C}$ of length n and dimension k is a k-dimensional subspace of $\mathbb{F}_2^n$. Such a code can be defined as the image of a generator matrix $G \in \mathbb{F}_2^{k \times n}$ or via the kernel of a parity check matrix $H \in \mathbb{F}_2^{(n-k)\times n}$. We use the parity check description of the code throughout this work. Note that since any codeword $\mathbf{c} \in \mathcal{C}$ satisfies $H\mathbf{c} = \mathbf{0}$ the task of decoding a faulty codeword $\mathbf{y} = \mathbf{c} + \mathbf{e}$ for some error $\mathbf{e}$ yields the identity

$$H\mathbf{y} = H(\mathbf{c} + \mathbf{e}) = H\mathbf{e} =: \mathbf{s} \ .$$

The vector $\mathbf{s}$ is usually called the *syndrome* of $\mathbf{y}$, while obtaining $\mathbf{e}$ from given H and $\mathbf{s}$ is called the *syndrome decoding problem.*

Definition 2.1 (Syndrome Decoding Problem). *Let $H \in \mathbb{F}_2^{(n-k)\times n}$ be the parity check matrix of a random linear code, $\mathbf{s} \in \mathbb{F}_2^{n-k}$ and $\omega \in [n]$. The* syndrome decoding problem *asks to find a vector $\mathbf{e} \in \mathbb{F}_2^n$ with $\mathrm{wt}(\mathbf{e}) = \omega$ satisfying $H\mathbf{e} = \mathbf{s}$.*

Nearest Neighbor. At the heart of all algorithms presented in this work lies a specific kind of nearest neighbor or approximate matching problem, which we define in the following.

Definition 2.2 (Approximate Matching Problem). *Let $M \in \mathbb{F}_2^{r\times m}$ be a random matrix, $\mathbf{s} \in \mathbb{F}_2^r$ and $\delta, p \in \mathbb{N}$. The* approximate matching problem *asks to find all solutions $\mathbf{e} \in \mathbb{F}_2^m$ satisfying*

$$\mathrm{wt}(\mathbf{e}) = p \text{ and } \mathrm{wt}(M\mathbf{e} + \mathbf{s}) = \delta.$$

We write

$$M\mathbf{e} \approx_\delta \mathbf{s} \ ,$$

to denote that $M\mathbf{e}$ matches $\mathbf{s}$ on all but δ coordinates and call this equation an approximate matching identity.

Usually, routines to solve the approximate matching problem exploit a direct reduction to the bichromatic nearest neighbor problem. In this problem we are given two lists of binary vectors and are asked to find all pairs between those lists with distance δ. Therefore split $\mathbf{e} = \mathbf{e}_1 + \mathbf{e}_2$ in the sum of two vectors. For now let us consider a meet-in-the-middle split and (without loss of generality) even m, where $\mathbf{e}_1 = (\mathbf{d}_1, 0^{\frac{m}{2}})$ and $\mathbf{e}_2 = (0^{\frac{m}{2}}, \mathbf{d}_2)$ with $\mathbf{d}_1, \mathbf{d}_2 \in \mathcal{B}_{p/2}^{m/2}$, but also other splittings are possible.[3] Then all $\mathbf{e}_1$, respectively $\mathbf{e}_2$, are enumerated and $M\mathbf{e}_1$ is stored in list L_1, respectively $M\mathbf{e}_2 + \mathbf{s}$ is stored in list L_2. Now, a pair with distance δ between those lists fulfills by definition the approximate matching identity

$$M(\mathbf{e}_1 + \mathbf{e}_2) \approx_\delta \mathbf{s} \ .$$

Also note that due to the chosen splitting $\mathbf{e} = \mathbf{e}_1 + \mathbf{e}_2$ has weight p by construction, as desired.

The asymptotically fastest known algorithm for solving the bichromatic nearest neighbor problem where the lists are of size $\tilde{\mathcal{O}}(2^{c\cdot m})$, for constant c, is by May-Ozerov [24]. While the algorithm achieves theoretically close to optimal complexities [21], it inherits a huge polynomial overhead limiting its practicality, despite recent efforts to reduce that overhead [14]. As one of the major goals of this work is to provide precise *practical* estimates we do not consider the algorithm by May-Ozerov. However, we use different, simpler but more practical approaches.

Let us briefly outline three techniques to solve the bichromatic nearest neighbor problem, where we measure all running times in vector operations in $\mathbb{F}_2^m$. The most basic variant is a naive enumeration, which we call BRUTEFORCE in the following. The algorithm simply enumerates all pairs of $L_1 \times L_2$ and checks if their distance is δ. Clearly this algorithm has running time

$$T_{\mathrm{B}} = |L_1 \times L_2|.$$

[3] Note that this splitting only allows to construct balanced solutions $\mathbf{e}$, which have exactly weight $\frac{p}{2}$ on the upper and lower half. While we take this into account when deriving our concrete estimates let us neglect this fact for now.

Meet-in-the-Middle. A slightly more sophisticated algorithm uses a meet-in-the-middle approach. First, the lists are enlarged by factor of the number of possible vectors of Hamming weight equal to δ. Thus, for every possible such vector, its sum with the original element is present in the enlarged list. To balance the complexities the δ-Hamming weight vector is again split in a meet-in-the-middle fashion among both lists. This implies that the algorithm can only find pairs of elements whose distance is balanced, i.e. splits equally on both sides of their sum. We will take this into account in our precise analysis later, but for know let us ignore this issue. The pseudocode of the algorithm is given in Algorithm 1. Note that after the addition of the $\delta/2$-weighted vectors the nearest neighbor problem degenerates to a search for equality.

Algorithm 1. MEET-IN-THE-MIDDLE

Input: $L_1, L_2 \in (\mathbb{F}_2^m)^*$, $\delta \in [m]$
Output: all $(\mathbf{x}, \mathbf{y}) \in L_1 \times L_2$ with $\mathrm{wt}(\mathbf{x}+\mathbf{y}) = \delta$

$L_1' = \{\mathbf{x} + (\mathbf{d}, \mathbf{0}) \mid \mathbf{x} \in L_1, \mathbf{d} \in \mathcal{B}_{\delta/2}^{m/2}\}$
$L_2' = \{\mathbf{y} + (\mathbf{0}, \mathbf{d}) \mid \mathbf{y} \in L_2, \mathbf{d} \in \mathcal{B}_{\delta/2}^{m/2}\}$
for $\mathbf{y}' \in L_2'$ **do**
    $L \leftarrow L \cup \{(\mathbf{x}, \mathbf{y}) \mid \mathbf{x}' = \mathbf{y}', \mathbf{x}' \in L_1'\}$
return L

Therefore note that for every pair $(\mathbf{x}, \mathbf{y}) \in L$ it holds that

$$\mathbf{x}' = \mathbf{y}' \Leftrightarrow \mathbf{x} + (\mathbf{d}_1, \mathbf{0}) = \mathbf{y} + (\mathbf{0}, \mathbf{d}_2) \Leftrightarrow \mathbf{x} + \mathbf{y} = (\mathbf{d}_1, \mathbf{d}_2) \Rightarrow \mathrm{wt}(\mathbf{x}+\mathbf{y}) = \delta.$$

The lists L_1' and L_2' are of size $\binom{m/2}{w/2} \cdot |L_1|$, while the output list L is of expected size $|L_1' \times L_2'|/2^m$. As we only need to search for equality the time complexity to construct L is linear in these lists sizes,[4] which gives a time complexity of

$$T_{\mathrm{MITM}} = 2 \cdot \binom{m/2}{w/2} \cdot |L_1| + \frac{|L_1|^2 \binom{m/2}{w/2}^2}{2^m} . \tag{1}$$

Indyk-Motwani. The third routine we consider for solving the nearest neighbor problem is based on locality sensitive hashing introduced by Indyk and Motwani [18]. Let $\mathbf{z} = \mathbf{x} + \mathbf{y}$ for $(\mathbf{x}, \mathbf{y}) \in L_1 \times L_2$ be an element with weight δ. Then the algorithm guesses $\lambda \in \mathbb{N}$ coordinates $I \subset [m]$ of $\mathbf{z}$ for which it assumes that $\mathbf{z}_I = \mathbf{0}$ holds. Now, an exact matching on these λ coordinates is performed between L_1 and L_2. For each match $(\mathbf{x}', \mathbf{y}')$, the algorithm then checks if $\mathrm{wt}(\mathbf{z}') = \delta$ for $\mathbf{z}' = \mathbf{x}' + \mathbf{y}'$ holds.

The algorithm relies on the fact that for elements whose sum has small weight, the projection to one of the coordinates of those elements is more likely to be equal then for elements whose sum has larger weight. Algorithm 2 gives a pseudocode description of the procedure.

[4] By using a hashing strategy.

Algorithm 2. INDYK-MOTWANI

Input: $L_1, L_2 \in (\mathbb{F}_2^m)^*$, $\delta \in [m]$
Output: all $(\mathbf{x}, \mathbf{y}) \in L_1 \times L_2$ with $\mathrm{wt}(\mathbf{x}+\mathbf{y}) = \delta$

```
λ := min(log L_1, m − 2δ), N := binom(m, δ) / binom(m−λ, δ)
for i = 1 to N do
    choose random I ⊆ [m] with |I| = λ
    for (x, y) ∈ {(x, y) ∈ L_1 × L_2 | x_I = y_I} do
        if wt(x + y) = δ then
            L ← L ∪ (x, y)
return L
```

Note that the probability that for a $\mathbf{z} \in \mathbb{F}_2^m$ with $\mathrm{wt}(\mathbf{z}) = \delta$ the projection to a random choice of λ distinct coordinates is the zero vector is

$$p := \Pr\left[\mathbf{z}_I = 0^\lambda \mid \mathbf{z} \in \mathbb{F}_2^m \wedge \mathrm{wt}(\mathbf{z}) = \delta\right] = \frac{\binom{m-\lambda}{\delta}}{\binom{m}{\delta}} .$$

Similar to the meet-in-the-middle approach the time for the construction of L is linear in the involved lists sizes, which results in an expected time complexity of

$$T_{\mathrm{IM}} = p^{-1} \cdot (2|L_1| + |L_1|^2/2^\lambda) = \frac{\binom{m}{\delta} \cdot (2|L_1| + |L_1|^2/2^\lambda)}{\binom{m-\lambda}{\delta}}, \tag{2}$$

assuming $|L_1| = |L_2|$. An approximation of the binomial coefficients via Stirling's formula and analytical analysis yields a global minimum at $\lambda = \min(\log|L_1|, m - 2\delta)$. Numerical computations show, that this value is also very close to the optimum when instead considering the more precise form of the runtime formula given in in Eq. (2).

3 ISD Algorithms from a Nearest Neighbor Perspective

Let us start with the ISD algorithm by Prange, which forms the foundation for all advanced techniques. The algorithm first applies a random permutation to the columns of the parity check matrix H. Note that for any permutation matrix $P \in \mathbb{F}_2^{n\times n}$ we have $(HP)(P^{-1}\mathbf{e}) = \mathbf{s}$. Now, by applying Gaussian elimination to its rows we transform HP into *systematic form*, modelled by the multiplication with an invertible matrix $Q \in \mathbb{F}_2^{(n-k)\times(n-k)}$

$$QHP = \left(\tilde{H}\ I_{n-k}\right), \text{ where } \tilde{H} \in \mathbb{F}_2^{(n-k)\times(k)}. \tag{3}$$

Note that for a random permutation matrix there exists such an invertible Q with constant probability. Further let $(P^{-1}\mathbf{e}) = (\mathbf{e}', \mathbf{e}'') \in \mathbb{F}_2^k \times \mathbb{F}_2^{n-k}$ and $Q\mathbf{s} = \tilde{\mathbf{s}} \in \mathbb{F}_2^{n-k}$, then the following identity holds

$$Q(HP)(P^{-1}\mathbf{e}) = (\tilde{H}\mathbf{e}' + \mathbf{e}'') = \tilde{\mathbf{s}}.$$

Assume that the permutation P induces a weight distribution of

$$\mathrm{wt}(\mathbf{e}') = p \text{ and hence } \mathrm{wt}(\mathbf{e}'') = \omega - p \;, \tag{4}$$

then it suffices to find an $\mathbf{e}' \in \mathbb{F}_2^k$ of weight p satisfying

$$\mathrm{wt}(\tilde{H}\mathbf{e}' + \tilde{\mathbf{s}}) = \mathrm{wt}(\mathbf{e}'') = \omega - p \;. \tag{5}$$

Once a suitable permutation P and a vector $\mathbf{e}'$ are found $\mathbf{e} = P(\mathbf{e}', \tilde{H}\mathbf{e}' + \tilde{\mathbf{s}})$ forms a solution to the syndrome decoding problem. Note that Eqs. (4) and (5) yield an approximate matching identity according to Definition 2.2

$$\tilde{H}\mathbf{e}' \approx_{\omega-p} \tilde{\mathbf{s}} \;. \tag{6}$$

While Prange's algorithm chooses the weight p of $\mathbf{e}'$ equal to zero and thus does not have to put any effort into solving the approximate matching problem,[5] all further improvements choose $p > 0$.

Choosing $p > 0$ and applying the bruteforce approach that simply enumerates all possible $\mathbf{e}'$ of weight p yields a polynomial improvement due to Lee and Brickell [22].

Applying instead the Indyk-Motwani or the meet-in-the-middle approaches results in algorithmic analogs of the well-known ISD improvements by Stern [31] and Dumer [11] respectively.

Stern's Original Algorithm. Stern [31] improved on the approach of Prange by introducing an ℓ-window of zero entries in the error $\mathbf{e}''$. Thus one considers $(P^{-1}\mathbf{e}) = (\mathbf{e}', \mathbf{e}'') \in \mathbb{F}_2^k \times \mathbb{F}_2^{n-k}$, where $\mathbf{e}'' = (0^\ell, \tilde{\mathbf{e}})$. Note that due to this weight distribution $\tilde{H}\mathbf{e}'$ matches the syndrome on the first ℓ coordinates, as we have

$$\tilde{H}\mathbf{e}' = \tilde{\mathbf{s}} + \mathbf{e}'' = \tilde{\mathbf{s}} + (0^\ell, \tilde{\mathbf{e}}) = (\tilde{\mathbf{s}}_1, \tilde{\mathbf{s}}_2 + \tilde{\mathbf{e}}) \;,$$

where $\tilde{\mathbf{s}} = (\tilde{\mathbf{s}}_1, \tilde{\mathbf{s}}_2) \in \mathbb{F}_2^\ell \times \mathbb{F}_2^{n-k-\ell}$. Now Stern's algorithm uses the identity $(\tilde{H}\mathbf{e}')_{[\ell]} = \tilde{\mathbf{s}}_1$ to perform a meet-in-the-middle search on $\mathbf{e}'$. Thus, it splits $\mathbf{e}' = (\mathbf{e}_1, 0^{\frac{k}{2}}) + (0^{\frac{k}{2}}, \mathbf{e}_2)$, constructs two lists containing $\tilde{H}(\mathbf{x}, 0^{\frac{k}{2}})$ and $\tilde{H}(0^{\frac{k}{2}}, \mathbf{y})$ respectively for all $\mathbf{x}, \mathbf{y} \in \mathcal{B}_{p/2}^{k/2}$ and searches between those lists for pairs that sum to $\tilde{\mathbf{s}}_1$ on their first ℓ coordinates. For every matching pair $((\mathbf{x}', \mathbf{0}), (\mathbf{0}, \mathbf{y}'))$ it is checked if $\tilde{H}(\mathbf{x}', \mathbf{y}') + \tilde{\mathbf{s}}$ has weight $\omega - p$, which is particularly satisfied when $(\mathbf{x}', \mathbf{y}') = (\mathbf{e}_1, \mathbf{e}_2)$.

NN-Perspective of Stern's Algorithm. Let us modify the permutation step by first aiming for the weight distribution of Prange (Eq. (4)) and then permuting the error $\mathbf{e}''$ separately several times until we may expect the desired ℓ-window. For every such permutation we continue with the meet-in-the-middle step of Stern's algorithm. First note that this does not change the expected amount

[5] For $p = 0$ a simple check if $\mathrm{wt}(\tilde{\mathbf{s}}) = \omega$ suffices to determine if the permutation distributes the weight correctly.

of necessary permutations until the weight is distributed as in Stern's original algorithm. However, it shows that the algorithm by Stern is actually solving the approximate matching identity from Eq. (6) via INDYK-MOTWANI. Here the matching on the first ℓ coordinates after the permutation corresponds to the matching on a random projection of ℓ coordinates used by INDYK-MOTWANI.

Dumer's Original Algorithm. Dumer [11] changed the procedure by increasing the dimension of $\mathbf{e}'$ to $k + \ell$, which allowed him to get rid of the ℓ-window of zeros in the permutation. Therefore he defines the systematic form as

$$QHP = \begin{pmatrix} H_1 & \mathbf{0} \\ H_2 & I_{n-k-\ell} \end{pmatrix}, \tag{7}$$

where $H_1 \in \mathbb{F}_2^{\ell \times (k+\ell)}$ and $H_2 \in \mathbb{F}_2^{(n-k-\ell)\times(k+\ell)}$. Again it is aimed for a weight distribution where for $P^{-1}\mathbf{e} = (\mathbf{e}', \mathbf{e}'') \in \mathbb{F}_2^{k+\ell} \times \mathbb{F}_2^{n-k-\ell}$ it holds $\mathrm{wt}(\mathbf{e}') = p$, and $\mathrm{wt}(\mathbf{e}'') = \omega - p$. Due to the increased dimension of $\mathbf{e}'$ we get

$$QHP(\mathbf{e}', \mathbf{e}'') = (H_1\mathbf{e}', H_2\mathbf{e}' + \mathbf{e}'') = (\tilde{\mathbf{s}}_1, \tilde{\mathbf{s}}_2) = \tilde{\mathbf{s}} \ ,$$

where $(\tilde{\mathbf{s}}_1, \tilde{\mathbf{s}}_2) \in \mathbb{F}_2^{\ell} \times \mathbb{F}_2^{n-k-\ell}$. The algorithm then uses the identity on the first ℓ bits again to search for $\mathbf{e}'$ using a meet-in-the-middle strategy. Again for each computed candidate $\mathbf{x}$ for $\mathbf{e}'$ satisfying the identity it checks if $\mathrm{wt}(H_2\mathbf{x} + \tilde{\mathbf{s}}_2) = \mathrm{wt}(\mathbf{e}'') = \omega - p$ and if so outputs the solution $P(\mathbf{x}, H_2\mathbf{x} + \tilde{\mathbf{s}}_2)$.

NN-Perspective of Dumer's Algorithm. Note that the original matrix used by Prange's algorithm (see Eq. (3)) is already in systematic form according to the definition of Dumer, since

$$\left(\tilde{H} \ I_{n-k}\right) = \begin{pmatrix} \tilde{H}_1 & I_\ell & \mathbf{0} \\ \tilde{H}_2 & \mathbf{0} & I_{n-k-\ell} \end{pmatrix}, \text{ where } \tilde{H} \in \mathbb{F}_2^{(n-k)\times(k)}.$$

Thus we obtain Eq. (7) by setting $H_1 = \left(\tilde{H}_1 \ I_\ell\right)$ and $H_2 = \left(\tilde{H}_2 \ \mathbf{0}\right)$. Now let us further split $\mathbf{e}' \in \mathbb{F}_2^{k+\ell}$ in two parts $\mathbf{e}' = (\mathbf{e}_1, \mathbf{e}_2) \in \mathbb{F}_2^k \times \mathbb{F}_2^\ell$ and reconsider the identity $H_1\mathbf{e}' = \tilde{\mathbf{s}}_1$, which now becomes

$$H_1\mathbf{e}' = \left(\tilde{H}_1 \ I_\ell\right)(\mathbf{e}_1, \mathbf{e}_2) = \tilde{H}_1\mathbf{e}_1 + \mathbf{e}_2 = \tilde{\mathbf{s}}_1 \ .$$

Thus we are facing again a nearest neighbor identity $\tilde{H}_1\mathbf{e}_1 \approx_{|\mathbf{e}_2|} \tilde{\mathbf{s}}_1$. Dumer's algorithm enforces only a joined weight distribution of $\mathrm{wt}((\mathbf{e}_1, \mathbf{e}_2)) = p$ and, hence, we do not exactly know the weight of the approximate matching problem we are facing. However, with inverse polynomial probability the weight distributes proportionally on both sides, giving $\mathrm{wt}(\mathbf{e}_1) = \frac{k \cdot p}{k+\ell}$ and $\mathrm{wt}(\mathbf{e}_2) = \frac{\ell \cdot p}{k+\ell}$. Now using the MEET-IN-THE-MIDDLE algorithm to solve this instance we obtain a version of Dumer's algorithm from a nearest neighbor perspective achieving the same asymptotic complexity.

A natural question which comes to mind when considering the nearest neighbor version of Dumer is: why should it be optimal to choose a joined weight distribution for $(\mathbf{e}_1, \mathbf{e}_2)$? By introducing two different weight parameters p_1 and p_2 for both sides of $\mathbf{e}'$ we obtain an algorithmic analogue of the improvement of Bernstein et al. [7] known as Ball Collision Decoding (BCD), which slightly improves on Dumer's algorithm.

Also one might question the optimality of Stern's procedure, which performs the nearest neighbor search on the whole $n-k$ coordinates of $\mathbf{e}''$ and weight $\omega - p$ instead of using a reduced instance of length ℓ_2 and weight p_2, like the BCD variant. We found that refining Stern's algorithm using the additional parameters ℓ_2 and p_2 yields a slight improvement similar to the BCD one.

The MMT Algorithm. Let us now turn our focus to the ISD improvements by May, Meurer and Thomae (MMT) [23] as well as by Becker, Joux, May and Meurer (BJMM) [4]. These algorithms first apply a permutation, similar to the previous algorithms. However, instead of splitting the vector $\mathbf{e}'$ in two addends, as done by Dumer, Stern or BCD, they split it in four (MMT) or eight (BJMM). Then all candidates for the addends are enumerated in a meet-in-the-middle fashion. A binary search tree (similar to Wagner's k-tree algorithm [35]) is subsequently used to construct the solution as sum of base list elements. Additionally, they do not use a disjoint splitting of the addends throughout the tree, which gives several different *representations* of the solution. For example the MMT algorithm represents $\mathbf{e}' = \mathbf{e}_1 + \mathbf{e}_2$ with $\mathbf{e}_1, \mathbf{e}_2 \in \mathbb{F}_2^n$ and then splits $\mathbf{e}_1$ and $\mathbf{e}_2$ in a meet-in-the-middle fashion (as before). This gives several different combinations of $(\mathbf{e}_1, \mathbf{e}_2)$ that sum up to $\mathbf{e}'$. As the binary search tree imposes restrictions on the exact form of the solution, a careful choice of parameters lets a single of these representations fulfill the constraints. Note that the knowledge of a single representation of $\mathbf{e}'$ suffices to solve the syndrome decoding problem.

As the structure of the BJMM and MMT algorithm is quite similar we stick with a description of the MMT algorithm for now, highlighting their differences later.

Let us explain the algorithm in a bit more detail. The MMT (as well as the BJMM) algorithm uses the same preprocessing step as Dumer, hence H is in systematic form according to Eq. (7) and the weight similarly distributes on $P^{-1}\mathbf{e} := (\mathbf{e}', \mathbf{e}'') \in \mathbb{F}_2^{k+\ell} \times \mathbb{F}_2^{n-k-\ell}$ as $\mathrm{wt}(\mathbf{e}') = p$ and $\mathrm{wt}(\mathbf{e}'') = \omega - p$. Now, as mentioned before, the algorithm splits

$$\mathbf{e}' = \underbrace{(\mathbf{a}_1, 0^{\frac{k+\ell}{2}}) + (0^{\frac{k+\ell}{2}}, \mathbf{a}_2)}_{\mathbf{e}_1} + \underbrace{(\mathbf{a}_3, 0^{\frac{k+\ell}{2}}) + (0^{\frac{k+\ell}{2}}, \mathbf{a}_4)}_{\mathbf{e}_2} ,$$

with $\mathbf{a}_i \in \mathcal{B}_{p/4}^{(k+\ell)/2}, i = 1, 2, 3, 4$, hence, by construction we have $\mathbf{e}_1, \mathbf{e}_2 \in \mathcal{B}_{p/2}^{k+\ell}$.

Next candidates for $\mathbf{a}_i$ are constructed by enumerating all possible values from $\mathcal{B}_{p/4}^{(k+\ell)/2}$ in the base lists L_i. Now, one chooses some random $\mathbf{t} \in \mathbb{F}_2^{\ell_1}$, for some optimized $\ell_1 \leq \ell$, and constructs a new list L_{12} by just considering those elements $(\mathbf{x}, \mathbf{y}) \in L_1 \times L_2$ for which it holds that

$$(H_1(\mathbf{x} + \mathbf{y}))_{[\ell_1]} = \mathbf{t} .$$

Now the same is done for the lists L_3 and L_4, thus they are merged in a new list L_{34} but using a modified target $\mathbf{t}' = \mathbf{t} + (\tilde{\mathbf{s}}_1)_{[\ell_1]}$. This choice of $\mathbf{t}'$ ensures that $(\mathbf{v}, \mathbf{w}) \in L_{12} \times L_{34}$ satisfy

$$H_1(\mathbf{v} + \mathbf{w}) = (\tilde{\mathbf{s}}_1)_{[\ell_1]} ,$$

i.e., the desired identity is already satisfied on the lower ℓ_1 coordinates. Finally the algorithm merges lists L_{12} and L_{34} in a list L_{1234} by enforcing the identity on all ℓ bits and then checks if for any $\mathbf{z} \in L_{1234}$ it holds that $\mathrm{wt}(\tilde{H}_2\mathbf{z} + \tilde{\mathbf{s}}_2) = \mathrm{wt}(\mathbf{e}'') = \omega - p$ and, if so, outputs the solution.

NN-Perspective and An Algorithmic Shortcoming of the MMT Algorithm. We show in the following that the MMT algorithm also uses a meet-in-the-middle strategy for solving nearest-neighbor equations. But contrary to the procedure given in Algorithm 1, too many vectors are enumerated in the base lists, which unnecessarily increases the list sizes and results in undesired list distributions for special inputs.

Similar to the NN-perspective of Dumer's algorithm, let H be in systematic form as given by Eq. (3), which is

$$H = \left(\tilde{H}\ I_{n-k}\right) = \begin{pmatrix} \tilde{H}_1 & I_\ell & \mathbf{0} \\ \tilde{H}_2 & \mathbf{0} & I_{n-k-\ell} \end{pmatrix}, \text{ where } \tilde{H} \in \mathbb{F}_2^{(n-k)\times(k)} .$$

Additionally, let $\mathbf{e}' = (\mathbf{e}'_1, \mathbf{e}'_2, \mathbf{e}'_3) \in \mathbb{F}_2^k \times \mathbb{F}_2^{\ell_1} \times \mathbb{F}_2^{\ell-\ell_1}$ and let the weight on each of the $\mathbf{e}'_i$ be $p_i := \frac{|\mathbf{e}'_i|\cdot p}{k+l}$. Also, for now consider the base list elements of the MMT algorithm to be formed as

$$\left(\mathcal{B}^{k/2}_{p_1/4} \times 0^{\frac{k}{2}} \times \mathcal{B}^{\ell_1/2}_{p_2/4} \times 0^{\frac{\ell_1}{2}} \times \mathcal{B}^{(\ell-\ell_1)/2}_{p_3/4} \times 0^{\frac{\ell-\ell_1}{2}}\right) \text{ and}$$
$$\left(0^{\frac{k}{2}} \times \mathcal{B}^{k/2}_{p_1/4} \times 0^{\frac{\ell_1}{2}} \times \mathcal{B}^{\ell_1/2}_{p_2/4} \times 0^{\frac{\ell-\ell_1}{2}} \times \mathcal{B}^{(\ell-\ell_1)/2}_{p_3/4}\right) ,$$

rather than

$$\left(\mathcal{B}^{(k+l)/2}_{p/4} \times 0^{\frac{k+\ell}{2}}\right) \text{ and } \left(0^{\frac{k+\ell}{2}} \times \mathcal{B}^{(k+l)/2}_{p/4}\right) .$$

Thus, each of the $\mathbf{e}'_i$ is getting enumerated in a meet-in-the-middle fashion in the base lists.[6] Additionally let us write H_1 as

$$H_1 := \left(\tilde{H}_1\ I_\ell\right) = \begin{pmatrix} \tilde{H}_{11} & I_{\ell_1} & \mathbf{0} \\ \tilde{H}_{12} & \mathbf{0} & I_{\ell-\ell_1} \end{pmatrix}$$

Now let us consider the first join of base lists. For this join only elements $\mathbf{x} \in L_1$ and $\mathbf{y} \in L_2$ are considered for which

$$\left(H_1(\mathbf{x} + \mathbf{y})\right)_{[\ell_1]} = \mathbf{t} . \tag{8}$$

[6] Note that both sets differ only in a polynomial fraction of their elements. Furthermore our argumentation also holds when using the original base lists, but the refinement allows for easier illustration by yielding approximate matching identities with fixed distances.

By letting $\mathbf{x} = (\mathbf{x}_1, \mathbf{x}_2, \mathbf{x}_3) \in \mathbb{F}_2^k \times \mathbb{F}_2^{\ell_1} \times \mathbb{F}_2^{\ell-\ell_1}$ and $\mathbf{y} = (\mathbf{y}_1, \mathbf{y}_2, \mathbf{y}_3)$, analogously, Eq. (8) becomes

$$\begin{aligned} & \tilde{H}_{11}(\mathbf{x}_1 + \mathbf{y}_1) + \mathbf{x}_2 + \mathbf{y}_2 = \mathbf{t} \\ \Leftrightarrow \quad & \tilde{H}_{11}(\mathbf{x}_1 + \mathbf{y}_1) = \mathbf{t} + \mathbf{x}_2 + \mathbf{y}_2 \ . \end{aligned} \tag{9}$$

Note that by construction $\mathrm{wt}(\mathbf{x}_1 + \mathbf{y}_1) = p_1/2$ and $\mathrm{wt}(\mathbf{x}_2 + \mathbf{y}_2) = p_2/2$, hence the newly constructed list L_{12} consists only of vectors having weight $p_1/2$, which are $p_2/2$ close to $\mathbf{t}$ when multiplied by $\tilde{H}_{11}$. Hence, this join solves the approximate matching problem given by the identity

$$H\mathbf{x} \approx_{p_2/2} \mathbf{t} \ ,$$

for $\mathbf{x}$ with $\mathrm{wt}(\mathbf{x}) = p_1/2$.

Contrary to the MEET-IN-THE-MIDDLE algorithm from Sect. 2 the MMT algorithm additionally enumerates all values for $\mathbf{x}_3$ (resp. $\mathbf{y}_3$) in the base lists even though they are not taken into account by the matching routine. Thus, whenever any element satisfies Eq. (9), it is added to L_{12} for any combination of $(\mathbf{x}_3, \mathbf{y}_3) \in \mathcal{B}_{p_3/4}^{(\ell-\ell_1)/2} \times \mathcal{B}_{p_3/4}^{(\ell-\ell_1)/2}$.

Thus, if $(\mathbf{z}_1, \mathbf{z}_2) = (\mathbf{x}_1 + \mathbf{y}_1, \mathbf{x}_2 + \mathbf{y}_2)$ describes an element satisfying Eq. (9), all elements of

$$\left\{ (\mathbf{z}_1, \mathbf{z}_2, \mathbf{z}_3) \mid \mathbf{z}_3 \in \left(\mathcal{B}_{p_3/4}^{(\ell-\ell_1)/2} \times \mathcal{B}_{p_3/4}^{(\ell-\ell_1)/2} \right) \right\} \tag{10}$$

are added to L_{12} (analogously the same holds for L_{34}).

The final join then solves the nearest neighbor identity on the upper $\ell - \ell_1$ bits for target $(\tilde{\mathbf{s}}_1)_{[\ell_1+1,\ell]}$ and distance p_3. But instead of using a disjoint split of the vectors with weight p_3, as done by Algorithm 1, the weight is distributed over the full $\ell - \ell_1$ coordinates (see $\mathbf{z}_3$ of Eq. (10)). Thus, there exist multiple different representations for every possible difference, resulting in as many duplicates being added to L_{1234} for every element fulfilling the approximate matching identity on the upper bits.

Not only would a single representation of the solution in L_{1234} suffice to solve the problem, but imagine there would be a subsequent level in the tree, which is e.g. the case for the BJMM algorithm. Then the degenerated list distribution would significantly affect the list sizes of following levels and, implicitly, the time complexity and correctness of the algorithm. We want to stress that this problem only occurs if the algorithm is provided with a parity-check matrix H as defined in Eq. (3). If the input matrix has the shape given in Eq. (7) with random H_1 this seems to re-randomize the duplicates such that the list sizes match their expectations, as experiments have shown [2,13]. Nevertheless, it enables us in the next section to improve on the standard MMT (respectively BJMM) algorithm by changing the way the base lists are constructed.

Other Advanced ISD Variants. Let us briefly outline the differences between the MMT algorithm and the improvements made by Becker-Joux-May-Meurer [4], May-Ozerov [24] and Both-May [8]. The BJMM algorithm works similar to the MMT algorithm but increases the weight of the candidates for the $\mathbf{a}_i$ to $p/4 + \varepsilon$. The parameter ε then accounts for ones that cancel during addition. While increasing list sizes, this also increases the amount of representations allowing for larger constraint choices (the length of ℓ_1). Additionally, the increased amount of representations yields a theoretically optimal search tree depth of three (instead of two), to cancel out the representations and balance the tree most effectively. The ideas introduced with the BJMM algorithm were adopted by both – May-Ozerov and Both-May. May and Ozerov exchanged the meet-in-the-middle strategy to solve the nearest neighbor problem on the last level by their own more efficient algorithm for nearest neighbor search. Both and May finally exploited the nearest neighbor search technique from May-Ozerov for the construction of all lists of the tree.

4 An ISD Framework Based on Nearest Neighbor Search

In this section we describe an algorithmic framework for ISD algorithms based explicitly on nearest neighbor search that resolves the shortcomings mentioned in the previous section. We are able to obtain variants of all major ISD improvements by choosing specific configurations of our framework. Additionally, we can easily exchange costly routines, such as May-Ozerov nearest neighbor search by more practical algorithms. Similar to the MMT algorithm, our framework uses a search tree to construct the solution. To obtain the lists of each level, nearest neighbor search is exploited. The framework then yields the basis for obtaining our practical security estimates.

Remark 4.1. Our complexity estimates show that, for the cryptographically interesting error regimes, a search tree depth of two is (almost) always optimal, regardless of the chosen instantiation of the framework. We find that this is the case in memory constrained and unconstrained settings, as well as under consideration of different memory access costs. Only in some rare cases, an increase to depth three gives minor improvements of a factor strictly less than two (for the proposed parameter sets of McEliece, BIKE and HQC). Hence, for didactic reasons we describe our framework only in depth two.

Let us assume the parity check matrix is in systematic form according to Eq. (3) and let us write the matrix as

$$H = (\tilde{H}\ I_{n-k}) = \begin{pmatrix} \tilde{H}_1 & I_{\ell_1} & \mathbf{0} & \mathbf{0} \\ \tilde{H}_2 & \mathbf{0} & I_{\ell_2} & \mathbf{0} \\ \tilde{H}_3 & \mathbf{0} & \mathbf{0} & I_{\ell_3} \end{pmatrix}, \text{ where } \tilde{H} \in \mathbb{F}_2^{(n-k)\times k}, \tag{11}$$

and let

$$\tilde{\mathbf{s}} := (\tilde{\mathbf{s}}_1, \tilde{\mathbf{s}}_2, \tilde{\mathbf{s}}_3) \in \mathbb{F}_2^{\ell_1} \times \mathbb{F}_2^{\ell_2} \times \mathbb{F}_2^{\ell_3} \tag{12}$$

be the corresponding syndrome (after the Gaussian elimination). The permutation is assumed to distribute the weight on $\mathbf{e} = (\mathbf{e}', \mathbf{e}_1'', \mathbf{e}_2'', \mathbf{e}_3'') \in (\mathbb{F}_2^k \times \mathbb{F}_2^{\ell_1} \times \mathbb{F}_2^{\ell_2} \times \mathbb{F}_2^{\ell_3})$ as

$$\mathrm{wt}(\mathbf{e}') = p \text{ and } \mathrm{wt}(\mathbf{e}_i'') = \omega_i \text{ for } i = 1, 2, 3, \tag{13}$$

where $\ell_1, \ell_2, \omega_1, \omega_2$ and p are optimized numerically and $\ell_3 := n - k - \ell_1 - \ell_2$, as well as $\omega_3 := \omega - p - \omega_1 - \omega_2$. Note that, by our formulation, the following three approximate matching identities hold[7]

$$\tilde{H}_i \mathbf{e}' \approx_{\omega_i} \tilde{\mathbf{s}}_i \text{ for } i = 1, 2, 3. \tag{14}$$

Again, we split $\mathbf{e}' = \mathbf{e}_1 + \mathbf{e}_2$ in two addends $\mathbf{e}_i \in \mathbb{F}_2^k$ with $\mathrm{wt}(\mathbf{e}_i) = p_1$ for some numerically optimized p_1.

In the base lists of the search tree (compare also to Fig. 1), we enumerate all candidates for $\mathbf{e}_1$, respectively $\mathbf{e}_2$, in a meet-in-the-middle fashion. To obtain the lists of the middle level, we combine two base lists by searching for pairs $(\mathbf{x}_1, \mathbf{x}_2) \in L_1 \times L_2$, respectively $(\mathbf{x}_3, \mathbf{x}_4) \in L_3 \times L_4$, fulfilling the identities

$$\begin{aligned} &\tilde{H}_1(\mathbf{x}_1 + \mathbf{x}_2) \approx_{\omega_{11}} 0^{\ell_1} \text{ and respectively} \\ &\tilde{H}_1(\mathbf{x}_3 + \mathbf{x}_4) \approx_{\omega_{11}} \tilde{\mathbf{s}}_1 \ , \end{aligned}$$

where ω_{11} is another parameter that has to be optimized numerically.

All resulting candidates for $\mathbf{e}_1$ and $\mathbf{e}_2$, namely $\mathbf{x}_{12} = \mathbf{x}_1 + \mathbf{x}_2$ and $\mathbf{x}_{34} = \mathbf{x}_3 + \mathbf{x}_4$, satisfying the above identities are stored in the lists L_{12} and L_{34} respectively. Finally, those two lists are merged in the list L_{1234} by finding all solutions to the identity

$$\tilde{H}_2(\mathbf{x}_{12} + \mathbf{x}_{34}) \approx_{\omega_2} \tilde{\mathbf{s}}_2 \ .$$

Eventually every element of L_{1234} is checked for yielding a solution.

We measure the time complexity of the proposed framework in vector additions in $\mathbb{F}_2^n$. Even though some of the used labels and vectors could be implemented using less than n coordinates, each addition contributes as one. On the one hand this simplifies the analysis and on the other hand it is highly implementation dependent if a vector is indeed implemented using less coordinates

Analysis of the Framework. Let us first analyze our framework. Later, we then compute the concrete complexity for different configurations. Let us start with the correctness. Assume the permutation distributes the error weight as desired (compare to Eq. (11)). Now consider the possible decomposition of $\mathbf{e}' = \mathbf{e}_1 + \mathbf{e}_2$ with $\mathrm{wt}(\mathbf{e}_i) = p_1$ and denote the amount of different such representations

[7] Note that the equation for $i = 3$ will not be used by the algorithm. It just enables us to perform the nearest neighbor search for $i = 2$ on a reduced sub-instance with flexible ℓ_2, ω_2; instead of being forced to operate always on the full $n - k - \ell_1$ coordinates with weight $\omega - p - \omega_1$.

Algorithm 3. ISD-NN-FRAMEWORK

Input: parity check matrix $H \in \mathbb{F}_2^{(n-k)\times n}$, syndrome $\mathbf{s}$, error weight $\omega \in [n]$
Output: $\mathbf{e} \in \mathbb{F}_2^n$: $H\mathbf{e} = \mathbf{s}$ and $\mathrm{wt}(\mathbf{e}) = \omega$
Optimize: $\ell_1, \ell_2, \omega_1, \omega_2, \omega_{11}, p_1, p$

1: Let $\tilde{H}_1, \tilde{H}_2, \tilde{\mathbf{s}}_1, \tilde{\mathbf{s}}_2$ and all parameters be as defined in Equations (11) to (13)
2: **repeat**
3: choose random permutation matrix $P \in \mathbb{F}_2^{n\times n}$
4: Transform HP to systematic form by multiplication of invertible matrix Q (compare to Equation (11)): $\tilde{H} \leftarrow (QHP)_{[k]}$, $\tilde{\mathbf{s}} \leftarrow Q\mathbf{s}$
5: $L_i = \{\mathbf{x}_i \mid \mathbf{x}_i = (\mathbf{y}, 0^{k/2}) : \mathbf{y} \in \mathcal{B}^{k/2}_{p_1/2}\}$ for $i = 1, 3$
6: $L_i = \{\mathbf{x}_i \mid \mathbf{x}_i = (0^{k/2}, \mathbf{y}) : \mathbf{y} \in \mathcal{B}^{k/2}_{p_1/2}\}$ for $i = 2, 4$
7: Compute L_{12}, L_{34} and L_{1234} using nearest neighbor algorithm
8: $L_{12} \leftarrow \{\mathbf{x}_1 + \mathbf{x}_2 \mid (\mathbf{x}_1, \mathbf{x}_2) \in L_1 \times L_2 \wedge \tilde{H}_1(\mathbf{x}_1 + \mathbf{x}_2) \approx_{\omega_{11}} \mathbf{0}\}$
9: $L_{34} \leftarrow \{\mathbf{x}_3 + \mathbf{x}_4 \mid (\mathbf{x}_3, \mathbf{x}_4) \in L_3 \times L_4 \wedge \tilde{H}_1(\mathbf{x}_3 + \mathbf{x}_4) \approx_{\omega_{11}} \tilde{\mathbf{s}}_1\}$
10: $L_{1234} \leftarrow \{\mathbf{x}_{12} + \mathbf{x}_{34} \mid (\mathbf{x}_{12}, \mathbf{x}_{34}) \in L_{12} \times L_{34} \wedge \tilde{H}_2(\mathbf{x}_{12} + \mathbf{x}_{34}) \approx_{\omega_2} \tilde{\mathbf{s}}_2\}$
11: **for** $\mathbf{x} \in L_{1234}$ **do**
12: $\tilde{\mathbf{e}} = (\mathbf{x}, \tilde{H}\mathbf{x} + \tilde{\mathbf{s}})$
13: **if** $\mathrm{wt}(\tilde{\mathbf{e}}) = \omega$ **then**
14: **break**
15: **until** $\mathrm{wt}(\tilde{\mathbf{e}}) = \omega$
16: **return** $P\tilde{\mathbf{e}}$

as R. Furthermore let the probability that any such representation fulfills the restrictions imposed by L_{12} and L_{34} be

$$q := \Pr\left[\mathrm{wt}(\tilde{H}_1\mathbf{e}_1) = \mathrm{wt}(\tilde{H}_1\mathbf{e}_2 + \tilde{\mathbf{s}}_1) = \omega_{11} \mid \mathbf{e}' = \mathbf{e}_1 + \mathbf{e}_2\right] .$$

Note that the computation of L_{1234} does not impose further constraints on the representations since, by Eq. (14), we already conditioned on

$$\tilde{H}_2(\mathbf{e}_1 + \mathbf{e}_2) = \tilde{H}_2\mathbf{e}' \approx_{\omega_2} \tilde{\mathbf{s}}_2 .$$

Hence, as long as we ensure $R \cdot q \geq 1$, we expect at least one representation to survive the restrictions imposed. Even if $R \cdot q < 1$, we can compensate for it by $\frac{1}{R \cdot q}$ randomized constructions of the tree (line 5 to 14 of Algorithm 3).[8]

Lets now turn our focus to the time complexity. We define T_P to be the expected number of random permutations until at least one of them distributes the weight as desired. For each of these T_P permutations we need to apply the Gaussian elimination at a cost of T_G as well as the computation of base lists,

[8] For example we can randomize by adding a random $\mathbf{r} \in \mathbb{F}_2^{n-k}$ to all labels in lists L_1 and L_3.

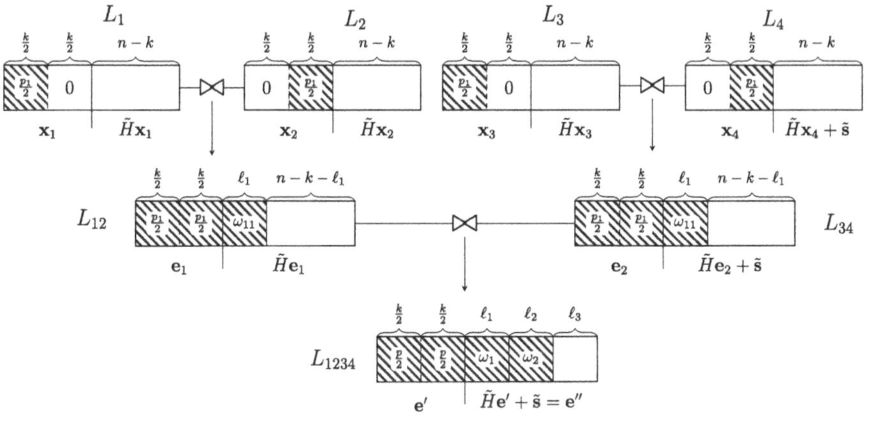

Fig. 1. Graphical representation of the computation tree used by the ISD framework.

three nearest neighbor computations and the weight check of elements of the final list.

Note that in our formulation of the lists they only hold the respective candidates $\mathbf{x}_i$ to keep the notation comprehensible. In a practical application one might also want to store the label $\tilde{H}\mathbf{x}_i$ in L_i for $i = 1, 2, 3$ and respectively $\tilde{H}\mathbf{x}_4 + \tilde{\mathbf{s}}$ in L_4 to avoid their re-computation at later levels. While these labels can be naively computed using matrix vector multiplication, a more sophisticated strategy enumerates the $\mathbf{x}_i$ in the base lists such that $\mathrm{wt}(\mathbf{x}_i + \mathbf{x}_{i+1}) = 2$. Then every label can be computed from the previous one using only two vector additions, yielding a total cost of roughly $\frac{p_1}{2} + 2L_1$ per base list. This is surpassed by the cost for the nearest neighbor search on the first level, which is why we neglect this term in the analysis. Let us denote the cost for nearest neighbor search on two lists of size $|L|$, for vectors of length ℓ and weight δ as $\mathcal{N}_{L,\ell,\delta}$. Finally observe, that the computation of L_{1234} comes at a much higher cost than the linear check of the list, which is why we disregard the linear pass through the list in the analysis.

Hence, in total the time complexity becomes

$$T = \underbrace{T_P}_{\text{permutations}} \cdot \Big(\underbrace{T_G}_{\text{Gaussian}} + \underbrace{\max\left(1, (R \cdot q)^{-1}\right)}_{\text{representations}} \cdot \underbrace{\left(2 \cdot \mathcal{N}_{|L_1|,\ell_1,\omega_{11}} + \mathcal{N}_{|L_{12}|,\ell_2,\omega_2}\right)}_{\text{tree computation}} \Big). \tag{15}$$

Note that from a memory point of view one can implement the procedure in a streaming manner rather than storing each list on every level, similar to the ones described in [26,35]. In this way we only need space for two base lists as well as one intermediate list, since the final list can be checked on-the-fly anyway. Additionally we need to store the matrix, thus we have

$$M = 2 \cdot |L_1| + |L_{12}| + n - k \ .$$

Using the above framework we obtain several ISD algorithms by changing the specific configuration. This includes improved and practical variants of all major ISD improvements (restricted to depth 2) such as MMT, BJMM, May-Ozerov as well as the latest improvement by Both and May.

Let us briefly sketch how to obtain these variants of known ISD algorithms before analyzing them in more detail. Let us start with the MMT/ BJMM algorithm[9]. Therefore let us instantiate our framework using the MEET-IN-THE-MIDDLE algorithm on both levels to directly obtain a variant of the MMT/ BJMM algorithm using disjoint weight distributions and resolving the shortcomings outlined in the previous section. If we instead choose MEET-IN-THE-MIDDLE on the first but May-Ozerov nearest neighbor search on the second level, set $\ell_2 = n - k - \ell_1$, $\omega_2 = \omega - p$ and hence $\ell_3 = \omega_3 = 0$ we obtain a variant of the May-Ozerov ISD algorithm using a disjoint weight distribution on the lower level. Observe that the choice of parameters ensures the nearest neighbor search on the final level being performed on all remaining coordinates. And finally if we choose the May-Ozerov nearest neighbor algorithm on both levels with the same choice of $\ell_2, \ell_3, \omega_2, \omega_3$ as for the May-Ozerov variant we obtain the ISD variant of Both and May.

4.1 Concrete Practical Instantiations of the Framework

So let us start the analysis with a variant where we instantiate the nearest neighbor routine by INDYK-MOTWANI. We credit this variant to Both and May, who first used explicit nearest neighbor search on all levels, by simply calling the variant BOTH-MAY in the following.

Remark 4.2 (Balanced Weight Distribution). As outlined in Sect. 2, the way we construct the solution only allows to obtain $\mathbf{e}'$ with balanced weight, i.e., vectors having weight $p/2$ on the upper and weight $p/2$ on the lower half of their coordinates. The amount of balanced vectors is a polynomial fraction of all vectors with weight p and hence it is usually disregarded in the theoretical analysis. However, for our practical estimates we account for this. Specifically this influences the amount of representations R as well as the amount of necessary permutations T_P.

BOTH-MAY Algorithm. Recall that for the Both-May algorithm we choose $\ell_2 = n - k - \ell_1$, $\omega_2 = \omega - p - \omega_1$ and $\ell_3 = \omega_3 = 0$. Thus the expected amount of iterations until we draw a permutation that distributes the weight according to Eq. (13) (under consideration of Remark 4.2) becomes

$$T_P = \frac{\binom{n}{\omega}}{\binom{\ell_2}{\omega_2}\binom{\ell_1}{\omega_1}\binom{k/2}{p/2}^2} = \frac{\binom{n}{\omega}}{\binom{n-k-\ell_1}{\omega-p-\omega_1}\binom{\ell_1}{\omega_1}\binom{k/2}{p/2}^2}.$$

[9] We do not differentiate between both algorithms, since in our setting the only difference of BJMM is the larger choice of $p_1 > p/2$. Hence, the bare optimization of p_1 determines which algorithm is chosen.

Further note, that the number of representations of one balanced vector $\mathbf{e}' \in \mathbb{F}_2^k$ with weight p as a sum of two balanced vectors with weight p_1 is

$$R = \binom{p/2}{p/4}^2 \binom{(k-p)/2}{p_1/2 - p/4}^2 .$$

Here the first factor counts the ones contributed to one half of $\mathbf{e}'$ from the first addend. The remaining $p/4$ ones are then contributed by the second addend. The second factor counts the possibilities how the remaining $p1/2 - p/4$ ones in one half can cancel out. Finally since every representation of the lower half can be combined with any representation of the upper half to obtain a valid representation of $\mathbf{e}'$, we square the result.

The probability q of a representation $(\mathbf{e}_1, \mathbf{e}_2)$ of $\mathbf{e}'$ fulfilling the restriction imposed by L_{12} and L_{34} is

$$\begin{aligned} q &:= \Pr\left[\mathrm{wt}(\tilde{H}_1\mathbf{e}_1) = \mathrm{wt}(\tilde{H}_1\mathbf{e}_2 + \tilde{\mathbf{s}}_1) = \omega_{11} \mid \mathbf{e}' = \mathbf{e}_1 + \mathbf{e}_2\right] \\ &= \frac{\binom{\omega_1}{\omega_1/2}\binom{\ell_1-\omega_1}{\omega_{11}-\omega_1/2}}{2^{\ell_1}} \end{aligned}$$

Therefore observe that for a representation $(\mathbf{e}_1, \mathbf{e}_2)$ of $\mathbf{e}'$ it holds that

$$\tilde{H}_1\mathbf{e}_1 + \tilde{H}_1\mathbf{e}_2 + \tilde{\mathbf{s}}_1 = \mathbf{e}_1'', \text{ where } \mathrm{wt}(\mathbf{e}_1'') = \omega_1 .$$

Now there are 2^{ℓ_1} different combinations of values for $\tilde{H}_1\mathbf{e}_1, \tilde{H}_1\mathbf{e}_2 + \tilde{\mathbf{s}}_1$ that satisfy the above identity. Out of these pairs $\binom{\omega_1}{\omega_1/2}\binom{\ell_1-\omega_1}{\omega_{11}-\omega_1/2}$ have the correct weight ω_{11}. Now by the randomness of $\tilde{H}_1$ the probability becomes the claimed fraction.

In the base lists we enumerate all vectors of length $k/2$ and weight $p_1/2$, hence it holds

$$|L_1| = \binom{k/2}{p_1/2} .$$

The intermediate lists hold all elements of the Cartesian product of two base lists which fulfill the weight restriction on ℓ_1 coordinates, thus

$$|L_{12}| = \frac{|L_1|^2\binom{\ell_1}{\omega_{11}}}{2^{\ell_1}}$$

Eventually the running time $\mathcal{N}_{|L_1|,\ell_1,\omega_{11}}$ for the nearest neighbor routine on the first level and $\mathcal{N}_{|L_{12}|,n-k-\ell_1,\omega-p-\omega_1}$ for the second level are given by Eq. (2).

BJMM-DW: BJMM / MMT with disjoint weight distribution. In comparison to our version of the Both-May algorithm the BJMM-DW algorithm uses MEET-IN-THE-MIDDLE for nearest neighbor search. Thus, we choose $\ell_2 < n-k-\ell_1$ and $\omega_2 < \omega - p - \omega_1$, which yields $\ell_3, \omega_3 > 0$.[10] Accordingly the time complexity for

[10] If we would perform the MEET-IN-THE-MIDDLE on the full $n - k - \ell_1$ coordinates as before, the blow-up due to the internal addition of the fixed Hamming weight vectors would be to huge and render this approach inefficient.

the nearest neighbor search on the first and second level, which are $\mathcal{N}_{|L_1|,\ell_1,\omega_{11}}$ and $\mathcal{N}_{|L_{12}|,\ell_2,\omega_2}$ are now given by Eq. (1). Note that the choice of the meet-in-the-middle approach only allows to find elements with balanced distances. Thus, we also need the balanced property on the ℓ_2 and ℓ_1 windows. Hence, the number of permutations and the probability of a representation matching the restrictions change to

$$T_P = \frac{\binom{n}{\omega}}{\binom{n-k-\ell_1-\ell_2}{\omega-\omega_1-\omega_2-p}\binom{\ell_2/2}{\omega_2/2}^2\binom{\ell_1/2}{\omega_1/2}^2\binom{k/2}{p/2}^2} \quad \text{and} \quad q = \frac{\binom{\omega_1/2}{\omega_1/4}^2\binom{\ell_1/2-\omega_1/2}{\omega_{11}/2-\omega_1/4}^2}{2^{\ell_1}} .$$

The rest stays as in the analysis of the Both-May variant.

4.2 Joint Weight Distributions

Since in practice ℓ_1 is comparably (to the code length) small and the error weight only sublinear, an optimization of parameters in some cases yields $\omega_{11} = 0$ and hence $\omega_1 = 0$. In these cases we find that a joint weight distribution on the base level, meaning an enumeration of vectors of length $\frac{k+\ell_1}{2}$ rather than $\frac{k}{2}$, as in the original algorithm by Dumer, can yield improvements. Recall that asymptotically the joint weight case is subsumed by the disjoint weight case when using proportional weight on both sides.

However, since our primary focus lies on the concrete hardness of cryptographic parameter sets, which all use a sublinear error weight, we now describe a variant of the framework using a joint weight distribution on the first level. Note that this description is also closer to the original descriptions of the May-Ozerov, BJMM and MMT algorithms, which all use joint weight distributions, the latter even over multiple levels.

First assume that the weight on the solution $\mathbf{e} = (\mathbf{e}', \mathbf{e}_1'', \mathbf{e}_2'', \mathbf{e}_3'') \in \mathbb{F}_2^k \times \mathbb{F}_2^{\ell_1} \times \mathbb{F}_2^{\ell_2} \times \mathbb{F}_2^{\ell_3}$ distributes as

$$\mathrm{wt}((\mathbf{e}', \mathbf{e}_1'')) = p,\ \mathrm{wt}(\mathbf{e}_2'') = \omega_2 \text{ and } \mathrm{wt}(\mathbf{e}_3'') = \omega_3 \ . \tag{16}$$

Also we re-randomize the identity part of size ℓ_1 by considering the parity check matrix being of form

$$H = (\tilde{H}\ I_{n-k-\ell_1}) = \begin{pmatrix} \tilde{H}_1 & \mathbf{0} & \mathbf{0} \\ \tilde{H}_2 & I_{\ell_2} & \mathbf{0} \\ \tilde{H}_3 & \mathbf{0} & I_{\ell_3} \end{pmatrix} ,$$

where $\tilde{H} \in \mathbb{F}_2^{(n-k)\times(k+\ell_1)}$ has random structure. This allows us to perform a meet-in-the-middle on $(\mathbf{e}', \mathbf{e}_1'')$ without splitting both parts individually. Therefore we change the definition of base lists to

$$L_i = \left\{\mathbf{x}_i \mid \mathbf{x}_i = (\mathbf{y}, 0^{(k+\ell_1)/2})\colon \mathbf{y} \in \mathcal{B}_{p_1/2}^{(k+\ell_1)/2}\right\} \text{ for } i = 1,3 \text{ and}$$
$$L_i = \left\{\mathbf{x}_i \mid \mathbf{x}_i = (0^{(k+\ell_1)/2}, \mathbf{y})\colon \mathbf{y} \in \mathcal{B}_{p_1/2}^{(k+\ell_1)/2}\right\} \text{ for } i = 2,4 \ .$$

Now we construct the lists L_{12} and L_{34} as

$$\begin{aligned} L_{12} &:= \{\mathbf{x}_1 + \mathbf{x}_2 \mid (\mathbf{x}_1, \mathbf{x}_2) \in L_1 \times L_2 \wedge \tilde{H}_1(\mathbf{x}_1 + \mathbf{x}_2) = \mathbf{0}\} \\ L_{34} &:= \{\mathbf{x}_3 + \mathbf{x}_4 \mid (\mathbf{x}_3, \mathbf{x}_4) \in L_3 \times L_4 \wedge \tilde{H}_1(\mathbf{x}_3 + \mathbf{x}_4) = \tilde{\mathbf{s}}_1\} \ . \end{aligned} \tag{17}$$

Finally list L_{1234} is constructed via nearest neighbor search, as before as

$$L_{1234} \leftarrow \{\mathbf{x}_{12} + \mathbf{x}_{34} \mid (\mathbf{x}_{12}, \mathbf{x}_{34}) \in L_{12} \times L_{34} \wedge \tilde{H}_2(\mathbf{x}_{12} + \mathbf{x}_{34}) \approx_{\omega_2} \tilde{\mathbf{s}}_2\} \ .$$

Adaptation of the Analysis. While most of the analysis stays the same as for the general nearest neighbor framework, our adaptations affect some of the details. Precisely the probability q of a representation surviving the imposed restrictions as well as the cost for the construction of L_{12} and L_{34}. First note that for lists as defined in Eq. (17) the probability q is defined as

$$q := \Pr\left[\tilde{H}_1\mathbf{e}_1 = \mathbf{0} \wedge \tilde{H}_1\mathbf{e}_2 = \tilde{\mathbf{s}}_1 \mid (\mathbf{e}', \mathbf{e}_1'') = \mathbf{e}_1 + \mathbf{e}_2\right] = 2^{-\ell_1} \ .$$

Since we already know that $\tilde{H}_1(\mathbf{e}', \mathbf{e}_1'') = \tilde{\mathbf{s}}_1$ by randomness of $\tilde{H}_1$ we have $q = \Pr\left[\tilde{H}_1\mathbf{e}_1 = \mathbf{0}\right] = 2^{-\ell_1}$. Now observe that the construction of L_{12} (resp. L_{34}) can be done in time $|L_1|+|L_2|+|L_{12}|$ as we only need to check for equality. Thus, the runtime can still be expressed via Eq. (15), where $\mathcal{N}_{|L_1|,\ell_1,\omega_{11}} := |L_1|+|L_2|+|L_{12}|$. Next we give two instantiations with joint weight distribution on the base level. The first is a variant of the BJMM algorithm using again Meet-in-the-Middle for the construction of L_{1234}, while the second uses Indyk-Motwani instead and can be seen as a variant of the May-Ozerov algorithm.

BJMM-p-dw: BJMM / MMTalgorithm with partially disjoint weight distribution. The expected amount of permutations until we may expect a weight distribution as given in Eq. (16) under consideration of the balanced property (see Remark 4.2) is

$$T_P = \frac{\binom{n}{\omega}}{\binom{n-k-\ell_1-\ell_2}{\omega-\omega_1-\omega_2-p}\binom{(k+\ell_1)/2}{p/2}^2\binom{\ell_2/2}{\omega_2/2}^2}$$

Note that the balanced property on the ℓ_2 windows stems from the fact that the BJMM algorithm uses Meet-in-the-Middle for the construction of L_{1234}. The base lists are now of increased size $|L_1| = \binom{(k+\ell_1)/2}{p_1/2}$ while $|L_{12}| = |L_{34}| = |L_1|^2/2^{\ell_1}$ since we perform an exact matching on ℓ_1 coordinates. On the upside we now have an increased amount of representations

$$R = \binom{p/2}{p/4}^2\binom{(k+\ell_1-p)/2)}{p_1/2-p/4}^2 \ .$$

The cost for the computation of L_{1234}, namely $\mathcal{N}_{|L_{12}|,\ell_2,\omega_2}$, is given by Eq. (1).

MAY-OZEROV The essential difference to the BJMM-P-DW lies in the usage of the INDYK-MOTWANI for the computation of L_{1234}. Also this variant chooses $\ell_2 = n - k - \ell_1$ and $\omega_2 = \omega - p$, which implies $\ell_3 = \omega_3 = 0$. Then the complexity of the final list computation $\mathcal{N}_{|L_{12}|,\ell_2,\omega_2}$ is given by Eq. (2). The rest stays as in the analysis of the BJMM-P-DW.

For completeness and comparisons we also state the running time of the original BJMM algorithm (in depth two). It uses a joint weight distribution over both levels, hence the vectors are enumerated on $(k + \ell_1 + \ell_2)/2$ coordinates in the base lists. This results in the final construction of list L_{1234} coming at a cost of $|L_{12}| + |L_{34}| + |L_{1234}|$. Referring to Eq. (15) this means we have $\mathcal{N}_{|L_{12}|,\ell_2,\omega_2} = |L_{12}| + |L_{34}| + |L_{1234}|$

BJMM: original BJMM algorithm. Let $\ell = \ell_1 + \ell_2$. The base list size of the BJMM algorithm is $|L_1| = \binom{(k+\ell)/2}{p_1/2}$. The matching is then performed again on ℓ_1 coordinates, which results in $|L_{12}| = |L_{34}| = |L_1|^2/2^{\ell_1}$. The amount of representations is

$$R = \binom{p/2}{p/4}^2 \binom{(k + \ell - p)/2}{p_1/2 - p/4}^2.$$

Now the construction of list L_{1234} is performed as a matching of L_{12} and L_{34} on $\ell - \ell_1 = \ell_2$ coordinates, thus we have $|L_{1234}| = |L_{12}|^2/2^{\ell_2}$. The rest stays as in the BJMM-P-DW algorithm.

5 Estimator

In this section we present our results on the bit security estimates for the suggested parameters of code based cryptographic submissions to the NIST PQC standardisation process, namely McEliece, BIKE and HQC.

A Cautious Note on Concrete Hardness Estimates. Concrete hardness estimates often give the impression of being highly accurate, not least because they are usually given up to the second or even third decimal place. In particular, following recent discussions (in the NIST PQC forum [33]), we want to emphasize that these concrete security estimates should always be taken with care. They heavily rely on implementation details, targeted platforms, possible hardware accelerations and many more factors. Thus, many assumptions must be made to obtain these estimates. The derived numbers should therefore be understood as *indicative* rather than precise. Following this line of thought we give our estimates rounded to the nearest integer and admit that they may inherit an inaccuracy of a few bits.

Before we discuss the security estimations let us briefly address some methodology aspects. All advanced algorithms we consider require an exponential amount of memory, which certainly slows down computations compared to memory-free algorithms like Prange. In [3] it was suggested to use a logarithmic memory access model, which accounts for the need of memory with an

Table 1. Parameter sets suggested by NIST PQC proposals.

	Category	n	k	ω
McEliece	1	3488	2720	64
	3	4608	3360	96
	5	6688	5024	128
	5	6960	5413	119
	5	8192	6528	128
BIKE (message)	1	24646	12323	134
	3	49318	24659	199
	5	81946	40973	264
BIKE (key)	1	24646	12323	142
	3	49318	24659	206
	5	81946	40973	274
HQC	1	35338	17669	132
	3	71702	35851	200
	5	115274	57637	262

additive $\log\log \texttt{memory}$ in the bit security estimate, where memory is the total memory consumed by the algorithm. We follow this suggestion and consider besides the more conservative constant memory access cost also this logarithmic model. Additionally, we consider a cube-root memory access cost, which results in an additive $\log \sqrt[3]{\texttt{memory}}$ in the respective algorithms bit complexity, which was recently suggested by Perlner [27].

Note that our estimator software also allows for a square-root access cost model as well as user defined cost functions. However, we believe that the constant, logarithmic and cube-root models already give a good overview.

The NIST defines five security categories, where most submissions focus on parameters for the categories one, three and five. A parameter set for a proposal is said to match the security level of category one, three or five if the scheme instantiated with the corresponding parameters is at least as hard to break as AES-128, AES-192 or AES-256 respectively. In Table 1 we list all corresponding parameters of each submission and their respective security category.

Remark 5.1 (Up-to-Date Estimates). Even though, we computed the presented estimates with the utmost care, we would like to encourage the reader to use our *Syndrome Decoding Estimator* rather than only relying on the estimates given in this paper. This is because the tool offers a wide variety of customization to make sure the estimates address the right setting. Also, we are constantly extending and improving the *Syndrome Decoding Estimator* such that the results obtained might slightly vary from the tables presented here.

Let us start with the Classic McEliece submission. Table 2 shows the bit complexity estimates for all suggested parameter sets. Besides the ISD variants obtained as instantiations of our framework we included the estimates for Prange and Stern for comparisons. It can be observed that the time complexity estimations for all advanced ISD algorithms, namely Both-May, May-Ozerov, BJMM, BJMM-dw and BJMM-p-dw are comparable, where the variants bring slight advantages over BJMM. However, the use of explicit nearest neighbor search and disjoint weight distributions pays off when turning the focus to the memory consumption. For the proposed parameter sets, our new BJMM variants for instance allow to decrease the memory consumption of plain BJMM by up to 30 bits. This partly stems form the advantage of not enumerating unnecessary vectors in the base lists as outlined in Sect. 3. Recall that this reduced memory consumption eventually also results in practical run time improvements when considering different memory access models.

Additionally we provide in Table 2 bit-security estimates where the available memory is limited to 60 and 80 bits (still in the constant memory access model). Under this memory restrictions the May-Ozerov algorithm performs best by entirely providing the best estimates for those regimes. This is an effect of the use of joined weight distributions on the lower level as well as memory-efficient nearest neighbor search in form of Indyk-Motwani.

Also we state the best complexities obtained when considering the logarithmic and cube-root memory access model.[11] For the logarithmic model it can be observed that the optimization suggests the same parameters as in the constant model. This results in all bit complexities being increased by a logarithm of the memory usage in the constant setting. Contrary, the optimization in the cube-root model avoids the use of memory almost completely, yielding significantly higher bit complexities.

We also used our estimator to approximate the hardness of an already solved McEliece instance reported online at decodingchallenge.org [2] and an instance that was attacked by Bernstein, Lange and Peters in [6]. Recently, Esser, May and Zweydinger reported the solution to an instance with parameters ($n = 1284, k = 1028, w = 24$) [2], for this instance our estimator yields a bit complexity of 65 bit. For the instance ($n = 1024, k = 525, w = 50$) attacked in [6] by Bernstein et al. we find a slightly lower bit complexity of 64 bit. Note that while these numbers might occur high, usually attacks are performed with a register-width of 64 bit. Thus, the actual operation count is reduced by six bit, yielding operation counts of 59 and 58 bits for those instances. These estimates seem to be coherent with the reported computational efforts made to solve those instances.

Next we give the security estimates for the BIKE scheme. Note that BIKE uses a quasi-cylic code allowing for polynomial speedups, which need to be considered in the security estimates.

This is also the reason why we have to distinguish the message and key security. Obtaining the message from a BIKE ciphertext requires the attacker

[11] Note that we take the number of necessary vector space elements that need to be stored as a measure to derive the penalty.

Table 2. Bit security estimates for the suggested parameter sets of the Classic McEliece scheme.

	Category 1 ($n = 3488$)		Category 3 ($n = 4608$)		Category 5 (n=6688)		Category 5 ($n = 6960$)		Category 5 ($n = 8192$)	
	T	M	T	M	T	M	T	M	T	M
PRANGE	173	22	217	23	296	24	297	24	334	24
STERN	151	50	193	60	268	80	268	90	303	109
BOTH-MAY	143	88	182	101	250	136	249	137	281	141
MAY-OZEROV	141	89	180	113	246	165	246	160	276	194
BJMM	142	97	183	121	248	160	248	163	278	189
BJMM-P-DW	143	86	183	100	249	160	248	161	279	166
BJMM-DW	144	97	183	100	250	130	250	160	282	164
$M \leq 60$	145	60	187	60	262	58	263	60	298	59
$M \leq 80$	143	74	183	77	258	76	258	74	293	77
$\log M$ access	147	89	187	113	253	165	253	160	283	194
$\sqrt[3]{M}$ access	156	25	199	26	275	36	276	36	312	47

to solve a syndrome decoding problem for a syndrome usually not equal to the zero vector. Opposed to that, attacking the secret key requires finding a low weight codeword or equivalently solving the syndrome decoding problem, where the syndrome is the zero vector. For these two cases different speed-ups can be obtained due to the cyclic structure.

In terms of message security, the cyclicity allows to derive $n-k = k$ syndrome decoding instances from an initial input instance out of which a single one has to be decoded to break the security of the system. This variant is known as decoding one out of many (DOOM). It has been shown in [30] that Stern's algorithm can be sped up in this setting by a factor of roughly $\sqrt{k}$. Even though, it has not been studied how to obtain this speed-up for advanced ISD algorithms, such as BJMM, it is commonly assumed to be obtainable similar to the case of Stern's algorithm. Hence, we also deducted $\frac{\log k}{2}$ from all our bit security estimates.

Considering key security the quasi cyclic code contains all k cyclic shifts of the searched codeword. Hence, without any adaptations the probability of choosing a permutation that distributes the weight as desired is enhanced by a factor of k. Thus, in this case we subtract $\log(k)$ from our bit security estimates.

Table 3 states the bit security estimates for the BIKE scheme. Note that BIKE in comparison to McEliece uses a decreased error weight of $\omega = \mathcal{O}(\sqrt{n})$ rather than $\omega = \mathcal{O}(\frac{n}{\log n})$. This reduced weight lets the advantage of enumeration based algorithms deteriorate, with the result that advanced algorithms only offer a slight advantage over basic STERN. However, when considering the logarithmic or cube-root model still our May-Ozerov variant provides the best complexities. For the BIKE setting we observe that already for a logarithmic penalty the optimization suggests to use low-memory configurations.

Table 3. Bit security estimates for the suggested parameter sets of the BIKE scheme.

		Category 1 ($n = 24646$)		Category 3 ($n = 49318$)		Category 5 ($n = 81946$)	
		T	M	T	M	T	M
message security	PRANGE	167	28	235	30	301	32
	STERN	146	40	211	43	277	45
	BOTH-MAY	147	38	212	41	276	63
	MAY-OZEROV	146	55	211	57	276	61
	BJMM	147	38	211	59	277	63
	BJMM-P-DW	147	37	211	56	276	61
	BJMM-DW	147	45	211	56	277	43
	$\log M$ access	150	31	215	33	281	34
	$\sqrt[3]{M}$ access	152	30	217	32	283	33
key security	PRANGE	169	28	234	30	304	32
	STERN	147	40	211	43	279	45
	BOTH-MAY	148	38	211	60	278	63
	MAY-OZEROV	147	55	210	57	278	61
	BJMM	147	54	211	59	279	63
	BJMM-P-DW	147	55	211	56	278	61
	BJMM-DW	147	55	211	56	279	43
	$\log M$ access	151	31	215	33	283	34
	$\sqrt[3]{M}$ access	153	30	217	32	285	33

Eventually we state in Table 4 our bit security estimates for the HQC scheme. Similar to the BIKE scheme HQC uses a cyclic structure allowing for a $\sqrt{k}$ speedup. Also HQC builds on the same asymptotically small error weight of $\omega = \mathcal{O}(\sqrt{n})$, but in comparison to BIKE uses even smaller constants. Thus, as the estimates show, the advantage of more involved procedures vanishes almost completely. Here most variants degenerate to a version of STERN, by choosing all intermediate weights equal to zero. Nevertheless, when considering memory access costs again our MAY-OZEROV algorithm yields the best time complexity.

The biggest solved instance reported to decodingchallenge.org in the quasi-cyclic setting has parameters $(n = 2918, k = 1459, w = 54)$ [2]. We estimate for this instance a bit complexity of 64 bit using our estimator tool, which corresponds to roughly 2^{58} necessary operations on a 64-bit architecture.

Interpretation of the Security Estimates. We observe that most bit security estimates match the required classical gate counts of 143, 207 and 272, corresponding to breaking AES-128, AES-192 and AES-256 according to NIST, surprisingly

Table 4. Bit security estimates for the suggested parameter sets of the HQC scheme.

	Category 1 ($n = 35338$)		Category 3 ($n = 71702$)		Category 5 ($n = 115274$)	
	T	M	T	M	T	M
PRANGE	166	29	237	31	300	33
STERN	145	41	213	44	276	46
BOTH-MAY	146	39	214	42	276	39
MAY-OZEROV	145	39	214	42	276	44
BJMM	146	39	214	42	276	44
BJMM-P-DW	146	39	214	42	276	43
BJMM-DW	146	39	214	42	276	40
$\log M$ access	150	32	218	34	280	36
$\sqrt[3]{M}$ access	151	31	220	33	282	35

well. Note that all submissions use the asymptotic complexity estimate of basic PRANGE as foundation for parameter selection. Hence, the exact match comes from the fact that the improvement due to advanced algorithms corresponds quite exactly to Prange's polynomial factors.

The McEliece submission team admits that advanced ISD algorithms yield a lower complexity count then required in the constant memory access model [10], which is confirmed by our estimates. However, they argue that the memory access costs faced in the real world will make up for the difference. Our estimates support this claim, when imposing a cube-root memory access cost.

Only the category three parameter set of the Classic McEliece scheme seems to fail the given security level slightly. Here, even when imposing a cube-root memory access cost it still deviates from the needed 207 bits by eight bits.

For BIKE and HQC the consideration of different memory access cost models is less significant. This is because already in the constant memory access setting the parameters do not allow advanced ISD techniques to leverage the use of memory. However, both schemes already match their security levels in the more conservative constant cost model. In the more realistic setting with logarithmic or cube-root access cost both schemes' parameter sets seem to inherit a slight margin of five to fifteen bits.

5.1 Quantum Security

The metric for quantum security provided by NIST is based on a `maxdepth` $\in \{40, 64, 96\}$ constraint, defining the maximum allowed depth of a quantum circuit used to attack the corresponding instantiation. Here the `maxdepth` constraint accounts for the difficulty of constructing large scale quantum computers.

A parameter set is said to match the quantum security definition of category one, three or five, if it is at least as hard to break as AES-128, AES-192 or AES-256 quantumly. Furthermore NIST defines the quantum security of AES as

- AES-128 corresponds to $2^{170-\texttt{maxdepth}}$ quantum gates,
- AES-192 corresponds to $2^{233-\texttt{maxdepth}}$ quantum gates,
- AES-256 corresponds to $2^{298-\texttt{maxdepth}}$ quantum gates.

In terms of quantum attacks Bernstein showed, that the search for a correct permutation in Prange's algorithm can be asymptotically accelerated by a square-root gain using a Grover search [5]. There has also been some research on how to quantize advanced ISD algorithms [19,20]. While resulting in slightly better asymptotic complexities than Bernstein's quantum Prange, we agree with the BIKE submission [1], that these procedures inherit huge overheads making them for practical security estimates irrelevant.

In the following we analyze the quantum security of the proposed parameter sets based on Bernstein's quantum Prange in a very optimistic way, disregarding any overhead caused by a real implementation. For an in-depth analysis of the necessary circuit required for launching a quantum ISD attack the reader is referred to [15]. Nevertheless, even with our analysis, which disregards a lot of the actual costs, we find that all parameter sets still match the quantum security definition of the respective categories.

Quantum Prange Under Depth Constraint. Let the Gaussian elimination circuit require a depth of $D_E = (n-k)^{\omega_M}$, where $\omega_M \in [\![2,3]\!]$. Now recall that the probability of drawing a random permutation that distributes the weight as desired (see Eq. (4)) is

$$q := \frac{\binom{n-k}{\omega}}{\binom{n}{\omega}} .$$

Hence, leveraging Grover search, finding a good permutation with one application of a single quantum circuit would require a depth of

$$D = \mathcal{O}(D_E\sqrt{q^{-1}}) .$$

Since we are limited in depth, following Zalka [36] we need to partition the search space in enough pieces such that the circuit performing a search on each partition does not exceed the depth constraint. Then the circuit has to be reapplied for each partition. Separating the search space in N equally large partitions results in a necessary quantum circuit depth of

$$D_N = \mathcal{O}(D_E\sqrt{(qN)^{-1}}) ,$$

for performing the search on a single partition. Now setting $D_N = 2^{\texttt{maxdepth}}$ results in

$$N = \frac{(D_E)^2 \cdot q^{-1}}{2^{2\cdot\texttt{maxdepth}}} .$$

Table 5. Quantum bit security margin of the corresponding schemes in comparison to breaking AES quantumly.

Scheme	Category	n	Quantum security margin
McEliece	1	3488	21
	3	4608	3
	5	6688	18
	5	6960	18
	5	8192	56
BIKE (message)	1	24646	41
	3	49318	47
	5	81946	53
BIKE (key)	1	24646	32
	3	49318	40
	5	81946	43
HQC	1	35338	33
	3	71702	43
	5	115274	44

Finally this gives a quantum circuit of depth $2^{\texttt{maxdepth}}$ which has to be reapplied N times to find the solution. Hence, the total time complexity becomes

$$T_Q = N \cdot 2^{\texttt{maxdepth}} = \frac{(D_E)^2}{q \cdot 2^{\texttt{maxdepth}}} .$$

In Table 5 we present the quantum bit security estimates for the NIST PQC schemes. Note that we do not state the security for every category and `maxdepth` combination. Rather we just state the difference of $\log T_Q$ and the quantum bit security of AES for the corresponding category, which is given in the above listing. Observe that this difference does not depend on the `maxdepth` constraint anymore. The table can now be read as *the quantum bit security of breaking the corresponding scheme is x bit higher than required*, where x is the value given in the column "quantum security margin". For obtaining these estimates we used the more than optimistic matrix multiplication constant of $\omega_M = 2.5$.

The estimates confirm our prior finding, that the McEliece parameter set for category three inherits a way smaller security margin compared to the other proposed parameter sets.

References

1. Aragon, N., et al.: BIKE: bit flipping key encapsulation (2020)
2. Aragon, N., Lavauzelle, J., Lequesne, M.: decodingchallenge.org (2019). https://decodingchallenge.org/
3. Baldi, M., Barenghi, A., Chiaraluce, F., Pelosi, G., Santini, P.: A finite regime analysis of information set decoding algorithms. Algorithms **12**(10), 209 (2019)
4. Becker, A., Joux, A., May, A., Meurer, A.: Decoding random binary linear codes in $2^{n/20}$: how $1 + 1 = 0$ improves information set decoding. In: Pointcheval, D., Johansson, T. (eds.) EUROCRYPT 2012. LNCS, vol. 7237, pp. 520–536. Springer, Heidelberg (2012). https://doi.org/10.1007/978-3-642-29011-4_31
5. Bernstein, D.J.: Grover vs. McEliece. In: Sendrier, N. (ed.) PQCrypto 2010. LNCS, vol. 6061, pp. 73–80. Springer, Heidelberg (2010). https://doi.org/10.1007/978-3-642-12929-2_6
6. Bernstein, D.J., Lange, T., Peters, C.: Attacking and defending the McEliece cryptosystem. In: Buchmann, J., Ding, J. (eds.) PQCrypto 2008. LNCS, vol. 5299, pp. 31–46. Springer, Heidelberg (2008). https://doi.org/10.1007/978-3-540-88403-3_3
7. Bernstein, D.J., Lange, T., Peters, C.: Smaller decoding exponents: ball-collision decoding. In: Rogaway, P. (ed.) CRYPTO 2011. LNCS, vol. 6841, pp. 743–760. Springer, Heidelberg (2011). https://doi.org/10.1007/978-3-642-22792-9_42
8. Both, L., May, A.: Decoding linear codes with high error rate and its impact for LPN security. In: Lange, T., Steinwandt, R. (eds.) PQCrypto 2018. LNCS, vol. 10786, pp. 25–46. Springer, Cham (2018). https://doi.org/10.1007/978-3-319-79063-3_2
9. Canteaut, A., Chabaud, F.: A new algorithm for finding minimum-weight words in a linear code: application to mceliece's cryptosystem and to narrow-sense bch codes of length 511. IEEE Trans. Inf. Theory **44**(1), 367–378 (1998)
10. Chou, T., et al.: Classic McEliece: conservative code-based cryptography 10 October 2020 (2020)
11. Dumer, I.: On minimum distance decoding of linear codes. In: Proceedings of the 5th Joint Soviet-Swedish International Workshop Information Theory, pp. 50–52 (1991)
12. Esser, A., Bellini, E.: Syndrome decoding estimator. Cryptology ePrint Archive (2021)
13. Esser, A., Kübler, R., May, A.: LPN decoded. In: Katz, J., Shacham, H. (eds.) CRYPTO 2017. LNCS, vol. 10402, pp. 486–514. Springer, Cham (2017). https://doi.org/10.1007/978-3-319-63715-0_17
14. Esser, A., Kübler, R., Zweydinger, F.: A faster algorithm for finding closest pairs in hamming metric. arXiv preprint arXiv:2102.02597 (2021)
15. Esser, A., Ramos-Calderer, S., Bellini, E., Latorre, J.I., Manzano, M.: An optimized quantum implementation of ISD on scalable quantum resources. Cryptology ePrint Archive (2021)
16. Finiasz, M., Sendrier, N.: Security bounds for the design of code-based cryptosystems. In: Matsui, M. (ed.) ASIACRYPT 2009. LNCS, vol. 5912, pp. 88–105. Springer, Heidelberg (2009). https://doi.org/10.1007/978-3-642-10366-7_6
17. Hamdaoui, Y., Sendrier, N.: A non asymptotic analysis of information set decoding. IACR Cryptol. ePrint Arch. **2013**, 162 (2013)
18. Indyk, P., Motwani, R.: Approximate nearest neighbors: towards removing the curse of dimensionality. In: Proceedings of the Thirtieth Annual ACM Symposium on Theory of Computing, pp. 604–613 (1998)

19. Kachigar, G., Tillich, J.-P.: Quantum information set decoding algorithms. In: Lange, T., Takagi, T. (eds.) PQCrypto 2017. LNCS, vol. 10346, pp. 69–89. Springer, Cham (2017). https://doi.org/10.1007/978-3-319-59879-6_5
20. Kirshanova, E.: Improved quantum information set decoding. In: Lange, T., Steinwandt, R. (eds.) PQCrypto 2018. LNCS, vol. 10786, pp. 507–527. Springer, Cham (2018). https://doi.org/10.1007/978-3-319-79063-3_24
21. Kirshanova, E., Laarhoven, T.: Lower bounds on lattice sieving and information set decoding. To appear at CRYPTO 2021 (2021)
22. Lee, P.J., Brickell, E.F.: An observation on the security of McEliece's public-key cryptosystem. In: Barstow, D., et al. (eds.) EUROCRYPT 1988. LNCS, vol. 330, pp. 275–280. Springer, Heidelberg (1988). https://doi.org/10.1007/3-540-45961-8_25
23. May, A., Meurer, A., Thomae, E.: Decoding random linear codes in $\tilde{\mathcal{O}}(2^{0.054n})$. In: Lee, D.H., Wang, X. (eds.) ASIACRYPT 2011. LNCS, vol. 7073, pp. 107–124. Springer, Heidelberg (2011). https://doi.org/10.1007/978-3-642-25385-0_6
24. May, A., Ozerov, I.: On computing nearest neighbors with applications to decoding of binary linear codes. In: Oswald, E., Fischlin, Marc (eds.) EUROCRYPT 2015. LNCS, vol. 9056, pp. 203–228. Springer, Heidelberg (2015). https://doi.org/10.1007/978-3-662-46800-5_9
25. Melchor, C.A., et al.: Hamming quasi-cyclic (HQC) (2020)
26. Naya-Plasencia, M., Schrottenloher, A.: Optimal merging in quantum k-xor and k-sum algorithms. In: EUROCRYPT 2020–39th Annual International Conference on the Theory and Applications of Cryptographic (2020)
27. Perlner, R.: pqc-forum: Round 3 official comment: classic mceliece (2021). https://groups.google.com/a/list.nist.gov/g/pqc-forum/c/EiwxGnfQgec/m/xBky_FKFDgAJ
28. Peters, C.: Information-set decoding for linear codes over **F** ¡Subscript¿ q ¡/Subscript¿. In: Sendrier, N. (ed.) PQCrypto 2010. LNCS, vol. 6061, pp. 81–94. Springer, Heidelberg (2010). https://doi.org/10.1007/978-3-642-12929-2_7
29. Prange, E.: The use of information sets in decoding cyclic codes. IRE Trans. Inf. Theory **8**(5), 5–9 (1962)
30. Sendrier, N.: Decoding one out of many. In: Yang, B.-Y. (ed.) PQCrypto 2011. LNCS, vol. 7071, pp. 51–67. Springer, Heidelberg (2011). https://doi.org/10.1007/978-3-642-25405-5_4
31. Stern, J.: A method for finding codewords of small weight. In: Cohen, G., Wolfmann, J. (eds.) Coding Theory 1988. LNCS, vol. 388, pp. 106–113. Springer, Heidelberg (1989). https://doi.org/10.1007/BFb0019850
32. Canto Torres, R., Sendrier, N.: Analysis of information set decoding for a sub-linear error weight. In: Takagi, T. (ed.) PQCrypto 2016. LNCS, vol. 9606, pp. 144–161. Springer, Cham (2016). https://doi.org/10.1007/978-3-319-29360-8_10
33. Various: pqc-forum: Round 3 official comment: classic mceliece (2021). https://groups.google.com/a/list.nist.gov/g/pqc-forum/c/EiwxGnfQgec
34. Various: pqc-forum: Security strength categories for code based crypto (and trying out crypto stack exchange) (2021). https://groups.google.com/a/list.nist.gov/g/pqc-forum/c/6XbG66gI7v0
35. Wagner, D.: A generalized birthday problem. In: Yung, M. (ed.) CRYPTO 2002. LNCS, vol. 2442, pp. 288–304. Springer, Heidelberg (2002). https://doi.org/10.1007/3-540-45708-9_19
36. Zalka, C.: Grover's quantum searching algorithm is optimal. Phys. Rev. A **60**(4), 2746 (1999)

On the Isogeny Problem with Torsion Point Information

Tako Boris Fouotsa[1(✉)], Péter Kutas[2,3(✉)], Simon-Philipp Merz[4(✉)], and Yan Bo Ti[5(✉)]

[1] Università Degli Studi Roma Tre, Rome, Italy
takoboris.fouotsa@uniroma3.it
[2] University of Birmingham, Birmingham, UK
p.kutas@bham.ac.uk
[3] Eötvös Loránd University, Budapest, Hungary
[4] Royal Holloway, University of London, Egham, UK
simon-philipp.merz.2018@rhul.ac.uk
[5] DSO, Singapore, Singapore
yanbo.ti@gmail.com

Abstract. It has recently been rigorously proven (and was previously known under certain heuristics) that the general supersingular isogeny problem reduces to the supersingular endomorphism ring computation problem. However, in order to attack SIDH-type schemes, one requires a particular isogeny which is usually not returned by the general reduction. At Asiacrypt 2016, Galbraith, Petit, Shani and Ti presented a polynomial-time reduction of the problem of finding the secret isogeny in SIDH to the problem of computing the endomorphism ring of a supersingular elliptic curve. Their method exploits the fact that secret isogenies in SIDH are of degree approximately $p^{1/2}$. The method does not extend to other SIDH-type schemes, where secret isogenies of larger degree are used and this condition is not fulfilled.

We present a more general reduction algorithm that generalises to all SIDH-type schemes. The main idea of our algorithm is to exploit available torsion point images together with the KLPT algorithm to obtain a linear system of equations over a certain residue class ring. We show that this system will have a unique solution that can be lifted to the integers if some mild conditions on the parameters are satisfied. This lift then yields the secret isogeny. One consequence of this work is that the choice of the prime p in B-SIDH is tight.

Keywords: post-quantum · isogeny-based cryptography · supersingular isogenies · endomorphism rings · SIDH

1 Introduction

Practical large scale quantum computers pose a threat to most cryptosystems currently in use [13,27]. Recent advances in quantum computing and the need for long-term security in cryptography has led to a surge of interest in developing

G. Hanaoka et al. (Eds.): PKC 2022, LNCS 13177, pp. 142–161, 2022.
https://doi.org/10.1007/978-3-030-97121-2_6

quantum secure replacements for these classical cryptographic algorithms. Moreover, NIST has started a procedure to determine new cryptographic standards for a post-quantum era [22].

Most of the standardisation candidates are based on lattices, codes or multivariate polynomial systems over finite fields. A more recent but promising area of post-quantum research is isogeny-based cryptography.

Couveignes was the first one to mention isogenies for cryptographic use in 1997 [6], and the area gained traction in the following decade with new developments such as collision-resistant hashing [3] and key exchange [26,29] based on isogeny problems. After Jao and De Feo introduced supersingular isogeny Diffie-Hellman (SIDH) [15], a predecessor of the isogeny-based submission to NIST's standardisation procedure SIKE [14], the area has enjoyed increasing popularity.

The central problem in most of isogeny-based cryptography is to find an isogeny $\varphi : E_1 \to E_2$, i.e. a morphism both in the sense of algebraic geometry and group theory, between two given supersingular elliptic curves defined over a finite field $\mathbb{F}_q$. For two supersingular elliptic curves E_1 and E_2, the problem of computing an arbitrary isogeny between them and the problem of computing their endomorphism rings $\mathrm{End}(E_1)$ and $\mathrm{End}(E_2)$ was recently proven to be equivalent under the assumption that the generalized Riemann hypothesis (GRH) holds by Wesolowski [34]. Yet, in the case where E_1 and E_2 are ordinary curves, it is usually much easier to determine $\mathrm{End}(E_i)$ of an arbitrary E_i than computing an isogeny between two arbitrary curves [19].

There are infinitely many isogenies $E_1 \to E_2$, but attacking isogeny-based primitives such as SIDH requires to recover an isogeny $\varphi : E_1 \to E_2$ of a specific degree. Generic algorithms are unlikely to return an isogeny of the correct degree given the endomorphism rings. In Section 4 of [12], it is shown how to recover secret isogenies in the case of SIDH. The attack exploits the observation that secret isogenies in SIDH are of degree $p^{1/2}$, which is relatively small. In the case where the isogeny one wishes to recover is not of particularly small degree, as is the case in B-SIDH [5], SÉTA [8] or instantiations of SIDH with secret isogenies of larger degree, this observation no longer holds and the algorithm due to Galbraith et al. no longer applies.

Our Contributions. Assuming the generalized Riemann hypothesis, this paper provides a polynomial-time (in $\log p$) algorithm that recovers an isogeny with certain torsion point images between two supersingular elliptic curves of a specific degree N_1, given their endomorphism rings and some torsion point images under the isogeny. More precisely, let d be the least degree of any isogeny between two isogenous supersingular elliptic curves E_1 and E_2. Then, our algorithm solves the following problem, whenever $N_1 < dN_2/16$.

Task 1.1. *Let N_1, N_2 be coprime integers and let $\varphi : E_1 \to E_2$ be a secret isogeny of degree N_1 between two supersingular elliptic curves. Let P_B, Q_B be a basis of $E_1[N_2]$. Given End(E_1), End(E_2), $\varphi(P_B)$, and $\varphi(Q_B)$, find an isogeny $\varphi' : E_1 \to E_2$ of degree N_1 such that $\varphi_{|E_1[N_2]} = \varphi'_{|E_1[N_2]}$.*

Since SIDH-type schemes such as B-SIDH tend to use balanced parameters, where $N_1 \approx N_2$, the condition that $N_1 < dN_2/16$ is very mild.

The main idea behind the algorithm is the following. Isogenies from E_1 to E_2 form a $\mathbb{Z}$-module M of rank 4. A basis of M can be computed using an algorithm due to Kirschmer and Voight [17] (or the KLPT algorithm [18]). Then, one computes an LLL-reduced basis $\psi_1, \psi_2, \psi_3, \psi_4$ of M. We show how to evaluate $\psi_i(P_B)$, $\psi_i(Q_B)$ for $i = 1, \ldots, 4$ and we are given $\phi(P_B)$ and $\phi(Q_B)$.

Since $\phi = x_1\psi_1 + x_2\psi_2 + x_3\psi_3 + x_4\psi_4$ for some $x_i \in \mathbb{Z}$, this yields 4 linear equations in 4 variables, x_1, x_2, x_3, x_4, modulo N_2 (torsion-point images can be represented by a 2×2 matrix with entries from $\mathbb{Z}/N_2\mathbb{Z}$ and each entry corresponds to an equation). We will show that this system of equations has a unique solution for x_i modulo N_2 which we also compute. Since the ψ_i form an LLL-reduced basis, we can bound the absolute value of the coefficients x_i by $N_2/2$ for $N_1 < dN_2/16$. This leads to a solution for $x_i \in \mathbb{Z}$.

The contribution of this paper can be seen as an extension of the reductions by Kohel, Lauter, Petit, and Tignol [18] and Wesolowski [34] which allow to compute an isogeny (of no specific degree) between two supersingular elliptic curves, whenever the endomorphism rings of the curves are known. Note that Kohel et al. provide a heuristic polynomial-time algorithm for this reduction, whereas Wesolowski shows that this reduction works in polynomial-time in general assuming only GRH.

Together with known results on the computation of endomorphism rings, a consequence of this work is an answer to the open question how small the size of the prime p in B-SIDH can be chosen. More precisely, this work implies that one cannot lower the size of the prime p in B-SIDH significantly, while maintaining the same security level. Current parameter sets are not threatened because parameters were selected in a cautious way (i.e., were larger than necessary if one only accounted for existing attacks). Our algorithm has a similar classical runtime to a generic meet-in-the-middle algorithm but is essentially memory-free whereas meet-in-the-middle requires an exponential amount of memory. Furthermore, the quantum version of our attack has a much better runtime than previously known quantum attacks ($O(p^{1/4})$ [10] compared to $O(p^{1/2})$ [16]), where the authors showed that the Tani's claw algorithm has better complexity quantumly, but suffers from quantum storage issues. The running time of our algorithms is dominated by the computation of the endomorphism rings.

Outline. In Sect. 2, we recall some necessary mathematical background, details of the SIDH key exchange as well as some related work. In Sect. 3, we give algorithms to evaluate non-smooth degree isogenies and to compute an isogeny of a specific degree between two supersingular elliptic curves with known endomorphism ring, if certain torsion point information is available. Moreover, we discuss the impact of this work on isogeny-based cryptography before concluding the paper in Sect. 5.

2 Preliminaries

In this section, we recall some relevant background on elliptic curves and isogeny-based cryptography. For further introductory reading, we refer to Silverman [28] and De Feo [7] respectively. Furthermore, we briefly recall some consequences of the KLPT algorithm [18] and the LLL lattice reduction [20]. Moreover, we sketch a related algorithm due to Galbraith et al. [12] which computes an isogeny of specific degree between two supersingular elliptic curves with known endomorphism ring, if this degree is sufficiently small.

2.1 Elliptic Curves and Isogenies

Let E_1, E_2 be elliptic curves defined over a field K. An isogeny between E_1 and E_2 is a non-constant rational map which is also a group homomorphism (or equivalently, fixes the point at infinity). The *degree* of an isogeny is its degree as a finite map of curves, i.e. the degree of the extension of function fields. An isogeny is called *separable* if the corresponding field extension is separable. For a separable isogeny, the degree equals the size of its kernel. Furthermore, for every finite subgroup G of an elliptic curve E, there exists a separable isogeny whose kernel is G. Up to post-composition with an isomorphism, the isogeny is unique. We denote the codomain of this isogeny by E/G. Given a finite subgroup $G \subset E$ the corresponding isogeny from E to E/G can be computed using Vélu's formulae [32].

Let $\phi : E_1 \to E_2$ be an isogeny of degree d. Then there exists a unique isogeny $\hat{\phi}$ with the property that $\phi \circ \hat{\phi} = [d]$, where $[d]$ denotes the multiplication by d. This isogeny $\hat{\phi}$ is called the *dual* of ϕ and it is also of degree d. An isogeny from E to itself is called an *endomorphism*. Together with the zero map, endomorphisms of E form a ring under addition and composition denoted by $\mathrm{End}(E)$.

Let E be defined over a finite field of characteristic p. Then $\mathrm{End}(E)$ is either an order in an imaginary quadratic field and E is called *ordinary*, or a maximal order in the rational quaternion algebra $B_{p,\infty}$ ramified at p and at infinity in which case E is called *supersingular*. For the rest of the paper we will restrict ourselves to supersingular elliptic curves.

For an elliptic curve $E : y^2 = x^3 + Ax + B$, its *j-invariant* is given by $j(E) = 1728 \frac{4A^3}{4A^3+27B^2}$ and two curves are isomorphic over $\overline{K}$ if and only if they share the same j-invariant.

Example 2.1. For the supersingular elliptic curve $E_0 : y^2 = x^3 + x$ the above formula yields the j-invariant $j(E_0) = 1728$. It is well-known that $\mathrm{End}(E_0)$ is the $\mathbb{Z}$-module generated by $1, \iota, \frac{1+\pi}{2}$ and $\frac{\iota+\iota\pi}{2}$, where ι denotes E_0's non-trivial automorphism, $(x, y) \mapsto (-x, iy)$, and π is the Frobenius endomorphism, $(x, y) \mapsto (x^p, y^p)$.

Let ℓ be a prime number and define the supersingular ℓ-isogeny *graph* as follows. The vertices of the graph are isomorphism classes of supersingular elliptic curves represented by their j-invariant and two vertices are connected by an edge if and only if they are ℓ-isogenous. The supersingular ℓ-isogeny graph is connected, $(\ell + 1)$-regular and a Ramanujan expander graph. The diameter of the graph is between $\log p$ and $2 \log p$ [25, Theorem 1]. The presumed hardness of path-finding in this graph is the hardness assumption underlying isogeny-based cryptography.

Remark 2.2. In the rest of this paper we will call an integer smooth if its smoothness bound is polynomial in $\log p$ for a fixed p.

2.2 SIDH and B-SIDH

We give a brief description of SIDH [15] and B-SIDH [5] key exchanges.

The public parameters of SIDH are two coprime smooth numbers N_1 and N_2, a prime p of the form $p = N_1 N_2 f - 1$, where f is a small cofactor, and a supersingular elliptic curve E_0 defined over $\mathbb{F}_{p^2}$ together with points P_A, Q_A, P_B, Q_B such that $E_0[N_1] = \langle P_A, Q_A \rangle$ and $E_0[N_2] = \langle P_B, Q_B \rangle$.

The protocol proceeds as follows:

1. Alice chooses a random cyclic subgroup of $E_0[N_1]$ as $G_A = \langle P_A + [x_A]Q_A \rangle$ and Bob chooses a random cyclic subgroup of $E_0[N_2]$ as $G_B = \langle P_B + [x_B]Q_B \rangle$.
2. Alice and Bob compute the isogeny $\phi_A : E_0 \to E_0/\langle G_A \rangle =: E_A$ and the isogeny $\phi_B : E_0 \to E_0/\langle G_B \rangle =: E_B$, respectively.
3. Alice sends the curve E_A and the two points $\phi_A(P_B), \phi_A(Q_B)$ to Bob. Mutatis mutandis, Bob sends $\big(E_B, \phi_B(P_A), \phi_B(Q_A)\big)$ to Alice.
4. Alice and Bob use the given torsion points to obtain the shared secret $j(E_0/\langle G_A, G_B \rangle)$. To do so, Alice computes $\phi_B(G_A) = \phi_B(P_A) + [x_A]\phi_B(Q_A)$ and uses the fact that $E_0/\langle G_A, G_B \rangle \cong E_B/\langle \phi_B(G_A) \rangle$. Bob proceeds analogously.

In practice N_1 and N_2 are chosen to be powers of 2 and 3, respectively, to maximize the efficiency of the scheme. However, choosing a prime of the form $N_1 N_2 f - 1$ with $N_1 \approx N_2$ implies that the curves E_A, E_B are much closer at E_0 than the diameter of the supersingular isogeny graph, i.e. the paths connecting E_0 with E_A and E_B are shorter than one would expect for randomly chosen isogenous curves.

In order to avoid walking only in a small subgraph and to reduce the size of the prime p, Costello introduced the variant B-SIDH [5]. The main differences between SIDH and B-SIDH are

- N_1 and N_2 are smooth coprime divisors of $p - 1$ and $p + 1$ (or vice versa) respectively. Hence, $p + 1$ and $p - 1$ both need to have large smooth factors as opposed to just one of them in SIDH.
- For the best parameter choice, we have $N_1 \approx N_2 \approx p$ as opposed to $N_1 \approx N_2 \approx \sqrt{p}$ in SIDH.
- Kernel generators are a priori $\mathbb{F}_{p^4}$-rational as opposed to $\mathbb{F}_{p^2}$-rational.

In B-SIDH the curves E_0 and E_A are no longer closer than expected in the isogeny graph, but parameter selection might be harder and it seems at first to come at the expense of working over larger field extensions. However, to every supersingular elliptic curve E defined over $\mathbb{F}_{p^2}$, there exists a quadratic twist (i.e., a curve defined over $\mathbb{F}_{p^2}$ which is isomorphic to E over $\mathbb{F}_{p^4}$ but not over $\mathbb{F}_{p^2}$). If E has $(p+1)^2$ rational points over $\mathbb{F}_{p^2}$, then its twist has $(p-1)^2$ rational points over $\mathbb{F}_{p^2}$. Thus, when computing an isogeny of degree N_1 dividing $p+1$ one can work with the curves having $p+1$ rational points, and before computing an isogeny of degree N_2 dividing $p-1$, one switches to twists that have $p-1$ rational points. Technically, the switch makes it possible to compute the isogenies using only operations over $\mathbb{F}_{p^2}$. For more details we refer to [5].

2.3 KLPT and LLL Lattice Reduction

In this subsection, we recall some facts about the Kohel-Lauter-Petit-Tignol (KLPT) algorithm [18] and the Lenstra-Lenstra-Lovász (LLL) lattice reduction [20].

Let $B_{p,\infty}$ be the quaternion algebra ramified at p and at infinity. Let $\mathcal{O}_1$ and $\mathcal{O}_2$ be maximal orders in $B_{p,\infty}$. Then the quaternion isogeny problem asks for a left ideal I connecting $\mathcal{O}_1$ and $\mathcal{O}_2$, i.e., a left ideal I of $\mathcal{O}_1$ which is also a right ideal of $\mathcal{O}_2$. By [18, Lemma 8], we have the following result.

Lemma 2.3. *Let $\mathcal{O}_1$ and $\mathcal{O}_2$ be maximal orders in $B_{p,\infty}$. Then the intersection $\mathcal{O}_1 \cap \mathcal{O}_2$ has the same index M in $\mathcal{O}_1$ and $\mathcal{O}_2$. Furthermore,*

$$I(\mathcal{O}_1, \mathcal{O}_2) = \{\alpha \in B_{p,\infty} \mid \alpha \mathcal{O}_2 \overline{\alpha} \subset M\mathcal{O}_1\}$$

is a left ideal of $\mathcal{O}_1$ and a right ideal of $\mathcal{O}_2$ of reduced norm M. $I(\mathcal{O}_1, \mathcal{O}_2)$ can be computed in polynomial time.

Lemma 2.3 shows that one can compute a connecting ideal between two maximal orders efficiently. However, this ideal will not have smooth norm in general. In [18], the main algorithm shows how to compute an equivalent left ideal of $\mathcal{O}_1$ of norm ℓ^k where ℓ is some small prime number.

Let E_1, E_2 be supersingular elliptic curves with endomorphism rings $\mathcal{O}_1$ and $\mathcal{O}_2$ respectively. Then the set of isogenies from E_1 to E_2 is a left $\mathcal{O}_1$-module and a right $\mathcal{O}_2$-module. In particular, they form a $\mathbb{Z}$-lattice of rank 4 [33, Lemma 42.1.11]. The $\mathbb{Z}$-lattice is isomorphic to a connecting left ideal I as an $\mathcal{O}_1$-module by the following lemma.

Lemma 2.4. *[33, 42.2.8] Let $Hom(E_2, E_1)$ denote the set of isogenies from E_2 to E_1 and let $\mathcal{O}_1$ and $\mathcal{O}_2$ denote the endomorphism rings of E_1 and E_2 respectively. Let I be a connecting ideal of $\mathcal{O}_1$ and $\mathcal{O}_2$ and let $\phi_I : E_2 \to E_1$ denote the corresponding isogeny. Then the map $\phi_I^* : Hom(E_1, E_2) \to I$, $\psi \mapsto \psi \circ \phi_I$ is an isomorphism of left $\mathcal{O}_1$-modules.*

Since the KLPT-algorithm computes a connecting ideal between two maximal orders, Lemma 2.4 implies that one can compute a $\mathbb{Z}$-basis of $\mathrm{Hom}(E_1, E_2)$. However, the degree of these isogenies might not be smooth and it is not obvious that one can evaluate them efficiently. In Algorithm 1, we will show that one can evaluate these isogenies on points efficiently using the KLPT algorithm.

Next, we recall some basic facts about lattice reduction, which aims to transform an arbitrary input basis into a basis of "higher quality". In the following, we are interested in bases that are close to orthogonal.

Let $B := (b_1, \ldots, b_n)$ be the basis of a lattice L, let π_i denote the projection onto $\text{span}(b_1, \ldots, b_{i-1})$ for $i = \{1, \ldots, n\}$ and let $B^* := (b_1^*, \ldots, b_n^*)$ be the *Gram-Schmidt orthogonalization* of B, where $b_i^* = \pi_i(b_i)$. Intuitively speaking, a good basis is one in which the sequence of Gram-Schmidt norms $\|b_1^*\|, \|b_2^*\|, \ldots, \|b_n^*\|$ does not decay too fast.

The Lenstra-Lenstra-Lovász (LLL) reduction calculates a short and nearly orthogonal lattice basis for any lattice in polynomial time [20]. We recall a more precise statement in the following proposition using the Gram-Schmidt coefficients $\mu_{i,j} := \frac{\langle b_i, b_j^* \rangle}{\langle b_j^*, b_j^* \rangle}$.

Proposition 2.5. *The LLL lattice reduction with factors (η, δ), where $\delta \in (0.25, 1)$ and $\eta \in [0.5, \sqrt{\delta}]$, provides in polynomial time a basis $B = (b_1, \ldots, b_n)$ that is size-reduced with $\mu_{i,j} < \eta$ for all $j < i$ and has Gram-Schmidt orthogonalization satisfying the Lovász condition $\delta \|b_i^*\|^2 \leq \|\mu_{i+1,i} b_i + b_{i+1}^*\|^2$.*

The default parameters for LLL-reduction in MAGMA, which we will use later in this paper, are $\delta = 0.75$ and $\eta = 0.501$. Since LLL-reduced bases are in some sense close to orthogonal, we can expect short vectors in the lattice to have rather small coefficients with respect to the basis. This is captured by the following lemma which is a consequence of [20, Equation (1.8)] and Cramer's rule.

Lemma 2.6. *Let L be a full rank lattice with LLL-reduced basis $b_1, \ldots, b_n$ with factors (η, δ) and let $v := \sum_{i=1}^n \gamma_i b_i \in L$. Then*

$$|\gamma_i| \leq \left(\frac{4}{(4\delta - 1)}\right)^{n(n-1)/4} \frac{|v|}{|b_i|}.$$

Proof. By [20, Equation (1.8)], an LLL-reduced basis $b_1, \ldots, b_n$ satisfies

$$\prod_{i=1}^n |b_i| \leq \left(\frac{4}{(4\delta - 1)}\right)^{n(n-1)/4} \det(L).$$

Therefore, using Cramer's rule we get

$$|\gamma_i| = \frac{\det(b_1, \ldots, b_{i-1}, v, b_{i+1}, \ldots, b_n)}{\det(L)} \leq \frac{|b_1| \cdots |b_{i-1}| \cdot |v| \cdot |b_{i+1}| \cdots |b_n|}{\det(L)} \cdot \frac{|b_i|}{|b_i|}$$
$$\leq \left(\frac{4}{(4\delta - 1)}\right)^{n(n-1)/4} \cdot \frac{|v| \cdot \det(L)}{|b_i| \cdot \det(L)} = \left(\frac{4}{(4\delta - 1)}\right)^{n(n-1)/4} \cdot \frac{|v|}{|b_i|}.$$

□

2.4 GPST

In [12, §4], Galbraith, Petit, Shani and Ti describe how to compute the secret isogeny of an SIDH instance efficiently, if the endomorphism rings of both the domain and the codomain of the isogeny are known (or can be computed). We summarize their results and we recall why the algorithm does not work as such outside of an SIDH setting.

Let $\varphi : E_1 \to E_2$ be a ℓ^n-degree isogeny one wishes to recover, given the two endomorphism rings $\mathcal{O}_1$ and $\mathcal{O}_2$ of E_1 and E_2 respectively. Since E_1 and E_2 are supersingular curves, their endomorphism rings are maximal orders in the rational quaternion algebra $B_{p,\infty}$. By Lemma 2.3, one can recover an ideal connecting $\mathcal{O}_1$ and $\mathcal{O}_2$. Such an ideal corresponds to one of infinitely many isogenies between E_1 and E_2. This isogeny is in general not of degree ℓ^n and, in particular, it is not the same as φ. Yet, to attack SIDH, the isogeny needs to be of the correct degree and should also have the correct action on the torsion points.

The secret isogenies in SIDH are of degree approximately $\sqrt{p}$. However, a pair of random supersingular elliptic curves over $\mathbb{F}_{p^2}$ is unlikely to be connected by an isogeny of degree significantly smaller than $\sqrt{p}$. In [12] the authors leverage this observation to recover the sought isogeny given the endomorphism rings of E_1 and E_2 as follows.

Given a connecting ideal I for the endomorphism rings, the authors compute a Minkowski reduced basis which is used to recover an element $\alpha \in I$ of minimal norm. By [18, Lemma 5], the ideal $I' := I\overline{\alpha}/\operatorname{Norm}(I)$ is another ideal connecting $\mathcal{O}_1$ and $\mathcal{O}_2$ of minimal norm, $\operatorname{Norm}(\alpha)$. Then, one can compute the isogeny $E_1 \to E_2$ of degree $\operatorname{Norm}(\alpha)$ corresponding to this ideal using Vélu's formulae. If the shortest isogeny between E_1 and E_2 is indeed of degree ℓ^n, this algorithm allows to recover such an isogeny of correct degree from the endomorphisms. The experimental results in [12] suggest that, by trying relatively few small elements α in the previous algorithm, one recovers an isogeny that can be used to attack SIDH with overwhelming probability.

Clearly, the approach outlined above relies crucially on the fact that the degree of the isogeny one wants to recover is among the smallest possible degrees of isogenies connecting E_1 and E_2. In schemes that do not use secret isogenies of relatively small degree (e.g., B-SIDH [5] or SÉTA [8]), the GPST approach is infeasible.

3 Computing Isogenies Using Torsion Information

In this section, we describe an algorithm to evaluate non-smooth degree isogenies; and an algorithm to compute a secret isogeny $\phi : E_1 \to E_2$ of degree N_1 between supersingular elliptic curves, provided that certain torsion images and the endomorphism rings of E_1 and E_2 are known.

3.1 Evaluating Non-smooth Degree Isogenies

In this subsection, we provide an algorithm for the following problem.

Task 3.1. *Let E_1 and E_2 be two curves with given endomorphism rings $\mathcal{O}_1$ and $\mathcal{O}_2$ respectively. Let I be an $\mathcal{O}_1$-left and $\mathcal{O}_2$-right ideal of norm N_1 and let $P \in E_1$. Evaluate $\phi_I(P)$, where ϕ_I is the isogeny corresponding to the ideal I.*

Remark 3.2. The isogeny ϕ_I corresponding to the left ideal I is only unique up to post-composition with isomorphisms. Here E_2 is a prescribed curve so one has only potential issues with automorphisms of E_2. The number of automorphisms of E_2 can be bounded by a constant (in most cases it is actually 2), so one has some slight amibguity in the end result of Task 3.1 which will eventually result in a constant overhead every time this subroutine is called.

To solve this task, we extend an algorithm due to Petit and Lauter [24, Algorithm 3] which evaluates endomorphisms. Note that a solution to Task 3.1 evaluates isogenies of non-smooth degree between curves with known endomorphism rings.

Petit-Lauter Algorithm [24, Alg. 3]**:** Let $(E_1, \mathcal{O}_1)$ denote a supersingular curve and its endomorphism ring, and let $w \in \mathcal{O}_1$. In order to evaluate the endomorphism $\phi_{\mathcal{O}_1 w}$ on a point $P \in E_1$, the algorithm by Petit and Lauter uses a curve $(E_0, \mathcal{O}_0)$ whose endomorphisms can be efficiently evaluated, e.g. the curve with j-invariant 1728 (see Example 2.1). The algorithm proceeds as follows.

Let $\{w_1, w_2, w_3, w_4\}$ be a basis of $\mathcal{O}_0$ and let $\{\phi_1, \phi_2, \phi_3, \phi_4\}$ be the corresponding basis of $\mathrm{End}(E_0)$. The core idea of the algorithm is to use the KLPT algorithm to compute a powersmooth isogeny $\varphi : E_1 \to E_0$ of degree N.

Then, we have $N\mathcal{O}_1 \subset \mathcal{O}_0$ and thus $Nw \in \mathcal{O}_0$. For $w = \frac{a_1 w_1 + a_2 w_2 + a_3 w_3 + a_4 w_4}{N}$ this implies

$$\phi_{w\mathcal{O}_1} = \varphi^{-1} \circ \frac{a_1\phi_1 + a_2\phi_2 + a_3\phi_3 + a_4\phi_4}{N} \circ \varphi,$$

where $\varphi^{-1} := \frac{1}{\deg \varphi}\widehat{\varphi}$. Since all the isogenies on the right-hand side can be evaluated efficiently, this allows to evaluate $\phi_{w\mathcal{O}_1}$.

Solving Task 3.1: Let $(E_2, \mathcal{O}_2)$ be a supersingular elliptic curve with its endomorphism ring, let I be an $\mathcal{O}_1$-left and $\mathcal{O}_2$-right ideal of non-smooth norm and let $P \in E_1$. We would like to evaluate the isogeny ϕ_I corresponding to the ideal I at the point P.

Using the KLPT algorithm, we compute an $\mathcal{O}_1$-right and $\mathcal{O}_2$-left ideal J whose smooth norm is coprime to that of I. Then, the ideal IJ represents an endomorphism $w \in \mathcal{O}_1$ of E_1. The element $w \in O_1$ can be recovered by computing the shortest vector in IJ. We obtain $IJ = w\mathcal{O}_1$ for some $w \in \mathcal{O}_1$. Using [24, Algorithm 3], we evaluate $Q = \phi_{w\mathcal{O}_1}(P)$, and compute $\phi_I(P) = \phi_J^{-1}(Q)$. We summarize the steps in Algorithm 1.

Lemma 3.3. *Assuming GRH, Algorithm 1 runs in polynomial time.*

Proof. The endomorphism rings of the curves E_0, E_1 and E_2 are known. For this case, Wesolowski gave a polynomial-time algorithm to compute a connecting smooth ideal in polynomial time assuming only GRH [34]. Previously, a similar (faster) polynomial-time algorithm, KLPT [18], was already known for this task, but it relies on heuristics. Thus, Steps 1 and 2 run in polynomial time.

The ideal I ($\mathcal{O}_1$-left and $\mathcal{O}_2$-right) and J ($\mathcal{O}_1$-right and $\mathcal{O}_2$-left) have coprime norms, hence the two-sided $\mathcal{O}_1$ ideal IJ corresponds to a non trivial endomorphism $w \in \mathcal{O}_1$ of E_1 that can be recovered by computing a Minkowski reduced

Algorithm 1: Evaluating non-smooth degree isogenies

Input: Elliptic curves E_1, E_2 with endomorphism rings $\mathcal{O}_1, \mathcal{O}_2$ and an $\mathcal{O}_1$-left and $\mathcal{O}_2$-right ideal I together with a point $P \in E_1$, an elliptic curve E_0 such that its endomorphism ring $\mathcal{O}_0$ is generated by endomorphisms $\phi_1, \phi_2, \phi_3, \phi_4$ that can be evaluated efficiently.

Output: $\phi_I(P)$.

1 Compute an $\mathcal{O}_1$-right and $\mathcal{O}_2$-left ideal J whose smooth norm is coprime to that of I using Wesolowski's algorithm [34] (or KLPT);

2 Compute an $\mathcal{O}_1$-left and $\mathcal{O}_0$-right ideal K of powersmooth norm N using Wesolowski's algorithm (or KLPT);

3 Set $IJ = w\mathcal{O}_1$ for some $w \in \mathcal{O}_1$ and find integers a_1, a_2, a_3 and a_4 such that $Nw = a_1w_1 + a_2w_2 + a_3w_3 + a_4w_4$;

4 Evaluate $Q = \phi_{IJ}(P) = \frac{\phi_K^{-1} \circ (a_1\phi_1 + a_2\phi_2 + a_3\phi_3 + a_4\phi_4) \circ \phi_K(P)}{N}$ using [24, Alg. 3];

5 **return** $\phi_J^{-1}(Q)$

basis of IJ. For lattices up to dimension 4, a Minkowski reduced basis can be computed in polynomial time [23]. The integers a_1, a_2, a_3 and a_4 are obtained by rewriting the quaternion Nw as an element of $\mathcal{O}_0$. Therefore, Step 3 runs in polynomial time. By hypothesis, the isogenies ϕ_1, ϕ_2, ϕ_3 and ϕ_4 can be evaluated efficiently. The ideals K and J have smooth norm, hence the isogenies ϕ_K, ϕ_K^{-1} and ϕ_J^{-1} have smooth degree and can also be evaluated efficiently. It follows that Step 4 and Step 5 run in polynomial time as well. □

3.2 Main Algorithm

Next, we generalise Algorithm 2 of [12]. In [12], an isogeny ϕ between two curves E_1 and E_2 with known endomorphism rings $\mathcal{O}_1$ and $\mathcal{O}_2$ is computed, if its degree is minimal (i.e., ϕ is the isogeny of smallest degree connecting E_1 and E_2). The algorithm in [12] applies to the SIDH setting where the degree of the secret isogenies are minimal with non-negligible probability (or otherwise at least of particularly small degree). Meanwhile, the torsion point information available in SIDH-like schemes is not used at all.

We will show in this section how the torsion point information in SIDH-like schemes can be exploited together with the knowledge of endomorphism rings to compute secret isogenies of arbitrary (larger but fixed) degree.

The strategy is as follows. Let $\phi : E_1 \to E_2$ be a secret isogeny, let P, Q be a basis of $E_1[N_2]$ and let $\phi(P)$, $\phi(Q)$ be the torsion information provided in SIDH-like schemes. Let $I(\mathcal{O}_1, \mathcal{O}_2)$ be a connecting ideal between the maximal orders $\mathcal{O}_1$ and $\mathcal{O}_2$. Instead of solving for a minimal norm element of the ideal $I(\mathcal{O}_1, \mathcal{O}_2)$ as in [12], we compute an LLL-reduced basis $\{\psi_1, \psi_2, \psi_3, \psi_4\}$ of I.

Using Algorithm 1, the isogenies ψ_i, $i = 1, \dots, 4$, can be evaluated at the points P and Q. Next, we want to write ϕ in terms of our LLL-reduced basis, i.e. we want to find $(x_1, \dots, x_4) \in \mathbb{Z}^4$ such that

$$\phi = x_1\psi_1 + x_2\psi_2 + x_3\psi_3 + x_4\psi_4, \tag{1}$$

Clearly, recovering x_i allows to compute the secret isogeny ϕ.

Note that Eq. 1 implies in particular

$$\sum_{i=1}^{4} x_i\psi_i(P) = \phi(P) \qquad \text{and} \qquad \sum_{i=1}^{4} x_i\psi_i(Q) = \phi(Q). \tag{2}$$

To compute x_1, x_2, x_3 and x_4, we first prove that a solution to Eq. 2 is unique modulo N_2. Then, we use simple linear algebra methods to recover it. Finally, we will show that knowing the x_i modulo N_2 is enough to recover them exactly (as integers).

Lemma 3.4. *Let E_1, E_2 be supersingular elliptic curves over $\mathbb{F}_{p^2}$ and let P, Q be a basis of $E_1[N_2]$. Let $\psi_1, \psi_2, \psi_3, \psi_4$ be a $\mathbb{Z}$-basis of Hom(E_1, E_2). The system of linear equations modulo N_2 corresponding to*

$$\sum_{i=1}^{4} x_i\psi_i(P) = \phi(P) \text{ and } \sum_{i=1}^{4} x_i\psi_i(Q) = \phi(Q)$$

has a unique solution $(x_1, x_2, x_3, x_4) \in (\mathbb{Z}/N_2\mathbb{Z})^4$.

Proof. Let P', Q' be a basis of $E_2[N_2]$. Every isogeny ϕ in $\text{Hom}(E_1, E_2)$ can be identified with a matrix $\begin{pmatrix} a & b \\ c & d \end{pmatrix} \in M_2(\mathbb{Z}/N_2\mathbb{Z})$ by writing its images on $E_1[N_2]$ as follows

$$\phi(P) = aP' + cQ', \ \phi(Q) = bP' + dQ'.$$

Let $A = \begin{pmatrix} a & b \\ c & d \end{pmatrix}$ be a matrix in $M_2(\mathbb{Z}/N_2\mathbb{Z})$. First, we prove that for any matrix A, there exists an isogeny $\phi \in \text{Hom}(E_1, E_2)$ such that representation of ϕ is A.

Let $\psi : E_1 \to E_2$ be an isogeny such that the degree of ψ is coprime to N_2. Note that such an isogeny exists as the ℓ-isogeny graph is connected for any prime ℓ. Let M be the matrix corresponding to ψ. Since the degree of ψ is coprime to N_2, it corresponds to an invertible matrix in $M_2(\mathbb{Z}/N_2\mathbb{Z})$.

It is known (see [33, Theorem 42.1.9.]) that $\text{End}(E_1)/N_2\,\text{End}(E_1)$ is isomorphic to $M_2(\mathbb{Z}/N_2\mathbb{Z})$ (the injection is clear, surjectivity is the key result). Note that the isomorphism depends on a choice of basis of $E_1[N_2]$. Consider the isomorphism corresponding to the basis P, Q. Then, there exists an endomorphism $\theta \in \text{End}(E_1)$ whose matrix representation is AM^{-1}. This implies that the matrix representation of $\phi = \theta \circ \psi$ is $AM^{-1}M = A$, i.e. there exists an isogeny from E_0 to E_1 that is represented by the matrix A.

Clearly, $\sum_{i=1}^{4} x_i\psi_i$ and $\sum_{i=1}^{4} y_i\psi_i$ are represented by the same matrix if $x_i \equiv y_i \pmod{N_2}$ for $i = 1, \ldots, 4$. Thus, there are at most $N_2^4 = |(\mathbb{Z}/N_2\mathbb{Z})^4|$ different matrices that one can obtain.

Now, the Lemma follows by a simple counting argument. Since every matrix in $M_2(\mathbb{Z}/N_2\mathbb{Z})$ is represented for an isogeny, every matrix must uniquely correspond to a sum of the form $\sum_{i=1}^{4} x_i\psi_i$ modulo N_2. Consequently, if a matrix has two different representations of the form $\sum_{i=1}^{4} x_i\psi_i$, then they are the same modulo N_2 which finishes the proof. □

Remark 3.5. Essentially the main result of the proof is that $\mathrm{Hom}(E_1, E_2)$ modulo N_2 is isomorphic to $M_2(\mathbb{Z}/N_2\mathbb{Z})$ as a $\mathbb{Z}/N_2\mathbb{Z}$-module [30]. Informally, the key idea is that $\mathrm{Hom}(E_1, E_2)$ is a left ideal in $\mathrm{End}(E_1)$, hence it will be a left ideal in $M_2(\mathbb{Z}/N_2\mathbb{Z})$ modulo N_2. Since isogenies between E_1 and E_2 of degree coprime to N_2 exist, this left ideal will contain invertible matrices, hence it must be the entire matrix ring.

Now we provide details on how to recover x_1, x_2, x_3, x_4. Given $\psi_i(P)$, $\psi_i(Q)$ for $i = 1, 2, 3, 4$ and $\phi(P)$, $\phi(Q)$, where $\{\psi_1, \psi_2, \psi_3, \psi_3\}$ is the LLL-reduced basis of $\mathrm{Hom}(E_1, E_2)$, we would like to compute $(x_1, \cdots, x_4) \in (\mathbb{Z}/N_2\mathbb{Z})^4$ such that

$$\sum_{i=1}^{4} x_i \psi_i(P) = \phi(P) \qquad \text{and} \qquad \sum_{i=1}^{4} x_i \psi_i(Q) = \phi(Q).$$

Note that N_2 is a smooth integer and that $\phi(P)$ and $\phi(Q)$ form a basis of $E_2[N_2]$ as $\deg(\phi)$ and N_2 are coprime. For $i = 1, 2, 3, 4$, we can compute the integers $a_i, b_i, c_i, d_i \in \mathbb{Z}/N_2\mathbb{Z}$ such that $\psi_i(P) = [a_i]\phi(P) + [b_i]\phi(Q)$ and $\psi_i(Q) = [c_i]\phi(P) + [d_i]\phi(Q)$ by using the Weil pairing and solving discrete logarithms in a group of smooth order. Now, the integers $(x_1, \cdots, x_4) \in (\mathbb{Z}/N_2\mathbb{Z})^4$ satisfy

$$\phi(P) = \left[\sum_{i=1}^{4} x_i a_i\right] \phi(P) + \left[\sum_{i=1}^{4} x_i b_i\right] \phi(Q)$$

and

$$\phi(Q) = \left[\sum_{i=1}^{4} x_i c_i\right] \phi(P) + \left[\sum_{i=1}^{4} x_i d_i\right] \phi(Q).$$

We obtain

$$\begin{pmatrix} 1\,0\,0\,1 \end{pmatrix} = \begin{pmatrix} x_1\ x_2\ x_3\ x_4 \end{pmatrix} \cdot \begin{pmatrix} a_1\ b_1\ c_1\ d_1 \\ a_2\ b_2\ c_2\ d_2 \\ a_3\ b_3\ c_3\ d_3 \\ a_4\ b_4\ c_4\ d_4 \end{pmatrix}.$$

By Lemma 3.4, there exists a unique solution $\begin{pmatrix} x_1\ x_2\ x_3\ x_4 \end{pmatrix}$ to the previous equation. Hence the matrix

$$M := \begin{pmatrix} a_1\ b_1\ c_1\ d_1 \\ a_2\ b_2\ c_2\ d_2 \\ a_3\ b_3\ c_3\ d_3 \\ a_4\ b_4\ c_4\ d_4 \end{pmatrix}$$

is invertible and the solution is given by $\begin{pmatrix} x_1\ x_2\ x_3\ x_4 \end{pmatrix} = \begin{pmatrix} 1\,0\,0\,1 \end{pmatrix} \cdot M^{-1}$. The latter operation corresponds to adding the first and the fourth row of M^{-1}. We summarize this process in Algorithm 2.

Lemma 3.6. *Algorithm 2 is correct and runs in polynomial time provided that* N_2 *is smooth.*

Algorithm 2: Computing the linear system

Input: $\psi_i(P)$ and $\psi_i(Q)$ for $i = 1, \ldots, 4$, where ψ_i are a $\mathbb{Z}$-basis of $\mathrm{Hom}(E_1, E_2)$; $\phi(P)$ and $\phi(Q)$ of smooth order N_2.

Output: x_1, x_2, x_3, x_4 such that $\sum_{i=1}^{4} x_i\psi_i(P) = \phi(P)$, and $\sum_{i=1}^{4} x_i\psi_i(Q) = \phi(Q)$.

```
for i = 1, ··· , 4 do
    Compute a_i, b_i, c_i, d_i ∈ Z/N_2Z such that ψ_i(P) = [a_i]φ(P) + [b_i]φ(Q) and
    ψ_i(Q) = [c_i]φ(P) + [d_i]φ(Q);
Set M to be the 4 × 4 matrix whose rows are (a_i b_i c_i d_i) for i = 1, 2, 3, 4;
Compute the inverse matrix M^{-1} of M;
Set (x_1 x_2 x_3 x_4) to be the sum of the first and the fourth rows of M^{-1};
return x_1, x_2, x_3, x_4 such that |x_i| < N_2/2.
```

Proof. Follows from the previous discussion. □

Lemma 3.7 gives a condition under which the solution computed in Algorithm 2 gives a solution to Eq. 1.

Lemma 3.7. *Let* $d := \min\{\deg(\varphi) \mid \varphi : E_1 \to E_2$ *is isogeny*$\}$. *If* $\frac{N_1}{N_2} < \frac{d}{16}$, *then given the solution* $x_1, \ldots, x_4$ *to the system of linear equations modulo* N_2 *returned by Algorithm 2* $\sum_{i=1}^{4} x_i\psi_i(P) = \phi(P)$, $\sum_{i=1}^{4} x_i\psi_i(Q) = \phi(Q)$, *we have* $\phi = \sum_{i=1}^{4} x_i\psi_i$ *in* $Hom(E_1, E_2)$.

Proof. By Lemma 2.6, setting $\delta = 0.75$ and $n = 4$, we have that $\phi = \sum_{i=1}^{4} \gamma_i\psi_i$ where $|\gamma_i| \le \frac{8\deg(\phi)}{\deg(\psi_i)} \le \frac{8N_1}{d}$. It follows that $|\gamma_i| \le \frac{8N_1}{d} < \frac{N_2}{2}$ since $\frac{N_1}{N_2} < \frac{d}{16}$ by hypothesis.

The solution (x_1, x_2, x_3, x_4) returned by Algorithm 2 satisfies $|x_i| < \frac{N_2}{2}$ for $i = 1, 2, 3, 4$. Moreover, by Lemma 3.4, this solution is unique modulo N_2. Thus, $\phi = \sum_{i=1}^{4} x_i\psi_i$ in $\mathrm{Hom}(E_1, E_2)$. □

The entire process of computing isogenies of a specific but arbitrary degree between two supersingular curves with known endomorphism ring is summarised in Algorithm 3.

Finally, we prove that Algorithm 3 succeeds in polynomial time.

Theorem 3.8. *Let* $d := \min\{\deg(\phi) \mid \phi : E_1 \to E_2$ *is isogeny*$\}$. *Assuming GRH, Algorithm 3 solves Problem 1.1 in polynomial time, whenever* $\frac{N_1}{N_2} < \frac{d}{16}$.

Proof. Correctness of the algorithm follows from Lemma 3.7 and the preceding discussion. We are left to show the polynomial running time. Step 1 could use the KLPT algorithm [18] or in fact the algorithm due to Kirschmer–Voight [17], as the connecting ideal does not need to have a smooth norm. This runs in polynomial time (to avoid heuristics we can also use the algorithm from [34]). Step 2 is the LLL lattice reduction algorithm which also runs in polynomial time. Step 3 and Step 4 run in polynomial time by Lemma 3.3 and Lemma 3.6 respectively. □

Algorithm 3: Computing isogeny with torsion-point information

---

Input: Supersingular elliptic curves E_1, E_2 with known endomorphism rings $\mathcal{O}_1, \mathcal{O}_2$ which are connected by an isogeny ϕ of degree N_1 and $\phi(P), \phi(Q)$, where P, Q are a basis of $E_1[N_2]$, such that $\frac{N_1}{N_2} < \frac{d}{16}$.
Output: ϕ.
Compute a basis of an $\mathcal{O}_1$-left and $\mathcal{O}_2$-right ideal I;
Compute an LLL-reduced basis $\psi_1, \psi_2, \psi_3, \psi_4$ of I;
Compute $\psi_i(P), \psi_i(Q)$ using Algorithm 1;
Use Algorithm 2 to solve for $|x_i| < N_2/2$ such that $\sum_{i=1}^4 x_i\psi_i(P) = \phi(P), \ \sum_{i=1}^4 x_i\psi_i(Q) = \phi(Q)$;
Compute isogeny from the relation $\phi = \sum_{i=1}^4 x_i\psi_i$;
return ϕ

Remark 3.9. We could also have required the condition $\frac{N_1}{N_2} \leq \frac{d}{16}$ and in that case we get the condition that $|x_i| \leq N_2/2$. However, when N_2 is even and x_i is congruent to $N_2/2$, then the lift to the above range is not unique (as $-N_2/2$ and $N_2/2$ represent the same residue class). This is not issue for Algorithm 3 as one will have multiple candidates (16 of them in the worst case) for ψ that can be tested. By looking at the degrees, the correct one can be chosen efficiently. More generally, one can actually relax the statement of Theorem 3.8 further by allowing non-unique lifts and adding a check step at the end of Algorithm 3.

Remark 3.10. As was shown in Lemma 3.7, Algorithm 3 requires an amount of torsion point information that depends on the degree d of the shortest isogeny between the supersingular elliptic curves E_1 and E_2.

For many applications of cryptographic interest balanced parameters are used where $N_1 \approx N_2$. Taking $\frac{N_1}{N_2} \approx 1$, the procedure above works whenever the two curves are not connected by an isogeny of degree smaller than 16. This can be checked easily with an exhaustive search.

Remark 3.11. One does not use the fact that N_1 is smooth in Algorithm 3. If one wants to retrieve the secret isogeny as a rational map (as a composition of small degree maps), then this is still important. However, if one wants only to be able to evaluate the secret isogeny at any point, then this can be accomplished by Algorithm 3 even if N_1 is not smooth.

3.3 Example

We will illustrate the attack with an example.

Consider the prime $p = 83701957499$, where we have $p + 1 = 2^2 \cdot 3^{14} \cdot 5^4 \cdot 7$. Let B be the quaternion algebra ramified at p and ∞ and generated over the rationals by i, j, k where $i^2 = -p$, $j^2 = -1$, and $k = ij$. Fix the finite field $\mathbb{F}_{p^2}$ where $\alpha^2 = -1$ generates $\mathbb{F}_{p^2}$ over $\mathbb{F}_p$.

Consider the elliptic curve given by $E_0 : y^2 = x^3 + x$ which has j-invariant 1728. The endomorphism ring of E_0 is generated by:

$$1, j, \frac{j+k}{2}, \frac{1+i}{2}.$$

We let the secret isogeny be a 3^{14}-isogeny $\theta : E_0 \to E$. We use θ to recover the endomorphism ring of E which is generated by

$$\frac{5159993 + i + 10319986j + 11800766447346k}{9565938}, \frac{2i + 6291065j + 7411685041437k}{9565938}, \frac{3j + 196249k}{2}, 1594323k.$$

Note that in the real attack, we have made the assumption that $\mathrm{End}(E)$ is known, so we have only used the secret to calculate a known quantity.

Now, using the knowledge of both endomorphism rings, we are able to compute a connecting ideal between them and also compute the reduced basis of the ideal to be

$$\frac{227049 + i + 154612j}{2}, \frac{154612 - 227049j + k}{2}, \frac{121127 - 9i + 4995744j + 14k}{2}, \frac{4995744 - 14i - 121127j - 9k}{2}.$$

We can interpret these endomorphisms and map the generators of the $E_0[5^4]$ through them.

We have chosen the points

$$\begin{aligned} P_5 &= (75854242840\alpha + 62002351922, 51107649030\alpha + 19190692821), \\ Q_5 &= (17857458337\alpha + 504604508, 77775481527\alpha + 25718537048) \end{aligned}$$

to be the generators of $E_0[5^4]$.

In particular, by naming the reduced basis elements as $\psi_1', \psi_2', \psi_3', \psi_4'$, we have that

$$\begin{aligned} \psi_1'(P_5) &= (9049577476\alpha + 26838535531, 9532248787\alpha + 18861270144) \\ \psi_1'(Q_5) &= (14085392798\alpha + 75272963133, 35152660085\alpha + 3705843319) \\ \psi_2'(P_5) &= (54148936824\alpha + 29574813, 27904476482\alpha + 79581351851) \\ \psi_2'(Q_5) &= (6218706354\alpha + 14437916419, 19897519544\alpha + 26853032937) \\ \psi_3'(P_5) &= (27253519435\alpha + 63921648196, 55371710596\alpha + 3587102479) \\ \psi_3'(Q_5) &= (6221393886\alpha + 23453138168, 81414672111\alpha + 63571818133) \\ \psi_4'(P_5) &= (20904892135\alpha + 45099774747, 32347928248\alpha + 14718113311) \\ \psi_4'(Q_5) &= (16837240041\alpha + 11444980635, 5815630261\alpha + 82050564219) \end{aligned}$$

Furthermore, we have the images of P_5 and Q_5 through the secret isogeny θ as given as part of the problem. Note that these ψ_i are not the same as the ones defined in the previous section as they are endomorphisms of E_0. However, they are just the original ψ_i composed with the isogeny between E_1 and E_0 coming from KLPT. We will denote the actual isogenies corresponding to them by ψ_i. They can be evaluated at P_5 and Q_5 by applying the connecting isogeny to them and multiplying it with the inverse of its degree modulo 5^4. These are points in

E, and in particular, they are in the subgroup $E[5^4]$. This allows us to express them in terms of $\theta(P_5)$ and $\theta(Q_5)$ which we are given.

This results in the following 4×4 matrix

$$\begin{pmatrix} 222 & 128 & 484 & 474 \\ 311 & 363 & 337 & 12 \\ 184 & 477 & 307 & 574 \\ 344 & 566 & 191 & 132 \end{pmatrix}$$

whose first row represents the four coefficients that expresses $\psi_1(P_5)$ as a linear combination of $\theta(P_5)$ and $\theta(Q_5)$, and $\psi_1(Q_5)$ as a linear combination of $\theta(P_5)$ and $\theta(Q_5)$. For example,

$$\psi_2(Q_5) = [337]\theta(P_5) + [12]\theta(Q_5).$$

Inverting this matrix and summing the first and fourth rows allow us to recover the coefficients x_i's providing the expression of the secret isogeny as a linear combination of ψ_1, ψ_2, ψ_3 and ψ_4. The result of the computation is that

$$\theta = 14\psi_1 + 9\psi_2 + \psi_4.$$

One can check that this is correct without actually computing the ψ_i by computing that the degree of this linear combination is indeed 3^{14} (as the action on the 5^4-torsion is already correct).

Remark 3.12. As one can see in this example, the secret isogeny is not the isogeny between E_0 and E of smallest degree, hence the algorithm from [12] would not have been sufficient for finding θ. However, the secret isogeny in this setting is still the smallest degree isogeny with the given action on the N_2-torsion.

4 Relevance to Isogeny-Based Cryptography

We use this section to summarize how Algorithm 3 impacts different isogeny-based constructions.

First, we recall the current state-of-the-art regarding endomorphism ring computations as it is clearly the most time consuming part when attacking an isogeny-based cryptosystem using the reduction given by this paper.

Given a supersingular elliptic curve E defined over a finite field of characteristic p, the problem is to find $\text{End}(E)$. The first algorithm to solve this is described in Kohel's thesis [19] and was later improved by Delfs-Galbraith [9] to a running time of $\tilde{O}(p^{1/2})$. The most recent algorithm is due to Eisenträger, Hallgren, Leonardi, Morrison, and Park [10] which runs in time $O(\log(p)^2 p^{1/2})$. The best known quantum algorithm is due to Biasse, Jao and Sankar [2] and has a running time of $\tilde{O}(p^{1/4})$.

The isogeny-based community for a long time considered the meet in the middle attack (MiTM) [11] as best attack when addressing the security level of isogeny-based schemes. Meanwhile, this MiTM attack requires exponential storage, hence may be unrealistic. Recently, [1] and [4] considered the van Oorschot-Wiener (vOW) parallel collision finding algorithm [31] for the isogeny computation problem. The vOW collision search allows for a space-time trade-off in the generic MiTM, leading to a larger time complexity when limited storage is used.

Estimating the security level of isogeny-based schemes using vOW, suggests that one can reduce the size of parameters that where previously fixed considering the generic MiTM attack with unrealistic memory requirements. For an SIDH-like scheme in which the secret isogenies have degree roughly N, the scheme is secured against the MiTM attack if $2^{2\lambda} < N$, where λ is the desired security level. When considering the vOW attack, N may be considerably smaller compared to $2^{2\lambda}$. See for instance a recent proposal for the reduction of parameters in SIKE by Cotello, Longa, Naehrig, Renes, and Virdia [21].

However, one also needs to take the attack into account where the endomorphism ring of curves is computed and then Algorithm 3 is used to attack the secret isogeny. Given the classical and quantum complexity $O(\log(p)^2 p^{1/2})$ and $\tilde{O}(p^{1/4})$ respectively, this implies that the parameter p must also satisfy $2^{2\lambda} < p$.

The complexity of our attack applied against SIDH instances is similar to the attack by Galbraith et al. [12]. It does not effect parameter choices, as SIDH isogenies are of small degrees and thus pathfinding algorithms are more efficient.

Our algorithm has more impact when isogeny degrees are larger relative to the size of the underlying finite field $\mathbb{F}_p$ (as the complexity of our algorithms depends on p and not on N_1).

For B-SIDH, the proposed prime p is roughly $2^{2\lambda}$. Provided the new analysis of the vOW collision search attack in [21], one may be tempted to propose smaller B-SIDH primes in order to improve on B-SIDH's efficiency. However, doing so would make the scheme vulnerable to attacks that compute endomorphism rings and use the results of this paper. This is because p would be smaller than $2^{2\lambda}$.

Hence, one consequence of this paper is that the current choice of the parameter p in B-SIDH is tight. Furthermore, one can also interpret this result differently. Namely, any SIDH-like construction has to use parameters at least as large as B-SIDH, otherwise they become vulnerable. In other words, proposing schemes with longer isogeny walks than in B-SIDH does not provide any security benefit. This is not unexpected, as walks in B-SIDH have lengths which are comparable to the diameter of the supersingular isogeny graph.

Another interpretation of our result is that when torsion point images are provided, then the problem of finding one isogeny between two supersingular elliptic curves becomes equivalent to finding an isogeny of a specific degree for a wide range of parameters.

5 Conclusion

In this paper, we showed how to compute an isogeny of a specific degree between two supersingular elliptic curves, given their endomorphism rings and the images of some torsion points under the isogeny. This can be seen as an extension of an algorithm due to Galbraith et al. [12] which did not use torsion point information but required the isogeny to be of small degree.

As a consequence, this paper allows us to estimate the security of schemes like B-SIDH, SÉTA and SIDH instantiated with larger degree isogenies, when considering an attack that computes endomorphism rings. In particular, our work provides a significant speed-up to existing quantum attacks on B-SIDH. We stress that this work does not allow to break any of the recommended parameter sets. However, our work shows that the prime chosen in B-SIDH cannot be lowered for the given security levels and also implies that any (reasonable) scheme that provides torsion point images has to use a 2λ-bit prime for security level λ.

Acknowledgements. We would like to thank Craig Costello and Christophe Petit for useful comments on a previous draft. Moreover, we thank the reviewers at PKC 2021 whose feedback helped improve the presentation of the paper. Péter Kutas and Simon-Philipp Merz were supported by EPSRC grants EP/S01361X/1 and EP/P009301/1 respectively. Further, Péter Kutas was supported by the Ministry of Innovation and Technology and the National Research, Development and Innovation Office within the Quantum Information National Laboratory of Hungary.

References

1. Adj, G., Cervantes-Vázquez, D., Chi-Domínguez, J.J., Menezes, A., Rodríguez-Henríquez, F.: On the cost of computing isogenies between supersingular elliptic curves. In: IACR Cryptol. ePrint Arch. (2018)
2. Biasse, J.-F., Jao, D., Sankar, A.: A quantum algorithm for computing isogenies between supersingular elliptic curves. In: Meier, W., Mukhopadhyay, D. (eds.) INDOCRYPT 2014. LNCS, vol. 8885, pp. 428–442. Springer, Cham (2014). https://doi.org/10.1007/978-3-319-13039-2_25
3. Charles, D.X., Lauter, K.E., Goren, E.Z.: Cryptographic hash functions from expander graphs. J. Cryptol. **22**(1), 93–113 (2009)
4. Costello, C., Longa, P., Naehrig, M., Renes, J., Virdia, F.: Improved classical cryptanalysis of SIKE in practice. In: Kiayias, A., Kohlweiss, M., Wallden, P., Zikas, V. (eds.) PKC 2020. LNCS, vol. 12111, pp. 505–534. Springer, Cham (2020). https://doi.org/10.1007/978-3-030-45388-6_18
5. Costello, C.: B-SIDH: supersingular isogeny Diffie-Hellman using twisted torsion. In: Moriai, S., Wang, H. (eds.) ASIACRYPT 2020, Part II. LNCS, vol. 12492, pp. 440–463. Springer, Cham (2020). https://doi.org/10.1007/978-3-030-64834-3_15
6. Couveignes, J.-M.: Hard homogeneous spaces (1999). Preprint at https://eprint.iacr.org/2006/291
7. De Feo, L.: Mathematics of isogeny based cryptography. arXiv preprint arXiv:1711.04062 (2017)
8. de Saint Guilhem, C.D., Kutas, P., Petit, C., Silva, J.: SéTA: supersingular encryption from torsion attacks. IACR Cryptol. ePrint Arch., 1291 (2019)
9. Delfs, C., Galbraith, S.D.: Computing isogenies between supersingular elliptic curves over $\mathbb{F}_p$. Des. Codes Cryptogr. **78**(2), 425–440 (2016)
10. Eisentraeger, K., Hallgren, S., Leonardi, C., Morrison, T., Park, J.: Computing endomorphism rings of supersingular elliptic curves and connections to pathfinding in isogeny graphs. arXiv preprint arXiv:2004.11495 (2020)

11. Galbraith, S.: Constructing isogenies between elliptic curves over finite fields. LMS J. Comput. Math. **2**, 118–138 (1999)
12. Galbraith, S.D., Petit, C., Shani, B., Ti, Y.B.: On the security of supersingular isogeny cryptosystems. In: Cheon, J.H., Takagi, T. (eds.) ASIACRYPT 2016. LNCS, vol. 10031, pp. 63–91. Springer, Heidelberg (2016). https://doi.org/10.1007/978-3-662-53887-6_3
13. Grover, L.K.: A fast quantum mechanical algorithm for database search. In: Proceedings of the Twenty-Eighth Annual ACM Symposium on the Theory of Computing, Philadelphia, Pennsylvania, USA, 22–24 May 1996, pp. 212–219 (1996)
14. Jao, D., et al.: SIKE: Supersingular isogeny key encapsulation (2017). http://sike.org/
15. Jao, D., De Feo, L.: Towards quantum-resistant cryptosystems from supersingular elliptic curve isogenies. In: Yang, B.-Y. (ed.) PQCrypto 2011. LNCS, vol. 7071, pp. 19–34. Springer, Heidelberg (2011). https://doi.org/10.1007/978-3-642-25405-5_2
16. Jaques, S., Schanck, J.M.: Quantum cryptanalysis in the RAM model: claw-finding attacks on SIKE. In: Boldyreva, A., Micciancio, D. (eds.) CRYPTO 2019. LNCS, vol. 11692, pp. 32–61. Springer, Cham (2019). https://doi.org/10.1007/978-3-030-26948-7_2
17. Kirschmer, M., Voight, J.: Algorithmic enumeration of ideal classes for quaternion orders. SIAM J. Comput. **39**(5), 1714–1747 (2010)
18. Kohel, D., Lauter, K., Petit, C., Tignol, J.-P.: On the quaternion ℓ-isogeny path problem. LMS J. Comput. Math. **17**(A), 418–432 (2014)
19. Kohel, D.R.: Endomorphism rings of elliptic curves over finite fields. Ph.D thesis, University of California, Berkeley (1996)
20. Lenstra, A.K., Lenstra, H.W., Lovász, L.: Factoring polynomials with rational coefficients. Mathematische Annalen **26**, 1:515–534 (1982)
21. Longa, P., Wang, W., Szefer, J.: The cost to break SIKE: a comparative hardware-based analysis with AES and SHA-3. Cryptology ePrint Archive, Report 2020/1457 (2020). https://eprint.iacr.org/2020/1457
22. National Institute for Standards and Technology (NIST). Post-quantum crypto standardization (2016). https://csrc.nist.gov/projects/post-quantum-cryptography
23. Nguyen, P.Q., Stehlé, D.: Low-dimensional lattice basis reduction revisited. In: Buell, D. (ed.) ANTS 2004. LNCS, vol. 3076, pp. 338–357. Springer, Heidelberg (2004). https://doi.org/10.1007/978-3-540-24847-7_26
24. Petit, C., Lauter, K.: Hard and easy problems for supersingular isogeny graphs. Cryptology ePrint Archive, Report 2017/962 (2017). https://eprint.iacr.org/2017/962
25. Pizer, A.K.: Ramanujan graphs and Hecke operators. Bull. Am. Math. Soc. **23**(1), 127–137 (1990)
26. Rostovtsev, A., Stolbunov, A.: Public-key cryptosystem based on isogenies. IACR Cryptology ePrint Archive 2006, 145 (2006)
27. Shor, P.W.: Polynomial-time algorithms for prime factorization and discrete logarithms on a quantum computer. SIAM J. Comput. **26**(5), 1484–1509 (1997)
28. Silverman, J.H.: The Arithmetic of Elliptic Curves, vol. 106. Springer, New York (2009). https://doi.org/10.1007/978-0-387-09494-6
29. Stolbunov, A.: Constructing public-key cryptographic schemes based on class group action on a set of isogenous elliptic curves. Adv. Math. Commun. **4**(2), 215–235 (2010)
30. Tate, J.: Endomorphisms of abelian varieties over finite fields. Invent. Math. **2**, 134–144 (1966)

31. Van Oorschot, P.C., Wiener, M.J.: Parallel collision search with cryptanalytic applications. J. Cryptol. **12**(1), 1–28 (1999)
32. Vélu, J.: Isogénies entre courbes elliptiques. CR Acad. Sci. Paris, Séries A **273**, 305–347 (1971)
33. Voight, J.: Quaternion algebras. preprint 13, 23–24 (2018)
34. Wesolowski, B.: The supersingular isogeny path and endomorphism ring problems are equivalent. Cryptology ePrint Archive, Report 2021/919 (2021). https://ia.cr/2021/919

MPC and Secret Sharing

Reusable Two-Round MPC from LPN

James Bartusek[1(✉)], Sanjam Garg[1,2], Akshayaram Srinivasan[3], and Yinuo Zhang[1]

[1] University of California, Berkeley, USA
{sanjamg,yinuo}@berkeley.edu
[2] NTT Research, Sunnyvale, USA
[3] Tata Institute of Fundamental Research, Mumbai, India
akshayaram.srinivasan@tifr.res.in

Abstract. We present a new construction of maliciously-secure, two-round multiparty computation (MPC) in the CRS model, where the first message is reusable an unbounded number of times. The security of the protocol relies on the Learning Parity with Noise (LPN) assumption with inverse polynomial noise rate $1/n^{1-\epsilon}$ for small enough constant ϵ, where n is the LPN dimension. Prior works on reusable two-round MPC required assumptions such as DDH or LWE that imply some flavor of homomorphic computation. We obtain our result in two steps:

- In the first step, we construct a two-round MPC protocol in the *silent pre-processing model* (Boyle et al. Crypto 2019). Specifically, the parties engage in a computationally inexpensive setup procedure that generates some correlated random strings. Then, the parties commit to their inputs. Finally, each party sends a message depending on the function to be computed, and these messages can be decoded to obtain the output. Crucially, the complexity of the pre-processing phase and the input commitment phase do not grow with the size of the circuit to be computed. We call this *multiparty silent NISC* (msNISC), generalizing the notion of two-party silent NISC of Boyle et al. (CCS 2019). We provide a construction of msNISC from LPN in the random oracle model.
- In the second step, we give a transformation that removes the pre-processing phase and use of random oracle from the previous protocol. This transformation additionally adds (unbounded) reusability of the first round message, giving the first construction of reusable two-round MPC from the LPN assumption. This step makes novel use of randomized encoding of circuits (Applebaum et al., FOCS 2004) and a variant of the "tree of MPC messages" technique of Ananth et al. and Bartusek et al. (TCC 2020).

1 Introduction

Consider a scenario where a consortium of oncologists wants to compute several statistical tests on the confidential genomic data of their patients, while preserving the privacy of their patients. To accomplish this, each oncologist first publishes an encryption of their private database on their website. Next, given

G. Hanaoka et al. (Eds.): PKC 2022, LNCS 13177, pp. 165–193, 2022.
https://doi.org/10.1007/978-3-030-97121-2_7

a proposed hypothesis F, the oncologists would like to figure out if this hypothesis is consistent with their joint databases. They would like to achieve this by sending a single message (that could grow with the size of the circuit computing F) to each other. Can they achieve this? What if they want to continue computing multiple hypotheses on the same data? Can they perform multiple tests at varying points in time while sending just one additional message for every new test? In other words, can they *reuse* the published encryptions of their data across multiple tests?

This scenario is a special case of the more general problem of constructing *reusable* two-round multiparty computation, whose feasibility was established in the work of Garg et al. [GGHR14] assuming the existence of indistinguishability obfuscation [BGI+01,GGH+13]. Starting with this work, an important line of research has been to weaken the computational assumptions required for constructing this primitive. The work of Mukherjee and Wichs [MW16] and a recent work of Ananth et al. [AJJM20] gave a construction from the Learning with Errors assumption [Reg05]. The work of Benhamouda and Lin [BL20] constructed such a protocol from standard assumptions on bilinear maps and the work of Bartusek et al. [BGMM20] provided a construction based on the DDH assumption.

Despite significant progress, our understanding of the assumptions necessary to realize two-round MPC protocols with reusability still lags behind the assumptions known to be sufficient for two-round MPC without reusability. In particular, while we know two-round MPC from any two-round OT [BL18, GS18a], known constructions of two-round MPC with reusability seem to require assumptions that support homomorphic computation—namely, LWE and DDH (which are known to imply various flavours of *homomorphic secret sharing* [BGI16]). In particular, these assumptions are known to imply some notion of *communication-efficient*[1] secure computation for a rich class of functions [MW16,BGI16,DHRW16]. In this work, we ask:

Can we realize reusable two-round MPC from assumptions that are not known to imply communication-efficient secure computation?

1.1 Our Results

We answer the above question in the affirmative by constructing a reusable two-round MPC protocol from the LPN assumption over binary fields with inverse polynomial noise rate $1/n^{1-\epsilon}$ for small enough constant ϵ, where n is the LPN dimension.

Our construction proceeds in two steps:

- **Multiparty Silent NISC:** We first consider the problem of constructing a two-round MPC protocol where the first round message is *succinct* (i.e., the

[1] By communication efficiency, we mean that the communication cost of the protocols do not grow with the circuit size of the functionality to be computed.

complexity of computing the first round message does not grow with the circuit size) in the silent pre-processing model [BCG+19b]. To give more details, there is a pre-processing phase run by a dealer that generates correlated random strings for each party. In the first round, the parties send a commitment to their inputs using the correlated randomness. In the second round, the parties send a message that can be later decoded to obtain the output of the function. For efficiency, we require the complexity of the pre-processing phase and the input commitment phase to be independent of the circuit size and only the second round computation can depend on this parameter. We call this *multiparty silent NISC*, and this naturally extends a similar notion defined by Boyle et al. [BCG+19a] for the two-party case. We give a construction of a multiparty silent NISC protocol in the random oracle model based on the LPN assumption.
- **Reusable Two-Round MPC:** In the second step, we transform the above protocol to a protocol in the CRS model that achieves unbounded reusability without increasing the number of rounds or requiring stronger assumptions. As a corollary, we obtain the first construction of reusable two-round MPC in the CRS model from the LPN assumption.

2 Technical Overview

In this section, we first discuss the notion of multiparty silent non-interactive secure computation (msNISC), which is a natural extension of the silent NISC primitive of [BCG+19a] to the multiparty setting. We then give an overview of our construction of msNISC from the LPN assumption in the random oracle model. This result mostly follows from a combination of ideas from [GIS18, BCG+19b], with a few necessary tweaks. Finally, we give an overview of the transformation from msNISC to reusable two-round MPC. This transformation forms the heart of our technical contribution.

2.1 Multi-party Silent NISC

In a silent NISC protocol [BCG+19a], two parties begin by interacting in a preprocessing phase that results in some shared correlated randomness. In addition, they send to each other encodings of their inputs x and y. So far, all computation and communication is "small", i.e. it does not grow with the size of the circuit C they will eventually want to compute on their inputs. At this point, one party may publish a *single* (large) message to the other party, allowing the latter to learn the value $C(x, y)$. Since all communication before this point was small, the parties will be required to "silently" expand their correlated randomness into useful correlations needed for the final non-interactive computation phase.

We naturally extend this interaction pattern to the multi-party setting. We outline a three-phase approach for computing an m-party functionality.

- *Preprocessing phase:* A trusted dealer computes correlated secrets $\{s_i\}_{i\in[m]}$ and sends s_i to party i.

- *Input commitment phase:* Party i, using secret s_i, computes and broadcasts a commitment c_i to its input x_i.
- *Compute phase:* Once a circuit C is known to all parties, they each compute and broadcast a single message m_i.
- *Recovery:* The protocol is publicly decodable. That is, the messages $\{m_i\}_{i \in [m]}$ can be combined by any party (inside or outside the system) to recover the output $Y \leftarrow C(x_1, \ldots, x_n)$.

Crucially, we require the computation and communication during the preprocessing and input commitment phases to only grow as a fixed polynomial in the input size and the security parameter, and not with the size of C (although an upper bound on the size of supported circuits may be known during these phases).

Starting Point: PCG. Based on prior works, we can construct a multiparty silent NISC protocol using either a multi-key fully-homomorphic encryption [MW16, DHRW16], or homomorphic secret sharing [BGMM20], or using a specialized type of witness encryption [BL20, GS17]. However, each of these approaches make use of assumptions that can support some (limited) form of homomorphic computation on encrypted data. Further, these protocols have a fairly inefficient compute phase. For example, the approach of [BGMM20] requires the parties to compute a PRF homomorphically under a HSS scheme - this non-black-box use of cryptography will be prohibitively inefficient in practice.

On the other hand, the works of [BCG+19b, BCG+19a] study methods for distributing short seeds to two parties which can then be silently and efficiently expanded into useful two-party correlations under the LPN assumption. For example, they show how to generate many random oblivious transfer (OT) correlations efficiently via short seeds, and they call the primitive that accomplishes this a *pseudorandom correlation generator* (PCG) for OT correlations.

Now, given pairwise random OT correlations between each pair of parties, [GIS18] shows how to implement the two-round MPC protocol of [GS18a] (which we refer to as GS18) in a black-box manner. Their approach would fit the template of multi-party silent NISC, except that their input commitment phase would also grow with the size of the circuit, and thus the resulting protocol would not be "succinct". In this work, we show how to use the PCG techniques of [BCG+19b, BCG+19a] in order to generate more sophisticated correlations that suffice to instantiate GS18 while keeping the input commitment phase independent of the circuit to be computed.

A PCG for GS18 Correlations. In [GIS18], the random OT correlations and first-round messages (which also function as input commitments) are essentially used to set up certain *structured* OT correlations that enable the parties to compute a circuit over their joint inputs with only one additional message. At a high level, these structured correlations allow parties to each output sequences of garbled circuits that communicate with each other in order to implement an MPC protocol among themselves, though the details of this will not be important for this discussion. Here, we directly describe the correlation which consists of pairwise correlations set up between each pair of parties, one acting as a sender and one as a receiver. The sender gets random OT messages $\{(m_{t,0}, m_{t,1})\}_{t\in[T]}$ and the receiver gets a random string v along with messages $\{m_{t,z_t}\}_{t\in[T]}$. Each z_t is *not* a uniformly random and independent bit, rather, each is computed as $z_t = \mathsf{NAND}(\mathsf{v}[f] \oplus \alpha, \mathsf{v}[g] \oplus \beta) \oplus \mathsf{v}[h]$ for some indices (f, g, h) and constants (α, β).

As we will see below, one can write what is described so far as a two-party bilinear correlation. This is good news, since the work of [BCG+19b] constructed a PCG for two-party bilinear correlations. However, we do not generically make use of their PCG, for two reasons. First, we will actually require a *multi-party* correlation, since each party's random string v must be shared among all of the two-party correlations it sets up with each other party. Next, we have a more stringent requirement on the complexity of expansion. In particular, parties must use some of their expanded randomness in the input commitment phase, which must be efficient. We set up the PCG so that parties can obtain some part of the expanded randomness without expanding the entire set of correlations, which is computation that would grow with the size of the circuit. Thus, we describe how to set up the multi-party correlations necessary for GS18 from basic building blocks. Although our construction and proof follow those of [BCG+19b] very closely, we give a full description of the scheme in the body for the sake of completeness.

Now we briefly review the PCG of [BCG+19b,BCG+19a] that produces a large number of (unstructured) random OT correlations. Fix parameters $n' > n$. The dealer first samples a sparse binary error vector $y \in \mathbb{F}_2^{n'}$ (with a compact description denoted by $\widetilde{y}$) and a random offset (shift) $\delta \in \mathbb{F}_{2^\lambda}$. Then, $y \cdot \delta$ is secret shared into shares k_0, k_1, which are vectors in $\mathbb{F}_{2^\lambda}^{n'}$ and also have compact descriptions $\widetilde{k}_0, \widetilde{k}_1$ (this step requires the use of Distributed Point Functions [GI14]). Finally, $(\widetilde{k}_0, \widetilde{y})$ is given to the receiver, $(\widetilde{k}_1, \delta)$ is given to the sender, and a n'-by-n random binary matrix H is made public. In order to expand these short seeds into n random OT correlations, the receiver first expands its compact descriptions into (k_0, y) and then computes $t_0 := k_0 \cdot H \in \mathbb{F}_{2^\lambda}^n$ and $z := y \cdot H \in \mathbb{F}_2^n$, and the sender expands its compact description into k_1 and computes $t_1 := k_1 \cdot H \in \mathbb{F}_{2^\lambda}^n$. It is easy to check that $t_0 = t_1 + z \cdot \delta$ and thus for each $i \in [n]$, $(z[i], t_0[i])$, $(t_1[i], t_1[i] + \delta)$ is a correlated random OT instance. The choice bits z are random due to the LPN assumption. In order to remove the correlated offset δ, the parties can use a correlation robust hash function [IKNP03] or a random oracle, to hash each OT string.

Recall that in our setting, we actually require some structure on the string z of choice bits. To implement this, we first write each expression $z_t = \mathsf{NAND}(\mathsf{v}[f] \oplus \alpha, \mathsf{v}[g] \oplus \beta) \oplus \mathsf{v}[h]$ as a degree-two equation over $\mathbb{F}_2$ whose variables are entries of v. That is, $z_t = \mathsf{v}[f]\mathsf{v}[g] + \alpha\mathsf{v}[g] + \beta\mathsf{v}[f] + \mathsf{v}[h] + \alpha\beta + 1$. In order to obtain these degree-two correlated OT, we follow the construction of

PCGs for constant-degree relations from [BCG+19b]. In particular, we define the error vector to be $y' := (1, y) \otimes (1, y) \in \mathbb{F}_2^{n' \cdot n'}$. Same as before, y' is secret shared into $k_0, k_1 \in \mathbb{F}_{2^\lambda}^{n' \cdot n'}$. Now, the receiver can compute $\mathsf{v} := y \cdot H$ and set $z := (1, \mathsf{v}) \otimes (1, \mathsf{v}) \in \mathbb{F}_2^{n \cdot n}$, and likewise the receiver and sender can compute vectors $t_0 := k_0 \cdot (H' \otimes H')$ and $t_1 := k_1 \cdot (H' \otimes H')$ respectively, where H' is $\begin{pmatrix} 1 & \\ & H \end{pmatrix}$. Both are vectors in $\mathbb{F}_{2^\lambda}^{n \cdot n}$, such that for any $f, g \in [n]$ and any degree-one or degree-two monomial $\mathsf{v}[f]\mathsf{v}[g]$ over the entries of v, there exists an index i such that $(z[i] := \mathsf{v}[f]\mathsf{v}[g], t_0[i]), (t_1[i], t_1[i] + \delta)$ is a valid correlated OT. One can then obtain any degree-two correlated OT by taking appropriate linear combinations. Correctness of this step crucially relies on the fact that all the "base" correlated OTs have the same shift δ. After taking the linear combinations, the parties can still apply a correlation robust hash function to get structured OT correlations with random sender strings.

In the body, we show that even in the setting where there is one receiver with a fixed error vector y, but multiple senders with different random offsets δ_i, one can still show security via reverse sampleability. In particular, for any one of n parties, their output correlation can be reverse sampled, given the output correlations of all other parties.

The Final Protocol. Given ideas from the previous section, we can complete our description of multiparty silent NISC from LPN in the random oracle model.

In the preprocessing phase, a trusted dealer sets up pairwise structured OT correlations between each pair of parties as described above. We include a random oracle in the CRS, which is used to generate the (large) matrix H and also used as a correlation robust hash function. In the input commitment phase, we have parties partially expand their correlated seeds into randomness that may be used to mask their inputs. Crucially, this step does not require fully expanding their seeds into the entire set of structured correlations that will be used in the compute phase, so we maintain the "silent" notion. To implement this, we actually sample two different H_1, H_2 matrices and two different error vectors y_1, y_2 of different sizes, and set $v = (y_1, y_2) \begin{pmatrix} H_1 & \\ & H_2 \end{pmatrix}$. As long as each y_b has sufficient error positions, we can still rely on LPN with inverse polynomial error rate. Finally, in the compute phase, the parties publish GS18 second round messages computed with respect to their expanded correlations, thus completing the protocol. Since the GS18 protocol is publicly decodable, so is our protocol.

As a final note, we can remove the random oracle at the cost of having a large CRS. In particular, given a bound on the size of the circuit to be computed, we can instantiate the protocol with a CRS that contains the H matrix (note that the size of this matrix must grow with the number of OT correlations generated and thus, the size of the circuit to be computed). Although this CRS is large, it can be *reused* across any number of input commitment and compute phases - a property that we take advantage of in the next section, which focuses on a construction of reusable two-round MPC from LPN. We will also have to replace the use of the random oracle as a correlation-robust hash function. As already observed in [BCG+19b], the role of correlation robust hash function can be replaced by an encryption scheme which is semantically secure against related-key attack for the class of linear functions. It is known that such an encryption scheme can be based on the LPN assumption [AHI11].

2.2 Reusable Two-Round MPC from LPN

We now turn to our main result - a reusable two-round MPC protocol from the LPN assumption. Our approach takes the multiparty silent NISC protocol from last section as a starting point and constructs from it a *first message succinct* two-round MPC (FMS-MPC). An FMS-MPC protocol satisfies the property that the size of computation and communication necessary in the first round only grows with the input size and security parameter, and not with the size of the circuit to be computed in the second round. The work of [BGMM20] shows that FMS-MPC implies reusable two-round MPC, so we appeal to their theorem to finish our construction. Our construction of FMS-MPC proceeds in two steps.

Step 1: Bounded FMS-MPC. In order to convert a multiparty silent NISC protocol into a two-round MPC, we need to remove the preprocessing phase, instantiating the dealer's computation in a distributed manner. A natural approach is to use a two-round MPC (e.g. GS18) to compute the preprocessing and input commitment phases, and after this is completed, have the parties compute and send their compute phases messages. However, this results in a three-round MPC protocol.

To collapse this protocol into two rounds, we use an idea from [BGMM20] - the two-round MPC which implements the dealer will compute *garbled labels* corresponding to the outputs of the preprocessing and input commitment phases, and in the second round, parties will also release *garbled circuits* that output their compute phase messages. Anyone can then combine the garbled inputs and garbled circuits to learn the entire set of compute phase messages, which will then allow one to recover the output of the circuit. Since the computation necessary for computing the preprocessing and input commitment phases is small, the first round of the resulting protocol is succinct.

However, recall that the multiparty silent NISC constructed in last section requires a *large* CRS if instantiated without the use of a random oracle. In an FMS-MPC, the size of CRS should only depend on the security parameter, not the circuit size. Thus, we do not quite obtain an FMS-MPC following the above approach. Rather, we obtain what we call a *bounded* FMS-MPC, which has a large (but reusable) CRS whose size grows with the size of the circuit to be computed. Meanwhile, this MPC protocol is bounded since the size of the CRS determines the bound on the circuit size that can be supported.

Step 2: From Bounded FMS-MPC to FMS-MPC. Thus, our task is to reduce the size of the CRS as well as to enable computation of unbounded polynomial-size circuits in the second round. This forms the main technical contribution of the second step.

To support unbounded circuit size, our idea is to use a *randomized encoding* in order to break down the computation of one large circuit into the computation of many small circuits. In particular, using results from [AIK05] for example, one can compute any a priori unbounded polynomial-size circuit with a number of "small" circuits, where this number depends on the original circuit size. Here "small" means that the size of each individual circuit is some fixed polynomial in the security parameter. Thus, the size of the CRS required to compute each of these small circuits only grows with the security parameter. Moreover, the CRS in our bounded FMS-MPC protocol is reusable, so the same small CRS can be used to compute each small circuit of randomized encodings.

However, computing each of the small circuits in parallel does not result in an FMS-MPC. Indeed, to maintain security this would require a different first round message for computing each randomized encoding circuit, and thus the total size of first round messages will still grow with the original circuit size. To remedy this, we use a variant of the tree-based approach from [AJJM20, BGMM20]. We construct a polynomial-size tree of bounded FMS-MPC instances, where each internal node computes two sets of fresh first round messages which are to be used to compute its two child nodes. Each leaf node corresponds to one of the small randomized encoding circuits. The first round message in our final FMS-MPC protocol will only consist of the first round messages for computing the *root* of this tree. In the second round, parties release garbled circuits that compute the second round message for each node in this tree. As before, to assist evaluation of these garbled circuits, each node will instead output *garbled labels* corresponding to the second round messages. This allows anyone to evaluate the entire tree, eventually learning the outputs of each leaf MPC, thus learning the randomized encoding of the original circuit that was computed.

Crucially, the small CRS can be reused to compute each node of this tree, so that each internal node does not need to generate a fresh CRS for its children. This allows the tree to grow to some unbounded polynomial size without each node computation becoming prohibitively large - each node just computes two sets of first round messages of the bounded FMS-MPC, which in total has some fixed polynomial size. Additional details of this construction can be found in Sect. 5.2.

On the LPN Assumption. In both the multiparty NISC and the reusable MPC results, we rely on LPN with inverse polynomial error rate $1/n^{1-\epsilon}$. In both cases, the reason is that we require the computation in the first phase to be polynomially smaller than the size of the circuits supported in the second phase. Indeed, as discussed above, in the reusable MPC case we only need to support circuits of some *fixed polynomial size* λ^c in order to allow parties to compute circuits of *unbounded* polynomial size. However, we require the size of the first-round message to be some fixed polynomial size in the security parameter λ, say λ^2, *independent* of the circuit size λ^c. That is, the size of the first round message should not depend on the constant c determining the fixed polynomial size of the circuits supported in the second round.[2]

We accomplish this as follows. In the first phase, parties perform computation that sets up the LPN error vector. We fix the number of error positions in this vector to be λ, so that the size of this computation does not grow with the size λ^c of circuits supported. Now, the number of LPN samples required in the second round must grow with λ^c. Thus, while the number of error positions is fixed to λ, we set the LPN dimension n to be roughly λ^c, and the number of samples to be, say, $2n$. In the two-round MPC setting without a random oracle, this corresponds to a CRS (consisting of the LPN matrix) that grows with the size of circuits supported. However, as discussed above, we can handle a large CRS on the way to our eventual reusable two-round MPC result, as long as the first round message satisfies our succinctness property. Finally, note that the error rate of the LPN samples is $\lambda/2n$, which is roughly $1/\lambda^{c-1} = 1/n^{1-1/c}$. Thus, setting $\epsilon \approx 1/c$, we see that our final results follows from LPN with inverse polynomial noise rate. We stress that while the constant ϵ that appears in the LPN noise rate does depend on the constant c that determines the size of circuits supported, this constant c can be some *fixed* constant in our final protocol, which nevertheless allows for computation of unbounded polynomial-size circuits.

3 Preliminaries

3.1 Learning Parity with Noise

We recall the decisional exact Learning Parity with Noise (LPN) assumption over binary fields. The word "exact" modifies the standard decisional Learning Parity with Noise problem by changing the sampling procedure for the error vector. Instead of setting each component of $e \in \mathbb{F}_2^n$ to be 1 with independent probability, we sample e uniformly from the set of error vectors with exactly t entries set to 1. We let $\mathcal{HW}_{n,t}$ denote the uniform distribution over binary strings of length n with Hamming weight t. The exact LPN problem is polynomially equivalent to the standard version following the search to decision reduction given in [AIK09], as noted in [JKPT12]. We give the precise definition in its dual formulation.

Definition 1 (Exact Learning Parity with Noise). *Let λ be the security parameter and let $n(\cdot), n'(\cdot), t(\cdot)$ be some polynomials. The (dual) Decisional Exact Learning Parity with Noise problem with parameters $(n(\cdot), n'(\cdot), t(\cdot))$ is hard if, for every probabilistic polynomial-time algorithm $\mathcal{A}$, there exists a negligible function μ such that*

$$\left| \Pr_{B,e}[\mathcal{A}(B, e \cdot B) = 1] - \Pr_{B,u}[\mathcal{A}(B, u) = 1] \right| \leq \mu(n)$$

[2] It should also suffice to require only that the first-round message is sufficiently sublinear in the size of circuits supported, though we achieve the stronger succinctness property described here.

where $B \leftarrow \mathbb{F}_2^{n'(\lambda)\times n(\lambda)}$, $e \leftarrow \mathcal{HW}_{n'(\lambda),t(\lambda)}$, *and* $u \leftarrow \mathbb{F}_2^{n(\lambda)}$.

Throughout this work, we will use the following flavor of LPN assumption. For a given security parameter λ and polynomial $p(\lambda)$, we will need to assume that LPN is hard when e has Hamming weight λ and $e \cdot B$ is a vector of length $p(\lambda)$. Thus, we can set $n = p(\lambda)$ and $n' = 2n$, which corresponds to a (primal) LPN assumption of dimension n and error rate $\lambda/2n = 1/n^{1-\epsilon}$ for some constant ϵ. This is referred to as "LPN with inverse polynomial error rate".

3.2 PCG

We recall the following definition of PCG from [BCG+19b]:

Definition 2 (Reverse-sampleable Correlation Generator). *Let C be a correlation generator, that is, $C(1^\lambda)$ outputs two random strings (R_0, R_1) according to some joint distribution. We say C is reverse sampleable if there exists a PPT algorithm* Rsample *such that for $b \in \{0,1\}$ the correlation obtained via:*

$$\{(R'_0, R'_1) \mid (R_0, R_1) \leftarrow C\left(1^\lambda\right), R'_b := R_b, R'_{1-b} \leftarrow \mathsf{Rsample}\left(b, R_b\right)\}$$

is indistinguishable from $\{(R_0, R_1) \leftarrow C\left(1^\lambda\right)\}$.

In this work, we primarily consider the following correlation generators:

- *Correlated OT:* $\{(R_0 := (\sigma, m_\sigma), R_1 := (m_0, m_1 := m_0 + \delta)) \leftarrow C(1^\lambda)\}$. Where δ is a random element in some field, each $\sigma \in \{0,1\}$ and each m_0 are uniformly sampled. This correlation generator is clearly reverse-sampleable. In this work we sometimes refer to R_0 as the receiver strings and R_1 as the sender strings.
- *Subfield-VOLE:* $\{(R_0 := (\vec{u}, \vec{v}), R_1 := (\delta, \vec{w})) \leftarrow C(1^\lambda)\}$. Where $(\vec{u}, \vec{v}) \in \mathbb{F}_2^n \times \mathbb{F}_{2^\lambda}^n$, $(\delta, \vec{w}) \in \mathbb{F}_{2^\lambda} \times \mathbb{F}_{2^\lambda}^n$, and where $\vec{u}, \vec{v}$, and δ are uniformly random, and $\vec{v} = \vec{u}\delta + \vec{w}$. This correlation generator is also reverse-sampleable.

Definition 3 (Pseudorandom Correlation Generator (PCG)). *Let C be a reverse-sampleable correlation generator. A pseudorandom correlation generator (PCG) for C is a pair of algorithms* (PCG.Gen, PCG.Expand) *with the following syntax:*

- $(\boldsymbol{s}_0, \boldsymbol{s}_1) \leftarrow \mathsf{PCG.Gen}\left(1^\lambda\right)$*: On input the security parameter λ, it outputs a pair of seeds $(\boldsymbol{s}_0, \boldsymbol{s}_1)$.*
- $R_b \leftarrow \mathsf{PCG.Expand}\left(b, \boldsymbol{s}_b\right)$*: On input an index $b \in \{0,1\}$, the seed $\boldsymbol{s}_b$, it outputs a string R_b.*

Correctness: *We require that the correlation obtained via:*

$$\{(R_0, R_1) \mid (\boldsymbol{s}_0, \boldsymbol{s}_1) \leftarrow \mathsf{PCG.Gen}\left(1^\lambda\right), R_b \leftarrow \mathsf{PCG.Expand}\left(b, \boldsymbol{s}_b\right)\}$$

is indistinguishable from $\{(R_0, R_1) \leftarrow C\left(1^\lambda\right)\}$.

Security: *For any $b \in \{0,1\}$, the following two distributions are computationally indistinguishable:*

$$\{(s_{1-b}, R_b) \mid (s_0, s_1) \leftarrow \mathsf{PCG.Gen}(1^\lambda),\ R_b \leftarrow \mathsf{PCG.Expand}(b, s_b)\},\ \textit{and}$$

$$\left\{(s_{1-b}, R_b) \middle| \begin{array}{r}(s_0, s_1) \leftarrow \mathsf{PCG.Gen}(1^\lambda), R_{1-b} \leftarrow \mathsf{PCG.Expand}(1-b, s_{1-b}),\\ R_b \leftarrow \mathsf{Rsample}(1-b, R_{1-b})\end{array}\right\}$$

where Rsample *is the reverse sampling algorithm for correlation C.*

We will also consider m-party PCGs, where $\mathsf{PCG.Gen}(1^\lambda)$ outputs an m-tuple of seeds $(\mathbf{s}_1, \ldots, \mathbf{s}_m)$. Here, security is defined against any subset of colluding parties. In particular, for any $T \subset [m]$, the following two distributions should be computationally indistinguishable:

$$\{(\{\mathbf{s}_j\}_{j\in T}, \{R_i\}_{i\notin T}) | (\mathbf{s}_1, \ldots, \mathbf{s}_m) \leftarrow \mathsf{PCG.Gen}(1^\lambda),\ \forall i \notin T, R_i \leftarrow \mathsf{PCG.Expand}(i, \mathbf{s}_i)\},\ \text{and}$$

$$\left\{(\{\mathbf{s}_j\}_{j\in T}, \{R_i\}_{i\notin T}) \middle| \begin{array}{r}(\mathbf{s}_1, \ldots, \mathbf{s}_m) \leftarrow \mathsf{PCG.Gen}(1^\lambda), \forall j \in T, R_j \leftarrow \mathsf{PCG.Expand}(j, \mathbf{s}_j),\\ \{R_i\}_{i\notin T} \leftarrow \mathsf{Rsample}(T, \{R_j\}_{j\in T})\end{array}\right\}.$$

PCG for Subfield-VOLE. One of the building blocks used in this work is a PCG protocol for subfield-VOLE correlation. It has been studied by the works of [BCG+19b,BCG+19a] and is known to be implied by a suitable choice of the LPN assumption. Our main construction is crucially inspired by such PCG so we give a brief overview of the protocol.

We denote this protocol specifically by $(\mathsf{PCG.Gen}_{\mathsf{sVOLE}}, \mathsf{PCG.Expand}_{\mathsf{sVOLE}})$. Due to the compressing nature of PCG, we also explicitly associate an algorithm sEval with this protocol. It takes as input any compressed vector $y \in \mathbb{F}_p^n$ and an evaluation domain of size $k \leq n$, and reconstructs the vector y restricted to $\mathbb{F}_p^k := \mathbb{F}_p^n[: k]$. We denote the compressed form of any vector y by $\widetilde{y}$. Therefore for correctness we always have $y = \mathsf{sEval}(\widetilde{y}, n)$.

In [BCG+19a], the algorithm $\mathsf{PCG.Gen}_{\mathsf{sVOLE}}$ begins by sampling a random sparse vector $\mathbf{y} \in \mathbb{F}_2^{n'}$ of Hamming weight w and a random offset $\delta \in \mathbb{F}_{2^\lambda}$, but here we alter the syntax so that $\mathsf{PCG.Gen}_{\mathsf{sVOLE}}$ takes these values as input. Since $\mathbf{y}$ is a sparse vector, it can be naturally represented in a compressed form using $O(w \cdot \log(n'))$ bits, which we denote by $\widetilde{\mathbf{y}}$. In this way, $\mathsf{PCG.Gen}_{\mathsf{sVOLE}}$ takes as input $(1^\lambda, \widetilde{\mathbf{y}}, \delta)$ and outputs a pair of compressed random seeds $(\widetilde{k_0}, \widetilde{k_1})$ where $(\widetilde{k_0}, \widetilde{k_1})$ can later be expanded using sEval into $k_0, k_1 \in \mathbb{F}_{2^\lambda}^{n'}$ such that $k_0 = k_1 + \mathbf{y} \cdot \delta$. In fact, $(\widetilde{k_0}, \widetilde{k_1})$ are the outputs of a Function Secret Sharing (FSS) scheme for the multi-point function induced by the sparse vector $\mathbf{y} \cdot \delta$. Their sizes only depend on $(\lambda, t, \log(n'))$. Furthermore, due to the security of FSS, there exists a simulator Sim so that for any PPT adversary who is given the description of $\mathbf{y} \cdot \delta$, and for each $b \in \{0,1\}$, the two distributions $\left\{(\widetilde{k_b}, \cdot) \leftarrow \mathsf{PCG.Gen}_{\mathsf{sVOLE}}(1^\lambda, \widetilde{\mathbf{y}}, \delta)\right\}$, $\left\{\widetilde{k_b'} \leftarrow \mathsf{Sim}(1^\lambda, \mathbb{F}_{2^\lambda}, n')\right\}$ are indistinguishable.

To expand these seeds into subfield-VOLE correlation, $\mathsf{PCG.Expand}_{\mathsf{sVOLE}}$ takes as input $\left(\widetilde{k_0}, \widetilde{k_1}\right)$ and a random n'-by-n binary code matrix $H_{n',n} \in \mathbb{F}_2^{n' \times n}$ (where $n < n'$), and computes $k_0 = \mathsf{sEval}\left(\widetilde{k_0}, n'\right)$, $k_1 = \mathsf{sEval}\left(\widetilde{k_1}, n'\right)$, $t_0 := k_0 \cdot H_{n',n}$, $t_1 := k_1 \cdot H_{n',n}$ and sets $\mathsf{v} := \mathbf{y} \cdot H_{n',n}$. This immediately gives the desired subfield-VOLE correlation where $t_0 = t_1 + \mathsf{v} \cdot \delta$. The vector v is random due to the LPN assumption.

4 Multiparty NISC with Silent Preprocessing

In this section we describe our first result: a multiparty silent NISC protocol from the LPN assumption in the random oracle model. We organize this section as follows. In Sect. 4.1, we give a definition of multiparty silent NISC. In Sect. 4.2, we revisit the GS18 compiler in the context of multiparty silent NISC and identify a specific type of correlation that we need for implementing this compiler. In Sect. 4.3 we give a PCG protocol for this correlation. The final construction is given in Sect. 4.4. Finally, in Sect. 4.5, we discuss some extensions to our basic protocol. The security proof of our protocol is given in the full version [BGSZ21].

The main result of this section is the following:

Assuming LPN with inverse polynomial error rate, there exists a multiparty silent NISC protocol in the random oracle model.

4.1 Multiparty Silent NISC: Definition

We introduce the notion of multiparty non-interactive secure computation with silent preprocessing, or *Multiparty Silent NISC*, which extends the two-party silent NISC primitive of [BCG+19a] to the multi-party setting.

An m-party silent NISC protocol begins with a preprocessing phase, where a CRS is sampled and a trusted dealer sets up m secret parameters and distributes them to each party. The computation performed by the dealer should be efficient, in the sense that it only grows with the security parameter, and not with the size of the circuit that the parties will eventually compute. After the preprocessing phase, each party broadcasts a commitment to its input. Finally, the parties compute a circuit C over their joint inputs by broadcasting *one* additional message. Anyone can recover the output of the computation based on these messages.

Definition 4 (Multiparty Silent NISC). *An m-party non-interactive secure computation with silent preprocessing (m-party silent NISC) is a protocol described by algorithms* (Gen, Setup, Commit, Compute, Recover) *with the following syntax and properties:*

- $\mathsf{CRS} \leftarrow \mathsf{Gen}(1^\lambda)$*: On input a security parameter λ, the* Gen *algorithm outputs a CRS.*

- $\{s_i\}_{i\in[m]} \leftarrow \mathsf{Setup}\left(1^\lambda, L, \mathsf{CRS}\right)$: *On input the security parameter* λ, *a bound* L *on the size of supported circuits, and* CRS, *the Setup algorithm outputs a set of secret parameters* $\{s_i\}_{i\in[m]}$. *Secret* s_i *is given to party* i.
- $c_i \leftarrow \mathsf{Commit}\left(i, x_i, s_i, \mathsf{CRS}\right)$: *On input an index* i, i^{th} *party's input* x_i, *its secret parameter* s_i *and* CRS, *the Commit algorithm outputs party* i*'s commitment* c_i *to its input* x_i.
- $m_i \leftarrow \mathsf{Compute}\left(i, x_i, s_i, \mathsf{CRS}, \{c_j\}_{j\in[m]}, C\right)$: *On input an index* i, i^{th} *party's input* x_i, *its secret parameter* s_i, *the* CRS, *all the commitments* $\{c_j\}_{j\in[m]}$ *and description of a circuit* C, *the Compute algorithm outputs party* i*'s message* m_i *for computing circuit* C.
- $Y \leftarrow \mathsf{Recover}\left(\{m_j\}_{j\in[m]}\right)$: *On input all messages* $\{m_j\}_{j\in[m]}$, *the Recover algorithm outputs* $Y \leftarrow C\left(x_1, \ldots, x_m\right)$.

Correctness. For any (deterministic) circuit C whose size is bounded by L, and any set of inputs $(x_1, \ldots, x_m)$, correctness requires that:

$$\Pr\left[Y = C\left(x_1, \ldots, x_m\right) \;\middle|\; \begin{array}{r} \mathsf{CRS} \leftarrow \mathsf{Gen}(1^\lambda), \\ \{s_i\}_{i\in[m]} \leftarrow \mathsf{Setup}\left(1^\lambda, L, \mathsf{CRS}\right) \\ c_i \leftarrow \mathsf{Commit}\left(i, x_i, s_i, \mathsf{CRS}\right) \\ m_i \leftarrow \mathsf{Compute}\left(i, x_i, s_i, \mathsf{CRS}, \{c_j\}_{j\in[m]}, C\right) \\ Y \leftarrow \mathsf{Recover}\left(\{m_j\}_{j\in[m]}\right) \end{array} \right] = 1.$$

Silent Preprocessing. A multi-party silent NISC satisfies the following properties.

- *Succinct setup*: The running time of the Setup algorithm is independent of the circuit size L. That is, we require that the setup algorithm runs in some fixed polynomial time poly (λ).
- *Circuit-independent commitment*: The running time of the Commit algorithm is independent of the circuit size, and only depends on the security parameter and input size.

Security. For defining security, we follow the standard real/ideal world paradigm. A formal definition may be found in the full version [BGSZ21].

4.2 A Strawman from GS18 Compiler

Recall that the GS18 compiler (see the full version [BGSZ21] for a description of the compiler and of the *conforming protocol* to which the compiler is applied) yields a two round MPC protocol $(\mathsf{MPC}_1, \mathsf{MPC}_2, \mathsf{MPC}_3)$, which can be presented in the syntax of multiparty NISC as follows:

- The Gen algorithm samples the CRS for GS18 compiler.
- In the setup phase, the setup algorithm samples a set of secret randomness $\{r_i\}_{i\in[m]}$. Then it sets $s_i := r_i$ for each $i \in [m]$.
- In the commit phase, given the description of circuit C, party i commits to its input x_i by running $\left(\mathsf{st}_i^{(1)}, \mathsf{msg}_i^{(1)}\right) \leftarrow \mathsf{MPC}_1\left(1^\lambda, \mathsf{CRS}, C, i, x_i, s_i\right)$. Then it sets $c_i := \mathsf{msg}_i^{(1)}$.
- In the compute phase, given all the previous commitments, i^{th} party computes $\mathsf{msg}_i^{(2)} \leftarrow \mathsf{MPC}_2\left(C, \mathsf{st}_i^{(1)}, \{c_j\}_{j\in[m]}\right)$. It then sets $m_i := \mathsf{msg}_i^{(2)}$.
- In the recover phase, given all messages, anyone can simply compute $Y \leftarrow \mathsf{MPC}_3\left(\{m_j\}_{j\in[m]}\right)$.

However, this naive construction does not achieve silent preprocessing (Sect. 4.1), due to the fact that MPC_1 takes as input a description of the circuit and that its running time is dependent on the size of this circuit. Thus, this construction does not achieve *circuit-independent commitment.*

To address this issue, we begin by taking a closer look to the MPC_1 algorithm. It outputs two things: an encoding of party i's input, which only depends on the input size, and a number of OT_1 messages that is comparable to the size of circuit C. Merely computing these messages already takes time $O(|C|)$ so we cannot hope to include them as part of the commitment.

The reason these OT_1 messages are required is that, combining with the subsequent OT_2 messages sent by each party's garbled circuits, they allow to set up OT correlations between any two parties (i, j) in the following way. For any round t where party i is the speaking party and party j is one of the listening parties,

- Party i has the receiver strings $R_0 := (\gamma_t, m_{\gamma_t})$. The choice bit γ_t is computed according to the description of action ϕ_t of the conforming protocol[3] Φ: $\gamma_t = \mathsf{NAND}(\mathsf{v}_f \oplus \alpha, \mathsf{v}_g \oplus \beta) \oplus \mathsf{v}_h$, where α and β are recorded in each party's public state, $\phi_t := (i, f, g, h)$ and $\mathsf{v} := \mathsf{v}_i$ are i^{th} party masking bits (secret state).
- Party j has the sender strings $R_1 := \left(m_0 := \mathbf{lab}_{h,0}^{i,t+1}, m_1 := \mathbf{lab}_{h,1}^{i,t+1}\right)$, where $\left(\mathbf{lab}_{h,0}^{i,t+1}, \mathbf{lab}_{h,1}^{i,t+1}\right)$ are input labels for input value γ_t of its next garbled circuit.

Then party i can simply output its string so that any party can recover the correct input label (c.f $\mathbf{lab}_{h,\gamma_t}^{i,t+1}$) for party j's next round garbled circuit.

We formalize those OT correlations by defining the more general GS18 correlations:

[3] See the full version [BGSZ21] for a description of the conforming protocol.

Definition 5 (GS18 correlation generator). *A GS18 correlation generator, denoted as* C_{GS}*, is an algorithm which takes as input the security parameter* λ *and a set* $\{\phi_t := (\cdot, f, g, h)\}_{t\in[q]}$[4]*, and outputs:*

$$\begin{pmatrix} R_0 := \left(\mathsf{v}, \left\{m_{t,(\alpha,\beta)}\right\}_{\alpha,\beta\in\{0,1\},t\in[q]}\right), \\ R_1 := \left(\delta, \left\{m_{t,(\alpha,\beta),0}\right\}_{\alpha,\beta\in\{0,1\},t\in[q]}\right) \end{pmatrix} \leftarrow C_{\mathsf{GS}}\left(1^\lambda, \{\phi_t\}_{t\in[q]}\right)$$

Where $\mathsf{v} \leftarrow \{0,1\}^n$ *is a random vector and* $\delta \leftarrow \mathbb{F}_{2^\lambda}$ *is a random offset.* $m_{t,(\alpha,\beta),0} \leftarrow \{0,1\}^\lambda$ *is a random string. Furthermore, for each* $t \in [q]$*,* $\phi_t := (\cdot, f, g, h)$*, and for any choice of* $\alpha, \beta \in \{0,1\}$*, let* $\gamma_{t,(\alpha,\beta)} = \mathit{NAND}(\mathsf{v}_f \oplus \alpha, \mathsf{v}_g \oplus \beta) \oplus \mathsf{v}_h$*, and* $m_{t,(\alpha,\beta),1} := m_{t,(\alpha,\beta),0} + \delta$*. Then* $m_{t,(\alpha,\beta)} = m_{t,(\alpha,\beta),\gamma_{t,(\alpha,\beta)}}$*. Notice that the GS18 correlation is also reverse-sampleable:*

- $\mathsf{Rsample}(0, R_0)$*: Sample* $\delta \leftarrow \mathbb{F}_{2^\lambda}$ *randomly, then for each* $t \in [q]$ *and each* $\alpha, \beta \in \{0,1\}$*, set* $m_{t,(\alpha,\beta),0} := m_{t,(\alpha,\beta)} + \gamma_{t,(\alpha,\beta)} \cdot \delta$*.*
- $\mathsf{Rsample}(1, R_1)$*: Sample* $\mathsf{v} \leftarrow \{0,1\}^n$ *randomly, then for each* $t \in [q]$ *and each* $\alpha, \beta \in \{0,1\}$*, compute* $\gamma_{t,(\alpha,\beta)}$ *as before and set* $m_{t,(\alpha,\beta)} := m_{t,(\alpha,\beta),0} + \gamma_{t,(\alpha,\beta)} \cdot \delta$*.*

Observe that we define GS18 correlation such that for each action ϕ_t, we obtain a set of four correlated OTs, one for each choice of α, β:

$$R_0 := \left(\gamma_{t,(\alpha,\beta)}, m_{t,(\alpha,\beta)}\right),\ R_1 := \left(m_{t,(\alpha,\beta),0}, m_{t,(\alpha,\beta),1} := m_{t,(\alpha,\beta),0} + \delta\right) \quad (1)$$

As first observed in [IKNP03], it suffices to use a correlation robust hash function to obtain random OTs from correlated OTs. In our construction we deploy a random oracle function ρ as correlation robust hash function.

Now suppose that before the compute phase, for each round t, party i is given R_0 whereas party j is given R_1, and additionally both parties agree on the choice of (α, β) in the compute phase. Thereby party i's garbled circuit can simply output $\left(\gamma_t := \gamma^i_{t,(\alpha,\beta)}, m_t := \rho\left(m^{i,j}_{t,(\alpha,\beta)}\right)\right)$, whereas party j's garbled circuit outputs:
$\left(a_0 := \mathbf{lab}^{i,t+1}_{h,0} \oplus \rho\left(m^{i,j}_{t,(\alpha,\beta),0}\right), a_1 := \mathbf{lab}^{i,t+1}_{h,1} \oplus \rho\left(m^{i,j}_{t,(\alpha,\beta),1}\right)\right)$. As a result, any party can recover the label $\mathbf{lab}^{i,t+1}_{h,\gamma_t} = a_{\gamma_t} \oplus m_t$.

But how can those parties obtain GS18 correlations before the compute phase? We cannot afford to generate them in the setup phase since its runtime should be succinct. To solve this problem, we specifically design a pseudorandom correlation generator (PCG) for GS18 correlations. With this tweak, the setup algorithm will include PCG seeds for each party in its secret parameter, so that each party can silently expand its seed to obtain desired GS18 correlations before the compute phase, hence making the preprocessing phase silent.

[4] We do not include the first argument to the description of the action $\phi_t = (i, f, g, h)$, since this will be constant (a single party) for each correlation that we generate. That is, we split the entire set of actions into one set per party, where each party's set consists of all actions in which they are the speaker.

4.3 A PCG Protocol for GS18 Correlation

As suggested in [BCG+19a], any subfield-VOLE correlation gives correlated OTs where for each $i \in [n]$, the receiver string is $R_0 := \left(\mathsf{v}[i], m_{\mathsf{v}[i]} := t_0[i]\right)$, and the sender string is $R_1 := (m_0 := t_1[i], m_1 := t_1[i] + \delta)$. One can then get random OTs by applying a correlation-robust hash function on these correlated OTs.

In order to generate desired OT correlations, first note that in the field $\mathbb{F}_2$, one can rewrite each NAND relation as a degree-two equation: $\mathsf{NAND}(\mathsf{v}_f \oplus \alpha, \mathsf{v}_g \oplus \beta) \oplus \mathsf{v}_h \equiv 1 + (\mathsf{v}_f + \alpha)(\mathsf{v}_g + \beta) + \mathsf{v}_h = (\mathsf{v}_f \mathsf{v}_g) + (\alpha \mathsf{v}_g + \beta \mathsf{v}_f + \mathsf{v}_h) + (\alpha\beta + 1)$. As a result of this, given random masking bits $\mathsf{v} \in \{0,1\}^n$, each choice bit γ_t can be viewed as a sum of a degree two relation over v, a degree one relation over v, and a constant which are parametrized by the choice of (α, β).

The subfield-VOLE correlation is itself a degree 1 relation. As before we set $\mathsf{v} := \mathbf{y} \cdot H_{n',n}$. In order to distinguish it from a degree 2 relation, we use the notation $((\widetilde{\mathbf{y}}, \widetilde{k_0^1}), (\widetilde{k_1^1}, \delta))$ to denote the degree 1 seeds for receiver ($R := 0$) and sender ($S := 1$) respectively, and propagate this notation to all other symbols in the natural way. For consistency with previous sections, we slightly abuse the notation by letting $\mathsf{v}_i := \mathsf{v}[i]$. Under this notation, the degree-1 correlated OT can be rewritten as follows: for each $i \in [n]$, $R_0^1 := \left(\mathsf{v}_i,\ m^1_{\mathsf{v}_i} := t_0^1[i]\right)$, $R_1^1 := \left(m_0^1 := t_1^1[i], m_1^1 := t_1^1[i] + \delta\right)$.

In order to deduce degree 2 relations, we take the tensor product of same error vector with itself and use it as the new error vector as suggested in [BCG+19a]: $\left(\widetilde{k_0^2}, \widetilde{k_1^2}\right) \leftarrow \mathsf{PCG.Gen_{sVOLE}}\left(1^\lambda, \widetilde{\mathbf{y} \otimes \mathbf{y}}, \delta\right)$. The expansion algorithm also needs to be modified as follows: $k_0^2 = \mathsf{sEval}\left(\widetilde{k_0^2}, n'\right)$, $t_0^2 := k_0^2 \cdot (H_{n',n} \otimes H_{n',n})$, $k_1^2 = \mathsf{sEval}\left(\widetilde{k_1^2}, n'\right)$, $t_1^2 := k_1^2 \cdot (H_{n',n} \otimes H_{n',n})$, where $t_0^2, t_1^2 \in \mathbb{F}_{2^\lambda}^{n^2}$. Viewing both t_1^2 and t_0^2 as n-by-n matrices over $\mathbb{F}_{2^\lambda}$, for any $i, j \in [n]$, observe that the following degree 2 relation holds: $t_0^2[i,j] = t_1^2[i,j] + \mathsf{v}_i \mathsf{v}_j \cdot \delta$. As before, this immediately gives a correlated OT where $R_0^2 := \left(\mathsf{v}_i \mathsf{v}_j, m^2_{\mathsf{v}_i \mathsf{v}_j} := t_0^2[i,j]\right)$, and $R_1^2 := \left(m_0^2 := t_1^2[i,j], m_1^2 := t_1^2[i,j] + \delta\right)$.

Now that we know how to generate degree 1 and degree 2 correlated OTs, we can easily derive the GS18 correlations by taking linear combinations of (R_0^1, R_0^2) (resp. (R_1^1, R_1^2)) over $\mathbb{F}_2$. This gives a PCG protocol for generating GS18 correlations. Now, the protocol we need is actually in the *multi-party* setting: that is, the receiver's choice bits v must be shared between all of their pairwise correlations with every other sender. This additional requirement can be ensured by reusing the same error vector $\mathbf{y}$ multiple times. Below we give a PCG protocol for GS18 correlations with one receiver and an arbitrary number m of senders. We denote this specific PCG protocol by $(\mathsf{PCG.Gen_{GS}}, \mathsf{PCG.Expand_{GS}})$, given in Protocol 1.

We prove the following theorem in the full version [BGSZ21].

Theorem 1. *Assuming LPN with noise rate λ/n', $(\mathsf{PCG.Gen_{GS}}, \mathsf{PCG.Expand_{GS}})$ in Protocol 1 is a multi-party PCG protocol for GS18 correlations satisfying PCG security (Definition 3).*

Protocol 1 (Multi-party PCG Protocol For GS18 Correlations)

- *Parameters: Let λ be the security parameter, m be the number of senders, q be the number of actions for the GS18 protocol, and n', n be integers such that $n' > n$.*
- *Output:*
  - ***For receiver:***
    - *Masking bits $\mathsf{v} \in \{0,1\}^n$;*
    - *For each $t \in [q]$, $\alpha, \beta \in \{0,1\}$, $i \in [m]$, a receiver string $m^i_{t,(\alpha,\beta)}$.*
  - ***For sender** $i \in [m]$:*
    - *A shift $\delta_i \in \mathbb{F}_{2^\lambda}$;*
    - *For each $t \in [q]$, $\alpha, \beta \in \{0,1\}$, a sender string $m^i_{t,(\alpha,\beta),0}$.*
- *Input:*
  - *A compressed random error vector $\mathbf{y} \in \{0,1\}^{n'}$ with hamming weight λ, denoted by $\widetilde{\mathbf{y}}$.*
  - *A random shift $\delta_i \in \mathbb{F}_{2^\lambda}$ for each $i \in [m]$.*
  - *An n'-by- n binary code matrix $H_{n',n}$.*
  - *A sequence of actions $\{\phi_t\}_{t\in[q]}$.*
- $\mathsf{Gen}_{\mathsf{GS}}\left(1^\lambda, \widetilde{\mathbf{y}}, \{\delta_i\}_{i\in[m]}\right)$:
  - *For each $i \in [m]$, compute $\left(\widetilde{k^1_{i,0}}, \widetilde{k^1_{i,1}}\right) \leftarrow \mathsf{PCG.Gen_{sVOLE}}\left(1^\lambda, \widetilde{\mathbf{y}}, \delta_i\right)$; $\left(\widetilde{k^2_{i,0}}, \widetilde{k^2_{i,1}}\right) \leftarrow \mathsf{PCG.Gen_{sVOLE}}\left(1^\lambda, \widetilde{\mathbf{y}\otimes\mathbf{y}}, \delta_i\right)$.*
  - *Set $\mathbf{s}^i_0 := \left(\widetilde{k^1_{i,0}}, \widetilde{k^2_{i,0}}, \widetilde{\mathbf{y}}\right)$, $\mathbf{s}^i_1 := \left(\widetilde{k^1_{i,1}}, \widetilde{k^2_{i,1}}, \delta_i\right)$.*
- $\mathsf{Expand}_{\mathsf{GS}}\left(1^\lambda, b, \{\mathbf{s}^i_b\}_{i\in[m]}, H_{n',n}, \{\phi_t\}_{t\in[q]}\right)$:
  - *If $b = 0$, set $\mathbf{y} = \mathsf{sEval}\left(\widetilde{\mathbf{y}}, n'\right)$, $\mathsf{v} = \mathbf{y} \cdot H_{n',n}$, and for each $i \in [m]$:*
    - *Parse $\mathbf{s}^i_0 = \left(k^1_{i,0}, k^2_{i,0}, \widetilde{\mathbf{y}}\right)$, and compute $k^1_{i,0} = \mathsf{sEval}\left(\widetilde{k^1_{i,0}}, n'\right)$, $k^2_{i,0} = \mathsf{sEval}\left(\widetilde{k^2_{i,0}}, n'\right)$.*
    - *Compute $t^1_{i,0} := k^1_{i,0} \cdot H_{n',n}$, $t^2_{i,0} := k^2_{i,0} \cdot (H_{n',n} \otimes H_{n',n})$.*
    - *For each $t \in [q]$, parse $\phi_t := (\cdot, f, g, h)$, and for each $\alpha, \beta \in \{0,1\}$ set $m^i_{t,(\alpha,\beta)} := t^2_{i,0}[f,g] + \alpha \cdot t^1_{i,0}[g] + \beta \cdot t^1_{i,0}[f] + t^1_{i,0}[h]$.*
  - *If $b = 1$, for each $i \in [m]$:*
    - *Parse $\mathbf{s}^i_1 = \left(k^1_{i,1}, k^2_{i,1}, \delta_i\right)$, and compute $k^1_{i,1} = \mathsf{sEval}\left(\widetilde{k^1_{i,1}}, n'\right)$, $k^2_{i,1} = \mathsf{sEval}\left(\widetilde{k^2_{i,1}}, n'\right)$.*
    - *Compute $t^1_{i,1} := k^1_{i,1} \cdot H_{n',n}$, $t^2_{i,1} := k^2_{i,1} \cdot (H_{n',n} \otimes H_{n',n})$.*
    - *For each $t \in [q]$, parse $\phi_t := (\cdot, f, g, h)$, and for each $\alpha, \beta \in \{0,1\}$, set $m^i_{t,(\alpha,\beta),0} := t^2_{i,1}[f,g] + \alpha \cdot t^1_{i,1}[g] + \beta \cdot t^1_{i,1}[f] + t^1_{i,1}[h] + (\alpha\beta + 1) \cdot \delta_i$.*

4.4 Multiparty Silent NISC: The Construction

Two-Step Seed Expansion. In our strawman protocol (see Sect. 4.2), each party's commitment contains an encoding of its input and a large number of OT_1 messages. Using PCG for GS18 correlations we are able to remove the OT_1 messages in this commitment. Nevertheless, recall that in GS18 compiler, party i's input encoding is computed as $z_i := x_i \oplus r_i$, where $r_i := \mathsf{v}_i[: l]$ (l is a bound on $|x_i|$). If party i does this naively and computes the whole masking bits v_i in the commit phase, it would take time $|\mathsf{v}_i|$ at least, which is dependent on the circuit size. To circumvent this problem, we slightly modify the receiver expansion algorithm to allow a two-step seed expansion.

First, instead of generating the code matrix $H_{n',n}$ uniformly at random, we let $H_{n',n}$ be a block diagonal matrix that consists of a small matrix $H^1_{l',l}$ and a big matrix $H^2_{n'-l',n-l}$ along its diagonal. The small matrix is only used to generate input masking bits whereas the big matrix is used to generate all of the remaining masking bits. Correspondingly, we also need to modify the error vector $\mathbf{y}$ now that $H_{n',n}$ is not a uniformly random matrix. The error vector will be split into two parts: $\mathbf{y} := \mathbf{y}'||\mathbf{y}^*$, where $|\mathbf{y}'| = l'$ and $|\mathbf{y}^*| = n' - l'$. We sample $\mathbf{y}' \leftarrow \mathcal{HW}_{l',\lambda}$ and $\mathbf{y}^* \leftarrow \mathcal{HW}_{n'-l',\lambda}$ independently. This ensures that both $\mathsf{v}' = \mathbf{y}' \cdot H^1_{l',l}$ and $\mathsf{v}^* = \mathbf{y}^* \cdot H^2_{n'-l',n-l}$ will both be indistinguishable from random due to the LPN assumption with inverse polynomial noise rate, showing that the multi-party PCG from last section remains secure.

Then, in the input commitment phase, each party computes $\mathbf{y}' = \mathsf{sEval}(\widetilde{\mathbf{y}'}, l')$ and then sets $\mathsf{v}' = \mathbf{y}' \cdot H^1_{l',l}$ and $c_i := z_i = x_i \oplus \mathsf{v}'$. This can be seen as the first-step seed expansion and it allows to remove dependency on circuit size. Finally, in the compute phase, each pair of parties silently expand the rest seeds just as before. This is the second-step seed expansion.

Protocol 2 (Multiparty Silent NISC)

- *Parameters: Let m be the number of parties. Let $(\mathsf{MPC}_1, \mathsf{MPC}_2, \mathsf{MPC}_3)$ be a set of algorithms in the GS18 compiler, and let $(\mathsf{PCG.Gen}_{\mathsf{GS}}, \mathsf{PCG.Expand}_{\mathsf{GS}})$ be a multi-party PCG protocol for GS18 correlations. Let $n' > n$ be integers that depend on the size L of the circuit to be computed, and let $l' > l$ be integers that depends on the size of inputs to the circuit.*
- $\mathsf{Gen}(1^\lambda)$: *Set $\mathsf{CRS} := \rho$, where ρ is a random oracle function.*
- $\mathsf{Setup}(1^\lambda, L)$:
  1. *For each $i \in [m]$, sample $\mathbf{y}'_i \leftarrow \mathcal{HW}_{l',\lambda}$, $\mathbf{y}^*_i \leftarrow \mathcal{HW}_{n'-l',\lambda}$ and set $\mathbf{y}_i = \mathbf{y}'_i||\mathbf{y}^*_i$.*
  2. *For each $i, j \in [m]$, sample shifts $\delta_{i,j} \leftarrow \mathbb{F}_p$.*
  3. *For each $i \in [m]$, compute $\left\{\boldsymbol{s}_0^{i,j}, \boldsymbol{s}_1^{i,j}\right\}_{j\neq i} \leftarrow \mathsf{PCG.Gen}_{\mathsf{GS}}\left(1^\lambda, \widetilde{\mathbf{y}}_i, \{\delta_{i,j}\}_{j\neq i}\right)$.*
  4. *Set secret parameter $s_i := \left(\left\{\boldsymbol{s}_0^{i,j}\right\}_{j\in[m]/\{i\}}, \left\{\boldsymbol{s}_1^{j,i}\right\}_{j\in[m]/\{i\}}\right)$.*
- $\mathsf{Commit}(i, x_i, s_i, \mathsf{CRS})$:
  1. *Parse $s_i := \left(\left\{\boldsymbol{s}_0^{i,j}\right\}_{j\in[m]/\{i\}}, \left\{\boldsymbol{s}_1^{j,i}\right\}_{j\in[m]/\{i\}}\right)$, then parse any $\boldsymbol{s}_0^{i,j} := \left(\widetilde{k_0^1}, \widetilde{k_0^2}, \widetilde{\mathbf{y}}_i\right)$ and $\widetilde{\mathbf{y}}_i = \widetilde{\mathbf{y}'_i}||\widetilde{\mathbf{y}^*_i}$.*
  2. *Compute $\mathbf{y}_i' = \mathsf{sEval}\left(\widetilde{\mathbf{y}'_i}, l'\right)$.*
  3. *Generate an l'-by- l random binary code matrix $H^1_{l',l} \leftarrow \rho(l, l')$ and compute $\mathsf{v}_i' = \mathbf{y}_i' \cdot H^1_{l',l}$, where $l \geq |x_i|$ and $l' > l$.*
  4. *Set commitment $c_i := x_i \oplus \mathsf{v}_i'$.*
- $\mathsf{Compute}$: *See algorithm 2.*
- $\mathsf{Recover}$: *See algorithm 3.*

Algorithm 2 (Compute)

- *Parameters: Let C be the description of a circuit and Φ be a T-round conforming protocol for computing C.*
- $\mathsf{Compute}\left(i, x_i, s_i, \mathsf{CRS}, \{c_j\}_{j\in[m]}, C\right)$:

1. *Parse* $s_i := \left(\left\{\boldsymbol{s}_0^{i,j}\right\}_{j\in[m]/\{i\}}, \left\{\boldsymbol{s}_1^{j,i}\right\}_{j\in[m]/\{i\}}\right)$.
2. *Generate a* $(n'-l')$*-by-*$(n-l)$ *random binary code matrix* $H^2_{n'-l',n-l} \leftarrow \rho(n',l')$, *and set*
$$H_{n',n} := \begin{bmatrix} H^1_{l',l} & \\ & H^2_{n'-l',n-l} \end{bmatrix}$$
3. $\left(\mathsf{v}_i, \left\{m^{i,j}_{t,(\alpha,\beta)}\right\}_{t,\alpha,\beta,j}\right) \leftarrow \mathsf{PCG.Expand}_{\mathsf{GS}}\left(1^\lambda, 0, \{\boldsymbol{s}_0^{i,j}\}_{j\neq i}, H_{n',n}, \{\phi_t\}_{t\in[q]}\right)$,
$\left(\delta_{j,i}, \left\{m^{j,i}_{t,(\alpha,\beta),0}\right\}_{t,\alpha,\beta,j}\right) \leftarrow \mathsf{PCG.Expand}_{\mathsf{GS}}\left(1^\lambda, 1, \{\boldsymbol{s}_1^{j,i}\}_{j\neq i}, H_{n',n}, \{\phi_t\}_{t\in[q]}\right)$.
4. *For each* $t \in T$ *such that* $\phi_t := (i, f, g, h)$, *and each* $j \in [m]/\{i\}$, *compute* $\left\{\widetilde{m}^{i,j}_{t,(\alpha,\beta)}\right\}_{t,\alpha,\beta} := \left\{\rho\left(m^{i,j}_{t,(\alpha,\beta)}\right)\right\}_{t,\alpha,\beta}$.
For each $t \in T$ *such that* $\phi_t := (j, f, g, h)$ *for* $j \neq i$,
   - *Set* $\left\{m^{j,i}_{t,(\alpha,\beta),1}\right\}_{t,\alpha,\beta} := \left\{m^{j,i}_{t,(\alpha,\beta),0} + \delta_{j,i}\right\}_{t,\alpha,\beta}$.
   - $\left\{\widetilde{m}^{j,i}_{(t,(\alpha,\beta),0)}, \widetilde{m}^{j,i}_{(t,(\alpha,\beta),1)}\right\}_{t,\alpha,\beta} := \left\{\rho\left(m^{j,i}_{(t,(\alpha,\beta),0)}\right), \rho\left(m^{j,i}_{(t,(\alpha,\beta),1)}\right)\right\}_{t,\alpha,\beta}$
5. *Parse* $\mathsf{v}_i := \mathsf{v}_i'||\mathsf{v}_i^*$ *and adjust* v_i^* *so that* $pq = |\mathsf{v}_i^*|$. *Initialize a computation tape* $\mathsf{st}_i := c_1||0^{pq}||\ldots||c_m||0^{pq}$. *Let* $N := |\mathsf{st}_i|$.
6. *Set* $\overline{\boldsymbol{lab}}^{i,T+1} := \left(\boldsymbol{lab}^{i,T+1}_{k,0}, \boldsymbol{lab}^{i,T+1}_{k,1}\right)_{k\in[N]}$ *where for each* $k \in [N]$ *and* $b \in \{0,1\}$ $\boldsymbol{lab}^{i,T+1}_{k,b} = 0^\lambda$.
7. *For each* t *from* T *to 1, compute:*
$$\left(\widetilde{\mathsf{P}}^{i,t}, \overline{\boldsymbol{lab}}^{i,t}\right) \leftarrow \mathsf{Garble}\left(1^\lambda, \mathsf{P}^{i,t}\right).$$
where the circuit $\mathsf{P}^{i,t}$ *hardcodes party* i*'s receiver and sender strings, as well as all input labels of* $\mathsf{P}^{i,t+1}$ *(see algorithm 4).*
8. *Set* $\widehat{\boldsymbol{lab}}^{i,1} := \left\{\boldsymbol{lab}^{i,1}_{k,\mathsf{st}_{i,k}}\right\}_{k\in[N]}$
9. *Set message* $m_i := \left(\left\{\widetilde{\mathsf{P}}^{i,t}\right\}_{t\in[T]}, \widehat{\boldsymbol{lab}}^{i,1}\right)$.

Algorithm 3 (Recover)

- *Parameters: Let Φ be the conforming protocol that computes circuit C. Let T be total number of rounds of Φ.*
- $\mathsf{Recover}\left(\{m_j\}_{j\in[m]}\right)$:
  1. *For each $j \in [m]$, parse $m_j := \left(\left\{\widetilde{\mathsf{P}}^{j,t}\right\}_{t\in[T]}, \widehat{\boldsymbol{lab}}^{j,1}\right)$.*
  2. *For each t from 1 to T, do:*
     (a) *Parse action $\phi_t := (i^*, f, g, h)$.*
     (b) *Compute $\left(\gamma_t, \left\{\widetilde{m}_t^{i^*,j}\right\}_{j\in[m]/\{i^*\}}, \widehat{\boldsymbol{lab}}^{i^*,t+1}\right) \leftarrow \mathsf{GEval}\left(\widetilde{\mathsf{P}}^{i^*,t}, \widehat{\boldsymbol{lab}}^{i^*,t}\right)$.*
     (c) *For each $j \neq i^*$, do:*
        i. *Compute $(a_0, a_1) \leftarrow \mathsf{GEval}\left(\widetilde{\mathsf{P}}^{j,t}, \widehat{\boldsymbol{lab}}^{j,t}\right)$.*
        ii. *Recover $\boldsymbol{lab}_h^{j,t+1} = a_{\gamma_t} \oplus \widetilde{m}_t^{i^*,j}$.*
        iii. *Reset $\widehat{\boldsymbol{lab}}^{j,t+1} := \left\{\{\boldsymbol{lab}_{k,\mathsf{st}_{j,k}}^{j,t+1}\}_{k\in[N]/\{h\}}, \boldsymbol{lab}_h^{j,t+1}\right\}$.*
  3. *Let $\mathsf{Z} := (\gamma_1, \ldots, \gamma_T)$, set $Y := \mathsf{post}(\mathsf{Z})$.*

Algorithm 4 (Circuit $\mathsf{P}^{i,t}$)
Input: st_i.
Hardwired inputs: Party i's masking bits v_i, its receiver and sender strings $\left\{\widetilde{m}_{t,(\alpha,\beta)}^{i,j}\right\}_{\alpha,\beta\in\{0,1\},j\in[m]/\{i\}}$, $\left\{\left(\widetilde{m}_{(t,(\alpha,\beta),0)}^{j,i}, \widetilde{m}_{(t,(\alpha,\beta),1)}^{j,i}\right)\right\}_{\alpha,\beta\in\{0,1\},j\in[m]/\{i\}}$, the input labels of the next garbled circuit $\widetilde{\mathsf{P}}^{i,t+1}$: $\overline{\boldsymbol{lab}}^{i,t+1}$, and the round action ϕ_t.

1. *Parse $\phi_t = (i^*, f, g, h)$.*
2. *Set $\alpha := \mathsf{st}_i[(i^*-1)(pq+l)+f]$, $\beta := \mathsf{st}_i[(i^*-1)(pq+l)+g]$.*
3. *If $i = i^*$, then:*
   (a) *Set $\mathsf{v} := \mathsf{v}_i$, and compute $\gamma_{t,(\alpha,\beta)}^i = \mathit{NAND}(\mathsf{v}_f \oplus \alpha, \mathsf{v}_g \oplus \beta) \oplus \mathsf{v}_h$.*
   (b) *Set $\mathsf{st}_i[(i-1)(pq+l)+h] := \gamma_{t,(\alpha,\beta)}^i$.*
   (c) *Set $\widehat{\boldsymbol{lab}}^{i,t+1} := \left\{\boldsymbol{lab}_{k,\mathsf{st}_{i,k}}^{i,t+1}\right\}_{k\in[N]}$.*
   (d) *Output $\left(\gamma_{t,(\alpha,\beta)}^i, \left\{\widetilde{m}_{t,(\alpha,\beta)}^{i,j}\right\}_{j\in[m]/\{i\}}, \widehat{\boldsymbol{lab}}^{i,t+1}\right)$.*
4. *If $i \neq i^*$, then:*
   (a) *Set $\widehat{\boldsymbol{lab}}^{i,t+1} := \left\{\boldsymbol{lab}_{k,\mathsf{st}_{i,k}}^{i,t+1}\right\}_{k\in[N]/\{h\}}$.*
   (b) *Output $\left(\boldsymbol{lab}_{h,0}^{i,t+1} \oplus \widetilde{m}_{t,(\alpha,\beta),0}^{i^*,i}, \boldsymbol{lab}_{h,1}^{i,t+1} \oplus \widetilde{m}_{t,(\alpha,\beta),1}^{i^*,i}, \widehat{\boldsymbol{lab}}^{i,t+1}\right)$, where the label $\boldsymbol{lab}_h^{i,t+1}$ is the input for the bit $\mathsf{st}_i[(i^*-1)(pq+l)+h]$ of the next garbled circuit.*

Theorem 5. *Fix any constant $\epsilon > 0$ and let $n = \lambda^{1/\epsilon}$ be a polynomial in the security parameter. Assuming LPN with inverse polynomial error rate $1/n^{1-\epsilon}$ (where n is the LPN dimension), Protocol 2 is a secure multiparty silent NISC protocol in the random oracle model for computing circuits C of size at most n.*[5]

See Sect. 3.1 for more details about how we set LPN parameters based on the (polynomial-size) circuit C to be computed. The proof of this theorem is given in the full version [BGSZ21].

4.5 Extensions

Removing the Random Oracle. Our construction of multiparty silent NISC relies on a random oracle. Nevertheless, we can remove the use of random oracle, at the cost of introducing a large (growing with the size of the computation) CRS. Below we define this notion as multiparty silent NISC with large reusable CRS.

To begin with, one can observe that the previous construction utilizes the random oracle in two following ways:

- Modeling it as a correlation robust hash function; This is used to obtain random OTs from correlated OTs.
- Generating random binary code matrices for PCG seed expansion.

As already observed in [BCG+19b], the role of correlation robust hash function can be replaced by an encryption scheme which is semantically secure against related-key attack (RKA) for the class of linear functions. It was also shown that this encryption scheme can be based on standard LPN assumptions (over $\mathbb{F}_2$) [AHI11]. Therefore we can effectively remove this use of random oracle without introducing new assumptions. In slightly more detail, rather than using the hash of each string $m^{i,j}_{t,\alpha,\beta,b}$ to mask the corresponding label $\mathbf{lab}_b$, we instead encrypt $\mathbf{lab}_b$ with an RKA-secure encryption scheme using key $m^{i,j}_{t,\alpha,\beta,b}$. Then, in Hybrid_2 in the proof of Theorem 5, we can appeal to the RKA-security of the encryption scheme rather than the corelation-robustness of the random oracle.

Without using the random oracle, an easy way to solve the second problem is to let the Gen algorithm sample a random block-diagonal code matrix, and directly includes it in the CRS. This, however, requires that the Gen algorithm must take as input the circuit size bound L since the dimension of this code matrix must exceed the size of circuit to be computed. Furthermore, the CRS is large since its size now depends on the circuit size. As a result, the commit algorithm cannot take the whole CRS as input. So instead we split the block-diagonal code matrix, and only supply the small code matrix as input to the commit algorithm so as to remove its dependency on the circuit size. To summarize, we set $\mathsf{CRS} := (\mathsf{CRS}', \mathsf{CRS}^*) \leftarrow \mathsf{Gen}(1^\lambda, L)$ where $\mathsf{CRS}' := H^1_{l',l}$ and $\mathsf{CRS}^* := H^2_{n'-l',n-l}$. Notice that the size of CRS' only depends on the input size whereas CRS^* depends on the circuit size $|C| \leq L$. The commit algorithm now takes as input $(i, x_i, s_i, \mathsf{CRS}')$

[5] Here, by "size" of C, we mean the number of actions in the conforming protocol used to compute C.

whereas the compute algorithm still takes as input $\left(i, x_i, s_i, \mathsf{CRS}, \{c_j\}_{j\in[m]}, C\right)$. We adopt these notations for CRS in all following sections.

Reusable CRS. Although the CRS in the resulting protocol is large, it can be *reused* across an arbitrary polynomial number of multiparty silent NISC executions. This property will be crucial for our construction next section, so we give more details here. After the CRS is sampled, an adversary may specify any polynomial $q(\lambda)$ number of multiparty silent NISC executions in which it would like to participate using the same fixed CRS (but fresh preprocessing, commitment, and compute phases). Security for each of these executions will still follow from the LPN assumption. To see why, recall that the CRS is a dual-LPN matrix H, and is only used in the security proof when appealing to the dual-LPN assumption. By a straightforward hybrid argument, dual-LPN will hold with respect to a single random matrix H for any polynomial $q(\lambda)$ number of samples.

5 Reusable Two-Round MPC from LPN

In this section, we build on top of our previous result and show a compiler that takes any multiparty silent NISC with large reusable CRS and produces a reusable two-round MPC protocol. This section is organized as follows: we divide our compiler into three parts, each part involving one specific transformation. We proceed and give constructions of these transformations one by one in each subsection:

1. We define the notion of bounded FMS-MPC and show that multiparty silent NISC with reusable large CRS implies bounded FMS-MPC.
2. We show that bounded FMS-MPC implies standard FMS-MPC
3. Finally, we appeal to [BGMM20], who show that FMS-MPC implies reusable two-round MPC.

5.1 Multiparty Silent NISC with Reusable Large CRS $\rightarrow$ Bounded FMS-MPC

We start by defining a relaxed notion of first message succinct MPC (FMS-MPC), which was introduced in [BGMM20]. We call this new primitive a bounded FMS-MPC, which can be naturally thought as a middle ground between a multiparty silent NISC and a standard FMS-MPC.

Definition 6 (Bounded FMS-MPC). *Let* Gen *be an algorithm that generates a* CRS. *We say that the protocol* $\pi^* = (\mathsf{Gen}, \mathsf{BFMS.MPC}_1, \mathsf{BFMS.MPC}_2, \mathsf{BFMS.MPC}_3)$ *is a bounded FMS-MPC protocol if it is a two-round MPC protocol with the following properties:*

- *Bounded circuit size: The* Gen *algorithm takes as input the security parameter* λ, *a circuit size bound* L, *and outputs a* $\mathsf{CRS} := (\mathsf{CRS}', \mathsf{CRS}^*)$. *The size of* CRS' *only depends on an upper bound on input size, whereas the size of* CRS^* *can be as large as* L. *Moreover, the protocol* π^* *only supports circuits such that* $|C| \leq L$.

- *Reusable CRS: The part* CRS^* *only needs to be set up once, and can be reused across an unbounded polynomial number of two-round MPC protocols.*
- *First message succinctness: The* $\mathsf{BFMS.MPC}_1$ *algorithm takes as input* $(1^\lambda, \mathsf{CRS}', i, x_i)$*. In particular, its runtime should not depend on the circuit size* $|C|$.

As our construction of bounded FMS-MPC from multiparty silent NISC is very similar to the transformation given in [BGMM20, Section 5], we defer the construction and security proof to the full version [BGSZ21]. In particular, we prove the following theorem.

Theorem 6. *Assuming a semi-honest multiparty silent NISC with large reusable CRS and a maliciously-secure vanilla two-round MPC in the CRS model, there exists a maliciously-secure bounded FMS-MPC protocol.*

Due to results from last section and [DGH+20], we have the following corollary.

Corollary 1. *Fix any constant* $\epsilon > 0$ *and let* $n = \lambda^{1/\epsilon}$ *be a polynomial in the security parameter. Assuming LPN with inverse polynomial error rate* $1/n^{1-\epsilon}$*, there exists a maliciously-secure bounded FMS-MPC protocol supporting circuits* C *of size at most* n.

5.2 Bounded FMS-MPC → FMS-MPC

In order to obtain standard FMS-MPC, we must allow for computation of a priori unbounded polynomial size circuits. That is, we must support the computation of unbounded polynomial size circuits using only a bounded polynomial size CRS. A natural idea is then to use *randomized encodings* to break down the computation of any unbounded polynomial size circuit into the computation of a number of *bounded* polynomial size circuits, and use a bounded size (reusable) CRS to compute each small circuit.

Indeed, any m-input polynomial-size circuit $C : \{0,1\}^{m \cdot \ell} \to \{0,1\}^{\ell'}$ admits a randomized encoding, which can be written as a sequence of small circuits $\{G_y : \{0,1\}^{m \cdot \ell} \times \{0,1\}^\lambda \to \{0,1\}^s\}_{y \in [n]}$, where n depends on the size of C, but each G_y has size $p(\lambda)$ for some a priori *fixed* polynomial $p(\cdot)$. The correctness of randomized encoding ensures that for any inputs $x_1, \ldots, x_m$ and random coins $v \leftarrow \{0,1\}^\lambda$, one can recover the output $Y := C(x_1, \ldots, x_m)$ just given $\{G_y(x_1, \ldots, x_m, v)\}_{y \in [n]}$. The security of randomized encoding guarantees that this distribution is simulatable just given the output Y.

Now, one could naively compute n bounded FMS-MPC protocols in parallel to determine the outputs of $G_1, \ldots, G_n$. However, the total number of first round messages would now depend on $|C|$, violating first message succinctness. To circumvent this issue, we delay the computation of those first round messages to the second round. Following the GGM approach, we define a complete binary tree based on the circuit being computed. This tree will have n leaves in total and will be of depth $d = \log(n)$. The y'th leaf is associated with the randomized encoding G_y. Each internal node is associated with an expansion circuit E. This circuit takes as input $(x_1, \ldots, x_m, v)$ and some additional secret randomness, and generates two sets of fresh first round messages, one for each child node. By computing all the expansion circuits using bounded FMS-MPC, we generate a set of fresh first round messages for each leaf node, enabling computation of all randomized encoding circuits using n more bounded FMS-MPC instances. Furthermore, since the CRS of the bounded FMS-MPC has unbounded reusability, it can be used by each node computation in this tree.

To fully compute this tree, each party needs to output its second round message for each node computation in each level, and read all other parties' second round messages. This allows it to recover a new set of first round messages which is required for node computations in the next level. If we implement this protocol naively, the number of rounds in total would match the depth of the tree. Nonetheless, one can still compress it to just two rounds by repeatedly applying the round collapsing transformation: In the first round, each party i outputs its first round message of a bounded FMS-MPC for computing the first expansion circuit (root node). In the second round, party i first outputs its second round message for this bounded FMS-MPC. Then for each level $k \in [2, d-1]$, party i outputs 2^{k-1} garbled circuits which realizes its MPC_2 functionality at this level. That is, for each $y \in [2^{k-1}]$, it computes a garbled circuit of $\mathsf{MPC}_2(\mathsf{E}, (\cdot, \mathsf{CRS}^*), \cdot, \cdot)$. This circuit hardwires the description of E and the part CRS^*. It takes as input the part CRS', party i's first round state and all first round messages for computing the yth expansion circuit in this level, and outputs its second round message. In the last level, for each $y \in [n]$, party i computes a garbled circuit of $\mathsf{MPC}_2(\mathsf{F}_y, (\cdot, \mathsf{CRS}^*), \cdot, \cdot)$, where F_y computes the randomized encoding G_y. These garbled circuits constitute party i's second round message.

In order to recover the input labels for each garbled circuit, we ask each expansion circuit E to output the input labels which correspond to the correct inputs for each party's next garbled circuit. Each party will actually output encryptions of all input labels along with each garbled circuit, and each expansion circuit will output keys that can be used to decrypt only the correct input labels for each party's next garbled circuit.

It is worth noting that this use of "tree of MPC messages" differs somewhat from how it is used in [AJJM20,BGMM20]. In particular, we build a tree of polynomial size. In order to compute a single large circuit in the second round, each party releases a garbled circuit for each node in the tree. During output reconstruction, the *entire* tree is evaluated. In [AJJM20,BGMM20], to obtain reusability, they set up a implicit tree of *exponential* size. Each time the parties wish to compute a circuit in the second round, they each release a sequence of garbled circuits that trace one root to leaf path in this exponentially-sized tree.

As a final point, since the size of the CRS in a FMS-MPC should only depend on the security parameter λ, we must argue that the CRS we are using is small. Notice that for every node in this tree, either the expansion circuit E or some randomized encoding G_y is computed. The size of either circuit only depends on λ. Therefore it suffices to set $L = \text{poly}(\lambda)$ for some fixed polynomial when instantiating the bounded FMS-MPC. As a result, the CRS only depends on λ, which is what is required for FMS-MPC.

Applying this transformation, we build a FMS-MPC (described in protocol 3) from bounded FMS-MPC.

Protocol 3 (FMS-MPC)
Let $(\mathsf{Gen}, \mathsf{MPC}_1, \mathsf{MPC}_2, \mathsf{MPC}_3)$ *be a bounded FMS-MPC protocol,* $(\mathsf{Garble}, \mathsf{GEval})$ *be a garbling scheme,* $(\mathsf{LabEnc}, \mathsf{LabDec})$ *be a label encryption scheme and* $(\mathsf{CRE.Enc}, \mathsf{CRE.Dec})$ *be a computational randomized encoding scheme. Let* $\mathsf{PRG} = (\mathsf{G}_0, \mathsf{G}_1, \mathsf{H}_0, \mathsf{H}_1)$ *be a length quadrupling PRG. The expansion circuit* E *is defined in algorithm 7 and circuit* F_y *is defined in algorithm 8. Let* $L = max(|\mathsf{E}|, |\mathsf{F}_y|)$ *and* $\mathsf{CRS} := (\mathsf{CRS}', \mathsf{CRS}^*) \leftarrow \mathsf{Gen}(1^\lambda, L)$.

- $\mathsf{FMS.MPC}_1\left(1^\lambda, \mathsf{CRS}', i, x_i\right)$:
  1. *Sample* $(r_i, v_i) \leftarrow \{0,1\}^\lambda \times \{0,1\}^\lambda$ *and compute* $\left(\mathsf{st}_i^{(1)}, \mathsf{msg}_i^{(1)}\right) \leftarrow \mathsf{MPC}_1\left(1^\lambda, \mathsf{CRS}', i, ((x_i, v_i), r_i)\right)$.
  2. *Set* $\mathsf{FMS.st}_i^{(1)} := \left(\mathsf{st}_i^{(1)}, r_i, v_i\right)$ *and* $\mathsf{FMS.msg}_i^{(1)} := \mathsf{msg}_i^{(1)}$.
- $\mathsf{FMS.MPC}_2\left(C, \mathsf{CRS}, \mathsf{FMS.st}_i^{(1)}, \left\{\mathsf{FMS.msg}_j^{(1)}\right\}_{j\in[m]}\right)$:
  1. *Compute* $[G_y]_{y\in[n]} \leftarrow \mathsf{CRE.Enc}\left(1^\lambda, C\right)$.
  2. *Define a complete binary tree of depth* $d = \log(n)$ *with* n *leaves. Associate the* y^{th} *leaf with the randomized encoding* G_y.
  3. *Let* $r_i^{(k,y)}$ *denotes party* i*'s secret randomness for computing the* y^{th} *node at level* k. *Set* $r_i^{(1,1)} := r_i$; *compute* $r_i^{(2,1)} := \mathsf{G}_0\left(r_i^{(1,1)}\right)$, $r_i^{(2,2)} := \mathsf{G}_1\left(r_i^{(1,1)}\right)$.
  4. *Compute* $k_i^{(2,1)} := \mathsf{H}_0\left(r_i^{(1,1)}\right)$, $k_i^{(2,2)} := \mathsf{H}_1\left(r_i^{(1,1)}\right)$.
  5. *Compute* $\mathsf{msg}_i^{(2)} \leftarrow \mathsf{MPC}_2\left(\mathsf{E}, \mathsf{CRS}, \mathsf{st}_i^{(1)}, \left\{\mathsf{msg}_j^{(1)}\right\}_{j\in[m]}\right)$.
  6. *For each level* $k \in [2, d-1]$ *and for each* $y \in [1, 2^{k-1}]$*:*
     (a) *Compute* $\left(\widetilde{C}_i^{(k,y)}, \overline{\boldsymbol{lab}}_i^{(k,y)}\right) \leftarrow \mathsf{Garble}\left(1^\lambda,\ \mathsf{MPC}_2\left(\mathsf{E},\ (\cdot\ ,\ \mathsf{CRS}^*),\ \cdot\ ,\ \cdot\right)\right)$.
     (b) *Compute* $\overline{\boldsymbol{elab}}_i^{(k,y)} \leftarrow \mathsf{LabEnc}\left(\overline{K}_i^{(k,y)}, \overline{\boldsymbol{lab}}_i^{(k,y)}\right)$, *where* $\overline{K}_i^{(k,y)} = \mathsf{PRF}\left(k_i^{(k,y)}, (t,b)\right)_{t\in[l], b\in\{0,1\}}$.
     (c) *Compute* $r_i^{(k+1,2y-1)} := \mathsf{G}_0\left(r_i^{(k,y)}\right)$, $r_i^{(k+1,2y)} := \mathsf{G}_1\left(r_i^{(k,y)}\right)$; $k_i^{(k+1,2y-1)} := \mathsf{H}_0\left(r_i^{(k,y)}\right)$, $k_i^{(k+1,2y)} := \mathsf{H}_1\left(r_i^{(k,y)}\right)$.
  7. *In the last level* d*, for each* $y \in [n]$*:*
     (a) *Compute* $\left(\widetilde{C}_i^{(d,y)}, \overline{\boldsymbol{lab}}_i^{(d,y)}\right) \leftarrow \mathsf{Garble}\left(1^\lambda,\ \mathsf{MPC}_2\left(\mathsf{F}_y,\ (\cdot\ ,\ \mathsf{CRS}^*),\ \cdot\ ,\ \cdot\right)\right)$;
     (b) *Compute* $\overline{\boldsymbol{elab}}_i^{(d,y)} \leftarrow \mathsf{LabEnc}\left(\overline{K}_i^{(d,y)}, \overline{\boldsymbol{lab}}_i^{(d,y)}\right)$ *where* $\overline{K}_i^{(d,y)} = \mathsf{PRF}\left(k_i^{(d,y)}, (t,b)\right)_{t\in[l], b\in\{0,1\}}$.
  8. *Set* $\mathsf{FMS.msg}_i^{(2)} := \left(\mathsf{msg}_i^{(2)}, \left\{\widetilde{C}_i^{(k,y)}, \overline{\boldsymbol{elab}}_i^{(k,y)}\right\}_{k\in[2,d], y\in[1,2^{k-1}]}\right)$.

- $\mathsf{FMS.MPC}_3\left(\left\{\mathsf{FMS.msg}_j^{(2)}\right\}_{j\in[m]}\right)$:
  1. *Compute* $\left\{\left(\widehat{K}_i^{(2,1)}, \widehat{K}_i^{(2,2)}\right)\right\}_{i\in[m]} \leftarrow \mathsf{MPC}_3\left(\left\{\mathsf{msg}_j^{(2)}\right\}_{j\in[m]}\right)$.
  2. *For each level* $k \in [2,d]$ *and each* $y \in [1, 2^{k-1}]$:
     (a) *For each* $j \in [m]$:
        i. *Compute* $\widehat{\boldsymbol{lab}}_j^{(k,y)} \leftarrow \mathsf{LabDec}\left(\widehat{K}_j^{(k,y)}, \overline{\boldsymbol{elab}}_j^{(k,y)}\right)$;
        ii. *Compute* $\left(\mathsf{msg}_j^{(2),(k,y)}\right) \leftarrow \mathsf{GEval}\left(\widetilde{C}_j^{(k,y)}, \widehat{\boldsymbol{lab}}_j^{(k,y)}\right)$.
     (b) *If* $k < d$, *then compute*
     $\left\{\left(\widehat{K}_i^{(k+1,2y-1)}, \widehat{K}_i^{(k+1,2y)}\right)\right\}_{i\in[m]} \leftarrow \mathsf{MPC}_3\left(\left\{\mathsf{msg}_j^{(2),(k,y)}\right\}_{j\in[m]}\right)$.
     (c) *If* $k = d$, *compute*
     $G_y((x_1,\ldots,x_m),v) \leftarrow \mathsf{MPC}_3\left(\left\{\mathsf{msg}_j^{(2),(d,y)}\right\}_{j\in[m]}\right)$.
  3. *Set* $Y \leftarrow \mathsf{CRE.Dec}\left(1^\lambda, C, \{G_y((x_1,\ldots,x_m),v)\}_{y\in[n]}\right)$.

Algorithm 7 (Circuit E**)**
Input: $\{(x_j,v_j),r_j\}_{j\in[m]}$.
Hardwired inputs: Description of a length-quadruple $\mathsf{PRG} : (\mathsf{G}_0,\mathsf{G}_1,\mathsf{H}_0,\mathsf{H}_1)$.

1. *For each* $i \in [m]$ *(Generating the left child):*
   (a) *Compute* $\mathsf{CRS'}^0 \leftarrow \mathsf{Gen}(1^\lambda)$.
   (b) *Compute* $\left(\mathsf{st}_i^{(1),0}, \mathsf{msg}_i^{(1),0}\right) \leftarrow \mathsf{MPC}_1\left(1^\lambda, \mathsf{CRS'}^0, i, ((x_i,v_i), \mathsf{G}_0(r_i))\right)$.
2. *For each* $i \in [m]$:
   (a) *Set* $k_i^0 := \mathsf{H}_0(r_i)$, $z_i^0 := \left(\mathsf{CRS'}^0, \mathsf{st}_i^{(1),0}, \left\{\mathsf{msg}_j^{(1),0}\right\}_{j\in[m]}\right)$.
   (b) *Let* $l := |z_i^0|$. *For* $t \in [l]$, *set* $K_{i,t}^0 := \mathsf{PRF}\left(k_i^0, (t, z_i^0[t])\right)$.
   (c) *Set* $\widehat{K}_i^0 := \{K_{i,t}^0\}_{t\in[l]}$.
3. *For each* $i \in [m]$ *(Generating the right child):*
   (a) *Compute* $\mathsf{CRS'}^1 \leftarrow \mathsf{Gen}(1^\lambda)$.
   (b) *Compute* $\left(\mathsf{st}_i^{(1),1}, \mathsf{msg}_i^{(1),1}\right) \leftarrow \mathsf{MPC}_1\left(1^\lambda, \mathsf{CRS'}^1, i, ((x_i,v_i), \mathsf{G}_1(r_i))\right)$.
4. *For each* $i \in [m]$:
   (a) *Set* $k_i^1 := \mathsf{H}_1(r_i)$, $z_i^1 := \left(\mathsf{CRS'}^1, \mathsf{st}_i^{(1),1}, \left\{\mathsf{msg}_j^{(1),1}\right\}_{j\in[m]}\right)$.
   (b) *Let* $l := |z_i^1|$. *For* $t \in [l]$, *set* $K_{i,t}^1 := \mathsf{PRF}\left(k_i^1, (t, z_i^1[t])\right)$.
   (c) *Set* $\widehat{K}_i^1 = \{K_{i,t}^1\}_{t\in[l]}$.
5. *Output* $\left\{\widehat{K}_i^0\right\}_{i\in[m]}$ *and* $\left\{\widehat{K}_i^1\right\}_{i\in[m]}$.

Algorithm 8 (Circuit F_y)
Input: $\{(x_j, v_j), r_j\}_{j\in[m]}$.
Hardwired input: the randomized encoding G_y.

1. *Set* $v := v_1 \oplus \cdots \oplus v_m$.
2. *Output* $G_y((x_1, \ldots, x_m), v)$.

In the full version [BGSZ21], we prove the following theorem, which, combined with Corollary 1, gives the following corollary.

Theorem 9. *There exists a polynomial* $p(\cdot)$ *such that, assuming a maliciously-secure bounded FMS-MPC protocol supporting circuits of size at most* $p(\lambda)$, *there exists a maliciously-secure FMS-MPC protocol in the CRS model.*

Corollary 2. *There exists a constant* $\epsilon > 0$ *such that, assuming LPN with inverse polynomial error rate* $1/n^{1-\epsilon}$, *there exists a maliciously-secure FMS-MPC protocol in the CRS model.*

5.3 FMS-MPC → Reusable Two-Round MPC

It has been shown in previous work [BGMM20] that any maliciously-secure FMS-MPC protocol in the CRS model implies a maliciously-secure reusable two-round MPC protocol in the CRS model. Thus, we immediately have the following theorem.

Theorem 10. *There exists a constant* $\epsilon > 0$ *such that, assuming LPN with inverse polynomial error rate* $1/n^{1-\epsilon}$, *there exists a maliciously-secure reusable two-round MPC protocol in the CRS model.*

The Semi-honest Case. We have presented all of our results in this section in the malicious-security setting, which requires a CRS. However, we remark here that we can also achieve semi-honest secure reusable MPC in the plain model from LPN. In fact, we claim that any maliciously-secure reusable MPC in the CRS model plus semi-honest secure vanilla two-round MPC in the plain model implies a semi-honest secure reusable MPC in the plain model. As this transformation is nearly identical to that of [BGMM20, Section 5], we do not provide a formal proof, but give the following sketch.

The vanilla two-round MPC can be used to compute a CRS and first round messages of the reusable MPC, and release *garbled labels* of the CRS and first round messages to all parties. In the second round, each party also releases a garbled circuit that computes their second round message of the reusable MPC. Anyone can combine the labels for the CRS and labels for the first round messages with these garbled circuits to compute the second round messages and thus the output.

Acknowledgments. JB and SG were supported in part by DARPA under Agreement No. HR00112020026, AFOSR Award FA9550-19-1-0200, NSF CNS Award 1936826, and research grants by the Sloan Foundation, Visa Inc., and Center for Long-Term Cybersecurity (CLTC, UC Berkeley). Any opinions, findings and conclusions or recommendations expressed in this material are those of the author(s) and do not necessarily reflect the views of the United States Government or DARPA.

References

[AHI11] Applebaum, B., Harnik, D., Ishai, Y.: Semantic security under related-key attacks and applications. In: Chazelle, B. (ed.) ICS 2011, pp. 45–60. Tsinghua University Press, January 2011

[AIK05] Applebaum, B., Ishai, Y., Kushilevitz, E.: Computationally private randomizing polynomials and their applications (extended abstract). In: 20th Annual IEEE Conference on Computational Complexity (CCC 2005), pp. 260–274 (2005)

[AIK09] Applebaum, B., Ishai, Y., Kushilevitz, E.: Cryptography with constant input locality. J. Cryptol. **22**(4), 429–469 (2009)

[AJJM20] Ananth, P., Jain, A., Jin, Z., Malavolta, G.: Multi-key fully-homomorphic encryption in the plain model. In: Pass, R., Pietrzak, K. (eds.) TCC 2020. LNCS, vol. 12550, pp. 28–57. Springer, Cham (2020). https://doi.org/10.1007/978-3-030-64375-1_2

[BCG+19a] Boyle, E.: Efficient two-round OT extension and silent non-interactive secure computation. In: ACM CCS 19, pp. 291–308. ACM Press (2019)

[BCG+19b] Boyle, E., Couteau, G., Gilboa, N., Ishai, Y., Kohl, L., Scholl, P.: Efficient pseudorandom correlation generators: silent OT extension and more. In: Boldyreva, A., Micciancio, D. (eds.) CRYPTO 2019. LNCS, vol. 11694, pp. 489–518. Springer, Cham (2019). https://doi.org/10.1007/978-3-030-26954-8_16

[BGI+01] Barak, B., et al.: On the (Im)possibility of obfuscating programs. In: Kilian, J. (ed.) CRYPTO 2001. LNCS, vol. 2139, pp. 1–18. Springer, Heidelberg (2001). https://doi.org/10.1007/3-540-44647-8_1

[BGI16] Boyle, E., Gilboa, N., Ishai, Y.: Breaking the circuit size barrier for secure computation under DDH. In: Robshaw, M., Katz, J. (eds.) CRYPTO 2016. LNCS, vol. 9814, pp. 509–539. Springer, Heidelberg (2016). https://doi.org/10.1007/978-3-662-53018-4_19

[BGMM20] Benhamouda, F., Jain, A., Komargodski, I., Lin, H.: Multiparty reusable non-interactive secure computation from LWE. In: Canteaut, A., Standaert, F.-X. (eds.) EUROCRYPT 2021. LNCS, vol. 12697, pp. 724–753. Springer, Cham (2021). https://doi.org/10.1007/978-3-030-77886-6_25

[BGSZ21] Bartusek, J., Garg, S., Srinivasan, A., Zhang, Y.: Reusable two-round MPC from LPN. Cryptology ePrint Archive, Report 2021/316 (2021). https://ia.cr/2021/316

[BL18] Benhamouda, F., Lin, H.: k-round multiparty computation from k-round oblivious transfer via garbled interactive circuits. In: Nielsen, J.B., Rijmen, V. (eds.) EUROCRYPT 2018. LNCS, vol. 10821, pp. 500–532. Springer, Cham (2018). https://doi.org/10.1007/978-3-319-78375-8_17

[BL20] Benhamouda, F., Lin, H.: Multiparty reusable non-interactive secure computation. In: TCC (2020)

[DGH+20] Döttling, N., Garg, S., Hajiabadi, M., Masny, D., Wichs, D.: Two-round oblivious transfer from CDH or LPN. In: Canteaut, A., Ishai, Y. (eds.) EUROCRYPT 2020. LNCS, vol. 12106, pp. 768–797. Springer, Cham (2020). https://doi.org/10.1007/978-3-030-45724-2_26

[DHRW16] Dodis, Y., Halevi, S., Rothblum, R.D., Wichs, D.: Spooky encryption and its applications. In: Robshaw, M., Katz, J. (eds.) CRYPTO 2016. LNCS, vol. 9816, pp. 93–122. Springer, Heidelberg (2016). https://doi.org/10.1007/978-3-662-53015-3_4

[GGH+13] Garg, S., Gentry, C., Halevi, S., Raykova, M., Sahai, A., Waters, B.: Candidate indistinguishability obfuscation and functional encryption for all circuits. In: 54th FOCS, pp. 40–49. IEEE Computer Society Press, October 2013

[GGHR14] Garg, S., Gentry, C., Halevi, S., Raykova, M.: Two-round secure MPC from indistinguishability obfuscation. In: Lindell, Y. (ed.) TCC 2014. LNCS, vol. 8349, pp. 74–94. Springer, Heidelberg (2014). https://doi.org/10.1007/978-3-642-54242-8_4

[GI14] Gilboa, N., Ishai, Y.: Distributed point functions and their applications. In: Nguyen, P.Q., Oswald, E. (eds.) EUROCRYPT 2014. LNCS, vol. 8441, pp. 640–658. Springer, Heidelberg (2014). https://doi.org/10.1007/978-3-642-55220-5_35

[GIS18] Garg, S., Ishai, Y., Srinivasan, A.: Two-round MPC: information-theoretic and black-box. In: Beimel, A., Dziembowski, S. (eds.) TCC 2018. LNCS, vol. 11239, pp. 123–151. Springer, Cham (2018). https://doi.org/10.1007/978-3-030-03807-6_5

[GS17] Garg, S., Srinivasan, A.: Garbled protocols and two-round MPC from bilinear maps. In: 58th FOCS, pp. 588–599. IEEE Computer Society Press (2017)

[GS18a] Garg, S., Srinivasan, A.: Two-round multiparty secure computation from minimal assumptions. In: Nielsen, J.B., Rijmen, V. (eds.) EUROCRYPT 2018. LNCS, vol. 10821, pp. 468–499. Springer, Cham (2018). https://doi.org/10.1007/978-3-319-78375-8_16

[IKNP03] Ishai, Y., Kilian, J., Nissim, K., Petrank, E.: Extending oblivious transfers efficiently (2003)

[JKPT12] Jain, A., Krenn, S., Pietrzak, K., Tentes, A.: Commitments and efficient zero-knowledge proofs from learning parity with noise. In: Wang, X., Sako, K. (eds.) ASIACRYPT 2012. LNCS, vol. 7658, pp. 663–680. Springer, Heidelberg (2012). https://doi.org/10.1007/978-3-642-34961-4_40

[MW16] Mukherjee, P., Wichs, D.: Two round multiparty computation via multi-key FHE. In: Fischlin, M., Coron, J.-S. (eds.) EUROCRYPT 2016. LNCS, vol. 9666, pp. 735–763. Springer, Heidelberg (2016). https://doi.org/10.1007/978-3-662-49896-5_26

[Reg05] Regev, O.: On lattices, learning with errors, random linear codes, and cryptography. In: Gabow, H.N., Fagin, R. (eds.) 37th ACM STOC, pp. 84–93. ACM Press, May 2005

On the Bottleneck Complexity of MPC with Correlated Randomness

Claudio Orlandi, Divya Ravi(✉), and Peter Scholl

Aarhus University, Aarhus, Denmark
{orlandi,divya,peter.scholl}@cs.au.dk

Abstract. At ICALP 2018, Boyle et al. introduced the notion of the *bottleneck complexity* of a secure multi-party computation (MPC) protocol. This measures the maximum communication complexity of any one party in the protocol, aiming to improve load-balancing among the parties.

In this work, we study the bottleneck complexity of MPC in the preprocessing model, where parties are given correlated randomness ahead of time. We present two constructions of *bottleneck-efficient* MPC protocols, whose bottleneck complexity is independent of the number of parties:

1. A protocol for computing abelian programs, based only on one-way functions.
2. A protocol for selection functions, based on any linearly homomorphic encryption scheme.

Compared with previous bottleneck-efficient constructions, our protocols can be based on a wider range of assumptions, and avoid the use of fully homomorphic encryption.

1 Introduction

Secure Multiparty Computation (MPC) [Yao86,GMW87,BGW88,CCD88] allows a set of mutually distrusting parties to jointly perform a computation on their private inputs in a way no information about their inputs is revealed, except the output of the computation.

There are various fundamental metrics with respect to which the efficiency of an MPC protocol can be measured such as round complexity, communication complexity and computation complexity. Among these, *communication complexity*, which measures the total number of bits communicated by honest parties in the protocol, is often cited as one of the most important ones in practical applications. In this work we study a particular flavour of communication

Research supported by: the Concordium Blockhain Research Center, Aarhus University, Denmark; the Carlsberg Foundation under the Semper Ardens Research Project CF18-112 (BCM); the European Research Council (ERC) under the European Unions's Horizon 2020 research and innovation programme under grant agreement No 803096 (SPEC); the Aarhus University Research Foundation (AUFF); the Independent Research Fund Denmark (DFF) under project number 0165-00107B; the Digital Research Centre Denmark (DIREC);.

G. Hanaoka et al. (Eds.): PKC 2022, LNCS 13177, pp. 194–220, 2022.
https://doi.org/10.1007/978-3-030-97121-2_8

complexity for MPC, namely *bottleneck complexity* ($\mathcal{BC}$). While there has been extensive research aimed at optimizing the communication complexity of MPC protocols, most of these works do not take into account the fact that parties may have asymmetric roles in the protocol, and communication may be unevenly distributed. The work of [BJPY18] addressed this concern by introducing *bottleneck complexity* as a new efficiency metric.

Informally, bottleneck complexity is the maximum communication required by any party within the protocol computation. To illustrate the difference between communication complexity and bottleneck complexity, consider two protocols – say, in the first protocol each party sends a bit to a central party while in the second one, the parties communicate in a chain-like fashion with party P_i sending one bit to P_{i+1} (for $i \in [1, n-1]$, where n is the number of parties). Both these protocols have total communication complexity $\Theta(n)$ but differ significantly in their bottleneck complexities. The first protocol has $\Theta(n)$ bottleneck complexity, while the second has $O(1)$ bottleneck complexity. If the receiving bandwidth of the central party in the first protocol becomes the bottleneck, the second protocol with low bottleneck complexity would be preferred in most practical scenarios. With this motivation, the work of [BJPY18] initiated the study of bottleneck complexity.

In the setting of bottleneck complexity, the focus is on protocols between large number of parties, and the goal is designing protocols with bottleneck complexity *independent of the number of parties.* Such protocols as thus referred as being *$\mathcal{BC}$-efficient.* On the lower bounds side, the work of [BJPY18] shows that, for general functions, achieving even sublinear (in the number of parties n) communication complexity is not always possible – even when no security is required! On the positive side, they present a generic compiler based on fully-homomorphic encryption (FHE) that transforms an insecure MPC protocol into a secure MPC protocol while preserving the bottleneck complexity.

It is well known that homomorphic encryption (in one or other of its many flavours) is a powerful tool for compiling protocols with low communication complexity (see for instance [NN01,IP07,DFH12,AJL+12,LNO13]). However, FHE is still relatively inefficient, and we only know how to construct it using the learning with errors (LWE) assumption [BV11] or the heavy machinery of indistinguishability obfuscation [CLTV15]. It is therefore very natural to ask the question:

For which functions can we achieve low bottleneck complexity without using FHE?

1.1 Our Contribution

In this work, we investigate the feasibility of $\mathcal{BC}$-efficient MPC without using heavy tools such as FHE. Instead, we focus on protocols which make use of correlated randomness and "traditional" assumptions such as one-way functions and (for one of our constructions) linearly homomorphic encryption (which can be instantiated with "90s" style assumptions based on discrete logarithms, factoring, etc.). All of our protocols are secure against a semi-honest (passive) adversary who may corrupt an arbitrary number of parties.

In this setting, we provide $\mathcal{BC}$-efficient protocols for the following classes of functions:

Abelian Programs. Abelian programs are defined as functions on the sum of the parties' inputs over an abelian group. More formally, an abelian program h takes n elements from an abelian group G as input and outputs $h(x_1, \ldots, x_n) = f(\sum_{i=1}^{n} x_i)$ for some function $f : G \rightarrow \{0, 1\}$. This is an expressive class of functions that can be used to securely perform e.g., voting or linear classifiers (see [EOYN21] for more details about applications of abelian programs).

As a warm-up, we design $\mathcal{BC}$-efficient protocols for simple boolean functions such as AND and XOR, which can be viewed as special cases of abelian programs. These protocols incur bottleneck complexity of $O(\lambda)$ and $O(1)$ respectively. We generalize the approach of these protocols and propose a $\mathcal{BC}$-efficient protocol for abelian programs that has bottleneck complexity $O(\lambda^2)$ (which is independent of n), where λ denotes the security parameter. Our construction is based on garbled circuits, and therefore can be built from one-way functions.

Selection Functions. A selection function is a function of the form $f(x_1 = \mathsf{q}, x_2, \ldots, x_n) = x_{\mathsf{q}}$, where P_1's input is a selection index $\mathsf{q} \in \{2, \ldots, n\}$ and the inputs of the other parties are in $\mathbb{Z}_M$ (set of integers modulo M).

We design a $\mathcal{BC}$-efficient protocol for selection functions that has bottleneck complexity $\mathsf{poly}(\lambda)$ (independent of n), where λ denotes the security parameter. Our construction uses additively homomorphic encryption and garbled circuits as the main tools, which can be instantiated under standard number-theoretic assumptions like decisional Diffie-Hellman, quadratic residuosity, N-th residuosity or learning with errors.

On the Communication Pattern of $\mathcal{BC}$-Efficient Protocols. We defer the detailed high-level overviews of the protocols to the respective technical section and highlight an important and common aspect of our $\mathcal{BC}$-efficient constructions below. As a starting point towards designing $\mathcal{BC}$-efficient protocols, we begin by analyzing what types of interaction patterns in MPC support the bottleneck complexity as being independent of the number of parties. The most common interaction pattern in MPC protocols is a complete network (where every pair of parties communicate with each other). Some other popular restricted interaction patterns include 'star' (where all parties interact with a central party) [BGI+14, HIJ+16] and 'chain' (where parties interact over a simple directed path traversing all nodes) [HIJ+16, IMO18]. It is easy to see that the 'chain' interaction pattern is promising to design $\mathcal{BC}$-efficient protocols. This is because it involves each party communicating with only a *constant* number of parties. However, we need two additional properties that a $\mathcal{BC}$-efficient protocol over a chain must satisfy: First, the number of communication traversals or passes over the chain must also be independent of n. Second, the size of the message communicated by each party to its neighbour must also be independent of n. All our protocols thereby entail a constant number of passes over a chain-like structure, where each message communicated is independent of n. We refer to the technical sections for further details.

Open Problems. As mentioned above, the study of bottleneck complexity in MPC is inherently tied to the bottleneck complexity of protocols *without security*, since not every function can be $\mathcal{BC}$-efficient [BJPY18]. It remains an open question to more thoroughly characterize which functions allow $\mathcal{BC}$-efficient protocols in the clear. With privacy, an interesting challenge is to obtain (even in the correlated randomness model) a compiler that transforms a (possibly insecure) protocol into a secure one with the same bottleneck complexity, while using non-FHE assumptions as considered in this work.

1.2 Related Work

The most relevant work to ours is the work of [BJPY18] which introduced the notion of bottleneck complexity. As mentioned previously, [BJPY18] presents a generic compiler based on fully-homomorphic encryption (FHE) that transforms an insecure MPC protocol into a secure MPC protocol while preserving the bottleneck complexity. For the two-party setting, such a compiler was proposed by the work of [NN01] (this compiler preserved communication complexity; however the notions of bottleneck and communication complexity align in the two-party case). The work of [FKLS20] in the massive parallel computation model focuses on minimizing the storage/communication of servers (which is similar to our goal of minimizing bottleneck complexity). However, similar to [BJPY18], their compiler from an insecure to secure protocol in the parallel computation model is based on FHE (which we wish to avoid).

Related to the setting of MPC with huge number of parties that we consider in this work, the study of scalable MPC was initiated by [DI06] and further explored in works of [DIK+08]. However, these works focus on optimizing communication complexity relative to the circuit size. Similarly, several works on optimizing communication complexity of MPC protocols such as [Cou19, DNPR16, IKM+13] in the information-theoretic setting with correlated randomness and [QWW18, ABJ+19] in the computational setting also focus on regulating the dependence on circuit size. The protocols in these works incur $\Omega(n)$ bottleneck complexity (which is inherent as shown by [BJPY18], since these protocols are for arbitrary functions).

Another related line of work is MPC protocols that involve a one-pass 'chain' interaction pattern, which includes works such as [HIJ+16]. Further, the protocols of [HLP11, GMRW13] that consider consider secure computation in a one-pass client server model can also be adapted to a one-pass chain-based interaction (as pointed out in [HIJ+16]). However, since these works restrict the interaction to a 'single' pass, their constructions achieve residual security (as opposed to standard security). The same holds for efficient non-interactive multiparty computation (NIMPC) constructions in [HIKR18, EOYN21, BGI+14].

Lastly, there are other notions that are related to bottleneck complexity such as communication locality (defined for a party as number of total other parties that the party communicates with) [BGT13] and message complexity (that captures the total number of messages sent in the protocol but does not focus on the size of the message) [IMO18]. However, the proposed protocols optimizing these metrics are for arbitrary functions and incurs $\Omega(n)$ bottleneck complexity.

2 Preliminaries

2.1 Notation

We denote the cryptographic security parameter as λ. We consider a set of $n = n(\lambda)$ parties $\{P_1, \ldots, P_n\}$, where n is polynomially-bounded. The parties are connected by pair-wise secure and authentic channels, and each party is modelled as a probabilistic polynomial time Turing (PPT) machine. We assume that there exists a PPT adversary $\mathcal{A}$, who can *passively* corrupt upto $n-1$ parties. The set of elements $\{1, \ldots, k\}$ is denoted as $[k]$.

2.2 Security Model

We prove the security of our protocols based on the standard real/ideal world paradigm. A reader who is familiar with this may skip to Sect. 2.3. Essentially, the security of a protocol is analyzed by comparing what an adversary can do in the real execution of the protocol to what it can do in an ideal execution, that is considered secure by definition (in the presence of an incorruptible trusted party). In an ideal execution, each party sends its input to the trusted party over a perfectly secure channel, the trusted party computes the function based on these inputs and sends to each party its respective output. Informally, a protocol is secure if whatever an adversary can do in the real protocol (where no trusted party exists) can be done in the above described ideal computation. In this work, the adversary is assumed to be *passive* (alternately, referred to as being semi-honest) – the corrupt parties must follow the protocol specifications. However, the adversary attempts to learn private information by observing the view of the passively corrupt parties. We refer to [Can00] for further details regarding the security model.

In more detail, let Π be a protocol and $\mathcal{F}$ be a functionality. Let $\mathcal{I}$ denote the set of parties that are corrupt (of size at most $n-1$). The "ideal" world execution involves parties $\{P_1, \ldots, P_n\}$, an ideal adversary $\mathcal{S}$ who controls the parties in $\mathcal{I}$. The "real" world execution involves the PPT parties $\{P_1, \ldots, P_n\}$, and a real world adversary $\mathcal{A}$ who corrupts the parties in $\mathcal{I}$ passively. The *view* of a party in the real world is defined to be its random tape, together with all messages received during the execution of the protocol. In the ideal world, the simulator $\mathcal{S}$ is given as input nothing but the corrupt parties' inputs sent to the trusted party and the outputs they receive from the trusted party. If $\mathcal{S}$ is able to 'simulate' the real-world view with just this information, intuitively, security must hold. This is formalized below.

We define the following distributions of random variables.

$\texttt{REAL}_{\Pi}(1^\lambda, \mathcal{I}; x_1, \ldots, x_n)$: suppose Π is run with security parameter λ where each party P_i runs the protocol honestly using private input x_i. Let V_i denote the view of party P_i at the end of the protocol execution and let y_i denote the output of P_i. Output $(\{V_i\}_{i \in \mathcal{I}}, (y_1, \ldots, y_n))$.

$\texttt{IDEAL}_{\mathcal{F},\mathcal{S}}(1^\lambda, \mathcal{I}; x_1, \ldots, x_n)$: Let $(y_1, \ldots, y_n) \leftarrow \mathcal{F}(x_1, \ldots, x_n)$. Output $(\mathcal{S}(I, \{x_i, y_i\}_{i \in \mathcal{I}}), (y_1, \ldots, y_n))$

A protocol is secure against passive adversaries if the corrupted parties in the real world have views that are indistinguishable from their views in the ideal world.

Definition 1. *A protocol Π securely realizes $\mathcal{F}$ if there exists a PPT ideal world adversary $\mathcal{S}$, such that for every subset of corrupt parties $\mathcal{I}$ and all inputs $x_1, \ldots, x_n$, the following two distributions are computationally indistinguishable:*

$$\texttt{REAL}_{\Pi}(1^\lambda, \mathcal{I}; x_1, \ldots, x_n) \stackrel{c}{\approx} \texttt{IDEAL}_{\mathcal{F},\mathcal{S}}(1^\lambda, \mathcal{I}; x_1, \ldots, x_n)$$

2.3 Definitions

Informally, the bottleneck complexity of a protocol is the maximum communication complexity required by any party in the protocol execution. More formally, we have:

Definition 2 (Bottleneck complexity of a Protocol [BJPY18]**).** *Let $\mathcal{CC}_i(\Pi)$ denote the expected number of bits sent or received by P_i in an execution of Π, with worst-case inputs. The bottleneck complexity of an n-party protocol Π is defined as $\mathcal{BC}(\Pi) = \max_{i \in [n]} \mathcal{CC}_i(\Pi)$*

We note that while we keep the $\mathcal{BC}$-complexity definition of [BJPY18] for consistency, all our protocols satisfy a stronger notion of worse-case (as opposed to expected) $\mathcal{BC}$-complexity.

Definition 3 (Bottleneck complexity of a Function [BJPY18]**).** *The bottleneck complexity of an n-input function f is the minimum value of $\mathcal{BC}(\Pi)$ when quantified over all n-party distributed protocols Π which securely evaluate f.*

We say that a protocol Π is $\mathcal{BC}$*-efficient*, if the bottleneck complexity of Π is independent of n. Formally, we require that there exists a polynomial $p(\lambda)$ such that for all $n(\lambda) \in \mathsf{poly}(\lambda)$, it holds that $\mathcal{BC}(\Pi) < p(\lambda)$.

Definition 4 (Abelian Programs). *Let G be an abelian group, $S_1, \ldots, S_n$ be subsets of G, and $\mathcal{H}^G_{S_1,\ldots,S_n}$ be the set of functions $h : S_1 \times \cdots \times S_n \to \{0,1\}$ of the form $h(x_1, \ldots, x_n) = f(\Sigma_{i=1}^n x_i)$, for some $f : G \to \{0,1\}$. We call such functions h abelian programs.*

Note that the simple boolean functions of $\texttt{AND}$ and $\texttt{XOR}$ are abelian programs, considering the abelian group G as $\mathbb{Z}_{n+1}$ (integers modulo $n+1$) and the subsets S_i ($i \in [n]$) as the set $\{0,1\}$. $\texttt{AND}(x_1,\ldots,x_n)$ can be expressed as $f(\sum_{i=1}^{n} x_i)$ where the addition is done modulo $(n+1)$ and $f(x)$ outputs 1 only when $x = n$ and 0 otherwise. On the other hand, $\texttt{XOR}(x_1,\ldots,x_n)$ can be expressed as $f(\sum_{i=1}^{n} x_i)$ where $f(x)$ outputs $x \mod 2$.

2.4 Primitives

Garbling Scheme. A garbling scheme, introduced by Yao [Yao82] and formalized by Bellare *et al.* [BHR12], enables a party to "encrypt" or "garble" a circuit in such a way that it can be evaluated on inputs—given tokens or "labels" corresponding to those inputs—without revealing what the inputs are.

Definition 5 (Garbling Scheme). *A projective garbling scheme is a tuple of efficient algorithms* $\mathtt{GC} = (\mathtt{garble}, \mathtt{eval})$ *defined as follows.*

$\mathtt{garble}(1^\lambda, \mathtt{C}) \rightarrow (\mathtt{GC}, \mathbf{K})$: *The garbling algorithm* $\mathtt{garble}$ *takes as input the security parameter* λ *and a boolean circuit* $\mathtt{C} : \{0,1\}^\ell \rightarrow \{0,1\}^m$*, and outputs a garbled circuit* $\mathtt{GC}$ *and* ℓ *pairs of garbled labels* $\mathbf{K} = (K_1^0, K_1^1, \ldots, K_\ell^0, K_\ell^1)$*. For simplicity we assume that for every* $i \in [\ell]$ *and* $b \in \{0,1\}$ *it holds that* $K_\ell^b \in \{0,1\}^\lambda$*.*
$\mathtt{eval}(\mathtt{GC}, K_1, \ldots, K_\ell) \rightarrow y$: *The evaluation algorithm* $\mathtt{eval}$ *takes as input the garbled circuit* $\mathtt{GC}$ *and* ℓ *garbled labels* $K_1, \ldots, K_\ell$*, and outputs a value* $y \in \{0,1\}^m$*.*

We require the following properties of a projective garbling scheme:

Correctness. We say $\mathtt{GC}$ satisfies *correctness* if for any boolean circuit $\mathtt{C} : \{0,1\}^\ell \rightarrow \{0,1\}^m$ and $x = (x_1, \ldots, x_\ell)$ it holds that

$$\Pr[\mathtt{eval}(\mathtt{GC}, \mathbf{K}[x]) \neq \mathtt{C}(x)] = negl(\lambda),$$

where $(\mathtt{GC}, \mathbf{K}) \leftarrow \mathtt{garble}(1^\lambda, \mathtt{C})$ with $\mathbf{K} = (K_1^0, K_1^1, \ldots, K_\ell^0, K_\ell^1)$, and $\mathbf{K}[x] = (K_1^{x_1}, \ldots, K_\ell^{x_\ell})$.

Next, we formally define the security notions we require for a garbling scheme. When garbled circuits are used in such a way that decoding information is used separately, *obliviousness* requires that a garbled circuit together with a set of labels reveals nothing about the input the labels correspond to, and *privacy* requires that the additional knowledge of the decoding information reveals only the appropriate output. In our work, we do not consider decoding information separately (but rather, consider it to be included in the garbled circuit), so we do not need obliviousness.

Privacy. Informally, privacy requires that a garbled circuit together with a set of labels reveal nothing about the input the labels correspond to (beyond the appropriate output and the side-information). For our constructions, we assume the side-information to be the topology of the circuit, denoted as $\theta(C)$.

More formally, we say that $\mathtt{GC}$ satisfies *privacy* if there exists a simulator $\mathtt{simGC}$ such that for every PPT adversary $\mathcal{A}$, it holds that

$$\Pr[\mathcal{A} \text{ wins}] \leq \frac{1}{2} + negl(\lambda)$$

in the following experiment:

Adversary $\mathcal{A}$		Challenger $\mathcal{C}$
	$\mathtt{C} : \{0,1\}^\ell \rightarrow \{0,1\}^m$ →	

	$\mathtt{x} = (\mathtt{x}_1, \ldots, \mathtt{x}_\ell) \in \{0,1\}^\ell$ →	$b \leftarrow \{0,1\}$
		if $b = 0$:
		$(\mathtt{GC}, (K_1^0, K_1^1, \ldots, K_\ell^0, K_\ell^1)) \leftarrow \mathtt{garble}(1^\lambda, \mathtt{C})$
		$K_i = K_i^{x_i}$ for $i \in [\ell]$
		if $b = 1$:
		$(\mathtt{GC}, K_1, \ldots, K_\ell) \leftarrow \mathtt{simGC}(1^\lambda, \theta(\mathtt{C}), \mathtt{C}(x))$

	← $\mathtt{GC}, \mathrm{K}_1, \ldots, \mathrm{K}_\ell$	
	b' →	
$\mathcal{A}$ wins if $b = b'$		

Lastly, we remark that one of our constructions requires the use of a slightly modified $\mathtt{garble}$ algorithm that takes as additional input, the labels of the garbled circuit. The modified syntax is as follows: $\mathtt{garble}(1^\lambda, \mathtt{C}, \mathbf{K} = (K_1^0, K_1^1, \ldots, K_\ell^0, K_\ell^1)) \rightarrow \mathtt{GC}$. Accordingly, the simulator of the garbling scheme $\mathtt{simGC}$ also takes as input one set of labels i.e. the syntax changes to $\mathtt{simGC}(1^\lambda, \theta(\mathtt{C}), \mathtt{C}(x), \{K_1, \ldots, K_\ell\}) \rightarrow \mathtt{GC}$. Note that most garbled circuits constructions, including Yao's original construction, can be used in this way.

Additively Homomorphic Encryption. We consider linearly homomorphic encryption over $(\mathbb{Z}_M, +)$, the ring of integers modulo M.

Definition 6 (Additively Homomorphic Encryption.). *Let* $(\mathbb{Z}_M, +)$ *be the ring of integers modulo* M. *An additively homomorphic encryption scheme over* $\mathbb{Z}_M$ *is a tuple* $\mathtt{AHE} = (\mathtt{Keygen}, \mathtt{Enc}, \mathtt{Dec}, \mathtt{Add}, \mathtt{ScalMul})$ *defined as:*

- **Key Generation.** *The algorithm* $\mathtt{Keygen}$ *is a randomized algorithm that takes as input the security parameter and outputs a public key* $\mathtt{pk}$ *and a secret key pair* $\mathtt{sk}$: $(\mathtt{pk}, \mathtt{sk}) \leftarrow \mathtt{Keygen}(1^\lambda)$.
- **Encryption.** *The randomized algorithm* $\mathtt{Enc}$ *takes as input the public key* $\mathtt{pk}$ *and the message* $m \in \mathbb{Z}_M$ *and outputs a ciphertext* c: $c \leftarrow \mathtt{Enc}(\mathtt{pk}, m; r)$ *(where* r *denotes the randomness used for encryption).*
- **Decryption.** *The algorithm* $\mathtt{Dec}$ *takes as input the secret key* $\mathtt{sk}$ *and the ciphertext* c *and outputs a plaintext* $m \in \mathbb{Z}_M$ *(or* $\perp$ *if the ciphertext is invalid):* $m \leftarrow \mathtt{Dec}(\mathtt{sk}, c)$.

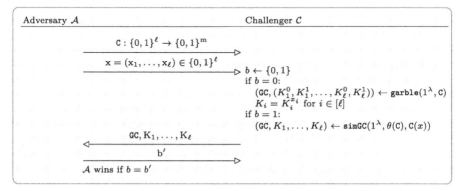

Homomorphic Addition. *The algorithm* Add *takes as input the public key* pk *and two ciphertexts* c_1 *and* c_2 *and outputs a ciphertext* $c^* : c^* \leftarrow \texttt{Add}(\texttt{pk}, c_1, c_2)$.
Scalar Multiplication. *The algorithm* ScalMul *takes as input the public key* pk, *a ciphertext* c *and an integer* $\alpha \in \mathbb{Z}_M$, *and outputs a ciphertext* $c' : c' \leftarrow \texttt{ScalMul}(\texttt{pk}, c, \alpha)$.

We require the following properties of an AHE*:*

Correctness. *An* AHE *is correct if for any* $m \in \mathbb{Z}_M$,

$$\Pr\left[\texttt{Dec}(\texttt{sk}, c) \neq m : \begin{array}{c}(\texttt{pk}, \texttt{sk}) \leftarrow \texttt{Keygen}(1^\lambda); \\ c \leftarrow \texttt{Enc}(\texttt{pk}, m)\end{array}\right] \leq negl(\lambda)$$

(where the randomness is taken over the random coins of the algorithms)
Additive Homomorphism. *An* AHE *satisfies additive homomorphism if for any* $m_1, m_2 \in \mathbb{Z}_M$, *the following holds:*

$$\Pr\left[\texttt{Dec}(\texttt{sk}, \texttt{Add}(\texttt{pk}, c_1, c_2)) \neq m_1 + m_2 \bmod M : \begin{array}{c}(\texttt{pk}, \texttt{sk}) \leftarrow \texttt{Keygen}(1^\lambda); \\ c_1 \leftarrow \texttt{Enc}(\texttt{pk}, m_1); \\ c_2 \leftarrow \texttt{Enc}(\texttt{pk}, m_2)\end{array}\right] \leq negl(\lambda)$$

$$\Pr\left[\texttt{Dec}(\texttt{sk}, \texttt{ScalMul}(\texttt{pk}, c, m_2)) \neq m_1 \cdot m_2 \bmod M : \begin{array}{c}(\texttt{pk}, \texttt{sk}) \leftarrow \texttt{Keygen}(1^\lambda); \\ c \leftarrow \texttt{Enc}(\texttt{pk}, m_1)\end{array}\right] \leq negl(\lambda)$$

(where the randomness is taken over the random coins of the algorithms)

CPA Security. *An* AHE *satisfies CPA security if for all PPT adversaries* $\mathcal{A}$, *for* $(\mathsf{msg}_0, \mathsf{msg}_1) \leftarrow \mathcal{A}(1^\lambda)$, *if* $|\mathsf{msg}_0| = |\mathsf{msg}_1|$,

$$\Pr\left[\mathcal{A}(\texttt{pk}, c) = b : \begin{array}{c}(\texttt{pk}, \texttt{sk}) \leftarrow \texttt{Keygen}(1^\lambda); b \leftarrow \{0,1\}; \\ c \leftarrow \texttt{Enc}(\texttt{pk}, \mathsf{msg}_b)\end{array}\right] \leq \frac{1}{2} + negl(\lambda)$$

(where the randomness is taken over the internal coin tosses of $\mathcal{A}$, Keygen *and* Enc*).*
Circuit Privacy. *An* AHE *satisfies circuit privacy if there exists a simulator* $\mathcal{S}$ *such that for any* $m_1, m_2 \in \mathbb{Z}_M$ *the distributions*

$$\{\texttt{sk}, \mathcal{S}(\texttt{pk}, m_1 + m_2 \bmod M)\} \text{ and } \{\texttt{sk}, \texttt{Add}(\texttt{pk}, \texttt{Enc}(\texttt{pk}, m_1), \texttt{Enc}(\texttt{pk}, m_2))\}$$

$$\{\texttt{sk}, \mathcal{S}(\texttt{pk}, m_1 \cdot m_2 \bmod M)\} \text{ and } \{\texttt{sk}, \texttt{ScalMul}(\texttt{pk}, \texttt{Enc}(\texttt{pk}, m_1), m_2)\}$$

where $(\texttt{pk}, \texttt{sk}) \leftarrow \texttt{Keygen}(1^\lambda)$ *are computationally indistinguishable.*

Note that our definition of circuit privacy implies that Add and ScalMul re-randomize the output ciphertext.

Additively-homomorphic encryption satisfying our requirements can be realized from a variety of assumptions, including QR, DDH, Paillier, learning with errors etc. In the case of DDH, we actually obtain AHE for small integer plaintexts, rather than $\mathbb{Z}_M$. However, this is enough for our application, since our construction never relies on wraparound modulo M, and we can always guarantee that messages are small by decomposing inputs into blocks and packing into several ciphertexts. Finally, note that standard LWE-based AHE constructions [Reg05] do not support an unbounded number of homomorphic operations; however, in our application this is limited to $O(n)$, so parameters can be chosen accordingly.

3 $\mathcal{BC}$-Efficient MPC for Abelian Programs

In this section, we present a $\mathcal{BC}$-efficient MPC protocol for abelian programs. As a warm-up, we begin with describing $\mathcal{BC}$-efficient protocols for basic boolean functions.

3.1 Protocol for AND

At a high-level, the $\mathcal{BC}$-efficient protocol for AND proceeds as follows. The setup maps the potential 1-input of each party to a random group element and distributes it to the respective party. In the online phase, the parties use either the element received as part of the setup or a random element (depending on whether their input is 1 or 0 respectively) to compute the sum incrementally over a chain. The basic idea is that if all parties' inputs are 1, the sum of these group elements would be a special element, say Y, which can also be given as part of the setup and thereby used to determine the output.

Unfortunately, the above protocol idea is susceptible to the residual function attack[1]– suppose the interaction over the chain occurs from P_1 to P_n and imagine the adversary corrupts a subset of parties towards the end of the chain, say P_k to P_n (where k could be any index between 2 to n). In such a case, it is easy to see that the adversary can always learn whether the logical AND of the honest parties' inputs is 1 or not, irrespective of the corrupt parties' inputs. This violates security because as per the ideal functionality, the adversary must not learn this information if any of the corrupt parties' input is 0.

To counter this residual attack, the online phase of our protocol performs an additional backwards pass over the chain i.e. from P_n to P_1. Suppose Y' denotes the sum computed at the end of the forward pass. The backward pass involves n applications of a PRF in a nested manner starting from Y', once by each party using its own PRF key (given as a part of the setup). Intuitively, this prevents the residual attack by the adversary for the following reason – when an honest party computes the PRF using its secret PRF key, the value Y' gets "fixed". It is no longer possible for the adversary to locally compute the output based on the scenario when $Y'' \neq Y'$ was computed at the end of the forward pass of the chain (as he does not know the secret PRF key of the honest party).

[1] However, this approach suffices for residual security, as shown in the NIMPC protocol of [HIKR18].

Lastly, our protocol does another forward pass over the chain to distribute the output. The formal description of the $\mathcal{BC}$-efficient protocol for AND appears in Fig. 1.

Private input. Each party P_i has input bit $x_i \in \{0, 1\}$.
Output. $y = x_1 \wedge x_2 \wedge \cdots \wedge x_n$.
Tools. Psuedorandom Function (PRF) $\mathsf{F} : \mathcal{K} \times \{0,1\}^\lambda \rightarrow \{0,1\}^\lambda$, where $\mathcal{K}$ refers to the key space
Correlated Randomness Setup. The setup involves the following:

1. For each $i \in [n]$, a uniformly random element $\mathsf{r}_i^1 \leftarrow G$ and a PRF key $\mathsf{s}_i \in \mathcal{K}$ is sampled.
2. Let $Y \leftarrow \Sigma_{i=1}^n \mathsf{r}_i^1$ and $Z \leftarrow \mathsf{F}\Big(\mathsf{s}_1, \mathsf{F}(\mathsf{s}_2, \mathsf{F}(\mathsf{s}_3, \ldots \mathsf{F}(\mathsf{s}_{n-2}, \mathsf{F}(\mathsf{s}_{n-1}, \mathsf{F}(\mathsf{s}_n, Y))) \ldots))\Big)$.
3. Output $(Z, \mathsf{r}_i^1, \mathsf{s}_i)$ to each P_i $(i \in [n])$.

The Protocol. The following steps are run in the online phase of the protocol –

Phase 1 (Round 1 to Round n). Each P_i chooses r_i^0 at random at the beginning of Phase 1. During round i, P_i does the following:

– If $i = 1$, set $Y_i = \mathsf{r}_i^{x_i}$.
– If $i \neq 1$, let Y_{i-1} denote the message received from P_{i-1} during the previous round. Compute $Y_i \leftarrow \mathsf{r}_i^{x_i} + Y_{i-1}$.
– If $i < n$, send Y_i to P_{i+1}. Else set $Y' = Y_n$.

Phase 2 (Round $n+1$ to Round $2n$). Each P_i does the following in sequence, starting from $i = n$ to 1:

– If $i = n$, compute $Z_n = \mathsf{F}(\mathsf{s}_n, Y')$.
– If $i \neq n$, receive Z_{i+1} from P_{i+1} in the previous round. Compute $Z_i \leftarrow \mathsf{F}(\mathsf{s}_i, Z_{i+1})$.
– If $i \neq 1$, send Z_i to P_{i-1}. Else set $Z' = Z_1$.

Output Computation. P_1 sets output $y = 1$ if $Z' == Z$ holds; else sets $y = 0$.

Phase 3 (Output Transfer). For i starting from 1 to n, each P_i does the following in sequence -

- If $i \neq 1$, let y denote the output received from P_{i-1} in previous round.
- If $i \neq n$, send y to P_{i+1}.
- Output y.

Fig. 1. Π_{AND}

Correctness. For correctness, note that when $x_i = 1$ for each $i \in [n]$, $Y' = \sum_{i=1}^{n} \mathsf{r}_i^1 = Y$. Therefore, $Z' == Z$ holds and the output y evaluates to 1 in such a case (which is the correct output). Next we consider the case when the input of at least one party is 0: $Y' \neq Y$ would hold (except with negligible probability) and consequently $Z' \neq Z$ holds (except with negligible probability). The parties output 0 (which is the correct output) in such a case with overwhelming probability.

Security. To argue security, consider the case when the adversary corrupts $n-1$ parties passively and P_i denotes the only honest party. Further, assume that at least one of the corrupt parties' input is 0 (which is the non-trivial case where adversary should learn nothing about x_i; else the input of P_i can be derived from the output itself). Firstly, the adversary learns nothing about x_i from Y_i, as both r_i^0 and r_i^1 are random elements in G. Next, we claim that the adversary learns no information about $Z_i'' = \mathsf{F}(\mathsf{s}_i, \mathsf{F}(\mathsf{s}_{i+1}, \mathsf{F}(\mathsf{s}_{i+2}, \ldots, \mathsf{F}(\mathsf{s}_n, Y'')\ldots)))$ computed on $Y'' \neq Y'$. This follows from security of the PRF – In more detail, such an adversary could use the query $Z_{i+1}'' = \mathsf{F}(\mathsf{s}_{i+1}, \mathsf{F}(\mathsf{s}_{i+2}, \ldots, \mathsf{F}(\mathsf{s}_n, Y'')\ldots))$ to distinguish between the PRF F (where the key sampled is s_i) and a truly random function; thereby breaking the security of the PRF. The above claim ensures that for any $Y'' \neq Y'$, the adversary cannot deduce whether $Z'' \leftarrow \mathsf{F}(\mathsf{s}_1, \mathsf{F}(\mathsf{s}_2, \ldots \mathsf{F}(\mathsf{s}_{n-2}, \mathsf{F}(\mathsf{s}_{n-1}, \mathsf{F}(\mathsf{s}_n, Y''))\ldots))$ computed at the end of Phase 2 with respect to Y'' would be identical to Z or not. We can thus conclude that the adversary learns nothing beyond the output 0 and the privacy of P_i's input is maintained. This completes the informal security argument.

$\mathcal{BC}$-Analysis. We analyze the communication incurred by a party, say P_i, in an execution of Π_{AND}. First, we observe that throughout Π_{AND}, each party communicates with at most two other parties (i.e. P_{i-1} and P_{i+1}). Further, the messages communicated (such as Y_i, Z_i, y) are of at most λ bits. It is therefore easy to see that the bottleneck complexity of Π_{AND} is $O(\lambda)$.

Extension to the Dual Case of OR *Function.* The above protocol extends naturally to the dual case of the OR function. For computation of the OR of all parties' input bits, the setup distributes random elements mapped to potential 0-inputs (instead of 1-inputs as in Π_{AND}) and computes Y, Z accordingly. The parties use the information received from the setup in case their input is 0 and sample a random group element otherwise. The rest of the protocol remains the same. It is easy to check that this yields a $\mathcal{BC}$-efficient protocol for OR.

3.2 Protocol for XOR

We present the $\mathcal{BC}$-efficient protocol Π_{XOR} for XOR in Fig. 2.

At a high-level, during Π_{XOR}, a correlated sharing of 0 is distributed as part of the setup. The parties mask their inputs using their respective share (received as part of the setup). In the online phase, the parties compute the XOR of their masked inputs in an incremental manner over a chain. It is easy to see that the XOR of the masked inputs evaluates to the XOR of the parties' inputs.

Note that, unlike the case of AND, $\Pi_{\mathtt{XOR}}$ does not need another pass over the chain before output distribution. This is because, in the case of the XOR function, standard security is the same as residual security. Lastly, we point that the correlated sharing of 0 and addition of masked inputs is also used in the NIMPC protocol for addition in [HIKR18]. While their protocol involves parties sending masked inputs to a central party, we carry out the computation in an incremental manner over a chain to preserve the $\mathcal{BC}$-efficiency.

Private input. Each party P_i has input bit $x_i \in \{0,1\}$.
Output. $y = x_1 \oplus x_2 \oplus \cdots \oplus x_n$.
Correlated Randomness Setup. The setup involves the following:

1. For each $i \in [n]$, sample a uniformly random bit $\mathsf{m}_i \leftarrow \{0,1\}$ such that $\oplus_{i=1}^{n} \mathsf{m}_i = 0$.
2. Output m_i to each P_i ($i \in [n]$).

The Protocol. The following steps are run in the online phase of the protocol:

Phase 1 (Round 1 to Round n). At the beginning of Phase 1, each P_i computes $M_i = x_i \oplus \mathsf{m}_i$. During round i, P_i does the following:

- If $i = 1$, set $X_i = M_i$.
- If $i \neq 1$, let X_{i-1} denote the message received from P_{i-1} during the previous round. Compute $X_i \leftarrow X_{i-1} \oplus M_i$.
- If $i < n$, send X_i to P_{i+1}.

Output Computation. P_n computes output y as $y = X_n$.

Phase 2 (Output Transfer). For i starting from n to 1, each P_i does the following in sequence -

- If $i \neq n$, let y denote the output received from P_{i+1} in previous round.
- If $i \neq 1$, send y to P_{i-1}.
- Output y.

Fig. 2. $\Pi_{\mathtt{XOR}}$

Correctness. For correctness, note that $X_n = \oplus_{i=1}^{n} M_i = \oplus_{i=1}^{n}(x_i \oplus \mathsf{m}_i) = \left(\oplus_{i=1}^{n} x_i\right) \oplus \left(\oplus_{i=1}^{n} \mathsf{m}_i\right) = \left(\oplus_{i=1}^{n} x_i\right) \oplus 0 = \oplus_{i=1}^{n} x_i$.

Security. For security, consider the case where there are at least two honest parties, say P_i and P_j (the case of single honest party is trivial as the party's input can be deduced from the output of XOR). During the protocol, the adversary learns $M_i = x_i \oplus \mathsf{m}_i$ and $M_j = x_j \oplus \mathsf{m}_j$. Further since $\oplus_{k=1}^{n} \mathsf{m}_i = 0$, the adversary can deduce $\mathsf{m}_i \oplus \mathsf{m}_j$. However, this leaks nothing beyond $x_i \oplus x_j$ which is allowed as per ideal realization of XOR. This completes the informal security argument.

$\mathcal{BC}$-Analysis. We analyze the communication incurred by a party, say P_i, in an execution of $\Pi_{\texttt{XOR}}$. First, we observe that throughout $\Pi_{\texttt{XOR}}$ each party communicates with at most two other parties (i.e. P_{i-1} and P_{i+1}). Further, the messages communicated (such as X_i, y) are a single bit. It is therefore easy to see that the bottleneck complexity of $\Pi_{\texttt{XOR}}$ is $O(1)$.

3.3 Protocol for Abelian Programs

Recall that an abelian program h can be expressed as $h(x_1, \ldots, x_n) = f(\Sigma_{i=1}^{n} x_i)$, for some $f : G \to \{0, 1\}$, where G denotes an abelian group (Definition 4). Towards securely computing such a function in a $\mathcal{BC}$-efficient manner, we begin with the following observation about the protocol design in Sect. 3.1 and Sect. 3.2 – At the end of the first forward pass, the parties obtain useful information related to the sum of their inputs. Roughly speaking, this is subsequently used to derive the output by applying some 'special' function. In the case of AND, this 'special' function essentially corresponds to checking if the sum is identical to a fixed value that is given to the parties in advance; in the case of XOR, the 'special' function turns out to be just the identity function (as the sum computed at the end of the first pass directly yields the output).

Extending this approach to an abelian program $h(x_1, \ldots, x_n) = f(\Sigma_{i=1}^{n} x_i) = f(Y)$, we first note that the useful information related to the sum of parties' inputs (that is computed at the end of the first forward pass) must be such that it does not allow the adversary to learn the sum of the parties' inputs i.e. Y. This is because the output of h may not necessarily reveal Y. For this reason, the first forward pass in our protocol computes a 'masked' sum of inputs, say $Z = Y + R$, where R corresponds to a random mask that is unknown to the parties. Now, the output of h can be derived from this masked sum by computing the 'special' function $f(Z - R)$.

To realize the above computation in a $\mathcal{BC}$-efficient manner, we use garbled circuits. The setup phase involves garbling the circuit corresponding to the 'special' function. In more detail, this circuit takes as input Z, has the mask R hard-coded and computes $f(Z - R)$. Further, to enable the parties to obtain labels for input wires corresponding to Z, the setup additively shares all the labels of the garbled circuit among the parties. Additive sharing of the input labels offers a two-fold advantage – Firstly, it ensures that during the execution of the protocol, the adversary learns at most one label per input wire. This counters residual attacks by the adversary and maintains privacy of honest parties' inputs. Specifically, privacy of garbling guarantees that the adversary is unable to learn the mask R (and therefore Y). Secondly, additive secret sharing supports reconstruction in an incremental fashion. This allows the parties to carry out the reconstruction of the appropriate label corresponding to Z while maintaining the $\mathcal{BC}$-efficiency.

Based on the above high-level ideas, our $\mathcal{BC}$-efficient construction $\Pi_{\texttt{abl}}$ has the following structure. It begins with a forward pass to compute the masked sum Z. Next, it does a backward pass where the parties use their respective additive shares (received as part of the setup) and reconstruct the labels corresponding to Z. Using these labels, the garbled circuit (received as a part of the setup) computing $f(Z - R)$ can be evaluated, which results in the output of h. The formal description of $\Pi_{\texttt{abl}}$ appears in Fig. 3.

Private input. Each party P_i has input $x_i \in G$, where G denotes an abelian group.
Output. $y = h(x_1, \ldots, x_n) = f(\Sigma_{i=1}^{n} x_i)$.
Tools. Garbling scheme ($\texttt{garble}, \texttt{eval}$)
Correlated Randomness Setup. The setup involves the following:

1. For each $i \in [n]$, sample $\mathsf{r}_i \in G$. Let $\Sigma_{i=1}^{n} \mathsf{r}_i = R$
2. Let $C_R(Z)$ denote a circuit that has $R \in \{0,1\}^\lambda$ [a] hard-coded, takes as input $Z \in \{0,1\}^\lambda$ and outputs $f(Z - R)$. Compute $(\mathtt{GC}, \{K_\alpha^{(0)}, K_\alpha^{(1)}\}_{\alpha \in [\lambda]}) \leftarrow \texttt{garble}(C, 1^\lambda)$ [b].
3. For each $\alpha \in [\lambda], b \in \{0,1\}$ – let $(K_{\alpha,1}^{(b)}, \ldots, K_{\alpha,n}^{(b)})$ denote the additive sharing of $K_\alpha^{(b)}$ i.e. $\Sigma_{i=1}^{n} K_{\alpha,i}^{(b)} = K_\alpha^{(b)}$.
4. Output $(\mathtt{GC}, \mathsf{r}_i, \{K_{\alpha,i}^{(0)}, K_{\alpha,i}^{(1)}\}_{\alpha \in [\lambda]})$ to P_i for each $i \in [n]$.

The Protocol. The following steps are run in the online phase of the protocol:
Phase 1 (Round 1 to Round n). Each P_i sets $M_i := x_i + \mathsf{r}_i$. During round i, P_i does the following:

- If $i = 1$, let $Y_i = M_i$.
- If $i \neq 1$, let Y_{i-1} denote the message received from P_{i-1} during the previous round. Compute $Y_i \leftarrow Y_{i-1} + M_i$.
- If $i < n$, send Y_i to P_{i+1}. Else, set $Z = Y_n$.

Phase 2 (Round $n+1$ to Round $2n$). Each P_i does the following in sequence, starting from $i = n$ to 1:

- If $i = n$, let $(z_1, z_2, \ldots, z_\lambda)$ denote the bits corresponding to Z. For each $\alpha \in [\lambda]$, set $K'_{\alpha,n} = K_{\alpha,n}^{(z_\alpha)}$.
- If $i \neq n$, parse the message received from P_{i+1} in the previous round as $\left(Z = (z_1, z_2, \ldots, z_\lambda), \{K'_{\alpha,i+1}\}_{\alpha \in [\lambda]}\right)$.
- For each $\alpha \in [\lambda]$, compute $K'_{\alpha,i} \leftarrow K'_{\alpha,i+1} + K_{\alpha,i}^{(z_\alpha)}$.
- If $i \neq 1$, send $\left(Z, \{K'_{\alpha,i}\}_{\alpha \in [\lambda]}\right)$ to P_{i-1}. Else, set $\vec{K} = \{K'_{\alpha,1}\}_{\alpha \in [\lambda]}$.

Output Computation. P_1 runs $y \leftarrow \texttt{eval}(\mathtt{GC}, \vec{K})$.

Phase 3 (Output Transfer). This phase is identical to Phase 3 of Figure 3.1.

[a] We assume a canonical mapping from elements in G to strings in $\{0,1\}^\lambda$.
[b] Here, we assume for simplicity that the garbling scheme has the property that the garbled circuit reveals no information about the hard-coded value R. This property holds for Yao's garbled circuits [Yao86]. However, this requirement can easily be removed by defining the circuit C to take an additional input R (instead of hard-coding R), for which the labels are given directly to the parties as part of the setup.

Fig. 3. $\Pi_{\mathtt{abl}}$

Correctness. For correctness, note that Z computed by P_n at the end of Phase 1 is $Z = \Sigma_{i=1}^n M_i = \Sigma_{i=1}^n (x_i + \mathsf{r}_i) = \Sigma_{i=1}^n x_i + \Sigma_{i=1}^n \mathsf{r}_i = \Sigma_{i=1}^n x_i + R$. Thus, the output computed via the evaluation of the garbled circuit as $f(Z - R) = f(\Sigma_{i=1}^n x_i) = h(x_1, \ldots, x_n)$ is indeed the correct output.
$\mathcal{BC}$-Analysis. We analyze the communication incurred by a party, say P_i, in an execution of $\Pi_{\mathtt{abl}}$. First, we observe that throughout $\Pi_{\mathtt{abl}}$ each party communicates with at most two other parties (i.e. P_{i-1} and P_{i+1}). Further, the messages communicated (such as $Y_i, Z, \{K'_{\alpha,i}\}_{\alpha \in [\lambda]}, y$) are of size at most λ^2. It is therefore easy to see that the bottleneck complexity of $\Pi_{\mathtt{abl}}$ is $O(\lambda^2)$.

We state the formal theorem below.

Theorem 1. *Protocol $\Pi_{\mathtt{abl}}$ securely computes the abelian program h against an adversary corrupting upto $n-1$ parties passively.*

Proof. Let $\mathcal{I}$ and $\mathcal{H} = \mathcal{P} \setminus \mathcal{I}$ denote the set of indices corresponding to corrupt and honest parties respectively. Let $j_{\min}$ and $j_{\max}$ denote the least and maximum index corresponding to an honest party, where the indices are in the range $\{1, \ldots, n\}$. To prove security, we define below a simulator $\mathcal{S}$ that simulates the real-world view of the parties. Recall that $\mathcal{S}$ is given $(\mathcal{I}, \{x_i\}_{i \in \mathcal{I}}, y)$ (see Sect. 2.2 for details about the security model).

Setup Simulation. Run $(\mathtt{GC}, \vec{K} = \{K_1, \ldots, K_\lambda\}) \leftarrow \mathtt{simGC}(1^\lambda, \theta(C), y)$, where $\mathtt{simGC}$ denotes the simulator of the garbling scheme and $\theta(C)$ denotes the topology of the circuit computing $f(Z - R)$ (note that the topology is independent of the hard-coded value R). For each $i \in \mathcal{I}$, sample $\left(\mathsf{r}_i, \{K_{\alpha,i}^{(0)}, K_{\alpha,i}^{(1)}\}_{\alpha \in [\lambda]}\right)$ at random. The view of corrupted P_i constructed by $\mathcal{S}$ at this stage comprises of $\left(\mathtt{GC}, \mathsf{r}_i, \{K_{\alpha,i}^{(0)}, K_{\alpha,i}^{(1)}\}_{\alpha \in [\lambda]}\right)$.

Phase 1 Simulation. Choose Y_j at random on behalf of each honest P_j ($j \in \mathcal{H}$). For $i \in \mathcal{I}$ and $j \in \mathcal{H}$, add Y_j to a corrupt party P_i's view if $i = j + 1$.

Phase 2 Simulation. Recall that for each $i \in \mathcal{I}$, $\mathcal{S}$ knows x_i and defined r_i (during the simulation of the setup) and therefore can compute M_i.

- Compute Z as $Z = Y_{j_{\max}} + \sum_{k=j+1}^{n} M_k$. Parse $Z = (z_1, z_2, \ldots, z_\lambda)$.
- For each $\alpha \in [\lambda]$ and $j \in \mathcal{H}$: If $j \neq j_{\min}$, sample $K'_{\alpha,j}$ at random. Else (i.e. for $j = j_{\min}$), set $K'_{\alpha,j_{\min}}$ such that $K'_{\alpha,j_{\min}} + \sum_{i=1}^{j_{\min}-1} K_{\alpha,i}^{(z_\alpha)} = K_\alpha$. Note that $K_{\alpha,i}^{(z_\alpha)}$ for $i \in [j_{\min} - 1]$ corresponds to additive shares of corrupt parties which were already defined by $\mathcal{S}$ during the setup.
- For $i \in \mathcal{I}$ and $j \in \mathcal{H}$, add $(Z, K'_{\alpha,j})$ to a corrupt party P_i's view if $i = j - 1$.

Phase 3 Simulation. For $i \in \mathcal{I}$ and $j \in \mathcal{H}$, add y to a corrupt party P_i's view if $i = j + 1$.

Below, we argue that the views of corrupt parties in the real and ideal world are indistinguishable via a series of intermediate hybrids.

- Hyb_0: Same as the real-world execution.
- Hyb_1: Same as Hyb_0, except that Y_j for $j \in \mathcal{H}$ is sampled at random. This is in contrast to the previous hybrid where Y_j is computed as $Y_j = Y_{j-1} + x_j + \mathsf{r}_j$. Since r_j is uniformly distributed in G, this is indistinguishable from the previous hybrid.
- Hyb_2: Same as Hyb_1, except for the way in which $K'_{\alpha,j}$ for $j \in \mathcal{H}, \alpha \in [\lambda]$ is computed – For $j \neq j_{\min}$, $K'_{\alpha,j}$ is chosen uniformly at random, whereas for $j = j_{\min}$, it is set such that $K'_{\alpha,j_{\min}} + \sum_{i=1}^{j_{\min}-1} K_{\alpha,i}^{(z_\alpha)} = K_\alpha^{(z_\alpha)}$. This is in contrast to the previous hybrid where $K'_{\alpha,j}$ is computed as $K'_{\alpha,j} \leftarrow K'_{\alpha,j+1} + K_{\alpha,j}^{(z_\alpha)}$. Since $K_{\alpha,j}^{(z_\alpha)}$ is distributed uniformly at random (conditioned on $\Sigma_{k=1}^{n} K_{\alpha,k}^{(z_\alpha)} = K_\alpha^{(z_\alpha)}$), this is indistinguishable from the previous hybrid.
- Hyb_3: Same as Hyb_2, except that $(\mathtt{GC}, \vec{K})$ is computed as $(\mathtt{GC}, \vec{K}) \leftarrow \mathtt{simGC}(1^\lambda, \theta(C), y)$, where $\theta(C)$ denotes the topology of the circuit computing $f(Z - R)$. This is in contrast to Hyb_2 where $(\mathtt{GC}, \vec{K})$ is computed as $(\mathtt{GC}, \{K_\alpha^{(z_\alpha)}\}_{\alpha \in [\lambda]})$, where $(\mathtt{GC}, \{K_\alpha^{(0)}, K_\alpha^{(1)}\}_{\alpha \in [\lambda]}) \leftarrow \mathtt{garble}(C, 1^\lambda)$. It follows from privacy of the garbling scheme (see Definition 5) that Hyb_3 is indistinguishable from Hyb_2.

Since Hyb_3 corresponds to the ideal execution and every pair of consecutive hybrids are indistinguishable, this completes the proof that the views of corrupt parties in the real and ideal world are indistinguishable.

4 $\mathcal{BC}$-Efficient Protocol for Selection Functions

In this section, we present a $\mathcal{BC}$-efficient protocol $\Pi_{\mathtt{sel}}$ for the selection function $f(x_1 = \mathsf{q}, x_2, \ldots, x_n) = x_{\mathsf{q}}$, where P_1's input is a selection index $\mathsf{q} \in \{2, \ldots, n\}$ and the inputs of the other parties are in $\mathbb{Z}_M$, the plaintext space of an additively homomorphic encryption scheme.

As a starting point, note that the output of the selection function can be viewed as $\sum_{i=2}^{n}(b_i \cdot x_i)$, where $b_i \in \{0, 1\}$ denotes an indicator bit showing whether $i = \mathsf{q}$ holds or not (i.e. $b_i = 1$ if $i = \mathsf{q}$ and 0 otherwise). This seems promising as such a computation can be carried out in a chain – each party P_i computes $(b_i \cdot x_i)$, and these values can be aggregated while preserving $\mathcal{BC}$-efficiency as seen in Sect. 3. Unfortunately, this direct approach requires P_i to know b_i, which must not be allowed (as it is not revealed by output of f). However, if P_i somehow had access to an encryption of b_i instead, then the above computation over the chain could be carried out under the hood of *additive homomorphic encryption*; maintaining that b_i remains private from P_i.

Next, we note that since b_i depends on the input of party P_1, it is not possible to distribute encryptions of b_i directly to P_i during the input-independent setup. Therefore, to account for each possible value of $x_1 = \mathsf{q}$ (where $\mathsf{q} \in [n]$), the setup distributes to each P_i $(i \geq 2)$ a look-up table containing n ciphertexts: among these ciphertexts, the one corresponding to $\mathsf{q} = i$ would be an encryption of $b_i = 1$, while the others would correspond to encryptions of $b_i = 0$. The idea is to 'point' P_i to the appropriate ciphertext in the look-up table without revealing b_i. For this, a random cyclic-shift can be used, say using an offset r (unknown to P_i). This offset r is given to P_1 to enable her to compute the 'pointer' $\mathsf{q}' = \mathsf{q} + r$. Lastly, the encryption is assumed to be randomized, otherwise P_i could learn b_i by simply inspecting her look-up table (since all but one ciphertexts correspond to encryptions of 0).

Based on the above ideas, we can obtain a $\mathcal{BC}$-efficient construction for securely computing the selection function, with $O(n)$ storage costs, as follows (in our final construction, we reduce the storage overhead). During the setup, each P_i $(i \geq 2)$ receives a look-up table containing a 'shifted' sequence of n ciphertexts (as explained above). Each of the look-up tables uses the same offset r for the shift and P_1 is given this offset r. The online phase begins with P_1 computing the appropriate pointer $\mathsf{q}' = x_1 + r = \mathsf{q} + r$, which is communicated over a forward pass of the chain to all. During this pass, each party P_i uses the ciphertext at index q' of her look-up table (which would correspond to an encryption of b_i) to homomorphically compute an encryption of $(b_i \cdot x_i)$. These encryptions are aggregated over the chain, resulting in the encryption of $\sum_{i=2}^{n}(b_i \cdot x_i) = x_{\mathsf{q}}$ at the end of the forward pass. The final step is to compute the output by decrypting this AHE output ciphertext. Possible ways to do this decryption in a $\mathcal{BC}$- efficient manner include either **(a)** incremental decryption (carried out over a chain) of this ciphertext or **(b)** use garbled circuits. We opt for approach **(b)** to avoid the additional requirement that the AHE used must support incremental decryption.

In the approach using garbled circuits for decryption, we consider a garbled circuit that takes as input the AHE ciphertext, has the secret key of AHE hard-coded and outputs the decryption. Similar to the protocol Π_{abl} (Fig. 3), the input labels of the garbled circuit are additively shared among the parties. This enables them to reconstruct (over a backward pass of the chain) the appropriate label corresponding to the output ciphertext and obtain the output via evaluation of the garbled circuit.

While the above construction is indeed $\mathcal{BC}$-efficient in the online phase, observe that the setup involves parties receiving look-up tables of size n. We avoid this in our final construction that achieves storage and computation complexity also independent of n. The main idea is to 'compress' the look-up table in a way that still allows party P_i to obtain the ciphertext corresponding to b_i (without revealing b_i).

Interestingly, this can be done using garbled circuits, thereby avoiding new primitives or assumptions over the above described construction. As part of the setup, each P_i is given a garbled circuit, say $\mathtt{GC}_i$ which garbles a circuit C described as follows: The circuit C has i, the public key of the AHE and the randomness used for encryption hard-coded; it takes as input the index j and outputs the encryption of b_i (where $b_i = 1$ if $\mathsf{q} = i$ holds and 0 otherwise). Further, P_1 is given the labels for input wires. The final construction differs from the previous construction in the following aspects: **(a)** the 'pointer' sent by P_1 is the appropriate label corresponding to q (instead of the index q' in the look-up table approach). **(b)** Each P_i obtains the encryption of b_i by evaluating $\mathtt{GC}_i$ using the label corresponding to q that it receives in the forward pass (instead of obtaining the appropriate encryption directly from the look-up table).

To make the above approach work while preserving $\mathcal{BC}$-efficiency, it is important that the 'pointer' label given by P_1 can be used by all parties to evaluate their respective garbled circuits (analogous to P_1 giving the same pointer index to all in the lookup-table approach). This is because we cannot afford to make P_1 give n different pointers, one for each garbled circuit as that would inflate the $\mathcal{BC}$ complexity. To enable the use of the same input label across the n garbled circuits, we use a slightly modified garbling algorithm that takes as input the labels corresponding to the input wires. The garbling algorithm of Yao [Yao86] easily supports this.

Lastly, we point out that it may seem problematic to give P_1 all the input labels of the garbled circuits (computing the encryptions) as this would compromise the privacy of garbling. However, we need to rely of privacy of garbling only when P_1 is honest. This is because an adversary corrupting P_1 and P_i ($i \geq 2$) already knows b_i. When P_1 is honest, a potentially corrupt P_i ($i \geq 2$) will have access to only one set of input labels of $\mathtt{GC}_i$ and privacy of garbling ensures that P_i cannot learn b_i. Thus, security is maintained.

The formal description of the protocol appears in Fig. 4.

Correctness. Correctness of garbling with respect to $\mathtt{GC}_i$ for each $P_i \in [n]$ and correctness of AHE ensures that Z computed at the end of the first forward pass corresponds to an encryption of $\sum_{i=2}^{n}(b_i \cdot x_i) = x_{\mathsf{q}}$ (where $b_i = 0$ for $i \neq \mathsf{q}$ and 1 otherwise). It now follows from correctness of garbling with respect to $\mathtt{GC}_{\mathtt{Dec}}$ (that computes the decryption of an input AHE ciphertext) that the output y computed is indeed the correct output x_{q}.

$\mathcal{BC}$-Analysis. We analyze the communication incurred by a party, say P_i, in an execution of $\Pi_{\mathtt{sel}}$. First, we observe that throughout $\Pi_{\mathtt{sel}}$ each party communicates with at most two other parties (i.e. P_{i-1} and P_{i+1}). Further, the messages communicated (such as $\mathbf{K}$, $\{K'_{\alpha,i}\}_{\alpha \in [\lambda]}, y$) are of size at most λ^2, for the GC wire label shares, plus the size of one AHE ciphertext, which is $\mathsf{poly}(\lambda)$. It is therefore easy to see that the bottleneck complexity of $\Pi_{\mathtt{sel}}$ is $\mathsf{poly}(\lambda)$ and independent of n.

Private input. P_1's input is a selection index $\mathsf{q} \in \{2,\ldots,n\}$ and the inputs of the other parties are $x_i \in \mathbb{Z}_M$.
Output. $f(x_1 = \mathsf{q}, x_2, \ldots, x_n)$.
Tools. Additively homomorphic Encryption over $\mathbb{Z}_M$ $\mathtt{AHE} = (\mathtt{Keygen}, \mathtt{Enc}, \mathtt{Dec}, \mathtt{Add}, \mathtt{ScalMul})$ (see Definition 6)[a], Garbling scheme $(\mathtt{garble}, \mathtt{eval})$ [b].
Correlated Randomness Setup. The setup involves the following:

1. Let $(\mathsf{pk}, \mathsf{sk}) \leftarrow \mathtt{Keygen}(1^\lambda)$.
2. For $i \in \{2,\ldots,n\}$:
   - Let $C_{i,\mathsf{pk},r_{i,\mathtt{Enc}}}(\mathsf{q})$ denote a circuit that has the value i, pk and the randomness used for encryption $r_{i,\mathtt{Enc}}$ hard-coded, takes as input an index q; outputs $c = \mathtt{Enc}(\mathsf{pk}, 1; r_{i,\mathtt{Enc}})$ if $\mathsf{q} = i$ holds and $c = \mathtt{Enc}(\mathsf{pk}, 0; r_{i,\mathtt{Enc}})$ otherwise.
   - Sample a set of input labels $\{\widetilde{K}_\alpha^{(0)}, \widetilde{K}_\alpha^{(1)}\}_{\alpha\in[\lambda]}$
   - Compute $\mathtt{GC}_i \leftarrow \mathtt{garble}(C_{i,\mathsf{pk},r_{\mathtt{Enc}}}, \{\widetilde{K}_\alpha^{(0)}, \widetilde{K}_\alpha^{(1)}\}_{\alpha\in[\lambda]}, 1^\lambda)$
3. Let $C_{\mathsf{sk}}(ct)$ denote a circuit that has a secret key value sk hard-coded, takes as input a ciphertext ct and outputs $z \leftarrow \mathtt{Dec}(\mathsf{sk}, ct)$.
4. Sample a set of input labels $\{K_\alpha^{(0)}, K_\alpha^{(1)}\}_{\alpha\in[\lambda]}$ and compute $\mathtt{GC}_{\mathtt{Dec}} \leftarrow \mathtt{garble}(C_{\mathsf{sk}}, \{K_\alpha^{(0)}, K_\alpha^{(1)}\}_{\alpha\in[\lambda]}, 1^\lambda)$. For each $\alpha \in [\lambda], b \in \{0,1\}$, let $(K_{\alpha,1}^{(b)}, \ldots, K_{\alpha,n}^{(b)})$ denote the additive sharing of $K_\alpha^{(b)}$.
5. Output $\left(\mathsf{pk}, \mathtt{GC}_i, \{K_{\alpha,i}^{(0)}, K_{\alpha,i}^{(1)}\}_{\alpha\in[\lambda]}\right)$ to P_i $(i \in \{2,\ldots,n\})$.
6. Output $\left(\mathsf{pk}, \{\widetilde{K}_\alpha^{(0)}, \widetilde{K}_\alpha^{(1)}\}_{\alpha\in[\lambda]}, \{K_{\alpha,1}^{(0)}, K_{\alpha,1}^{(1)}\}_{\alpha\in[\lambda]}, \mathtt{GC}_{\mathtt{Dec}}\right)$ to P_1.

The Protocol. The following steps are run in the online phase of the protocol:
Phase 1 (Round 1 to Round n). During round i, P_i does the following:

- If $i = 1$: let $(b_1, \ldots, b_\lambda)$ denote the bits corresponding to $x_1 = \mathsf{q}$. Sample randomness r and compute $ct_1 = \mathtt{Enc}(\mathsf{pk}, 0; r)$.
  Set $\mathbf{K} = \{\widetilde{K}_\alpha^{(b_\alpha)}\}_{\alpha\in[\lambda]}$. Send $(\mathbf{K}, ct_1)$ to P_{i+1}.
- If $i \neq 1$: let $(\mathbf{K}, ct_{i-1})$ denote the message received from P_{i-1} during the previous round.
  - Compute $c_i' = \mathtt{eval}(\mathtt{GC}_i, \mathbf{K})$.
  - Compute $c_i^* = \mathtt{ScalMul}(\mathsf{pk}, c_i', x_i)$.
  - Compute $ct_i = \mathtt{Add}(\mathsf{pk}, ct_{i-1}, c_i^*)$.
- If $i < n$, send $(\mathbf{K}, ct_i)$ to P_{i+1}. Else, set $Z = ct_n$.

Phase 2 (Round $n+1$ to Round $2n$). In this phase, parties use their additive shares of the labels of $\mathtt{GC}_{\mathtt{Dec}}$ to reconstruct the input label (say $\vec{K}$) corresponding to Z. The steps are identical to Phase 2 of Figure 3.3 .

Output Computation. P_1 runs $y \leftarrow \mathtt{eval}(\mathtt{GC}_{\mathtt{Dec}}, \vec{K})$.

Phase 3 (Output Transfer). This phase is identical to Phase 3 of Figure 3.1.

[a] Here we assume for simplicity that $M \geq 2^\lambda$ so the input of the parties can be encrypted using the $\mathtt{AHE}$. As described in the preliminaries, if $M < 2^\lambda$, one can simply perform the encryption of the inputs e.g., in a bit by bit fashion.
[b] In this construction, we assume the modified $\mathtt{garble}$ algorithm which takes as additional input, the labels of the garbled circuit. Yao's garbling supports this requirement easily.

Fig. 4. $\Pi_{\mathtt{sel}}$

Extension to Larger Inputs. The protocol $\Pi_{\mathtt{sel}}$ can be extended for the case where the inputs of $P_2, \ldots P_n$ are arbitary-length vectors i.e. $x_i \in \mathbb{Z}_M^k$, by running the scalar multiplication on each entry of the input vector. In more detail, each P_i is still given a single garbled circuit $\mathtt{GC}_i$ which he uses to compute c'_i. However, each P_i would now compute a set of k ciphertexts $\{c^*_{i,\alpha} \leftarrow \mathtt{ScalMul}(\mathtt{pk}, c'_i, x_{i,\alpha})\}_{\alpha \in [k]}$ and $\{ct_{i,\alpha} = \mathtt{Add}(\mathtt{pk}, ct_{i-1,\alpha}, c^*_{i,\alpha})\}_{\alpha \in [k]}$ accordingly, where $x_{i,\alpha}$ denotes the α'th entry of x_i. This would introduce a multiplicative factor of k (which is independent of n) in the $\mathcal{BC}$ complexity of $\Pi_{\mathtt{sel}}$, thereby maintaining the $\mathcal{BC}$-efficiency.

We state the formal theorem below.

Theorem 2. *Protocol $\Pi_{\mathtt{sel}}$ securely computes the selection function $f(x_1 = j, x_2, \ldots, x_n) = x_j$ (where $x_1 \in \{2, \ldots, n\}$ and $x_i \in \mathbb{Z}_M$, $i \geq 2$) against an adversary corrupting upto $n-1$ parties passively.*

Proof. Let $\mathcal{I}$ and $\mathcal{H} = \mathcal{P} \setminus \mathcal{I}$ denote the set of indices corresponding to corrupt and honest parties respectively. Let $j_{\min}$ and $j_{\max}$ denote the least and maximum index corresponding to an honest party, where the indices are in the range $\{1, \ldots, n\}$. To prove security, we define below a simulator $\mathcal{S}$ that simulates the real-world view of the parties. Recall that $\mathcal{S}$ is given $(\mathcal{I}, \{x_i\}_{i \in \mathcal{I}}, y)$ (we refer to Sect. 2.2 for details about the security model).

Since the parties' roles are asymmetric, we describe the simulation in two parts based on whether $P_1 \in \mathcal{I}$ or not. First, we describe the simulation for the case when $P_1 \in \mathcal{I}$. As discussed previously, we do not rely on privacy of garbling with respect to $\mathtt{GC}_i$ ($i \in \mathcal{I}$) in this case. However, privacy of garbling with respect to $\mathtt{GC}_{\mathtt{Dec}}$ is crucial.

Setup Simulation.

- Compute the values $\mathtt{pk}$, $\mathtt{GC}_i$, $\{\widetilde{K}_\alpha^{(0)}, \widetilde{K}_\alpha^{(1)}\}_{\alpha \in [\lambda]}$ for each $i \in \mathcal{I}$ as per the protocol steps in Fig. 4.
- Sample $\vec{K} = \{K_1, \ldots, K_\lambda\}$ and run $\mathtt{GC}_{\mathtt{Dec}} \leftarrow \mathtt{simGC}(1^\lambda, \theta(C), y, \vec{K})$, where $\mathtt{simGC}$ denotes the simulator of the garbling scheme and $\theta(C)$ denotes the circuit computing the decryption of an $\mathtt{AHE}$ input ciphertext. (Note that the topology of the circuit is independent of the hard-coded values).
- For each $i \in \mathcal{I}$, sample $\left(\{K_{\alpha,i}^{(0)}, K_{\alpha,i}^{(1)}\}_{\alpha \in [\lambda]}\right)$ at random.

The view of corrupted P_i ($i \geq 2$) constructed by $\mathcal{S}$ at this stage comprises of $\left(\mathtt{pk}, \mathtt{GC}_i, \{K_{\alpha,i}^{(0)}, K_{\alpha,i}^{(1)}\}_{\alpha \in [\lambda]}\right)$. The view of corrupted P_1 constructed by $\mathcal{S}$ at this stage comprises of $\left(\mathtt{pk}, \{\widetilde{K}_\alpha^{(0)}, \widetilde{K}_\alpha^{(1)}\}_{\alpha \in [\lambda]}, \{K_{\alpha,1}^{(0)}, K_{\alpha,1}^{(1)}\}_{\alpha \in [\lambda]}, \mathtt{GC}_{\mathtt{Dec}}\right)$.

Phase 1 Simulation.

- Recall that $\mathcal{S}$ knows $x_1 = (b_1, \ldots, b_\lambda)$ and defined $\{\widetilde{K}_\alpha^{(0)}, \widetilde{K}_\alpha^{(1)}\}_{\alpha \in [\lambda]}$ during the setup simulation and can therefore compute $\mathbf{K} = \{\widetilde{K}_\alpha^{(b_\alpha)}\}_{\alpha \in \lambda}$.
- On behalf of each honest P_j ($j \in \mathcal{H}$), compute $ct_j \leftarrow \mathcal{S}_{\mathtt{AHE}}(\mathtt{pk}, m)$, where $m = y$ if $x_1 = \mathsf{q} \leq j$ and $m = 0$ otherwise. Here, $\mathcal{S}_{\mathtt{AHE}}$ refers to the simulator of the AHE for circuit privacy (Definition 6).

For $i \in \mathcal{I}$ and $j \in \mathcal{H}$, add $(\mathbf{K}, ct_j)$ to a corrupt party P_i's view if $i = j + 1$.

Phase 2 Simulation. This is similar to Phase 2 simulation of Theorem 1, which we describe below for completeness. Recall that for each $i \in \mathcal{I}$, $\mathcal{S}$ knows x_i and distributed $\mathtt{GC}_i$ (during the simulation of the setup) and can therefore can compute c_i^*.

- Compute Z by homomorphic addition of $ct_{j_{\max}}$ and each c_k^* for $k \in [j+1, n]$. Parse $Z = (z_1, z_2, \ldots, z_\lambda)$.
- For each $\alpha \in [\lambda]$ and $j \in \mathcal{H}$: If $j \neq j_{\min}$, sample $K'_{\alpha,j}$ at random. Else (i.e. for $j = j_{\min}$), set $K'_{\alpha,j_{\min}}$ such that $K'_{\alpha,j_{\min}} + \sum_{i=1}^{j_{\min}-1} K_{\alpha,i}^{(z_\alpha)} = K_\alpha$. Note that $K_{\alpha,i}^{(z_\alpha)}$ for $i \in [j_{\min} - 1]$ corresponds to additive shares of corrupt parties which were already defined by $\mathcal{S}$ during the setup.
- For $i \in \mathcal{I}$ and $j \in \mathcal{H}$, add $(Z, K'_{\alpha,j})$ to a corrupt party P_i's view if $i = j - 1$.

Phase 3 Simulation. For $i \in \mathcal{I}$ and $j \in \mathcal{H}$, add y to a corrupt party P_i's view if $i = j + 1$.

Below, we argue that the views of corrupt parties in the real and ideal world are indistinguishable via a series of intermediate hybrids.

-Hyb_0: Same as the real-world execution.
-Hyb_1: Same as the previous hybrid except that c_j^* for $j \in \mathcal{H}$ and $j \neq \mathsf{q}$ is computed as $\mathcal{S}_{\mathtt{AHE}}(\mathtt{pk}, 0)$.
This is in contrast to the previous hybrid where c_j^* for $j \in \mathcal{H}$ and $j \neq \mathsf{q}$ is computed as $\mathtt{ScalMul}(\mathtt{pk}, \mathtt{Enc}(\mathtt{pk}, 0), x_j)$. Indistinguishability follows from circuit privacy of the AHE.
-Hyb_2: Same as the previous hybrid except that ct_j for $j \in \mathcal{H}$ is computed as $\mathcal{S}_{\mathtt{AHE}}(\mathtt{pk}, m)$, where $m = y$ if $x_1 = \mathsf{q} \leq j$ and $m = 0$ otherwise.

This is in contrast to the previous hybrid where ct_j for $j \in \mathcal{H}$ is computed as $\mathtt{Add}(\mathtt{pk}, \mathtt{Enc}(\mathtt{pk}, 0), \mathtt{Enc}(\mathtt{pk}, m))$, where $m = y$ if $x_1 = \mathsf{q} \leq j$ and $m = 0$ otherwise. Indistinguishability follows from circuit privacy of the AHE.
-Hyb_3: Same as Hyb_2, except for the way in which $K'_{\alpha,j}$ for $j \in \mathcal{H}, \alpha \in [\lambda]$ is computed – For $j \neq j_{\min}$, $K'_{\alpha,j}$ is chosen uniformly at random, whereas for $j = j_{\min}$, it is set such that $K'_{\alpha,j_{\min}} + \sum_{i=1}^{j_{\min}-1} K_{\alpha,i}^{(z_\alpha)} = K_\alpha^{(z_\alpha)}$.

This is in contrast to the previous hybrid where $K'_{\alpha,j}$ is computed as $K'_{\alpha,j} \leftarrow K'_{\alpha,j+1} + K_{\alpha,j}^{(z_\alpha)}$. Since $K_{\alpha,j}^{(z_\alpha)}$ is distributed uniformly at random (conditioned on $\Sigma_{k=1}^{n} K_{\alpha,k}^{(z_\alpha)} = K_\alpha^{(z_\alpha)}$), this is indistinguishable from the previous hybrid.

-Hyb_4: Same as Hyb_3, except that $(\mathtt{GC_{Dec}}, \vec{K})$ is computed as $\mathtt{GC_{Dec}} \leftarrow \mathtt{simGC}(1^\lambda, \theta(C), y, \vec{K})$, where $\vec{K} = \{K_1, \ldots, K_\lambda\}$ is sampled at random and $\theta(C)$ denotes the topology of the circuit computing the decryption of an AHE input ciphertext.

This is in contrast to Hyb_3 where $\mathtt{GC_{Dec}}$ is computed as $\mathtt{GC_{Dec}} \leftarrow \mathtt{garble}(C_{\mathtt{sk}}, \{K_\alpha^{(0)}, K_\alpha^{(1)}\}_{\alpha\in[\lambda]}, 1^\lambda)$ where $\{K_\alpha^{(0)}, K_\alpha^{(1)}\}_{\alpha\in[\lambda]}$ is sampled at random and $\vec{K} = \{K_\alpha^{(z_\alpha)}\}_{\alpha\in[\lambda]}$ It follows from privacy of the garbling scheme (see Definition 5) that Hyb_4 is indistinguishable from Hyb_3.

Since Hyb_4 corresponds to the ideal execution and every pair of consecutive hybrids are indistinguishable, this completes the proof that the views of corrupt parties in the real and ideal world are indistinguishable for the case when $P_1 \in \mathcal{I}$.

Next, we describe the simulation for the case when $P_1 \in \mathcal{H}$. The main difference is that in this case we rely on privacy of garbling with respect to $\mathtt{GC}_i$ $(i \in \mathcal{I})$. On the other hand, simulation of $\mathtt{GC_{Dec}}$ is not relevant here as the adversary (who does not corrupt P_1) does not have access to $\mathtt{GC_{Dec}}$ in the real-world execution of the protocol.

Setup Simulation.

- For each $i \in \mathcal{I}$: Sample $\mathtt{pk}, r_{i,\mathtt{Enc}}$ and compute $c_i' = \mathtt{Enc}(\mathtt{pk}, 0; r_{i,\mathtt{Enc}})$. Run $\mathtt{GC}_i \leftarrow \mathtt{simGC}(1^\lambda, \theta(C), c_i', \{\widetilde{K}_1, \ldots, \widetilde{K}_\lambda\})$, where $\mathtt{simGC}$ denotes the simulator of the garbling scheme, $\{\widetilde{K}_1, \ldots, \widetilde{K}_\lambda\}$ are chosen at random and $\theta(C)$ denotes the topology of the circuit $C_{i,\mathtt{pk},r_{i,\mathtt{Enc}}}$ described in $\Pi_{\mathtt{sel}}$ (Fig. 4). Note that the topology of the circuit is independent of the hard-coded values.
- For each $i \in \mathcal{I}$, sample $(\{K_{\alpha,i}^{(0)}, K_{\alpha,i}^{(1)}\}_{\alpha\in[\lambda]})$ at random.

The view of corrupted P_i $(i \geq 2)$ constructed by $\mathcal{S}$ at this stage comprises of $\left(\mathtt{pk}, \mathtt{GC}_i, \{K_{\alpha,i}^{(0)}, K_{\alpha,i}^{(1)}\}_{\alpha\in[\lambda]}\right)$.

Phase 1 Simulation. On behalf of each honest P_j $(j \in \mathcal{H})$, compute $ct_j \leftarrow \mathcal{S}_{\mathtt{AHE}}(\mathtt{pk}, 0)$, where $\mathcal{S}_{\mathtt{AHE}}$ refers to the simulator of the AHE for circuit privacy (Definition 6). For $i \in \mathcal{I}$ and $j \in \mathcal{H}$, add $(\mathbf{K} = \{\widetilde{K}_1, \ldots, \widetilde{K}_\lambda\}, ct_j)$ to a corrupt party P_i's view if $i = j + 1$.

Phase 2 Simulation. Recall that for each $i \in \mathcal{I}$, $\mathcal{S}$ knows x_i and c_i' (during the simulation of the setup) and can therefore compute c_i^*.

- Compute Z by homomorphic addition of $ct_{j_{\max}}$ and each c_k^* for $k \in [j+1, n]$. Parse $Z = (z_1, z_2, \ldots, z_\lambda)$.
- For each $\alpha \in \lambda$ and $j \in \mathcal{H}$: Sample $K_{\alpha,j}'$ at random.
- For $i \in \mathcal{I}$ and $j \in \mathcal{H}$, add $(Z, K_{\alpha,j}')$ to a corrupt party P_i's view if $i = j - 1$.

Phase 3 Simulation. For $i \in \mathcal{I}$ and $j \in \mathcal{H}$, add y to a corrupt party P_i's view if $i = j + 1$.

Below, we argue that the views of corrupt parties in the real and ideal world are indistinguishable via a series of intermediate hybrids.

- Hyb_0: Same as the real-world execution.
- Hyb_1: Same as the previous hybrid, except that y is sent by P_1 in Phase 3 directly, without evaluating $\mathtt{GC}_{\mathtt{Dec}}$.

This is indistinguishable from the previous hybrid as the adversary's view is identical.

- Hyb_2: Same as the previous hybrid except that $\mathtt{GC}_i$ for $i \in \mathcal{I}$ outputs $\mathtt{Enc}(\mathtt{pk}, 0; r_{i,\mathtt{Enc}})$.

This hybrid differs from the previous one only if $i = \mathsf{q}$ holds. In such a case, c'_i corresponds to an encryption of 1 in the previous hybrid (as opposed to encryption of 0 in Hyb_2). This is indistinguishable from the previous hybrid due to CPA security of $\mathtt{AHE}$.

- Hyb_3: Same as the previous hybrid except that honest parties P_j $(j \in \mathcal{H})$ compute c'_j as $c'_j \leftarrow \mathtt{Enc}(\mathtt{pk}, 0; r_{j,\mathtt{Enc}})$.

This hybrid differs from the previous one only if $j = \mathsf{q}$ holds. In such a case, c'_j corresponds to an encryption of 1 in the previous hybrid (as opposed to encryption of 0 in Hyb_3). This is indistinguishable from the previous hybrid due to CPA security of $\mathtt{AHE}$.

- Hyb_4: Same as the previous hybrid except that c^*_j for $j \in \mathcal{H}$ is computed as $\mathcal{S}_{\mathtt{AHE}}(\mathtt{pk}, 0)$.

This is in contrast to the previous hybrid where c^*_j is computed as $c^*_j \leftarrow \mathtt{ScalMul}(\mathtt{pk}, \mathtt{Enc}(\mathtt{pk}, 0), x_j)$. Indistinguishability follows from circuit privacy of the $\mathtt{AHE}$.

- Hyb_5: Same as the previous hybrid except that ct_j for $j \in \mathcal{H}$ is computed as $\mathcal{S}_{\mathtt{AHE}}(\mathtt{pk}, 0)$.

This is in contrast to the previous hybrid where ct_j is computed as $\mathtt{Add}(\mathtt{pk}, \mathtt{Enc}(\mathtt{pk}, 0), \mathtt{Enc}(\mathtt{pk}, 0))$. Indistinguishability follows from circuit privacy of the $\mathtt{AHE}$.

-Hyb_6: Same as Hyb_5, except that $\mathtt{GC}_i$ for $i \in \mathcal{I}$ is computed as $\mathtt{GC}_i \leftarrow \mathtt{simGC}(1^\lambda, \theta(C), c_i', \{\widetilde{K}_1, \ldots, \widetilde{K}_\lambda\})$, where $\{\widetilde{K}_1, \ldots, \widetilde{K}_\lambda\}$ are chosen at random and $\theta(C)$ denotes the topology of the circuit $C_{i,\mathtt{pk},r_{i,\mathtt{Enc}}}$ described in $\Pi_{\mathtt{sel}}$ (Fig. 4).
This is in contrast to Hyb_5 where $\mathtt{GC}_i, \{\widetilde{K}_1, \ldots, \widetilde{K}_\lambda\}$ are computed as $\mathtt{GC}_i \leftarrow \mathtt{garble}(C_{i,\mathtt{pk},r_{i,\mathtt{Enc}}}, \{\widetilde{K}_\alpha^{(0)}, \widetilde{K}_\alpha^{(1)}\}_{\alpha \in [\lambda]}, 1^\lambda)$. Here, $\{\widetilde{K}_\alpha^{(0)}, \widetilde{K}_\alpha^{(1)}\}_{\alpha \in [\lambda]}$ is sampled at random and $\{\widetilde{K}_1, \ldots, \widetilde{K}_\lambda\} = \{K_\alpha^{(b_\alpha)}\}_{\alpha \in [\lambda]}$ where $\mathsf{q} = (b_1, \ldots, b_\lambda)$. It follows from privacy of the garbling scheme (see Definition 5) that Hyb_6 is indistinguishable from Hyb_5.

Since Hyb_6 corresponds to the ideal execution and every pair of consecutive hybrids are indistinguishable, this completes the proof that the views of corrupt parties in the real and ideal world are indistinguishable for the case when $P_1 \in \mathcal{H}$.

References

[ABJ+19] Ananth, P., Badrinarayanan, S., Jain, A., Manohar, N., Sahai, A.: From FE combiners to secure MPC and back. In: Hofheinz, D., Rosen, A. (eds.) TCC 2019. LNCS, vol. 11891, pp. 199–228. Springer, Cham (2019). https://doi.org/10.1007/978-3-030-36030-6_9

[AJL+12] Asharov, G., Jain, A., López-Alt, A., Tromer, E., Vaikuntanathan, V., Wichs, D.: Multiparty computation with low communication, computation and interaction via threshold FHE. In: Pointcheval, D., Johansson, T. (eds.) EUROCRYPT 2012. LNCS, vol. 7237, pp. 483–501. Springer, Heidelberg (2012). https://doi.org/10.1007/978-3-642-29011-4_29

[BGI+14] Beimel, A., Gabizon, A., Ishai, Y., Kushilevitz, E., Meldgaard, S., Paskin-Cherniavsky, A.: Non-interactive secure multiparty computation. In: Garay, J.A., Gennaro, R. (eds.) CRYPTO 2014. LNCS, vol. 8617, pp. 387–404. Springer, Heidelberg (2014). https://doi.org/10.1007/978-3-662-44381-1_22

[BGT13] Boyle, E., Goldwasser, S., Tessaro, S.: Communication locality in secure multi-party computation. In: Sahai, A. (ed.) TCC 2013. LNCS, vol. 7785, pp. 356–376. Springer, Heidelberg (2013). https://doi.org/10.1007/978-3-642-36594-2_21

[BGW88] Ben-Or, M., Goldwasser, S., Wigderson, A.: Completeness theorems for non-cryptographic fault-tolerant distributed computation (extended abstract). In: 20th ACM STOC, pp. 1–10. ACM Press, May 1988

[BHR12] Bellare, M., Hoang, V.T., Rogaway, P.: Foundations of garbled circuits. In: Yu, T., Danezis, G., Gligor, V.D. (eds.) ACM CCS 2012, pp. 784–796. ACM Press, October 2012

[BJPY18] Boyle, E., Jain, A., Prabhakaran, M., Yu, C.-H.: The bottleneck complexity of secure multiparty computation. In: Chatzigiannakis, I., Kaklamanis, C., Marx, D., Sannella, D. (eds.) ICALP 2018, LIPIcs, vol. 107, pp. 24:1–24:16. Schloss Dagstuhl, July 2018

[BV11] Brakerski, Z., Vaikuntanathan, V.: Efficient fully homomorphic encryption from (standard) LWE. In: Ostrovsky, R. (ed.) 52nd FOCS, pp. 97–106. IEEE Computer Society Press, October 2011

[Can00] Canetti, R.: Security and composition of multiparty cryptographic protocols. J. Cryptol. **13**(1), 143–202 (2000)

[CCD88] Chaum, D., Crépeau, C., Damgård, I.: Multiparty unconditionally secure protocols (extended abstract). In: 20th ACM STOC, pp. 11–19. ACM Press, May 1988

[CLTV15] Canetti, R., Lin, H., Tessaro, S., Vaikuntanathan, V.: Obfuscation of probabilistic circuits and applications. In: Dodis, Y., Nielsen, J.B. (eds.) TCC 2015. LNCS, vol. 9015, pp. 468–497. Springer, Heidelberg (2015). https://doi.org/10.1007/978-3-662-46497-7_19

[Cou19] Couteau, G.: A note on the communication complexity of multiparty computation in the correlated randomness model. In: Ishai, Y., Rijmen, V. (eds.) EUROCRYPT 2019. LNCS, vol. 11477, pp. 473–503. Springer, Cham (2019). https://doi.org/10.1007/978-3-030-17656-3_17

[DFH12] Damgård, I., Faust, S., Hazay, C.: Secure two-party computation with low communication. In: Cramer, R. (ed.) TCC 2012. LNCS, vol. 7194, pp. 54–74. Springer, Heidelberg (2012). https://doi.org/10.1007/978-3-642-28914-9_4

[DI06] Damgård, I., Ishai, Y.: Scalable secure multiparty computation. In: Dwork, C. (ed.) CRYPTO 2006. LNCS, vol. 4117, pp. 501–520. Springer, Heidelberg (2006). https://doi.org/10.1007/11818175_30

[DIK+08] Damgård, I., Ishai, Y., Krøigaard, M., Nielsen, J.B., Smith, A.: Scalable multiparty computation with nearly optimal work and resilience. In: Wagner, D. (ed.) CRYPTO 2008. LNCS, vol. 5157, pp. 241–261. Springer, Heidelberg (2008). https://doi.org/10.1007/978-3-540-85174-5_14

[DNPR16] Damgård, I., Nielsen, J.B., Polychroniadou, A., Raskin, M.: On the communication required for unconditionally secure multiplication. In: Robshaw, M., Katz, J. (eds.) CRYPTO 2016. LNCS, vol. 9815, pp. 459–488. Springer, Heidelberg (2016). https://doi.org/10.1007/978-3-662-53008-5_16

[EOYN21] Eriguchi, R., Ohara, K., Yamada, S., Nuida, K.: Non-interactive secure multiparty computation for symmetric functions, revisited: more efficient constructions and extensions. In: Malkin, T., Peikert, C. (eds.) CRYPTO 2021. LNCS, vol. 12826, pp. 305–334. Springer, Cham (2021). https://doi.org/10.1007/978-3-030-84245-1_11

[FKLS20] Fernando, R., Komargodski, I., Liu, Y., Shi, E.: Secure Massively parallel computation for dishonest majority. In: Pass, R., Pietrzak, K. (eds.) TCC 2020. LNCS, vol. 12551, pp. 379–409. Springer, Cham (2020). https://doi.org/10.1007/978-3-030-64378-2_14

[GMRW13] Gordon, S.D., Malkin, T., Rosulek, M., Wee, H.: Multi-party computation of polynomials and branching programs without simultaneous interaction. In: Johansson, T., Nguyen, P.Q. (eds.) EUROCRYPT 2013. LNCS, vol. 7881, pp. 575–591. Springer, Heidelberg (2013). https://doi.org/10.1007/978-3-642-38348-9_34

[GMW87] Goldreich, O., Micali, S., Wigderson, A.: How to play any mental game or A completeness theorem for protocols with honest majority. In: Aho, A. (ed.) 19th ACM STOC, pp. 218–229. ACM Press, May 1987

[HIJ+16] Halevi, S., Ishai, Y., Jain, A., Kushilevitz, E., Rabin, T.: Secure multiparty computation with general interaction patterns. In: Sudan, M. (ed.) ITCS 2016, pp. 157–168. ACM, January 2016

[HIKR18] Halevi, S., Ishai, Y., Kushilevitz, E., Rabin, T.: Best possible information-theoretic MPC. In: Beimel, A., Dziembowski, S. (eds.) TCC 2018. LNCS, vol. 11240, pp. 255–281. Springer, Cham (2018). https://doi.org/10.1007/978-3-030-03810-6_10

[HLP11] Halevi, S., Lindell, Y., Pinkas, B.: Secure computation on the web: computing without simultaneous interaction. In: Rogaway, P. (ed.) CRYPTO 2011. LNCS, vol. 6841, pp. 132–150. Springer, Heidelberg (2011). https://doi.org/10.1007/978-3-642-22792-9_8

[IKM+13] Ishai, Y., Kushilevitz, E., Meldgaard, S., Orlandi, C., Paskin-Cherniavsky, A.: On the power of correlated randomness in secure computation. In: Sahai, A. (ed.) TCC 2013. LNCS, vol. 7785, pp. 600–620. Springer, Heidelberg (2013). https://doi.org/10.1007/978-3-642-36594-2_34

[IMO18] Ishai, Y., Mittal, M., Ostrovsky, R.: On the message complexity of secure multiparty computation. In: Abdalla, M., Dahab, R. (eds.) PKC 2018. LNCS, vol. 10769, pp. 698–711. Springer, Cham (2018). https://doi.org/10.1007/978-3-319-76578-5_24

[IP07] Ishai, Y., Paskin, A.: Evaluating branching programs on encrypted data. In: Vadhan, S.P. (ed.) TCC 2007. LNCS, vol. 4392, pp. 575–594. Springer, Heidelberg (2007). https://doi.org/10.1007/978-3-540-70936-7_31

[LNO13] Lindell, Y., Nissim, K., Orlandi, C.: Hiding the input-size in secure two-party computation. In: Sako, K., Sarkar, P. (eds.) ASIACRYPT 2013. LNCS, vol. 8270, pp. 421–440. Springer, Heidelberg (2013). https://doi.org/10.1007/978-3-642-42045-0_22

[NN01] Naor, M., Nissim, K.: Communication preserving protocols for secure function evaluation. In: 33rd ACM STOC, pp. 590–599. ACM Press, July 2001

[QWW18] Quach, W., Wee, H., Wichs, D.: Laconic function evaluation and applications. In: Thorup, M. (ed.) 59th FOCS, pp. 859–870. IEEE Computer Society Press, October 2018

[Reg05] Regev, O.: On lattices, learning with errors, random linear codes, and cryptography. In: Gabow, H.N., Fagin, R. (eds.) 37th ACM STOC, pp. 84–93. ACM Press, May 2005

[Yao82] Yao, A.C.-C.: Protocols for secure computations (extended abstract). In: 23rd FOCS, pp. 160–164. IEEE Computer Society Press, November 1982

[Yao86] Yao, A.C.-C.: How to generate and exchange secrets (extended abstract). In: 27th FOCS, pp. 162–167. IEEE Computer Society Press, October 1986

Low-Communication Multiparty Triple Generation for SPDZ from Ring-LPN

Damiano Abram(✉) and Peter Scholl

Aarhus University, Aarhus, Denmark
{damiano.abram,peter.scholl}@cs.au.dk

Abstract. The SPDZ protocol for multi-party computation relies on a correlated randomness setup consisting of authenticated, multiplication triples. A recent line of work by Boyle et al. (Crypto 2019, Crypto 2020) has investigated the possibility of producing this correlated randomness in a *silent preprocessing* phase, which involves a "small" setup protocol with less communication than the total size of the triples being produced. These works do this using a tool called a *pseudorandom correlation generator* (PCG), which allows a large batch of correlated randomness to be compressed into a set of smaller, correlated seeds. However, existing methods for compressing SPDZ triples only apply to the 2-party setting.

In this work, we construct a PCG for producing SPDZ triples over large prime fields in the multi-party setting. The security of our PCG is based on the ring-LPN assumption over fields, similar to the work of Boyle et al. (Crypto 2020) in the 2-party setting. We also present a corresponding, actively secure setup protocol, which can be used to generate the PCG seeds and instantiate SPDZ with a silent preprocessing phase. As a building block, which may be of independent interest, we construct a new type of 3-party distributed point function supporting outputs over arbitrary groups (including large prime order), as well as an efficient protocol for setting up our DPF keys with active security.

1 Introduction

Multi-party computation (MPC) allows a set of parties to securely compute on private inputs, while learning nothing but the desired result of the computation. Modern MPC protocols often use a source of secret, *correlated randomness*, which can be distributed to the parties ahead of time, and used to help improve efficiency of the protocol. This is especially important in the dishonest majority setting, where up to $n-1$ out of n parties may be corrupted, since these types of protocols rely on expensive, 'public key'-type cryptographic primitives.

For instance, the SPDZ family of protocols [DPSZ12, DKL+13], which achieves active security with a dishonest majority, uses preprocessed, authenticated multiplication triples, to achieve a very fast online phase where the computation takes place. Multiplication triples, coming from the work of

Supported by the Aarhus University Research Foundation and Independent Research Fund Denmark (DFF) under project number 0165-00107B (C3PO).

G. Hanaoka et al. (Eds.): PKC 2022, LNCS 13177, pp. 221–251, 2022.
https://doi.org/10.1007/978-3-030-97121-2_9

Beaver [Bea92], are triples of random, secret-sharings of values a, b, c over some ring, where $c = a \cdot b$, and allow protocols to offload the heavy work of MPC multiplication to the preprocessing phase. Unfortunately, producing these triples, although it can be done ahead of time, is still an expensive process in terms of computation, communication and storage costs, since typically a very large number of triples is required, for any reasonably complex computation.

Most current techniques for triple generation are either based on homomorphic encryption [DPSZ12, DKL+13, KPR18] or oblivious transfer [KOS16]. Homomorphic encryption is computationally expensive and also incurs moderately high communication costs (especially due to the use of zero-knowledge proofs for active security), while oblivious transfer is much cheaper computationally, but requires a large amount of bandwidth.

More recently, Boyle et al. [BCG+19b] proposed using *pseudorandom correlation generators* to produce a large amount of correlated randomness without interaction, starting from only a short set of correlated seeds. More concretely, a PCG consists of a seed-generation algorithm, Gen, which outputs a set of correlated seeds $\kappa_0, \ldots, \kappa_{n-1}$, one given to each party. There is then an Expand algorithm, which deterministically expands κ_i into a large amount of correlated randomness R_i. The security requirements are that the expanded outputs $(R_i)_i$ should be indistinguishable from a sample from the target correlation, and furthermore, knowing a subset of the keys should not reveal any information about the missing outputs (beyond what can be deduced from their evaluation). This paradigm offers the potential to greatly reduce communication in the preprocessing of MPC protocols, while also reducing storage costs for the necessary correlated randomness, since the PCG seeds need only be expanded "on-demand".

The first construction of a PCG for authenticated triples [BCG+19b] was based on homomorphic encryption, and not so efficient in practice. However, more recently, the authors proposed another construction [BCG+20] based on a variant of the *ring learning parity with noise* (ring-LPN) assumption. By using distributed point functions [GI14, BGI15] to compress secret-shared, sparse vectors, this construction achieves much better concrete efficiency, as well as a good compression rate.

Unfortunately, both of these PCGs for authenticated, SPDZ-style triples are restricted to the 2-party setting. Note that *unauthenticated* triples, as used in passively secure protocols, can be generated with a PCG in the multi-party setting, with a transformation from [BCG+19b], however, this does not apply to the more complex task of authenticated sharings.

1.1 Our Contributions

In this work, we investigate the possibility of constructing PCGs for SPDZ-style, authenticated triples in the multi-party setting. As our main contributions, we construct such a PCG based on the ring-LPN assumption over large prime fields, and design an actively secure protocol for distributing the PCG seeds among the parties. Our PCG allows expanding short, correlated seeds of size $O(n^3\sqrt{N})$ into N SPDZ triples for n parties. Meanwhile, our actively secure setup protocol produces N SPDZ triples for n parties with $O(n^4\sqrt{N})$ communication. Compared with previous protocols for SPDZ [KPR18,KOS16], which use $O(n^2N)$ communication, our protocol scales sublinearly in the number of triples, but is less suitable for a large number of parties. (In the above, we ignore asymptotic factors that only depend on the security parameter.)

Below, we expand on our results in a little more detail.

Background: Construction of [BCG+20]**.** We first briefly recall the 2-party PCG for authenticated triples from [BCG+20]. Their construction relies on a variant of the ring-LPN (or module-LPN) assumption, which works over the polynomial ring $R = \mathbb{F}[X]/(F(X))$, for some finite field $\mathbb{F}$ and fixed polynomial $F(X)$. The assumption, for noise weight t and dimension c, states that the distribution

$$\{\boldsymbol{a}, \langle \boldsymbol{a}, \boldsymbol{e} \rangle \,|\boldsymbol{a} \leftarrow R^c, \boldsymbol{e} \leftarrow R^c \text{ s.t. } \mathrm{wt}(e_i) = t\}$$

is indistinguishable from random, when each $e_i \in R$ is a sparse polynomial of degree $< N$, with up to t non-zero coefficients. In typical parameters, N will be very large, while c is a small constant, and t the order of the security parameter.

The goal will be to produce a PCG that outputs 2-party, additive shares of a random tuple $(x, y, z, \alpha x, \alpha y, \alpha z)$, where $\alpha \in \mathbb{F}$, $x, y \leftarrow R$ and $z = x \cdot y \in R$. When R is chosen appropriately, such an authenticated triple over R can be locally converted into a large batch of N triples over $\mathbb{F}$.

To obtain a PCG, the construction picks vectors of sparse polynomials $\boldsymbol{u}, \boldsymbol{v} \in R^c$, and computes the tensor product $\boldsymbol{u} \otimes \boldsymbol{v} \in R^{c^2}$. Each of these polynomial products is still somewhat sparse, having at most t^2 non-zero coordinates. The idea is that the sparse $\boldsymbol{u}, \boldsymbol{v}$, as well as their products, can be secret-shared using distributed point functions (DPFs) [GI14,BGI15,BGI16], which provide a way to share sparse vectors in a succinct manner.

Given shares of these values, the parties can locally compute inner products with the public vector $\boldsymbol{a}$, to transform the sparse vectors $\boldsymbol{u}, \boldsymbol{v}$ into pseudorandom polynomials $x = \langle \boldsymbol{a}, \boldsymbol{u} \rangle$ and $y = \langle \boldsymbol{a}, \boldsymbol{v} \rangle$. Similarly, the shares of $\boldsymbol{u} \otimes \boldsymbol{v}$ can be locally transformed into shares of xy, due to bilinearity of the tensor product.

The above blueprint gives additive shares of the (x, y, z) components of the triple. This easily extends to obtain shares of $(\alpha x, \alpha y, \alpha z)$, since multiplying each sparse vector by $\alpha \in \mathbb{F}$ preserves its sparsity, so these can be distributed in the same way.

Using 3-Party Distributed Point Functions. A natural approach to extend the above to more than two parties, is to simply use multi-party DPFs. Unfortunately, existing n-party DPFs [BGI15] scale badly, with a key size growing exponentially in the number of parties. Instead, in the full version of [BCG+20], Boyle et al. sketched an approach using *3-party DPFs*, based on the observation that the product αxy can be broken down into a sum of $\alpha_i x_j y_k$, over parties $i, j, k \in [n]$. This means that each of these terms only needs to be shared between 3 parties, so 3-party DPFs suffice.

However, it turns out this approach is not so straightforward. An immediate challenge is that existing 3-party DPFs only output shares that are XOR-sharings, or shares over $\mathbb{Z}_p$ for small primes p; this excludes the important case of $\mathbb{F}_p$ where p is a large prime, as often used in protocols like SPDZ. Therefore, our first contribution is to construct a 3-party DPF suitable for this setting, by modifying the DPF of Bunn et al. [BKKO20] to work with outputs over any abelian group. Our modification introduces some leakage into the construction: when two specific parties are corrupted, they now learn some information about the secret index of the point function that is being hidden. Fortunately, it turns out that for our application to SPDZ, this leakage is harmless, since it translates to corrupt parties $\{P_j, P_k\}$ learning information on the product $x_j y_k$, which P_j and P_k already know if they collude.

An additional benefit of our DPF, beyond supporting more general outputs, is that our key sizes are smaller than the 3-party DPF of [BKKO20] by around a factor of 3.

PCG for Authenticated Triples. Given our 3-party DPF, we give the full construction of a multi-party PCG for authenticated triples over a large field $\mathbb{F}$. The basic construction for producing N triples with n parties has seeds of size $O(n^3 t^2 \sqrt{N} \lambda)$ bits, where λ is the security parameter and t is roughly λ, although this can be optimized slightly with a more aggressive assumption. Compared with the 2-party PCG of [BCG+20], we incur some extra costs moving to the multi-party setting, since theirs scales with $O(\log N)$ and not $O(\sqrt{N})$. This is due to the $O(\sqrt{N})$ seed size in our DPF, which is also inherited from previous 3-party DPFs [BGI15,BKKO20][1].

Efficient, Actively Secure Distributed Setup for 3-Party DPF. To obtain our triple generation protocol, we need a way of securely setting up the PCG seeds among the parties. The main necessary ingredient is a protocol for distributing the keys in our 3-party DPF. Previously, Bunn et al. [BKKO20] gave a secure protocol for setting up their 3-party DPF keys; however, as well as being very complex, their protocol only has passive security and tolerates 1 out of 3 corruptions. We therefore set out to design an *actively secure* protocol for our 3-party DPF, tolerating any number of corruptions, while only introducing a minimal communication overhead relative to the size of the underlying DPF keys. Our starting point is a lightweight, passively secure setup protocol based on OT and 2-party DPFs, which we combine with a recursive step to generate the necessary "correction word" in the DPF keys. Using recursion here helps to keep the communication overhead down in our protocol. We add active security, by first replacing OT with *authenticated OT*, whereby the receiver's choice bits are authenticated using MACs. We then apply several consistency checks on the DPF keys, including one inspired by a recent OT extension protocol [YWL+20],

[1] In the 2-party setting, there are efficient DPFs with logarithmic key size [BGI15, BGI16].

to prove that the parties behaved honestly. Here, we exploit the fact that the OT choice bits were authenticated, which allows us to reliably perform linear tests on these bits as part of our checks.

Our final setup protocol is very lightweight, and only communicates a small constant factor (2–3x) more information than the size of the DPF keys. On top of the inherent leakage in our DPF, the protocol introduces a small amount of leakage, in the form of allowing the adversary to try and guess some information about the secret point function. This is similar to leakage from other PCG setup protocols based on LPN [BCG+19a, YWL+20], and essentially only translates into an average of one bit of leakage on the (ring)-LPN secret.

Concrete Efficiency. We analyse the concrete efficiency of our actively secure protocol for setting up the PCG seeds, and producing authenticated triples. The main bottleneck is the distributed execution of the 3-party DPF, the only part of the protocol with $\Omega(\sqrt{N})$ complexity. We measure the efficiency of the construction by considering its "stretch", the ratio between the size of the produced triples and the total communication. We observed that the stretch becomes greater than 1 when N is above 2^{24}, meaning producing more than 16 million multiplication triples. When N increases, the stretch improves, reaching values close to 8 for $N = 2^{28}$. This comes, however, at a greater computational cost as the latter scales as $O(N \log(N))$. On the other hand, even for $N = 2^{20}$, our construction performs significantly better than alternative approaches such as Overdrive [KPR18], improving the communication complexity by at least a factor of 10. In this parameter regime, the 2-party PCG of [BCG+20] has practical computational cost, and although we have not implemented our construction, we believe the same will hold since it uses similar building blocks.

2 Notation and Preliminaries

We denote the multiplicative group of a finite field by $\mathbb{F}^\times$. The ideal generated by a polynomial $F(X) \in \mathbb{F}[X]$ is $\big(F(X)\big)$.

When dealing with bit sequences, with an abuse of notation, we identify the sets $\{0,1\}^k$, $\mathbb{F}_2^k$ and $\mathbb{F}_{2^k}$ as different representations of the finite field with 2^k elements. For this reason, when multiplying two elements $a, b \in \{0,1\}^k$, we mean multiplication in $\mathbb{F}_{2^k}$.

Throughout the paper, we will deal with protocols between an ordered set of n parties, $P_1, \ldots, P_n$. We let $\mathcal{H}$ be the set of indices of honest parties, and $\mathcal{C}$ the set of indices of corrupt ones.

The symbol $[m]$ indicates the set $\{0, 1, 2, \ldots, m-1\}$ and $\lfloor \cdot \rfloor$ denotes the integral part of a real number. We represent vectors using bold font, the j-th entry of a vector $\boldsymbol{v}$ is denoted by v_j or $v[j]$. We indicate the scalar product by $\langle \cdot, \cdot \rangle$ The function $\delta_y(\cdot)$ denotes the Kronecker delta function, that is,

$$\delta_y(x) := \begin{cases} 1 & \text{if } x = y, \\ 0 & \text{otherwise.} \end{cases}$$

Given two vectors $\boldsymbol{u}$ and $\boldsymbol{v}$ of dimensions l and m respectively, we denote their outer product by $\boldsymbol{u} \otimes \boldsymbol{v}$. Observe that this is an ml-dimensional vector whose $(im + j)$-th entry is $u_i \cdot v_j$. In a similar way, we define their outer sum $\boldsymbol{u} \boxplus \boldsymbol{v}$ as the ml-dimensional vector whose $(im + j)$-th entry is $u_i + v_j$.

We write $a \stackrel{\$}{\leftarrow} S$, where S is a set, to mean that a is randomly sampled from S. Finally, λ denotes the security parameter and $\mathbb{P}$ represents a probability measure.

Polynomial Rings. Let p be prime and N a positive integer. We will work with the ring $R := \mathbb{F}_p[X]/(F(X))$, where $F(X)$ is an irreducible, degree-N polynomial in $\mathbb{Z}[X]$. Similarly to the case of homomorphic encryption [SV14], we will be interested in the case where $F(X)$ factors completely modulo p into a product of distinct, linear terms. In this case, we say that R is fully splittable, and have the isomorphism $R \cong \mathbb{F}_p^N$. This can be ensured, for instance, by choosing N to be a power of 2 and the cyclotomic polynomial $F(X) = X^N + 1$, with $p = 1 \bmod (2N)$.

2.1 Module-LPN

The security of our triple generation protocol relies on the Module-LPN assumption with static leakage, a generalisation of Ring-LPN that was recently studied by Boyle et al. [BCG+20]. We recap here its definition.

Definition 1 (Module-LPN with static leakage). *Let $R := \mathbb{F}_p[X]/(F(X))$, for a prime p and $F(X)$ of degree N. Let t and c be two positive integers with $c \geq 2$. Let $\mathcal{HW}_t$ be the distribution that samples t noise positions $\omega[i] \stackrel{\$}{\leftarrow} [N]$ and t payloads $\beta[i] \stackrel{\$}{\leftarrow} \mathbb{F}_p$, outputting the polynomial*

$$e(X) := \sum_{i \in [t]} \beta[i] \cdot X^{\omega[i]}$$

embedded in the ring R. Let $\mathcal{A}$ be a PPT adversary and consider the game $\mathcal{G}^{\text{Module-LPN}}_{R,t,c,\mathcal{A}}(\lambda)$ described in Fig. 1. We say that the R^c-LPN$_t$ problem with static leakage is hard if, for PPT adversary $\mathcal{A}$, the advantage

$$Adv^{\text{Module-LPN}}_{R,t,c,\mathcal{A}}(\lambda) := \left| \mathbb{P}\left(\mathcal{G}^{\text{Module-LPN}}_{R,t,c,\mathcal{A}}(\lambda) = 1\right) - \frac{1}{2} \right|$$

is negligible in the security parameter λ.

Clearly, in the definition, we assume that the ring R and the values c and t depends on the security parameter λ. Observe that the greater c and t are, the harder the distinguishability becomes. A thorough analysis of the assumption

$\mathcal{G}_{R,t,c,\mathcal{A}}^{\text{Module-LPN}}(\lambda)$

Initialisation. The challenger activates $\mathcal{A}$ with $1\!\!1^\lambda$ and samples a random bit $b \xleftarrow{\$} \{0,1\}$. Then, it samples c elements of the ring $e_0, e_1, \ldots, e_{c-1} \leftarrow \mathcal{HW}_t$. Let the j-th noise positions of e_i be $\omega_i[j]$.
Query. The adversary is allowed to adaptively issue a polynomial number of queries of the form (i, j, I) where $i \in [c]$, $j \in [t]$ and $I \subseteq [N]$. If $\omega_i[j] \in I$, the challenger answers with SUCCESS, otherwise, it sends ABORT and halts.
Challenge. After the Query phase, for every $i \in [c-1]$, the challenger samples $a_i \xleftarrow{\$} R$ and sets

$$u_1 \leftarrow \sum_{i=0}^{c-2} a_i \cdot e_i + e_{c-1}.$$

Moreover, it samples $u_0 \xleftarrow{\$} R$. Finally, it gives $(a_0, a_1, \ldots, a_{c-2}, u_b)$ to the $\mathcal{A}$. The adversary replies with a bit b'. The final output of the game is 1 if and only if $b = b'$.

Fig. 1. The Module-LPN game.

can be found in [BCG+20], including for the case when the polynomial $F(X)$ splits completely into linear factors over $\mathbb{F}$, i.e. when $R \cong \mathbb{F}^N$.

Regarding the leakage, note that in Fig. 1, the adversary's guesses are restricted to *before* it learns the ring-LPN challenge; thus, even though there may be many queries, the resulting leakage is very small: just 1 bit of information on the secret (that is, the fact that all guesses were correct).

Choice of Error Distribution. The basic module-LPN definition assumes each error polynomial is chosen uniformly, subject to having t non-zero coefficients. We can also improve efficiency with more structured errors, such as *regular errors*, where the non-zero coordinates are more evenly spaced out, so that each is guaranteed to lie in a unique interval of size N/t. We use this variant in our efficiency estimates to improve parameters. Note that it has also been used previously [BCG+19b, BCG+20, YWL+20], and is conjectured to have essentially the same security as the standard assumption.

2.2 Pseudorandom Correlation Generators

To obtain a low communication complexity, our protocol uses pseudorandom correlation generators (PCGs) [BCG+19a, BCG+19b, BCG+20]. An n-party PCG is a pair of algorithms, the first of which outputs n correlated seeds of relatively small size. These can be, later on, locally expanded by the parties to obtain a large amount of desired correlated randomness. Since the expansion phase does not require any communication between the parties and the seed size is small compared to the output, the hope is to design low-communication protocols that securely generate and distribute the seeds to the parties. This allows the secure generation of large amounts of correlated randomness with low communication complexity.

The syntax of a PCG is given firstly by the algorithm Gen, which on input the security parameter, outputs n correlated keys κ_i, for $i \in [n]$. Secondly, the Expand algorithm takes as input (i, κ_i), and produces an expanded output R_i. The formal definition of a PCG, shown in the full-version of this work [AS21], requires both a correctness property and a security property.

Essentially, correctness requires that the joint distribution of the parties' outputs $(R_1, \ldots, R_n)$ is indistinguishable from the target correlation $\mathcal{C}_{\mathrm{corr}}$. The security property states that the knowledge of a subset of the seeds leaks no information about the other outputs, that could not already be inferred from the knowledge of the expansion of the given seeds.

2.3 Distributed Point Functions

In [GI14], Gilboa and Ishai introduced distributed point functions (DPFs). A point function is a function f whose support (i.e. the elements which have non-zero image) contains at most one element. Therefore, if the domain has size N, we can regard f as an N-dimensional vector with at most one non-zero entry, whose i-th entry, for $i \in [N]$, corresponds to the evaluation $f(i)$. We call such vector a unit vector, and often refer to the index of the non-zero entry as the *special position* and its value as the *non-zero element.*

An n-party DPF consists of a pair of algorithms, the first of which takes as input the description of a point function f and outputs n succinct keys. These can be, later on, locally evaluated by the parties on input x to obtain a secret-sharing of $f(x)$. DPFs and PCGs have some similarity, in that in both cases, we have an initial phase in which correlated, succinct keys are generated, followed by an evaluation phase that locally produces the desired output. The analogy between the two notions is the reason why DPFs are often a key building block of PCGs. Our protocol is no exception.

Definition 2 (DPF with leakage). *Let $(\mathbb{G}, +)$ be an abelian group and let N be a positive integer. An n-party distributed point function (DPF) for $(N, \mathbb{G})$ with leakage function* Leak *is a pair of PPT algorithms* $(\mathsf{DPF}^n_N.\mathsf{Gen}, \mathsf{DPF}^n_N.\mathsf{Eval})$ *with the following syntax:*

- *On input $\mathbb{1}^\lambda$, $\omega \in [N]$ and $\beta \in \mathbb{G}$,* $\mathsf{DPF}^n_N.\mathsf{Gen}$ *outputs n keys $\kappa_0, \kappa_1, \ldots, \kappa_{n-1}$.*
- *On input (i, κ_i, x) for $i \in [n]$ and $x \in [N]$,* $\mathsf{DPF}^n_N.\mathsf{Eval}$ *outputs a value $v_i \in \mathbb{G}$.*

Moreover, the following properties are satisfied

- ***(Correctness)****. For every $x, \omega \in [N]$ and $\beta \in \mathbb{G}$,*

$$\mathbb{P}\left(\sum_{i=0}^{n-1} v_i = \beta \cdot \delta_\omega(x) \,\middle|\, \begin{array}{l} (\kappa_0, \kappa_1, \ldots, \kappa_{n-1}) \leftarrow \mathsf{DPF}^n_N.\mathsf{Gen}(\mathbb{1}^\lambda, \omega, \beta) \\ v_i \leftarrow \mathsf{DPF}^n_N.\mathsf{Eval}(i, \kappa_i, x) \quad \forall i \in [n] \end{array}\right) = 1.$$

– ***(Security)**. There exists a PPT simulator* Sim *such that for every $T \subsetneq [n]$, $\omega \in [N]$ and $\beta \in \mathbb{G}$, the following distributions are computationally indistinguishable*

$$\left\{(\kappa_i)_{i\in T} | (\kappa_0, \kappa_1, \ldots, \kappa_{n-1}) \leftarrow \mathsf{DPF}^n_N.\mathsf{Gen}(1\!\!1^\lambda, \omega, \beta)\right\} \equiv_C$$
$$\left\{(\kappa_i)_{i\in T} \leftarrow \mathsf{Sim}\big(1\!\!1^\lambda, T, \mathsf{Leak}(T, \omega, \beta)\big)\right\}.$$

Essentially, correctness requires that the evaluation of the keys on x is a secret-sharing of β if $x = \omega$, or of 0 otherwise. Security instead states that the information inferable from a subset of the keys is bounded by the leakage function Leak, which takes as input the special position ω, the non-zero value β and the set of corrupted parties T. In most cases, Leak just outputs the domain size N and the codomain $\mathbb{G}$ of the point function. However, this will not happen in the DPF on which our protocol relies.

We write $\mathsf{DPF}^n_N.\mathsf{FullEval}(i, \kappa_i)$ to mean the result of calling Eval on the entire domain of the function, obtaining a secret-sharing of the full length-N unit vector.

State-of-the-Art. Actually, very little is known about DPFs. In [BGI15], the authors presented a 2-party DPF with $O(\log(N))$ key size and an n-party construction with $O(\sqrt{N})$ key size. In both cases, the only leakage is N and $\mathbb{G}$, however, while the 2-party construction allows outputs in any group $\mathbb{G}$, the multiparty DPF essentially works only when $\mathbb{G} = (\{0,1\}^l, \oplus)$, or when $\mathbb{G}$ has polynomial order. In [BKKO20], Bunn et al. presented an improved version of the second algorithm for the 3-party case, however, obtaining again $O(\sqrt{N})$ key size. As we will show in Sect. 3, this construction is also limited to outputs in $\mathbb{G} = (\{0,1\}^l, \oplus)$, and does not extend to e.g. $\mathbb{F}_p$ for a large prime p.

Distributed Sum of Point Functions. We use a simple extension of DPFs to sums of point functions, as also done in [BCG+20]. A DSPF scheme $\mathsf{DSPF}^n_{N,t}$ consists of algorithms ($\mathsf{DSPF}^n_{N,t}.\mathsf{Gen}$, $\mathsf{DSPF}^n_{N,t}.\mathsf{Eval}$), just as a DPF, except now Gen takes as input a pair of length-t vectors $\boldsymbol{\omega}, \boldsymbol{\beta} \in [N]^t \times \mathbb{G}^t$, which define the sum of point functions

$$f_{\boldsymbol{\omega},\boldsymbol{\beta}}(x) = \sum_{i\in[t]} \boldsymbol{\beta}[i] \cdot \delta_{\boldsymbol{\omega}[i]}(x)$$

Observe that $f_{\boldsymbol{\omega},\boldsymbol{\beta}}$ can be represented as a sum of unit vectors. We will refer to the latter as a multi-point vector.

The correctness property of a DSPF is then the same as a DPF, except we require that $\sum_{i\in[n]} v_i = f_{\boldsymbol{\omega},\boldsymbol{\beta}}(x)$, where $v_i = \mathsf{DSPF}^n_{N,t}.\mathsf{Eval}(i, \kappa_i, x)$. The security property is defined the same way as in a DPF.

Given a DPF, constructing a t-point DSPF can be done in the natural way, using one DPF instance for each of the t points, and summing up the t outputs of $\mathsf{DPF}^n_N.\mathsf{Eval}$ to evaluate the DSPF.

3 Generalisation of the 3-Party DPF to Prime Fields

In this section, we first recap the 3-party DPF of [BKKO20], and then describe our extension of this to support outputs modulo p for any prime p.

High-Level Description of [BKKO20]. The scheme assumes N, the domain size, is a perfect square, and the codomain is $\mathbb{F}_{2^l}$. It uses a PRG $G : \{0,1\}^\lambda \longrightarrow \mathbb{F}_{2^l}^{\sqrt{N}}$. DPF keys in their construction do not leak anything beyond the domain and codomain, namely, the leakage function is given by $\mathsf{Leak}(T, \omega, \beta) = (N, \mathbb{F}_{2^l})$ for every subset of parties $T \subsetneq [3]$, special position $\omega \in [N]$ and non-zero value $\beta \in \mathbb{F}_{2^l}$.

During key generation, the unit vector representing the point function is rearranged into a $\sqrt{N} \times \sqrt{N}$ matrix M. If we rewrite $x \in [N]$ as $x'\sqrt{N} + x''$ with $0 \leq x', x'' < \sqrt{N}$, the x-th element of the unit vector is moved to the x'-th row and x''-th column of the matrix M. We call the row containing β the special row.

$$M := \begin{bmatrix} 0\ 0 \cdots\cdots 0 \cdots\cdots\cdots 0 \\ 0\ 0 \cdots\cdots 0 \cdots\cdots\cdots 0 \\ \vdots\ \vdots \qquad\ \ \vdots \qquad\qquad \vdots \\ 0\ 0 \qquad\ \ 0 \qquad\qquad 0 \\ 0\ 0 \cdots\ 0\ \beta\ 0\ \cdots\cdots 0 \\ 0\ 0 \qquad\ \ 0 \qquad\qquad 0 \\ \vdots\ \vdots \qquad\ \ \vdots \qquad\qquad \vdots \\ 0\ 0 \cdots\cdots 0 \cdots\cdots\cdots 0 \end{bmatrix} \leftarrow \omega'$$

$$\uparrow$$
$$\omega''$$

The algorithm is essentially based on the observation that it is possible to compress a 3-party secret-sharing of a row of zeros. Indeed, it suffices to sample 3 random PRG seeds a_j, b_j, c_j for every row j and give $\{a_j, b_j\}$ to P_0, $\{b_j, c_j\}$ to P_1 and $\{c_j, a_j\}$ to P_2. To decompress, each party just has to evaluate the seeds and XOR the results. We obtain a secret-sharing of zero since

$$\Big(G(a_j) \oplus G(b_j)\Big) \oplus \Big(G(b_j) \oplus G(c_j)\Big) \oplus \Big(G(c_j) \oplus G(a_j)\Big) = \mathbf{0}.$$

In order to not leak ω', the parties need to obtain similar seeds for the special row too. Observe that for every row, an adversary controlling two parties sees two sets of seeds with only one element in common, therefore, security requires that the property to hold for the special row too. For this reason, the algorithm samples 4 PRG seeds $a_{\omega'}, b_{\omega'}, c_{\omega'}, d_{\omega'}$ and gives $\{a_{\omega'}, d_{\omega'}\}$ to P_0, $\{b_{\omega'}, d_{\omega'}\}$ to P_1 and $\{c_{\omega'}, d_{\omega'}\}$ to P_2. Observe how the property is still satisfied.

Although security is guaranteed, the seeds $a_{\omega'}, b_{\omega'}, c_{\omega'}, d_{\omega'}$ are not a compression of the special row. Indeed, by expanding them ad XORing the results as for the other rows, we obtain a secret-sharing of a random vector

$$r := G(a_{\omega'}) \oplus G(b_{\omega'}) \oplus G(c_{\omega'}) \oplus G(d_{\omega'}).$$

Observe that when there exists at least one honest party, one of the seeds remains unknown to the adversary, therefore, $\boldsymbol{r}$ is always indistinguishable from random. The DPF exploits this fact to include the correction word

$$\boldsymbol{CW} := \boldsymbol{r} \oplus \underbrace{(\overbrace{0, 0, \ldots, 0}^{\omega''}, \beta, 0, 0, \ldots, 0)}_{\sqrt{N} \text{ elements}}$$

to the key of every party. By adding the correction word to the expansion of the seeds of the special row, we obtain exactly what we desire, however, we must find a way to perform this operation without leaking the position ω'. The algorithm solves the problem by including in the keys a secret-sharing $[[\boldsymbol{y}]]_2$ of the unit vector having 1 in the special position ω'. Let $y_i[x']$ denote the x'-th bit of P_i's share of $\boldsymbol{y}$. By summing $y_i[x'] \cdot \boldsymbol{CW}$ to the expansion of the seeds, we add the correction word only to the special row. To summarise, the evaluation algorithm retrieves the row corresponding to the point that has to be evaluated, expands the associated seeds and obliviously adds the correction word when necessary.

Prime Field Generalisation. In order to generate multiplication triples over large prime fields $\mathbb{F}$ following the blueprint described in the introduction, we needed a 3-party DPF with codomain $\mathbb{F}$. Therefore, the first necessary step was to generalise the construction of [BKKO20]. As we have already mentioned, our modification requires weakening security, by introducing additional leakage.

The Issue. The main cause of problems is that large prime fields have characteristic different from 2 and therefore addition and subtraction are different operations. Referring to the roadmap in the previous section, we can still compress a secret-sharing of zero by sampling 3 PRG seeds a_j, b_j, c_j and giving $\{a_j, b_j\}$ to P_0, $\{b_j, c_j\}$ to P_1 and $\{c_j, a_j\}$ to P_2. However, the decompression requires attention, indeed, when two parties have a seed in common, one of them has to add its expansion to its secret-sharing, the other one has to subtract it. It is therefore necessary to associate every seed in the keys with a bit, which will be set if and only if the expansion of the seed has to be added. Whenever two parties have a seed in common, the associated bits will be opposites.

This property has to be satisfied by the seeds of the special row too. One possibility would be of course to do exactly the same as for the normal rows, obtaining a secret-sharing of zero. However, that would not allow us to use the correction word $\boldsymbol{CW}$ as it would leak the non-zero value β. The only other possibility would be to sample 4 PRG seeds $a_{\omega'}, b_{\omega'}, c_{\omega'}, d_{\omega'}$ as before and give $\{a_{\omega'}, d_{\omega'}\}$ to P_0, $\{b_{\omega'}, d_{\omega'}\}$ to P_1 and $\{c_{\omega'}, d_{\omega'}\}$ to P_2. Clearly, we have to associate every seed with a bit expressing whether its expansion has to be added or subtracted, but whatever way we do it for $d_{\omega'}$, there will always be two parties with the same bit. If those two parties are corrupted, the value of ω' is leaked to them, compromising security of the DPF. On the other hand, this leakage turned out not to be problematic for our application.

Our Solution. We decided to generate the sign bits so that ω' is leaked when the last two parties are corrupted. Since these bits do not need to be random, it is enough to ensure that the first party always subtracts the expansion of its seeds, the second party always adds them and the last party always adds the expansion of the first seed and subtracts the expansion of the second one. This means that the seeds of the second and the third party now have to be ordered. For instance, when $j \neq \omega'$, we can give $\{a_j, b_j\}$ to P_0, (b_j, c_j) to P_1 and (a_j, c_j) to P_2. When instead $j = \omega'$, we can give $\{a_j, d_j\}$ to P_0, (d_j, b_j) to P_1 and (d_j, c_j) to P_2. The construction is secure as long as the seeds in common with the first party are always in the first position of P_1 and P_2's pairs (which are ordered). On the other hand, it is crucial that the seeds of P_0 are an unordered set, otherwise ω' would be leaked to the adversary when P_0 and P_1, or P_0 and P_2 are both corrupted.

The fact that we do not need to protect ω' from an adversary corrupting the last two parties allows us to further improve the efficiency of the construction. For instance, we can secret-share $\boldsymbol{y}$ only between the second and the third party and remove the correction word from the key of the first party. Actually, since $\boldsymbol{y}$ is a unit vector, we can further compress the secret-sharing using the 2-party DPF of [BGI15], which has logarithmic key size.

Also, the seeds (a_j, b_j, c_j) can be somewhat compressed. If we consider the last seeds of the second and the third party, we observe that they coincide for every $j \neq \omega'$. When instead $j = \omega'$, the two seeds are independent. Essentially, they form a secret-sharing over $\mathbb{F}_{2^\lambda}$ of a $\sqrt{N}$-dimensional unit vector having special position ω' and random non-zero element. Such a secret-sharing can again be compressed using a 2-party DPF, such as from [BGI15,BGI16].

As a final optimization, it turns out the remaining seeds can also be compressed by roughly a factor of 2. This technique relies on the fact that we can generate the missing seeds using Random-OT tuples[2], which can themselves be compressed using a PCG based on the LPN assumption with *logarithmic* overhead [BCG+19b]. We omit the details here for ease of presentation, but the technique is used in our 3-party DPF protocol in Sect. 5.

Construction and Concrete Efficiency. Our 3-party DPF following the above ideas is given in Fig. 2. The construction assumes the domain size is a perfect square and has a prime field $\mathbb{F}$ as codomain. The size of the key κ_0 is $\sqrt{N} \cdot 2\lambda$ bits, while the size of κ_1 and κ_2 is dominated by $\sqrt{N} \cdot (\lambda + \log|\mathbb{F}|) + O(\log(N) \cdot \lambda)$ bits. When $|\mathbb{F}| \approx 2^\lambda$, this gives a total of around $6\sqrt{N}\lambda$ bits for all three keys. If we additionally apply the optimization mentioned above, and compress the seeds using random OT and LPN, the total key size falls to $3\sqrt{N}\lambda$ bits (ignoring small $\log N$ terms), which is around 3x smaller than that of [BKKO20] (which only works in groups of small characteristic, but on the other hand, does not leak any information on ω).

[2] Tuples $\big((X_0, X_1), (b, X_b)\big)$ where $X_0, X_1 \xleftarrow{\$} \{0,1\}^\lambda$ and $b \xleftarrow{\$} \{0,1\}$.

Prime field 3-party DPF

Let N be a perfect square and suppose that $\mathbb{G} = \mathbb{F}$. Let $G : \{0,1\}^\lambda \longrightarrow \mathbb{F}^{\sqrt{N}}$ be a PRG and let $\mathsf{DPF}^2_{\sqrt{N}}$ denote a 2-party DPF with domain size $\sqrt{N}$.

DPF.Gen. On input $1\!\!1^\lambda$, $\omega \in [N]$ and $\beta \in \mathbb{F}$, perform the following operations:

1. Rewrite ω as $\omega' \cdot \sqrt{N} + \omega''$ where $0 \leq \omega', \omega'' < \sqrt{N}$.
2. Sample $\Delta \xleftarrow{\$} \mathbb{F}_{2^\lambda}$ and compute

$$(\widehat{\kappa}_1^1, \widehat{\kappa}_1^2) \leftarrow \mathsf{DPF}^2_{\sqrt{N}}.\mathsf{Gen}(1\!\!1^\lambda, \omega', 1), \qquad (\widehat{\kappa}_2^1, \widehat{\kappa}_2^2) \leftarrow \mathsf{DPF}^2_{\sqrt{N}}.\mathsf{Gen}(1\!\!1^\lambda, \omega', \Delta).$$

3. For every $j \in [\sqrt{N}]$ with $j \neq \omega'$, sample $a_j, b_j \xleftarrow{\$} \{0,1\}^\lambda$ and set

$$S_j^0 \leftarrow \{a_j, b_j\}, \qquad S_j^1 \leftarrow b_j, \qquad S_j^2 \leftarrow a_j.$$

4. Sample $a_{\omega'}, d_{\omega'} \xleftarrow{\$} \{0,1\}^\lambda$ and set

$$S_{\omega'}^0 \leftarrow \{a_{\omega'}, d_{\omega'}\}, \qquad S_{\omega'}^1 \leftarrow d_{\omega'}, \qquad S_{\omega'}^2 \leftarrow d_{\omega'}.$$

5. Compute

$$b_{\omega'} \leftarrow \mathsf{DPF}^2_{\sqrt{N}}.\mathsf{Eval}(1, \widehat{\kappa}_2^1, \omega'), \qquad c_{\omega'} \leftarrow \mathsf{DPF}^2_{\sqrt{N}}.\mathsf{Eval}(2, \widehat{\kappa}_2^2, \omega'),$$

$$\boldsymbol{CW} \leftarrow G(a_{\omega'}) - G(b_{\omega'}) + G(c_{\omega'}) - G(d_{\omega'}) + \underbrace{(\overbrace{0, 0, \ldots, 0}^{\omega''}, \beta, 0, 0, \ldots, 0)}_{\sqrt{N}\ \text{elements}}.$$

6. Output $(\kappa_0, \kappa_1, \kappa_2)$ where

$$\kappa_0 := (S_j^0)_{j \in [\sqrt{N}]}, \qquad \kappa_i := \left(\widehat{\kappa}_1^i, \widehat{\kappa}_2^i, (S_j^i)_{j \in [\sqrt{N}]}, \boldsymbol{CW}\right) \quad \text{if } i \in \{1, 2\}.$$

DPF.Eval. On input $i \in [3]$, the key κ_i and a point $x \in [N]$, perform the following operations:

1. Rewrite x as $x' \cdot \sqrt{N} + x''$ where $0 \leq x', x'' < \sqrt{N}$.
2. If $i = 0$, pick an arbitrary ordering and rewrite $S_{x'}^0$ as (w_1^0, w_2^0).
3. If $i \in \{1, 2\}$, set $w_1^i \leftarrow S_{x'}^i$ and compute

$$y_i[x'] \leftarrow \mathsf{DPF}^2_{\sqrt{N}}.\mathsf{Eval}(i, \widehat{\kappa}_1^i, x'), \qquad w_2^i \leftarrow \mathsf{DPF}^2_{\sqrt{N}}.\mathsf{Eval}(i, \widehat{\kappa}_2^i, x').$$

4. Compute

$$\boldsymbol{v}_{x'}^i \leftarrow \begin{cases} -G(w_1^0) - G(w_2^0) & \text{if } i = 0, \\ y_i[x'] \cdot \boldsymbol{CW} + G(w_1^1) + G(w_2^1) & \text{if } i = 1, \\ y_i[x'] \cdot \boldsymbol{CW} + G(w_1^2) - G(w_2^2) & \text{if } i = 2. \end{cases}$$

5. Output $v_{x'}^i[x'']$.

Fig. 2. The prime field 3-party DPF

Theorem 1. *The construction described in Fig. 2 is a 3-party DPF for* $(N, \mathbb{F})$ *with leakage*

$$\mathsf{Leak}(T, \omega, \beta) = \begin{cases} (N, \mathbb{F}) & \text{if } T \neq \{1, 2\}, \\ \left(N, \mathbb{F}, \lfloor \omega/\sqrt{N} \rfloor\right) & \text{if } T = \{1, 2\}. \end{cases}$$

The proof of Theorem 1 can be found in [AS21, Appendix A].

Extension to Distributed Sum of Point Functions. In later sections, we will use a distributed *sum of* point functions, built on top of our 3-party DPF in the naive way, as described in Sect. 2.3. Here, the leakage function is extended to output $\lfloor \omega_i/\sqrt{N} \rfloor$, for each special position ω_i, for $i \in [t]$, when the set of corruptions is $T = \{1, 2\}$.

4 Multiparty PCG for Triple Generation

In this section, we show how to use our 3-party DPF to construct a multi-party, pseudorandom correlation generator for authenticated triple generation.

Authenticated Secret-Sharing. We produce additively secret-shared values with information-theoretic MACs, as used in SPDZ [DPSZ12, DKL+13]. Here, an n-party secret-sharing of $x \in \mathbb{F}$ is given by a tuple

$$[\![x]\!] := (\alpha_i, x_i, m_{x,i})_{i \in [n]}$$

where (α_i, x_i, m_{x_i}) are known to the i-th party. Each $\alpha_i \in \mathbb{F}$ is fixed for every sharing x, and is a share of the global MAC key $\alpha = \sum_i \alpha_i$. The shares $x_i \in \mathbb{F}$ and MAC shares $m_{x,i} \in \mathbb{F}$ then satisfy

$$\sum_i x_i = x, \quad \sum_i m_{x,i} = \alpha \cdot x$$

We construct a PCG for the correlation which samples a random triple $([\![x]\!], [\![y]\!], [\![z]\!])$, where x, y are random elements of the ring $R = \mathbb{F}[X]/F(X)$, and $z = x \cdot y$ (while the MAC key α is a scalar in $\mathbb{F}$). As discussed in Sect. 2, when p is a suitable prime and $F(X)$ is e.g. a cyclotomic polynomial of degree N, this is equivalent to a batch of N triples over $\mathbb{F}$, thanks to the CRT isomorphism $R \cong \mathbb{F}^N$.

Note that it is easy to see that this correlation satisfies the reverse-samplable requirement.

4.1 Construction

Our construction is given in Figs. 3 and 4. We combine 3-party DPFs with the ring-LPN assumption, following the outline in the introduction (also sketched in [BCG+20]).

In more detail, we will compress the x, y terms of the triple using sparse, random polynomials $u^r(X), v^r(X) \in R$, for $r \in [c]$. Recall that if $\boldsymbol{a} \in R^c$ is a public, random vector over R, then

$$x = \langle \boldsymbol{a}, \boldsymbol{u} \rangle, \quad y = \langle \boldsymbol{a}, \boldsymbol{v} \rangle$$

are computationally indistinguishable from random R elements, under the module-LPN assumption.

We sample the u^r, v^r polynomials by first picking sparse u_i^r, v_i^r for each party, and summing up these shares. These are implicitly defined in steps 2 of Fig. 3, which sample the non-zero coefficients and values of the polynomials.

Then, we use 2-party distributed (sums of) point functions to compress additive shares of the cross-products $\alpha_j \cdot u_i^r, \alpha_j \cdot v_i^r$ and $u_i^r \cdot v_j^s$, in steps 3–4. This allows the parties to obtain shares of the MACs $\alpha x, \alpha y$, as well as the product xy.

Finally, to obtain shares of αxy, we decompose this into a sum of products $\alpha_i \cdot x_j \cdot y_k$, for every $i, j, k \in [n]$. By distributing shares of each term $\alpha_i \cdot u_j^r \cdot v_k^s$ using the 3-party DPF from Sect. 3, the parties can locally recover shares of αxy in the evaluation stage.

Note that due to the leakage in our 3-party DPF, if P_j and P_k are both corrupted, they learn something about the indices of the non-zero entries in $\alpha_i \cdot u_j^r \cdot v_k^s$. However, since these indices are independent of α_i, this leakage does not give away anything that wasn't already known to P_j and P_k.

In [AS21, Appendix B], we prove the following.

Theorem 2. *Suppose that* $\mathsf{DSPF}^2_{N,t}$, DSPF^2_{2N,t^2} *and* DSPF^3_{2N,t^2} *are secure distributed sums of point functions, and the* R^c*-LPN*$_t$ *assumption (Definition 1) holds. Then the construction in Figs. 3 and 4 is a secure PCG for* n*-party authenticated triples over* $R = \mathbb{F}[X]/F(X)$.

Efficiency. Note that we can optimize the construction slightly, with the observation that in any 3-party DPF instance where two of i, j, k are equal, we can instead use a 2-party DPF. This reduces the total number of 3-party DSPFs from $c^2n^2(n-1)$ down to $c^2n(n-1)(n-2)$. Each DSPF has t^2 points and a domain of size $2N$. There are also $O(c^2n^2)$ 2-party DSPFs, however, since these have logarithmic key size, their cost is dominated by the 3-party instances.

As a further optimization, we can rely on module-LPN with a *regular error distribution* [BCG+20], where each of the t non-zero entries in an error vector is sampled to be within a fixed range of length N/t. This reduces the domain size of the DPFs from $2N$ and N down to $2N/t$ and N/t, respectively.

In Sect. 6, we analyze the concrete parameters of our PCG, and the efficiency of our protocol for securely setting up the seeds and producing triples.

5 Distributed Setup for the 3-Party DPF

We now present an actively secure protocol that permits to distribute the keys of the 3-party DPF described in Sect. 3. We start by giving an overview of the

PCG$_{\text{triple}}$

Let $\mathbb{F}$ be a prime field and let N be the number of generated triples. Let t and c be the parameters of the Module-LPN assumption.

Gen: On input $1\!\!1^\lambda$, do the following:

1. Sample MAC key shares $\alpha_i \xleftarrow{\$} \mathbb{F}$, for every $i \in [n]$.
2. For every $i \in [n]$, $r \in [c]$, sample $\boldsymbol{\omega}_i^r, \boldsymbol{\eta}_i^r \xleftarrow{\$} [N]^t$ and $\boldsymbol{\beta}_i^r, \boldsymbol{\gamma}_i^r \xleftarrow{\$} \mathbb{F}^t$.
3. For every $i, j \in [n]$ with $i \neq j$, $r \in [c]$, compute

$$\left(U_{i,j}^{r,0}, U_{i,j}^{r,1}\right) \leftarrow \mathsf{DSPF}_{N,t}^2.\mathsf{Gen}\left(1\!\!1^\lambda,\ \boldsymbol{\omega}_i^r,\ \alpha_j \cdot \boldsymbol{\beta}_i^r\right),$$
$$\left(V_{i,j}^{r,0}, V_{i,j}^{r,1}\right) \leftarrow \mathsf{DSPF}_{N,t}^2.\mathsf{Gen}\left(1\!\!1^\lambda,\ \boldsymbol{\eta}_i^r,\ \alpha_j \cdot \boldsymbol{\gamma}_i^r\right).$$

4. For every $i, j \in [n]$ with $i \neq j$, $r, s \in [c]$, compute

$$\left(C_{i,j}^{r,s,h}\right)_{h \in [2]} \leftarrow \mathsf{DSPF}_{2N,t^2}^2.\mathsf{Gen}\left(1\!\!1^\lambda,\ \boldsymbol{\omega}_i^r \boxplus \boldsymbol{\eta}_j^s,\ \boldsymbol{\beta}_i^r \otimes \boldsymbol{\gamma}_j^s\right).$$

5. For every $i, j, k \in [n]$ with i, j, k not all equal, for $r, s \in [c]$, compute

$$\left(W_{i,j,k}^{r,s,h}\right)_{h \in [3]} \leftarrow \mathsf{DSPF}_{2N,t^2}^3.\mathsf{Gen}\left(1\!\!1^\lambda,\ \boldsymbol{\omega}_j^r \boxplus \boldsymbol{\eta}_k^s,\ \alpha_i \cdot (\boldsymbol{\beta}_j^r \otimes \boldsymbol{\gamma}_k^s)\right).$$

6. For every $i \in [n]$, output the seed

$$\kappa_i \leftarrow \begin{pmatrix} \alpha_i, \left(\boldsymbol{\omega}_i^r, \boldsymbol{\beta}_i^r\right)_{r \in [c]}, \left(\boldsymbol{\eta}_i^r, \boldsymbol{\gamma}_i^r\right)_{r \in [c]}, \left(U_{i,j}^{r,0}, U_{j,i}^{r,1}\right)_{\substack{j \neq i \\ r \in [c]}}, \left(V_{i,j}^{r,0}, V_{j,i}^{r,1}\right)_{\substack{j \neq i \\ r \in [c]}} \\ \left(C_{i,j}^{r,s,0}, C_{j,i}^{r,s,1}\right)_{\substack{j \neq i, \\ r,s \in [c]}}, \left(W_{i,j,k}^{r,s,0}, W_{k,i,j}^{r,s,1}, W_{j,k,i}^{r,s,2}\right)_{\substack{(j,k) \neq (i,i), \\ r,s \in [c]}} \end{pmatrix}$$

Eval: On input the seed κ_i, do the following:

1. For every $r \in [c]$, define the two polynomials

$$u_i^r(X) = \sum_{l \in [t]} \boldsymbol{\beta}_i^r[l] \cdot X^{\boldsymbol{\omega}_i^r[l]}, \quad v_i^r(X) = \sum_{l \in [t]} \boldsymbol{\gamma}_i^r[l] \cdot X^{\boldsymbol{\eta}_i^r[l]}$$

2. For every $r \in [c]$, compute

$$\widetilde{u_i^r} = \alpha_i \cdot u_i^r + \sum_{j \neq i} \left(\mathsf{DSPF}_{N,t}^2.\mathsf{FullEval}(U_{i,j}^{r,0}) + \mathsf{DSPF}_{N,t}^2.\mathsf{FullEval}(U_{j,i}^{r,1})\right)$$
$$\widetilde{v_i^r} = \alpha_i \cdot v_i^r + \sum_{j \neq i} \left(\mathsf{DSPF}_{N,t}^2.\mathsf{FullEval}(V_{i,j}^{r,0}) + \mathsf{DSPF}_{N,t}^2.\mathsf{FullEval}(V_{j,i}^{r,1})\right)$$

(viewing outputs of FullEval as degree $N-1$ polynomials over $\mathbb{F}$)

Fig. 3. PCG$_{\text{triple}}$ - Part 1

3. For every $r, s \in [c]$, compute

$$w_i^{r,s} = u_i^r \cdot v_i^s + \sum_{j \neq i} \left(\mathsf{DSPF}^2_{2N,t^2}.\mathsf{FullEval}(C_{i,j}^{r,s,0}) + \mathsf{DSPF}^2_{2N,t^2}.\mathsf{FullEval}(C_{j,i}^{r,s,1}) \right)$$

4. For every $r, s \in [c]$, compute

$$\widetilde{w}_i^{r,s} = \sum_{\substack{j,k \\ (i,i) \neq (j,k)}} \Big(\mathsf{DSPF}^3_{2N,t^2}.\mathsf{FullEval}(W_{i,j,k}^{r,s,0}) + \mathsf{DSPF}^3_{2N,t^2}.\mathsf{FullEval}(W_{k,i,j}^{r,s,1}) + \mathsf{DSPF}^3_{2N,t^2}.\mathsf{FullEval}(W_{j,k,i}^{r,s,2}) \Big) + \alpha_i \cdot u_i^r(X) \cdot v_i^s(X)$$

5. Define the vectors of polynomials $\boldsymbol{u}_i = (u_i^1, \ldots, u_i^c)$, $\boldsymbol{v}^i = (v_i^1, \ldots, v_i^c)$, similarly for $\widetilde{\boldsymbol{u}}_i, \widetilde{\boldsymbol{v}}_i$.
   Let $\boldsymbol{w}_i = (w_i^{0,0}, \ldots, w_i^{c-1,0}, w_i^{0,1}, \ldots, w_i^{c-1,1}, \ldots, w_i^{c-1,c-1})$, and similarly define $\widetilde{\boldsymbol{w}}_i$.
6. Compute the final shares

$$x_i = \langle \boldsymbol{a}, \boldsymbol{u}_i \rangle, y_i = \langle \boldsymbol{a}, \boldsymbol{v}_i \rangle, z_i = \langle \boldsymbol{a} \otimes \boldsymbol{a}, \boldsymbol{w}_i \rangle \quad \text{and}$$
$$m_{x,i} = \langle \boldsymbol{a}, \widetilde{\boldsymbol{u}}_i \rangle, m_{y,i} = \langle \boldsymbol{a}, \widetilde{\boldsymbol{v}}_i \rangle, m_{z,i} = \langle \boldsymbol{a} \otimes \boldsymbol{a}, \widetilde{\boldsymbol{w}}_i \rangle$$

   in $\mathbb{F}_p[X]/(F(X))$.
7. Output $(\alpha_i, x_i, y_i, z_i, m_{x,i}, m_{y,i}, m_{z,i})$.

Fig. 4. $\mathbf{PCG}_{\text{triple}}$ - Part 2

passively secure approach; later we will delve into the details, including active security.

High-Level Overview. The protocol permits to derive a 3-party secret-sharing of the unit-vector

$$\underbrace{(\overbrace{0, 0, \ldots, 0}^{\omega}, \beta, 0, 0, \ldots, 0)}_{N}$$

given secret-shared special position and non-zero value $[[\omega]]_2$ and $[[\beta]]$. Writing $\omega = \omega'\sqrt{N} + \omega''$, and following the blueprint of our 3-party DPF, the protocol samples a random $\Delta \in \mathbb{F}_{2^\lambda}$ and shares the unit vectors

$$\boldsymbol{y} = \underbrace{(\overbrace{0, 0, \ldots, 0}^{\omega'}, 1, 0, 0, \ldots, 0)}_{\sqrt{N}}, \qquad \boldsymbol{Y} = \underbrace{(\overbrace{0, 0, \ldots, 0}^{\omega'}, \Delta, 0, 0, \ldots, 0)}_{\sqrt{N}}$$

between the last two parties using a 2-party DPF. The shares of $\boldsymbol{Y}$ are regarded as vectors of seeds.

As we mentioned in Sect. 3, to derive the remaining seeds, we rely on oblivious transfer (OT). Observe that for every position $j \in [\sqrt{N}]$, the first party has to generate two random seeds. Moreover, for every j, the last two parties have to learn one of these seeds each. The discovered seeds coincide if and only if $j = \omega'$. We setup these seeds by running two sets of OTs, where the first party is sender in both, and the other two parties play receiver in one set each. The receivers' choice bits are determined based on the shares of $\boldsymbol{y}$, which are random bits that coincide if and only if $j = \omega'$.

Assuming the availability of a 3-party secret sharing of

$$\boldsymbol{v} = \underbrace{(\overbrace{0, 0, \ldots, 0}^{\omega''}, \beta, 0, 0, \ldots, 0)}_{\sqrt{N}},$$

the generation of the correction word is very simple: each party can just retrieve its share of $\boldsymbol{v}$ and add or subtract the expansions of its seeds. The correction word is obtained by broadcasting and adding the results. Once we have the correction word, the DPF setup phase is complete. The only remaining question, then, is how to derive the secret-sharing of $\boldsymbol{v}$: since it is a unit-vector, we will use recursion.

We now discuss the protocol more in detail, including the details of recursion and active security. To simplify the presentation, we introduce some notation and building blocks.

Double Exponential Representation. We assume that N is a double exponential, that is, $N = 2^{2^h}$ for some $h \in \mathbb{N}$. In practice, this choice is rather restrictive as the value of N grows very quickly. However, we only make this assumption to simplify the description of a recursive step in our protocol, and this step can easily be adapted to the case $N = 2^m$ without significantly affecting the overall complexity[3].

We define the double exponential function $\mathrm{dE}(\cdot)$ as

$$\mathrm{dE}(k) := \begin{cases} 2 & \text{if } k = -1, \\ 2^{2^k} & \text{otherwise.} \end{cases}$$

We also use the following decomposition of integers, using a double exponential basis. Its proof can be found in [AS21, Appendix C].

Lemma 1. *Any $\omega \in [N]$ can be written in a unique way as*

$$\omega = x(-1) + \sum_{i \in [h]} x(i) \cdot \mathrm{dE}(i)$$

for some $x(i) \in [\mathrm{dE}(i)]$ (depending on ω), for $i \in [h] \cup \{-1\}$, i.e. $0 \leq x(i) < 2^{2^i}$ if $i \in [h]$ and $x(-1) \in \{0, 1\}$.

[3] The protocol is more efficient when m is divisible by a power of 2.

Notation. Given a number $\omega \in [N]$, we denote its j-th bit by ω_j, whereas the j-th element of its double exponential notation is indicated by $\omega(j)$. Let $\mathcal{K} := [h] \cup \{-1\}$ and define

$$\mathcal{T} := \Big\{ (k, j) \mid k \in \mathcal{K}, j \in [\mathrm{dE}(k)] \Big\}.$$

In the protocol we use h PRGs. The k-th one will be $G_k : \{0,1\}^\lambda \longrightarrow \mathbb{F}^{\mathrm{dE}(k)}$. We will also rely on a tweakable correlation-robust hash function

$$H : \{0,1\}^\lambda \times \{0,1\}^* \longrightarrow \{0,1\}^\lambda.$$

An important fact is that the protocol requires the cardinality of the field $\mathbb{F}$ to be sufficiently close to 2^λ. More specifically, consider the map $\mathrm{Enc} : \{0,1\}^\lambda \longrightarrow \mathbb{F}$ sending every string $(x_0, x_1, \ldots, x_{\lambda-1})$ to $\sum_{i\in[\lambda]} x_i \cdot 2^i$. Let U be the uniform distribution over $\{0,1\}^\lambda$ and let V be the uniform distribution over $\mathbb{F}$. In order to be secure, the protocol requires the statistical distance between V and $\mathrm{Enc}(U)$ to be negligible in the security parameter. It is possible to prove that this condition is satisfied if and only if $|p - 2^\lambda|/2^\lambda$, where $p = |\mathbb{F}|$, is negligible in λ.

We also define a set of sign bits u_i^l with $i \in [3]$ and $l \in \{0,1\}$, by

$$u_i^l := \begin{cases} 1 & \text{if } i = 1, \text{ or } i = 2 \text{ and } l = 0 \\ -1 & \text{otherwise.} \end{cases}$$

These parameters will indicate whether we need to add or subtract the expansion of the seeds in the 3-party DPF keys (see Sect. 3).

Finally, we define some matrices used to translate between different representations. In the protocol, we use the set of matrices $(B_k)_{k\in\mathcal{K}}$, which allow us to map an N-dimensional unit vector having special position $\omega \in [N]$ into a $\mathrm{dE}(k)$-dimensional unit vector with special position $\omega(k)$ and the same non-zero value. We also use a matrix $C \in \mathbb{F}_2^{\log(N)\times|\mathcal{T}|}$. This allows us to retrieve a binary representation of $\eta \in [N]$, given the unit-vector

$$\underbrace{(\overbrace{0, 0, \ldots, 0}^{\eta(k)}, 1, 0, 0, \ldots, 0)}_{\mathrm{dE}(k)}$$

for every $k \in \mathcal{K}$. A formal description of the matrices $(B_k)_k$ and C can be found in [AS21, Appendix D].

5.1 Resources

The protocol we are going to present relies on an authenticated Random-OT functionality, which we instantiate using similar techniques to the TinyOT protocol [NNOB12]. We assume that every pair of parties (P_i, P_j) has access to an instance $\mathcal{F}^{i,j}_{\text{auth-ROT}}$ of this resource. The functionality $\mathcal{F}^{i,j}_{\text{auth-ROT}}$ provides

Random-OT tuples, i.e. upon every call, P_i, the sender, obtains two random values $X_0, X_1 \in \{0,1\}^\lambda$, whereas P_j, the receiver, obtains a random choice bit b and the value X_b. Additionally, $\mathcal{F}^{i,j}_{\text{auth-ROT}}$ permits to perform linear operations on the choice bits it stored. The results of these computations are output to P_i and their correctness is guaranteed even when P_j is corrupted. Finally, the resource can output random bits to P_j. The latter can be used in combination with the choice bits in the computations. A formal description of $\mathcal{F}^{i,j}_{\text{auth-ROT}}$ can be found in [AS21, Appendix F], where we also show how to implement it with low communication complexity using a Correlated-OT functionality.

In the protocol, we also use a black-box multiparty computation functionality $\mathcal{F}_{\text{MPC}}$ which allows n parties to perform computations over the prime field $\mathbb{F}$ and over $\mathbb{F}_2$. A complete description can be found in [AS21, Figure 13]. The functionality stores the inputs and results of the computations internally, providing the parties with handles. Each of the stored values is associated with one of the domains $\mathbb{F}$ and $\mathbb{F}_2$ to which the element must belong. In the first case, the handle of x is denoted by $[[x]]$, whereas in the second case, the handle is denoted by $[[x]]_2$. Sometimes, we will abuse the notation and we will write $[[x]]_2$ even if $x \notin \{0,1\}$, in that case, it is understood that the functionality stored x bit by bit and the number of such bits depends only on the actual domain of x. The functionality $\mathcal{F}_{\text{MPC}}$ also features a 2-party DPF functionality, which, on input the indexes of two parties i, j, a value $[[\beta]]$ in $\mathbb{F}$ or $\mathbb{F}_{2^\lambda}$, a power of 2 M and $[[\omega]]_2 \in [M]$, outputs to P_i and P_j a 2-party secret-sharing of the M-dimensional unit vector having β in the ω-th position. The group on which the secret-sharing is defined coincides with the field to which β belongs.

Finally, we will use a functionality $\mathcal{F}_{\text{Rand}}$ which provides all the parties with random values sampled from the queried domains.

5.2 The Protocol

The functionality that our construction is going to implement is described in Fig. 5. Observe that when the second and the third party are both corrupted the special position of the unit vector is leaked to the adversary. Since the protocol is based on the 3-party DPF described in Sect. 3, a leakage of this type was unavoidable. The functionality also allows the adversary to test the inputs in several occasions, every incorrect guess leading to an abort. In the triple generation protocol, the non-zero value β will be uniformly distributed in $\mathbb{F}^\times$, so any attempt of the adversary to guess it will fail with overwhelming probability. The leakage about the special position will not instead constitute a problem as it will be absorbed by the hardness of Module-LPN.

We can finally present our protocol. Its formal description can be found in Figs. 6, 7 and 8.

Recursion. The protocol uses the 3-party DPF described in Fig. 2 recursively in h levels indexed by $k = 0, 1, \dots, h-1$. Once the k-th level is completed, the parties obtain a secret-sharing over $\mathbb{F}$ of the unit vector

$\mathcal{F}_{\text{3-DPF}}$

MPC Functionality. The functionality features the procedures Input, LinComb, Mult, Output, 2-DPF and Abort as in $\mathcal{F}_{\text{MPC}}$.

3-DPF. On input $[[\beta]] \in \mathbb{F}$, $[[\omega]]_2 \in [N]$ and three indexes $\sigma_0, \sigma_1, \sigma_2 \in [n]$:

1. If P_{σ_0}, P_{σ_1} and P_{σ_2} are all corrupted, send ω and β to the adversary. If only P_{σ_1} and P_{σ_2} are corrupted, send ω to the adversary.
2. If there exists $i \in [3]$ such that P_{σ_i} is corrupted, for three times, wait for $I \subseteq [N]$ from the adversary. If $\omega \notin I$, send ω to the adversary and abort.
3. If $\beta = 0$, output ZERO to the parties and to the adversary and stop.
4. If there exists $i \in [3]$ such that P_{σ_i} is corrupted, wait for the adversary.
   - If the latter sends $(\beta_\eta, \boldsymbol{v}'_\eta)_{\eta \in [N]}$, check whether $\beta_\omega = \beta$. If this is the case, set $\widehat{\boldsymbol{v}} \leftarrow \boldsymbol{v}'_\omega$. Otherwise, send (ω, β) to the adversary and abort.
   - If the latter sends $(I''', \widehat{\boldsymbol{v}})$, check whether $\omega \in I'''$. If this is not the case, send ω to the adversary and abort.
5. If P_{σ_0}, P_{σ_1} and P_{σ_2} are all honest, set $\widehat{\boldsymbol{v}} \leftarrow \boldsymbol{0}$.
6. For every $\sigma_i \in \mathcal{H}$, sample a random $\boldsymbol{v_i} \in \mathbb{F}^N$ subject to

$$\sum_{\sigma_i \in \mathcal{H}} \boldsymbol{v_i} + \widehat{\boldsymbol{v}} = \underbrace{(\overbrace{0, 0, \dots, 0}^{\omega \text{ elements}}, \beta, 0, 0, \dots, 0)}_{N \text{ elements}}.$$

7. Output $\boldsymbol{v_i}$ to party P_{σ_i} for every $\sigma_i \in \mathcal{H}$.

Fig. 5. The 3-party DPF functionality

$$\boldsymbol{v}_{k+1} := \underbrace{(\overbrace{0, 0, \dots, 0}^{\widehat{\omega}(k+1)}, \beta, 0, 0, \dots, 0)}_{\text{dE}(k+1)},$$

$$\text{where} \qquad \widehat{\omega}(k+1) := \omega(-1) + \sum_{i=0}^{k} \omega(i) \cdot \text{dE}(i).$$

Observe that $\widehat{\omega}(h) = \omega$.

More in detail, suppose that the parties possess a secret-sharing over $\mathbb{F}$ of $\boldsymbol{v}_k$. We aim to use it to securely generate 3-party DPF keys for the unit vector $\boldsymbol{v}_{k+1}$ (see Fig. 2). Using the evaluation algorithm, the parties can then expand the keys to obtain a secret-sharing of $\boldsymbol{v}_{k+1}$.

Rearranging $\boldsymbol{v}_{k+1}$ into a Matrix. First of all, observe that $\boldsymbol{v}_{k+1}$ is an $N_k :=$ dE$(k+1)$-dimensional unit vector, whose special position is $\widehat{\omega}(k+1)$. Notice that

$$\widehat{\omega}(k+1) = \omega(k) \cdot \sqrt{N_k} + \widehat{\omega}(k) \quad \text{and} \quad 0 \le \omega(k), \widehat{\omega}(k) < \text{dE}(k) = \sqrt{N_k}.$$

In other words, when we rearrange $\boldsymbol{v}_{k+1}$ into a square matrix, following the procedure described in Sect. 3, the special position ends up at the intersection between the $\omega(k)$-th row and the $\widehat{\omega}(k)$-th column. Observe that it is easy to obtain a secret-sharing of $\omega(k)$ over $\mathbb{F}_2$ given a secret-sharing of ω over $\mathbb{F}_2$. Indeed, $\omega(k)$ is described by a 2^k-bit substring of the bit representation of ω.

The vectors $\boldsymbol{y_0}$, $\boldsymbol{y_1}$ *and* $\boldsymbol{y_2}$. Following the blueprint of the 3-party DPF described in Sect. 3, the first ingredient needed to generate $\boldsymbol{v_{k+1}}$ is the vectors $\boldsymbol{y_{k,1}}$ and $\boldsymbol{y_{k,2}}$, i.e. a secret-sharing over $\mathbb{F}$ of

$$\boldsymbol{y^k} := \underbrace{(\overbrace{0,0,\ldots,0}^{\omega(k)},1,0,0,\ldots,0)}_{\mathrm{dE}(k)} = \boldsymbol{y_{k,1}} + \boldsymbol{y_{k,2}}.$$

At the beginning of our protocol, using the 2-party DPF procedure in $\mathcal{F}_{\mathrm{MPC}}$, the second and third party obtain a secret-sharing of the unit vector

$$\boldsymbol{y} := \underbrace{(\overbrace{0,0,\ldots,0}^{\omega},1,0,0,\ldots,0)}_{N}.$$

By locally applying the matrix B_k on the shares, this also gives the shares $\boldsymbol{y_{k,1}}$ and $\boldsymbol{y_{k,2}}$. We recall that B_k maps an N-dimensional unit vector having special position $\omega \in [N]$ into a $\mathrm{dE}(k)$-dimensional unit vector with special position $\omega(k)$ and the same non-zero value.

From $\mathbb{F}$*-Secret-Sharing to Binary Secret-Sharing.* In the previous paragraph, we described how it is possible to obtain a 2-party secret-sharing over $\mathbb{F}$ of the unit vector $\boldsymbol{y^k}$. In order to securely generate the seeds in the DPF key, we will need to convert this to a 2-party secret-sharing over the binary field $\mathbb{F}_2$. Using a standard trick, we can do this conversion without any interaction.

Recall that $|\mathbb{F}| = p$ for a large prime p. Suppose that the two parties have shares $b_1, b_2 \in [p]$, where $b_1 + b_2 \equiv b \bmod p$, for some $b \in \{0,1\}$, as we do for each entry of $\boldsymbol{y^k}$. If the shares are random, then with overwhelming probability both of them are non-zero, so over the integers, $2 \leq b_1 + b_2 < 2p$ and therefore $b_1 + b_2 = b + p$. Reducing both sides modulo 2, we get that $(b_1 \bmod 2) \oplus (b_2 \bmod 2) = b \oplus 1$. In other words, for every $j \in [\mathrm{dE}(k)]$, the second and the third parties can obtain bits $b^j_{k,1} := y^j_{k,1} \bmod 2$ and $b^j_{k,2} := y^j_{k,2} \bmod 2$ that coincide if and only if $j = \omega(k)$.

This procedure works only if both b_1 and b_2 are non-zero, and for that reason, the parties abort if this is not satisfied. When the second and the third party are both honest, the property condition holds with overwhelming probability. If one of the parties is corrupted, however, $\mathcal{F}_{\mathrm{MPC}}$ allows the adversary to choose its shares. An attacker can exploit this fact to retrieve information about ω, indeed, it can select its shares so that the protocol aborts only if ω assumes particular values (selective failure attack). The corresponding leakage is modelled in step 2 of $\mathcal{F}_{3\text{-DPF}}$ (see Fig. 5).

$\Pi_{\text{3-DPF}}$

The environment has access to the the procedures Input, LinComb, Mult, Output and 2-DPF of $\mathcal{F}_{\text{MPC}}$.

3-DPF. On input a number $[[\omega]]_2 \in [N]$, $[[\beta]] \in \mathbb{F}$ and indexes $\sigma_0, \sigma_1, \sigma_2 \in [n]$:

Generation of $\boldsymbol{y}_{k,0}$, $\boldsymbol{y}_{k,1}$ and $\boldsymbol{y}_{k,2}$.

1. The parties call 2-DPF over $\mathbb{F}$ with special position $[[\omega]]_2$, non-zero element 1 and indexes σ_1 and σ_2. If the latter aborts, the parties abort. Let $\boldsymbol{y}_i$ be the output received by P_{σ_i} for $i \in \{1, 2\}$.
2. For every $k \in \mathcal{K}$ and $i \in \{1, 2\}$, P_{σ_i} computes $\boldsymbol{y}_{k,i} \leftarrow B_k \cdot \boldsymbol{y}_i$. P_{σ_0} sets $\boldsymbol{y}_{k,0} \leftarrow \boldsymbol{0}$.

From $\mathbb{F}$ secret-sharing to binary secret-sharing.

3. If there exists $(k, j) \in \mathcal{T}$ and $i \in \{1, 2\}$ such that $y^j_{k,i} = 0$, P_{σ_i} aborts.
4. For every $k \in \mathcal{K}$ and $i \in \{1, 2\}$, P_{σ_i} sets $\boldsymbol{b}_{k,i} \leftarrow \boldsymbol{y}_{k,i} \bmod 2$.

Seed generation - Part 1.

5. The parties generate $[[\Delta]]_2 \leftarrow \mathsf{Rand}(\mathbb{F}_{2^\lambda})$.
6. The parties call 2-DPF over $\mathbb{F}_{2^\lambda}$ with special position $[[\omega]]_2$, non-zero element $[[\Delta]]_2$ and indexes σ_1 and σ_2. If the latter aborts, the parties abort. Let $\boldsymbol{T}_i$ be the output received by P_{σ_i} for $i \in \{1, 2\}$.
7. For every $k \in \mathcal{K}$ and $i \in \{1, 2\}$, P_{σ_i} computes $\boldsymbol{T}_{k,i} \leftarrow B_k \cdot \boldsymbol{T}_i$.
8. For every $(k, j) \in \mathcal{T}$ and $i \in \{1, 2\}$, P_{σ_i} computes $Y^j_{k,i} \leftarrow H\big(T^j_{k,i}, (k, j)\big)$.

Seed generation - Part 2.

9. For ever $(k, j) \in \mathcal{T}$:
   (a) P_{σ_0} and P_{σ_1} call $\mathcal{F}^{\sigma_0,\sigma_1}_{\text{auth-ROT}}$ with P_{σ_0} as sender. P_{σ_0} obtains $(X^j_k[0], X^j_k[1]) \in \mathbb{F}_{2^\lambda} \times \mathbb{F}_{2^\lambda}$, P_{σ_1} receives $(t^j_{k,1}, X^j_k[2]) \in \mathbb{F}_2 \times \mathbb{F}_{2^\lambda}$, where $X^j_k[2] = X^j_k[t^j_{k,1}]$.
   (b) P_{σ_1} sends $w^j_{k,1} \leftarrow b^j_{k,1} \oplus t^j_{k,1}$ to P_{σ_0}.
   (c) P_{σ_0} and P_{σ_2} call $\mathcal{F}^{\sigma_0,\sigma_2}_{\text{auth-ROT}}$ with P_{σ_0} as sender. P_{σ_0} obtains $(W^j_k[0], W^j_k[1]) \in \mathbb{F}_{2^\lambda} \times \mathbb{F}_{2^\lambda}$, P_{σ_2} receives $(t^j_{k,2}, W^j_k) \in \mathbb{F}_2 \times \mathbb{F}_{2^\lambda}$, where $W^j_k = W^j_k[t^j_{k,2}]$.
   (d) P_{σ_2} sends $w^j_{k,2} \leftarrow b^j_{k,2} \oplus t^j_{k,2}$ to P_{σ_0}.
   (e) P_{σ_0} sends to P_{σ_2}
   $$Z^j_k[0] \leftarrow W^j_k[w^j_{k,2}] \oplus X^j_k[w^j_{k,1}], \qquad Z^j_k[1] \leftarrow W^j_k[w^j_{k,2} \oplus 1] \oplus X^j_k[w^j_{k,1} \oplus 1].$$
   (f) P_{σ_2} computes $X^j_k[3] \leftarrow W^j_k \oplus Z^j_k[b^j_{k,2}]$
10. For every $(k, j) \in \mathcal{T}$
    - P_{σ_0} sets $S^j_{k,0,0} \leftarrow X^j_k[0]$ and $S^j_{k,0,1} \leftarrow X^j_k[1]$.
    - P_{σ_1} sets $S^j_{k,1,0} \leftarrow X^j_k[2]$ and $S^j_{k,1,1} \leftarrow Y^j_{k,1}$.
    - P_{σ_2} sets $S^j_{k,2,0} \leftarrow X^j_k[3]$ and $S^j_{k,2,1} \leftarrow Y^j_{k,2}$.

Fig. 6. $\Pi_{\text{3-DPF}}$ - Part 1

First check.

11. For every $i \in \{1,2\}$ and $k \in \mathcal{K}$, P_{σ_0} and P_{σ_i} call LinearCombination in $\mathcal{F}^{\sigma_0,\sigma_i}_{\text{auth-ROT}}$ to compute
$$t_{k,i} \leftarrow \bigoplus_{j\in[\mathrm{dE}(k)]} [[t^j_{k,i}]]_2.$$
12. For every $k \in \mathcal{K}$, P_{σ_0} computes
$$\psi_k \leftarrow t_{k,1} \oplus t_{k,2} \oplus \bigoplus_{j\in[\mathrm{dE}(k)]} (w^j_{k,1} \oplus w^j_{k,2}).$$
If any of them is different from 1, it makes the protocol abort.

Second check.

13. For every $i \in \{1,2\}$, P_{σ_0} and P_{σ_i} call Random in $\mathcal{F}^{\sigma_0,\sigma_i}_{\text{auth-ROT}}$ for λ times. Let $R_i \in \{0,1\}^\lambda$ be the binary string obtained by P_{σ_i}.
14. For every $i \in \{1,2\}$, P_i inputs R_i into $\mathcal{F}_{\text{MPC}}$ with domain $\mathbb{F}_2$.
15. The parties call $\mathcal{F}_{\text{Rand}}$ to obtain a random matrix $V \in \mathbb{F}_2^{\lambda\times\log(N)}$
16. For every $i \in \{1,2\}$, P_{σ_0} and P_{σ_i} call LinearCombination in $\mathcal{F}^{\sigma_0,\sigma_i}_{\text{auth-ROT}}$ to compute $\Phi_i \leftarrow [[R_i]]_2 \oplus V \cdot C \cdot [[\boldsymbol{t_i}]]_2$ where $\boldsymbol{t_i}$ is the $|\mathcal{T}|$-dimensional vector having $t^j_{k,i}$ in the $(\mathrm{dE}(k)+j)$-th position.
17. P_{σ_0} computes $\Phi \leftarrow \Phi_1 \oplus \Phi_2 \oplus V \cdot C \cdot (\boldsymbol{w} \oplus \boldsymbol{1})$ where $\boldsymbol{w} \oplus \boldsymbol{1}$ is the $|\mathcal{T}|$-dimensional vector having $w^j_{k,1} \oplus w^j_{k,2} \oplus 1$ in the $(\mathrm{dE}(k)+j)$-th position.
18. Using $\mathcal{F}_{\text{MPC}}$ the parties open $\Phi' \leftarrow [[R_1]]_2 \oplus [[R_2]]_2 \oplus V \cdot [[\omega]]_2$. If $\Phi \neq \Phi'$, P_{σ_0} makes the protocol abort.

Base case.

19. For every $j \in [2]$ the parties set
$$x^j_0 \leftarrow \mathrm{Enc}(X^j_{-1}[0]), \quad x^j_1 \leftarrow \mathrm{Enc}(X^j_{-1}[1]), \quad x^j_2 \leftarrow \mathrm{Enc}(X^j_{-1}[2]),$$
$$x^j_3 \leftarrow \mathrm{Enc}(X^j_{-1}[3]), \quad x^j_4 \leftarrow \mathrm{Enc}(Y^j_{-1,1}), \quad x^j_5 \leftarrow \mathrm{Enc}(Y^j_{-1,2}).$$
P_{σ_0} sets $s^j_0 \leftarrow -x^j_0 - x^j_1$. P_{σ_1} sets $s^j_1 \leftarrow x^j_2 + x^j_4$. P_{σ_2} sets $s^j_2 \leftarrow x^j_3 - x^j_5$. Then, for each $i \in [3]$, P_{σ_i} sets $z_i \leftarrow s^0_i \oplus s^1_i$.
20. The parties perform the following operations
$$[[z_i]] \leftarrow \mathsf{Input}(P_{\sigma_i}, z_i) \quad \forall i \in [3]$$
$$[[CW]] \leftarrow ([[z_0]] + [[z_1]] + [[z_2]])^{-1} \cdot [[\beta]]$$
$$CW \leftarrow \mathsf{Output}([[CW]])$$
If $CW = 0$, the parties stop and output ZERO. If the operation cannot be performed due to a zero denominator, all the parties stop and output $\perp$.
21. Each party P_{σ_i} sets $v^j_{0,i} \leftarrow s^j_i \cdot CW$ for $j \in \{0,1\}$. Let $\boldsymbol{v_{0,i}} := (v^0_{0,i}, v^1_{0,i})$ for every $i \in [3]$.

Fig. 7. $\Pi_{3\text{-DPF}}$ - Part 2

Generation of the correction words.

22. For each $k \in [h]$ the parties compute the following operations
    (a) For every $i \in [3]$, P_{σ_i} broadcasts

$$\boldsymbol{CW_{k,i}} \leftarrow \boldsymbol{v_{k,i}} - \sum_{j \in [\mathrm{dE}(k)]} u_i^0 \cdot G_k(S^j_{k,i,0}) - \sum_{j \in [\mathrm{dE}(k)]} u_i^1 \cdot G_k(S^j_{k,i,1}).$$

    (b) The parties set $\boldsymbol{CW_k} \leftarrow \boldsymbol{CW_{k,0}} + \boldsymbol{CW_{k,1}} + \boldsymbol{CW_{k,2}}$.
    (c) Each party P_{σ_i} sets for every $j \in [\mathrm{dE}(k)]$

$$\boldsymbol{v^j_{k+1,i}} \leftarrow u_i^0 \cdot G_k(S^j_{k,i,0}) + u_i^1 \cdot G_k(S^j_{k,i,1}) + y^j_{k,i} \cdot \boldsymbol{CW_k}.$$

    Let $\boldsymbol{v_{k+1,i}} := (\boldsymbol{v^0_{k+1,i}} \parallel \boldsymbol{v^1_{k+1,i}} \parallel \cdots \parallel \boldsymbol{v^{\mathrm{dE}(k)-1}_{k+1,i}})$.

Final check.

23. The parties call $\mathcal{F}_{\mathrm{Rand}}$ to sample $\boldsymbol{\chi} = (\chi_0, \chi_1, \ldots, \chi_{N-1}) \in \mathbb{F}^N$.
24. Perform the following operations
    (a) $[[d_i]] \leftarrow \mathsf{Input}(P_{\sigma_i}, \langle \boldsymbol{\chi}, \boldsymbol{y_i} \rangle)$ for each $i \in \{1, 2\}$.
    (b) $[[\zeta_i]] \leftarrow \mathsf{Input}(P_{\sigma_i}, \langle \boldsymbol{\chi}, \boldsymbol{v_{h,i}} \rangle)$ for each $i \in [3]$.
    (c) $[[\rho]] \leftarrow [[\zeta_0]] + [[\zeta_1]] + [[\zeta_2]] - ([[d_1]] + [[d_2]]) \cdot [[\beta]]$
    (d) $\rho \leftarrow \mathsf{Output}([[\rho]])$
    (e) If $\rho \neq 0$, P_{σ_i} outputs ABORT and stops. Otherwise, P_{σ_i} outputs $\boldsymbol{v_{h,i}}$.

Fig. 8. $\Pi_{3\text{-DPF}}$ - Part 3

The Seed Generation - Part 1. We now turn to the task of generating the PRG seeds used in the DPF. We start with the method for obtaining the last seeds of the second and the third party, which, following the idea from Sect. 3, we compress using a 2-party DPF. Recall that these seeds coincide for every position $j \neq \omega(k)$, whereas, when $j = \omega(k)$, they are independent. Using the 2-party DPF command of $\mathcal{F}_{\mathrm{MPC}}$, we can obtain a 2-party secret-sharing over $\mathbb{F}_{2^\lambda}$ of

$$\underbrace{(\overbrace{0, 0, \ldots, 0,}^{\omega} \Delta, 0, 0, \ldots, 0)}_{N}.$$

where Δ is sampled randomly by $\mathcal{F}_{\mathrm{MPC}}$. Then, by applying the matrix B_k, this can be translated into shares of

$$\underbrace{(\overbrace{0, 0, \ldots, 0,}^{\omega(k)} \Delta, 0, 0, \ldots, 0)}_{\mathrm{dE}(k)}.$$

for any $k \in \mathcal{K}$. The only problem is that, in this way, the entries of the shares in the special position are not independent, due to the fixed correlation Δ. Therefore, to turn these shares into independent, random seeds, we apply the correlation-robust hash function H to each entry.

The Seed Generation - Part 2. Generating and distributing the remaining seeds is more complex. We have previously explained how the second and third parties derive, for each $j \in [\mathrm{dE}(k)]$, bits $b_{k,1}^j$ and $b_{k,2}^j$ that coincide if and only if $j = \omega(k)$. Now, for every $j \in [\mathrm{dE}(k)]$, the second and the third party must learn one of the seeds of the first party. The discovered seeds will coincide if and only if $j = \omega(k)$. We can therefore generate and distribute the remaining seeds using oblivious transfer (OT). Specifically, for every $j \in [\mathrm{dE}(k)]$, the first and the second party can obtain their missing seeds by means of a "sender-random" OT, i.e. an OT where the sender's messages, corresponding to the seeds of the first party, are random, while the receiver can choose its input. The first party will be the sender, while the second party will be the receiver with choice bit $b_{k,1}^j$. The third party can then receive its missing seed by means of another, now standard, OT. The sender, corresponding to the first party, will choose its messages to be the same as in the "sender-random" OT, while the choice bit of the receiver, the third party, will be $b_{k,2}^j$. The two OTs are implemented using the random-OT functionality $\mathcal{F}_{\text{auth-ROT}}$. Note that this functionality ensures that the choice bits are authenticated, which we rely on later, to check consistency of this stage and achieve active security.

The Correction Word (Fig. 8). After obtaining the seeds, the only missing piece of the DPF key is the correction word. Computing it is rather straightforward as each party can just retrieve its share of $\boldsymbol{v_k}$ and add or subtract the expansions of its seeds using G_k[4]. The correction word is obtained by broadcasting and adding the results. Observe that if recursion had not been used, at this point of the protocol, the parties would have needed to generate a secret-sharing of the $\sqrt{N}$-dimensional vector $\boldsymbol{v_{h-1}}$. Direct approaches would have required $O(\sqrt{N})$ communication, recursion instead allows us to compute that with $O(\sqrt[4]{N})$ complexity.

The Base Case $k = 0$. We have explained how to derive a secret-sharing of $\boldsymbol{v_{k+1}}$ given a secret-sharing of $\boldsymbol{v_k}$. It remains to describe how to deal with the base case, i.e. how to derive a secret-sharing of $\boldsymbol{v_0}$. Observe that $\boldsymbol{v_0}$ is a 2-dimensional unit vector, where β occupies the $\omega(-1)$-th position.

By using the same procedure described in the seed generation, for each position of $\boldsymbol{v_0}$, the parties can obtain pairs of elements in $\{0,1\}^\lambda$ of the form

$$\begin{array}{llll}\textbf{if } \boldsymbol{j \neq \omega(-1)}: & \{a_{-1}^j, b_{-1}^j\}, & (b_{-1}^j, c_{-1}^j), & (a_{-1}^j, c_{-1}^j),\\ \textbf{if } \boldsymbol{j = \omega(-1)}: & \{a_{-1}^j, d_{-1}^j\}, & (d_{-1}^j, b_{-1}^j), & (d_{-1}^j, c_{-1}^j).\end{array}$$

This time, we do not regard them as seeds anymore, but using the encoding map Enc, we convert them into random elements in the field $\mathbb{F}$. Observe that by combining the elements with the coefficients u_i^b, we can derive a secret-sharing of zero when $j \neq \omega(-1)$ and a secret-sharing of a random value $z \in \mathbb{F}$ when $j = \omega(-1)$. Obtaining a secret-sharing of $\boldsymbol{v_0}$ is now easy, we simply need to multiply each secret-sharing we have just computed by $\beta \cdot z^{-1}$. The operation can be performed using $\mathcal{F}_{\text{MPC}}$.

[4] Whether we need to add or subtract is specified by the sign multipliers u_i^b.

Achieving Active Security. The protocol we just described allows the adversary to deviate in several points. In order to regain control on the execution, we relied on three different checks. Only the combination of all of them guarantees security.

The first issue we encounter is in the seed generation. An adversary corrupting both the second and third party can indeed discover all the seeds of the first party by always inputting different choice bits in the OTs. With this attack, the adversary would be able to retrieve β once the correction word is computed. So, we designed the first check to fail in these situations. Specifically, using $\mathcal{F}_{\text{auth-ROT}}$, the check recomputes the sum of the OT bits input by the receivers for every recursion level k. If the result is different from 1, the protocol aborts.

When the second or third party are corrupted, by cleverly choosing the choice bits of the OTs, the adversary can move the non-zero value β to a different position $\eta \neq \omega$. The second check makes sure that this attack fails with overwhelming probability. This is achieved by recomputing η from the OT inputs using the matrix C and $\mathcal{F}_{\text{auth-ROT}}$. The result is obliviously compared to ω using $\mathcal{F}_{\text{MPC}}$, the protocol aborts when they do not match.

The third check, inspired by [YWL+20], is probably the most important. Essentially, it draws a random N-dimensional vector $\boldsymbol{\chi} \in \mathbb{F}^N$ and checks that the result of the linear combination $\langle \boldsymbol{\chi}, \boldsymbol{v_h} \rangle$ coincides with $\chi_\omega \cdot \beta$. The procedure counteracts any malicious behaviour in the generation of the correction words. Moreover, in combination with the first check, it makes sure that, for every level k, there exists only one position for which the choice bits of the OTs coincide. On the other hand, the third check causes some leakage which is modelled in step 4 of $\mathcal{F}_{\text{3-DPF}}$ (see Fig. 5). We prove the following in [AS21, Appendix D].

Theorem 3. *Let $N = \mathrm{dE}(h)$ be a double power of 2 and assume that $\mathbb{F}$ is a security-parameter-dependent prime field of cardinality p such that $|p - 2^\lambda|/2^\lambda$ is negligible in λ. Let $G_k : \{0,1\}^\lambda \longrightarrow \mathbb{F}^{\mathrm{dE}(k)}$ be a PRG for every $k \in [h]$ and let $H : \{0,1\}^\lambda \times \{0,1\}^* \longrightarrow \{0,1\}^\lambda$ be a tweakable correlation-robust hash function. Then the protocol $\Pi_{\text{3-DPF}}$ UC-realises $\mathcal{F}_{\text{3-DPF}}$ in the $(\mathcal{F}_{\text{MPC}}, \mathcal{F}_{\text{auth-ROT}}, \mathcal{F}_{\text{Rand}})$-hybrid model. Moreover, if all the parties are honest, $\Pi_{\text{3-DPF}}$ aborts with negligible probability.*

Complexity. The protocol $\Pi_{\text{3-DPF}}$ achieves low communication complexity. As a matter of fact, in [BCG+20], the authors described how to implement the 2-party DPF procedure of $\mathcal{F}_{\text{MPC}}$ with $O(\log(N)\cdot \mathsf{poly}(\lambda))$ communication. We also observe that the seed generation needs $O(\sqrt{N})$ OTs. Hence, $\Pi_{\text{3-DPF}}$ has $O(\sqrt{N}\cdot \mathsf{poly}(\lambda))$ communication complexity. A more detailed analysis of efficiency can be found in [AS21, Section 7.1].

6 Offline Phase

We can finally describe our Offline phase protocol Π_{Offline}, which achieves sublinear communication complexity. It can be broken down into 3 procedures: an initialisation procedure in which the MAC key α is generated and secret-shared, a triple generation procedure and an input mask generation procedure. The latter is used to produce, for every $j \in [n]$, random authenticated secret-shared elements $[\![a_j]\!]$ whose value is known only to party P_j. As for multiplication triples, input masks constitute an essential part of SPDZ as they are needed to provide the inputs of the computation.

The protocol Π_{Offline} closely resembles $\mathsf{PCG}_{\text{triple}}$. For this reason, we now give only an informal description of its operation and we refer to [AS21, Section 6.1] for a more thorough analysis. The protocol permits to generate N multiplication triples with $O(\sqrt{N} \cdot \mathsf{poly}(\lambda))$ communication complexity and N input masks with $O(\log(N) \cdot \mathsf{poly}(\lambda))$ communication complexity. The bottleneck of the triple generation is the 3-party DPF. If future research proves the existence of 3-party DPFs with logarithmic key size, we will probably be able to design multiparty triple generation protocols with logarithmic communication complexity.

Multiplication Triples. The protocol uses the functionality $\mathcal{F}_{\text{3-DPF}}$ as a black box. During the initialisation procedure, each party P_i samples a random share α_i for the MAC key and inputs it in $\mathcal{F}_{\text{3-DPF}}$, fundamentally committing to its choice.

The multiplication triples are derived by executing the seed generation and the evaluation of $\mathsf{PCG}_{\text{triple}}$ inside $\mathcal{F}_{\text{3-DPF}}$: at the very beginning, each party P_i samples random special positions $\boldsymbol{\omega}_i^r, \boldsymbol{\eta}_i^r \in [N]^t$ and random non-zero elements $\boldsymbol{\beta}_i^r, \boldsymbol{\gamma}_i^r \in \mathbb{F}^t$ for every $r \in [c]$. These values are input in $\mathcal{F}_{\text{3-DPF}}$. Using 2-DPF and 3-DPF, it is then possible for P_i to obtain $\boldsymbol{u}_i, \widetilde{\boldsymbol{u}}_i, \boldsymbol{v}_i, \widetilde{\boldsymbol{v}}_i, \boldsymbol{w}_i$ and $\widetilde{\boldsymbol{w}}_i$. Finally, by sampling a random $\boldsymbol{a} \in R^c$ using $\mathcal{F}_{\text{Rand}}$, the parties can compute the final output, i.e. random authenticated secret-shared elements $[\![x]\!], [\![y]\!], [\![z]\!] \in R$ such that $z = x \cdot y$. We recall that $R = \mathbb{F}[X]/(F(X))$ where $F(X)$ is a degree-N polynomial. If $F(X)$ has N distinct roots in $\mathbb{F}$, the tuple $([\![x]\!], [\![y]\!], [\![z]\!])$ can be converted into N random multiplication triples by evaluating the shares[5] over the roots of $F(X)$.

Input Masks. The generation of inputs masks is very similar but simpler. At the beginning, the party P_j to which the masks are addressed samples random special positions $\boldsymbol{\omega}^r \in [N]^t$ and random non-zero elements $\boldsymbol{\beta}^r \in \mathbb{F}^t$ for every $r \in [c]$, inputting them in $\mathcal{F}_{\text{3-DPF}}$. These values will be used to define the sparse polynomial

$$u^r(X) \leftarrow \sum_{l \in [t]} \beta^r[l] \cdot X^{\omega^r[l]}$$

Later on, for every $i \neq j$, P_i and P_j can obtain a secret-sharing of $\alpha_i \cdot u^r(X)$ using 2-DPF. Finally, by sampling a random $\boldsymbol{a} \in R^c$ using $\mathcal{F}_{\text{Rand}}$ and relying on the hardness of Module LPN, the shares can be converted into a random authenticated secret-shared element $[\![x]\!] \in R$. Since P_j knows $u^r(X)$ for every $r \in [c]$, it can also learn x. As a last operation, the shares are rerandomised using a PRG. Observe that from $[\![x]\!]$, we can derive N masks using the same trick described for the multiplication triples.

[5] The shares are elements of R and therefore polynomials.

Leakage. The main difference between Π_{Offline} and $\mathsf{PCG}_{\mathsf{triple}}$ is that every execution of 2-DPF and 3-DPF has additional leakage. At first, it might seem that the main issue arises when the last two players P_j and P_k of the 3-party DPF procedure are corrupted. In such cases, the special positions $(\boldsymbol{\omega}_j^r \boxplus \boldsymbol{\eta}_k^s)_{r,s\in[c]}$ are indeed revealed to the adversary. Notice, however, that this is no problem at all, as the leaked values were chosen by the adversary itself at the beginning of the protocol.

Regarding the remaining leakage, observe that when the adversary tries the guess any non-zero element during 3-DPF, the procedure aborts with overwhelming probability. Indeed, the non-zero values are uniformly distributed in $\mathbb{F}^\times$, assuming that at least one party involved in 3-DPF is honest. Moreover, any leakage concerning the special positions is absorbed by the hardness of module-LPN with static leakage. For a formal discussion, see [AS21, Appendix E].

6.1 Concrete Efficiency

Table 1. Estimated seed size for producing N triples with the 3-party PCG over a 128-bit field, with 80-bit computational security.

N	2^{20}			2^{24}			2^{28}		
c	2	4	8	2	4	8	2	4	8
$w = ct$	96	40	32	96	40	32	96	40	32
Comm. (MB)	308	114	109	1120	417	418	4329	1641	1650
Stretch	0.16	0.44	0.46	0.72	1.93	1.92	2.98	7.85	7.81

In Table 1, we estimate the concrete communication cost of our protocol, for several sets of parameters with $n = 3$ parties and 80-bit computational security. For further details and parameters for 128-bit security, we refer to the full version [AS21, Section 7.2]. The "stretch" of the protocol is defined as the ratio of the size of the uncompressed triples ($3N$ field elements) and the total communication cost. We see that, when producing around a million triples ($N = 2^{20}$), the stretch is still less than 1, meaning that the PCG does not achieve a good compression factor. Nevertheless, even at this level, we do achieve a protocol for generating triples with much lower communication than methods based on alternative techniques. For instance, using the Overdrive protocol based on homomorphic encryption [KPR18] requires almost 2GB of communication to generate the same number of triples, which is more than 10x our protocol.

When moving to larger batch sizes, the stretch improves, going up to almost 8x with $N = 2^{28}$ and $c \in \{4, 8\}$. This gives a strong saving in communication, but comes with larger computational costs due to the higher degree polynomial operations needed for arithmetic in the ring R. In practice, since these operations cost $O(N \log N)$, it seems likely that the smaller sizes of $N \leq 2^{24}$ will be preferable.

Acknowledgements. We thank the anonymous reviewers for their feedback, which helped to improve the paper.

References

[AS21] Abram, D., Scholl, P.: Low-Communication Multiparty Triple Generation for SPDZ from Ring-LPN. Cryptology ePrint Archive, 2021 (2021)

[BCG+19a] Boyle, E., et al.: Efficient two-round OT extension and silent non-interactive secure computation. In: ACM CCS 2019. ACM Press, November 2019

[BCG+19b] Boyle, E., Couteau, G., Gilboa, N., Ishai, Y., Kohl, L., Scholl, P.: Efficient pseudorandom correlation generators: silent OT extension and more. In: Boldyreva, A., Micciancio, D. (eds.) CRYPTO 2019, Part III. LNCS, vol. 11694, pp. 489–518. Springer, Cham (2019). https://doi.org/10.1007/978-3-030-26954-8_16

[BCG+20] Boyle, E., Couteau, G., Gilboa, N., Ishai, Y., Kohl, L., Scholl, P.: Efficient pseudorandom correlation generators from ring-LPN. In: Micciancio, D., Ristenpart, T. (eds.) CRYPTO 2020, Part II. LNCS, vol. 12171, pp. 387–416. Springer, Cham (2020). https://doi.org/10.1007/978-3-030-56880-1_14

[Bea92] Beaver, D.: Efficient multiparty protocols using circuit randomization. In: Feigenbaum, J. (ed.) CRYPTO 1991. LNCS, vol. 576, pp. 420–432. Springer, Heidelberg (1992). https://doi.org/10.1007/3-540-46766-1_34

[BGI15] Boyle, E., Gilboa, N., Ishai, Y.: Function secret sharing. In: Oswald, E., Fischlin, M. (eds.) EUROCRYPT 2015, Part II. LNCS, vol. 9057, pp. 337–367. Springer, Heidelberg (2015). https://doi.org/10.1007/978-3-662-46803-6_12

[BGI16] Boyle, E., Gilboa, N., Ishai, Y.: Function secret sharing: improvements and extensions. In: ACM CCS 2016. ACM Press, October 2016

[BKKO20] Bunn, P., Katz, J., Kushilevitz, E., Ostrovsky, R.: Efficient 3-party distributed ORAM. In: Galdi, C., Kolesnikov, V. (eds.) SCN 2020. LNCS, vol. 12238, pp. 215–232. Springer, Cham (2020). https://doi.org/10.1007/978-3-030-57990-6_11

[DKL+13] Damgård, I., Keller, M., Larraia, E., Pastro, V., Scholl, P., Smart, N.P.: Practical covertly secure MPC for dishonest majority – or: breaking the SPDZ limits. In: Crampton, J., Jajodia, S., Mayes, K. (eds.) ESORICS 2013. LNCS, vol. 8134, pp. 1–18. Springer, Heidelberg (2013). https://doi.org/10.1007/978-3-642-40203-6_1

[DPSZ12] Damgård, I., Pastro, V., Smart, N., Zakarias, S.: Multiparty computation from somewhat homomorphic encryption. In: Safavi-Naini, R., Canetti, R. (eds.) CRYPTO 2012. LNCS, vol. 7417, pp. 643–662. Springer, Heidelberg (2012). https://doi.org/10.1007/978-3-642-32009-5_38

[GI14] Gilboa, N., Ishai, Y.: Distributed point functions and their applications. In: Nguyen, P.Q., Oswald, E. (eds.) EUROCRYPT 2014. LNCS, vol. 8441, pp. 640–658. Springer, Heidelberg (2014). https://doi.org/10.1007/978-3-642-55220-5_35

[KOS16] Keller, M., Orsini, E., Scholl, P.: MASCOT: faster malicious arithmetic secure computation with oblivious transfer. In: ACM CCS 2016. ACM Press, October 2016

[KPR18] Keller, M., Pastro, V., Rotaru, D.: Overdrive: making SPDZ great again. In: Nielsen, J.B., Rijmen, V. (eds.) EUROCRYPT 2018, Part III. LNCS, vol. 10822, pp. 158–189. Springer, Cham (2018). https://doi.org/10.1007/978-3-319-78372-7_6

[NNOB12] Nielsen, J.B., Nordholt, P.S., Orlandi, C., Burra, S.S.: A new approach to practical active-secure two-party computation. In: Safavi-Naini, R., Canetti, R. (eds.) CRYPTO 2012. LNCS, vol. 7417, pp. 681–700. Springer, Heidelberg (2012). https://doi.org/10.1007/978-3-642-32009-5_40

[SV14] Smart, N.P., Vercauteren, F.: Fully homomorphic SIMD operations. Des. Codes Cryptogr. **71**(1), 57–81 (2014)

[YWL+20] Yang, K., Weng, C., Lan, X., Zhang, J., Wang, X.: Ferret: fast extension for correlated OT with small communication. In: ACM CCS 20. ACM Press, November 2020

Storing and Retrieving Secrets on a Blockchain

Vipul Goyal[1,2], Abhiram Kothapalli[1], Elisaweta Masserova[1(✉)], Bryan Parno[1], and Yifan Song[1]

[1] Carnegie Mellon University, Pittsburgh, USA
vipul@cmu.edu, elisawem@cs.cmu.edu
[2] NTT Research, Sunnyvale, USA

Abstract. A *secret sharing* scheme enables one party to distribute shares of a secret to n parties and ensures that an adversary in control of t out of n parties will learn no information about the secret. However, traditional secret sharing schemes are often insufficient, especially for applications in which the set of parties who hold the secret shares might change over time. To achieve security in this setting, *dynamic proactive secret sharing* (DPSS) is used. DPSS schemes proactively update the secret shares held by the parties and allow changes to the set of parties holding the secrets. We propose FaB-DPSS (FAst Batched DPSS) – a new and highly optimized batched DPSS scheme. While previous work on batched DPSS [BDLO15] focuses on a single client submitting a batch of secrets and does not allow storing and releasing secrets independently, we allow multiple *different* clients to dynamically share and release secrets. FaB-DPSS is the most efficient robust DPSS scheme that supports the highest possible adversarial threshold of $\frac{1}{2}$. We prove FaB-DPSS secure and implement it. All operations complete in seconds, and we outperform a prior state-of-the-art DPSS scheme [MZW+19] by over 6×.

Additionally, we propose new applications of DPSS in the context of blockchains. Specifically, we propose a protocol that uses blockchains and FaB-DPSS to provide conditional secret storage. The protocol allows parties to store secrets along with a release condition, and once a (possibly different) party satisfies this release condition, the secret is privately released to that party. This functionality is similar to *extractable witness encryption.* While there are numerous compelling applications (e.g., time-lock encryption, one-time programs, and fair multi-party computation) which rely on extractable witness encryption, there are no known efficient constructions (or even constructions based on any well-studied assumptions) of extractable witness encryption. However, by utilizing blockchains and FaB-DPSS, we can easily build all those applications. We provide an implementation of our conditional secret storage protocol as well as several applications building on top of it.

1 Introduction

In recent years, secret sharing schemes have received considerable attention. While traditional secret sharing is a well-known cryptographic primitive which has been extensively used in the context of secure multi-party computation,

G. Hanaoka et al. (Eds.): PKC 2022, LNCS 13177, pp. 252–282, 2022.
https://doi.org/10.1007/978-3-030-97121-2_10

recently *proactive secret sharing* has become increasingly important. Similar to traditional secret sharing, proactive secret sharing schemes enable one party to distribute shares of a secret to n parties such that any $t + 1$ shares are enough to reconstruct the secret, and an adversary in possession of t out of n shares learns no information about the secret. In contrast to traditional secret sharing, proactive secret sharing additionally considers the setting where the adversary may eventually corrupt *all* participants over time, while corrupting no more than a certain threshold at any given time. In the context of blockchains, proactive secret sharing has proven a useful alternative to central storage for securing secret keys (which are used to sign transactions, access cryptocurrency wallets, etc.). As pointed out in CHURP [MZW+19], since blockchain nodes are typically allowed to freely leave or join a system at any time, in this context it is critical to allow for *dynamic* changes in the secret sharing committee. This is supported by *dynamic proactive secret sharing* (DPSS) [DJ97, MZW+19, SLL08, BDLO15, ZSVR05, WWW02] which proactively updates the secret shares held by the parties and allows changes to the set of parties holding the secrets.

Scheme	Dynamic setting	Adversary	Threshold	Network	Comm. (amort.)	Comm. (non-amort.)
[HJKY95]	No	Active	$t/n < 1/2$	synch.	$O(n^2)$	$O(n^2)$
[CKLS02]	No	Active	$t/n < 1/3$	asynch.	$O(n^4)$	$O(n^4)$
[DJ97]	Yes	Passive	$t/n < 1/3$	asynch.	$O(n^2)$	$O(n^2)$
[WWW02]	Yes	Active	$t/n < 1/2$	synch.	$exp(n)$	$exp(n)$
[ZSVR05]	Yes	Active	$t/n < 1/3$	asynch.	$exp(n)$	$exp(n)$
[SLL08]	Yes	Active	$t/n < 1/3$	asynch.	$O(n^4)$	$O(n^4)$
[BDLO15]	Yes	Active	$t/n < 1/2 - \epsilon$	synch.	$O(1)$	$O(n^3)$
[MZW$^+$19]	Yes	Active	$t/n < 1/2$	synch.	$O(n^2)$	$O(n^2)$
This work	Yes	Active	$t/n < 1/2$	synch.	$O(n)$	$O(n^2)$

Fig. 1. Comparison of PSS Schemes. The Comm. columns show the communication cost/secret in a hand-off round.

We introduce FaB-DPSS (FAst Batched DPSS) – a highly optimized batched DPSS scheme. Especially in the context of secret storage on blockchains, batching is crucial as thousands of secrets might be stored and updated in parallel at any given time. FaB-DPSS improves over prior work in multiple dimensions. In contrast to previous work on batched DPSS [BDLO15], which focuses on a single client submitting a batch of secrets and does not allow storing and releasing secrets independently, we allow multiple *different* clients to dynamically and independently share and release secrets. Among the robust schemes which allow the highest-possible adversarial threshold of $\frac{1}{2}$ (see Fig. 1), our protocol has the best communication complexity. It is also the most concretely efficient scheme – all operations complete in seconds (Sect. 8), and we outperform a prior state-of-the-art DPSS scheme [MZW+19] by over 6×. These improvements are possible because of our entirely new approach to the hand-off phase of the DPSS – instead of relying on bivariate polynomials as is done in prior work [MZW+19], we use a technique we dub "coupled sharings".

In addition to FaB-DPSS, we propose a number of blockchain-based DPSS applications, thus expanding the reach of DPSS in the context of blockchains. The most important one can be seen as a blockchain-based alternative to *extractable witness encryption*. Introduced by Garg et al. [GGSW13], a witness encryption scheme is, roughly, a primitive that allows one to encrypt a message with respect to a problem instance. Such a problem instance could be a sudoku puzzle in a newspaper or an allegedly bug-free program, or more generally, any NP search problem. If the decryptor knows a valid witness for the corresponding problem instance, such as a sudoku solution or a bug in the program, she can decrypt the ciphertext. Moreover, if a witness encryption scheme is *extractable*, then an adversary able to learn any non-trivial information about the encrypted message is also able to provide a witness for the corresponding problem instance.

Unfortunately, existing proposals for extractable witness encryption typically rely on *differing-inputs* obfuscation [BGI+12, ABG+13], a technique that is computationally expensive and relies on strong cryptographic assumptions. Responding to the lack of extractable witness encryption schemes based on standard assumptions, Garg et al. [GGHW14] suggest that it may be impossible.

Building upon blockchains and FaB-DPSS with a threshold of $t/n < \frac{1}{2}$, we design eWEB – an efficient alternative to extractable witness encryption. It uses only standard cryptographic assumptions, while respecting prior impossibility results: Instead of resorting to expensive cryptographic machinery, it relies on interaction with a dynamic set of nodes with an honest majority. We believe this a favorable trade-off, as the honest majority setting has been repeatedly used in practice, most notably in blockchains[1]. For simplicity, in the following we will use the terms "dynamic set of nodes with an honest majority" and "blockchain" interchangeably, and the same for "nodes" and "miners". Roughly, we allow users to encode a secret along with a release condition. A predefined set of n nodes jointly and securely store the encoding and later *privately* release the secret to a user who demonstrably satisfies the release condition. We provide a formal proof of security of our construction, relying on the guarantees provided by the blockchain setting (specifically, we will assume a set of miners such that the majority of the selected miners are honest). As pointed out by Goyal and Goyal [GG17], one way to select such a set of miners is by selecting miners who were responsible for mining the last n blocks (where n is large enough). While it might seem like using secret sharing in combination with a blockchain directly provides a solution for conditional secret sharing, achieving a formally secure solution is subtle and requires careful design, as well as a few tricks we introduce in Sect. 5.2.

We note that the combination of blockchains and witness encryption has proven remarkably powerful. Indeed, Liu et al. [LJKW18] propose a time-lock encryption scheme that allows one to encrypt a message such that it can only be decrypted once a certain deadline has passed, without relying on trusted third parties or imposing high computational overhead on the receiver. The construction of Choudhuri et al. [CGJ+17] achieves fairness in multi-party computation

[1] Other instantiations are possible as well, see Sect. 5.1.

against a dishonest majority. Goyal and Goyal [GG17] present the first construction for one-time programs (that run only once and then "self-destruct") that does not use tamper-proof hardware.

Using our DPSS- and blockchain based eWEB scheme, practitioners can easily implement all these applications. Note that many of them [LJKW18, CGJ+17, GG17] already rely on blockchains, implying that using eWEB does not add any additional assumptions. We explain in detail how a number of these applications can be achieved, and we implement and evaluate a few of them.

We also note that eWEB has already formed the basis of a follow-up work on non-interactive MPC [GMPS21].

1.1 Our Results

As explained above, one of our main contributions is a new and highly efficient DPSS scheme. More specifically, we achieve the following:

Theorem 1. *Assuming secure point-to-point channels and assuming that the t-SDH assumption holds, our construction satisfies the DPSS security definition (Definition 1) for a fully malicious adversary satisfying a corruption threshold* $t < \frac{1}{2}n$*, where* n *is the total number of parties holding the secrets. The adversary has the power to adaptively corrupt parties at any time. Our construction achieves amortized complexity of* $O(n)$ *and non-amortized complexity of* $O(n^2)$*.*

Here, Definition 1 is a DPSS security definition which is based on an ideal functionality, which behaves as follows:

- The functionality keeps track of the current committee.
- Upon receiving a secret storage request, the functionality stores the secret and notifies the current committee about the storage request.
- Upon receiving a release request from more than t (the adversarial threshold) number of parties in the current committee, the functionality either sends the corresponding secret to the client if the release request was private, or to the public otherwise.

Intuitively, this security definition requires that an adversary corrupting no more than the allowed threshold of parties does not learn any information about the secret through our protocol (secrecy) and cannot prevent an eligible party from learning the secret (robustness).

We present and formally prove secure FaB-DPSS in Sect. 3. We note that among the robust DPSS schemes which provide the highest-possible adversarial threshold of $t < \frac{1}{2}n$ our batched construction achieves the best amortized complexity – $O(n)$, while the state of the art CHURP [MZW+19] achieves $O(n^2)$ (see Fig. 1 for comparison). Simultaneously, we achieve the same non-amortized complexity as CHURP – both works achieve $O(n^2)$. Our evaluation shows (see Fig. 2 as well as Sect. 8.1) that FaB-DPSS outperforms CHURP in practice.

Next, we propose eWEB – a new cryptographic primitive which can be seen as a blockchain-based alternative to extractable witness encryption. We give a formal syntax for eWEB in Sect. 4.

Building upon FaB-DPSS and blockchains, we design and formally prove secure an eWEB construction. For this, we assume that an adversary controls some number of users and miners subject to the constraint that at any time the majority of miners who are eligible to participate in the protocol are honest (we explain how such a miner committee is chosen in Sect. 5.2). We assume that eWEB is a core functionality for the underlying blockchain. We use blockchain also for a PKI infrastructure and assume that each party has a unique identifier that is known to other parties. Finally, we assume authenticated IND-CCA secure encryption, collision-resistant hash functions and simulation extractable non-interactive zero knowledge proofs of knowledge.

We implement and evaluate our eWEB protocol (Sect. 7).

Finally, we explain how time-lock encryption, dead-man's switch, fair MPC, one-time programs and proofs of receipts can be achieved using eWEB (Sect. 6). As a more involved example, we propose an eWEB-based proof-of-concept voting protocol (Sect. 6.1). We implement and evaluate several of these applications (Sect. 8.3).

1.2 Related Work

We elaborate on the prior work of both DPSS and conditional secret release.

Prior Work on DPSS. Since the introduction of proactive secret sharing by Herzberg et al. [HJKY95], many PSS schemes have been developed. These schemes vary in terms of security guarantees, network assumptions (synchronous or asynchronous), communication complexity and whether they can handle dynamic changes in the committee membership. In Fig. 1 we provide a comparison.

Below, we compare FaB-DPSS in detail with the two constructions (Baron et al. [BDLO15], CHURP [MZW+19]) that are most closely related to our protocol, as they are also the most efficient robust DPSS schemes to date.

In the best case, CHURP [MZW+19] achieves communication complexity $O(n^2)$ plus $O(n) \cdot \mathcal{B}$ to refresh each secret in the hand-off phase, where n is the number of parties and $\mathcal{B}$ denotes the cost of broadcasting a bit. In the worst case (where some corrupted party deviates from the protocol), it requires $O(n^2) \cdot \mathcal{B}$ communication per secret.

In the single-secret setting, our protocol achieves the same asymptotic communication complexity as CHURP. However, our protocol achieves *amortized* communication complexity $O(n)$ plus $O(1) \cdot \mathcal{B}$ per secret in the best case, and $O(n^2)$ plus $O(n) \cdot \mathcal{B}$ per secret in the worst case. Batching is crucially important in eWEB since there may be thousands of secrets stored at any given time.

While CHURP uses asymmetric bivariate polynomials to refresh a secret during hand-off, we use a modified version of a technique of Damgård et al. [DN07] to prepare a batch of random secret sharings. Generating random secret sharings is much more efficient than generating bivariate polynomials. Specifically, each bivariate polynomial requires $O(n)$ communication per party; i.e., $O(n^2)$

in total. On the other hand, we can prepare $O(n)$ random sharings with the same communication cost as preparing one bivariate polynomial. To benefit from it, we use an entirely different way to refresh secrets.

The work of Baron et al. [BDLO15] focuses on a slightly different setting from ours: they consider unconditionally secure DPSS with a $(1/2-\epsilon)$ corruption threshold, where ϵ is a constant. Their scheme has $O(1)$ amortized communication per secret. However, in the single-secret setting, it requires $O(n^3)$ communication to refresh a secret. The authors use the party virtualization technique where every virtual party is simulated by a set of real parties running a maliciously secure MPC protocol. As discussed in [MZW+19], a high constant is hidden in the big O notation. For example, if $\epsilon = 1/6$, i.e., the scheme is only secure with a $1/3$ corruption threshold, the virtualization requires to simulate at least 576 virtual parties with each using a set of 576 real parties running a maliciously secure MPC protocol, rendering the scheme very inefficient in practice.

Baron et al. use *packed* secret sharing [FY92] (in contrast to our *batched* secret sharing), which allows the same client to store $O(n)$ secrets in one sharing by encoding multiple secrets as distinct points of a single polynomial. Thus, refreshing each sharing effectively refreshes a batch of $O(n)$ secrets submitted by the same client at the same time. However, this means that secrets in the same batch come from a *single* client and can only be refreshed or reconstructed together. It is unclear if merging batches submitted by different clients is possible. Thus, even if in eWEB some secrets submitted by different clients were to be released at the same time, Baron et al.'s scheme would not allow us to join these secrets in one batch to profit from their low amortized communication complexity. Our scheme has one secret per sharing: only supplementary random sharings are generated in a batch. This allows to refresh (and release) each secret individually.

To reach $O(1)$ amortized communication per secret, Baron et al. need a $(1/2 - \epsilon)$ corruption threshold. Our scheme does not suffer from this corruption threshold loss.

Extractable Witness Encryption and Conditional Secret Release. The notion of witness encryption was introduced by Garg et al. [GGSW13]. Goldwasser et al. [GKP+13] proposed extractable security for witness encryption. In their work a candidate construction was introduced that requires very strong assumptions over multilinear maps. According to Liu et al. [LJKW18], existing witness encryption schemes have no efficient extraction methods. Garg et al. [GGHW14] suggest that it even might be impossible to achieve extractable witness encryption with arbitrary auxiliary inputs.

Nevertheless, as mentioned in Sects. 1 and 6, the notion of extractable witness encryption has been extensively used in various cryptographic protocols [CGJ+17, GG17, BH15, LJKW18], especially in conjunction with blockchains.

Concurrently to our preprint, Benhamouda et al. [BGG+20] published a manuscript that also proposes conditionally storing secrets on a blockchain. Unlike eWEB, their work is specific to proof-of-stake blockchains. Like us, they design a new DPSS scheme, but they target a very specific (albeit intriguing) use case—in their setting, the members of a committee must remain anonymous, even to the previous committee. They consider a stronger adversary who can corrupt and uncorrupt previously honest parties, but they only tolerate 25% corruption, versus 50% for our scheme. They do not explain how to release secrets without revealing witnesses to the miners. This is not trivial, as one would not want to release the secret publicly or allow an adversary to reuse an honest user's witness. Finally, they do not provide a formal security definition or implementation. Our work closes this gap.

Recently, a preprint by Gentry et al. [GHM+20] improved the adversarial threshold of Benhamouda et al., allowing it to tolerate $\frac{1}{2} - \epsilon$ corruptions – fewer than eWEB. While our amortized communication complexity is $O(n)$, the amortized complexity of Gentry et al. (building upon Benhamouda et al.'s work) is an unspecified polynomial. Their setting and focus is different from ours.

Kokoris-Kogias et al. proposed Calypso [KKAS+18], a verifiable data management solution that relies on blockchains and threshold encryption. Calypso targets a different use case than our eWEB system: it allows verifiable sharing of data to parties that are explicitly authorized (either by the depositor or by a committee of authorized parties) to have access rather than specifying a general secret release condition that allows anyone who is able to satisfy this condition to get the data. Kokoris-Kogias et al. do not provide a formal security definition or formal security proof of their system. The major part of their work focuses on the static committee of parties holding the secrets; the dynamic committee setting is only discussed very briefly.

eWEB could be seen as a special case of proactive secure multi-party computation (PMPC) [OY91,BEDLO14,EOPY18]. However, while our DPSS scheme could be used for PMPC, eWEB targets a different use case than general PMPC. This allows for a much more efficient and largely non-interactive construction compared to PMPC protocols, which typically have very high round complexity.

2 Preliminaries

In this section, we introduce the DPSS security definition. In the interest of space, we introduce further building blocks in the full version of this paper [GKM+20].

2.1 DPSS Security Definition

A dynamic proactive secret-sharing scheme (DPSS) scheme allows a client to distribute shares of a secret to n parties, so that an adversary in control of some threshold number of parties t learns no information about the secret. The set of parties holding secrets is constantly changing, and the adversary can "release" some parties (users regain control of their systems) and corrupt new ones.

A DPSS scheme consists of the following three phases.

Setup. In each setup phase, one or more independent clients secret-share a total of m secrets to a set of n parties, known as a committee, denoted by

$\mathcal{C} = \{P_1, \ldots, P_n\}$. After each setup phase, each committee member holds one share for each secret s distributed during this phase.

Hand-off. As the protocol runs, the hand-off phase is periodically invoked to provide the new committee with updated shares in such a way that the adversary cannot use information from multiple committees to learn anything about the secret. This process reflects parties leaving and joining the committee. After the hand-off phase, all parties in the old committee delete their shares, and all parties in the new committee hold a sharing for each secret s. The hand-off phase is particularly challenging, since during the hand-off a total of $2t$ parties may be corrupted (t parties in the old committee and t parties in the new committee).

Reconstruction. When a client (which need not be one who stored the secret) asks for the secret reconstruction, that client and the current committee engage in a reconstruction process to allow the client learn the secret.

At a high-level, the security of the DPSS scheme requires that it should always be possible to recover the secret, and an adversary should not learn any further information about the secret beyond what has been learned before running the protocol. We formally model the security in $\mathsf{Ideal}_{\mathsf{safe}}$. Note that we slightly generalize the typical DPSS definition by supporting not only private release to a client, but also a public release of the secret. In this case, the secret is broadcast to all parties.

Ideal Secrecy: $\mathsf{Ideal}_{\mathsf{safe}}$

1. $\mathsf{Ideal}_{\mathsf{safe}}$ receives a list $\mathcal{C}$ of parties as the first committee, and a corruption threshold t. $\mathsf{Ideal}_{\mathsf{safe}}$ initializes an empty list $\mathcal{L}$ for the secrets.
2. Upon receiving a storage request (store, s) from a client, $\mathsf{Ideal}_{\mathsf{safe}}$ adds the secret s to the end of list $\mathcal{L}$, and sets the identifier id of the secret s to be the number of secrets in $\mathcal{L}$. $\mathsf{Ideal}_{\mathsf{safe}}$ sends id to all parties in the current committee.
3. Upon receiving $(\mathsf{change\text{-}committee}, \mathcal{C}')$ from more than t parties in the current committee $\mathcal{C}$, $\mathsf{Ideal}_{\mathsf{safe}}$ changes the committee to the parties in $\mathcal{C}'$ and sends the identities of $\mathcal{C}'$ to all the parties in $\mathcal{C}$.
4. Upon receiving $(\mathsf{release}, \mathsf{id}, \mathsf{client})$ from more than t parties in the current committee, $\mathsf{Ideal}_{\mathsf{safe}}$ scans list $\mathcal{L}$ for the secret $s^\star$ that corresponds to the identifier id. If such a secret does not exist, $\mathsf{Ideal}_{\mathsf{safe}}$ sets $s^\star = \perp$.
   - If $\mathsf{client} \neq \mathsf{public}$, $\mathsf{Ideal}_{\mathsf{safe}}$ sends $s^\star$ to the client.
   - Otherwise, $\mathsf{Ideal}_{\mathsf{safe}}$ broadcasts $s^\star$.

Definition 1. *A dynamic proactive secret-sharing scheme is secure if for any PPT adversary $\mathcal{A}$ and threshold t, there exists a simulator $\mathcal{S}$ with access to Ideal_{safe} (described in Ideal Secrecy), such that the view of $\mathcal{A}$ interacting with $\mathcal{S}$ is computationally indistinguishable from the view in the real execution.*

2.2 DPSS Definition Discussion

Our definition is slightly different from the original definition of PSS [OY91]. In that definition, there is an additional "Recovery" phase where a party infected by a virus reboots itself to remove the virus and recovers its share jointly with all other parties. In our definition, however, we assume that a party regains control automatically when the adversary releases it, and such a party can use fresh randomness afterwards. To adapt to the original definition where a reboot is needed for a party to remove the virus, this party backs up its share and reboots itself before the next handoff phase. The backup guarantees that an honest party does not lose its shares during the reboot. If this party is corrupted before the reboot, then since the handoff phase will generate a new sharing for all parties, there is no need to recover its old share.

3 Technical Overview – FaB-DPSS

In the following section we give an overview of our FaB-DPSS scheme and security proof. We give the entire construction in the full version of this paper.

FaB-DPSS is based on Shamir Secret Sharing [Sha79]. In the following, we assume the corruption threshold for each committee is fixed to t. We use $[x]_d$ to denote a degree-d sharing, i.e., $(d+1)$-out-of-n Shamir sharing. It requires at least $d+1$ shares to reconstruct the secret, any d or fewer shares leak no information about the secret. Note that Shamir's scheme is additively homomorphic.

In the following, first we outline the adversarial model. Then we discuss the hand-off phase of our scheme in the semi-honest case (Sect. 3.1) and explain how it can be modified for the fully malicious case (Sect. 3.2). We solve the semi-honest case through the introduction of the techique we dub "coupled sharings" combined with the careful use of ideas from the MPC literature [DN07] and a few additional tricks which allow us to achieve good amortized communication complexity. For the fully malicious case, unlike in the MPC world, we must marry these techniques with polynomial commitment schemes. We present the setup phase (Sect. 3.3) as a special case of our hand-off phase, summarize our reconstruction phase (Sect. 3.4), and provide intuition for our construction's security proof (Sect. 3.5).

Adversary Model. We consider a computationally bounded fully malicious adversary $\mathcal{A}$ with the power to adaptively choose parties to corrupt at any time. $\mathcal{A}$ can corrupt any number of clients distributing secrets and learn the secrets held by the corrupted clients. For each committee $\mathcal{C}$ with a threshold $t < |\mathcal{C}|/2$, $\mathcal{A}$ can corrupt at most t parties in $\mathcal{C}$. When a party P_i is corrupted by $\mathcal{A}$, $\mathcal{A}$ fully controls the behavior of P_i and can modify P_i's memory state. Even if $\mathcal{A}$ releases its control of P_i, its memory may have already been modified; e.g., P_i's share might have been erased.

For a party P_i in both the old committee $\mathcal{C}$ and the new committee $\mathcal{C}'$, if $\mathcal{A}$ has the control of P_i during the hand-off phase, then P_i is considered to be corrupted in both committees. If $\mathcal{A}$ releases its control before the hand-off phase in which the secret sharing is passed from $\mathcal{C}$ to $\mathcal{C}'$, then P_i is only considered corrupted in the old committee $\mathcal{C}$. If $\mathcal{A}$ only corrupts P_i after the hand-off phase, P_i is only considered corrupted in the new committee $\mathcal{C}'$.

For simplicity, in the following, we assume that there exist secure point-to-point channels between the parties and the corruption threshold is a fixed value t. Our protocol can be easily adapted to allow different thresholds for different committees (see the full version of this paper).

3.1 FaB-DPSS: Semi-honest Case

We first explain the high-level idea of our protocol in the semi-honest setting; i.e., all parties honestly follow the protocol. The foundational idea in FaB-DPSS is the introduction of so-called *coupled sharings*. By this, we mean two sharings $([r]_t, [\tilde{r}]_t)$ which have the same *value* $(r = \tilde{r})$, even though the particular shares which lead to this value are different for the two sharings. Now, imagine a coupled sharing $([r]_t, [\tilde{r}]_t)$ of a uniformly random value r. We let $[r]_t$ be held by the old committee, and $[\tilde{r}]_t$ be held by the new committee. Suppose the secret sharing we want to refresh is $[s]_t$, held by the old committee. Then the old committee will compute the sharing $[s+r]_t = [s]_t + [r]_t$ and reconstruct the secret $s + r$. Since r is uniformly random, $s+r$ does not leak any information about s. Now, the new committee can compute $[\tilde{s}]_t = (s+r) - [\tilde{r}]_t$. Since $\tilde{r} = r$, we have $\tilde{s} = s$. This whole process is split into *preparation* and *refresh* phases:

- In the preparation phase, parties in the new committee prepare the coupled sharing: two degree-t sharings of the same random value $r(=\tilde{r})$, denoted by $[r]_t$ and $[\tilde{r}]_t$. The old committee receives the shares of $[r]_t$ and the new committee holds the shares of $[\tilde{r}]_t$.
- In the refresh phase, the old committee reconstructs the sharing $[s]_t + [r]_t$ and publishes the result. The new committee sets $[\tilde{s}]_t = (s+r) - [\tilde{r}]_t$.

The rest of our protocol builds around this idea. We need to solve the following challenges:

- How can committees prepare the coupled sharings?
- How can this preparation step be done as efficiently as possible?
- How can these sharings be used efficiently during the refresh step?

We start by answering the first two questions. In the following, let $\mathcal{C}$ denote the old committee and $\mathcal{C}'$ denote the new committee. Intuitively, the straw man solution which allows to obtain one coupled sharing is the following:

1. Each party $P'_i \in \mathcal{C}'$ prepares a coupled sharing $([u^{(i)}]_t, [\tilde{u}^{(i)}]_t)$ of a random value and distributes $[u^{(i)}]_t$ to the old committee and $[\tilde{u}^{(i)}]_t$ to the new committee.
2. All parties in the old committee compute $[r]_t = \sum_{i=1}^{n} [u^{(i)}]_t$. All parties in the new committee compute $[\tilde{r}]_t = \sum_{i=1}^{n} [\tilde{u}^{(i)}]_t$.

Since for each i, $u^{(i)} = \tilde{u}^{(i)}$, we have $r = \tilde{r}$.

Unfortunately, this way of preparing coupled sharings is wasteful since at least $(n-t)$ coupled sharings are generated by honest parties, which appear uniformly random to corrupted parties. In order to get $(n-t)$ random coupled sharings instead of just 1, we borrow an idea from Damgård and Nielsen [DN07].

In their work, parties need to prepare a batch of random sharings which will be used in an MPC protocol. All parties first agree on a fixed and public Vandermonde matrix $\boldsymbol{M}^{\mathrm{T}}$ of size $n \times (n-t)$. An important property of a Vandermonde matrix is that any $(n-t) \times (n-t)$ submatrix of $\boldsymbol{M}^{\mathrm{T}}$ is *invertible*. To prepare a batch of random sharings, each party P_i generates and distributes a random sharing $[u^{(i)}]_t$. Next, all parties compute

$$([r^{(1)}]_t, [r^{(2)}]_t, \ldots, [r^{(n-t)}]_t)^{\mathrm{T}} = \boldsymbol{M}([u^{(1)}]_t, [u^{(2)}]_t, \ldots, [u^{(n)}]_t)^{\mathrm{T}},$$

and take $[r^{(1)}]_t, [r^{(2)}]_t, \ldots, [r^{(n-t)}]_t$ as output. Since any $(n-t) \times (n-t)$ submatrix of $\boldsymbol{M}$ is invertible, given the sharings provided by corrupted parties, there is a one-to-one map from the output sharings to the sharings distributed by honest parties. Since the input sharings of the honest parties are uniformly random, the one-to-one map ensures that the output sharings are uniformly random as well [DN07].

Note that any linear combination of a set of coupled sharings is also a valid coupled sharing. Thus, in our protocol, instead of computing $([r]_t, [\tilde{r}]_t) = \sum_{i=1}^{n}([u^{(i)}]_t, [\tilde{u}^{(i)}]_t)$, parties in the old committee can compute

$$([r^{(1)}]_t, [r^{(2)}]_t, \ldots, [r^{(n-t)}]_t)^{\mathrm{T}} = \boldsymbol{M}([u^{(1)}]_t, [u^{(2)}]_t, \ldots, [u^{(n)}]_t)^{\mathrm{T}}$$

and parties in the new committee can compute

$$([\tilde{r}^{(1)}]_t, [\tilde{r}^{(2)}]_t, \ldots, [\tilde{r}^{(n-t)}]_t)^{\mathrm{T}} = \boldsymbol{M}([\tilde{u}^{(1)}]_t, [\tilde{u}^{(2)}]_t, \ldots, [\tilde{u}^{(n)}]_t)^{\mathrm{T}}$$

Now all parties get $(n-t)$ random coupled sharings. The amortized communication cost per such sharing is $O(n)$.

We now describe the *refresh phase*. For each sharing $[s]_t$ of a client secret which needs to be refreshed, one random coupled sharing $([r]_t, [\tilde{r}]_t)$ is consumed. Parties in the old committee first select a special party $P_{\texttt{king}}$. To reconstruct $[s]_t + [r]_t$, parties in the old committee locally compute their shares of $[s]_t + [r]_t$, and then send the shares to $P_{\texttt{king}}$. Then, $P_{\texttt{king}}$ uses these shares to reconstruct $s+r$ and publishes the result. Finally, parties in the new committee can compute $[\tilde{s}]_t = (s+r) - [\tilde{r}]_t$.

3.2 Moving to a Fully-Malicious Setting

In a fully-malicious setting, three problems might arise.

- During preparation, a party distributes an inconsistent degree-t sharing or incorrect coupled sharing.
- During refresh, a party provides an incorrect share to $P_{\texttt{king}}$, causing a reconstruction failure.
- $P_{\texttt{king}}$ provides an incorrectly reconstructed value.

We address these problems by checking the correctness of coupled sharings in the preparation phase and relying on polynomial commitments to transform a plain Shamir secret sharing into a verifiable one.

Checking the Correctness of Coupled Sharings. While it is possible to check the correctness of each coupled sharing separately, we can increase efficiency by utilizing the following trick: check if *all* of them are correct by checking their *random linear combination*. It works since any linear combination of coupled sharings is also a valid coupled sharing.

Note that in the process we need to to protect the privacy of every coupled sharing $([u^{(i)}]_t, [\tilde{u}^{(i)}]_t)$ generated by a party P_i'. We achieve it by having P_i' generate one additional random coupled sharing as a random mask, which is denoted by $([\mu^{(i)}]_t, [\tilde{\mu}^{(i)}]_t)$.

Consider the following two sharings of polynomials of degree-$(2n-1)$:

$$[F(X)]_t = \sum_{i=1}^{n}([\mu^{(i)}]_t + [u^{(i)}]_t \cdot X)X^{2(i-1)},$$

$$[\tilde{F}(X)]_t = \sum_{i=1}^{n}([\tilde{\mu}^{(i)}]_t + [\tilde{u}^{(i)}]_t \cdot X)X^{2(i-1)}.$$

These two sharings have the following benefitial properties:

1. If *all* coupled sharings are correct, then $([F(\lambda)]_t, [\tilde{F}(\lambda)]_t)$ is also a coupled sharing for any λ. Otherwise, the number of λ such that $([F(\lambda)]_t, [\tilde{F}(\lambda)]_t)$ is a coupled sharing is bounded by $2n-1$. Thus, in order to test whether all sharings are correct, it is sufficient to test $([F(\lambda)]_t, [\tilde{F}(\lambda)]_t)$ at a random evaluation point λ.
2. The coupled sharing $([u^{(i)}]_t, [\tilde{u}^{(i)}]_t)$ generated by P_i' is masked by a random coupled sharing $([\mu^{(i)}]_t, [\tilde{\mu}^{(i)}]_t)$ which is also generated by P_i'. Thus, the secrecy of $([u^{(i)}]_t, [\tilde{u}^{(i)}]_t)$ is preserved during the check of $([F(\lambda)]_t, [\tilde{F}(\lambda)]_t)$.

Therefore, we first let all parties generate a random challenge λ. Parties in the old committee compute $[F(\lambda)]_t$ and publish their shares. Parties in the new committee compute $[\tilde{F}(\lambda)]_t$ and publish their shares. Finally, all parties check whether $([F(\lambda)]_t, [\tilde{F}(\lambda)]_t)$ is a valid coupled sharing.

If the check fails (not all sharings are correct), we need to pinpoint parties who distributed incorrect coupled sharings. Since each coupled sharing $([u^{(i)}]_t, [\tilde{u}^{(i)}]_t)$ is masked by $([\mu^{(i)}]_t, [\tilde{\mu}^{(i)}]_t)$, it is safe to open the whole sharing $([\mu^{(i)}]_t + [u^{(i)}]_t \cdot \lambda, [\tilde{\mu}^{(i)}]_t + [\tilde{u}^{(i)}]_t \cdot \lambda)$ and check whether it is a valid coupled sharing. Since $([F(\lambda)]_t, [\tilde{F}(\lambda)]_t)$ is a linear combination of the coupled sharings $\{([\mu^{(i)}]_t + [u^{(i)}]_t \cdot \lambda, [\tilde{\mu}^{(i)}]_t + [\tilde{u}^{(i)}]_t \cdot \lambda)\}_{i=1}^n$, at least one coupled sharing of $\{([\mu^{(i)}]_t + [u^{(i)}]_t \cdot \lambda, [\tilde{\mu}^{(i)}]_t + [\tilde{u}^{(i)}]_t \cdot \lambda)\}_{i=1}^n$ is inconsistent. In fact, we can find all inconsistent coupled sharings with overwhelming probability with the help of polynomial commitments introduced later. For each i, parties in the old committee compute $[\mu^{(i)}]_t + [u^{(i)}]_t \cdot \lambda$ and publish their shares, and parties in the new committee compute $[\tilde{\mu}^{(i)}]_t + [\tilde{u}^{(i)}]_t \cdot \lambda$ and publish their shares. This way, we can tell which coupled sharings are inconsistent. This inconsistency in the coupled sharing distributed by some party P_i' (in the following, *dealer*) has two possible causes:

- The dealer P'_i distributed an invalid coupled sharing (either the secrets were not the same or one of the degree-t sharings was invalid).
- Some corrupted party $P_j \in C \cup C'$ provided an incorrect share during the verification of the sharing distributed by the dealer P'_i.

The first case implies that the dealer is a corrupted party. To distinguish the first case from the second, we will rely on *polynomial commitments*, which can be used to transform a plain Shamir secret sharing into a verifiable one so that an incorrect share (e.g., in case 2) can be identified and rejected by all parties.

Relying on Polynomial Commitments. A degree-t Shamir secret sharing corresponds to a degree-t polynomial $f(\cdot)$ such that: **(a)** the secret is $f(0)$, and **(b)** the i-th share is $f(i)$. Thus, each dealer can commit to f by using a polynomial commitment scheme to add verifiability.

A polynomial commitment scheme allows the dealer to open one evaluation of f (which corresponds to one share of the Shamir secret sharing) and the receiver can verify the correctness of this evaluation value. Essentially, whenever a dealer distributes a share it also provides a *witness* which can be used to verify this share. Informally, a polynomial commitment scheme satisfies three properties:

- Polynomial Binding: A commitment cannot be opened to two different polynomials.
- Evaluation Binding: A commitment cannot be opened to two different values at the same evaluation point.
- Hiding: A commitment should not leak any information about the committed polynomial.

We use polynomial commitments as follows: in the beginning, each dealer first commits to the sharings it generated and opens the shares to corresponding parties. To ensure that each party is satisfied with the shares it received, there is a following accusation-and-response phase:

1. Each party publishes $(\texttt{accuse}, P'_i)$ if the share received from P'_i does not pass the verification algorithm.
2. For each accusation made by P_j, P'_i opens the j-th share to all parties, and P_j uses the new share published by P'_i if it passes the verification. Otherwise, P'_i is regarded as a corrupted party by everyone else.

Note that an honest party will never accuse another honest party. Also, if a malicious party accuses an honest party, no more information is revealed to the adversary than what the adversary knew already. Thus, it is safe to reveal the share sent from P'_i to P_j. *After this step, all parties should always be able to provide valid witnesses for their shares.*

Recall that parties need to do various linear operations on the shares. In FaB-DPSS we use the KZG commitment scheme [KZG10], which is linearly homomorphic. Thus, even if a share is a result of a number of linear operations, it is still possible for a party to compute the witness for this share. From now on, each time a party sends or publishes a share, this party also provides *the associated witness* to allow other parties verify the correctness of the share. Since honest parties will always provide shares with valid witnesses and there are at least $n - t \geq t + 1$ honest parties, all parties will only use shares that pass verification. Intuitively, this solves the problem of incorrect shares provided by corrupted parties since corrupted parties cannot provide valid witnesses for those shares. Similarly, it should solve the problem of a malicious $P_{\texttt{king}}$, since he cannot provide a valid witness for the incorrectly reconstructed value. However, due to a subtle limitation of the KZG commitment scheme, we actually need to add an additional minor verification step (see [GKM+20] for details).

See [GKM+20] for a complete description of the hand-off process.

3.3 FaB-DPSS Setup Phase

The setup phase uses a similar approach to the hand-off phase. First, the committee prepares random sharings. As in the hand-off phase, the validity of the distributed shares is verified using the KZG commitment scheme. For each secret s distributed by a client, one random sharing $[r]_t$ is consumed. The client receives the whole sharing $[r]_t$ from the committee and reconstructs the value r. Finally, the client publishes $s + r$. The committee then computes $[s]_t = s + r - [r]_t$. See [GKM+20] for details.

3.4 FaB-DPSS Reconstruction Phase

When a client asks for the reconstruction of some secret $s^\star$, all parties in the current committee simply send their shares of $[s^\star]_t$ and the associated witnesses to the client. The client then reconstructs the secret using the first $t + 1$ shares that pass the verification checks. See [GKM+20] for details.

3.5 Security of Our Construction

We give a high-level idea of our proof. The goal is to construct a simulator to simulate the behaviour of honest parties. For each sharing, corrupted parties receive at most t shares, which are independent of the secret. Thus, when an honest party needs to distribute a random sharing, the simulator can send random elements to corrupted parties as their shares without fixing the shares of honest parties. Since we use the perfectly hiding variant of the KZG commitment, the commitment is independent of the secret, and can be generated using the trapdoor of the KZG scheme. Furthermore, we can adaptively open t shares chosen by the adversary after the commitment is generated. This makes our scheme secure against adaptive corruptions. We present the full formal security proof of our scheme in [GKM+20].

4 DPSS Applications – eWEB Primitive

Our next goal is to expand the reach of DPSS. We ask the following question:

Is it possible to let users store secrets and specify release conditions for these secrets in a way that allows (other) users to retrieve these secrets later on if and only if they are able to satisfy the release condition?

Our goal is to achieve this without relying on trusted third parties. Instead, we imagine a distributed storage of secrets which would allow for a high adversarial threshold. We refine our question as follows:

Is it possible to let users store secrets with some group of parties and specify release conditions for these secrets in a way that allows (other) users to retrieve these secrets later on if and only if they are able to satisfy the release condition? Furthermore, is it possible to achieve this if the adversary is able to corrupt up to $t < \frac{1}{2}n$ number of parties storing the secrets?

We are able to answer these questions positively by utilizing DPSS and a dynamic set with honest majority, PKI, and authenticated broadcast. We utilize blockchains as a real-world system which provides the latter three primitives. While we emphasize that technically our solution can be based on any other set of parties with honest majority (supplemented with a PKI and authenticated broadcast), for ease of exposition, in the following we will use "dynamic set with honest majority" and "blockchains" interchangeably.

We now formally introduce the extractable witness encryption on a blockchain (*eWEB*) primitive. We distinguish between users who deposit secrets (depositors), users who request that a secret be released (requesters), and a changing set of blockchain nodes (miners) who are executing these requests.

An eWEB system consists of the following, possibly randomized and interactive, subroutines:

$\mathit{SecretStore}(M, F) \rightarrow (id, \{\mathit{frag}_1, .., \mathit{frag}_n\}, F)$: A depositor stores a secret M which can be released to a requester who knows a witness w s.t. $F(w)$ is true. After interacting with the depositor, each of the n miners obtains a "fragment", frag_i, of the secret that is associated with the secret storage request with the identifier id.

$\mathit{SecretsHandoff}(\{\mathit{frag}_1^1, .., \mathit{frag}_n^1\}, .., \{\mathit{frag}_1^m, .., \mathit{frag}_n^m\}) \rightarrow (\{\widetilde{\mathit{frag}_1^1}, .., \widetilde{\mathit{frag}_n^1}\}, .., \{\widetilde{\mathit{frag}_1^m}, .., \widetilde{\mathit{frag}_n^m}\})$: Miners periodically execute this function to hand over all m stored secrets from the old committee to the new committee. Each miner i of the old committee possesses m fragments (one for each secret) $\mathit{frag}_i^1, .., \mathit{frag}_i^m$ at the start of the hand-off protocol. Each miner i of the new committee possesses m fragments (one for each secret) $\widetilde{\mathit{frag}_i^1}, .., \widetilde{\mathit{frag}_i^m}$ at the end of the protocol.

$\mathit{SecretRelease}(id, w) \rightarrow M$ or $\perp$: A requester uses this function to request the release of the secret with the identifier id. The requester specifies the witness w to the release condition. Miners check whether the requester holds a valid witness and if so, as a result of the interaction with the miners, the requester obtains the secret M. Otherwise the function returns $\perp$ (i.e., attempt failed).

Security Definition. We provide a formal game-based secrecy definition in [GKM+20]. Practically, this definition states that if an adversary is able to distinguish between the protocol executed with secret M_0 and the protocol executed with secret M_1, then we can extract a valid witness for the release condition F using this adversary. Intuitively, this notion is quite similar to the extractable security of witness encryption, which states that if an adversary can distinguish between two ciphertexts, then he can also extract a witness from the corresponding problem instance. For robustness, intuitively we require that it is always possible for an honest requester to reconstruct a secret dealt by an honest depositor.

Remark 1. We also propose a variant of eWEB with a slightly relaxed security notion we dub *Public Witness* security. Here, the secret is made public after a single successful secret release. As we show in Sect. 6, this notion proves quite useful in a number of applications.

5 Our eWEB Protocol Design

Before we introduce our eWEB construction, we provide an overview of the assumptions that we rely on in our scheme (Sect. 5.1).

5.1 Assumptions

Adversary Model. We rely on blockchains and assume that eWEB is a core functionality, which allows us to focus on the fundamental construction without worrying about selfish mining or bribery attacks. The adversary is able to control a polynomial number of users and miners, subject to the constraint that the blockchain has $(\frac{n}{2}+1, n)$-chain quality, meaning that for each n or more continuous blocks mined in the system, more than half were mined by honest parties. As noted by [GG17], for proof of work blockchains, where the probability of successful mining is proportional to the amount of computational power, this assumption follows from the assumption that honest miners possess the majority of the computational power in the system. We assume this majority is "significant enough" (to, for example, defeat selfish mining attacks [ES14] that would threaten Bitcoin's security). For proof of stake blockchains, where the probability of successful mining is proportional to the amount of coins possessed by the miner, it follows from the assumption that honest miners possess the majority of stake in the system. In practice, we pick an n that is big enough to provide this property with only a very small error probability. Honest majority assumptions are very common in the blockchain space [GG17,CGJ+17,MZW+19,GHM+17,KKAS+18], especially in permissioned blockchains, which often rely on BFT replication protocols, which in turn usually assume an honest supermajority [ABB+18]. We assume that the blockchain is an append-only log, and it is hard to modify or erase its contents.

We assume that once an adversary corrupts a party it remains corrupted. The adversary cannot adaptively corrupt previously honest parties. When a party is corrupted by the adversary, the adversary fully controls this party's behaviour and internal memory state. We do not distinguish between adversarial and honest parties who behave maliciously unintentionally; e.g., those who have connection issues and cannot access the blockchain to participate.

Infrastructure Model. It is common for public keys to be known in blockchains. We require that additionally each party p_i has a *unique identifier*, denoted by pid_i, that is known to all other parties. In practice, this identifier can be the hash of the party's public key. For simplicity, we present the scheme as if there were authenticated channels between all parties in the system. In practice, these channels can be realized using standard techniques such as signatures.

Communication Model. Our DPSS scheme assumes secure point-to-point communication channels. In the decentralized blockchain setting of eWEB we prefer not to make such an assumption, since using point-to-point channels could compromise nodes' anonymity and lead to targeted attacks [MZW+19]. Instead, we assume that parties communicate via an existing blockchain. We distinguish between posting a message on the blockchain (expensive) and using the blockchain's peer-to-peer network for broadcast (cheap). Point-to-point channels can be simulated using IND-CCA secure encryption and broadcasting the ciphertexts.

Storage. We assume that, in addition to parties' internal storage, there exists some publicly accessible off-chain storage that is cheaper than on-chain one. Thus, we store data off-chain and save only data *hashes* on-chain. Our system's robustness depends on the robustness of the off-chain storage. Thus, storage systems with a reputation for high availability should be chosen. However malicious off-chain storage does not impact the secrecy properties of our system (see [GKM+20]. Alternatively, at a higher cost, we can use on-chain storage for everything.

Cryptographic Assumptions. In addition to the assumptions outlined above, we assume IND-CCA secure encryption, collision-resistant hash functions, simulation extractable non-interactive zero knowledge proofs of knowledge, and (for DPSS) the t-SDH assumption.

Blockchain Setting. eWEB can be built atop of any node set with honest majority supplemented by a PKI. We present eWEB in the blockchain setting simply because it is a system which already exists in practice (and because multiple applications which rely on extractable witness encryption and which we try to achieve already rely on blockchains [LJKW18, CGJ+17, GG17]).

We note that miners that behave honestly w.r.t. the blockchain protocol might need further incentivization to behave honestly w.r.t. eWEB; otherwise they might try to disrupt the execution of the eWEB protocol or leak their secret shares. Our DPSS scheme has numerous checks that identify parties disrupting correct protocol execution (see Sect. 3.2), which could translate to economic disincentivization. Traitor-tracing secret sharing [GSS21] as well as trusted hardware that can verify correct share deletion could be used as mechanisms that ensure that miners are punished for leaking secrets entrusted to them. We leave exploring these directions for future work.

5.2 Our eWEB Construction

We now describe our eWEB scheme. Its key building block is a DPSS scheme used in a black-box way. The initial committee are miners who mined the most recent n blocks in the underlying blockchains.

Given a secret message M and a release condition F, the depositor stores the release condition F on the blockchain and secret-shares M among the miners using the secret storage (setup) algorithm of the DPSS scheme.

During the protocol's periodically executed hand-off phase, the secrets are passed from the miners of the old committee to the miners of the new committee using the DPSS hand-off algorithm. The new committee consists of the miners who mined the most recent n blocks. This keeps the size of the committee constant and allows all parties to determine the current committee by looking at the blockchain state. It is possible that some committee members receive more information about the secrets than others - roughly, if a party mined m out of the last n blocks, this party receives $\frac{m}{n}$ of all the shares. This reflects the distribution of the computing power (for POW blockchains) or stake (for POS blockchains) in the system [GG17].

To retrieve a stored secret, a requester U needs to prove that they are eligible to do so. This poses a challenge. An insecure solution is to just send a valid witness w ($F(w) = true$) to the miners. One obvious problem with this solution is that a malicious miner can use the provided witness to construct a new secret release request and retrieve the secret himself. To solve this problem, instead of sending the witness in clear, the user *proves that they know a valid witness.* Thus, while the committee members are able to check the validity of the request and privately release the secret to U, the witness remains hidden. In our scheme we rely on non-interactive zero knowledge proofs (NIZKs) [BFM88]. Such proofs allow one party (the prover) to prove validity of some statement to another party (the verifier), such that nothing except for the validity of the statement is revealed. In eWEB we specifically use simulation extractable non-interactive zero knowledge *proofs of knowledge*, which allow the prover convince the verifier that they know a witness to some statement. Note that extractability can be added to any NIZK [ARS20,KZM+15]. We use NIZKs for relation $R = \{(pk, w) \mid F(w) = true \text{ and } pk = pk\}$, where $F(\cdot)$ is the release condition specified by the depositor and pk is the public key of user U and is used to identify the user eligible to receive the secret. After the miners verify the validity of the request, they engage in the DPSS's secret reconstruction with requester U to release the secret to U.

We provide the full secret storage protocol in Fig. 3. The hand-off protocol is given in Fig. 4. The secret release protocol is in Fig. 5. Note that the asymptotics of eWEB match those of our underlying DPSS scheme. Below, we elaborate on additional details of our construction.

Subtleties of Point-to-Point Channels. As mentioned in Sect. 5.1, while FaB-DPSS assumes secure point-to-point channels, we do not make such an assumption in eWEB. Instead, we rely on authenticated encryption and Protocols 1 and 2, executed whenever a message needs to be securely sent from one party to another. It is used for all messages exchanged in eWEB, including the underlying DPSS protocol. Whenever a party receives an encrypted message, it performs an authentication check to ensure that a ciphertext received from some party was generated by that party. This prevents the following malleability issue - a malicious user desiring to learn a secret with the identifier id could generate a new secret storage request with a function $\tilde{F}$ for which he knows a witness, copy the DPSS messages sent by the user who created the storage request id to the miners and later on prove his knowledge of a witness for $\tilde{F}$ to release the corresponding secret. Without the authentication check, our scheme would be insecure, and our security proof (see [GKM+20]) would not go through.

Protocol 1. MESSAGEPREPARATION

1. For a message m to be sent by party P_s to party P_r, P_s computes the ciphertext $c \leftarrow Enc_{pk_r}(m|pid_s)$, where pk_r is the public key of P_r and pid_s is the party identifier of P_s.
2. P_s prepends the storage identifier id of his request and sends the tuple (id, c) to P_r.

Protocol 2. AUTHENTICATEDDECRYPTION

1. Upon receiving a tuple (id, c) from party P_s over an authenticated channel, the receiving party P_r decrypts c using its secret key sk to obtain $m \leftarrow Dec_{sk}(c)$.
2. P_r verifies that m is of the form $m'|pid_s$ for some message m', where pid_s is the identifier of party P_s.
3. If the verification check fails, P_r stops processing c and outputs an error message.

Storage Identifiers. Each storage request has a unique identifier id. This can be, e.g., the address of this particular transaction in the blockchain. It is used for practical reasons, and is not relevant for the security of our construction.

Handling Large Secrets. Since the secret itself might be very large, it is also possible to first encrypt the secret using a symmetric encryption scheme, store the ciphertext publicly off chain and then secret-share the symmetric key instead. Also, we store request parameters (such as release conditions or proofs) off-chain, saving only the hash of the message on-chain.

5.3 Security Proof Intuition

We provide a formal proof of security in [GKM+20], showing that our scheme satisfies the security definition for eWEB given in [GKM+20]. In this proof, we rely on the zero-knowledge and simulation-sound extractability properties of the NIZK scheme to switch from providing honest proofs to using simulated

Protocol 3. SecretStore

1. The depositor executes NIZK's KeyGen protocol to obtain a CRS: $\sigma \leftarrow \mathsf{KeyGen}(1^k)$.
2. The depositor computes hash $\mathsf{requestHash} \leftarrow H(F|\sigma)$, and publishes $\mathsf{requestHash}$ on the blockchain. Let id be the storage identifier of the published request.
3. The depositor stores the tuple $(id, F|\sigma)$ offchain.
4. The depositor and the current members of the miner committee engage in the DPSS **Setup Phase**.
5. Each committee member retrieves $\mathsf{requestHash}$ from the blockchain, $F|\sigma$ from the offchain storage, and verifies that $\mathsf{requestHash}$ is indeed the hash of $F|\sigma$:

$$\mathsf{requestHash} \stackrel{?}{=} H(F|\sigma)$$

   If this is not the case, the committee member aborts.
6. C_i stores $(id, \mathsf{dpss\text{-}data}_i)$ internally, where $\mathsf{dpss\text{-}data}_i$ is the data obtained from the DPSS **Setup Phase**.

Protocol 4. SecretsHandoff

1. For each secret storage identifier id, the miners of the old and the new committee engage in the DPSS **Handoff Phase** for the corresponding secret. Let $\mathsf{dpss\text{-}data}_i^{id}$ denote the resulting DPSS data corresponding to the storage identifier id of party C_i of the new committee after the handoff phase.
2. For each secret storage identifier id, each miner of the new committee stores $(id, \mathsf{dpss\text{-}data}_i^{id})$ internally.

proofs. Next, we rely on the collision-resistance of the hash function to show that any modification of the data stored offchain will be detected. Then, we rely on the multi-message IND-CCA security of the encryption scheme to change all encrypted messages exchanged between honest parties to encryptions of zero. Finally, we rely on the security of our DPSS scheme to switch from honestly executing the DPSS protocol to using a DPSS simulator. At this point, we can show that either the adversary was able to provide a valid secret release request for the challenge's secret-release function, in which case we are able to extract a witness from the provided NIZK proof (relying on the NIZK's proof-of-knowledge property), or the adversary did not provide a valid secret release request and in this case we are able to "forget" the secret altogether, since it is never used.

Protocol 5. SecretRelease

1. To request the release of a secret with identifier id, the requester retrieves $\mathsf{requestHash}$ from the blockchain, $F|\sigma$ from off-chain storage, and verifies that $\mathsf{requestHash}$ is indeed the hash of $F|\sigma$:

   $$\mathsf{requestHash} \stackrel{?}{=} H(F|\sigma)$$

   If this is not the case, the requester aborts.
2. The requester computes a NIZK proof of knowledge of the witness for F and his identifier p_{id}:

   $$\pi \leftarrow P(\sigma, p_{id}, w),$$

3. The requester computes hash of the storage identifier, his identifier and the proof to obtain $\mathsf{requestHash}^* \leftarrow H(id|p_{id}|\pi)$ and publishes $\mathsf{requestHash}^*$ on blockchain. Let id^* be the identifier of the published request.
4. The requester stores $(id^*, id|p_{id}|\pi)$ offchain.
5. Each committee member retrieves $\mathsf{requestHash}^*$ from the blockchain request with the identifier id^*, $id|p_{id}|\pi$ from the offchain storage, and verifies that:

   $$\mathsf{requestHash}^* \stackrel{?}{=} H(id|p_{id}|\pi)$$

   If not, the committee member aborts.
6. Each committee member retrieves $\mathsf{requestHash}$ from the blockchain request with the identifier id, $F|\sigma$ from the offchain storage, and verifies that:

   $$\mathsf{requestHash} \stackrel{?}{=} H(F|\sigma)$$

   If not, the committee member aborts.
7. Each committee member C_i retrieves its share of the secret, $\mathsf{dpss\text{-}data}_i$, from its internal storage.
8. Each committee member C_i checks if π is a valid proof using the NIZK's verification algorithm V:

   $$V(\sigma, p_{id}, \pi) \stackrel{?}{=} true$$

   If so, C_i and party p_{id} engage in the DPSS **Reconstruction** using $\mathsf{dpss\text{-}data}_i$.

6 Application Examples

In this section, we present some motivational application examples and briefly explain the key ideas behind implementing each of them using our construction.

Time-Lock Encryption. Time-lock encryption, related to timed-release encryption introduced by Rivest et al. [RSW96], allows one to encrypt a message such that it can only be decrypted after a certain deadline has passed. Time-lock encryption must satisfy a number of properties [LJKW18], such as the encrypter needs not be available for decryption and trusted parties are not allowed. Time-lock encryption can be easily implemented using the PUBLICWITNESS scheme (see [GKM+20]). Using this scheme, the encrypter executes *SecretStore* with a secret release condition F specifying the time t when the data can be released. Once the time has passed, a user who wishes to see the message submits a *SecretRelease* request with the witness "The deadline has passed". Miners check whether the time is indeed past t and if so, release their fragments of the secret. With a slight modification to our scheme, it is also possible to enable automatic decryption - upon receiving a secret storage request with an "automatic" tag, miners would place the identifier in a list and periodically check whether the release condition holds for any request in this list.

Note that we evade the issue that some time-lock schemes [LJKW18] have: even if the adversary becomes computationally more powerful, it does not allow him to receive the secret message earlier. Additionally, we avoid the computational waste of timed-release encryption schemes [RSW96], which often require the decrypter to, say, compute a long series of repeated modular squarings.

Dead-Man's Switch. A dead-man's switch is designed to be activated when the human operator becomes incapacitated. Software versions of the dead-man's switch typically trigger a process such as making public (or deleting) some secret data. The triggering event, for centralized software versions, can be a user failing to log in for three days, a GPS-enabled mobile phone that does not move for a period of time, or a user failing to respond to an automated email. A dead-man's switch can be seen as insurance for journalists and whistleblowers.

A dead-man's switch can use our PUBLICWITNESS protocol as follows: the user who wishes to setup the switch generates a SECRETSTORE request with the desired release condition. Such condition can be failing to post a signed message on the blockchain for several days or anything publicly verifiable. As in the time-lock example, we can either use the standard scheme where a person (e.g., a relative or a friend) proves to the miners that the release condition has been satisfied or define an "automatic" request where the miners periodically check the release condition.

Fairness. eWEB can be used to support fair exchange, which ensures that two parties receive each other's inputs atomically. Using eWEB, Alice specifies a release condition that requires a signature from her and from Bob, while Bob's release condition requires only a signature from Bob. Once both secrets are posted, Alice verifies Bob's release condition and posts her signature. When Bob posts his signature, the committee releases both their secrets atomically. Fair exchange can be used to build fair MPC [Yao82, GHY87].

Multi-party computation (MPC) is considered fair if it ensures that either all parties receive the output of the protocol, or none. In the standard model, fair MPC was proven to be impossible to achieve for general functions when a majority of the parties are dishonest [Cle86]. However, we can achieve it by simply adapting the construction of Choudhuri et al. [CGJ+17] to use our eWEB protocol, instead of traditional witness encryption. Conveniently, Choudhuri et al.'s scheme relies on a public bulletin board, which is most readily realized in practice via a blockchain-based ledger. Thus, by replacing witness encryption with our blockchain-based scheme, we do not add any extra assumptions to Choudhuri et al.'s construction.

One-Time Programs. A one-time program, introduced by Goldwasser et al. [GKR08], is a program that runs only once and then "self-destructs". In the same work they presented a proof of concept construction that relies on tamper-proof hardware. Considerable work on one-time programs followed [GIS+10, BHR12, AIKW15, DDKZ13], but all such schemes relied on tamper-proof hardware. Goyal and Goyal [GG17], however, present the first construction for one-time programs that does not rely on tamper-proof hardware (but does rely on extractable witness encryption). As with fair MPC and Choudhuri et al.'s construction, by replacing the witness encryption scheme with our eWEB protocol in the Goyal and Goyal's one-time program construction with public inputs, we are not adding any extra assumptions since they already rely on blockchains. Since eWEB reveals whether a secret was retrieved, additional mechanisms are needed when the inputs submitted to the one-time program must be kept private.

Non-repudiation/Proof of Receipt. A protocol allows *repudiation* if one of the entities involved can deny participating in all or part of the communication. With eWEB, it is easy to provide a proof that a person received certain data. In this case, the user providing the data stores it using the SecretStore protocol. To satisfy the release condition F, a user with public identifier *pid* publishes a signed message "User *pid* requests the message". The miners then securely release a secret to the user *pid* as specified by SecretRelease. The publicly verifiable signature on the message "User *pid* requests the message" then serves as a proof that party *pid* indeed received the data.

6.1 Voting Protocol

As a more detailed example, we show how eWEB can support a "yes-no" voting application. Specifically, using eWEB, each voter can independently and asynchronously cast their vote by secret sharing a -1 for a "no" or a 1 for a "yes" (note that $(0, 1)$ voting can be supported as well). When voting closes, the miners release an aggregate of the votes. The vote of any specific client must be kept private (guaranteed by eWEB's secrecy), and no client should be able to manipulate the result more than with his own vote.

To prevent improper votes, the committee must verify the correctness of the secrets shared by the clients; i.e., that each $s \in \{-1, 1\}$. Our key idea is to let each client first commit to its secret and then prove its correctness to the miners. However, this requires the client to prove that the committed value is the same as the value the client shared to the committee. To avoid this expensive check, committee members instead *compute* the necessary commitment using the secret shares they receive from the client (guaranteeing consistency by construction).

In [GKM+20], we show that the committee members can prepare Pedersen commitments [Ped92] for all of the clients with constant amortized cost. For a client's secret s, the resulting commitment is of the form $c = g^s h^z$, where z is a random value (known to the client) and g, h are publicly known generators with $h = g^{\beta}$ for some unknown β.

With such a commitment, the user can prove $s \in \{-1, 1\}$ by proving $s^2 = 1$. To prove that $s^2 = 1$, the client (who knows s and z) computes $w = g^{2sz} h^{z^2}$ and publishes w to all parties. To check that $s^2 = 1$, anyone can check that:

$$e(c, c) = e(g, g) \cdot e(h, w).$$

Correctness. To show correctness, note that

$$\begin{aligned} \text{LHS} &= e(g^{s+\beta z}, g^{s+\beta z}) = e(g, g)^{s^2 + 2\beta s z + \beta^2 z^2} \\ \text{RHS} &= e(g, g) \cdot e(g^{\beta}, g^{2sz + \beta z^2}) = e(g, g)^{1 + 2\beta s z + \beta^2 z^2}. \end{aligned}$$

If the equation holds, then $s^2 = 1$ and thus the client's vote is valid.

To compute the voting result the committee computes the sharing of the result relying on the linear homomorphism of KZG commitments and Shamir's secret sharing, and then follows the usual *SecretRelease* procedure.

7 Implementation

We implement both FaB-DPSS and our eWEB scheme in about 2000 lines of Python code. To perform the underlying field and curve operations, we add Python wrappers around the C++ code of the Ate-Pairings library [Shi10]. For networking, we rely on gRPC [gRP], and for hashing, we use SHA256. For our NIZK scheme, we currently use Schnorr's proof of knowledge [Sch90]. We make it non-interactive via the Fiat-Shamir heuristic [FS86], thus simultaneously making it simulation extractable [FKMV12].

Polynomial arithmetic is done over the polynomial ring $\mathbb{F}_p[X]$ for a 254-bit prime p. For the KZG commitment scheme [KZG10], we use an ate pairing over Barreto-Naehrig curves of the form $y^2 = x^3 + b$ for constant b over $\mathbb{F}_p$ with a 254-bit prime p. We implement polynomial interpolation for polynomials of degree n in time $O(n \log^2 n)$ using an algorithm presented by Aho et al. [AHU74].

8 Experimental Evaluation

We evaluate FaB-DPSS and eWEB and show that:

1. FaB-DPSS outperforms the state-of-the-art (Sect. 8.1).
2. eWEB's performance is dominated by FaB-DPSS.
3. Our eWEB prototype's performance matches the expected asymptotics with small constants (Sect. 8.2), making it practical to integrate with existing blockchains.

We discuss microbenchmarks in [GKM+20].

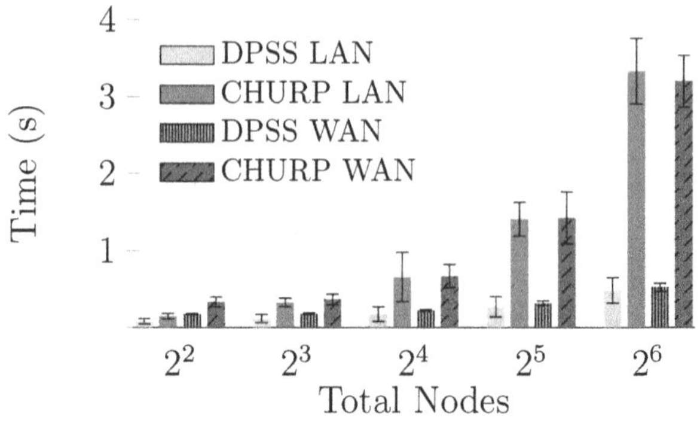

Fig. 2. Handoff Times for our DPSS vs. CHURP. Error bars represent 95% confidence interval.

Setup. We run experiments using CloudLab [DRM+19], an NSF-sponsored testbed that provides compute nodes along with a configurable networking substrate. We run experiments in both a LAN setting (~0.2 ms ping) to focus on the CPU overhead of our cryptography and a WAN setting (~40 ms ping) to demonstrate the networking overhead. In the LAN setting we use up to 128 machines each with 8-core 2.00 GHz CPUs and 4 GB RAM. In the WAN setting we use up to 128 machines split between Salt Lake City, Utah and Madison, Wisconsin. These machines have 8–10 cores and 2.00–2.4 GHz CPUs with 2–4 GB RAM.

Since eWEB is compatible with a wide range of blockchains, we abstract away the blockchain and simulate it via a single trusted node. In practice, writes to the blockchain will incur additional blockchain-specific latency.

8.1 DPSS Comparison

As Sect. 1.2 discusses, the most efficient prior DPSS schemes are CHURP [MZW+19] and that of Baron et al. [BDLO15]. Since CHURP reports [MZW+19, §6.3] that their performance dominates that of Baron et al., we focus on CHURP.

In our experiment, we measure the time required for each scheme to handoff secrets to a new committee in the optimistic case where parties behave honestly. Both schemes have a fallback path for when malfeasance is detected; it adds an $O(n)$ factor to both schemes.

Figure 2 summarizes the average time for 50 runs. As expected from our asymptotic analysis, FaB-DPSS increasingly out-performs CHURP as the number of nodes increases, to the point where our scheme is ~7× faster than CHURP with 64 nodes. The absolute difference will increase as committee sizes grow.

Note that the additional networking overhead in the WAN setting (~40 ms latency) only significantly affects the end-to-end latency for committees with less than 8 members for both FaB-DPSS and CHURP. For larger committees, computation dominates networking costs even with realistic latencies.

8.2 eWEB Performance

We measure the costs of eWEB's top-level operations (*SecretStore*, *SecretsHandoff*, and *SecretRelease*) for the minimal Schnorr identification application over an increasing number of committee members. In particular, given a public key, committee members release the secret if a client proves (in zero-knowledge) that they possess the associated secret key.

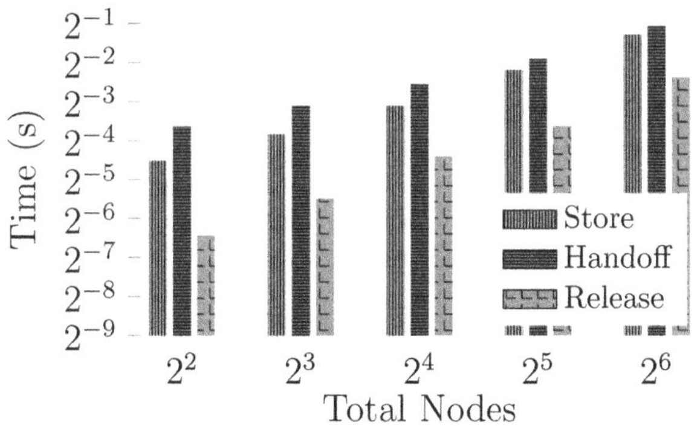

Fig. 3. Time required for high-level eWEB steps on a LAN. Non-DPSS operations are too small to see.

Figure 3 summarizes the average time for 150 runs (note the log-log scale). Each bar shows the split between eWEB operations (e.g., preparing the NIZK proof) and the underlying DPSS operations. Note that the time for *SecretsHandoff* includes the amortized cost for the preparation phase that produces coupled sharings of random value used during the refresh phase. Similiarly the time for *SecretStore* includes the amortized cost for the preparation phase that produces sharings for random values used to distribute the initial secret.

The DPSS costs dominate, to the point where the time for eWEB operations cannot be seen. The performance results match our expectation of linear asymptotic growth, and concretely costs ~7.3 milliseconds/node, ~10.7 milliseconds/node, and ~3.0 milliseconds/node for the store, refresh, and release secret operations respectively. This suggests if CloudLab allowed us to scale beyond 64 nodes per committee, we would expect eWEB to store, refresh, release secrets in 7.3 s, 10.7 s, and 3.0 s respectively, even with a 1000-node committee.

8.3 Applications

We implement several applications on top of our eWEB protocol in order to demonstrate practicality and efficiency for common use cases. As a baseline we implement the minimal Schorr identification application: Given a public key, committee members release a secret when provided a (zero-knowledge) proof that a client possess the associated private key. Because the Schnorr identification protocol only requires a few additional group operations for both the client and committee members, this gives us the best view of eWEB's core operational cost.

We additionally implement *time-lock encryption* and *dead-man's switch* as described in Sect. 6. In both applications, a claim that the prescribed amount of time has passed is treated as the "witness". In the latter application, we additionally implement an update functionality that allows an operator to extend the secret-release timeout if they provide a valid signature.

We implement the *fair exchange* (Sect. 6), where given valid signatures from two clients, the committee releases both their secrets atomically.

Table 1 outlines the cost of eWEB applications for various committee sizes.

Table 1. Cost of eWEB applications. End-to-end latency including secret store, a single handoff, and secret release. (50 trials)

	Committee Size				
	4	8	16	32	64
Schnorr Identification	0.15 s	0.22 s	0.37 s	0.67 s	1.22 s
Time Lock Encryption	0.15 s	0.22 s	0.36 s	0.66 s	1.25 s
Dead-man's Switch	0.15 s	0.23 s	0.37 s	0.68 s	1.23 s
Fair Exchange	0.19 s	0.27 s	0.44 s	0.78 s	1.45 s

9 Conclusion

We have introduced a new and highly efficient batched DPSS protocol – FaB-DPSS. We also proposed eWEB – a new cryptographic primitive which allows the blockchain to store and release secrets. We designed a proof of concept eWEB protocol based on FaB-DPSS and implemented it. Additionally, we implemented and evaluated several applications atop eWEB.

Acknowledgements. We thank Emanuel Jöbstl for helping us with the experimental evaluation of this work.

Bryan Parno, Abhiram Kothapalli and Elisaweta Masserova were supported by a fellowship from the Alfred P. Sloan Foundation, a gift from Bosch, NSF Grant No. 1801369, and by the CONIX Research Center, one of six centers in JUMP, a Semiconductor Research Corporation (SRC) program sponsored by DARPA. Vipul Goyal and Yifan Song were supported by the NSF award 1916939, the DARPA SIEVE program, a Cylab Presidential Fellowship, a gift from Ripple, a DoE NETL award, a JP Morgan Faculty Fellowship, a PNC center for financial services innovation award, and a Cylab seed funding award.

References

[ABB+18] Androulaki, E., et al.: Hyperledger fabric: a distributed operating system for permissioned blockchains. In: Proceedings of the Thirteenth EuroSys Conference (2018)

[ABG+13] Ananth, P., Boneh, D., Garg, S., Sahai, A., Zhandry, M.: Differing-inputs obfuscation and applications. IACR ePrint, 2013/689 (2013)

[AHU74] Aho, A., Hopcroft, J., Ulman, J.: The Design and Analysis of Computer Algorithms (1974)

[AIKW15] Applebaum, B., Ishai, Y., Kushilevitz, E., Waters, B.: Encoding functions with constant online rate, or how to compress garbled circuit keys. SIAM J. Comput. **44**(2), 433–466 (2015)

[ARS20] Abdolmaleki, B., Ramacher, S., Slamanig, D.: Lift-and-shift: obtaining simulation extractable subversion and updatable SNARKs generically. IACR ePrint, 2020:62 (2020)

[BDLO15] Baron, J., Defrawy, K.E., Lampkins, J., Ostrovsky, R.: Communication-optimal proactive secret sharing for dynamic groups. In: Malkin, T., Kolesnikov, V., Lewko, A.B., Polychronakis, M. (eds.) ACNS 2015. LNCS, vol. 9092, pp. 23–41. Springer, Cham (2015). https://doi.org/10.1007/978-3-319-28166-7_2

[BEDLO14] Baron, J., El Defrawy, K., Lampkins, J., Ostrovsky, R.: How to withstand mobile virus attacks, revisited. In: Proceedings of the 2014 ACM Symposium on Principles of Distributed Computing (2014)

[BFM88] Blum, M., Feldman, P., Micali, S.: Non-interactive zero-knowledge and its applications. In: Proceedings of the Twentieth Annual ACM Symposium on Theory of Computing (1988)

[BGG+20] Benhamouda, F., et al.: Can a public blockchain keep a secret? In: Pass, R., Pietrzak, K. (eds.) TCC 2020. LNCS, vol. 12550, pp. 260–290. Springer, Cham (2020). https://doi.org/10.1007/978-3-030-64375-1_10

[BGI+12] Barak, B., et al.: On the (im) possibility of obfuscating programs. J. ACM (JACM) **59**(2), 1–48 (2012)

[BH15] Bellare, M., Hoang, V.T.: Adaptive witness encryption and asymmetric password-based cryptography. In: Katz, J. (ed.) PKC 2015. LNCS, vol. 9020, pp. 308–331. Springer, Heidelberg (2015). https://doi.org/10.1007/978-3-662-46447-2_14

[BHR12] Bellare, M., Hoang, V.T., Rogaway, P.: Adaptively secure garbling with applications to one-time programs and secure outsourcing. In: Wang, X., Sako, K. (eds.) ASIACRYPT 2012. LNCS, vol. 7658, pp. 134–153. Springer, Heidelberg (2012). https://doi.org/10.1007/978-3-642-34961-4_10

[CGJ+17] Choudhuri, A.R., Green, M., Jain, A., Kaptchuk, G., Miers, I.: Fairness in an unfair world: fair multiparty computation from public bulletin boards. In: Proceedings of the 2017 ACM Conference on Computer and Communications Security (2017)

[CKLS02] Cachin, C., Kursawe, K., Lysyanskaya, A., Strobl, R.: Asynchronous verifiable secret sharing and proactive cryptosystems. In: Proceedings of the 9th ACM Conference on Computer and Communications Security (2002)

[Cle86] Cleve, R.: Limits on the security of coin flips when half the processors are faulty. In: Proceedings of the Eighteenth Annual ACM Symposium on Theory of Computing (1986)

[DDKZ13] Durnoga, K., Dziembowski, S., Kazana, T., Zając, M.: One-time programs with limited memory. In: Lin, D., Xu, S., Yung, M. (eds.) Inscrypt 2013. LNCS, vol. 8567, pp. 377–394. Springer, Cham (2014). https://doi.org/10.1007/978-3-319-12087-4_24

[DJ97] Desmedt, Y., Jajodia, S.: Redistributing secret shares to new access structures and its applications. Technical report, Citeseer (1997)

[DN07] Damgård, I., Nielsen, J.B.: Scalable and unconditionally secure multiparty computation. In: Menezes, A. (ed.) CRYPTO 2007. LNCS, vol. 4622, pp. 572–590. Springer, Heidelberg (2007). https://doi.org/10.1007/978-3-540-74143-5_32

[DRM+19] Duplyakin, D., et al.: The design and operation of CloudLab. In: Proceedings of the USENIX Annual Technical Conference (ATC), July 2019

[EOPY18] Eldefrawy, K., Ostrovsky, R., Park, S., Yung, M.: Proactive secure multiparty computation with a dishonest majority. In: Catalano, D., De Prisco, R. (eds.) SCN 2018. LNCS, vol. 11035, pp. 200–215. Springer, Cham (2018). https://doi.org/10.1007/978-3-319-98113-0_11

[ES14] Eyal, I., Sirer, E.G.: Majority is not enough: bitcoin mining is vulnerable. In: Christin, N., Safavi-Naini, R. (eds.) FC 2014. LNCS, vol. 8437, pp. 436–454. Springer, Heidelberg (2014). https://doi.org/10.1007/978-3-662-45472-5_28

[FKMV12] Faust, S., Kohlweiss, M., Marson, G.A., Venturi, D.: On the non-malleability of the Fiat-Shamir transform. In: Galbraith, S., Nandi, M. (eds.) INDOCRYPT 2012. LNCS, vol. 7668, pp. 60–79. Springer, Heidelberg (2012). https://doi.org/10.1007/978-3-642-34931-7_5

[FS86] Fiat, A., Shamir, A.: How to prove yourself: practical solutions to identification and signature problems. In: Odlyzko, A.M. (ed.) CRYPTO 1986. LNCS, vol. 263, pp. 186–194. Springer, Heidelberg (1987). https://doi.org/10.1007/3-540-47721-7_12

[FY92] Franklin, M., Yung, M.: Communication complexity of secure computation. In: Proceedings of the Twenty-Fourth Annual ACM Symposium on Theory of Computing (1992)

[GG17] Goyal, R., Goyal, V.: Overcoming cryptographic impossibility results using blockchains. In: Kalai, Y., Reyzin, L. (eds.) TCC 2017. LNCS, vol. 10677, pp. 529–561. Springer, Cham (2017). https://doi.org/10.1007/978-3-319-70500-2_18

[GGHW14] Garg, S., Gentry, C., Halevi, S., Wichs, D.: On the implausibility of differing-inputs obfuscation and extractable witness encryption with auxiliary input. In: Garay, J.A., Gennaro, R. (eds.) CRYPTO 2014. LNCS, vol. 8616, pp. 518–535. Springer, Heidelberg (2014). https://doi.org/10.1007/978-3-662-44371-2_29

[GGSW13] Garg, S., Gentry, C., Sahai, A., Waters, B.: Witness encryption and its applications. In: Proceedings of the Forty-Fifth Annual ACM Symposium on Theory of Computing (2013)

[GHM+17] Gilad, Y., Hemo, R., Micali, S., Vlachos, G., Zeldovich, N.: Algorand: scaling byzantine agreements for cryptocurrencies. In: Proceedings of the 26th Symposium on Operating Systems Principles (2017)

[GHM+20] Gentry, C., Halevi, S., Magri, B., Nielsen, J.B., Yakoubov, S.: Random-index PIR and applications. Cryptology ePrint Archive, Report 2020/1248 (2020)

[GHY87] Galil, Z., Haber, S., Yung, M.: Cryptographic computation: secure fault-tolerant protocols and the public-key model (extended abstract). In: Pomerance, C. (ed.) CRYPTO 1987. LNCS, vol. 293, pp. 135–155. Springer, Heidelberg (1988). https://doi.org/10.1007/3-540-48184-2_10

[GIS+10] Goyal, V., Ishai, Y., Sahai, A., Venkatesan, R., Wadia, A.: Founding cryptography on tamper-proof hardware tokens. In: Micciancio, D. (ed.) TCC 2010. LNCS, vol. 5978, pp. 308–326. Springer, Heidelberg (2010). https://doi.org/10.1007/978-3-642-11799-2_19

[GKM+20] Goyal, V., Kothapalli, A., Masserova, E., Parno, B., Song, Y.: Storing and retrieving secrets on a blockchain. Cryptology ePrint Archive, Report 2020/504 (2020). https://eprint.iacr.org/2020/504

[GKP+13] Goldwasser, S., Kalai, Y.T., Popa, R.A., Vaikuntanathan, V., Zeldovich, N.: How to run turing machines on encrypted data. In: Canetti, R., Garay, J.A. (eds.) CRYPTO 2013. LNCS, vol. 8043, pp. 536–553. Springer, Heidelberg (2013). https://doi.org/10.1007/978-3-642-40084-1_30

[GKR08] Goldwasser, S., Kalai, Y.T., Rothblum, G.N.: One-time programs. In: Wagner, D. (ed.) CRYPTO 2008. LNCS, vol. 5157, pp. 39–56. Springer, Heidelberg (2008). https://doi.org/10.1007/978-3-540-85174-5_3

[GMPS21] Goyal, V., Masserova, E., Parno, B., Song, Y.: Blockchains enable non-interactive MPC. In: Nissim, K., Waters, B. (eds.) TCC 2021. LNCS, vol. 13043, pp. 162–193. Springer, Cham (2021). https://doi.org/10.1007/978-3-030-90453-1_6

[gRP] gRPC: A high performance, open-source universal RPC framework. https://grpc.io/

[GSS21] Goyal, V., Song, Y., Srinivasan, A.: Traceable secret sharing and applications. In: Malkin, T., Peikert, C. (eds.) CRYPTO 2021. LNCS, vol. 12827, pp. 718–747. Springer, Cham (2021). https://doi.org/10.1007/978-3-030-84252-9_24

[HJKY95] Herzberg, A., Jarecki, S., Krawczyk, H., Yung, M.: Proactive secret sharing or: how to cope with perpetual leakage. In: Coppersmith, D. (ed.) CRYPTO 1995. LNCS, vol. 963, pp. 339–352. Springer, Heidelberg (1995). https://doi.org/10.1007/3-540-44750-4_27

[KKAS+18] Kokoris-Kogias, E., et al.: Verifiable management of private data under byzantine failures. IACR ePrint, 2018/209 (2018)

[KZG10] Kate, A., Zaverucha, G.M., Goldberg, I.: Constant-size commitments to polynomials and their applications. In: Abe, M. (ed.) ASIACRYPT 2010. LNCS, vol. 6477, pp. 177–194. Springer, Heidelberg (2010). https://doi.org/10.1007/978-3-642-17373-8_11

[KZM+15] Kosba, A., et al.: CØCØ: a framework for building composable zero-knowledge proofs. IACR ePrint, 2015/1093 (2015)

[LJKW18] Liu, J., Jager, T., Kakvi, S.A., Warinschi, B.: How to build time-lock encryption. Des. Codes Crypt. **86**(11), 2549–2586 (2018)

[MZW+19] Maram, S.K.D., et al.: Churp: dynamic-committee proactive secret sharing. In: Proceedings of the 2019 ACM Conference on Computer and Communications Security (2019)

[OY91] Ostrovsky, R., Yung, M.: How to withstand mobile virus attacks. In: Proceedings of the ACM Symposium on Principles of Distributed Computing (1991)

[Ped92] Pedersen, T.P.: Non-interactive and information-theoretic secure verifiable secret sharing. In: Feigenbaum, J. (ed.) CRYPTO 1991. LNCS, vol. 576, pp. 129–140. Springer, Heidelberg (1992). https://doi.org/10.1007/3-540-46766-1_9

[RSW96] Rivest, R.L., Shamir, A., Wagner, D.A.: Time-lock puzzles and timed-release crypto (1996)

[Sch90] Schnorr, C.P.: Efficient identification and signatures for smart cards. In: Brassard, G. (ed.) CRYPTO 1989. LNCS, vol. 435, pp. 239–252. Springer, New York (1990). https://doi.org/10.1007/0-387-34805-0_22

[Sha79] Shamir, A.: How to share a secret. Commun. ACM **22**(11), 612–613 (1979)

[Shi10] Shigeo, M.: High-speed software implementation of the optimal ate pairing over Barreto-Naehrig curves. In: International Conference on Pairing-Based Cryptography (2010). https://github.com/herumi/ate-pairing

[SLL08] Schultz, D.A., Liskov, B., Liskov, M.: Mobile proactive secret sharing. In: Proceedings of the Twenty-Seventh ACM Symposium on Principles of Distributed Computing (2008)

[WWW02] Wong, T.M., Wang, C., Wing, J.M.: Verifiable secret redistribution for archive systems. In: IEEE Security in Storage Workshop (2002)

[Yao82] Yao, A.C.: Protocols for secure computations. In: Foundations of Computer Science (1982)

[ZSVR05] Zhou, L., Schneider, F.B., Van Renesse, R.: APSS: proactive secret sharing in asynchronous systems. ACM Trans. Inf. Syst. Secur. **8**(3), 259–286 (2005)

CNF-FSS and Its Applications

Paul Bunn[1(✉)], Eyal Kushilevitz[2], and Rafail Ostrovsky[3]

[1] Stealth Software Technologies, Inc., Los Angeles, USA
paul@stealthsoftwareinc.com
[2] Computer Science Department, Technion, Haifa, Israel
eyalk@cs.technion.ac.il
[3] Department of Computer Science and Department of Mathematics, University of California, Los Angeles, USA
rafail@cs.ucla.edu

Abstract. Function Secret Sharing (FSS), introduced by Boyle, Gilboa and Ishai [BGI15], extends the classical notion of secret-sharing a *value* to secret sharing a *function*. Namely, for a secret function f (from a class $\mathcal{F}$), FSS provides a sharing of f whereby *succinct* shares ("keys") are distributed to a set of parties, so that later the parties can non-interactively compute an additive sharing of $f(x)$, for any input x in the domain of f. Previous work on FSS concentrated mostly on the two-party case, where highly efficient schemes are obtained for some simple, yet extremely useful, classes $\mathcal{F}$ (in particular, FSS for the class of point functions, a task referred to as DPF – Distributed Point Functions [GI14,BGI15]).

In this paper, we concentrate on the multi-party case, with $p \geq 3$ parties and t-security ($1 \leq t < p$). First, we introduce the notion of CNF-DPF (or, more generally, CNF-FSS), where the scheme uses the CNF version of secret sharing (rather than additive sharing) to share each value $f(x)$. We then demonstrate the utility of CNF-DPF by providing several applications. Our main result shows how CNF-DPF can

P. Bunn—This work was supported by DARPA and NIWC Pacific under contract N66001-15-C-4065. The U.S. Government is authorized to reproduce and distribute reprints for Governmental purposes not withstanding any copyright notation thereon. The views, opinions, and/or findings expressed are those of the author(s) and should not be interpreted as representing the official views or policies of the Department of Defense or the U.S. Government.

E. Kushilevitz—Supported by ISF grant 2774/20, BSF grant 2018393, and NSF-BSF grant 2015782.

R. Ostrovsky—Supported in part by DARPA under Cooperative Agreement HR0011-20-2-0025, by DARPA and NIWC Pacific under contract N66001-15-C-4065, NSF grant CNS-2001096, US-Israel BSF grant 2015782, Google Faculty Award, JP Morgan Faculty Award, IBM Faculty Research Award, Xerox Faculty Research Award, OKAWA Foundation Research Award, B. John Garrick Foundation Award, Teradata Research Award, Lockheed-Martin Research Award and Sunday Group. The U.S. Government is authorized to reproduce and distribute reprints for governmental purposes not withstanding any copyright annotation therein. The views, opinions, and/or findings expressed are those of the author(s) and should not be interpreted as representing the official views or policies of the Department of Defense or the U.S. Government.

G. Hanaoka et al. (Eds.): PKC 2022, LNCS 13177, pp. 283–314, 2022.
https://doi.org/10.1007/978-3-030-97121-2_11

be used to achieve substantial asymptotic improvement in communication complexity when using it as a building block for constructing *standard* (t,p)-DPF protocols that tolerate $t > 1$ (semi-honest) corruptions (of the p parties). For example, we build a 2-out-of-5 secure (standard) DPF scheme of communication complexity $O(N^{1/4})$, where N is the domain size of f (compared with the current best-known of $O(N^{1/2})$ for $(2,5)$-DPF). More generally, with $p > dt$ parties, we give a (t,p)-DPF whose communication grows as $O(N^{1/2d})$ (rather than $O(\sqrt{N})$ that follows from the $(p-1,p)$-DPF scheme of [BGI15]). (We ignore here terms that depend on the number of parties, p, the security parameter, etc. See precise statements in the main body of the paper below)

We also present a 1-out-of-3 secure CNF-DPF scheme, in which each party holds two of the three keys, with poly-logarithmic communication complexity. These results have immediate implications to scenarios where (multi-server) DPF was shown to be applicable. For example, we show how to use such a scheme to obtain asymptotic improvement ($O(\log^2 N)$ versus $O(\sqrt{N})$) in communication complexity over the 3-party protocol of [BKKO20].

Keywords: Secret Sharing · Function Secret Sharing (FSS) · Replicated Secret Sharing (CNF)

1 Introduction

Function Secret Sharing (FSS) [BGI15] provides a sharing of a secret function f, from a class of functions $\mathcal{F}$, between p parties, such that each party's share of f (also termed "key") is *succinct* (in terms of the size of the truth-table representing f) and such that the parties can locally compute (additive) shares of $f(x)$, for any input x, without further interaction. While efficient FSS schemes are currently known only for limited classes of functions (and impossibility results demonstrate other classes of functions for which no efficient FSS scheme can exist), FSS has found enormous utility in distributed and multi-party protocols, due to its low communication overhead. Indeed, the FSS paradigm has proven to be incredibly powerful even for the most basic of function classes: Point Functions, which output a non-zero value at only a single point in their domain. FSS for the class of point functions is known as DPF (Distributed Point Functions). Since DPF and FSS were introduced [GI14,BGI15], they have found applications in many areas of cryptography (see Sect. 1.3 below for more details). For the case of $p = 2$ parties, highly efficient (both theoretically and practically) DPF schemes, with poly-logarithmic communication (in N) are known [GI14,BGI15,BGI16a], based on the minimal assumption that one-way functions (OWF) exist. This clearly implies $(1,p)$-DPF schemes for any $p > 2$. Obtaining similar results for the multiparty case, with $t > 1$, is an open problem and, to the best of our knowledge, the only known result in the FSS setting, based on OWF alone, is a $(p-1,p)$-DPF scheme of communication proportional to $\sqrt{N}$ from [BGI15] (and a protocol with similar communication for the special case of $(2,3)$-DPF in [BKKO20]).

CNF secret-sharing [ISN87] (also known as "replication-based secret-sharing" in [GI99]) has found great utility in a variety of applications, including: Verifiable Secret Sharing and MPC protocols [Mau02], PIR [BIK05] and others.[1] A (t,p)-CNF secret-sharing works by first additively breaking the secret value s to $\ell = \binom{p}{t}$ random shares $\{s_T\}_{T\in\binom{[p]}{t}}$, subject to their sum satisfying $\sum_{T\in\binom{[p]}{t}} s_T = s$, and then distributing each share s_T to all parties *not* in T. It satisfies t-secrecy since, for any set T of t parties, all parties in T miss the share s_T.[2] In the present work, we adapt the same approach in the context of FSS and introduce the notion of CNF-FSS (and the analogous notion of CNF-DPF, when the class of functions being shared are point functions) whereby, given an input x, the parties obtain a CNF-secret-sharing of $f(x)$.[3] We then explore the power of this new notion by constructing CNF-DPF schemes and by getting applications of these constructions. Specifically, in Sect. 1.1 we describe our main result – for the case of p parties and $1 < t < p$, we show how to use CNF-DPF schemes to obtain improved *standard* DPF schemes; then, in Sect. 1.2, we deal with the special case $p = 3, t = 1$, where CNF-sharing is useful in some applications.

1.1 Improved Multiparty DPF with $t > 1$ from CNF-DPF

As mentioned, [GI14] and subsequent works demonstrated highly efficient 1-out-of-2 DPF schemes (with logarithmic communication in the size of the DPF domain), but much less is known for the $p > 2$ and secrecy threshold $t > 1$ case. A trivial solution for $(p-1)$-out-of-p DPF is to additively share the truth-table of the point function $f_{x,v} : [N] \to \mathbb{F}$ as a string. However, this approach has communication complexity $O(N \cdot m)$, where N is the size of the domain of $f_{x,v}$ and m is its output length (note that this trivial solution is, in fact, information-theoretic). A more efficient $(p-1)$-out-of-p DPF solution is given by [BGI15] and has communication of essentially $O(\sqrt{N})$ (more precisely $O(\sqrt{N} \cdot 2^p \cdot (\lambda + m))$, where λ is the security parameter).[4] For the special case $p = 3$, a scheme with $O(\sqrt{N})$ communication was also pointed out in [BKKO20]. When making stronger assumptions than the existence of OWF, additional results are known: for example, using PK assumptions and operations, specifically seed-homomorphic PRG, [CBM15] also achieve a scheme with communication that depends on $\sqrt{N}$, but has better dependency on p and, under the LWE assumption, a $(p-1,p)$-FSS scheme for all functions can be constructed [DHRW16].

1 In fact, CNF secret sharing is a special case of formula-based secret sharing [BL88]; similar generalizations are in principle possible also in the context of FSS.

2 CNF sharing immediately implies additive sharing, by arbitrarily assigning each share s_T to one of the parties who hold it (i.e., a party not in T), and each party's share being the sum of all (at least one) shares assigned to it.

3 In our constructions, this is often achieved by having each party receive multiple overlapping keys, in CNF form, that encode the DPF function; however, in general, this is not a requirement. For formal definitions, see Sect. 2 (including Remark 1).

4 In [BGI15], the range may be a group, as they only need the additive structure. However, we require a Ring structure for the range, since we will also use multiplication. For concreteness, we can think of the field $GF[2^m]$, represented by m-bit strings.

In this paper, we show how to get better communication complexity, when one can settle for smaller values of t. The high-level idea is as follows. First, we construct, as an intermediate tool, a (t,p)-CNF-DPF scheme. The key-generation algorithm Gen of our (t,p)-CNF-DPF scheme, produces $\ell = \binom{p}{t}$ keys $\{K_T\}_{T\in\binom{[p]}{t}}$ and gives each key K_T to each party not in T (i.e., to each party in $[p]\setminus T$). This is done by invoking the key-generation algorithm of [BGI15] for the $(\ell-1,\ell)$-DPF case. Algorithm Eval of [BGI15] can be applied to any input y and any key K_T, and together these ℓ values give an additive sharing of $f_{x,v}(y)$ with ℓ values.

Our next idea is to view the domain $[N]$ of the point function as a d-dimensional cube, where each dimension is of size $M = N^{1/d}$. This allows to express the point function $f_{x,v}$ as the product of d point functions $f_1,\ldots,f_d$, on much smaller domain of size M and apply CNF-DPF sharing to each f_i. Finally, the property of CNF sharing is that with the right relations between p,t and d (specifically, when $p > td$) non-interactive multiplication is possible, since the replication guarantees that each term in the product is known to some party.

These results are presented in detail in Sect. 3. As an example, we get a (standard) $(2,5)$-DPF scheme with communication $O(N^{1/4})$ (instead of $O(N^{1/2})$) and, more generally, with $p > dt$ parties, we get a (t,p)-DPF with communication $O(N^{1/2d}\cdot\sqrt{2^{p^t}}\cdot p^t\cdot d\cdot(\lambda+m))$. In fact, one can also obtain a scheme with information-theoretic security and communication complexity $O(N^{1/d}\cdot p^t\cdot d\cdot m)$ by just replacing the CNF-DPF above (based on [BGI15]) with a naive CNF sharing of the truth table of each f_i.

Our results may be useful in several cases where DPF was already shown to be relevant. For instance, consider Binary CPIR (i.e., Computational Private Information Retrieval schemes where servers' answers are a single bit) or, more generally, CPIR with constant answer length. Binary PIR schemes are useful in the context of retrieving long records, and have connections with locally decodable codes (LDC). The fact that DPF schemes imply Binary CPIR schemes with the same complexity was shown in [GI14,BGI15] and this connection holds also for the t-private version of DPF and CPIR schemes. Hence, our (t,p)-DPF schemes with communication $\approx O(N^{1/2d})$ (for $p = dt+1$ parties) imply (t,p)-binary-CPIR with similar complexity. Before, to get (t,p)-binary-CPIR, one could use a number of servers p that is exponential in t, to get much better communication complexity. Specifically, one could get information-theoretic Binary PIR with communication $N^{o(1)}$ using $p = 3^t$ servers (by combining [BIW07] with [Efr09]), or Binary CPIR of poly-logarithmic communication using $p = 2^t$ servers (by combining [BIW07] with a 2-server DPF, as pointed out in [GI14]). Or, with a moderate number of servers p, one could use a binary (information theoretic) PIR with communication $\approx O(N^{1/d})$ (again, for $p = dt+1$) [DIO98,BIK05]. We essentially get a quadratic improvement in this regime of parameters. Similar improvements can be applied also to the PIR writing model [OS97].

1.2 1-out-of-3 CNF-DPF

Motivated by applications, we give a special treatment for the 3-party case. A $(1,3)$ standard DPF scheme of poly-logarithmic communication complexity is easy to achieve just by using solutions for the $(1,2)$-case and not utilizing the third party at all. However, in some settings, (2,3)-DPF may be required, for which only schemes of communication $O(\sqrt{N})$ are known. For example, in [BKKO20] a so-called *Distributed ORAM* (DORAM) scheme is presented that relies on $(2,3)$-DPF. We observe that [BKKO20] does not need the full strength of (2,3)-security and, instead, can rely on a $(1,3)$-DPF, provided an appropriate "CNF" replication of keys between the 3 parties (i.e., there are still 3 keys, as in the $(2,3)$ case, but each of them is known to 2 of the parties, which can clearly only give 1-security). Note that this does not seem trivial to achieve: if we start from a (2,3)-DPF scheme then we can easily get a $(1,3)$-CNF-DPF but with much higher communication than what we aim for, and if we start from a $(1,3)$-DPF and give each key to 2 parties, then security is lost. Nevertheless, we show (in Sect. 4) how to construct a $(1,3)$-CNF-DPF scheme, while still maintaining poly-logarithmic communication. Hence, improving the asymptotic communication of the scheme from [BKKO20].[5]

While we focus on the case of 1-out-of-3 CNF-DPF, as our construction is similar in spirit to the 2-party DPF scheme of [BGI15], the same modifications that are proposed in [BGI15] to extend DPF to FSS for related function classes (e.g. "sparse" vectors or matrices, step functions, interval functions, etc.) are applicable for our 1-out-of-3 scheme as well; details and additional discussion will be provided in the full version.

Additionally, $(1,3)$-CNF-DPF schemes have features that may be useful in other applications. The most basic one is the ability to perform *multiplication*; that is, given two point functions f and g that are shared using a $(1,3)$-CNF-DPF scheme, and any evaluation points x and y, the parties can (non-interactively) generate additive shares of the product[6] $f(x) \cdot g(y)$. The reason is that $f(x)$ is the sum of 3 values, each of which is known to 2 parties, and similarly $g(y)$ is the sum of 3 values, each known to 2 parties, so their product contains 9 terms each known to (at least) one party. (A similar observation is what we use for the general (t,p)-case (see below), and what is used in other contexts where CNF secret sharing is used; see, e.g., [BIK05].) Similarly, we can multiply a point function by a (secret-shared) value a to get additive shares of $a \cdot f(x)$, as well as other generalizations. We note that the ability to perform non-interactive multiplication(s), in CNF-FSS schemes, can be used to extend the known function

[5] In order to use our $(1,3)$-CNF-DPF scheme as a subprotocol of [BKKO20], it must be converted into a distributed (*dealerless*) protocol. While generic techniques exist to perform this conversion, using these would decrease overall performance of the resulting protocol. In the full version we show how our $(1,3)$-CNF-DPF can be converted into a distributed protocol in a black-box manner, while maintaining polylog communication (though this conversion does incur a hit in round-complexity over the protocol of [BKKO20]: log rounds versus constant-round).

[6] As mentioned, for the product to be defined we need the range of the functions to be a ring rather than just a group.

classes for which *standard* FSS is available. For example, FSS for functions that involve the product of two sparse matrices, or of a sparse vector times a (secret-shared) pseudo-random matrix, can be readily built using CNF-FSS. (See below for comparison with a related notion from [BGI16b].)

1.3 Related Work

Distributed point functions (DPF) were introduced by Gilboa and Ishai [GI14] who gave efficient constructions of (2-party) DPF schemes, based on the minimal assumption of OWF, together with a spectrum of useful applications, such as improved schemes for 2-server (computational) PIR, "PIR writing" (PIW) and related problems. Boyle, Gilboa and Ishai [BGI15], generalized this notion to other classes of functions, obtaining the notion of *Function Secret Sharing* (FSS). They present various FSS schemes, for DPF and other classes and, of particular relevance to the present work, they presented the first non-trivial solution for *multi-party* DPF. Further extension and optimizations of FSS are given in [BGI16b]. In particular, this paper presents the notion of *FSS product operator*, that allows to combine FSS schemes for classes $\mathcal{F}_1, \mathcal{F}_2$ to an FSS for the class of their products. For a more detailed discussion and a comparison of this operator with our construction, see Sect. 3.2.

The related notion of *Homomorphic Secret Sharing* (HSS), which is "dual" to FSS (in the sense that it switches roles between functions and inputs), was introduced in [BGI16a] and further studied in [BGI+18b]. It allows for sharing a value x between p parties, so that given a function $f \in \mathcal{F}$, each party may (non-interactively) apply Eval to its share of x (and a representation of f) so as to get a sharing of $f(x)$. In particular, [BGI16a] gives a 2-party FSS for a wide class of functions such as branching programs (though, under a stronger assumption, DDH, and with 1/poly error probability). This result yields 2-party secure computation protocols with communication sub-linear in the circuit size. Other applications of FSS include *silent OT extension* and *pseudorandom correlation generation* for simple correlations [BCG+19], and many more.

Another application that makes use of DPF for $p > 2$ parties is Distributed ORAM (DORAM), where read/write operations into memory are done obliviously (see, e.g., [LO13, ZWR+16, DS17, GKW18, JW18, KM19, BKKO20, HV20]). Concretely, [BKKO20] use a $(2,3)$-DPF scheme in order to construct efficient 3-party DORAM. They use overlaps between the keys of pairs of servers, to invoke PIR/PIW schemes that rely on replication of information. This serves as one motivation for the study of CNF-sharing in the present paper. Before the work of [BKKO20], Doerner and Shelat [DS17] used 2-party DPF to construct what can be viewed as a DORAM protocol in the two-party setting. In comparing [DS17] and [BKKO20] as multiparty DORAM protocols: the former has superior communication complexity (polylog N versus $\sqrt{N}$) but inferior round-complexity (logarithmic in N versus constant-round). Applying the results in the current paper to [BKKO20], the communication complexity improves from $\sqrt{N}$ to polylog (albeit with a cost of logarithmic round-complexity), thus matching the asymptotic communication complexity of [DS17][7].

[7] This is demonstrated in the full version.

In [CBM15], the authors describe a multi-server system called Riposte for anonymous broadcast messaging, with various features. They use the general notion of (t, p)-DPF, hence giving motivation for improving the communication complexity of such schemes. While concentrating on a 3-server system (using 2-party DPF), they also present a $(p-1, p)$-DPF scheme of $O(\sqrt{N})$ communication. (It differs from the scheme of [BGI15] by using also PK assumptions and operations, specifically seed-homomorphic PRGs, and also their scheme does not have the 2^p term for communication.) A follow-up paper describes the Express system [ECZB19], in a 2-server setting and using 2-party DPF. They also mention the need for improved multi-party DPFs. Finally, Blinder [APY20] is a scalable system for so-called *Anonymous Committed Broadcast*. As with the previous systems, Blinder also uses DPF as a building block but concentrates on the multi-server case.

As mentioned, the CNF version of secret sharing [ISN87] is useful in many applications, including VSS and MPC (e.g. [Mau02,IKKP15,AFL+16, FLNW17]), PIR [BIK05], etc. In the context of *share conversion*, it was shown in [CDI05] that shares from the CNF scheme can be locally converted to shares of the same secret from any other linear scheme realizing the same access structure (e.g., shares from the (t, p)-CNF scheme can be converted to shares for the t-out-of-p Shamir scheme).

1.4 Organization

We provide the requisite definitions and notation in Sect. 2. We then describe our improved t-out-of-p secure DPF schemes in Sect. 3, and our 1-out-of-3 secure CNF-DPF construction, with poly-logarithmic communication complexity, in Sect. 4.

2 Model and Definitions

Notation: We use $[a..b]$ to denote the integers in the (closed) interval from a to b, and $[b]$ to denote $[1..b]$. We further denote by $\binom{[b]}{t}$ the collection of all subsets of $[b]$ of size t.

Definition 1 ***FSS*** *[BGI15, BGI16a]. A t-out-of-p Function Secret Sharing scheme ((t, p)-FSS, for short) for a class of functions $\mathcal{F} = \{f : D \to \mathbb{G}\}$, with input domain D and output domain an abelian group $(\mathbb{G}, +)$, is a pair of PPT algorithms $FSS = (\mathsf{Gen}, \mathsf{Eval})$ with the following syntax:*

- $\mathsf{Gen}(1^\lambda, f)$*: On input the security parameter λ and a description of a function $f \in \mathcal{F}$, outputs p keys: $\{\kappa_1, \ldots, \kappa_p\}$;*
- $\mathsf{Eval}(i, \kappa_i, x)$*: On input an index $i \in [p]$, key κ_i, and input string $x \in D$, outputs a value ("share") $y_i \in \mathbb{G}$;*

satisfying the following correctness and secrecy requirements:

Correctness. *For all $f \in \mathcal{F}$, $x \in D$:*

$$Pr\left[\{\kappa_1,\ldots,\kappa_p\} \leftarrow_R \mathsf{Gen}(1^\lambda, f) \ : \sum_{i=1}^{p} \mathsf{Eval}(i,\kappa_i,x) = f(x)\right] = 1.$$

Security. *For any subset of indices $\mathcal{I} \subset [p]$ with size $|\mathcal{I}| \leq t$, there exists a PPT simulator Sim such that for any polynomial-size function sequence $f_\lambda \in \mathcal{F}$, the following distributions are computationally indistinguishable:*

$$\left\{\{\kappa_1,\ldots,\kappa_p\} \leftarrow_R \mathsf{Gen}(1^\lambda, f) \ : \ \{\kappa_i\}_{i\in\mathcal{I}}\right\} \approx_C \left\{\{\kappa_1,\ldots,\kappa_{|\mathcal{I}|}\} \leftarrow_R \mathsf{Sim}(1^\lambda,\ D,\mathbb{G})\right\}.$$

We now extend the original FSS definition to *Conjunctive Normal Form (CNF) FSS.* This is similar to Definition 1, except that the output of Eval, over all p parties, should be a legal (t,p)-CNF secret-sharing of $f(x)$ (rather than additive secret sharing). That is, let $\mathcal{S}_t$ denote the set of subsets of $[p]$ of size t (there are $\binom{p}{t}$ such subsets) and, for any $i \in [p]$, let $\mathcal{T}_t^{\mathcal{P}_i} \subset \mathcal{S}_t$ denote the subsets of $\mathcal{S}_t$ that do *not* contain index i (there are $\binom{p-1}{t}$ such subsets). Then the algorithm Eval of a (t,p)-CNF-FSS scheme produces, for each party $i \in [p]$, all the shares of $f(x)$ corresponding to $\mathcal{T}_t^{\mathcal{P}_i}$.

Definition 2. *A t-out-of-p CNF-FSS (also denoted (t,p)-CNF-FSS) scheme for a class of functions $\mathcal{F} = \{f : D \to \mathbb{G}\}$ with input domain D and output domain an abelian group $(\mathbb{G},+)$ is a pair of PPT algorithms CNF-FSS = (Gen, Eval) with the following syntax:*

- $\mathsf{Gen}(1^\lambda, f)$*: On input the security parameter λ and a description of a function $f \in \mathcal{F}$, outputs p keys: $\{\kappa_1,\ldots,\kappa_p\}$;*
- $\mathsf{Eval}(i,\kappa_i,x)$*: On input an index $i \in [p]$, key κ_i, and input string $x \in D$, outputs a sequence of $a = \binom{p-1}{t}$ values $\mathcal{Y}_i := \{y_T\}_{T\in\mathcal{T}_t^{\mathcal{P}_i}}$ in $\mathbb{G}^a$;*

satisfying the following consistency, correctness and secrecy requirements:

Consistency. *For every function $f \in \mathcal{F}$, input $x \in D$, pair of distinct parties $i, i' \in [p]$, and set $T \in \mathcal{S}_t$ that does not contain i or i' (i.e. $T \in \mathcal{T}_t^{\mathcal{P}_i} \cap \mathcal{T}_t^{\mathcal{P}_{i'}}$), when producing keys $\{\kappa_1,\ldots,\kappa_p\} \leftarrow_R \mathsf{Gen}(1^\lambda,\ f)$ and getting $y_{i,T} \in \mathcal{Y}_i$ for this $T \in \mathcal{T}_t^{\mathcal{P}_i}$ from $\mathsf{Eval}(i,\kappa_i,x)$ (among other outputs) and, similarly, $y_{i',T} \in \mathcal{Y}_{i'}$ for this same $T \in \mathcal{T}_t^{\mathcal{P}_{i'}}$ from $\mathsf{Eval}(i',\kappa_{i'},x)$ then, with probability 1, we have $y_{i,T} = y_{i',T}$. Denote by y_T this common share value held by all parties $i \notin T$.* ***Correctness.*** *For all $f \in \mathcal{F}$, $x \in D$: let $\{\kappa_1,\ldots,\kappa_p\} \leftarrow_R \mathsf{Gen}(1^\lambda,\ f)$ and let y_T, for all $T \in \mathcal{S}_t$, as defined above. Then, with probability 1, we have: $\sum_{T\in\mathcal{S}_t} y_T = f(x)$.*

Security. *For any subset of indices $\mathcal{I} \subset [p]$ with size $|\mathcal{I}| \leq t$, there exists a PPT simulator Sim such that for any polynomial-size function sequence $f_\lambda \in \mathcal{F}$, the following distributions are computationally indistinguishable:*

$$\left\{\{\kappa_1,\ldots,\kappa_p\} \leftarrow_R \mathsf{Gen}(1^\lambda,\ f) \ : \ \{\kappa_i\}_{i\in\mathcal{I}}\right\} \approx_C \left\{\{\kappa_1,\ldots,\kappa_{|\mathcal{I}|}\} \leftarrow_R \mathsf{Sim}(1^\lambda,\ D,\mathbb{G})\right\}.$$

Remark 1. The above definition requires only that the outputs of Eval, i.e. $\mathcal{Y}_i = \{y_T\}_{T \in \mathcal{T}_t^{P_i}}$, over all parties i, is a legal CNF secret sharing (of $f(x)$). A stricter requirement that some of our constructions satisfy is that: (1) the keys themselves are in a CNF form, i.e. that each party i receives keys $\mathcal{K}_i := \{\kappa_T\}_{T \in \mathcal{T}_t^{P_i}}$; and (2) each share y_T is computed only from κ_T. Satisfying (1) and (2) immediately implies that the shares are consistent and are in CNF form. Our CNF-DPF schemes in Sect. 3 have this property; while the (1,3)-CNF-DPF scheme of Sect. 4 satisfies (1) but not (2). That is, for the (1,3)-CNF-DPF scheme of Sect. 4, the keys are in CNF format, but Eval needs to operate on *both* keys of each party in order to produce its two shares.

Additionally, we will require the definitions of several variants of standard DPF for our (1,3)-CNF-DPF scheme of Sect. 4, which for clarity are defined as they are needed in Sect. 4.2.

3 t-out-of-p DPF from CNF-DPF

In this section, we discuss *standard* (i.e. non-CNF) DPF for $p > 2$ parties, and security threshold $t > 1$. As mentioned in Sect. 1.1, in contrast to the case $t = 1$, where very efficient poly-logarithmic solutions are known, even with $p = 2$ parties, the communication complexity in the general case of (t,p)-DPF (and more generally (t,p)-FSS) is much less understood.

We begin with a fixed choice of parameters $t = 2$ and $p = 5$ and demonstrate in Sect. 3.1 below how CNF-DPF can be used to construct an improved (standard) $(2,5)$-DPF scheme. We then generalize this approach in Sect. 3.2 to show how to construct (t,p)-DPF from CNF-DPF for a variety of parameters t and p.

3.1 Example: 2-out-of-5 DPF

To demonstrate our ideas, we start with a concrete example of $t = 2$ and $p = 5$, and present a $(2,5)$-DPF of communication $O(N^{1/4})$. As a first step towards this goal, we construct a (2,5)-CNF-DPF scheme B with communication $O(\sqrt{N})$. For this, we use the (standard) $(q-1,q)$-DPF scheme of [BGI15], with $q = \binom{5}{2} = 10$. This gives 10 keys $K_1, \ldots, K_{10}$ so that any set of 9 keys gives no information about the point function f, and those keys allow for producing additive shares for the value $f(y)$, for any input y. Next, associate with each key K_i ($i \in [10]$) a distinct subset $T \in \binom{[5]}{2}$ and give K_i to the 3 parties outside the set T (or, equivalently, do not give K_i only to the 2 parties in T). In other words, the key κ_j of party j in our scheme B consists of all the keys K_i that correspond to sets T with $j \notin T$ (there are $6 = \binom{4}{2}$ such sets). Our B.Eval algorithm, on input κ_j, simply works by applying the Eval algorithm of [BGI15] to each K_i that κ_j contains, separately. This gives a $(2,5)$-CNF scheme B as needed: 10 shares/keys $K_1, \ldots, K_{10}$, where each pair of parties misses exactly one of them. Therefore, the view of this pair of parties in B is identical to the view of a corresponding set of 9 parties in the [BGI15] scheme, which is 9-secure (for $q = 10$).

Next, assume for convenience, that $N = M^2$. In this case, we can view points in the domain $[N]$ as *pairs* of elements in $[M]$ (e.g., we can view the point $x \in [N]$ as $(x_1, x_2) \in [M] \times [M]$). Similarly, we can view the truth table of the function $f_{x,v} : [N] \to \mathbb{F}$ as an $M \times M$ matrix, with v in position (x_1, x_2) and 0's elsewhere. With this view, we can write the point function $f_{x,v}$ as the product of two point functions (on a smaller domain) $f_{x_1,v}, f_{x_2,1} : [M] \to \mathbb{F}$. That is, for every $y = (y_1, y_2)$, we have $f_{x,v}(y) = f_{x_1,v}(y_1) \cdot f_{x_2,1}(y_2)$ (because if $y = x$ then $y_1 = x_1$ and $y_2 = x_2$ so the product will be $v \cdot 1 = v$ and, otherwise if $y \neq x$, the product will be 0 as either the row satisfies $y_1 \neq x_1$ or the column satisfies $y_2 \neq x_2$). The Gen algorithm will apply the B.Gen algorithm twice to generate 10 keys $\{K_1, \ldots, K_{10}\}$ for $f_{x_1,v}$, and 10 keys $\{K'_1, \ldots, K'_{10}\}$ for $f_{x_2,1}$; and then, distribute each set of keys, $\{K_i\}$ and $\{K'_i\}$, to the 5 parties according to the CNF associations, as described above. The Eval algorithm, on input $y = (y_1, y_2)$, is applied with those keys to get additive sharing of $f_{x_1,v}(y_1)$ (into 10 shares that we denote $u_1, \ldots, u_{10}$); and similarly to get additive sharing of $f_{x_2,1}(y_2)$ (into 10 shares that we denote $v_1, \ldots, v_{10}$). That is, we have:

$$f_{x,v}(y) = f_{x_1,v}(y_1) \cdot f_{x_2,1}(y_2) = \sum_{i=1}^{10} u_i \cdot \sum_{j=1}^{10} v_j = \sum_{i,j \in [10]} u_i \cdot v_j.$$

Finally, we observe that because B is a CNF-DPF scheme, the CNF sharing guarantees that for each pair (i, j), there is (at least one) party that knows both values u_i, v_j (since u_i is not known only to 2 parties and v_j is not known only to 2 parties but we have $p = 5$ parties). Hence, we can allocate the product $u_i \cdot v_j$, for each pair (i, j), to one of the 5 parties, which will compute it and include it in its share. So letting a_k denote party k's sum of all the pairs (i, j) allocated to it, the desired output value $f_{x,v}(y)$ is additively shared across the 5 parties as: $a_1 + \ldots + a_5$, as desired.

Correctness of the above scheme follows by the description. 2-security follows since the information known to each pair of parties T is only what they got in two invocations of the CNF-DPF scheme B. Since B is 2-secure this keeps the functions $f_{x_1,v}, f_{x_2,1}$ secret. Other than that, everything else is local computations that each party does on its own while applying Eval. As for the communication complexity (i.e., key sizes), both invocations of B and our final scheme have communication of $O(\sqrt{M} \cdot (\lambda + m)) = O(N^{1/4} \cdot (\lambda + m))$ where, as above, m denotes the output length of the point function and λ is the security parameter.

3.2 Extending to General t-out-of-p DPF

Next, we generalize the above example. Suppose one wants to secret-share a point function with security threshold t, and has $p \geq dt + 1$ parties available for the sharing, for some d (e.g., in the example, $p = 5$ and $t = d = 2$). Then, our next result shows how this can be done with communication complexity $\approx O(N^{1/2d})$.

Theorem 3. *Let t, p, d be such that $p = dt + 1$. Then, assuming OWF exists, there is a (standard, computational) (t, p)-DPF scheme Π with communication* $O(N^{1/2d} \cdot \sqrt{2^{p^t}} \cdot p^t \cdot d \cdot (\lambda + m))$.

Note that we usually think of p (and hence also t and d) as being "small" and of N as being the main parameter, so the not-so-good dependency on p (which is inherited from [BGI15]) is secondary.

Remark 2. Our result uses the $(p-1)$-out-of-p DPF protocol of [BGI15] and, as such, the result is limited to DPF functions where the range is a group $\mathbb{G}$ of characteristic two. Concretely, they consider functions with range $\{0, 1\}^m$ which we view as $\mathbb{F} = GF[2^m]$, as we require a ring structure. While it is not explicitly stated in the conference version of [BGI15], the full version will include a generalization of the $(p-1)$-out-of-p DPF protocol for more general groups $\mathbb{G}$ (private communication with authors of [BGI15]), and this generality is transferrable to our constructions. Specifically, for "small" q, a simple modification allows generalization to $\mathbb{G} = \mathbb{Z}_q$, and this can be further generalized to larger groups $\mathbb{Z}_m$ for m that is a product of distinct primes, by utilizing the Chinese Remainder Theorem in the Eval algorithm. Note that these ranges are what is needed for most applications of DPFs in the literature.

Proof. Assume for concreteness that $N = M^d$, and view each input in the domain as a vector of d values, e.g. $x = (x_1, \ldots, x_d) \in [M]^d$. Then the truth table of the point function $f_{x,v}$ can be viewed as a d-dimensional cube with v at position $x = (x_1, \ldots, x_d)$, and 0's elsewhere. Next, view the point function $f_{x,v} : [N] \to \mathbb{F}$ as the product of d point functions $f_{x_i,v_i} : [M] \to \mathbb{F}$, where $v = \prod_{i=1}^{d} v_i$ (e.g., $v_1 = v, v_2 = \ldots = v_d = 1$). Hence, we have, for all input $y = (y_1, \ldots, y_d)$ in the domain of $f_{x,v}$:

$$f_{x,v}(y) = \prod_{i=1}^{d} f_{x_i,v_i}(y_i).$$

As in the example, the idea will be to share each of the d "smaller" point functions f_{x_i,v_i} separately, using a CNF-DPF scheme B_i, in such a way that during the evaluation stage we can combine the outcomes of the d evaluations to obtain a (standard) additive sharing of $f_{x,v}(y)$. To construct each B, we use as a building block the $(q-1, q)$-DPF scheme of [BGI15], with $q = \binom{p}{t}$. Invoking the [BGI15] scheme with these parameters generates q keys, which we denote $\{K_T\}_{T \in \binom{[p]}{t}}$, and each B.Gen distributes each K_T to all parties in $[p] \setminus T$. Meanwhile, each B.Eval works by applying the Eval algorithm of the [BGI15] scheme for each key K_T separately. By construction, this is indeed a CNF-sharing scheme. The t-security of B follows from the fact that each set T of t parties misses the share K_T and by the $(q-1)$-security of the [BGI15] scheme (assuming OWF). The size of the keys in the [BGI15] scheme (on domain of size M) is $O(\sqrt{M} \cdot 2^q \cdot (\lambda + m))$ and each of the p parties gets $\binom{p-1}{t} < p^t$ of them, and also $q < p^t$ so all together $O(\sqrt{M} \cdot 2^{p^t} \cdot p^t \cdot (\lambda + m))$. The key-generation algorithm of our scheme, Π.Gen, works by invoking the algorithm B.Gen d times, once for each point function f_{x_i,v_i}. Denote the keys generated by the i-th invocation by $\{K_{i,T}\}_{i\in[d],T\in\binom{[p]}{t}}$.

The algorithm Π.Eval, on input $y=(y_1,\ldots,y_d)$, works as follows: Denote by $S_{i,T}$ the share obtained by applying the Eval algorithm of [BGI15] on $K_{i,T}$ and y_i. By the correctness of the underlying [BGI15] scheme, we have that $f_{x_i,v_i}(y_i)=\sum_{T_i\in\binom{[p]}{t}} S_{i,T_i}$, and hence:

$$f_{x,v}(y)=\prod_{i=1}^{d} f_{x_i,v_i}(y_i)=\prod_{i=1}^{d}\left(\sum_{T_i\in\binom{[p]}{t}} S_{i,T_i}\right)=\sum_{T_1,\ldots,T_d\in\binom{[p]}{t}}\left(\prod_{i=1}^{d} S_{i,T_i}\right).$$

Consider any term of the form $\prod_{i=1}^{d} S_{i,T_i}$. Each of the shares S_{i,T_i} is not known only to the t parties in T_i, so all together at most $d\cdot t$ parties miss any of d shares of this term. Since $p>d\cdot t$, there is (at least) one party that knows all the shares of this term and can compute it. Assign each term to, say, the lexicographically first party (by index) that knows this term, and let a_j, for $j\in[p]$, be the sum of all terms assigned to the j-th party. We get that, as needed:

$$\sum_{j=1}^{p} a_j=\sum_{T_1,\ldots,T_d\in\binom{[p]}{t}}\left(\prod_{i=1}^{d} S_{i,T_i}\right)=f_{x,v}(y),$$

In terms of t-security: this follows since we invoke d times (independently) the t-secure scheme B. The size of keys is therefore d times larger than the size of keys in B, i.e. $O(\sqrt{M\cdot 2^{p^t}}\cdot p^t\cdot(\lambda+m)\cdot d)=O(N^{1/2d}\cdot\sqrt{2^{p^t}}\cdot p^t\cdot d\cdot(\lambda+m))$. □

Remark 3. We observe that setting e.g. $v_1=v$, and then insisting that for all $i>1$: $\{f_{x_i,v_i}\}$ has range $\{0,1\}$ instead of $\mathbb{F}$ (with $v_i:=1$ for all such i), removes the factor of m in the communication complexity of all of the $\{f_{x_i,v_i}\}$ (except for f_{x_1,v_1}), and consequently the overall complexity of Π in Theorems 3 and 4 can be reduced (by a factor of m for Theorem 4 below, and by a factor of m in one of the additive terms for Theorem 3, which is meaningful when $m>>\lambda$).

Note that the above scheme, as with most FSS/DPF schemes, provides computational security. However, it is possible to get *information-theoretic* security with only a relatively small loss (essentially replacing the $N^{1/2d}$ term in the communication of the above scheme with $N^{1/d}$) and, in fact, getting a slightly better dependency on p. More precisely:

Theorem 4. *Let t,p,d be such that $p=dt+1$. Then, there is a (standard,* ***information-theoretically****-secure) (t,p)-DPF scheme Π with communication complexity $O(N^{1/d}\cdot p^t\cdot d\cdot m)$.*

Proof. The proof is very similar to the previous construction above, except that we replace all invocations of the (computational) scheme from [BGI15] for creating $q=\binom{p}{t}$ key shares, with the naive (but information-theoretically secure) scheme where the truth table is just CNF-shared as a string (with parameters (t, p)). When applied to point functions with domain size M and output length m, the key size of each of the p parties is at most $M \cdot m \cdot q = M \cdot m \cdot \binom{p}{t}$. The scheme then proceeds as above, by CNF-sharing the d point functions on domain of size $M = N^{1/d}$. The correctness and security arguments are similar to the above. The key size is $O(M \cdot p^t \cdot d \cdot m) = O(N^{1/d} \cdot p^t \cdot d \cdot m)$. □

Similarly, one can plug the $(p-1, p)$-DPF scheme of [CBM15] to the construction of CNF-DPF in Theorem 3. This scheme relies on the existence of seed-homomorphic PRG [BLMR13] (compared to the minimal assumption of OWF, as in standard DPF schemes), and has better dependency on p, i.e., communication of $O(\sqrt{N} \cdot poly(p) \cdot (\lambda + m))$. Hence, we can get a (t, p)-DPF scheme, like in Theorem 3, under the same assumption as [CBM15], with somewhat better communication of $O(N^{1/2d} \cdot poly(p^t) \cdot d \cdot (\lambda + m))$.

It is instructive to compare our technique with that of [BGI16b] (and its full version in [BGI18a]). Concretely, [BGI18a, Thm. 3.22] shows how to combine (t, p_1)-FSS for a class $\mathcal{F}_1$ and a (t, p_2)-FSS for a class $\mathcal{F}_2$ into a $(t, p_1 \cdot p_2)$-FSS for the class of products (they term this "FSS product operator"). The main difference between our construction and their transformation is that the number of parties in their transformation grows very quickly. This means that, even if combined with our idea of decomposing the point function $f_{x,v} : [N] \to \mathbb{F}$ to a product of d point functions with smaller domains, $f_{x_i,v_i} : [M] \to \mathbb{F}$, the [BGI16b] product will require number of parties which is exponential in d, while we only use $p = dt + 1$ parties. For example, in the case $t = 2$ we get, in Sect. 3.1 above, (2,5)-DPF with communication $O(N^{1/4})$, while combining two $(2, 3)$-DPFs, using [BGI16b], will result in a (2,9)-scheme (with communication $O(N^{1/4})$, using our decomposition). Also, [BGI18a, Thm. 3.23] can be viewed as a special case of our construction for $t = 1$; note that we focus in this paper on $t \geq 2$, as for $t = 1$ highly efficient DPF constructions are already known.

Determining the exact communication complexity of multi-party DPF, as a function of t and p, remains an intriguing open problem. This holds even in concrete special cases, such as $p = 4, t = 2$, where we do not know of a $(2, 4)$-DPF scheme with complexity $o(\sqrt{N})$ (while, as mentioned in the Introduction, $(2, 4)$-Binary-*CPIR* has a very efficient solution by combining DPF with [BIW07]).

4 1-out-of-3 CNF-DPF

In this section we present a 1-out-of-3 secure CNF-DPF protocol that achieves poly-log communication (in the domain size $N := |D|$). Our construction combines ideas from the original 1-out-of-2 protocol of [BGI15] with the 2-out-of-3 protocol of [BKKO20], whereby we seek to get the communication efficiency of the former, but extended to the 3-party setting as is treated by the latter. Before giving the formal presentation of our construction, we provide some insight on the main ideas of how we convert the $O(\sqrt{N})$ protocol of [BKKO20] into the poly-log(N) protocol presented below.

4.1 Overview of Construction

In [BKKO20], the Gen algorithm partitions the domain size N into $\sqrt{N}$ "blocks" of size $\sqrt{N}$, and to each block $1 \leq j \leq \sqrt{N}$, each key will be assigned a pair of PRG seeds $\{x_j, y_j\}$. In the notation below, the superscript $\mathcal{P}_i$ for $i \in [3]$ denotes the key index,[8] and $\mathcal{P}_R$ (respectively $\mathcal{P}_L$) refers to a PRG seed associated with a key to the "right" (respectively, to the "left") of key $\mathcal{P}$, where we view the key indices as a cycle: $\mathcal{P}_1 \to \mathcal{P}_2 \to \mathcal{P}_3 \to \mathcal{P}_1$, e.g. for $\mathcal{P} = \mathcal{P}_1$, we have: $\mathcal{P}_R = \mathcal{P}_2$ and $\mathcal{P}_L = \mathcal{P}_3$. Also, for the DPF scheme of [BKKO20], the terminology "on-block" index $j \in [\sqrt{N}]$ refers to the index of the unique block that contains $\alpha \in D$ that defines the point function. Similarly, in a binary tree partitioning of $[N]$ used in our construction, a node ν in this binary tree is "on-path" if the leaf-node with index $\alpha \in [N]$ is a descendent of ν.

With this notation, the PRG seeds in [BKKO20] satisfy:[9]

For *On-Block* Indices j	For *Off-Block* Indices j
$x_j^{\mathcal{P}_1} \neq x_j^{\mathcal{P}_2} \neq x_j^{\mathcal{P}_3}$	$x_j^{\mathcal{P}} = y_j^{\mathcal{P}_L}$
$y_j^{\mathcal{P}_1} = y_j^{\mathcal{P}_2} = y_j^{\mathcal{P}_3}$	$y_j^{\mathcal{P}} = x_j^{\mathcal{P}_R}$

(1)

In this paper, to avoid the $\sqrt{N}$ cost of dealing the seeds as per (1), as motivated by the paradigm of [BGI15] we "partition" the domain D via a binary tree, where the leaf-level has $N = |D|$ nodes. Then, instead of dealing the PRG seeds for *every* node in the binary tree, we only deal seeds at the root, and then describe a process (which uses extra auxiliary information dealt for each level) to generate PRG seeds for the rest of the nodes in the binary tree. This process is described formally in Sect. 4.3 below, but we mention here the important invariant that is maintained at every node ν in the binary tree:

For *On-Path* Nodes ν	For *Off-Path* Nodes ν
$x_\nu^{\mathcal{P}} = z_\nu^{\mathcal{P}_L}$	$x_\nu^{\mathcal{P}} = y_\nu^{\mathcal{P}_L} = z_\nu^{\mathcal{P}_R}$
$y_\nu^{\mathcal{P}_1} = y_\nu^{\mathcal{P}_2} = y_\nu^{\mathcal{P}_3}$	$y_\nu^{\mathcal{P}} = z_\nu^{\mathcal{P}_L} = x_\nu^{\mathcal{P}_R}$
$z_\nu^{\mathcal{P}} = x_\nu^{\mathcal{P}_R}$	$z_\nu^{\mathcal{P}} = x_\nu^{\mathcal{P}_L} = y_\nu^{\mathcal{P}_R}$

(2)

In comparing (2) to (1), notice first that instead of each key consisting of two PRG seeds, they each have *three* PRG seeds now: $\{x_j, y_j, z_j\}$. To clarify the nature of this extra seed, it will be convenient to (temporarily) modify the notation slightly: for an off-path block, in (1) the first key has PRG seeds $\{a, b\}$,

---

[8] We write the key index as a superscript (not a subscript) to avoid confusion with the node index ν (denoted as a subscript). The choice of $\mathcal{P}$ over a simpler index $i \in [3]$ is to avoid confusion with an exponent (since it is a superscript), and the specific choice of "P" is for "Party," as FSS typically associates each key κ with a party $\mathcal{P}$.

[9] The on-block property that seeds $\{x_j^{\mathcal{P}}\}_{\mathcal{P}}$ are not equal to each other, as described in (1), is intended to capture intuition. More formally, the requirement is that the on-block seeds $\{x_j^{\mathcal{P}}\}_{\mathcal{P}}$ are independent and (pseudo-)randomly generated.

the second key has seeds $\{b, c\}$, and the third key has seeds $\{c, a\}$.[10] So there are a total of three distinct seeds $\{a, b, c\}$ across all keys, and each key is missing exactly one of these three seeds for (1). Then the extra seed in each key of (2) is simply the third "missing seed."

Meanwhile, for the on-path block, in (1) the first key has PRG seeds $\{a, d\}$, the second key has seeds $\{b, d\}$, and the third key has seeds $\{c, d\}$.[11] So there are a total of *four* distinct seeds $\{a, b, c, d\}$ across all keys, with seed d being common to all three keys, and each of the other three seeds appearing in exactly one key. Thus, unlike in off-block positions where each key was missing *one* of the *three* seeds, in the on-block position each key is missing *two* of the *four* seeds. Then, in (2), each key is given one of the two missing seeds, namely the missing seed of the key on their "right." In sticking with the present notation, we can view the extra seed z included with each key as: $z^{\mathcal{P}_1} = b$, $z^{\mathcal{P}_2} = c$, and $z^{\mathcal{P}_3} = a$.

The two main points here are:

(i) Including an extra seed as part of the keys is necessary in order to iteratively generate the seeds on lower nodes in the binary tree. In [BKKO20], there was no iterative (tree) structure, but rather everything was flat: The domain D was partitioned into $\sqrt{N}$ blocks of $\sqrt{N}$ elements. But in following the binary tree approach of [BGI15] in attempt to minimize communication of the Gen algorithm, we need an iterative procedure to generate seeds on lower nodes in the binary tree. As in [BGI15], the difficult step is when the procedure attempts to specify the seeds on the children nodes of an on-path parent: one child node remains on-path, while the other becomes off-path. Maintaining the proper invariant (that on-path seeds should look like the left column of (2), while off-path seeds should look like the right column of (2)) will require keys to have partial information about the two "missing" seeds, which is why our algorithm provides one of the missing seeds as part of each key.

(ii) On the other hand, including one of the "missing" seeds as part of each key is exactly why the 2-out-of-3 security of [BKKO20] is reduced to 1-out-of-3 security in our protocol: If any two parties collude, they can easily link their own extra/missing seed that they were dealt with the node for which their partner also has that seed, and thus the secret path is revealed. However, even though this restricts our protocol to 1-out-of-3 security, we observe that providing one of the two "missing seeds" as part of each key is exactly the property we require for CNF sharing of the Gen keys.

---

[10] The overlapping nature of the PRG seeds, in a CNF format, is the important point; formally, to link the notations, set $a = x^{\mathcal{P}_1} = y^{\mathcal{P}_3}$, $b = x^{\mathcal{P}_2} = y^{\mathcal{P}_1}$, and $c = x^{\mathcal{P}_3} = y^{\mathcal{P}_2}$.

[11] The fact that there is one common seed "d" across all three keys, and that the other seeds are all distinct, is the important point here; formally, to link the two notations, set $a = x^{\mathcal{P}_1}$, $b = x^{\mathcal{P}_2}$, $c = x^{\mathcal{P}_3}$, and $d = y^{\mathcal{P}_1} = y^{\mathcal{P}_2} = y^{\mathcal{P}_3}$.

Expanding more on (i) above, we provide an overview of how the two child nodes of an on-path node have correct values (i.e. values satisfying the invariant of (2)). Fix an on-path node μ on level l, and denote as the three sets of values on μ (as would be obtained by invoking the Eval algorithm using each of the three keys):

$$\begin{aligned} &\kappa^{\mathcal{P}_1} \text{ seeds for on-path parent node } \mu: && \{a, d, b\} \\ &\kappa^{\mathcal{P}_2} \text{ seeds for on-path parent node } \mu: && \{b, d, c\} \\ &\kappa^{\mathcal{P}_3} \text{ seeds for on-path parent node } \mu: && \{c, d, a\} \end{aligned} \tag{3}$$

where we have used in (3) that invariant (2) applies on the on-path node μ. Then in generating values on the children nodes of μ, the on-path child has keys:[12]

$$\begin{aligned} &\kappa^{\mathcal{P}_1} \text{ seeds for } \mu \text{ 's on-path child:} && \{q \oplus G_*(a),\ q \oplus G_*(d),\ q \oplus G_*(b)\} \\ &\kappa^{\mathcal{P}_2} \text{ seeds for } \mu \text{ 's on-path child:} && \{q \oplus G_*(b),\ q \oplus G_*(d),\ q \oplus G_*(c)\} \\ &\kappa^{\mathcal{P}_3} \text{ seeds for } \mu \text{ 's on-path child:} && \{q \oplus G_*(c),\ q \oplus G_*(d),\ q \oplus G_*(a)\} \end{aligned} \tag{4}$$

where q is a random length-λ bit string and $G_* \in \{G_L, G_R\}$ (which of these G_* equals depends on whether the on-path child of μ is the left or right child). Meanwhile, the off-path child will have keys:

$$\begin{aligned} &\kappa^{\mathcal{P}_1} \text{ seeds for } \mu \text{ 's off-path child:} && \{q \oplus G_*(b),\ q \oplus G_*(c),\ q \oplus G_*(a)\} \\ &\kappa^{\mathcal{P}_2} \text{ seeds for } \mu \text{ 's off-path child:} && \{q \oplus G_*(c),\ q \oplus G_*(a),\ q \oplus G_*(b)\} \\ &\kappa^{\mathcal{P}_3} \text{ seeds for } \mu \text{ 's off-path child:} && \{q \oplus G_*(a),\ q \oplus G_*(b),\ q \oplus G_*(c)\} \end{aligned} \tag{5}$$

Notice that both (4) and (5) satisfy the appropriate invariant in (2). Also notice that the values in (4) can be generated directly from the same key's corresponding values on parent node μ (from (3)), whereas the values in (5) cannot (e.g. each of the new y values require knowledge of the "missing" seed value on parent node μ). Namely, the ability for each key to generate the center ("y") seed values as in (5) will come from extra information that is provided by the "Correction Word" component of each Gen key (see (7), and notice the $x^{\mathcal{P}_L}$ term, which to emphasize is *not* $x^{\mathcal{P}}$ but rather is the x seed value from the "left" key $\kappa^{\mathcal{P}_L}$, and this exactly corresponds to the "missing" seed value for key $\kappa^{\mathcal{P}}$).

4.2 Variants of DPF

We introduce (somewhat informally) a few variants of DPF that will be used as building blocks for our protocol below. Formal definitions, as well as concrete instantiations of these, can be found in the full version.

[12] The formulas used for (4) and (5) come from (16), where we assumed "sibling control bit" values $b^{\mathcal{P}_1} = b^{\mathcal{P}_2} = b^{\mathcal{P}_3} = 0$ for the on-path child of μ, and that $b^{\mathcal{P}_1} = b^{\mathcal{P}_2} = b^{\mathcal{P}_3} = 1$ for the off-path child of μ. The other cases for valid sibling control bits would produce different key values, but the intuition for how values match or not is similar.

Definition 5 ***(Informal).*** *A 1-out-of-p* Matching-Share DPF (MS-DPF) *is defined analogously as ordinary DPF, except that instead of the requirement that* $\sum_i \mathsf{Eval}(i, \kappa_i, \beta) = 0$ *for every* $\beta \neq \alpha$ *in the domain of the point function* $f_{\alpha,v}$, *we require:* $\forall \beta \neq \alpha : \mathsf{Eval}(1, \kappa_1, \beta) = \mathsf{Eval}(2, \kappa_2, \beta) = \cdots = \mathsf{Eval}(p, \kappa_p, \beta)$, *where* p *is the number of parties.*

Remark 4. Note that MS-DPF as defined above is strictly speaking *not* FSS for the class of point functions: because all Eval shares match on every input $\beta \neq \alpha$, the actual function that an MS-DPF protocol represents looks random. However, based on the close relation to point functions (indeed, for the two-party case ($p = 2$) with $(\mathbb{G}, +) = (\mathbb{Z}_2^m, XOR)$, MS-DPF is identical to ordinary DPF), we stick with the "DPF" terminology.

Definition 6 ***(Informal).*** *A t-out-of-p* DPF$^+$ *is defined analogously as ordinary DPF, except that instead of the requirement that* $\sum_i \mathsf{Eval}(i, \kappa_i, \alpha) = v$, *for the point function* $f_{\alpha,v}$, *we have a concrete specification of the exact value of* $\mathsf{Eval}(i, \kappa_i, \alpha)$ *for each* i. *Namely,* DPF$^+$ *allows specification of* p *values* $\{v_1, \ldots, v_p\}$, *such that* $\forall i : \mathsf{Eval}(i, \kappa_i, \alpha) = v_i$.

Finally, we combine the two definitions above, of MS-DPF and DPF^+, and get:

Definition 7 ***(Informal).*** *A 1-out-of-p* MS-DPF$^+$ *scheme has Correctness properties:* $\forall \beta \neq \alpha : \mathsf{Eval}(1, \kappa_1, \beta) = \mathsf{Eval}(2, \kappa_2, \beta) = \cdots = \mathsf{Eval}(p, \kappa_p, \beta)$, *and meanwhile at the special input point* $\alpha \in D$: $\forall i : \mathsf{Eval}(i, \kappa_i, \alpha) = v_i$.

We use MS-DPF$^+$ in our $(1,3)$-CNF-DPF construction (constructions of each of the DPF variants is straightforward; see the full version).

Claim 8. *Assuming OWF, there exists a* $(1,3)$*-MS-DPF*$^+$ *scheme with communication* $O(\lambda \log(N))$.

4.3 Detailed Construction of 1-out-of-3 CNF-DPF

For any point function $f_{\alpha,v} \in \mathcal{F}$ with domain D (of size $N := |D|$) and range a finite abelian group[13] $(\mathbb{G}, +)$ (of size $m := |\mathbb{G}|$), we demonstrate the following:

Theorem 9. *Assuming OWF, there is a* $(1,3)$*-CNF-DPF scheme with communication* $O(m + \lambda \log^2(N))$.

We prove Theorem 9 constructively: the Gen and Eval algorithms are presented in this section, and Appendix A details the proof that the resulting scheme enjoys the stated complexity and satisfies the consistency, correctness, and security requirements of Definition 2. Our construction assumes the existence of a

[13] For most applications, $\mathbb{G} = \mathbb{Z}_2^B$, so addition (XOR over a bitstring) and multiplication are defined. While Sect. 4.3 focuses on characteristic two groups, which covers the majority of applications in the literature, extending to arbitrary (finite, abelian) groups is straightforward (only (17) and the definition of final correction word W require modification). A demonstration of this fact is presented in the full version.

PRG $G : \{0,1\}^\lambda \rightarrow \{0,1\}^{2\lambda+4}$ for security parameter λ, and a pseudorandom "convert" function $\widehat{G} : \{0,1\}^\lambda \rightarrow \mathbb{G}$. To fix notation, when G is applied to a seed x on a node μ, it stretches that seed to two new seeds plus four more bits, with one new seed and two bits going to each child node of node μ. To emphasize this, we write $G(x_\mu) = \Big(G_L(x_\mu), H_L(x_\mu), \widehat{H}_L(x_\mu)\Big), \Big(G_R(x_\mu), H_R(x_\mu), \widehat{H}_R(x_\mu)\Big)$, where $G_L, G_R : \{0,1\}^\lambda \rightarrow \{0,1\}^\lambda$ are zero stretch PRGs; and $H_L, \widehat{H}_L, H_R, \widehat{H}_R : \{0,1\}^\lambda \rightarrow \{0,1\}$ all output a single bit. The L and R subscripts on each PRG emphasize how the outputs of the PRGs will be applied, namely when generating values on the *Left* and *Right* child nodes of a given parent node μ.

Gen **Algorithm.**

1. Values at Root (level 0). At the root node of the tree, for each index $\mathcal{P} \in [3]$, choose PRG seeds $\{x^{\mathcal{P}}, y^{\mathcal{P}}, z^{\mathcal{P}}\}$ which are random subject to the constraints of the left (On-Path) column of (2). Our algorithm will also require that, for each key $\mathcal{P}$, each node ν in the binary tree has "control bits" $\{c_\nu^{\mathcal{P}}\}$ associated with it. These "on-path" control bits should appear random, subject to the constraint that they sum to one if and only if node ν is on-path. We will also associate a second set of control bits $\{b_\nu^{\mathcal{P}}\}$ to each node; these will satisfy a similar property as the "on-path" control bits, except with the condition that they sum to one if and only if ν's *sibling* is on-path (for the root node ν, which has no sibling, we demand the "sibling" control bits sum to zero).
Thus, at the root node, also choose sibling control bits $\{b^{\mathcal{P}}\}$ and on-path control bits $\{c^{\mathcal{P}}\}$ which are random subject to the constraints of (6). Each key will actually include four total control bits (as these are CNF-shared across keys) at the root: $\{b^{\mathcal{P}}, b^{\mathcal{P}_R}, c^{\mathcal{P}}, c^{\mathcal{P}_R}\}$.

"Sibling" Control Bit b	"On-Path" Control Bit c	
$\bigoplus_{\mathcal{P}} b_\nu^{\mathcal{P}} = \begin{cases} 0 & \text{if } \nu\text{'s } \textit{sibling} \text{ is } \textit{off-path} \\ 1 & \text{if } \nu\text{'s } \textit{sibling} \text{ is } \textit{on-path} \end{cases}$	$\bigoplus_{\mathcal{P}} c_\nu^{\mathcal{P}} = \begin{cases} 0 & \text{if } \nu \text{ is } \textit{off-path} \\ 1 & \text{if } \nu \text{ is } \textit{on-path} \end{cases}$	(6)

2. Correction Words. For each level $1 \leq l \leq \log(N)$ and each $\mathcal{P} \in [3]$, let $\{\kappa_l^{\mathcal{P}}\}$ denote the keys to a MS-DPF$^+$ protocol for $f_l = f_{(\alpha)_{l-1}, \{v_l^{\mathcal{P}_1}, v_l^{\mathcal{P}_2}, v_l^{\mathcal{P}_3}\}}$, and let $\{\widehat{\kappa}_l^{\mathcal{P}}\}$ denote the keys to a MS-DPF$^+$ protocol for $\widehat{f}_l = \widehat{f}_{(\alpha)_l, \{\widehat{v}_l^{\mathcal{P}_1}, \widehat{v}_l^{\mathcal{P}_2}, \widehat{v}_l^{\mathcal{P}_3}\}}$, for functions f_l and $\widehat{f}_l$ defined as follows.[14] First, for each level l, the Gen algorithm will generate uniformly random λ-bit strings $\{p_l, q_l\}$. Then, if $\nu = \nu_l$ denotes the unique on-path node at level l, and $\mu = \mu_l$ denotes its parent node, then f_l is the MS-DPF$^+$ function:

[14] Recall that MS-DPF+ functions f_l and $\widehat{f}_l$ are *not* technically point functions (see Definition 5 and the ensuing remark). Also, for notation, $(\alpha)_{l-1}$ (as the special point in the domain of $f_l = f_{(\alpha)_l, \{v_l^{\mathcal{P}_1}, v_l^{\mathcal{P}_2}, v_l^{\mathcal{P}_3}\}}$) and $(\alpha)_l$ (for $\widehat{f}_l = \widehat{f}_{(\alpha)_l, \{\widehat{v}_l^{\mathcal{P}_1}, \widehat{v}_l^{\mathcal{P}_2}, \widehat{v}_l^{\mathcal{P}_3}\}}$) denote the first $l-1$ bits (respectively l bits) of α; whereas α_l (as it appears in (7) and (8)) denotes the lth bit of α.

$$f_{(\alpha)_{l-1},\{v_l^{\mathcal{P}_1},v_l^{\mathcal{P}_2},v_l^{\mathcal{P}_3}\}} : \{0,1\}^{l-1} \rightarrow \{0,1\}^{2\lambda}, \quad \text{with } v_l^{\mathcal{P}} = (v_L^{\mathcal{P}}, v_R^{\mathcal{P}}), \text{ where:}$$
$$(v_L^{\mathcal{P}}, v_R^{\mathcal{P}}) = \left(G_L(x_\mu^{\mathcal{P}_L}) \oplus (1 \oplus \alpha_l)\cdot(q_l \oplus p_l),\ G_R(x_\mu^{\mathcal{P}_L}) \oplus \alpha_l \cdot (q_l \oplus p_l)\right) \quad (7)$$

where $x_\mu^{\mathcal{P}_L}$ is the first on-path seed of $\mathcal{P}_L$ (see Step 3 below), and α_l is the lth bit of α. Meanwhile, $\widehat{f}_l$ is the MS-DPF$^+$ function:

$$\widehat{f}_{(\alpha)_l,\{\widehat{v}_l^{\mathcal{P}_1},\widehat{v}_l^{\mathcal{P}_2},\widehat{v}_l^{\mathcal{P}_3}\}} : \{0,1\}^{l} \rightarrow \{0,1\}^{\lambda}, \quad \text{with } \widehat{v}_l^{\mathcal{P}} = \begin{cases} p_l \text{ if } b_\nu^{\mathcal{P}_L} = 0 \\ q_l \text{ if } b_\nu^{\mathcal{P}_L} = 1 \end{cases} \quad (8)$$

The above MS-DPF$^+$ keys will serve as the "correction words" for the PRG seeds. Notice that we use MS-DPF+ (instead of just dealing correction words directly as a common term across all three keys) because we require each key use a slightly different correction word. Indeed, as motivated in Sect. 4.1, the first correction word (corresponding to f_l and keys $\{\kappa_l^{\mathcal{P}}\}$) encodes the "missing" seed information that allows each key to overlap (as per CNF sharing) with the values from the other key(s). Meanwhile, the second correction word (corresponding to $\widehat{f}_l$ and keys $\{\widehat{\kappa}_l^{\mathcal{P}}\}$) ensures that for the next on-path node at the next level l, each key is still missing information on exactly one of the four distinct seeds on that node.

In addition to the correction words, the Gen algorithm will produce "correction bits," which will ensure correct (i.e. respecting (6)) values for $\{b^{\mathcal{P}}\}$ and $\{c^{\mathcal{P}}\}$ on each level. To simplify notation in the definition of the correction bits, we define the following values:[15]

$$\begin{aligned} h_L &:= H_L(x_\mu^{\mathcal{P}_1}) \oplus H_L(x_\mu^{\mathcal{P}_2}) \oplus H_L(x_\mu^{\mathcal{P}_3}) \oplus H_L(y_\mu^{\mathcal{P}_1}) \\ h_R &:= H_R(x_\mu^{\mathcal{P}_1}) \oplus H_R(x_\mu^{\mathcal{P}_2}) \oplus H_R(x_\mu^{\mathcal{P}_3}) \oplus H_R(y_\mu^{\mathcal{P}_1}) \\ \widehat{h}_L &:= \widehat{H}_L(x_\mu^{\mathcal{P}_1}) \oplus \widehat{H}_L(x_\mu^{\mathcal{P}_2}) \oplus \widehat{H}_L(x_\mu^{\mathcal{P}_3}) \oplus \widehat{H}_L(y_\mu^{\mathcal{P}_1}) \\ \widehat{h}_R &:= \widehat{H}_R(x_\mu^{\mathcal{P}_1}) \oplus \widehat{H}_R(x_\mu^{\mathcal{P}_2}) \oplus \widehat{H}_R(x_\mu^{\mathcal{P}_3}) \oplus \widehat{H}_R(y_\mu^{\mathcal{P}_1}) \end{aligned} \quad (9)$$

where μ denotes the on-path node on level $l-1$. Now, for each level l, each key will include four "correction bits" $\{r_l, s_l, t_l, u_l\}$, defined as follows:

$$\begin{aligned} r_l &= \begin{cases} h_L & \text{if } \alpha_l = 0 \\ 1 \oplus h_L & \text{if } \alpha_l = 1 \end{cases} \qquad & s_l &= \begin{cases} 1 \oplus h_R & \text{if } \alpha_l = 0 \\ h_R & \text{if } \alpha_l = 1 \end{cases} \\ t_l &= \begin{cases} 1 \oplus \widehat{h}_L & \text{if } \alpha_l = 0 \\ \widehat{h}_L & \text{if } \alpha_l = 1 \end{cases} \qquad & u_l &= \begin{cases} \widehat{h}_R & \text{if } \alpha_l = 0 \\ 1 \oplus \widehat{h}_R & \text{if } \alpha_l = 1 \end{cases} \end{aligned} \quad (10)$$

3. Compute On-Path Seed Values. For each level l, use the correction words and bits (from the previous step) to generate seeds for the following level, as per the formulas in (15) and (16) (see Step 1c of the Eval Algorithm).
4. Final Correction Word. Define the final correction word $W := v \oplus_{\mathbb{G}} Q \in \mathbb{G}$, where v is the non-zero value of the target point function $f_{\alpha,v}$, and Q is:

$$Q := \widehat{G}(x_{\widehat{\nu}}^{\mathcal{P}_1}) \oplus_{\mathbb{G}} \widehat{G}(x_{\widehat{\nu}}^{\mathcal{P}_2}) \oplus_{\mathbb{G}} \widehat{G}(x_{\widehat{\nu}}^{\mathcal{P}_3}) \ominus_{\mathbb{G}} 3 \cdot \widehat{G}(y_{\widehat{\nu}}^{\mathcal{P}_1}) \in \mathbb{G}, \quad (11)$$

[15] For clarity, we suppress the level l in the subscript in the notation of (9).

where $\ominus_{\mathbb{G}}$ denotes the negation of the group operation in $\mathbb{G}$,[16] and $\widehat{G}$: $\{0,1\}^\lambda \rightarrow \mathbb{G}$ is a map that converts a random λ-bit string into a pseudo-random group element in $\mathbb{G}$.

As the final output, for each $\mathcal{P} \in [3]$, the Gen algorithm outputs keys:

$$\kappa^{\mathcal{P}} := \Big(\{x^{\mathcal{P}}, y^{\mathcal{P}}, z^{\mathcal{P}}\},\ \{b^{\mathcal{P}}, b^{\mathcal{P}_R}, c^{\mathcal{P}}, c^{\mathcal{P}_R}\},\ W \\ \forall 1 \le l \le \log(N) :\ \{\kappa_l^{\mathcal{P}}\},\ \{\widehat{\kappa}_l^{\mathcal{P}}\},\ \{r_l, s_l, t_l, u_l\}\Big) \tag{12}$$

Eval Algorithm.

The Eval($\kappa^{\mathcal{P}}$, i, β) algorithm is an iterative procedure where we start at the root of the binary tree, and define a procedure for traversing the tree (along the path of input $\beta \in D$)[17] whereby, at each step, we use the current node's values (plus the Gen key) to compute the values of the next node on the path. Formally, for any current node μ on level l of the path of β, with seed values $\{x_\mu^{\mathcal{P}}, y_\mu^{\mathcal{P}}, z_\mu^{\mathcal{P}}\}$ and (CNF-shared) control bits $\{b_\mu^{\mathcal{P}}, b_\mu^{\mathcal{P}_R}, c_\mu^{\mathcal{P}}, c_\mu^{\mathcal{P}_R}\}$, we demonstrate how to generate corresponding values for the next node ν on the path of β, corresponding to node μ's left or right child (depending on whether β_l is zero or one).

1. Traverse Tree per $\beta \in D$. For each level $1 \le l \le \log(N)$, let ν denote the current node on the path[18] of β at level l, and let μ denote ν's parent node. The previous iteration[19] of this step output values on parent node μ: $\{x_\mu^{\mathcal{P}}, y_\mu^{\mathcal{P}}, z_\mu^{\mathcal{P}}\}$ and $\{b_\mu^{\mathcal{P}}, b_\mu^{\mathcal{P}_R}, c_\mu^{\mathcal{P}}, c_\mu^{\mathcal{P}_R}\}$. Also, recall from (12) that for the current level l the Gen algorithm output the MS-DPF$^+$ keys $\kappa_l^{\mathcal{P}}$ and $\widehat{\kappa}_l^{\mathcal{P}}$; as well as the correction bits $\{r_l, s_l, t_l, u_l\}$. Output the following corresponding values for node ν as follows:
   (a) Generating CNF-sharing of sibling control bits: $\{b_\nu^{\mathcal{P}}, b_\nu^{\mathcal{P}_R}\}$.
   Set $\{b_\nu^{\mathcal{P}}, b_\nu^{\mathcal{P}_R}\}$ as follows:

$$b_\nu^{\mathcal{P}} = \begin{cases} c_\mu^{\mathcal{P}} \cdot r_l \oplus H_L(x_\mu^{\mathcal{P}}) \oplus H_L(y_\mu^{\mathcal{P}}) & \text{if } \nu \text{ is } \textit{left} \text{ child of } \mu \\ c_\mu^{\mathcal{P}} \cdot s_l \oplus H_R(x_\mu^{\mathcal{P}}) \oplus H_R(y_\mu^{\mathcal{P}}) & \text{if } \nu \text{ is } \textit{right} \text{ child of } \mu \end{cases}$$
$$b_\nu^{\mathcal{P}_R} = \begin{cases} c_\mu^{\mathcal{P}_R} \cdot r_l \oplus H_L(y_\mu^{\mathcal{P}}) \oplus H_L(z_\mu^{\mathcal{P}}) & \text{if } \nu \text{ is } \textit{left} \text{ child of } \mu \\ c_\mu^{\mathcal{P}_R} \cdot s_l \oplus H_R(y_\mu^{\mathcal{P}}) \oplus H_R(z_\mu^{\mathcal{P}}) & \text{if } \nu \text{ is } \textit{right} \text{ child of } \mu \end{cases} \tag{13}$$

[16] For characteristic two groups, $\ominus_{\mathbb{G}} = \oplus_{\mathbb{G}}$; but we use this notation in (11) so as to minimize changes when we extend to arbitrary finite abelian groups $\mathbb{G}$.

[17] The binary representation $\beta = \beta_1\beta_2 \ldots \beta_{\log(N)}$ of input $\beta \in D$ naturally defines a path down a binary tree (of depth $\log(N)$) by interpreting $\beta_l = 0$ to indicate going to the *left* child of the current node at level l, and moving right at level l if $\beta_l = 1$.

[18] Formally, if we index (0-based) the nodes on any level l, then the (binary representation of the) index of ν is: $\beta_1\beta_2 \ldots \beta_l$.

[19] If $l = 1$ then μ is the root node and the values on μ are directly from the Gen key.

(b) Generating CNF-sharing of on-path control bits: $\{c_\nu^{\mathcal{P}}, c_\nu^{\mathcal{P}_R}\}$.
Set $\{c_\nu^{\mathcal{P}}, c_\nu^{\mathcal{P}_R}\}$ as follows:

$$c_\nu^{\mathcal{P}} = \begin{cases} c_\mu^{\mathcal{P}} \cdot t_l \oplus \widehat{H}_L(x_\mu^{\mathcal{P}}) \oplus \widehat{H}_L(y_\mu^{\mathcal{P}}) & \text{if } \nu \text{ is } \textit{left} \text{ child of } \mu \\ c_\mu^{\mathcal{P}} \cdot u_l \oplus \widehat{H}_R(x_\mu^{\mathcal{P}}) \oplus \widehat{H}_R(y_\mu^{\mathcal{P}}) & \text{if } \nu \text{ is } \textit{right} \text{ child of } \mu \end{cases}$$
$$c_\nu^{\mathcal{P}_R} = \begin{cases} c_\mu^{\mathcal{P}_R} \cdot t_l \oplus \widehat{H}_L(y_\mu^{\mathcal{P}}) \oplus \widehat{H}_L(z_\mu^{\mathcal{P}}) & \text{if } \nu \text{ is } \textit{left} \text{ child of } \mu \\ c_\mu^{\mathcal{P}_R} \cdot u_l \oplus \widehat{H}_R(y_\mu^{\mathcal{P}}) \oplus \widehat{H}_R(z_\mu^{\mathcal{P}}) & \text{if } \nu \text{ is } \textit{right} \text{ child of } \mu \end{cases} \tag{14}$$

(c) Generating Seeds $\{x_\nu^{\mathcal{P}}, y_\nu^{\mathcal{P}}, z_\nu^{\mathcal{P}}\}$. First, to set notation: Let $G_* = G_L$ (respectively $G_* = G_R$) if ν is the *left* (respectively *right*) child of μ. Also, let $w_\nu^{\mathcal{P}} := \mathsf{Eval}(\kappa_l^{\mathcal{P}}, \mu)$ and let $\widehat{w}_\nu^{\mathcal{P}} := \mathsf{Eval}(\widehat{\kappa}_l^{\mathcal{P}}, \nu)$.[20] Recall from (7) that $w_\nu^{\mathcal{P}} \in \{0,1\}^{2\lambda}$, so let $w_*^{\mathcal{P}}$ be the first (respectively the last) λ bits of $w_\nu^{\mathcal{P}}$ if ν is the left (respectively right) child of its parent. We condition on the $\{b_\nu^{\mathcal{P}}, b_\nu^{\mathcal{P}_R}\}$ values that were output in Step 1a above:
Case I: $b_\nu^{\mathcal{P}} \neq b_\nu^{\mathcal{P}_R}$. Then set $\{x_\nu^{\mathcal{P}}, y_\nu^{\mathcal{P}}, z_\nu^{\mathcal{P}}\}$ as follows:

$$\begin{aligned} x_\nu^{\mathcal{P}} &= G_*(y_\mu^{\mathcal{P}}) \oplus b_\nu^{\mathcal{P}} \cdot (G_*(y_\mu^{\mathcal{P}}) \oplus w_*^{\mathcal{P}}) \oplus \widehat{w}_\nu^{\mathcal{P}} \\ y_\nu^{\mathcal{P}} &= G_*(x_\mu^{\mathcal{P}}) \oplus b_\nu^{\mathcal{P}} \cdot (G_*(x_\mu^{\mathcal{P}}) \oplus G_*(z_\mu^{\mathcal{P}})) \oplus \widehat{w}_\nu^{\mathcal{P}} \\ z_\nu^{\mathcal{P}} &= w_*^{\mathcal{P}} \oplus b_\nu^{\mathcal{P}} \cdot (w_*^{\mathcal{P}} \oplus G_*(y_\mu^{\mathcal{P}})) \oplus \widehat{w}_\nu^{\mathcal{P}} \end{aligned} \tag{15}$$

Case II: $b_\nu^{\mathcal{P}} = b_\nu^{\mathcal{P}_R}$. Then set $\{x_\nu^{\mathcal{P}}, y_\nu^{\mathcal{P}}, z_\nu^{\mathcal{P}}\}$ as follows:

$$\begin{aligned} x_\nu^{\mathcal{P}} &= G_*(x_\mu^{\mathcal{P}}) \oplus b_\nu^{\mathcal{P}} \cdot (G_*(x_\mu^{\mathcal{P}}) \oplus G_*(z_\mu^{\mathcal{P}})) \oplus \widehat{w}_\nu^{\mathcal{P}} \\ y_\nu^{\mathcal{P}} &= G_*(y_\mu^{\mathcal{P}}) \oplus b_\nu^{\mathcal{P}} \cdot (G_*(y_\mu^{\mathcal{P}}) \oplus w_*^{\mathcal{P}}) \oplus \widehat{w}_\nu^{\mathcal{P}} \\ z_\nu^{\mathcal{P}} &= G_*(z_\mu^{\mathcal{P}}) \oplus b_\nu^{\mathcal{P}} \cdot (G_*(z_\mu^{\mathcal{P}}) \oplus G_*(x_\mu^{\mathcal{P}})) \oplus \widehat{w}_\nu^{\mathcal{P}} \end{aligned} \tag{16}$$

2. Apply Final Correction Word. After terminating the above step at the leaf node ν on level $l = \log(N)$, the above iterative procedure has output values on ν: $\{x_\nu^{\mathcal{P}}, y_\nu^{\mathcal{P}}, z_\nu^{\mathcal{P}}\}$ and $\{b_\nu^{\mathcal{P}}, b_\nu^{\mathcal{P}_R}, c_\nu^{\mathcal{P}}, c_\nu^{\mathcal{P}_R}\}$. Then, as per the definition of $(1,3)$-CNF-FSS, $\mathsf{Eval}(\mathcal{P}, \kappa^{\mathcal{P}}, \beta)$ outputs $\binom{3-1}{1} = 2$ values in $\mathbb{G}$, which are:

$$\mathsf{Eval}(\mathcal{P}, \kappa^{\mathcal{P}}, \beta) := \left(\widehat{G}(x_\nu^{\mathcal{P}}) \ominus_{\mathbb{G}} \widehat{G}(y_\nu^{\mathcal{P}}) \oplus_{\mathbb{G}} c_\nu^{\mathcal{P}} \cdot W,\ \widehat{G}(z_\nu^{\mathcal{P}}) \ominus_{\mathbb{G}} \widehat{G}(y_\nu^{\mathcal{P}}) \oplus_{\mathbb{G}} c_\nu^{\mathcal{P}_R} \cdot W\right) \tag{17}$$

[20] Recall that $\{\kappa_l^{\mathcal{P}}, \widehat{\kappa}_l^{\mathcal{P}}\}$ were output as part of the Gen key, and they correspond to the MS-DPF$^+$ protocols described by (7)–(8). Also, notice that $w_\nu^{\mathcal{P}}$ comes from evaluating MS-DPF$^+$ key $\kappa_l^{\mathcal{P}}$ at point μ (the location of the *parent* node), whereas $\widehat{w}_\nu^{\mathcal{P}}$ comes from evaluating MS-DPF$^+$ key $\widehat{\kappa}_l^{\mathcal{P}}$ at point ν; this is why the domains of the two MS-DPF$^+$ functions $\{f_l, \widehat{f}_l\}$ differ by a factor of two (one extra bit for $\widehat{f}_l$).

A Proof of Theorem 9

We argue how the scheme described in Sect. 4.3 enjoys the stated communication complexity and satisfies each of the requisite properties of CNF-DPF (see Definition 2).

Communication. The size of each Gen key is $O(m + \lambda \log^2(N))$:

- $O(\lambda)$ for each of the original PRG seeds $\{x^{\mathcal{P}}, y^{\mathcal{P}}, z^{\mathcal{P}}\}$.
- $O(1)$ for the four control bits on the root node $\{b^{\mathcal{P}}, b^{\mathcal{P}_R}, c^{\mathcal{P}}, c^{\mathcal{P}_R}\}$.
- $O(m)$ for the $W \in \mathbb{G}$ (recall $m = \log(|\mathbb{G}|)$).
- For each $1 \leq l \leq \log(N)$: $O(\lambda \log(N))$ for the collection of MS-DPF$^+$ keys $\{\kappa_l^{\mathcal{P}}, \widehat{\kappa}_l^{\mathcal{P}}\}$ (see Claim 8). Adding these costs for each level l yields total cost of these keys: $O(\lambda \log^2(N))$.

Consistency. That the protocol of Sect. 4.3 satisfies the Consistency property of CNF-FSS (see Definition 2) requires showing, among other things, that for each $\mathcal{P} \in [3]$ and for each $\widehat{P} := \mathcal{P}_R$, that the control bits observe CNF-sharing:

$$b_\nu^{\mathcal{P}_R} = b_\nu^{\widehat{\mathcal{P}}} \quad \text{and} \quad c_\nu^{\mathcal{P}_R} = c_\nu^{\widehat{\mathcal{P}}} \tag{18}$$

In other words, (18) is emphasizing that the formulas for $b_\nu^{\mathcal{P}_R}$ and $c_\nu^{\mathcal{P}_R}$ in (the bottom equations of) (13) and (14) generate the same bits as (the top equations of) the corresponding formulas for $b_\nu^{\widehat{\mathcal{P}}}$ and $c_\nu^{\widehat{\mathcal{P}}}$ in (13) and (14), for $\widehat{\mathcal{P}} = \mathcal{P}_R$. For example, when computing the bottom formulas of (13) and (14) for $\mathcal{P} = \mathcal{P}_1$, the values output there (which are for $\mathcal{P}_R = \mathcal{P}_2$) match the values that are output for key $\mathcal{P}_2$ in (the top part of) the equations (13) and (14).

We make an inductive argument to demonstrate CNF-sharing of the control bits (as per (18)) holds for all nodes ν. At the root, (18) is true by construction of values $\{b_\nu^{\mathcal{P}}\}$ and $\{c_\nu^{\mathcal{P}}\}$ in Step 1 of the Gen algorithm. Now for any non-root node ν, let μ denote its parent, and assume that (18); we use the formulas in (13) and (14) to demonstrate that (18) also holds for ν. To fix notation, fix $\mathcal{P} \in [3]$, and let $\widehat{\mathcal{P}} = \mathcal{P}_R$ denote the *right* key of $\mathcal{P}$.

<u>Case1 : μ is *off-path*.</u> In the Correctness argument above, we demonstrated that (2) is satisfied for the seeds on every node. Since μ is off-path: $x_\mu^{\mathcal{P}} = z_\mu^{\widehat{\mathcal{P}}}$, $y_\mu^{\mathcal{P}} = x_\mu^{\widehat{\mathcal{P}}}$, and $z_\mu^{\mathcal{P}} = y_\mu^{\widehat{\mathcal{P}}}$. Plugging in these relations into (13) for $b_\nu^{\mathcal{P}_R}$:

$$\begin{aligned}
\underline{\text{If } \nu \text{ is } \textit{left} \text{ child of } \mu\text{:}} \quad b_\nu^{\mathcal{P}_R} &= c_\mu^{\mathcal{P}_R} \cdot r_l \oplus H_L(y_\mu^{\mathcal{P}}) \oplus H_L(z_\mu^{\mathcal{P}}) \\
&= c_\mu^{\widehat{\mathcal{P}}} \cdot r_l \oplus H_L(x_\mu^{\widehat{\mathcal{P}}}) \oplus H_L(y_\mu^{\widehat{\mathcal{P}}}) = b_\nu^{\widehat{\mathcal{P}}} \\
\underline{\text{If } \nu \text{ is } \textit{right} \text{ child of } \mu\text{:}} \quad b_\nu^{\mathcal{P}_R} &= c_\mu^{\mathcal{P}_R} \cdot s_l \oplus H_R(y_\mu^{\mathcal{P}}) \oplus H_R(z_\mu^{\mathcal{P}}) \\
&= c_\mu^{\widehat{\mathcal{P}}} \cdot s_l \oplus H_R(x_\mu^{\widehat{\mathcal{P}}}) \oplus H_R(y_\mu^{\widehat{\mathcal{P}}}) = b_\nu^{\widehat{\mathcal{P}}}
\end{aligned}$$

where we have applied the inductive argument that $c_\mu^{\mathcal{P}_R} = c_\mu^{\widehat{\mathcal{P}}}$ for parent node μ for the center equality of each case above.

Case 2: μ is *on-path*. Since μ is on-path: $z_\mu^{\mathcal{P}} = x_\mu^{\widehat{\mathcal{P}}}$ and $y_\mu^{\mathcal{P}} = y_\mu^{\widehat{\mathcal{P}}}$. Plugging in these relations into (13) for $b_\nu^{\mathcal{P}_R}$:

$$\begin{aligned}
\underline{\text{If } \nu \text{ is } \textit{left} \text{ child of } \mu\text{:}} \quad b_\nu^{\mathcal{P}_R} &= c_\mu^{\mathcal{P}_R} \cdot r_l \oplus H_L(y_\mu^{\mathcal{P}}) \oplus H_L(z_\mu^{\mathcal{P}}) \\
&= c_\mu^{\widehat{\mathcal{P}}} \cdot r_l \oplus H_L(y_\mu^{\widehat{\mathcal{P}}}) \oplus H_L(x_\mu^{\widehat{\mathcal{P}}}) = b_\nu^{\widehat{\mathcal{P}}} \\
\underline{\text{If } \nu \text{ is } \textit{right} \text{ child of } \mu\text{:}} \quad b_\nu^{\mathcal{P}_R} &= c_\mu^{\mathcal{P}_R} \cdot s_l \oplus H_R(y_\mu^{\mathcal{P}}) \oplus H_R(z_\mu^{\mathcal{P}}) \\
&= c_\mu^{\widehat{\mathcal{P}}} \cdot s_l \oplus H_R(y_\mu^{\widehat{\mathcal{P}}}) \oplus H_R(x_\mu^{\widehat{\mathcal{P}}}) = b_\nu^{\widehat{\mathcal{P}}}
\end{aligned}$$

The argument that $c_\nu^{\mathcal{P}_R} = c_\nu^{\widehat{\mathcal{P}}}$ is similar, using t_l fori r_l, u_l for s_l, and $\widehat{H}$ for H.

With (18) verified, Consistency follows immediately from the invariants of (2), both for the case ν is on-path (i.e. $\beta = \alpha$) and off-path (i.e. $\beta \neq \alpha$); see (17).

Security. We provide a sketch of the proof here, which captures the intuition of the argument; the full proof is relegated to the extended version.

We argue that the components of any Gen key $\kappa^{\mathcal{P}}$ (see (12)) are independent from each other and either truly random or masked with pseudorandom values whose seeds are known only to other parties (and not to party $\mathcal{P}$). In fact, the information of $\kappa^{\mathcal{P}}$ related to the root node is randomly chosen, and the information related to the other levels of the tree is masked using pseudorandom values not known to $\mathcal{P}$. Based on this, a simulator that simply outputs random values according to the key structure will satisfy Definition 2, which we recall here (updated for our case of security threshold $t = 1$):

$$\left\{\{\kappa_1, \ldots, \kappa_p\} \leftarrow_R \mathsf{Gen}(1^\lambda,\ f_{\alpha,v}) \ :\ \kappa_i\right\} \approx_C \left\{\kappa \leftarrow_R \mathsf{Sim}(1^\lambda,\ D, \mathbb{G})\right\}. \quad (19)$$

The proof follows an inductive argument (on the depth of the binary tree), and argues that assuming a simulator that outputs random values satisfies (19) for depth $l-1$, the extra values output by Gen in (12) for level l do not threaten the validity of the same simulator (i.e. one that is simply outputting random values) for the extra layer of the tree. More concretely, we will demonstrate the existence of a related simulator[21]:

$$\begin{aligned}
\forall 1 \le l \le \log N: \quad &\left\{\{\kappa^{\mathcal{P}_1}, \kappa^{\mathcal{P}_2}, \kappa^{\mathcal{P}_3}\} \leftarrow_R \mathsf{Gen}(1^\lambda,\ f_{\alpha,v}) \ :\ ((\kappa^{\mathcal{P}})_l,\ x_{\nu_l}^{\mathcal{P}_L})\right\} \approx_C \\
&\left\{(\kappa)_l \leftarrow_R \mathsf{Sim}(1^\lambda,\ D, \mathbb{G}),\ x \leftarrow_R \{0,1\}^\lambda \ :\ ((\kappa)_l,\ x)\right\}, \quad (20)
\end{aligned}$$

where ν_l refers to the on-path node at level l, $(\kappa^{\mathcal{P}})_l$ refers to the components of key $\kappa^{\mathcal{P}}$ from Gen steps 1–3 through level l (i.e. everything from (12) *except*

[21] The existence of a simulator as in (20) is actually *stronger* than what we need to argue (19). Technically, it would be sufficient to argue the existence of a simulator:

$$\begin{aligned}
\forall 1 \le l \le \log N: \quad &\left\{\{\kappa^{\mathcal{P}_1}, \kappa^{\mathcal{P}_2}, \kappa^{\mathcal{P}_3}\} \leftarrow_R \mathsf{Gen}(1^\lambda,\ f_{\alpha,v}) \ :\ ((\kappa^{\mathcal{P}})_l,\ x_{\nu_l}^{\mathcal{P}_L})\right\} \approx_C \\
&\left\{((\kappa)_l,\ x) \leftarrow_R \mathsf{Sim}(1^\lambda,\ D, \mathbb{G})\right\}
\end{aligned}$$

and then to prove that $x_{\nu_l}^{\mathcal{P}_L}$ is (computationally) independent of $(\kappa^{\mathcal{P}})_l$. While this is possible, our proof demonstrates the existence of the stronger simulator of (20).

the final correction word W and the per-level values for levels in $[l+1..\log N]$), and $x_{\nu_l}^{\mathcal{P}_L}$ refer to the seed values x on node ν_l that are associated with the key $\kappa^{\mathcal{P}_L}$ to the *left* of the provided key $\kappa^{\mathcal{P}}$.[22] The reason that the existence of a simulator as per (20) (and more specifically, where this simulator simply outputs random values as per the structure of $(\kappa^{\mathcal{P}})_l$) implies the existence of a simulator as per (19) is based on the formulas dictating how the Gen algorithm computes the extra seed values on level l: $\{\kappa_l^{\mathcal{P}}\}$, $\{\widehat{\kappa}_l^{\mathcal{P}}\}$, $\{r_l, s_l, t_l, u_l\}$. Namely, investigating the formulas for these extra values on level l ((7), (8), (9), and (10)), each formula has a term involving $x_\mu^{\mathcal{P}_L}$ for the value of $x^{\mathcal{P}_L}$ on node μ on level $l-1$, and consequently as long as the value of $x_\mu^{\mathcal{P}_L}$ on parent level $l-1$ cannot be distinguished from uniform, the new Gen key values on level l: $\{\kappa_l^{\mathcal{P}}\}$, $\{\widehat{\kappa}_l^{\mathcal{P}}\}$, $\{r_l, s_l, t_l, u_l\}$ will also be indistinguishable from uniform. Notice that for each $1 \le l \le \log N$, (20) explicitly excludes the final correction word W from both sides. However, the last step of the argument has the same spirit, whereby the existence of the $x_\nu^{\mathcal{P}_L}$ term (for on-path leaf node ν) in W implies that W is indistinguishible from uniform.

We proceed with an inductive argument, demonstrating that all the values output by the Gen algorithm respect the security invariant, and then demonstrate how the security invariant implies that all values output by the Gen algorithm appear uniformly random (and independent of one another).

- Step 1: Values at Root. The seeds $\{x^{\mathcal{P}}_, y^{\mathcal{P}}_, z^{\mathcal{P}}\}$ are chosen uniformly at random (subject to the constraint in (2), i.e. that there is a single common seed $y^{\mathcal{P}}$ that is common across all three keys, and that the other two seeds of each key overlap with exactly one of the seeds from each of the other two keys) and, in particular, the seeds are chosen independently from the point function $f_{\alpha,v}$ parameters, α and v. Similarly, the sibling control bits $\{b^{\mathcal{P}}_, b^{\mathcal{P}_R}\}$ and on-path control bits $\{c^{\mathcal{P}}_, c^{\mathcal{P}_R}\}$ are also chosen uniformly at random (subject to the constraint in (6)) and independently from the parameters α and v.
- Step 2.i: For each$1 \le l \le \log(N)$: $\mathrm{MS}-\mathrm{DPF}^+$keys $\{\kappa_l^{\mathcal{P}}, \widehat{\kappa}_l^{\mathcal{P}}\}$.

  Note that the security of the underlying MS-DPF$^+$ schemes for f_l and $\widehat{f_l}$ ensure that $\{v_l^{\mathcal{P}_L}, v_l^{\mathcal{P}_R}\}$ and $\{\widehat{v}_l^{\mathcal{P}_L}, \widehat{v}_l^{\mathcal{P}_R}\}$ cannot be distinguished from random even for someone holding $(\kappa^{\mathcal{P}})_l$ (and thus holding $\kappa_l^{\mathcal{P}}$ and $\widehat{\kappa}_l^{\mathcal{P}}$, which in particular reveals $v_l^{\mathcal{P}} = (v_L^{\mathcal{P}}, v_R^{\mathcal{P}})$ and $\widehat{v}_l^{\mathcal{P}}$; see (7)–(8)). That $\widehat{v}_l^{\mathcal{P}}$ do not leak information about parameters α or v follows from the fact that (8) indicates that $\widehat{v}_l^{\mathcal{P}}$ is uniformly random. Meanwhile, that $v_l^{\mathcal{P}} = (v_L^{\mathcal{P}}, v_R^{\mathcal{P}})$ does not leak information about parameters α or v is argued as follows: For the base case ($l = 1$), the formula for $v^{\mathcal{P}_L}$ indicates dependence on $G_L(x_\mu^{\mathcal{P}_L})$ (respectively $v^{\mathcal{P}_R}$ depends on $G_R(x_\mu^{\mathcal{P}_L})$), where μ is the on-path node on the parent level, i.e. μ is the root node if $l = 1$. Since (as mentioned in Step 1 above)

[22] Note that (20) is motivated by the CNF-sharing of the keys (or more precisely, the seeds), whereby each key $\kappa^{\mathcal{P}}$ has overlapping information from one of the other keys (in this case $\kappa^{\mathcal{P}_R}$), but is missing information from the third key (in this case $\kappa^{\mathcal{P}_L}$). In particular, this is why it is the seed of the *left* key $x^{\mathcal{P}_L}$ that is referenced in (20), as well as in (7) and (8).

$x_\mu^{\mathcal{P}_L}$ cannot be distinguished from uniform by information in $\kappa^{\mathcal{P}}$, it follows that $v_l^{\mathcal{P}}$ also cannot be distinguished from uniform (also, pseudorandomness of $G = (G_L, G_R)$ implies there is no dependence on the two components $(v_L^{\mathcal{P}}, v_R^{\mathcal{P}})$ of $v_l^{\mathcal{P}}$). For the inductive case $(1 < l \leq \log N)$, we follow the same argument, except now we use the Security Invariant (20) (plus pseudorandomness of the PRG G) inductively to argue that $x_\mu^{\mathcal{P}_L}$ from the parent level $l-1$ cannot be distinguished from uniform, and therefore $v_l^{\mathcal{P}}$ also appears uniformly random.

- Step 2.ii: For each$1 \leq l \leq \log(N)$: CorrectionBits $\{r_l, s_l, t_l, u_l\}$.
  As can be seen in (10), each correction bit depends on one of the values $\{h_L, h_R, \widehat{h}_L, \widehat{h}_R\}$, and, as per (9), each of these values in turn appears uniformly random due to its dependence on $x_\mu^{\mathcal{P}_L}$ for parent node μ (as was argued above in Step 2.i). Furthermore, pseudorandomness of $H, \widehat{H}$ implies that there is no dependency between the correction bit values and any other values dealt as part of the Gen key $\kappa^{\mathcal{P}}$.
- Step 3: Final Correction Word W.
  While $W = v \oplus \widehat{G}(x_{\widehat{\nu}}^{\mathcal{P}_1}) \oplus \widehat{G}(x_{\widehat{\nu}}^{\mathcal{P}_2}) \oplus \widehat{G}(x_{\widehat{\nu}}^{\mathcal{P}_3}) \oplus \widehat{G}(y_{\widehat{\nu}}^{\mathcal{P}_1})$ involves the secret parameter v, the Security Invariant applied to on-path leaf node $\widehat{\nu}$ implies that W contains a term $(x_{\widehat{\nu}}^{\mathcal{P}_L})$ that cannot be distinguished from random by $\mathcal{P}$, and therefore v remains completely hidden. Furthermore, pseudorandomness of $\widehat{G}$ implies that there is no dependency between W and any other values dealt as part of the Gen key $\kappa^{\mathcal{P}}$.

Correctness. We demonstrate for any input $\beta \in D$ and for each $\mathcal{P} \in [3]$:

$$\sum_{\mathcal{P}} \mathsf{Eval}(\mathcal{P}, \kappa^{\mathcal{P}}, \beta) = \begin{cases} (0_{\mathbb{G}}, 0_{\mathbb{G}}) & \text{if } \beta \neq \alpha \\ (v, v) & \text{if } \beta = \alpha \end{cases} \tag{21}$$

(Recall that in a (1, 3)-CNF scheme, Eval outputs for each party a pair of values, one per key, and the sum of all left values and the sum of all right values should both equal $f(\beta)$, which for DPF is either $0_{\mathbb{G}}$ or v, depending on whether input β equals α.) To show (21) holds, we first show that at every iteration of Step 1 of the Eval procedure, that the values $\{x_\nu^{\mathcal{P}}, y_\nu^{\mathcal{P}}, z_\nu^{\mathcal{P}}\}$ and $\{b_\nu^{\mathcal{P}}, b_\nu^{\mathcal{P}_R}, c_\nu^{\mathcal{P}}, c_\nu^{\mathcal{P}_R}\}$ respect the invariants listed in tables (2) and (6), respectively. Then, once this is shown, (21) follows immediately since:

$$\text{First coordinate of } \bigoplus_{\mathcal{P}}{}_{\mathbb{G}} \mathsf{Eval}(\mathcal{P}, \kappa^{\mathcal{P}}, \beta):$$

$$= \bigoplus_{\mathcal{P}}{}_{\mathbb{G}} \left(\widehat{G}(x_\nu^{\mathcal{P}}) \ominus_{\mathbb{G}} \widehat{G}(y_\nu^{\mathcal{P}}) \oplus_{\mathbb{G}} c_\nu^{\mathcal{P}} \cdot W \right)$$

$$= \left(\left(\widehat{G}(x_\nu^{\mathcal{P}_1}) \ominus_{\mathbb{G}} \widehat{G}(y_\nu^{\mathcal{P}_1}) \right) \oplus_{\mathbb{G}} \left(\widehat{G}(x_\nu^{\mathcal{P}_2}) \ominus_{\mathbb{G}} \widehat{G}(y_\nu^{\mathcal{P}_2}) \right) \oplus_{\mathbb{G}} \left(\widehat{G}(x_\nu^{\mathcal{P}_3}) \ominus_{\mathbb{G}} \widehat{G}(y_\nu^{\mathcal{P}_3}) \right) \right) \oplus_{\mathbb{G}}$$
$$W \cdot \bigoplus_{\mathcal{P}}{}_{\mathbb{G}} c_\nu^{\mathcal{P}}$$

$$= \left(\left(\widehat{G}(x_\nu^{\mathcal{P}_1}) \ominus_{\mathbb{G}} \widehat{G}(y_\nu^{\mathcal{P}_1}) \right) \oplus_{\mathbb{G}} \left(\widehat{G}(x_\nu^{\mathcal{P}_2}) \ominus_{\mathbb{G}} \widehat{G}(y_\nu^{\mathcal{P}_2}) \right) \oplus_{\mathbb{G}} \left(\widehat{G}(x_\nu^{\mathcal{P}_3}) \ominus_{\mathbb{G}} \widehat{G}(y_\nu^{\mathcal{P}_3}) \right) \right) \oplus_{\mathbb{G}}$$

$$(v \oplus_{\mathbb{G}} Q) \cdot \bigoplus_{\mathcal{P}} {}_{\mathbb{G}}\, c_\nu^{\mathcal{P}} \tag{22}$$

Notice from (2) that:

$$\left(\widehat{G}(x_\nu^{\mathcal{P}_1}) \ominus_{\mathbb{G}} \widehat{G}(y_\nu^{\mathcal{P}_1})\right) \oplus_{\mathbb{G}} \left(\widehat{G}(x_\nu^{\mathcal{P}_2}) \ominus_{\mathbb{G}} \widehat{G}(y_\nu^{\mathcal{P}_2})\right) \oplus_{\mathbb{G}} \left(\widehat{G}(x_\nu^{\mathcal{P}_3}) \ominus_{\mathbb{G}} \widehat{G}(y_\nu^{\mathcal{P}_3})\right)$$
$$= \begin{cases} \widehat{G}(x_\nu^{\mathcal{P}_1})) \oplus_{\mathbb{G}} \widehat{G}(x_\nu^{\mathcal{P}_2})) \oplus_{\mathbb{G}} \widehat{G}(x_\nu^{\mathcal{P}_3})) \ominus_{\mathbb{G}} 3 \cdot \widehat{G}(y_\nu^{\mathcal{P}_1})) = Q & \text{if } \beta = \alpha \\ 0_{\mathbb{G}} & \text{if } \beta \neq \alpha \end{cases}$$

Also, notice that (6) implies that[23]:

$$\bigoplus_{\mathcal{P}} {}_{\mathbb{G}}\, c_\nu^{\mathcal{P}} = \begin{cases} 1 \text{ if } \widehat{\nu} = \nu \text{ is } \textit{on-path} \Leftrightarrow \beta = \alpha \\ 0 \text{ if } \widehat{\nu} \neq \nu \text{ is } \textit{off-path} \Leftrightarrow \beta \neq \alpha \end{cases} \tag{23}$$

Thus (22) becomes:

$$\text{First coordinate of } \bigoplus_{\mathcal{P}} {}_{\mathbb{G}}\, \mathsf{Eval}(\mathcal{P}, \kappa^{\mathcal{P}}, \beta):$$
$$= \begin{cases} Q \oplus_{\mathbb{G}} (v \oplus_{\mathbb{G}} Q) \cdot 1 = v & \text{if } \beta = \alpha \\ 0_{\mathbb{G}} \oplus_{\mathbb{G}} (v \oplus_{\mathbb{G}} Q) \cdot 0 = 0_{\mathbb{G}} & \text{if } \beta \neq \alpha \end{cases} \tag{24}$$

Meanwhile, the case for the second coordinate of $\sum_{\mathcal{P}} \mathsf{Eval}(\mathcal{P}, \kappa^{\mathcal{P}}, \beta)$ is similar, since the $\{c_\nu^{\mathcal{P}_R}\}$ obey (6) in the same way that $\{c_\nu^{\mathcal{P}}\}$ do, and the symmetry (in terms of (2)) of each key's first two PRG seeds $\{x_\nu^{\mathcal{P}}, y_\nu^{\mathcal{P}}\}$ and each key's second two PRG seeds $\{y_\nu^{\mathcal{P}}, z_\nu^{\mathcal{P}}\}$.

Thus, it remains to show that the invariants of (2) and (6) apply at every node in the binary tree. We argue this fact recursively, by demonstrating that as long as the invariants (2) and (6) hold on a parent node μ, then these invariants will continue to hold for both of μ's children. We kick off the recursive argument by noting that the root note (which is necessarily on-path) satisfies (2) and (6) by construction (see Step 1 of the Gen algorithm). For the inductive step, consider an arbitrary node ν on level $1 \leq l \leq \log(N)$, and let μ denote ν's parent. We do a case analysis based on whether ν is the left or right child of μ:

CASE 1: ν IS THE LEFT CHILD OF μ.

Sibling Control Bits $\{b_\nu^{\mathcal{P}}\}$.
Looking at formula (13) for generating the sibling control bits $\{b_\nu^{\mathcal{P}}, b_\nu^{\mathcal{P}_R}\}$ on ν:

$$\sum_{\mathcal{P}} b_\nu^{\mathcal{P}} = \sum_{\mathcal{P}} \left(c_\mu^{\mathcal{P}} \cdot r_l \oplus H_L(x_\mu^{\mathcal{P}}) \oplus H_L(y_\mu^{\mathcal{P}})\right)$$
$$= r_l \cdot \sum_{\mathcal{P}} c_\mu^{\mathcal{P}} \quad \oplus$$
$$\left(\left(H_L(x_\mu^{\mathcal{P}_1}) \oplus H_L(y_\mu^{\mathcal{P}_1})\right) \oplus \left(H_L(x_\mu^{\mathcal{P}_2}) \oplus H_L(y_\mu^{\mathcal{P}_2})\right) \oplus \left(H_L(x_\mu^{\mathcal{P}_3}) \oplus H_L(y_\mu^{\mathcal{P}_3})\right)\right)$$
$$= \begin{cases} r_l \oplus h_L & \text{if } \mu \text{ is } \textit{on-path} \\ 0 & \text{if } \mu \text{ is } \textit{off-path} \end{cases} \tag{25}$$

[23] (23) assumes $\mathbb{G}$ has characteristic two, so that (6), $\oplus_{\mathbb{G}}$.

where we have used in (25) that $\sum_{\mathcal{P}} c_\mu^{\mathcal{P}} = 1$ if parent node μ is *on-path* and otherwise the sum equals zero (as per (6)); and from (2) that:

$$\begin{aligned}&\big(H_L(x_\mu^{\mathcal{P}_1}) \oplus H_L(y_\mu^{\mathcal{P}_1})\big) \oplus \big(H_L(x_\mu^{\mathcal{P}_2}) \oplus H_L(y_\mu^{\mathcal{P}_2})\big) \oplus \big(H_L(x_\mu^{\mathcal{P}_3}) \oplus H_L(y_\mu^{\mathcal{P}_3})\big)\\ &= \begin{cases} H_L(x_\mu^{\mathcal{P}_1})) \oplus H_L(x_\mu^{\mathcal{P}_2})) \oplus H_L(x_\mu^{\mathcal{P}_3})) \oplus H_L(y_\mu^{\mathcal{P}_1})) = h_L & \text{if } \mu \text{ is } \textit{on-path} \\ 0 & \text{if } \mu \text{ is } \textit{off-path} \end{cases}\end{aligned}$$

Thus, if μ is off-path, then both ν and its sibling are also off-path, and $\{b_\nu^{\mathcal{P}}\}$ satisfies the requisite property of (6). Meanwhile, if μ is on-path, then exactly one of ν or its sibling is on-path. Since we are in the case that ν is the *left* child of μ, then ν is on-path if and only if $\alpha_l = 0$. In particular if μ is on-path:

$$\sum_{\mathcal{P}} b_\nu^{\mathcal{P}} = r_l \oplus h_L = \begin{cases} h_L \oplus h_L = 0 & \text{if } \alpha_l = 0 \Leftrightarrow \nu\text{'s } \textit{sibling} \text{ is off-path} \\ 1 \oplus h_L \oplus h_L = 1 & \text{if } \alpha_l = 1 \Leftrightarrow \nu\text{'s } \textit{sibling} \text{ is on-path} \end{cases}$$

where we used (10) to replace r_l conditioned on whether α_l is 0 or 1. The argument for the "right" sibling control bits $\{b_\nu^{\mathcal{P}_R}\}$ mirrors the above argument, since $\sum_{\mathcal{P}} c_\mu^{\mathcal{P}} = \sum_{\mathcal{P}} c_\mu^{\mathcal{P}_R}$ (per (18)) and $\{(x_\mu^{\mathcal{P}}, y_\mu^{\mathcal{P}})\}_{\mathcal{P}} = \{(y_\mu^{\mathcal{P}}, z_\mu^{\mathcal{P}})\}_{\mathcal{P}}$ (per (2)).

On-Path Control Bits $\{c_\nu^{\mathcal{P}}\}$.

Looking at formula (14) for generating the on-path control bits $\{c_\nu^{\mathcal{P}}, c_\nu^{\mathcal{P}_R}\}$ on ν:

$$\begin{aligned}\sum_{\mathcal{P}} c_\nu^{\mathcal{P}} &= \sum_{\mathcal{P}} \left(c_\mu^{\mathcal{P}} \cdot t_l \oplus \widehat{H}_L(x_\mu^{\mathcal{P}}) \oplus \widehat{H}_L(y_\mu^{\mathcal{P}})\right)\\ &= t_l \cdot \sum_{\mathcal{P}} c_\mu^{\mathcal{P}} \quad \oplus \\ &\quad \left(\left(\widehat{H}_L(x_\mu^{\mathcal{P}_1}) \oplus \widehat{H}_L(y_\mu^{\mathcal{P}_1})\right) \oplus \left(\widehat{H}_L(x_\mu^{\mathcal{P}_2}) \oplus \widehat{H}_L(y_\mu^{\mathcal{P}_2})\right) \oplus \left(\widehat{H}_L(x_\mu^{\mathcal{P}_3}) \oplus \widehat{H}_L(y_\mu^{\mathcal{P}_3})\right)\right)\\ &= \begin{cases} t_l \oplus \widehat{h}_L & \text{if } \mu \text{ is } \textit{on-path} \\ 0 & \text{if } \mu \text{ is } \textit{off-path} \end{cases}\end{aligned} \tag{26}$$

where we have used in (26) that $\sum_{\mathcal{P}} c_\mu^{\mathcal{P}} = 1$ if parent node μ is *on-path* and otherwise the sum equals zero (per (6)); and from (2) that:

$$\begin{aligned}&\left(\widehat{H}_L(x_\mu^{\mathcal{P}_1}) \oplus \widehat{H}_L(y_\mu^{\mathcal{P}_1})\right) \oplus \left(\widehat{H}_L(x_\mu^{\mathcal{P}_2}) \oplus \widehat{H}_L(y_\mu^{\mathcal{P}_2})\right) \oplus \left(\widehat{H}_L(x_\mu^{\mathcal{P}_3}) \oplus \widehat{H}_L(y_\mu^{\mathcal{P}_3})\right)\\ &= \begin{cases} \widehat{H}_L(x_\mu^{\mathcal{P}_1})) \oplus \widehat{H}_L(x_\mu^{\mathcal{P}_2})) \oplus \widehat{H}_L(x_\mu^{\mathcal{P}_3})) \oplus \widehat{H}_L(y_\mu^{\mathcal{P}_1})) = \widehat{h}_L & \text{if } \mu \text{ is } \textit{on-path} \\ 0 & \text{if } \mu \text{ is } \textit{off-path} \end{cases}\end{aligned}$$

Thus, if μ is off-path, then both ν and its sibling are also off-path, and $\{c_\nu^{\mathcal{P}}\}$ satisfies the requisite property of (6). Meanwhile, if μ is on-path, then exactly one of ν or its sibling is on-path. Since we are in the case that ν is the *left* child of μ, then ν is on-path if and only if $\alpha_l = 0$. In particular if μ is on-path:

$$\sum_{\mathcal{P}} c_\nu^{\mathcal{P}} = t_l \oplus \widehat{h}_L = \begin{cases} 1 \oplus \widehat{h}_L \oplus \widehat{h}_L = 1 & \text{if } \alpha_l = 0 \Leftrightarrow \nu \text{ is on-path} \\ \widehat{h}_L \oplus \widehat{h}_L = 0 & \text{if } \alpha_l = 1 \Leftrightarrow \nu \text{ is off-path} \end{cases}$$

where we used (10) to replace t_l conditioned on whether $\alpha_l = 0$ or $\alpha_l = 1$. The argument for the "right" sibling control bits $\{c_\nu^{\mathcal{P}_R}\}$ mirrors the above argument, since $\sum_{\mathcal{P}} c_\mu^{\mathcal{P}} = \sum_{\mathcal{P}} c_\mu^{\mathcal{P}_R}$ (per (18)) and $\{(x_\mu^{\mathcal{P}}, y_\mu^{\mathcal{P}})\}_{\mathcal{P}} = \{(y_\mu^{\mathcal{P}}, z_\mu^{\mathcal{P}})\}_{\mathcal{P}}$ (per (2)).

Seeds $\{x_\nu^{\mathcal{P}}, y_\nu^{\mathcal{P}}, z_\nu^{\mathcal{P}}\}$.
Demonstrating that the formulas for the next-level seeds in (15)–(16) maintain the seed invariants of (2) is straightforward, but requires a case analysis based on whether the current node is on-path or off-path.

Case Analysis of Correctness for 1-out-of-3 CNF-DPF.
We prove the new seed values on ν, computed as per (15)–(16), obey (2) by doing a case analysis, broken down by ν's location (on-path, sibling is on-path, both self and sibling are off-path), as well as on the $\{b_\nu^{\mathcal{P}}, b_\nu^{\mathcal{P}_R}\}$ values on ν. Before proceeding, recall the notation for $w_*^{\mathcal{P}}$ (see Step (1c) of the Eval algorithm): the first (respectively last) λ bits of $\mathsf{Eval}(\kappa_l^{\mathcal{P}}, \nu)$ if ν is the left (respectively right) child of its parent, where $\kappa_l^{\mathcal{P}}$ denotes the MS-DPF$^+$ key for level l (see (7) in Step 2 of the Gen algorithm); and also the notation for $\widehat{w}_\nu^{\mathcal{P}} = \mathsf{Eval}(\widehat{\kappa}_l^{\mathcal{P}}, \nu)$, and for $G_* = G_L$ (resp. G_R) if ν is the *left* (resp. *right*) child of its parent.

For each case below, we present a table which shows what each key's new seed values on node ν will be, given ν's position (on/off path) and the seed values that were present on ν's parent node μ. The tables indicate, for each key, which seed formula ((15) vs. (16)) are used to derive the new seed values on ν.

Case A: Parent μ is off-path. Because parent node μ is off-path, its position (at depth $l-1$) does *not* correspond to the DPF index $(\alpha)_{l-1}$ of MS-DPF$^+$ function f_l; and similarly, neither of its children nodes are at position $(\alpha)_l$, and therefore they do not correspond to the DPF index of $\widehat{f_l}$. Therefore, $w_*^{\mathcal{P}_1} = w_*^{\mathcal{P}_2} = w_*^{\mathcal{P}_3}$ and $\widehat{w}_\nu^{\mathcal{P}_1} = \widehat{w}_\nu^{\mathcal{P}_2} = \widehat{w}_\nu^{\mathcal{P}_3}$ (by definition of f_l and $\widehat{f_l}$; see Step 2 of the Gen algorithm), and so we suppress player superscripts and write simply w_* and $\widehat{w}_\nu$. Also, since μ is off-path, the seeds on μ satisfy invariant (2), and for convenience we will denote the three keys' seeds on off-path parent node μ as: $\kappa^{\mathcal{P}_1} = \{a, b, c\}$, $\kappa^{\mathcal{P}_2} = \{b, c, a\}$, $\kappa^{\mathcal{P}_3} = \{c, a, b\}$. Finally, since μ is off-path, so is ν and its sibling, and thus by the invariant of (6), we have that $\bigoplus_{\mathcal{P}} b_\nu^{\mathcal{P}} = 0$. Thus, there are four possibilities for the values of $(b_\nu^{\mathcal{P}_1}, b_\nu^{\mathcal{P}_2}, b_\nu^{\mathcal{P}_3})$: $(0,0,0)$, $(0,1,1)$, $(1,0,1)$, or $(1,1,0)$. We do a case-analysis just of the first two; the latter two are similar to the second:

Case A.1: $\{b_\nu^{\mathcal{P}}\} = (0,0,0)$:

	$\kappa^{\mathcal{P}_1}$ (via (16))	$\kappa^{\mathcal{P}_2}$ (via (16))	$\kappa^{\mathcal{P}_3}$ (via (16))
$x_\nu^{\mathcal{P}}$	$G_*(a) \oplus \widehat{w}_\nu$	$G_*(b) \oplus \widehat{w}_\nu$	$G_*(c) \oplus \widehat{w}_\nu$
$y_\nu^{\mathcal{P}}$	$G_*(b) \oplus \widehat{w}_\nu$	$G_*(c) \oplus \widehat{w}_\nu$	$G_*(a) \oplus \widehat{w}_\nu$
$z_\nu^{\mathcal{P}}$	$G_*(c) \oplus \widehat{w}_\nu$	$G_*(a) \oplus \widehat{w}_\nu$	$G_*(b) \oplus \widehat{w}_\nu$

Case A.2: $\{b_\nu^{\mathcal{P}}\} = (0,1,1)$:

	$\kappa^{\mathcal{P}_1}$ (via (15))	$\kappa^{\mathcal{P}_2}$ (via (16))	$\kappa^{\mathcal{P}_3}$ (via (15))
$x_\nu^{\mathcal{P}}$	$G_*(b) \oplus \widehat{w}_\nu$	$G_*(a) \oplus \widehat{w}_\nu$	$w_* \oplus \widehat{w}_\nu$
$y_\nu^{\mathcal{P}}$	$G_*(a) \oplus \widehat{w}_\nu$	$w_* \oplus \widehat{w}_\nu$	$G_*(b) \oplus \widehat{w}_\nu$
$z_\nu^{\mathcal{P}}$	$w_* \oplus \widehat{w}_\nu$	$G_*(b) \oplus \widehat{w}_\nu$	$G_*(a) \oplus \widehat{w}_\nu$

Case B: Parent μ is on-path; ν is on-path. Because parent node μ is on-path, its position (at depth $l-1$) corresponds to the DPF index $(\alpha)_{l-1}$ of MS-DPF$^+$ function f_l; and similarly ν on-path means that its position is $(\alpha)_l$ which corresponds to the DPF index of $\widehat{f}_l$. Therefore, $w_*^{\mathcal{P}}$ follows (7) and $\widehat{w}_\nu^{\mathcal{P}}$ follows (8):

$$w_*^{\mathcal{P}} = \begin{cases} v_L^{\mathcal{P}} = G_L(x_\mu^{\mathcal{P}_L}) \oplus q_l \oplus p_l \text{ if } \nu \text{ is the } \textit{left} \text{ child} \\ v_R^{\mathcal{P}} = G_R(x_\mu^{\mathcal{P}_L}) \oplus q_l \oplus p_l \text{ if } \nu \text{ is the } \textit{right} \text{ child} \end{cases} \tag{27}$$

$$\widehat{w}_\nu^{\mathcal{P}} = \widehat{v}_l^{\mathcal{P}} = \begin{cases} p_l \text{ if } b_\nu^{\mathcal{P}} = 0 \\ q_l \text{ if } b_\nu^{\mathcal{P}} = 1 \end{cases} \tag{28}$$

where $\{p_l, q_l\}$ are uniform random values chosen for each level $1 \le l \le \log(N)$, and we have used that, since ν is on-path, then $\alpha_l = 1$ (respectively $\alpha_l = 0$) when ν is the *left* child (respectively *right* child) of μ. Also, since μ is on-path, the seeds on μ satisfy invariant (2), and for convenience we will denote the three keys' seeds on on-path parent node μ as: $\kappa^{\mathcal{P}_1} = \{a, d, b\}$, $\kappa^{\mathcal{P}_2} = \{b, d, c\}$, $\kappa^{\mathcal{P}_3} = \{c, d, a\}$. Finally, since ν is on-path, its sibling is off-path, and thus by the invariant of (6), we have that $\bigoplus_{\mathcal{P}} b_\nu^{\mathcal{P}} = 0$. Thus, there are four possibilities for the values of $(b_\nu^{\mathcal{P}_1}, b_\nu^{\mathcal{P}_2}, b_\nu^{\mathcal{P}_3})$: $(0,0,0)$, $(0,1,1)$, $(1,0,1)$, or $(1,1,0)$. We do a case-analysis just of the first two; the latter two are similar to the second:

Case B.1: $\{b_\nu^{\mathcal{P}}\} = (0,0,0)$:

	$\kappa^{\mathcal{P}_1}$ (via (16))	$\kappa^{\mathcal{P}_2}$ (via (16))	$\kappa^{\mathcal{P}_3}$ (via (16))
$x_\nu^{\mathcal{P}}$	$G_*(a) \oplus p_l$	$G_*(b) \oplus p_l$	$G_*(c) \oplus p_l$
$y_\nu^{\mathcal{P}}$	$G_*(d) \oplus p_l$	$G_*(d) \oplus p_l$	$G_*(d) \oplus p_l$
$z_\nu^{\mathcal{P}}$	$G_*(b) \oplus p_l$	$G_*(c) \oplus p_l$	$G_*(a) \oplus p_l$

Case B.2: $\{b_\nu^{\mathcal{P}}\} = (0,1,1)$:

	$\kappa^{\mathcal{P}_1}$ (via (15))	$\kappa^{\mathcal{P}_2}$ (via (16))	$\kappa^{\mathcal{P}_3}$ (via (15))
$x_\nu^{\mathcal{P}}$	$G_*(d) \oplus q_l$	$G_*(c) \oplus p_l$	$G_*(b) \oplus p_l$
$y_\nu^{\mathcal{P}}$	$G_*(a) \oplus q_l$	$G_*(a) \oplus q_l$	$G_*(a) \oplus q_l$
$z_\nu^{\mathcal{P}}$	$G_*(c) \oplus p_l$	$G_*(b) \oplus p_l$	$G_*(d) \oplus q_l$

Case C:μ is on-path, ν is off-path. Because parent node μ is on-path, its position (at depth $l-1$) corresponds to the DPF index $(\alpha)_{l-1}$ of MS-DPF$^+$ function f_l; and similarly ν off-path means that its position is does *not* correspond to $(\alpha)_l$, the DPF index of $\widehat{f}_l$. Therefore, $\widehat{w}_\nu^{\mathcal{P}_1} = \widehat{w}_\nu^{\mathcal{P}_2} = \widehat{w}_\nu^{\mathcal{P}_3}$ (by definition of $\widehat{f}_l$; see Step 2 of the Gen algorithm), and so we suppress player superscripts and write simply $\widehat{w}_\nu$. Meanwhile, per (7) we have that $w_*^{\mathcal{P}} = v_L^{\mathcal{P}} = G_L(x_\mu^{\mathcal{P}_L})$ if ν is the *left* child, and otherwise $w_*^{\mathcal{P}} = v_R^{\mathcal{P}} = G_R(x_\mu^{\mathcal{P}_L})$, since ν is off-path and parent μ is on-path, then $\alpha_l = 1$ (respectively $\alpha_l = 0$) when ν is the *left* child (respectively *right* child) of μ. Also, since μ is on-path, the seeds on μ satisfy invariant (2), and for convenience we will denote the three keys' seeds as above. Finally, since ν is off-path but parent node μ is on-path, the sibling of ν must be on-path, and thus by the invariant of (6), we have that $\bigoplus_{\mathcal{P}} b_\nu^{\mathcal{P}} = 1$. Thus, there are four possibilities for the values of $(b_\nu^{\mathcal{P}_1}, b_\nu^{\mathcal{P}_2}, b_\nu^{\mathcal{P}_3})$: $(1,1,1)$, $(0,0,1)$, $(0,1,0)$, or $(1,0,0)$. We do a case-analysis just of the first two; the latter two are similar to the second:

Case C.1: $\{b_\nu^{\mathcal{P}}\} = (1,1,1)$:

	$\kappa^{\mathcal{P}_1}$ (via (16))	$\kappa^{\mathcal{P}_2}$ (via (16))	$\kappa^{\mathcal{P}_3}$ (via (16))
$x_\nu^{\mathcal{P}}$	$G_*(b) \oplus \widehat{w}_\nu$	$G_*(c) \oplus \widehat{w}_\nu$	$G_*(a) \oplus \widehat{w}_\nu$
$y_\nu^{\mathcal{P}}$	$G_*(c) \oplus \widehat{w}_\nu$	$G_*(a) \oplus \widehat{w}_\nu$	$G_*(b) \oplus \widehat{w}_\nu$
$z_\nu^{\mathcal{P}}$	$G_*(a) \oplus \widehat{w}_\nu$	$G_*(b) \oplus \widehat{w}_\nu$	$G_*(c) \oplus \widehat{w}_\nu$

Case C.2: $\{b_\nu^{\mathcal{P}}\} = (0,0,1)$:

	$\kappa^{\mathcal{P}_1}$ (via (16))	$\kappa^{\mathcal{P}_2}$ (via (15))	$\kappa^{\mathcal{P}_3}$ (via (15))
$x_\nu^{\mathcal{P}}$	$G_*(a) \oplus \widehat{w}_\nu$	$G_*(d) \oplus \widehat{w}_\nu$	$G_*(b) \oplus \widehat{w}_\nu$
$y_\nu^{\mathcal{P}}$	$G_*(d) \oplus \widehat{w}_\nu$	$G_*(b) \oplus \widehat{w}_\nu$	$G_*(a) \oplus \widehat{w}_\nu$
$z_\nu^{\mathcal{P}}$	$G_*(b) \oplus \widehat{w}_\nu$	$G_*(a) \oplus \widehat{w}_\nu$	$G_*(d) \oplus \widehat{w}_\nu$

CASE 2: ν IS THE RIGHT CHILD OF μ.
The argument for this case is essentially identical to Case 1, making the symmetric replacements of $H_L \to H_R$, $r_l \to s_l$, and $t_l \to u_l$. Details are provided in the full version. □

References

[AFL+16] Araki, T., Furukawa, J., Lindell, Y., Nof, A., Ohara, K.: High-throughput semi-honest secure three-party computation with an honest majority. In: CCS, pp. 805–817. ACM Press (2016)

[APY20] Abraham, I., Pinkas, B., Yanai, A.: Blinder: MPC based scalable and robust anonymous committed broadcast. In: CCS. ACM Press (2020)

[BCG+19] Boyle, E., Couteau, G., Gilboa, N., Ishai, Y., Kohl, L., Scholl, P.: Efficient pseudorandom correlation generators: silent OT extension and more. In: Boldyreva, A., Micciancio, D. (eds.) CRYPTO 2019. LNCS, vol. 11694, pp. 489–518. Springer, Cham (2019). https://doi.org/10.1007/978-3-030-26954-8_16

[BGI15] Boyle, E., Gilboa, N., Ishai, Y.: Function secret sharing. In: Oswald, E., Fischlin, M. (eds.) EUROCRYPT 2015. LNCS, vol. 9057, pp. 337–367. Springer, Heidelberg (2015). https://doi.org/10.1007/978-3-662-46803-6_12

[BGI16a] Boyle, E., Gilboa, N., Ishai, Y.: Breaking the circuit size barrier for secure computation under DDH. In: Robshaw, M., Katz, J. (eds.) CRYPTO 2016. LNCS, vol. 9814, pp. 509–539. Springer, Heidelberg (2016). https://doi.org/10.1007/978-3-662-53018-4_19

[BGI16b] Boyle, E., Gilboa, N., Ishai, Y.: Function secret sharing: improvements and extensions. In: CCS, pp. 1292–1303. ACM Press (2016)

[BGI18a] Boyle, E., Gilboa, N., Ishai, Y.: Function secret sharing: improvements and extensions (2018). https://eprint.iacr.org/2018/707.pdf

[BGI+18b] Boyle, E., Gilboa, N., Ishai, Y., Lin, H., Tessaro, S.: Foundations of homomorphic secret sharing. In: ITCS, pp. 21:1–21:21 (2018)

[BIK05] Beimel, A., Ishai, Y., Kushilevitz, E.: General constructions for information-theoretic private information retrieval. J. Comput. Syst. Sci. **71**(2), 213–247 (2005)

[BIW07] Barkol, O., Ishai, Y., Weinreb, E.: On locally decodable codes, self-correctable codes, and t-private PIR. In: Charikar, M., Jansen, K., Reingold, O., Rolim, J.D.P. (eds.) APPROX/RANDOM -2007. LNCS, vol. 4627, pp. 311–325. Springer, Heidelberg (2007). https://doi.org/10.1007/978-3-540-74208-1_23

[BKKO20] Bunn, P., Katz, J., Kushilevitz, E., Ostrovsky, R.: Efficient 3-party distributed ORAM. In: Galdi, C., Kolesnikov, V. (eds.) SCN 2020. LNCS, vol. 12238, pp. 215–232. Springer, Cham (2020). https://doi.org/10.1007/978-3-030-57990-6_11

[BL88] Benaloh, J., Leichter, J.: Generalized secret sharing and monotone functions. In: Goldwasser, S. (ed.) CRYPTO 1988. LNCS, vol. 403, pp. 27–35. Springer, New York (1990). https://doi.org/10.1007/0-387-34799-2_3

[BLMR13] Boneh, D., Lewi, K., Montgomery, H., Raghunathan, A.: Key homomorphic PRFs and their applications. In: Canetti, R., Garay, J.A. (eds.) CRYPTO 2013. LNCS, vol. 8042, pp. 410–428. Springer, Heidelberg (2013). https://doi.org/10.1007/978-3-642-40041-4_23

[CBM15] Corrigan-Gibbs, H., Boneh, D., Mazières, D.: Riposte: an anonymous messaging system handling millions of users. In: IEEE SP, pp. 321–338. IEEE Computer Society (2015)

[CDI05] Cramer, R., Damgård, I., Ishai, Y.: Share conversion, pseudorandom secret-sharing and applications to secure computation. In: Kilian, J. (ed.) TCC 2005. LNCS, vol. 3378, pp. 342–362. Springer, Heidelberg (2005). https://doi.org/10.1007/978-3-540-30576-7_19

[DHRW16] Dodis, Y., Halevi, S., Rothblum, R.D., Wichs, D.: Spooky encryption and its applications. In: Robshaw, M., Katz, J. (eds.) CRYPTO 2016. LNCS, vol. 9816, pp. 93–122. Springer, Heidelberg (2016). https://doi.org/10.1007/978-3-662-53015-3_4

[DIO98] Di-Crescenzo, G., Ishai, Y., Ostrovsky, R.: Universal service-providers for database private information retrieval. In: PODC, pp. 91–100. ACM Press (1998)

[DS17] Doerner, J., Shelat, A.: Scaling ORAM for secure computation. In: CCS, pp. 523–535. ACM Press (2017)

[ECZB19] Eskandarian, S., Corrigan-Gibbs, H., Zaharia, M., Boneh, D.: Express: lowering the cost of metadata-hiding communication with cryptographic privacy. CoRR, abs/1911.09215(v1) (2019)

[Efr09] Efremenko, E.: 3-query locally decodable codes of subexponential length. In: STOC, pp. 39–44. ACM Press (2009)

[FLNW17] Furukawa, J., Lindell, Y., Nof, A., Weinstein, O.: High-throughput secure three-party computation for malicious adversaries and an honest majority. In: Coron, J.-S., Nielsen, J.B. (eds.) EUROCRYPT 2017. LNCS, vol. 10211, pp. 225–255. Springer, Cham (2017). https://doi.org/10.1007/978-3-319-56614-6_8

[GI99] Gilboa, N., Ishai, Y.: Compressing cryptographic resources. In: Wiener, M. (ed.) CRYPTO 1999. LNCS, vol. 1666, pp. 591–608. Springer, Heidelberg (1999). https://doi.org/10.1007/3-540-48405-1_37

[GI14] Gilboa, N., Ishai, Y.: Distributed point functions and their applications. In: Nguyen, P.Q., Oswald, E. (eds.) EUROCRYPT 2014. LNCS, vol. 8441, pp. 640–658. Springer, Heidelberg (2014). https://doi.org/10.1007/978-3-642-55220-5_35

[GKW18] Gordon, S.D., Katz, J., Wang, X.: Simple and efficient two-server ORAM. In: Peyrin, T., Galbraith, S. (eds.) ASIACRYPT 2018. LNCS, vol. 11274, pp. 141–157. Springer, Cham (2018). https://doi.org/10.1007/978-3-030-03332-3_6

[HV20] Hamlin, A., Varia, M.: Two-server distributed ORAM with sublinear computation and constant rounds (2020). https://eprint.iacr.org/2020/1547

[IKKP15] Ishai, Y., Kumaresan, R., Kushilevitz, E., Paskin-Cherniavsky, A.: Secure computation with minimal interaction, revisited. In: Gennaro, R., Robshaw, M. (eds.) CRYPTO 2015. LNCS, vol. 9216, pp. 359–378. Springer, Heidelberg (2015). https://doi.org/10.1007/978-3-662-48000-7_18

[ISN87] Ito, M., Saito, A., Nishizeki, T.: Secret sharing schemes realizing general access structure. In: Globecom, pp. 99–102. IEEE (1987)

[JW18] Jarecki, S., Wei, B.: 3pc ORAM with low latency, low bandwidth, and fast batch retrieval (2018). https://eprint.iacr.org/2018/347.pdf

[KM19] Kushilevitz, E., Mour, T.: Sub-logarithmic distributed oblivious RAM with small block size. In: Lin, D., Sako, K. (eds.) PKC 2019. LNCS, vol. 11442, pp. 3–33. Springer, Cham (2019). https://doi.org/10.1007/978-3-030-17253-4_1

[LO13] Lu, S., Ostrovsky, R.: Distributed oblivious RAM for secure two-party computation. In: Sahai, A. (ed.) TCC 2013. LNCS, vol. 7785, pp. 377–396. Springer, Heidelberg (2013). https://doi.org/10.1007/978-3-642-36594-2_22

[Mau02] Maurer, U.: Secure multi-party computation made simple. In: SCN, pp. 14–28 (2002)

[OS97] Ostrovsky, R., Shoup, V.: Private information storage. In: STOC, pp. 294–303. ACM Press (1997)

[ZWR+16] Zahur, S., et al.: Revisiting square-root ORAM: efficient random access in multi-party computation. In: IEEE Symposium on Security and Privacy, pp. 218–234. IEEE (2016)

Cryptographic Protocols

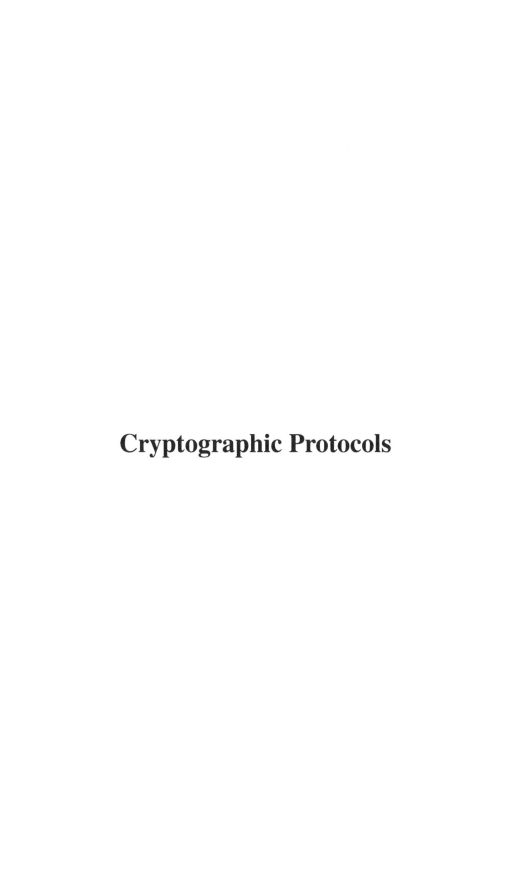

Efficient Verifiable Partially-Decryptable Commitments from Lattices and Applications

Muhammed F. Esgin[1,2(✉)], Ron Steinfeld[1], and Raymond K. Zhao[1]

[1] Faculty of Information Technology, Monash University, Clayton, Australia
{Muhammed.Esgin,Ron.Steinfeld,Raymond.Zhao}@monash.edu
[2] CSIRO's Data61, Melbourne, Australia

Abstract. We introduce *verifiable partially-decryptable commitments* (VPDC), as a building block for constructing efficient privacy-preserving protocols supporting *auditability* by a trusted party. A VPDC is an extension of a commitment along with an accompanying proof, convincing a verifier that (i) the given commitment is well-formed and (ii) a certain *part* of the committed message can be decrypted using a (secret) trapdoor known to a trusted party.

We first formalize VPDCs and then introduce a general decryption feasibility result that overcomes the challenges in *relaxed* proofs arising in the lattice setting. Our general result can be applied to a wide class of Fiat-Shamir based protocols and may be of independent interest.

Next, we show how to extend the commonly used lattice-based 'Hashed-Message Commitment' (HMC) scheme into a succinct and efficient VPDC. In particular, we devise a novel 'gadget'-based Regev-style (partial) decryption method, compatible with efficient relaxed lattice-based zero-knowledge proofs. We prove the soundness of our VPDC in the setting of adversarial proofs, where a prover tries to create a valid VPDC output that fails in decryption.

To demonstrate the effectiveness of our results, we extend a private blockchain payment protocol, MatRiCT, by Esgin et al. (ACM CCS '19) into a formally auditable construction, which we call MatRiCT-Au, with very low communication and computation overheads over MatRiCT.

Keywords: Lattice · Zero Knowledge · Verifiable Partially-Decryptable Commitment · Auditable RingCT · Accountable Ring Signature

1 Introduction

Commitment schemes and accompanying zero-knowledge proofs (ZKPs) have become crucial tools used in countless privacy-preserving protocols. For example, they are extensively used in privacy-aware blockchain applications such as Monero and Zcash cryptocurrencies to hide sensitive information such as user

G. Hanaoka et al. (Eds.): PKC 2022, LNCS 13177, pp. 317–348, 2022.
https://doi.org/10.1007/978-3-030-97121-2_12

identities and transaction amounts. In many such privacy-preserving applications, there is a need for *auditability*, i.e., the ability of a trusted third-party to revoke the privacy or anonymity of the protocol, in order to catch or punish misbehaving entities. For instance, it is well known that the privacy features of cryptocurrencies have been exploited by cyber criminals to hide their illegal financial activities, and some level of government oversight may be required in future to allow such activities to be traced by law authorities. Many applications where such an auditability feature is needed exist, including group signatures [5], fair exchange [1], key escrow [23] and e-voting. To enable the auditability property of the privacy protocol, we would like the protocol to use a *decryptable* commitment scheme, supporting a trapdoor decryption algorithm that enables the authority with some trapdoor to recover a message from a given commitment.[1] At the same time, to prevent malicious parties from escaping the auditability property, the protocol must support a *verifiable* decryptable commitment, which allows protocol parties to verify that a commitment is decryptable by the authority, while still hiding its contents from all other parties.

A problem similar to constructing verifiable decryptable commitments has been previously studied under the name of *verifiable encryption* [4] in the classical setting of DL-based and factoring-based public-key cryptography. The approach here is to use a public-key encryption scheme as the commitment (with the secret key known to the authority), and attach to it a zero-knowledge proof of plaintext knowledge in order to turn it into a verifiable commitment. This approach was extended to the post-quantum lattice-based setting in [18], instantiating the encryption scheme by a variant of Regev's encryption scheme [21] based on (Ring/Module)-LWE. We note that Regev's encryption scheme can also be viewed as a decryptable *short message* variant of the 'Unbounded-Message Commitment' (UMC) scheme [3] (see the full version of this paper on IACR's ePrint archive). Despite allowing Regev-style decryption, UMC also has the practical efficiency drawbacks we discuss below.

The use of verifiable Regev encryption as in [18] can result in very long commitments and communication overheads in typical applications. This is because both the randomness length and commitment length of Regev-encryption commitments have an additive term proportional to the dimension of the message vector. In typical lattice-based ZKPs such as [7,9,10,12], the structure of the protocol requires the prover to send commitments to a large number of messages including masking randomness values as well as auxiliary terms, in addition to the commitment of the 'real' message which needs to be decrypted by the opening authority (e.g., the payment amount, or payer/payee identity in cryptocurrencies). The protocol also requires the prover to send masked variants of the commitment randomness. Both those factors lead to long proofs with Regev encryption commitments. To illustrate, in the MatRiCT cryptocurrency protocol of [12], an aggregated binary proof is used (see [12, Section 1.2]) to significantly

[1] We note here that our notion of a decryptable commitment is different from a *trapdoor* commitment. For a given commitment and a message, the latter allows a trapdoor holder to find a properly distributed opening randomness for the commitment.

reduce the proof length. In this proof, it is necessary to commit to individual bits of integers by separate ring elements so that each bit can be manipulated independently. As a result, the total message dimension in a commitment over the underlying polynomial ring R_q is in the order of several hundreds (the 'real' message is still a few hundreds dimensional). If one were to use a Regev-style encryption for this commitment, the commitment *alone* would cost around 100–200 KB. In comparison, this commitment costs only about 13 KB in MatRiCT thanks to the use of a *compressing* commitment.

To reduce the length of commitments/proofs, an alternative approach (used in [12]) to Regev-encryption commitments is to instead use lattice-based 'Hashed-Message Commitments' (HMC), where message hashing leads to a short commitment dimension independent of the total dimension of the committed messages. In HMC, message hashing is achieved by multiplying the (long) message vector by a *random* 'fat' (i.e., compressing) matrix and one relies on the hardness of (Ring/Module)-SIS to accomplish the binding property. However, in our context of *decryptable* commitments, the lack of a unique decryption for such HMC commitments (due to compression) makes them not directly suitable. Therefore, we study HMC in the *partial* decryption setting where the committed message has two parts: (i) a decryptable message (that contains the 'real' message the authority wants to recover), and (ii) a non-decryptable/auxiliary message (that contains other auxiliary terms that need not be recovered). This way, we can achieve both of our succinctness and (partial) decryptability goals simultaneously. We note that a straightforward combination of using UMC for the decryptable part of the message and HMC for the non-decryptable message part, although it deals with the auxiliary terms, still suffers from an overhead of at least two commitments plus the large cost of a UMC commitment. In contrast to HMC, the latter UMC commitment dimension over R_q is linear in the message dimension over R_q, which is over 100 in the context of MatRiCT discussed above.

An initial attempt to overcome the above-mentioned efficiency issues of UMC-like commitments in constructing VPDCs, was proposed in [12, Section 6.1], where a method of incorporating a lightweight Regev-style decryption trapdoor into an HMC commitment was proposed. However, although a promising direction to combine the best of both HMC and Regev encryption commitments, the work of [12] does not give a full solution to the problem, as it does not address two main technical challenges that we now explain.

Firstly, the decryption algorithm in [12] is only analyzed for *honestly-created* commitments *without* a rigorous framework. The analysis against *adversarially-created* commitments/proofs that pass the verification check, which is an important requirement in the auditability setting of VPDCs, is missing. We recall that for the underlying efficient ZKPs of opening for the HMC scheme we study in this work (see, e.g., [9,10]), the ZKP soundness only guarantees the existence of a *relaxed* commitment opening $(\boldsymbol{m}, \boldsymbol{r}, y)$ of a commitment C, satisfying the relaxed opening relation

$$(yC = \mathsf{Com}_{ck}(y\boldsymbol{m}; \boldsymbol{r})) \wedge (y \in \Delta\mathcal{C}) \wedge (\boldsymbol{m} \in \mathcal{M}), \quad (1)$$

where y is a short non-zero relaxation factor, $\Delta\mathcal{C}$ is the set of challenge differences and $\mathcal{M}$ is a public message space. Observe that the message opening $\boldsymbol{m}$ is proven to be in some set $\mathcal{M}$, which is important for our analysis, and for example, $\mathcal{M} = \{0,1\}^v$ for some $v \geq 1$ for the proof systems in [9,10,12]. Also, note that the relaxation factor y is *unknown* to the decryption algorithm as it is part of the prover's secret. Thus, it is not clear how one could enable such a decryption feature in the setting of relaxed proofs as the decryptor does not even know what to decrypt exactly. The work by Lyubashevsky and Neven [18] addresses this problem in the setting of verifiable Regev encryption. Particularly in [18], it is shown that choosing a random y from the set of possible relaxation factors is in fact a good way to go, and the *expected* running time for their decryption algorithm is shown to be proportional to the number of random oracle queries made by the prover to generate the protocol transcript[2]. However, this result is specific to the Fiat-Shamir (FS) protocol[3] and the Regev-style decryption described in [18].

A second technical challenge in constructing an HMC-based partially decryptable commitment following the approach of [12] is that even if a suitable relaxation factor y is known by the decryption algorithm, decrypting the commitment with the Regev-style trapdoor key does not directly yield the decryptable message, but reveals a noisy inner-product (over the underlying polynomial ring R_q) of the message with a known *random* vector $\boldsymbol{a}$, of the form $\langle y\boldsymbol{a}, \boldsymbol{m}\rangle + e$ for some short noise term e (and y the relaxation factor). This leaves the question of how to efficiently recover the message $\boldsymbol{m}$ from this noisy information. The work of [12] addressed this issue only for *small* message spaces (and honestly generated commitments) by performing an exhaustive search over all possible messages, which is very restrictive and computationally expensive. How to make decryption work *efficiently* for *exponentially large* message spaces and guarantee the decryption soundness even against adversarially constructed commitments having such a relaxed opening has since remained unaddressed.

1.1 Our Contributions

Verifiable Partially-Decryptable Commitments. In this work, we first formalize the notion of a *Verifiable Partially-Decryptable Commitment* (VPDC), which is closely related to proofs of plaintext knowledge and verifiable encryption. In particular, a VPDC extends a commitment scheme C and a matching Non-Interactive Zero-Knowledge Proof (NIZK) Σ of opening for C by adding a trapdoor key generation algorithm CAddTd and a matching decryption algorithm

[2] We refer to [18] for methods that can be used to restrict an attacker from making a lot of random oracle queries.

[3] We call a public-coin proof made non-interactive via the Fiat-Shamir transformation as a Fiat-Shamir (FS) protocol.

CDec for C. The VPDC ensures that any valid commitment-proof pair (C, π) can be (partially) decrypted using the (secret) trapdoor td output by CAddTd.

The above notion is similar to verifiable encryption except that C is not an encryption, but rather a commitment. The differences, as pointed out in the introduction, are as follows. First, a commitment scheme in general allows for a more *succinct* encoding of a message (i.e., can be compressing unlike an encryption) and is readily compatible with many existing proof systems (see, e.g., [2,3,9–12]), hence has a matching NIZK already available. Second, in a VPDC, there are two message spaces: (i) a *decryptable* message space $\mathcal{D}$, whose elements can be committed *and* recovered in decryption, and (ii) an *auxiliary* message space $\mathcal{U}$, whose elements can be used to create a commitment, but are not decryptable. As a result, a VPDC eliminates the need for an additional set of requirements due to an encryption scheme, avoids potential compatibility issues and enables partial decryption while still permitting a succinct encoding of the whole message (together with additional auxiliary terms). We therefore believe VPDCs can serve as an important building block in constructing *efficient* cryptographic schemes supporting accountability, such as group signatures, fair exchange protocols, key escrow and e-voting.

Generalized Analysis of Decryption Feasiblity for *relaxed* ZKPs. To address the first main technical challenge of handling relaxed ZKPs in decryption of VPDCs, we show how to abstract and generalize the decryption algorithm of [18] that works only for the specific Regev-based (UMC-like) encryption considered therein, to design an efficient decryption algorithm for *any* VPDC satisfying a few natural properties. In particular, the expected number of iterations until the decryption function terminates is about the number of random oracle queries made by the prover in generating the transcript to be decrypted as in [18]. Our general result is applicable to any VPDC whose underlying NIZK is derived via the Fiat-Shamir transform in the random oracle model from a Sigma protocol satisfying a variant of special soundness that is satisfied by all known instantiations of such Sigma protocols.

A Novel Gadget-Based Regev-Style Decryption for HMC. Building on the above general foundations, we construct a VPDC extending one of the most commonly used lattice-based commitment schemes, namely HMC[4]. For example, the HMC scheme is an integral part of one of the most efficient post-quantum ring signatures and set membership proofs in [11], arising from [9,12], as well as sublinear-sized arithmetic circuit satisfiability proofs in [2].

In particular, to address the second main technical challenge, we introduce an HMC-compatible trapdoor decryption method that works even when the decryptable message opening is proven to be in a set of exponential size (such as 2^{256}). We analyze this method in the setting of adversarially-created VPDC outputs and provide decryption soundness guarantees. As opposed to the trapdoor decryption of [12], where the trapdoor decryption yields $\langle y\boldsymbol{a}, \boldsymbol{m}\rangle + e$ for a *ran-*

[4] This distinguishes our VPDC construction from the verifiable encryption scheme of [18], that extends a UMC-type commitment scheme.

dom vector $\boldsymbol{a}$, small noise e and relaxation factor y (which is hard to decrypt), our new Regev-style partial trapdoor embeds a *structured* 'gadget' vector $\bar{t}\boldsymbol{g}$ in place of $\boldsymbol{a}$ in the HMC submatrix corresponding to the decryptable message. With this, trapdoor decryption of a commitment yields $\bar{t}y\langle \boldsymbol{g}, \boldsymbol{m}\rangle + e$ for a 'large' integer $\bar{t}$, which is efficiently decryptable by exploiting the structure of the gadget vector $\bar{t}\boldsymbol{g}$ using a rounding procedure similar to standard Regev decryption. The runtime of our new trapdoor decryption is polylogarithmic in the message space size $|\mathcal{D}|$ and we prove that it works correctly even against adversarially-generated commitments and ZKPs, as long as the system modulus q is sufficiently large and the message is proven to be a part of a decryptable message space $\mathcal{D}$.

Our lightweight Regev-style 'partial trapdoor' also avoids the heavyweight machinery of 'full' lattice trapdoors a-la [19], and still supports SIS-style HMC commitment, compatible with efficient ZKP techniques used in [9,12]. Using the 'full' trapdoors in [19] in our commitments (with ternary coordinate trapdoor vectors) requires SIS matrices with n rows and $m \geq n \log q$ columns over the underlying ring, while the 'partial trapdoor' commitments we use, $m = 2n$ columns are sufficient (still with ternary coordinate trapdoor vectors). We save a significant factor $\approx \log q$ in both public parameter length and the length of masked messages in the ZKP protocol, for the same security level.

MatRiCT-Au: Auditable RingCT Based on Standard Lattice Assumptions. As an application of our compact lattice-based VPDC, we show how it can enable an extension of the lattice-based RingCT-like private cryptocurrency protocol MatRiCT [12] easily and efficiently into an auditable variant we call MatRiCT-Au, where an auditor with access to a (secret) trapdoor can revoke the anonymity of certain users (e.g., in case of misbehaviour). The auditability feature can be optional (i.e., each user individually decides whether and by whom she wants to be audited) or enforced by a simple public check. Our construction allows *adversarially-generated* transactions to be audited, whereas, in [12], the discussion about auditability is incomplete, as the decryption method given there may fail in the adversarial transaction setting, potentially allowing adversaries to avoid auditability. Furthermore, the proposal in [12] requires an exhaustive-search-based approach while we can very efficiently run **Audit** function over a message space of size $> 2^{128}$. To analyze auditability formally in confidential transactions, we also extend the formal model for RingCT-like protocols in [12] to add the *auditability* property and prove formally that MatRiCT-Au is auditable. We compute concrete parameters for MatRiCT-Au and present implementation results[5]. Our evaluation demonstrates the practicality of MatRiCT-Au, and in particular there are very little communication and computation overheads introduced over the original MatRiCT protocol [12] as shown in Table 1 (see the full version of this paper for more run-time results).

We believe that our new techniques will find further applications in the settings where accountable anonymity is desired. Particularly, our extension of HMC into a VPDC with soundness against adversarially-created outputs

[5] The source code of our MatRiCT-Au implementation is available at https://gitlab.com/raykzhao/matrict_au.

Table 1. Comparison between MatRiCT [12] and MatRiCT-Au (this work).

Anonymity level		1/10		1/100	
# of inputs → # of outputs		1 → 2	2 → 2	1 → 2	2 → 2
Proof	MatRiCT [12]	93	110	103	120
Size	**MatRiCT-Au**	**96**	**113**	**106**	**123**
Spend/Verify	MatRiCT [12]	242/20	375/23	360/31	610/40
Runtimes	**MatRiCT-Au**	**233/21**	**414/25**	**402/33**	**654/42**
Parameters	MatRiCT [12]	PK Size: 4.36 KB	Moduli: $< 2^{53.0}$		
	MatRiCT-Au	PK Size: 4.36 KB	Moduli: $< 2^{55.3}$		

extends the group (or accountable ring) signature in [12] so as to enable *efficient* anonymity revocation (i.e., opening of a group signature) against *cheating* signers. Interesting research directions from here would be, for example, to design efficient post-quantum e-voting, auction and anonymous credential schemes by exploiting the accountable anonymity provided by our VPDC.

1.2 Our Results and Techniques

A Novel Gadget-Based Regev-Style Decryption for HMC. Suppose that we work over a cyclotomic ring $R_q = \mathbb{Z}_q[X]/(X^d + 1)$, and have a *binary* secret vector $\boldsymbol{b} \in \{0,1\}^v \subset R_q^v$ that forms the decryptable message to be recovered in decryption. As explained above, in a typical application protocol, we commit to this message $\boldsymbol{b}$ together with a non-decryptable message $\boldsymbol{u}$ as $C = \mathsf{Com}_{ck}(\boldsymbol{b}, \boldsymbol{u}; \boldsymbol{r})$ under some commitment randomness $\boldsymbol{r}$. The application protocol also proves knowledge of a *relaxed* opening of C (i.e., knowledge of $(y, \boldsymbol{b}', \boldsymbol{u}', \boldsymbol{r}')$ such that $yC = \mathsf{Com}_{ck}(y\boldsymbol{b}', \boldsymbol{u}'; \boldsymbol{r}')$ and $\boldsymbol{b}' \in \{0,1\}^v$). For simplicity, let us consider the case $y = 1$. After dealing with this case, we will discuss how we lift the restriction of $y = 1$ using our generalized decryption analysis results from Sect. 4.

The HMC commitment we use has the form $C = \mathsf{Com}_{ck}(\boldsymbol{b}, \boldsymbol{u}; \boldsymbol{r}) = \boldsymbol{A}\boldsymbol{r} + \boldsymbol{B}\boldsymbol{b} + \boldsymbol{C}\boldsymbol{u}$ and we recover the decrypted message as an element of R_t for some $t \geq 1$. To allow trapdoor decryption of $\boldsymbol{b}$, but not $\boldsymbol{r}$ and $\boldsymbol{u}$, our trapdoor key generation algorithm embeds a Regev-style '*gadget trapdoor*' into the last row $\boldsymbol{t}_B^\top$ of matrix $\boldsymbol{B}$ and a Regev-style '*error trapdoor*' into the last row $\boldsymbol{t}_A^\top$ (resp. $\boldsymbol{t}_C^\top$) of matrix $\boldsymbol{A}$ (resp. $\boldsymbol{C}$). That is, for the 'gadget trapdoor' matrix, we have $\boldsymbol{B} = \begin{pmatrix} \boldsymbol{B}' \\ \boldsymbol{t}_B^\top \end{pmatrix}$ with 'gadget trapdoor' row $\boldsymbol{t}_B^\top = \boldsymbol{s}'^\top \boldsymbol{B}' + \boldsymbol{e}_B^\top + \bar{t}\boldsymbol{g}^\top$, where $\bar{t} = \lfloor q/t \rfloor$, $\boldsymbol{e}_B$ is a short error, $\boldsymbol{s}'$ is a random secret, and $\boldsymbol{g}^\top$ is a 'gadget' vector with coordinates of the form $(2^i X^j)_{i<\tau, j<d}$ where $2^\tau \leq t$. While for the 'error trapdoor' matrices, we have $\boldsymbol{A} = \begin{pmatrix} \boldsymbol{A}' \\ \boldsymbol{t}_A^\top \end{pmatrix}$ and $\boldsymbol{C} = \begin{pmatrix} \boldsymbol{C}' \\ \boldsymbol{t}_C^\top \end{pmatrix}$ with 'error trapdoor' rows $\boldsymbol{t}_A^\top = \boldsymbol{s}'^\top \boldsymbol{A}' + \boldsymbol{e}_A^\top$ and $\boldsymbol{t}_C^\top = \boldsymbol{s}'^\top \boldsymbol{C}' + \boldsymbol{e}_C^\top$, where $\boldsymbol{e}_A, \boldsymbol{e}_C$ are short errors. Let $\boldsymbol{s}^\top = (-\boldsymbol{s}'^\top, 1)$ be the trapdoor. We remark that in the prior work [12], the matrix $\boldsymbol{B}$ was a random

SIS matrix with no decryption trapdoor, which led to an inefficient exhaustive search decryption over the message space.

Now, it is easy to observe that $C' := \langle \boldsymbol{s}, C\rangle = e + \langle \bar{t}\boldsymbol{g}, \boldsymbol{b}\rangle$, where $e := (\langle \boldsymbol{e}_A, \boldsymbol{r}\rangle + \langle \boldsymbol{e}_B, \boldsymbol{b}\rangle + \langle \boldsymbol{e}_C, \boldsymbol{u}\rangle)$ is a small error. Thanks to the structure of the gadget vector $\bar{t}\boldsymbol{g}^\top$, the integer coefficients of $\langle \bar{t}\boldsymbol{g}, \boldsymbol{b}\rangle$ are multiples of the large integer $\bar{t}$ and encode the bits of the decryptable message $\boldsymbol{b}$ in their binary representation. Thus, $\boldsymbol{b}$ can be recovered from C' in the decryption algorithm by rounding out the small error term e to a multiple of $\bar{t}$ and performing binary decomposition, whereas the non-decryptable message/randomness $\boldsymbol{u}, \boldsymbol{r}$ only contribute to the error term e.

To apply our gadget-based Regev-style decryption for HMC to adverserially-generated commitments with a relaxed proof of opening, we apply the general result of Theorem 1. To apply the latter theorem, we give a generalized decryption algorithm for our Regev-style HMC trapdoor and analyse (in Theorem 2 in Sect. 5.5) its correctness and soundness against (i) 'false rejection' decryption errors (where the algorithm fails to recover a decryptable message opening, even though the latter exists), as well as (ii) 'false acceptance' decryption errors (where the algorithm recovers a different decryptable message than the one in the valid opening), respectively. For (i), to recover the decryptable message $\boldsymbol{b}$ even for adverserial commitments C with a non-trivial relaxed opening $yC = \mathsf{Com}_{ck}(y\boldsymbol{b}, \boldsymbol{u}; \boldsymbol{r})$ with some short relaxation factor y, our decryption algorithm recovers $y\langle \boldsymbol{g}, \boldsymbol{b}\rangle \bmod t$ after rounding $\langle \boldsymbol{s}, yC\rangle$ to a multiple of $\bar{t}$, and we rely on invertibility of relaxation factors $y \bmod t$ to recover $\boldsymbol{b}$. For (ii), we show that a mildly larger choice of modulus q than needed for (i) guarantees that incorrect (non-unique) decryptable messages are never returned by our decryption algorithm, even with adverserial commitments/proofs and relaxation factors y.

We remark that the high-level structure of our HMC gadget-based Regev-style decryption trapdoor is similar to the full LWE inversion trapdoor of [19], but there are several important technical differences due to our HMC setting that are crucial to our scheme's efficiency and security. First, our use of the gadget during decryption is in some sense 'dual' to its use in [19]: in the LWE inversion problem considered in [19], the LWE secret $\boldsymbol{s}$ is assumed to be *uniformly random* mod q (rather than 'short'), so that trapdoor decryption yields $\boldsymbol{c} = \boldsymbol{G}\cdot\boldsymbol{s}+\boldsymbol{e}'$ for a gadget matrix $\boldsymbol{G}$ and short error vector $\boldsymbol{e}'$. Here, to efficiently recover the 'large' coordinate secret $\boldsymbol{s}$ from $\boldsymbol{c}$, the gadget matrix $\boldsymbol{G}$ is constructed to have $\log q$ powers of 2 (up to $q/2$) along each of its *columns* so that the mapping $\boldsymbol{s} \mapsto \boldsymbol{G}\cdot\boldsymbol{s}$ effectively performs *bit decomposition* of the coordinates of $\boldsymbol{s}$. This approach *expands* the dimension of $\boldsymbol{s}$ by a factor $\log q$ to allow recovery of each bit of each coordinate of $\boldsymbol{s}$ from the corresponding row of $\boldsymbol{G}\boldsymbol{s}$. Whereas in our 'dual' HMC decryption algorithm, the decryptable message $\boldsymbol{s}$ is binary (and hence 'short'), so that when our trapdoor decryption similarly yields $\boldsymbol{c} = \boldsymbol{G}\cdot\boldsymbol{s}+\boldsymbol{e}'$, we can choose the gadget matrix $\boldsymbol{G} = \boldsymbol{g}^\top$ to have powers of 2 along its *row* so that the mapping $\boldsymbol{s} \mapsto \boldsymbol{G}\cdot\boldsymbol{s}$ performs *binary reconstruction* of integers whose bits are the coordinates of $\boldsymbol{s}$. Our approach *compresses* the dimension of $\boldsymbol{s}$ to a single element over the underlying ring, and minimises the dimension of the underlying matrices/commitments. Hence, our algorithm can also be viewed as a more efficient inversion trapdoor for LWE in 'dual' *knapsack* form ($\boldsymbol{c} = \boldsymbol{B}\boldsymbol{b}$ for 'short' $\boldsymbol{b}$ and 'fat' $\boldsymbol{B}$) rather than the more usual 'primal' form ($\boldsymbol{c} = \boldsymbol{A}\boldsymbol{s} + \boldsymbol{e}$ for 'short' $\boldsymbol{e}$ and 'tall' $\boldsymbol{A}$) addressed in [19]. A second difference from [19] is our use of *error trapdoors* for the HMC submatrices corresponding to non-decryptable message/randomness. And thirdly, as outlined above, our decryption algorithm analysis handles the adverserial commitment case with relaxed opening proofs, whereas [19] only analyses decryption for honestly created LWE samples.

MatRiCT-Au Application. To show the usefulness of our novel decryption method in practice, we apply it in the setting of MatRiCT [12]. In MatRiCT, a commitment B encodes (i) an index in binary form that identifies the real user creating the transaction, and (ii) the bits of the transaction amount. Therefore, we can apply our novel decryption method to decrypt this commitment. Overall, in addition to revoking the anonymity, we can enable an auditor to recover the hidden transaction amount. This is similar in spirit to traceable range proofs [15] (though the techniques are completely different).

Recently, a newer version of MatRiCT was published in [11]. Our techniques apply also to this newer version, called MatRiCT^{+}, and the overhead of extending MatRiCT^{+} to support auditability is just an increase of about 20% in proof size. We discuss further details in the full version of this paper.

Organization of the Paper. Section 2 covers preliminaries. We introduce the formal definitions of a VPDC in Sect. 3. Our generalized analysis of decryption runtime for relaxed ZKPs is introduced in Sect. 4. Then, in Sect. 5, we provide, along with the ordinary HMC scheme, the details of our new lattice-based VPDC, its decryption algorithm, and its adversarial soundness and run-time analyses. We discuss how VPDC can be used to construct MatRiCT-Au in Sect. 6 and, due to limited space, provide the full details relating to MatRiCT-Au in the full version of this paper on IACR's ePrint archive. Particularly, our extended formal model for RingCT-like protocols, the full description of MatRiCT-Au (including parameter setting and implementation details), and the security discussions of MatRiCT-Au are provided in the full version.

2 Preliminaries

For an odd modulus q, the ring of integers modulo q, $\mathbb{Z}_q = \mathbb{Z}/q\mathbb{Z}$, is represented by the range $\left[-\frac{q-1}{2}, \frac{q-1}{2}\right]$. To denote column vectors and matrices, we use bold-face lower-case letters such as $\boldsymbol{x}$ and bold-face capital letters such as $\boldsymbol{V}$, respectively (hence, $\boldsymbol{x}^\top$ denotes a row vector). $(\boldsymbol{x}, \boldsymbol{y})$ is used to denote concatenation of the two vectors $\boldsymbol{x}$ and $\boldsymbol{y}$ to form a single longer vector. For a vector $\boldsymbol{x} = (x_0, \ldots, x_{n-1})$, we define the following norms $\|\boldsymbol{x}\| = \sqrt{\sum_{i=0}^{n-1} x_i^2}$, $\|\boldsymbol{x}\|_\infty = \max_i |x_i|$ and $\|\boldsymbol{x}\|_1 = \sum_{i=0}^{n-1} |x_i|$. When considering a norm of a polynomial f, we define the same norms on the coefficient vector of f. For a vector $\boldsymbol{f} = (f_0, \ldots, f_{s-1})$ of polynomials, we further define $\|\boldsymbol{f}\| = \sqrt{\sum_{i=0}^{s-1} \|f_i\|^2}$,

$\|\boldsymbol{f}\|_1 = \sum_{i=0}^{s-1} \|f_i\|_1$, $\|\boldsymbol{f}\|_\infty = \max_i \|f_i\|_\infty$. The Hamming weight of the (concatenated) coefficient vector of $\boldsymbol{f}$ is denoted by $\mathsf{HW}(\boldsymbol{f})$. $\mathcal{U}(S)$ denotes uniform distribution on a set S.

Capital letters such as C denote commitments, and we write $\mathcal{S}^{d \cdot k}$ when a total of kd coefficients are sampled from a set $\mathcal{S}$ in order to generate k polynomials in $R = \mathbb{Z}[X]/(X^d + 1)$ of a power-of-2 degree d. $\mathbb{S}_{\mathcal{B}}$ denotes the set of polynomials in R, where each coefficient has an absolute value bounded by $\mathcal{B} \in \mathbb{Z}^+$.

2.1 Security Assumptions

In our applications, we use a commitment scheme whose security relies on the following well-known lattice problems.

Definition 1 (M-SIS$_{n,m,q,\beta_{SIS}}$). *Given $\boldsymbol{A} \leftarrow R_q^{n \times m}$ sampled uniformly at random, the Module-SIS (M-SIS) problem asks to find a* short *$\boldsymbol{x} \in R_q^m$ such that $\boldsymbol{A}\boldsymbol{x} = \boldsymbol{0}$ over R_q and $0 < \|\boldsymbol{x}\| \le \beta_{SIS}$.*

Definition 2 (M-LWE$_{n,m,q,\mathcal{B}}$). *The Module-LWE (M-LWE) problem asks to distinguish between the following two cases: (i) $(\boldsymbol{A}, \boldsymbol{A}\boldsymbol{s} + \boldsymbol{e})$ for $\boldsymbol{A} \leftarrow R_q^{m \times n}$, a secret vector $\boldsymbol{s} \leftarrow \mathbb{S}_{\mathcal{B}}^n$ and an error vector $\boldsymbol{e} \leftarrow \mathbb{S}_{\mathcal{B}}^m$, and (ii) $(\boldsymbol{A}, \boldsymbol{t})$ for $\boldsymbol{A} \leftarrow R_q^{m \times n}$ and $\boldsymbol{t} \leftarrow R_q^m$.*

It is known that the secret $\boldsymbol{s}$ can equivalently be sampled from $\mathcal{U}(R_q^n)$.

2.2 Zero-Knowledge Proofs

A Relaxed NIZK $\Sigma = (\mathsf{K}, \mathsf{P}, \mathsf{V})$ for relation R_σ and its relaxed counterpart R'_σ with $\mathsf{R}_\sigma \subseteq \mathsf{R}'_\sigma$ (parameterized by a common reference string σ) and their corresponding languages $L_\sigma = \{u : \exists r \text{ s.t. } (u, r) \in \mathsf{R}_\sigma\}$ and $L'_\sigma = \{u : \exists r \text{ s.t. } (u, r) \in \mathsf{R}'_\sigma\}$ respectively, consists of the following algorithms (here, u denotes a language member and r denotes a witness):

$\sigma \leftarrow \mathsf{K}(1^\lambda)$: is the PPT common reference string generation algorithm of Σ that outputs a common reference string σ.

$\pi \leftarrow \mathsf{P}^{\mathcal{H}}(\sigma, u, r)$: is the PPT prover algorithm of Σ that, given a common reference string σ, access to a random oracle $\mathcal{H}$ and a language member u and a witness r with $(u, r) \in \mathsf{R}_\sigma$, outputs a proof π.

$0/1 \leftarrow \mathsf{V}^{\mathcal{H}}(\sigma, u, \pi)$: is the PPT verification algorithm of Σ that, given a common reference string σ, access to a random oracle $\mathcal{H}$ and a language member u and proof π, outputs 0 (invalid) or 1 (valid).

We remark that our lattice-based constructions regard the commitment key as part of the CRS σ (a similar issue arises in both DL-based Pedersen and lattice-based commitments). We refer to the full version of this paper for the standard definitions of completeness, soundness and zero-knowledge for NIZK proofs.

Our VDPC construction is based on a NIZK obtained using the Fiat-Shamir (FS) transform [13] applied to an interactive Zero-Knowledge Sigma protocol $\Sigma_{\mathsf{I}} = (\mathsf{K}_{\mathsf{I}}, \mathsf{P}_{\mathsf{I}}, \mathsf{V}_{\mathsf{I}})$ for relations $\mathsf{R}_\sigma, \mathsf{R}'_\sigma$ (parameterised by a common reference string σ) with a challenge space $\mathcal{C}$ and public-private inputs (u, r) with same notations for relations as above. We refer to the full version of this paper for the standard definitions of completeness, special soundness and honest-verifier zero-knowledge for Sigma protocols. The FS heuristic transforms Σ_{I} into a NIZK using a random oracle $\mathcal{H}$, by letting the prove algorithm compute the verifier's challenge from the common reference string σ, public input u, and commitment message w, setting $x = \mathcal{H}(\sigma, u, w)$.

2.3 Commitment Schemes

A commitment scheme $\mathsf{C} = (\mathsf{CKeygen}, \mathsf{Commit}, \mathsf{COpen})$ consists of three algorithms:

$pp = (ck, \mathcal{M}, \mathcal{R}) \leftarrow \mathsf{CKeygen}(1^\lambda)$: is a PPT key generation algorithm returning pp containing a commitment key ck and descriptions of message space $\mathcal{M}$ and randomness space $\mathcal{R}$. Note pp is an implicit input to the remaining algorithms.

$(C, \mathsf{o}) \leftarrow \mathsf{Commit}(\mathsf{m})$: is a PPT commitment algorithm which for message $\mathsf{m} \in \mathcal{M}$, outputs a commitment C to m together with an opening o.

$0/1 \leftarrow \mathsf{COpen}(C, \mathsf{o})$: is a deterministic poly-time opening algorithm that given commitment C and opening o, checks whether o is a valid opening of C.

An opening o of a commitment is a tuple containing a message m, randomness r, and possibly also relaxation factors used by the opening algorithm (e.g., the relaxation factor y used in the lattice-based HMC commmitment in Sect. 5.1). We write $\mathsf{m}(\mathsf{o})$ to denote the message part of opening o. We refer to the full version of this paper for standard definitions of correctness, hiding and binding properties of commitment schemes.

3 VPDC: Verifiable Partially-Decryptable Commitments

A VPDC is an extension of two building blocks: (1) a (non-decryptable) commitment scheme C, and (2) a NIZK relaxed proof of opening protocol Σ for C. The VPDC adds a new trapdoor key generation algorithm CAddTd to embed a hidden partial decryption trapdoor td in the commitment key of C, such that with this trapdoor, efficient partial decryption of commitments accompanied by a valid relaxed proof of opening is possible, using the VPDC's partial decryption algorithm CDec. In particular, for VPDC, we view the commitment scheme's message space $\mathcal{M}$ as the product of two sets $\mathcal{D}$ and $\mathcal{U}$, where $\mathcal{D}$ is the *decryptable* message space and $\mathcal{U}$ is the *auxiliary* message space. For a commitment opening o, we let $\mu(\mathsf{o})$ denote the decryptable message part of o.

Formally, a Verifiable Partially-Decryptable Commitment scheme $\mathsf{VPDC} = (\mathsf{C}, \Sigma, \mathsf{CAddTd}, \mathsf{CDec})$ consists of a (non-decryptable) commitment scheme $\mathsf{C} =$

$(\mathsf{CKeygen}, \mathsf{Commit}, \mathsf{COpen})$ with message space $\mathcal{M} = \mathcal{D} \times \mathcal{U}$ (the decryptable message space $\mathcal{D}$ and auxiliary message space $\mathcal{U}$ respectively), and a *matching* NIZK relaxed proof of opening protocol $\Sigma = (\mathsf{K}, \mathsf{P}, \mathsf{V})$ for C, a trapdoor key generation algorithm CAddTd and a partial decryption algorithm CDec.

We say that the underlying NIZK Σ is a *matching* NIZK relaxed proof of opening for C if:

- On input 1^λ, the CRS generation algorithm K returns a CRS of the form $\sigma = (pp, \sigma')$, where $pp = (ck, \mathcal{M}, \mathcal{R})$ is C's public parameters $pp \leftarrow \mathsf{CKeygen}(1^\lambda)$. (i.e. Σ has pp in its CRS).
- Σ satisfies the standard completeness, soundness and zero-knowledge properties with respect to the following commitment opening relations $\mathsf{R}_{\mathsf{C},pp} \subseteq \mathsf{R}'_{\mathsf{C},pp}$ (parameterised by the commitment key pp from the CRS):

$$\mathsf{R}_{\mathsf{C},pp} = \{(C, \mathsf{o}) : \exists(\mathsf{m}, r) \in (\mathcal{M} \times \mathcal{R}) \text{ with } (C, \mathsf{o}) = \mathsf{Commit}(m; r)\}$$

and

$$\mathsf{R}'_{\mathsf{C},pp} \subseteq \mathsf{R}^{\mathsf{COpen}}_{\mathsf{C},pp} := \{(C, \mathsf{o}) : \mathsf{COpen}(C, \mathsf{o}) = 1\}.$$

In addition to the algorithms $(\mathsf{CKeygen}, \mathsf{Commit}, \mathsf{COpen})$ of C and the algorithms $(\mathsf{K}, \mathsf{P}, \mathsf{V})$ of Σ, VPDC adds two new algorithms to enable decryptability, with the following syntax:

$(ck^{\mathsf{td}}, \mathsf{td}) \leftarrow \mathsf{CAddTd}(ck, \mathcal{D}, \mathcal{U})$: a PPT algorithm that on input a commitment key ck and a description of the decryptable and auxiliary message spaces $\mathcal{D}$ and $\mathcal{U}$ such that $\mathcal{M} = \mathcal{D} \times \mathcal{U}$, outputs a 'trapdoored' commitment key ck^{td} and a partial decryption trapdoor td.

$\mu' \leftarrow \mathsf{CDec}_{\mathsf{td}}(C, \pi)$: is a probabilistic algorithm that on input a commitment C with a corresponding proof π and a trapdoor td, outputs a message $\mu' \in \mathcal{D}$.

We now list several additional properties for a VPDC, all of which are enjoyed by our construction:

Succinctness: The bit length of the commitment should depend only polylogarithmically on the bit length of the auxiliary message.[6]

Additive Homomorphism: The commitment message and randomness spaces are subsets of modules with operations $(+, \cdot)$ over some underlying scalar ring $\mathfrak{R}$, the commitment space is a subset of a module with operations $(\oplus, \otimes)$ over $\mathfrak{R}$, and there exists a set $S \subseteq \mathfrak{R}$ of scalars, such that for all messages $\mathsf{m}_1, \mathsf{m}_2 \in \mathcal{M}$, randomness $r_1, r_2 \in \mathcal{R}$ and scalar $\alpha \in S$, we have $C = \alpha \otimes C_1 \oplus C_2$ for $(C, \cdot) := \mathsf{Commit}(\alpha \cdot \mathsf{m}_1 + \mathsf{m}_2; \alpha \cdot r_1 + r_2)$, $(C_1, \cdot) := \mathsf{Commit}(\mathsf{m}_1; r_1)$ and $(C_2, \cdot) := \mathsf{Commit}(\mathsf{m}_2; r_2)$.

Small Integer Decryptable Message Space: The decryptable message space $\mathcal{D} \subset \mathfrak{R}^v$ is of the form $\mathcal{D} := Z_{\mathcal{B}}^v$, where $Z_{\mathcal{B}} \subseteq \mathbb{Z}$ is a set of *integers* of small maximum absolute value $\mathcal{B} = \lambda^{o(1)}$, and v is the decryptable message dimension over the underlying scalar ring $\mathfrak{R}$.

[6] Note that succinctness cannot be achieved for the *decryptable* message.

The succinctness property is essential for the efficient application of our VPDC in ZKPs. For our concrete VPDC construction, $\mathcal{U}$ is a much bigger set than $\mathcal{D}$. Thus, one can commit to auxiliary terms together with the target message to be decrypted under a single succinct commitment to save significant communication thanks to the commitment's compression feature (which is not available in encryption-based commitments). Here, we stress that *partial* decryption (as opposed to *full* decryption) is an important feature, not a drawback. If we required full decryption, then we would not be able to achieve succinctness. Similarly, the additively homomorphic property is needed to support efficient (e.g., 'Schnorr-like' [22]) ZKPs that rely on this property. Note that such a homomorphism is needed also for the non-decryptable message parts. This precludes a simple VPDC solution that would commit by hashing the auxiliary message part with a non-homomorphic collision-resistant hash function. The 'Small Integer Decryptable Message Space' property is required to efficiently support certain classes of ZK proofs needed in applications, such as the binary proofs, range proofs and 1-out-of-N proofs in [9,12,14]. Here, the fact that the message coordinates are integers, rather than general ring elements, allows for independent manipulation of the committed decryptable message coordinates (e.g., for computing an integer vector inner-product or independent evaluation of a quadratic function on all message coordinates) as needed in the verification of such ZK proofs. Their smallness bound (size $\mathcal{B} = \lambda^{o(1)}$) allows the length of such proofs to be kept short.

It is important to note that our VPDC model allows all of the following three properties *together* within the same environment:

- one can commit to any message in $\mathcal{M}$, where decryption is (computationally) infeasible. Such commitments are simply ordinary commitments and in this case, the commitment key ck should be used.
- one can commit to any message μ in $\mathcal{D}$ together with an auxiliary message in $\mathcal{U}$, where recovery of μ is possible using td. In this case, the commitment key ck^{td} should be used.
- one can commit to any message in $\mathcal{M}$, where decryption is not necessarily needed. Here, both commitment keys ck or ck^{td} can be used and commitments created this way are easily compatible with the rest of the protocol.

We require that C satisfies the standard correctness, hiding and binding properties of commitment schemes. Furthermore, we recall that NIZK proof Σ is required to be a matching NIZK for C (see above), and so satisfies the completeness, (relaxed) soundness and zero-knowledge properties for relations $(\mathsf{R}_{\mathsf{C},pp}, \mathsf{R}'_{\mathsf{C},pp})$ defined above.

In addition, as a partially-decryptable extension of a given commitment scheme C and matching ZK proof Σ, we would like the VPDC's trapdoor key generation algorithm for C to preserve the functionality and security properties of C and Σ. Accordingly, we say that C (resp. Σ) satisfies the *VPDC trapdoor key variants* of correctness, hiding, and binding properties for C (respectively, the trapdoor key variants of completeness, (relaxed) soundness and zero-knowledge for Σ) if the properties are still satisfied when the commitment key generation calls $pp = (ck, \mathcal{M}, \mathcal{R}) \leftarrow \mathsf{CKeygen}$ in C (resp. its call in K of Σ) are followed by the trapdoor commitment key generation calls $(ck^{\mathsf{td}}, \mathsf{td}) \leftarrow \mathsf{CAddTd}(ck)$ and $pp' = (ck^{\mathsf{td}}, \mathcal{M}, \mathcal{R})$ replaces pp. For ease of reference, we define from hereon $(ck^{\mathsf{td}}, \mathsf{td}, \mathcal{M}, \mathcal{R}) \leftarrow \mathsf{CKeygenTd}(1^\lambda)$ as the function that runs $(ck, \mathcal{M}, \mathcal{R}) \leftarrow \mathsf{CKeygen}(1^\lambda)$ and $(ck^{\mathsf{td}}, \mathsf{td}) \leftarrow \mathsf{CAddTd}(ck)$, and returns $(ck^{\mathsf{td}}, \mathsf{td}, \mathcal{M}, \mathcal{R})$. The following commitment Key Indistinguishability property for a VPDC suffices for this purpose (see Proposition 1).

Key Indistinguishability. A VPDC scheme is said to satisfy *key indistinguishability* if any PPT adversary $\mathcal{A}$ wins the following game with probability $1/2 + \text{negl}(\lambda)$:

1. $pp_0 = (ck, \mathcal{M}, \mathcal{R}) \leftarrow \mathsf{CKeygen}(1^\lambda)$,
2. $pp_1 \leftarrow (ck^{\mathsf{td}}, \mathcal{M}, \mathcal{R})$, where $(ck^{\mathsf{td}}, \mathsf{td}) \leftarrow \mathsf{CAddTd}(ck)$.
3. $b \xleftarrow{\$} \{0, 1\}$,
4. $b' \leftarrow \mathcal{A}(pp_b)$.
5. $\mathcal{A}$ wins the game if $b' = b$.

The following proposition is immediate from the fact that the trapdoor key td does not appear in the view of the adversary in the security games defining the trapdoor key variants of the C and Σ properties. Therefore, by key indistinguishability, any attack against the VPDC trapdoor key variant properties of C (resp. Σ) would imply a corresponding attack contradicting the assumed (non trapdoor key variant) property of C (resp. Σ).

Proposition 1. *If a VPDC scheme* $\mathsf{VPDC} = (\mathsf{C}, \Sigma, \mathit{CAddTd}, \mathit{CDec})$ *satisfies key indistinguishability, then* C *(resp.* Σ*) satisfies the* VPDC *trapdoor key variants of correctness, hiding, and binding properties for* C *(respectively, the* VPDC *trapdoor key variants of completeness, (relaxed) soundness and zero-knowledge for* Σ*).*

In some applications, it is desirable to strengthen the binding requirement for the VDPC so it holds even against attackers that are given the partial decryption trapdoor key td (e.g. in our blockchain application as we do not want auditors to create fake proofs). We call this requirement *trapdoor-binding.*

Trapdoor-Binding. A VPDC is *(computationally) trapdoor-binding* if, for $(pp, \mathsf{td}) \leftarrow \mathsf{CKeygenTd}(1^\lambda)$, the following probability (over the randomness of PPT $\mathcal{A}$ and $\mathsf{CKeygen}$) is negligible

$$\Pr[(C, \mathsf{o}, \mathsf{o}') \leftarrow \mathcal{A}(pp, \mathsf{td}) : \mathsf{m}(\mathsf{o}) \neq \mathsf{m}'(\mathsf{o}) \wedge \mathsf{COpen}(C, \mathsf{o}) = \mathsf{COpen}(C, \mathsf{o}') = 1].$$

We capture the decryptability requirements for VPDC by the *Decryption Soundness* and *Decryption Feasibility* properties defined as follows.

Decryption Soundness. A VPDC scheme is said to satisfy *Decryption Soundness* if any PPT adversary wins the following `Exp:Soundness` game with $\text{negl}(\lambda)$ probability.

1. $P := (ck^{\mathsf{td}}, \mathsf{td}, \mathcal{M}, \mathcal{R}) \leftarrow \mathsf{CKeygenTd}(1^\lambda)$
2. $(C, \pi) \leftarrow \mathcal{A}(P)$,
3. $b \leftarrow \mathsf{V}_{ck^{\mathsf{td}}}(C, \pi)$,
4. $\mu' \leftarrow \mathsf{CDec}_{\mathsf{td}}(C, \pi)$.

$\mathcal{A}$ wins the game if $b = 1$ and one of the following conditions holds

(i) There exists no opening o such that $\mathsf{COpen}(C, \mathsf{o}) = 1$, or
(ii) There exists an opening o such that $\mathsf{COpen}(C, \mathsf{o}) = 1$ and $\mu(\mathsf{o}) \neq \mu'$.

Decryption Feasibility. A VPDC scheme is said to satisfy *Decryption Feasibility* if, for any $\alpha \geq 1$ and any PPT adversary $\mathcal{A}$, if $b = 1$ in Step 3 of game `Exp:Soundness` above, the running time of $\mathsf{CDec}_{\mathsf{td}}(C, \pi)$ in Step 4 of game `Exp:Soundness` is at most $\alpha \cdot T_{\mathcal{A}} \cdot \mathrm{poly}(\lambda)$, except with probability $\leq \frac{1}{\alpha} + \mathrm{poly}\left(\frac{T_{\mathcal{A}}}{2^\lambda}\right)$, where $T_{\mathcal{A}}$ is the runtime of $\mathcal{A}$.

Remark 1 (Decryption Soundness). The decryption soundness property captures the informal requirement that it should be infeasible for an attacker to output a maliciously-created commitment and proof (C, π) that passes the V verification check, but where C cannot be decrypted into the correct decryptable message μ using the trapdoor decryption algorithm $\mathsf{CDec}_{\mathsf{td}}$. The latter may occur either because of the non-existence of a decryptable message opening (case i), or because of the existence multiple decryptable message openings that may cause a 'false accept' decryption error (case ii).

Remark 2 (Decryption Feasibility). The decryption feasibility requirement captures the property that the decryption algorithm does not run for 'too long'. Here, a too long decryption time corresponds to exceeding the attacker runtime by a super-polynomial factor. Jumping ahead to our construction, similarly to [18], this attacker time corresponds to the number of queries made by the attacker to a certain random oracle. Such a runtime as given in our decryption feasibility definition (arising from our results generalizing those of [18]) is currently the best one can achieve for relaxed proofs, where the relaxation factor is unknown to the decryptor.

There are examples of VPDC-like constructions in the literature satisfying some but not all of our desired properties. For example, the proofs of plaintext knowledge in general are an example, where the commitment is an encryption scheme and $\mathcal{U} = \emptyset$. For a lattice-based construction, one may see the discussions in [18, Section 3.3] and [7]. The "extractable" commitment scheme in [12] is another (weaker) example, where the decryption soundness holds only against *honest* provers and decryption runtime is linear in $|\mathcal{D}|$. The main motivation for our VPDC notion is that we want the additional properties of succinctness (i.e., C should be compressing, which is not possible for encryption) and decryption feasibility and soundness against *cheating* provers. These properties are achieved by our concrete construction $\mathsf{VPDC}_{\mathsf{HMC}}$ (Sect. 5).

4 Generalized Decryption Feasibility for Relaxed Proofs

In this section, we study the decryption algorithms for relaxed NIZK proofs and show a general result on the Partial-Decryption Feasibility of any VPDC in which the underlying NIZK Σ is derived from a suitable interactive Sigma protocol Σ_I using the Fiat-Shamir (FS) transform. Our result generalizes previous results of [18]. The discussion is kept abstract in this section to preserve the generality of our results. Our concrete lattice-based instantiation of decryption algorithms is given in the next section.

The questions we focus on are as follows. If one is given a valid transcript $\mathsf{tr} = (C, w, x, z)$ for Σ and a trapdoor td that enables recovering a message from a *well-formed* commitment of the form $\bar{x}C$ for an *unknown* relaxed opening factor $\bar{x}$ (also known as a relaxation factor) and a known commitment C, how should one precisely design the overall decryption algorithm? Moreover, what is the *expected* number of iterations until the decryption algorithm terminates?

To answer these questions, we prove the general result in Theorem 1 below for the generic decryption algorithm given in Algorithm 1. This approach first allows us to put our decryption methodology into a general framework. Then, we identify the connections between the components of Algorithm 1 that must be satisfied so that the decryption runs in polynomial time. As the result can be applied to *any* suitable functions F, Rec, V' in Algorithm 1, we can use this result to analyze the run-time of different decryption methods. Besides the Partial-Decryption Feasibility, there is, of course, also the Partial-Decryption Soundness aspect that depends on the concrete instantiation of CDec, which will be analyzed in the next section.

Our Partial-Decryption Feasibility result applies to VPDCs in which the underlying NIZK Σ is derived via the FS transform from an interactive Sigma protocol with the following mild variant of the special soundness property, that we call *existential special-soundness*. This property relaxes the standard PPT efficiency requirement for extractor $\mathcal{E}$, but requires that the extracted witness contains a component (relaxation factor $\bar{x} = x - x'$ in Schnorr-like protocols) depending on only the two input transcript challenges via a poly-time computable function F (the latter syntactic requirement is used in our decryption compatibility definition below). Therefore, the existential special-soundness is directly implied by the standard special-soundness property for a large class of known Schnorr-like Sigma protocols, in which $\mathcal{E}$ is efficient, and $F(x, x') = x - x'$.

Definition 3 (Existential Special-Soundness). *We say that a Sigma protocol* $\Sigma_\mathsf{I} = (\mathsf{K_I}, \mathsf{P_I}, \mathsf{V_I})$ *for relations* $\mathsf{R}_{\mathsf{C},pp}, \mathsf{R}'_{\mathsf{C},pp}$ *(parameterised by a common reference string pp) with a challenge space* $\mathcal{C}$ *and public-private inputs* (C, o), *satisfies* existential special-soundness *if the following holds.*

- ***Existential special-soundness:*** *There exists an* extractor $\mathcal{E}$ *and a deterministic poly-time algorithm* F *such that, given* $(pp, \sigma') \leftarrow \mathsf{K_I}(1^\lambda)$ *and two accepting protocol transcripts* $\mathsf{tr} = (C, w, x, z)$ *and* $\mathsf{tr}' = (C, w, x', z')$ *with* $x \neq x'$, *computes an extracted witness of the form* $\bar{\mathsf{o}} = (\bar{x}, \bar{\mathsf{o}}')$ *where*

Algorithm 1. $\mathsf{CDec_{td}}(\mathsf{tr})$

INPUT: $\mathsf{tr} = (C, \pi = (w, x, z))$ Σ_I protocol transcript; td trapdoor
OUTPUT: (m', x') such that $V'(m') = 1$ for some validity check V'

```
1: loop
2:     x' ←$ C                        ▷ Choose a random challenge
3:     x̄ = F(x, x')                   ▷ F(x, x') = x − x' for 2-sound FS proofs
4:     m' = Rec(x̄, tr, td)            ▷ Tries to decrypt a well-formed commitment
5:     if V'(m') = 1 then             ▷ Check if the recovered message is "valid"
6:         return (m', x')
7:     end if
8: end loop
```

$\bar{x} = F(x, x')$, satisfying $(C, \bar{\mathsf{o}}) \in \mathsf{R}'_{\mathsf{C},pp}$ with probability $1 - negl(\lambda)$ over the choice of σ.

The following definition captures the properties of a decryption algorithm CDec that are sufficient to ensure it terminates in feasible time, if the underlying Sigma protocol Σ_I satisfies existential special-soundness.

Definition 4 (Compatible *CDec***).** *Let* $\mathsf{VPDC} = (\mathsf{C}, \Sigma, \mathit{CAddTd}, \mathit{CDec})$ *with* Σ *a matching NIZK relaxed proof of opening for* C*, and* Σ *is obtained from a Sigma protocol* Σ_I *using the Fiat-Shamir transform.*

We say that CDec is compatible *with* Σ *if it satisfies the following properties:*

P$_1$: *CDec has a structure as in Algorithm 1, where* Rec *is a PPT algorithm.*
P$_2$: *On input* td *(generated by running* $(ck^{\mathsf{td}}, \mathsf{td}, \mathcal{M}, \mathcal{R}) \leftarrow \mathit{CKeygenTd}(1^\lambda)$*) and any* tr*, if, for some loop iteration, Step 3 of CDec computes a "good"* $\bar{x}$ *(such that there exists an opening of the form* $\bar{\mathsf{o}} = (\bar{x}, \bar{\mathsf{o}}')$ *satisfying* $(C, \bar{\mathsf{o}}) \in \mathsf{R}'_{\mathsf{C},pp}$*), then CDec terminates in this loop iteration, i.e.* Rec *recovers a message* m' *deemed "valid" by* $V'(m') = 1$.

The function Rec in Algorithm 1 is a procedure that recovers the message from a well-formed commitment and will be instantiated depending on our decryption method. One may imagine it being similar to the decryption of Regev encryption scheme. However, the Rec function always returns a message m' that may simply be useless. Therefore, there is an additional check V' to make sure that the given message is "valid" (where "valid" is protocol-dependent).

Theorem 1 below shows that the only task required to use our results is to design a compatible decryption algorithm as in Definition 4 (as existential special-soundness is implied by special-soundness). In essence, this task itself reduces to making sure that the message recovery algorithm Rec returns a "valid" message from any given "good" $\bar{x}$ for the relaxed relation $\mathsf{R}'_{\mathsf{C},pp}$. In the next section, we will show how our VPDC allows the recovery of the *same* message used to create the proof transcript.

To make it easier to read Theorem 1, let us interpret it in the case of 'Schnorr-like' FS proofs that work as follows. For a homomorphic commitment Commit (we use additive notation as it is the case in the lattice setting), let $C = \mathsf{Commit}(r)$ be an input commitment whose opening the prover wants to prove knowledge of. The prover computes a 'masking' commitment $w = \mathsf{Commit}(\rho)$ for some masking value ρ. Then, she computes a challenge $x \leftarrow \mathcal{H}(pp, C, w)$, followed by a response $z = \rho + x \cdot r$, where r is the prover's witness. The verification V in this case checks $w + x \cdot C \stackrel{?}{=} \mathsf{Commit}(z)$. It is easy to see from here that this proof has the '2-soundness' property, i.e., a *knowledge extractor* can extract a (relaxed) opening of C given two 'rewinded' accepting transcripts with distinct challenges. In particular, given accepting (C, w, x, z) and (C, w, x', z') with $x \neq x'$, we have $\bar{x}C = \mathsf{Commit}(\bar{z})$ for $\bar{x} := x - x'$ and $\bar{z} := z - z'$. Therefore, the concrete functions in this case are $F(x, x') = x - x'$ and $(C, (\bar{x}, \bar{z})) \in \mathsf{R}'_{\mathsf{C},pp}$ iff $\bar{x}C = \mathsf{Commit}(\bar{z})$, i.e., $\mathsf{R}'_{\mathsf{C},pp}$ in Theorem 1 corresponds to the *relaxed* commitment opening relation $\mathsf{COpen}(C, (\bar{x}, \bar{m}, \bar{r}))$ where $\bar{z} = (\bar{m}, \bar{r})$. Here, $(\bar{x}, \bar{z})$ serves as an *extracted* witness/opening for C. It is easy to see that the existential special-soundness property follows from the special-soundness of the 'Schnorr-like' protocol. Although in the setting of the Schnorr proof of knowledge of discrete-log [22], one may further recover an *exact* opening of u by computing $\bar{z}/\bar{x}$, this approach does not work in the lattice variants [16,17] as $\bar{z}/\bar{x}$ must be *short* (relative to the system modulus q), which cannot be guaranteed unless some costly measures are implemented[7].

Theorem 1. *Let* $\mathsf{VPDC} = (\mathsf{C}, \Sigma, \mathit{CAddTd}, \mathit{CDec})$ *with* Σ *a matching NIZK relaxed proof of opening for* C*, and* Σ *is obtained from a Sigma protocol* Σ_{I} *using the Fiat-Shamir transform with random oracle* $\mathcal{H} : \{0,1\}^* \to \mathcal{C}$.

If Σ_{I} *satisfies Existential Special Soundness (Definition 3),* CDec *is compatible with* Σ *(Definition 4) and* $|\mathcal{C}| \geq 2^\lambda$*, then* VPDC *satisfies Decryption Feasibility.*

Concretely, let $\hat{H}$ *and* $\hat{D}$ *be the random coins of* $\mathcal{H}$ *and* CDec*, respectively, and* T *be the number of loop iterations in the execution of* CDec *in Step 6 of game* **Exp:Soundness** *when* $b = 1$*. Then, for any* $\mathcal{A}$ *that makes at most* $q_H - 1$ *queries to* $\mathcal{H}$ *and any positive* α,

$$\Pr_{\hat{H},\hat{D}}\left[T \geq \alpha \cdot q_H\right] \leq \frac{1}{\alpha} + 2 \cdot \sqrt{\frac{q_H}{\alpha \cdot |\mathcal{C}|}} + \frac{q_H}{|\mathcal{C}|}. \tag{2}$$

Proof (Theorem 1). The proof follows essentially the same blueprint as in the proof of [18, Lemma 3.2], but we show precisely where the properties in the theorem statement are needed.

Let pp be some public parameters. For a given $\mathsf{tr} = (C, w, x, z)$ of Σ_{I}, define the set of "good" challenges $\mathcal{G}_{\mathsf{tr}}$ as follows

$$\mathcal{G}_{\mathsf{tr}} = \{\, x' \in \mathcal{C} \;:\; \exists z' \;:\; \mathsf{V}_{\mathsf{I}}(C, w, x', z') = 1 \,\}. \tag{3}$$

Here, V_{I} denotes the verification algorithm of Σ_{I}. Let G be the event that $\mathcal{A}$ produces tr with $|\mathcal{G}_{\mathsf{tr}}| > f$ for $f = \left\lceil \sqrt{\frac{|\mathcal{C}|}{\alpha q_H}} \right\rceil$.

[7] For example, *exact* lattice proofs (see, e.g., [7]) require around 40–50 KB in comparison to 2–3 KB for *relaxed* lattice proofs.

Claim: For any valid $\mathsf{tr} = (C, w, x, z)$, if CDec chooses x' with $x' \in \mathcal{G}_{\mathsf{tr}} \setminus \{x\}$, then CDec terminates.
The claim follows from the following facts. If the assumption of the claim holds, then there exist (C, w, x, z) (as the input) and (C, w, x', z') such that $\mathsf{V}_{\mathsf{I}}(C, w, x, z) = \mathsf{V}_{\mathsf{I}}(C, w, x', z') = 1$ by the definition of $\mathcal{G}_{\mathsf{tr}}$. Then, by the existential special soundness of Σ_{I}, there exists $(\bar{x}, \bar{\mathsf{o}}')$ such that $\bar{x} = F(x, x')$ and $(C, (\bar{x}, \mathsf{o}')) \in \mathsf{R}'_{\mathsf{C},pp}$. Now, by the property $\mathbf{P}_2$ of CDec, the claim follows.

As a result, the probability that CDec terminates in one iteration is at least $\frac{|\mathcal{G}_{\mathsf{tr}}|-1}{|\mathcal{C}|}$. Therefore, we have

$$\mathrm{Exp}_{\hat{D}}\left[\, T \mid \mathcal{A}^{\mathcal{H}} \text{ outputs } \mathsf{tr} \,\right] \le \frac{|\mathcal{C}|}{|\mathcal{G}_{\mathsf{tr}}| - 1}, \quad \text{and also} \tag{4}$$

$$\mathrm{Exp}_{\hat{D}}\left[\, T \mid \mathcal{A}^{\mathcal{H}} \text{ outputs } \mathsf{tr} \wedge G \,\right] \le \frac{|\mathcal{C}|}{f}. \tag{5}$$

We say that "$\mathcal{A}^{\mathcal{H}}$ outputs tr_i" if $\mathcal{A}^{\mathcal{H}}$ outputs $\mathsf{tr} = (C, w, x, z)$ such that the output of $\mathcal{A}$'s i-th random oracle query is x. As in [18], without loss of generality, we consider an adversary $\mathcal{A}$ that (1) makes q_H random oracle queries, (2) uses one of the random oracle outputs in his output transcript and (3) only makes random oracle queries for transcripts tr_i with $|\mathcal{G}_{\mathsf{tr}_i}| > f$ as we are conditioning on G. Then, similar to [18], we have the following

$$\mathrm{Exp}_{\hat{H},\hat{D}}\left[T \mid G\right] = \sum_{i=1}^{q_H} \Pr_{\hat{H}}\left[\mathcal{A}^{\mathcal{H}} \text{ outputs } \mathsf{tr}_i \mid G\right] \mathrm{Exp}_{\hat{D}}\left[T \mid \mathcal{A}^{\mathcal{H}} \text{ outputs } \mathsf{tr}_i \wedge G\right]. \tag{6}$$

For each random oracle query made by $\mathcal{A}$ for a transcript tr_i, the probability (over $\hat{H}$) that $\mathcal{A}$ outputs tr_i is at most the probability that the random oracle query output is in $\mathcal{G}_{\mathsf{tr}_i}$, as otherwise there exists no response z such that $\mathsf{V}_{\mathsf{I}}(C, w, x, z) = 1$. Therefore, each tr_i can be output with probability at most $\frac{|\mathcal{G}_{\mathsf{tr}_i}|}{|\mathcal{C}|}$. Then, using this fact and (4), we get

$$\mathrm{Exp}_{\hat{H},\hat{D}}\left[\, T \mid G \,\right] \le \sum_{i=1}^{q_H} \frac{|\mathcal{G}_{\mathsf{tr}_i}|}{|\mathcal{C}|} \frac{|\mathcal{C}|}{|\mathcal{G}_{\mathsf{tr}_i}| - 1} \le q_H \cdot \max_{i=1,\ldots,q_H} \left(\frac{|\mathcal{G}_{\mathsf{tr}_i}|}{|\mathcal{G}_{\mathsf{tr}_i}| - 1} \right) \le \frac{q_H(f+1)}{f}.$$

For any random oracle query, the probability that $\mathcal{A}$ outputs a transcript with $|\mathcal{G}_{\mathsf{tr}}| \le f$ is at most $f/|\mathcal{C}|$. Therefore, we have

$$\Pr_{\hat{H},\hat{D}}\left[\, \neg G \,\right] \le \frac{f \cdot q_H}{|\mathcal{C}|}. \tag{7}$$

Using now Markov's inequality and (7), we get

$$\begin{aligned}\Pr_{\hat{H},\hat{D}}\left[T \ge \alpha q_H\right] &= \Pr_{\hat{H},\hat{D}}\left[T \ge \alpha q_H \mid G\,\right] \Pr_{\hat{H},\hat{D}}\left[\, G \,\right] + \Pr_{\hat{H},\hat{D}}\left[T \ge \alpha q_H \mid \neg G\,\right] \Pr_{\hat{H},\hat{D}}\left[\, \neg G \,\right] \\ &\le \frac{\mathrm{Exp}_{\hat{H},\hat{D}}\left[\, T \mid G \,\right]}{\alpha \cdot q_H} + \Pr_{\hat{H},\hat{D}}\left[\, \neg G \,\right] \le \frac{f+1}{\alpha \cdot f} + \frac{f \cdot q_H}{|\mathcal{C}|} = \frac{1}{\alpha} \cdot \left(1 + \frac{1}{f}\right) + \frac{f \cdot q_H}{|\mathcal{C}|}.\end{aligned}$$

Plugging in the value of $f = \left\lceil \sqrt{\frac{|\mathcal{C}|}{\alpha q_H}} \right\rceil$ proves the result. □

5 HMC-Based VPDC from Lattices

5.1 Instantiation of (Ordinary) HMC

We start by describing the (ordinary) Hashed-Message Commitment (HMC) scheme C underlying our lattice-based VPDC. Let n, m, q be positive integers with $m > n$. If we want to commit to a v_1-dimensional 'real' message over R_q for $v_1 \geq 1$ together with a v_2-dimensional auxiliary message for $v_2 \geq 0$, then HMC is instantiated as follows.

- $\mathsf{CKeygen}(1^\lambda)$: Sample $\boldsymbol{A} \leftarrow R_q^{n\times m}$, $\boldsymbol{B} \leftarrow R_q^{n\times v_1}$ and $\boldsymbol{C} \leftarrow R_q^{n\times v_2}$. Output $ck = \boldsymbol{G} = [\,\boldsymbol{A} \,\|\, \boldsymbol{B} \,\|\, \boldsymbol{C}\,] \in R_q^{n\times(m+v_1+v_2)}$, message space $\mathcal{M} = \mathcal{D} \times \mathcal{U}$ with $\mathcal{D} := \mathbb{S}_\alpha^{v_1}$ and $\mathcal{U} := \mathbb{S}_\beta^{v_2}$, and $\mathcal{R} := \mathbb{S}_\mathcal{B}^m$ for some $\alpha, \beta, \mathcal{B} \geq 1$.
- $\mathsf{Commit}_{ck}(\boldsymbol{m}, \boldsymbol{u})$: Sample $\boldsymbol{r} \leftarrow \mathbb{S}_\mathcal{B}^m$. Output C and $\mathsf{o} = (1, \boldsymbol{m}, \boldsymbol{u}, \boldsymbol{r})$, where

$$C =, \boldsymbol{m}, \boldsymbol{u}\boldsymbol{r} = \boldsymbol{G} \cdot (\boldsymbol{r}, \boldsymbol{m}, \boldsymbol{u})^\top = \boldsymbol{A} \cdot \boldsymbol{r} + \boldsymbol{B} \cdot \boldsymbol{m} + \boldsymbol{C} \cdot \boldsymbol{u}.$$

- $\mathsf{COpen}_{ck}(C, (y, \boldsymbol{m}', \boldsymbol{u}', \boldsymbol{r}'))$: If $yC =, y\boldsymbol{m}', \boldsymbol{u}'\boldsymbol{r}'$, $\|(\boldsymbol{r}', y\boldsymbol{m}', \boldsymbol{u}')\| \leq \gamma_{\text{com}}$, and $\dim(\boldsymbol{m}') = v_1$, $\dim(\boldsymbol{u}') = v_2$ and $\dim(\boldsymbol{r}') = m$ over R_q, return 1. Otherwise, return 0.

One can easily observe that HMC is additively homomorphic. Moreover, note that the opening algorithm is relaxed, where an additional *relaxation factor* $y \in R_q$ is involved. This relaxation is needed to obtain *efficient* lattice-based ZKPs. For classical commitment schemes such as Pedersen commitment, the relaxation factor is always 1. The same is true for *honestly-created* lattice-based commitments. However, *efficient* lattice-based ZKPs do not always prove that this is the case. For example, for the *exact* proof of knowledge of a commitment opening with $y = 1$ as in [7], the proof length is more than 40 KB while a *relaxed* variant leads to a proof length of only a few KBs. Therefore, the relaxation factor can be a non-trivial value when created by a cheating prover (that still succeeds in the ZKP verification). For HMC used within our VPDC below, we say that the trapdoor-binding property is *satisfied w.r.t. to the same relaxation factor* if the relaxation factors in o and o' in the binding definition in Sect. 3 are restricted to be the same. This same-relaxation trapdoor-binding property is sufficient for our applications as well as many prior ones, e.g., [9,10,12], and can be based on a harder variant of the MSIS problem than the general trapdoor-binding property (see Lemma 1).

We remark that in some applications, the COpen algorithm checks a slightly different relation than above, of the form $yC = \mathsf{Com}_{ck}(\boldsymbol{m}', \boldsymbol{u}'; \boldsymbol{r}')$, where the relaxation factor y does not multiply the decryptable message. However, in this paper, we need the stronger variant in the above definition. Despite the relaxation factor, HMC defined above is still (computationally) binding and hiding as we will discuss in Lemma 1.

5.2 Instantiation of NIZK

Our lattice-based VPDC can be instantiated with any suitable Schnorr-like lattice-based relaxed NIZK proofs of opening for HMC commitments derived from a Sigma protocol via the Fiat-Shamir transform, such as the one-shot relaxed binary proof protocols in [9,11,12]. For compatibility with such protocols, we define the challenge space

$$\mathcal{C}^d_{w,p} = \{x \in \mathbb{Z}[X] : \deg(x) < d \wedge \mathsf{HW}(x) = w \wedge \|x\|_\infty \leq p\}.$$

The same set is also defined in [9] and $|\mathcal{C}^d_{w,p}| = \binom{d}{w}(2p)^w$. Thus, given d, it is easy to set (w, p) such that $|\mathcal{C}^d_{w,p}| > 2^{256}$. Throughout the manuscript, we assume that (d, w, p) is set so that $|\mathcal{C}^d_{w,p}|$ is exponentially large. We also let $\Delta\mathcal{C}^d_{w,p}$ denote the set of differences of challenges in $\mathcal{C}^d_{w,p}$ except for the zero element. We design our VPDC to work with the following definition of relaxed "well-formedness" of a commitment relation. We refer the reader to Lemma 2 in the Sect. 6 for a concrete example of such a relaxed NIZK protocol Σ in our cryptocurrency protocol application.

Definition 5 (γ-valid commitment opening relation $\mathsf{R}'_{\mathsf{C},pp}$). *We say that* $\mathsf{o} := (y, (\boldsymbol{m}, \boldsymbol{u}, \boldsymbol{r}))$ *is a γ-valid opening of a commitment C with a decryptable message space $\mathcal{D}$, denoted by $(C, \mathsf{o}) \in \mathsf{R}'_{\mathsf{C},pp}$, if the following holds:*

- $y \in \Delta\mathcal{C}^d_{w,p}$,
- $\boldsymbol{m} \in \mathcal{D}$,
- $yC = \mathsf{Com}_{ck}(y\boldsymbol{m}, \boldsymbol{u}; \boldsymbol{r})$,
- $\|(y\boldsymbol{m}, \boldsymbol{u}, \boldsymbol{r})\| \leq \gamma$ *for* $\gamma \in \mathbb{R}^+$,
- $\dim(\boldsymbol{m}) = v_1$, $\dim(\boldsymbol{u}) = v_2$ *and* $\dim(\boldsymbol{r}) = m$ *over* R_q.

The above relation definition is very similar to COpen except that we additionally have the first two requirements. For our proof systems (as in Schnorr-like proofs), the commitment w of the Fiat-Shamir protocol as given in Sect. 4 is uniquely determined by the rest of the proof output. Hence, it need not be included in the non-interactive proof transcript and therefore its notation is omitted in the rest of the paper.

5.3 VPDC Trapdoor for HMC

Now, we present our gadget-based Regev-style VPDC trapdoor algorithm CAddTd for our lattice-based VPDC based on the HMC commitment described in Sect. 5.1.

Our trapdoor $\boldsymbol{s}$ is designed to allow partial decryption of the latter HMC commitment, i.e., to recover the decryptable binary message $\boldsymbol{m} \in \{0,1\}^{v_1}$ from the commitment $C = \mathsf{Com}_{ck}(\boldsymbol{m}, \boldsymbol{u}; \boldsymbol{r}) = \boldsymbol{G} \cdot \begin{pmatrix} \boldsymbol{r} \\ \boldsymbol{m} \\ \boldsymbol{u} \end{pmatrix}$, where $\boldsymbol{G} = [\boldsymbol{A} \,\|\, \boldsymbol{B} \,\|\, \boldsymbol{C}] \in R_q^{n\times(m+v_1+v_2)}$ is the commitment key matrix, and $\boldsymbol{r}$ and $\boldsymbol{u}$

are the short non-decryptable commitment randomness and auxiliary message, respectively. Our trapdoor $\boldsymbol{s}$ is embedded into the matrix $\boldsymbol{G}$ such that $\boldsymbol{s}^\top \cdot \boldsymbol{G} \approx [\boldsymbol{0}, \bar{t}\boldsymbol{g}^\top, \boldsymbol{0}] \in R_q^{m+v_1+v_2}$ (with the approximate equality up to a 'short' error vector) where $\bar{t}\boldsymbol{g}^\top$ (with $\bar{t} = \lfloor q/t \rfloor$) is a large gadget vector of the form $\bar{t} \cdot (1, 2, 2^2, \ldots, 2^{\tau-1}, X, X \cdot 2, \ldots, X \cdot 2^{\tau-1}, \ldots)$. This means that VPDC partial decryption of the commitment C can be carried out by computing $\boldsymbol{s}^\top C \approx \bar{t}\boldsymbol{g}^\top \boldsymbol{m}$. The (approximately) 0 entries in $\boldsymbol{s}^\top \cdot \boldsymbol{G}$ annihilate the non-decryptable $\boldsymbol{r}$ and $\boldsymbol{u}$ vectors in decryption (these vectors only contribute to the short error terms in the approximate equality), whereas the gadget vector $\bar{t}\boldsymbol{g}^\top$ entry of $\boldsymbol{s}^\top \cdot \boldsymbol{G}$ 'selects' the decryptable message $\boldsymbol{m}$ and compresses its dimension by reconstructing and packing groups of τ bits in $\boldsymbol{m}$ into the integer coefficients of $1, X, X^2, \ldots$ in the ring element $\boldsymbol{g}^\top \boldsymbol{m}$. To achieve the desired trapdoor condition $\boldsymbol{s}^\top [\boldsymbol{A} \,\|\, \boldsymbol{B} \,\|\, \boldsymbol{C}] \approx [\boldsymbol{0}, \bar{t}\boldsymbol{g}^\top, \boldsymbol{0}]$, for the 'selection' gadget, we embed a Regev-style LWE decryption '*gadget trapdoor*' into the last row $\boldsymbol{t}_B^\top$ of matrix $\boldsymbol{B}$, setting $\boldsymbol{t}_B^\top \approx \boldsymbol{s}'^\top \boldsymbol{B}' + \bar{t}\boldsymbol{g}^\top$, where $\boldsymbol{B}'$ consists of the top $n-1$ rows of $\boldsymbol{B}$ and $\boldsymbol{s}' \in R_q^{n-1}$ is random, and we use the form $\boldsymbol{s} = (-\boldsymbol{s}', 1)$ for the trapdoor. For the annihilating 0 entries of $\boldsymbol{s}^\top \cdot \boldsymbol{G}$, we embed a Regev-style '*error trapdoor*' into the last rows $\boldsymbol{t}_A^\top$ (resp. $\boldsymbol{t}_C^\top$) of matrices $\boldsymbol{A}$ (resp. $\boldsymbol{C}$), setting them to $\approx \boldsymbol{s}'^\top \boldsymbol{A}'$ (resp. $\approx \boldsymbol{s}'^\top \boldsymbol{C}'$), where $\boldsymbol{A}'$ (resp. $\boldsymbol{C}'$) denote the top $n-1$ rows of $\boldsymbol{A}$ (resp. $\boldsymbol{C}$). Due to the errors in the above approximate equalities, to an attacker not knowing the secret trapdoor $\boldsymbol{s}'$, the trapdoor rows of matrix $\boldsymbol{G}$ are indistinguishable from uniformly random rows, assuming the hardness of the rank-$(n-1)$ M-LWE problem with respect to the secret $\boldsymbol{s}'$.

We now summarise our new gadget-based Regev-style HMC VPDC construction and start with instantiating CAddTd.

- $\mathsf{CAddTd}(ck)$: Let $ck = [\boldsymbol{A} \,\|\, \boldsymbol{B} \,\|\, \boldsymbol{C}] \in R_q^{n \times (m+v_1+v_2)}$ where $\boldsymbol{A} = \begin{bmatrix} \boldsymbol{A}' \\ \boldsymbol{a}^\top \end{bmatrix}$ for $\boldsymbol{A}' \in R_q^{(n-1)\times m}$ and $\boldsymbol{a} \in R_q^m$, $\boldsymbol{B} = \begin{bmatrix} \boldsymbol{B}' \\ \boldsymbol{b}^\top \end{bmatrix}$ for $\boldsymbol{B}' \in R_q^{(n-1)\times v_1}$ and $\boldsymbol{b} \in R_q^{v_1}$, and $\boldsymbol{C} = \begin{bmatrix} \boldsymbol{C}' \\ \boldsymbol{c}^\top \end{bmatrix}$ for $\boldsymbol{C}' \in R_q^{(n-1)\times v_2}$ and $\boldsymbol{c} \in R_q^{v_2}$. Sample $\boldsymbol{s}' \leftarrow R_q^{n-1}$, $\boldsymbol{e}_0 \leftarrow \mathbb{S}_{\mathcal{B}_e}^m$, $\boldsymbol{e}_1 \leftarrow \mathbb{S}_{\mathcal{B}_e}^{v_1}$, and $\boldsymbol{e}_2 \leftarrow \mathbb{S}_{\mathcal{B}_e}^{v_2}$, and set $\boldsymbol{A}^{\mathrm{td}} = \begin{bmatrix} \boldsymbol{A}' \\ \boldsymbol{t}_0^\top \end{bmatrix}$, $\boldsymbol{B}^{\mathrm{td}} = \begin{bmatrix} \boldsymbol{B}' \\ \boldsymbol{t}_1^\top \end{bmatrix}$, $\boldsymbol{C}^{\mathrm{td}} = \begin{bmatrix} \boldsymbol{C}' \\ \boldsymbol{t}_2^\top \end{bmatrix}$ where $\boldsymbol{t}_0 = \boldsymbol{A}'^\top \boldsymbol{s}' + \boldsymbol{e}_0$, $\boldsymbol{t}_1 = \boldsymbol{B}'^\top \boldsymbol{s}' + \boldsymbol{e}_1 + \bar{t}\boldsymbol{g}$ and $\boldsymbol{t}_2 = \boldsymbol{C}'^\top \boldsymbol{s}' + \boldsymbol{e}_2$, with
$$\boldsymbol{g}^\top := (2^0X^0, \ldots, 2^{\tau-1}X^0, 2^0X^1, \ldots, 2^{\tau-1}X^1, \ldots, 2^0X^{d'}, \ldots, 2^{\ell-1}X^{d'}) \in R^{v_1},$$
$\tau := \lceil \frac{v_1}{d} \rceil$, $d' := \lfloor \frac{v_1}{\tau} \rfloor$ (note that $d' \leq d$) and $\ell := v_1 \bmod \tau \in \{0, \ldots, \tau-1\}$. Output $(ck^{\mathrm{td}}, \mathsf{td}) = ([\boldsymbol{A}^{\mathrm{td}} \,\|\, \boldsymbol{B}^{\mathrm{td}} \,\|\, \boldsymbol{C}^{\mathrm{td}}], \boldsymbol{s})$ where $\boldsymbol{s} = \begin{pmatrix} -\boldsymbol{s}' \\ 1 \end{pmatrix}$.

The following lemma follows from the hiding/binding properties of standard HMC commitments, and the M-LWE based key indistinguishability property of CAddTd. The proof is given in the full version of this paper.

Lemma 1. *Let the ring R_q split into s fields $\mathbb{F}_{p_1}, \ldots, \mathbb{F}_{p_s}$ with $p = \min\{p_1, \ldots, p_s\}$. If $\frac{n \cdot s}{p^{m-n+1}}$ is negligible, then HMC under 'trapdoored' commitment keys as output by* CAddTd *defined above is*

- *correct if $\gamma_{com} \geq \sqrt{\mathcal{B}^2 md + (\gamma_y \alpha d)^2 v_1 + \beta^2 v_2 d}$,*
- *computationally trapdoor γ_{com}-binding with respect to the same relaxation factor (resp. γ_{com}-binding) if M-$SIS_{n-1,m+v_1+v_2,q,2\gamma_{com}}$ is hard (resp. if M-$SIS_{n-1,m+v_1+v_2,q,2\sqrt{d}\gamma_Y \cdot \gamma_{com}}$ is hard, where $\gamma_Y := max_{y \in Y} \|y\|$, and Y is the set of valid relaxation factors accepted by* COpen*; for our VPDC, it suffices to use $Y := \Delta C^d_{w,p}$ as in Definition 5).*
- *computationally hiding if M-$LWE_{m-n,m,q,\mathcal{B}}$ and M-$LWE_{n-1,m+v_1+v_2,q,\mathcal{B}}$ problems are hard.*

Additionally, if M-$LWE_{m-n,m,q,\mathcal{B}}$ and M-$LWE_{n-1,m+v_1+v_2,q,\mathcal{B}}$ problems are hard, any commitment vector is computationally indistinguishable from a uniformly random element in R_q^n.

Note that there are two main differences in Lemma 1 compared to the assumptions required for standard HMC (see [12, Lemma 2.3],[6, Lemma 3.4]): (i) the module rank of M-SIS is reduced by 1 (from n to $n-1$), and (ii) the hardness of M-LWE$_{n-1,m+v_1+v_2,q,\mathcal{B}}$ is additionally required. As mentioned before, binding w.r.t. the same relaxation factor is sufficient for many applications (including ours) since the reduction creates a challenge commitment with a known *exact* opening (i.e., $y = 1$) and recovers another *relaxed* opening by rewinding the adversary. The former exact opening can be multiplied by the relaxation factor of the latter to solve an M-SIS problem.

5.4 Gadget-Based Regev-Style Decryption for HMC

We now present the decryption algorithm CDecGR for our lattice-based VPDC. When a commitment key with a trapdoor is used to generate a proof, the ZKPs we use prove knowledge of an opening $(y, \boldsymbol{m}, \boldsymbol{u}, \boldsymbol{r})$ of a commitment C such that

$$yC = \mathsf{Com}_{ck^{\mathsf{td}}}(y\boldsymbol{m}, \boldsymbol{u}; \boldsymbol{r}) = \boldsymbol{A}^{\mathsf{td}}\boldsymbol{r} + \boldsymbol{B}^{\mathsf{td}}y\boldsymbol{m} + \boldsymbol{C}^{\mathsf{td}}\boldsymbol{u}. \quad (8)$$

Note that the opening message is also multiplied by the relaxation factor y. From here, we can try to eliminate the randomness $\boldsymbol{r}$ and the auxiliary message $\boldsymbol{u}$ by multiplying both sides by the secret trapdoor $\boldsymbol{s}$. However, the decryptor does not know what y is. For an honest user, we simply have $y = 1$, but for adversarially-generated proofs, that may not be the case. Thankfully, we can use our new results from Sect. 4 to overcome this problem. Let us first present the full procedure in Algorithm 2. In this algorithm, the decrypted message is encoded as an element of R_t for some positive integer t, and we define the integer $\bar{t} := \lfloor q/t \rfloor$. We also use the following two functions. The function $\mathsf{BD}_{\tau,v_1}(m'')$ performs bit decomposition of the coefficients of the R_t-encoded message $m'' = m''_0 + m''_1 X + \cdots + m''_{d-1} X^{d-1}$ and returns the resulting binary vector message $\boldsymbol{m}' = (m'_0, \ldots, m'_{v_1-1}) \in \{0,1\}^{v_1}$. Namely, for $j \in \{0, \ldots, v_1 - 1\}$, it sets m'_j to

Algorithm 2. $\mathsf{CDecGR}(C, x, \mathsf{td}, v_1)$

INPUT: a commitment $C \in R_q^n$; a challenge $x \in \mathcal{C}_{w,p}^d$; trapdoor $\mathsf{td} = \boldsymbol{s} \in R_q^n$; the dimension v_1 such that $\mathcal{D} = \{0,1\}^{v_1}$
OUTPUT: $(\boldsymbol{m}', x') \in \mathcal{D} \times \mathcal{C}_{w,p}^d$

1: **loop**
2: $\quad x' \leftarrow \mathcal{C}_{w,p}^d$
3: $\quad y' = x - x'$ ▷ $y' = 1$ is assumed to be tried first
4: $\quad C' = \langle \boldsymbol{s}, y'C \rangle$
5: $\quad C'' = \mathsf{Rnd}_{\bar{t}}(C')$ where $\bar{t} = \lfloor q/t \rfloor$
6: $\quad \bar{m}' = (\bar{t})^{-1} \cdot C'' \in R$ ▷ Note that C'' is a multiple of $\bar{t}$ in R
7: $\quad m'' = (y')^{-1} \cdot \bar{m}' \in R_t$ ▷ If y' is not invertible in R_t, restart from Step 2
8: $\quad \boldsymbol{m}' = \mathsf{BD}_{\tau,v_1}(m'')$
9: $\quad e' = C' - C''$
10: $\quad$ **if** $(\|e'\|_\infty < \|e\|_{bnd,\infty})$ **and** $(m'' \in [0,\ldots,2^\tau - 1]^d)$ **then**
11: $\quad\quad$ **return** $(\boldsymbol{m}', x')$
12: $\quad$ **end if**
13: **end loop**

the k-th bit of the coefficient $m''_{\lfloor j/\tau \rfloor}$ where $k := j \bmod \tau$. The function $\mathsf{Rnd}_{\bar{t}}(C')$ rounds each coefficient of $C' \in R$ to the nearest integer multiple of $\bar{t}$.

As mentioned in Sect. 4, an important task is to prove that the message returned by the decryption algorithm (Algorithm 2) is "valid". We prove this in Theorem 2 below so that, for a commitment C with a valid NIZK relaxed proof of opening and a sufficiently large q, the message output by Algorithm 2 is the same as the one used to generate the commitment C. In the theorem below, we show the decryption feasibility (which relies on the results from Sect. 4) and also the decryption soundness of our construction.

Theorem 2 (HMC Decryption). *Let* $\mathsf{VPDC_{HMC}} = (\mathsf{C}, \Sigma, \mathit{CAddTd}, \mathit{CDecGR})$ *denote our lattice-based VPDC construction with HMC commitment scheme* C, Σ *a matching NIZK relaxed proof of* γ*-valid opening relation* $\mathsf{R}'_{\mathsf{C},pp}$ *as in Definition 5, with* $\mathcal{D} := \{0,1\}^{v_1}$. *Suppose that* Σ *is obtained from a Sigma protocol* Σ_I *using the Fiat-Shamir transform with random oracle* $\mathcal{H} : \{0,1\}^* \to \mathcal{C}$, Σ_I *satisfies Existential Special Soundness (Definition 3), that for any fixed* $x \in \mathcal{C}_{w,p}^d$, $x - x' \in \Delta\mathcal{C}_{w,p}^d$ *is invertible in* R_t *except with negligible probability* p_{ni} *over the uniformly random choice of* $x' \in \mathcal{C}_{w,p}^d$ *and* $|\mathcal{C}_{w,p}^d| \geq 2^\lambda$.

For an adversary $\mathcal{A}$ *against soundness game* ***Exp:Soundness*** *making* $q_H - 1$ *queries to its random oracle, let*

$$\|e\|_{bnd,\infty} := \sqrt{(m + v_1 + v_2)d\mathcal{B}_e\gamma} + 2pw(2^\tau - 1) + t/2. \tag{9}$$

Suppose that $t \geq 2^\tau$ *and*

$$\bar{t} := \lfloor q/t \rfloor > 4pw\|e\|_{bnd,\infty} + t(1/2 + 2pw). \tag{10}$$

Then the following holds:

1. ***Decryption Feasibility:*** *The scheme* $\mathsf{VPDC}_{\mathsf{HMC}}$ *satisfies Decryption Feasibility. Concretely, the number of iterations* T *of the loop over* x' *in* CDecGR *is upper bounded by* $\alpha \cdot q_H$*, except with probability at most* $\frac{1}{\alpha} + 2\sqrt{\frac{q_H}{\alpha \cdot |\mathcal{C}^d_{w,p}|}} + \frac{q_H}{|\mathcal{C}^d_{w,p}|} + \alpha q_H p_{\mathrm{ni}}$.
2. ***Decryption soundness:*** *The scheme* $\mathsf{VPDC}_{\mathsf{HMC}}$ *satisfies Decryption Soundness. Concretely, we have*

$$Adv_{\mathit{Exp:Soundness}}(\mathcal{A}) \leq q_H / |\mathcal{C}^d_{w,p}|.$$

Proof (Theorem 2). **Decryption Feasibility:** To prove the run-time claim, we apply Theorem 1. For this, we need to show that the assumptions of Theorem 1 are satisfied. First, by our assumption on Σ_{I}, the existential special-soundness property is satisfied. For the compatibility of CDecGR and Σ_{I}, the property $\mathbf{P}_1$ is satisfied by structure of the algorithm CDecGR. For the property $\mathbf{P}_2$, we show that if y' in some iteration of the loop in Step 3 of Algorithm CDecGR is 'good' in the sense that y' is invertible in R_t and there exists a γ-valid opening $(y', \boldsymbol{m}, \boldsymbol{u}, \boldsymbol{r})$ of C as in Definition 5, then decryption will terminate and return $\boldsymbol{m}' = \boldsymbol{m}$. Let us denote by E_0 the bad event that y' is not invertible in R_t. We first observe that E_0 occurs with negligible probability, i.e. $\Pr[E_0] \leq \alpha q_H p_{\mathrm{ni}}$ over at most αq_H iterations of CDecGR, since at each iteration $y' = x - x'$ where x' sampled uniformly from $\mathcal{C}^d_{w,p}$ independently of x. Now we show that $\mathbf{P}_2$ holds if E_0 does not occur. Indeed, by γ-validity of $(y', \boldsymbol{m}, \boldsymbol{u}, \boldsymbol{r})$, we have $y'C = \boldsymbol{A}^{\mathsf{td}}\boldsymbol{r} + \boldsymbol{B}^{\mathsf{td}}y'\boldsymbol{m} + \boldsymbol{C}^{\mathsf{td}}\boldsymbol{u}$ and $\boldsymbol{m} \in \{0,1\}^{v_1}$.

Multiplying the γ-valid relation by $\boldsymbol{s}^\top$, defining $\langle \boldsymbol{e}_0, \boldsymbol{r}\rangle + \langle \boldsymbol{e}_1, y'\boldsymbol{m}\rangle + \langle \boldsymbol{e}_2, \boldsymbol{u}\rangle := e$, and using $\boldsymbol{s}^\top \cdot \boldsymbol{A}^{\mathsf{td}} = \boldsymbol{e}_0^\top$, $\boldsymbol{s}^\top \cdot \boldsymbol{B}^{\mathsf{td}} = \bar{t}\boldsymbol{g}^\top + \boldsymbol{e}_1^\top$ and $\boldsymbol{s}^\top \cdot \boldsymbol{C}^{\mathsf{td}} = \boldsymbol{e}_2^\top$, we have $\langle \boldsymbol{s}, y'C\rangle = \bar{t}y'\langle \boldsymbol{g}, \boldsymbol{m}\rangle + e$ over R_q. Writing $y'\langle \boldsymbol{g}, \boldsymbol{m}\rangle = (y'\langle \boldsymbol{g}, \boldsymbol{m}\rangle \bmod t) + t\lfloor \frac{y'\langle \boldsymbol{g}, \boldsymbol{m}\rangle}{t}\rceil$, we get the following equality over R_q:

$$\langle \boldsymbol{s}, y'C\rangle = \bar{t}(y'\langle \boldsymbol{g}, \boldsymbol{m}\rangle \bmod t) + e + \tilde{e}, \tag{11}$$

where $\tilde{e} := \bar{t}t \cdot \lfloor \frac{y'\langle \boldsymbol{g}, \boldsymbol{m}\rangle}{t}\rceil \bmod q$. We have $\|\bar{t}(y'\langle \boldsymbol{g}, \boldsymbol{m}\rangle \bmod t)\|_\infty \leq \lfloor q/t\rfloor (t-1)/2 \leq q/2 - \bar{t}/2$. Hence, if $\|e + \tilde{e}\|_\infty < \bar{t}/2$, there is no wraparound mod q on the right hand side of (11), and since $\bar{t}y'\langle \boldsymbol{g}, \boldsymbol{m}\rangle$ is a multiple of $\bar{t}$ in R, the rounded polynomial $C'' = \mathsf{Rnd}_{\bar{t}}(C')$ (recall $C' = \langle \boldsymbol{s}, y'C\rangle \bmod q$) will be equal to $\bar{t}(y'\langle \boldsymbol{g}, \boldsymbol{m}\rangle \bmod t)$ and decryption will succeed and return $\boldsymbol{m}$. It remains to show that $\|e + \tilde{e}\|_\infty < \bar{t}/2$. By the Schwartz inequality, $\|e\|_\infty \leq \|(\boldsymbol{e}_0, \boldsymbol{e}_1, \boldsymbol{e}_2)\| \cdot \|(\boldsymbol{r}, y\boldsymbol{m}, \boldsymbol{u})\| \leq \sqrt{(m + v_1 + v_2)d}\mathcal{B}_{\mathrm{e}}\gamma$ using $\|(\boldsymbol{r}, y\boldsymbol{m}, \boldsymbol{u})\| \leq \gamma$ by γ-validity. Also, writing $\bar{t} = q/t - \epsilon$ for $0 \leq \epsilon < 1$, we have $\|\tilde{e}\|_\infty = \|(q/t - \epsilon)t \cdot \lfloor \frac{y'\langle \boldsymbol{g}, \boldsymbol{m}\rangle}{t}\rceil \bmod q\|_\infty = \|\epsilon t \cdot \lfloor \frac{y'\langle \boldsymbol{g}, \boldsymbol{m}\rangle}{t}\rceil\|_\infty \leq \|t\lfloor \frac{y'\langle \boldsymbol{g}, \boldsymbol{m}\rangle}{t}\rceil\|_\infty \leq t/2 + \|y'\langle \boldsymbol{g}, \boldsymbol{m}\rangle\|_\infty$, and $\|y'\langle \boldsymbol{g}, \boldsymbol{m}\rangle\|_\infty \leq \|y'\|_1 \|\langle \boldsymbol{g}, \boldsymbol{m}\rangle\|_\infty \leq (2pw)(2^\tau - 1)$ using $\|y'\|_1 \leq 2pw$ and $\|\langle \boldsymbol{g}, \boldsymbol{m}\rangle\|_\infty \leq 2^\tau - 1$ since $\boldsymbol{m} \in \{0,1\}^{v_1}$. Overall, we have $\|e + \tilde{e}\|_\infty \leq \|e\|_\infty + \|\tilde{e}\|_\infty \leq \sqrt{(m + v_1 + v_2)d}\mathcal{B}_{\mathrm{e}}\gamma + (2pw)(2^\tau - 1) + t/2 := \|e\|_{bnd,\infty}$, which is less than $\bar{t}/2$ by condition (10), as required.

Decryption Soundness: To show the decryption soundness claim, let E_1 denote the event that $\mathcal{A}$ wins and case (i) in `Exp:Soundness` occurs, i.e.,

$\mathsf{V}(C, x, \boldsymbol{z}) = 1$ but a γ-valid opening $(C, y, (\boldsymbol{m}, \boldsymbol{u}, \boldsymbol{r}))$ of C with $y = x - x''$ and $x'' \in \mathcal{C}^d_{w,p}$ does *not* exist. Similarly, let E_2 be the event that $\mathcal{A}$ wins and case (ii) in Exp:Soundness occurs, i.e., $\mathsf{V}(C, x, \boldsymbol{z}) = 1$ and a γ-valid opening $(C, y, (\boldsymbol{m}, \boldsymbol{u}, \boldsymbol{r}))$ of C with $y = x - x''$ and $x'' \in \mathcal{C}^d_{w,p}$ exists, but CDecGR returns the wrong message $\boldsymbol{m'} \neq \boldsymbol{m}$. We show that $\Pr[E_1] + \Pr[E_2] \leq \frac{q_H}{|\mathcal{C}^d_{w,p}|}$.

We first claim that $\Pr[E_1] \leq \frac{q_H}{|\mathcal{C}^d_{w,p}|}$. Indeed, for each $\mathcal{H}$-query of $\mathcal{A}$ of the form $(pp, C, \cdot)$, we have that for any query answer $x' \neq x$, there does not exist a $\boldsymbol{z}'$ such that $\mathsf{V}(C, x', \boldsymbol{z}') = 1$ (otherwise, by existential special-soundness of the protocol Σ_{I}, a γ-valid opening $(C, y, (\boldsymbol{m}, \boldsymbol{u}, \boldsymbol{r}))$ of C with $y = x - x'$ would exist, a contradiction with E_1). It follows that $\Pr[E_1]$ is upper bounded by the probability that $\mathcal{A}$ receives the special challenge x for which a $\boldsymbol{z}$ exists in one of the $\leq q_H$ queries to $\mathcal{H}$. Since the special challenge is returned with probability $1/|\mathcal{C}^d_{w,p}|$ in each query, the claimed bound on $\Pr[E_1]$ follows.

Next, we claim that $\Pr[E_2] = 0$. On the one hand, if E_2 occurs, then the existence of the γ-valid opening $(C, y, (\boldsymbol{m}, \boldsymbol{u}, \boldsymbol{r}))$ of C with $y = x - x''$ means that $yC = \boldsymbol{A}^{\mathsf{td}}\boldsymbol{r} + \boldsymbol{B}^{\mathsf{td}}y\boldsymbol{m} + \boldsymbol{C}^{\mathsf{td}}\boldsymbol{u}$. Similarly to (11), multiplying the latter by $\boldsymbol{s}^\top$ gives us the following relation over R_q:

$$\langle \boldsymbol{s}, yC\rangle = \bar{t}(y\langle \boldsymbol{g}, \boldsymbol{m}\rangle \bmod t) + e + \tilde{e}, \tag{12}$$

where $e := \langle \boldsymbol{e}_0, \boldsymbol{r}\rangle + \langle \boldsymbol{e}_1, y\boldsymbol{m}\rangle + \langle \boldsymbol{e}_2, \boldsymbol{u}\rangle$ and $\tilde{e} := \bar{t}t \cdot \lfloor \frac{y\langle \boldsymbol{g}, \boldsymbol{m}\rangle}{t} \rceil \bmod q$. The same bound $\|e\|_{bnd,\infty}$ on $\|e + \tilde{e}\|$ applies by the same argument as in the run-time proof, based on Schwartz inequality. On the other hand, let $y' = x - x'$ be the value chosen in the iteration of the loop in CDecGR for which the message $\boldsymbol{m}'$ is returned. Then $\bar{m}' = \bar{t}(y'\langle \boldsymbol{g}, \boldsymbol{m}'\rangle \bmod t) \in R$, and we get the following relation over R_q:

$$\langle \boldsymbol{s}, yC\rangle = \bar{t}(y'\langle \boldsymbol{g}, \boldsymbol{m}'\rangle \bmod t) + e', \tag{13}$$

where $\|e'\|_\infty < \|e\|_{bnd,\infty}$ by the decryption check of CDecGR.

We now multiply (12) by y' and subtract (13) multiplied by y. Let $b_1 := y'(y\langle \boldsymbol{g}, \boldsymbol{m}\rangle \bmod t) \in R$, $b_2 := y(y'\langle \boldsymbol{g}, \boldsymbol{m}'\rangle \bmod t) \in R$. Note that $b_1 - b_2 = y'y\langle \boldsymbol{g}, \boldsymbol{m} - \boldsymbol{m}'\rangle \bmod t$. Writing $b_1 - b_2 = (y'y\langle \boldsymbol{g}, \boldsymbol{m} - \boldsymbol{m}'\rangle \bmod t) + t\lfloor \frac{b_1 - b_2}{t}\rceil$ gives the following relation over R_q:

$$\bar{t}(y'y\langle \boldsymbol{g}, \boldsymbol{m} - \boldsymbol{m}'\rangle \bmod t) = y'(e + \tilde{e}) - ye' - \tilde{e}', \tag{14}$$

where $\tilde{e}' := \bar{t}t\lfloor \frac{b_1 - b_2}{t}\rceil \bmod q$. We claim that the relation (14) leads to a contradiction, so that $\Pr[E_2] = 0$. To see this, first observe that the relation actually holds over R, not just R_q. Indeed, there is no wraparound mod q in the left hand side of (14), since the left hand side norm is at most $\|\lfloor q/t\rfloor \cdot t/2\|_\infty < q/2$. Since $\boldsymbol{m} - \boldsymbol{m'} \neq 0$, and $\boldsymbol{m} - \boldsymbol{m'} \in \{-1, 0, 1\}^{v_1}$, we have $\|\langle \boldsymbol{g}, \boldsymbol{m} - \boldsymbol{m}'\rangle\|_\infty \leq 2^\tau - 1 < t$ so $\langle \boldsymbol{g}, \boldsymbol{m} - \boldsymbol{m}'\rangle \neq 0 \bmod t$. Note that y is non-zero in R (since γ-validity of $(C, y, (\boldsymbol{m}, \boldsymbol{u}, \boldsymbol{r}))$ implies $y \in \Delta\mathcal{C}^d_{w,p}$) and y' is also non-zero in R (since it caused termination of CDecGR and hence is invertible in R_t) and R is an integral domain, the left hand side of (14) is a non-zero multiple of $\bar{t}$ in R. But the norm of the error terms on the right-hand side of (14) is bounded as follows. First, $\|y'(e+\tilde{e}) - ye'\|_\infty < \|y'\|_1\|e+\tilde{e}\|_\infty + \|y\|_1\|e'\|_\infty \leq 4pw\|e\|_{bnd,\infty}$ using $\|y'\|_1 \leq 2pw$, $\|y\|_1 \leq 2pw$, $\|e+\tilde{e}\|_\infty < \|e\|_{bnd,\infty}$ and $\|e'\|_\infty < \|e\|_{bnd,\infty}$. Also, $\|\tilde{e}'\|_\infty = \|\bar{t}t\lfloor\frac{b_1-b_2}{t}\rceil \bmod q\|_\infty \leq t\lfloor\frac{b_1-b_2}{t}\rceil \leq t(\frac{1}{2}+2pw)$ using $|\bar{t}t \mod q| < t$, and $\|\lfloor\frac{b_1-b_2}{t}\rceil\|_\infty \leq \frac{1}{2} + 2pw$ using $\|b_1\|_\infty \leq \|y'\|_1\|y\langle \boldsymbol{g}, \boldsymbol{m}\rangle \bmod t\|_\infty \leq (2pw)(t/2) \leq pw$, and similarly, $\|b_2\|_\infty \leq pw$. Overall, the norm of the right-hand side of (14) is bounded as $\|y'(e+\tilde{e}) - ye' - \tilde{e}'\|_\infty < 4pw\|e\|_{bnd,\infty} + t(\frac{1}{2}+2pw)$, which is smaller than $\bar{t}$ by condition (10). So, the left-hand side cannot be a non-zero multiple of $\bar{t}$ in R, implying the claimed contradiction. This completes the proof that $\Pr[E_2] = 0$ and the claimed soundness bound. □

5.5 Generalized Decryption

Our gadget-based Regev-style decryption trapdoor presented in the previous section, which handles a binary decryptable message space $\mathcal{D} = \{0,1\}^{v_1}$, can be readily generalised to handle more general decryptable message spaces $\mathcal{D} = (\{0,\ldots,\beta-1\}[X]^{<\delta})^{v_1}$ whose coordinates are polynomials in the ring R of degree $< \delta$ with β-ary coefficients for some positive integers $\delta, \beta > 1$. This generalisation can naturally be achieved via the appropriate generalisation of the reconstruction gadget vector $\boldsymbol{g}$, by setting

$$\boldsymbol{g}^\top := (\beta^0X^0,\ldots,\beta^{\tau-1}X^0,\beta^0X^\delta,\ldots,\beta^{\tau-1}X^\delta,\ldots,\beta^0X^{d'\delta},\ldots,\beta^{\ell-1}X^{d'\delta}) \in R^{v_1},$$

with $\tau := \left\lceil\frac{v_1}{\lfloor d/\delta\rfloor}\right\rceil$, $d' := \lfloor\frac{v_1}{\tau}\rfloor \leq \lfloor d/\delta\rfloor$. The decryption soundness result, Theorem 2, directly extends to this generalised case with the term 2^τ replaced by β^τ.

5.6 Succinctness of Our HMC-Based VPDC

An HMC commitment C as defined in Sect. 5.1 costs $nd\log q$ bits, i.e.,

$$\mathsf{bitlen}(C) = nd\log q. \tag{15}$$

We show that we can choose parameters such that succinctness of the VPDC is satisfied, i.e., $\mathsf{bitlen}(C) = \log^{O(1)}(\mathsf{bitlen}(\boldsymbol{u}))$, where $\mathsf{bitlen}(\boldsymbol{u})$ is the bit length of *honestly generated* auxiliary messages, assuming the following very mild assumptions: (i) $v_1/d = O(\log\lambda)$ and (ii) $\gamma = (\lambda\|\boldsymbol{u}\|)^{O(1)}$, a condition that is typically satisfied by the soundness extractor of the associated ZKP. The auxiliary message space is defined as $\mathcal{U} := \mathbb{S}_{\mathcal{B}}^{v_2}$ with $\mathcal{B} = \lambda^{O(1)}$. Then $\mathsf{bitlen}(\boldsymbol{u}) := dv_2\log(2\mathcal{B})$. Set $d = \Theta(\lambda)$, $v_1 = \Theta(\lambda)$ (with $v_1/d = O(\log\lambda)$), $v_2 = \lambda^{O(1)}$, $p = O(1)$, $w = \Theta(\lambda)$ (so that $|\mathcal{C}_{w,p}^d| \geq (d/w-1)^w \geq 2^\lambda$), $\mathcal{B}_e = \Theta(1)$ and $n, m = \Theta(\log\gamma)$. As a result, we have $t = O(2^\tau) = O(2^{v_1/d}) = \lambda^{O(1)}$.

In general, we require two conditions to be satisfied: decryption soundness requirements and M-SIS security requirements (note that M-LWE security affects the number of columns of the commitment matrix, and thus not the commitment size). Let us analyze these two aspects.

(1) Partial-Decryption Soundness and Feasibility (Theorem 2):

$$q > \Omega(tpw\gamma B_e\sqrt{d(m+v_1+v_2)} + t^2pw) = \Omega(\lambda^{O(1)}\gamma\log\gamma). \tag{16}$$

(2) M-SIS security (Lemma 1): The hardness of M-SIS$_{n,m,q,\beta_{\mathrm{SIS}}}$ requires (see [9, Section 1.2]):

$$nd\log q \geq \Omega(\lambda\log^2(\beta_{\mathrm{SIS}})) = \Omega(\lambda\log^2(\gamma)). \tag{17}$$

Note that $\beta_{\mathrm{SIS}} = 2\gamma$ as given in Lemma 1. We can satisfy both conditions with some $\log q = \Theta(\log(\lambda\gamma))$ (ignoring $\log\log\gamma$). With this choice, we get commitment length $\mathsf{bitlen}(C) = nd\log q = \Theta(\lambda\log^2(\gamma))$. To show it is polylog in $\mathsf{bitlen}(\boldsymbol{u})$, it suffices to show that $\log\gamma = \log^{O(1)}(\mathsf{bitlen}(\boldsymbol{u}))$. Assuming that $\gamma = (\lambda\|\boldsymbol{u}\|)^{O(1)}$, we have $\log\gamma \leq O(\log(\lambda\|\boldsymbol{u}\|)) = O(\log\lambda + \log(dv_2) + \log\mathcal{B}) = \log^{O(1)}(\mathsf{bitlen}(\boldsymbol{u}))$, as required.

6 Extending MatRiCTto Auditable Setting

Having dealt with the core task of constructing and analysing a VPDC, we now explain how our VPDC construction can be applied to extend a privacy-preserving confidential transaction blockchain protocol MatRiCT [12] to the auditable setting. Unlike the auditability feature of the original MatRiCT protocol, where auditing may fail against adversarially-created transactions, our auditable MatRiCT variant, called MatRiCT-Au, takes advantage of our VPDC to efficiently provide auditability soundness guarantees against adverserial transactions. More specifically, we show that only minor modifications to MatRiCT are sufficient to add the auditability feature. As the whole MatRiCT protocol is quite involved, in this section, we only briefly review MatRiCT, focusing on the specific parts of the protocol which we modify.

MatRiCT follows the blueprint of RingCT-like [20] private blockchain payment protocols, in which there are two main entities: (i) *spenders/payers*, who create transactions together with a proof of validity, and (ii) *verifiers*, who check that the proof and transaction is valid. The goal of the private payment protocol is to enable users to conduct transactions on blockchain while hiding sensitive transaction information such as the payer/payee identities and the payment amount. Once such information is concealed from the verifiers, it gets harder to validate transactions as we cannot, for example, simply check that the transaction amount is positive and the total balance of the transaction is zero (i.e., the amount spent equals the amount received). To this end, the payers create a NIZK proof showing that they are not creating an invalid transaction, for example, by proving that the balance is preserved.

To hide the payer identity, MatRiCT makes use of a 1-out-of-N NIZK proof (or a ring signature), where the identity of the real payer is hidden within a set of possible payers. This involves committing to the unary representation of an index $\ell \in [0, N-1]$. To hide the payment amount, a commitment to the bits of the transaction amount is used. In fact, the bits representing the user index and those representing the transaction amount are committed in a single commitment. To enable an authority to recover these two critical data pieces, we apply our new VPDC from Sect. 5 for this commitment, so that the VPDC decryption algorithm recovers (i) the real payer's index among N users, and (ii) the transaction amount. Let us investigate more details.

In MatRiCT, an HMC commitment $B = \mathsf{Com}_{ck}(\boldsymbol{b}, \boldsymbol{u}; \boldsymbol{r})$ is computed, where $\boldsymbol{b}$ is a binary vector over $R_{\hat{q}}$ for some $\hat{q} \in \mathbb{Z}^+$ (i.e., $\boldsymbol{b} = (b_0, b_1, \ldots)$ such that $b_i \in \{0, 1\} \subset R_{\hat{q}}$), $\boldsymbol{u}$ is some short auxiliary message and $\boldsymbol{r}$ is some short randomness. Here, the binary vector $\boldsymbol{b}$ is comprised of three components: (i) the unary representation of an index ℓ that identifies the real payer (i.e., spender) index among N parties in a ring signature or a 1-out-of-N proof, (ii) the bits in the binary representation of all output amounts, and (iii) the bits in the so-called "corrector values". Our target is to recover the first two components in decryption so that the authority can learn the two hidden data pieces mentioned above. Note that the payer indeed proves in zero-knowledge that she owns the ℓ-th public key and that certain bits (with known indices) in $\boldsymbol{b}$ construct the output coins. Hence, recovering $\boldsymbol{b}$ guarantees that the real payer index and the output amounts (and thus the transaction amount) are revealed.

As it is expensive to perform an *exact* binary proof on B, MatRiCT performs a *relaxed* binary proof on B. Let us recall a simplified version of the relation proven in MatRiCT for the commitment B, which also applies to our variant MatRiCT-Au.

Lemma 2. *Assume that $\hat{q}$ is sufficiently large and that HMC is γ_{bin}-binding for some γ_{bin} that depends on the system parameters. For an input commitment $B \in R_{\hat{q}}^{\hat{n}}$ and a commitment key $ck = \hat{\boldsymbol{G}} = [\,\boldsymbol{A} \,\|\, \boldsymbol{B} \,\|\, \boldsymbol{C}\,]$ defined over $R_{\hat{q}}$, our binary proof proves knowledge of $(y, \boldsymbol{b}, \hat{\boldsymbol{c}}, \hat{\boldsymbol{r}})$ such that*

- *$y \in \Delta\mathcal{C}^d_{w,p}$, $\hat{\boldsymbol{c}} \in R_{\hat{q}}^{v_2}$ and $\hat{\boldsymbol{r}} \in R_{\hat{q}}^{\hat{m}}$ for some $v_2, \hat{m} \geq 1$,*
- *$yB = \mathsf{Com}_{ck}(y\boldsymbol{b}, \hat{\boldsymbol{c}}; \hat{\boldsymbol{r}}) = \boldsymbol{A}\hat{\boldsymbol{r}} + \boldsymbol{B}y\boldsymbol{b} + \boldsymbol{C}\hat{\boldsymbol{c}}$,*
- *All coordinates b_i of $\boldsymbol{b}$ are in $\{0,1\}$, i.e., $\boldsymbol{b} \in \{0,1\}^{v_1} \subset R_{\hat{q}}^{v_1}$, where $v_1 = k\beta + Sr + \lceil \log(M + S - 1) \rceil (r - 1)$ for parameters k, β satisfying $N = \beta^k$, M, S denoting the number of input/output accounts and r denoting the bit length of each amount,*
- *$\|(y\boldsymbol{b}, \hat{\boldsymbol{c}}, \hat{\boldsymbol{r}})\| \leq \gamma_B$ for some $\gamma_B \in \mathbb{R}^+$ with $\gamma_B < \hat{q}$.*

The above relation is effectively what we study in Definition 5 with $\mathcal{D} = \{0,1\}^{v_1}$. So, the extension we need to make over MatRiCT is to let the spender use the VPDC from Sect. 5 for the commitment B. In particular, the spender just needs to update $ck = \hat{\boldsymbol{G}}$ with a 'trapdoored' commitment key ck^{td} generated by CAddTd. This simply means that the spender replaces the last row of $ck = \hat{\boldsymbol{G}}$ with trapdoor rows published by an authority. This way, the authority in possession of the corresponding trapdoor td can execute CDecGR (Algorithm 2) to recover the vector $\boldsymbol{b}$, which in turn reveals the real payer index $\ell \in [0, N-1]$ and the transaction amount, which is equal to the sum of the output amounts. In particular, since the commitment algorithm for our VPDC remains exactly the same as the standard HMC commitment algorithm used in MatRiCT, our VPDC can be directly plugged in and used with the same efficient NIZK proof of transaction well-formedness used in MatRiCT. For the invertibility of challenge differences in R_t as required in Theorem 2, we use the results of [8,11].

For the concrete parameter setting in MatRiCT with $N = 100$, we have $\dim(\boldsymbol{b}) = v_1 = 291$ as $(k, \beta) = (1, N)$ and $(M, S, r) = (1, 2, 64)$ with the first $k\beta = 100$ bits having exactly a single '1'. As a result, there are more than 2^{191} possibilities for $\boldsymbol{b}$ (i.e., $|\mathcal{D}| > 2^{191}$). Hence, it is infeasible to do an exhaustive search over $\mathcal{D}$ (as done in [12]) for decryption. As our new decryption's run-time is *polylogarithmic* in $|\mathcal{D}|$, we can efficiently execute it. In particular, as we discuss in the full version of this paper, to guarantee auditability soundness against adversarially-created commitments based on our VPDC security bounds while maintaining the same security level as MatRiCT against best-known lattice attacks, we only need to increase (i) the system modulus $\hat{q}$ to a 55-bit value from a 53-bit value and (ii) the commitment matrix dimensions slightly. As shown in the full version of this paper, the decryption runs very fast despite the exponentially large message space.

It is important to note here that MatRiCT and MatRiCT-Au crucially relies on an *aggregate* binary proof for compactness, where many messages are committed together inside a single commitment B. Therefore, the additional succinctness feature of VPDC plays an important role. If one were to replace this HMC commitment with an encryption (or an encryption-like commitment as in [3]), the proof/commitment length would significantly increase (as also discussed in the introduction) due to the large input message dimension (several hundreds) over the polynomial ring $R_{\hat{q}}$.

In the full version of this paper, we describe MatRiCT-Au in full details, and show that addition of a trapdoor as in CAddTd is effectively the only modification required over MatRiCT. We instantiated MatRiCT-Au concretely and implemented it in C/C++ (see the full version). We compare MatRiCT and MatRiCT-Au in Table 1. Our results show that the overhead of MatRiCT-Au over MatRiCT is very small in both communication and computation.

References

1. Bao, F., Deng, R.H., Mao, W.: Efficient and practical fair exchange protocols with off-line TTP. In: IEEE S&P, pp. 77–85. IEEE Computer Society (1998)
2. Baum, C., Bootle, J., Cerulli, A., del Pino, R., Groth, J., Lyubashevsky, V.: Sublinear lattice-based zero-knowledge arguments for arithmetic circuits. In: Shacham, H., Boldyreva, A. (eds.) CRYPTO 2018. LNCS, vol. 10992, pp. 669–699. Springer, Cham (2018). https://doi.org/10.1007/978-3-319-96881-0_23
3. Baum, C., Damgård, I., Lyubashevsky, V., Oechsner, S., Peikert, C.: More efficient commitments from structured lattice assumptions. In: Catalano, D., De Prisco, R. (eds.) SCN 2018. LNCS, vol. 11035, pp. 368–385. Springer, Cham (2018). https://doi.org/10.1007/978-3-319-98113-0_20
4. Camenisch, J., Shoup, V.: Practical verifiable encryption and decryption of discrete logarithms. In: Boneh, D. (ed.) CRYPTO 2003. LNCS, vol. 2729, pp. 126–144. Springer, Heidelberg (2003). https://doi.org/10.1007/978-3-540-45146-4_8

5. Chaum, D., van Heyst, E.: Group signatures. In: Davies, D.W. (ed.) EUROCRYPT 1991. LNCS, vol. 547, pp. 257–265. Springer, Heidelberg (1991). https://doi.org/10.1007/3-540-46416-6_22
6. Esgin, M.F.: Practice-oriented techniques in lattice-based cryptography. Ph.D. thesis, Monash University (2020). https://doi.org/10.26180/5eb8f525b3562
7. Esgin, M.F., Nguyen, N.K., Seiler, G.: Practical exact proofs from lattices: new techniques to exploit fully-splitting rings. In: Moriai, S., Wang, H. (eds.) ASIACRYPT 2020. LNCS, vol. 12492, pp. 259–288. Springer, Cham (2020). https://doi.org/10.1007/978-3-030-64834-3_9
8. Esgin, M.F., Steinfeld, R., Liu, D., Ruj, S.: Efficient hybrid exact/relaxed lattice proofs and applications to rounding and VRFs. Cryptology ePrint Archive, Report 2022 (2022)
9. Esgin, M.F., Steinfeld, R., Liu, J.K., Liu, D.: Lattice-based zero-knowledge proofs: new techniques for shorter and faster constructions and applications. In: Boldyreva, A., Micciancio, D. (eds.) CRYPTO 2019. LNCS, vol. 11692, pp. 115–146. Springer, Cham (2019). https://doi.org/10.1007/978-3-030-26948-7_5
10. Esgin, M.F., Steinfeld, R., Sakzad, A., Liu, J.K., Liu, D.: Short lattice-based one-out-of-many proofs and applications to ring signatures. In: Deng, R.H., Gauthier-Umaña, V., Ochoa, M., Yung, M. (eds.) ACNS 2019. LNCS, vol. 11464, pp. 67–88. Springer, Cham (2019). https://doi.org/10.1007/978-3-030-21568-2_4
11. Esgin, M.F., Steinfeld, R., Zhao, R.K.: MatRiCT$^+$: more efficient post-quantum private blockchain payments. Cryptology ePrint Archive, Report 2021/545 (2021). http://ia.cr/2021/545. (to appear at IEEE S&P 2022)
12. Esgin, M.F., Zhao, R.K., Steinfeld, R., Liu, J.K., Liu, D.: MatRiCT: efficient, scalable and post-quantum blockchain confidential transactions protocol. In: ACM CCS, CCS 2019, pp. 567–584. ACM (2019). (Full version at http://ia.cr/2019/1287)
13. Fiat, A., Shamir, A.: How to prove yourself: practical solutions to identification and signature problems. In: Odlyzko, A.M. (ed.) CRYPTO 1986. LNCS, vol. 263, pp. 186–194. Springer, Heidelberg (1987). https://doi.org/10.1007/3-540-47721-7_12
14. Groth, J., Kohlweiss, M.: One-out-of-many proofs: or how to leak a secret and spend a coin. In: Oswald, E., Fischlin, M. (eds.) EUROCRYPT 2015. LNCS, vol. 9057, pp. 253–280. Springer, Heidelberg (2015). https://doi.org/10.1007/978-3-662-46803-6_9
15. Li, W., Wang, Y., Chen, L., Lai, X., Zhang, X., Xin, J.: Fully auditable privacy-preserving cryptocurrency against malicious auditors (2019). http://ia.cr/2019/925
16. Lyubashevsky, V.: Fiat-Shamir with aborts: applications to lattice and factoring-based signatures. In: Matsui, M. (ed.) ASIACRYPT 2009. LNCS, vol. 5912, pp. 598–616. Springer, Heidelberg (2009). https://doi.org/10.1007/978-3-642-10366-7_35
17. Lyubashevsky, V.: Lattice signatures without trapdoors. In: Pointcheval, D., Johansson, T. (eds.) EUROCRYPT 2012. LNCS, vol. 7237, pp. 738–755. Springer, Heidelberg (2012). https://doi.org/10.1007/978-3-642-29011-4_43
18. Lyubashevsky, V., Neven, G.: One-shot verifiable encryption from lattices. In: Coron, J.-S., Nielsen, J.B. (eds.) EUROCRYPT 2017. LNCS, vol. 10210, pp. 293–323. Springer, Cham (2017). https://doi.org/10.1007/978-3-319-56620-7_11
19. Micciancio, D., Peikert, C.: Trapdoors for lattices: simpler, tighter, faster, smaller. In: Pointcheval, D., Johansson, T. (eds.) EUROCRYPT 2012. LNCS, vol. 7237, pp. 700–718. Springer, Heidelberg (2012). https://doi.org/10.1007/978-3-642-29011-4_41

20. Noether, S.: Ring signature confidential transactions for monero. Cryptology ePrint Archive, Report 2015/1098 (2015). http://ia.cr/2015/1098
21. Regev, O.: On lattices, learning with errors, random linear codes, and cryptography. J. ACM **56**(6), 34:1–34:40 (2009). Preliminary version in STOC 2005
22. Schnorr, C.P.: Efficient identification and signatures for smart cards. In: Brassard, G. (ed.) CRYPTO 1989. LNCS, vol. 435, pp. 239–252. Springer, New York (1990). https://doi.org/10.1007/0-387-34805-0_22
23. Young, A., Yung, M.: Auto-recoverable auto-certifiable cryptosystems. In: Nyberg, K. (ed.) EUROCRYPT 1998. LNCS, vol. 1403, pp. 17–31. Springer, Heidelberg (1998). https://doi.org/10.1007/BFb0054114

Making Private Function Evaluation Safer, Faster, and Simpler

Yi Liu[1,3], Qi Wang[1,2(✉)], and Siu-Ming Yiu[3]

[1] Research Institute of Trustworthy Autonomous Systems and Guangdong Provincial Key Laboratory of Brain-Inspired Intelligent Computation, Department of Computer Science and Engineering, Southern University of Science and Technology, Shenzhen 518055, China
liuy7@mail.sustech.edu.cn, wangqi@sustech.edu.cn

[2] National Center for Applied Mathematics Shenzhen, Southern University of Science and Technology, Shenzhen 518055, China

[3] Department of Computer Science, The University of Hong Kong, Pokfulam, Hong Kong SAR, China
smyiu@cs.hku.hk

Abstract. In the problem of two-party *private function evaluation* (PFE), one party $\mathsf{P_A}$ holds a *private function* f and (optionally) a private input x_A, while the other party $\mathsf{P_B}$ possesses a private input x_B. Their goal is to evaluate f on x_A and x_B, and one or both parties may obtain the evaluation result $f(x_A, x_B)$ while no other information beyond $f(x_A, x_B)$ is revealed.

In this paper, we revisit the two-party PFE problem and provide several enhancements. We propose the *first* constant-round actively secure PFE protocol with linear complexity. Based on this result, we further provide the *first* constant-round publicly verifiable covertly (PVC) secure PFE protocol with linear complexity to gain better efficiency. For instance, when the deterrence factor is $\epsilon = 1/2$, compared to the passively secure protocol, its communication cost is very close and its computation cost is around 2.6×. In our constructions, as a by-product, we design a specific protocol for proving that a list of ElGamal ciphertexts is derived from an *extended permutation* performed on a given list of elements. It should be noted that this protocol greatly improves the previous result and may be of independent interest. In addition, a reusability property is added to our two PFE protocols. Namely, if the same function f is involved in multiple executions of the protocol between $\mathsf{P_A}$ and $\mathsf{P_B}$, then the protocol could be executed more efficiently from the second execution. Moreover, we further extend this property to be *global*, such that it supports multiple executions for the same f in a reusable fashion between $\mathsf{P_A}$ and *arbitrary* parties playing the role of $\mathsf{P_B}$.

Keywords: Extended permutation · Private function evaluation · Publicly verifiable covert security · Secure two-party computation

G. Hanaoka et al. (Eds.): PKC 2022, LNCS 13177, pp. 349–378, 2022.
https://doi.org/10.1007/978-3-030-97121-2_13

1 Introduction

The two-party *private function evaluation* (PFE) problem considers the scenario where a party $\mathsf{P_A}$ holds a *private function* f and (optionally) a private input x_A while the other party $\mathsf{P_B}$ has another private input x_B. These two parties intend to compute $f(x_A, x_B)$ without the existence of a third party. Finally, one or both parties may obtain $f(x_A, x_B)$, while they cannot deduce any other information beyond their specified outputs during the interaction. As a special case of secure computation, note that PFE is different from the notion of standard *secure function evaluation* (SFE). The key difference is that the function f is *commonly known* by participants in SFE, while f should *remain private* in PFE, in the sense that *everything* about the function, except an upper bound on its size and the lengths of both input and output, is hidden.

Both data and algorithms are valuable in numerous real-world scenarios, such as medical and commercial applications. For instance, we consider the following business scenario between a traditional enterprise and an algorithm-driven company. The traditional enterprise has a dataset, while the algorithm-driven company holds a powerful data mining algorithm that can process this dataset. On the one hand, the algorithm-driven company does not intend to disclose the algorithm. On the other hand, since the dataset may contain sensitive data, the traditional enterprise is unwilling to reveal the dataset to others. We note that this dilemma can be solved by a PFE protocol that allows the traditional enterprise to receive the result of privately running the algorithm on the dataset.

It is trivial to design a PFE protocol based on fully homomorphic encryption (FHE) schemes [17]. However, the efficiency of FHE schemes is still prohibitive, and researchers attempted to design PFE in the setting of traditional multi-party computation (MPC). In the literature, some PFE protocols specify a *limited* set of functions, such as polynomials [12,31,35] and low-depth circuits [38], while others are *general-purpose*, focusing on functions implemented by arbitrary (polynomial-size) circuits [1]. In this paper, we work on general-purpose PFE protocols, and thus the PFE protocols mentioned in the rest of this paper are assumed to be general-purpose.

To construct general-purpose PFE protocols, there exist two main approaches. The first approach reduces the PFE problem to the problem of secure computation for universal circuits (UC) (see [2,18,24,26,29,30,40,42]). UC refers to a sequence of circuits $\mathsf{U} = \{\mathsf{U}_n\}_{n \in \mathbb{N}}$, each of which can take as input (the description of) a circuit C of size n and a valid input x, and output $C(x) \leftarrow \mathsf{U}_n(C, x)$. Therefore, we can combine UC with traditional MPC techniques, such as Yao's garbled circuits [28,41], to obtain PFE protocols. The major goal of this line of work is to reduce the size of UC and improve the traditional MPC techniques. However, a noted barrier of UC-based PFE protocol is that a (Boolean) UC has (optimal) size $|\mathsf{U}_n| = \Theta(n \log n)$ [40], where the constant factor (more than 12 for the state-of-the-art result [30]) and the low-order terms are significant. Hence, when the size of a circuit used for evaluation is relatively large, the considerable expansion of its size caused by the use of UC makes UC-based PFE prohibitive.

The second approach avoids the usage of UC. In 2011, Katz and Malka [22] proposed a constant-round passively secure two-party PFE protocol applied on Boolean circuits, and the protocol achieves linear complexity in circuit size. This linear-complexity PFE protocol has asymptotically less computation and communication complexity than UC-based PFE protocols that have complexity $\Theta(n \log n)$. Very recently, an implementation [20] of the passively secure PFE protocol [22] showed that this protocol outperforms the state-of-the-art UC-based PFE protocol not only in communication but also in total running time, *e.g.*, it is $\sim 3.3\times$ faster in a LAN and $\sim 7.0\times$ faster in a WAN for private circuits of size 10^6. Subsequently, the work [33] introduced a general framework for designing PFE protocols. This general framework captures the idea of [22] and provides a slight improvement in communication cost. In addition, a PFE protocol based on *oblivious evaluation of switching networks* (OSN) was provided in [33] and was later improved in [8]. However, it is shown [2,7] that OSN-based PFE protocols have $\Theta(n \log n)$ computation and communication complexities limit their usage when the size of circuits is considerable. More recently, a passively secure re-executable PFE protocol with linear complexity was proposed in [7]. With this reusability property, it is shown [7] that this protocol has significantly better performance than the PFE protocol in [22] and [33] when the protocol is executed any number (more than one) of times for the same function by the same two parties.

Since parties may deviate from the protocol to gain more advantages, such as learning the other party's input and affecting the output of the protocol, it is more realistic to consider PFE protocols that are secure under stronger security models. Unfortunately, even though the line of work for PFE protocols with linear complexity has better performance theoretically and experimentally, existing protocols are mainly focused on the semi-honest model, and very few results managed to provide protocols in stronger security models.

To the best of our knowledge, only two papers considered PFE protocols with linear complexity that are secure against malicious adversaries. The seminal work [22] introduced how to compile their passively secure PFE protocol to be secure against malicious $\mathsf{P_B}$, *i.e.*, the party that provides the private input x_B, via specific efficient zero-knowledge protocols. However, the security of the compiled protocol is not full-fledged, and the function provider $\mathsf{P_A}$ is required to be semi-honest. The subsequent work [34] proposed an actively secure PFE framework with linear complexity based on the results in [33]. However, the number of rounds in this protocol is equal to the number of gates for the evaluated circuit. This will simply become a bottleneck when the size of the circuit is considerable.

Besides the malicious model, there is no PFE protocol with linear complexity in other security models. We notice that the *publicly verifiable covert* (PVC) model is particularly useful for many scenarios that PFE protocols may apply to. *Covert security* was introduced by Aumann and Lindell [4]. It serves as a compromise between semi-honest and malicious security definitions, and thereby provides a more realistic security guarantee than semi-honest security and has significantly less overhead than malicious security. Informally, a malicious party is still allowed to covertly deviate from the protocol execution in this model. However, this misbehavior will be detected by honest parties with a certain probability ϵ, which is called *deterrence factor*. The fear of being caught will deter participants from acting maliciously and deviating from the protocol. The PVC security notion that enhances the covert security model was introduced by Asharov and Orlandi in 2012 [3]. PVC security guarantees that once the misbehavior of a malicious party is caught, honest parties could generate a publicly verifiable certificate to persuade others, including those outside the protocol, that the malicious party is cheating. Meanwhile, it should be guaranteed that this malicious party learns no information about the inputs of honest parties even when the certificate is given. This notion significantly strengthens the covert security model especially when parties' reputations are important. A general PVC-secure two-party computation protocol was proposed in [3] based on garbled circuits and the Signed-OT technique. Then the Signed-OT protocol was improved in [25] to obtain a more efficient PVC-secure protocol. Subsequently, an elegant protocol [21] using a derandomized approach was proposed in 2019. Avoiding the use of costly Signed-OT, this protocol is more efficient than the previous protocols. In the meantime, another protocol [43] introduced a notion called financially secure computation that combines a PVC-secure protocol with blockchain. Very recently, compilers that can transform a two-party passively secure protocol to a PVC-secure protocol were introduced [14,15,39]. It is easy to see that PVC security is useful for two-party PFE protocols in many realistic scenarios. Note that all existing results for two-party PVC security [3,14,15,21,25,39] are only designed for SFE, *i.e.*, the function f is *publicly known*. Although UC can be integrated into these frameworks to derive a PVC-secure PFE protocol, so far there is no PVC-secure PFE protocol with linear complexity.

Therefore, the following question is open so far:

> *Can we construct a constant-round actively secure and a constant-round PVC-secure PFE protocols with linear complexity in the two-party setting while avoiding strong primitives such as FHE?*

In this paper, we answer this question. In addition, we borrow the idea of [7] to realize a reusability property for our protocols and further extend it *globally*. A comparison of main properties for all PFE protocols *with linear complexity* is summarized in Table 1.

1.1 Our Results

We summarize our results and main contributions in this paper as follows.

Active security. We provide the *first* constant-round actively secure PFE protocol with linear complexity in the two-party setting. More precisely, we design a constant-round two-party PFE protocol that is secure against malicious function owner $\mathsf{P_A}$ and semi-honest private input provider $\mathsf{P_B}$. Then by leveraging classical MPC results for security against malicious $\mathsf{P_B}$ providing private input values, such as the approach used in [22], we can automatically

Table 1. Comparison of the main properties for all PFE protocols with linear complexity.

Paper	Security	# Round	Reusable?
[22]	Passive	Constant	No.
[33]	Passive	Constant	No.
[34]	Active	# Gates	No.
[7]	Passive	Constant	Yes, for two parties.
This paper	Active	Constant	Yes, global reusability.
This paper	PVC	Constant	Yes, global reusability.

obtain the desirable actively secure protocol. Our protocol is composed of an *initiation* phase and an *evaluation* phase.

PVC security. Based on the techniques of our actively secure PFE protocol, we design the *first* constant-round PVC-secure PFE protocol with linear complexity in the two-party setting to gain much better efficiency. This protocol inherits the two-phase structure. It is noted that the additional overhead to achieve PVC security is very light from both computation and communication aspects, *e.g.*, when the deterrence factor is $\epsilon = 1/2$, compared to the passively secure protocol, its communication cost is very close and its computation cost is around 2.6×.

Efficiency improvement. We provide the sub-protocol $\Pi_{\mathsf{zk}}^{\mathsf{EncEP}}$ as a core component for our actively secure and PVC-secure protocols. This protocol is designed for proving that a list of ElGamal [16] ciphertexts is derived from an *extended permutation* (see Definition 3) performed on a given list of elements. A generic construction for such a purpose was originally given in [34], and it is left open whether it is possible to construct such a protocol in a specific approach to gaining better performance. Our protocol answers this open problem, and improves the generic construction [34] significantly: the communication cost of our protocol is less than 1/56 of the generic construction, and the computation cost is less than 36%.

Reusability (simplified follow-up executions). The reusability property is added to both of our two PFE protocols. When two specified parties intend to evaluate the same private function f on different private inputs, they only need to go through the initiation phase at one time and then execute the evaluation phase multiple times with different inputs. Moreover, we extend this property *globally*. Namely, once an initiation for a private f is performed by the function owner $\mathsf{P_A}$, *arbitrary* private input providers playing the role of $\mathsf{P_B}$ can benefit from the reusability property for f.

2 Preliminaries

We use $|S|$ to denotes the size of a set S and $||S||$ to denote the number of bits required to represent elements in the set S. We write $x \leftarrow_{\$} S$ for uniformly sampling an element x from the set S. For a positive integer n, let $[n] = \{1, \ldots, n\}$. For a bit string x, we use $x[i]$ to represent the ith bit of x. We write a vector named a as $\vec{a} = (a_1, \ldots, a_n)$, and use $\vec{0}$ and $\vec{1}$ to denote a vector where all entries are equal to 0 and 1 when its dimension is clear in the context, respectively. Let $\vec{a}\vec{b} = (a_1 b_1, \ldots, a_n b_n)$ denote the Hadamard product of two vectors $\vec{a}$ and $\vec{b}$, $\vec{a} \circ \vec{b} = (a_1, \ldots, a_{n_a}, b_1, \ldots, b_{n_b})$ the concatenation of vectors, $\vec{a}^{\mathrm{T}}\vec{b} = \sum_i a_i b_i$ the inner product, and $\vec{g}^{\vec{a}} = \prod_i g_i^{a_i}$ the multi-exponentiation. For a scalar c and a vector $\vec{a}$, the scalar product is $c\vec{a} = (ca_1, \ldots, ca_n)$.

Let κ be the computational security parameter, and κ is written in unary as input to all algorithms. A function f in a variable κ mapping natural numbers to $[0, 1]$ is *negligible* if $f(\kappa) = \mathcal{O}(\kappa^{-c})$ for every constant $c > 0$. We say that $1 - f$ is *overwhelming* if f is negligible.

Given a $\mathsf{seed} \in \{0, 1\}^{\kappa}$, we can use a pseudorandom function with seed as the key in the CTR mode to derive sufficiently many pseudorandom numbers and use them as random coins for operations in protocols.

We use Com to denote the (non-interactive) commitment scheme. We write decom as the random coins for a commitment, which can be used to open this commitment. The commitment scheme Com achieves (computationally) binding and hiding properties. We will use a signature scheme $(\mathsf{KGen}, \mathsf{Sig}, \mathsf{Vf})$ that is existentially unforgeable under chosen-message attacks (EUF-CMA) for our PVC-secure protocol in Sect. 4.

The oblivious transfer (OT) functionality $\mathcal{F}_{\mathsf{OT}}$ is presented below. Let Π_{OT} be the protocol that securely realizes a parallel version of $\mathcal{F}_{\mathsf{OT}}$.

Functionality $\mathcal{F}_{\mathsf{OT}}$

Private inputs: $\mathsf{P_A}$ has input $x \in \{0, 1\}^{\lambda}$ and $\mathsf{P_B}$ has input $\{(A_{i,0}, A_{i,1})\}_{i \in [\lambda]}$.

Upon receiving $x \in \{0, 1\}^{\lambda}$ from $\mathsf{P_A}$ and $\{(A_{i,0}, A_{i,1})\}_{i \in [\lambda]}$ from $\mathsf{P_B}$, the functionality sends $\{A_{i,x[i]}\}_{i \in [\lambda]}$ to $\mathsf{P_A}$.

The security of our protocol relies on the decisional Diffie-Hellman (DDH) assumption as follows.

Definition 1. *The decisional Diffie-Hellman (DDH) assumption in a cyclic group $\mathbb{G} = \langle g \rangle$ of prime order $q \in \Theta(2^{\kappa})$ is that given (g^a, g^b) for $a, b \leftarrow_{\$} \mathbb{Z}_q$, g^{ab} is computationally indistinguishable from a random element in $\mathbb{G}$.*

Under the DDH assumption, we have the following lemma.

Lemma 1 ([36]). *Under the DDH assumption for the cyclic group $\mathbb{G}$ of prime order $q \in \Theta(2^{\kappa})$, for any positive integer $n = \mathsf{poly}(\kappa)$, given $g_1, \ldots, g_n \leftarrow_{\$} \mathbb{G}$, we have that $(g_1^{\alpha_1}, \ldots, g_n^{\alpha_n})$ is computationally indistinguishable from $(g_1^{\alpha}, \ldots, g_n^{\alpha})$ for $\alpha, \alpha_1, \ldots, \alpha_n \leftarrow_{\$} \mathbb{Z}_q$.*

It is well-known that the DDH assumption implies the discrete logarithm assumption, which is equivalent to the following assumption.

Definition 2. *The discrete logarithm relation assumption in a cyclic group* $\mathbb{G}$ *of prime order* $q \in \Theta(2^\kappa)$ *is that for any positive integer* $n = \mathsf{poly}(\kappa)$*, given* $g_1, \ldots, g_n \leftarrow_\$ \mathbb{G}$*, it is computationally hard to find* $a_1, \ldots, a_n \in \mathbb{Z}_q$*, such that* $\exists a_i \neq 0 \in \mathbb{Z}_q \wedge \prod_{i=1}^n g_i^{a_i} = 1$*. We call* $\prod_{i=1}^n g_i^{a_i} = 1$ *a nontrivial discrete logarithm relation.*

We use the ElGamal encryption scheme in our protocol. This encryption scheme is over the cyclic group $\mathbb{G} = \langle g \rangle$ of prime order q, and it is indistinguishable under chosen plaintext attack (IND-CPA) under the DDH assumption for $\mathbb{G}$. We provide the description of algorithms for the scheme as follows.

Key Generation. This algorithm takes as input the security parameter 1^κ, picks $s \leftarrow_\$ \mathbb{Z}_q$, and sets $h \leftarrow g^s$. Then the algorithm outputs the public key $\mathsf{pk} \leftarrow (\mathbb{G}, q, g, h)$ and the private key $\mathsf{sk} \leftarrow s$.

Encryption. This algorithm takes as input a message $m \in \mathbb{G}$ and a public key pk, and returns the ciphertext $c \leftarrow (c^{(0)} = g^r, c^{(1)} = mh^r)$ for $r \leftarrow_\$ \mathbb{Z}_q$.

Decryption. This algorithm takes as input a ciphertext $c = (c^{(0)}, c^{(1)})$ and a key pair $(\mathsf{pk}, \mathsf{sk})$, and returns $m \leftarrow c^{(1)}/(c^{(0)})^s$.

The ElGamal encryption scheme is multiplicatively homomorphic, such that the multiplication result of two ciphertexts is the ciphertext of the multiplication result of the two corresponding plaintexts. Computing the power of a ciphertext c also derives the ciphertext for the power of the corresponding plaintext of c.

2.1 Circuit Representation and Extended Permutation

Here, we introduce an approach to describing Boolean circuits with arbitrary fan-out (see an example circuit C_f in Fig. 1). For a circuit, we call a wire *outgoing wire* (denoted by OW) if it is an input wire of the circuit or output wire of a gate. Meanwhile, a wire is called *incoming wire* (denoted by IW) if it is the input wire of a gate. Outgoing wires are connected with incoming wires, in the sense that each incoming wire connects with exactly one outgoing wire while an outgoing wire may connect with an arbitrary number (including 0) of incoming wires. Suppose that a circuit consists of θ gates, n input bits, and m output bits. Then this circuit has $n + \theta$ outgoing wires and 2θ incoming wires. For a gate G_i, its output wire is the outgoing wire OW_{n+i} and its two input wires are the incoming wires IW_{2i-1} and IW_{2i}. The last m gates are the output gates of the circuit. Figure 1(b) lists all gates $(G_i)_i$ inside the circuit C_f. A formal description of the connections between incoming wires and outgoing wires is captured by [33] via extended permutation.

Definition 3 ([33])**.** *For positive integers* N *and* M*, a mapping* $\pi : [N] \to [M]$ *is an extended permutation (EP) if for every* $x \in [N]$*, there exists one* $y \in [M]$*, such that* $y = \pi(x)$*.*

Given an index of an incoming wire, π maps it to the index of the outgoing wire that connects with this incoming wire (see example in Fig. 1(c)). Note that different from the one-to-one correspondence mapping of the standard permutation, EP allows to replicate or omit elements during the mapping.

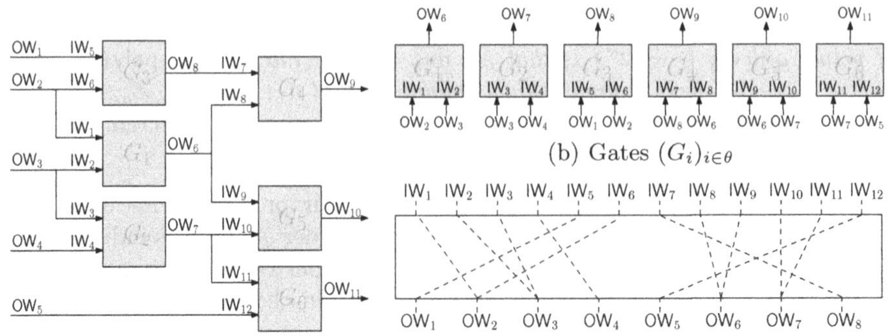

(a) Circuit C_f assembled by $(G_i)_{i\in\theta}$ (b) Gates $(G_i)_{i\in\theta}$ (c) Wire connections and EP π_f

Fig. 1. A circuit C_f and the illustration of its wire connections and EP π_f.

Given a set of gates $(G_i)_{i\in[\theta]}$, the circuit owner $\mathsf{P_A}$ holding the description of a circuit C_f can follow the (randomized) procedure below to assign $(G_i)_{i\in[\theta]}$ to positions of gates in C_f and derive an EP π_f from the resulting circuit assembled by this set of gates.

1. Sort indices for non-output gate positions of C_f in a topological order, such that if the output wire of the ith gate is connected with the input wire of the jth gate, then i must be smaller than j. The indices of output gates are from $\theta - m + 1$ to θ.
2. Pick a random standard permutation π_R. For non-output gates with indices $i \in [\theta - m]$, the position for the ith gate of C_f is assigned to gate $G_{\pi_R(i)}$.
3. For all output gates with indices $i = \theta - m + 1, \ldots, \theta$, assign gate G_i to the position of the ith gate.
4. Extract the EP π_f for connections of outgoing wires and incoming wires from the resulting circuit.

When we consider a circuit that only includes one type of gates, *e.g.*, NAND gates, the circuit can be exactly described by the corresponding EP. Now given π_f, it is easy to derive the description of the circuit. Our protocol indeed leverages this idea and assumes that circuits only consist of NAND gates for simplicity.

2.2 Building Blocks

In Table 2, we present two zero-knowledge ideal functionalities $\mathcal{F}_{\mathsf{zk}}^{\mathsf{DH}}$ and $\mathcal{F}_{\mathsf{zk}}^{\mathsf{EncEP}}$ associated with the relations R_{DH} and R_{EncEP} for the cyclic group $\mathbb{G} = \langle g \rangle$ of prime order q as building blocks for our protocols. We will introduce how to instantiate them in Sect. 3.

3 PFE Protocol for Active Security

In this section, we introduce our constant-round two-party PFE protocol. This protocol is secure against malicious $\mathsf{P_A}$ and semi-honest $\mathsf{P_B}$. Note that it is

Table 2. Relations and their zero-knowledge ideal functionalities.

Relation	Functionality
$R_{\mathsf{DH}} = \{(\mathbb{G}, q, \{g_i\}_{i\in[N]}, \{h_i\}_{i\in[N]}) \mid \exists x, s.t. \bigwedge_{i\in[N]}(h_i = g_i^x)\}$	$\mathcal{F}_{\mathsf{zk}}^{\mathsf{DH}}$
$R_{\mathsf{EncEP}} = \{(\mathbb{G}, q, g, h, \{g_i\}_{i\in[M]}, \{(c_i^{(0)}, c_i^{(1)})\}_{i\in[N]}) \mid \exists \{r_i\}_{i\in[N]}, \pi, s.t.$ $c_i^{(0)} = g^{r_i} \wedge c_i^{(1)} = g_{\pi(i)} h^{r_i} \wedge \pi$ is an EP. $\}$	$\mathcal{F}_{\mathsf{zk}}^{\mathsf{EncEP}}$

straightforward to obtain a constant-round actively secure PFE protocol with linear complexity by leveraging classical MPC results, such as the approach used in [22], to compile the protocol to be secure against malicious (circuit grabler) $\mathsf{P_B}$ providing private input values.

In PFE, a party $\mathsf{P_A}$ has a private Boolean circuit input C_f (implementing a function f) and private input $x_A \in \{0,1\}^{n_A}$, whereas the other party $\mathsf{P_B}$ has private input $x_B \in \{0,1\}^{n_B}$. We present the ideal functionality $\mathcal{F}_{\mathsf{activePFE}}$ for our protocol in the following. Here we consider the more general case that the circuit holder $\mathsf{P_A}$ has an input $x_A \in \{0,1\}^{n_A}$, and it is not difficult to modify the protocols to the case that $\mathsf{P_A}$ has the private input C_f only. For the sake of simplicity, we assume that only one party will receive the evaluation result. It is also possible to modify the protocol such that both parties can receive the final result (see [19, Section 2.5.2]).

Functionality $\mathcal{F}_{\mathsf{activePFE}}$

Pre-agreement: The circuit consists of θ gates, m output wires, and $n(= n_A + n_B)$ input wires.
Private inputs: $\mathsf{P_A}$ has a Boolean circuit input C_f and input $x_A \in \{0,1\}^{n_A}$, whereas the other party $\mathsf{P_B}$ has input $x_B \in \{0,1\}^{n_B}$.

1. If an input of the form abort_i from the party P_i for $i \in \{A, B\}$ is received, the ideal functionality sends $\perp$ to both parties and terminates.
2. If an input circuit C_f satisfying the pre-agreement from $\mathsf{P_A}$ is received, store C_f.
3. If $x_A \in \{0,1\}^{n_A}$ from $\mathsf{P_A}$ and $x_B \in \{0,1\}^{n_B}$ from $\mathsf{P_B}$ are received and an input circuit C_f is stored, the ideal functionality computes $C_f(x_A, x_B)$.
   (a) If P_i (which is corrupted by $\mathcal{A}$) is allowed to learn $C_f(x_A, x_B)$, then it sends $C_f(x_A, x_B)$ to P_i.
   (b) Otherwise, the ideal functionality sends $\mathsf{nothing}$ to the corrupted P_i. Then if the message $\mathsf{continue}$ from $\mathcal{A}$ is received, the ideal functionality sends $C_f(x_1, x_2)$ to the honest party. Otherwise, if abort_i is received from $\mathcal{A}$ on behalf of the corrupted P_i, it sends $\perp$ to the honest party.

3.1 Full Description of the Protocol

We now give a full description of our protocol $\Pi_{\mathsf{activePFE}}$. Our protocol consists of two phases: initiation and evaluation. In the initiation phase, two parties prepare required data for later evaluations of C_f. Then given the preprocessed data from the initiation phase, $\mathsf{P_A}$ and $\mathsf{P_B}$ evaluate C_f on their inputs x_A and

x_B in the evaluation phase. At the end of the protocol, parties obtain their outputs specified by $\mathcal{F}_{\mathsf{activePFE}}$, *i.e.*, the evaluation result $C_f(x_A, x_B)$ or nothing. For the first execution of the protocol, $\mathsf{P_A}$ and $\mathsf{P_B}$ together execute the initiation phase and evaluation phase sequentially. Then, if the two parties would like to evaluate the same circuit C_f on different inputs, they now only need to execute the evaluation phase using the information previously generated in the initiation phase. This reusability property will be further extended to global reusability (see Remark 2). Note that in our protocols, we consider the Boolean circuit C_f only consists of NAND gates for simplicity. We use the cyclic group $\mathbb{G} = \langle g \rangle$ of prime order q as above.

Here, we briefly present the main flow of the protocol. In the initiation phase, $\mathsf{P_A}$ derives an EP from her private circuit C_f and establishes connections of wire labels between incoming and outgoing wires, while $\mathsf{P_B}$'s tasks are to assist $\mathsf{P_A}$ and ensure that $\mathsf{P_A}$ honestly follows the protocol. Then in the evaluation phase, different from the standard paradigm of garbled circuits, we let $\mathsf{P_B}$ *obliviously* garble (all gates of) the circuit for $\mathsf{P_A}$. Then $\mathsf{P_A}$ can evaluate the corresponding garbled circuit, since she knows the topology of her circuit and the connections of wire labels established in the initiation phase.

In this initiation phase, $\mathsf{P_B}$ first chooses a list G of $M = n + \theta - m$ different elements from $\mathbb{G}$ and sends G to $\mathsf{P_A}$. This list G will be used to derive the labels of outgoing wires except those that are output wires of the circuit. After receiving the list G, $\mathsf{P_A}$ generates an ElGamal encryption key pair. Then $\mathsf{P_A}$ derives the EP π_f from the circuit C_f following the procedure in Sect. 2.1. Now $\mathsf{P_A}$ performs the EP π_f on G and encrypts all elements of the resulting list to obtain the list Φ, where the ith encrypted elements in Φ are of the form $g_{\pi(i)}$. The list Φ is then sent to $\mathsf{P_B}$. The EP here is to establish the connections between the outgoing wires (except output wires of the circuit since they do not connect with other wires) and the incoming wires for the further generation of wire labels, and the resulting list is encrypted to hide the EP from $\mathsf{P_B}$. Then $\mathsf{P_A}$ picks a list $T = [t_1, \ldots, t_N]$ for $t_i \in \mathbb{Z}_q$ as the *blinding factors.* Using the homomorphic property, $\mathsf{P_A}$ can compute the t_ith power of the plaintext of c_i for all c_i's in Φ and obtain the resulting list Φ', where the ith element is the encryption of $g^{t_i}_{\pi_f(i)}$. We note that here t_i is used to blind the encrypted values in Φ, such that $\mathsf{P_B}$ still does not know the base $g_{\pi_f(i)}$ when the element $g^{t_i}_{\pi_f(i)}$ is given later, and thus π_f and C_f are hidden. Finally, $\mathsf{P_A}$ helps $\mathsf{P_B}$ to decrypt all elements of Φ' to derive $P = [p_1, \ldots, p_N]$, where $p_i = g^{t_i}_{\pi_f(i)}$. In Fig. 2, we give an illustration of the procedure that the circuit owner $\mathsf{P_A}$ will go through in the initiation phase for the previous example (Fig. 1).

During this procedure, to gain active security, it is important that $\mathsf{P_A}$ should prove in zero-knowledge that her operations are valid using the building blocks in Sect. 2.2. After the initiation phase, $\mathsf{P_B}$ holds the two lists G and P, while $\mathsf{P_A}$ holds the list T, together with lists G and P.

At the beginning of the evaluation phase, $\mathsf{P_B}$ generates labels for all wires. For the output wires of the circuit, $\mathsf{P_B}$ randomly generates wire labels representing 0 and 1 from $\mathbb{G}$. For labels of other wires, $\mathsf{P_B}$ first picks randomly two values $\alpha_0 \in$

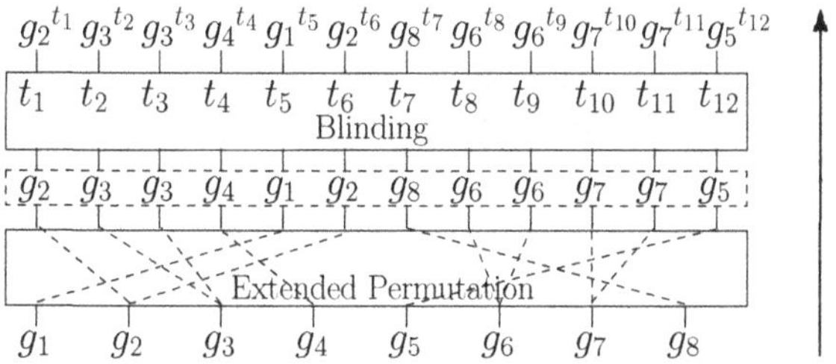

Fig. 2. Procedure of the circuit owner $\mathsf{P_A}$ in the initiation phase. The values in the dotted-line box are encrypted values that are hidden from $\mathsf{P_B}$.

$\mathbb{Z}_q$ and $\alpha_1 \in \mathbb{Z}_q$. Then, all incoming-wire and outgoing-wire labels, except the outgoing wires that are output wires of the circuit (whose have been generated), are generated via computing the values in the lists P and G to the power of α_0 and α_1, respectively, for values 0 and 1. Here, each element p_i in P is for an incoming wire IW_i, and the pair of its wire labels is computed via $(v_i^0, v_i^1) \leftarrow (p_i^{\alpha_0}, p_i^{\alpha_1})$, *i.e.*, $(v_i^0, v_i^1) = (g_{\pi_f(i)}^{t_i\alpha_0}, g_{\pi_f(i)}^{t_i\alpha_1})$. Similarly, for an outgoing wire OW_i, the pair of wire labels $(w_i^0, w_i^1) \leftarrow (g_i^{\alpha_0}, g_i^{\alpha_1})$ is computed using g_i in G. $\mathsf{P_B}$ now can garble all θ gates of the circuit that are composed solely of NAND gates for $\mathsf{P_A}$ one by one using these labels via a classical approach for garbling gates as we will introduce later. Then $\mathsf{P_B}$ sends these garbled gates to $\mathsf{P_A}$. Note that $\mathsf{P_B}$ is unaware of the EP π_f (and the topology of C_f). An illustration for wire labels with respect to garbled gates for the previous example (Fig. 1) is given in Fig. 3. Note that all input-wire labels of the circuit are generated and possessed by $\mathsf{P_B}$, and thus $\mathsf{P_B}$ picks out the input-wire labels corresponding to his input x_B and sends his garbled inputs to $\mathsf{P_A}$. Meanwhile, $\mathsf{P_A}$ could retrieve the garbled inputs corresponding to her input x_A from $\mathsf{P_B}$ through OT. This approach inherits from the standard approach of gabled circuits. Now since $\mathsf{P_A}$ knows the topology of the circuit, the list of blinding factors T, and input-wire labels, she can re-construct

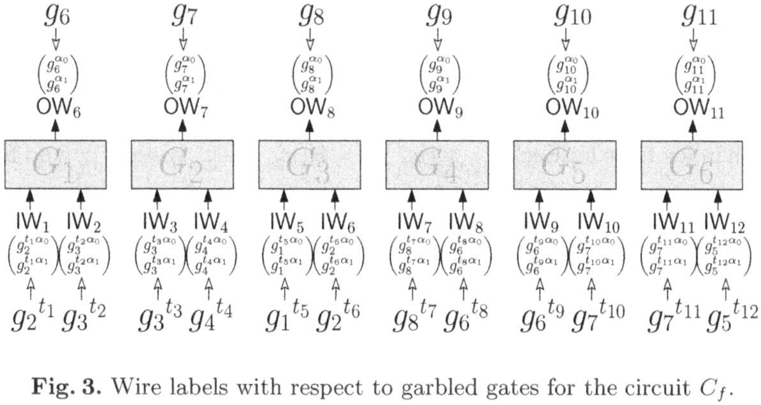

Fig. 3. Wire labels with respect to garbled gates for the circuit C_f.

the garbled circuit assembled by the received garbled gates and evaluate the garbled circuit using both parties' input-wire labels $\{\mathsf{x}_i\}_{i\in[n]}$.

We now introduce the approach to garbling gates and evaluating the garbled circuit assembled by garbled gates. Two algorithms $(\mathsf{Gb}, \mathsf{Eval})$ are involved here.

The algorithm Gb is invoked by $\mathsf{P_B}$ to generate garbled gates (in a one-by-one manner) for $\mathsf{P_A}$. According to the circuit representation approach in Sect. 2.1, a gate G_i consists of two input wires, *i.e.*, incoming wires, with indices $2i-1$ and $2i$, and one output wire, *i.e.*, an outgoing wire, with index $n+i$. For such a gate, Gb takes as input the gate index i, the two pairs of input-wire labels (v_{2i-1}^0, v_{2i-1}^1) and (v_{2i}^0, v_{2i}^1), together with the pair of output-wire labels (w_{n+i}^0, w_{n+i}^1), and prepares four ciphertexts: $c_i^{a,b} \leftarrow \mathsf{Enc}^i_{v^a_{2i-1}, v^b_{2i}}(w_{n+i}^{\overline{a\cdot b}})$ for $a, b \in \{0,1\}$ for a dual-key cipher Enc. Gb outputs the set of garbled gates $\{\mathsf{GG}_i\}_{i\in[\theta]}$. Here $\mathsf{GG}_i = \{c_i^{a,b}\}_{a,b\in\{0,1\}}$, where $c_i^{a,b}$ are randomly permuted.

Eval is invoked by $\mathsf{P_A}$ to evaluate the garbled circuit that consists of garbled gates generated by $\mathsf{P_B}$. It takes as input a set of garbled gates $\{\mathsf{GG}_i\}_{i\in[\theta]}$, a set of input-wire labels $\{\mathsf{x}_i\}_{i\in[n]}$, the list of blinding factors $T = \{t_i\}_{i\in[N]}$, and an EP π_f. This algorithm first derives the description of the corresponding circuit C_f from π_f. Now starting from (outgoing-wire) labels $\{\mathsf{x}_i\}_{i\in[n]}$, Eval computes incoming-wire labels from the corresponding outgoing-wire labels and evaluates garbled gates one by one following the topographical order of the circuit to obtain the final output-wire labels. Without loss of generality, for an outgoing wire OW_i, we denote its label in hand by w_i^b, where $b \in \{0,1\}$. Note that each outgoing wire may connect with some incoming wires that are the input wires of some gates. Assume that an incoming wire IW_j is connected with OW_i, *i.e.*, $i = \pi_f(j)$. $\mathsf{P_A}$ can obtain the wire label of IW_j by computing the t_jth power of w_i^b, *i.e.*, $(w_i^b)^{t_j}$. It is easy to verify that $(w_i^b)^{t_j} = g_i^{\alpha_b t_j} = p_j^{\alpha_b} = v_j^b$, *i.e.*, the result is the input-wire (incoming-wire) label we want. When having two input-wire (incoming-wire) labels $(v_{2i-1}^b, v_{2i}^{b'})$, where $b, b' \in \{0,1\}$, for a garbled gate GG_i, the algorithm can decrypt GG_i using these two labels as keys (via a simple reverse approach of Enc) and obtain the non-$\perp$ resulting output-wire (outgoing-wire) label $w_{n+i}^{\overline{b\cdot b'}}$. It is easy to see that the values of the wire b and b' are hidden from $\mathsf{P_A}$ during this procedure. Since Eval follows the topology of the circuit, input-wire labels of a gate are always ready when we proceed to evaluate that gate. Finally, Eval returns the decrypted output-wire labels of the output gates.

The dual-key cipher Enc here can be constructed based on the random oracle (denoted by $\mathsf{H}\colon \mathbb{G}\times\mathbb{G}\times\{0,1\}^* \to \{0,1\}^{\|\mathbb{G}\|\times\tau}$) in a standard way: to garble a gate with index i, we let $\mathsf{Enc}^i_{v^a_{2i-1}, v^b_{2i}}(w_{n+i}^{\overline{a\cdot b}}) = \mathsf{H}(v_{2i-1}^a, v_{2i}^b, i) \oplus w_{n+i}^{\overline{a\cdot b}}$,[1] and further optimizations exist, *e.g.*, a variant of the point-and-permute optimization [6] (see [7]). This garbling scheme is secure under the random oracle model, and we refer readers to see more information in the full version [32].

We provide the formal descriptions of the protocol below.

[1] The operator $\oplus$ here is applied on the bit-representation of the right group element, and τ specifies the length of proper padding to ensure the check of correct decryption.

Protocol $\Pi_{\mathsf{activePFE}}$

Pre-agreement: Both parties agree on a cyclic group $\mathbb{G} = \langle g \rangle$ of prime order q, where DDH assumption holds. They also have the pre-agreement that C_f consists of θ gates, m output wires, and $n(= n_A + n_B)$ input wires. We denote the number of incoming wires by $N \leftarrow 2\theta$ and the number of outgoing wires except those that are output wires of the circuit by $M \leftarrow n + \theta - m$.
Private inputs: $\mathsf{P_A}$ has a Boolean circuit input C_f and input $x_A \in \{0,1\}^{n_A}$, whereas the other party $\mathsf{P_B}$ has input $x_B \in \{0,1\}^{n_B}$.

Initiation Phase

In this phase, $\mathsf{P_A}$ has private circuit input C_f, while $\mathsf{P_B}$ has no input.

1. $\mathsf{P_B}$ picks $g_i \leftarrow_{\$} \mathbb{G}$ for $i \in [M]$, such that all g_i's are different, and collects them as a list $G = [g_1, \ldots, g_M]$. Then, $\mathsf{P_B}$ sends G to $\mathsf{P_A}$.
2. $\mathsf{P_A}$ picks $s \leftarrow_{\$} \mathbb{Z}_q$ and computes $h \leftarrow g^s$. The public key and private key of the ElGamal encryption then is denoted by $\mathsf{pk} = (\mathbb{G}, q, g, h)$ and $\mathsf{sk} = s$, respectively.
   $\mathsf{P_A}$ derives an EP π_f from C_f. Then $\mathsf{P_A}$ performs π_f on the elements of G and encrypts all resulting elements using pk to derive the list $\Phi = [c_1, c_2, \ldots, c_N]$, where c_i is the encryption of $g_{\pi_f(i)}$ for $i \in [N]$.
   $\mathsf{P_A}$ picks $t_i \leftarrow_{\$} \mathbb{Z}_q$ for $i \in [N]$, such that all t_i's are different, and stores the list $T = [t_1, \ldots, t_N]$ for the evaluation phase. $\mathsf{P_B}$ computes the t_ith power of each plaintext $g_{\pi_f(i)}$ of c_i via the multiplicatively homomorphic property of the ElGamal encryption to obtain c'_i. Let the resulting list $\Phi' = [c'_1, \ldots, c'_N]$.
   $\mathsf{P_A}$ computes the information for decryption of all ciphertexts c'_i (remember that $c'_i = (c'^{(0)}_i, c'^{(1)}_i))$, *i.e.*, $\mathsf{P_A}$ computes $d_i \leftarrow (c'^{(0)}_i)^s$ for $i \in [N]$.
   $\mathsf{P_A}$ sends h, Φ, Φ', and $\{d_i\}_{i \in [N]}$ to $\mathsf{P_B}$. Then $\mathsf{P_A}$ uses the functionalities $\mathcal{F}^{\mathsf{EncEP}}_{\mathsf{zk}}$ to prove to $\mathsf{P_B}$ that she has performed a valid EP on G to obtain Φ. Meanwhile, $\mathsf{P_A}$ uses $\mathcal{F}^{\mathsf{DH}}_{\mathsf{zk}}$ to prove to $\mathsf{P_B}$ her knowledge of s, *i.e.*, the private key, for $(g, \{c'^{(0)}_i\}_{i \in [N]})$ and $(h, \{d_i\}_{i \in [N]})$, together with her knowledge of t_i for the two-tuple ciphertexts c_i and c'_i for all $i \in [N]$.
3. $\mathsf{P_B}$ decrypts all c'_i's to obtain the plaintexts $p_i \leftarrow c'^{(1)}_i \cdot d_i^{-1}$, and stores a list $P = [p_1, \ldots, p_N]$ for the evaluation phase.

Evaluation phase

In this phase, $\mathsf{P_A}$ has private input π_f (for C_f) and x_A, and $\mathsf{P_B}$ has private input x_B. $\mathsf{P_B}$ holds the two lists G and P derived in the initiation phase, while $\mathsf{P_A}$ holds the lists T, G, and P. This phase could be executed multiple times for different input x_A and x_B once the two parties finish the initiation phase.

1. For output wires of the circuit, $\mathsf{P_B}$ picks $w_i^0, w_i^1 \leftarrow_{\$} \mathbb{G}$ for $i = M+1, \ldots, M+m$ as the wire labels. Then $\mathsf{P_B}$ picks $\alpha_0, \alpha_1 \leftarrow_{\$} \mathbb{Z}_q$. For input wires of the circuit and output wires of non-output gates, *i.e.*, all outgoing wires except output wires of the circuit, $\mathsf{P_B}$ computes labels $w_i^0 \leftarrow g_i^{\alpha_0}$ and $w_i^1 \leftarrow g_i^{\alpha_1}$ for $i \in [M]$. For all incoming wires, $\mathsf{P_B}$ computes labels $v_i^0 \leftarrow p_i^{\alpha_0}$ and $v_i^1 \leftarrow p_i^{\alpha_1}$ for $i \in [N]$. $\mathsf{P_B}$ computes $\{\mathsf{GG}_i\}_{i \in [\theta]} \leftarrow \mathsf{Gb}(\{i, (v_{2i-1}^0, v_{2i-1}^1), (v_{2i}^0, v_{2i}^1), (w_{n+i}^0, w_{n+i}^1)\}_{i \in [\theta]})$. Here, for a gate with index i, (v_{2i-1}^0, v_{2i-1}^1) and (v_{2i}^0, v_{2i}^1) are the labels of the two input wires, and (w_{n+i}^0, w_{n+i}^1) are the labels of the output wire.

2. $\mathsf{P_A}$ and $\mathsf{P_B}$ execute $\mathcal{F}_{\mathsf{OT}}$. $\mathsf{P_B}$ uses as input $\{(w_i^0, w_i^1)\}_{i\in[n_A]}$, while $\mathsf{P_A}$ uses as input all bits of $x_A \in \{0,1\}^{n_A}$. At the end, $\mathsf{P_A}$ receives her garbled inputs $\{\mathsf{x}_i = w_i^{x_A[i]}\}_{i\in[n_A]}$.
3. $\mathsf{P_B}$ derives $\mathsf{x}_{n_A+i} \leftarrow w_{n_A+i}^{x_B[i]}$ for $i \in [n_B]$ as his garbled inputs. Then $\mathsf{P_B}$ sends $\mathsf{GC} = \{\mathsf{GG}_i\}_{i\in[\theta]}$ and $\{\mathsf{x}_{n_A+i}\}_{i\in[n_B]}$ to $\mathsf{P_A}$. If $\mathsf{P_A}$ is allowed to know the evaluation result, $\mathsf{P_B}$ also sends the garbled output mapping $\{(w_{M+i}^0, w_{M+i}^1)\}_{i\in[n]}$ to $\mathsf{P_A}$.
4. $\mathsf{P_A}$ computes the garbled output: $\{\mathsf{y}_i\}_{i\in[m]} \leftarrow \mathsf{Eval}(\mathsf{GC}, \{\mathsf{x}_i\}_{i\in[n_A+n_B]}, T, \pi_f)$. If $\mathsf{P_A}$ is allowed to know the evaluation result $y \in \{0,1\}^m$, $\mathsf{P_A}$ can derive and output y from the garbled output mapping he has received. If $\mathsf{P_B}$ is allowed to know the evaluation result, $\mathsf{P_A}$ sends $\{\mathsf{y}_i\}_{i\in[m]}$ to $\mathsf{P_B}$ so that $\mathsf{P_B}$ could derive and output the final result. If the output-wire labels are not consistent with those $\mathsf{P_B}$ generated, $\mathsf{P_B}$ outputs $\perp$.

We present the theorem for the security of the protocol $\Pi_{\mathsf{activePFE}}$ below.

Theorem 1. *If the dual-key cipher is constructed based on the random oracle as above and the DDH assumption of* $\mathbb{G}$ *holds, the protocol* $\Pi_{\mathsf{activePFE}}$ *securely realizes* $\mathcal{F}_{\mathsf{activePFE}}$ *in the presence of malicious* $\mathsf{P_A}$ *and semi-honest* $\mathsf{P_B}$ *in the* $(\mathcal{F}_{\mathsf{OT}}, \mathcal{F}_{\mathsf{zk}}^{\mathsf{EncEP}}, \mathcal{F}_{\mathsf{zk}}^{\mathsf{DH}})$*-hybrid world.*

The proof of this theorem can be found in the full version [32].

We note that there exist protocols that securely realize $\mathcal{F}_{\mathsf{OT}}$ (*e.g.*, [11,23]), such that these protocols can be executed in parallel with constant-round and have linear complexity in the number of $\mathsf{P_B}$'s input wires $n_A (\leq n \ll \theta)$. Meanwhile, there exist protocols (*e.g.*, [13] that can be compiled by Fiat-Shamir heuristic to be non-interactive) that securely realizes $\mathcal{F}_{\mathsf{zk}}^{\mathsf{DH}}$, such that the complexity of the total execution of the protocols is linear in $N(=2\theta)$, *i.e.*, linear in the number of gates θ. In Sect. 3.2, we will give a realization of $\mathcal{F}_{\mathsf{zk}}^{\mathsf{EncEP}}$ that can also be compiled to be non-interactive and has linear complexity. Therefore, the protocol $\Pi_{\mathsf{activePFE}}$ can be instantiated as a constant-round PFE protocol with linear complexity. By leveraging classical MPC results, such as the approach used in [22], our protocol can be compiled to be secure against malicious $\mathsf{P_B}$ and still preserves constant-round and linear complexity. Hence, we obtain a constant-round actively secure PFE protocol in the two-party setting with linear complexity.

Remark 1. The approach in [22] consider the case that $\mathsf{P_A}$ only provides a circuit C_f, while in some scenarios, $\mathsf{P_A}$ may also provide a private input x_A. For this case, we could simply use standard techniques, such as XOR-tree [27], to prevent malicious $\mathsf{P_B}$ launching selective-failure attacks.

In the following theorem, we show that executing the evaluation phase multiple times when the protocol involves the same circuit C_f (and EP π_f) does not sacrifice the security of the protocol $\Pi_{\mathsf{activePFE}}$. The proof of this theorem is put in the full version [32].

Theorem 2. *The evaluation phase of* $\Pi_{\mathsf{activePFE}}$ *can be securely executed multiple times for a fixed circuit* C_f*. In other words, the protocol that executes one initiation phase and multiple evaluation phases is secure against malicious* $\mathsf{P_A}$ *and semi-honest* $\mathsf{P_B}$.

We note that every execution of the evaluation phase in the view of $\mathsf{P_B}$ is to generate a set of new garbled gates, and the efforts to achieve reusability are mainly devoted to preventing $\mathsf{P_A}$ from learning additional information. Therefore, when we use classical MPC results, such as the approach used in [22], for the protocol, it is obvious that this reusability property still holds.

Remark 2. It is important that all messages from $\mathsf{P_B}$ in the initiation phase, including those from $\mathsf{P_B}$ in the protocols that securely realize $\mathcal{F}_{\mathsf{zk}}^{\mathsf{DH}}$ and $\mathcal{F}_{\mathsf{zk}}^{\mathsf{EncEP}}$ (in Sect. 3.2) are all random. Meanwhile, after the initiation phase, $\mathsf{P_B}$ does not possess any private information. Therefore, we can make the initiation phase non-interactive via borrowing the idea of Fiat-Shamir heuristic. Now $\mathsf{P_A}$ can use the random oracle to generate messages of $\mathsf{P_B}$ (using all previous messages), simulate the interaction, and publish her messages in this simulated interaction at one time. Via this approach, the protocol is *globally* reusable for the same circuit C_f. This means that *all* parties playing the role of $\mathsf{P_B}$ can retrieve $\mathsf{P_A}$'s messages and verify the correctness of these published messages. Then it is sufficient for them to directly start the evaluation phase with $\mathsf{P_A}$ for the fixed private circuit C_f multiple times using P and G derived in this simulated interaction. No interaction for initiation phase is needed between $\mathsf{P_A}$ and a potential party playing the role of $\mathsf{P_B}$. This is a new feature, since the reusability of previous PFE protocols with linear complexity [7] is *locally* reusable, such that $\mathsf{P_A}$ needs to interactively perform a setup for a fixed circuit with a specified $\mathsf{P_B}$, and the reusability only works for the two parties that perform such a setup together.

3.2 Realization of Functionality $\mathcal{F}_{\mathsf{zk}}^{\mathsf{EncEP}}$

In this section, we introduce an approach securely realizing the functionality $\mathcal{F}_{\mathsf{zk}}^{\mathsf{EncEP}}$. We would like to note that although EP is a generalization of permutation (shuffle), it seems that its corresponding zero-knowledge protocol cannot be constructed by simply modifying or invoking a shuffle protocol, *e.g.*, [5,9]. That may be the main reason why [34] failed to provide such a specific protocol for EP by extending shuffle protocols (see Appendix B of [34] for their thoughts on failed attempts) and they only provided a protocol in a generic approach. In what follows, we provide an efficient and specific protocol for $\mathcal{F}_{\mathsf{zk}}^{\mathsf{EncEP}}$.

We firstly introduce the basic idea of our protocol. The job of the prover in $\mathcal{F}_{\mathsf{zk}}^{\mathsf{EncEP}}$ is to convince the verifier that the plaintexts of a list of ciphertexts $\Phi = [c_1, \ldots, c_N]$ is derived from an EP that performs on a list of elements $G = [g_1, \ldots, g_M]$. In other words, the plaintext of each ciphertext in Φ is one of the elements in G. Notice that this is equivalent to saying that the plaintext of a ciphertext c_i is $\vec{g}^{\vec{e}_i} = \prod_{j=1}^{M} g_j^{e_{ij}}$, where the vector $\vec{e}_i = (e_{i1}, \ldots, e_{iM})$ is of the form that exact one entry is 1 and all other entries are 0, *i.e.*,

$$e_{ij} = \begin{cases} 1 & \text{if } c_i \text{ encrypts } g_j\,, \\ 0 & \text{otherwise.} \end{cases}$$

The vector $\vec{e}_i$ satisfies such a condition if and only if $\vec{1}^{\mathrm{T}}\vec{e}_i = 1$ and $\vec{e}_i\vec{e}_i = \vec{e}_i$. The condition $\vec{1}^{\mathrm{T}}\vec{e}_i = 1$ implies that the sum of all entries of $\vec{e}_i$ is equal to 1. The condition $\vec{e}_i\vec{e}_i = \vec{e}_i$ implies that $\vec{e}_i(\vec{e}_i - \vec{1}) = \vec{0}$, *i.e.*, each entry of the vector is either 0 or 1. These two conditions conclude that $\vec{e}_i$ is of the form that exact one entry is 1 and all other entries are 0. In addition, the corresponding ciphertext c_i is of the form $(g^{r_i}, \vec{g}^{\vec{e}_i} h^{r_i})$, which is reminiscent of ElGamal or Pedersen [37] commitment schemes and can be regarded as a commitment to the vector $\vec{e}_i$. Therefore, the prover's goal is to prove that each "committed" vector $\vec{e}_i$ satisfies $\vec{1}^{\mathrm{T}}\vec{e}_i = 1$ and $\vec{e}_i\vec{e}_i = \vec{e}_i$, in a zero-knowledge manner. We note that it is possible for the prover to simultaneously prove the conditions for all $\vec{e}_i$'s.

For the proof of the condition $\vec{1}^{\mathrm{T}}\vec{e}_i = 1$, let the verifier pick a challenge $\omega \leftarrow_{\$} \mathbb{Z}_q$. Then using the homomorphic property, both parties compute $C = (\prod_{i=1}^{N}(c_i^{(0)})^{\omega^i}, \prod_{i=1}^{N}(c_i^{(1)})^{\omega^i})$, which can be regarded as a commitment to the vector $\vec{e} = \sum_{i=1}^{N}\omega^i\vec{e}_i$. Since ω is random, if $\sum_{i=1}^{N}\omega^i(\vec{1}^{\mathrm{T}}\vec{e}_i) = \sum_{i=1}^{N}\omega^i$ holds, then $\vec{1}^{\mathrm{T}}\vec{e}_i = 1$ holds for all $i \in [M]$ with an overwhelming probability. Let $\Omega \leftarrow \sum_{i=1}^{N}\omega^i$. Since $\sum_{i=1}^{N}\omega^i(\vec{1}^{\mathrm{T}}\vec{e}_i) = \vec{1}^{\mathrm{T}}\vec{e}$ and $\vec{e}$ is committed in C, it is enough for the prover to prove that $\vec{1}^{\mathrm{T}}\vec{e} = \Omega$ holds if the prover is computationally bounded.

We could follow a similar approach for the proof of the condition $\vec{e}_i\vec{e}_i = \vec{e}_i$. Let the verifier pick a random challenge $x \in \mathbb{Z}_q$. Then, using the homomorphic property, both parties compute $c_{\vec{d}} = (\prod_{i=1}^{N}(c_i^{(0)})^{x^i}, \prod_{i=1}^{N}(c_i^{(1)})^{x^i})$, which can be regarded as a commitment to $\vec{d} = \sum_{i=1}^{N}x^i\vec{e}_i$. Since x is randomly chosen, if $\sum_{i=1}^{N}x^i\vec{e}_i\vec{e}_i - \vec{d} = \vec{0}$ holds, then $\vec{e}_i\vec{e}_i = \vec{e}_i$ holds for all $i \in [N]$ with an overwhelming probability. Moreover, let the verifier pick another random challenge $y \in \mathbb{Z}_q$ and define a bilinear map $* : \mathbb{Z}_q^M \times \mathbb{Z}_q^M \to \mathbb{Z}_q$ by $(a_1, \ldots, a_M) * (b_1, \ldots, b_M) = \sum_{j=1}^{M}a_jb_jy^j$. Similarly, if $\vec{e}_i * \vec{e}_i - \vec{1} * \vec{e}_i = 0$, then $\vec{e}_i\vec{e}_i = \vec{e}_i$ holds with an overwhelming probability. Hence, since the vectors $\vec{e}_i$'s and $\vec{d}$ have been committed in c_i's and $c_{\vec{d}}$, it is enough for the prover to prove that $\sum_{i=1}^{N}x^i\vec{e}_i * \vec{e}_i - \vec{1} * \vec{d} = 0$ holds if the prover is computationally bounded.

It is important to note that all g_i's are generated by $\mathsf{P_B}$, and thus a computationally bounded $\mathsf{P_A}$ cannot find a non-trivial discrete logarithm relation for $\{g_i\}_{i\in[M]}$ except a negligible probability. This guarantees the soundness of the protocols. Now we present the protocol $\Pi_{\mathsf{zk}}^{\mathsf{EncEP}}$ between a prover P and a verifier V below. Two sub-protocols $\Pi_{\mathsf{zk}}^{\mathsf{Sum}}$ and $\Pi_{\mathsf{zk}}^{\mathsf{Zero}}$ then follow respectively. In these protocols, V always verifies whether the received messages are of correct form, and rejects once they are not. These protocols are all public-coin honest-verifier zero-knowledge, and we can compile them to be non-interactive and secure via Fiat-Shamir heuristic to obtain the protocols we want.

Protocol $\Pi_{\mathsf{zk}}^{\mathsf{EncEP}}$

Public Inputs: A cyclic group $\mathbb{G} = \langle g \rangle$ of prime order q, where DDH assumption holds. The public key of the ElGamal encryption scheme $\mathsf{pk} = (\mathbb{G}, q, g, h)$. A list of elements $G = [g_1, \ldots, g_M]$. A list of ElGamal ciphertexts $\Phi = [c_1, \ldots, c_N]$, where $c_i = (c_i^{(0)}, c_i^{(1)})$. Elements in G and Φ all belong to the group $\mathbb{G}$.

Witness: P has an EP π and a list $R = [r_1, \ldots, r_N]$ that are random coins of ciphertexts in Φ, where $r_i \in \mathbb{Z}_q$.

1. For $i \in [N]$, P derives a vector $\vec{e_i} = (e_{i,1}, \ldots, e_{i,M}) \in \mathbb{Z}_q^M$ from π, such that the encrypted value of c_i can be represented by $\vec{g}^{\vec{e_i}}$. For the EP π, this vector is of the form where exact one entry is 1 and all other entries are all 0.
2. V picks an element $\omega \leftarrow_\$ \mathbb{Z}_q$ and sends it to P. Both parties compute $C \leftarrow (C^{(0)} = \prod_{i=1}^N (c_i^{(0)})^{\omega^i}, C^{(1)} = \prod_{i=1}^N (c_i^{(1)})^{\omega^i})$. P computes $\vec{e} \leftarrow \sum_{i=1}^N \omega^i \vec{e_i}$ and $r_{\vec{e}} \leftarrow \sum_{i=1}^N \omega^i r_i$. Both parties compute $\Omega \leftarrow \sum_{i=1}^N \omega^i$. P proves to V the following relation R_{Sum} for $\vec{y} = \vec{1}$ via the protocol $\Pi_{\mathsf{zk}}^{\mathsf{Sum}}$:
$$\{(\mathbb{G}, q, g, h, G, C, \Omega, \vec{y}) \mid \exists(\vec{e}, r_{\vec{e}}) : C^{(0)} = g^{r_{\vec{e}}} \wedge C^{(1)} = \vec{g}^{\vec{e}} h^{r_{\vec{e}}} \wedge \vec{y}^{\mathrm{T}} \vec{e} = \Omega\}.$$
3. V picks two elements $x, y \leftarrow_\$ \mathbb{Z}_q$ and sends them to P. Both parties compute $c_{\vec{d_i}} \leftarrow (c_{\vec{d_i}}^{(0)} = (c_i^{(0)})^{x^i}, c_{\vec{d_i}}^{(1)} = (c_i^{(1)})^{x^i})$ for $i \in [N]$ and also $c_{\vec{d}} \leftarrow (c_{\vec{d}}^{(0)} = \prod_{i=1}^N (c_i^{(0)})^{x^i}, c_{\vec{d}}^{(1)} = \prod_{i=1}^N (c_i^{(1)})^{x^i})$ and $c_{-\vec{1}} \leftarrow (\prod_{i=1}^M g_i^{-1}, 1)$. P computes $\vec{d_i} \leftarrow x^i \vec{e_i}$ and $r_{\vec{d_i}} \leftarrow x^i r_i$ for $i \in [N]$, $\vec{d} \leftarrow \sum_{i=1}^N \vec{d_i}$, and $r_{\vec{d}} = \sum_{i=1}^N r_{\vec{d_i}}$. Define a bilinear map $* : \mathbb{Z}_q^M \times \mathbb{Z}_q^M \to \mathbb{Z}_q$ by $(a_1, \ldots, a_M) * (b_1, \ldots, b_M) = \sum_{j=1}^M a_j b_j y^j$. P proves to V the following relation R_{Zero} via the protocol $\Pi_{\mathsf{zk}}^{\mathsf{Zero}}$:
$$\{(\mathbb{G}, q, g, h, G, \Phi, \{c_{\vec{d_i}}\}_{i \in [N]}, c_{\vec{d}}, c_{-\vec{1}}) \mid \exists(\{\vec{e_i}, r_i, \vec{d_i}, r_{d_i}\}_{i \in [N]}, \vec{d}, r_{\vec{d}}) :$$
$$(\forall i \in [N], c_i^{(0)} = g^{r_i} \wedge c_i^{(1)} = \vec{g}^{\vec{e_i}} h^{r_i} \wedge c_{\vec{d_i}}^{(0)} = g^{r_{\vec{d_i}}} \wedge c_{\vec{d_i}}^{(1)} = \vec{g}^{\vec{d_i}} h^{r_{\vec{d_i}}})$$
$$\wedge c_{\vec{d}}^{(0)} = g^{r_{\vec{d}}} \wedge c_{\vec{d}}^{(1)} = \vec{g}^{\vec{d}} h^{r_{\vec{d}}} \wedge \sum_{i=1}^N \vec{e_i} * \vec{d_i} - \vec{1} * \vec{d} = 0\}.$$

Theorem 3. *The protocol $\Pi_{\mathsf{zk}}^{\mathsf{EncEP}}$ is an honest-verifier zero-knowledge argument of knowledge for R_{EncEP}.*

The proof of this theorem can be found in the full version [32].

The protocol $\Pi_{\mathsf{zk}}^{\mathsf{Sum}}$ between a prover P and a verifier V below uses the idea mentioned in [10] for recursing the protocol and halving the statement in each recursion. Thus, $\Pi_{\mathsf{zk}}^{\mathsf{Sum}}$ has logarithmic communication cost. Throughout this protocol, we assume that the parameter M is a power of 2. If needed, one can easily pad the inputs to ensure that this holds as in [10].

Protocol $\Pi_{\mathsf{zk}}^{\mathsf{Sum}}$

Public Inputs: A cyclic group $\mathbb{G} = \langle g \rangle$ of prime order q, where DDH assumption holds. The public key of the ElGamal encryption scheme $\mathsf{pk} = (\mathbb{G}, q, g, h)$. An ElGamal ciphertexts $C = (C^{(0)}, C^{(1)})$. An element $\Omega \in \mathbb{Z}_q$. Two vectors $\vec{g} = (g_1, \ldots, g_M)$ and $\vec{y} = (y_1, \ldots, y_M)$ of length M. Denote the length of vectors $\vec{g}$ and $\vec{y}$ by $\ell = M$. Let $c_{\vec{e}} \leftarrow C^{(1)}$. Both parties initiate an element $c'_{\vec{e}} \leftarrow g^{\Omega}$.
Witness: The prover P has witness $\vec{e}$, $r_{\vec{e}}$.
Statement: There exist $\vec{e}$ and $r_{\vec{e}}$, such that $C^{(0)} = g^{r_{\vec{e}}} \wedge c_{\vec{e}} = \vec{g}^{\vec{e}} h^{r_{\vec{e}}} \wedge c'_{\vec{e}} = g^{\vec{y}^{\mathrm{T}} \vec{e}}$.

- V picks $u \leftarrow_\$ \mathbb{G}$ and sends u to P. P initiates $\rho_{\vec{e}} = 0$, and $\rho'_{\vec{e}} = 0$. Then two parties engage in the procedure below to prove the statement:
  There exist $\vec{e}$, $r_{\vec{e}}$, $\rho_{\vec{e}}$, *and* $\rho'_{\vec{e}}$, *such that* $C^{(0)} = g^{r_{\vec{e}}} \wedge c_{\vec{e}} = \vec{g}^{\vec{e}} u^{\rho_{\vec{e}}} h^{r_{\vec{e}}} \wedge c'_{\vec{e}} = g^{\vec{y}^{\mathrm{T}}\vec{e}} u^{\rho'_{\vec{e}}}$.
- If $\ell = 1$, we denote the only element in $\vec{e}$, $\vec{g}$, and $\vec{y}$ by $\bar{e}$, $\bar{g}$, and $\bar{y}$, respectively. Let $\gamma \leftarrow g^{\bar{y}}$. Now $c_{\vec{e}}$, $c'_{\vec{e}}$, and $C^{(0)}$ are of the form $c_{\vec{e}} = \bar{g}^{\bar{e}} u^{\rho_{\vec{e}}} h^{r_{\vec{e}}}$, $c'_{\vec{e}} = \gamma^{\bar{e}} u^{\rho'_{\vec{e}}}$, and $C^{(0)} = g^{r_{\vec{e}}}$, respectively. P and V follow the procedure as follows.
  1. P picks $x_1, x_2, x_3, x_4 \leftarrow_\$ \mathbb{Z}_q$, and sends $a_1 \leftarrow \bar{g}^{x_1} u^{x_2} h^{x_3}$, $a_2 \leftarrow \gamma^{x_1} u^{x_4}$, $a_3 \leftarrow g^{x_3}$ to V.
  2. V sends $\alpha \leftarrow_\$ \mathbb{Z}_q$ to P.
  3. P sends $z_1 \leftarrow x_1 + \alpha\bar{e}$, $z_2 \leftarrow x_2 + \alpha\rho_{\vec{e}}$, $z_3 \leftarrow x_3 + \alpha r_{\vec{e}}$, and $z_4 \leftarrow x_4 + \alpha\rho'_{\vec{e}}$ to V.
  4. V verifies whether equations $\bar{g}^{z_1} u^{z_2} h^{z_3} = a_1 c_{\vec{e}}^{\alpha}$, $\gamma^{z_1} u^{z_4} = a_2 (c'_{\vec{e}})^{\alpha}$, and $g^{z_3} = a_3 (C^{(0)})^{\alpha}$ hold. If they all hold, V outputs accept. Otherwise, V outputs reject.
- If $\ell \neq 1$, P and V follow the following procedure.
  1. We write $\vec{e} = \vec{e}_L \circ \vec{e}_R$, $\vec{g} = \vec{g}_L \circ \vec{g}_R$, and $\vec{y} = \vec{y}_L \circ \vec{y}_R$. P computes $v_L \leftarrow \vec{g}_R^{\vec{e}_L} u^{\rho_L}$, $v_R \leftarrow \vec{g}_L^{\vec{e}_R} u^{\rho_R}$, $v'_L \leftarrow g^{\vec{y}_R^{\mathrm{T}}\vec{e}_L} u^{\rho'_L}$, and $v'_R \leftarrow g^{\vec{y}_L^{\mathrm{T}}\vec{e}_R} u^{\rho'_R}$, where $\rho_L, \rho_R, \rho'_L, \rho'_R \leftarrow_\$ \mathbb{Z}_q$. Then P sends v_L, v_R, v'_L, and v'_R to V.
  2. V sends $\alpha \leftarrow_\$ \mathbb{Z}_q$ to P.
  3. P computes $\vec{e}' = \alpha\vec{e}_L + \alpha^{-1}\vec{e}_R$ of length $\ell' = \ell/2$, and also computes $\rho_{\vec{e}'} \leftarrow \rho_{\vec{e}} + \alpha^2\rho_L + \alpha^{-2}\rho_R$ and $\rho'_{\vec{e}'} \leftarrow \rho'_{\vec{e}} + \alpha^2\rho'_L + \alpha^{-2}\rho'_R$. Both parties compute $c_{\vec{e}'} \leftarrow c_{\vec{e}} v_L^{\alpha^2} v_R^{\alpha^{-2}}$ and $c'_{\vec{e}'} \leftarrow c'_{\vec{e}} (v'_L)^{\alpha^2} (v'_R)^{\alpha^{-2}}$, and two vectors $\vec{g}' \leftarrow \vec{g}_L^{\alpha^{-1}} \vec{g}_R^{\alpha}$ and $\vec{y}' \leftarrow \alpha^{-1}\vec{y}_L + \alpha\vec{y}_R$ of length $\ell' = \ell/2$. It is easy to verify that $c_{\vec{e}'} = \vec{g}'^{\vec{e}'} u^{\rho_{\vec{e}'}} h^{r_{\vec{e}}}$ and $c'_{\vec{e}'} = g^{\vec{y}'^{\mathrm{T}}\vec{e}'} u^{\rho'_{\vec{e}'}}$.
  4. Both parties recurse on $\Pi_{\mathsf{zk}}^{\mathsf{Sum}}$ for the same $C^{(0)}$, $(\mathbb{G}, q, g, h)$, u but using $c_{\vec{e}'}$, $c'_{\vec{e}'}$, $\vec{g}'$, $\vec{y}'$ in place of $c_{\vec{e}}$, $c'_{\vec{e}}$, $\vec{g}$, $\vec{y}$. P in the recursion uses the same $r_{\vec{e}}$, but uses $\rho_{\vec{e}'}$, $\rho'_{\vec{e}'}$, $\vec{e}'$ in place of $\rho_{\vec{e}}$, $\rho'_{\vec{e}}$, $\vec{e}$. We use $\ell' = \ell/2$ in place of ℓ to denote the length of vector $\vec{g}'$, $\vec{y}'$, and $\vec{e}'$.

Theorem 4. *The protocol* $\Pi_{\mathsf{zk}}^{\mathsf{Sum}}$ *is an honest-verifier zero-knowledge argument of knowledge for the relation* R_{Sum}.

The proof of this theorem can be found in the full version [32].

The protocol $\Pi_{\mathsf{zk}}^{\mathsf{Zero}}$ between a prover P and a verifier V below borrows the idea of the *zero argument* in [5]. We tailor the protocol to support the ElGamal encryption scheme and introduce how to further reduce the communication cost in Remark 3.

Protocol $\Pi_{\mathsf{zk}}^{\mathsf{Zero}}$

Public Inputs: A cyclic group $\mathbb{G} = \langle g \rangle$ of prime order q, where DDH assumption holds. The public key of the ElGamal encryption scheme $\mathsf{pk} = (\mathbb{G}, q, g, h)$. A list $G = [g_1, \ldots, g_M]$. Two lists of ElGamal ciphertexts $\{c_{\vec{u}_i}^{(0)}, c_{\vec{u}_i}^{(1)}\}_{i\in[\ell]}$, $\{c_{\vec{v}_i}^{(0)}, c_{\vec{v}_i}^{(1)}\}_{i\in[\ell]}$. The description of the bilinear map $*$ for a variable y.
Witness: The prover P has witness $\{\vec{u}_i, r_{\vec{u}_i}\}_{i\in[\ell]}$, $\{\vec{v}_i, r_{\vec{v}_i}\}_{i\in[\ell]}$.

Statement: There exist $\{\vec{u}_i, r_{\vec{u}_i}\}_{i\in[\ell]}$ and $\{\vec{v}_i, r_{\vec{v}_i}\}_{i\in[\ell]}$, such that $c^{(0)}_{\vec{u}_i} = g^{r_{\vec{u}_i}}$, $c^{(1)}_{\vec{u}_i} = \vec{g}^{\vec{u}_i} h^{r_{\vec{u}_i}}$, $c^{(0)}_{\vec{v}_i} = g^{r_{\vec{v}_i}}$, $c^{(1)}_{\vec{v}_i} = \vec{g}^{\vec{v}_i} h^{r_{\vec{v}_i}}$ for all $i \in [\ell]$, and $\sum_{i=1}^{\ell} \vec{u}_i * \vec{v}_i = 0$.

1. P picks $\vec{u}_0, \vec{v}_{\ell+1} \leftarrow_\$ \mathbb{Z}_q^M$ and $r_{\vec{u}_0}, r_{\vec{v}_{\ell+1}} \leftarrow_\$ \mathbb{Z}_q$. Then P computes $c_{\vec{u}_0} \leftarrow (c^{(0)}_{\vec{u}_0} = g^{r_{\vec{u}_0}}, c^{(1)}_{\vec{u}_0} = \vec{g}^{\vec{u}_0} h^{r_{\vec{u}_0}})$ and $c_{v_{\vec{\ell+1}}} \leftarrow (c^{(0)}_{v_{\vec{\ell+1}}} = g^{r_{\vec{v}_{\ell+1}}}, c^{(1)}_{v_{\vec{\ell+1}}} = \vec{g}^{\vec{v}_{\ell+1}} h^{r_{\vec{v}_{\ell+1}}})$. P computes for $\phi = 0, \dots, 2\ell$
$$d_\phi \leftarrow \sum_{\substack{0\le i\le \ell, 1\le j\le \ell+1 \\ j=\ell+1-\phi+i}} \vec{u}_i * \vec{v}_j \,.$$
P picks $r_{d_\phi} \leftarrow_\$ \mathbb{Z}_q$ for $\phi \in \{0,\dots,2\ell\}\backslash\{\ell+1\}$ and computes $c_{d_\phi} \leftarrow g^{d_\phi} h^{r_{d_\phi}}$ for $\phi \in \{0,\dots,2\ell\}\backslash\{\ell+1\}$. For $\phi = \ell+1$, both parties set $r_{d_{\ell+1}} \leftarrow 0$ and $c_{d_{\ell+1}} \leftarrow 1$, After the computation, P sends $c_{\vec{u}_0}$, $c_{\vec{v}_{\ell+1}}$, and $\{c_{d_\phi}\}_{\phi\in\{0,\dots,2\ell\}\backslash\{\ell+1\}}$ to V.
2. V sends $x \leftarrow_\$ \mathbb{Z}_q$ to P.
3. P computes $\vec{u} \leftarrow \sum_{i=0}^{\ell} x^i \vec{u}_i$, $r_{\vec{u}} \leftarrow \sum_{i=0}^{\ell} x^i r_{\vec{u}_i}$, $\vec{v} \leftarrow \sum_{j=1}^{\ell+1} x^{\ell-j+1} \vec{v}_j$, $r_{\vec{v}} \leftarrow \sum_{j=1}^{\ell+1} x^{\ell+1-j} r_{\vec{v}_j}$, and $t \leftarrow \sum_{\phi=0}^{2\ell} x^\phi r_{d_\phi}$, and sends $\vec{u}$, $r_{\vec{u}}$, $\vec{v}$, $r_{\vec{v}}$, t to V.
4. V outputs accept if all equations $\prod_{i=0}^{\ell} (c^{(0)}_{\vec{u}_i})^{x^i} = g^{r_{\vec{u}}}$, $\prod_{i=0}^{\ell} (c^{(1)}_{\vec{u}_i})^{x^i} = \vec{g}^{\vec{u}} h^{r_{\vec{u}}}$, $\prod_{j=1}^{\ell+1} (c^{(0)}_{\vec{v}_j})^{x^{\ell+1-j}} = g^{r_{\vec{v}}}$, $\prod_{j=1}^{\ell+1} (c^{(1)}_{\vec{v}_j})^{x^{\ell+1-j}} = \vec{g}^{\vec{v}} h^{r_{\vec{v}}}$, and $\prod_{\phi=0}^{2\ell} c_{d_\phi}^{x^\phi} = g^{\vec{u}*\vec{v}} h^t$ hold. Otherwise, V outputs reject.

Theorem 5. *The protocol $\Pi^{\mathsf{Zero}}_{\mathsf{zk}}$ is an honest-verifier zero-knowledge argument of knowledge for the relation R_{Zero}.*

The proof of this theorem can be found in the full version [32].

Remark 3. We can further reduce the communication cost of $\Pi^{\mathsf{Zero}}_{\mathsf{zk}}$. Notice that in Step 1, P needs to commit to all elements in $\{d_\phi\}_{\phi=0,\dots,2\ell}$. We could include a list of $2\ell+1$ random elements of $\mathbb{G}$, *e.g.*, $H = \{h_\phi\}_{\phi=0,\dots,2\ell}$, in the common reference string. P can thus commit to $\{d_\phi\}_{\phi=0,\dots,2\ell}$ by computing $c_{\vec{d}} \leftarrow (g^{r_{\vec{d}}}, \sum_{\phi=0}^{2\ell} h_\phi^{d_\phi} h^{r_{\vec{d}}})$ for $r_{\vec{d}} \leftarrow_\$ \mathbb{Z}_q$. P now only needs to send $c_{\vec{d}}$ to verifier instead of $\{c_{d_\phi}\}_{\phi\in\{2,\dots,2\ell\}\backslash\{\ell+1\}}$, and does not need to send t to V in Step 3. Alternatively, P proves to V the following statement for $\vec{y} = [x^0, \dots, x^\ell, 0, x^{\ell+2}, x^{2\ell}]$ and $D = \vec{u} * \vec{v}$ via the protocol $\Pi^{\mathsf{Sum}}_{\mathsf{zk}}$ in Step 4:
$$\{(\mathbb{G}, q, g, h, H, c_{\vec{d}}, D, \vec{y}) \mid \exists(\vec{d}, r_{\vec{d}}) : c^{(0)}_{\vec{d}} = g^{r_{\vec{d}}} \wedge c^{(1)}_{\vec{d}} = \vec{h}^{\vec{d}} h^{r_{\vec{d}}} \wedge \vec{y}^{\mathrm{T}} \vec{d} = D\}\,.$$
Following this approach, we reduce the linear communication cost of sending d_ϕ's to the logarithmic communication cost of using $\Pi^{\mathsf{Sum}}_{\mathsf{zk}}$. Similarly, P can avoid directly sending $\vec{v}$ and $r_{\vec{v}}$, *i.e.*, the opening for $c_{\vec{v}} = (c^{(0)}_{\vec{v}}, c^{(1)}_{\vec{v}}) = (\prod_{j=1}^{\ell+1} (c^{(0)}_{\vec{v}_j})^{x^{\ell+1-j}}, \prod_{j=1}^{\ell+1} (c^{(1)}_{\vec{v}_j})^{x^{\ell+1-j}})$. Now P only sends $\vec{u}$ and $r_{\vec{u}}$ in Step 3, and V only verifies the two equations related to $\vec{u}$ and $r_{\vec{u}}$ in Step 4. Then, P sends $D = \vec{u} * \vec{v}$ to V and proves the following statement for $\vec{y} = [y^1 u_1, \dots, y^M u_M]$ via the protocol $\Pi^{\mathsf{Sum}}_{\mathsf{zk}}$ in Step 4:
$$\{(\mathbb{G}, q, g, h, G, c_{\vec{v}}, D, \vec{y}) \mid \exists(\vec{v}, r_{\vec{v}}) : c^{(0)}_{\vec{v}} = g^{r_{\vec{v}}} \wedge c^{(1)}_{\vec{v}} = \vec{g}^{\vec{v}} h^{r_{\vec{v}}} \wedge \vec{y}^{\mathrm{T}} \vec{v} = D\}\,.$$

4 PFE Protocol for PVC Security

In this section, we introduce the *first* constant-round PVC-secure PFE protocol with linear complexity in the two-party setting based on the results in Sect. 3. The corresponding ideal functionality $\mathcal{F}_{\mathsf{covertPFE}}$ is given in the following.

Functionality $\mathcal{F}_{\mathsf{covertPFE}}$

Pre-agreement: The circuit C_f consists of θ gates, m output wires, and $n(= n_A + n_B)$ input wires.
Private inputs: $\mathsf{P_A}$ has a Boolean circuit input C_f and input $x_A \in \{0,1\}^{n_A}$, whereas the other party $\mathsf{P_B}$ has input $x_B \in \{0,1\}^{n_B}$.

1. If an input of the form abort_i from the party P_i for some $i = \{A, B\}$ is received, the ideal functionality sends $\perp$ to both parties and the ideal execution terminates.
2. If a circuit C_f satisfying the pre-agreement from $\mathsf{P_A}$ is received, store C_f.
3. If an input of the form blatantCheat from $\mathsf{P_B}$ is received, the ideal functionality sends corrupted to both parties and terminates.
4. If an input of the form cheat from $\mathsf{P_B}$ is received and $\mathsf{P_A}$'s inputs C_f and x_A were received previously:
   - With probability ϵ, the ideal functionality sends corrupted to both parties and terminates.
   - With probability $1 - \epsilon$, the ideal functionality sends $(\mathsf{undetected}, x_A, C_f)$ to $\mathsf{P_B}$. If $\mathsf{P_A}$ is allowed to receive the output, the ideal functionality waits for $y \in \{0,1\}^m$ from the adversary $\mathcal{A}$, sends y to $\mathsf{P_A}$, and terminates.
5. If input $x_A \in \{0,1\}^{n_A}$ from $\mathsf{P_A}$ and $x_B \in \{0,1\}^{n_B}$ from $\mathsf{P_B}$ are received and an input circuit C_f is stored, the ideal functionality computes $C_f(x_A, x_B)$.
   (a) If $\mathsf{P_A}$ (when she is corrupted by $\mathcal{A}$) is allowed to learn $C_f(x_A, x_B)$, then it sends $C_f(x_A, x_B)$ to $\mathsf{P_A}$.
   (b) Otherwise, the ideal functionality sends nothing to $\mathsf{P_A}$. Then if continue from $\mathcal{A}$ is received, the ideal functionality sends $C_f(x_1, x_2)$ to the honest $\mathsf{P_B}$. Otherwise, if abort_A is received from $\mathcal{A}$ on behalf of the corrupted $\mathsf{P_A}$, it sends $\perp$ to the honest $\mathsf{P_B}$.

We give the PVC-security definition for our PFE protocol $\Pi_{\mathsf{covertPFE}}$ as follows.

Definition 4. *A two-party PFE protocol* $\Pi_{\mathsf{covertPFE}}$ *along with algorithms* Blame *and* Judge *is publicly verifiable covert secure with* ϵ*-deterrent if the following conditions hold.*

PVC security *The protocol* $\Pi_{\mathsf{covertPFE}}$*, which might output* cert *if the honest party detects covert cheating, securely realizes* $\mathcal{F}_{\mathsf{covertPFE}}$ *with* ϵ*-deterrent.*
Public verifiability *If the honest party outputs* cert *during the protocol execution, then the output of the algorithm* Judge *for* cert *is* 1*, except a negligible probability.*
Defamation freeness *If one party is honest, the probability that the other malicious party generates a certificate* cert *for which* Judge *outputs* 1 *is negligible.*

4.1 Full Description of the Protocol

In the two-party case, active security implies covert security with public verifiability, since we could regard attempts to cheat as abortions. Therefore, techniques for dealing with malicious $\mathsf{P_A}$ are workable for the PVC-secure setting.

Here we briefly introduce the main idea of our PVC-secure protocol $\Pi_{\mathsf{covertPFE}}$. Recall that in Remark 2, we describe how to make the initiation phase non-interactive. This approach can also be adopted here in $\Pi_{\mathsf{covertPFE}}$. Thus, we now do not need to consider malicious $\mathsf{P_B}$ in the initiation phase. We can reuse the initiation phase of $\Pi_{\mathsf{activePFE}}$ for $\Pi_{\mathsf{covertPFE}}$, with the exception that we include G in the common reference string to simplify the proof of security. Note that this small change does not hinder the protocol from achieving global reusability.

In the evaluation phase of $\Pi_{\mathsf{activePFE}}$, $\mathsf{P_A}$ receives the garbled circuit and garbled inputs, evaluates the garbled circuit, and derives the resulting outputs or sends garbled outputs back to $\mathsf{P_B}$. It is easy to see that $\mathsf{P_A}$ has no chance to cheat in the protocol. Even if $\mathsf{P_A}$ sends incorrect garbled outputs to $\mathsf{P_B}$, the incorrect garbled outputs will still be rejected by $\mathsf{P_B}$ due to the authenticity of the garbling. Hence, we only need to focus on the security against covert $\mathsf{P_B}$.

To achieve covert security, we follow the same paradigm of all existing work, *i.e.*, parties generate λ instances of a passively secure protocol, check the correctness of $\lambda - 1$ randomly chosen instances, and take the result of the unopened one. In addition, we use a derandomized approach to supporting efficient correctness check in our protocol. More concretely, $\mathsf{P_B}$ needs to pick for each instance a seed to generate random coins during the execution of that instance (including the circuit garbling and OT protocol). $\mathsf{P_A}$ then uses OT protocol to retrieve all but one of the seeds, such that $\mathsf{P_B}$ is unaware of which instances are checked. Now given the seeds, $\mathsf{P_A}$ can easily check the correctness of the corresponding instances. To prevent $\mathsf{P_B}$ leaking inputs, $\mathsf{P_B}$ commits to his pairs of input-wire labels in random order with randomness derived from the seed and send these two commitments to $\mathsf{P_A}$ for each instance. Hence, $\mathsf{P_A}$ can effectively check the correctness of these commitments using the seed for opened instance, while $\mathsf{P_B}$'s inputs are preserved. After the check, $\mathsf{P_A}$ points out the unopened instance, and now one of the two commitments for her input wires needs to be opened by $\mathsf{P_B}$ as his garbled input to enable $\mathsf{P_A}$ to evaluate the unopened garbled circuit.

To add public verifiability to the approach above, we let $\mathsf{P_B}$ sign all transcripts that have been produced before the time when $\mathsf{P_A}$ reveals the index of the unopened instance. In addition, for each instance, let $\mathsf{P_A}$ commit to a random seed at the beginning of the protocol and uses this seed to derived random coins during her execution of the instance. This commitment will be included in $\mathsf{P_B}$'s transcript and signed by $\mathsf{P_B}$, such that it can prevent $\mathsf{P_A}$ from defaming honest $\mathsf{P_B}$. If $\mathsf{P_B}$ deviates from an instance checked by $\mathsf{P_A}$, $\mathsf{P_A}$ can generate a certificate that includes related transcripts and $\mathsf{P_B}$'s signature on them for that instance, such that it allows a third party to verify this proof of misbehavior. Since $\mathsf{P_B}$ cannot realize in time that the instance in which he deviates from the protocol has been checked by $\mathsf{P_A}$, he cannot abort before $\mathsf{P_A}$ has collected enough materials to generate the certificate.

Our protocol $\Pi_{\mathsf{covertPFE}}$ is given in the following. Since parties need to commit to transcripts of the OT executions in the protocol, the description directly uses the protocol Π_{OT} that securely realizes a parallel version of $\mathcal{F}_{\mathsf{OT}}$.

Protocol $\Pi_{\mathsf{covertPFE}}$

Pre-agreement: Both parties agree on a cyclic group $\mathbb{G} = \langle g \rangle$ of prime order q, where DDH assumption holds. They also have the pre-agreement about C_f: θ gates, m output wires, $n(= n_A + n_B)$ input wires, $N = 2\theta$ incoming wires, and $M = n + \theta - m$ outgoing wires except output wires of the circuit. The common reference string includes a list $G = [g_1, \ldots, g_M] \in \mathbb{G}^M$, where all g_i's are different.
Private inputs: $\mathsf{P_A}$ has a Boolean circuit input C_f and input $x_A \in \{0,1\}^{n_A}$, whereas the other party $\mathsf{P_B}$ has input $x_B \in \{0,1\}^{n_B}$ and keys $(\mathsf{vk}, \mathsf{sigk})$ for a signature scheme. $\mathsf{P_A}$ knows the verification key vk.

Initiation Phase

1. $\mathsf{P_A}$ picks $s \leftarrow_\$ \mathbb{Z}_q$ and computes $h \leftarrow g^s$. Denote the public and private keys of the ElGamal encryption by $\mathsf{pk} = (\mathbb{G}, q, g, h)$ and $\mathsf{sk} = s$, respectively.
   $\mathsf{P_A}$ derives an EP π_f from C_f. Then $\mathsf{P_A}$ permutes elements of G according to π_f and encrypts all resulting elements using pk to derive the list $\Phi = [c_1, c_2, \ldots, c_N]$, where c_i is the encryption of $g_{\pi_f(i)}$ for $i \in [N]$.
   $\mathsf{P_A}$ picks $t_i \leftarrow_\$ \mathbb{Z}_q$ for $i \in [N]$, such that all t_i's are different, and stores the list $T = [t_1, \ldots, t_N]$ for the evaluation phase. $\mathsf{P_B}$ computes the t_ith power of each plaintext $g_{\pi_f(i)}$ of c_i via the multiplicatively homomorphic property of the ElGamal encryption (using pk) to obtain c'_i. Let the resulting list $\Phi' = [c'_1, \ldots, c'_N]$. $\mathsf{P_A}$ computes the information for decryption of all ciphertexts c'_i (remember that $c'_i = (c'^{(0)}_i, c'^{(1)}_i)$), *i.e.*, $\mathsf{P_A}$ computes $d_i \leftarrow (c'^{(0)}_i)^s$ for $i \in [N]$. $\mathsf{P_A}$ sends h, Φ, Φ', and $\{d_i\}_{i\in[N]}$ to $\mathsf{P_B}$. Then $\mathsf{P_A}$ uses the functionality $\mathcal{F}_{\mathsf{zk}}^{\mathsf{EncEP}}$ to prove to $\mathsf{P_B}$ that she has performed a valid EP on G to obtain the list of ciphertexts Φ. Meanwhile, $\mathsf{P_A}$ uses $\mathcal{F}_{\mathsf{zk}}^{\mathsf{DH}}$ to prove to $\mathsf{P_B}$ her knowledge of s, *i.e.*, sk, for $(g, \{c'^{(0)}_i\}_{i\in[N]})$ and $(h, \{d_i\}_{i\in[N]})$, together with her knowledge of t_i for the two-tuple ciphertexts c_i and c'_i for all $i \in [N]$.
2. $\mathsf{P_B}$ decrypts all c'_i's to obtain the plaintexts via $p_i \leftarrow c'^{(1)}_i \cdot d_i^{-1}$. $\mathsf{P_B}$ stores a list $P = [p_1, \ldots, p_N]$ for the evaluation phase.

Evaluation phase

0. $\mathsf{P_A}$ chooses uniform κ-bit strings $\{\mathsf{seed}^A_j\}_{j\in[\lambda]}$, computes $\mathsf{c}^{\mathsf{seed}^A_j} \leftarrow \mathsf{Com}(\mathsf{seed}^A_j)$ and sends $\{\mathsf{c}^{\mathsf{seed}^A_j}\}_{j\in[\lambda]}$ to $\mathsf{P_B}$.
   $\mathsf{P_B}$ chooses uniform κ-bit strings $\{\mathsf{seed}^B_j, \mathsf{witness}_j\}_{j\in[\lambda]}$, while $\mathsf{P_A}$ picks $\hat{\jmath} \leftarrow_\$ [\lambda]$ and sets $b_{\hat{\jmath}} = 1$ and $b_j = 0$ for $j \neq \hat{\jmath}$. $\mathsf{P_B}$ and $\mathsf{P_A}$ run λ executions of Π_{OT}. In the jth execution, $\mathsf{P_B}$ uses as input $(\mathsf{seed}^B_j, \mathsf{witness}_j)$ and $\mathsf{P_A}$ uses as input b_j with randomness derived from seed^A_j. At the end, $\mathsf{P_A}$ has $\{\mathsf{seed}^B_j\}_{j\neq\hat{\jmath}}$ and $\mathsf{witness}_{\hat{\jmath}}$. Let us denote the transcript of the jth execution by trans_j.
1. For $j \in [\lambda]$, using the randomness derived from seed^B_j, $\mathsf{P_B}$ picks $w^0_{i,j}, w^1_{i,j} \leftarrow_\$ \mathbb{G}$ for $i = M+1, \ldots, M+m$ and $\alpha_{0,j}, \alpha_{1,j} \leftarrow_\$ \mathbb{Z}_q$. $\mathsf{P_B}$ also computes wire labels and produces garbled gates as in $\Pi_{\mathsf{activePFE}}$. At the end, $\mathsf{P_B}$ obtains the resulting collection of garbled gates $\mathsf{GC}_j = \{\mathsf{GG}_{i,j}\}_{i\in[\theta]}$, $\mathsf{P_A}$'s input-wire

labels $\{(w^0_{i,j}, w^1_{i,j})\}_{i\in[n_A]}$, $\mathsf{P_B}$'s input-wire labels $\{(w^0_{n_A+i,j}, w^1_{n_A+i,j})\}_{i\in[n_B]}$, and output-wire labels of the garbled circuit $\{(w^0_{M+i,j}, w^1_{M+i,j})\}_{i=1,\ldots,m}$.

2. $\mathsf{P_A}$ and $\mathsf{P_B}$ are involved in λ executions of Π_{OT}. In the jth execution, $\mathsf{P_B}$ uses as input $(w^0_{i,j}, w^1_{i,j})_{i\in[n_A]}$, while $\mathsf{P_A}$ uses as input x_A if $j = \hat{\jmath}$ and 0^{n_A} otherwise, and random coins of $\mathsf{P_A}$ and $\mathsf{P_B}$ are derived from seed^A_j and seed^B_j, respectively. At the end, $\mathsf{P_A}$ obtains her garbled input $\{\mathsf{x}_i = w^{x_A[i]}_{i,\hat{\jmath}}\}_{i\in[n_A]}$. Let $\mathtt{h}^{\mathsf{OT}}_j$ denote the hash value of the transcript for the jth execution of Π_{OT}.
3. (a) For all $j \in [\lambda]$, $\mathsf{P_B}$ computes $\mathsf{c}^{x_B}_{i,j,b} \leftarrow \mathsf{Com}(w^b_{n_A+i,j})$ for all $i \in [n_B]$ and $b \in \{0,1\}$. Let $\mathtt{h}^{\mathsf{O}}_j$ be the hash value of $\{(w^0_{M+i,j}, w^1_{M+i,j})\}_{i=1,\ldots,m}$. $\mathsf{P_B}$ then computes $\mathsf{c}_j \leftarrow \mathsf{Com}(\mathsf{GC}_j, \{\mathsf{c}^{x_B}_{i,j,b}\}_{i\in[n_B],b\in\{0,1\}}, \mathtt{h}^{\mathsf{O}}_j)$, where two elements in each pair $(\mathsf{c}^{x_B}_{i,j,0}, \mathsf{c}^{x_B}_{i,j,1})$ are permuted in random order. The random coins of commitments and permutations are derived from seed^B_j.

   (b) $\mathsf{P_B}$ generates $\sigma_j \leftarrow \mathsf{Sig}_{\mathsf{sigk}}(G, P, j, \mathsf{c}^{\mathsf{seed}^A_j}, \mathsf{trans}_j, \mathsf{h}^{\mathsf{OT}}_j, \mathsf{c}_j)$ for $j \in [\lambda]$.

   Then $\mathsf{P_B}$ sends $\{\mathsf{c}_j, \sigma_j\}_{j\in[\lambda]}$ to $\mathsf{P_A}$.
4. $\mathsf{P_A}$ verifies that whether all σ_j's are valid. If not, $\mathsf{P_A}$ halts and outputs $\perp$. Then $\mathsf{P_A}$ calls $\mathsf{Blame}(\{\mathsf{h}^{\mathsf{OT}}_j, \mathsf{c}_j\}_{j\in[\lambda]\setminus\{\hat{\jmath}\}})$. If the output is cert, $\mathsf{P_B}$ sends cert to $\mathsf{P_B}$, outputs corrupted, and halts. Otherwise, $\mathsf{P_A}$ sends $(\hat{\jmath}, \{\mathsf{seed}^B_j\}_{j\neq\hat{\jmath}}, \mathsf{witness}_{\hat{\jmath}})$ to $\mathsf{P_B}$. $\mathsf{P_B}$ verifies that these values are all consistent with those he has sent in Step 0 and aborts if not.
5. $\mathsf{P_B}$ assigns $\mathsf{x}_{n_A+i} \leftarrow w^{x_B[i]}_{n_A+i,\hat{\jmath}}$ for $i \in [n_B]$. Then $\mathsf{P_B}$ sends $\mathsf{GC}_{\hat{\jmath}}$, $\{\mathsf{x}_{n_A+i}\}_{i\in[n_B]}$, $\{\mathsf{c}^{x_B}_{i,\hat{\jmath},b}\}_{i\in[n_B],b\in\{0,1\}}$ (in the same order as Step 3a), and $\mathtt{h}^{\mathsf{O}}_{\hat{\jmath}}$, together with $\mathsf{decom}^{\mathsf{c}_{\hat{\jmath}}}$ and $\{\mathsf{decom}^{\mathsf{c}^{x_B}_{i,\hat{\jmath},x_B[i]}}\}_{i\in[n_B]}$, to $\mathsf{P_A}$. If $\mathsf{P_A}$ is allowed to know the evaluation result, $\mathsf{P_B}$ also sends the garbled output mapping $\{(w^0_{M+i}, w^1_{M+i})\}_{i\in[m]}$ to $\mathsf{P_A}$.
6. $\mathsf{P_A}$ outputs $\perp$ and aborts if $\mathsf{Com}(\mathsf{GC}_j, \{\mathsf{c}^{x_B}_{i,\hat{\jmath},b}\}_{i\in[n_B],b\in\{0,1\}}, \mathtt{h}^{\mathsf{O}}_{\hat{\jmath}}; \mathsf{decom}^{\mathsf{c}_{\hat{\jmath}}}) \neq \mathsf{c}_{\hat{\jmath}}$, for some $i \in [n_B]$, $\mathsf{Com}(\mathsf{x}_{n_A+i}; \mathsf{decom}^{\mathsf{c}^{x_B}_{i,\hat{\jmath},x_B[i]}}) \notin \{\mathsf{c}^{x_B}_{i,\hat{\jmath},0}, \mathsf{c}^{x_B}_{i,\hat{\jmath},1}\}$, or $\mathtt{h}^{\mathsf{O}}_{\hat{\jmath}}$ is not consistent (if it is verifiable).

   $\mathsf{P_A}$ computes $\{\mathsf{y}_i\}_{i\in[m]} \leftarrow \mathsf{Eval}(\mathsf{GC}_{\hat{\jmath}}, \{\mathsf{x}_i\}_{i\in[n]}, T, \pi_f)$. If $\mathsf{P_A}$ is allowed to know the evaluation result, $\mathsf{P_A}$ can thereby derive the output. If $\mathsf{y}_i \notin \{w^0_i, w^1_i\}$ for some $i \in \{M+1, \ldots, M+m\}$, $\mathsf{P_A}$ outputs $\perp$. If $\mathsf{P_B}$ is allowed to know the evaluation result, $\mathsf{P_A}$ sends $\{\mathsf{y}_i\}_{i\in[m]}$ to $\mathsf{P_B}$ so that $\mathsf{P_B}$ could derive the result. If the output-wire labels are not consistent with those $\mathsf{P_B}$ generated, $\mathsf{P_B}$ outputs $\perp$.

In the following, we provide the algorithms Blame and Judge used in $\Pi_{\mathsf{covertPFE}}$.

Algorithm Blame

Specified parameters: G, P, $\{\mathsf{trans}_j, \sigma_j, \mathsf{seed}^A_j, \mathsf{decom}^{\mathsf{seed}^A_j}, \mathsf{seed}^B_j\}_{j\in[\lambda]\setminus\{\hat{\jmath}\}}$.
Inputs: $\{\mathsf{h}^{\mathsf{OT}}_j, \mathsf{c}_j\}_{j\in[\lambda]\setminus\{\hat{\jmath}\}}$.

1. For all $j \neq \hat{\jmath}$, simulate $\mathsf{P_B}$'s computation in steps 1, 2, and 3a, and particularly compute $\hat{\mathsf{h}}^{\mathsf{OT}}_j$ and $\hat{\mathsf{c}}_j$. Let J be the set of indices, such that for $j \in J$, $(\hat{\mathsf{h}}^{\mathsf{OT}}_j, \hat{\mathsf{c}}_j) \neq (\mathsf{h}^{\mathsf{OT}}_j, \mathsf{c}_j)$.
2. (a) If $|J| = 0$, the algorithm returns accept.

(b) If $|J| \geq 1$, the algorithm picks $j \leftarrow_\$ J$ and outputs a certificate $\mathsf{cert} = (P, j, \mathsf{trans}_j, \mathsf{h}_j^{\mathsf{OT}}, \mathsf{c}_j, \sigma_j, \mathsf{seed}_j^A, \mathsf{decom}^{\mathsf{seed}_j^A})$.

Algorithm Judge

Inputs: A verification key vk for the signature scheme, a certificate $\mathsf{cert} = (P, j, \mathsf{trans}_j, \mathsf{h}_j^{\mathsf{OT}}, \mathsf{c}_j, \sigma_j, \mathsf{seed}_j^A, \mathsf{decom}^{\mathsf{seed}_j^A})$, common reference string G.

1. Compute $\mathsf{c}^{\mathsf{seed}_j^A} \leftarrow \mathsf{Com}(\mathsf{seed}_j^A; \mathsf{decom}^{\mathsf{seed}_j^A})$.
2. If $\mathsf{Vf}((G, P, j, \mathsf{c}^{\mathsf{seed}_j^A}, \mathsf{trans}_j, \mathsf{h}_j^{\mathsf{OT}}, \mathsf{c}_j), \sigma_j) = 0$, output 0.
3. Simulate the execution of Π_{OT} that involves trans_j (Step 0 of the evaluation phase). In this simulation, the input of $\mathsf{P_A}$ is 0, random coins are derived from seed_j^A, and the incoming messages of $\mathsf{P_B}$ are those included in trans_j. Check whether messages sent by $\mathsf{P_A}$ are consistent with that of trans_j and output 0 if not. Otherwise, denote $\mathsf{P_A}$'s output of this simulation of Π_{OT} by seed_j^B.
4. Use seed_j^A and seed_j^B to simulate the execution of Steps 1, 2, and 3a of the evaluation phase, and particularly compute $\hat{\mathsf{h}}_j^{\mathsf{OT}}$ and $\hat{\mathsf{c}}_j$.
5. (a) If $(\hat{\mathsf{h}}_j^{\mathsf{OT}}, \hat{\mathsf{c}}_j) = (\mathsf{h}_j^{\mathsf{OT}}, \mathsf{c}_j)$, output 0.
   (b) If $\hat{\mathsf{c}}_j \neq \mathsf{c}_j$, output 1.
   (c) If the first message for which $\hat{\mathsf{h}}_j^{\mathsf{OT}} \neq \mathsf{h}_j^{\mathsf{OT}}$ corresponds to $\mathsf{P_A}$, output 0. Otherwise, output 1.

We present the theorem for the security of the protocol $\Pi_{\mathsf{covertPFE}}$ as follows.

Theorem 6. *If the commitment algorithm* Com *is computationally binding and hiding, the hash function is modeled as a random oracle, the garbling scheme is secure under the random oracle model, the DDH assumption of* $\mathbb{G}$ *holds, perfectly correct protocol* Π_{OT} *UC-realizes* $\mathcal{F}_{\mathsf{OT}}$*, and the signature scheme* $(\mathsf{KGen}, \mathsf{Sig}, \mathsf{Vf})$ *is* EUF-CMA*, then the protocol* $\Pi_{\mathsf{CovertPFE}}$ *along with* Blame *and* Judge *is publicly verifiable covert secure with deterrence factor* $\epsilon = 1 - \frac{1}{\lambda}$ *in the* $(\mathcal{F}_{\mathsf{zk}}^{\mathsf{EncEP}}, \mathcal{F}_{\mathsf{zk}}^{\mathsf{DH}})$*-hybrid world.*

The proof of this theorem can be found in the full version [32]. Following the same discussion as $\Pi_{\mathsf{activePFE}}$, it is easy to see that $\Pi_{\mathsf{covertPFE}}$ could be instantiated as a constant-round PVC-secure PFE protocol with linear complexity. Similarly, it is straightforward that we have the theorem below, and Remark 2 is also applicable to $\Pi_{\mathsf{covertPFE}}$ to achieve global reusability.

Theorem 7. *Once the initiation phase for a private circuit* C_f *is executed, every subsequent execution of the evaluation phase of* $\Pi_{\mathsf{covertPFE}}$ *does not degenerate the security of* $\Pi_{\mathsf{covertPFE}}$.

5 Analysis

5.1 Performance of $\Pi_{\mathsf{zk}}^{\mathsf{EncEP}}$

In Table 3, we provide from two directions the communication cost of each part of $\Pi_{\mathsf{zk}}^{\mathsf{EncEP}}$ for one execution of $\Pi_{\mathsf{zk}}^{\mathsf{EncEP}}$ with parameters M and N in the honest-verifier zero-knowledge setting. Note that $\Pi_{\mathsf{zk}}^{\mathsf{Zero+}}$ is the optimized protocol of

$\Pi_{\mathsf{zk}}^{\mathsf{Zero}}$ according to the idea introduced in Remark 3. The row of remaining is for the communication cost of $\Pi_{\mathsf{zk}}^{\mathsf{EncEP}}$ excluding the cost of sub-protocols. Since messages sent from V to P are random messages in all protocols, we can leverage the random oracle and compile these protocols to be non-interactive via the Fiat-Shamir heuristic. Using this approach, the communication cost now only takes into account the cost from P to V.

Table 3. Communication cost of each part of $\Pi_{\mathsf{zk}}^{\mathsf{EncEP}}$ with parameters M and N.

Protocols	Bits from P to V	Bits from V to P
$\Pi_{\mathsf{zk}}^{\mathsf{Sum}}$	$(4\lceil\log_2 M\rceil + 3)\|\mathbb{G}\| + 4\|\mathbb{Z}_q\|$	$\|\mathbb{G}\| + (\lceil\log_2 M\rceil + 1)\|\mathbb{Z}_q\|$
$\Pi_{\mathsf{zk}}^{\mathsf{Zero}}$	$(2N+4)\|\mathbb{G}\| + (2M+3)\|\mathbb{Z}_q\|$	$\|\mathbb{Z}_q\|$
$\Pi_{\mathsf{zk}}^{\mathsf{Zero+}}$	$(4\lceil\log_2(2N+3)\rceil + 4\lceil\log_2 M\rceil + 12)\|\mathbb{G}\| + (M+10)\|\mathbb{Z}_q\|$	$2\|\mathbb{G}\| + (\lceil\log_2(2N+3) + \lceil\log_2 M\rceil + 3)\|\mathbb{Z}_q\|$
Remaining	0	$3\|\mathbb{Z}_q\|$

We give comparisons between the previous generic work [34] and our protocol $\Pi_{\mathsf{zk}}^{\mathsf{EncEP}}$ (using the optimized protocol $\Pi_{\mathsf{zk}}^{\mathsf{Zero+}}$) in Tables 4 and 5. From Table 4, we can see that the (non-interactive) communication cost of our protocol is around $M\|\mathbb{Z}_q\|$. In comparison, the protocol in [34] cannot be compiled to be non-interactive. Its total communication cost is around $(34N\|\mathbb{G}\| + 22N\|\mathbb{Z}_q\|)$ bits. For a regular circuit, we always have $M < N$. Meanwhile, we have $\|\mathbb{G}\| > \|\mathbb{Z}_q\|$. Hence, the number of the transmitted bits of the previous generic protocol is at least 56× larger than ours.

Table 4. Communication cost comparison between the previous generic work [34] and $\Pi_{\mathsf{zk}}^{\mathsf{EncEP}}$ in this paper with parameters M and N.

Protocols	Bits from P to V	Bits from V to P
[34]	$\sim(32N\|\mathbb{G}\| + 12N\|\mathbb{Z}_q\|)$	$\sim(2N\|\mathbb{G}\| + 10N\|\mathbb{Z}_q\|)$
This paper	$\sim(4\lceil\log_2(N)\rceil + 8\lceil\log_2 M\rceil)\|\mathbb{G}\| + M\|\mathbb{Z}_q\|$	$\sim(\lceil\log_2 N\rceil + 2\lceil\log_2 M\rceil)\|\mathbb{Z}_q\|$

Table 5. Computation cost comparison between the previous generic work [34] and $\Pi_{\mathsf{zk}}^{\mathsf{EncEP}}$ in this paper with parameters M and N.

Protocols	Time P Expos	Time V Expos
[34]	$\sim 59N$	$\sim 52N$
This paper	$\sim(16N + 11M)$	$\sim(10N + 3M)$

In Table 5, we count the total number of exponentiations that P and V need to perform in these two protocols. It is easy to see that the execution of our protocol should be much faster than the protocol in [34].

5.2 Performance of Our PFE Protocols

In this paper, we provide the *first* constant-round actively secure PFE protocol with linear complexity and the *first* constant-round PVC-secure PFE protocol with linear complexity in the two-party setting. Furthermore, our constructions have comparably good performance with existing passively secure PFE protocols.

The same initiation phase of the two protocols can be compiled to be non-interactive, and the resulting non-interactive information for the initiation phase is around $(8N\|\mathbb{G}\| + 2M\|\mathbb{Z}_q\|)$ bits. The linear constant-round passively secure PFE protocols in [22] and [33] do not achieve reusability, but we can still divide them into the same two phases, such that the phase for preprocessing the circuit C_f is the initiation phase, and the phase for generating, sending the garbled circuit, and evaluating that circuit is the evaluation phase. The communication cost of the initiation phase of the optimized protocol in [22], the protocol in [33], and the protocol in [7] are $(2M + 6N)\|\mathbb{G}\|$ bits, $(2M + 4N)\|\mathbb{G}\|$ bits, and $(M + N)\|\mathbb{G}\|$ bits, respectively. We can see that our protocol is competitive, even if it is actively secure. We also remark that since the protocols in [22] and [33] do not achieve reusability. Their initiation phases require to be executed every time when the same circuit C_f is involved, while the cost of the initiation phase can be amortized to multiple executions if a protocol achieves reusability. Meanwhile, the initiation phase of the protocol in [7] is interactive, and it does not achieve global reusability. In comparison, the initiation phase of our protocol could be non-interactive, and it achieves global reusability.

It is shown that the linear passively secure PFE protocol in [7] outperforms the protocols in [22] and [33] when it is executed any number (more than one) of time for a fixed private circuit. Here, we reason that our PVC-secure protocol does not have too much overhead compared with the passively secure protocol in [7] in the evaluation phase. The additional communication cost of $\Pi_{\mathsf{covertPFE}}$ compared with the passively secure protocol in [7] mainly includes the following.

1. The λ executions of Π_{OT} in Step 0 for seed transmission.
2. The extra $\lambda - 1$ executions of Π_{OT} for input-wire labels retrieval in Step 2.
3. The λ tuples of $\{\mathsf{c}_j, \sigma_j\}$ sent in Step 3.
4. The messages $\{\mathsf{c}_{i,j,b}^{x_B}\}_{i\in[n_B],b\in\{0,1\}}$, $\mathsf{h}_{\hat{j}}^{\mathsf{O}}$, $\mathsf{decom}^{\mathsf{c}_{\hat{j}}}$, and $\{\mathsf{decom}^{\mathsf{c}_{i,j,x_B[i]}^{x_B}}\}_{i\in[n_B]}$ sent in Step 5.

Let us analyze the cost of $\Pi_{\mathsf{covertPFE}}$ for the deterrence factor $\epsilon = 1/2$, *i.e.*, $\lambda = 2$. The additional communication cost of Step 1 and Step 3 is constant now. Meanwhile, the additional communication cost of Step 2 and Step 4 now only depends on the input length n of the circuit. For most regular circuits, this cost is significantly smaller than the dominant communication cost of transmitting the garbled gates, which is bounded by $\mathcal{O}(\theta)$ for circuit size θ. The additional computation cost for both parties is mainly from the cost of generating the corresponding GC_j's to compute the commitments c_j's for checked instances. Therefore, for the evaluation phase, the computation cost of both parties in our PVC-secure PFE protocol with $\epsilon = 1/2$ is only around 2.6× that of the passively secure PFE protocol [7], and thus it is acceptable.

Finally, let us see the size of the certificate in our PVC-secure PFE protocol. Note that all elements other than the list P inside a certificate do not depend on the size of the private circuit C_f. If the initiation phase is compiled to be non-interactive, we can assume that all parties have already held the messages generated in the initiation phase, including P. Now we do not need to include P in the certificate, and the size of the certificate is constant.

Acknowledgments. We thank the reviewers for their detailed and helpful comments. Y. Liu and Q. Wang were partially supported by the Shenzhen fundamental research programs under Grant no. 20200925154814002 and Guangdong Provincial Key Laboratory (Grant No. 2020B121201001). Y. Liu and S.-M. Yiu were also partially supported by ITF, Hong Kong (ITS/173/18FP) and the funding from HKU-SCF FinTech Academy.

References

1. Abadi, M., Feigenbaum, J.: Secure circuit evaluation. J. Cryptol. **2**(1), 1–12 (1990). https://doi.org/10.1007/BF02252866
2. Alhassan, M.Y., Günther, D., Kiss, Á., Schneider, T.: Efficient and scalable universal circuits. J. Cryptol. **33**(3), 1216–1271 (2020)
3. Asharov, G., Orlandi, C.: Calling out cheaters: covert security with public verifiability. In: Wang, X., Sako, K. (eds.) ASIACRYPT 2012. LNCS, vol. 7658, pp. 681–698. Springer, Heidelberg (2012). https://doi.org/10.1007/978-3-642-34961-4_41
4. Aumann, Y., Lindell, Y.: Security against covert adversaries: efficient protocols for realistic adversaries. J. Cryptol. **23**(2), 281–343 (2010)
5. Bayer, S., Groth, J.: Efficient zero-knowledge argument for correctness of a shuffle. In: Pointcheval, D., Johansson, T. (eds.) EUROCRYPT 2012. LNCS, vol. 7237, pp. 263–280. Springer, Heidelberg (2012). https://doi.org/10.1007/978-3-642-29011-4_17
6. Beaver, D., Micali, S., Rogaway, P.: The round complexity of secure protocols (extended abstract). In: Ortiz, H. (ed.) Proceedings of the 22nd Annual ACM Symposium on Theory of Computing, Baltimore, Maryland, USA, 13–17 May 1990, pp. 503–513. ACM (1990)
7. Bicer, O., Bingol, M.A., Kiraz, M.S., Levi, A.: Highly efficient and re-executable private function evaluation with linear complexity. IEEE Trans. Dependable Secure Comput. https://doi.org/10.1109/TDSC.2020.3009496
8. Bingöl, M.A., Biçer, O., Kiraz, M.S., Levi, A.: An efficient 2-party private function evaluation protocol based on half gates. Comput. J. **62**(4), 598–613 (2019)
9. Bootle, J., Cerulli, A., Chaidos, P., Groth, J., Petit, C.: Efficient zero-knowledge arguments for arithmetic circuits in the discrete log setting. In: Fischlin, M., Coron, J.-S. (eds.) EUROCRYPT 2016. LNCS, vol. 9666, pp. 327–357. Springer, Heidelberg (2016). https://doi.org/10.1007/978-3-662-49896-5_12
10. Bünz, B., Bootle, J., Boneh, D., Poelstra, A., Wuille, P., Maxwell, G.: Bulletproofs: short proofs for confidential transactions and more. In: 2018 IEEE Symposium on Security and Privacy, SP 2018, Proceedings, 21–23 May 2018, San Francisco, California, USA, pp. 315–334. IEEE Computer Society (2018)

11. Canetti, R., Sarkar, P., Wang, X.: Blazing fast OT for three-round UC OT extension. In: Kiayias, A., Kohlweiss, M., Wallden, P., Zikas, V. (eds.) PKC 2020. LNCS, vol. 12111, pp. 299–327. Springer, Cham (2020). https://doi.org/10.1007/978-3-030-45388-6_11
12. Chang, Y., Lu, C.: Oblivious polynomial evaluation and oblivious neural learning. Theor. Comput. Sci. **341**(1–3), 39–54 (2005)
13. Chaum, D., Pedersen, T.P.: Wallet databases with observers. In: Brickell, E.F. (ed.) CRYPTO 1992. LNCS, vol. 740, pp. 89–105. Springer, Heidelberg (1993). https://doi.org/10.1007/3-540-48071-4_7
14. Damgård, I., Orlandi, C., Simkin, M.: Black-box transformations from passive to covert security with public verifiability. In: Micciancio, D., Ristenpart, T. (eds.) CRYPTO 2020. LNCS, vol. 12171, pp. 647–676. Springer, Cham (2020). https://doi.org/10.1007/978-3-030-56880-1_23
15. Faust, S., Hazay, C., Kretzler, D., Schlosser, B.: Generic compiler for publicly verifiable covert multi-party computation. In: Canteaut, A., Standaert, F.-X. (eds.) EUROCRYPT 2021. LNCS, vol. 12697, pp. 782–811. Springer, Cham (2021). https://doi.org/10.1007/978-3-030-77886-6_27
16. Gamal, T.E.: A public key cryptosystem and a signature scheme based on discrete logarithms. In: Blakley, G.R., Chaum, D. (eds.) CRYPTO 1984. LNCS, vol. 196, pp. 10–18. Springer, Heidelberg (1985). https://doi.org/10.1007/3-540-39568-7_2
17. Gentry, C.: Fully homomorphic encryption using ideal lattices. In: Mitzenmacher, M. (ed.) Proceedings of the 41st Annual ACM Symposium on Theory of Computing, STOC 2009, Bethesda, MD, USA, 31 May–2 June 2009, pp. 169–178. ACM (2009)
18. Günther, D., Kiss, Á., Schneider, T.: More efficient universal circuit constructions. In: Takagi, T., Peyrin, T. (eds.) ASIACRYPT 2017. LNCS, vol. 10625, pp. 443–470. Springer, Cham (2017). https://doi.org/10.1007/978-3-319-70697-9_16
19. Hazay, C., Lindell, Y.: Efficient Secure Two-Party Protocols - Techniques and Constructions. Information Security and Cryptography, Springer, Heidelberg (2010). https://doi.org/10.1007/978-3-642-14303-8
20. Holz, M., Kiss, Á., Rathee, D., Schneider, T.: Linear-complexity private function evaluation is practical. In: Chen, L., Li, N., Liang, K., Schneider, S. (eds.) ESORICS 2020. LNCS, vol. 12309, pp. 401–420. Springer, Cham (2020). https://doi.org/10.1007/978-3-030-59013-0_20
21. Hong, C., Katz, J., Kolesnikov, V., Lu, W., Wang, X.: Covert security with public verifiability: faster, leaner, and simpler. In: Ishai, Y., Rijmen, V. (eds.) EUROCRYPT 2019. LNCS, vol. 11478, pp. 97–121. Springer, Cham (2019). https://doi.org/10.1007/978-3-030-17659-4_4
22. Katz, J., Malka, L.: Constant-round private function evaluation with linear complexity. In: Lee, D.H., Wang, X. (eds.) ASIACRYPT 2011. LNCS, vol. 7073, pp. 556–571. Springer, Heidelberg (2011). https://doi.org/10.1007/978-3-642-25385-0_30
23. Keller, M., Orsini, E., Scholl, P.: Actively secure OT extension with optimal overhead. In: Gennaro, R., Robshaw, M. (eds.) CRYPTO 2015. LNCS, vol. 9215, pp. 724–741. Springer, Heidelberg (2015). https://doi.org/10.1007/978-3-662-47989-6_35
24. Kiss, Á., Schneider, T.: Valiant's universal circuit is practical. In: Fischlin, M., Coron, J.-S. (eds.) EUROCRYPT 2016. LNCS, vol. 9665, pp. 699–728. Springer, Heidelberg (2016). https://doi.org/10.1007/978-3-662-49890-3_27

25. Kolesnikov, V., Malozemoff, A.J.: Public verifiability in the covert model (almost) for free. In: Iwata, T., Cheon, J.H. (eds.) ASIACRYPT 2015. LNCS, vol. 9453, pp. 210–235. Springer, Heidelberg (2015). https://doi.org/10.1007/978-3-662-48800-3_9
26. Kolesnikov, V., Schneider, T.: A practical universal circuit construction and secure evaluation of private functions. In: Tsudik, G. (ed.) FC 2008. LNCS, vol. 5143, pp. 83–97. Springer, Heidelberg (2008). https://doi.org/10.1007/978-3-540-85230-8_7
27. Lindell, Y., Pinkas, B.: An efficient protocol for secure two-party computation in the presence of malicious adversaries. In: Naor, M. (ed.) EUROCRYPT 2007. LNCS, vol. 4515, pp. 52–78. Springer, Heidelberg (2007). https://doi.org/10.1007/978-3-540-72540-4_4
28. Lindell, Y., Pinkas, B.: A proof of security of Yao's protocol for two-party computation. J. Cryptol. **22**(2), 161–188 (2009)
29. Lipmaa, H., Mohassel, P., Sadeghian, S.: Valiant's universal circuit: improvements, implementation, and applications. Cryptology ePrint Archive, Report 2016/017 (2016). https://ia.cr/2016/017
30. Liu, H., Yu, Yu., Zhao, S., Zhang, J., Liu, W., Hu, Z.: Pushing the limits of valiant's universal circuits: simpler, tighter and more compact. In: Malkin, T., Peikert, C. (eds.) CRYPTO 2021. LNCS, vol. 12826, pp. 365–394. Springer, Cham (2021). https://doi.org/10.1007/978-3-030-84245-1_13
31. Liu, Y., Wang, Q., Yiu, S.-M.: Blind polynomial evaluation and data trading. In: Sako, K., Tippenhauer, N.O. (eds.) ACNS 2021. LNCS, vol. 12726, pp. 100–129. Springer, Cham (2021). https://doi.org/10.1007/978-3-030-78372-3_5
32. Liu, Y., Wang, Q., Yiu, S.M.: Making private function evaluation safer, faster, and simpler. Cryptology ePrint Archive, Report 2021/1682 (2021). https://ia.cr/2021/1682
33. Mohassel, P., Sadeghian, S.: How to hide circuits in MPC an efficient framework for private function evaluation. In: Johansson, T., Nguyen, P.Q. (eds.) EUROCRYPT 2013. LNCS, vol. 7881, pp. 557–574. Springer, Heidelberg (2013). https://doi.org/10.1007/978-3-642-38348-9_33
34. Mohassel, P., Sadeghian, S., Smart, N.P.: Actively secure private function evaluation. In: Sarkar, P., Iwata, T. (eds.) ASIACRYPT 2014. LNCS, vol. 8874, pp. 486–505. Springer, Heidelberg (2014). https://doi.org/10.1007/978-3-662-45608-8_26
35. Naor, M., Pinkas, B.: Oblivious polynomial evaluation. SIAM J. Comput. **35**(5), 1254–1281 (2006)
36. Naor, M., Reingold, O.: Number-theoretic constructions of efficient pseudo-random functions. J. ACM **51**(2), 231–262 (2004)
37. Pedersen, T.P.: Non-interactive and information-theoretic secure verifiable secret sharing. In: Feigenbaum, J. (ed.) CRYPTO 1991. LNCS, vol. 576, pp. 129–140. Springer, Heidelberg (1992). https://doi.org/10.1007/3-540-46766-1_9
38. Sander, T., Young, A.L., Yung, M.: Non-interactive cryptocomputing for nc^1. In: 40th Annual Symposium on Foundations of Computer Science, FOCS 1999, 17–18 October 1999, New York, NY, USA, pp. 554–567. IEEE Computer Society (1999)
39. Scholl, P., Simkin, M., Siniscalchi, L.: Multiparty computation with covert security and public verifiability. Cryptology ePrint Archive, Report 2021/366 (2021). https://ia.cr/2021/366
40. Valiant, L.G.: Universal circuits (preliminary report). In: Chandra, A.K., Wotschke, D., Friedman, E.P., Harrison, M.A. (eds.) Proceedings of the 8th Annual ACM Symposium on Theory of Computing, Hershey, Pennsylvania, USA, 3–5 May 1976, pp. 196–203. ACM (1976)

41. Yao, A.C.: How to generate and exchange secrets (extended abstract). In: 27th Annual Symposium on Foundations of Computer Science, Toronto, Canada, 27–29 October 1986, pp. 162–167. IEEE Computer Society (1986)
42. Zhao, S., Yu, Yu., Zhang, J., Liu, H.: Valiant's universal circuits revisited: an overall improvement and a lower bound. In: Galbraith, S.D., Moriai, S. (eds.) ASIACRYPT 2019. LNCS, vol. 11921, pp. 401–425. Springer, Cham (2019). https://doi.org/10.1007/978-3-030-34578-5_15
43. Zhu, R., Ding, C., Huang, Y.: Efficient publicly verifiable 2PC over a blockchain with applications to financially-secure computations. In: Cavallaro, L., Kinder, J., Wang, X., Katz, J. (eds.) Proceedings of the 2019 ACM SIGSAC Conference on Computer and Communications Security, CCS 2019, London, UK, 11–15 November 2019, pp. 633–650. ACM (2019)

Two-Round Oblivious Linear Evaluation from Learning with Errors

Pedro Branco[1(✉)], Nico Döttling[2], and Paulo Mateus[1]

[1] SQIG - IT, University of Lisbon, Lisbon, Portugal
[2] Helmholtz Center for Information Security (CISPA), Saarbrücken, Germany

Abstract. Oblivious Linear Evaluation (OLE) is the arithmetic analogue of the well-know oblivious transfer primitive. It allows a sender, holding an affine function $f(x) = a + bx$ over a finite field or ring, to let a receiver learn $f(w)$ for a w of the receiver's choice. In terms of security, the sender remains oblivious of the receiver's input w, whereas the receiver learns nothing beyond $f(w)$ about f. In recent years, OLE has emerged as an essential building block to construct efficient, reusable and maliciously-secure two-party computation.

In this work, we present efficient two-round protocols for OLE over large fields based on the Learning with Errors (LWE) assumption, providing a full arithmetic generalization of the oblivious transfer protocol of Peikert, Vaikuntanathan and Waters (CRYPTO 2008). At the technical core of our work is a novel extraction technique which allows to determine if a non-trivial multiple of some vector is close to a q-ary lattice.

1 Introduction

Oblivious Linear Evaluation (OLE) is a cryptographic primitive between a sender and a receiver, where the sender inputs an affine function $f(x) = a + bx$ over a finite field $\mathbb{F}$, the receiver inputs an element $w \in \mathbb{F}$, and in the end the receiver learns $f(w)$. The sender remains oblivious of the receiver's input w and the receiver learns nothing beyond $f(w)$ about f. OLE can be seen as a generalization of the well-known Oblivious Transfer (OT) primitive.[1] In fact, just as secure computation of *Boolean* circuits can be based on OT, secure computation of *arithmetic* circuits can be based on OLE [2,20,22].

In recent years, OLE has emerged as one of the most promising avenues to realize efficient two-party secure computation in different settings [1,2,6,11,13, 21,22]. Interestingly, OLE has found applications, not just in the secure computation of generic functions, but also in specific tasks such as Private Set Intersection [18,19] or Machine Learning related tasks [23,28].

[1] It is easy to see that, if we consider the affine function $f : \{0,1\} \to \{0,1\}$ such that $f(b) = m_0 + b(m_1 - m_0)$, OLE trivially implements OT.

G. Hanaoka et al. (Eds.): PKC 2022, LNCS 13177, pp. 379–408, 2022.
https://doi.org/10.1007/978-3-030-97121-2_14

Other aspects that set OLE apart from OT are reusability, meaning that the first message of a protocol is reusable across multiple executions,[2] and the fact that even a semi-honest secure OLE can be used to realize maliciously secure two-party computation [21].

Although OLE secure against semi-honest adversaries is complete for maliciously-secure two-party computation [21], this comes at the cost of efficiency and, thus, is it always preferable to start with a maliciously-secure one. Moreover, some applications of OLE even ask specifically for a maliciously-secure one [18]. Given this state of affairs and the importance of OLE in constructing two-party secure computation protocols, we ask the following question:

Can we build efficient and maliciously-secure two-round OLE protocols from (presumed) post-quantum hardness assumptions?

1.1 Our Results

In this work, we give an affirmative answer to the question above. Specifically, we present two simple, efficient and round-optimal protocols for OLE based on the hardness of the Learning with Errors (LWE) assumption [31], which is conjectured to be post-quantum secure.

Before we start, we clarify what type of OLE we obtain. OLE comes in many flavors, one of the most useful being *vector OLE* where the sender inputs two vectors $a = \mathbf{a}, b = \mathbf{b} \in \mathbb{F}^\ell$ and the receiver obtains a linear combination of them $\mathbf{z} = \mathbf{a} + w\mathbf{b} \in \mathbb{F}^\ell$ [6]. For simplicity, we just refer to this variant as OLE.

Both of our protocols implement the functionality in just two-rounds and have the following properties:

- Our first protocol (Sect. 5) for OLE achieves statistical security against a corrupted receiver and computational semi-honest security against a corrupted sender based on LWE. Additionally, we show how we can extend this protocol to implement *batch OLE*, a functionality similar to OLE where the receiver can input a batch of values $\{x_i\}_{i\in[k']}$, instead of just one value.
- Our main technical innovation is a new extraction technique which allows to determine if a vector $\mathbf{z} \in \mathbb{Z}_q^n$ is of the form $\mathbf{z} = \mathbf{s}\mathbf{A} + \alpha\mathbf{e}$, where the matrix $\mathbf{A} \in \mathbb{Z}_q^{k\times n}$ is given, and the unknown $\mathbf{s} \in \mathbb{Z}_q^k$, $\alpha \in \mathbb{Z}_q$ and short vector $\mathbf{e}$ are to be determined. We provide an algorithm which solves this problem efficiently given a trapdoor for the lattice $\Lambda_q^\perp(\mathbf{A})$. We believe that this contribution is of independent interest. In particular, our extractor immediately leads to an efficient simulation strategy for the PVW protocol [29] even for super-polynomial moduli q.

[2] While two-party *reusable* non-interactive secure computation (NISC) is impossible in the OT-hybrid model [11], reusable NISC for general Boolean circuits is known to be possible in the (reusable) OLE-hybrid model assuming one-way functions [11]. The result stated above is meaningful only if we have access to a reusable two-round OLE protocol. The only efficient realizations of this primitive are based on the Decisional Composite Residuosity (DCR) and the Quadratic Residuosity assumptions [11].

- We then show how to extend our OLE protocol to provide malicious security for both parties (Sect. 6). The protocol makes λ invocations of a two-round Oblivious Transfer protocol (which exists under LWE [29,30]), where λ is the security parameter. By instantiating the OT with the LWE-based protocols of [29,30], we preserve statistical security against a malicious receiver.

1.2 Related Work and Comparison

In the following, we briefly review some proposals from prior work and compare them with our proposal. We only consider schemes that are provable UC-secure as our protocols. OLE can be trivially implemented using Fully/Somewhat Homomorphic Encryption (e.g., [23]) but these solutions are usually just proven secure against semi-honest adversaries and it is unclear how to extend security against malicious adversaries without relying on generic approaches such as Non-Interactive Zero-Knowledge (NIZK) proofs.[3] OLE can also be trivially implemented using generic solutions for two-party secure computation (via OT) such as [32]. However, these solutions fall short in achieving an *acceptable* level of efficiency.

The work of Döttling et al. [14,15] proposed an OLE protocol with unconditional security, in the stateful tamper-proof hardware model. The protocol takes only two rounds, however further interaction with the token is needed by the parties.

In [22], a semi-honest protocol for oblivious multiplication was proposed, which can be easily extended to a OLE protocol. The protocol is based on noisy encodings. Based on the same assumption, [17] proposed a maliciously-secure OLE protocol, which extends the techniques of [22]. However, their protocol takes eight rounds of interaction.

Chase et al. [11] presented a round-optimal reusable OLE protocol based on the Decisional Composite Residuosity (DCR) and the Quadratic Residuosity (QR) assumptions. The protocol is maliciously-secure and, to the best of our knowledge, it is the most efficient protocol for OLE proposed so far. However, it is well-known that both the DCR and the QR problems are quantumly insecure.

Recently, two new protocols for OLE based on the Ring LWE assumption were presented in [5,10]. Both protocols run in two rounds but the protocol of [5] either requires a PKI or a setup phase, and the protocol of [10] is secure only against semi-honest adversaries.

We also remark that our protocols implement vector OLE where the sender's input are vectors over a field, as in [17].

In Table 1, a brief comparison between several UC-secure OLE protocols is presented.

[3] As an example consider the work of [11], where the Paillier cryptosystem is extended into an OLE protocol with malicious security and the construction is highly non-trivial.

Table 1. Comparison between different OLE schemes.

	Hardness Assumption	Setup Assumption	Rounds	Reusability	Security
[22]	Noisy Encodings	OT	3	-	semi-honest
[14]	-	Stateful tamper proof hardware	2	✗	malicious
[17]	Noisy Encodings	OT	8	-	malicious
[11]	DCR & QR	CRS	2	✓	malicious
[5]	RLWE	PKI/Setup	2	✗	malicious
[10]	RLWE	-	2	-	semi-honest
This work	LWE	CRS	2	✓	malicious receiver
	LWE	CRS & OT	2	✗	malicious

1.3 Open Problems

Our first protocol is secure against semi-honest senders and, thus, it is trivially reusable. However, our fully maliciously-secure protocol (in Sect. 6) does not have reusability of the first message. Hence, the main open problem left in our work is the following: Can we construct a reusable maliciously-secure two-round OLE protocol based on the LWE assumption?

2 Technical Outline

We will now give a brief overview of our protocol. In abuse of notation, we drop the transposition operator for transposed vectors and always assume that vectors multiplied from the right side are transposed.

2.1 The PVW Protocol

Our starting point is the LWE-based oblivious transfer protocol of Peikert, Vaikuntanathan and Waters [29], which is based on Regev's encryption scheme [31]. Since our goal is to construct an OLE protocol, we will describe the PVW scheme as a $\mathbb{F}_2$ OLE rather than the standard OT functionality. Assume for simplicity that the LWE modulus q is even.

The PVW scheme uses a common reference string which consists of a random matrix $\mathbf{A} \in \mathbb{Z}_q^{n \times m}$ and a vector $\mathbf{a} \in \mathbb{Z}_q^m$, which together syntactically form a Regev public key. Given the CRS $(\mathbf{A}, \mathbf{a})$, the receiver, whose input is a choice bit $b \in \{0, 1\}$ chooses a uniformly random $\mathbf{s} \in \mathbb{Z}_q^n$ and a $\mathbf{e} \in \mathbb{Z}_q^m$ from a (short) LWE error distribution, e.g. a discrete gaussian. The receiver now sets $\mathbf{z} = \mathbf{s}\mathbf{A} + \mathbf{e} - b \cdot \mathbf{a}$. In other words, if $b = 0$ then $(\mathbf{A}, \mathbf{z})$ is a well-formed Regev public key, whereas if $b = 1$ then $(\mathbf{A}, \mathbf{z} + \mathbf{a})$ is a well-formed Regev public key.

The receiver now sends $\mathbf{z}$ to the sender who proceeds as follows. Say the sender's input are $v_0, v_1 \in \{0, 1\}$. The sender now encrypts v_0 under the public key $(\mathbf{A}, \mathbf{z})$ and v_1 under $(\mathbf{A}, \mathbf{a})$ *using the same randomness* $\mathbf{r}$. Specifically, the sender chooses $\mathbf{r} \in \mathbb{Z}^m$ from a wide enough discrete gaussian, sets $\mathbf{c} = \mathbf{A}\mathbf{r}$, $c_0 = \mathbf{z}\mathbf{r} + \frac{q}{2} v_0$ and $c_1 = \mathbf{a}\mathbf{r} + \frac{q}{2} v_1$. Now the sender sends $(\mathbf{c}, c_0, c_1)$ back to the receiver. The receiver then computes and outputs $y = \lceil b \cdot c_1 + c_0 - \mathbf{s}\mathbf{c} \rfloor_2$. Here $\lceil \cdot \rfloor_2$ denotes the rounding operation with respect to $q/2$.

To see that this scheme is correct, note that

$$\begin{aligned} b \cdot c_1 + c_0 - \mathbf{s}\mathbf{c} &= b\mathbf{a}\mathbf{r} + b \cdot \frac{q}{2} v_1 + \mathbf{z}\mathbf{r} + \cdot \frac{q}{2} v_0 - \mathbf{s}\mathbf{A}\mathbf{r} \\ &= b\mathbf{a}\mathbf{r} + b \cdot \frac{q}{2} v_1 + (\mathbf{s}\mathbf{A} + \mathbf{e} - b\mathbf{a})\mathbf{r} + \cdot \frac{q}{2} v_0 - \mathbf{s}\mathbf{A}\mathbf{r} \\ &= \frac{q}{2}(b v_1 + v_0) + \mathbf{e}\mathbf{r}. \end{aligned}$$

Since both $\mathbf{e}$ and $\mathbf{r}$ are short, $\mathbf{e}\mathbf{r}$ is also short and we can conclude that $y = \lceil b \cdot c_1 + c_0 - \mathbf{s}\mathbf{c} \rfloor_2 = b v_1 + v_0$.

Security. Security against semi-honest senders follows routinely from the hardness of LWE. We will omit the discussion on security against malicious senders for now and focus on security against malicious receivers.

The basic issue here is that a malicious receiver may choose $\mathbf{z}$ not of the form $\mathbf{z} = \mathbf{s}\mathbf{A} + \mathbf{e} - b\mathbf{a}$ but rather arbitrarily.

It can now be argued that except with negligible probability over the choice of $\mathbf{a}$, one of the matrices $\mathbf{A}_0 = \begin{pmatrix} \mathbf{A} \\ \mathbf{z} \end{pmatrix}$ or $\mathbf{A}_1 = \begin{pmatrix} \mathbf{A} \\ \mathbf{z} + \mathbf{a} \end{pmatrix}$ does not have a short vector in its row-span. We can then invoke the Smoothing Lemma [27] to argue that given $\mathbf{c} = \mathbf{A}\mathbf{r}$ either $\mathbf{z}\mathbf{r}$ or $(\mathbf{z} + \mathbf{a})\mathbf{r}$ is statistically close to uniform. In the first case we get that $(\mathbf{c}, c_0, c_1)$ statistically hides $v_0 = v_0 + 0 \cdot v_1$, in the second case $v_0 + v_1 = v_0 + 1 \cdot v_1$ is statistically hidden. In order to simulate, we must determine which one of the two cases holds.

In [29] this is achieved as follows. First, the matrix $\mathbf{A}$ is chosen together with a *lattice trapdoor* [16,26] which allows to efficiently *decode* a point $\mathbf{x} \in \mathbb{Z}_q^m$ to the point in the row-span of $\mathbf{A}$ closest to $\mathbf{x}$ (given that $\mathbf{x}$ is sufficiently close to the row-span of $\mathbf{A}$). The PVW extractor now tries to determine whether there is a short vector in the row-span of $\mathbf{A}_0$ by going through all multiples $\alpha\mathbf{z}$ of $\mathbf{z}$ (for $\alpha \in \mathbb{Z}_q$) and testing whether $\alpha\mathbf{z}$ is close to the row-span of $\mathbf{A}$. If such an α is found, we know by the above argument that given $\mathbf{A}\mathbf{r}$ and $\mathbf{z}\mathbf{r}$ it must hold that $(\mathbf{z} + \mathbf{a})\mathbf{r}$ is statistically close to uniform, and the simulator can set the extracted choice bit b to 0. On the other hand, if no such α is found, it sets the extracted choice bit to 1 since we know that in this case $\mathbf{z}\mathbf{r}$ is statistically close to uniform given $\mathbf{A}\mathbf{r}$ and $(\mathbf{z} + \mathbf{a})\mathbf{r}$.

A severe drawback of this method is that the extractor must iterate over all $\alpha \in \mathbb{Z}_q$. Consequently, for the extractor to be efficient q must be of polynomial size. A recent work of Quach [30] devised an extraction method for superpolynomial modulus q by using Hash Proof Systems (HPS)[4]. To make this approach work the underlying Regev encryption scheme must be modified in a way that unfortunately deteriorates correctness and prohibits linear homomorphism.

[4] Despite numerous efforts, HPS in the lattice setting fall short in efficiency when comparing to their group-based counterpart.

2.2 An Oblivious Linear Evaluation Protocol Based on PVW

We will now discuss our OLE modification of the PVW scheme. The basic idea is very simple: We will modify the underlying Regev encryption scheme to support a larger plaintext space, namely $\mathbb{Z}_{q_1}$ for a modulus q_1 and exploit linear homomorphism over $\mathbb{Z}_{q_1}$, which will lead to an OLE over $\mathbb{Z}_{q_1}$.

Concretely, let $q = q_1 \cdot q_2$ for a sufficiently large q_2. We have the same CRS as in the PVW scheme, i.e. a random matrix $\mathbf{A} \in \mathbb{Z}_q^{n \times m}$ and a random vector $\mathbf{a} \in \mathbb{Z}_q^m$. Now the receiver's input is a $x \in \mathbb{Z}_{q_1}$, and he computes $\mathbf{z}$ by $\mathbf{z} = \mathbf{sA} + \mathbf{e} - x \cdot \mathbf{a}$ (where $\mathbf{s}$ and $\mathbf{e}$ are as above). The sender's input is now a pair $v_0, v_1 \in \mathbb{Z}_{q_1}$, and the sender computes $\mathbf{c} = \mathbf{Ar}$, $c_0 = \mathbf{zr} + q_2 v_0$ and $c_0 = \mathbf{ar} + q_2 v_1$ (again $\mathbf{r}$ as above). Given $(\mathbf{c}, c_0, c_1)$ the receiver can recover y by computing $y = \lceil x \cdot c_1 + c_0 - \mathbf{sc} \rfloor_{q_1}$. Here $\lceil \cdot \rfloor_{q_1}$ is as usual defined by $\lceil u \rfloor_{q_1} = \cdot \lceil u/q_2 \rfloor$. We can establish correctness as above:

$$\begin{aligned} x \cdot c_1 + c_0 - \mathbf{sc} &= x\mathbf{ar} + x \cdot q_2 v_1 + \mathbf{zr} + q_2 v_0 - \mathbf{sAr} \\ &= x\mathbf{ar} + x q_2 v_1 + (\mathbf{sA} + \mathbf{e} - x\mathbf{a})\mathbf{r} + q_2 v_0 - \mathbf{sAr} \\ &= q_2(x v_1 + v_0) + \mathbf{er}. \end{aligned}$$

Now, given that $\mathbf{e}$ and $\mathbf{r}$ are sufficiently short, specifically such that $\mathbf{er}$ is shorter than $q_2/2$ it holds that $y = \lceil x \cdot c_1 + c_0 - \mathbf{sc} \rfloor_{q_1} = x v_1 + v_0$ and correctness follows.

A detailed description of the protocol is presented in Sect. 5.[5] The protocol described there directly implements *vector OLE*, instead of just OLE as presented above.

Security. Security against semi-honest senders follows, just as above, routinely from the LWE assumption. But for superpolynomial moduli q_1 (which, in the OLE setting, is the case we are mostly interested in) we are seemingly at an impasse when it comes to proving security against malicious receivers: In this case, the PVW extractor is not efficient and Quach's technique [30] is incompatible with our reliance on linear homomorphism of the Regev encryption scheme.

Consequently, we need to devise an alternative method of extracting the receiver's input x. The core idea of our extractor is surprisingly simple: While PVW choose the matrix $\mathbf{A}$ together with a lattice trapdoor, we will instead choose the matrix $\mathbf{A}' = \begin{pmatrix} \mathbf{A} \\ \mathbf{a} \end{pmatrix}$ together with a lattice trapdoor $\mathbf{T} \in \mathbb{Z}^{m \times m}$ (i.e. a short square matrix $\mathbf{T}$ such that $\mathbf{A}'\mathbf{T} = 0$). This is possible as the vector $\mathbf{a}$ is also provided in the CRS.

How does this help us to extract a $\tilde{x} \in \mathbb{Z}_q$ from the malicious receiver's message $\mathbf{z}$? Let $\mathbf{z} \in \mathbb{Z}_q^m$ be arbitrary, write $\mathbf{z}$ as $\mathbf{z} = \mathbf{sA} - x \cdot \mathbf{a} + \alpha \mathbf{d}$ for some $\mathbf{s} \in \mathbb{Z}_q^n$, $x \in \mathbb{Z}_q$, $\alpha \in \mathbb{Z}_q$ and a $\mathbf{d} \in \mathbb{Z}^m$ of minimal length. In other words, there exists no $\mathbf{d}^*$ with $\|\mathbf{d}^*\| < \|\mathbf{d}\|$ such that $\mathbf{z}$ can be written as $\mathbf{z} = \mathbf{s}^*\mathbf{A} + \alpha^*\mathbf{d}^* - x^*\mathbf{a}$ for some $\mathbf{s}^*$, x^* and α^*.

[5] The protocol presented in Sect. 5 is presented in a slightly, but equivalent, form.

Then it holds that

$$\begin{aligned}(\mathbf{c}, c_0, c_1) &= (\mathbf{Ar}, \mathbf{zr} + q_2 v_0, \mathbf{ar} + q_2 v_1) &(1)\\ &= (\mathbf{Ar}, (\mathbf{sA} - x \cdot \mathbf{a} + \alpha\mathbf{d})\mathbf{r} + q_2 v_0, \mathbf{ar} + q_2 v_1) &(2)\\ &= (\mathbf{Ar}, \mathbf{sAr} - x\mathbf{ar} + \alpha\mathbf{dr} + q_2 v_0, \mathbf{ar} + q_2 v_1) &(3)\\ &\approx_s (\mathbf{u}, \mathbf{su} - xu + \alpha\mathbf{dr} + q_2 v_0, u + q_2 v_1) &(4)\\ &\equiv (\mathbf{u}, \mathbf{su} - xu' + xq_2 v_1 + \alpha\mathbf{dr} + q_2 v_0, u') &(5)\\ &= (\mathbf{u}, \mathbf{su} + \alpha\mathbf{dr} - xu' + q_2(xv_1 + v_0), u') &(6)\\ &\approx_s (\mathbf{Ar}, \mathbf{sAr} + \alpha\mathbf{dr} - x\mathbf{ar} + q_2(xv_1 + v_0), \mathbf{ar}) &(7)\\ &= (\mathbf{Ar}, \mathbf{zr} + q_2(xv_1 + v_0), \mathbf{ar}). &(8)\end{aligned}$$

In other words, we can simulate $(\mathbf{c}, c_0, c_1)$ given only $xv_1 + v_0$. In the above derivation, (4) holds as by the partial smoothing lemma [7] as $(\mathbf{Ar}, \mathbf{ar}, \mathbf{dr}) = (\mathbf{A}'\mathbf{r}, \mathbf{dr}) \approx_s (\mathbf{u}', \mathbf{dr}) = (\mathbf{u}, u, \mathbf{dr})$ where $\mathbf{u} \in \mathbb{Z}_q^m$ and $u \in \mathbb{Z}_q$ are uniformly random. Equation (5) follows by a simple substitution $u \to u' - q_2 v_1$, where $u' \in \mathbb{Z}_q$ is also uniformly random. Equation (7) follows analogously to (4) via the smoothing lemma.

Efficient Extraction. It remains to be discussed how we can *efficiently* recover x from $\mathbf{z}$ given the lattice trapdoor $\mathbf{T}$ for $\Lambda_q^{\perp}(\mathbf{A}')$. We will recover the representation $\mathbf{z} = \mathbf{s}^*\mathbf{A} + \alpha^*\mathbf{d}^* - x^*\mathbf{a}$. Note that we can write $\mathbf{z} = \mathbf{s}'\mathbf{A}' + \alpha\mathbf{d}$, where $\mathbf{s}' = (\mathbf{s}, -x)$. Setting $\mathbf{f} = \mathbf{zT}$ we get

$$\mathbf{f} = \mathbf{zT} = (\mathbf{s}'\mathbf{A}' + \alpha\mathbf{d})\mathbf{T} = \alpha\mathbf{dT}.$$

Assuming that $\mathbf{d}$ is sufficiently short, it holds that $\mathbf{d}' = \mathbf{dT}$ is also short. We will now solve the equation system $\alpha\mathbf{d}' = \mathbf{f}$, in which $\mathbf{f}$ is known, for α and $\mathbf{d}'$. Write $\mathbf{f} = (f_1, \ldots, f_m)$ and $\mathbf{d}' = (d_1', \ldots, d_m')$. Then we get the equation system

$$f_1 = \alpha d_1', \ldots, f_m = \alpha d_m'.$$

We can eliminate α using the first equation and obtain the equations

$$-f_2 d_1' + f_1 d_2' = 0, \ldots, -f_m d_1' + f_1 d_m' = 0.$$

Now assume for simplicity f_1 is invertible, i.e. $f_1 \in \mathbb{Z}_q^{\times}$. Then we can express the above equations as

$$-(f_2/f_1) \cdot d_1' + d_2' = 0, \ldots, -(f_m/f_1) \cdot d_1' + d_m' = 0.$$

Consequently, it is sufficient to find the first coordinate d_1' to find all other $d_j' = (f_j/f_1) \cdot d_1'$.

To find the first coordinate d_1', we rely on the fact that solving the Shortest Vector Problem (SVP) in a two-dimensional lattice can actually be done in polynomial time (and essentially independently of the modulus q) [24]. Consider the lattice Λ_j defined by $\Lambda_j = \Lambda_q^{\perp}(\mathbf{b}_j)$, where $\mathbf{b}_j = (-f_j/f_1, 1)$. First note that

$\mathbf{d}'_j = (d'_1, d'_j)$ is a short vector in Λ_i. Furthermore, notice that $\det(\Lambda_j) = q$ as the second component of $\mathbf{b}_j$ is 1 ($\mathbf{b}_j$ is *primitive*). Letting $B = \|\mathbf{d}'_j\|$, we can then argue via Hadamard's inequality that any vector $\mathbf{v} \in \Lambda_i$ shorter than q/B *must* be linearly dependent with $\mathbf{d}'_j$.

By applying a SVP solver, we are able to find the shortest vector $\mathbf{g}_j = (g_j^{(1)}, g_j^{(2)})$ in Λ_i. Observe that d'_1 must be a multiple of $g_j^{(1)}$ for all $j = 2, \ldots, n$ (otherwise, $\mathbf{g}_j$ would not be the shortest solution of the SVP instance). Hence, d'_1 can be computed by taking the least common multiple of $g_1^{(1)}, \ldots, g_n^{(1)}$.

Having recovered $\mathbf{d}' \in \mathbb{Z}^m$, we can recover $\mathbf{d}$ by solving the linear equation system $\mathbf{dT} = \mathbf{d}'$ over $\mathbb{Z}$ to recover $\mathbf{d}$. Finally, given $\mathbf{d}$ we can efficiently find $\mathbf{s}' \in \mathbb{Z}_q^{n+1}$ and $\alpha \in \mathbb{Z}_q$ using basic linear algebra by solving the equation system $\mathbf{s}'\mathbf{A}' = \mathbf{z} - \alpha\mathbf{d}$. Given $\mathbf{s}'$ we can set x to s'_{n+1}. If no solution is found in this process we set $x = 0$ by default. Now notice that we can write

$$\mathbf{z} = \mathbf{s}'\mathbf{A}' + \alpha\mathbf{d} = \mathbf{sA} + x\mathbf{a} + \alpha\mathbf{d},$$

where $\mathbf{s} = (s'_1, \ldots, s'_n)$. We remark that for a prime modulus q the above analysis readily applies, whereas for composite moduli we need to take into account several fringe cases.

Using a variant of the Smoothing Lemma [7] we can finally argue that $(\mathbf{Ar}, \mathbf{zr} + q_2 v_0, \mathbf{ar} + q_2 v_1)$ only contains information about $x v_1 + v_0$, but leaks otherwise no information about v_0, v_1.

2.3 Applications to PVW OT

Note that by setting $q_1 = 2$ our OLE protocol realizes exactly the PVW protocol [29]. Thus, our new extraction mechanism immediately improves the PVW protocol by allowing the modulus q to be superpolynomial. Furthermore, we can combine our extractor with the smoothing technique of Quach [30] to obtain a UC-secure variant of the PVW protocol with reusable CRS without the correctness and efficiency penalties incurred by Quach's protocol.

2.4 Extending to Malicious Adversaries

It might seem that Quach's smoothing technique [30] immediately allows us to prove security against malicious senders as well. And indeed, by choosing $\mathbf{a}$ as a well-formed LWE sample $\mathbf{a} = \mathbf{s}^*\mathbf{A} + \mathbf{e}^*$ we can extract the sender's input v_0, v_1 from $\mathbf{c}, c_0, c_1$. However, the issue presents itself slightly different: In the real protocol the receiver computes and outputs $y = \lceil x \cdot (c_1 - \mathbf{s}^*\mathbf{c}) + c_0 - \mathbf{sc} \rfloor_{q_1}$. If $\mathbf{c}, c_0, c_1$ are well-formed this is indeed a linear function in x. However, if $c_1 - \mathbf{s}^*\mathbf{c}$ or $c_0 - \mathbf{sc}$ is *not close to a multiple of* q_2, then this is a non-linear function! But by the functionality of OLE in the ideal model we have to compute a linear function. Observe that this is not an issue in the case of OT (i.e. $q_1 = 2$), as in this case any 1-bit input function is a linear function. To overcome this issue for OLE, we need to deploy a technique which ensures that $\mathbf{c}, c_0, c_1$ are well-formed.

In a nutshell, the idea to make the protocol secure against malicious senders is to use a *cut-and-choose*-style approach using a two-round OT protocol[6], which exists under various assumptions [12,29,30]. Using the OT, the receiver is able to check if the vectors $\mathbf{c}_j = \mathbf{A}\mathbf{r}_j$ provided by the sender are well-formed. More precisely, our augmented protocol works as follows:[7]

1. The receiver computes $\mathbf{z} = \mathbf{s}\mathbf{A} + \mathbf{e} - x\mathbf{a}$ for a uniform input x (in Sect. 6 we show how to remove the condition of x being uniform). Additionally, it runs λ instances of the OT in parallel (playing the role of the receiver), with input bits $(b_1, \ldots, b_\lambda) \leftarrow_\$ \{0,1\}^\lambda$ chosen uniformly at random; and sends the first messages of each instance.
2. For $j \in [\lambda]$, the sender (with input (v_0, v_1)) computes $\mathbf{c}_j = \mathbf{A}\mathbf{r}_j$, $c_{0,j} = \mathbf{z}\mathbf{r}_j + q_2 u_{0,j}$ and $c_{1,j} = \mathbf{a}\mathbf{r}_j + q_2 u_{1,j}$ for a gaussian $\mathbf{r}_j$ and uniform $(u_{0,j}, u_{1,j}$. It sets $M_{0,j} = (\mathbf{r}_j, u_{0,j}, u_{1,j})$ and $M_{1,j} = (\bar{v}_{0,j} = v_0 + u_{0,j}, \bar{v}_{1,j} = v_1 + u_{1,j})$ and inputs $(M_{0,j}, M_{1,j})$ into the OT. Moreover, $\mathbf{c}_j, c_{0,j}, c_{1,j}$ are sent to the receiver in the plain.
3. If $b_j = 0$, the receiver can check that the values $\mathbf{c}_j, c_{0,j}, c_{1,j}$ are indeed well-formed, i.e. it holds $\mathbf{c}_j = \mathbf{A}\mathbf{r}_j$, $c_{0,j} = \mathbf{z}\mathbf{r}_j + q_2 u_{0,j}$, $c_{1,j} = \mathbf{a}\mathbf{r}_j + q_2 u_{1,j}$ and $\mathbf{r}_j$ is short. If $b_j = 1$, the receiver obtains a random OLE $u_{0,j} + x u_{1,j}$ (which can be obtained by computing $y = \lceil x \cdot c_{1,j} + c_{0,j} - \mathbf{s}\mathbf{c}_j \rfloor_{q_1}$). This random OLE instance can be derandomized by computing $y_j = \bar{v}_{0,j} + x\bar{v}_{0,j} - (u_{0,j} + x u_{1,j})$. If y_j coincides at all the positions where $b_j = 1$, then it outputs this value. Else, it aborts.

Security against an unbounded receiver in the OT-hybrid model essentially follows the same reasoning as in the previous protocol.

We now argue how we can build the simulator Sim against a corrupted sender. Sim checks for which of the positions j, the message $M_{0,j}$ is well-formed. If all but a small number of them are well-formed, Sim proceeds; else, it aborts. Then, having recovered the randomness $(\mathbf{r}_j, u_{0,j}, u_{1,j})$, Sim can extract a pair $(v_{0,j}, v_{0,1})$ from $(\mathbf{c}_j, c_{0,j}, c_{1,j})$. If $(v_{0,j}, v_{0,1})$ coincides in at least half of the positions, then Sim outputs this pair; else, if no such pair exists, Sim aborts.

3 Preliminaries

Throughout this work, λ denotes the security parameter and PPT stands for "probabilistic polynomial-time".

Let $\mathbf{A} \in \mathbb{Z}_q^{k \times n}$ and $\mathbf{x} \in \mathbb{Z}_q^n$. Then $\|\mathbf{x}\|$ denotes the usual ℓ_2 norm of a vector $\mathbf{x}$. Moreover, $\|\mathbf{A}\| = \max_{i \in [m]}\{\|\mathbf{a}^{(i)}\|\}$ where $\mathbf{a}^{(i)}$ is the i-th column of $\mathbf{A}$. For a vector $\mathbf{b} \in \{0,1\}^k$, we denote its weight, that is the number of non-null coordinates, by $wt(\mathbf{b})$.

[6] The approach is similar in spirit as previous works, e.g. [25].

[7] The construction actually works for any OLE scheme that is secure against semi-honest senders and malicious receivers. In the technical sections we present the generic construction.

If S is a (finite) set, we denote by $x \leftarrow_{\$} S$ an element $x \in S$ sampled according to a uniform distribution. Moreover, we denote by $U(S)$ the uniform distribution over S. If D is a distribution over S, $x \leftarrow_{\$} D$ denotes an element $x \in S$ sampled according to D. If $\mathcal{A}$ is an algorithm, $y \leftarrow \mathcal{A}(x)$ denotes the output y after running $\mathcal{A}$ on input x.

A negligible function $\mathsf{negl}(n)$ in n is a function that vanishes faster than the inverse of any polynomial in n.

Given two distributions D_1 and D_2, we say that they are ε-statistically indistinguishable, denoted by $D_1 \approx_{\varepsilon} D_2$, if the statistical distance is at most ε.

The function $\mathsf{lcm}(i_1, \ldots, i_j)$ between j integers $i_1, \ldots, i_j$ is the smallest integer $a \in \mathbb{Z}$ such that a is divisible by all $i_1, \ldots, i_j$.

Error-Correcting Codes. We define Error-Correcting Codes (ECC). An ECC over $\mathbb{Z}_q$ is composed by the following algorithms $\mathsf{ECC}_{q',q,\ell,k,\delta} = (\mathsf{Encode}, \mathsf{Decode})$ such that: i) $\mathbf{c} \leftarrow \mathsf{Encode}(\mathbf{m})$ takes as input a message $\mathbf{m} \in \mathbb{Z}_{q'}^{\ell}$ and outputs a codeword $\mathbf{c} \in \mathbb{Z}_q^k$; ii) $\mathbf{m} \leftarrow \mathsf{Decode}(\tilde{\mathbf{c}})$ takes as input corrupted codeword $\tilde{\mathbf{c}} \in \mathbb{Z}_q^k$ and outputs a message $\mathbf{m} \in \mathbb{Z}_{q'}^{\ell}$ if $\|\tilde{\mathbf{c}} - \mathbf{c}\| \leq \delta$ where $\mathbf{c} \leftarrow \mathsf{Encode}(\mathbf{m})$. In this case, we say that ECC corrects up to δ errors. We say that ECC is linear if any linear combination of codewords of ECC is also a codeword of ECC.

An example of such code is the primitive lattice of [26] which allows for efficient decoding and fulfills all the properties that we need. In this code, $q = q'$ and $\ell < k$.

Alternatively, if $\mathbf{m} \in \mathbb{Z}_{q'}^{\ell}$ for $q't = q$ for some $t \in \mathbb{N}$, we can use the encoding $\mathbf{c} = t \cdot \mathbf{m}$ which is usually used in lattice-based cryptography (e.g., [4]). Decoding a corrupted codeword $\tilde{\mathbf{c}}$ works by rounding $\lceil \tilde{\mathbf{c}} \rfloor_{q'} = \lceil (1/t) \cdot \tilde{\mathbf{c}} \rfloor \mod q'$.

3.1 Universal Composability

UC-framework [9] allows to prove security of protocols even under arbitrary composition with other protocols. Let $\mathcal{F}$ be a functionality, π a protocol that implements $\mathcal{F}$ and $\mathcal{Z}$ be a environment, an entity that oversees the execution of the protocol in both the real and the ideal worlds. Let $\mathsf{IDEAL}_{\mathcal{F},\mathsf{Sim},\mathcal{Z}}$ be a random variable that represents the output of $\mathcal{Z}$ after the execution of $\mathcal{F}$ with adversary Sim. Similarly, let $\mathsf{REAL}^{\mathcal{G}}_{\pi,\mathcal{A},\mathcal{Z}}$ be a random variable that represents the output of $\mathcal{Z}$ after the execution of π with adversary $\mathcal{A}$ and with access to the functionality $\mathcal{G}$.

A protocol π *UC-realizes $\mathcal{F}$ in the $\mathcal{G}$-hybrid model* if for every PPT adversary $\mathcal{A}$ there is a PPT simulator Sim such that for all PPT environments $\mathcal{E}$, the distributions $\mathsf{IDEAL}_{\mathcal{F},\mathsf{Sim},\mathcal{Z}}$ and $\mathsf{REAL}^{\mathcal{G}}_{\pi,\mathcal{A},\mathcal{Z}}$ are computationally indistinguishable.

In this work, we only consider *static* adversaries. That is, parties involved in the protocol are corrupted at the beginning of the execution.

We now present the ideal functionalities that we will use in this work.

CRS functionality. This functionality generates a crs and distributes it between all the parties involved in the protocol. Here, we present the ideal functionality as in [29].

$\mathcal{G}_{\mathsf{CRS}}$ functionality

Parameters: An algorithm D.

- Upon receiving $(\mathsf{sid}, \mathsf{P}_i, \mathsf{P}_j)$ from P_i, $\mathcal{G}_{\mathsf{CRS}}$ runs $\mathsf{crs} \leftarrow \mathsf{D}(1^\kappa)$ and returns $(\mathsf{sid}, \mathsf{crs})$ to P_i.
- Upon receiving $(\mathsf{sid}, \mathsf{P}_i, \mathsf{P}_j)$ from P_j, $\mathcal{G}_{\mathsf{CRS}}$ returns $(\mathsf{sid}, \mathsf{crs})$ to P_j.

OT functionality. Oblivious Transfer (OT) can be seen as a particular case of OLE. We show the ideal OT functionality below.

$\mathcal{F}_{\mathsf{OT}}$ functionality

Parameters: $\mathsf{sid} \in \mathbb{N}$ known to both parties.

- Upon receiving $(\mathsf{sid}, (M_0, M_1))$ from S, $\mathcal{F}_{\mathsf{OT}}$ stores (M_0, M_1) and ignores future messages from S with the same sid;
- Upon receiving $(\mathsf{sid}, b \in \{0, 1\})$ from R, $\mathcal{F}_{\mathsf{OT}}$ checks if it has recorded $(\mathsf{sid}, (M_0, M_1))$. If so, it returns (sid, M_b) to R and $(\mathsf{sid}, \mathsf{receipt})$ to S, and halts. Else, it sends nothing, but continues running.

OLE functionality. We now present the OLE functionality. This functionality involves two parties: the sender S and the receiver R.

$\mathcal{F}_{\mathsf{OLE}}$ functionality

Parameters: $\mathsf{sid}, q, k \in \mathbb{N}$ and a finite field $\mathbb{F}$ known to both parties.

- Upon receiving $\left(\mathsf{sid}, (\mathbf{a}, \mathbf{b}) \in \mathbb{F}^k \times \mathbb{F}^k\right)$ from S, $\mathcal{F}_{\mathsf{OLE}}$ stores $(\mathbf{a}, \mathbf{b})$ and ignores future messages from S with the same sid;
- Upon receiving $(\mathsf{sid}, x \in \mathbb{F})$ from R, $\mathcal{F}_{\mathsf{OLE}}$ checks if it has recorded $(\mathsf{sid}, (\mathbf{a}, \mathbf{b}))$. If so, it returns $(\mathsf{sid}, \mathbf{z} = \mathbf{a} + x\mathbf{b})$ to R and $(\mathsf{sid}, \mathsf{receipt})$ to S, and halts. Else, it sends nothing but continues running.

Batch OLE functionality. Here we define a batch version of the functionality defined above. In this functionality, the receiver inputs several OLE inputs at the same time. The sender can then input an affine function together with an index corresponding to which input the receiver should receive the linear combination. The formal description of the functionality is presented in the full version of the paper [8].

3.2 Lattices and Hardness Assumptions

Notation. Let $\mathbf{B} \in \mathbb{R}^{k \times n}$ be a matrix. We denote the lattice generated by $\mathbf{B}$ by $\Lambda = \Lambda(\mathbf{B}) = \{\mathbf{xB} : \mathbf{x} \in \mathbb{Z}^k\}$.[8] The dual lattice Λ^* of a lattice Λ is defined by $\Lambda^* = \{\mathbf{x} \in \mathbb{R}^n : \forall y \in \Lambda, \mathbf{x} \cdot \mathbf{y} \in \mathbb{Z}\}$. It holds that $(\Lambda^*)^* = \Lambda$.

[8] The matrix $\mathbf{B}$ is called a basis of $\Lambda(\mathbf{B})$.

We denote by $\gamma\mathcal{B}$ the ball of radius γ centered on zero. That is

$$\gamma\mathcal{B} = \{\mathbf{x} \in \mathbb{Z}^n : \|\mathbf{x}\| \leq \gamma\}.$$

A lattice Λ is said to be q-ary if $(q\mathbb{Z})^n \subseteq \Lambda \subseteq \mathbb{Z}^n$. For every q-ary lattice Λ, there is a matrix $\mathbf{A} \in \mathbb{Z}_q^{k\times n}$ such that

$$\Lambda = \Lambda_q(\mathbf{A}) = \{y \in \mathbb{Z}^n : \exists \mathbf{x} \in \mathbb{Z}_q^k, \mathbf{y} = \mathbf{x}\mathbf{A} \mod q\}.$$

The orthogonal lattice $\Lambda_q^\perp$ is defined by $\{\mathbf{y} \in \mathbb{Z}^n : \mathbf{A}\mathbf{y}^T = 0 \mod q\}$. It holds that $\frac{1}{q}\Lambda_q^\perp = \Lambda_q^*$.

Let $\rho_s(\mathbf{x})$ be probability distribution of the Gaussian distribution over $\mathbb{R}^n$ with parameter s and centered in 0. We define the discrete Gaussian distribution $D_{S,s}$ over S and with parameter s by the probability distribution $\rho_s(\mathbf{x})/\rho(S)$ for all $\mathbf{x} \in S$ (where $\rho_s(S) = \sum_{\mathbf{x}\in S} \rho_s(\mathbf{x})$).

For $\varepsilon > 0$, the smoothing parameter $\eta_\varepsilon(\Lambda)$ of a lattice Λ is the least real number $\sigma > 0$ such that $\rho_{1/\sigma}(\Lambda^* \setminus \{0\}) \leq \varepsilon$ [27].

Useful Lemmata. The following lemmas are well-known results on discrete Gaussians over lattices.

Lemma 1 **([3]).** *Let $\sigma > 0$ and $\mathbf{x} \leftarrow_\$ D_{\mathbb{Z}^n,\sigma}$. Then we have that*

$$\Pr\left[\|\mathbf{x}\| \geq \sigma\sqrt{n}\right] \leq \mathsf{negl}(n).$$

The next lemma is a consequence of the smoothing lemma [27] and it tells us that $\mathbf{A}\mathbf{e}^T$ is uniform, when $\mathbf{e}$ is sampled from a discrete Gaussian for a proper choice of parameters.

Lemma 2 **([16]).** *Let $q \in \mathbb{N}$ and $\mathbf{A} \in \mathbb{Z}_q^{k\times n}$ be a matrix such that $n = \mathsf{poly}(k \log q)$. Moreover, let $\varepsilon \in (0, 1/2)$ and $\sigma \geq \eta_\varepsilon(\Lambda_q^\perp(\mathbf{A}))$. Then, for $\mathbf{e} \leftarrow_\$ D_{\mathbb{Z}^m,\sigma}$,*

$$\mathbf{A}\mathbf{e}^T \mod q \approx_{2\varepsilon} \mathbf{u}^T \mod q$$

where $\mathbf{u} \leftarrow_\$ \mathbb{Z}_q^k$.

The *partial smoothing lemma* tells us that the famous *smoothing lemma* [27] still holds even given a small leak.

Lemma 3 (Partial Smoothing **[7]).** *Let $q \in \mathbb{N}$, $\gamma > 0$ be a real number, $\mathbf{A} \in \mathbb{Z}_q^{k\times n}$ and $\sigma, \varepsilon > 0$ be such that $\rho_{q/\sigma}(\Lambda_q(\mathbf{A}) \setminus \gamma\mathcal{B}) \leq \varepsilon$. Moreover, let $\mathbf{D} \in \mathbb{Z}_q^{m\times k}$ be a full-rank matrix with $\Lambda_q^\perp(\mathbf{D}) = \{\mathbf{x} \in \mathbb{Z}^n : \mathbf{x} \cdot \mathbf{y}^T = 0, \forall \mathbf{y} \in \Lambda_q(\mathbf{A}) \cap \gamma\mathcal{B}\}$. Then we have that*

$$\mathbf{A}\mathbf{x}^T \mod q \approx_\varepsilon \mathbf{A}(\mathbf{x} + \mathbf{u})^T \mod q$$

where $\mathbf{x} \leftarrow_\$ D_{\mathbb{Z}^n,\sigma}$ and $\mathbf{u} \leftarrow_\$ \Lambda_q^\perp(\mathbf{D}) \mod q$.

Recall Hadamard's inequality.

Theorem 1 (Hadamard's inequality). *Let $\Lambda \subseteq \mathbb{R}^n$ be a lattice and let $\mathbf{e}_1, \ldots, \mathbf{e}_n$ be a basis of Λ. Then it holds that*

$$\det(\Lambda) \leq \prod_{i=1}^{n} \|\mathbf{e}_i\|.$$

The following two lemmas give us an upper-bound on and the value of the determinant of a two-dimensional lattice $\Lambda_q^{\perp}(\mathbf{a})$ for $\mathbf{a} \in \mathbb{Z}_q^2$.

Lemma 4. *Let $q \in \mathbb{N}$, $B \in \mathbb{R}$ and $\mathbf{a} \in \mathbb{Z}_q^2$ such that $\mathbf{a} \neq 0$. Let $\mathbf{e}, \mathbf{e}' \in \mathbb{Z}^2$ such that $\mathbf{e}, \mathbf{e}' \in \Lambda_q^{\perp}(\mathbf{a})$, $\|\mathbf{e}\|, \|\mathbf{e}'\| < B$ and $\mathbf{e}, \mathbf{e}'$ are linearly independent over $\mathbb{Z}$. Then $\det\left(\Lambda_q^{\perp}(\mathbf{a})\right) \leq B^2$.*

The proof is presented in the full version of the paper [8].

We will need the following simple Definition and Lemma.

Definition 1. *Let q be a modulus. We say that a vector $\mathbf{a} \in \mathbb{Z}_q^n$ is* primitive, *if the row-span of of $\mathbf{a}^\top$ is $\mathbb{Z}_q$. In other words it holds that every $z \in \mathbb{Z}_q$ can be expressed as $z = \langle \mathbf{a}, \mathbf{x} \rangle$ for some $\mathbf{x} \in \mathbb{Z}_q^n$.*

Lemma 5. *Let q be a modulus an let $\mathbf{a} \in \mathbb{Z}_q^n$ be primitive. Then it holds that* $\det(\Lambda^{\perp}(\mathbf{a})) = q$.

The proof is presented in the full version of the paper [8].

The following lemma states that, for two-dimensional lattices, we can efficiently find the shortest vector of the lattice.

Lemma 6 ([24]). *Let $q \in \mathbb{N}$, and let $\Lambda \subseteq \mathbb{Z}^2$ be a q-ary lattice. There exists an algorithm* SolveSVP *that takes as input (a basis of) Λ and outputs the shortest vector $\mathbf{e} \in \Lambda$. This algorithm runs it time $\mathcal{O}(\log q)$.*

We will also need the following lemma which states that any sufficiently short vector of the lattice $\Lambda_q^{\perp}(\mathbf{a})$ must be a multiple of the shortest vector $\mathbf{e}' \leftarrow \mathsf{SolveSVP}(\mathbf{a})$.

Lemma 7. *Let $q \in \mathbb{N}$, $B < \sqrt{q}$, $\mathbf{a} \in \mathbb{Z}_q^2$ be a primitive 2-dimensional vector such that $\mathbf{a} \neq 0$, and $\mathbf{e} \in \mathbb{Z}^2$ be the shortest vector of the lattice $\Lambda_q^{\perp}(\mathbf{a})$. If $\|\mathbf{e}\| < B$ then for any $\mathbf{e}' \in \mathbb{Z}^2$ such that $\mathbf{e}' \in \Lambda_q^{\perp}(\mathbf{a})$ and $\|\mathbf{e}'\| < B$ we have that $\mathbf{e}' = t\mathbf{e}$ for some $t \in \mathbb{Z}$, i.e., $\mathbf{e}'$ is a multiple of $\mathbf{e}$ over $\mathbb{Z}$.*

Proof. We have that $\mathbf{e}, \mathbf{e}' \in \Lambda_q^{\perp}(\mathbf{a})$ and $\|\mathbf{e}\|, \|\mathbf{e}'\| < B$. Assume towards contradiction that $\mathbf{e}, \mathbf{e}'$ are linearly dependent over $\mathbb{Z}$. Then by Lemma 4 $\det\left(\Lambda_q^{\perp}(\mathbf{a}_i)\right) \leq B^2$.

On the other hand, we have that $\det\left(\Lambda_q^{\perp}(\mathbf{a})\right) = q$ by Lemma 5. Then $q \leq B^2$ and thus $\sqrt{q} \leq B$, which contradicts the assumption that $B < \sqrt{q}$. We conclude that $\mathbf{e}$ must be a multiple of $\mathbf{e}'$ over the integers.

The LWE Assumption. The Learning with Errors assumption was first presented in [31]. The assumption roughly states that it should be hard to solve a set linear equations by just adding a little noise to it.

Definition 2 (Learning with Errors). *Let $q, k \in \mathbb{N}$ where $k \in \mathsf{poly}(\lambda)$, $\mathbf{A} \in \mathbb{Z}_q^{k\times n}$ and $\beta \in \mathbb{R}$. For any $n = \mathsf{poly}(k \log q)$, the $\mathsf{LWE}_{k,\beta,q}$ assumption holds if for every PPT algorithm $\mathcal{A}$ we have*

$$|\Pr[1 \leftarrow \mathcal{A}(\mathbf{A}, \mathbf{sA} + \mathbf{e})] - \Pr[1 \leftarrow \mathcal{A}(\mathbf{A}, \mathbf{y})]| \leq \mathsf{negl}(\lambda)$$

for $\mathbf{s} \leftarrow_\$ \{0,1\}^k$, $\mathbf{e} \leftarrow_\$ D_{\mathbb{Z}^n,\beta}$ and $\mathbf{y} \leftarrow_\$ \{0,1\}^n$.

Regev proved in [31] that there is a (quantum) worst-case to average-case reduction from some problems on lattices which are believed to be hard even in the presence of a quantum computer.

Trapdoors for Lattices. Recent works [16,26] have presented trapdoors functions based on the hardness of LWE.

Lemma 8 ([16,26]). *Let $\tau(k) \in \omega\left(\sqrt{\log k}\right)$ be a function. There is a pair of algorithms* ($\mathsf{TdGen}, \mathsf{Invert}$) *such that if* $(\mathbf{A}, \mathsf{td}) \leftarrow \mathsf{TdGen}(1^\lambda, n, k, q)$ *then:*

- $\mathbf{A} \in \mathbb{Z}_q^{k\times n}$ *where $n \in \mathcal{O}(k \log q)$ is a matrix whose distribution is 2^{-k} close to the uniform distribution over $\mathbb{Z}_q^{k\times n}$.*
- *For any $\mathbf{s} \in Z_q^k$ and $\mathbf{e} \in \mathbb{Z}_q^n$ such that $\|\mathbf{e}\| < q/(\sqrt{n}\tau(k))$, we have that*

$$\mathbf{s} \leftarrow \mathsf{Invert}(\mathsf{td}, \mathbf{sA} + \mathbf{e}).$$

In the lemma above, td corresponds to a *short* matrix $\mathbf{T} \in \mathbb{Z}^{n\times n}$ (that is, $\|\mathbf{T}\| < B$, for some $B \in \mathbb{R}$ and B determines the trapdoor *quality* [16,26]) such that $\mathbf{AT} = 0$ and $\mathbf{T}^{-1}$ can be easily computed. To invert a sample of the form $\mathbf{y} = \mathbf{sA} + \mathbf{e}$, we simply compute $\mathbf{yT} = \mathbf{sAT} + \mathbf{eT} = \mathbf{eT}$. The error vector $\mathbf{e}$ can be easily recovered by multiplying by $\mathbf{T}^{-1}$.

Observe that, if $(\mathbf{A}, \mathsf{td}_\mathbf{A}) \leftarrow \mathsf{TdGen}(1^\lambda, n, k, q)$, then $\Lambda(\mathbf{A})$ has no *short* vectors. That is, for all $\mathbf{y} \in \Lambda(\mathbf{A})$, then $\|\mathbf{y}\| > B = q/(\sqrt{n}\tau(k))$ [26]. If this does not happen, then the algorithm Invert would not output the right $\mathbf{s}$ for a non-negligible number of cases.

4 Finding Short Vectors in a Lattice with a Trapdoor

In this section, we provide an algorithm that, given a matrix $\mathbf{A} \in \mathbb{Z}_q^{k\times n}$ together with the corresponding lattice trapdoor $\mathsf{td}_\mathbf{A}$ (in the sense of Lemma 8), we can decide if a vector $\mathbf{a} \in \mathbb{Z}_q^n$ is close to the row-span of $\mathbf{A}$, i.e. if $\mathbf{a}$ is close to the lattice $\Lambda_q(\mathbf{A})$, and even find the closest vector in $\Lambda_q(\mathbf{A})$.

To keep things simple, we will only consider the case where q is either a prime or the product of a "small" prime q_1 and a "large" prime q_2.

Before providing the algorithm, we will first prove the following structural result about equation systems of the form $\mathbf{y} = r\mathbf{e}(\mod q)$, where $\mathbf{y} \in \mathbb{Z}_q^n$ is given and $r \in \mathbb{Z}_q$ and a short $\mathbf{e} \in \mathbb{Z}^n$ are to be determined.

Lemma 9. *Let q be a modulus and let $B^2 \leq q$. Let $\mathbf{y} \in \mathbb{Z}_q^n$ be a vector such that there is an index i for which $y_i \in \mathbb{Z}_q^*$. Assume* wlog *that $y_1 \in \mathbb{Z}_q^*$. Define the q-ary lattice Λ as the set of all $\mathbf{x} = (x_1, \ldots, x_n) \in \mathbb{Z}^n$ for which it holds that $-y_i/y_1 \cdot x_1 + x_i = 0(\mod q)$ for $i = 2, \ldots, n$. Now let $r \in \mathbb{Z}_q$ and $\mathbf{e} \in \mathbb{Z}^n$ be such that $\mathbf{y} = r \cdot \mathbf{e}$. Then $\mathbf{e} \in \Lambda$. Furthermore, all $\mathbf{x} \in \Lambda$ with $\|\mathbf{x}\| \leq B$ are linearly dependent. In other words, if there exists a $\mathbf{x} \in \Lambda \backslash \{0\}$ with $\|\mathbf{x}\| \leq B$, then there exists a $\mathbf{x}^* \in \Lambda$ such that every $\mathbf{x} \in \Lambda$ with $\|\mathbf{x}\| \leq B$ can be written as $\mathbf{x} = t \cdot \mathbf{x}^*$ for a $t \in \mathbb{Z}$.*

Proof. First not that if $\mathbf{y} = r \cdot \mathbf{e}$ for an $r \in \mathbb{Z}_q$ and an $\mathbf{e} \in \mathbb{Z}^n$, then it holds routinely that $-y_i/y_1 \cdot e_1 + e_i = 0$ for all $i = 2, \ldots, n$. We will now show the second part of the lemma, namely that if there exists an $\mathbf{x} \in \Lambda \backslash \{0\}$ with $\|\mathbf{x}\| \leq B$, then any such $\mathbf{x}$ can be written as $\mathbf{x} = t \cdot \mathbf{x}^*$ for a $\mathbf{x}' \in \Lambda$, which is the shortest non-zero vector in Λ. Let $\mathbf{x} = (x_1, \ldots, x_n) \in \mathbb{Z}^n$ and define the shortened vectors $\mathbf{x}_i = (x_1, x_i) \in \mathbb{Z}^2$. Note that since $\|\mathbf{x}\| \leq B$, it also holds that $\|\mathbf{x}_i\| \leq B$. Further define the lattices $\Lambda_i \subseteq \mathbb{Z}^2$ (for $i = 2, \ldots, n$) via the equation $-y_i/y_1 x_1 + x_i = 0$, and observe that $\mathbf{x}_i \in \Lambda_i$. Further let $\mathbf{x}_i^* = (x_{1,i}^*, x_i^*)$ be the shortest non-zero vector in Λ_i. Set $x_1^\dagger = \mathsf{lcm}(x_{1,2}^*, \ldots, x_{1,n}^*)$ and $x_i^\dagger = x_i^* \cdot x_1^\dagger / x_{1,i}^*$, and set set $\mathbf{x}^\dagger = (x_1^\dagger, \ldots, x_n^\dagger)$. Note that $\mathbf{x}^\dagger \in \Lambda$. We claim that $\mathbf{x}$ can be written as $\mathbf{x} = t \cdot \mathbf{x}^\dagger$, hence $\mathbf{x}^\dagger$ is the shortest vector in Λ.

Since $\|\mathbf{x}_i\| \leq B$ it follows by Lemma 7 that we can write $\mathbf{x}_i$ as $\mathbf{x}_i = t_i \cdot \mathbf{x}_i^*$ for a $t_i \in \mathbb{Z}$. That is $x_1 = t_i \cdot x_{1,i}^*$ and $x_i = t_i \cdot x_i^*$. Now, since $x_{1,i}^*$ divides x_1 for $i = 2, \ldots, n$, it also holds that $x_1^\dagger = \mathsf{lcm}(x_{1,2}^*, \ldots, x_{1,n}^*)$ divides x_1. Thus write $x_1 = t^\dagger \cdot x_1^\dagger$ for some $t^\dagger$, and it follows that

$$\begin{aligned}
t^\dagger \cdot x_i^\dagger &= t^\dagger \cdot x_i^* \cdot x_1^\dagger / x_{1,i}^* \\
&= x_i^* \cdot x_1 / x_{1,i}^* \\
&= x_i^* \cdot t_i \\
&= x_i,
\end{aligned}$$

for $i = 2, \ldots, n$. We conclude that $\mathbf{x} = t^\dagger \cdot \mathbf{x}^\dagger$.

The proof of Lemma 9 suggest an approach to recover $\mathbf{e}$ for $\mathbf{y}$: Compute the shortest vectors of the two-dimensional lattices Λ_i and use them to find the shortest vector $\mathbf{e}^\dagger$ in Λ. Since $\mathbf{e}$ is a multiple of $\mathbf{e}^\dagger$, $\mathbf{e}^\dagger$ also must be a short solution to $\mathbf{y} = r^\dagger \mathbf{e}^\dagger$.

The following algorithm receives as input a vector $\mathbf{y}$ and allows us to find $(r, \mathbf{e})$ such that $r\mathbf{e} = \mathbf{y} \mod q$ and $\mathbf{e}$ is a short vector (if such a vector exists).

Construction 1. *Let q be a modulus and let $n = \mathsf{poly}(\lambda)$. Let $\mathbf{y} \in \mathbb{Z}_q^n$ be such that at least one component y_i is invertible, i.e. $y_i \in \mathbb{Z}_q^*$. Without loss of generality, we assume that this component is y_1.*

$\mathsf{RecoverError}_{q,n}(\mathbf{y}, B)$*:*

- *Parse $\mathbf{y} \in \mathbb{Z}_q^n$ as $(y_1, \ldots, y_n)$ and $B > 0$. If $\|\mathbf{y}\| \leq B$ output $\mathbf{y}$.*

- *Since* $y_i \in \mathbb{Z}_q^*$, *compute for all* $i = 2, \ldots, n$ $v_i = y_i \cdot (y_1)^{-1}$ *over* $\mathbb{Z}_q$, *and set* $\mathbf{a}_i = (v_i \ \ -1)$.
- *For* $i = 2, \ldots, n$ *consider the lattice* $\Lambda_i = \Lambda_q^{\perp}(\mathbf{a}_i) \subseteq \mathbb{Z}^2$ *and run* $\mathsf{SolveSVP}(\Lambda_i)$ *to obtain* $\mathbf{e}_i^* \in \Lambda_i$. *Parse* $\mathbf{e}_i = (e_{1,i}^*, e_i^*)$.
- *Compute* $e_1^{\dagger} = \mathsf{lcm}\,(e_{1,2}, \ldots, e_{1,n})$.
- *For all* $i = 2, \ldots, n$, *set* $\alpha_i = e_1^{\dagger}/e_{1,i} \in \mathbb{Z}$
- *Set* $e_i^{\dagger} = \alpha_i \cdot e_i^*$.
- *Set* $\mathbf{e}^{\dagger} = (e_1^{\dagger}, \ldots, e_n^{\dagger})$ *and* $r^{\dagger} = y_1 \cdot (e_1^{\dagger})^{-1} \in \mathbb{Z}_q$
- *If* $\|\mathbf{e}^{\dagger}\|_{\infty} < B$, *output* $(r^{\dagger}, \mathbf{e}^{\dagger})$. *Else, output* $\perp$.

Lemma 10. *Given that* $B^2 \leq q$ *and the vector* $\mathbf{y}$ *is of the form* $\mathbf{y} = r\mathbf{e}$ *for some* $r \in \mathbb{Z}_q$ *and* $\mathbf{e} \in \mathbb{Z}^n$ *with* $\|\mathbf{e}\|_{\infty} \leq B$, *and further there exists an* $y_i \in \mathbb{Z}_q^*$, *then* $\mathsf{RecoverError}_{q,n}(\mathbf{y}, B)$ *outputs a pair* $(r^{\dagger}, \mathbf{e}^{\dagger})$ *with* $\mathbf{y} = r^{\dagger} \cdot \mathbf{e}^{\dagger}$ *for an* $r^{\dagger} \in Z_q$ *and* $\mathbf{e}^{\dagger} \in \mathbb{Z}^n$ *with* $\|\mathbf{e}^{\dagger}\| \leq B$. *Furthermore,* $\mathbf{e}$ *is a short* $\mathbb{Z}$*-multiple of* $\mathbf{e}^{\dagger}$, *i.e.* $\mathbf{e}$ *and* $\mathbf{e}^{\dagger}$ *are linearly dependent. The algorithm runs in time* $\mathsf{poly}(\log q, n)$.

Proof. We first analyze the runtime of the algorithm. Note that, since Λ_i has dimension 2, then $\mathsf{SolveSVP}$ runs in time $\mathcal{O}(\log q)$ by Lemma 6. All other procedures run in time $\mathsf{poly}(\log q, n)$.

We will now show that algorithm $\mathsf{RecoverError}$ is correct. Let

$$\mathbf{y} = r \cdot \mathbf{e} \in \mathbb{Z}_q^n \tag{9}$$

for an $r \in \mathbb{Z}_q$ and a $\mathbf{e} \in \mathbb{Z}^n$ with $\|\mathbf{e}\|_{\infty} \leq B$. We claim that algorithm $\mathsf{RecoverError}$, on input $\mathbf{y}$ outputs an $r^* \in \mathbb{Z}_q$ and a $\mathbf{e}^* \in \mathbb{Z}^n$ with $\|\mathbf{e}^*\|_{\infty} \leq \|\mathbf{e}\|_{\infty}$.

We can expand (9) as the following *non-linear equation system*:

$$\begin{aligned} y_1 &= r \cdot e_1 \\ &\vdots \\ y_n &= r \cdot e_n. \end{aligned}$$

Eliminating r via the first equation, using that $y_1 \in \mathbb{Z}_q^*$ we obtain the equation system

$$\begin{aligned} -y_2 \cdot y_1^{-1} \cdot e_1 + e_2 &= 0 \\ &\vdots \\ -y_n \cdot y_1^{-1} \cdot e_1 + e_n &= 0, \end{aligned}$$

i.e. we conclude that any solution to the above problem must also satisfy this *linear* equation system. Now write $v_i = y_i/y_1$ and set $\mathbf{a}_i = (-v_i, 1)$ and $\mathbf{e}_i = (e_1, e_i)$. The above equation system can be restated as for all $i = 2, \ldots, n$ that $\mathbf{e}_i \in \Lambda_i = \Lambda^{\perp}(\mathbf{a}_i)$.

Since $\|\mathbf{e}\|_{\infty} \leq B$, it immediately follows that $\|\mathbf{e}_i\|_{\infty} \leq B$. Note further that all vectors $\mathbf{a}_i \in \mathbb{Z}_q^2$ are primitive (as their second component is 1). Now, let $\mathbf{e}_i^*$

be the shortest (non-zero) vector in Λ_i. As by the above argument $\mathbf{e}_i \in \Lambda_i$ and $\|\mathbf{e}_i\|_\infty < B$, it follows by Lemma 7 that $\mathbf{e}_i$ must be of the form $\mathbf{e}_i = r_i \cdot \mathbf{e}_i^*$ for an $r_i \in \mathbb{Z}$.

Parsing $\mathbf{e}_i^*$ as $\mathbf{e}_i^* = (e_{i,1}^*, e_i^*)$, the above implies for all i that $e_1 = r_i \cdot e_{i,1}^*$, in other words $e_{i,1}^*$ divides e_1. But this means that also the least common multiple $e_1^\dagger$ of the $e_{i,1}^*$ divides e_1, i.e. $e_1 = t_i e_1^\dagger$. Consequently, it holds that $|e_1^\dagger| \leq |e_1|$. Now set $\alpha_i = e_1^\dagger / e_{1,i}^*$ and $\mathbf{e}_i^\dagger = \alpha_i \cdot \mathbf{e}_i^*$. Since $|e_1^\dagger| \leq |e_1|$, it must hold that $\alpha_i \leq r_i$ (as the linear combination $\mathbf{e}_i = r_i \cdot \mathbf{e}_i^*$ is unique) and therefore $\left\|\mathbf{e}_i^\dagger\right\|_\infty \leq \|\mathbf{e}_i\|_\infty$. Now parse $\mathbf{e}_i^\dagger = (e_1^\dagger, e_i^\dagger)$ and set $\mathbf{e}^\dagger = (\mathbf{e}_1^\dagger, \ldots, \mathbf{e}_n^\dagger)$. It follows that $\left\|\mathbf{e}^\dagger\right\|_\infty \leq B$. By the above it follows that $\mathbf{e}^\dagger$ is a B-short solution to the linear equation system. It follows that $r^\dagger = y_1 \cdot (e_1^\dagger)^{-1} \in \mathbb{Z}_q$ provides us a solution to the non-linear system.

Algorithm RecoverError requires that the vector $\mathbf{y}$ has a component in $\mathbb{Z}_q^*$. If the modulus q is prime, then the existence of such a component follows from $\mathbf{y} \neq 0$. However, this is generally not the case for composite moduli q. We will now present an algorithm RecoverError$^+$ which also covers composite moduli of the form q is of the form $q = q_1 \cdot q_2$, where q_2 is a "large" prime and q_1 is either 1 or a small prime.

Construction 2. *Let q be a modulus of the form $q = q_1 \cdot q_2$ (where the factors q_1 and q_2 are explicitly known) and let $n = \mathsf{poly}(\lambda)$. Let $\mathbf{y} \in \mathbb{Z}_q^n$.*

RecoverError$^+_{q,q_1,q_2,n}(\mathbf{y}, B)$:

- *If it holds for all i that $q_1 | y_i$, proceed as follows:*
  - *Compute $\bar{\mathbf{y}} = \mathbf{y} \mod q_2$ (i.e. $\bar{\mathbf{y}} \in \mathbb{Z}_{q_2}^n$)*
  - *Compute $(r_0, \mathbf{e}) =$ RecoverError$_{q_2,n}(\bar{\mathbf{y}})$*
  - *Set $r_1 = (q_1)^{-1} r_0$*
  - *Let r_1' be the lifting of r_1 to $\mathbb{Z}_q$ and set $r = q_1 \cdot r_1' \in \mathbb{Z}_q$.*
  - *Output $(r, \mathbf{e})$*
- *Otherwise, if it holds for all i that $q_2 | y_i$ proceed as follows:*
  - *Compute $\bar{\mathbf{y}} = \mathbf{y} \mod q_1$ (i.e. $\bar{\mathbf{y}} \in \mathbb{Z}_{q_1}^n$)*
  - *Set $\bar{\mathbf{e}} = (q_2)^{-1} \cdot \bar{\mathbf{y}} \in \mathbb{Z}_{q_2}^n$ (Note that q_2 has an inverse modulo q_1 as q_1 and q_2 are co-prime).*
  - *Lift $\bar{\mathbf{e}}$ to an $\mathbf{e} \in [-q_1/2, q_2/2]^n \subseteq \mathbb{Z}^n$ for which $\mathbf{e} \mod q_1 = \bar{\mathbf{e}}$.*
  - *Set $r = q_2$.*
  - *Output $(r, \mathbf{e})$.*
- *In the final case, there must exist components y_i and y_j such that $q_1 \nmid y_i$ and $q_2 \nmid y_j$. Proceed as follows:*
  - *If $q_2 \nmid y_i$ it holds that $y_i \in \mathbb{Z}_q^*$. Likewise, if $q_1 \nmid y_j$ it holds that $y_j \in \mathbb{Z}_q^*$. If one of these two trivial cases happen compute and output $(r, e) =$ RecoverError$_{q,n}(\mathbf{y})$.*
  - *Otherwise, set $y_{n+1} = y_i + y_j$ and $\mathbf{y}' = (\mathbf{y}, y_{n+1}) \in \mathbb{Z}_q^{n+1}$. Compute $(r, \mathbf{e}') =$ RecoverError$_{q,n+1}(\mathbf{y}')$. Set $\mathbf{e} = \mathbf{e}'_{1,\ldots,n} \in \mathbb{Z}^n$. If $\|\mathbf{e}\| \leq B$ Output $(r, \mathbf{e})$, otherwise try this step again for $y_{n+1} = y_i - y_j$ and output $(r, \mathbf{e})$.*

Lemma 11. *Let $q = q_1 \cdot q_2$, where $q_1 \leq 2B$ is either 1 or a prime and $q_2 > B^2$ is a prime. If $\mathbf{y}$ is of the form $\mathbf{y} = r'\mathbf{e}'$ for some $r' \in \mathbb{Z}_q$ and $\mathbf{e}' \in \mathbb{Z}^n$ with $\|\mathbf{e}'\|_\infty \leq B$, then $\mathsf{RecoverError}^+_{q,q_1,q_2,n}(\mathbf{y}, B)$ outputs a pair $(r, \mathbf{e})$ with $\|\mathbf{e}\|_\infty \leq B$ such that $\mathbf{y} = r \cdot \mathbf{e}$. The algorithm runs in time $\mathsf{poly}(\log q, n)$.*

Proof. It follows routinely that $\mathsf{RecoverError}^+_{q,q_1,q_2,n}(\mathbf{y}, B)$ runs in polynomial time. We will proceed to the correctness analysis and distinguish the same cases as $\mathsf{RecoverError}^+$.

- In the first case, given that $\mathbf{y} = r' \cdot \mathbf{e}'$ (for a $\mathbf{e}' \in \mathbb{Z}^n$ with $\|\mathbf{e}'\|_\infty \leq B$) it holds that $\bar{\mathbf{y}} = \bar{r}' \cdot \mathbf{e}'$, where $\bar{r}' = r \mod q_2$. Consequently, as $q_2 > B^2$ it holds that $\mathsf{RecoverError}_{q_2,n}(\bar{\mathbf{y}})$ will output a pair $(r_0, \mathbf{e})$ with $\|\mathbf{e}\|_\infty \leq B$ such that $r_0 \cdot \mathbf{e} \mod q_2 = \bar{\mathbf{y}}$. Now it holds that

$$(r \cdot \mathbf{e}) \mod q_2 = q_1 \cdot (q_1)^{-1} \cdot r_0 \cdot \mathbf{e} = r_0 \cdot \mathbf{e} = \bar{\mathbf{y}} = \mathbf{y} \mod q_2.$$

  Furthermore, it holds that $(r \cdot \mathbf{e}) \mod q_1 = q_1 \cdot r_1' \cdot \mathbf{e} = 0 = \mathbf{y} \mod q_1$. Thus, by the Chinese remainder theorem it holds that $r \cdot \mathbf{e} = \mathbf{y}$.
- In the second case, if for all i that $q_2 | y_i$, then it holds that $\|\mathbf{e}\|_\infty \leq q_1/2 \leq B$. Furthermore, it holds that $(r \cdot \mathbf{e}) \mod q_1 = (q_2 \cdot (q_2)^{-1}\bar{\mathbf{e}}) \mod q_1 = \bar{\mathbf{e}} = \mathbf{y} \mod q_1$ and $(r \cdot \mathbf{e}) \mod q_2 = (q_2 \cdot \mathbf{e}) \mod q_2 = 0 = \mathbf{y} \mod q_2$. Consequently, by the Chinese remainder theorem it holds that $r \cdot \mathbf{e} = \mathbf{y}$.
- In the third case, if $q_2 \nmid y_i$ or $q_1 \nmid y_j$ correctness follows immediately from the correctness of $\mathsf{RecoverError}$, as in this case either y_i or y_j is the required invertible component. Thus, assume that $q_1 | y_i$ but $q_2 \nmid y_i$ and $q_2 | y_j$ but $q_1 \nmid y_j$. It holds that $(y_i \pm y_j) \mod q_2 = y_i \mod q_2 \neq 0$ and $(y_i \pm y_j) \mod q_1 = \pm y_j \mod q_1 \neq 0$. Consequently, $y_i \pm y_j \in \mathbb{Z}_q^*$. Finally given that $y_i = r \cdot e_i$ and $y_j = r \cdot e_j$ with $|e_i|, |e_j| \leq B$, it holds that $y_i \pm y_j = r \cdot (e_i \pm e_j)$ and either $|e_i + e_j| \leq B$ or $|e_i - e_j| \leq B$. Consequently, for one of these two cases correctness follows from the correctness of $\mathsf{RecoverError}$, as in this case $\mathbf{y}'$ is of the form $\mathbf{y}' = r \cdot \mathbf{e}'$ for an $\mathbf{e}' \in \mathbb{Z}^n$ with $\|\mathbf{e}'\|_\infty \leq B$.

We now present the main result of this section. The algorithm presented in Construction 3 allows us decide if a given vector $\mathbf{a}$ is close to the row-span of $\mathbf{A}$, if $\mathbf{A}$ is generated together with a lattice trapdoor.

Construction 3. *Let $q = q_1 \cdot q_2$ be a product of primes, $(\mathbf{A}, \mathsf{td}_\mathbf{A}) \leftarrow \mathsf{TdGen}(1^\lambda, n, k, q)$ and let $\mathsf{RecoverError}^+$ be the algorithm from Construction 2.*

$\mathsf{InvertCloseVector}(\mathsf{td}_\mathbf{A}, \mathbf{a}, B)$:

- *Parse $\mathsf{td}_\mathbf{A} = \mathbf{T} \in \mathbb{Z}^{n \times n}$, $\mathbf{a} \in \mathbb{Z}_q^n$ and $B > 0$. Let $C \in \mathbb{R}$ be such that $\|\mathbf{T}\| < C$.*
- *Compute $\mathbf{z} = \mathbf{aT}$.*
- *Run $\Gamma \leftarrow \mathsf{RecoverError}^+_{q,q_1,q_2,n}(\mathbf{z}, B')$ where $B' = BC\sqrt{n}$. If $\Gamma = \perp$, abort the protocol. Else, parse $\Gamma = (r^\dagger, \mathbf{e}^\dagger)$.*
- *Let $t \in \mathbb{Z}$ be the smallest integer for which $\tilde{\mathbf{e}} = t \cdot \mathbf{e}^\dagger \mathbf{T}^{-1} \in \mathbb{Z}^n$ (t is the least common multiple of the denominators of $\mathbf{e}^\dagger \mathbf{T}^{-1}$).*

- *Check if* $\|\tilde{\mathbf{e}}\| < B$ *and recover* $\mathbf{x}', r$ *such that* $\mathbf{x}'\mathbf{A} + r \cdot \tilde{\mathbf{e}} = \mathbf{a}$ *(using gaussian elimination).*
- *If* $\|\mathbf{e}\| > B$ *output* $\perp$. *Else, output* $(\mathbf{x}', r, \tilde{\mathbf{e}})$.

Theorem 2. *Let* $C = C(\lambda) > 0$ *be a parameter, let* $q = q_1 \cdot q_2$, *where* $q_1 \leq 2BC\sqrt{n}$ *is either 1 or a prime and* $q_2 > B^2C^2n$ *is a prime. Let* TdGen *be the algorithm from Lemma 8 and* $\mathsf{RecoverError}_{q,n}$ *be the algorithm of Construction 1. Let* $(\mathbf{A}, \mathsf{td}_{\mathbf{A}}) \leftarrow \mathsf{TdGen}(q, k)$ *where* $\mathbf{A} \in \mathbb{Z}_q^{k\times n}$ *and* $\mathsf{td}_{\mathbf{A}} = \mathbf{T} \in \mathbb{Z}^{n\times n}$ *with* $\|\mathbf{T}\| < C$. *If there are* $\mathbf{x} \in \mathbb{Z}_q^k$ *and* $r \in \mathbb{Z}_q$ *such that* $\mathbf{a} = \mathbf{x}\mathbf{A} + r\mathbf{e}$ *for some* $\mathbf{e} \in \mathbb{Z}^n$ *such that* $\|\mathbf{e}\| \leq B$ *(where* $\mathbf{e}$ *is the shortest vector with this property), then the algorithm* $\mathsf{InvertCloseVector}$ *outputs* $(\mathbf{x}, r, \mathbf{e})$.

Proof. Assume now that $\mathbf{e}$ is the shortest vector for which we can write $\mathbf{a} = \mathbf{x}\mathbf{A} + r\mathbf{e}$ for some $\mathbf{x}$ and r. Then it holds that

$$\mathbf{y} = \mathbf{a}\mathbf{T} = \mathbf{x}\mathbf{A}\mathbf{T} + r\mathbf{e}\mathbf{T} = r\mathbf{e}' \mod q$$

where $\mathbf{e}' = \mathbf{e}\mathbf{T}$ and where the last equality holds because $\mathbf{A}\mathbf{T} = 0 \mod q$. Note that $\|\mathbf{e}'\| < \|\mathbf{e}\|\,\|\mathbf{T}\|\,\sqrt{n} \leq BC\sqrt{n} = B'$.

By Lemma 10, $\mathsf{RecoverError}(\mathbf{y}, B')$ will recover a pair $(r^\dagger, \mathbf{e}^\dagger)$ satisfying $\mathbf{y} = r^\dagger \cdot \mathbf{e}^\dagger$, and $\mathbf{e}^\dagger$ is the shortest vector with this property. By Lemma 9 it holds that $\mathbf{e}'$ and $\mathbf{e}^\dagger$ are linearly dependent, i.e. it holds that $\mathbf{e}' = t^\dagger \cdot \mathbf{e}^\dagger$. Thus, it holds that $\mathbf{e} = \mathbf{e}'\mathbf{T}^{-1} = t^\dagger \cdot \mathbf{e}^\dagger\mathbf{T}^{-1}$. Since the t computed by $\mathsf{RecoverError}(\mathbf{y}, B')$ is the shortest integer for which $t \cdot \mathbf{e}^\dagger\mathbf{T}^{-1} \in \mathbb{Z}^n$, it must hold that $t = t^\dagger$. Thus it holds that $\tilde{\mathbf{e}} = \mathbf{e}$. This concludes the proof.

5 Oblivious Linear Evaluation Secure Against a Corrupted Receiver

In this section, we present a semi-honest protocol for OLE based on the hardness of the LWE assumption. The protocol implements functionality $\mathcal{F}_{\mathsf{OLE}}$ defined in Sect. 3.

5.1 Protocol

We begin by presenting the protocol.

Construction 4. *The protocol is composed by the algorithms* $(\mathsf{GenCRS}, \mathsf{R}_1, \mathsf{S}, \mathsf{R}_2)$. *Let* $k, n, \ell, \ell', q \in \mathbb{Z}$ *such that* q *is as in Theorem 2,* $n = \mathsf{poly}(k \log q)$ *and* $\ell' \leq \ell$, *and let* $\beta, \delta, \xi \in \mathbb{R}$ *such that* $q/C > \beta\sqrt{n}$ *(where* $C \in \mathbb{R}$ *is as in Theorem 2),* $\delta > \beta > 1$ *and* $\beta > q/\delta$. *Additionally, let* $\mathsf{ECC}_{\ell',\ell,\xi} = (\mathsf{ECC.Encode}, \mathsf{ECC.Decode})$ *be an ECC over* $\mathbb{Z}_q$. *We present the protocol in full detail.*

$\mathsf{GenCRS}(1^\lambda)$*:*

- *Sample* $\mathbf{A} \leftarrow_\$ \mathbb{Z}_q^{k\times n}$ *and* $\mathbf{a} \leftarrow_\$ \mathbb{Z}_q^n$.
- *Output* $\mathsf{crs} = (\mathbf{A}, \mathbf{a})$.

$\mathsf{R}_1\,(\mathsf{crs}, x \in \mathbb{Z}_q)$:

- *Parse* crs *as* $(\mathbf{A}, \mathbf{a})$.
- *Sample* $\mathbf{s} \leftarrow_\$ \mathbb{Z}_q^k$ *and an error vector* $\mathbf{e} \leftarrow_\$ D_{\mathbb{Z}^n,\beta}$.
- *Compute* $\mathbf{a}' = \mathbf{s}\mathbf{A} + \mathbf{e} - x\mathbf{a}$.
- *Output* $\mathsf{ole}_1 = \mathbf{a}'$ *and* $\mathsf{st} = (\mathbf{s}, x)$.

$\mathsf{S}\left(\mathsf{crs}, (\mathbf{z}_0, \mathbf{z}_1) \in \left(\mathbb{Z}_q^{\ell'}\right)^2, \mathsf{ole}_1\right)$:

- *Parse* crs *as* $(\mathbf{A}, \mathbf{a})$ *and* ole_1 *as* $\mathbf{a}'$.
- *Sample* $\mathbf{R} \leftarrow_\$ D_{\mathbb{Z}^{n\times\ell},\delta}$.
- *Compute* $\mathbf{C} = \mathbf{A}\mathbf{R} \in \mathbb{Z}_q^{k\times\ell}$, $\mathbf{t}_0 = \mathbf{a}'\mathbf{R} + \mathsf{ECC.Encode}(\mathbf{z}_0)$ *and* $\mathbf{t}_1 = \mathbf{a}\mathbf{R} + \mathsf{ECC.Encode}(\mathbf{z}_1)$.
- *Output* $\mathsf{ole}_2 = (\mathbf{C}, \mathbf{t}_0, \mathbf{t}_1)$.

$\mathsf{R}_2\,(\mathsf{crs}, \mathsf{st}, \mathsf{ole}_2)$:

- *Parse* ole_2 *as* $(\mathbf{C}, \mathbf{t}_0, \mathbf{t}_1)$ *and* st *as* $(\mathbf{s}, x) \in \mathbb{Z}_q^k \times \mathbb{Z}_q$.
- *Compute* $\mathbf{y} \leftarrow \mathsf{ECC.Decode}(x\mathbf{t}_1 + \mathbf{t}_0 - \mathbf{s}\mathbf{C})$. *If* $\mathbf{y} = \perp$, *abort the protocol.*
- *Output* $\mathbf{y} \in \mathbb{Z}_q^{\ell'}$.

5.2 Analysis

Theorem 3. (Correctness). *Let* $\mathsf{ECC}_{\ell',\ell,\xi}$ *be a linear ECC where* $\xi \geq \sqrt{\ell}\beta\delta n$. *Then the protocol presented in Construction 4 is correct.*

Proof. To prove correctness, we have to prove that R_2 outputs $\mathbf{z}_0 + x\mathbf{z}_1$, where $(\mathbf{z}_0, \mathbf{z}_1)$ is the input of S.

We have that

$$\begin{aligned}\tilde{\mathbf{y}} &= x\mathbf{t}_1 + \mathbf{t}_0 - \mathbf{s}\mathbf{C}\\ &= x\mathbf{a}\mathbf{R} + x\hat{\mathbf{z}}_1 + \mathbf{a}'\mathbf{R} + \hat{\mathbf{z}}_0 - \mathbf{s}\mathbf{A}\mathbf{R}\\ &= x\mathbf{a}\mathbf{R} + x\hat{\mathbf{z}}_1 + (\mathbf{s}\mathbf{A} + \mathbf{e} - x\mathbf{a})\mathbf{R} + \hat{\mathbf{z}}_0 - \mathbf{s}\mathbf{A}\mathbf{R}\\ &= x\hat{\mathbf{z}}_1 + \hat{\mathbf{z}}_0 + \mathbf{e}'\end{aligned}$$

where $\mathbf{e}' = \mathbf{e}\mathbf{R}$, $\hat{\mathbf{z}}_1 \leftarrow \mathsf{ECC.Encode}(\mathbf{z}_1)$ and $\hat{\mathbf{z}}_0 \leftarrow \mathsf{ECC.Encode}(\mathbf{z}_0)$. Now since ECC is a linear code over $\mathbb{Z}_{q'}$, then

$$\begin{aligned}x\hat{\mathbf{z}}_1 + \hat{\mathbf{z}}_0 &= x \cdot \mathsf{ECC.Encode}(\mathbf{z}_1) + \mathsf{ECC.Encode}(\mathbf{z}_0)\\ &= \mathsf{ECC.Encode}(x\mathbf{z}_1 + \mathbf{z}_0)\end{aligned}$$

Finally, by Lemma 1, we have that $\|\mathbf{e}\| \leq \beta\sqrt{n}$. Moreover, if $\mathbf{r}^{(i)}$ is a column of $\mathbf{R}$, then $\left\|\mathbf{r}^{(i)}\right\| \leq \delta\sqrt{n}$. Therefore, each coordinate of $\mathbf{e}'$ has norm at most $\|\mathbf{e}\| \cdot \left\|\mathbf{r}^{(i)}\right\| \leq \beta\delta n$. We conclude that $\|\mathbf{e}'\| \leq \sqrt{\ell}\beta\delta n$. Since ECC corrects errors with norm up to $\xi \geq \sqrt{\ell}\beta\delta n$, the output of $\mathsf{ECC.Decode}(\tilde{\mathbf{y}})$ is exactly $\mathbf{z}_0 + x_1\mathbf{z}_1$.

Theorem 4 (Security). *Assume that the* $\mathsf{LWE}_{k,\beta,q}$ *assumption holds,* q *is as in Theorem 2,* $q/C > \beta\sqrt{n}$ *(where* $C \in \mathbb{R}$ *is as in Theorem 2),* $\delta > \beta > 1$, $\beta > q/\delta$ *and* $n = \mathsf{poly}(k \log q)$*. The protocol presented in Construction 4 securely realizes the functionality* $\mathcal{F}_{\mathsf{OLE}}$ *in the* $\mathcal{G}_{\mathsf{CRS}}$*-hybrid model against:*

- *a semi-honest sender given that the* $\mathsf{LWE}_{k,\beta,q}$ *assumption holds;*
- *a malicious receiver where security holds statistically.*

Proof. We begin by proving security against a computationally unbounded corrupted receiver.

Simulator for corrupted receiver: We describe the simulator Sim. Let (TdGen, Invert) be the algorithms described in Lemma 8 and InvertCloseVector be the algorithm of Theorem 2.

- **CRS generation:** Sim generates $(\mathbf{A}', \mathsf{td}_{\mathbf{A}'}) \leftarrow \mathsf{TdGen}(1^\lambda, k+1, n, q)$ and parse $\mathbf{A}' = \begin{pmatrix} \mathbf{A} \\ \mathbf{a} \end{pmatrix}$ where $\mathbf{A} \in \mathbb{Z}_q^{k \times n}$ and $\mathbf{a} \in \mathbb{Z}_q^n$. Additionally, parse $\mathsf{td}_{\mathbf{A}'}$ as $\mathbf{T} \in \mathbb{Z}^{n \times n}$ and let $C \in \mathbb{R}$ be such that $\|\mathbf{T}\| < C$. It publishes $\mathsf{crs} = (\mathbf{A}, \mathbf{a})$ and keeps $\mathsf{td}_{\mathbf{A}'}$ to itself.
- Upon receiving a message $\mathbf{a}'$ from R, Sim runs $(\tilde{\mathbf{s}}, \alpha, \mathbf{e}) \leftarrow \mathsf{InvertCloseVector}$ $(\mathsf{td}_{\mathbf{A}'}, \mathbf{a}', B)$ where $B = \beta\sqrt{n}$. There are two cases to consider:
  - If $\tilde{\mathbf{s}} = \perp$, then Sim samples $\mathbf{t}_0, \mathbf{t}_1 \leftarrow_\$ \mathbb{Z}_q^\ell$ and $\mathbf{C} \leftarrow_\$ \mathbb{Z}_q^{k \times \ell}$. It sends $\mathsf{ole}_2 = (\mathbf{C}, \mathbf{t}_0, \mathbf{t}_1)$.
  - Else if $\tilde{\mathbf{s}} \neq \perp$, then Sim sets $x = \tilde{s}_{k+1}$ where $\tilde{s}_{k+1}$ is the $(k+1)$-th coordinate of $\tilde{\mathbf{s}}$. It sends x to $\mathcal{F}_{\mathsf{OLE}}$. When it receives a $\mathbf{y} \in \mathbb{Z}_q^{\ell'}$ from $\mathcal{F}_{\mathsf{OLE}}$, Sim samples a uniform matrix $\mathbf{U}' \leftarrow_\$ \mathbb{Z}_q^{(k+1) \times \ell}$, which is parsed as $\mathbf{U}' = \begin{pmatrix} \mathbf{U} \\ \mathbf{u} \end{pmatrix}$, and a matrix $\mathbf{R} \leftarrow_\$ D_{\mathbb{Z}^{n \times \ell}, \delta}$. It sets

$$\mathbf{C} = \mathbf{U}$$
$$\mathbf{t}_0 = \tilde{\mathbf{s}}\mathbf{U}' + \alpha\mathbf{e}\mathbf{R} + \mathsf{ECC.Encode}(\mathbf{y})$$
$$\mathbf{t}_1 = \mathbf{u}.$$

  It sends $\mathsf{ole}_2 = (\mathbf{C}, \mathbf{t}_0, \mathbf{t}_1)$.

We now proceed to show that the real-world and the ideal-world executions are indistinguishable. The following lemma shows that the CRS generated in the simulation is indistinguishable from one generated in the real-world execution. Then, the next two lemmas deal with the two possible cases in the simulation.

Lemma 12. *The CRS generated above is statistically indistinguishable from a CRS generated according to* GenCRS.

Proof. The only thing that differs in both CRS's is that the matrix $\mathbf{A}' = \begin{pmatrix} \mathbf{A} \\ \mathbf{a} \end{pmatrix}$ is generated via TdGen in the simulation (instead of being chosen uniformly). By Lemma 8, it follows that the CRS is statistically indistinguishable from one generated using GenCRS.

Lemma 13. *Assume that* $\tilde{\mathbf{s}} = \perp$*. Then, the simulated execution is indistinguishable from the real-world execution.*

Proof. We prove that no (computationally unbounded) adversary can distinguish both executions, except with negligible probability. First, note that, if $\tilde{\mathbf{s}} = \perp$ where $(\tilde{\mathbf{s}}, \alpha, \mathbf{e}) \leftarrow \mathsf{InvertCloseVector}(\mathsf{td}_{\mathbf{A}'}, \mathbf{a}', B)$, then for any $(\alpha, \mathbf{s}, x) \in \mathbb{Z}_q \times \mathbb{Z}_q^k \times \mathbb{Z}_q$ we have that $\mathbf{a}' = \mathbf{s}\mathbf{A} + x\mathbf{a} + \alpha\mathbf{e}$ for an $\mathbf{e}$ with $\|\mathbf{e}\| > \beta\sqrt{n}$ since, by Theorem 2, only in this case algorithm $\mathsf{InvertCloseVector}$ fails to *invert* $\mathbf{a}'$. In other words, consider the matrix $\hat{\mathbf{A}} = \begin{pmatrix} \mathbf{A}' \\ \mathbf{a}' \end{pmatrix}$. If $\mathbf{a}'$ is of the form described above, then the matrix $\hat{\mathbf{A}}$ has no *short* vectors in its row-span. That is, there is no vector $\mathbf{v} \neq 0$ in $\Lambda_q(\hat{\mathbf{A}})$ such that $\|\mathbf{v}\| \leq \beta\sqrt{n}$. This is a direct consequence of the definition of algorithm $\mathsf{InvertCloseVector}$ of Theorem 2.

Hence $\rho_\beta(\Lambda_q(\hat{\mathbf{A}}) \setminus \{0\}) \leq \mathsf{negl}(\lambda)$. Moreover, we have that

$$\begin{aligned}
\rho_\beta(\Lambda_q(\hat{\mathbf{A}}) \setminus \{0\}) &\geq \rho_{1/\beta}(\Lambda_q(\hat{\mathbf{A}}) \setminus \{0\}) \\
&\geq \rho_{1/\delta}(\Lambda_q(\hat{\mathbf{A}}) \setminus \{0\}) \\
&\geq \rho_{1/(q\delta)}(\Lambda_q(\hat{\mathbf{A}}) \setminus \{0\}) \\
&= \rho_{1/\delta}(q\Lambda_q(\hat{\mathbf{A}}) \setminus \{0\}) \\
&= \rho_{1/\delta}((\Lambda_q^\perp(\hat{\mathbf{A}}))^* \setminus \{0\})
\end{aligned}$$

where the first and the second inequalities hold because $\delta > \beta > 1$ by hypothesis and the last equality holds because $\frac{1}{q}\Lambda_q^\perp(\hat{\mathbf{A}}) = \Lambda_q(\hat{\mathbf{A}})^*$. Since

$$\rho_{1/\delta}((\Lambda_q^\perp(\hat{\mathbf{A}}))^* \setminus \{0\}) \leq \mathsf{negl}(\lambda)$$

then $\delta \geq \eta_\varepsilon(\Lambda^\perp(\hat{\mathbf{A}}))$, for $\varepsilon = \mathsf{negl}(\lambda)$. Moreover $n = \mathsf{poly}(k \log q)$ by assumption. Thus the conditions of Lemma 2 are met.

Therefore, we can switch to a hybrid experiment where $\hat{\mathbf{A}}\mathbf{R} \bmod q$ is replaced by $\hat{\mathbf{U}} \leftarrow_\$ \mathbb{Z}^{(k+2)\times\ell}$ incurring only negligible statistical distance. That is,

$$\begin{pmatrix} \mathbf{C} \\ \mathbf{t}_1 \\ \mathbf{t}_0 \end{pmatrix} = \begin{pmatrix} \mathbf{A} \\ \mathbf{a} \\ \mathbf{a}' \end{pmatrix} \mathbf{R} + \begin{pmatrix} 0 \\ \hat{\mathbf{z}}_1 \\ \hat{\mathbf{z}}_0 + \tilde{\mathbf{e}} \end{pmatrix} \approx_{\mathsf{negl}(\lambda)} \hat{\mathbf{U}} + \begin{pmatrix} 0 \\ \hat{\mathbf{z}}_1 \\ \hat{\mathbf{z}}_0 + \tilde{\mathbf{e}} \end{pmatrix} \approx_{\mathsf{negl}(\lambda)} \mathbf{U}$$

where $\hat{\mathbf{z}}_j$ is the encoding $\mathsf{ECC.Encode}(\mathbf{z}_j)$ for $j \in \{0, 1\}$.

We conclude that, in this case, the real-world and the ideal-world execution (where Sim just sends a uniformly chosen triple $(\mathbf{C}, \mathbf{t}_0, \mathbf{t}_1)$) are statistically indistinguishable.

Lemma 14. *Assume that* $\tilde{\mathbf{s}} \neq \perp$*. Then, the simulated execution is indistinguishable from the real-world execution.*

Proof. In this case, $\mathbf{a}' = \tilde{\mathbf{s}}\mathbf{A} + \alpha\mathbf{e}$ for some $\tilde{\mathbf{s}} \in \mathbb{Z}_1^k$ and $\mathbf{e} \in \mathbb{Z}^n$ such that $\|\mathbf{e}\| < \beta\sqrt{n}$. The proof follows the following sequence of hybrids:

Hybrid $\mathcal{H}_0$. This is the real-world protocol. In particular, in this hybrid, the simulator behaves as the honest sender and computes

$$\begin{aligned} \mathbf{t}_0 &= \mathbf{a}'\mathbf{R} + \mathsf{ECC.Encode}(\mathbf{z}_0) = \tilde{\mathbf{s}}\mathbf{A}'\mathbf{R} + \alpha\mathbf{e}\mathbf{R} + \mathsf{ECC.Encode}(\mathbf{z}_0) \mod q \\ \mathbf{t}_1 &= \mathbf{a}\mathbf{R} + \mathsf{ECC.Encode}(\mathbf{z}_1) \mod q \\ \mathbf{C} &= \mathbf{A}\mathbf{R} \mod q \end{aligned}$$

for some $\alpha \in \mathbb{Z}_q \setminus \{0\}$ and where $\mathbf{A}' = \begin{pmatrix} \mathbf{A} \\ \mathbf{a} \end{pmatrix}$.

Hybrid $\mathcal{H}_1$. This hybrid is similar to the previous one, except that Sim computes $\mathbf{t}_0 = \tilde{\mathbf{s}}\mathbf{U}' + \alpha\mathbf{e}\mathbf{R} + \mathsf{ECC.Encode}(\mathbf{z}_0)$, $\mathbf{C} = \mathbf{U}$ and $\mathbf{t}_1 = \mathbf{u} + \mathsf{ECC.Encode}(\mathbf{z}_1)$, where $\mathbf{U}' = \begin{pmatrix} \mathbf{U} \\ \mathbf{u} \end{pmatrix} \leftarrow_\$ \mathbb{Z}_q^{(k+1)\times\ell}$.

Claim 1. $|\Pr[1 \leftarrow \mathcal{A} : \mathcal{A} \text{ plays } \mathcal{H}_0] - \Pr[1 \leftarrow \mathcal{A} : \mathcal{A} \text{ plays } \mathcal{H}_1]| \leq \mathsf{negl}(\lambda)$.

To prove this claim, we will resort to the partial smoothing lemma (Lemma 3). Using the same notation as in Lemma 3, consider $\gamma = \beta\sqrt{n}$. Then, we have that

$$\mathsf{negl}(\lambda) \geq \rho_\beta(\Lambda_q(\mathbf{A}') \setminus \gamma\mathcal{B}) \geq \rho_{q/\delta}(\Lambda_q(\mathbf{A}') \setminus \gamma\mathcal{B})$$

since, by assumption, $\beta > q/\delta$ and where $\mathbf{A}' = \begin{pmatrix} \mathbf{A} \\ \mathbf{a} \\ \mathbf{a}' \end{pmatrix}$.

Hence, by applying Lemma 3, we obtain

$$\mathbf{A}'\mathbf{R} \mod q \approx_{\mathsf{negl}(\lambda)} \mathbf{A}'(\mathbf{R} + \mathbf{X}) \mod q$$

for $\mathbf{X} \leftarrow_\$ \Lambda^\perp(\mathbf{e})$ (here, in the notation of Lemma 3, we consider $\mathbf{D} = \mathbf{e}$).

We now argue that $\mathbf{A}'\mathbf{X} \mod q \approx_{\mathsf{negl}(\lambda)} \mathbf{U}'$ for $\mathbf{U}' \leftarrow_\$ \mathbb{Z}_q^{(k+1)\times\ell}$. Let $\mathbf{B} \in \mathbb{Z}_q^{n\times k'}$ be a basis of $\Lambda^\perp(\mathbf{e})$, that is, $\mathbf{e}\mathbf{B} = 0$. Let us assume for the sake of contradiction that $\mathbf{A}'\mathbf{B}$ does not have full rank (hence, $\mathbf{A}'\mathbf{X} \mod q$ is not uniform over $\mathbb{Z}_q^{(k+1)\times\ell}$). Then, there is a vector $\mathbf{v} \in \mathbb{Z}_q^{k+1}$ such that $\mathbf{v}\mathbf{A}'\mathbf{B} = 0$.

Since $\mathbf{B}$ is a basis of $\Lambda^\perp(\mathbf{e})$, this means that $\mathbf{v}\mathbf{B} \in (\Lambda^\perp(\mathbf{e}))^\perp = \Lambda(\mathbf{e})$. In other words, $\mathbf{v}\mathbf{A}' = t \cdot \mathbf{e}$ for some $t \in \mathbb{Z}_q$. Consequently, we have $\mathbf{e} = t^{-1}\mathbf{v}\mathbf{A}'$ and thus $\mathbf{e}$ is in the row-span of $\mathbf{A}'$, that is, $\Lambda(\mathbf{A}')$ has a vector of norm shorter than $\beta\sqrt{n}$. However, this happens only with negligible probability over the uniform choice of $\mathbf{A}$ and, thus, we reach a contradiction. We conclude that $\mathbf{A}'\mathbf{B}$ needs to have full rank. Now, since $\mathbf{X}$ is sampled uniformly from $\Lambda^\perp(\mathbf{e})$, we have that $\mathbf{A}'\mathbf{X}$ is uniform over $\mathbb{Z}_q^{(k+1)\times\ell}$. Thus, $\mathbf{A}'\mathbf{X} \mod q \approx_{\mathsf{negl}(\lambda)} \mathbf{U}'$ where $\mathbf{U}' \leftarrow_\$ \mathbb{Z}_q^{(k+1)\times\ell}$.

Hybrid $\mathcal{H}_2$. This hybrid is similar to the previous one, except that Sim computes $\mathbf{t}_0 = \tilde{\mathbf{s}}\mathbf{U}' + \alpha\mathbf{e}\mathbf{R} + \mathsf{ECC.Encode}(\mathbf{y})$, $\mathbf{C} = \mathbf{U}$ and $\mathbf{t}_1 = \mathbf{u}$, where $\mathbf{U}' = \begin{pmatrix} \mathbf{U} \\ \mathbf{u} \end{pmatrix} \leftarrow_\$ \mathbb{Z}_q^{k\times\ell}$.

This hybrid corresponds to the simulator for the corrupted receiver.

Claim 2. $|\Pr[1 \leftarrow \mathcal{A} : \mathcal{A} \textit{ plays } \mathcal{H}_1] - \Pr[1 \leftarrow \mathcal{A} : \mathcal{A} \textit{ plays } \mathcal{H}_2]| \leq \mathsf{negl}(\lambda)$.

Since $\mathbf{u}$ is uniformly at random, then it is statistically indistinguishable from $\mathbf{u}' - \mathsf{ECC.Encode}(\mathbf{z}_1)$ where $\mathbf{u}' \leftarrow_\$ \mathbb{Z}_q^\ell$ is a uniformly random vector. Thus, replacing the occurrences of $\mathbf{u}$ by $\mathbf{u}' - \mathsf{ECC.Encode}(\mathbf{z}_1)$, we obtain

$$\begin{aligned}(\mathbf{C}, \mathbf{t}_0, \mathbf{t}_1) &= (\mathbf{U}, \tilde{\mathbf{s}}\mathbf{U}' + \alpha\mathbf{e}\mathbf{R} + \mathsf{ECC.Encode}(\mathbf{z}_0), \mathbf{u} + \mathsf{ECC.Encode}(\mathbf{z}_1)) \\ &\approx_{\mathsf{negl}(\lambda)} \left(\mathbf{U}, \tilde{\mathbf{s}}\overline{\mathbf{U}}' + \alpha\mathbf{e}\mathbf{R} + \mathsf{ECC.Encode}(\mathbf{z}_0), \mathbf{u}'\right) \\ &= \left(\mathbf{U}, \tilde{\mathbf{s}}_{-(k+1)}\mathbf{U} + \alpha\mathbf{e}\mathbf{R} + \mathsf{ECC.Encode}(\mathbf{z}_0) + x\mathsf{ECC.Encode}(\mathbf{z}_1), \mathbf{u}'\right) \\ &= (\mathbf{U}, \mathbf{x}\mathbf{U} + \alpha\mathbf{e}\mathbf{R} + \mathbf{y}, \mathbf{u}')\end{aligned}$$

where $\overline{\mathbf{U}}'$ is the matrix whose rows are equal to $\mathbf{U}'$, except for the $(k+1)$-th which is equal to $\mathbf{u}' - \mathsf{ECC.Encode}(\mathbf{z}_1)$, $x = \tilde{s}_{k+1}$ is the $(k+1)$-th coordinate of $\tilde{\mathbf{s}}$ and $\tilde{\mathbf{s}}_{-(k+1)} \in \mathbb{Z}_q^k$ is the vector $\tilde{\mathbf{s}}$ with the $(k+1)$-th coordinate removed.

This concludes the description of the simulator for the corrupted receiver. We now resume the proof of Theorem 4 by presenting the simulator for the semi-honest sender.

Simulator for corrupted sender. We describe how the simulator Sim proceeds: It takes S's inputs $(\mathbf{z}_0, \mathbf{z}_1)$ and sends them to the ideal functionality $\mathcal{F}_{\mathsf{OLE}}$, which returns nothing. It simulates the dummy R by sampling $\mathbf{a}' \leftarrow_\$ \mathbb{Z}_q^n$ and sending it to the corrupted sender.

It is trivial to see that both the ideal and the real-world executions are indistinguishable given that the $\mathsf{LWE}_{k,q,\beta}$ assumption holds.

5.3 Batch OLE

We now show how we can extend the protocol described above in order to implement a batch reusable OLE protocol, that is, in order to implement the functionality $\mathcal{F}_{\mathsf{bOLE}}$ described in Sect. 3.

This variant improves the efficiency of the protocol since the receiver R can *commit* to a batch of inputs $\{x_i\}_{i\in[k']}$, and not just one input, using the same first message of the two-round OLE. Hence, the size of the first message can be amortized over the number of R's inputs, to achieve a better communication complexity.

Construction 5. *The protocol is composed by the algorithms* $(\mathsf{GenCRS}, \mathsf{R}_1, \mathsf{S}, \mathsf{R}_2)$. *Let* $k, n, \ell, \ell', q, k' \in \mathbb{Z}$ *such that* q *is as in Theorem 2 and* $n = \mathsf{poly}((k+k')\log q)$, *and let* $\beta, \delta, \xi \in \mathbb{R}$ *such that* $\frac{q}{\sqrt{n\tau(k)}} > \beta$ *(where* $\tau(k) = \omega(\sqrt{\log k})$ *as in Lemma 8),* $\delta > \beta > 1$, $\beta > q/\delta$ *and* $n = \mathsf{poly}((k+k')\log q)$. *Additionally, let* $\mathsf{ECC}_{\ell',\ell,\xi} = (\mathsf{ECC.Encode}, \mathsf{ECC.Decode})$ *be an ECC over* $\mathbb{Z}_q$.

$\mathsf{GenCRS}(1^\lambda)$: *This algorithm is similar to the one described in Construction 4 except that* $\mathsf{crs} = (\mathbf{A}, \mathbf{a}_1, \ldots, \mathbf{a}_{k'})$ *where* $\mathbf{a}_i \leftarrow_\$ \mathbb{Z}_q^n$ *for* $i \in [k']$

$\mathsf{R}_1\left(\mathsf{crs}, \{x_j\}_{j\in[k']} \in \mathbb{Z}_q\right)$: *The algorithm is similar to the one described in Construction 4, except that it outputs* $\mathsf{ole}_1 = \mathbf{a}'$ *and* $\mathsf{st} = (\mathbf{s}, \{x_i\}_{i\in[k']})$, *where* $\mathbf{a}' = \mathbf{sA} + \mathbf{e} - \left(\sum_{i=1}^{k'} x_i \mathbf{a}_i\right)$.

$\mathsf{S}\left(\mathsf{crs}, (\mathbf{z}_0, \mathbf{z}_1) \in \left(\mathbb{Z}_q^{\ell'}\right)^2, \mathsf{ole}_1, j \in [k']\right)$: *This algorithm is similar to the one described in Construction 4, except that; i) it computes* $\mathbf{t}_1 = -\mathbf{a}_j\mathbf{R}$; *ii) It computes* $\mathbf{w}_i = \mathbf{a}_i\mathbf{R}$ *for all* $i \in [k']$ *such that* $i \neq j$; *and iii) it outputs* $\mathsf{ole}_2 = (\mathbf{C}, \mathbf{t}_0, \mathbf{t}_1, \{\mathbf{w}_i\}_{i\neq j}, j)$ *(where* j *corresponds to which* x_j *the receiver* R *is supposed to use in that particular execution of the protocol) and* $\{\}$.

$\mathsf{R}_2(\mathsf{crs}, \mathsf{st}, \mathsf{ole}_2)$: *This algorithm is similar to the one described in Construction 4, except that it outputs*

$$\mathbf{z}_0 + x_j\mathbf{z}_1 = \mathbf{y} \leftarrow \mathsf{ECC.Decode}\left(\mathbf{t}_0 + x_j\mathbf{t}_1 - \left(\mathbf{sC} + \sum_{i\neq j} x_i \mathbf{w}_i\right)\right).$$

It is easy to see that correctness holds following a similar analysis as the one of Theorem 3. We now state the theorem that guarantees security of the scheme.

Theorem 5 (Security). *Assume that the* $\mathsf{LWE}_{k,\beta,q}$ *assumption holds,* $q \in \mathbb{N}$ *is as in Theorem 2,* $q/C > \beta\sqrt{n}$ *(where* $C \in \mathbb{R}$ *is as in Lemma 8),* $\delta > \beta > 1$, $\beta > q/\delta$ *and* $n = \mathsf{poly}((k + k')\log q)$. *The protocol presented in Construction 5 securely realizes the functionality* $\mathcal{F}_{\mathsf{bOLE}}$ *in the* $\mathcal{G}_{\mathsf{CRS}}$*-hybrid model against:*

- *a semi-honest sender given that the* $\mathsf{LWE}_{k,\beta,q}$ *assumption holds;*
- *a malicious receiver where security holds statistically.*

The proof of the theorem stated above essentially follows the same blueprint as the proof of Theorem 4, except that the simulator for the corrupted receiver extracts the first k' coordinates $\{x_j\}_{j\in[k']}$ of $\mathbf{x}$ and sends these values to $\mathcal{F}_{bOLE}$. From now on, it behaves exactly as the simulator in the proof of Theorem 4. Indistinguishability of executions follows exactly the same reasoning.

Communication Efficiency Comparison. Comparing with the protocol presented in Construction 4, this scheme achieves the same communication complexity for the receiver (that is, the receiver message is of the same size in both constructions). On the other hand, the sender's message now depends on k'.

6 OLE from LWE Secure Against Malicious Adversaries

In this section, we extend the construction of the previous section to support malicious sender. The idea is to use a *cut-and-choose* approach via the use of an OT scheme in two rounds and extract the sender's input via the OT simulator.

6.1 Protocol

Construction 6. *The protocol is composed by the algorithms* $(\mathsf{GenCRS}, \mathsf{R}_1, \mathsf{S}, \mathsf{R}_2)$. *Let* $\mathsf{OLE} = (\mathsf{GenCRS}, \mathsf{R}_1, \mathsf{S}, \mathsf{R})$ *be a two-round OLE protocol which is secure against malicious receivers and semi-honest senders and* $\mathsf{OT} = (\mathsf{GenCRS}, \mathsf{R}_1, \mathsf{S}, \mathsf{R}_2)$ *be a two-round OT protocol. We now present the protocol in full detail.*

$\mathsf{GenCRS}(1^\lambda)$:

- *Run* $\mathsf{crs}_{\mathsf{OLE}} \leftarrow \mathsf{OLE.GenCRS}(1^\lambda)$ *and* $\mathsf{crs}_{\mathsf{OT}} \leftarrow \mathsf{OT.GenCRS}(1^\lambda)$.
- *Output* $\mathsf{crs} = (\mathsf{crs}_{\mathsf{OLE}}, \mathsf{crs}_{\mathsf{OT}})$.

$\mathsf{R}_1(\mathsf{crs}, x \in \mathbb{Z}_q)$:

- *Parse* crs *as* $(\mathsf{crs}_{\mathsf{OLE}}, \mathsf{crs}_{\mathsf{OT}})$.
- *Sample* $x_1, x_2 \leftarrow_\$ \mathbb{Z}_q$ *such that* $x_1 + x_2 = x$.
- *Compute* $(\mathsf{ole}_{1,1}, \mathsf{st}_{1,1}) \leftarrow \mathsf{OLE.R}_1(\mathsf{crs}_{\mathsf{OLE}}, x_1)$ *and* $(\mathsf{ole}_{1,2}, \mathsf{st}_{1,2}) \leftarrow \mathsf{OLE.R}_1(\mathsf{crs}_{\mathsf{OLE}}, x_2)$.
- *Additionally, choose uniformly at random* $\mathbf{b} = (b_1, \ldots, b_\lambda) \leftarrow_\$ \{0,1\}^\lambda$ *and compute* $(\mathsf{ot}_{1,i}, \tilde{\mathsf{st}}_i) \leftarrow \mathsf{OT.R}_1(\mathsf{crs}_{\mathsf{OT}}, b_i)$ *for all* $i \in [\lambda]$.
- *Output* $\mathsf{ole}_1 = (\mathsf{ole}_{1,1}, \mathsf{ole}_{1,2}, \{\mathsf{ot}_{1,i}\}_{i \in [\lambda]})$ *and* $\mathsf{st} = \left(\mathsf{st}_{1,1}, \mathsf{st}_{1,2}, \{\tilde{\mathsf{st}}_i\}_{j \in [\lambda]}\right)$.

$\mathsf{S}\left(\mathsf{crs}, (\mathbf{z}_0, \mathbf{z}_1) \in \mathbb{Z}_q^\ell, \mathsf{ole}_1\right)$:

- *Parse* crs *as* $(\mathsf{crs}_{\mathsf{OLE}}, \mathsf{crs}_{\mathsf{OT}})$ *and* ole_1 *as* $(\mathsf{ole}_{1,1}, \mathsf{ole}_{1,2}, \{\mathsf{ot}_{1,i}\}_{i \in [\lambda]})$.
- *Sample* $\mathbf{z}_{1,1}, \mathbf{z}_{1,2} \leftarrow_\$ \mathbb{Z}_q^\ell$ *such that* $\mathbf{z}_{1,1} + \mathbf{z}_{1,1} = \mathbf{z}_1$.
- *For all* $j \in [\lambda]$, *do the following:*
  - *Sample random coins* $r_{j,1}, r_2 \leftarrow_\$ \{0,1\}^\lambda$.
  - *Compute* $\mathsf{ole}_{2,j,1} \leftarrow \mathsf{OLE.S}(\mathsf{crs}_{\mathsf{OLE}}, \mathsf{ole}_{1,1}, (\mathbf{u}_{0,j,1}, \mathbf{u}_{1,j,1}); r_{j,1})$ *for uniformly chosen* $\mathbf{u}_{0,j,1}, \mathbf{u}_{1,j,1} \leftarrow_\$ \mathbb{Z}_q^{\ell'}$. *Additionally, compute* $\mathsf{ole}_{2,j,2} \leftarrow \mathsf{OLE.S}(\mathsf{crs}_{\mathsf{OLE}}, \mathsf{ole}_{1,2}, (\mathbf{u}_{0,j,2}, \mathbf{u}_{1,j,2}); r_{j,2})$ *for uniformly chosen* $\mathbf{u}_{0,j,2}, \mathbf{u}_{1,j,2} \leftarrow_\$ \mathbb{Z}_q^{\ell'}$.
  - *Set* $M_{0,j} = (r_{j,1}, r_{j,2}, \mathbf{u}_{0,j,1}, \mathbf{u}_{1,j,1}, \mathbf{u}_{0,j,2}, \mathbf{u}_{1,j,2})$ *and* $M_{1,j} = (\mathbf{u}_{0,j,1} + \mathbf{z}_0, \mathbf{u}_{1,j,1} + \mathbf{z}_{1,1}, \mathbf{u}_{0,j,2} + \mathbf{z}_0, \mathbf{u}_{1,j,2} + \mathbf{z}_{1,2})$. *Compute* $\mathsf{ot}_{2,j} \leftarrow \mathsf{OT.S}(\mathsf{crs}_{\mathsf{OT}}, \mathsf{ot}_{1,j}, (M_{0,j}, M_{1,j}))$.
- *Output* $\mathsf{ole}_2 = \{\mathsf{ole}_{2,j,1}, \mathsf{ole}_{2,j,2}, \mathsf{ot}_{2,j}\}_{j \in [\lambda]}$.

$\mathsf{R}_2(\mathsf{crs}, \mathsf{st}, \mathsf{ole}_2)$:

- *Parse* ole_2 *as* $\{\mathsf{ole}_{2,j,1}, \mathsf{ole}_{2,j,2}, \mathsf{ot}_{2,j}\}_{j \in [\lambda]}$ *and* st *as* $\left(\mathsf{st}_{1,1}, \mathsf{st}_{1,2}, \{\tilde{\mathsf{st}}_i\}_{j \in [\lambda]}\right)$.
- *For all* $j \in [\lambda]$, *do the following:*
  - *Recover* $M_{b_j,j} \leftarrow \mathsf{OT.R}_2(\mathsf{crs}_{\mathsf{OT}}, \tilde{\mathsf{st}}_i)$.
  - *If* $b_j = 0$, *parse* $M_{0,j} = (r_{j,1}, r_{j,2}, \mathbf{u}_{0,j,1}, \mathbf{u}_{1,j,1}, \mathbf{u}_{0,j,2}, \mathbf{u}_{1,j,2})$. *Compute*

$$\mathsf{ole}'_{2,j,1} \leftarrow \mathsf{OLE.S}(\mathsf{crs}_{\mathsf{OLE}}, \mathsf{ole}_{1,1}, (\mathbf{u}_{0,j,1}, \mathbf{u}_{1,j,1}); r_{j,1})$$

  and

$$\mathsf{ole}'_{2,j,2} \leftarrow \mathsf{OLE.S}(\mathsf{crs}_{\mathsf{OLE}}, \mathsf{ole}_{1,2}, (\mathbf{u}_{0,j,2}, \mathbf{u}_{1,j,2}); r_{j,2}).$$

  If $\mathsf{ole}'_{2,j,1} \neq \mathsf{ole}_{2,j,1}$ *or if* $\mathsf{ole}'_{2,j,1} \neq \mathsf{ole}_{2,j,1}$, *abort the protocol.*

  - *If* $b_j = 1$*, parse* $M_{1,j}$ *as* $(\mathbf{v}_{0,j,1}, \mathbf{v}_{1,j,1}, \mathbf{v}_{0,j,2}, \mathbf{v}_{1,j,2})$*. Compute* $\mathbf{y}_{j,1} \leftarrow \mathsf{OLE.R}_2(\mathsf{crs}_{\mathsf{OLE}}, \mathsf{ole}_{2,j,1}, \mathsf{st}_{j,1})$ *and* $\mathbf{y}_{j,2} \leftarrow \mathsf{OLE.R}_2(\mathsf{crs}_{\mathsf{OLE}}, \mathsf{ole}_{2,j,2}, \mathsf{st}_{j,2})$*. Compute* $\mathbf{w}_{j,1} = \mathbf{v}_{0,j,1} + x_1\tilde{\mathbf{v}}_{1,j,1} - \mathbf{y}_{j,1}$ *and* $\mathbf{w}_{j,2} = \mathbf{v}_{0,j,2} + x_2\tilde{\mathbf{v}}_{1,j,2} - \mathbf{y}_{j,2}$*.*
- *Let* $I_1 \subseteq [\lambda]$ *be the set of indices* j *such that* $b_j = 1$ *and let* $\{\mathbf{w}_{j,1}, \mathbf{w}_{j,2}\}_{j \in I_1}$*. If* $\mathbf{w}_1 = \mathbf{w}_{j,1} = \mathbf{w}_{j',1}$*,* $\mathbf{w}_2 = \mathbf{w}_{j,2} = \mathbf{w}_{j',2}$ *and* $\mathbf{w} = \mathbf{w}_{j,1} + w_{j,2} = \mathbf{w}_{j',1} + \mathbf{w}_{j',2}$ *for all pairs* $(j, j') \in I_1^2$ *then output* $\mathbf{w}$*. Else abort the protocol.*

6.2 Analysis

We now proceed to the analysis of the protocol described above.

Theorem 6 (Correctness). *Assume* OLE *and* OT *implement the functionalities* $\mathcal{F}_{\mathsf{OLE}}$ *and* $\mathcal{F}_{\mathsf{OT}}$*. Then the protocol presented in Construction 6 is correct.*

Theorem 7 (Security). *Let* $q = 2^{\omega}(\log \lambda)$*. Assume that* OLE *implements* $\mathcal{F}_{\mathsf{OLE}}$ *against malicious receivers and semi-honest sender and that* OT *implements the functionality* $\mathcal{F}_{\mathsf{OT}}$*. The protocol presented in Construction 6 securely realizes the functionality* $\mathcal{F}_{\mathsf{OLE}}$ *in the* $\mathcal{G}_{\mathsf{CRS}}$*-hybrid model against static malicious adversaries.*

The proof of the theorem is presented in the full version of the paper available at [8].

On the choice of the modulus q*.* The scheme presented above is only secure if q is chosen to be superpolynomial in λ. The scheme can be adapted to support fields of polynomial size by running λ instances of the underlying OLE, instead of running only two instances.

6.3 Instantiating the Functionalities

We now discuss how we can instantiate the underlying functionalities $\mathcal{F}_{\mathsf{OT}}$ and $\mathcal{F}_{\mathsf{OLE}}$ (secure against semi-honest receivers) used in the protocol described above.

When we instantiate $\mathcal{F}_{\mathsf{OT}}$ with the OT schemes from [29,30] and $\mathcal{F}_{\mathsf{OLE}}$ (secure against semi-honest receivers) with the scheme from Sect. 5, we obtain a maliciously secure OLE protocol with the following properties:

1. It has two rounds;
2. It is statistically secure against a malicious receiver since the the OT of [29, 30] and the scheme from Sect. 5 are statistically secure against a malicious receiver.
3. Security against a malicious sender holds under the LWE assumption since both the schemes of [29,30] are secure against malicious senders and the scheme from Sect. 5 is secure against semi honest senders under the LWE assumption.

Acknowledgment. Pedro Branco thanks the support from DP-PMI and FCT (Portugal) through the grant PD/BD/135181/2017. Part of the work was done while the author was at CISPA.

Pedro Branco and Paulo Mateus are partially supported by national funds through Fundação para a Ciência e a Tecnologia (FCT) with reference UIDB/50008/2020 (Instituto de Telecomunicações via actions QuRUNNER, QUESTS) and Projects Quantum-Mining POCI-01-0145-FEDER-031826, PREDICT PTDC/CCI-CIF/29877/2017 and QuantumPrime PTDC/EEI-TEL/8017/2020.

Nico Döttling was supported by the Helmholtz Association within the project "Trustworthy Federated Data Analytics" (TFDA) (funding number ZT-I- OO1 4).

References

1. Applebaum, B., Damgård, I., Ishai, Y., Nielsen, M., Zichron, L.: Secure arithmetic computation with constant computational overhead. In: Katz, J., Shacham, H. (eds.) CRYPTO 2017. LNCS, vol. 10401, pp. 223–254. Springer, Cham (2017). https://doi.org/10.1007/978-3-319-63688-7_8
2. Applebaum, B., Ishai, Y., Kushilevitz, E.: How to garble arithmetic circuits. In: 2011 IEEE 52nd Annual Symposium on Foundations of Computer Science, pp. 120–129 (2011)
3. Banaszczyk, W.: New bounds in some transference theorems in the geometry of numbers. Math. Ann. **296**(4), 625–636 (1993). http://eudml.org/doc/165105
4. Banerjee, A., Peikert, C., Rosen, A.: Pseudorandom functions and lattices. In: Pointcheval, D., Johansson, T. (eds.) EUROCRYPT 2012. LNCS, vol. 7237, pp. 719–737. Springer, Heidelberg (2012). https://doi.org/10.1007/978-3-642-29011-4_42
5. Baum, C., Escudero, D., Pedrouzo-Ulloa, A., Scholl, P., Troncoso-Pastoriza, J.R.: Efficient protocols for oblivious linear function evaluation from ring-LWE. In: Galdi, C., Kolesnikov, V. (eds.) SCN 2020. LNCS, vol. 12238, pp. 130–149. Springer, Cham (2020). https://doi.org/10.1007/978-3-030-57990-6_7
6. Boyle, E., Couteau, G., Gilboa, N., Ishai, Y.: Compressing vector OLE. In: Proceedings of the 2018 ACM SIGSAC Conference on Computer and Communications Security, CCS 2018, pp. 896–912. Association for Computing Machinery, New York (2018). https://doi.org/10.1145/3243734.3243868
7. Brakerski, Z., Döttling, N.: Two-message statistically sender-private OT from LWE. In: Beimel, A., Dziembowski, S. (eds.) TCC 2018. LNCS, vol. 11240, pp. 370–390. Springer, Cham (2018). https://doi.org/10.1007/978-3-030-03810-6_14
8. Branco, P., Döttling, N., Mateus, P.: Two-round oblivious linear evaluation from learning with errors. Cryptology ePrint Archive, Report 2020/635 (2020). https://ia.cr/2020/635
9. Canetti, R.: Universally composable security: a new paradigm for cryptographic protocols. In: Proceedings 42nd IEEE Symposium on Foundations of Computer Science, pp. 136–145 (2001)
10. de Castro, L., Juvekar, C., Vaikuntanathan, V.: Fast vector oblivious linear evaluation from ring learning with errors. Cryptology ePrint Archive, Report 2020/685 (2020). https://eprint.iacr.org/2020/685
11. Chase, M., et al.: Reusable non-interactive secure computation. In: Boldyreva, A., Micciancio, D. (eds.) CRYPTO 2019. LNCS, vol. 11694, pp. 462–488. Springer, Cham (2019). https://doi.org/10.1007/978-3-030-26954-8_15

12. Döttling, N., Garg, S., Hajiabadi, M., Masny, D., Wichs, D.: Two-round oblivious transfer from CDH or LPN. In: Canteaut, A., Ishai, Y. (eds.) EUROCRYPT 2020. LNCS, vol. 12106, pp. 768–797. Springer, Cham (2020). https://doi.org/10.1007/978-3-030-45724-2_26
13. Döttling, N., Ghosh, S., Nielsen, J.B., Nilges, T., Trifiletti, R.: TinyOLE: efficient actively secure two-party computation from oblivious linear function evaluation. In: Proceedings of the 2017 ACM SIGSAC Conference on Computer and Communications Security, CCS 2017, pp. 2263–2276. Association for Computing Machinery, New York (2017). https://doi.org/10.1145/3133956.3134024
14. Döttling, N., Kraschewski, D., Müller-Quade, J.: Statistically secure linear-rate dimension extension for oblivious affine function evaluation. In: Smith, A. (ed.) ICITS 2012. LNCS, vol. 7412, pp. 111–128. Springer, Heidelberg (2012). https://doi.org/10.1007/978-3-642-32284-6_7
15. Döttling, N., Kraschewski, D., Müller-Quade, J.: David & Goliath oblivious affine function evaluation - asymptotically optimal building blocks for universally composable two-party computation from a single untrusted stateful tamper-proof hardware token. Cryptology ePrint Archive, Report 2012/135 (2012). https://eprint.iacr.org/2012/135
16. Gentry, C., Peikert, C., Vaikuntanathan, V.: Trapdoors for hard lattices and new cryptographic constructions. In: Proceedings of the Fortieth Annual ACM Symposium on Theory of Computing, STOC 2008, pp. 197–206. ACM, New York (2008). https://doi.org/10.1145/1374376.1374407
17. Ghosh, S., Nielsen, J.B., Nilges, T.: Maliciously secure oblivious linear function evaluation with constant overhead. In: Takagi, T., Peyrin, T. (eds.) ASIACRYPT 2017. LNCS, vol. 10624, pp. 629–659. Springer, Cham (2017). https://doi.org/10.1007/978-3-319-70694-8_22
18. Ghosh, S., Nilges, T.: An algebraic approach to maliciously secure private set intersection. In: Ishai, Y., Rijmen, V. (eds.) EUROCRYPT 2019. LNCS, vol. 11478, pp. 154–185. Springer, Cham (2019). https://doi.org/10.1007/978-3-030-17659-4_6
19. Ghosh, S., Simkin, M.: The communication complexity of threshold private set intersection. In: Boldyreva, A., Micciancio, D. (eds.) CRYPTO 2019. LNCS, vol. 11693, pp. 3–29. Springer, Cham (2019). https://doi.org/10.1007/978-3-030-26951-7_1
20. Goldreich, O., Micali, S., Wigderson, A.: How to play any mental game, or a completeness theorem for protocols with honest majority. In: Providing Sound Foundations for Cryptography: On the Work of Shafi Goldwasser and Silvio Micali, pp. 307–328 (2019)
21. Hazay, C., Ishai, Y., Marcedone, A., Venkitasubramaniam, M.: LevioSA: lightweight secure arithmetic computation. In: Proceedings of the 2019 ACM SIGSAC Conference on Computer and Communications Security, CCS 2019, pp. 327–344. Association for Computing Machinery, New York (2019). https://doi.org/10.1145/3319535.3354258
22. Ishai, Y., Prabhakaran, M., Sahai, A.: Secure arithmetic computation with no honest majority. In: Reingold, O. (ed.) TCC 2009. LNCS, vol. 5444, pp. 294–314. Springer, Heidelberg (2009). https://doi.org/10.1007/978-3-642-00457-5_18
23. Juvekar, C., Vaikuntanathan, V., Chandrakasan, A.: GAZELLE: a low latency framework for secure neural network inference. In: Proceedings of the 27th USENIX Conference on Security Symposium, SEC 2018, pp. 1651–1668. USENIX Association, USA (2018)

24. Lempel, M., Paz, A.: An algorithm for finding a shortest vector in a two-dimensional modular lattice. Theor. Comput. Sci. **125**(2), 229–241 (1994). http://www.sciencedirect.com/science/article/pii/030439759200021I
25. Lindell, Y., Pinkas, B.: An efficient protocol for secure two-party computation in the presence of malicious adversaries. In: Naor, M. (ed.) EUROCRYPT 2007. LNCS, vol. 4515, pp. 52–78. Springer, Heidelberg (2007). https://doi.org/10.1007/978-3-540-72540-4_4
26. Micciancio, D., Peikert, C.: Trapdoors for lattices: simpler, tighter, faster, smaller. In: Pointcheval, D., Johansson, T. (eds.) EUROCRYPT 2012. LNCS, vol. 7237, pp. 700–718. Springer, Heidelberg (2012). https://doi.org/10.1007/978-3-642-29011-4_41
27. Micciancio, D., Regev, O.: Worst-case to average-case reductions based on gaussian measures. SIAM J. Comput. **37**(1), 267–302 (2007). https://doi.org/10.1137/S0097539705447360
28. Mohassel, P., Zhang, Y.: SecureML: a system for scalable privacy-preserving machine learning. In: 2017 IEEE Symposium on Security and Privacy (SP), pp. 19–38 (2017)
29. Peikert, C., Vaikuntanathan, V., Waters, B.: A framework for efficient and composable oblivious transfer. In: Wagner, D. (ed.) CRYPTO 2008. LNCS, vol. 5157, pp. 554–571. Springer, Heidelberg (2008). https://doi.org/10.1007/978-3-540-85174-5_31
30. Quach, W.: UC-secure OT from LWE, revisited. In: Galdi, C., Kolesnikov, V. (eds.) SCN 2020. LNCS, vol. 12238, pp. 192–211. Springer, Cham (2020). https://doi.org/10.1007/978-3-030-57990-6_10
31. Regev, O.: On lattices, learning with errors, random linear codes, and cryptography. In: Proceedings of the Thirty-Seventh Annual ACM Symposium on Theory of Computing, STOC 2005, pp. 84–93. ACM, New York (2005). https://doi.org/10.1145/1060590.1060603
32. Yao, A.C.: Protocols for secure computations. In: 23rd Annual Symposium on Foundations of Computer Science (SFCS 1982), pp. 160–164 (1982)

Improved Constructions of Anonymous Credentials from Structure-Preserving Signatures on Equivalence Classes

Aisling Connolly[1(✉)], Pascal Lafourcade[2(✉)], and Octavio Perez Kempner[3,4(✉)]

[1] Worldline Global, Paris, France
aislingmconnolly@gmail.com
[2] LIMOS, University Clermont Auvergne, Clermont-Ferrand, France
pascal.lafourcade@uca.fr
[3] DIENS, École normale supérieure, CNRS, PSL University, Paris, France
[4] be-ys Research, Clermont-Ferrand, France
octavio.perez.kempner@ens.fr

Abstract. Anonymous attribute-based credentials (ABCs) are a powerful tool allowing users to authenticate while maintaining privacy. When instantiated from structure-preserving signatures on equivalence classes (SPS-EQ) we obtain a controlled form of malleability, and hence increased functionality and privacy for the user. Existing constructions consider equivalence classes on the message space, allowing the joint randomization of credentials and the corresponding signatures on them.

In this work, we additionally consider equivalence classes on the signing-key space. In this regard, we obtain a *signer-hiding* notion, where the issuing organization is not revealed when a user shows a credential. To achieve this, we instantiate the ABC framework of Fuchsbauer, Hanser, and Slamanig (FHS, Journal of Cryptology '19) with a recent SPS-EQ scheme (ASIACRYPT '19) modified to support a fully adaptive NIZK from the framework of Couteau and Hartmann (CRYPTO '20). We also show how to obtain Mercurial Signatures (CT-RSA, 2019), extending the application of our construction to anonymous delegatable credentials.

To further increase functionality and efficiency, we augment the set-commitment scheme of FHS19 to support openings on attribute sets disjoint from those possessed by the user, while integrating a proof of exponentiation to allow for a more efficient verifier. Instantiating in the CRS model, we obtain an efficient credential system, anonymous under malicious organization keys, with increased expressiveness and privacy, proven secure in the standard model.

Keywords: Anonymous credentials · Mercurial signatures · SPS-EQ

1 Introduction

Considering access to online services, designing protocols to manage the information users can be requested to present is of utmost importance to protect the user. A first step in the literature developed the concept of *attribute-based*

G. Hanaoka et al. (Eds.): PKC 2022, LNCS 13177, pp. 409–438, 2022.
https://doi.org/10.1007/978-3-030-97121-2_15

credentials (ABC), to model how users could show a credential, containing a set of attributes, to access different services.

Subsequently, the development of *anonymous* attribute-based credentials made it possible protect the holders identity when showing a credential. Users could present a credential disclosing no information other than that revealed by the attributes they choose to show (*anonymity*), while also ensuring that the provided information is authentic (*unforgeability*). Proposed alternatives consider a third property *unlinkability* which ensures that multiple showings of the same credential cannot be linked. Credential systems that support an arbitrary number of unlinkable showings are said to be *multi-show*. In contrast, those that only allow a single use of an issued credential in an unlinkable fashion are called *one-show*.

Initial progress was made with respect to one-show constructions. Here, *blind signatures* are issued on commitments to attributes so that users can later show the signature and disclose some of the attributes, while proving knowledge of those left unrevealed. Examples include [4,9], and [30].

In the multi-show setting, pioneering constructions (based on Camenisch and Lysyanskaya's (CL) signatures [12,13]) such as the one underlying the Idemix credential system [52] rely on randomizing the signature to then prove in zero-knowledge the correspondence between the set of attributes (disclosed and undisclosed), and the signature.

A major drawback from such an approach is that the zero-knowledge proof used during showings is of variable-length and may require multiple sub-proofs On the other hand, more recent constructions (*e.g.*, [11,14,24,32,38,46,49]) apply other techniques based on different lines of work to adapt the signature and the message without using Zero-Knowledge Proofs of Knowledge (ZKPoK), providing constant-size showings.

The concept of ABC has been recently extended to consider multi-authority credentials (*e.g.*, [23,38,48]), where users obtain a single credential for a set of attributes not necessarily issued by a single authority. In this work we consider the *classical* setting (single authority issuance).

1.1 Limitations of State-of-the-art ABCs

Constructions in the classical setting differentiate from each other by the expressiveness they provide, their efficiency, on whether or not they provide non-interactive features, on their security model, and on how and if they manage revocation features. Achieving all these properties simultaneously has been challenging and tends to rely on complex or non-standard assumptions.

When considering state-of-the-art credential systems, there are five lines of work with respect to the underlying signature scheme that is used to build them; (1) CL signatures [13]: Idemix [52] and [49]. (2) Aggregatable signatures: [14] and [38]. (3) Sanitizable signatures: [15]. (4) Redactable signatures: [11] and [46]. (5) Structure-Preserving Signatures on Equivalence Classes (SPS-EQ): [32].

PROOF SETTINGS. All previous work with the exception of [49] rely on security proofs in the Generic Group Model (GGM) [47]. Our first motivation is to provide an alternative to [49], building on [32] without relying on the GGM.

Table 1. Signatures comparison including pairings and exponentiations.

Scheme	$\lvert\sigma\rvert$	$\lvert\mathsf{pk}\rvert$	Sign	Verify	ChgRep	Assumptions
[40]	$8\lvert\mathbb{G}_1\rvert + 9\lvert\mathbb{G}_2\rvert$	$(2+\ell)\lvert\mathbb{G}_2\rvert$	29E	11P	19P+38E	SXDH
Section 5	$9\lvert\mathbb{G}_1\rvert + 4\lvert\mathbb{G}_2\rvert$	$(2+\ell)\lvert\mathbb{G}_2\rvert$	10E	11P	19P+21E	extKerMDH, SXDH

Signer-hiding properties. Showing protocols of previous constructions (including [49]), verify signatures with a key that belongs to the authority that issued the credential. This restricts the use of ABC in scenarios where one would like to verify a valid credential without linking it to a particular authority.

Concrete efficiency. Most alternatives provide similar efficiency at the asymptotic level. Yet, an up-to-date fine-grained analysis on their concrete efficiency lacks in the literature.

1.2 Summary of Contributions

We follow the ABC and SPS-EQ line of work from Fuchsbauer, Hanser and Slamanig [32], improving over prior work in the following ways:

1. We extend the set-commitment scheme from [32] to build a more expressive credential system allowing the generation of witnesses for disjoint sets ([32] allows only selective disclosure of attributes).
2. We instantiate the ABC from [32], with a new SPS-EQ scheme based on the one from [40] also using a CRS, a tight reduction, and under weaker assumptions. Thus, we move away from a security proof in the GGM when compared to the work from [32], and obtain a more efficient ABC than the one resulting from instantiating [32] with [40] (see Table 1).
3. We incorporate a proof of exponentiation to outsource part of computational cost from the verifier to the prover, which can be useful in some settings.
4. We adapt the signature scheme to build an SPS-EQ where one not only can randomize the message together with the signature, but also the corresponding public key used to verify the signature using a proof of well-formedness. Thus, users can hide the identity of the *signer* during showings.

By doing so, the verifier can check a signature using a randomized public key, knowing that it comes from a valid authority but not which one. Unlike solutions using ring signatures where it is the signer (credential issuer) who chooses the ring size, we let users do it independently (relying on SPS-EQ and an efficient proof of correct randomization alone). Hence, once users get a credential from a valid authority they can decide on the anonymity set themselves whenever they use their credential. This approach is better aligned with the concept of self sovereign identity and related applications that seek to empower users giving them full control on their identity.

Along the way, we also describe how to build *mercurial signatures* [20] with security proofs in the standard model (assuming a CRS). All the previous ones [20,21] have security proofs in the GGM. Consequently, our signature construction can also be used to build delegatable anonymous credentials [5,17] as well.

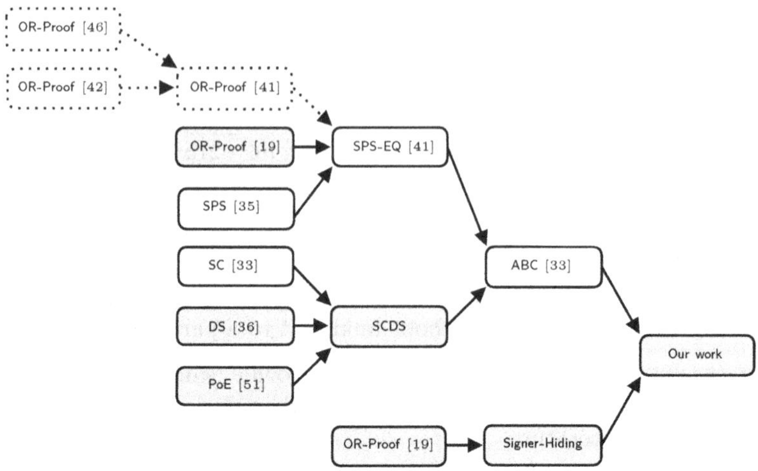

Fig. 1. Summary of building blocks used in this work. Dashed boxes represent replaced building blocks while grey boxes are used to highlight our contributions. When applicable, references inside each box indicate the related previous work.

1.3 Roadmap

We begin by presenting related work with a focus on the development of SPS-EQ and set-commitment schemes (Sect. 2) followed by the required cryptographic background in Sect. 3. Our *first* contribution, extending the set-commitment scheme (SC) in [32] to support non-membership proofs for disjoint sets (DS), is presented in Sect. 4. We also define here the proof of exponentiation (PoE), which can be seen as an optional *plug-in* to gain efficiency in this new set-commitment scheme (SCDS).

In Sect. 5 we present our SPS-EQ scheme. It uses a new malleable NIZK argument based on a recent work from Couteau and Hartmann [19], which we use to replace the one underlying [40].

In [32] the authors discuss a concurrently secure variant of their ABC based on a trapdoor commitment scheme to implement ZKPoK, assuming the existence of one-way functions and a CRS. Since our SPS-EQ makes use of a CRS, we instantiate the previous variant with it, incorporate a Pedersen commitment scheme to compute the relevant ZKPoK, and adapt the rest to our set-commitment scheme and the proof of exponentiation (*second* and *third* contributions). Thus, we dedicate Sect. 6 to present the resulting ABC.

Subsequently, we extend the previous construction to support another NIZK argument that allows to hide the identity of the signer during showings. This allows us to build another ABC as our *fourth* contribution. Furthermore, we also outline in this section how to perform revocation and build mercurial signatures.

In Fig. 1 we summarize the dependencies between the different building blocks used in the previously mentioned sections highlighting our contributions.

Finally, a detailed comparison on the concrete efficiency of our constructions when compared to other state-of-the-art alternatives is provided in Sect. 8, while the conclusions of this work are presented in Sect. 9.

2 Background and Related Work

2.1 Structure-Preserving Signatures on Equivalence Classes

In [36], Hanser and Slamanig introduced a novel structure preserving signature (SPS) scheme that allowed joint randomization of messages and their corresponding signatures, coining Structure-Preserving Signatures on Equivalence Classes (SPS-EQ). They observed that if one considers a prime-order group $\mathbb{G}$ and defines the projective vector space $(\mathbb{G}^*)^\ell$, there is a partition into equivalence classes given by the following relation $\mathcal{R}$: $\mathbf{m} \in (\mathbb{G}^*)^\ell \sim_\mathcal{R} \mathbf{m}^* \in (\mathbb{G}^*)^\ell \iff \exists\ \mu \in \mathbb{Z}_p^* : \mathbf{m}^* = \mu\mathbf{m}$. If the discrete logarithm problem is hard in $\mathbb{G}$ and one restricts the vector components to be non-zero, given two vectors $\mathbf{m}$ and $\mathbf{m}^*$, it is difficult to distinguish whether they were randomly sampled or if they belong to the same equivalence class. Hence, Hanser and Slamanig defined SPS-EQ as SPS that produce signatures on an equivalence class instead of messages alone. Given a message and its corresponding signature, SPS-EQ provides a *controlled form of malleability* in which one can publicly (without requiring access to the secret key) adapt a signature to change the representative (message). The equivalence relation provides indistinguishability on the message space if the DDH assumption holds. If additionally, updated signatures are distributed like fresh signatures, message-signature pairs falling into the same class are unlinkable. For unlinkability to hold, signatures should also be randomized when adapting them to a new representative of the class. As described in [32], given a representative and its corresponding signature, a random representative of the same class with an adapted signature are indistinguishable from a random message-signature pair.

Since their introduction, SPS-EQ have been used to build several cryptographic protocols (*e.g.*, [2,3,10,26,29–31]). They have been used in anonymous credentials [24,32,36], and delegatable anonymous credential systems, in this case under the name of mercurial signatures [20,21], which are an extension of the equivalence classes to the signing keys. State-of-the-art constructions focus on building schemes under weaker assumptions and with tight security. The first step was the work from Fuchsbauer and Gay [28]. Subsequently, Khalili *et al.* [40] proposed a new SPS-EQ which is, to the best of our knowledge, the only one under standard assumptions and with a tight security reduction to date.

The construction of [28] is based on the family of Matrix-Diffie-Hellman assumptions [27]. They first modify an affine MAC from [6] to obtain a linear structure-preserving MAC, which is made publicly verifiable using a known technique in the context of SPS [41]. This allows to use a *tag* to randomize both the signature and message.

The resulting scheme is secure under a weaker notion of unforgeability (EUF-CoMA). In [40], authors observe that using a structure-preserving MAC such as the one from [28] has an inherent problem in the security game. As messages and Matrix Decision Diffie-Hellman challenges belong to the same source group of the bilinear group, one cannot do better than EUF-CoMA security following this approach. Consequently, they proposed to use an OR-Proof based on that in [34] to then construct tightly secure structure-preserving MACs based on the key encapsulation mechanism of Gay *et al.* in [33]. This allows to circumvent the previous issue and obtain the first EUF-CMA secure SPS-EQ scheme with a tight security reduction under standard assumptions.

In this work, we present an SPS-EQ scheme where the OR-based proof in [40] is replaced by the one in [19], while adapting other building blocks accordingly.

2.2 Accumulators and Set-Commitments

In [25], Derler, Hanser and Slamanig revisited the notion of cryptographic accumulators and proposed a unified formal model which included the notions of undeniability and indistinguishability for accumulators, complementing the classical ones of correctness and collision-freeness. They showed how to construct a commitment scheme using an indistinguishable accumulator in a black-box manner. The relation stems from the fact that indistinguishability and collision-freeness of accumulators resemble those of hiding and binding for commitments.

In subsequent work [36], Hanser and Slamanig built an ABC with constant-size credentials and constant-size showings (for selective disclosure of attributes) based on a polynomial commitment scheme with factor openings. They departed from the work of Kate *et al.* on constant-size polynomial commitments [39] with the following observations; (1) If a credential is seen as a set of attributes mapped to roots of a monic polynomial, then one can generate a polynomial commitment of constant-size to represent the credential using the approach from [39]. (2) Instead of evaluating the polynomial at certain points, what is important to prove possession of an attribute is to open factors of the polynomial instead. (3) If one can open multiple factors in constant-size, a showing involving a selective disclosure of attributes can be done in constant-size as well.

As a result they proposed an indistinguishable bilinear accumulator ([43]) with batch membership proofs (*i.e.,* factor opening), which was subsequently re-stated as a *set-commitment* scheme in a follow-up work [32].

A drawback of the ABC from [32] is that the achieved level of *expressiveness* is limited. It allows only to show proofs for the conjunction of attributes in arbitrary subsets of attributes encoded in the credential (selective disclosure). Another potential issue is that verification involves a number of exponentiations that are linear in the size of the subset to be verified. This is undesirable when verification of the credential should be fast.

Thakur [50] proposed a series of protocols for batch membership and non-membership proofs for bilinear accumulators using *proofs of exponentiation* (an idea previously introduced for accumulators in groups of unknown order by Boneh et al. [8] and by Wesolowski [51]) to shift the computational cost from the verifier to the prover. The main idea is to replace some of the exponentiations by a single polynomial division and to use of a non-interactive proof obtained via the Fiat-Shamir transform.

Batch proofs in the bilinear accumulator setting can be traced back to the works by Papamanthou *et al.* [44] and by Ghosh *et al.* [35]. The latter presents the same underlying ideas of the (non)membership proofs provided by Thakur, and a *Zero-Knowledge Dynamic Universal Accumulator*, which strengthens the notion of indistinguishability using the randomization ideas from [25].

Table 2. Asymptotic complexities of ABC systems where n is the number of attributes in the credential and k the number of disclosed ones during a showing.

Scheme	[13]	[14]	[15]	[11] & [32]	[49]	[46]	[38]	Section 6
	Issuing n-attr. credential							
Comm.	$O(n)$	$O(n)$	$O(n)$	$\mathbf{O(1)}$	$O(n)$	$\mathbf{O(1)}$	$O(n)$	$\mathbf{O(1)}$
User	$O(n)$	$O(n)$	$O(n)$	$O(n)$	$O(n)$	$O(n)$	$O(n)$	$O(n)$
Issuer	$O(n)$	$O(n)$	$O(n)$	$O(n)$	$O(n)$	$O(n)$	$O(n)$	$O(n)$
	Showing k-of-n attributes (selective disclosure)							
$\vert\mathsf{ek}\vert$	$O(n)$	$O(n)$	$O(n)$	$O(n)$	$O(n)$	$O(n^2)$	$O(n)$	$O(n)$
Comm.	$O(n)$	$O(1)$	$O(k)$	$O(1)$	$O(1)$	$O(1)$	$O(1)$	$O(1)$
User	$O(n)$	$O(n)$	$O(k)$	$O(n-k)$	$O(n-k)$	$O(n-k)$	$\mathbf{O(1)}$	$O(\max\{n-k,k\})$
Verifier	$O(n)$	$O(n)$	$O(k)$	$O(k)$	$O(k)$	$O(k)$	$O(n)$	$\mathbf{O(1)}$

More recently, a new set-commitment scheme including set intersection and set difference operations was proposed in [49]. It provides more expressiveness when compared to the one from [32] but under a weaker hiding notion.

We incorporate the previous ideas from [25,35], and [50] to extend the set-commitment scheme from [32] to support disjoint sets (batch non-membership proofs), while also allowing a faster verification and a stronger hiding notion. Thus, we obtain a set-commitment scheme that is more expressive than the one in [32] and almost as expressive as [49] (but better in efficiency and strength).

2.3 Attribute-Based Credentials

We recall in Table 2 the asymptotic complexities for the issuing and showing protocols, considering recent credential systems from each of the lines of work mentioned in the introduction, and our construction in Sect. 6. For showing protocols we consider the selective disclosure of attributes (*i.e.*, the ability to show multiple attributes while hiding others during a showing). While the work from [38] (based on aggregatable signatures) is the only one with $O(1)$ complexity for the user during a showing, this is obtained at the cost of a more expensive verifier. Our work achieves $O(1)$ complexity for the verifier but keeping better asymptotics for the user. A more detailed comparison on the concrete efficiency of ABC's (as well as an implementation benchmark) was provided in [49], but the recent works from [46] and [38] were not included. Therefore, we provide an updated comparison for the most efficient ones in Sect. 8.

2.4 Signer-Hiding

Independent and concurrent work by Bobolz *et al.* [7] also addressed the problem of hiding the identity of a credential issuer/signer under the notion of *issuer-hiding*. There, the authors propose a sligthly different setting to avoid using an OR-like proof as done in this work. In brief, the authors consider access policies of the form $\{\sigma_i, \mathsf{pk}_i\}_{i\in[n]}$, where σ_i is a signature on a given authority's public key pk_i produced by the verifier. As a result, users can prove the correspondence between a public key (defined in the policy) and the credential verification under that public key in zero knowledge, using a NIZK independent to the number of public keys defined in the policy. In this regard, we note that our work is compatible with their formalization and, furthermore, under the previous setting such NIZK can be avoided in our case. Since we use mercurial signatures, it would suffice to randomize the access policy and the user credential consistently.

3 Preliminaries

NOTATION. Let BGGen be a p.p.t algorithm that on input 1^λ with λ the security parameter, returns a description $\mathsf{BG} = (p, \mathbb{G}_1, \mathbb{G}_2, \mathbb{G}_T, P_1, P_2, e)$ of an asymmetric bilinear group where $\mathbb{G}_1, \mathbb{G}_2, \mathbb{G}_T$ are cyclic groups of prime order p with $\lceil \log_2 p \rceil = \lambda$, P_1 and P_2 are generators of $\mathbb{G}_1$ and $\mathbb{G}_2$, and $e : \mathbb{G}_1 \times \mathbb{G}_2 \rightarrow \mathbb{G}_T$ is an efficiently computable (non-degenerate) bilinear map. BG is said to be of Type-3 if no efficiently computable isomorphisms between $\mathbb{G}_1$ and $\mathbb{G}_2$ are known. For all $a \in \mathbb{Z}_p$, we denote by $[a]_s = aP_s \in \mathbb{G}_s$ the implicit representation of a in $\mathbb{G}_s$ for $s \in \{1, 2, T\}$. For matrices (or vectors) $\mathbf{A}, \mathbf{B}$ we extend the pairing notation to $e([\mathbf{A}]_1, [\mathbf{B}]_2) := [\mathbf{AB}]_T \in \mathbb{G}_T$. Sampling r from set $\mathcal{S}$ uniformly at random is denoted by $r \overset{\$}{\leftarrow} \mathcal{S}$. Finally, we use the notation $\mathcal{A}(x; y)$ to indicate that a value y (usually computed internally by $\mathcal{A}$), is being passed directly to $\mathcal{A}$ on input x.
ASSUMPTIONS. We recall the Diffie-Hellman assumptions in the billinear group setting and the algebraic framework from [27] and [42], including a generalization of the Strong Diffie-Hellman assumption from [32], in the full version (Appendix A from [18]). Besides, we will also use the following generalization of the KerMDH assumption introduced in [19]. It allows an adversary to extend the given matrix but requiring it to output multiple, linearly independent vectors in the kernel.

$\mathcal{D}_k$-$\mathsf{extKerMDH}$ASSUMPTION. Let $\mathcal{D}_k$ be a matrix distribution, $l, k \in \mathbb{N}$, and $s \in \{1, 2\}$. We say that the $\mathcal{D}_k$-$\mathsf{extKerMDH}$ *assumption* holds in $\mathbb{G}_s$ relative to BGGen, if for every $\mathsf{BG} \overset{\$}{\leftarrow} \mathsf{BGGen}(1^\lambda)$, $\mathbf{D} \overset{\$}{\leftarrow} \mathcal{D}_k$, and all p.p.t. adversaries $\mathcal{A}$ the following probability is negligible.

$$\Pr\left[\begin{array}{c|c} [\mathbf{C}]_{3-s} \in \mathbb{G}_3^{l+1 \times k+l+1} \wedge [\mathbf{B}]_s \in \mathbb{G}_s^{l \times k} & \mathsf{BG} \overset{\$}{\leftarrow} \mathsf{BGGen}(1^\lambda); \mathbf{D} \overset{\$}{\leftarrow} \mathcal{D}_k \\ \wedge\ [\mathbf{C}]_{3-s}[\mathbf{D}']_s = 0 & ([\mathbf{C}]_{3-s}, [\mathbf{B}]_s) \overset{\$}{\leftarrow} \mathcal{A}(\mathsf{BG}, [\mathbf{D}]_s) \\ \wedge\ \mathsf{rank}(\mathbf{C}) \geq l + 1 & [\mathbf{D}']_s := \left[\begin{smallmatrix}\mathbf{D} \\ \mathbf{B}\end{smallmatrix}\right]_s \end{array}\right]$$

CHARACTERISTIC POLYNOMIAL. For a set $\mathcal{X}$ with elements in $\mathbb{Z}_p$, we refer to $\mathsf{Ch}_{\mathcal{X}}(X) = \prod_{x \in \mathcal{X}}(X + x) = \sum_{i=0}^{i=n} c_i \cdot X^i$ (a monic polynomial of degree $n = |\mathcal{X}|$ and defined over $\mathbb{Z}_p[X]$) as its *characteristic polynomial.* For a group generator P, $\mathsf{Ch}_{\mathcal{X}}(s)P$ can be efficiently computed (*e.g.*, using the Fast Fourier Transform) when given $(s^i P)_{i=0}^{|\mathcal{X}|}$ but not s. This is because $\mathsf{Ch}_{\mathcal{X}}(s)P = \sum_{i=0}^{i=n}(c_i \cdot s^i)P$.

In addition to exploiting properties of characteristic polynomials, we will also use the Schwartz-Zippel lemma and the Extended Euclidean Algorithm (EEA) in our constructions following the ideas from [35].

Lemma 1 (Schwartz-Zippel). *Let $q_1(x), q_2(x)$ be two d-degree polynomials from $\mathbb{Z}_p[X]$ with $q_1(x) \neq q_2(x)$, then for $s \overset{\$}{\leftarrow} \mathbb{Z}_p$, the probability that $q_1(x) = q_2(x)$ is at most d/p, and the equality can be tested in time $O(d)$.*

3.1 Non-interactive Zero-Knowledge Arguments and Malleable Proof Systems

We next define fully adaptive NIZK arguments (*i.e.*, the crs does not depend on the language distribution or language parameters), and the notions of malleable proof systems given in [16] and [40] respectively.

NIZK SYNTAX. A fully adaptive NIZK Π for a family of language distribution $\{\mathcal{D}_{\mathsf{pp}}\}_{\mathsf{pp}}$ consists of four probabilistic algorithms:

$\mathsf{PGen}(1^\lambda)$: On input 1^λ generates public parameters pp, a crs and a trapdoor td.
$\mathsf{Prove}(\mathsf{crs}, \rho, x, w)$: On input a crs, a language description $\rho \in \mathcal{D}_{\mathsf{pp}}$ and a statement x with witness w, outputs a proof π for $x \in \mathcal{L}_\rho$.
$\mathsf{Verify}(\mathsf{crs}, \rho, x, \pi)$: On input a crs, a language description $\rho \in \mathcal{D}_{\mathsf{pp}}$, a statement x and a proof π, accepts or rejects the proof.
$\mathsf{SimProve}(\mathsf{crs}, \mathsf{td}, \rho, x)$: Given a crs, the trapdoor td, a language description $\rho \in \mathcal{D}_{\mathsf{pp}}$ and a statement x, outputs a simulated proof for the statement $x \in \mathcal{L}_\rho$.

The following properties need to hold for NIZK arguments with respect to a family of language distributions $\mathcal{D}_{\mathsf{pp}}$.

PERFECT COMPLETENESS.

$$\Pr\left[\mathsf{Verify}(\mathsf{crs}, \rho, x, \pi) = 1 \;\middle|\; \begin{array}{c}(\mathsf{pp}, \mathsf{crs}, \mathsf{td}) \xleftarrow{\$} \mathsf{PGen}(1^\lambda); \rho \in \mathsf{Supp}(\mathcal{D}_{\mathsf{pp}});\\ (x, w) \in R_\rho; \pi \xleftarrow{\$} \mathsf{Prove}(\mathsf{crs}, \rho, x, w)\end{array}\right] = 1$$

COMPUTATIONAL SOUNDNESS. For every efficient adversary $\mathcal{A}$,

$$\Pr\left[\begin{array}{c}\mathsf{Verify}(\mathsf{crs}, \rho, x, \pi) = 1\\ \wedge\, x \notin \mathcal{L}_\rho\end{array} \;\middle|\; \begin{array}{c}(\mathsf{pp}, \mathsf{crs}, \mathsf{td}) \xleftarrow{\$} \mathsf{PGen}(1^\lambda);\\ \rho \in \mathsf{Supp}(\mathcal{D}_{\mathsf{pp}}); (\pi, x) \xleftarrow{\$} \mathcal{A}(\mathsf{crs}, \rho)\end{array}\right] \approx 0$$

where the probability is taken over PGen.

PERFECT ZERO-KNOWLEDGE. For all λ, all $(\mathsf{pp}, \mathsf{crs}, \mathsf{td}) \in \mathsf{Supp}(\mathsf{PGen}(1^\lambda))$, all $\rho \in \mathsf{Supp}(\mathcal{D}_{\mathsf{pp}})$ and all $(x, w) \in R_\rho$, the distributions $\mathsf{Prove}(\mathsf{crs}, \rho, x, w)$ and $\mathsf{SimProve}(\mathsf{crs}, \mathsf{td}, \rho, x)$ are identical.

Let $\mathcal{R}_\mathcal{L}$ be the witness relation associated to a language $\mathcal{L}$, then a controlled malleable proof system is accompanied by a family of efficiently computable n-ary transformations $T = (T_x, T_w)$ such that for any n-tuple $\{(x_1, w_1), \ldots, (x_n, w_n)\} \in \mathcal{R}_\mathcal{L}^n$ it holds that $(T_x(x_1, \ldots, x_n), T_w(w_1, \ldots, w_n)) \in \mathcal{R}_\mathcal{L}$. Intuitively, such a proof system allows when given valid proofs $\{\Omega_i\}_{i\in[n]}$ for words $\{x_i\}_{i\in[n]}$ with associated witnesses $\{w_i\}_{i\in[n]}$ to publicly compute a valid proof Ω for word $x := T_x(x_1, \ldots, x_n)$ corresponding to witness $w := T_w(w_1, \ldots, w_n)$ using an additional algorithm ZKEval which is defined as follows:

$\mathsf{ZKEval}(\mathsf{crs}, \mathcal{T}, (x_i, \Omega_i)_{i\in[n]})$ takes as input a common reference string crs, a transformation $T \in \mathcal{T}$, words $x_1, \ldots, x_n$ and their corresponding proofs $\Omega_1, \ldots, \Omega_n$, and outputs a new word $x' := T_x(x_1, \ldots, x_n)$ and proof Ω'.

Proofs computed by ZKEval should be indistinguishable from freshly computed proofs for the resulting word x' and corresponding witness w'. This notion is captured by the following definition.

Derivation Privacy. A NIZK proof system Π, malleable with respect to a set of transformations $\mathcal{T}$ defined on some relation $\mathcal{R}$ is *derivation private*, if for all p.p.t adversaries $\mathcal{A}$, the following probability is negligible,

$$\Pr\left[\begin{array}{l}\mathsf{crs} \xleftarrow{\$} \mathsf{PGen}(1^\lambda), b \xleftarrow{\$} \{0,1\} \\ (\mathsf{st}, ((x_i, w_i), \Omega_i)_{i\in[q]}, T) \xleftarrow{\$} \mathcal{A}(\mathsf{crs}), \\ \textbf{if } (T \notin \mathcal{T} \vee (\exists\, i \in [q] : (\mathsf{Verify}(\mathsf{crs}, x_i, \Omega_i) = 0) \vee (x_i, w_i) \notin \mathcal{R}) \\ \textbf{return } \bot, \\ \textbf{else if } b = 0 : \Omega \leftarrow \mathsf{Prove}(\mathsf{crs}, T_x((x_i)_{i\in[q]}), T_w((w_i)_{i\in[q]})), \\ \textbf{else if } b = 1 : \Omega \leftarrow \mathsf{ZKEval}(\mathsf{crs}, T, (x_i, \pi_i)_{i\in[q]}), \\ b' \xleftarrow{\$} \mathcal{A}(\mathsf{st}, \Omega)\end{array} : b = b'\right]$$

4 A Set-Commitment Scheme Supporting Disjoint Sets

We extend the set-commitment scheme in [32] to support *non-membership proofs* for disjoint sets, while also including an optional *proof of exponentiation* to replace most of the exponentiations in the verifier (outsourcing them to the prover) with a single polynomial division. To do so, we borrow the previously mentioned ideas in [25,35,50], and adapt them to the Type-3 setting.

SCDS Syntax. A *set-commitment scheme supporting disjoint sets* (SCDS) consists of the following p.p.t algorithms:

$\mathsf{Setup}(1^\lambda, 1^q)$ is a probabilistic algorithm which takes as input a security parameter λ and an upper bound q for the cardinality of committed sets, both in unary form. It outputs public parameters pp (including an evaluation key ek), and discards the trapdoor key s used to generate them. $\mathbb{Z}_p^* \setminus \{s\}$ defines the domain of set elements for sets of maximum cardinality q.

$\mathsf{TSetup}(1^\lambda, 1^q)$ is equivalent to Setup but also returns the trapdoor key.

$\mathsf{Commit}(\mathsf{pp}, \mathcal{X})$ is a probabilistic algorithm which takes as input pp and a set $\mathcal{X}$ with $1 \le |\mathcal{X}| \le q$. It outputs a commitment C on set $\mathcal{X}$ and opening information O.

$\mathsf{Open}(\mathsf{pp}, C, \mathcal{X}, O)$ is a deterministic algorithm which takes as input pp, a commitment C, a set $\mathcal{X}$, and opening information O. It outputs 1 if and only if O is a valid opening of C on $\mathcal{X}$.

$\mathsf{OpenSS}(\mathsf{pp}, C, \mathcal{X}, O, \mathcal{S})$ is a deterministic algorithm which takes as input pp, a commitment C, a set $\mathcal{X}$, opening information O, and a non-empty set $\mathcal{S}$. If $\mathcal{S}$ is a subset of $\mathcal{X}$ committed to in C, OpenSS outputs a witness wit that attests to it. Otherwise, outputs $\bot$.

$\mathsf{OpenDS}(\mathsf{pp}, C, \mathcal{X}, O, \mathcal{D})$ is a deterministic algorithm which takes as input pp, a commitment C, a set $\mathcal{X}$, opening information O, and a non-empty set $\mathcal{D}$. If $\mathcal{D}$ is disjoint from $\mathcal{X}$ committed to in C, OpenDS outputs a witness $\underline{\mathsf{wit}}$ that attests to it. Otherwise, outputs $\bot$.

$\mathsf{VerifySS}(\mathsf{pp}, C, \mathcal{S}, \mathsf{wit})$ is a deterministic algorithm which takes as input pp, a commitment C, a non-empty set $\mathcal{S}$, and a witness wit. If wit is a valid witness for $\mathcal{S}$ a subset of the set committed to in C, it outputs 1 and otherwise $\bot$.

$\mathsf{VerifyDS}(\mathsf{pp}, C, \mathcal{D}, \underline{\mathsf{wit}})$ takes as input pp, a commitment C, a non-empty set $\mathcal{D}$, and a witness wit. If $\underline{\mathsf{wit}}$ is a valid witness for $\mathcal{D}$ being disjoint from the set committed to in C, it outputs 1 and otherwise $\perp$.

$\mathsf{PoE}(\mathsf{pp}, \mathcal{X}, \alpha)$ takes as input pp, a non-empty set $\mathcal{X}$, and a randomly-chosen value α. It computes a proof of exponentiation for the characteristic polynomial of $\mathcal{X}$ and outputs a proof π_Q and a witness Q.

A SCDS scheme is *secure* if it satisfies the properties of correctness, binding, hiding, and soundness. These notions are defined next, modified to suit the scheme, but following the usual convention.

CORRECTNESS. An SCDS scheme is *correct* if for all $q > 0$, all $\lambda > 0$, all $\mathsf{pp} \in [\mathsf{Setup}(1^\lambda, 1^q)]$, all non-empty $\mathcal{S} \subseteq \mathcal{X}$ and all non-empty $\mathcal{D} : \mathcal{D} \cap \mathcal{X} = \emptyset$, the following probabilities equal 1:

1. $\Pr\left[(C, O) \xleftarrow{\$} \mathsf{Commit}(\mathsf{pp}, \mathcal{X}) : \mathsf{Open}(\mathsf{pp}, C, \mathcal{X}, O) = 1\right]$
2. $\Pr\left[\begin{array}{l}(C, O) \xleftarrow{\$} \mathsf{Commit}(\mathsf{pp}, \mathcal{X});\\ \mathsf{wit} \leftarrow \mathsf{OpenSS}(\mathsf{pp}, C, \mathcal{X}, O, \mathcal{S})\end{array} : \mathsf{VerifySS}(\mathsf{pp}, C, \mathcal{S}, \mathsf{wit}) = 1\right]$
3. $\Pr\left[\begin{array}{l}(C, O) \xleftarrow{\$} \mathsf{Commit}(\mathsf{pp}, \mathcal{X});\\ \underline{\mathsf{wit}} \leftarrow \mathsf{OpenDS}(\mathsf{pp}, C, \mathcal{X}, O, \mathcal{D})\end{array} : \mathsf{VerifyDS}(\mathsf{pp}, C, \mathcal{D}, \underline{\mathsf{wit}}) = 1\right]$

BINDING. An SCDS scheme is *binding* if for all $q > 0$ and all p.p.t adversaries $\mathcal{A}$, the following probability is negligible,

$$\Pr\left[\begin{array}{l}\mathsf{pp} \xleftarrow{\$} \mathsf{Setup}(1^\lambda, 1^q),\\ (C, \mathcal{X}, O, \mathcal{X}', O') \xleftarrow{\$} \mathcal{A}(\mathsf{pp})\end{array} : \begin{array}{r}\mathsf{Open}(\mathsf{pp}, C, \mathcal{X}, O) = 1 \wedge\\ \mathsf{Open}(\mathsf{pp}, C, \mathcal{X}', O') = 1 \ \wedge \ \mathcal{X} \neq \mathcal{X}'\end{array}\right]$$

HIDING. We say that an SCDS scheme is *hiding* if for all $q > 0$ and all p.p.t adversaries $\mathcal{A}$ with access to $\mathcal{O}_{\mathsf{SS}}$, an opening oracle which allows queries for sets $\mathcal{X}' \subseteq \mathcal{X}_0 \cap \mathcal{X}_1$, and to $\mathcal{O}_{\mathsf{DS}}$, for sets $\mathcal{X}'$ s.t. $\mathcal{X}' \cap \{\mathcal{X}_0 \cup \mathcal{X}_1\} = \emptyset$, there is a negligible function $\epsilon(\cdot)$ such that:

$$\Pr\left[\begin{array}{l}b \xleftarrow{\$} \{0,1\}; \mathsf{pp} \xleftarrow{\$} \mathsf{Setup}(1^\lambda, 1^q);\\ (\mathcal{X}_0, \mathcal{X}_1, \mathsf{st}) \xleftarrow{\$} \mathcal{A}(\mathsf{pp});\\ (C, O) \xleftarrow{\$} \mathsf{Commit}(\mathsf{pp}, \mathcal{X}_b);\\ b^* \xleftarrow{\$} \mathcal{A}^{\mathcal{O}_{\mathsf{SS}}(\mathsf{pp}, C, \mathcal{X}_b, O, \cdot), \mathcal{O}_{\mathsf{DS}}(\mathsf{pp}, C, \mathcal{X}_b, O, \cdot)}(\mathsf{st}, C)\end{array} : b^* = b\right] - \frac{1}{2} \leq \epsilon(k).$$

where $\mathcal{X}_0$ and $\mathcal{X}_1$ are two distinct sets s.t. $1 \leq |\mathcal{X}_b| \leq q$.
If the above holds for $\epsilon \equiv 0$, the scheme is said to be perfectly hiding.

SOUNDNESS. An SCDS scheme is sound if for all $q > 0$ and all p.p.t adversaries $\mathcal{A}$, the following probabilities are negligible,

1. $\Pr\left[\begin{array}{l}\mathsf{pp} \xleftarrow{\$} \mathsf{Setup}(1^\lambda, 1^q);\\ (C, \mathcal{X}, O, \mathcal{S}, \mathsf{wit}) \xleftarrow{\$} \mathcal{A}(\mathsf{pp})\end{array} : \begin{array}{r}\mathcal{S} \not\subseteq \mathcal{X} \ \wedge \ \mathsf{OpenSS}(C, \mathcal{X}, O) = 1\\ \wedge \ \mathsf{VerifySS}(C, \mathcal{S}, \mathsf{wit}) = 1\end{array}\right]$

2. $\Pr\left[\begin{array}{l}\mathsf{pp} \xleftarrow{\$} \mathsf{Setup}(1^\lambda, 1^q);\\ (C, \mathcal{X}, O, \mathcal{D}, \underline{\mathsf{wit}}) \xleftarrow{\$} \mathcal{A}(\mathsf{pp})\end{array} : \begin{array}{r}\mathcal{D} \cap \mathcal{X} \neq \emptyset \ \wedge \ \mathsf{OpenDS}(C, \mathcal{X}, O) = 1\\ \wedge \ \mathsf{VerifyDS}(C, \mathcal{D}, \underline{\mathsf{wit}}) = 1\end{array}\right]$

$\mathsf{SCDS.Setup}(1^\lambda, 1^q)$:
$\mathsf{BG} \xleftarrow{\$} \mathsf{BGGen}(1^\lambda)$; $s \xleftarrow{\$} \mathbb{Z}_p^*$
$\mathsf{pp} \leftarrow (\mathsf{BG}, (s^i P_1, s^i P_2)_{i \in [q]})$
return pp

$\mathsf{SCDS.TSetup}(1^\lambda, 1^q)$:
$\mathsf{BG} \xleftarrow{\$} \mathsf{BGGen}(1^\lambda)$; $s \xleftarrow{\$} \mathbb{Z}_p^*$
$\mathsf{pp} \leftarrow (\mathsf{BG}, (s^i P_1, s^i P_2)_{i \in [q]})$
return (pp, s)

$\mathsf{SCDS.PoE}(\mathsf{pp}, \mathcal{X}, \alpha)$:
$Q \leftarrow \mathsf{Ch}_{\mathcal{X}}(s) P_2$; Let $h(X)$ and β s.t.
$\mathsf{Ch}_{\mathcal{X}}(X) = (X+\alpha) \cdot h(X) + \beta$; $\pi_Q \leftarrow h(s) P_2$
return (π_Q, Q)

$\mathsf{SCDS.Commit}(\mathsf{pp}, \mathcal{X})$:
if $|\mathcal{X}| > q$ **return** $\bot$; $r \xleftarrow{\$} \mathbb{Z}_p^*$
if $\exists\, s' \in \mathcal{X} : s' P_1 = s P_1$
  $C \leftarrow r P_1$; $O \leftarrow (1, (r, s'))$
else $C \leftarrow r \cdot \mathsf{Ch}_{\mathcal{X}}(s) P_1$; $O \leftarrow (0, r)$
return (C, O)

$\mathsf{SCDS.Open}(\mathsf{pp}, C, \mathcal{X}, O)$:
if $O = (1, (r, s')) \wedge s' P_1 = s P_1$
  if $C = r P_1$ **return** 1 **else** 0
if $O = (0, r)$
  if $C = r \cdot \mathsf{Ch}_{\mathcal{X}}(s) P_1$ **return** 1 **else** 0

$\mathsf{SCDS.OpenSS}(\mathsf{pp}, C, \mathcal{X}, O, \mathcal{S})$:
if $\mathsf{SCDS.Open}(C, \mathcal{X}, O) = 0 \vee$
  $\mathcal{S} \not\subseteq \mathcal{X} \vee \mathcal{S} = \emptyset$ **return** $\bot$
if $O = (1, (r, s'))$
  if $s' \notin \mathcal{S}$ **return** $\mathsf{Ch}_{\mathcal{S}}(s')^{-1} C$
if $O = (0, r)$ **return** $r \cdot \mathsf{Ch}_{\mathcal{X} \setminus \mathcal{S}}(s) P_1$
else return $\bot$

$\mathsf{SCDS.VerifySS}(\mathsf{pp}, C, \mathcal{S}, \mathsf{wit}, [\mathsf{PoE}])$:
if $(\mathcal{S} = \emptyset \wedge \mathsf{wit} = \bot)$ **return** 1
if $\exists\, s' \in \mathcal{S} : s' P_1 = s P_1$
  if $\mathsf{wit} = \bot$ **return** 1 **else** 0
if $\mathsf{PoE} = \bot$
  return $e(\mathsf{wit}, \mathsf{Ch}_{\mathcal{S}}(s) P_2) = e(C, P_2)$
else
  parse $\mathsf{PoE} = (\alpha, \pi_Q, Q)$
  $\beta \leftarrow \mathsf{Ch}_{\mathcal{S}}(X) (\mathrm{mod}\ (X + \alpha))$
  return $e(sP_1 + \alpha P_1, \pi_Q) + e(\beta P_1, P_2)$
  $= e(P_1, Q) \wedge e(\mathsf{wit}, Q) = e(C, P_2)$

$\mathsf{SCDS.OpenDS}(\mathsf{pp}, C, \mathcal{X}, O, \mathcal{D})$:
if $(t = 0 \vee |\mathcal{D} \cap \mathcal{X}| > 0)$ **return** $\bot$
if $O = (1, (r, s'))$
  if $s' \in \mathcal{D}$ **return** $\bot$ **else**
  $\gamma \xleftarrow{\$} \mathbb{Z}_p^*$; $(w_0, w_1) \leftarrow (\gamma P_2, \frac{1 - \gamma \cdot r}{\mathsf{Ch}_{\mathcal{D}}(s)} P_1)$
if $O = (0, r)$
  $\gamma \xleftarrow{\$} \mathbb{Z}_p^*$; Let $q_1(X)$ and $q_2(X)$ s.t.
  $\mathsf{Ch}_{\mathcal{X}}(X) \cdot q_1(X) + \mathsf{Ch}_{\mathcal{D}}(X) \cdot q_2(X) = 1$
  $q_1'(s) \leftarrow q_1(s) + \gamma \cdot \mathsf{Ch}_{\mathcal{D}}(s)$
  $q_2'(s) \leftarrow q_2(s) - \gamma \cdot \mathsf{Ch}_{\mathcal{X}}(s)$
  $(w_0, w_1) \leftarrow ((r^{-1} \cdot q_1'(s)) P_2, q_2'(s) P_1)$
return (w_0, w_1)

$\mathsf{SCDS.VerifyDS}(\mathsf{pp}, C, \mathcal{D}, \underline{\mathsf{wit}}, [\mathsf{PoE}])$:
if $(\mathcal{D} = \emptyset \wedge \underline{\mathsf{wit}} = \bot)$ **return** 1
if $\exists\, s' \in \mathcal{D} : s' P_1 = s P_1$
  if $\underline{\mathsf{wit}} = \bot$ **return** 1 **else** 0
parse $\underline{\mathsf{wit}} = (w_0, w_1)$
if $\mathsf{PoE} = \bot$ **return**
  $e(C, w_0) + e(w_1, \mathsf{Ch}_{\mathcal{D}}(s) P_2) = e(P_1, P_2)$
else
  parse $\mathsf{PoE} = (\alpha, \pi_Q, Q)$
  $\beta \leftarrow \mathsf{Ch}_{\mathcal{D}}(X) (\mathrm{mod}\ (X + \alpha))$
  return $e(sP_1 + \alpha P_1, \pi_Q) + e(\beta P_1, P_2)$
  $= e(P_1, Q) \wedge e(C, w_0) + e(w_1, Q) = e(P_1, P_2)$

Fig. 2. Our SCDS construction

4.1 Construction

Our construction is presented in Fig. 2. As in [32] we use a special opening for the case in which the commited set contains the trapdoor to achieve perfect correctness and perfect hiding. To prove that a given set is disjoint with respect to the commited set, the EEA is computed to obtain the Bézout coefficients. This way, equality is checked randomizing q_1, q_2 and using a single PPE. Finally, the PoE computes a polynomial division, and produces the corresponding proof.

Theorem 1. The SCDS construction from Fig. 2 is correct and perfectly hiding. Furthermore, if the q-co-DL (resp. q-co-GSDH) assumption holds, SCDS is computationally binding (resp. sound).

Proof. The proof strategy follows closely that of [32]. We extend these proofs in a similar manner to consider disjoint sets. The full proof is provided in [18] (Appendix B).

5 Our SPS-EQ Construction

The starting point for the SPS-EQ construction in [40] was the tightly secure SPS from [34], which builds on a structure-preserving MAC (based on the works from [33] and [37]) and a NIZK OR-Proof from [45]. To couple with equivalence classes, the authors proposed a way to adapt the OR-Proof so that it could be randomized and malleable. Unfortunately, as the CRS used in the OR-Proof from [45] was incompatible with the required randomization properties, the authors were forced to build a QA-NIZK on top to overcome the limitation.

In this section we introduce a new SPS-EQ scheme based on the one from [40], which we obtain replacing the underlying OR-Proof from [45] with one given in [19], while adapting accordingly. As a result we obtain a more efficient signature scheme based on a new malleable OR-NIZK argument. Before giving the intuition of our construction, we recall the syntax and security properties for SPS-EQ introduced in [32] and [40].

SPS-EQ SYNTAX. An SPS-EQ consists of the following p.p.t algorithms:

$\mathsf{ParGen}(1^\lambda)$ is a probabilistic algorithm which takes as input a security parameter λ and returns public parameters pp including an asymmetric bilinear group, but without the related trapdoor.

$\mathsf{TParGen}(1^\lambda)$ is like the ParGen algorithm but it also returns the trapdoor.

$\mathsf{KGen}(\mathsf{pp}, \ell)$ is a probabilistic algorithm which takes as input pp and a vector length $\ell > 1$, and outputs a key pair $(\mathsf{sk}, \mathsf{pk})$.

$\mathsf{Sign}(\mathsf{pp}, \mathsf{sk}, \mathbf{m})$ is a probabilistic algorithm which takes as input pp, a representative $\mathbf{m} \in (\mathbb{G}_i^*)^\ell$ for class $[\mathbf{m}]_\mathcal{R}$, a secret key sk, and outputs a signature $\sigma' = (\sigma, \tau)$ (potentially including a tag τ) on the message $\mathbf{m}$.

$\mathsf{ChgRep}(\mathsf{pp}, \mathbf{m}, (\sigma, \tau), \mu, \mathsf{pk})$ is a probabilistic algorithm which takes as input pp, a representative message $\mathbf{m} \in (\mathbb{G}_i^*)^\ell$, a signature σ (and potentially a tag τ), a scalar μ and a public key pk. It computes an updated signature σ' on new representative $\mathbf{m}^* = \mu\mathbf{m}$ and returns $(\mathbf{m}^*, \sigma')$.

$\mathsf{Verify}(\mathsf{pp}, \mathbf{m}, (\sigma, \tau), \mathsf{pk})$ is a deterministic algorithm which takes as input pp, a representative message $\mathbf{m}$, a signature σ (potentially including a tag τ) and public key pk. If σ is a valid signature on $\mathbf{m}$ it outputs 1 and 0 otherwise.

CORRECTNESS. An SPS-EQ scheme over $(\mathbb{G}_i^*)^\ell$ is correct if for any $\lambda \in \mathbb{N}$, any $\ell > 1$, any $\mathsf{pp} \xleftarrow{\$} \mathsf{ParGen}(1^\lambda)$, any pair $(\mathsf{sk}, \mathsf{pk})$, any message $\mathbf{m} \in (\mathbb{G}_i^*)^\ell$, and any $\mu \in \mathbb{Z}_p^*$, the following holds:

$$\mathsf{Pr}\big[\mathsf{Verify}(\mathbf{m}, \mathsf{Sign}(\mathsf{sk}, \mathbf{m}), \mathsf{pk}) = 1\big] = 1, \text{ and}$$
$$\mathsf{Pr}\big[\mathsf{Verify}(\mathsf{ChgRep}(\mathbf{m}, \mathsf{Sign}(\mathsf{sk}, \mathbf{m}), \mu, \mathsf{pk}), \mathsf{pk}) = 1\big] = 1.$$

EUF-CMA. An SPS-EQ scheme over $(\mathbb{G}_i^*)^\ell$ is existentially unforgeable under adaptively chosen-message attacks, if for all $\ell > 1$ and p.p.t adversaries $\mathcal{A}$ with access to a signing oracle SIGN, the following probability is negligible,

$$\mathsf{Pr}\left[\begin{array}{l} \mathsf{pp} \xleftarrow{\$} \mathsf{ParGen}(1^\lambda), \\ (\mathsf{sk}, \mathsf{pk}) \xleftarrow{\$} \mathsf{KGen}(\mathsf{pp}, \ell), \\ ([\mathbf{m}]_i^*, \sigma^*) \xleftarrow{\$} \mathcal{A}^{\mathrm{SIGN}(\mathsf{sk},\cdot)}(\mathsf{pk}) \end{array} : \begin{array}{r} [\mathbf{m}^*]_{\mathcal{R}} \neq [\mathbf{m}]_{\mathcal{R}} \ \forall\ [\mathbf{m}]_i \in \mathsf{Q}\ \wedge \\ \mathsf{Verify}([\mathbf{m}]_i^*, \sigma^*, \mathsf{pk}) = 1 \end{array}\right],$$

where Q is the set of queries that $\mathcal{A}$ has issued to the signing oracle SIGN. Note that in the tag-based case this oracle returns (σ_i, τ_i).

The following notion is based on Definition 10 from [40], which defines perfect adaption of signatures in the CRS model. Perfect adaption mandates that signatures output by the algorithm ChgRep are distributed identically to new signatures on the respective representative. When this notion is defined considering adversaries who could maliciously generate signing keys, one obtains the strongest possible notion for perfect adaption. Unlike [40], we opt to explicitly state that perfect adaption is defined with respect to the message space. We do this, as later on we will introduce a new a definition for perfect adaption with respect to the *key space*.

PERFECT ADAPTION OF SIGNATURES (under malicious keys in the honest parameters model) with respect to the *message space*: An SPS-EQ over $\mathcal{S}_{\mathbf{m}}$ perfectly adapts signatures with respect to the message space if for all tuples $(\mathsf{pp}, \mathsf{pk}, [\mathbf{m}]_i, \sigma, \mu)$ where $\mathsf{pp} \xleftarrow{\$} \mathsf{ParGen}(1^\lambda)$, $[\mathbf{m}]_i \in \mathcal{S}_{\mathbf{m}}$, $\mu \in \mathbb{Z}_p^*$, and $\mathsf{Verify}([\mathbf{m}]_i, \sigma, \mathsf{pk}) = 1$, we have that the output of $\mathsf{ChgRep}([\mathbf{m}]_i, (\sigma, \tau), \mu, \mathsf{pk})$ is $([\mu \cdot \mathbf{m}]_i, \sigma^*)$, with σ^* being a uniformly random element in the space of signatures, conditioned on $\mathsf{Verify}([\mu \cdot \mathbf{m}]_i, \sigma^*, \mathsf{pk}) = 1$.

5.1 Our Malleable NIZK Argument

Our malleable NIZK argument is based solely on the fully-adaptive OR-Proof from [19]. This allows us to circumvent the randomization problem in the OR-Proof from [45], and to avoid the need to build a QA-NIZK atop.

As a result, we reduce the number of exponentiations required in the proving and ZKEval algorithms, which leads to a more efficient signature scheme. This comes at the cost of relying on the $\mathcal{L}_1$-1-extKerMDH assumption. We argue that the change is justified as the extKerMDH is a natural extension of the KerMDH assumption and in this case, the assumption is also falsifiable.

INTUITION. We look for a NIZK proof which can be randomizable and malleable so that randomized proofs look like fresh proofs, while the malleability allows to update the proof statements. The goal is to obtain derivation privacy, which is crucial to perform the change of representative in the signature scheme.

The fully-adaptive NIZK argument from [19] is based on a challenge $z = z_0 + z_1$, where z is in the CRS, and z_0 and z_1 are elements of the proof and

$\underline{\mathsf{PGen}(1^\lambda):}$

$\mathsf{BG} \xleftarrow{\$} \mathsf{BGGen}(1^\lambda);\ z \xleftarrow{\$} \mathbb{Z}_p$

$\textbf{return}\ ((\mathsf{BG}, [z]_2), z)$

$\underline{\mathsf{PPro}(\mathsf{crs}, [\mathbf{x}_1]_1, \mathbf{w}_1, [\mathbf{x}_2]_1, \mathbf{w}_2):}$

$//\ [\mathbf{x}_j]_1 = \mathbf{A}_i \mathbf{w}_j \text{ with } \mathbf{A} \in \mathcal{M}^{2k \times k}$

$\mathbf{s}_j \xleftarrow{\$} \mathbb{Z}_p^k;\ z_{1-i} \xleftarrow{\$} \mathbb{Z}_p^*;\ \delta \xleftarrow{\$} \mathbb{Z}_p^*$

$[z_i]_2 \leftarrow \delta[z]_2 - [z_{1-i}]_2$

$[\mathbf{d}_i^j]_2 \leftarrow [z_i]_2 \mathbf{w}_j + [\mathbf{s}_j]_2$

$[\mathbf{a}_i^j]_1 \leftarrow [\mathbf{A}_i] \mathbf{s}_j$

$\mathbf{d}_{1-i}^j \xleftarrow{\$} \mathbb{Z}_p^k$

$[\mathbf{a}_{1-i}^j]_1 \leftarrow \mathbf{A}_{1-i} \mathbf{d}_{1-i}^j - z_{1-i} \mathbf{x}_j$

$\textbf{return}\ ([\mathbf{a}_i^j]_1, [\mathbf{d}_i^j]_2, [z_i]_2, \delta P_1)_{i \in \{0,1\}}^{j \in \{1,2\}}$

$\underline{\mathsf{PSim}(\mathsf{crs}, z, [\mathbf{x}_1]_1, [\mathbf{x}_2]_1):}$

$z_0 \xleftarrow{\$} \mathbb{Z}_p;\ \delta \xleftarrow{\$} \mathbb{Z}_p^*;\ z_1 \leftarrow \delta z - z_0$

$\textbf{for all}\ i \in \{0,1\},\ j \in \{1,2\}\ \textbf{do}$

$\quad \mathbf{d}_i^j \xleftarrow{\$} \mathbb{Z}_p^k;\ [\mathbf{a}_i^j]_1 \leftarrow \mathbf{A}_i \mathbf{d}_i^j - z_i \mathbf{x}_j$

$\textbf{return}\ ([\mathbf{a}_i^j]_1, [\mathbf{d}_i^j]_2, [z_i]_2, \delta P_1)_{i \in \{0,1\}}^{j \in \{1,2\}}$

$\underline{\mathsf{PRVer}(\mathsf{crs}, [\mathbf{x}]_1, \pi):}$

$\textbf{parse}\ \pi = ([\mathbf{a}_i]_1, [\mathbf{d}_i]_2, [z_i]_2, Z_1)_{i \in \{0,1\}}$

$\textbf{check}\ e(Z_1, [z]_2) = e([1]_1, [z_0]_2 + [z_1]_2)$

$\textbf{for all}\ i \in \{0,1\}\ \textbf{check}$

$\quad e([\mathbf{A}_i]_1, [\mathbf{d}_i]_2) = e([\mathbf{x}]_1, [z_i]_2) + e([\mathbf{a}_i]_1, [1]_2)$

$\underline{\mathsf{PVer}(\mathsf{crs}, [\mathbf{x}_1]_1, [\mathbf{x}_2]_1, \Omega):}$

$\textbf{parse}\ \Omega = ([\mathbf{a}_i^j]_1, [\mathbf{d}_i^j]_2, [z_i]_2, Z_1)_{i \in \{0,1\}}^{j \in \{1,2\}}$

$\textbf{check}\ e(Z_1, [z]_2) = e([1]_1, [z_0]_2 + [z_1]_2)$

$\textbf{for all}\ i \in \{0,1\},\ j \in \{1,2\}\ \textbf{check}$

$\quad e([\mathbf{A}_i]_1, [\mathbf{d}_i^j]_2) = e([\mathbf{x}_j]_1, [z_i]_2) + e([\mathbf{a}_i^j]_1, [1]_2)$

$\underline{\mathsf{ZKEval}(\mathsf{crs}, [\mathbf{x}_1]_1, [\mathbf{x}_2]_1, \Omega):}$

$\textbf{parse}\ \Omega = ([\mathbf{a}_i^j]_1, [\mathbf{d}_i^j]_2, [z_i]_2, Z_1)_{i \in \{0,1\}}^{j \in \{1,2\}}$

$\textbf{check}\ \mathsf{PVer}(\mathsf{crs}, [\mathbf{x}_1]_1, [\mathbf{x}_2]_1, \Omega)$

$\alpha, \beta \xleftarrow{\$} \mathbb{Z}_p^*;\ Z_1' \leftarrow \alpha Z_1$

$\textbf{for all}\ i \in \{0,1\}$

$\quad [z_i']_2 \leftarrow \alpha [z_i]_2;\ [\mathbf{a}_i']_1 \leftarrow \alpha [\mathbf{a}_i^1]_1 + \alpha\beta [\mathbf{a}_i^2]_1$

$\quad [\mathbf{d}_i']_2 \leftarrow \alpha [\mathbf{d}_i^1]_2 + \alpha\beta [\mathbf{d}_i^2]_2$

$\textbf{return}\ ([\mathbf{a}_i']_1, [\mathbf{d}_i']_2, [z_i']_2, Z_1')$

Fig. 3. Malleable NIZK argument for language $\mathcal{L}_{\mathbf{A}_0, \mathbf{A}_1}^{\vee}$

chosen such that the equation holds. To randomize a proof we need to randomize z_0 and z_1 and so, instead of checking the original equation we will check for linear combinations of the equation $\alpha z = z_0 + z_1$. We modify the original proof to compute a random α and add an extra element $Z = \alpha P_1$ to the proof. Consequently, the verification algorithm will now check an extra pairing.

As observed in [40], the malleability of the OR-NIZK proof can be achieved by using a tag and a second NIZK for that tag with shared randomness. We follow the same approach. The resulting malleable NIZK argument for the OR-language (for fixed $\mathbf{A}_0$ and $\mathbf{A}_1$) is defined below and presented in Fig. 3.

$$\mathcal{L}_{\mathbf{A}_0, \mathbf{A}_1}^{\vee} = \{[\mathbf{x}]_1 \in \mathbb{G}_1^{2k} | \exists\ \mathbf{w} \in \mathbb{Z}_p^k : [\mathbf{x}]_1 = [\mathbf{A}_0]_1 \cdot \mathbf{w} \vee [\mathbf{x}]_1 = [\mathbf{A}_1]_1 \cdot \mathbf{w}\},$$

Theorem 2. The protocol in Fig. 3 is a fully adaptive NIZK argument for the OR-language $\mathcal{L}_{\mathbf{A}_0, \mathbf{A}_1}^{\vee}$ if the falsifiable $\mathcal{L}_1$-$(4k+1)$-$\mathsf{extKerMDH}$ assumption holds in $\mathbb{G}_2$.

Proof. The proof follows [19] and is provided in [18] (Appendix C).

5.2 Signature Construction

Our construction is shown in Fig. 4, where the higlighted sections note the main differences to the scheme presented in [40]. In [18] (Appendix H), we also show how to extend it to obtain mercurial signatures (later explained in Section 7.1).

$\mathsf{SPS\text{-}EQ.ParGen}(1^\lambda)$:

$\mathsf{BG} \xleftarrow{\$} \mathsf{BGGen}(1^\lambda)$; $\mathbf{A}, \mathbf{A}_0, \mathbf{A}_1 \xleftarrow{\$} \mathcal{D}_1$
$(\mathsf{crs}, \mathsf{td}) \xleftarrow{\$} \mathsf{PGen}(1^\lambda; \mathsf{BG})$
return $(\mathsf{BG}, [\mathbf{A}]_2, [\mathbf{A}_0]_1, [\mathbf{A}_1]_1, \mathsf{crs})$

$\mathsf{SPS\text{-}EQ.TParGen}(1^\lambda)$:

$\mathsf{BG} \xleftarrow{\$} \mathsf{BGGen}(1^\lambda)$; $\mathbf{A}, \mathbf{A}_0, \mathbf{A}_1 \xleftarrow{\$} \mathcal{D}_1$
$(\mathsf{crs}, \mathsf{td}) \xleftarrow{\$} \mathsf{PGen}(1^\lambda; \mathsf{BG})$
$\mathsf{pp} \leftarrow (\mathsf{BG}, [\mathbf{A}]_2, [\mathbf{A}_0]_1, [\mathbf{A}_1]_1, \mathsf{crs})$
return $(\mathsf{pp}, \mathsf{td})$

$\mathsf{SPS\text{-}EQ.KGen}(\mathsf{pp}, 1^\lambda)$:

$\mathbf{K}_0 \xleftarrow{\$} \mathbb{Z}_p^{2\times 2}$; $\mathbf{K} \xleftarrow{\$} \mathbb{Z}_p^{\ell \times 2}$
$[\mathbf{B}]_2 \leftarrow [\mathbf{K}_0]_2[\mathbf{A}]_2$; $[\mathbf{C}]_2 \leftarrow [\mathbf{K}]_2[\mathbf{A}]_2$
$\mathsf{sk} \leftarrow (\mathbf{K}_0, \mathbf{K})$; $\mathsf{pk} \leftarrow ([\mathbf{B}]_2, [\mathbf{C}]_2)$
return $(\mathsf{sk}, \mathsf{pk})$

$\mathsf{SPS\text{-}EQ.Sign}(\mathsf{pp}, \mathsf{sk}, [\mathbf{m}]_1)$:

$r_1, r_2 \xleftarrow{\$} \mathbb{Z}_p$
$[\mathbf{t}]_1 \leftarrow [\mathbf{A}_0]_1 r_1$; $[\mathbf{w}]_1 \leftarrow [\mathbf{A}_0]_1 r_2$
$\Omega \leftarrow \mathsf{PPro}(\mathsf{crs}, [\mathbf{t}]_1, r_1, [\mathbf{w}]_1, r_2)$
parse $\Omega = (\Omega_1, \Omega_2, [z_0]_2, [z_1]_2, Z_1)$
$\mathbf{u}_1 \leftarrow \mathbf{K}_0^\top [\mathbf{t}]_1 + \mathbf{K}^\top [\mathbf{m}]_1$; $\mathbf{u}_2 \leftarrow \mathbf{K}_0^\top [\mathbf{w}]_1$
$\sigma \leftarrow ([\mathbf{u}_1]_1, [\mathbf{t}]_1, \Omega_1, [z_0]_2, [z_1]_2, Z_1)$
$\tau \leftarrow ([\mathbf{u}_2]_1, [\mathbf{w}]_1, \Omega_2)$
return (σ, τ)

$\mathsf{SPS\text{-}EQ.Verify}(\mathsf{pp}, [\mathbf{m}]_1, (\sigma, \tau), \mathsf{pk})$:

parse $\sigma = ([\mathbf{u}_1]_1, [\mathbf{t}]_1, \Omega_1, [z_0]_2, [z_1]_2, Z_1)$
parse $\tau \in \{([\mathbf{u}_2]_1, [\mathbf{w}]_1, \Omega_2) \cup \bot\}$
check $\mathsf{PRVer}(\mathsf{crs}, [\mathbf{t}]_1, \Omega_1, [z_0]_2, [z_1]_2, Z_1)$
check $e([\mathbf{u}_1]_1^\top, [\mathbf{A}]_2) =$
  $e([\mathbf{t}]_1^\top, [\mathbf{B}]_2) + e([\mathbf{m}]_1^\top, [\mathbf{C}]_2)$
if $\tau \neq \bot$ **check**
  $\mathsf{PRVer}(\mathsf{crs}, [\mathbf{w}]_1, \Omega_2, [z_0]_2, [z_1]_2, Z_1)$
  $e([\mathbf{u}_2]_1^\top, [\mathbf{A}_2]) = e([\mathbf{w}]_1^\top, [\mathbf{B}]_2)$

$\mathsf{SPS\text{-}EQ.ChgRep}(\mathsf{pp}, [\mathbf{m}]_1, \sigma, \tau, \mu, \mathsf{pk})$:

parse $\sigma = ([\mathbf{u}_1]_1, [\mathbf{t}]_1, \Omega_1, [z_0]_2, [z_1]_2, Z_1)$
parse $\tau \in \{([\mathbf{u}_2]_1, [\mathbf{w}]_1, \Omega_2) \cup \bot\}$
$\Omega \leftarrow (\Omega_1, \Omega_2, [z_0]_2, [z_1]_2, Z_1)$
check $\mathsf{PVer}(\mathsf{crs}, [\mathbf{t}]_1, [\mathbf{w}]_1, \Omega)$
check $e([\mathbf{u}_2]_1^\top, [\mathbf{A}]_2) \neq e([\mathbf{w}]_1^\top, [\mathbf{B}]_2)$
check $e([\mathbf{u}_1]_1^\top, [\mathbf{A}]_2) \neq$
$e([\mathbf{t}]_1^\top, [\mathbf{B}]_2) + e([\mathbf{m}]_1^\top, [\mathbf{C}]_2)$
$\alpha, \beta \xleftarrow{\$} \mathbb{Z}_p^*$
$[\mathbf{u}_1']_1 \leftarrow \mu[\mathbf{u}_1]_1 + \beta[\mathbf{u}_2]_1$
$[\mathbf{t}']_1 \leftarrow \mu[\mathbf{t}]_1 + \beta[\mathbf{w}]_1 = [\mathbf{A}_0]_1(\mu r_1 + \beta r_2)$
for all $i \in \{0, 1\}$
  $[z_i']_2 \leftarrow \alpha[z_i]_2$
  $[\mathbf{a}_i']_2 \leftarrow \alpha\mu[\mathbf{a}_i^1]_2 + \alpha\beta[\mathbf{a}_i^2]_2$
  $[d_i']_1 \leftarrow \alpha\mu[d_i^1]_1 + \alpha\beta[d_i^2]_1$
$\Omega' \leftarrow (([\mathbf{a}_i']_1, [d_i']_2, [z_i']_2)_{i\in\{0,1\}}, \alpha Z_1)$
$\sigma' \leftarrow ([\mathbf{u}_1']_1, [\mathbf{t}']_1, \Omega')$
return $(\mu[\mathbf{m}]_1, \sigma')$

Fig. 4. Our SPS-EQ scheme.

Theorem 3. The SPS-EQ in Fig. 4 perfectly adapts signatures (under malicious keys in the honest parameter model) with respect to the message space.

To prove Theorem 3 we follow almost verbatim the original proof from [40].

Proof. For all $[\mathbf{m}]_1$ and $\mathsf{pk} = ([\mathbf{K}_0\mathbf{A}]_2, [\mathbf{K}\mathbf{A}]_2)$, a signature σ=($[\mathbf{u}_1]_1$, $[\mathbf{t}]_1$, Ω_1, $[z_0]_2$, $[z_1]_2$, Z_1) generated according to the CRS ($[\mathbf{A}]_2, [\mathbf{A}_0]_1, [\mathbf{A}_1]_1, [z]_2$) satisfying the verification algorithm must be of the form: $\sigma = (\mathbf{K}_0^\top[\mathbf{A}_0]_1 r_1 + \mathbf{K}^\top[\mathbf{m}]_1$, $[\mathbf{A}_0]_1 r_1$, $[\mathbf{A}_0]s_1$, $[\mathbf{A}_1]d_1^1 - z_1[\mathbf{A}_0]_1 r_1$, $[z_0]_2 r_1 + [s_1]_2$, $[d_1^1]_2$, $[z_0]_2$, $[z_1]_2$, $Z_1)$. A signature output by ChgRep has the form $\sigma = (\mathbf{K}_0^\top[\mathbf{A}_0]_1(\mu r_1 + \beta r_2) + \mathbf{K}^\top[\mu\mathbf{m}]_1$, $[\mathbf{A}_0]_1(\mu r_1 + \beta r_2)$, $[\mathbf{A}_0]\alpha(\mu s_1 + \beta s_2)$, $[\mathbf{A}_1]\alpha(\mu d_1^1 + \beta d_1^2) - z_1[\mathbf{A}_0]_1\alpha(\mu r_1 + \beta r_2)$, $\alpha([z_0]_2(\mu r_1 + \beta r_2) + \mu[s_1]_2 + \beta[s_2]_2)$, $\alpha(\mu[d_1^1]_2 + \beta[d_1^2]_2)$, $\alpha[z_0]_2$, $\alpha[z_1]_2$, $\alpha Z_1)$, for new independent randomness α, β and μ so is a random element in the space of all signatures. Furthermore, the signature output by ChgRep is distributed identically to a fresh signature on message $[\mathbf{m}]_1$ output by Sign. □

Theorem 4. If the KerMDH and MDDH assumptions hold, the SPS-EQ in Fig. 4 is unforgeable.

Proof. The proof is provided in [18] (Appendix D).

6 Extending the ABC Model from [32]

In this section we present a new ABC model which extends [32] to consider NAND showing proofs and the use of a CRS (denoted as pp). A NAND showing proof allows users to demonstrate that a given set of attributes is not present in their credential. The core differences in this extended ABC model follow naturally from (1) the addition of disjoint sets in the SCDS scheme in Sect. 4, and (2) the removal of the key verification algorithm (as we work with a CRS).
ABC SYNTAX. An ABC scheme consists of the following p.p.t algorithms:

$\mathsf{Setup}(1^\lambda, 1^q)$ takes a security parameter λ and an upper bound q for the size of attribute sets, and outputs public parameters pp discarding any trapdoor.
$\mathsf{TSetup}(1^\lambda, 1^q)$ similar to Setup but it also returns a trapdoor (if any).
$\mathsf{OrgKeyGen}(\mathsf{pp})$ takes pp as input and outputs an organization key pair $(\mathsf{osk}, \mathsf{opk})$.
$\mathsf{UserKeyGen}(\mathsf{pp})$ takes pp as input and outputs a user key pair $(\mathsf{usk}, \mathsf{upk})$.
$\mathsf{Obtain}(\mathsf{pp}, \mathsf{usk}, \mathsf{opk}, \mathcal{X})$ and $\mathsf{Issue}(\mathsf{pp}, \mathsf{upk}, \mathsf{osk}, \mathcal{X})$ are run by a user and the organization respectively, who interact during execution. Obtain takes as input pp, the user's secret key usk, an organization's public key opk, and an attribute set $\mathcal{X}$ of size $|\mathcal{X}| < t$. Issue takes as input pp, a user public key upk, the organization's secret key osk, and an attribute set $\mathcal{X}$ of size $|\mathcal{X}| < t$. At the end of this protocol, Obtain outputs a credential cred on $\mathcal{X}$ for the user or $\perp$ if the execution failed.
$\mathsf{Show}(\mathsf{pp}, \mathsf{opk}, \mathcal{X}, \mathcal{S}, \mathcal{D}, \mathsf{cred})$ and $\mathsf{Verify}(\mathsf{pp}, \mathsf{opk}, \mathcal{S}, \mathcal{D})$ are run by a user and a verifier respectively, who interact during execution. Show takes as input pp, an organization public key opk, a credential cred for the attribute set $\mathcal{X}$, potentially non-empty sets $\mathcal{S} \subseteq \mathcal{X}$, $\mathcal{D} \not\subseteq \mathcal{X}$ representing attributes sets being a subset ($\mathcal{S}$) or disjoint ($\mathcal{D}$) to the attribute set ($\mathcal{X}$) committed in the credential. Verify takes as input pp, an organization public key opk, the sets $\mathcal{S}$ and $\mathcal{D}$. At the end, Verify outputs 1 or 0 indicating whether or not the credential showing was accepted.

6.1 Security Properties

The following notions are based on the security model from [32] (Sect. 5.1), which we adapt to consider the use of a crs (pp) and NAND showing proofs. Informally, an ABC scheme is secure if it has the following properties:

Correctness. A showing of a credential with respect to a non-empty sets $\mathcal{S}$ and $\mathcal{D}$ of attributes always verify if the credential was issued honestly on some attribute set $\mathcal{X}$ with $\mathcal{S} \subset \mathcal{X}$ and $\mathcal{D} \not\subseteq \mathcal{X}$.

Unforgeablility. Given at least one non-empty set $\mathcal{S} \subset \mathcal{X}$ or $\mathcal{D} \not\subset \mathcal{X}$, a user in possession of a credential for the attribute set $\mathcal{X}$ cannot perform a valid showing for $\mathcal{D} \subset \mathcal{X}$ nor for $\mathcal{S} \not\subset \mathcal{X}$. Moreover, no coalition of malicious users can combine their credentials and prove possession of a set of attributes which no single member has. This holds even after seeing showings of arbitrary credentials by honest users (thus, covering replay attacks).

Anonymity. During a showing, no verifier and no (malicious) organization (even if they collude) is able to identify the user or learn anything about the user, except that she owns a valid credential for the shown attributes. Furthermore, different showings of the same credential are unlinkable.

To introduce the corresponding formal definitions, the following global variables and oracles are listed below.

Global variables. At the beginning of each experiment, either the experiment computes an organization key pair $(\mathsf{osk}, \mathsf{opk})$ or the adversary outputs opk. In the anonymity game there is a bit b, which the adversary must guess.

In order to keep track of all honest and corrupt users, we introduce the sets $\mathtt{HU}$, and $\mathtt{CU}$, respectively. We use the lists $\mathtt{UPK}$, $\mathtt{USK}$, $\mathtt{CRED}$, $\mathtt{ATTR}$ and $\mathtt{OWNR}$ to track user public and secret keys, issued credentials and corresponding attributes and to which user they were issued. Furthermore, we use the sets J_{LoR} and I_{LoR} to store which issuance indices and corresponding users have been set during the first call to the left-or-right oracle in the anonymity game.

Oracles. Considering an adversary $\mathcal{A}$ the oracles are as follows:

$\mathcal{O}_{\mathtt{HU}}(i)$ takes as input a user identity i. If $i \in \mathtt{HU} \cup \mathtt{CU}$, it returns $\perp$. Otherwise, it creates a new honest user i by running $(\mathtt{USK}[i], \mathtt{UPK}[i]) \xleftarrow{\$} \mathsf{UsrKGen}(\mathsf{opk})$, adding i to the honest user list $\mathtt{HU}$ and returning $\mathtt{UPK}[i]$.

$\mathcal{O}_{\mathtt{CU}}(i, \mathsf{upk})$ takes as input a user identity i and (optionally) a user public key upk; if user i does not exist, a new corrupt user with public key upk is registered, while if i is honest, its secret key and all credentials are leaked. In particular, if $i \in \mathtt{CU}$ or if $i \in I_{\mathsf{LoR}}$ (that is, i is a challenge user in the anonymity game) then the oracle returns $\perp$. If $i \in \mathtt{HU}$ then the oracle removes i from $\mathtt{HU}$ and adds it to $\mathtt{CU}$; it returns $\mathtt{USK}[i]$ and $\mathtt{CRED}[j]$ for all j with $\mathtt{OWNR}[j] = i$. Otherwise ($i.e.$, $i \notin \mathtt{HU} \cup \mathtt{CU}$), it adds i to $\mathtt{CU}$ and sets $\mathtt{UPK}[i] \leftarrow \mathsf{upk}$.

$\mathcal{O}_{\mathsf{ObtIss}}(i, \mathcal{X})$ takes as input a user identity i and a set of attributes $\mathcal{X}$. If $i \notin \mathtt{HU}$, it returns $\perp$. Otherwise, it issues a credential to i by running

$$(\mathsf{cred}, \top) \xleftarrow{\$} \mathsf{Obtain}(\mathsf{pp}, \mathtt{USK}[i], \mathsf{opk}, \mathcal{X}), \mathsf{Issue}(\mathsf{pp}, \mathtt{UPK}[i], \mathsf{osk}, \mathcal{X}).$$

If $\mathsf{cred} = \perp$, it returns $\perp$. Else, it appends $(i, \mathsf{cred}, \mathcal{X})$ to $(\mathtt{OWNR}, \mathtt{CRED}, \mathtt{ATTR})$ and returns $\top$.

$\mathcal{O}_{\mathsf{Obtain}}(i, \mathcal{X})$ lets the adversary $\mathcal{A}$, who impersonates a malicious organization, issue a credential to an honest user. It takes as input a user identity i and a set of attributes $\mathcal{X}$. If $i \notin \mathtt{HU}$, it returns $\perp$. Otherwise, it runs

$$(\mathsf{cred}, \cdot) \xleftarrow{\$} \mathsf{Obtain}(\mathsf{pp}, \mathtt{USK}[i], \mathsf{opk}, \mathcal{X}), \cdot),$$

where the Issue part is executed by $\mathcal{A}$. If $\mathsf{cred} = \perp$, it returns $\perp$. Else, it appends $(i, \mathsf{cred}, \mathcal{X})$ to $(\mathtt{OWNR}, \mathtt{CRED}, \mathtt{ATTR})$ and returns $\top$.

$\mathcal{O}_{\mathsf{Issue}}(i, \mathcal{X})$ lets the adversary $\mathcal{A}$, who impersonates a malicious user, obtain a credential from an honest organization. It takes as input a user identity i and a set of attributes $\mathcal{X}$. If $i \notin \mathtt{CU}$, it returns $\perp$. Otherwise, it runs

$$(\cdot, I) \xleftarrow{\$} (\cdot, \mathsf{Issue}(\mathsf{pp}, \mathtt{UPK}[i], \mathsf{osk}, \mathcal{X})),$$

where the Obtain part is executed by $\mathcal{A}$. If $\mathrm{I} = \perp$, it returns $\perp$. Else, it appends $(i, \perp, \mathcal{X})$ to $(\mathtt{OWNR}, \mathtt{CRED}, \mathtt{ATTR})$ and returns $\top$.

$\mathcal{O}_{\mathsf{Show}}(j, \mathcal{S}, \mathcal{D})$ lets the adversary $\mathcal{A}$ play a dishonest verifier during a showing by an honest user. It takes as input an index of an issuance j and attributes sets $\mathcal{S}$ and $\mathcal{D}$. Let $i \xleftarrow{\$} \mathtt{OWNR}[j]$. If $i \notin \mathtt{HU}$, it returns $\perp$. Otherwise, it runs

$$(S, \cdot) \xleftarrow{\$} \mathsf{Show}(\mathsf{pp}, \mathsf{opk}, \mathtt{ATTR}[j], \mathcal{S}, \mathcal{D}, \mathtt{CRED}[j]), \cdot)$$

where the Verify part is executed by $\mathcal{A}$.

$\mathcal{O}_{\mathsf{LoR}}(j_0, j_1, \mathcal{S}, \mathcal{D})$ is the challenge oracle in the anonymity game where $\mathcal{A}$ must distinguish (multiple) showings of two credentials $\mathtt{CRED}[j_0]$ and $\mathtt{CRED}[j_1]$. The oracle takes two issuance indices j_0 and j_1 and attribute sets $\mathcal{S}$ and $\mathcal{D}$. If $J_{\mathsf{LoR}} \neq \emptyset$ and $J_{\mathsf{LoR}} \neq \{j_0, j_1\}$, it returns $\perp$. Let $i_0 \xleftarrow{\$} \mathtt{OWNR}[j_0]$ and $i_1 \xleftarrow{\$} \mathtt{OWNR}[j_1]$. If $J_{\mathsf{LoR}} \neq \emptyset$ then it sets $J_{\mathsf{LoR}} \xleftarrow{\$} \{j_0, j_1\}$ and $I_{\mathsf{LoR}} \xleftarrow{\$} \{i_0, i_1\}$. If $i_0, i_1 \neq \mathtt{HU} \vee \mathcal{S} \nsubseteq \mathtt{ATTR}[j_0] \cap \mathtt{ATTR}[j_1] \vee \mathcal{D} \cap \{\mathtt{ATTR}[j_0] \cup \mathtt{ATTR}[j_1]\} \neq \emptyset$, it returns $\perp$. Else, it runs

$$(S, \cdot) \xleftarrow{\$} (\mathsf{Show}(\mathsf{opk}, \mathtt{ATTR}[j_b], \mathcal{S}, \mathcal{D}, \mathtt{CRED}[j_b]), \cdot),$$

(with b set by the experiment) where the Verify part is executed by $\mathcal{A}$.

Correctness. An ABC system is correct, if for all $\lambda > 0$, all $t > 0$, all $\mathcal{X}$ with $0 < |\mathcal{X}| \leq t$ and all $\emptyset \neq \mathcal{S} \subset \mathcal{X}$ and $\emptyset \neq \mathcal{D} \nsubseteq \mathcal{X}$ with $0 < |\mathcal{D}| \leq t$ it holds that:

$$\Pr\left[\begin{array}{l} \mathsf{pp} \xleftarrow{\$} \mathsf{Setup}(1^\lambda, 1^q); \\ (\mathsf{osk}, \mathsf{opk}) \xleftarrow{\$} \mathsf{OrgKGen}(\mathsf{pp}); \\ (\mathsf{usk}, \mathsf{upk}) \xleftarrow{\$} \mathsf{UsrKGen}(\mathsf{pp}); \\ (\mathsf{cred}, \top) \xleftarrow{\$} (\mathsf{Obtain}(\mathsf{pp}, \mathsf{usk}, \mathsf{opk}, \mathcal{X}), \\ \mathsf{Issue}(\mathsf{pp}, \mathsf{upk}, \mathsf{osk}, \mathcal{X})) \end{array} : \begin{array}{l} (\top, 1) \xleftarrow{\$} (\mathsf{Show}(\mathsf{pp}, \mathsf{opk}, \mathcal{X}, \mathcal{S}, \\ \mathcal{D}, \mathsf{cred}), \mathsf{Verify}(\mathsf{pp}, \mathsf{opk}, \mathcal{S}, \mathcal{D})) \end{array}\right] = 1.$$

Unforgeability. An ABC system is unforgeable, if for all $\lambda > 0$, all $q > 0$ and p.p.t adversaries $\mathcal{A}$ having oracle access to $\mathcal{O} := \{\mathcal{O}_{\mathtt{HU}}, \mathcal{O}_{\mathtt{CU}}, \mathcal{O}_{\mathsf{ObtIss}}, \mathcal{O}_{\mathsf{Issue}}, \mathcal{O}_{\mathsf{Show}}\}$ the following probability is negligible.

$$\Pr\left[\begin{array}{l} \mathsf{pp} \xleftarrow{\$} \mathsf{Setup}(1^\lambda, 1^q); \\ (\mathsf{osk}, \mathsf{opk}) \xleftarrow{\$} \mathsf{OrgKGen}(\mathsf{pp}); \\ (\mathcal{S}, \mathcal{D}, \mathsf{st}) \xleftarrow{\$} \mathcal{A}^{\mathcal{O}}(\mathsf{pp}, \mathsf{opk}); \\ (\cdot, b^*) \xleftarrow{\$} (\mathcal{A}(\mathsf{st}), \mathsf{Verify}(\mathsf{pp}, \mathsf{opk}, \mathcal{S}, \mathcal{D})) \end{array} : \begin{array}{l} b^* = 1 \wedge \\ \forall j : \mathtt{OWNR}[j] \in \mathtt{CU} \implies \\ (\mathcal{S} \notin \mathtt{ATTR}[j] \vee \mathcal{D} \in \mathtt{ATTR}[j]) \end{array}\right]$$

Anonymity. An ABC system is anonymous, if for all $\lambda > 0$, all $q > 0$ and all p.p.t adversaries $\mathcal{A}$ having oracle access to $\mathcal{O} := \{\mathcal{O}_{\mathtt{HU}}, \mathcal{O}_{\mathtt{CU}}, \mathcal{O}_{\mathsf{Obtain}}, \mathcal{O}_{\mathsf{Issue}}, \mathcal{O}_{\mathsf{Show}}, \mathcal{O}_{\mathsf{LoR}}\}$ the following probability is negligible.

$$\Pr\left[\begin{array}{l} \mathsf{pp} \xleftarrow{\$} \mathsf{Setup}(1^\lambda, 1^q); b \xleftarrow{\$} \{0,1\}; (\mathsf{opk}, \mathsf{st}) \xleftarrow{\$} \mathcal{A}(\mathsf{pp}); \\ b^* \xleftarrow{\$} \mathcal{A}^{\mathcal{O}}(\mathsf{st}) \end{array} : b^* = b\right] - \frac{1}{2}$$

7 Our ABC Construction

As previously explained in Sect. 1.3, our ABC scheme is based on the one from [32]. The main changes are the following:

- As we use a signature scheme that relies on a CRS, we move the parameters of the set-commitment scheme from the organization's key pair to the public parameters pp that include the previous CRS. Furthermore, we instantiate the ZKPoK's using Pedersen commitments and the construction from [22], as suggested in [32] (Remark 1).
- Our showing protocol can be instantiated with two sets $\mathcal{S}$ and $\mathcal{D}$, one to compute AND proofs (selective disclosure) and one to compute NAND proofs.
- We integrate the proof of exponentiation to the showing protocol[1].

INTUITION. We begin explaining the difference to [32] with respect to malicious organizations as it clarifies the changes introduced in the issuing protocol. We recall that in this context the term *malicious organizations* refers to organizations whose key-pairs are generated in a way that trapdoor information is included. Such trapdoor information could later be used by an organization to break anonymity, provided that extra information (a transcript of a given showing protocol containing a credential issued by the organization) is available. The ABC scheme from [32] defines a ZKPoK in the issuing protocol ($\Pi^{\mathcal{R}_O}$) for which the organization needs to prove knowledge of the corresponding secret key to avoid the previous scenario. Since the signing keys in our SPS-EQ need to be generated using the CRS (which includes the matrix $\mathbf{A}$), we do not need to request a ZKPoK from the organization in the issuing protocol as the signature's verification algorithm a pairing involving the matrix $\mathbf{A}$ and the organization's public key $\mathsf{opk} = (\mathbf{B}, \mathbf{C})$ is used to check the signature. Hence, a signature that verifies rules out that 1) someone impersonated the issuer signing with a different secret key, and 2) that the public key was maliciously generated. Regarding the showing protocol, the only changes are the addition of NAND and exponentiation proofs. For the latter, we require the verifier to randomly pick the challenge and send it to the user.

For ease of exposition, we present the resulting construction (Scheme 1) in Fig. 5 considering selective disclosures only. We highlight in gray the required changes to do NAND proofs, but both types of proofs could be computed while executing a single showing. If so, a NAND proof increases bandwidth by 4 elements (two from $\mathbb{G}_1$ and two from $\mathbb{G}_2$), as the PoE can reuse the same challenge.

Theorem 5. Scheme 1 is correct.

Theorem 6. If the q-co-DL assumption holds, the ZKPoK's have perfect ZK, SCDS is sound, and $\mathsf{SPS\text{-}EQ}$ is EUF-CMA secure, then Scheme 1 is unforgeable.

Theorem 7. If the DDH assumption holds, the ZKPoK's have perfect ZK, and the $\mathsf{SPS\text{-}EQ}$ perfectly adapts signatures, then Scheme 1 is anonymous.

[1] The security of this integration is discussed in [18] (Appendix J).

Proof. Proof of Theorem 6 follows closely to that presented in [32] but extended to include disjoint sets. Proof of Theorem 7 also follows that in [32] with the exception that we work with a CRS and an accordingly modified definition of perfect adaption. All proofs are provided in [18] (Appendix E).

7.1 Revocation Strategies

The natural approach to revocation would be to follow that described in [24] where they use the fact that randomization of a credential is compatible with the randomization of the accumulator and its corresponding witness. This approach requires the revocation authority to compute and maintain the witness list. As it uses the accumulator from [1], the cost of non-membership proofs is linear in the size of the accumulator (*i.e.*, revoked users), and this should be done at least once by the manager for every user. If, instead, the dynamic variant is used (as discussed in [24]), then users could be given their non-membership witness once and subsequently update it with a single constant size operation. Other approaches for revocation are discussed in [18] (Appendix F).

7.2 Signer-Hiding

We recall that our signature scheme is based on the one from [40] and that we are using the credential framework of [32]. Therefore, as we have $k = 1$ and $\ell = 3$, the public keys consist of two vectors $[\mathbf{B}]_2 \in (\mathbb{G}_2^*)^2$ and $[\mathbf{C}]_2 \in (\mathbb{G}_2^*)^3$, where the secret keys have the form $\mathsf{sk} = (\mathbf{K}_0, \mathbf{K})$ with $\mathbf{K}_0 \xleftarrow{\$} (\mathbb{Z}_p^*)^{2\times 2}$ and $\mathbf{K} \xleftarrow{\$} (\mathbb{Z}_p^*)^{3\times 2}$. With this in mind, we can naturally define equivalence relationships on the key spaces $\mathcal{S}_{\mathsf{sk}} = \{(\mathbb{Z}_p^*)^{2\times 2} \times (\mathbb{Z}_p^*)^{3\times 2}\}$ and $\mathcal{S}_{\mathsf{pk}} = \{(\mathbb{G}_2^*)^2 \times (\mathbb{G}_2^*)^3\}$ as follows:

$$\mathcal{R}_{\mathsf{sk}} = \{(\mathsf{sk}, \tilde{\mathsf{sk}}) \in \mathcal{S}_{\mathsf{sk}} \times \mathcal{S}_{\mathsf{sk}} \mid \exists\, \rho \in \mathbb{Z}_p^* \text{ s.t } \tilde{\mathsf{sk}} = \rho \cdot \mathsf{sk}\}$$
$$\mathcal{R}_{\mathsf{pk}} = \{(\mathsf{pk}, \tilde{\mathsf{pk}}) \in \mathcal{S}_{\mathsf{pk}} \times \mathcal{S}_{\mathsf{pk}} \mid \exists\, \rho \in \mathbb{Z}_p^* \text{ s.t } \tilde{\mathsf{pk}} = \rho \cdot \mathsf{pk}\}$$

If we have a list of public keys $(\mathbf{B}_1, \mathbf{C}_1), ..., (\mathbf{B}_n, \mathbf{C}_n)$ and define the equivalence class of each public key as before $((\mathbf{B}'_i, \mathbf{C}'_i) = (\mathbf{B}_i, \mathbf{C}_i)\cdot\rho)$, we can efficiently prove that a given public key $(\mathbf{B}'_i, \mathbf{C}'_i)$ belongs to the equivalence class of one of the public keys $(\mathbf{B}_1, \mathbf{C}_1), ..., (\mathbf{B}_n, \mathbf{C}_n)$ for some $(\mathbf{B}_i, \mathbf{C}_i)$. The idea is to use a generalized version of the OR-Proof from [19], and building a generalized NIZK OR-Proof for the AND statements of the two components. The new language is defined as follows (remember we use $\ell = 3$):

$$\mathcal{L}_{\bigvee(\mathbf{B}_i \wedge \mathbf{C}_i)_{i\in[n]}} = \{(\mathbf{B}'_i, \mathbf{C}'_i) \in \mathbb{G}_2^{2\times\ell} \mid \exists\, \rho \in \mathbb{Z}_p^* : \vee\ (\mathbf{B}'_i = \mathbf{B}_i \cdot \rho \wedge \mathbf{C}'_i = \mathbf{C}_i \cdot \rho)_{i\in[n]}\}$$

The resulting NIZK argument is given in Fig. 6.

Theorem 8. The proof system given in Fig. 6 is a fully-adaptive NIZK argument for the language $\mathcal{L}_{\bigvee(\mathbf{B}_i \wedge \mathbf{C}_i)_{i\in[n]}}$.

Proof. The proof follows from Theorem 19 in [19]. The only difference is that we rely on the AND composition for sigma protocols to compile the one in [19] using the same challenge for both proofs.

$\underline{\mathsf{ABC.Setup}(1^\lambda, 1^q)}$:

$(\mathsf{BG}, \mathsf{scds_{pp}}) \xleftarrow{\$} \mathsf{SCDS.Setup}(1^\lambda, q)$; $(\mathsf{sps_{pp}}) \xleftarrow{\$} \mathsf{SPS\text{-}EQ.ParGen}(1^\lambda; \mathsf{BG})$;
$r \xleftarrow{\$} \mathbb{Z}_p^*$; $\mathsf{ck} \leftarrow (P_1, rP_1)$; **return** $(\mathsf{BG}, \mathsf{scds_{pp}}, \mathsf{sps_{pp}}, \mathsf{ck})$

$\underline{\mathsf{ABC.TSetup}(1^\lambda, 1^q)}$:

$(\mathsf{BG}, \mathsf{scds_{pp}}, \mathsf{scds_{td}}) \xleftarrow{\$} \mathsf{SCDS.TSetup}(1^\lambda, q)$; $(\mathsf{sps_{pp}}, \mathsf{sps_{td}}) \xleftarrow{\$} \mathsf{SPS\text{-}EQ.TParGen}(1^\lambda; \mathsf{BG})$;
$r \xleftarrow{\$} \mathbb{Z}_p^*$; $\mathsf{ck} \leftarrow (P_1, rP_1)$; $\mathsf{ck_{td}} \leftarrow r$; **return** $((\mathsf{BG}, \mathsf{scds_{pp}}, \mathsf{sps_{pp}}, \mathsf{ck}), (\mathsf{scds_{td}}, \mathsf{sps_{td}}, \mathsf{ck_{td}}))$

$\underline{\mathsf{ABC.OrgKGen}(\mathsf{pp})}$:	$\underline{\mathsf{ABC.UsrKGen}(\mathsf{pp})}$:
return $\mathsf{SPS\text{-}EQ.KGen}(\mathsf{BG}, \mathsf{sps_{pp}}, 3)$	$\mathsf{usk} \xleftarrow{\$} \mathbb{Z}_p^*$; $\mathsf{upk} \leftarrow \mathsf{usk}P_1$ **return** $(\mathsf{usk}, \mathsf{upk})$

$\mathsf{ABC.Obtain}(\mathsf{pp}, \mathsf{usk}, \mathsf{opk}, \mathcal{X})$		$\mathsf{ABC.Issue}(\mathsf{pp}, \mathsf{upk}, \mathsf{osk}, \mathcal{X})$
$r_1, r_2 \xleftarrow{\$} \mathbb{Z}_p^*$; $a \leftarrow r_1 P_1$		
$c \leftarrow \mathsf{Commit}(\mathsf{ck}, a, r_2)$	$\xrightarrow{c}$	
$z \leftarrow r_1 + e \cdot \mathsf{usk}$	$\xleftarrow{e}$	$e \xleftarrow{\$} \mathbb{Z}_p^*$
$(C, O) \leftarrow \mathsf{SCDS.Commit}(\mathsf{scds_{pp}}, \mathcal{X}; \mathsf{usk})$		
$r_3 \xleftarrow{\$} \mathbb{Z}_p^*$; $R \leftarrow r_3 C$	$\xrightarrow{C, R, z, a, r_2}$	**if** $(zP_1 \neq a + e \cdot \mathsf{upk} \vee$ $c \neq \mathsf{Commit}(\mathsf{ck}, a, r_2))$ **return** $\bot$ **if** $(e(C, P_2) \neq e(\mathsf{upk}, \mathsf{Ch}_{\mathcal{X}}(s)P_2)$ $\wedge\ \forall\, x \in \mathcal{X} : xP_1 \neq \mathsf{ek}_1^0)$ **return** $\bot$
	$\xleftarrow{(\sigma, \tau)}$	$(\sigma, \tau) \leftarrow \mathsf{SPS\text{-}EQ.Sign}((C, R, P_1), \mathsf{osk})$
check $\mathsf{SPS\text{-}EQ.Verify}(\mathsf{sps_{pp}}, (C, R, P_1), (\sigma, \tau), \mathsf{opk})$ **return** $\mathsf{cred} = (C, (\sigma, \tau), r_3, O)$		

$\mathsf{ABC.Show}(\mathsf{pp}, \mathsf{usk}, \mathsf{opk}, \mathsf{ek}, \mathcal{S}, \mathsf{cred})$		$\mathsf{ABC.Verify}(\mathsf{pp}, \mathsf{opk}, \mathcal{S})$
parse $\mathsf{cred} = (C, \sigma, r, O)$; $\mu \xleftarrow{\$} \mathbb{Z}_p^*$ **if** $O = (1, (o_1, o_2))$ **then** $O' = (1, (\mu \cdot o_1, o_2))$ **else** $O' = \mu O$ $\sigma' \xleftarrow{\$} \mathsf{SPS\text{-}EQ.ChgRep}(\mathsf{sps_{pp}}, (C, rC, P_1), \sigma, \tau, \mu, \mathsf{opk})$ $(C_1, C_2, C_3) \leftarrow \mu \cdot (C, rC, P_1)$ $\mathsf{cred}' \leftarrow (C_1, C_2, C_3, \sigma')$ $\mathsf{wit} \leftarrow \mathsf{SCDS.OpenSS}(\mathsf{scds_{pp}}, \mu C, \mathcal{S}, \mathsf{ek}, O')$ $r_1, r_2, r_3, r_4 \xleftarrow{\$} \mathbb{Z}_p^*$; $a_1 \leftarrow r_1 C_1$; $a_2 \leftarrow r_3 P_1$ $c_1 \leftarrow \mathsf{Commit}(\mathsf{ck}, a_1, r_2)$		
$c_2 \leftarrow \mathsf{Commit}(\mathsf{ck}, a_2, r_4)$	$\xrightarrow{\mathsf{cred}', \mathsf{wit}, c_1, c_2}$	**parse** $\mathsf{cred}' = (C_1, C_2, C_3, \sigma)$
$\pi \leftarrow \mathsf{SCDS.PoE}(\mathsf{scds_{pp}}, \mathcal{S}, \tilde{e})$	$\xleftarrow{e, \tilde{e}}$	$e, \tilde{e} \xleftarrow{\$} \mathbb{Z}_p^*$
$z_1 \leftarrow r_1 + e \cdot (r \cdot \mu)$; $z_2 \leftarrow r_3 + e \cdot \mu$		
$\Omega = ((z_i, a_i, r_i)_{i \in \{1,2\}}, \pi)$	$\xrightarrow{\Omega}$	**parse** $\Omega = ((z_i, a_i, r_i)_{i \in \{1,2\}}, \pi)$ **check** $z_1 C_1 = a_1 + eC_2$; $z_2 P_1 = a_2 + eC_3$ $c_1 = \mathsf{Commit}(\mathsf{ck}, a_1, r_2)$ $c_2 = \mathsf{Commit}(\mathsf{ck}, a_2, r_4)$ $\mathsf{SPS\text{-}EQ.Verify}(\mathsf{sps_{pp}}, \mathsf{cred}', \mathsf{opk})$ $\mathsf{SCDS.VerifySS}(\mathsf{scds_{pp}}, C_1, \mathcal{S}, \mathsf{wit}; \pi, \tilde{e})$

Fig. 5. Scheme 1.

$\mathsf{PGen}(1^\lambda)$:

$\mathsf{BG} \xleftarrow{\$} \mathsf{BGGen}(1^\lambda);\ z \xleftarrow{\$} \mathbb{Z}_p;\ \mathsf{crs} \leftarrow (\mathsf{BG}, [z]_1);$
$\quad \mathsf{td} \leftarrow z$
return $(\mathsf{crs}, \mathsf{td})$

$\mathsf{PPrv}(\mathsf{crs}, (\mathbf{B}_i, \mathbf{C}_i)_{i\in[n]}, (\mathbf{B}'_i, \mathbf{C}'_i), \rho)$:

$//\ \mathbf{B}'_i = \mathbf{B}_i \cdot \rho \wedge \mathbf{C}'_i = \mathbf{C}_i \cdot \rho$
$s_1, s_2, z_1, \ldots, z_{n-1} \xleftarrow{\$} \mathbb{Z}_p$
$[z_n]_1 \leftarrow [z]_1 - \sum_{j=1}^{j=n-1}[z_j]_1$
$[\mathbf{a}_i^1]_2 \leftarrow s_1\mathbf{B}_i;\ [\mathbf{a}_i^2]_2 \leftarrow s_2\mathbf{C}_i$
$[d_i^1]_1 \leftarrow \rho[z_i]_1+[s_1]_1;\ [d_i^2]_1 \leftarrow \rho[z_i]_1+[s_2]_1$
for all $j \neq i \in [n]$ **do**
$\quad d_j^1, d_j^2 \xleftarrow{\$} \mathbb{Z}_p$
$\quad [\mathbf{a}_j^1]_2 \leftarrow d_j^1\mathbf{B}_j\text{-}z_j\mathbf{B}'_j;\ [\mathbf{a}_j^2]_2 \leftarrow d_j^2\mathbf{C}_j\text{-}z_j\mathbf{C}'_j$
return $(([\mathbf{a}_n^k]_2, [d_n^k]_1)_{n\in[n]}^{k\in[2]}, ([z_j]_1)_{j\in[n-1]})$

$\mathsf{PSim}(\mathsf{crs}, \mathsf{td}, (\mathbf{B}_i, \mathbf{C}_i)_{i\in[n]}, (\mathbf{B}'_i, \mathbf{C}'_i))$:

$z_1, \ldots, z_{n-1} \xleftarrow{\$} \mathbb{Z}_p$
$[z_n]_1 \leftarrow [\mathsf{td}]_1 - \sum_{j=1}^{j=n-1}[z_j]_1$
for all i $\in [n]$ **do**
$\quad d_i^1, d_i^2 \xleftarrow{\$} \mathbb{Z}_p$
$\quad [\mathbf{a}_i^1]_2 \leftarrow d_i^1\mathbf{B}_i\text{-}z_i\mathbf{B}'_i;\ [\mathbf{a}_i^2]_2 \leftarrow d_i^2\mathbf{C}_i\text{-}z_i\mathbf{C}'_i$
return $(([\mathbf{a}_n^k]_2, [d_n^k]_1)_{n\in[n]}^{k\in[2]}, ([z_j]_1)_{j\in[n-1]})$

$\mathsf{PVer}(\mathsf{crs}, (\mathbf{B}_i, \mathbf{C}_i)_{i\in[n]}, (\mathbf{B}'_i, \mathbf{C}'_i), \pi)$:

parse $\pi=(([\mathbf{a}_n^k]_2, [d_n^k]_1)_{n\in[n]}^{k\in[2]}, ([z_j]_1)_{j\in[n-1]})$
$[z_n]_1 = [z]_1 - \sum_{j=1}^{j=n-1}[z_j]_1$
for all i $\in [n]$ **check**
$\quad e([d_i^1]_1, \mathbf{B}_i)=e([z_i]_1, \mathbf{B}'_i)+e([1]_1, [\mathbf{a}_i^1]_2)$
$\quad e([d_i^2]_1, \mathbf{C}_i)=e([z_i]_1, \mathbf{C}'_i)+e([1]_1, [\mathbf{a}_i^2]_2)$

Fig. 6. Fully adaptive NIZK argument for $\mathcal{L}^{\vee}_{(\mathbf{B}_i \wedge \mathbf{C}_i)_{i\in[n]}}$

We now explain how the above NIZK can be used to hide the identity of a signer. First, we need to consider a scenario in which n-authorities can issue credentials to different sets of users. As we are in the classical setting, we also assume that every user gets a credential from one of the n-authorities and that the organization keys are certified and publicly available.

When showing a credential, the verifier needs to check the signature using the corresponding public key. The idea is to use the above NIZK proof so that a user can randomize the public key and present this randomized key to the verifier, which in turn will check the NIZK to verify that the public key is valid (*i.e.*, it belongs to the equivalence class of one of the n-authorities).

Signatures need to be adapted by the users so that they can be verified with the randomized public key. Therefore, we consider the definition of mercurial signatures [20], which includes algorithms ConvertPK, ConvertSK and ConvertSig, and introduce the following notion.

PERFECT ADAPTION OF SIGNATURES (under malicious keys in the honest parameters model) with respect to the *key space*; An SPS-EQ over a message space $\mathcal{S}_\mathbf{m}$ perfectly adapts signatures with respect to the key space $\mathcal{S}_{\mathsf{pk}}$ if for all tuples $(\mathsf{pp},[\mathsf{pk}]_j,[\mathbf{m}]_i,(\sigma,\tau),\rho)$ where $\mathsf{pp} \xleftarrow{\$} \mathsf{ParGen}(1^\lambda)$, $[\mathsf{pk}]_j \in \mathcal{S}_{\mathsf{pk}}$, $[\mathbf{m}]_i \in \mathcal{S}_\mathbf{m}$, $\mathsf{Verify}([\mathbf{m}]_i, (\sigma, \tau), [\mathsf{pk}]_j) = 1$ and $\rho \in \mathbb{Z}_p^*$, we have that the output of $\mathsf{ConvertSig}([\mathbf{m}]_i, (\sigma, \tau), \rho, [\mathsf{pk}]_j)$ is σ^*, with σ^* being a random element in the space of signatures, conditioned on $\mathsf{Verify}([\mathbf{m}]_i, \sigma^*, \mathsf{ConvertPK}([\mathsf{pk}]_j, \rho)) = 1$.

ConvertSig is analogous to the ChgRep algorithm, but restricted to act on the equivalence class defined by the key space. The algorithms ConvertPK and ConvertSK are just defined to abstract the computation of new representatives.

As our signature construction is compatible with the joint executions of the algorithms ChgRep and ConvertSig, we define below a general notion for perfect adaption where the ChgRep algorithm acts on all the equivalence classes.

PERFECT ADAPTION OF SIGNATURES (under malicious keys in the honest parameters model); An SPS-EQ over $\mathcal{S}_{\mathbf{m}}$ perfectly adapts signatures with respect to the key space $\mathcal{S}_{\mathsf{pk}}$ if for all tuples $(\mathsf{pp}, [\mathsf{pk}]_j, [\mathbf{m}]_i, (\sigma, \tau), \mu, \rho)$ where $\mathsf{pp} \xleftarrow{\$} \mathsf{ParGen}(1^\lambda)$, $[\mathsf{pk}]_j \in \mathcal{S}_{\mathsf{pk}}$, $[\mathbf{m}]_i \in \mathcal{S}_{\mathbf{m}}$, $\mathsf{Verify}([\mathbf{m}]_i, (\sigma, \tau), [\mathsf{pk}]_j) = 1$ and $\mu, \rho \in \mathbb{Z}_p^*$ we have that the output of $\mathsf{ChgRep}([\mathbf{m}]_i, (\sigma, \tau), \mu, \rho, [\mathsf{pk}]_j)$ is $([\mu \cdot \mathbf{m}]_i, \sigma^*)$, with σ^* being a random element in the space of signatures, conditioned on $\mathsf{Verify}([\mu \cdot \mathbf{m}]_i, \sigma^*, \mathsf{ConvertPK}([\mathsf{pk}]_j, \rho)) = 1$.

Theorem 9. The above extension applied to the SPS-EQ from Fig. 4 perfectly adapts signatures (under malicious keys in the honest parameter model).

Proof. It follows from the security of SPS-EQ and the definition of perfect adaption for mercurial signatures (Appendix D and H from [18]).

We now formalize the signer-hiding notion and show that our construction satisfies it as it perfectly adapts signatures.

SIGNER-HIDING. An ABC system supports signer-hiding if for all $\lambda > 0$, all $q > 0$, all $n > 0$, all $t > 0$, all $\mathcal{X}$ with $0 < |\mathcal{X}| \leq t$, all $\emptyset \neq \mathcal{S} \subset \mathcal{X}$ and $\emptyset \neq \mathcal{D} \nsubseteq \mathcal{X}$ with $0 < |\mathcal{D}| \leq t$, and p.p.t adversaries $\mathcal{A}$, the following holds.

$$\Pr\left[\begin{array}{l} \mathsf{pp} \xleftarrow{\$} \mathsf{Setup}(1^\lambda, 1^q); \\ \forall\, i \in [n] : (\mathsf{osk}_i, \mathsf{opk}_i) \xleftarrow{\$} \mathsf{OrgKGen}(\mathsf{pp}); \\ (\mathsf{usk}, \mathsf{upk}) \xleftarrow{\$} \mathsf{UsrKGen}(\mathsf{pp}); j \xleftarrow{\$} [n]; \\ (\mathsf{cred}, \top) \xleftarrow{\$} (\mathsf{Obtain}(\mathsf{usk}, \mathsf{opk}_j, \mathcal{X}), \mathsf{Issue}(\mathsf{upk}, \mathsf{osk}_j, \mathcal{X})); \\ j^* \xleftarrow{\$} \mathcal{A}^{\mathcal{O}_{\mathsf{Show}}}(\mathsf{pp}, \mathcal{S}, \mathcal{D}, (\mathsf{opk}_i)_{i \in [n]}) \end{array} : j^* = j \right] \leq \frac{1}{n}$$

where the oracle $\mathcal{O}_{\mathsf{Show}}$ is defined as in Sect. 6.

Theorem 10. If the underlying signature scheme is a SPS-EQ which perfectly adapts signatures (under malicious keys in the honest parameter model), the resulting ABC from Sect. 7.2 supports signer-hiding.

Proof. Let us first observe that the adversary can guess the bit j^* with probability $1/n$. By definition of perfect adaption, for all tuples $(\mathsf{pp}, [\mathsf{opk}]_j, [\mathbf{m}]_i, (\sigma, \tau), \mu, \rho)$ s.t $(\sigma, \tau) \xleftarrow{\$} \mathsf{Sign}(\mathsf{pp}, \mathsf{osk}_j, [\mathbf{m}]_i)$, we have that $[\mu \cdot \mathbf{m}]_i$ and $[\rho \cdot \mathsf{opk}]_j$ are identically distributed in the message and key spaces, where $([\mu \cdot \mathbf{m}]_i, \sigma^*) \leftarrow \mathsf{ChgRep}([\mathbf{m}]_i, (\sigma, \tau), \mu, \rho, [\mathsf{opk}]_j)$ and $[\rho \cdot \mathsf{opk}]_j \leftarrow \mathsf{ConvertPK}(\mathsf{opk}_j, \rho)$. Furthermore, we also have that σ^* is a random element in the space of signatures conditioned on $\mathsf{Verify}([\mu \cdot \mathbf{m}]_i, \sigma^*, [\rho \cdot \mathsf{opk}]_j) = 1$. Therefore, an adversary with access to $[\mu \cdot \mathbf{m}]_i$, σ^* and $[\rho \cdot \mathsf{opk}]_j$ can only guess the bit j^* with probability at most $1/n$. □

INTEGRATION WITH OUR ABC SCHEME. As our NIZK argument is fully adaptive, users can choose the size of the anonymity set (*i.e.*, the set of public keys in the OR-Proof). We find this approach much simpler than using delegatable credentials to achieve a similar result as users do not need to interact with the organizations to compute the NIZK proof nor to adapt the signature. Moreover, there is no need to use pseudonyms for public and secret keys. We essentially compute public key's pseudonyms "on-the-fly" guaranteeing that the signature adaption is done with respect to a valid public key. In other words, our NIZK argument is a proof of correct randomization, where the same randomizer is used to adapt the signature and generate a pseudonymous public key. A complete figure for the proposed ABC, including the signer-hiding extension as well as NAND proofs, is given in [18] (Appendix I).

EFFICIENCY ANALYSIS. As the proof size is $9n - 1$ for an anonymity set of n-authorities, communication bandwidth will no longer be constant. Nevertheless, given the previously mentioned advantages we believe that this is a fair trade-off for the added functionality. In terms of computational cost, it is also substantially more efficient than similar variants (see, for instance, Table 2 from [19]).

8 Comparison of State-of-the-art ABC

We provide comparisons on the efficiency of state-of-the-art ABC and ours (Sect. 7) on Table 3. For ease of exposition, we list the work from [32] next to ours, and consider an instantiation of it in the CRS model, and using the same ZKPoK's as the ones used in Sect. 7.

When looking at a whole, the work from Sanders [46] presents very good results while also allowing showings to prove relationships between attributes and to consider malicious keys. Nevertheless, security of the related construction is proven in the GGM model and thus, falls short in that aspect. The same also applies to the works from [38] and [32].

While for the comparisons only the classical setting (credentials are issued by a single authority) was considered, it is worth to mention that [38] does consider multi-authorities. As authors point out, in order to allow multi-authorities they base their construction on aggregate signatures, and obtain the most efficient showing for the users. Their security model follows the game-based approach from [32] but because of the multi-authority setting, they also consider malicious credential issuers, with adaptive corruptions, and collusions with malicious users. Unfortunately, this is done assuming that the keys are *honestly* generated.

[49] uses a set-commitment scheme which alongside an SDH-based signature, leads to a credential system that supports a variety of show proofs for complex statements among which AND and NAND are included. For this reason, we also compare our work with the one from [49] considering NAND showings. In terms of security models, authors provide a formalization for impersonation attacks and prove their scheme secure against impersonation under active and concurrent attacks. The security of their ABC scheme is proven in the standard model and providing a tight reduction.

Considering the different trade-offs, our ABC provides very similar performance when compared to [32] and it is not too distant from the most efficient ones either. Unlike the rest, it can be adapted to different scenarios in case that reducing the verification cost is not needed, and it can also be efficiently adapted to provide revocation features. Furthermore, as for many practical applications

Table 3. Efficiency of ABCs considering issuing and showing interactions (the number of pairings is marked in bold).

ABC	[46]	[38]	[49]	[32]	Section 7
			Parameters size (n-attributes)		
ek	$(\frac{n^2+n+2}{2})_{\mathbb{G}_1} + n_{\mathbb{G}_2}$	$(2n+2)_{\mathbb{G}_2}$	$(n+1)_{\mathbb{G}_1} + (n+1)_{\mathbb{G}_2}$	$(n+1)_{\mathbb{G}_1} + (n+1)_{\mathbb{G}_2}$	$(n+1)_{\mathbb{G}_1} + (n+1)_{\mathbb{G}_2}$
Cred	$2_{\mathbb{G}_2}$	$4_{\mathbb{G}_1}$	$1_{\mathbb{G}_1} + 6_{\mathbb{Z}_p}$	$3_{\mathbb{G}_1} + 1_{\mathbb{G}_2} + 2_{\mathbb{Z}_p}$	$18_{\mathbb{G}_1} + 6_{\mathbb{G}_2} + 3_{\mathbb{Z}_p}$
			Bandwidth		
Issue	$4_{\mathbb{G}_2} + 2_{\mathbb{Z}_p}$	$n_{\mathbb{G}_1}$	$3_{\mathbb{G}_1}+(n+3)_{\mathbb{Z}_p}$	$12_{\mathbb{G}_1} + 1_{\mathbb{G}_2} + 8_{\mathbb{Z}_p}$	$14_{\mathbb{G}_1} + 11_{\mathbb{G}_2} + 7_{\mathbb{Z}_p}$
Show	$2_{\mathbb{G}_1} + 2_{\mathbb{G}_2} + 1_{\mathbb{G}_T} + 2_{\mathbb{Z}_p}$	$3_{\mathbb{G}_1} + 1_{\mathbb{Z}_p}$	$3_{\mathbb{G}_1} + 5_{\mathbb{Z}_p}$	$10_{\mathbb{G}_1} + 1_{\mathbb{G}_2} + 8_{\mathbb{Z}_p}$	$18_{\mathbb{G}_1} + 14_{\mathbb{G}_2} + 4_{\mathbb{Z}_p}$
			k-of-n attributes (AND)		
Usr	$(2(n\text{-}k)+2)_{\mathbb{G}_1}, 2_{\mathbb{G}_2}$, **1**	$6_{\mathbb{G}_1}$	$(6+n\text{-}k)_{\mathbb{G}_1}$	$(11+n\text{-}k)_{\mathbb{G}_1}, 1_{\mathbb{G}_2}$**8**,	$(20+n\text{-}k)_{\mathbb{G}_1}$, $(k\text{-}1)_{\mathbb{G}_2}$,**19**
Ver	$(k{+}1)_{\mathbb{G}_1}, 1_{\mathbb{G}_T}$,**5**	$4_{\mathbb{G}_1}, 2n_{\mathbb{G}_2}$,**3**	$5_{\mathbb{G}_1}, (k+1)_{\mathbb{G}_2}$,**3**	$4_{\mathbb{G}_1}, (k+1)_{\mathbb{G}_2}$,**10**	$10_{\mathbb{G}_1}$,**16**
			k-of-n attributes (NAND)		
Usr	N/A	N/A	$(6+n)_{\mathbb{G}_1}$	N/A	$(31+n)_{\mathbb{G}_1}$, $(9+2k)_{\mathbb{G}_2}$,**19**
Ver	N/A	N/A	$(2k+5)_{\mathbb{G}_1}$, $(k+3)_{\mathbb{G}_2}$,**3**	N/A	$10_{\mathbb{G}_1}$,**17**

the ability to perform AND and NAND showings suffices, we also achieve a good level of expressiveness too. Finally, the signer-hiding feature makes it suitable for scenarios in which the rest of the alternatives struggle.

9 Conclusions and Future Work

Our results explore multiple paths to extend the ABC framework of [32] to include more applications and scenarios where it can be used. In order to improve expressiveness of the set-commitment scheme in [32] we allow openings on sets of attributes disjoint from those possessed by a user. We also enhance efficiency by employing the trick of allowing the prover to compute a proof of exponentiation leaving the verifier only to compute a polynomial division.

Our signature scheme is based on [40] where we adapt the SPS-EQ scheme by alleviating the need to build a QA-NIZK incorporating results from the recent framework of [19]. With this fully adaptive NIZK, we find further interesting applications by looking at equivalence classes on the key-space. We develop a signer-hiding notion to allow a credential-bearing user to hide their issuing organization upon presentation of the credential. As we increasingly see cases of (algorithmic) bias against users, notions such as this are of growing importance. Moreover, we also present interesting directions to integrate revocation features.

We worked in the classical setting where each credential is issued by a single authority. It would be interesting to follow the related work on aggregatable signatures to see if we could lift SPS-EQ to the multi-authority setting.

While our set-commitment scheme is more expressive than [32] it is still less expressive than [49]. Hence, it would be interesting to see if the set-commitment scheme introduced there would yield greater expressiveness to the ABC scheme from this work. Likewise, to verify if the stronger security notions presented here, could enhance the construction in [49].

Acknowledgements. We thank the anonymous reviewers for their valuable feedback. The European Commission partially supported Octavio Perez Kempner's work as part of the CUREX project (H2020-SC1-FA-DTS-2018-1 under grant agreement No 826404).

References

1. Au, M.H., Tsang, P.P., Susilo, W., Mu, Y.: Dynamic universal accumulators for DDH groups and their application to attribute-based anonymous credential systems. In: Fischlin, M. (ed.) CT-RSA 2009. LNCS, vol. 5473, pp. 295–308. Springer, Heidelberg (2009). https://doi.org/10.1007/978-3-642-00862-7_20
2. Backes, M., Hanzlik, L., Kluczniak, K., Schneider, J.: Signatures with flexible public key: introducing equivalence classes for public keys. In: Peyrin, T., Galbraith, S. (eds.) ASIACRYPT 2018. LNCS, vol. 11273, pp. 405–434. Springer, Cham (2018). https://doi.org/10.1007/978-3-030-03329-3_14
3. Backes, M., Hanzlik, L., Schneider-Bensch, J.: Membership privacy for fully dynamic group signatures. In: Proceedings of the 2019 ACM SIGSAC Conference on Computer and Communications Security, pp. 2181–2198. CCS 2019, Association for Computing Machinery, New York, NY, USA (2019)
4. Baldimtsi, F., Lysyanskaya, A.: Anonymous credentials light. In: Proceedings of the ACM Conference on Computer and Communications Security, pp. 1087–1098, November 2013
5. Belenkiy, M., Camenisch, J., Chase, M., Kohlweiss, M., Lysyanskaya, A., Shacham, H.: Randomizable proofs and delegatable anonymous credentials. In: Halevi, S. (ed.) CRYPTO 2009. LNCS, vol. 5677, pp. 108–125. Springer, Heidelberg (2009). https://doi.org/10.1007/978-3-642-03356-8_7
6. Blazy, O., Kiltz, E., Pan, J.: (Hierarchical) identity-based encryption from affine message authentication. In: Garay, J.A., Gennaro, R. (eds.) CRYPTO 2014. LNCS, vol. 8616, pp. 408–425. Springer, Heidelberg (2014). https://doi.org/10.1007/978-3-662-44371-2_23
7. Bobolz, J., Eidens, F., Krenn, S., Ramacher, S., Samelin, K.: Issuer-hiding attribute-based credentials. In: Conti, M., Stevens, M., Krenn, S. (eds.) Cryptology and Network Security, pp. 158–178. Springer, Cham (2021)
8. Boneh, D., Bünz, B., Fisch, B.: Batching techniques for accumulators with applications to IOPs and stateless blockchains. In: Boldyreva, A., Micciancio, D. (eds.) CRYPTO 2019. LNCS, vol. 11692, pp. 561–586. Springer, Cham (2019). https://doi.org/10.1007/978-3-030-26948-7_20
9. Brands, S.A.: Rethinking Public Key Infrastructures and Digital Certificates: Building in Privacy. MIT Press, Cambridge (2000)
10. Bultel, X., Lafourcade, P., Lai, R.W.F., Malavolta, G., Schröder, D., Thyagarajan, S.A.K.: Efficient invisible and unlinkable sanitizable signatures. In: Lin, D., Sako, K. (eds.) PKC 2019. LNCS, vol. 11442, pp. 159–189. Springer, Cham (2019). https://doi.org/10.1007/978-3-030-17253-4_6
11. Camenisch, J., Dubovitskaya, M., Haralambiev, K., Kohlweiss, M.: Composable and modular anonymous credentials: definitions and practical constructions. In: Iwata, T., Cheon, J.H. (eds.) ASIACRYPT 2015. LNCS, vol. 9453, pp. 262–288. Springer, Heidelberg (2015). https://doi.org/10.1007/978-3-662-48800-3_11

12. Camenisch, J., Lysyanskaya, A.: A signature scheme with efficient protocols. In: Cimato, S., Persiano, G., Galdi, C. (eds.) SCN 2002. LNCS, vol. 2576, pp. 268–289. Springer, Heidelberg (2003). https://doi.org/10.1007/3-540-36413-7_20
13. Camenisch, J., Lysyanskaya, A.: Signature schemes and anonymous credentials from bilinear maps. In: Franklin, M. (ed.) CRYPTO 2004. LNCS, vol. 3152, pp. 56–72. Springer, Heidelberg (2004). https://doi.org/10.1007/978-3-540-28628-8_4
14. Canard, S., Lescuyer, R.: Anonymous credentials from (Indexed) aggregate signatures. In: Proceedings of the 7th ACM Workshop on Digital Identity Management, DIM 2011, pp. 53–62. Association for Computing Machinery, New York, NY, USA (2011)
15. Canard, S., Lescuyer, R.: Protecting privacy by sanitizing personal data: a new approach to anonymous credentials. In: Proceedings of the 8th ACM SIGSAC Symposium on Information, Computer and Communications Security, ASIA CCS 2013, pp. 381–392. Association for Computing Machinery, New York, NY, USA (2013)
16. Chase, M., Kohlweiss, M., Lysyanskaya, A., Meiklejohn, S.: Malleable proof systems and applications. In: Pointcheval, D., Johansson, T. (eds.) EUROCRYPT 2012. LNCS, vol. 7237, pp. 281–300. Springer, Heidelberg (2012). https://doi.org/10.1007/978-3-642-29011-4_18
17. Chase, M., Lysyanskaya, A.: On signatures of knowledge. In: Dwork, C. (ed.) CRYPTO 2006. LNCS, vol. 4117, pp. 78–96. Springer, Heidelberg (2006). https://doi.org/10.1007/11818175_5
18. Connolly, A., Lafourcade, P., Perez Kempner, O.: Improved constructions of anonymous credentials from structure-preserving signatures on equivalence classes. Cryptology ePrint Archive, Report 2021/1680 (2021). https://ia.cr/2021/1680
19. Couteau, G., Hartmann, D.: Shorter non-interactive zero-knowledge arguments and ZAPs for algebraic languages. In: Micciancio, D., Ristenpart, T. (eds.) CRYPTO 2020. LNCS, vol. 12172, pp. 768–798. Springer, Cham (2020). https://doi.org/10.1007/978-3-030-56877-1_27
20. Crites, E.C., Lysyanskaya, A.: Delegatable anonymous credentials from mercurial signatures. In: Matsui, M. (ed.) CT-RSA 2019. LNCS, vol. 11405, pp. 535–555. Springer, Cham (2019). https://doi.org/10.1007/978-3-030-12612-4_27
21. Crites, E.C., Lysyanskaya, A.: Mercurial signatures for variable-length messages. Proc. Privacy Enhancing Technol. **2021**(4), 441–463 (2021)
22. Damgård, I.: Efficient concurrent zero-knowledge in the auxiliary string model. In: Preneel, B. (ed.) EUROCRYPT 2000. LNCS, vol. 1807, pp. 418–430. Springer, Heidelberg (2000). https://doi.org/10.1007/3-540-45539-6_30
23. Datta, P., Komargodski, I., Waters, B.: Decentralized multi-authority ABE for DNFs from LWE. In: Canteaut, A., Standaert, F.-X. (eds.) EUROCRYPT 2021. LNCS, vol. 12696, pp. 177–209. Springer, Cham (2021). https://doi.org/10.1007/978-3-030-77870-5_7
24. Derler, D., Hanser, C., Slamanig, D.: A new approach to efficient revocable attribute-based anonymous credentials. In: Groth, J. (ed.) IMACC 2015. LNCS, vol. 9496, pp. 57–74. Springer, Cham (2015). https://doi.org/10.1007/978-3-319-27239-9_4
25. Derler, D., Hanser, C., Slamanig, D.: Revisiting cryptographic accumulators, additional properties and relations to other primitives. In: Nyberg, K. (ed.) CT-RSA 2015. LNCS, vol. 9048, pp. 127–144. Springer, Cham (2015). https://doi.org/10.1007/978-3-319-16715-2_7

26. Derler, D., Slamanig, D.: Highly-efficient fully-anonymous dynamic group signatures. In: Proceedings of the 2018 on Asia Conference on Computer and Communications Security, ASIACCS 2018, pp. 551–565. Association for Computing Machinery, New York, NY, USA (2018)
27. Escala, A., Herold, G., Kiltz, E., Ràfols, C., Villar, J.: An algebraic framework for Diffie-Hellman assumptions. In: Canetti, R., Garay, J.A. (eds.) CRYPTO 2013. LNCS, vol. 8043, pp. 129–147. Springer, Heidelberg (2013). https://doi.org/10.1007/978-3-642-40084-1_8
28. Fuchsbauer, G., Gay, R.: Weakly secure equivalence-class signatures from standard assumptions. In: Abdalla, M., Dahab, R. (eds.) PKC 2018. LNCS, vol. 10770, pp. 153–183. Springer, Cham (2018). https://doi.org/10.1007/978-3-319-76581-5_6
29. Fuchsbauer, G., Gay, R., Kowalczyk, L., Orlandi, C.: Access control encryption for equality, comparison, and more. In: Fehr, S. (ed.) PKC 2017. LNCS, vol. 10175, pp. 88–118. Springer, Heidelberg (2017). https://doi.org/10.1007/978-3-662-54388-7_4
30. Fuchsbauer, G., Hanser, C., Kamath, C., Slamanig, D.: Practical round-optimal blind signatures in the standard model from weaker assumptions. In: Zikas, V., De Prisco, R. (eds.) SCN 2016. LNCS, vol. 9841, pp. 391–408. Springer, Cham (2016). https://doi.org/10.1007/978-3-319-44618-9_21
31. Fuchsbauer, G., Hanser, C., Slamanig, D.: Practical round-optimal blind signatures in the standard model. In: Gennaro, R., Robshaw, M. (eds.) CRYPTO 2015. LNCS, vol. 9216, pp. 233–253. Springer, Heidelberg (2015). https://doi.org/10.1007/978-3-662-48000-7_12
32. Fuchsbauer, G., Hanser, C., Slamanig, D.: Structure-preserving signatures on equivalence classes and constant-size anonymous credentials. J. Cryptol. **32**(2), 498–546 (2018). https://doi.org/10.1007/s00145-018-9281-4
33. Gay, R., Hofheinz, D., Kohl, L.: Kurosawa-Desmedt meets tight security. In: Katz, J., Shacham, H. (eds.) CRYPTO 2017. LNCS, vol. 10403, pp. 133–160. Springer, Cham (2017). https://doi.org/10.1007/978-3-319-63697-9_5
34. Gay, R., Hofheinz, D., Kohl, L., Pan, J.: More efficient (Almost) tightly secure structure-preserving signatures. In: Nielsen, J.B., Rijmen, V. (eds.) EUROCRYPT 2018. LNCS, vol. 10821, pp. 230–258. Springer, Cham (2018). https://doi.org/10.1007/978-3-319-78375-8_8
35. Ghosh, E., Ohrimenko, O., Papadopoulos, D., Tamassia, R., Triandopoulos, N.: Zero-knowledge accumulators and set algebra. In: Cheon, J.H., Takagi, T. (eds.) ASIACRYPT 2016. LNCS, vol. 10032, pp. 67–100. Springer, Heidelberg (2016). https://doi.org/10.1007/978-3-662-53890-6_3
36. Hanser, C., Slamanig, D.: Structure-preserving signatures on equivalence classes and their application to anonymous credentials. In: Sarkar, P., Iwata, T. (eds.) ASIACRYPT 2014. LNCS, vol. 8873, pp. 491–511. Springer, Heidelberg (2014). https://doi.org/10.1007/978-3-662-45611-8_26
37. Hofheinz, D.: Adaptive partitioning. In: Coron, J.-S., Nielsen, J.B. (eds.) EUROCRYPT 2017. LNCS, vol. 10212, pp. 489–518. Springer, Cham (2017). https://doi.org/10.1007/978-3-319-56617-7_17
38. Hébant, C., Pointcheval, D.: Traceable constant-size multi-authority credentials. Cryptology ePrint Archive, Report 2020/657 (2020)
39. Kate, A., Zaverucha, G.M., Goldberg, I.: Constant-size commitments to polynomials and their applications. In: Abe, M. (ed.) ASIACRYPT 2010. LNCS, vol. 6477, pp. 177–194. Springer, Heidelberg (2010). https://doi.org/10.1007/978-3-642-17373-8_11

40. Khalili, M., Slamanig, D., Dakhilalian, M.: Structure-preserving signatures on equivalence classes from standard assumptions. In: Galbraith, S.D., Moriai, S. (eds.) Advances in Cryptology - ASIACRYPT 2019, pp. 63–93. Springer, Cham (2019). https://doi.org/10.1007/978-3-030-34618-8_3
41. Kiltz, E., Pan, J., Wee, H.: Structure-preserving signatures from standard assumptions, revisited. In: Gennaro, R., Robshaw, M. (eds.) CRYPTO 2015. LNCS, vol. 9216, pp. 275–295. Springer, Heidelberg (2015). https://doi.org/10.1007/978-3-662-48000-7_14
42. Morillo, P., Ràfols, C., Villar, J.L.: The Kernel matrix Diffie-Hellman assumption. In: Cheon, J.H., Takagi, T. (eds.) ASIACRYPT 2016. LNCS, vol. 10031, pp. 729–758. Springer, Heidelberg (2016). https://doi.org/10.1007/978-3-662-53887-6_27
43. Nguyen, L.: Accumulators from bilinear pairings and applications. In: Menezes, A. (ed.) CT-RSA 2005. LNCS, vol. 3376, pp. 275–292. Springer, Heidelberg (2005). https://doi.org/10.1007/978-3-540-30574-3_19
44. Papamanthou, C., Tamassia, R., Triandopoulos, N.: Optimal verification of operations on dynamic sets. In: Rogaway, P. (ed.) CRYPTO 2011. LNCS, vol. 6841, pp. 91–110. Springer, Heidelberg (2011). https://doi.org/10.1007/978-3-642-22792-9_6
45. Ràfols, C.: Stretching Groth-Sahai: Nizk proofs of partial satisfiability. In: Dodis, Y., Nielsen, J.B. (eds.) Theory of Cryptography, pp. 247–276. Springer, Heidelberg (2015). https://doi.org/10.1007/978-3-662-46497-7_10
46. Sanders, O.: Efficient redactable signature and application to anonymous credentials. In: Kiayias, A., Kohlweiss, M., Wallden, P., Zikas, V. (eds.) PKC 2020. LNCS, vol. 12111, pp. 628–656. Springer, Cham (2020). https://doi.org/10.1007/978-3-030-45388-6_22
47. Shoup, V.: Lower bounds for discrete logarithms and related problems. In: Fumy, W. (ed.) EUROCRYPT 1997. LNCS, vol. 1233, pp. 256–266. Springer, Heidelberg (1997). https://doi.org/10.1007/3-540-69053-0_18
48. Sonnino, A., Al-Bassam, M., Bano, S., Meiklejohn, S., Danezis, G.: Coconut: threshold issuance selective disclosure credentials with applications to distributed ledgers. In: The Network and Distributed System Security Symposium (NDSS) (2019)
49. Tan, S.-Y., Groß, T.: MoniPoly—an expressive q-SDH-based anonymous attribute-based credential system. In: Moriai, S., Wang, H. (eds.) ASIACRYPT 2020. LNCS, vol. 12493, pp. 498–526. Springer, Cham (2020). https://doi.org/10.1007/978-3-030-64840-4_17
50. Thakur, S.: Batching non-membership proofs with bilinear accumulators. IACR Cryptol. ePrint Arch. **2019**, 1147 (2019)
51. Wesolowski, B.: Efficient verifiable delay functions (extended version). J. Cryptol. **33**(4), 2113–2147 (2020)
52. Zurich, I.R.: Specification of the identity mixer cryptographic library v2.3.0. (2013)

Traceable PRFs: Full Collusion Resistance and Active Security

Sarasij Maitra[1] and David J. Wu[2](✉)

[1] University of Virginia, Charlottesville, VA, USA
sm3vg@virginia.edu
[2] University of Texas at Austin, Austin, TX, USA
dwu4@cs.utexas.edu

Abstract. The main goal of traceable cryptography is to protect against unauthorized redistribution of cryptographic functionalities. Such schemes provide a way to embed identities (i.e., a "mark") within cryptographic objects (e.g., decryption keys in an encryption scheme, signing keys in a signature scheme). In turn, the tracing guarantee ensures that any "pirate device" that successfully replicates the underlying functionality can be successfully traced to the set of identities used to build the device.

In this work, we study traceable pseudorandom functions (PRFs). As PRFs are the workhorses of symmetric cryptography, traceable PRFs are useful for augmenting symmetric cryptographic primitives with strong traceable security guarantees. However, existing constructions of traceable PRFs either rely on strong notions like indistinguishability obfuscation or satisfy weak security guarantees like single-key security (i.e., tracing only works against adversaries that possess a *single* marked key).

In this work, we show how to use fingerprinting codes to upgrade a single-key traceable PRF into a *fully collusion resistant* traceable PRF, where security holds regardless of how many keys the adversary possesses. We additionally introduce a stronger notion of security where tracing security holds even against *active adversaries* that have oracle access to the tracing algorithm. In conjunction with known constructions of single-key traceable PRFs, we obtain the first fully collusion resistant traceable PRF from standard lattice assumptions. Our traceable PRFs directly imply new lattice-based secret-key traitor tracing schemes that are CCA-secure and where tracing security holds against active adversaries that have access to the tracing oracle.

1 Introduction

Traitor tracing [CFN94] and software watermarking schemes [BGI+01,BGI+12] are cryptographic primitives for protecting against the unauthorized distribution

D. J. Wu—Research supported by NSF CNS-1917414, CNS-2045180, and a Microsoft Research Faculty Fellowship.

G. Hanaoka et al. (Eds.): PKC 2022, LNCS 13177, pp. 439–469, 2022.
https://doi.org/10.1007/978-3-030-97121-2_16

of software. In both settings, a content distributor can embed some special information (e.g., a "mark" or a "tag") into a program in a way that preserves the functionality of the program while ensuring that it is difficult for an adversary to remove the tag from the program without destroying its functionality. Schemes that provide strong security guarantees have typically focused on cryptographic programs. Specifically, traitor tracing schemes focus on protecting the decryption functionality in a (public-key) encryption scheme [CFN94,BSW06,BN08, GKW18,Zha20] while software watermarking has focused on symmetric primitives like pseudorandom functions (PRFs) [CHN+16,KW17,QWZ18,YAYX20] and on public-key primitives such as public-key encryption or digital signatures [GKM+19,Nis20].

Traceable PRFs. In this work, we study traceable PRFs, a notion recently introduced by Goyal et al. [GKWW21]. Recall first that a PRF [GGM84] is a keyed function $\mathsf{PRF}(k, \cdot)$ whose input/output behavior is computationally indistinguishable from a truly random function. As PRFs are the workhorses of symmetric cryptography, traceable PRFs are sufficient to augment a wide range of symmetric primitives with tracing capabilities: this can include notions such as symmetric encryption (which corresponds to secret-key traitor tracing), message authentication codes, or symmetric challenge-response authentication systems.

In a traceable PRF, the holder of the PRF key k can issue "marked" keys k_{id} associated with an identity id. First, the marked key k_{id} can be used to evaluate the PRF almost everywhere: namely, there is an efficient evaluation algorithm Eval where $\mathsf{Eval}(k_{\mathsf{id}}, x) = \mathsf{PRF}(k, x)$ for all but a negligible fraction of elements in the domain. Moreover, there is a tracing algorithm Trace that takes any "useful" program D and outputs at least one of the identity keys k_{id} that was used to construct D. More precisely, if an adversary that has keys $k_{\mathsf{id}_1}, \ldots, k_{\mathsf{id}_q}$ manages to create a "useful" program D, the tracing algorithm on program D should successfully output at least one of the identities $\mathsf{id}_1, \ldots, \mathsf{id}_q$.[1]

The question is how to define the "usefulness" of a program D. In the setting of watermarkable PRFs [CHN+16], a program D is considered useful only if $D(x) = \mathsf{PRF}(k, x)$ on at least a $(1/2 + \varepsilon)$-fraction of elements in the domain; in other words, programs are considered useful if they *exactly* preserve the output of the original PRF on most inputs. Goyal et al. [GKWW21] showed that this security notion is inadequate in settings where an adversarial program can break the security of a particular application without necessarily replicating the exact input/output behavior of the PRF. To address the weaknesses of the prevailing security notions for watermarking, Goyal et al. strengthened the "usefulness" definition on a program D to capture *all* programs that can successfully break (weak) pseudorandomness of the PRF. Specifically, any efficient program D that is able to distinguish a sequence $(x_1, \mathsf{PRF}(k, x_1)), \ldots, (x_n, \mathsf{PRF}(k, x_n))$ from $(x_1, f(x_1)), \ldots, (x_n, f(x_n))$ with probability $1/2 + \varepsilon$, where $x_1, \ldots, x_n$ are

[1] While it might seem more natural to require that Trace outputs all of the identities $\mathsf{id}_1, \ldots, \mathsf{id}_q$, this requirement is impossible since an adversary can build its program D from just one of the keys it requested (and ignore all of the other ones).

random domain elements, f is a truly random function, and ε is non-negligible, is considered to be useful. In other words, the tracing algorithm should successfully extract an identity from any efficient distinguisher D that can *distinguish* PRF evaluations on random domain elements.

Collusion Resistance. An important property in the study of traceable cryptography is collusion resistance, which requires that tracing security holds even if the adversary obtains *multiple* marked keys. We say a scheme is "fully collusion resistant" if security holds against adversaries that can obtain any unbounded polynomial number of keys.

Goyal et al. [GKWW21] gave two constructions of traceable PRFs: (1) a *single-key* construction from standard lattice assumptions where security holds against an adversary that holds a *single* marked key; and (2) a collusion resistant construction from indistinguishability obfuscation [BGI+01]. A natural question is whether we can obtain a collusion resistant traceable PRF from standard lattice assumptions. Such a construction would have the advantage of being plausibly post-quantum secure and also provides a more direct instantiation than going through the full power of indistinguishability obfuscation.

Fully collusion resistant constructions of related notions such as traitor tracing (i.e., traceable encryption) [GKW18, CVW+18] and watermarkable PRFs [YAYX20] are known from standard lattice assumptions.

Active security. Traceable PRFs and traitor tracing schemes come in several varieties. Some schemes support *public tracing* where anyone is able to run the tracing algorithm, while others only support *secret tracing* where knowledge of a secret key is needed to run the tracing algorithm. Existing lattice-based constructions of traceable PRFs and traitor tracing only support secret tracing.

In the secret tracing setting, existing security models only consider adversaries that do *not* have access to the tracing key. However, in practical scenarios where traitor tracing schemes may be deployed, it makes sense to consider *active adversaries* that may make multiple attempts to try and evade the tracing algorithm (or even worse, cause the tracing algorithm to falsely implicate an honest user). Certainly, any scheme that supports public tracing ensures robustness against such active adversaries, but the same does not hold in the secret-tracing setting. In this work, we model the capabilities of an active adversary by introducing a stronger security model in the secret tracing setting where we additionally allow the adversary to make queries to the tracing oracle. We view our notion to be an intermediate notion between secret tracing and public tracing. A similar intermediary notion was previously considered in the setting of watermarkable PRFs [QWZ18, KW19, YAL+19].

This Work. In this work, we show how to *generically* augment traceable PRFs with collusion resistance and active security through the use of fingerprinting codes [BS95].[2] We summarize our main results below and provide a more detailed technical overview in Sect. 1.1.

- **Collusion resistance:** We describe a generic transformation that transforms any single-key traceable PRF with domain $\mathcal{X}$, range $\{0,1\}^\rho$, and polynomial-size identity space $\mathcal{I}$ into a fully collusion resistant traceable PRF over the same domain, range, and identity space. A limitation of our construction is that the marked keys k_{id} are long: $|k_{\mathsf{id}}|$ scales polynomially with the size $|\mathcal{I}|$ of the identity space.
  We note that collusion resistance is meaningful and non-trivial to achieve even when the identity space is polynomial. For example, existing lattice-based traceable PRFs [GKWW21] are *completely* insecure if the adversary obtains just *two* marked keys (in fact, the adversary can recover the PRF secret key from any two marked keys). Moreover, in the closely-related setting of traitor tracing, many existing schemes only achieve full collusion resistance assuming a polynomial number of identities (e.g., [BSW06, GKSW10, Zha20, GQWW19]); in each of these examples, at least one of the scheme parameters grows *polynomially* with the number of identities, thus limiting the size of the identity space supported by the scheme.
- **Active Security:** We describe a generic transformation that takes any single-key traceable PRF and compiles it into a traceable PRF with *active* security (i.e., where the adversary is allowed to have access to the tracing oracle). Combined with collusion resistant fingerprinting codes that support tracing queries [YAYX20], we obtain collusion resistant traceable PRFs with active security. We note that existing constructions of collusion resistant fingerprinting codes only support an a priori bounded polynomial number of tracing queries. The same limitation extends to our collusion resistant traceable PRFs with active security.

We capture these results in the following (informal) theorem:

Theorem 1.1 (Informal). *Let λ be a security parameter and take any polynomial $n = n(\lambda)$. Let TPRF_0 be a single-key secretly-traceable PRF with domain $\mathcal{X}$, range $\{0,1\}^\rho$, and any identity space containing at least two identities. Then there exists a fully collusion resistant secretly-traceable PRF TPRF with domain $\mathcal{X}$, range $\{0,1\}^\rho$, and identity space $\{1,\ldots,n\}$. Moreover, for any polynomial $Q = Q(\lambda)$, TPRF is fully collusion resistant against an active adversary that makes up to Q queries to the tracing oracle. The size of the marked keys in TPRF is $\mathsf{poly}(\lambda, n, Q) \cdot |k_0|$, where $|k_0|$ denotes the size of a marked key in TPRF_0.*

Applying the above transformation to the single-key traceable PRF of Goyal et al. [GKWW21], we obtain the first fully collusion resistant traceable PRF from standard lattice assumptions. This puts traceable PRFs on par with the best-known results for watermarkable PRFs [YAYX20], while retaining the

[2] The fingerprinting codes we rely on in this work [BS95, Tar03, YAL+19] are information-theoretic objects and do *not* require making additional computational assumptions.

benefits of the significantly stronger tracing security provided by traceable PRFs. We summarize this instantiation in the following corollary to Theorem 1.1:

Corollary 1.2 (Collusion Resistant Traceable PRF). *Under the sub-exponential hardness of LWE (with a sub-exponential modulus-to-noise ratio), there exists a fully collusion resistant traceable PRF with secret tracing and a polynomial identity space. The traceable PRF is secure against active adversaries making up to Q tracing queries, for any a priori bounded polynomial $Q = Q(\lambda)$.*

Applications to Traitor Tracing. As noted in Goyal et al. [GKWW21], traceable PRFs immediately give rise to symmetric traitor tracing schemes. Here, we note that if the underlying traceable PRFs provide active security, we obtain fully collusion resistant traitor tracing schemes with security against active adversaries. We also note that since PRFs can be directly used to construct a CCA-secure symmetric encryption scheme (and more generally, an authenticated encryption scheme [BN00]), our traceable PRF immediately implies a traitor tracing scheme for an authenticated encryption scheme. Previous constructions of traitor tracing (e.g., [GKW18, CVW+18]) typically only consider chosen plaintext security (CPA-security) for the underlying encryption scheme. At the same time, the existing lattice-based traitor tracing schemes have the advantage that they support public encryption and have short marked keys. We provide more details in Sect. 4.

1.1 Construction Overview

In this section, we provide a high-level overview of our generic transformations (Theorem 1.1). We provide the technical details in Sect. 3.

Fingerprinting Codes. Our construction combines a single-key (i.e., non-collusion-resistant) traceable PRF with a collusion resistant fingerprinting code [BS95]. A fingerprinting code is an information-theoretic primitive defined over an alphabet Σ and an identity space $\mathcal{I}$. Here, we consider binary codes so $\Sigma = \{0,1\}$ and a polynomial-sized identity space $\mathcal{I} = [n] = \{1,\ldots,n\}$. A fingerprinting code is described by two main algorithms $(\mathsf{Gen}, \mathsf{Trace})$:

- The code generator algorithm Gen is a randomized algorithm that outputs a codebook $\Gamma = \{\bar{w}^{(i)}\}_{i\in[n]}$ together with a tracing key tk. We say that $\bar{w}^{(i)} \in \{0,1\}^\ell$ is the "codeword" associated with the ith identity and we refer to its length ℓ as the length of the code.
- The trace algorithm Trace takes as input the tracing key tk and a word $\bar{w}^* \in \{0,1\}^\ell$ and outputs a subset $S \subseteq [n]$.

Given a collection of codewords $W = \{\bar{w}^{(\mathsf{id}_1)}, \ldots, \bar{w}^{(\mathsf{id}_t)}\} \subseteq \Gamma$, we say that a word $\bar{w} \in \{0,1\}^\ell$ is *feasible* for W if for all $i \in [\ell]$, there exists $j \in [t]$ such that $\bar{w}_i = \bar{w}_i^{(\mathsf{id}_j)}$. In words, every bit in $\bar{w}$ agrees with the corresponding bit in one of the codewords in W. We define the feasible set $F(W) \subseteq \{0,1\}^\ell$ for W to be the set of words that are feasible for W.

Security for a fingerprinting code is defined by the following game between an adversary and a challenger. The challenger starts by sampling a codebook Γ and a tracing key tk. The adversary is allowed to adaptively request for codewords $\bar{w}^{(\mathsf{id})} \in \Gamma$ on identities $\mathsf{id} \in \mathcal{I}$ of its choosing. Let $T \subseteq \mathcal{I}$ be the set of identities queried by the adversary and let $W = \{\bar{w}^{(\mathsf{id})}\}_{\mathsf{id} \in T} \subseteq \Gamma$ be the set of associated codewords the adversary receives. At the end of the game, the adversary outputs a word $\bar{w}^* \in F(W)$ and wins if $\mathsf{Trace}(\mathsf{tk}, \bar{w}^*)$ outputs a set S where either $S = \varnothing$ or $S \not\subseteq T$. We say that a fingerprinting code is secure if no adversary $\mathcal{A}$ can win this game with non-negligible probability (taken over the code-generation and tracing randomness).

We note that fingerprinting codes can be used to directly construct collusion resistant *traitor tracing* [BN08,BP08]. In these settings, the resulting scheme satisfies a weaker *threshold* notion of traitor tracing where tracing succeeds only if the adversary outputs a decoder that succeeds with probability at least $1/2+\varepsilon$ for a *predetermined* and fixed ε. In contrast, the standard tracing definitions used for traceable PRFs and traitor tracing allows tracing a decoder that succeeds for arbitrary inverse polynomial ε. In this work, we show how to use fingerprinting codes to *upgrade* a non-collusion-resistant traceable PRF to a collusion resistant one *without* weakening the traceability guarantee. Recently, Zhandry [Zha20] introduced new techniques to compile a threshold traitor tracing scheme into one without the threshold limitation. It is not clear whether those techniques extend to the traceable PRF setting (in fact, it does not seem straightforward to even construct a traceable PRF with a threshold security notion directly from fingerprinting codes).

Collusion Resistant Traceable PRFs. Our main construction relies on the simple observation that the xor function is a "combiner" for PRFs. Namely, if $\mathsf{PRF}_1, \ldots, \mathsf{PRF}_\ell \colon \mathcal{K} \times \mathcal{X} \to \{0,1\}^\rho$ are PRF candidates, then $\mathsf{PRF}((k_1, \ldots, k_\ell), x) := \bigoplus_{i \in [\ell]} \mathsf{PRF}_i(k_i, x)$ is a secure PRF as long as *at least one* of the PRF_i is secure.

Let $\mathsf{TPRF}_{\mathsf{nc}}$ be a single-key (i.e., *non-collusion-resistant*) traceable PRF, and let $\Gamma = \{\bar{w}^{(i)}\}_{i \in [n]}$ be a fingerprinting code for the set $[n]$, where each codeword $\bar{w}^{(i)} \in \{0,1\}^\ell$. Our construction will use ℓ independent copies of $\mathsf{TPRF}_{\mathsf{nc}}$, where each copy is used to embed a *single* bit of the codeword. In more detail, the PRF key is a tuple of ℓ independent PRF keys $(\mathsf{msk}_1, \ldots, \mathsf{msk}_\ell)$ for $\mathsf{TPRF}_{\mathsf{nc}}$. The PRF evaluation is defined to be

$$\mathsf{Eval}((\mathsf{msk}_1, \ldots, \mathsf{msk}_\ell), x) = \bigoplus_{i \in [\ell]} \mathsf{TPRF}_{\mathsf{nc}}.\mathsf{Eval}(\mathsf{msk}_i, x).$$

A marked key for an identity id consists of a tuple of marked keys $(\mathsf{sk}_1, \ldots, \mathsf{sk}_\ell)$ where each sk_i is msk_i marked with the bit $\bar{w}_i^{(\mathsf{id})}$. Pseudorandomness of this construction also follows from pseudorandomness of $\mathsf{TPRF}_{\mathsf{nc}}$.

To trace a distinguisher D, we use the above combiner property: any algorithm that can break (weak) pseudorandomness of $\bigoplus_{i \in [\ell]} \mathsf{TPRF}_{\mathsf{nc}}.\mathsf{Eval}(\mathsf{msk}_i, \cdot)$ can also break (weak) pseudorandomness of $\mathsf{TPRF}_{\mathsf{nc}}.\mathsf{Eval}(\mathsf{msk}_j, \cdot)$ for every

$j \in [\ell]$. In particular, it is straightforward to take a distinguisher D and convert it into a distinguisher D_j for $\mathsf{TPRF}_{\mathsf{nc}}.\mathsf{Eval}(\mathsf{msk}_j, \cdot)$; recall here that in the secret-tracing setting, the tracing algorithm has the master secret key of the traceable PRF. The tracing algorithm runs the underlying single-key tracing algorithm on each distinguisher D_j to obtain sets $T_1, \ldots, T_\ell$. It uses the sets T_j to construct a codeword $\bar{w}^* \in \{0,1\}^\ell$ as follows: if $0 \in T_j$, then set $\bar{w}^*_j = 0$. Otherwise, set $\bar{w}^*_j = 1$. The final output of the tracing algorithm is obtained by running the decoding algorithm for the fingerprinting code on the extracted word $\bar{w}^*$.[3]

We argue that tracing security reduces to security of the underlying single-key traceable PRF and of the fingerprinting code. Suppose the adversary asks for keys on identities $\mathsf{id}_1, \ldots, \mathsf{id}_q$ and manages to produce a useful distinguisher D. The argument then proceeds as follows:

- Let $W = \{\bar{w}^{(\mathsf{id}_1)}, \ldots, \bar{w}^{(\mathsf{id}_q)}\}$ be the set of codewords for the fingerprinting code that are associated with the identities queried by the adversary. As long as the word $\bar{w}^*$ extracted by the tracing algorithm is contained in the feasible set of W, then security of the fingerprinting code guarantees that tracing security holds.
- By construction, $\bar{w}^* \in \{0,1\}^\ell$. This means that $\bar{w}^* \in F(W)$ as long as for every index $i \in [\ell]$ where $\bar{w}_i^{(\mathsf{id}_j)} = \bar{w}_i^{(\mathsf{id}_1)}$ for all $j \in [q]$, $\bar{w}^*_i = \bar{w}_i^{(\mathsf{id}_1)}$. In other words, if *all* of the codewords corresponding to identities requested by the adversary have the same bit in a particular position, then the corresponding bit in $\bar{w}^*$ must also match. But this property directly follows by *single-key* tracing security. Namely, if the codewords corresponding to identities requested by the adversary all match in a particular index $i \in [\ell]$, then the adversary only obtains *one* marked version of msk_i.[4] As described above, if D is a useful distinguisher, then it can be used to obtain a useful distinguisher for *any* of the underlying traceable PRFs. We use D to obtain a useful distinguisher D_i for the ith traceable PRF. Since the adversary only possesses a single marked key for the ith PRF (marked with the bit $\bar{w}_i^{(\mathsf{id}_1)}$), single-key tracing security ensures that tracing distinguisher D_i correctly recovers $\bar{w}_i^{(\mathsf{id}_1)}$.

Essentially, single-key security of the traceable PRF binds the adversary to strategies that conform to the restrictions of the fingerprinting code model. This in turn yields a fully collusion resistant traceable PRF.

Active Security. The second security property we consider in this work is active security, where tracing security holds even if an adversary has oracle access to the tracing algorithm. We start by considering active security in the *single-key* setting. Intuitively, security in this setting should *almost* follow from single-key tracing security. This is because if a distinguisher is "useful," then security requires that the tracing algorithm outputs the single identity id that the

---

[3] To avoid falsely implicating an honest user, we also run a statistical test to check that the distinguisher is "sufficiently good." We refer to Sect. 3 for more details.

[4] For this step to work, we need to first *derandomize* the key-generation algorithm. This can be done via the standard approach of deriving the key-generation randomness from a PRF. We refer to Sect. 3 for the full construction and analysis.

adversary requested. Conversely, if the distinguisher is "useless" (e.g., outputs a random guess), the tracing algorithm should output $\varnothing$ to avoid false implication of an honest user.

In some sense then, the adversary in the single-key security game should be able to "predict" the output of the tracing function in advance. If this is true, then the tracing oracle is no longer useful to the adversary and security reduces to the setting without tracing queries. However, the catch is handling distinguishers which are somewhere in between "useful" and "useless." For instance, the adversary might start with a useful distinguisher and construct distinguishers with progressively decreasing distinguishing advantage until it observes a change in the behavior of the tracing algorithm; where this occurs can leak information about the secret tracing key.

More precisely, the tracing algorithm in a traceable PRF takes a distinguisher D and a threshold ε as input. The requirement is that if D has distinguishing advantage at least $1/2 + \varepsilon$, then running the tracing algorithm with threshold ε will correctly identify at least one corrupted user. However, if D's distinguishing advantage is less than $1/2 + \varepsilon$, then the only guarantee provided by the tracing algorithm is that it does not falsely implicate an honest user; in this case, it can either output a compromised identity or the empty set.

Our approach to achieving active security is through introducing an efficient statistical test $\mathsf{CheckDis}$ for deciding whether a distinguisher is "useful" (in which case the tracing algorithm always outputs the single corrupted identity) or "not useful" (in which case the tracing algorithm always outputs $\varnothing$). Importantly, this test can be run by the adversary itself, so the tracing oracle does not provide the adversary additional information. The $\mathsf{CheckDis}$ algorithm is very simple: it takes a distinguisher D and a threshold ε and estimates the distinguishing advantage of D. The algorithm satisfies two properties:

- If the distinguishing advantage of D is at least $1/2+\varepsilon$, then $\mathsf{CheckDis}$ outputs 1 with overwhelming probability.
- If $\mathsf{CheckDis}$ outputs 1, then the distinguishing advantage of D is at least $1/2 + \varepsilon/4$ with overwhelming probability.

We now modify the tracing algorithm to first run $\mathsf{CheckDis}$ on the distinguisher. If $\mathsf{CheckDis}$ fails, then the tracing algorithm always outputs $\varnothing$; the first property guarantees that this will never happen to a "good" distinguisher. If $\mathsf{CheckDis}$ succeeds, then run the tracing algorithm with distinguishing threshold $\varepsilon/4$; the second property ensures that the tracing algorithm correctly outputs the compromised identity in this case. Finally, since $\mathsf{CheckDis}$ can be computed by the adversary, it is possible for the adversary to simulate for itself the output of the tracing queries without access to the tracing oracle. Thus, in the single-key setting, it is straightforward to achieve active security essentially for free.

To obtain a collusion resistant traceable PRF with active security, we can apply our generic transformation based on fingerprinting codes. While the general transformation still applies, security will require that the underlying fingerprinting code remains secure in the presence of tracing queries. Currently, there exist collusion resistant fingerprinting codes that are secure against adversaries that make an *a priori* bounded polynomial number of tracing queries [YAYX20]. In conjunction with our compilers, this yields a collusion resistant traceable PRF that is secure against adversaries that can make a bounded number of tracing queries. Constructing fingerprinting codes that are secure against an unbounded polynomial number of tracing queries is an interesting open problem, and a construction would immediately yield traceable PRFs (and correspondingly, traitor tracing schemes) with active security.

1.2 Additional Related Work

In this section, we discuss some additional results on traitor tracing and watermarking.

Traitor Tracing. Traitor tracing has been studied extensively and numerous constructions of traitor tracing have been proposed based on combinatorial techniques [CFN94,NP98,SSW01,CFNP00,SSW01,BN08] as well as algebraic techniques [BSW06,GKSW10,LPSS14,KT15,NWZ16,GKW18,CVW+18, GKW19,GQWW19]. Some of these schemes are secure against bounded collusions [CFN94,SSW01,LPSS14,KT15,NWZ16] while others are fully collusion resistant [BSW06,GKSW10,GKW18,CVW+18,GQWW19,Zha20]. We refer to these works and the references therein for further information.

Traitor Tracing from Fingerprinting Codes. Fingerprinting codes can be directly combined with public-key encryption to obtain traitor tracing schemes (though not traceable PRFs) [BN08]. As noted earlier, the resulting traitor tracing scheme satisfies a weaker threshold tracing guarantee. Our work shows that by combining fingerprinting codes with an existing (non-collusion-resistant) tracing scheme, it is possible to obtain full collusion resistance *without* the threshold restriction.

In the setting of watermarkable PRFs, Yang et al. [YAL+19] showed how to use fingerprinting codes to upgrade a non-collusion-resistant watermarkable PRF to a collusion resistant one. Their approach relies on concatenating the outputs of many watermarkable PRFs and only supports tracing adversaries that preserve the entirety of the PRF output (i.e., this precludes applications from truncating the PRF output). Overall, both the size of the marked keys and the length of the PRF output of their scheme scale polynomially with the number of identities. Our collusion resistant traceable PRF has long keys, but the length of the PRF output is independent of the number of identities. For instance, this property enables symmetric traitor tracing with short ciphertexts.

Watermarking. Barak et al. [BGI+01,BGI+12] and Hopper et al. [HMW07] provided the first rigorous definitions of software watermarking. Multiple works have subsequently studied constructions of watermarking for symmetric primitives [CHN+16,BLW17,KW17,YAL+18,QWZ18,KW19,YAL+19, YAYX20] and public-key primitives [GKM+19,Nis20]. Goyal et al. [GKWW21] recently highlighted some definitional issues with watermarking for PRFs and introduced the notion of traceable PRFs.

2 Preliminaries

Notation. We write λ (oftentimes implicitly) to denote the security parameter. For a positive integer $n \in \mathbb{N}$, we write $[n]$ to denote the set $\{1, \ldots, n\}$. For a finite set S, we write $x \xleftarrow{R} S$ to denote that x is sampled uniformly from S. For a distribution $\mathcal{D}$, we write $x \leftarrow \mathcal{D}$ to denote that x is sampled from $\mathcal{D}$. For an event E, we write $\neg E$ to denote its complement. For finite sets $\mathcal{X}$ and $\mathcal{Y}$, we write $\mathsf{Funs}[\mathcal{X}, \mathcal{Y}]$ to denote the set of all functions from $\mathcal{X}$ to $\mathcal{Y}$.

We say that a function f is negligible in the parameter λ if $f(\lambda) = o(1/\lambda^c)$ for all $c \in \mathbb{N}$. We denote this by writing $f(\lambda) = \mathsf{negl}(\lambda)$. We write $\mathsf{poly}(\lambda)$ to denote a function bounded by a fixed polynomial in λ. We say an event E (parameterized by a security parameter λ) happens with negligible probability if $\Pr[E] = \mathsf{negl}(\lambda)$ and that it happens with overwhelming probability if $\Pr[\neg E] = \mathsf{negl}(\lambda)$. We say an algorithm $\mathcal{A}$ is efficient if it runs in probabilistic polynomial time in the length of its input. We say that two families of distributions $\mathcal{D}_1 = \{\mathcal{D}_{1,\lambda}\}_{\lambda \in \mathbb{N}}$ and $\mathcal{D}_2 = \{\mathcal{D}_{2,\lambda}\}_{\lambda \in \mathbb{N}}$ are computationally indistinguishable if no efficient adversary can distinguish samples from $\mathcal{D}_1$ and $\mathcal{D}_2$ except with negligible probability. We will also use standard Chernoff/Hoeffding bounds in our analysis:

Fact 2.1 (Hoeffding's Inequality [Hoe63]**).** Let $X_1, \ldots, X_n$ be independent random variables where $0 \leq X_i \leq 1$ for all $i \in [n]$. Let $S = \sum_{i \in [n]} X_i$ and let $\mathbb{E}[S]$ denote the expected value of S. Then, for any $t \geq 0$,

$$\Pr[|S - \mathbb{E}[S]| \geq nt] \leq 2^{-\Omega(nt^2)}.$$

Finally, we recall the definition of a pseudorandom function [GGM84]:

Definition 2.2 (Pseudorandom Function [GGM84]**).** *A pseudorandom function (PRF) with key-space $\mathcal{K}$, domain $\mathcal{X}$ and range $\mathcal{Y}$ is an efficiently-computable function* $\mathsf{PRF} \colon \mathcal{K} \times \mathcal{X} \to \mathcal{Y}$ *with the property that for all efficient adversaries $\mathcal{A}$, there exists a negligible function* $\mathsf{negl}(\cdot)$ *such that*

$$\Pr[\mathcal{A}^{O_b(\cdot)}(1^\lambda) = b : k \xleftarrow{R} \mathcal{K}, f \xleftarrow{R} \mathsf{Funs}[\mathcal{X}, \mathcal{Y}], b \xleftarrow{R} \{0,1\}] \leq \frac{1}{2} + \mathsf{negl}(\lambda),$$

where $O_b(x)$ outputs $\mathsf{PRF}(k, x)$ *if $b = 0$ and $f(x)$ if $b = 1$.*

2.1 Fingerprinting Codes

In this section, we recall the formal definition of a fingerprinting code from Boneh and Shaw [BS95]. To construct traceable PRFs with active security, we require the fingerprinting code to satisfy collusion resistance against adversaries that are allowed to make tracing queries [YAYX20].

Definition 2.3 (Feasible Set [BS95]**).** *Let $W = \{\bar{w}^{(1)}, \ldots, \bar{w}^{(t)}\} \subseteq \{0,1\}^\ell$. We say that a word $\bar{w} \in \{0,1\}^\ell$ is* feasible *for W if for all $i \in [\ell]$, there exists $j \in [t]$ such that $\bar{w}_i = \bar{w}_i^{(j)}$. We define the* feasible set *$F(W) \subseteq \{0,1\}^\ell$ of W to be the set of all words in $\{0,1\}^\ell$ that are feasible for W.*

Definition 2.4 (Fingerprinting Code [BS95, adapted]**).** *A fingerprinting code* FC *with n codewords is a pair of efficient algorithms* (Gen, Trace) *with the following properties:*

- $\mathsf{Gen}(1^\lambda) \rightarrow (\mathsf{tk}, \Gamma)$: *On input the security parameter $\lambda \in \mathbb{N}$, the code-generation algorithm outputs a tracing key* tk *and a dictionary $\Gamma = \{\bar{w}^{(i)}\}_{i\in[n]}$. Here, $\bar{w}^{(i)} \in \{0,1\}^\ell$ for some parameter $\ell > 0$. We refer to ℓ as the* code length.
- $\mathsf{Trace}(\mathsf{tk}, \bar{w}^*) \rightarrow S$: *On input the tracing key* tk *and a word $\bar{w}^* \in \{0,1\}^\ell$, the decoding algorithm outputs a set $S \subseteq [n]$.*

Definition 2.5 (Collusion Resistance with Tracing Queries [YAYX20, adapted]**).** *Let* $\mathsf{FC} = (\mathsf{Gen}, \mathsf{Trace})$ *be a fingerprinting code with n codewords. For an adversary $\mathcal{A}$, we define the fingerprinting code experiment* $\mathsf{ExptFC}_{\mathcal{A}}^{\mathsf{FC}}(\lambda)$ *as follows:*

Experiment $\mathsf{ExptFC}_{\mathcal{A}}^{\mathsf{FC}}(\lambda)$:

- *The challenger starts by sampling* $(\mathsf{tk}, \Gamma = \{\bar{w}^{(i)}\}_{i\in[n]}) \leftarrow \mathsf{Gen}(1^\lambda)$. *It also initializes an empty set $W \leftarrow \varnothing$.*
- *The adversary is given access to the following oracles:*
  - ***Encode query:*** *On input an index $i \in [n]$, the challenger replies with $\bar{w}^{(i)} \in \{0,1\}^\ell$. The challenger adds $\bar{w}^{(i)}$ to W.*
  - ***Tracing query:*** *On input a word $\bar{w}^* \in \{0,1\}^\ell$, if $\bar{w}^* \notin F(W)$, the challenger replies with $\perp$. Otherwise, if $\bar{w}^* \in F(W)$, then the challenger computes* $S \leftarrow \mathsf{Trace}(\mathsf{tk}, \bar{w}^*)$. *If $S \neq \varnothing$ and $\bar{w}^{(\mathsf{id})} \in W$ for all* $\mathsf{id} \in S$, *the challenger replies with S. Otherwise, the experiment halts with output* 1.
- *After the adversary $\mathcal{A}$ finishes making its queries, the experiment halts with output* 0 *(if it has not already halted).*

We say that FC *is fully collusion resistant in the presence of Q tracing queries if for all security parameters $\lambda \in \mathbb{N}$ and all adversaries $\mathcal{A}$ making up to Q tracing queries, there exists a negligible function* $\mathsf{negl}(\cdot)$ *such that*

$$\Pr[\mathsf{ExptFC}_{\mathcal{A}}^{\mathsf{FC}}(\lambda) = 1] \leq \mathsf{negl}(\lambda).$$

When we allow Q to be an arbitrary polynomial, we say that FC *is fully collusion resistant in the presence of tracing queries.*

Fact 2.6 (Fingerprinting Codes). We recall the following results on the existence of collusion resistant fingerprinting codes (with and without tracing queries):

- For all $\lambda \in \mathbb{N}$ and $n \in \mathbb{N}$, there exists a fingerprinting code that is fully collusion resistant *without* tracing queries (i.e., $Q = 0$) with code length $\ell = \mathsf{poly}(n, \lambda)$ [BS95, Tar03]. Specifically, the Tardos instantiation [Tar03] yields a construction with code-length $\ell = O(\lambda n^2 \log n)$.

- For all $\lambda \in \mathbb{N}$, $n \in \mathbb{N}$, and $Q = \mathsf{poly}(\lambda)$ there exists a fingerprinting code that is fully collusion resistant in the presence of Q tracing queries with code length $\ell = \mathsf{poly}(n, \lambda, Q)$ [YAYX20].

2.2 Traceable PRFs

In this section, we recall the formal definition of a traceable PRF from [GKWW21]. We note that our transformations will rely on a stronger notion of tracing security we call "strong tracing" (see Definition 2.12). Existing constructions of traceable PRFs [GKWW21] satisfy this security notion (Remark 2.13). Finally, we introduce our notion of tracing security against active adversaries that have oracle access to the tracing algorithm (Definition 2.14).

Definition 2.7 (Traceable PRFs [GKWW21]). *Let λ be a security parameter. A traceable PRF scheme (in the secret-tracing setting) with domain $\mathcal{X}$, range $\mathcal{Y}$, and identity space $[n]$ where $n = n(\lambda)$ is a tuple of four algorithms* $\mathsf{TPRF} = (\mathsf{Setup}, \mathsf{KeyGen}, \mathsf{Eval}, \mathsf{Trace})$ *with the following properties:*

- $\mathsf{Setup}(1^\lambda) \to \mathsf{msk}$: *The setup algorithm takes as input the security parameter λ and outputs a master secret key* msk.
- $\mathsf{KeyGen}(\mathsf{msk}, \mathsf{id}) \to \mathsf{sk}_{\mathsf{id}}$: *The key generation algorithm takes as input the master secret key* msk *and an identity* $\mathsf{id} \in [n]$, *and outputs a secret key* $\mathsf{sk}_{\mathsf{id}}$.
- $\mathsf{Eval}(\mathsf{sk}, x) \to y$: *The evaluation algorithm takes as input a secret key* sk *(which could be the master key* msk*), an input $x \in \mathcal{X}$, and outputs a value $y \in \mathcal{Y}$.*
- $\mathsf{Trace}^D(\mathsf{msk}, 1^z) \to T$: *The tracing algorithm has oracle access to an oracle-aided distinguisher D^O and takes as input the master secret key* msk *and a parameter z. It outputs a set of identities $T \subseteq [n]$. Note that the tracing algorithm must includes a description of how to implement the oracle O used by the oracle-aided distinguisher.*

Correctness. The basic correctness requirement for a traceable PRF is that the behavior of the marked key agrees with the original key on all but a negligible fraction of the domain. We recall this below:

Definition 2.8 (Key Similarity). *A traceable PRF* $\mathsf{TPRF} = (\mathsf{Setup}, \mathsf{KeyGen}, \mathsf{Eval}, \mathsf{Trace})$ *with domain $\mathcal{X}$, range $\mathcal{Y}$, and identity space $[n]$ satisfies key similarity if for every security parameter $\lambda \in \mathbb{N}$, every identity* $\mathsf{id} \in [n]$, *there exists a negligible function* $\mathsf{negl}(\cdot)$ *where*

$$\Pr\left[\mathsf{Eval}(\mathsf{msk}, x) \neq \mathsf{Eval}(\mathsf{sk}_{\mathsf{id}}, x) : \begin{array}{c} \mathsf{msk} \leftarrow \mathsf{Setup}(1^\lambda) \\ \mathsf{sk}_{\mathsf{id}} \leftarrow \mathsf{KeyGen}(\mathsf{msk}, \mathsf{id}), x \xleftarrow{\mathrm{R}} \mathcal{X} \end{array}\right] \leq \mathsf{negl}(\lambda).$$

Remark 2.9 (Stronger Notions of Correctness). Definition 2.8 requires that marked keys agree with unmarked keys on all but a negligible fraction of the domain. Goyal et al. [GKWW21] also consider a stronger notion of key indistinguishability that requires that it is computationally difficult to *find* domain elements where the marked key and the unmarked key differ. We note that our generic transformations in Sect. 3 can be shown to preserve this stronger notion of correctness. For ease of exposition in this work, we focus on the simpler notion of key similarity.

Definition 2.10 (Weak Pseudorandomness). *A traceable PRF* $\mathsf{TPRF} = (\mathsf{Setup}, \mathsf{KeyGen}, \mathsf{Eval}, \mathsf{Trace})$ *with domain* $\mathcal{X}$*, range* $\mathcal{Y}$*, and identity space* $[n]$ *satisfies weak pseudorandomness if for all efficient adversaries* $\mathcal{A}$*, there exists a negligible function* $\mathsf{negl}(\cdot)$ *such that*

$$\Pr\left[\mathcal{A}^{O_b}(1^\lambda) = b : \mathsf{msk} \leftarrow \mathsf{Setup}(1^\lambda), f \xleftarrow{R} \mathsf{Funs}[\mathcal{X}, \mathcal{Y}], b \xleftarrow{R} \{0,1\}\right] \leq \mathsf{negl}(\lambda),$$

where the weak PRF challenge oracle O_b *samples* $x \xleftarrow{R} \mathcal{X}$ *and outputs* $(x, \mathsf{Eval}(\mathsf{msk}, x))$ *if* $b = 0$ *and* $(x, f(x))$ *if* $b = 1$.

Remark 2.11 (On Weak Pseudorandomness). Similar to Goyal et al. [GKWW21], we use weak pseudorandomness as our primary security notion for traceable PRFs. As discussed in [GKWW21, §3.1], tracing is only feasible against adversarial strategies that contain "global" information about the behavior of the PRF (i.e., adversaries that can break weak pseudorandomness). We do note that it is still possible for traceable PRFs to independently satisfy the usual notion of strong pseudorandomness (and indeed, the constructions of Goyal et al. do). All of the transformations developed in this work preserve strong pseudorandomness.

Definition 2.12 (Secure Tracing). *Let* $\mathsf{TPRF} = (\mathsf{Setup}, \mathsf{KeyGen}, \mathsf{Eval}, \mathsf{Trace})$ *be a traceable PRF with domain* $\mathcal{X}$ *and range* $\mathcal{Y}$ *and identity space* $[n]$*. For a function* $\varepsilon = \varepsilon(\lambda)$ *and adversary* $\mathcal{A}$*, we define the tracing experiment* $\mathsf{ExptTPRF}^{\mathsf{TPRF}}_{\mathcal{A},\varepsilon}(\lambda)$ *as follows:*

> **Experiment** $\mathsf{ExptTPRF}^{\mathsf{TPRF}}_{\mathcal{A},\varepsilon}(\lambda)$:
>
> - $\mathsf{msk} \leftarrow \mathsf{Setup}(1^\lambda)$
> - $D \leftarrow \mathcal{A}^{\mathsf{Eval}(\mathsf{msk},\cdot), \mathsf{KeyGen}(\mathsf{msk},\cdot)}(1^\lambda)$
> - $T \leftarrow \mathsf{Trace}^D(\mathsf{msk}, 1^{1/\varepsilon(\lambda)})$

Let S_{id} *be the set of identities* $\mathcal{A}$ *submits to the key-generation oracle* $\mathsf{KeyGen}(\mathsf{msk}, \cdot)$*. Based on the output of* $\mathsf{ExptTPRF}^{\mathsf{TPRF}}_{\mathcal{A},\varepsilon}$*, we define the following set of (probabilistic) events and their corresponding probabilities (which are a functions of* λ *and parameterized by* $\mathcal{A}, \varepsilon$*):*

- $\mathsf{GoodDis}_{\mathcal{A},\varepsilon}$*: This is the event where* $\Pr[D^{O_b}(1^\lambda) = b : b \xleftarrow{R} \{0,1\}, f \xleftarrow{R} \mathsf{Funs}[\mathcal{X}, \mathcal{Y}]] \geq 1/2 + \varepsilon(\lambda)$*, where the probability is taken over the coins of* D*, and the oracle* O_b *is the weak PRF challenge oracle: namely,* O_b *samples* $x \xleftarrow{R} \mathcal{X}$ *and outputs* $(x, \mathsf{Eval}(\mathsf{msk}, x))$ *if* $b = 0$ *and* $(x, f(x))$ *if* $b = 1$*. Intuitively, this says that a distinguisher* D *is an* ε*-good distinguisher if* D *can break weak pseudorandomness of the underlying PRF with advantage* $\varepsilon = \varepsilon(\lambda)$*.*

- $\mathsf{CorrectTr}_{\mathcal{A},\varepsilon}$: *This is the event where* $T \neq \varnothing \wedge T \subseteq S_{\mathsf{id}}$. *This event corresponds to the tracing algorithm successfully outputting one or more of the keys the adversary possesses.*
- $\mathsf{BadTr}_{\mathcal{A},\varepsilon}$: *This is the event where* $T \not\subseteq S_{\mathsf{id}}$. *This event corresponds to the tracing algorithm outputting a key that the adversary did not request (i.e., falsely implicating an honest user).*

We say that an adversary $\mathcal{A}$ *is admissible for the secure tracing experiment if the distinguisher* D *it outputs is efficiently-computable. A traceable PRF scheme* TPRF *satisfies* secure tracing *if for every* $\lambda \in \mathbb{N}$, *and every efficient and admissible adversary* $\mathcal{A}$, *and every inverse polynomial function* $\varepsilon(\lambda) = 1/\mathsf{poly}(\lambda)$, *there exists a negligible function* $\mathsf{negl}(\cdot)$ *such that*

$$\Pr[\mathsf{BadTr}_{\mathcal{A},\varepsilon}] \leq \mathsf{negl}(\lambda) \text{ and } \Pr[\mathsf{CorrectTr}_{\mathcal{A},\varepsilon}] \geq \Pr[\mathsf{GoodDis}_{\mathcal{A},\varepsilon}] - \mathsf{negl}(\lambda). \quad (2.1)$$

The first property states that the tracing algorithm cannot falsely implicate an honest user with non-negligible probability and the second property requires that the probability of the tracing algorithm correctly identifying at least one corrupt user be at least as high as the probability that the adversary outputs an ε*-good distinguisher. We say that* TPRF *satisfies* strongly-secure tracing *if for every* $\lambda \in \mathbb{N}$, *every efficient and admissible adversary* $\mathcal{A}$, *and every inverse polynomial function* $\varepsilon(\lambda) = 1/\mathsf{poly}(\lambda)$, *there exists a negligible function* $\mathsf{negl}(\cdot)$ *where*

$$\Pr[\mathsf{BadTr}_{\mathcal{A},\varepsilon}] \leq \mathsf{negl}(\lambda) \text{ and } \Pr[\mathsf{GoodDis}_{\mathcal{A},\varepsilon} \wedge \neg\mathsf{CorrectTr}_{\mathcal{A},\varepsilon}] \leq \mathsf{negl}(\lambda).$$

Remark 2.13 (Strong Tracing). Strong tracing requires that the probability that the adversary outputs an ε-good distinguisher and yet, tracing fails, be negligible. This means that if the adversary outputs an ε-good distinguisher with non-negligible probability, then tracing succeeds with overwhelming probability. This is *not* required by the standard tracing definition. A simple calculation shows that strong tracing security implies standard secure tracing. First,

$$\Pr[\mathsf{GoodDis}_{\mathcal{A},\varepsilon}] = \Pr[\mathsf{GoodDis}_{\mathcal{A},\varepsilon} \wedge \mathsf{CorrectTr}_{\mathcal{A},\varepsilon}] + \Pr[\mathsf{GoodDis}_{\mathcal{A},\varepsilon} \wedge \neg\mathsf{CorrectTr}_{\mathcal{A},\varepsilon}].$$

Strong secure tracing implies that $\Pr[\mathsf{GoodDis}_{\mathcal{A},\varepsilon} \wedge \neg\mathsf{CorrectTr}_{\mathcal{A},\varepsilon}] \leq \mathsf{negl}(\lambda)$. Thus,

$$\Pr[\mathsf{CorrectTr}_{\mathcal{A},\varepsilon}] \geq \Pr[\mathsf{CorrectTr}_{\mathcal{A},\varepsilon} \wedge \mathsf{GoodDis}_{\mathcal{A},\varepsilon}] \geq \Pr[\mathsf{GoodDis}_{\mathcal{A},\varepsilon}] - \mathsf{negl}(\lambda).$$

Existing construction of traceable PRFs [GKWW21] all satisfy this stronger notion. In fact, the analysis of existing constructions show that $\Pr[\mathsf{CorrectTr}_{\mathcal{A},\varepsilon} \mid \mathsf{GoodDis}_{\mathcal{A},\varepsilon}] \geq 1 - \mathsf{negl}(\lambda)$; namely, whenever the adversary outputs a useful distinguisher, the tracing algorithm successfully recovers one of the identities.

Definition 2.14 (Secure Tracing against Active Adversaries). *We say a traceable PRF* $\mathsf{TPRF} = (\mathsf{Setup}, \mathsf{KeyGen}, \mathsf{Eval}, \mathsf{Trace})$ *satisfies secure tracing against active adversaries (i.e., is actively secure) if Definition 2.12 holds even if the adversary* $\mathcal{A}$ *in experiment* $\mathsf{ExptTPRF}^{\mathsf{TPRF}}_{\mathcal{A},\varepsilon}$ *has oracle access to a tracing oracle* $\mathcal{O}(\mathsf{msk}, \cdot, \cdot)$ *that takes as input the description of an efficiently-computable* *distinguisher D and the tracing parameter 1^z (encoded in unary) and outputs* $\mathsf{Trace}^D(\mathsf{msk}, 1^z)$. *We say* TPRF *satisfies secure tracing against Q-bounded active adversaries if Definition 2.12 holds against all efficient adversaries $\mathcal{A}$ that makes at most Q queries to the tracing oracle $\mathcal{O}(\mathsf{msk}, \cdot, \cdot)$ in* $\mathsf{ExptTPRF}_{\mathcal{A},\varepsilon}^{\mathsf{TPRF}}$.

Remark 2.15 (Comparison with [GKWW21]*).* Definition 2.12 is slightly simpler than the corresponding definition from [GKWW21]. Namely, the definition in [GKWW21] required that for all efficient adversaries $\mathcal{A}$, every polynomial q, and non-negligible function ε, there exists a negligible function $\mathsf{negl}(\cdot)$ such that for all $\lambda \in \mathbb{N}$ where $\varepsilon(\lambda) > 1/q(\lambda)$, Eq. 2.1 holds. Our formulation is equivalent; we refer to [Zha20, Remark 4] for a similar type of modification in the context of traitor tracing.

Remark 2.16 (Special Evaluation Queries). The secure tracing definition from Goyal et al. [GKWW21] also allows the adversary to make *special evaluation queries* where the adversary can request evaluations on inputs $x \in \mathcal{X}$ under different identity keys. We do not focus on this setting since existing constructions of (non-collusion-resistant) traceable PRFs based on standard lattice assumptions do *not* support special evaluation queries. Special evaluation queries are not essential to realizing applications like traitor tracing from traceable PRFs.

3 Traceable PRF Constructions

In this section, we introduce our generic transformations (Constructions 3.3 and 3.6) for constructing traceable PRFs with active security and full collusion resistance (based on any single-key traceable PRF). In both of our constructions, we need an algorithm to estimate the success probability of a distinguisher. We use a standard approach based on Chernoff/Hoeffding bounds (Fact 2.1):

Definition 3.1 (CheckDis)**.** *Let λ be a security parameter, and let* $\mathsf{TPRF} = (\mathsf{Setup}, \mathsf{KeyGen}, \mathsf{Eval}, \mathsf{Trace})$ *be a traceable PRF with domain $\mathcal{X}$, range $\mathcal{Y}$, and identity space $[n]$. Given a distinguisher D, we define the algorithm* CheckDis*:*

- $\mathsf{CheckDis}^D(\mathsf{msk}, 1^z)$*: On input the master secret key* msk*, a parameter $z \in \mathbb{N}$, and given oracle access to a distinguisher D, the* CheckDis *algorithm proceeds as follows:*
  - *Let $N = \lambda z^2$. For each $i \in [N]$, sample $b_i \xleftarrow{R} \{0,1\}$, initialize an empty table* T*, and compute $b_i' \leftarrow D^{O_{b_i}(\mathsf{msk})}(1^\lambda)$, where the oracle O_{b_i} is implemented as follows:*
    - * *If $b_i = 0$, sample $x \xleftarrow{R} \mathcal{X}$, compute $y \leftarrow \mathsf{Eval}(\mathsf{msk}, x)$, and output (x, y).*
    - * *If $b_i = 1$, sample $x \xleftarrow{R} \mathcal{X}$ and check if there is already a mapping of the form $x \mapsto y$ in* T*. If so, output (x, y). Otherwise, sample $y \xleftarrow{R} \mathcal{Y}$, add (x, y) to* T*, and output (x, y).*
  - *Let t be the number of indices $i \in [N]$ where $b_i = b_i'$. If $t > N(1/2 + 1/(2z))$ occurs, then output 1. Otherwise, output 0.*

Lemma 3.2 (Distinguisher Success Probability). *Take any* $z = z(\lambda)$. *Let* $\mathsf{TPRF} = (\mathsf{Setup}, \mathsf{KeyGen}, \mathsf{Eval}, \mathsf{Trace})$ *be a traceable PRF, and sample* $\mathsf{msk} \leftarrow \mathsf{Setup}(1^\lambda)$. *Take any candidate distinguisher* D, *and let* O_b *be the weak PRF challenge oracle from Definition 2.12. Then the following properties hold:*

- *Suppose* $\Pr[D^{O_b(\mathsf{msk})}(1^\lambda) = b \colon b \xleftarrow{\text{R}} \{0,1\}] \geq 1/2 + 1/z$. *Then,* $\Pr[\mathsf{CheckDis}^D(\mathsf{msk}, 1^z) = 1] \geq 1 - \mathsf{negl}(\lambda)$.
- *Suppose* $\mathsf{CheckDis}^D(\mathsf{msk}, 1^{1/\varepsilon}) = 1$. *Then, with overwhelming probability over the randomness of* $\mathsf{CheckDis}$, *we have that* $\Pr[D^{O_b(\mathsf{msk})}(1^\lambda) = b \colon b \xleftarrow{\text{R}} \{0,1\}] \geq 1/2 + 1/(4z)$.

Proof. Both properties follow via Chernoff/Hoeffding bounds (Fact 2.1).

3.1 Tracing Security with Active Adversaries

We first show how to generically transform any single-key traceable PRF satisfying strong tracing security into a single-key traceable PRF with strong tracing security against active adversaries (Definition 2.14).

Construction 3.3 (Actively Secure Single-Key Traceable PRF). Let $\lambda \in \mathbb{N}$ be a security parameter. Let $\mathsf{TPRF}_0 = (\mathsf{Setup}_0, \mathsf{KeyGen}_0, \mathsf{Eval}_0, \mathsf{Trace}_0)$ be a secret-key traceable PRF with domain $\mathcal{X}$, range $\mathcal{Y}$ and identity space $[n]$. We construct a traceable PRF $\mathsf{TPRF} = (\mathsf{Setup}, \mathsf{KeyGen}, \mathsf{Eval}, \mathsf{Trace})$ with the same domain, range, and identity space as follows:

- $\mathsf{Setup}(1^\lambda) \to \mathsf{msk}$: On input the security parameter λ, the setup algorithm samples $\mathsf{msk} \leftarrow \mathsf{Setup}_0(1^\lambda)$.
- $\mathsf{Eval}(\mathsf{sk}, x) \to y$: Output $y \leftarrow \mathsf{Eval}_0(\mathsf{sk}, x)$.
- $\mathsf{KeyGen}(\mathsf{msk}, \mathsf{id}) \to \mathsf{sk}_{\mathsf{id}}$: Output $\mathsf{sk}_{\mathsf{id}} \leftarrow \mathsf{KeyGen}_0(\mathsf{msk}, \mathsf{id})$.
- $\mathsf{Trace}^D(\mathsf{msk}, 1^z) \to T$: On input the master secret key msk and the parameter z, the tracing algorithm outputs $\varnothing$ if $\mathsf{CheckDis}^D(\mathsf{msk}, 1^z)$ outputs 0. Otherwise, output $\mathsf{Trace}_0^D(\mathsf{msk}, 1^{4z})$.

Theorem 3.4 (Correctness and Weak Pseudorandomness). *If* TPRF_0 *satisfies weak pseudorandomness (resp., key similarity), then* TPRF *in Construction 3.3 also satisfies weak pseudorandomness (resp., key similarity).*

Proof. This is immediate since Setup, KeyGen, and Eval simply invokes the corresponding algorithm in TPRF_0.

Theorem 3.5 (Tracing Security). *If* TPRF_0 *is a single-key strongly-secure traceable PRF, then* TPRF *in Construction 3.3 is a single-key strongly-secure traceable PRF with active security.*

Due to space limitations, we defer the proof of Theorem 3.5 to the full version of this paper [MW21].

3.2 Collusion Resistant Traceable PRFs

We now introduce our main construction of a fully collusion resistant traceable PRF from any single-key traceable PRF (in conjunction with a fingerprinting code). We refer to Sect. 1.1 for an overview of the construction.

Construction 3.6 (Collusion Resistant Traceable PRF). Let $\lambda \in \mathbb{N}$ be a security parameter and $n = n(\lambda)$ be the number of identities. Our construction relies on the following ingredients:

- Let $\mathsf{TPRF}_{\mathsf{nc}} = (\mathsf{TPRF}_{\mathsf{nc}}.\mathsf{Setup}, \mathsf{TPRF}_{\mathsf{nc}}.\mathsf{KeyGen}, \mathsf{TPRF}_{\mathsf{nc}}.\mathsf{Eval}, \mathsf{TPRF}_{\mathsf{nc}}.\mathsf{Trace})$ be a (single-key) secret-key traceable PRF with domain $\mathcal{X}$, range $\{0,1\}^\rho$ and identity space $\{0,1\}$.
- Let $\mathsf{FC} = (\mathsf{FC.Gen}, \mathsf{FC.Trace})$ be a fingerprinting code with n codewords and code length ℓ.
- Let $\mathcal{R}$ be the randomness space for $\mathsf{TPRF}_{\mathsf{nc}}.\mathsf{KeyGen}$ and let $\mathsf{PRF}\colon \mathcal{K} \times ([\ell] \times \{0,1\}) \to \mathcal{R}$ be a pseudorandom function (with key-space $\mathcal{K}$ and domain $[\ell] \times \{0,1\}$).

We construct a fully collusion resistant secret-key traceable PRF $\mathsf{TPRF} = (\mathsf{Setup}, \mathsf{KeyGen}, \mathsf{Eval}, \mathsf{Trace})$ with domain $\mathcal{X}$, range $\{0,1\}^\rho$, and identity space $[n]$ as follows:

- $\mathsf{Setup}(1^\lambda) \to \mathsf{msk}$: On input the security parameter λ, the setup algorithm starts by sampling $\mathsf{msk}_i \leftarrow \mathsf{TPRF}_{\mathsf{nc}}.\mathsf{Setup}(1^\lambda)$ for each $i \in [\ell]$. In addition, it samples $k \xleftarrow{\text{R}} \mathcal{K}$ and $(\mathsf{tk}_{\mathsf{FC}}, \Gamma) \leftarrow \mathsf{FC.Gen}(1^\lambda)$. It outputs $\mathsf{msk} = (\mathsf{msk}_1, \ldots, \mathsf{msk}_\ell, \Gamma, \mathsf{tk}_{\mathsf{FC}}, k)$.
- $\mathsf{Eval}(\mathsf{sk}, x) \to y$: On input a secret key $\mathsf{sk} = (\mathsf{sk}_1, \ldots, \mathsf{sk}_\ell, \Gamma, \mathsf{tk}_{\mathsf{FC}}, k)$ and an input $x \in \mathcal{X}$, the evaluation algorithm computes $y_i \leftarrow \mathsf{TPRF}_{\mathsf{nc}}.\mathsf{Eval}(\mathsf{sk}_i, x)$ for each $i \in [\ell]$, and outputs $y \leftarrow \bigoplus_{i \in [\ell]} y_i$.
- $\mathsf{KeyGen}(\mathsf{msk}, \mathsf{id}) \to \mathsf{sk}_{\mathsf{id}}$: On input the master secret key $\mathsf{msk} = (\mathsf{msk}_1, \ldots, \mathsf{msk}_\ell, \Gamma = \{\bar{w}^{(i)}\}_{i \in [n]}, \mathsf{tk}_{\mathsf{FC}}, k)$ and an identity $\mathsf{id} \in [n]$, the key-generation algorithm computes randomness $r_i \leftarrow \mathsf{PRF}(k, (i, \bar{w}_i^{(\mathsf{id})}))$ and samples $\mathsf{sk}_i \leftarrow \mathsf{TPRF}_{\mathsf{nc}}.\mathsf{KeyGen}(\mathsf{msk}_i, \bar{w}_i^{(\mathsf{id})}; r_i)$ for each $i \in [\ell]$. It outputs $\mathsf{sk} = (\mathsf{sk}_1, \ldots, \mathsf{sk}_\ell, \bot, \bot, \bot)$.[5]
- $\mathsf{Trace}^D(\mathsf{msk}, 1^z) \to T$: On input the master secret key $\mathsf{msk} = (\mathsf{msk}_1, \ldots, \mathsf{msk}_\ell, \Gamma, \mathsf{tk}_{\mathsf{FC}}, k)$ and the parameter z, the tracing algorithm proceeds as follows:
  - If $\mathsf{CheckDis}^D(\mathsf{msk}, 1^z)$ outputs 0, output $\varnothing$.
  - Otherwise, define the oracle-aided distinguisher D_i^O as follows:
    * On input the security parameter λ, start running algorithm $D^{O'}(1^\lambda)$.
    * Whenever D makes a query to its oracle O', the distinguisher D_i makes a query to its own oracle O to obtain a sample (x, y). Algorithm D_i computes $y' \leftarrow y \oplus \left(\bigoplus_{j \neq i} \mathsf{TPRF}_{\mathsf{nc}}.\mathsf{Eval}(\mathsf{msk}_j, x)\right)$ and replies to D with the sample (x, y').

[5] The $\bot$'s are added so that msk and sk have the same format (and can both be used as an input to the evaluation algorithm).

- For each $i \in [\ell]$, run $T_i \leftarrow \mathsf{TPRF_{nc}.Trace}^{D_i}(\mathsf{msk}_i, 1^{4z})$. If $0 \in T_i$, set $\bar{w}_i^* = 0$; otherwise, set $\bar{w}_i^* = 1$.
- Output $\mathsf{FC.Trace}(\mathsf{tk_{FC}}, \bar{w}^*)$.

Theorem 3.7 (Weak Pseudorandomness). *If* $\mathsf{TPRF_{nc}}$ *satisfies weak pseudorandomness, then* TPRF *in Construction 3.6 also satisfies weak pseudorandomness.*

Proof. This follows from the fact that xor-ing the outputs of a (weak) PRF preserves (weak) pseudorandomness. More formally, suppose there exists an efficient adversary $\mathcal{A}$ that breaks weak pseudorandomness of Construction 3.6. We use $\mathcal{A}$ to construct an adversary $\mathcal{B}$ that breaks the weak pseudorandomness of $\mathsf{TPRF_{nc}}$ as follows:

1. For $i \in [\ell - 1]$, algorithm $\mathcal{B}$ samples a key $\mathsf{msk}_i \leftarrow \mathsf{TPRF_{nc}.Setup}(1^\lambda)$.
2. Whenever $\mathcal{A}$ makes an oracle query, algorithm $\mathcal{B}$ queries its own oracle to obtain an output (x, y). It compute $y' \leftarrow y \oplus \left(\bigoplus_{i \in [\ell-1]} \mathsf{Eval}(\mathsf{msk}_i, x)\right)$ and replies to $\mathcal{A}$ with (x, y).

The weak PRF challenger is used to simulate the evaluations of the ℓth copy of $\mathsf{TPRF_{nc}}$. If the challenger replies with PRF evaluations, then $\mathcal{B}$ perfectly simulates the pseudorandom distribution for $\mathcal{A}$ while if the challenger replies with uniform random value, then $\mathcal{B}$ perfectly simulates the truly random distribution.

Theorem 3.8 (Key Similarity). *If* $\mathsf{TPRF_{nc}}$ *satisfies key similarity, then* TPRF *in Construction 3.6 also satisfies key similarity.*

Proof. Take any identity $\mathsf{id} \in [n]$, and sample $\mathsf{msk} \leftarrow \mathsf{Setup}(1^\lambda)$, $\mathsf{sk_{id}} \leftarrow \mathsf{KeyGen}(\mathsf{msk}, \mathsf{id})$, $x \xleftarrow{\text{R}} \mathcal{X}$. In this case, $\mathsf{msk} = (\mathsf{msk}_1, \ldots, \mathsf{msk}_\ell, \Gamma, \mathsf{tk_{FC}}, k)$ where $\mathsf{msk}_i \leftarrow \mathsf{TPRF_{nc}.Setup}(1^\lambda)$ and $\mathsf{sk_{id}} = (\mathsf{sk}_1, \ldots, \mathsf{sk}_\ell, \bot, \bot, \bot)$ where $\mathsf{sk}_i \leftarrow \mathsf{TPRF_{nc}.KeyGen}(\mathsf{msk}_i, \mathsf{id})$. Key similarity of $\mathsf{TPRF_{nc}}$ implies that

$$\Pr[\mathsf{TPRF_{nc}.Eval}(\mathsf{msk}_i, x) \neq \mathsf{TPRF_{nc}.Eval}(\mathsf{sk}_i, x)] \leq \mathsf{negl}(\lambda).$$

By a union bound, with probability $1 - \mathsf{negl}(\lambda)$, $\mathsf{Eval}(\mathsf{msk}_i, x) = \mathsf{Eval}(\mathsf{sk}_i, x)$ for all $i \in [\ell]$, and the claim follows. □

Theorem 3.9 (Tracing Security). *Let $Q = Q(\lambda)$ be an arbitrary polynomial. If* $\mathsf{TPRF_{nc}}$ *is a strongly-secure single-key traceable PRF with security against Q-bounded active adversaries,* FC *is a fully collusion resistant fingerprinting code in the presence of Q tracing queries, and* PRF *is a secure PRF, then Construction 3.6 is a fully collusion resistant strongly-secure traceable PRF with security against Q-bounded active adversaries. If* $\mathsf{TPRF_{nc}}$ *and* FC *are both secure against adversaries that can make an unbounded number of tracing queries, then the same holds for Construction 3.6.*

Proof. Fix a security parameter $\lambda \in \mathbb{N}$ and take any inverse polynomial function $\varepsilon(\lambda) = 1/\mathsf{poly}(\lambda)$. Consider an execution of experiment $\mathsf{ExptTPRF}_{\mathcal{A},\varepsilon}^{\mathsf{TPRF}}$. We now define the following sequence of hybrid experiments:

- Hyb_0: This is the real security experiment $\mathsf{ExptTPRF}^{\mathsf{TPRF}}_{\mathcal{A},\varepsilon}(\lambda)$.
- Hyb_1: Same as Hyb_0 except the challenger samples $f \xleftarrow{\text{R}} \mathsf{Funs}[[\ell] \times \{0,1\}, \mathcal{R}]$ and computes $f(\cdot)$ instead of $\mathsf{PRF}(k, \cdot)$.
- Hyb_2: Same as Hyb_1, except on every tracing query and at the end of the game when $\mathcal{A}$ outputs its distinguisher, the experiment additionally checks the following two conditions. Let $(D, 1^z)$ be the distinguisher and tracing parameter the adversary submits in its tracing query (or outputs at the end of the experiment[6]).
    - $\mathsf{CheckDis}^D(\mathsf{msk}, 1^z)$ outputs 1.
    - The word $\bar{w}^* \in \{0,1\}^\ell$ computed by $\mathsf{Trace}^D(\mathsf{msk}, 1^z)$ satisfies $\bar{w}^* \notin F(W)$, where $F(W)$ is the feasible set of $W = \{\bar{w}^{(\mathsf{id}_j)}\}_{j \in [Q]}$, $\mathsf{id}_1, \ldots, \mathsf{id}_Q \in [n]$ are the identities $\mathcal{A}$ submitted to the key-generation oracle *prior* to outputting D, and $\Gamma = \{\bar{w}^{(i)}\}_{i \in [n]}$ is the set of codewords sampled by Setup.

  If both conditions hold, then the experiment sets the Bad flag and aborts with output $\perp$.

For an event E, we write $\mathsf{Hyb}_i[E]$ to denote the indicator random variable that is 1 if event E occurs in an execution of Hyb_i and 0 otherwise. In the following, we will consider events E that are functions of the "experiment's messages:" these include the adversary's queries, the challenger's responses, and the adversary's output in the experiment.

Lemma 3.10. *Let E be an efficiently-checkable event that is a function of $(\mathsf{msk}_1, \ldots, \mathsf{msk}_\ell, \Gamma, \mathsf{tk}_{\mathsf{FC}})$ and the experiment's messages in $\mathsf{ExptTPRF}^{\mathsf{TPRF}}_{\mathcal{A},\varepsilon}$. If PRF is secure, then for all efficient adversaries $\mathcal{A}$, we have that $|\Pr[\mathsf{Hyb}_0[E] = 1] - \Pr[\mathsf{Hyb}_1[E] = 1]| \le \mathsf{negl}(\lambda)$.*

Proof. Suppose there exists efficient $\mathcal{A}$ where $|\Pr[\mathsf{Hyb}_0[E] = 1] - \Pr[\mathsf{Hyb}_1[E] = 1]| \ge \varepsilon'$ for some non-negligible ε'. We use $\mathcal{A}$ to construct an adversary $\mathcal{B}$ that breaks security of PRF as follows:

1. Algorithm $\mathcal{B}$ starts by sampling a key $\mathsf{msk}_i \leftarrow \mathsf{TPRF}_{\mathsf{nc}}.\mathsf{Setup}(1^\lambda)$ for each $i \in [\ell]$. It also samples $(\mathsf{tk}_{\mathsf{FC}}, \Gamma = \{\bar{w}^{(i)}\}_{i \in [\ell]}) \leftarrow \mathsf{FC}.\mathsf{Gen}(1^\lambda)$.
2. Algorithm $\mathcal{B}$ starts running $\mathcal{A}$. Whenever $\mathcal{A}$ makes an evaluation or a trace query, algorithm $\mathcal{B}$ responds according to the specification of the real scheme (Construction 3.6). Observe that neither of these queries depend on the PRF key k.
3. When $\mathcal{A}$ makes a key-generation query on an identity $\mathsf{id} \in [n]$, algorithm $\mathcal{B}$ queries the PRF challenger on input $(i, \bar{w}_i^{(\mathsf{id})})$ and obtains output $r_i \in \mathcal{R}$ for each $i \in [\ell]$. It then computes $\mathsf{sk}_i \leftarrow \mathsf{TPRF}_{\mathsf{nc}}.\mathsf{KeyGen}(\mathsf{msk}_i, \bar{w}_i^{(\mathsf{id})}; r_i)$ and replies to $\mathcal{A}$ with $(\mathsf{sk}_1, \ldots, \mathsf{sk}_\ell, \perp, \perp, \perp)$.
4. At the end of the game, algorithm $\mathcal{B}$ outputs 1 if event E occurs and 0 otherwise.

[6] The tracing parameter for the final output is set to be $z = 1/\varepsilon$.

Algorithm $\mathcal{B}$ is efficient since deciding E can be efficiently computed as a function of $(\mathsf{msk}_1, \ldots, \mathsf{msk}_\ell, \Gamma, \mathsf{tk}_{\mathsf{FC}})$ and the experiment's messages. All of these quantities are known to $\mathcal{B}$. By construction, if $r_i \leftarrow \mathsf{PRF}(k, (i, \bar{w}_i^{(\mathsf{id})}))$ where $k \xleftarrow{\text{R}} \mathcal{K}$, then $\mathcal{B}$ perfectly simulates the distribution in Hyb_0. If $r_i \leftarrow f(i, \bar{w}_i^{(\mathsf{id})})$ where $f \xleftarrow{\text{R}} \mathsf{Funs}[[\ell] \times \{0,1\}, \mathcal{R}]$, then $\mathcal{B}$ perfectly simulates the distribution in Hyb_1. Thus, algorithm $\mathcal{B}$'s distinguishing advantage is exactly ε'.

Lemma 3.11. *Let E be any event that depends only on the experiment's messages and* msk. *If* $\mathsf{TPRF}_{\mathsf{nc}}$ *is a strongly secure single-key traceable PRF with security against Q-bounded active adversaries, then for all efficient Q-bounded active adversaries $\mathcal{A}$,* $|\Pr[\mathsf{Hyb}_1[E] = 1] - \Pr[\mathsf{Hyb}_2[E] = 1]| \le \mathsf{negl}(\lambda)$.

Proof. Suppose there exists efficient $\mathcal{A}$ where $|\Pr[\mathsf{Hyb}_1[E] = 1] - \Pr[\mathsf{Hyb}_2[E] = 1]| = \varepsilon'$ for some non-negligible ε'. Since the only difference between Hyb_1 and Hyb_2 is the additional checks in Hyb_2, it must be the case that in an execution of Hyb_1 or Hyb_2, algorithm $\mathcal{A}$ outputs a distinguisher D and a tracing parameter 1^z (either as part of a tracing query or at the end of the experiment) that causes Hyb_2 to set the Bad flag. We use $\mathcal{A}$ to construct an algorithm $\mathcal{B}$ for experiment $\mathsf{ExptTPRF}^{\mathsf{TPRF}_{\mathsf{nc}}}_{\mathcal{B},1/(4z)}$:

1. Algorithm $\mathcal{B}$ begins by sampling an index $i^* \xleftarrow{\text{R}} [\ell]$ and a bit $b^* \xleftarrow{\text{R}} \{0,1\}$. It makes a key-generation query to its challenger on the bit b^* to obtain a key sk^*.
2. For all $i \ne i^*$, algorithm $\mathcal{B}$ samples a key $\mathsf{msk}_i \leftarrow \mathsf{TPRF}_{\mathsf{nc}}.\mathsf{Setup}(1^\lambda)$. It also samples $(\mathsf{tk}_{\mathsf{FC}}, \Gamma = \{\bar{w}^{(i)}\}_{i \in [\ell]}) \leftarrow \mathsf{FC.Gen}(1^\lambda)$.
3. Algorithm $\mathcal{B}$ initializes an empty table T and starts running $\mathcal{A}$. Whenever $\mathcal{A}$ makes an oracle query, algorithm $\mathcal{B}$ responds as follows:
   - **Evaluation queries:** On input $x \in \mathcal{X}$, algorithm $\mathcal{B}$ computes $y_i \leftarrow \mathsf{TPRF}_{\mathsf{nc}}.\mathsf{Eval}(\mathsf{msk}_i, x)$ for all $i \ne i^*$. It makes an evaluation query to its challenger on input x to obtain a value $y_{i^*} \in \{0,1\}^\rho$. It replies to $\mathcal{A}$ with $y_{i^*} \oplus \left(\bigoplus_{i \ne i^*} y_i\right)$.
   - **Key-generation queries:** If $\bar{w}_{i^*}^{(\mathsf{id})} \ne b^*$, then algorithm $\mathcal{B}$ aborts the experiments and outputs $\perp$. Otherwise, algorithm $\mathcal{B}$ sets $\mathsf{sk}_{i^*} \leftarrow \mathsf{sk}^*$. Next, for each $i \ne i^*$, $\mathcal{B}$ checks if there exists a mapping $(i, \bar{w}_i^{(\mathsf{id})}) \mapsto r_{i, \bar{w}_i^{(\mathsf{id})}}$ in T. If not, it samples a random $r_{i, \bar{w}_i^{(\mathsf{id})}} \xleftarrow{\text{R}} \mathcal{R}$ and adds $(i, \bar{w}_i^{(\mathsf{id})}) \mapsto r_{i, \bar{w}_i^{(\mathsf{id})}}$ to T. Algorithm $\mathcal{B}$ then computes $\mathsf{sk}_i \leftarrow \mathsf{TPRF}_{\mathsf{nc}}.\mathsf{KeyGen}(\mathsf{msk}_i, \bar{w}_i^{(\mathsf{id})}; r_{i, \bar{w}_i^{(\mathsf{id})}})$ for each $i \ne i^*$. Algorithm $\mathcal{B}$ gives $\mathcal{A}$ the tuple $(\mathsf{sk}_1, \ldots, \mathsf{sk}_\ell, \perp, \perp, \perp)$.
   - **Tracing queries:** On input a distinguisher D and a tracing parameter 1^z, algorithm $\mathcal{B}$ starts by computing $\mathsf{CheckDis}^D(\mathsf{msk}, 1^z)$, where it uses the procedure for simulating evaluation queries to compute $\mathsf{Eval}(\mathsf{msk}, x)$ in $\mathsf{CheckDis}$. If $\mathsf{CheckDis}$ outputs 0, then $\mathcal{B}$ replies to $\mathcal{A}$ with $\varnothing$.

     Otherwise, if $\mathsf{CheckDis}$ outputs 1, for $i \ne i^*$, algorithm $\mathcal{B}$ computes T_i by emulating an execution of $\mathsf{TPRF}_{\mathsf{nc}}.\mathsf{Trace}^{D_i}(\mathsf{msk}_i, 1^{4z})$. Whenever $\mathsf{TPRF}_{\mathsf{nc}}.\mathsf{Trace}^{D_i}$ makes a query to the oracle-aided algorithm D_i^O, algorithm $\mathcal{B}$ implements the logic as follows:

- When $\mathsf{TPRF_{nc}.Trace}$ makes an oracle query to D_i on input 1^λ, algorithm $\mathcal{B}$ starts running $D^{O'}(1^\lambda)$.
- When D makes an oracle query to its oracle O', algorithm $\mathcal{B}$ treats it as if D_i made a query to O, and computes the oracle's response (x, y) according to the specification in $\mathsf{TPRF_{nc}.Trace}$. Algorithm $\mathcal{B}$ then makes an evaluation query to its challenger on input x to receive y_{i^*} and computes $y' \leftarrow y \oplus \big(\bigoplus_{j \neq i, i^*} \mathsf{TPRF_{nc}.Eval}(\mathsf{msk}_j, x)\big) \oplus y_{i^*}$, and gives the pair (x, y') to D as the response from O'.

Let T_i be the output of this emulated execution of $\mathsf{TPRF_{nc}.Trace}^{D_i}(\mathsf{msk}_i, 1^{4z})$. Next, to compute T_{i^*}, algorithm $\mathcal{B}$ defines the oracle-aided algorithm $D_{i^*}^O$ according to the specification of the real tracing algorithm:

- On input the security parameter λ, run $D^{O'}(1^\lambda)$.
- Whenever D makes a query to its oracle O', the distinguisher D_{i^*} makes a query to its own oracle to obtain a sample (x, y). Algorithm D_{i^*} computes $y' \leftarrow y \oplus \big(\bigoplus_{j \neq i^*} \mathsf{TPRF_{nc}.Eval}(\mathsf{msk}_j, x)\big)$ and replies to D with the same (x, y').

Algorithm $\mathcal{B}$ submits a tracing query on $D_{i^*}^O$ to its challenger to obtain a set T_{i^*}. If $T_{i^*} \neq \{b^*\}$, algorithm $\mathcal{B}$ halts and outputs $D_{\mathsf{nc}} = D_{i^*}$. Otherwise, for each $i \in [\ell]$, if $0 \in T_i$, it sets $\bar{w}_i^* = 0$, and otherwise, it sets $\bar{w}_i^* = 1$. It replies to $\mathcal{A}$ with $\mathsf{FC.Trace}(\mathsf{tk_{FC}}, \bar{w}^*)$.

4. After $\mathcal{A}$ has finished making queries (and assuming $\mathcal{B}$ has not yet aborted), then $\mathcal{A}$ outputs a distinguisher D. Algorithm $\mathcal{B}$ constructs the oracle-aided algorithm D_{nc}^O using the same procedure as in $D_{i^*}^O$ in the above description for simulating tracing queries. Finally, it outputs D_{nc} as its distinguisher.

By construction, algorithm $\mathcal{B}$ perfectly simulates an execution of experiment Hyb_1 for $\mathcal{A}$ unless $\mathcal{A}$ makes a key-generation query that causes $\mathcal{B}$ to abort. By assumption, in an execution of Hyb_1, algorithm $\mathcal{A}$ will output a distinguisher D and a tracing parameter 1^z (either as part of a tracing query or at the end of the experiment) that satisfies the following properties:

- $\mathsf{CheckDis}^D(\mathsf{msk}, 1^z)$ outputs 1.
- Let $\mathsf{id}_1, \ldots, \mathsf{id}_q \in [n]$ be the identities $\mathcal{A}$ submitted to the key-generation oracle prior to outputting $(D, 1^z)$ and let $\Gamma = \{\bar{w}^{(i)}\}_{i \in [n]}$ be the set of codewords $\bar{w}^{(i)} \in \{0,1\}^\ell$ sampled by Setup. Then, there exists an index $j \in [\ell]$ with the following two properties:
  - $\bar{w}_j^{(\mathsf{id}_i)} = \bar{w}_j^{(\mathsf{id}_1)}$ for all $i \in [q]$; and
  - $T_j \neq \{\bar{w}_j^{(\mathsf{id}_1)}\}$, where $T_j \leftarrow \mathsf{TPRF_{nc}.Trace}^{D_j}(\mathsf{msk}_j, 1^{4z})$, and D_j is the oracle-aided distinguisher as defined in Construction 3.6.

Algorithm $\mathcal{B}$ samples the index i^* and the bit b^* uniformly at random (and independently of the view of the adversary). Observe that if $i^* = j$ and $b^* = \bar{w}_j^{(\mathsf{id}_1)}$, algorithm $\mathcal{B}$ does not abort the simulation, and instead, outputs the distinguisher D_{i^*}. Thus, with probability at least $\varepsilon'/(2\ell)$, algorithm $\mathcal{B}$ does not abort and successfully outputs a distinguisher D_{nc}. We now argue that this implies events $\mathsf{GoodDis}_{\mathcal{B},1/(4z)}$ and $\neg\mathsf{CorrectTr}_{\mathcal{B},1/(4z)}$. In the following, we write msk_{i^*} to denote the master secret key sampled by the challenger in $\mathsf{ExptTPRF}^{\mathsf{TPRF}_{\mathsf{nc}}}_{\mathcal{B},1/(4z)}$. By construction, algorithm $\mathcal{B}$ simulates an execution of Hyb_1 with $\mathsf{msk} = (\mathsf{msk}_1, \ldots, \mathsf{msk}_\ell, \Gamma, \mathsf{tk}_{\mathsf{FC}}, \perp)$.

- Let $O_{\mathcal{A},b}(\mathsf{msk})$ and $O_{\mathcal{B},b}(\mathsf{msk}_{i^*})$ be the weak PRF challenge oracles from Definition 2.12 in $\mathsf{ExptTPRF}^{\mathsf{TPRF}}_{\mathcal{A},\varepsilon}$ and $\mathsf{ExptTPRF}^{\mathsf{TPRF}_{\mathsf{nc}}}_{\mathcal{B},1/(4z)}$, respectively. Since $\mathsf{CheckDis}^D(\mathsf{msk}, 1^z) = 1$, we appeal to Lemma 3.2 and conclude that with probability $1 - \mathsf{negl}(\lambda)$,

$$\Pr[D^{O_{\mathcal{A},b}}(1^\lambda) = b : b \xleftarrow{\text{R}} \{0,1\}] \geq 1/2 + 1/(4z).$$

  Consider the probability that $\Pr[D_{\mathsf{nc}}^{O_{\mathcal{B},b}(\mathsf{msk}_{i^*})}(1^\lambda) = b : b \xleftarrow{\text{R}} \{0,1\}]$. By construction, for any oracle O, $D^O_{\mathsf{nc}}(1^\lambda)$ outputs $D^{O'}(1^\lambda)$, where D_{nc} simulates oracles queries to O' by issuing a query to O to obtain (x, y), computing $y' \leftarrow y \oplus \big(\bigoplus_{j \neq i^*} \mathsf{TPRF}_{\mathsf{nc}}.\mathsf{Eval}(\mathsf{msk}_j, x)\big)$, and replying with (x, y'). We claim that if $O \equiv O_{\mathcal{B},b}(\mathsf{msk}_{i^*})$, then the oracle O' that D_{nc} simulates for D is precisely $O' \equiv O_{\mathcal{A},b}(\mathsf{msk})$.
  - Suppose $O \equiv O_{\mathcal{B},0}(\mathsf{msk}_{i^*})$. The output of O is a pair (x, y) where $x \xleftarrow{\text{R}} \mathcal{X}$ and $y \leftarrow \mathsf{Eval}(\mathsf{msk}_{i^*}, x)$. By construction of D_{nc}, the output of O' is then a pair (x, y') where $x \xleftarrow{\text{R}} \mathcal{X}$ and

$$y' = \mathsf{TPRF}_{\mathsf{nc}}.\mathsf{Eval}(\mathsf{msk}_{i^*}, x) \oplus \left(\bigoplus_{i \neq i^*} \mathsf{TPRF}_{\mathsf{nc}}.\mathsf{Eval}(\mathsf{msk}_i, x)\right) = \mathsf{Eval}(\mathsf{msk}, x).$$

    This is precisely the output distribution of $O_{\mathcal{A},0}(\mathsf{msk})$.
  - Suppose $O \equiv O_{\mathcal{B},1}(\mathsf{msk}_{i^*})$. The output of O is a pair (x, y) where $x \xleftarrow{\text{R}} \mathcal{X}$ and $y \xleftarrow{\text{R}} \{0,1\}^\rho$. In this case, the distribution of $y' = y \oplus \big(\bigoplus_{i \neq i^*} \mathsf{TPRF}_{\mathsf{nc}}.\mathsf{Eval}(\mathsf{msk}_i, x)\big)$ is uniform over $\{0,1\}^\rho$ since y is sampled independently of msk_i and x for all i. As such, the output distribution of O' precisely coincides with the output distribution of $O_{\mathcal{A},1}(\mathsf{msk})$.

  By the above analysis,

$$\Pr[D_{\mathsf{nc}}^{O_{\mathcal{B},b}(\mathsf{msk}_{i^*})}(1^\lambda) = b : b \xleftarrow{\text{R}} \{0,1\}] = \Pr[D^{O_{\mathcal{A},b}(\mathsf{msk})}(1^\lambda) = b : b \xleftarrow{\text{R}} \{0,1\}] \geq 1/2 + 1/(4z).$$

  Thus, the event $\mathsf{GoodDis}_{\mathcal{B},1/(4z)}$ holds.
- Next, let $T \leftarrow \mathsf{TPRF}_{\mathsf{nc}}.\mathsf{Trace}^{D_{i^*}}(\mathsf{msk}_{i^*}, 1^{4z})$ where D_{i^*} is constructed from D as specified in Construction 3.6. In the reduction, algorithm $\mathcal{B}$ constructs D_{nc} from D in exactly the same way. By assumption, we have that $T \neq \{b^*\}$. This means that the output of $\mathsf{TPRF}_{\mathsf{nc}}.\mathsf{Trace}^{D_{\mathsf{nc}}}(\mathsf{msk}_{i^*}, 1^{4z})$ is also not $\{b^*\}$. However, since $\mathcal{B}$ makes a single key-generation query to its challenger on identity b^*, this means that event $\neg\mathsf{CorrectTr}_{\mathcal{B},1/(4z)}$ occurs.

We conclude that $\Pr[\mathsf{GoodDis}_{\mathcal{B},1/(4z)} \wedge \neg\mathsf{CorrectTr}_{\mathcal{B},1/(4z)}] \geq \varepsilon'/(2\ell) - \mathsf{negl}(\lambda)$, which is non-negligible.

Lemma 3.12. *Let D be the distinguisher the adversary outputs at the end of the experiment. We define* $\mathsf{ProbGoodDis}$ *to be the event where* $\mathsf{CheckDis}^D(\mathsf{msk}, 1^{1/\varepsilon}) = 1$*. If* FC *is fully collusion resistant in the presence of $Q+1$ tracing queries, then for all adversaries $\mathcal{A}$ in* Hyb_2, $\Pr[\mathsf{ProbGoodDis} \wedge \neg\mathsf{CorrectTr}_{\mathcal{A},\varepsilon}] \leq \mathsf{negl}(\lambda)$.

Proof. Suppose there is an adversary $\mathcal{A}$ in Hyb_2 where $\Pr[\mathsf{Hyb}_2[\mathsf{ProbGoodDis} \wedge \neg\mathsf{CorrectTr}_{\mathcal{A},\varepsilon}] = 1] = \varepsilon'$ for some non-negligible ε'. We use $\mathcal{A}$ to construct an adversary $\mathcal{B}$ for the fingerprinting code security game:

1. Algorithm $\mathcal{B}$ samples $\mathsf{msk}_i \leftarrow \mathsf{TPRF}_{\mathsf{nc}}.\mathsf{Setup}(1^\lambda)$ for each $i \in [\ell]$. It also initializes an initially empty table T.
2. Algorithm $\mathcal{B}$ starts running $\mathcal{A}$. Whenever $\mathcal{A}$ makes an oracle query, algorithm $\mathcal{B}$ does the following:
   - **Evaluation queries:** On input $x \in \mathcal{X}$, $\mathcal{B}$ computes $y_i \leftarrow \mathsf{TPRF}_{\mathsf{nc}}.\mathsf{Eval}(\mathsf{msk}_i, x)$ and replies to $\mathcal{A}$ with $y \leftarrow \bigoplus_{i\in[\ell]} y_i$.
   - **Key-generation queries:** On input $\mathsf{id} \in [n]$, $\mathcal{B}$ makes an encode query to its oracle to obtain a codeword $\bar{w}^{(\mathsf{id})} \in \{0,1\}^\ell$. Then, for each $i \in [\ell]$, algorithm $\mathcal{B}$ checks if there exists a mapping $(i, \bar{w}_i^{(\mathsf{id})}) \mapsto r_{i,\bar{w}_i^{(\mathsf{id})}}$ in T. If not, it samples a random $r_{i,\bar{w}_i^{(\mathsf{id})}} \xleftarrow{\text{R}} \mathcal{R}$ and adds $(i, \bar{w}_i^{(\mathsf{id})}) \mapsto r_{i,\bar{w}_i^{(\mathsf{id})}}$ to T. Algorithm $\mathcal{B}$ then computes $\mathsf{sk}_i \leftarrow \mathsf{TPRF}_{\mathsf{nc}}.\mathsf{KeyGen}(\mathsf{msk}_i, \bar{w}_i^{(\mathsf{id})}; r_{i,\bar{w}_i^{(\mathsf{id})}})$ for each i and replies to $\mathcal{A}$ with the tuple $(\mathsf{sk}_1, \ldots, \mathsf{sk}_\ell, \bot, \bot, \bot)$
   - **Tracing queries:** On input a distinguisher D and a tracing parameter 1^z, algorithm $\mathcal{B}$ first runs $\mathsf{CheckDis}^D(\mathsf{msk}, 1^z)$ where $\mathsf{msk} = (\mathsf{msk}_1, \ldots, \mathsf{msk}_\ell, \bot, \bot, \bot)$. If $\mathsf{CheckDis}$ outputs 0, output $\varnothing$. Otherwise, algorithm $\mathcal{B}$ computes the bits $\bar{w}_i^*$ using the same procedure as in Trace^D for each $i \in [\ell]$. It then submits a tracing query $\bar{w}^* \in \{0,1\}^\ell$ to its challenger. If the challenger replies with $\bot$, then $\mathcal{B}$ halts and outputs $\bot$. Otherwise, if the challenger replies with a set $S \subseteq [n]$, algorithm $\mathcal{B}$ replies to $\mathcal{A}$ with S.
3. After $\mathcal{A}$ finishes making its queries, algorithm $\mathcal{A}$ outputs a distinguisher D. Algorithm $\mathcal{B}$ again computes $\bar{w}_i^*$ using the same procedure as in Trace^D for each $i \in [\ell]$. It submits a tracing query $\bar{w}^* \in \{0,1\}^\ell$ to its challenger.

We claim that $\mathcal{B}$ either *perfectly* simulates an execution of Hyb_2 for $\mathcal{A}$ or the experiment $\mathsf{ExptFC}_{\mathcal{B}}^{\mathsf{FC}}$ outputs 1. First, algorithm $\mathcal{B}$ perfectly simulates the evaluation and key-generation queries. We consider the tracing queries. Let D be the distinguisher and 1^z be the tracing parameter that $\mathcal{A}$ submits to the tracing oracle.

- If $\mathsf{CheckDis}^D(\mathsf{msk}, 1^{1/\varepsilon})$ outputs 0, then the output in Hyb_2 is $\varnothing$, which matches the behavior of $\mathcal{B}$.
- Alternatively, if $\mathsf{CheckDis}^D(\mathsf{msk}, 1^z)$ outputs 1, then the word $\bar{w}^* \in \{0,1\}^\ell$ is computed using the same procedure as in Hyb_2. If $\bar{w}^* \in F(W)$, where $W = \{\bar{w}^{(\mathsf{id}_j)}\}_{j\in[Q]}$, $\mathsf{id}_1, \ldots, \mathsf{id}_Q \in [n]$ are the identities $\mathcal{A}$ submitted to the

key-generation oracle prior to outputting D, and $\Gamma = \{\bar{w}^{(i)}\}_{i \in [n]}$ is the codebook sampled by the challenger for the fingerprinting code, then either the simulation is correct or experiment $\mathsf{ExptFC}_{\mathcal{B}}^{\mathsf{FC}}$ outputs 1. If $\bar{w}^* \notin F(W)$, then the output in Hyb_2 is $\perp$, which matches the behavior of $\mathcal{B}$.

Thus, either $\mathcal{B}$ perfectly simulates an execution of Hyb_2 for $\mathcal{A}$ or the experiment $\mathsf{ExptFC}_{\mathcal{B}}^{\mathsf{FC}}$ outputs 1.

It suffices to show that in the case where $\mathcal{B}$ perfectly simulates the execution of Hyb_2, the experiment $\mathsf{ExptFC}_{\mathcal{B}}^{\mathsf{FC}}$ also outputs 1 with probability at least ε'. By assumption, in Hyb_2, with probability ε', algorithm $\mathcal{A}$ will output a distinguisher D that satisfies $\mathsf{ProbGoodDis}$ and $\neg\mathsf{CorrectTr}_{\mathcal{A},\varepsilon}$ (and the experiment does not abort). Since $\mathsf{ProbGoodDis}$ occurs (and the experiment does not abort), $\mathsf{Trace}^D(\mathsf{msk}, 1^{1/\varepsilon})$ computes a word $\bar{w}^* \in \{0,1\}^\ell$ where $\bar{w}^* \in F(W)$, where $W = \{\bar{w}^{(\mathsf{id}_j)}\}_{j \in [Q]}$ and $\mathsf{id}_1, \ldots, \mathsf{id}_Q \in [n]$ are the identities algorithm $\mathcal{B}$ makes to the encode oracle (when responding to $\mathcal{A}$'s key-generation queries). Since the output of $\mathsf{Trace}^D(\mathsf{msk}, 1^{1/\varepsilon})$ in this case is $\mathsf{FC.Trace}(\mathsf{tk}_{\mathsf{FC}}, \bar{w}^*)$, and $\neg\mathsf{CorrectTr}_{\mathcal{A},\varepsilon}$ occurs, this means that $\mathsf{FC.Trace}(\mathsf{tk}_{\mathsf{FC}}, \bar{w}^*)$ outputs a non-empty set S that contains an identity id' where $\mathsf{id}' \notin \{\mathsf{id}_1, \ldots, \mathsf{id}_Q\}$. In this case, experiment $\mathsf{ExptFC}_{\mathcal{B}}^{\mathsf{FC}}$ outputs 1 and the claim holds.

Lemma 3.13. *If* FC *is a fully collusion resistant in the presence of* $Q+1$ *tracing queries, then for all adversaries* $\mathcal{A}$ *in* Hyb_2, $\Pr[\mathsf{BadTr}_{\mathcal{A},\varepsilon}] \le \mathsf{negl}(\lambda)$.

Proof. Take an adversary $\mathcal{A}$ in Hyb_2, and let D be the distinguisher that $\mathcal{A}$ outputs at the end of Hyb_2. Let $S_{\mathsf{id}} \subseteq [n]$ be the set of identities that $\mathcal{A}$ submits to the key-generation oracle in Hyb_2. Consider the output of $\mathsf{Trace}^D(\mathsf{msk}, 1^{1/\varepsilon})$. We consider two possibilities:

- Suppose $\mathsf{CheckDis}^D(\mathsf{msk}, 1^{1/\varepsilon})$ outputs 0. Then the Trace algorithm outputs $\varnothing$ and $\mathsf{BadTr}_{\mathcal{A},\varepsilon}$ does not occur.
- Suppose $\mathsf{CheckDis}^D(\mathsf{msk}, 1^{1/\varepsilon})$ outputs 1. For $\mathsf{BadTr}_{\mathcal{A},\varepsilon}$ to occur in this case, the Trace algorithm must output a set T where $\varnothing \neq T \not\subseteq S_{\mathsf{id}}$. But this means $\neg\mathsf{CorrectTr}_{\mathcal{A},\varepsilon}$ occurs in addition to the event $\mathsf{ProbGoodDis}$ (from Lemma 3.12). By Lemma 3.12, this event occurs with negligible probability. pagination ☐

Combining Lemmas 3.10–3.13, we have that in $\mathsf{Hyb}_0 \equiv \mathsf{ExptTPRF}_{\mathcal{A},\varepsilon}^{\mathsf{TPRF}}$, for all efficient adversaries $\mathcal{A}$,

$$\Pr[\mathsf{CheckDis}^D(\mathsf{msk}, 1^{1/\varepsilon}) = 1 \wedge \neg\mathsf{CorrectTr}_{\mathcal{A},\varepsilon}] \le \mathsf{negl}(\lambda) \text{ and } \Pr[\mathsf{BadTr}_{\mathcal{A},\varepsilon}] \le \mathsf{negl}(\lambda),$$

where D is the distinguisher $\mathcal{A}$ outputs at the end of the experiment. To complete the proof, we compute the probability of the event $\mathsf{GoodDis}_{\mathcal{A},\varepsilon} \wedge \neg\mathsf{CorrectTr}_{\mathcal{A},\varepsilon}$. By Lemma 3.2, if $\mathsf{GoodDis}_{\mathcal{A},\varepsilon}$ holds, then $\mathsf{CheckDis}^D(\mathsf{msk}, 1^{1/\varepsilon}) = 1$ with probability $1 - \mathsf{negl}(\lambda)$. Correspondingly,

$$\Pr[\mathsf{GoodDis}_{\mathcal{A},\varepsilon} \wedge \neg\mathsf{CorrectTr}_{\mathcal{A},\varepsilon}] \le \mathsf{negl}(\lambda),$$

and the claim follows. ☐

4 An Application: Traitor Tracing with Active Security

In this section, we introduce stronger security notions for traitor tracing in the secret-key setting, and then show that our new traceable PRFs directly yields constructions of these notions. We strengthen existing definitions along two main axis:

- **CCA-security:** We require that the underlying encryption scheme itself is secure against chosen-ciphertext attacks (i.e., "CCA-secure") [NY90, RS91, DDN00]. CCA-security (and in the symmetric setting, authenticated encryption), is essential for guaranteeing security against active adversaries. Previous definitions of traitor tracing only required that the underlying encryption scheme be secure against chosen plaintext attacks (i.e., "CPA-secure"), which is inadequate in the presence of active adversaries.
- **Secure tracing against active adversaries:** Like many recent works [GKW18, CVW+18, Zha20], our construction only supports secret tracing. Analogous to the setting of traceable PRFs, we can consider a stronger tracing requirement where secure tracing holds even if the adversary has access to a tracing oracle. This models active adversaries that can make multiple attempts to try and evade the traitor tracing algorithm (and can observe the behavior of the tracing authority in response to each of those attempts).

We first recall the definition of traitor tracing, specialized to the secret-key setting. Our definitions are adapted from those of Goyal et al. [GKW18] and Zhandry [Zha20].

Definition 4.1 (Traitor Tracing [GKW18, Zha20, adapted]**).** *Let λ be a security parameter. A secret-key traitor tracing scheme with message space $\mathcal{M}$ and identity space $[n]$ where $n = n(\lambda)$ is a tuple of five algorithms* $\mathsf{TT} = (\mathsf{Setup}, \mathsf{KeyGen}, \mathsf{Enc}, \mathsf{Dec}, \mathsf{Trace})$ *with the following properties:*[7]

- $\mathsf{Setup}(1^\lambda) \to \mathsf{msk}$*: The setup algorithm takes as input the security parameter λ, and outputs a master secret key* msk.
- $\mathsf{KeyGen}(\mathsf{msk}, \mathsf{id}) \to \mathsf{sk}_{\mathsf{id}}$*: The key-generation algorithm takes the master secret key* msk *and an identity* $\mathsf{id} \in [n]$ *and outputs a secret key* $\mathsf{sk}_{\mathsf{id}}$.
- $\mathsf{Enc}(\mathsf{msk}, m) \to \mathsf{ct}$. *The encryption algorithm takes the master secret key* msk *and a message $m \in \mathcal{M}$ and outputs a ciphertext* ct.
- $\mathsf{Dec}(\mathsf{sk}, \mathsf{ct}) \to m$. *The decryption algorithm takes as input a secret key* sk *(which could be the master key* msk*) and a ciphertext* ct *and outputs a message $m \in \mathcal{M} \cup \{\perp\}$.*
- $\mathsf{Trace}^D(\mathsf{msk}, 1^z, m_0, m_1) \to T$. *The tracing algorithm has oracle access to a program D, and takes as input the master secret key* msk*, a parameter z, and two messages $m_0, m_1 \in \mathcal{M}$. It outputs a set $T \subseteq [n]$.*

Moreover, the traitor tracing scheme should satisfy the following correctness property:

[7] More generally, the message space $\mathcal{M} = \{\mathcal{M}_\lambda\}_{\lambda \in \mathbb{N}}$ can also be parameterized by the security parameter λ. For simplicity of notation, we omit this parameterization here.

- ***Correctness:*** *For all polynomials $n = n(\lambda)$, there exists a negligible function* $\mathsf{negl}(\cdot)$ *such that for all $\lambda \in \mathbb{N}$, all identities* $\mathsf{id} \in [n]$ *and all messages $m \in \mathcal{M}$,*

$$\Pr[\mathsf{Dec}(\mathsf{msk}, \mathsf{Enc}(\mathsf{msk}, m)) \neq m : \mathsf{msk} \leftarrow \mathsf{Setup}(1^\lambda)] \leq \mathsf{negl}(\lambda)$$

and

$$\Pr[\mathsf{Dec}(\mathsf{KeyGen}(\mathsf{msk}, \mathsf{id}), \mathsf{Enc}(\mathsf{msk}, m)) \neq m : \mathsf{msk} \leftarrow \mathsf{Setup}(1^\lambda)] \leq \mathsf{negl}(\lambda).$$

Security. There are two main security requirements on a traitor tracing scheme. The first is that the underlying encryption scheme is semantically secure and the second is tracing security. As noted above, most existing definitions of traitor tracing only consider these notions in a "passive setting" (i.e., CPA security and tracing security where the adversary does not have access to the tracing oracle). In this work, we consider *active* notions of both security notions. Namely, we require that the underlying encryption scheme satisfy CCA-security and that tracing security holds even if the adversary has access to the tracing oracle. We define these notions formally below:

Definition 4.2 (CCA Security). *A secret-key traitor tracing scheme* $\mathsf{TT} = (\mathsf{Setup}, \mathsf{KeyGen}, \mathsf{Enc}, \mathsf{Dec}, \mathsf{Trace})$ *is CCA-secure if for every efficient and admissible algorithm $\mathcal{A}$, there exists a negligible function* $\mathsf{negl}(\cdot)$ *such that for all $\lambda \in N$,*

$$\Pr\left[\mathcal{A}^{\mathcal{O}_b(\mathsf{msk},\cdot,\cdot),\mathsf{Dec}(\mathsf{msk},\cdot)}(1^\lambda) = b : \mathsf{msk} \leftarrow \mathsf{Setup}(1^\lambda), b \xleftarrow{\text{R}} \{0,1\}\right] \leq \frac{1}{2} + \mathsf{negl}(\lambda),$$

where $\mathcal{O}_b(\mathsf{msk}, m_0, m_1)$ outputs $\mathsf{Enc}(\mathsf{msk}, m_b)$. We say that $\mathcal{A}$ is admissible if for all queries ct *that algorithm $\mathcal{A}$ submits to the decryption oracle $\mathsf{Dec}(\mathsf{msk}, \cdot)$, it is the case that* ct *was* not *previously output by the encryption oracle $\mathcal{O}_b$.*

Definition 4.3 (Tracing Security against Active Adversaries). *Let* $\mathsf{TT} = (\mathsf{Setup}, \mathsf{KeyGen}, \mathsf{Enc}, \mathsf{Dec}, \mathsf{Trace})$ *be a secret-key traitor tracing scheme with message space $\mathcal{M}$ and identity space $[n]$ where $n = n(\lambda)$. For a function $\varepsilon = \varepsilon(\lambda)$ and adversary $\mathcal{A}$, we define the tracing experiment $\mathsf{ExptTT}^{\mathsf{TT}}_{\mathcal{A},\varepsilon}(\lambda)$ as follows:*

> **Experiment** $\mathsf{ExptTT}^{\mathsf{TT}}_{\mathcal{A},\varepsilon}(\lambda)$
>
> - $\mathsf{msk} \leftarrow \mathsf{Setup}(1^\lambda)$.
> - $(D, m_0, m_1) \leftarrow \mathcal{A}^{\mathsf{KeyGen}(\mathsf{msk},\cdot),\mathsf{Enc}(\mathsf{msk},\cdot),\mathsf{Dec}(\mathsf{msk},\cdot)}$
> - $T \leftarrow \mathsf{Trace}^D(\mathsf{msk}, 1^{1/\varepsilon(\lambda)}, m_0, m_1)$.

Let S_{id} be the set of identities algorithm $\mathcal{A}$ submits to the key-generation oracle. Based on the output of $\mathsf{ExptTT}^{\mathsf{TT}}_{\mathcal{A},\varepsilon}$ above experiment, we define the following set of (probabilistic) events and the corresponding probabilities (which are functions of λ and parameterized by $\mathcal{A}, \varepsilon$):

- $\mathsf{GoodDis}_{\mathcal{A},\varepsilon}$: *This is the event where* $\Pr[D^{O_b}(1^\lambda) = b : b \xleftarrow{R} 0, 1] \geq 1/2 + \varepsilon(\lambda)$, *where oracle* O_b *is the semantic security challenge oracle (with* msk *hard-wired) that outputs* $\mathsf{Enc}(\mathsf{msk}, m_b)$. *This property says that the distinguisher* D *output by* $\mathcal{A}$ *can successfully distinguish between encryptions of* m_0 *and* m_1.[8]
- $\mathsf{CorrectTr}_{\mathcal{A},\varepsilon}$: *This is the event where* $T \neq \varnothing \wedge T \subseteq S$. *This event corresponds to the tracing algorithm successfully outputting one or more of the keys the adversary possesses.*
- $\mathsf{BadTr}_{\mathcal{A},\varepsilon}$: $T \nsubseteq S$. *This event corresponds to the tracing algorithm outputting a key that the adversary did not request.*

A traitor tracing scheme $\mathcal{T}$ *satisfies secure tracing if for every* $\lambda \in \mathbb{N}$, *every efficient adversary* $\mathcal{A}$, *and every inverse polynomial function* $\varepsilon(\lambda) = 1/\mathsf{poly}(\lambda)$, *there exists a negligible function* $\mathsf{negl}(\cdot)$ *such that*

$$\Pr[\mathsf{BadTr}_{\mathcal{A},\varepsilon}] \leq \mathsf{negl}(\lambda) \text{ and } \Pr[\mathsf{CorrectTr}_{\mathcal{A},\varepsilon}] \geq \Pr[\mathsf{GoodDis}_{\mathcal{A},\varepsilon}] - \mathsf{negl}(\lambda). \quad (4.1)$$

Similar to the case with traceable PRFs (Definition 2.14), we say that TT *satisfies secure tracing against active adversaries if Eq. 4.1 holds even if the adversary* $\mathcal{A}$ *in* $\mathsf{ExptTT}^{\mathsf{TT}}_{\mathcal{A},\varepsilon}$ *has oracle access to a tracing oracle* $\mathcal{O}(\mathsf{msk}, \cdot, \cdot, \cdot, \cdot)$ *that takes as input the description of a distinguisher* D, *the tracing parameter* 1^z, *and two messages* m_0 *and* m_1, *and outputs* $\mathsf{Trace}^D(\mathsf{msk}, 1^z, m_0, m_1)$. *We say* TT *satisfies secure tracing against* Q*-bounded active adversaries if secure tracing holds against all efficient adversaries that makes at most* Q *queries to the tracing oracle* $\mathcal{O}(\mathsf{msk}, \cdot, \cdot, \cdot, \cdot)$.

4.1 Traceable PRFs to Traitor Tracing

It is well known that PRFs can be used to construct authenticated encryption schemes (e.g., via the "encrypt-then-MAC" paradigm [BN00]). Not surprising, instantiating the encryption scheme with a traceable PRF and composing with an arbitrary MAC (*without* any tracing guarantees) directly yields a traitor tracing scheme where the underlying encryption scheme is an authenticated encryption (and hence, trivially satisfies CCA-security). Moreover, if the underlying traceable PRF is secure against (Q-bounded) active adversaries, then the resulting traitor tracing scheme is also secure against (Q-bounded) active adversaries. We state the construction below:

Construction 4.4 (Secret-Key Traitor Tracing with Active Security). Let $\lambda \in \mathbb{N}$ be a security parameter. Let $\mathsf{TPRF} = (\mathsf{TPRF.Setup}, \mathsf{TPRF.KeyGen}, \mathsf{TPRF.Eval}, \mathsf{TPRF.Trace})$ be a traceable PRF with domain $\mathcal{X}$, range $\{0,1\}^\rho$, and identity space $[n]$. Let $\mathsf{PRF}\colon \mathcal{K} \times (\mathcal{X} \times \{0,1\}^\rho) \to \{0,1\}^\lambda$ be a secure PRF. We construct a secret-key traitor tracing scheme with message space $\{0,1\}^\rho$ as follows:

[8] In the public-key setting considering in previous works, it is unnecessary to give D oracle access to the encryption algorithm, since the distinguisher can simulate encryption queries itself using the public key. In the secret-key setting, we provide the adversary oracle access to the encryption algorithm.

- $\mathsf{Setup}(1^\lambda)$: Run $\mathsf{TPRF.msk} \leftarrow \mathsf{TPRF.Setup}(1^\lambda)$ and $k \xleftarrow{R} \mathcal{K}$. Output $\mathsf{msk} = (\mathsf{TPRF.msk}, k)$.
- $\mathsf{KeyGen}(\mathsf{msk}, \mathsf{id})$: On input $\mathsf{msk} = (\mathsf{TPRF.msk}, k)$, output $\mathsf{sk}_{\mathsf{id}} = (\mathsf{TPRF.sk}_{\mathsf{id}}, k)$ where $\mathsf{TPRF.sk}_{\mathsf{id}} \leftarrow \mathsf{TPRF.KeyGen}(\mathsf{TPRF.msk}, \mathsf{id})$.
- $\mathsf{Enc}(\mathsf{msk}, m)$: On input $\mathsf{msk} = (\mathsf{TPRF.msk}, k)$, sample $x \xleftarrow{R} \mathcal{X}$, and compute $y \leftarrow \mathsf{TPRF.Eval}(\mathsf{TPRF.msk}, x) \oplus m$, $\tau \leftarrow \mathsf{PRF}(k, (x, y))$. Output the ciphertext $\mathsf{ct} \leftarrow (x, y, \tau)$.
- $\mathsf{Dec}(\mathsf{sk}, \mathsf{ct})$: On input $\mathsf{sk} = (\mathsf{TPRF.sk}, k)$ and $\mathsf{ct} = (x, y, \tau)$, check if $\mathsf{PRF}(k, (x, y)) = \tau$. If the check fails, output $\perp$. Otherwise, output $\mathsf{TPRF.Eval}(\mathsf{TPRF.sk}, x) \oplus y$.
- $\mathsf{Trace}^D(\mathsf{msk}, 1^z, m_0, m_1)$: On input $\mathsf{msk} = (\mathsf{TPRF.msk}, k)$, the parameter z, messages $m_0, m_1 \in \{0,1\}^\rho$, and a distinguisher D, define the oracle-aided traceable PRF distinguisher $\hat{D}^{\hat{O}}$ that operates as follows:
  - Sample a bit $\beta \xleftarrow{R} \{0,1\}$.
  - Run the distinguisher D. Whenever D makes a query to its encryption oracle, algorithm $\hat{D}$ makes a query to its oracle $\hat{O}$ to obtain a value (x, y).
  - Compute $z \leftarrow y \oplus m_\beta$ and $\tau \leftarrow \mathsf{PRF}(k, (x, z))$. Algorithm $\hat{D}$ replies to D's query with the ciphertext $\mathsf{ct} = (x, z, \tau)$.
  - Eventually, algorithm D outputs a bit $\beta' \in \{0,1\}$. Algorithm $\hat{D}$ outputs 0 if $\beta = \beta'$ and 1 otherwise.

  Output $\mathsf{TPRF.Trace}^{\hat{D}}(\mathsf{TPRF.msk}, 1^{2z})$.

Correctness and Security Analysis. Correctness and security of Construction 4.4 follows directly from correctness and security of the underlying traceable PRF. We state the formal theorems here.

Theorem 4.5 (Correctness). *If* TPRF *satisfies key similarity, then* TT *from Construction 4.4 is correct.*

Proof. Take any message $m \in \mathcal{M}$. Sample $\mathsf{msk} \leftarrow \mathsf{Setup}(1^\lambda)$, and let $\mathsf{ct} = (x, y, \tau) \leftarrow \mathsf{Enc}(\mathsf{msk}, m)$. If we write $\mathsf{msk} = (\mathsf{TPRF.msk}, k)$, then $y = \mathsf{TPRF.Eval}(\mathsf{msk}, x) \oplus m$. Clearly, decryption with the master secret key correctly recovers m. For any identity $\mathsf{id} \in [n]$, decryption with $\mathsf{sk}_{\mathsf{id}} \leftarrow \mathsf{KeyGen}(\mathsf{msk}, \mathsf{id})$ succeeds as long as $\mathsf{TPRF.Eval}(\mathsf{TPRF.sk}_{\mathsf{id}}, x) = \mathsf{TPRF.Eval}(\mathsf{TPRF.msk}, x)$ where $\mathsf{TPRF.sk}_{\mathsf{id}} \leftarrow \mathsf{TPRF.KeyGen}(\mathsf{TPRF.msk}, \mathsf{id})$. Since x is uniform over $\mathcal{X}$, this follows by key similarity of TPRF. □

We now state the security theorems, but defer their proofs to the full version of this paper [MW21].

Theorem 4.6 (Authenticated Encryption). *If* TPRF *satisfies weak pseudorandomness and* PRF *is secure, then* TT *from Construction 4.4 is an authenticated encryption scheme, and correspondingly, CCA-secure.*

Theorem 4.7 (Tracing Security). *If* TPRF *satisfies secure tracing, then* TT *from Construction 4.4 also satisfies secure tracing. If* TPRF *is secure against (Q-bounded) active adversaries, then so is* TT.

Remark 4.8 (Longer Message Space). While Construction 4.4 only suffices to encrypt messages whose length ρ coincides with the output length of the PRF, as long as $\rho = \Omega(\lambda)$, it is easy to extend to arbitrary-length messages using standard key encapsulation techniques. Namely, we would use Construction 4.4 to encrypt a symmetric key k for an authenticated encryption scheme (that supports long messages), and then encrypt the message with the authenticated encryption scheme. As long as the key encapsulation mechanism supports tracing, the same extends to the composed scheme.

Acknowledgments. We thank the anonymous reviewers for helpful feedback on the presentation.

References

BGI+01. Barak, B., et al.: On the (im)possibility of obfuscating programs. In: Kilian, J. (ed.) CRYPTO 2001. LNCS, vol. 2139, pp. 1–18. Springer, Heidelberg (2001). https://doi.org/10.1007/3-540-44647-8_1

BGI+12. Barak, B., et al.: On the (im)possibility of obfuscating programs. J. ACM **59**(2), 1–48 (2012)

BLW17. Boneh, D., Lewi, K., Wu, D.J.: Constraining pseudorandom functions privately. In: PKC, pp. 494–524 (2017)

BN00. Bellare, M., Namprempre, C.: Authenticated encryption: relations among notions and analysis of the generic composition paradigm. In: Okamoto, T. (ed.) ASIACRYPT 2000. LNCS, vol. 1976, pp. 531–545. Springer, Heidelberg (2000). https://doi.org/10.1007/3-540-44448-3_41

BN08. Boneh, D., Naor, M.: Traitor tracing with constant size ciphertext. In: ACM CCS, pp. 501–510 (2008)

BP08. Billet, O., Phan, D.H.: Efficient traitor tracing from collusion secure codes. In: Safavi-Naini, R. (ed.) ICITS 2008. LNCS, vol. 5155, pp. 171–182. Springer, Heidelberg (2008). https://doi.org/10.1007/978-3-540-85093-9_17

BS95. Boneh, D., Shaw, J.: Collusion-secure fingerprinting for digital data. In: Coppersmith, D. (ed.) CRYPTO 1995. LNCS, vol. 963, pp. 452–465. Springer, Heidelberg (1995). https://doi.org/10.1007/3-540-44750-4_36

BSW06. Boneh, D., Sahai, A., Waters, B.: Fully collusion resistant traitor tracing with short ciphertexts and private keys. In: Vaudenay, S. (ed.) EUROCRYPT 2006. LNCS, vol. 4004, pp. 573–592. Springer, Heidelberg (2006). https://doi.org/10.1007/11761679_34

CFN94. van Tilborg, H.C.A., Jajodia, S. (eds.): Encyclopedia of Cryptography and Security. Springer, Boston (2011). https://doi.org/10.1007/978-1-4419-5906-5

CFNP00. Chor, B., Fiat, A., Naor, M., Pinkas, B.: Tracing traitors. IEEE Trans. Information Theory **46**(3), 893–910 (2000)

CHN+16. Cohen, A., Holmgren, J., Nishimaki, R., Vaikuntanathan, V., Wichs, D.: Watermarking cryptographic capabilities. In: STOC, pp. 1115–1127 (2016)

CVW+18. Chen, Y., Vaikuntanathan, V., Waters, B., Wee, H., Wichs, D.: Traitor-tracing from LWE made simple and attribute-based. In: Beimel, A., Dziembowski, S. (eds.) TCC 2018. LNCS, vol. 11240, pp. 341–369. Springer, Cham (2018). https://doi.org/10.1007/978-3-030-03810-6_13

DDN00. Dolev, D., Dwork, C., Naor, M.: Nonmalleable cryptography. SIAM J. Comput. **30**(2), 391–437 (2000)

GGM84. Goldreich, O., Goldwasser, S., Micali, S.: How to construct random functions (extended abstract). In: FOCS, pp. 464–479 (1984)

GKM+19. Goyal, R., Kim, S., Manohar, N., Waters, B., Wu, D.J.: Watermarking public-key cryptographic primitives. In: Boldyreva, A., Micciancio, D. (eds.) CRYPTO 2019. LNCS, vol. 11694, pp. 367–398. Springer, Cham (2019). https://doi.org/10.1007/978-3-030-26954-8_12

GKSW10. Garg, S., Kumarasubramanian, A., Sahai, A., Waters, B.: Building efficient fully collusion-resilient traitor tracing and revocation schemes. In: ACM CCS, pp. 121–130 (2010)

GKW18. Goyal, R., Koppula, V., Waters, B.: Collusion resistant traitor tracing from learning with errors. In: STOC, pp. 660–670 (2018)

GKW19. Goyal, R., Koppula, V., Waters, B.: New approaches to traitor tracing with embedded identities. In: Hofheinz, D., Rosen, A. (eds.) TCC 2019. LNCS, vol. 11892, pp. 149–179. Springer, Cham (2019). https://doi.org/10.1007/978-3-030-36033-7_6

GKWW21. Goyal, R., Kim, S., Waters, B., Wu, D.J.: Beyond software watermarking: traitor-tracing for pseudorandom functions. In: Tibouchi, M., Wang, H. (eds.) Advances in Cryptology – ASIACRYPT 2021. ASIACRYPT 2021. LNCS, vol. 13092. Springer, Cham (2021). https://doi.org/10.1007/978-3-030-92078-4_9

GQWW19. Goyal, R., Quach, W., Waters, B., Wichs, D.: Broadcast and trace with N^{ε} ciphertext size from standard assumptions. In: Boldyreva, A., Micciancio, D. (eds.) CRYPTO 2019. LNCS, vol. 11694, pp. 826–855. Springer, Cham (2019). https://doi.org/10.1007/978-3-030-26954-8_27

HMW07. Hopper, N., Molnar, D., Wagner, D.: From weak to strong watermarking. In: Vadhan, S.P. (ed.) TCC 2007. LNCS, vol. 4392, pp. 362–382. Springer, Heidelberg (2007). https://doi.org/10.1007/978-3-540-70936-7_20

Hoe63. Hoeffding, W.: Probability inequalities for sums of bounded random variables. J. Am. Stat. Assoc. **58**(301), 13–30 (1963)

KT15. Kiayias, A., Tang, Q.: Traitor deterring schemes: using bitcoin as collateral for digital content. In: ACM CCS, pp. 231–242 (2015)

KW17. Kim, S., Wu, D.J.: Watermarking cryptographic functionalities from standard lattice assumptions. In: Katz, J., Shacham, H. (eds.) CRYPTO 2017. LNCS, vol. 10401, pp. 503–536. Springer, Cham (2017). https://doi.org/10.1007/978-3-319-63688-7_17

KW19. Kim, S., Wu, D.J.: Watermarking PRFs from lattices: stronger security via extractable PRFs. In: Boldyreva, A., Micciancio, D. (eds.) CRYPTO 2019. LNCS, vol. 11694, pp. 335–366. Springer, Cham (2019). https://doi.org/10.1007/978-3-030-26954-8_11

LPSS14. Ling, S., Phan, D.H., Stehlé, D., Steinfeld, R.: Hardness of k-LWE and applications in traitor tracing. In: Garay, J.A., Gennaro, R. (eds.) CRYPTO 2014. LNCS, vol. 8616, pp. 315–334. Springer, Heidelberg (2014). https://doi.org/10.1007/978-3-662-44371-2_18

MW21. Maitra, S., Wu, D.J.: Traceable PRFs: full collusion resistance and active security. Cryptology ePrint Archive, Report 2021/1675 (2021). https://ia.cr/2021/1675

Nis20. Nishimaki, R.: Equipping public-key cryptographic primitives with watermarking (or: a hole is to watermark). In: Pass, R., Pietrzak, K. (eds.) TCC 2020. LNCS, vol. 12550, pp. 179–209. Springer, Cham (2020). https://doi.org/10.1007/978-3-030-64375-1_7

NP98. Naor, M., Pinkas, B.: Threshold traitor tracing. In: Krawczyk, H. (ed.) CRYPTO 1998. LNCS, vol. 1462, pp. 502–517. Springer, Heidelberg (1998). https://doi.org/10.1007/BFb0055750

NWZ16. Nishimaki, R., Wichs, D., Zhandry, M.: Anonymous traitor tracing: how to embed arbitrary information in a key. In: Fischlin, M., Coron, J.-S. (eds.) EUROCRYPT 2016. LNCS, vol. 9666, pp. 388–419. Springer, Heidelberg (2016). https://doi.org/10.1007/978-3-662-49896-5_14

NY90. Naor, M., Yung, M.: Public-key cryptosystems provably secure against chosen ciphertext attacks. In: STOC, pp. 427–437 (1990)

QWZ18. Quach, W., Wichs, D., Zirdelis, G.: Watermarking PRFs under standard assumptions: public marking and security with extraction queries. In: Beimel, A., Dziembowski, S. (eds.) TCC 2018. LNCS, vol. 11240, pp. 669–698. Springer, Cham (2018). https://doi.org/10.1007/978-3-030-03810-6_24

RS91. Rackoff, C., Simon, D.R.: Non-interactive zero-knowledge proof of knowledge and chosen ciphertext attack. In: Feigenbaum, J. (ed.) CRYPTO 1991. LNCS, vol. 576, pp. 433–444. Springer, Heidelberg (1992). https://doi.org/10.1007/3-540-46766-1_35

SSW01. Staddon, J., Stinson, D.R., Wei, R.: Combinatorial properties of frameproof and traceability codes. IEEE Trans. Information Theory **47**(3), 1042–1049 (2001)

Tar03. Tardos, G.: Optimal probabilistic fingerprint codes. In: STOC, pp. 116–125 (2003)

YAL+18. Yang, R., Au, M.H., Lai, J., Xu, Q., Yu, Z.: Unforgeable watermarking schemes with public extraction. In: Catalano, D., De Prisco, R. (eds.) SCN 2018. LNCS, vol. 11035, pp. 63–80. Springer, Cham (2018). https://doi.org/10.1007/978-3-319-98113-0_4

YAL+19. Yang, R., Au, M.H., Lai, J., Xu, Q., Yu, Z.: Collusion resistant watermarking schemes for cryptographic functionalities. In: Galbraith, S.D., Moriai, S. (eds.) ASIACRYPT 2019. LNCS, vol. 11921, pp. 371–398. Springer, Cham (2019). https://doi.org/10.1007/978-3-030-34578-5_14

YAYX20. Yang, R., Au, M.H., Yu, Z., Xu, Q.: Collusion resistant watermarkable PRFs from standard assumptions. In: Micciancio, D., Ristenpart, T. (eds.) CRYPTO 2020. LNCS, vol. 12170, pp. 590–620. Springer, Cham (2020). https://doi.org/10.1007/978-3-030-56784-2_20

Zha20. Zhandry, M.: New techniques for traitor tracing: size $N^{1/3}$ and more from pairings. In: Micciancio, D., Ristenpart, T. (eds.) CRYPTO 2020. LNCS, vol. 12170, pp. 652–682. Springer, Cham (2020). https://doi.org/10.1007/978-3-030-56784-2_22

Tools

Radical Isogenies on Montgomery Curves

Hiroshi Onuki(✉) and Tomoki Moriya

Department of Mathematical Informatics, The University of Tokyo, Tokyo, Japan
{onuki,tomoki_moriya}@mist.i.u-tokyo.ac.jp

Abstract. We work on some open problems in radical isogenies. Radical isogenies are formulas to compute chains of N-isogenies for small N and proposed by Castryck, Decru, and Vercauteren in Asiacrypt 2020. These formulas do not need to generate a point of order N generating the kernel and accelerate some isogeny-based cryptosystems like CSIDH. On the other hand, since these formulas use Tate normal forms, these need to transform Tate normal forms to curves with efficient arithmetic, e.g., Montgomery curves. In this paper, we propose radical-isogeny formulas of degrees 3 and 4 on Montgomery curves. Our formulas compute some values determining Montgomery curves, from which one can efficiently recover Montgomery coefficients. And our formulas are more efficient for some cryptosystems than the original radical isogenies. In addition, we prove a conjecture left open by Castryck et al. that relates to radical isogenies of degree 4.

Keywords: Post-quantum cryptography · Radical isogenies · Montgomery curves · CSIDH

1 Introduction

Recent developments in quantum computers raise the importance of research on post-quantum cryptography (PQC), which is resistant to attacks using quantum computers. Isogeny-based cryptography is one of the promising candidates for PQC. Indeed, an isogeny-based cryptosystem SIKE is one of the 3rd-round alternate candidates in the NIST PQC competition [1]. An advantage of isogeny-based cryptography is that it has smaller public and private keys and ciphertext than other candidates for PQC. On the other hand, the computational costs of encryption and decryption in isogeny-based cryptography are relatively high.

The first isogeny-based cryptosystem was proposed by Couveignes [11] and by Rostovtsev and Stolbunov [20,22] independently. Their cryptosystem uses an action of the ideal class group of an order of an imaginary quadratic field on a set of ordinary elliptic curves. The action is calculated by isogenies between these elliptic curves. Isogenies between supersingular elliptic curves were brought to cryptography by Charles, Lauter, and Goren [9]. They proposed a cryptographic hash function based on supersingular isogenies. The security of their hash function is based on the hardness of path-finding in supersingular isogeny

G. Hanaoka et al. (Eds.): PKC 2022, LNCS 13177, pp. 473–497, 2022.
https://doi.org/10.1007/978-3-030-97121-2_17

graphs. Subsequently, Jao and De Feo [16] constructed a key-exchange protocol based on the hardness of a similar problem. Their protocol, SIDH (Supersingular Isogeny Diffie-Hellman), underlies SIKE. Castryck, Lange, Martindale, Panny, and Renes [7] proposed another key-exchange protocol using supersingular isogenies, CSIDH (commutative SIDH). As the scheme of Couveignes and Rostovtsev-Stolbunov, CSIDH uses an action of the ideal class group of an order of an imaginary quadratic field. On the other hand, CSIDH uses a set of $\mathbb{F}_p$-isomorphism classes of supersingular elliptic curves, and the action is calculated by isogenies defined over $\mathbb{F}_p$, where p is a large prime number. There are many protocols based on CSIDH, e.g., signature schemes, SeaSign [12] and CSI-FiSh [2]. In addition, public-key encryption schemes, SiGamal [19] and InSIDH [15], use the group action in CSIDH.

It is known that an isogeny can be computed from points in its kernel by using Vélu's formulas [24]. For accelerating the computation of isogeny-based cryptosystems, many variants of Vélu's formulas are considered. There are the formulas on Montgomery curves [10,13], Edwards curves [8,17], and Hessian curves [4]. In addition, Bernstein, De Feo, Leroux, and Smith [4] proposed a new algorithm that reduces the cost to compute an isogeny of degree ℓ from $O(\ell)$ to $\tilde{O}(\sqrt{\ell})$.

Castryck, Decru, and Vercauteren [6] proposed new formulas, radical isogenies, that compute a chain of isogenies of the same degree. They showed that radical isogenies are more efficient for small degrees than other isogeny formulas. In particular, they showed that radical isogenies accelerate a variant of CSIDH.

In CSIDH, we need to compute isogenies of small degrees over $\mathbb{F}_p$ repeatedly. These isogenies correspond to the actions of ideal classes. To compute an isogeny by Vélu's formula, we need a generator of the kernel of the isogeny. We obtain the generator from a random point on the domain of the isogeny by scalar multiplication. Let E be an elliptic curve such that $(0,0)$ on E has order ℓ and φ an isogeny with kernel generated by $(0,0)$. Then a radical-isogeny formula gives the codomain E' of φ such that an isogeny with kernel generated by $(0,0)$ on E' is not the dual isogeny $\hat{\varphi}$. The coefficients of E' are in the smallest field containing the coefficients of E and an ℓ-th root of a rational expression in the coefficients of E. In CSIDH, if ℓ is odd, then there is only one ℓ-th root in $\mathbb{F}_p$. Therefore, we can determine the codomain uniquely and apply radical isogenies iteratively.

On the other hand, if ℓ is even, then there are two choices of an ℓ-th root in $\mathbb{F}_p$, i.e., x and $-x$ have the same ℓ-th power. Castryck, Decru, and Vercauteren [6] conjectured a radical-isogeny formula of degree 4 that corresponds to the action of an ideal of norm 4 and left it as an open problem.

Another crucial open problem is to reduce the costs of transformations between elliptic curves in radical isogenies. Radical isogenies need to transform an elliptic curve to another curve on which the point $(0,0)$ has order ℓ. In particular, the calculation of radical isogenies are as follows:

1. Take a starting curve E as a Montgomery curve.
2. Find a point $P \in E$ of order ℓ.

Table 1. The costs of radical isogenies in CSIDH and CSURF. The formulas of degree 4 are only applied to CSURF. The letters **E**, **M**, **A**, and **I** denote exponentiation, multiplication, addition, and inversion on $\mathbb{F}_p$, respectively. The latter α in the table represents $2\mathbf{E}+2\mathbf{M}+6\mathbf{A}+\mathbf{I}$ if the exponent of the ideal of norm two is negative, and zero otherwise.

	Degree 3		Degree 4	
	Formulas in [6]	**Our formula**	Formulas in [6]	**Our formula**
Isogeny	$\mathbf{E}+3\mathbf{M}+12\mathbf{A}$	$\mathbf{E}+5\mathbf{M}+12\mathbf{A}$	$\mathbf{E}+3\mathbf{M}+5\mathbf{A}+\mathbf{I}$	$\mathbf{E}+3\mathbf{M}+4\mathbf{A}+\mathbf{I}$
Transform from Montgomery($^-$)	$>\mathbf{E}$	None	$>3\mathbf{E}$	$3\mathbf{A}+\alpha$
Transform to Montgomery($^-$)	$>3\mathbf{E}$	$>3\mathbf{M}+9\mathbf{A}+\mathbf{I}$	$>3\mathbf{E}$	$\mathbf{E}+4\mathbf{M}+6\mathbf{A}$

3. Transform E to a curve F such that the image of P in F is $(0,0)$.
4. Apply radical isogenies of degree ℓ to F iteratively.
5. Transform the last codomain of the radical isogenies to a Montgomery curve.
6. Calculate isogenies of another degree.

The reason to use Montgomery curves is that Montgomery curves have efficient point addition formulas. Furthermore, if the degree ℓ is large, then the formulas on Montgomery curves is more efficient than radical isogenies. The computational costs of the transformations between Montgomery curves and curves used in radical isogenies are relatively high. Therefore, it is important to reduce these costs.

Contribution

We work on some open problems in radical isogenies. In particular, we propose radical-isogeny formulas of degrees 3 and 4 on Montgomery curves and prove the conjecture on radical isogenies of degree 4. Since our formulas have an efficient method to calculate Montgomery coefficients, our formulas reduce the costs of the transformations. Table 1 summarizes the computational costs of our formulas and the formulas in [6] in CSIDH and CSURF, a variant of CSIDH by [5].

Let E be a Montgomery curve, P a point on E of order 3 with x-coordinate t, and E' a Montgomery curve that is the codomain of an isogeny with kernel generated by P. Our formula of degree 3 gives the x-coordinate of a point of order 3 on E' by a rational expression in a cube root of t. Though the computational cost of our formula is higher than that of the original radical isogeny of degree 3, there is a simple formula to compute the Montgomery coefficient of E from t. Therefore, our formula could improve the computational cost in some cases.

For degree 4, we give a radical-isogeny formula between Montgomery coefficients. In addition, our formula can be simplified by using a *modified Montgomery coefficient*, which is defined by $4(A+2)$ or $4(-A+2)$, where A is a Montgomery coefficient. The computational cost of our formula is slightly less than that of the original radical isogeny of degree 4. In CSURF, we need a transformation between Montgomery curves if the action of an ideal of norm two with a negative exponent. This transformation occurs in half of the keys in CSURF. Although the cost of this transformation is relatively high, it is less than the cost of transformation in the original radical isogenies of degree 4.

In addition, our formula of degree 4 proves the conjecture on radical isogenies of degree 4 by [6]. We obtain this result using the explicit formula to transform a Tate normal form to a Montgomery curve.

Organization

Section 2 introduces mathematical tools and previous works we refer to in this paper. Section 3 gives new formulas over arbitrary fields. In Sect. 4, we attempt to obtain a simpler form of radical isogenies. In particular, we consider a pair of a curve and its ℓ-cyclic subgroup instead of a pair of a curve and an order-ℓ point on it. Section 5 applies the formulas in Sect. 3 to isogenies over $\mathbb{F}_p$. We compare the computational costs of our formulas and that of the original radical isogenies. In addition, we prove the conjecture on radical isogenies of degree 4. Finally, Sect. 6 concludes this paper.

2 Preliminaries

This section gives a summary of the mathematical background of this paper and introduces previous works. We refer the reader to Silverman [21] for Sect. 2.1 and Diamond and Shurman [14] for Sect. 2.2.

2.1 Elliptic Curves and Isogenies

Let K be a field. An *elliptic curve over* K is a smooth projective curve over K of genus one with a specified base point over K. For an elliptic curve E, we denote its specified base point by O_E. An elliptic curve E has an abelian group structure with identity O_E. For an extension field L over K, we denote the set of points on E defined over L by $E(L)$. Then $E(L)$ is a subgroup of E. For an integer n, we denote the multiplication-by-n map on an elliptic curve by $[n]$. The *n-torsion subgroup of* E is $\{P \in E \mid [n]P = O_E\}$ and denoted by $E[n]$. If the characteristic $\mathrm{char}(K)$ is coprime to n, we can define the *Tate pairing*, which is a bilinear map

$$t_n : E(K)[n] \times E(K)/nE(K) \to K^\times/(K^\times)^n,$$

where $E(K)[n]$ is the set of points defined over K in $E[n]$.

Let E and E' be elliptic curves over K. An *isogeny* $\varphi : E \to E'$ is a non-constant morphism such that $\varphi(O_E) = O_{E'}$. The isogeny φ induces an injection $\varphi^* : \overline{K}(E') \to \overline{K}(E)$ between the function fields of the curves. The *degree* of φ

is the degree of the field extension $\overline{K}(E)/\varphi^*(\overline{K}(E'))$. We denote this by $\deg\varphi$. We say that φ is *separable (resp. inseparable)* if the extension $\overline{K}(E)/\varphi^*(\overline{K}(E'))$ is separable (resp. inseparable). The degree of φ is finite, and the cardinality of $\ker\varphi$ is less than or equal to $\deg\varphi$. Furthermore, if φ is separable, then we have $\#\ker\varphi = \deg\varphi$. Conversely, given a finite subgroup Ψ of E, there exists a separable isogeny with kernel Ψ. In addition, the codomain of an isogeny with kernel Ψ is unique up to isomorphism. We denote the codomain by E/Ψ. We call a separable isogeny whose kernel is an n-cyclic group an *n-isogeny*. For an isogeny $\varphi : E \to E'$, there exists the unique isogeny $\hat{\varphi} : E' \to E$ such that $\hat{\varphi} \circ \varphi$ is the multiplication-by-$\deg\varphi$ map on E. We call $\hat{\varphi}$ the *dual isogeny of* φ. We have $\deg\hat{\varphi} = \deg\varphi$ and that the dual isogeny of $\hat{\varphi}$ is φ.

2.2 Congruence Subgroups and Enhanced Elliptic Curves

Let N be a positive integer. The *principal congruence subgroup of level* N is

$$\Gamma(N) = \left\{ \begin{pmatrix} a & b \\ c & d \end{pmatrix} \in \mathrm{SL}_2(\mathbb{Z}) \mid \begin{pmatrix} a & b \\ c & d \end{pmatrix} \equiv \begin{pmatrix} 1 & 0 \\ 0 & 1 \end{pmatrix} \pmod{N} \right\},$$

where $\mathrm{SL}_2(\mathbb{Z})$ is the special linear group of degree 2 over $\mathbb{Z}$, i.e., the set of 2-by-2 matrices over $\mathbb{Z}$ having determinant 1. A *congruence subgroup of level* N is a subgroup of $\mathrm{SL}_2(\mathbb{Z})$ that includes $\Gamma(N)$. We define two congruence subgroups

$$\Gamma_0(N) = \left\{ \begin{pmatrix} a & b \\ c & d \end{pmatrix} \in \mathrm{SL}_2(\mathbb{Z}) \mid \begin{pmatrix} a & b \\ c & d \end{pmatrix} \equiv \begin{pmatrix} * & * \\ 0 & * \end{pmatrix} \pmod{N} \right\},$$

$$\Gamma_1(N) = \left\{ \begin{pmatrix} a & b \\ c & d \end{pmatrix} \in \mathrm{SL}_2(\mathbb{Z}) \mid \begin{pmatrix} a & b \\ c & d \end{pmatrix} \equiv \begin{pmatrix} 1 & * \\ 0 & 1 \end{pmatrix} \pmod{N} \right\},$$

where $*$ means unspecified. We define an action of $\mathrm{SL}_2(\mathbb{Z})$ on the upper half plane $\mathcal{H}$ in $\mathbb{C}$ by

$$\begin{pmatrix} a & b \\ c & d \end{pmatrix} z = \frac{az+b}{cz+d}.$$

Then we define sets $Y(N) = \Gamma(N)\backslash\mathcal{H}$, $Y_0(N) = \Gamma_0(N)\backslash\mathcal{H}$, and $Y_1(N) = \Gamma_1(N)\backslash\mathcal{H}$. Furthermore, we can extend the action of $\mathrm{SL}_2(\mathbb{Z})$ to $\mathcal{H}^* := \mathcal{H} \cup \mathbb{Q} \cup \{\infty\}$, and define $X(N) = \Gamma(N)\backslash\mathcal{H}^*$, $X_0(N) = \Gamma_0(N)\backslash\mathcal{H}^*$, and $X_1(N) = \Gamma_1(N)\backslash\mathcal{H}^*$. The sets $X(N)$, $X_0(N)$, and $X_1(N)$ have structures of compact Riemann surfaces and are called *Modular curves*. The points in $Y(N)$, $Y_0(N)$, and $Y_1(N)$ correspond to enhanced elliptic curves over $\mathbb{C}$. An *enhanced elliptic curve for* $\Gamma_0(N)$ is an ordered pair (E, C), where E is an elliptic curve over $\mathbb{C}$ and C is an N-cyclic subgroup of E. Two enhanced elliptic curves (E, C) and (E', C') for $\Gamma_0(N)$ are *equivalent* if there exists an isomorphism $E \to E'$ that takes C to C'. We write this as $(E, C) \sim (E', C')$. The set of equivalence classes is denoted by

$$S_0(N) = \{\text{enhanced elliptic curves for } \Gamma_0(N)\}/\sim.$$

The equivalence class of an enhanced elliptic curve (E, C) is denoted by $[E, C]$. We define an enhanced elliptic curve for $\Gamma_1(N)$ as a pair of an elliptic curve over

$\mathbb{C}$ and a point of order N on the curve, and an enhanced elliptic curve for $\Gamma(N)$ as a pair of an elliptic curve over $\mathbb{C}$ and an ordered pair of points that generates the N-torsion subgroup of the curve. Sets $S_1(N)$ and $S(N)$ are defined similarly to $S_0(N)$. Then there are one-to-one correspondences

$$Y_0(N) \leftrightarrow S_0(N),\ Y_1(N) \leftrightarrow S_1(N),\quad \text{and } Y(N) \leftrightarrow S(N).$$

In these correspondences, the natural projections in residues correspond to the natural projection in enhanced elliptic curves. For example, consider the natural projection $Y_0(p) \to Y(1)$ for a prime p. This projection corresponds to omitting the p-cyclic subgroup from an enhanced elliptic curve. Here, the index $[\Gamma(1) : \Gamma_0(p)] = p+1$ corresponds to the number of p-cyclic subgroups of an elliptic curve.

For an arbitrary algebraically closed field, we can define enhanced elliptic curves and the sets $S_0(N)$, $S_1(N)$, and $S(N)$ in the same way. We use the same notation for these as over $\mathbb{C}$.

2.3 Montgomery Curves

We give the definition and basic properties of Montgomery curves [18]. In this subsection, we let K be a field with $\mathrm{char}(K) \neq 2$.

A *Montgomery curve over* K is an elliptic curve E defined by $y^2 = x^3 + Ax^2 + x$, where $A \in K$ such that $A^2 \neq 4$. We call A the *Montgomery coefficient* of E. We denote a point of x-coordinate $a \in K$ on a Montgomery curve by $(a, -)$. The j-invariant of E is

$$256\frac{(A^2-3)^3}{A^2-4}.$$

This formula means that there are exactly six isomorphic Montgomery curves over $\overline{K}$ (counted with multiplicity). The number six comes from the index $[\Gamma_0(1) : \Gamma_0(4)]$. In other words, a Montgomery curve represents a class in $S_0(4)$. To explain this fact, we define a specified 4-cyclic subgroup of a Montgomery curve. By the arithmetic in Montgomery curves (see [18]), we obtain that the point $(0,0)$ on a Montgomery curve has order 2, and the x-coordinates of its halves are 1 and -1. For a Montgomery curve E, we denote the cyclic subgroup of E generated by $(1,-) \in E$ by $C_E^{(4)}$. Then we have the following.

Proposition 1. *Let E and E' be two Montgomery curves over K of Montgomery coefficients A and A', respectively. Then $(E, C_E^{(4)}) \sim (E', C_{E'}^{(4)})$ if and only if $A = A'$. Furthermore, we have $(E, \langle(0,0)\rangle) \sim (E', \langle(0,0)\rangle)$ if and only if $A^2 = A'^2$.*

Proof. From Proposition III.3.1 in [21], every isomorphism between Montgomery curves is of the form $(x,y) \mapsto (u^2x + r, u^3y)$, where $r \in \overline{K}$ and $u \in \overline{K}^{\times}$.

Let $\iota : E \to E'$ be an isomorphism that preserves $(0,0)$. Then we have $\iota(x,y) = (u^2x, u^3y)$, where $u \in \overline{K}$ such that $u^4 = 1$, and $A' = u^2A$. Therefore, we conclude $A' = \pm A$, i.e., $A^2 = A'^2$. In addition, if ι takes $C_E^{(4)}$ to $C_{E'}^{(4)}$, then $\iota((1,-)) = (1,-)$ thus $u^2 = 1$. This means $A = A'$.

Conversely, we assume $A' = -A$. Then there exists an isomorphism $\iota : E \to E'$, $(x, y) \mapsto (-x, iy)$, where i is a square root of -1 in $\overline{K}$. Since $\iota((0,0)) = (0,0)$, we have $(E, \langle(0,0)\rangle) \sim (E', \langle(0,0)\rangle)$. □

It is easy to verify that for an enhanced elliptic curve (E, C) over $\overline{K}$ for $\Gamma_0(4)$, there exist a Montgomery curve E' and an isomorphism $E \to E'$ that takes C to $C_{E'}^{(4)}$. Therefore, we can define a bijection $A : S_0(4) \to \overline{K}\backslash\{\pm 2\}$ by sending $[E, C]$ to the Montgomery coefficient of a Montgomery curve in the class $[E, C]$. The following corollary summarizes our discussion.

Corollary 2. *We have the following commutative diagram*

$$\begin{array}{ccccc} S_0(4) & \longrightarrow & S_0(2) & \longrightarrow & S_0(1) \\ {\scriptstyle A}\downarrow & & {\scriptstyle A^2}\downarrow & & {\scriptstyle j}\downarrow \\ \overline{K}\backslash\{\pm 2\} & \longrightarrow & \overline{K}\backslash\{4\} & \longrightarrow & \overline{K}, \end{array}$$

where the top arrows are the natural projections, and the bottom arrows are defined by

$$A \mapsto A^2 \text{ and } a \mapsto 256\frac{(a-3)^3}{a-4}.$$

2.4 Vélu's Formulas

Vélu [24] gave explicit formulas for isogenies between elliptic curves represented as Weierstrass forms. Vélu's formulas take an elliptic curve E and a finite subgroup C of E as input and output an elliptic curve E' and a separable isogeny $\varphi : E \to E'$ with kernel C. We display some of the variants of Vélu's formulas that we need later.

Proposition 3 (Theorem 1 in [10]). *Let K be a field with* $\mathrm{char}(K) \neq 2$, *E a Montgomery curve over K of coefficient A, and P a point on E of order $\ell = 2d+1$. We write the x-coordinate of $[i]P$ for $i = 1, \dots, d$ as x_i. Then the Montgomery curve $y^2 = x^3 + A'x^2 + x$ with*

$$A' = \left(6\sum_{i=1}^{d}\left(\frac{1}{x_i} - x_i\right) + A\right)\left(\prod_{i=1}^{d} x_i\right)^2 \tag{1}$$

is the codomain of a separable isogeny φ with kernel $\langle P\rangle$, which is defined by

$$\varphi : (x, y) \mapsto \left(f(x), yf'(x)\prod_{i=1}^{d} x_i\right), \tag{2}$$

where

$$f(x) = x\prod_{i=1}^{d}\left(\frac{xx_i - 1}{x - x_i}\right)^2, \tag{3}$$

and $f'(x)$ is its derivative.

Note that φ in Proposition 3 sends $(1, -)$ on E to $(1, -)$ on the codomain. As we showed in Sect. 2.3, the coefficient A' is unique as we take an isogeny with this property.

For an isogeny whose kernel includes the point $(0,0)$, we need to choose a Montgomery coefficient of its codomain. Jao and De Feo [13] gave a formula for 2-isogenies that sends $(1, -)$ to $(0,0)$.

Proposition 4 **([13]).** *Let K be a field with $\mathrm{char}(K) \neq 2$ and E a Montgomery curve over K of coefficient A. Then the Montgomery curve $y^2 = x^3 + A'x^2 + x$ with*

$$A' = \frac{A+6}{2\alpha}, \tag{4}$$

where α is a square root of $A+2$, is the codomain of a 2-isogeny φ that sends $(1, -)$ to $(0,0)$, which is defined by

$$\varphi : (x, y) \mapsto \left(\frac{(x-1)^2}{2\alpha x}, \frac{1}{\beta^3} y \left(1 - \frac{1}{x^2} \right) \right), \tag{5}$$

where β is a square root of 2α.

Note that there are two choices of a Montgomery coefficient of the codomain, which corresponds to the sign of the square root α. The sign of the square root β is not essential since the change of the sign corresponds to the composition with the multiplication by -1.

2.5 Radical Isogenies

Let N be a positive integer, K a field with $\mathrm{char}(K) \nmid N$, E an elliptic curve over K, and P a point in $E(K)$ of order N. Then there exists an isogeny $\varphi : E \to E/\langle P \rangle$ with kernel $\langle P \rangle$. We can choose a model of $E/\langle P \rangle$ to be defined over K. Let E' be such a model. Let P' be a point on E' such that $\hat{\varphi}(P') = P$. Castryck, Decru, and Vercauteren [6] showed that P' is defined over $K(\sqrt[N]{\rho})$, where ρ is a representative of the Tate pairing $t_N(P, -P)$. The N choices of an N-th root of ρ correspond to N-isogenies different from $\hat{\varphi}$. By taking models of E and $E/\langle P \rangle$ such that P and P' are $(0,0)$, they gave explicit formulas to compute $E/\langle P \rangle$ from E, and called these *radical isogenies.* A radical isogeny can be seen as a map on $S_1(N)$; $(E, (0,0)) \mapsto (E/\langle (0,0) \rangle, (0,0))$. For curve models, they used Tate normal forms [23] for $N \geq 4$. We write some of their formulas that we refer to later.

$N = 3$. We use the model $E : y^2 + a_1 xy + a_3 y = x^3$ and $P = (0,0)$. Then a model of $E/\langle P \rangle$ such that $P' = (0,0)$ is $E' : y^2 + a_1' xy + a_3' y = x^3$ with

$$a_1' = -6\alpha + a_1 \text{ and } a_3' = 3a_1\alpha^2 - a_1^2\alpha + 9a_3, \tag{6}$$

where α is a cube root of $-a_3$.

$N = 4$. We use the Tate normal form $E : y^2 + xy - by = x^3 - bx^2$ and $P = (0, 0)$. Then a Tate normal form of $E/\langle P\rangle$ such that $P' = (0, 0)$ is $E' : y^2 + xy - b'y = x^3 - b'x^2$ with

$$b' = -\frac{\alpha(4\alpha^2 + 1)}{(2\alpha + 1)^4}, \tag{7}$$

where α is a fourth root of $-b$.

$N = 5$. We use the Tate normal form $E : y^2 + (1 - b)xy - by = x^3 - bx^2$ and $P = (0, 0)$. Then a Tate normal form of $E/\langle P\rangle$ such that $P' = (0, 0)$ is $E' : y^2 + (1 - b')xy - b'y = x^3 - b'x^2$ with

$$b' = \alpha\frac{\alpha^4 + 3\alpha^3 + 4\alpha^2 + 2\alpha + 1}{\alpha^4 - 2\alpha^3 + 4\alpha^2 - 3\alpha + 1}, \tag{8}$$

where α is a fifth root of b.

3 Radical-Isogeny Formulas on Montgomery Curves

In this section, we introduce radical-isogeny formulas of degrees 3 and 4 on Montgomery curves. In addition, we give some consideration for that of degree ≥ 5.

3.1 Degree 3

Let K be a field with $\mathrm{char}(K) \neq 2, 3$.

As we showed in Sect. 2.2, a Montgomery coefficient represents a class in $S_0(4)$. A 3-cyclic subgroup of a Montgomery curve is represented by the x-coordinate of its generator. Therefore, a class in $S_0(12)$ can be represented by a pair of a Montgomery coefficient and the x-coordinate of a point of order 3. However, the genus of $X_0(12)$ is zero, so a class in $S_0(12)$ can be parametrized by one variable. Indeed, we show that the x-coordinate of a point of order 3 determines the Montgomery coefficient of the curve on which the point is.

From the arithmetic in Montgomery curves, we obtain the 3rd division polynomial of the Montgomery curve with coefficient $A \in K$:

$$x^4 + \frac{4}{3}Ax^3 + 2x^2 - \frac{1}{3}.$$

Let t be the x-coordinate of a point of order 3 on the Montgomery curve with coefficient A. Then we have

$$A = \frac{-3t^4 - 6t^2 + 1}{4t^3}. \tag{9}$$

From the condition that $A \neq \pm 2, \infty$, we have $t \neq 0, \pm 1, \pm\frac{1}{3}$. For $t \in \overline{K}\backslash\{0, \pm 1, \pm\frac{1}{3}\}$, we denote the Montgomery curve with coefficient defined by (9) by E_t, and the 3-cyclic subgroup of E_t generated by $(t, -)$ by $C_t^{(3)}$. The subgroup $C_{E_t}^{(4)} + C_t^{(3)} := \{P + Q \mid P \in C_{E_t}^{(4)}, Q \in C_t^{(3)}\}$ is cyclic of order 12. Then we have an analogue of Proposition 1.

Proposition 5. *The map*

$$T:\overline{K}\backslash\left\{0,\pm 1,\pm\frac{1}{3}\right\}\to S_0(12),\ t\mapsto[E_t,C_{E_t}^{(4)}+C_t^{(3)}]$$

is a well-defined bijection.

Proof. As we explained above, the map T is well-defined.

First, we show the surjectivity. Let (E,C) be an enhanced elliptic curve for $\Gamma_0(12)$ over $\overline{K}$. We decompose C to C_3+C_4, where C_3 is cyclic of order 3 and C_4 is cyclic of order 4. From Proposition 1, there exists a Montgomery curve E' such that $(E',C_{E'}^{(4)})\sim(E,C_4)$. Let $\iota:E\to E'$ be an isomorphism taking C_4 to $C_{E'}^{(4)}$, and t the x-coordinate of a generator of $\iota(C_3)$. Then $t\neq 0,\pm 1,\pm\frac{1}{3}$ and $E'=E_t$. Therefore we have $(E,C)\sim(E_t,C_{E_t}^{(4)}+C_t^{(3)})$.

Next, we show the injectivity. Let t and t' be elements in $\overline{K}\backslash\left\{0,\pm 1,\pm\frac{1}{3}\right\}$ such that there exists an isomorphism $\iota:E_t\to E_{t'}$ taking $C_{E_t}^{(4)}+C_t^{(3)}$ to $C_{E_{t'}}^{(4)}+C_{t'}^{(3)}$. From the proof of Proposition 1, we have $E_t=E_{t'}$ and $\iota((x,y))=(x,y)$ or $(x,-y)$. Therefore, we conclude $t=t'$. □

As in the case of Montgomery curves, we have the following corollary.

Corollary 6. *We have the following commutative diagram*

$$\begin{array}{ccc} S_0(12) & \longrightarrow & S_0(4) \\ {\scriptstyle T^{-1}}\downarrow & & \downarrow{\scriptstyle A} \\ \overline{K}\backslash\{0,\pm 1,\pm\frac{1}{3}\} & \longrightarrow & \overline{K}\backslash\{\pm 2\}, \end{array}$$

where the top arrow is the natural projection, the left vertical arrow is the inverse of the map in Proposition 5, and the bottom arrow is defined by

$$t\mapsto\frac{-3t^4-6t^2+1}{4t^3}.$$

Using this parametrization of $S_0(12)$, we can derive a radical-isogeny formula of degree 3.

Theorem 7. *Let $t\in\overline{K}\backslash\{0,\pm 1,\pm\frac{1}{3}\}$, E be a Montgomery curve over $\overline{K}$, and $\varphi:E_t\to E$ an isogeny taking $C_{E_t}^{(4)}$ to $C_E^{(4)}$ with kernel $C_t^{(3)}$. Then the x-coordinate of a generator of $\ker\hat{\varphi}$ is $-\frac{1}{3t}$, and the x-coordinates of other points of order 3 on E are*

$$3t\alpha^2+(3t^2-1)\alpha+3t^3-2t, \tag{10}$$

where α is a cube root of $t(t^2-1)$.

Proof. From Proposition 3, the Montgomery coefficient of E is

$$\frac{-27t^4+18t^2+1}{4t}.$$

The 3rd division polynomial of E is decomposed as

$$\left(x+\frac{1}{3t}\right)(x^3+(-9t^3+6t)x^2+3t^2x-t). \tag{11}$$

It is easy to verify that $(-\frac{1}{3t}, -)$ on E generates the kernel of the dual isogeny $\hat{\varphi}$.

Let $P = (t, -)$ on E_t. An easy calculation shows that the y-coordinate of P is $\frac{t^2-1}{2\beta}$, where β is a square root of t. By the theory of radical isogenies (see Sect. 3 in [6]), a root of the latter factor in (11) has a rational expression in β and a cube root of the Tate pairing $t_3(P, -P)$. The isogeny φ is unchanged by replacing P with $-P$, i.e., β with $-\beta$. Therefore, the root should be in a radical extension of $\mathbb{Q}(t)$ of degree 3. Indeed, the Tate paring can be computed as

$$t_3(P, -P) = t(t^2-1) \bmod \mathbb{Q}(\beta)^{\times 3}.$$

Let α be a cube root of $t(t^2-1)$. Then the latter factor in (11) decomposes into linear factors in $\mathbb{Q}(t, \alpha)$ and has a root of the form (10). This proves the theorem. □

The computational cost of this formula is worse than that of the original radical-isogeny formula (6). An advantage of this formula is that one can use the simple formula (9) to calculate the Montgomery coefficient from the representation t. In isogeny-based cryptosystems, Montgomery curves are used because of computational efficiency. Therefore, we need transformation between a Montgomery curve and a curve used in radical isogenies. In the case of (6), the transformation needs calculating radicals. On the other hand, our transformation formula (9) does not need any radicals. We discuss the detail of this point in Sect. 5.3.

3.2 Degree 4

Let K be a field with $\mathrm{char}(K) \neq 2$.

Since a Montgomery coefficient represents a class in $S_0(4) = S_1(4)$, it must be true that there exists a radical-isogeny formula of degree 4 between Montgomery coefficients. Indeed, we have the following.

Theorem 8. *Let E be a Montgomery curve with coefficient $A \in K$, E' a Montgomery curve, $\varphi : E \to E'$ an isogeny with kernel $C_E^{(4)}$, and ψ an isogeny from E' with kernel $\langle (0,0) \rangle$. If the kernel of the composition $\psi \circ \varphi$ is cyclic, then the Montgomery coefficient A' of E' is*

$$\frac{(\beta+2)^4}{4\beta(\beta^2+4)} - 2, \tag{12}$$

where β is a fourth root of $4(A+2)$.

Proof. We decompose φ into the composition of two 2-isogenies $\varphi_2 \circ \varphi_1$. We can assume that φ_1 takes $(1, -)$ to $(0, 0)$. Let A'' be the Montgomery coefficient of $\varphi_1(E)$. From Proposition 4, we have

$$A'' + 2 = \frac{(\alpha + 2)^2}{2\alpha}, \tag{13}$$

where α is a square root of $A + 2$. Again, from Proposition 4, The Montgomery coefficient of E' is

$$\frac{((\alpha + 2)/\beta + 2)^2}{2(\alpha + 2)/\beta} - 2, \tag{14}$$

where β is a square root of 2α, i.e., a fourth root of $4(A + 2)$. We can obtain (12) by an easy calculation. □

By putting $a = 4(A + 2)$ and $a' = 4(A' + 2)$, we have a simpler formula

$$a' = \frac{(\beta + 2)^4}{\beta(\beta^2 + 4)}, \tag{15}$$

where β is a fourth root of a. The computational cost of this formula is slightly less than that of the original radical-isogeny formula (7). In addition, as in degree 3, it is easy to transform our new representation a into the Montgomery coefficient.

3.3 Degree ≥ 5

We could not generalize our method to the case that $N \geq 5$. Since the genus of $X_0(4N)$ is greater than 0 for $N \geq 5$, we cannot represent an element in $S_0(4N)$ by one parameter. Furthermore, we have $S_0(N) \neq S_1(N)$ for $N \geq 5$, unlike in the case that $N = 3$ or 4. As we discuss in the next section, we cannot obtain radical-isogeny formulas of degree N for a model of $S_0(N)$ for $N \geq 5$. Therefore, we have to work on a model of $S_1(N)$. A natural parametrization for the case that $N \geq 5$ is a pair of a Montgomery coefficient and the x-coordinate of a point of order N. However, even for the case that $N = 5$, the calculation is too complicated, and we could not derive any formula.

4 Consideration to Formulas on $S_0(N)$

As we stated in Sect. 2.5, radical isogenies of degree N can be seen as a map on $S_1(N)$. For example, for $N = 3$, consider two curves $E : y^2 + a_1xy + a_3y = x^3$ and $E' : y^2 + a_1'xy + a_3'y = x^3$. In these curves, the point $(0, 0)$ has order 3. It is easy to verify that $(E, (0, 0)) \sim (E', (0, 0))$ if and only if $a_1^3/a_3 = {a_1'}^3/a_3'$. Note that $a_3, a_3' \neq 0$ since the curves are smooth. By putting $T = a_1^3/a_3$ and $T' = {a_1'}^3/a_3'$, one can transform (6) to

$$T' = \frac{(\beta - 6)^3}{-\beta^2 + 3\beta - 9},$$

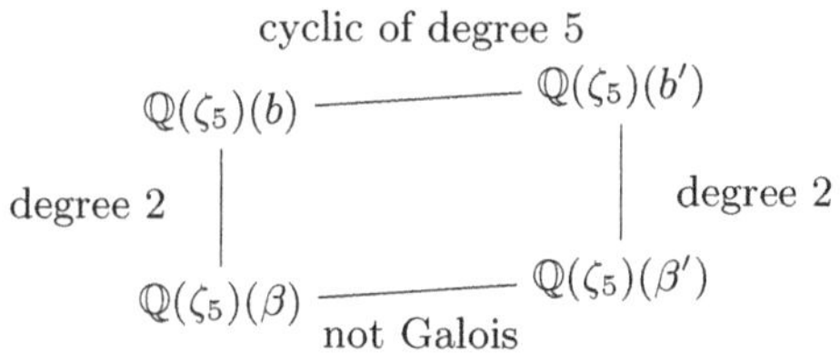

Fig. 1. The tower of field extensions

where β is a cube root of $-T$. (This formula is more costly than (6) because of the inversion and the cubic calculation.)

As we stated in the previous section, we have $S_0(N) = S_1(N)$ for $N \leq 4$ since there is the isomorphism $[-1]$. For the case that $N \geq 5$, we could obtain a simpler isogeny formula on a parametrization of $S_0(N)$ than that of $S_1(N)$. However, in general, we cannot obtain radical formulas on a parametrization of $S_0(N)$. We explain this in the following.

Consider the case that $N = 5$. Let K be a field with $\mathrm{char}(K) \neq 5$, and consider two elliptic curves over K defined by

$$\begin{aligned} E &: y^2 + (1-b)xy - by = x^3 - bx, \\ E' &: y^2 + (1-b')xy - b'y = x^3 - b'x. \end{aligned}$$

These curves are in Tate normal form, and the points $(0,0)$ on these curves have order 5. The cyclic subgroup of E generated by $(0,0)$ is

$$\{O_E, (0,0), (b, b^2), (b, 0), (0, b)\}.$$

From this, it is easy to verify that $(E, (0,0)) \sim (E', (0,0))$ if and only if $b = b'$ and that $(E, \langle(0,0)\rangle) \sim (E', \langle(0,0)\rangle)$ if and only if $b = b'$ or $b = -\frac{1}{b'}$, i.e., $\frac{b^2-1}{b} = \frac{b'^2-1}{b'}$. Therefore, $\frac{b^2-1}{b}$ is a parametrization of $S_0(5)$. Note that b and $-\frac{1}{b}$ are the roots of $x^2 - \frac{b^2-1}{b}x - 1$.

Let E and E' be elliptic curves defined by the equations above. We define $\beta = \frac{b^2-1}{b}$ and $\beta' = \frac{b'^2-1}{b'}$. From the radical-isogeny formula (8), we have $\mathbb{Q}(b') = \mathbb{Q}(\sqrt[5]{b})$. In this setting, we show that $\beta' := \frac{b'^2-1}{b'}$ does not have any rational expression in a fifth root of any element in $\mathbb{Q}(\beta)$.

As we mentioned above, the field extension $\mathbb{Q}(b)/\mathbb{Q}(\beta)$ is of degree 2. Let $\zeta_5 \in \mathbb{C}$ be a primitive fifth root of unity. By adjoining ζ_5 to the field extension $\mathbb{Q}(b')/\mathbb{Q}(\beta)$, we obtain the Galois extension $\mathbb{Q}(\zeta_5)(b')/\mathbb{Q}(\zeta_5)(\beta)$ of degree 10. The Galois group $\mathrm{Gal}(\mathbb{Q}(\zeta_5)(b')/\mathbb{Q}(\zeta_5)(\beta))$ is generated by automorphisms $\sigma : b' \mapsto -\frac{1}{b'}$ and $\tau : b' \mapsto \zeta_5 b'$. The fixed field of σ is $\mathbb{Q}(\zeta_5)(\beta')$, and that of τ is $\mathbb{Q}(\zeta_5)(b)$. It is easy to verify that $\tau^{-1}\sigma\tau \neq \sigma$. Therefore, the group $\langle\sigma\rangle$ is not a normal subgroup of $\mathrm{Gal}(\mathbb{Q}(\zeta_5)(b')/\mathbb{Q}(\zeta_5)(\beta))$, i.e., the extension $\mathbb{Q}(\zeta_5)(\beta')/\mathbb{Q}(\zeta_5)(\beta)$ is not a Galois extension. This means that β' cannot be expressed as any rational expression in any element in $\mathbb{Q}(\zeta_5)(\beta)$. The diagram in Fig. 1 summarizes the discussion.

To obtain a radical-isogeny formula for $S_0(N)$, we need to find a parametrization for $S_0(N)$ that makes the bottom extension in the diagram in Fig. 1 a Galois extension. We do not have any result for the existence of such parametrization. However, it seems to be complicated to find it. We leave this as an open problem.

5 Application to Cryptography

In this section, we consider the application of our formulas in Sect. 3 to CSIDH and its variants.

CSIDH uses the action of the ideal class group of an order of an imaginary quadratic field on supersingular elliptic curves. The action is calculated by isogenies defined over a finite prime field $\mathbb{F}_p$. Therefore, we consider formulas of such isogenies.

Let $\mathcal{O}$ be $\mathbb{Z}[\sqrt{-p}]$ or $\mathbb{Z}[\frac{1+\sqrt{-p}}{2}]$, and $\mathcal{E}\ell\ell_p(\mathcal{O})$ the set of $\mathbb{F}_p$-isomorphism classes of supersingular elliptic curves over $\mathbb{F}_p$ whose $\mathbb{F}_p$-endomorphism ring is isomorphic to $\mathcal{O}$. Note that the p-th power Frobenius endomorphism π corresponds to $\sqrt{-p}$ or $-\sqrt{-p}$. We identify the $\mathbb{F}_p$-endomorphism ring of a curve with $\mathcal{O}$ under the former isomorphism. If $\mathcal{E}\ell\ell_p(\mathcal{O})$ is nonempty, then the ideal class group $\mathrm{cl}(\mathcal{O})$ acts freely and transitively on $\mathcal{E}\ell\ell_p(\mathcal{O})$ (Theorem 7 in [7]). The group action is defined as follows: Let $E \in \mathcal{E}\ell\ell_p(\mathcal{O})$, and $[\mathfrak{a}]$ be an ideal class in $\mathrm{cl}(\mathcal{O})$ represented by an integral ideal $\mathfrak{a}$. Then the action of $[\mathfrak{a}]$ on E is defined by $[\mathfrak{a}] * E = E/E[\mathfrak{a}]$, where $E[\mathfrak{a}]$ is the $\mathfrak{a}$-torsion subgroup of E, which is defined by $\{P \in E \mid \alpha(P) = O_E \text{ for all } \alpha \in \mathfrak{a}\}$, and we take an isogeny with kernel $E[\mathfrak{a}]$ defined over $\mathbb{F}_p$. We denote the ideal in $\mathcal{O}$ generated by a, b by (a, b) and the ideal class of (a, b) by $[a, b]$.

We restrict our attention to the case that $p \equiv 3 \pmod 4$ since there is no supersingular Montgomery curve over $\mathbb{F}_p$ if $p \equiv 1 \pmod 4$ [5]. We fix a square root of -1 in $\mathbb{F}_{p^2}$ and denote it by i. Note that $i \notin \mathbb{F}_p$ in our case.

5.1 Degree-3 Isogenies

Assume that $3 \mid p + 1$ so that a supersingular elliptic curve over $\mathbb{F}_p$ has an $\mathbb{F}_p$-rational point of order 3. Then the map $\mathbb{F}_p \to \mathbb{F}_p; a \mapsto a^3$ is bijective. Therefore, there is only one cube root of an element of $\mathbb{F}_p$. For $a \in \mathbb{F}_p$, the cube root of a in $\mathbb{F}_p$ is computed by the exponentiation a^e, where e is an integer such that $e \equiv 3^{-1} \pmod{p-1}$.

Let E be a Montgomery curve in $\mathcal{E}\ell\ell_p(\mathcal{O})$. The role of 3-isogenies in CSIDH is to compute the actions of prime ideals $(3, \sqrt{-p} - 1)$ and $(3, \sqrt{-p} + 1)$. The torsion subgroup $E[3, \sqrt{-p} - 1]$ is generated by a point P of order 3 such that $\pi(P) = P$, and $E[3, \sqrt{-p} + 1]$ is generated by a point Q of order 3 such that $\pi(Q) = -Q$. Note that the x-coordinates of P and Q are in $\mathbb{F}_p$. We can use Theorem 7 to compute the actions of these ideals.

Corollary 9. *Let E be a Montgomery curve in $\mathcal{E}\ell\ell_p(\mathcal{O})$, and t the x-coordinate of a generator of $E[3, \sqrt{-p} - 1]$ (resp. $E[3, \sqrt{-p} + 1]$). Then $[3, \sqrt{-p} - 1] * E$*

(resp. $[3, \sqrt{-p}+1] * E$*) can be defined as a Montgomery curve* E' *over* $\mathbb{F}_p$ *such that the* x*-coordinate of a generator of* $E'[3, \sqrt{-p}-1]$ *(resp.* $E'[3, \sqrt{-p}+1]$*) is*

$$3t\alpha^2 + (3t^2 - 1)\alpha + 3t^3 - 2t, \tag{16}$$

where α *is the cube root of* $t(t^2-1)$ *in* $\mathbb{F}_p$*.*

Proof. We prove the case for $E[3, \sqrt{-p}-1]$. The other case can be proved in the same way.

Let t' be an element in $\mathbb{F}_p$ defined by the equation (16), and E' a Montgomery curve that has an order-3 point with x-coordinate t'. From Theorem 7, E' is the codomain of the isogeny φ in Proposition 3 with kernel generated by $(t, -)$. Because $t \in \mathbb{F}_p$, the isogeny φ is defined over $\mathbb{F}_p$. Therefore, E' is a representative of the $\mathbb{F}_p$-isomorphism class $[3, \sqrt{-p}-1] * E$. Because α is only one cube root of $t(t^2-1)$ in $\mathbb{F}_p$, the element t' is only one element such that the point $(t', -)$ on E' has order 3 and generates the kernel of an isogeny different from $\hat{\varphi}$. This means that t' is the x-coordinate of a generator of $E'[3, \sqrt{-p}-1]$. □

A Formula for Montgomery$^-$ Curves. A *Montgomery$^-$ curve* over a field K with $\mathrm{char}(K) \neq 2$ is an elliptic curve defined by $y^2 = x^3 + Ax^2 - x$, where $A \in K$ such that $A^2 \neq -4$.

Castryck and Decru [5] introduced Montgomery$^-$ curves for a model of a variant of CSIDH they proposed, CSURF. CSURF uses Montgomery$^-$ curves since there is a one-to-one correspondence between Montgomery$^-$ coefficients of supersingular elliptic curves and classes in $\mathcal{E}\ell\ell_p(\mathbb{Z}[\frac{1+\sqrt{-p}}{2}])$.

The arithmetic and isogeny formulas on Montgomery$^-$ curves are given in [5]. Like Montgomery curves, the x-coordinate t of a point of order 3 on a Montgomery$^-$ curve determines the Montgomery$^-$ coefficient A. Indeed, we have

$$A = \frac{-3t^4 + 6t^2 + 1}{4t^3}. \tag{17}$$

From the conditions $A^2 \neq -4$ and $A \neq \infty$, we have $t \neq 0, \pm i, \pm\frac{i}{3}$. For $t \in \mathbb{F}_p \backslash \{0\}$, we denote the Montgomery$^-$ curve with coefficient defined by (17) by E_t^-, and the 3-cyclic subgroup of E_t^- generated by $(t, -)$ by $C_t^{(3-)}$.

The point $(0, 0)$ on Montgomery$^-$ curve has order 2, and the x-coordinates of halves of $(0, 0)$ are $\pm i$. Therefore, it is natural to use isogenies that send $(i, -)$ to $(i, -)$ between Montgomery$^-$ curves. However, if we use curves in $\mathcal{E}\ell\ell_p(\mathcal{O})$, such isogenies are not defined over $\mathbb{F}_p$ in general. A formula of isogenies over $\mathbb{F}_p$ between Montgomery$^-$ curves is given by Proposition 2 in [5]. By combining the formula in [5] and the proof of Theorem 7, we obtain the following formula for Montgomery$^-$ curves.

Theorem 10. *Let* $t \in \mathbb{F}_p \backslash \{0\}$*,* E *be a Montgomery curve$^-$ over* $\mathbb{F}_p$*, and* $\varphi : E_t^- \to E$ *an isogeny with kernel* $C_t^{(3-)}$ *defined over* $\mathbb{F}_p$ *that sends* $(0, 0)$ *to* $(0, 0)$*.*

Then the x-coordinate of a generator of $\ker\hat{\varphi}$ *is* $-\frac{1}{3t}$, *and the x-coordinates of other points of order* 3 *on* E *are expressed by*

$$3t\alpha^2 + (3t^2+1)\alpha + 3t^3 + 2t, \tag{18}$$

where α *is a cube root of* $t(t^2+1)$.

By choosing α in $\mathbb{F}_p$, we can obtain a similar result to Corollary 9.

5.2 Degree-4 Isogenies

We consider the case that $p \equiv 7 \pmod 8$ and $\mathcal{O} = \mathbb{Z}[\frac{1+\sqrt{-p}}{2}]$, which is the setting in CSURF. In this case, the prime 2 splits as the product of $\left(2, \frac{1-\sqrt{-p}}{2}\right)$ and $\left(2, \frac{1+\sqrt{-p}}{2}\right)$ in $\mathbb{Z}[\frac{1+\sqrt{-p}}{2}]$. As in [5], for $a \in (\mathbb{F}_p^\times)^2$, we denote the square root of a that is a square in $\mathbb{F}_p$ by $\sqrt{a}$ and define $\sqrt[4]{a} := \sqrt{\sqrt{a}}$. Note that $\sqrt{a}$ can be computed as $a^{\frac{p+1}{4}}$ and $\sqrt[4]{a}$ as $a^{\frac{p+1}{8}}$.

Our purpose is to apply Theorem 8 to computing the actions of the squares of the prime ideals above 2. Unlike the case of degree 3, the squaring map in $\mathbb{F}_p$ is not bijective. Therefore, we need to determine a square root (or a fourth root) that corresponds to the action of an ideal class we want to compute.

As considered in [5], every class in $\mathcal{E}\ell\ell_p(\mathbb{Z}[\frac{1+\sqrt{-p}}{2}])$ contains exactly two Montgomery curves over $\mathbb{F}_p$. In one of them, the point $(0,0)$ generates the $\left(2, \frac{1-\sqrt{-p}}{2}\right)$-torsion subgroup, and in the other curve, the point $(0,0)$ generates the $\left(2, \frac{1+\sqrt{-p}}{2}\right)$-torsion subgroup.

In the following, we let E be a Montgomery curve over $\mathbb{F}_p$ in $\mathcal{E}\ell\ell_p(\mathbb{Z}[\frac{1+\sqrt{-p}}{2}])$, and A the Montgomery coefficient of E. First, we show how to determine which ideal the point $(0,0)$ generates.

Lemma 11. *The point* $(0,0)$ *on* E *generates* $E[2, \frac{1-\sqrt{-p}}{2}]$ *if and only if* $A+2 \in (\mathbb{F}_p^\times)^2$ *and* $E[2, \frac{1+\sqrt{-p}}{2}]$ *if and only if* $-A+2 \in (\mathbb{F}_p^\times)^2$

Proof. From Lemma 5 in [5], the point $(0,0)$ generates $E[2, \frac{1-\sqrt{-p}}{2}]$ if and only if $(0,0)$ has half in $E(\mathbb{F}_p)$. Furthermore, if $(0,0)$ has half in $E(\mathbb{F}_p)$, then all halves of $(0,0)$ are in $E(\mathbb{F}_p)$ since $E \in \mathcal{E}\ell\ell_p(\mathbb{Z}[\frac{1+\sqrt{-p}}{2}])$ implies $E[2] \subset E(\mathbb{F}_p)$.

Let $P = (1, -)$ on E. Then P is half of $(0,0)$, and the y-coordinate of P is a square root of $A+2$. Therefore, P has half in $E(\mathbb{F}_p)$ if and only if $A+2 \in (\mathbb{F}_p^\times)^2$.

Because $E[2] \subset E(\mathbb{F}_p)$, the all roots of $x^3 + Ax^2 + x$ are in $\mathbb{F}_p$. This means that $A^2 - 4 \in (\mathbb{F}_p^\times)^2$. Therefore, if $A+2 \notin (\mathbb{F}_p^\times)^2$, then $-A+2 \in (\mathbb{F}_p^\times)^2$. This proves the latter of the lemma. □

We define the *modified Montgomery coefficient* a *of* E as $a = 4(A+2)$ if $A+2 \in (\mathbb{F}_p^\times)^2$ and $a = 4(-A+2)$ if $-A+2 \in (\mathbb{F}_p^\times)^2$. Note that a is always in $(\mathbb{F}_p^\times)^2$. To simplify notation, we let $\mathfrak{a} = \left(2, \frac{1-\sqrt{-p}}{2}\right)$ if $A+2 \in (\mathbb{F}_p^\times)^2$ and

$\mathfrak{a} = \left(2, \frac{1+\sqrt{-p}}{2}\right)$ if $-A+2 \in (\mathbb{F}_p^\times)^2$. Then we can compute the action of $\mathfrak{a}$ as follows.

Lemma 12. *Let E' be a representative of the $\mathbb{F}_p$-isomorphism class $[\mathfrak{a}] * E$ that is expressed as the Montgomery curve over $\mathbb{F}_p$ such that $(0,0)$ on E' generates $E'[\mathfrak{a}]$. Then the modified Montgomery coefficient of E' is*

$$\frac{(\sqrt{a}+4)^2}{\sqrt{a}}. \tag{19}$$

Proof. If $A+2 \in (\mathbb{F}_p^\times)^2$, then the isogeny φ in Proposition 4 is defined over $\mathbb{F}_p$ by taking $\alpha = \sqrt{A+2}$. Let E'' be the codomain of φ and A'' the Montgomery coefficient of E''. Then we have $A''+2 = \frac{(\sqrt{A+2}+2)^2}{2\sqrt{A+2}} \in (\mathbb{F}_p^\times)^2$. Therefore, we conclude that $E' = E''$ as a Montgomery curve because E' is the unique Montgomery curve satisfying the property by which it is defined. By multiplying $A''+2$ by 4, we obtain the formula in the lemma for the case that $A+2 \in (\mathbb{F}_p^\times)^2$.

In the case that $-A+2 \in (\mathbb{F}_p^\times)^2$, we use quadratic twists. Let $E^{(t)}$ be the quadratic twist of E, i.e., the Montgomery curve with coefficient $-A$. Then there exists an isomorphism $\tau : E \to E^{(t)}; (x,y) \mapsto (-x, iy)$. Let φ be the isogeny in Proposition 4 from $E^{(t)}$ with $\alpha = \sqrt{-A+2}$, and E'' the codomain of φ. Let $E''^{(t)}$ be the quadratic twist of E'' and $\tau' : E'' \to E''^{(t)}$ be the isomorphism defined by $(x,y) \mapsto (-x, iy)$. Then the composition

$$E \xrightarrow{\ \tau\ } E^{(t)} \xrightarrow{\ \varphi\ } E'' \xrightarrow{\ \tau'\ } E''^{(t)}$$

is defined over $\mathbb{F}_p$. An easy calculation shows that the modified Montgomery coefficient of $E''^{(t)}$ is equal to (19). This proves the lemma. □

Remark 1. If $A+2 \in (\mathbb{F}_p^\times)^2$, then the isogeny in Lemma 12 sends $(1,-)$ to $(0,0)$. On the other hand, if $-A+2 \in (\mathbb{F}_p^\times)^2$, then the isogeny sends $(-1,-)$ to $(0,0)$ because we use the composition with the twist maps in this case. This means that $E[\mathfrak{a}^2]$ is generated by $(1,-)$ if $A+2 \in (\mathbb{F}_p^\times)^2$ and $(-1,-)$ if $-A+2 \in (\mathbb{F}_p^\times)^2$. Note that $\mathfrak{a}$ is different in each case.

By using this lemma twice, we obtain a formula for the action of $\mathfrak{a}^2$. The obtained formula includes the square root of (19) in $(\mathbb{F}_p^\times)^2$. Therefore, we need to determine whether $\sqrt{a}+4$ is a square in $\mathbb{F}_p$. The following lemma answers it.

Lemma 13. *$\sqrt{a}+4$ is a square in $\mathbb{F}_p$ if and only if $p \equiv 15 \pmod{16}$.*

Proof. From Lemma 3 in [5], the subgroup $E(\mathbb{F}_p)[4]$ is isomorphic to $\mathbb{Z}/2\mathbb{Z} \oplus \mathbb{Z}/4\mathbb{Z}$. This subgroup has order 8, so $E(\mathbb{F}_p)$ contains a point of order 8 if and only if $p \equiv 15 \pmod{16}$.

Assume $A+2 \in (\mathbb{F}_p^\times)^2$. Let $P = (1,-)$ on E. As we mentioned in Remark 1, P generates $E[\mathfrak{a}^2]$. Therefore, we have

$$\left(\frac{1-\sqrt{-p}}{2}\right)^2 P = O_E.$$

A straightforward calculation shows that

$$\frac{1-\sqrt{-p}}{2}P = \frac{p+1}{4}P.$$

Because P has order 4, this equation implies that half of P is in $E(\mathbb{F}_p)$ if and only if $p \equiv 15 \pmod{16}$. From the arithmetic of Montgomery curves, the x-coordinate of half of P is a root of

$$x^4 - 4x^3 - (4A+2)x^2 - 4x + 1.$$

This is decomposed as

$$(x^2 + (\sqrt{a}-2)x + 1)(x^2 + (-\sqrt{a}-2)x + 1). \tag{20}$$

The discriminant of the left factor is $\sqrt{a}(\sqrt{a}-4)$ and that of the right factor is $\sqrt{a}(\sqrt{a}+4)$. Since $(\sqrt{a}-4)(\sqrt{a}+4) = a - 16 \in (\mathbb{F}_p^\times)^2$, the polynomial (20) has a root in $\mathbb{F}_p$ if and only if $\sqrt{a}+4 \in (\mathbb{F}_p^\times)^2$. Assume (20) has a root x_0 in $\mathbb{F}_p$, and let Q be $(x_0, -)$ on E. Then we have $2Q = P$. Because $x_0 \in \mathbb{F}_p$, the image $\pi(Q)$ of the Frobenius is Q or $-Q$. If $\pi(Q) = -Q$, we obtain $\pi(P) = -P$ by multiplying both sides by 2. This contradicts the fact that $P \in E(\mathbb{F}_p)$. Therefore, we have $\pi(Q) = Q$, i.e., $Q \in E(\mathbb{F}_p)$. This proves the lemma for the case that $A+2 \in (\mathbb{F}_p^\times)^2$.

For the case that $-A+2 \in (\mathbb{F}_p^\times)^2$, we can prove the lemma by applying the same discussion to the quadratic twist of E. □

Now we obtain the following radical-isogeny formula for the action of $\mathfrak{a}^2$.

Theorem 14. *Let E' be a representative of the $\mathbb{F}_p$-isomorphism class $[\mathfrak{a}^2] * E$ that is expressed as the Montgomery curve over $\mathbb{F}_p$ such that $(0,0)$ on E' generates $E'[\mathfrak{a}]$. Then the modified Montgomery coefficient of E' is*

$$\frac{(\varepsilon\sqrt[4]{a}+2)^4}{\varepsilon\sqrt[4]{a}(\sqrt{a}+4)}, \tag{21}$$

where $\varepsilon = -1$ if $p \equiv 7 \pmod{16}$ or $\varepsilon = 1$ if $p \equiv 15 \pmod{16}$.

Proof. From Lemma 13, we have

$$\sqrt{\frac{(\sqrt{a}+4)^2}{\sqrt{a}}} = \frac{\varepsilon(\sqrt{a}+4)}{\sqrt[4]{a}}.$$

By applying Lemma 12 twice, we obtain the formula in the theorem. □

As a corollary of Theorem 14, we prove a conjecture stated by [6]. In particular, we prove the following.

Corollary 15 (Conjecture 2 in [6]). *Let E be an elliptic curve defined by a Tate normal form $y^2 + xy - by = x^3 - bx^2$, $b \in \mathbb{F}_p$, let $P = (0,0) \in E$, and let $\mathfrak{a} = \left(2, \frac{1-\sqrt{-p}}{2}\right)$. Assume that* $\mathrm{End}(E) \cong \mathbb{Z}[\frac{1+\sqrt{-p}}{2}]$ *and P generates $E[\mathfrak{a}^2]$. Then $-b$ is a square in $\mathbb{F}_p$. Moreover, the elliptic curve $E' : y^2 + xy - b'y = x^3 - b'x^2$ with*

$$b' = -\frac{\alpha(4\alpha^2+1)}{(2\alpha+1)^4}, \tag{22}$$

where $\alpha = -\sqrt[4]{-b}$ if $p \equiv 7 \pmod{16}$ or $\alpha = \sqrt[4]{-b}$ if $p \equiv 15 \pmod{16}$, is a representative of the $\mathbb{F}_p$-isomorphism class $[\mathfrak{a}^2] * E$ such that $(0,0)$ on E' generates $E'[\mathfrak{a}^2]$.

Proof. Note that $b \neq 0$ because E is smooth. We also note that P has order 4.

Let E_+ be the Montgomery curve with coefficient $2 + \frac{1}{4b}$ and E_- the Montgomery curve with coefficient $-(2 + \frac{1}{4b})$. There are two isomorphisms $\iota_+ : E \to E_+$ defined by

$$(x, y) \mapsto \left(\frac{1}{b}(x-b), \frac{1}{b\sqrt{b}}\left(y + \frac{x-b}{2}\right)\right)$$

and $\iota_- : E \to E_-$ defined by

$$(x, y) \mapsto \left(-\frac{1}{b}(x-b), -\frac{1}{b\sqrt{-b}}\left(y + \frac{x-b}{2}\right)\right).$$

(Here, we extend the symbol $\sqrt{\ }$ to $\mathbb{F}_p$. A choice of a square root is not essential since it corresponds to the composition with $[-1]$.)

Assume that $-b$ is not a square in $\mathbb{F}_p$. Then b is a square in $\mathbb{F}_p$, so the isomorphism ι_+ is defined over $\mathbb{F}_p$. Therefore we have $E_+ \in \mathcal{E}\ell\ell_p(\mathbb{Z}[\frac{1+\sqrt{-p}}{2}])$. From the assumption, the point $\iota_+(P)$ generates $E_+[\mathfrak{a}^2]$. However, the x-coordinate of $\iota_+(P)$ is -1. This contradicts Remark 1. Thus we conclude that $-b$ is a square in $\mathbb{F}_p$.

Because the isomorphism τ_- is defined over $\mathbb{F}_p$ and the x-coordinate of $\iota_-(P)$ is 1, the Montgomery curve E_- is in $\mathcal{E}\ell\ell_p(\mathbb{Z}[\frac{1+\sqrt{-p}}{2}])$, and the modified Montgomery coefficient of E_- is $-\frac{1}{b}$. Let E'_- be the Montgomery curve obtained by applying Theorem 14 to E_-. Then it is easy to verify that E' is $\mathbb{F}_p$-isomorphic to E'_- by an isomorphism defined as ι_-, which sends $(0,0)$ on E' to $(1, -)$ on E'_-. This completes the proof. □

5.3 Computational Efficiency

We discuss the computational efficiency of our formulas in application to CSIDH and its variants. As in [6], we evaluate the costs of formulas by the number of exponentiations, multiplications, additions, and inversions on $\mathbb{F}_p$ and denote these by **E**, **M**, **A**, and **I**, respectively. Note that the exponent of **E** is almost the same size as p and that its cost is about $1.5\log_2(p)\mathbf{M}$.

Table 2. The costs of 3-isogenies and transformations

	Formula in [6]	Our formula
Isogeny	$\mathbf{E} + 3\mathbf{M} + 12\mathbf{A}$	$\mathbf{E} + 5\mathbf{M} + 12\mathbf{A}$
Transform from Montgomery	$> \mathbf{E}$	None
Transform to Montgomery	$> 3\mathbf{E}$	$3\mathbf{M} + 9\mathbf{A} + \mathbf{I}$

Degree 3. We compare the cost of our formula (16) with the original radical isogeny (6). The cost of our formula is $\mathbf{E} + 5\mathbf{M} + 12\mathbf{A}$, and that of the original is $\mathbf{E} + 3\mathbf{M} + 12\mathbf{A}$. Note that we count the multiplication by 2, 3, and 9 as $\mathbf{A}$, $2\mathbf{A}$, and $4\mathbf{A}$, respectively. Our cost is $2\mathbf{M}$ higher than the original. However, our parametrization t has the transformation formula (9) to recover a Montgomery coefficient, which is easy to compute. On the other hand, the original radical isogeny needs transformations between a Montgomery curve and a curve used in radical isogenies of degree 3. The costs of these transformations are relatively high since these include some exponentiations. From this, our formula could be more efficient than the original in some parameters of cryptosystems. We explain this in detail below.

Let $E \in \mathcal{E}\ell\ell_p(\mathcal{O})$, ℓ be an odd prime dividing $p+1$, and $\mathfrak{l}$ be a prime ideal above ℓ in $\mathcal{O}$. The method to compute the action of $\mathfrak{l}^n$ on E by [6] is as follows:

1. Find a generator P of $E[\mathfrak{l}]$ on a Montgomery curve.
2. Transform the Montgomery curve to a curve with the image of P is $(0,0)$.
3. Compute an ℓ-isogeny $n-1$ times by iterating the radical-isogeny formula.
4. Compute an ℓ-isogeny with kernel $\langle(0,0)\rangle$ by Vélu's formula.
5. Transform the curve to a Montgomery form.

In the implementation[1] in [6] of CSURF, Step 2 contains $\mathbf{E}$, and Step 5 contains $3\mathbf{E}$. On the other hand, by using our formula, we do not need Step 2 and obtain the objective Montgomery coefficient by (9) instead of Step 5. The cost of (9) is $3\mathbf{M} + 9\mathbf{A} + \mathbf{I}$.

Table 2 shows the costs of the 3-isogenies and the transformations. (Table 2 redisplays the left half of Table 1.) Because the cost of $\mathbf{I}$ is less than that of $\mathbf{E}$, our formula reduces the cost of the transformations at least $3\mathbf{E}$. In addition, if we use the projective coordinate on Montgomery curves, then the inversion in (9) vanishes. While the exceeding cost of our formula in Step 3 is $3(n-1)\mathbf{M}$. In Step 4, both methods use Vélu's formulas. However, our method is slightly faster because Vélu's formulas on Montgomery curves are efficient. Therefore, if the exponent n of the ideal is less than about $1.5\log_2(p)$, then our formula accelerates the action of an ideal of norm 3.

[1] https://github.com/KULeuven-COSIC/Radical-Isogenies.

Remark 2. The implementation in [6] uses 9-isogenies instead of 3-isogenies for CSURF-512, a parameter set of CSURF proposed by [5]. Since the characteristic p of the base field in CSURF-512 satisfies $9 \mid p+1$, the elliptic curves in $\mathcal{E}\ell\ell_p(\mathcal{O})$ have a point of order 9 over $\mathbb{F}_p$. In this case, using 9-isogenies reduces the cost of the action of an ideal of norm 3 since the number of $\mathbf{E}$ in Step 3 is halved. Consequently, our formula does not improve the efficiency in this case. However, our formula could do in the case that $9 \nmid p+1$, for example, CSIDH-512 proposed in [7].

Degree 4. As in Sect. 5.2, we let $p \equiv 7 \pmod 8$ for considering 4-isogenies corresponding to the ideal actions. We say curves in $\mathcal{E}\ell\ell_p(\mathbb{Z}[\frac{1+\sqrt{-p}}{2}])$ are *on the surface*, and curves in $\mathcal{E}\ell\ell_p(\mathbb{Z}[\sqrt{-p}])$ are *on the floor.*

First, we recall the computing method of CSURF in the previous works.

The original CSURF [5] uses Montgomery$^-$ curves since these curves are always on the surface, and there is a one-to-one correspondence between Montgomery$^-$ coefficients of supersingular elliptic curves and the classes in $\mathcal{E}\ell\ell_p(\mathbb{Z}[\frac{1+\sqrt{-p}}{2}])$ if $p \equiv 7 \pmod 8$. All the computation in the original CSURF, thus, is done on the surface.

On the other hand, the CSURF using radical isogenies [6] uses curves both on the surface and the floor. There are two reasons to use curves on the floor. First, their transformations from Tate normal forms to Montgomery curves for degrees greater than four use the properties that these curves have exactly one point of order 2 over $\mathbb{F}_p$. Second, the arithmetic on Montgomery curves is slightly faster than that on Montgomery$^-$ curves. The computation of ideal class actions is as follows:

1. Take a Montgomery$^-$ curve as an input.
2. Transform the curve to a Tate normal form and compute 4-radical isogenies.
3. Transform the resulting curve to a Montgomery curve on the floor.
4. Compute radical isogenies of degrees less than 17.
5. Compute the action of the remaining ideal as in the original CSIDH [7].
6. Transform the resulting Montgomery curve to Montgomery$^-$ curve.

Here, we propose a computing method of CSURF that does not use Montgomery$^-$ curves at all. Table 1 in [5] shows that there are exactly two $\mathbb{F}_p$-isomorphic Montgomery curves on the surface. On one of these, the point $(0,0)$ generates the ideal $\left(2, \frac{1-\sqrt{-p}}{2}\right)$ (we call a Montgomery curve with this property by *positive type*). On the other, the point $(0,0)$ generates the ideal $\left(2, \frac{1+\sqrt{-p}}{2}\right)$ (we call a Montgomery curve with this property by *negative type*). In short, there is a one-to-one correspondence between positive-type Montgomery curves and the classes in $\mathcal{E}\ell\ell_p(\mathbb{Z}[\frac{1+\sqrt{-p}}{2}])$. Lemma 11 allows us to determine which type of curve is by computing a Legendre symbol. A Montgomery curve with coefficient A is on the surface if and only if $A^2-4 \in (\mathbb{F}_p^\times)^2$. Therefore, by adding two Legendre symbol computations to key validation in CSURF, we can use Montgomery coefficients of positive-type curves as public keys and shared secrets.

Unfortunately, we need to transform a Montgomery curve from positive type to negative type for computing the action of $\left(2, \frac{1+\sqrt{-p}}{2}\right)$, which is the inverse of $\left(2, \frac{1-\sqrt{-p}}{2}\right)$ as an ideal class, and the cost of the transformation needs two exponentiations. Let E be a positive-type Montgomery curve with coefficient A. Lemma 4 in [5] shows that the negative-type curve that is $\mathbb{F}_p$-isomorphic to E is obtained by an isomorphism between Montgomery curves sending $\left(\frac{-A-\sqrt{A^2-4}}{2}, 0\right)$ to $(0, 0)$. Therefore, the coefficient of the negative-type curve is

$$\frac{-A - 3\sqrt{A^2-4}}{\sqrt{2\sqrt{A^2-4}(A + \sqrt{A^2-4})}}.$$

We use this transformation if the exponent of the ideal $\left(2, \frac{1-\sqrt{-p}}{2}\right)$ is negative. Furthermore, we have to move to the floor from the surface for using radical isogenies of degrees greater than four. This can be computed by a 2-isogeny.

Consequently, the computation of ideal class actions using our radical isogenies of degree 4 is as follows:

1. Take a positive-type Montgomery curve as an input.
2. Transform to negative type if the exponent of $\left(2, \frac{1-\sqrt{-p}}{2}\right)$ is negative.
3. Transform to the modified Montgomery coefficient.
4. Compute 4-radical isogenies by (21).
5. Transform to the Montgomery coefficient.
6. Transform to the floor.
7. Compute radical isogenies of other degrees.
8. Compute the action of the remaining ideal as in the original CSIDH [7].
9. Transform to the surface.

We can compute 9 by $A \mapsto \frac{A+6}{2\sqrt{A+2}}$. It is easy to check that the resulting curve is always positive type. The computational cost is slightly less than transforming a Montgomery curve on the floor to a Montgomery$^-$ curve.

Table 3 compares the costs related to 4-isogenies of our method with the original radical isogenies. This shows that our method is more efficient even if we need to transform to a negative-type curve.

We implemented CSURF using our formulas on Magma [3]. Our implementation is based on that by [6] and available at https://github.com/hiroshi-onuki/Montgomery-Radical-Isogenies.

Table 3. The costs of 4-isogenies and transformations. The costs of transformations in our formulas include the cost of transformations between Montgomery coefficients and modified Montgomery coefficients. In the second line, we need the cost $(2\mathbf{E} + 2\mathrm{M} + 6\mathbf{A} + \mathbf{I})^*$ only in the case that the exponent of the ideal $[2, \frac{1-\sqrt{-p}}{2}]$ is negative.

	Formula in [6]	Our formula
Isogeny	$\mathbf{E} + 3\mathrm{M} + 5\mathbf{A} + \mathbf{I}$	$\mathbf{E} + 3\mathrm{M} + 4\mathbf{A} + \mathbf{I}$
Transform to computation forms	$> 3\mathbf{E}$	$3\mathbf{A} + (2\mathbf{E} + 2\mathrm{M} + 6\mathbf{A} + \mathbf{I})^*$
Transform to the floor	$> 3\mathbf{E}$	$\mathbf{E} + 4\mathrm{M} + 6\mathbf{A}$

6 Conclusion

We proposed the radical-isogeny formulas of degrees 3 and 4 on Montgomery curves. We analyzed those computational efficiencies in application to CSIDH and its variants. Because our formulas reduce the cost of transformations between elliptic curves, these could improve the efficiency of CSIDH and its variants. In particular, we showed that our formulas of degree 3 could be efficient in some cases. Our formula of degree 4 is more efficient than the original radical isogenies. In addition, we proved the conjecture on radical isogenies of degree 4, which was left open in [6].

Acknowledgements. This study was supported by the Ministry of Internal Affairs and Communications, Japan (JPJ000254) and JSPS KAKENHI Grant Numbers JP21K17739, JP21J10711.

References

1. National Institute of Standards and Technology (NIST): NIST post-quantum cryptography standardization. https://csrc.nist.gov/Projects/Post-Quantum-Cryptography
2. Beullens, W., Kleinjung, T., Vercauteren, F.: CSI-FiSh: efficient isogeny based signatures through class group computations. In: Galbraith, S.D., Moriai, S. (eds.) ASIACRYPT 2019. LNCS, vol. 11921, pp. 227–247. Springer, Cham (2019). https://doi.org/10.1007/978-3-030-34578-5_9
3. Bosma, W., Cannon, J., Playoust, C.: The Magma algebra system. I. The user language. J. Symbolic Comput. **24**(3–4), 235–265 (1997). https://doi.org/10.1006/jsco.1996.0125, Computational algebra and number theory (London, 1993)
4. Broon, F.L.P., Dang, T., Fouotsa, E., Moody, D.: Isogenies on twisted Hessian curves. J. Math. Cryptol. **15**(1), 345–358 (2021). https://doi.org/10.1515/jmc-2020-0037
5. Castryck, W., Decru, T.: CSIDH on the surface. In: Ding, J., Tillich, J.P. (eds.) Post-Quantum Cryptography, pp. 111–129. Springer, Cham (2020)
6. Castryck, W., Decru, T., Vercauteren, F.: Radical isogenies. In: Moriai, S., Wang, H. (eds.) ASIACRYPT 2020. LNCS, vol. 12492, pp. 493–519. Springer, Cham (2020). https://doi.org/10.1007/978-3-030-64834-3_17

7. Castryck, W., Lange, T., Martindale, C., Panny, L., Renes, J.: CSIDH: an efficient post-quantum commutative group action. In: Peyrin, T., Galbraith, S. (eds.) ASIACRYPT 2018. LNCS, vol. 11274, pp. 395–427. Springer, Cham (2018). https://doi.org/10.1007/978-3-030-03332-3_15
8. Cervantes-Vázquez, D., Chenu, M., Chi-Domínguez, J.-J., De Feo, L., Rodríguez-Henríquez, F., Smith, B.: Stronger and faster side-channel protections for CSIDH. In: Schwabe, P., Thériault, N. (eds.) LATINCRYPT 2019. LNCS, vol. 11774, pp. 173–193. Springer, Cham (2019). https://doi.org/10.1007/978-3-030-30530-7_9
9. Charles, D.X., Lauter, K.E., Goren, E.Z.: Cryptographic hash functions from expander graphs. J. Cryptol. **22**(1), 93–113 (2009). https://doi.org/10.1007/s00145-007-9002-x
10. Costello, C., Hisil, H.: A simple and compact algorithm for SIDH with arbitrary degree isogenies. In: Takagi, T., Peyrin, T. (eds.) ASIACRYPT 2017. LNCS, vol. 10625, pp. 303–329. Springer, Cham (2017). https://doi.org/10.1007/978-3-319-70697-9_11
11. Couveignes, J.M.: Hard homogeneous spaces. Cryptology ePrint Archive, Report 2006/291 (2006). https://eprint.iacr.org/2006/291
12. De Feo, L., Galbraith, S.D.: SeaSign: compact isogeny signatures from class group actions. In: Ishai, Y., Rijmen, V. (eds.) EUROCRYPT 2019. LNCS, vol. 11478, pp. 759–789. Springer, Cham (2019). https://doi.org/10.1007/978-3-030-17659-4_26
13. De Feo, L., Jao, D., Plût, J.: Towards quantum-resistant cryptosystems from supersingular elliptic curve isogenies. J. Math. Cryptol. **8**(3), 209–247 (2014)
14. Diamond, F., Shurman, J.: A First Course in Modular Forms. Graduate Texts in Mathematics. Springer, New York (2006). https://doi.org/10.1007/978-0-387-27226-9
15. Fouotsa, T.B., Petit, C.: InSIDH: a simplification of sigamal. Cryptology ePrint Archive, Report 2021/218 (2021). https://eprint.iacr.org/2021/218
16. Jao, D., De Feo, L.: Towards quantum-resistant cryptosystems from supersingular elliptic curve isogenies. In: Yang, B.Y. (ed.) Post-Quantum Cryptography, pp. 19–34. Springer, Heidelberg (2011)
17. Kim, S., Yoon, K., Park, Y.-H., Hong, S.: Optimized method for computing odd-degree isogenies on Edwards curves. In: Galbraith, S.D., Moriai, S. (eds.) ASIACRYPT 2019. LNCS, vol. 11922, pp. 273–292. Springer, Cham (2019). https://doi.org/10.1007/978-3-030-34621-8_10
18. Montgomery, P.L.: Speeding the Pollard and elliptic curve methods of factorization. Math. Comput. **48**(177), 243–264 (1987)
19. Moriya, T., Onuki, H., Takagi, T.: SiGamal: a supersingular isogeny-based PKE and its application to a PRF. In: Moriai, S., Wang, H. (eds.) ASIACRYPT 2020. LNCS, vol. 12492, pp. 551–580. Springer, Cham (2020). https://doi.org/10.1007/978-3-030-64834-3_19
20. Rostovtsev, A., Stolbunov, A.: Public-key cryptosystem based on isogenies. Cryptology ePrint Archive, Report 2006/145 (2006). https://eprint.iacr.org/2006/145
21. Silverman, J.H.: The Arithmetic of Elliptic Curves. Graduate Texts in Mathematics, 2nd edn. Springer, New York (2009). https://doi.org/10.1007/978-1-4757-1920-8
22. Stolbunov, A.: Constructing public-key cryptographic schemes based on class group action on a set of isogenous elliptic curves. Adv. Math. Commun. **4**(2), 215 (2010). http://aimsciences.org//article/id/e8001706-6615-4b24-b499-8ea9d348dabb

23. Streng, M.: Generators of the group of modular units for $\Gamma^1(N)$ over the rationals. arXiv:1503.08127v2 (2019)
24. Vélu, J.: Isogénies entre courbes elliptiques. Comptes-Rendues de l'Académie des Sciences **273**, 238–241 (1971)

Towards a Simpler Lattice Gadget Toolkit

Shiduo Zhang[1] and Yang Yu[2(✉)]

[1] Institute for Advanced Study, Tsinghua University, Beijing, China
[2] BNRist, Tsinghua University, Beijing, China
yu-yang@mail.tsinghua.edu.cn

Abstract. As a building block, gadgets and associated algorithms are widely used in advanced lattice cryptosystems. The gadget algorithms for power-of-base moduli are very efficient and simple, however the current algorithms for arbitrary moduli are still complicated and practically more costly despite several efforts. Considering the necessity of arbitrary moduli, developing simpler and more practical gadget algorithms for arbitrary moduli is crucial to improving the practical performance of lattice based applications.

In this work, we propose two new gadget sampling algorithms for arbitrary moduli. Our first algorithm is for gadget Gaussian sampling. It is simple and efficient. One distinguishing feature of our Gaussian sampler is that it does not need floating-point arithmetic, which makes it better compatible with constrained environments. Our second algorithm is for gadget subgaussian sampling. Compared with the existing algorithm, it is simpler, faster, and requires asymptotically less randomness. In addition, our subgaussian sampler achieves an almost equal quality for different practical parameters. Overall these two algorithms provide simpler options for gadget algorithms and enhance the practicality of the gadget toolkit.

1 Introduction

Lattice based cryptography is not only a strong contender in the NIST post-quantum standardization, but also offers powerful versatility leading to the constructions of various advanced cryptographic primitives ranging from identity based encryption (IBE) [1,13], attribute based encryption (ABE) [27], group signatures [29,34,36] to fully homomorphic encryption (FHE) [15,24,26], functional encryption [2,3,35] and much more [7,28]. Many advanced lattice cryptosystems rely on strong *lattice trapdoors* that allow to sample lattice points from Gaussian-like distributions. The notion of lattice trapdoor was introduced in [25] along with a sampling algorithm. Later a series of works [14,18–20,37] proposed improved trapdoor constructions and sampling algorithms.

Currently, the state-of-the-art lattice trapdoor framework is developed by Micciancio and Peikert [37]. Following the idea of [39], the trapdoor sampling in this framework is decomposed into online and offline two phases, and the online sampling is accomplished by the sampling over a special lattice $\Lambda^{\perp}(\mathbf{g}^t) = \{\mathbf{z} \in$

G. Hanaoka et al. (Eds.): PKC 2022, LNCS 13177, pp. 498–520, 2022.
https://doi.org/10.1007/978-3-030-97121-2_18

$\mathbb{Z}^k : \mathbf{g}^t\mathbf{z} = 0 \bmod q\}$ defined by the *gadget* $\mathbf{g} = (1, b, \cdots, b^{k-1})$. Thanks to the good structure of the short basis of $\Lambda^{\perp}(\mathbf{g}^t)$, the sampling over $\Lambda^{\perp}(\mathbf{g}^t)$ is convenient and fast, which improves the efficiency of the online sampling. As a building block of lattice based cryptography, gadgets have been in effect used in much more applications, e.g. [11,12,26]. In summary, the use of the gadget is mainly based on four algorithms:

- **Digit Decomposition:** Given $u \in \mathbb{Z}_q$, find a short $\mathbf{x}$ such that $\langle \mathbf{x}, \mathbf{g} \rangle = u \bmod q$. This is the most widely used case, identifying a number of size $O(b^k)$ with a vector of norm $O(b\sqrt{k})$.
- **LWE Decoding:** Given $s\mathbf{g}+\mathbf{e} \bmod q$ for a sufficiently small $\mathbf{e}$, recover s. This algorithm is deterministic as the digit decomposition and a representative usecase is in the decryption of LWE cryptosystems.
- **Gaussian Sampling:** Given $u \in \mathbb{Z}_q$, sample $\mathbf{x}$ from a discrete Gaussian on a lattice coset $\Lambda_u^{\perp}(\mathbf{g}^t) = \{\mathbf{z} \in \mathbb{Z}^k : \mathbf{g}^t\mathbf{z} = u \bmod q\}$. This algorithm is randomized unlike the digit decomposition and LWE decoding. It is the main component of the Micciancio-Peikert trapdoor [37] and used in lattice based signatures, IBE and many other primitives.
- **Subgaussian Sampling:** Given $u \in \mathbb{Z}_q$, sample a subgaussian $\mathbf{x}$ in $\Lambda_u^{\perp}(\mathbf{g}^t)$. This algorithm is also randomized and can work with much less randomness than the Gaussian sampling. It is used in some FHE schemes as an alternative to the digit decomposition for tighter parameters [4].

Micciancio and Peikert gave very efficient gadget Gaussian sampling and LWE decoding algorithms in [37] but mainly for the special case where the modulus $q = b^k$. Genise and Micciancio later proposed an equally efficient (in an asymptotic sense) gadget Gaussian sampler for arbitrary moduli [21]. Genise, Micciancio and Polyakov also devised gadget subgaussian sampling and LWE decoding algorithms applicable to an arbitrary modulus q [23]. With these efforts, recent years have seen significant progress in bringing advanced lattice cryptosystems in practice [8,9,16,17,30].

Despite the same asymptotic complexity, there still exist some gaps between the practicalities of the gadget algorithms for the special $q = b^k$ and for an arbitrary modulus $q < b^k$. The specialized algorithms for $q = b^k$ are very simple and only require integer operations. In contrast, the existing algorithms for $q < b^k$ are complicated, and particularly the Gaussian sampler has to resort to high-precision arithmetic, which limits the use of gadget algorithms on some constrained devices. To close these gaps is not only of theoretical interest but also crucial for practical applications: many lattice cryptosystems require the modulus q to support the NTT/RNS/CRT techniques for better performance, hence $q < b^k$ in these cases.

Our contribution. Towards better practicality of the gadget toolkit, we improve on two randomized gadget algorithms, i.e. Gaussian sampling and subgaussian sampling, for arbitrary moduli.

We present a new gadget Gaussian sampler that avoids the floating-point arithmetic in existing algorithms. Compared with the previous algorithms, our sampler achieves the same quality and asymptotic complexity, but is simpler and highly parallelizable. Verified by experiments (see Figs. 1 and 2), our sampler is as fast as the original Genise-Micciancio sampler [21] for practical parameters, but slower than an improved variant of the Genise-Micciancio sampler [16] in which continuous Gaussian sampling is heavily used.

We also propose a new gadget subgaussian sampler. It does not use any linear transformation and most computations are identical to those in the specialized algorithm for $q = b^k$. Consequently, the new sampler is simpler, faster and only requires $O(k \log b)$-bits of randomness, which improves the previous (considered essentially optimal) result by $O(k)$. Indeed the subgaussian parameter achieved by our algorithm may be $\sqrt{2}$ times as large as that by the previous algorithm in the worst case. But it is convenient to get an almost equal quality in practice by selecting proper parameters without speed and security loss.

In summary, we provide the gadget toolkit with simpler algorithmic options. Due to the absence of high-precision arithmetic, the new gadget Gaussian sampler is of some interest when side-channel protections and constrained devices are taken into account. The new subgaussian sampler can be used to improve the efficiency and simplicity of the implementation of advanced lattice schemes.

Techniques. We now briefly explain the used techniques. In this work, we focus on the gadget $\mathbf{g} = (1, b, \cdots, b^{k-1})$ and the gadget lattice $\Lambda^{\perp}(\mathbf{g}^t) = \{\mathbf{z} \in \mathbb{Z}^k : \mathbf{g}^t\mathbf{z} = 0 \mod q\}$.

Our gadget Gaussian sampling algorithm follows Peikert's approach [39]: it first generates a perturbation vector of certain covariance and then generates a Gaussian sample from an easy-to-sample lattice. Concretely, we represent the basis $\mathbf{B}_q$ of $\Lambda^{\perp}(\mathbf{g}^t)$ as $\mathbf{B}_q = \mathbf{TD}$ where $\mathbf{T}$, $\mathbf{D}$ were first suggested in [21]. With such a factorization, the sampling over $\Lambda^{\perp}(\mathbf{g}^t)$ is decomposed into the sampling over $\mathcal{L}(\mathbf{D})$ that is easy and over integers and the perturbation sampling of covariance $\mathbf{\Sigma} = s^2\mathbf{I} - \mathbf{TT}^t$ that introduces floating-point arithmetic. To avoid floating-point arithmetic, we exploit an integral matrix decomposition $\mathbf{\Sigma} = \mathbf{AJA}^t$ with $\mathbf{A} \in \mathbb{Z}^{k \times k'}$ and $\mathbf{J}$ being diagonal, which is inspired by [18]. But a technical difference is that the middle matrix $\mathbf{J}$ is a diagonal but not identity matrix, which allows to reduce the size of $\mathbf{A}$, that is only $k \times (k+2)$ much smaller than the size of the Gram root given in [18], while keeping $\mathbf{A}$ integral. With such a compact integral decomposition, the perturbation sampling can be done by applying a linear transformation of $\mathbf{A}$ on $D_{\mathbb{Z}^{k'}, \sqrt{\mathbf{J}}}$, which is simple, fast and highly parallelizable.

Our gadget subgaussian algorithm is very different from the one proposed by Genise, Micciancio and Polyakov [23]. The Genise-Micciancio-Polyakov algorithm relies on the factorization $\mathbf{B}_q = \mathbf{TD}$ used in the previous gadget Gaussian sampler [21]: it first performs subgaussian sampling with respect to $\mathbf{D}$ and then multiplies by $\mathbf{T}$ to get the final result. The subgaussian sampling with respect to $\mathbf{D}$ requires $O(k^2 \log b)$-bits of randomness while the specialized algorithm sampling directly over $\mathbf{B}_{b^k}$ needs only $O(k \log b)$-bits. The linear transformation $\mathbf{T}$

also introduces extra computational overhead. Consequently, a performance gap occurs between the Genise-Micciancio-Polyakov algorithm for $q = b^k$ and $q < b^k$. To close this gap, our idea is to convert the sampling for $q < b^k$ into the sampling for a power-of-b modulus. In a nutshell, we propose to first sample the $(k-1)$ lower digits by calling the subgaussian algorithm for the modulus b^{k-1} and then to compute the highest digit. Specifically, we sample within two sets $S_0 = \{\mathbf{x} \mid \langle \mathbf{x}, \mathbf{g} \rangle = u\}$ and $S_1 = \{\mathbf{x} \mid \langle \mathbf{x}, \mathbf{g} \rangle = u - q\}$ and in each set the highest digit x_{k-1} is basically fixed and so is $\langle \mathbf{x}', \mathbf{g}' \rangle \bmod b^{k-1}$ where $\mathbf{x}' = (x_0, \cdots, x_{k-2})$ and $\mathbf{g}' = (1, b, \cdots, b^{k-2})$. Our sampler proceeds in three steps. First, it chooses either S_0 or S_1 to which the output belongs. Once the set is fixed, it then calls the specialized algorithm to output a subgaussian $\mathbf{x}'$ given $\langle \mathbf{x}', \mathbf{g}' \rangle \bmod b^{k-1}$. Finally it computes x_{k-1} according to the chosen S_i and the exact value of $\langle \mathbf{x}', \mathbf{g}' \rangle$. To ensure $\mathbf{x}$ is subgaussian, it suffices to show the expectation of the output $\mathbf{x}$ is $\mathbf{0}$. To this end, we figure out the probability of S_i should be chosen according to u. As a consequence, we prove the subgaussian parameter of the output is at most $\sqrt{(b-1)^2 + \alpha^2}\sqrt{2\pi}$ with $\alpha = \lfloor q/b^{k-1} \rfloor + 1$, which can be close to even better than the previous result $(b+1)\sqrt{2\pi}$ for some practical (q, b). Thanks to the ease of the specialized algorithm, our subgaussian algorithm achieves better practical performance (see Fig. 3) and requires $O(k \log b)$ random bits which asymptotically improves the previous result and is essentially identical to the case $q = b^k$.

Roadmap. We start in Sect. 2 with some preliminary material. Section 3 is devoted to recalling the state of the art of the gadget Gaussian and subgaussian samplers. We present our new gadget Gaussian and subgaussian sampling algorithms in Sects. 4 and 5 respectively. Finally, we conclude in Sect. 6.

2 Preliminaries

2.1 Notation

A number is denoted by a lower case letter, e.g. $z \in \mathbb{Z}$. A vector is denoted by a bold lower case letter, e.g. $\mathbf{v}$, and in column form ($\mathbf{v}^t$ is a row vector). The inner product of two vectors is $\langle \mathbf{x}, \mathbf{y} \rangle = \mathbf{x}^t \mathbf{y}$. Let $\mathbb{Z}_q = \{0, 1, \cdots, q-1\}$ for a positive integer q. For integers $b > 0$ and $u < b^k$, the b-ary decomposition of u is $[u]_b^k = (u_0, \cdots, u_{k-1}) \in \mathbb{Z}_b^k$ such that $\sum_i b^i u_i = u$. We denote matrices with bold upper case letters, e.g. $\mathbf{B}$. Let $\mathbf{B}^t$ be the transpose of $\mathbf{B}$. Unless otherwise stated, the norm of a vector is the ℓ_2 norm. Let $\|\mathbf{B}\|_{col} = max_i \|\mathbf{b}_i\|$. We use log and ln to denote the base 2 logarithm and the natural logarithm respectively. Let $\epsilon > 0$ be some very small number. We use the notational shortcut $\hat{\epsilon} = \epsilon + O(\epsilon^2)$. Then $\frac{1+\epsilon}{1-\epsilon} = 1 + 2\hat{\epsilon}$ and $\ln(\frac{1+\epsilon}{1-\epsilon}) = 2\hat{\epsilon}$.

A random variable x sampled from a distribution D is written as $x \leftarrow D$. A random variable distributed as D is denoted $x \sim D$. The *max-log distance* between two distributions D_1 and D_2 over the same support S is

$$\Delta_{ML}(D_1, D_2) = \max_{x \in S} |\ln(D_1(x)) - \ln(D_2(x))|.$$

As shown in [38], $\Delta_{ML}(D_1, D_2) \leq \Delta_{ML}(D_1, D_3) + \Delta_{ML}(D_2, D_3)$.

2.2 Linear Algebra

For $\mathbf{T} \in \mathbb{R}^{n \times k}$, let $\text{span}(\mathbf{T})$ be the linear span of the columns of $\mathbf{T}$ and $\ker(\mathbf{T})$ be the kernel of $\mathbf{T}$. The (foreward) *Gram-Schmidt orthogonalization* of an ordered set of linearly independent vectors $\mathbf{B} = \{\mathbf{b}_1, \cdots, \mathbf{b}_k\}$ is $\tilde{\mathbf{B}} = \{\tilde{\mathbf{b}}_1, \cdots, \tilde{\mathbf{b}}_k\}$ where each $\tilde{\mathbf{b}}_i$ is the component of $\mathbf{b}_i$ orthogonal to $\text{span}(\mathbf{b}_1, \cdots, \mathbf{b}_{i-1})$.

We write $\mathbf{\Sigma} > 0$ (resp., $\mathbf{\Sigma} \geq 0$) when a symmetric matrix $\mathbf{\Sigma} \in \mathbb{R}^{n \times n}$ is *positive definite* (resp. *semidefinite*), i.e. $\mathbf{x}^t \mathbf{\Sigma} \mathbf{x} > 0$ (resp., $\mathbf{x}^t \mathbf{\Sigma} \mathbf{x} \geq 0$) for all nonzero $\mathbf{x} \in \mathbb{R}^n$. We write $\mathbf{\Sigma}_1 \geq \mathbf{\Sigma}_2$ or $\mathbf{\Sigma}_2 \leq \mathbf{\Sigma}_1$ if $\mathbf{\Sigma}_1 - \mathbf{\Sigma}_2 \geq 0$, and similarly for $\mathbf{\Sigma}_1 > \mathbf{\Sigma}_2$. It holds that $\mathbf{\Sigma}_1 > \mathbf{\Sigma}_2 > 0$ if and only if $\mathbf{\Sigma}_2^{-1} > \mathbf{\Sigma}_1^{-1} > 0$. If $\mathbf{\Sigma} = \mathbf{A}\mathbf{A}^t$, we call $\mathbf{A}$ a *Gram root* of $\mathbf{\Sigma}$. Let $\sqrt{\mathbf{\Sigma}}$ denote any Gram root of $\mathbf{\Sigma}$ when the context permits it.

2.3 Lattices

A lattice is the set of all integer combinations of linearly independent vectors $\mathbf{b}_1, \cdots, \mathbf{b}_n \in \mathbb{R}^m$. We call $\mathbf{B} = (\mathbf{b}_1, \cdots, \mathbf{b}_n)$ a basis and n the dimension of the lattice. The lattice is *full-rank* if $n = m$. We denote by $\mathcal{L}(\mathbf{B})$ the lattice generated by the basis $\mathbf{B}$. A coset of a lattice Λ is a set of the form $\{\mathbf{v} + \mathbf{a} | \mathbf{v} \in \Lambda\} := \Lambda + \mathbf{a}$. Let $\Lambda^* = \{\mathbf{x} \in \text{span}(\Lambda) | \langle \mathbf{x}, \Lambda \rangle \subseteq \mathbb{Z}\}$ be the dual lattice of Λ.

2.4 Gaussian

The n-dimensional *Gaussian* function $\rho : \mathbb{R}^n \to (0, 1]$ is defined as $\rho(\mathbf{x}) := \exp(-\pi \|\mathbf{x}\|^2)$. Let $\rho_{\mathbf{B}}(\mathbf{x}) = \exp(-\pi \mathbf{x}^t \mathbf{\Sigma}^{-1} \mathbf{x})$ where $\mathbf{\Sigma} = \mathbf{B}\mathbf{B}^t$. Since $\rho_{\mathbf{B}}(\mathbf{x})$ is completely determined by $\mathbf{\Sigma} = \mathbf{B}\mathbf{B}^t$, we also write $\rho_{\sqrt{\mathbf{\Sigma}}}(\mathbf{x}) = \rho_{\mathbf{B}}(\mathbf{x})$. Let $\rho_{\sqrt{\mathbf{\Sigma}}, \mathbf{c}}(\mathbf{x}) = \rho_{\sqrt{\mathbf{\Sigma}}}(\mathbf{x} - \mathbf{c})$ for $\mathbf{c} \in \text{span}(\mathbf{\Sigma})$. When $\mathbf{c} = \mathbf{0}$, we omit the subscript $\mathbf{c}$. For a countable set of $S \subset \mathbb{R}^n$, let $\rho_{\sqrt{\mathbf{\Sigma}}}(S) = \sum_{\mathbf{s} \in S} \rho_{\sqrt{\mathbf{\Sigma}}}(\mathbf{s})$. The *discrete Gaussian* over a lattice Λ with center $\mathbf{c}$ and covariance matrix $\mathbf{\Sigma}$ is defined by the probability function

$$D_{\Lambda, \sqrt{\mathbf{\Sigma}}, \mathbf{c}}(\mathbf{x}) = \frac{\rho_{\sqrt{\mathbf{\Sigma}}, \mathbf{c}}(\mathbf{x})}{\rho_{\sqrt{\mathbf{\Sigma}}, \mathbf{c}}(\Lambda)} \propto \rho_{\sqrt{\mathbf{\Sigma}}, \mathbf{c}}(\mathbf{x}).$$

The discrete Gaussian on $\Lambda + \mathbf{c}$, for $\mathbf{c} \in \text{span}(\Lambda)$, is defined by $D_{\Lambda + \mathbf{c}, \sqrt{\mathbf{\Sigma}}}(\mathbf{x}) = \rho_{\sqrt{\mathbf{\Sigma}}}(\mathbf{x}) / \rho_{\sqrt{\mathbf{\Sigma}}}(\Lambda + \mathbf{c})$ for all $\mathbf{x} \in \Lambda + \mathbf{c}$. When $\mathbf{\Sigma} = s^2 \mathbf{I}$, we call the Gaussian *spherical* of *width* s and write the subscript $\sqrt{\mathbf{\Sigma}}$ as s simply.

For a lattice Λ and $\epsilon > 0$, $\eta_\epsilon(\Lambda) = \min\{s > 0 \mid \rho_{\frac{1}{s}}(\Lambda^*) \leq 1 + \epsilon\}$ is called the *smoothing parameter*. The following definition is a generalized version.

Definition 1 ([39], Definition 2.3). *Let* $\mathbf{\Sigma} > 0$ *and lattice* $\Lambda \in \text{span}(\mathbf{\Sigma})$. *We write* $\sqrt{\mathbf{\Sigma}} \geq \eta_\epsilon(\Lambda)$ *if* $\eta_\epsilon(\sqrt{\mathbf{\Sigma}}^{-1} \cdot \Lambda) \leq 1$ *i.e.* $\eta_{\sqrt{\mathbf{\Sigma}^{-1}}}(\Lambda^*) \leq 1 + \epsilon$.

Notice that for two lattices of the same rank $\Lambda_1 \subseteq \Lambda_2$, the denser lattice always has the smaller smoothing parameter, i.e. $\eta_\epsilon(\Lambda_2) \leq \eta_\epsilon(\Lambda_1)$. Let $\overline{\eta_\epsilon}(\mathbb{Z}^n) = \sqrt{\frac{\ln(2n(1+1/\epsilon))}{\pi}}$. Here we recall several facts to be used later.

Lemma 1 **([25], Lemma 3.1).** *Let $\Lambda \subset \mathbb{R}^n$ be a lattice with a basis $\mathbf{B}$, then $\eta_\epsilon(\Lambda) \leq \|\tilde{\mathbf{B}}\|_{col} \cdot \overline{\eta_\epsilon}(\mathbb{Z}^n)$.*

Theorem 1 (Adapted from Theorem 3.1 [22]). *For any $\epsilon \in [0,1)$, matrix $\mathbf{S}$ of full column rank, lattice $\Lambda \subset \mathsf{span}(\mathbf{S})$, and matrix $\mathbf{T}$ such that $\mathsf{ker}(\mathbf{T})$ is a Λ-subspace and $\eta_\epsilon(\Lambda \cap \mathsf{ker}(\mathbf{T})) \leq \mathbf{S}$, then $\Delta_{ML}(\mathbf{T} \cdot D_{\Lambda,\mathbf{S}}, D_{\mathbf{T}\Lambda,\mathbf{TS}}) \leq 2\hat{\epsilon}$.*

Theorem 2 (Adapted from Theorem 3.1 [39]). *Let $\mathbf{\Sigma}_1, \mathbf{\Sigma}_2 \in \mathbb{R}^{n\times n}$ be positive definite matrices. Let $\mathbf{\Sigma} = \mathbf{\Sigma}_1 + \mathbf{\Sigma}_2$ and let $\mathbf{\Sigma}_3 \in \mathbb{R}^{n\times n}$ be such that $\mathbf{\Sigma}_3^{-1} = \mathbf{\Sigma}_1^{-1} + \mathbf{\Sigma}_2^{-1}$. Let Λ_1, Λ_2 be two full-rank lattices in $\mathbb{R}^n$ such that $\sqrt{\mathbf{\Sigma}_1} \geq \eta_\epsilon(\Lambda_1)$ and $\sqrt{\mathbf{\Sigma}_3} \geq \eta_\epsilon(\Lambda_2)$ for $\epsilon \in (0,1/2)$. Let $\mathbf{c}_1, \mathbf{c}_2 \in \mathbb{R}^n$, then the distribution of $\mathbf{x} \leftarrow D_{\Lambda_1,\sqrt{\mathbf{\Sigma}_1},\mathbf{p}-\mathbf{c}_2+\mathbf{c}_1}$ where $\mathbf{p} \leftarrow D_{\Lambda_2,\sqrt{\mathbf{\Sigma}_2},\mathbf{c}_2}$ is within max-log distance $4\hat{\epsilon}$ of $D_{\Lambda_1,\sqrt{\mathbf{\Sigma}},\mathbf{c}_1}$.*

2.5 Subgaussian Random Variables

A random variable X over $\mathbb{R}$ is *subgaussian* with parameter $\alpha > 0$ if for all $t \in \mathbb{R}$, its (scaled) moment generating function satisfies

$$\mathbb{E}[\exp(2\pi t X)] \leq \exp(\pi \alpha^2 t^2).$$

Scaling a subgaussian X with parameter α by any $c \in \mathbb{R}$ to $c \cdot X$ yields a subgaussian random variable with parameter $|c|\alpha$. If X is subgaussian with parameter α, then $\Pr[|X| \geq t] \leq 2\exp(-\pi t^2/\alpha^2)$. If X is a random variable with $\mathbb{E}(X) = 0$ and $|X| \leq b$ for some $b > 0$, then X is subgaussian with parameter $b\sqrt{2\pi}$ [40]. Moreover, if X is subgaussian variable, then $\mathbb{E}[X] = 0$. An important property of subgaussian called *Pythagorean additivity* is defined as follow.

Lemma 2. *Let X, Y be discrete random variables over $\mathbb{R}$ such that X is subgaussian with parameter α and Y conditioned on X taking any value is subgaussian with parameter β. Then, $X + Y$ is subgaussian with parameter $\sqrt{\alpha^2 + \beta^2}$.*

A random vector $\mathbf{x}$ over $\mathbb{R}^n$ is subgaussian with parameter $\alpha > 0$ if $\langle \mathbf{x}, \mathbf{u} \rangle$ is subgaussian with parameter α for all unit vectors $\mathbf{u}$.

Lemma 3. *Let $\mathbf{x}$ be a discrete random vector over $\mathbb{R}^n$ such that each coordinate x_i is subgaussian with parameter α_i given the previous coordinates take any values. Then, $\mathbf{x}$ is a subgaussian vector with parameter $\max_i\{\alpha_i\}$.*

3 Recall the Gadget Sampling

The gadget Gaussian and subgaussian samplings are two primary algorithms associated to the lattice gadget. For better completeness and comparisons, let us briefly recall the state of the art of these two algorithms.

Throughout the paper, we focus on the most widely used gadget defined by $\mathbf{g} = (1, b, \cdots, b^{k-1})$ where $b \in \mathbb{N}$ such that the global modulus $q \leq b^k$. The lattice $\Lambda^\perp(\mathbf{g}^t) = \{\mathbf{z} \in \mathbb{Z}^k : \mathbf{g}^t\mathbf{z} = 0 \bmod q\}$ is called the gadget lattice.

3.1 Gadget Gaussian Sampling

The goal of gadget Gaussian sampling is to generate a sample from a discrete Gaussian on a lattice coset $\Lambda_u^{\perp}(\mathbf{g}^t) = \{\mathbf{z} \in \mathbb{Z}^k : \mathbf{g}^t\mathbf{z} = u \bmod q\}$. The associated algorithms were developed by Micciancio and Peikert [37] to construct an efficient and powerful lattice trapdoor framework. As shown in [37], the gadget Gaussian sampling is convenient thanks to a good basis of $\Lambda^{\perp}(\mathbf{g}^t)$ as follows:

$$\mathbf{B}_q = \begin{pmatrix} b & & & & q_0 \\ -1 & b & & & q_1 \\ & -1 & \ddots & & \vdots \\ & & \ddots & b & q_{k-2} \\ & & & -1 & q_{k-1} \end{pmatrix} \tag{1}$$

where $q = \sum_{i=0}^{k-1} b^i q_i$. Particularly, when $q = b^k$, $\mathbf{B}_q$ is bi-diagonal and thus its Gram-Schmidt orthogonalization in reverse order is diagonal, which leads to a very simple sampler that runs in $O(k)$ and is implemented over integers. But the sampler for $q < b^k$ proposed in [37] requires $O(k^2)$ complexity even with pre-computation.

Later, Genise and Micciancio proposed in [21] an improved gadget Gaussian sampler for $q < b^k$ that achieves the complexity of $O(k)$ as well. Their approach is build upon the Gaussian convolution technique [39]. In more details, they noticed a factorization $\mathbf{B}_q = \mathbf{TD}$ with

$$\mathbf{T} = \begin{pmatrix} b & & & & \\ -1 & b & & & \\ & -1 & \ddots & & \\ & & \ddots & b & \\ & & & -1 & b \end{pmatrix} \quad \text{and} \quad \mathbf{D} = \begin{pmatrix} 1 & & & & d_0 \\ & 1 & & & d_1 \\ & & \ddots & & \vdots \\ & & & 1 & d_{k-2} \\ & & & & d_{k-1} \end{pmatrix} \tag{2}$$

and then decomposed the sampling into two steps: generating $\mathbf{p} \leftarrow D_{\mathcal{L},r\sqrt{\mathbf{\Sigma}_2}}$ and outputting $\mathbf{T} \cdot D_{\mathcal{L}(\mathbf{D}),r,-\mathbf{c}}$ with $\mathbf{\Sigma}_2 = (s/r)^2\mathbf{I} - \mathbf{TT}^t$, $\mathbf{c} = \mathbf{T}^{-1}(\mathbf{u} - \mathbf{p})$. Originally, [21] proposed to set $\mathcal{L} = \mathcal{L}(\mathbf{\Sigma}_2)$ to simplify the sampling of $\mathbf{p}$. Later, [16] suggested to sample $\mathbf{p}$ via continuous Gaussian sampling, which turns out practically efficient given some high-precision arithmetic library.

Hu and Jia also gave a gadget Gaussian sampler for $q < b^k$ [32]: instead of sampling a spherical Gaussian, they proposed to sample a non-spherical one over $\Lambda^{\perp}(\mathbf{g}^t)$. This improves the efficiency of the gadget Gaussian sampling at the cost of complicating the offline sampling in the Micciancio-Peikert framework, which defeats some optimization techniques [18,21]. In this paper, we are interested in spherical gadget Gaussian sampling as in [21,37] that gives a better overall performance.

3.2 Gadget Subgaussian Sampling

The gadget subgaussian sampling produces a subgaussian vector on a lattice coset $\Lambda_u^{\perp}(\mathbf{g}^t)$. It has advantages over digit decomposition and gadget Gaussian sampling: the subgaussian has a "pythagorean additivity" property, which gives rise to tighter parameters than digit decomposition; the subgaussian sampling is faster and requires less randomness than the Gaussian one.

Genise, Micciancio and Polyakov initiated the study of gadget subgaussian sampling [23] and proposed two algorithms for $q = b^k$ and $q < b^k$ respectively. When $q = b^k$, the algorithm is in effect a specialized version of the Babai's nearest plane algorithm [5] on $\mathbf{B}_q$ (Eq. (1)). This algorithm achieves subgaussian parameter at most $(b-1)\sqrt{2\pi}$ with $O(k)$ operations and $\log q$ random bits.

The gadget subgaussian algorithm for arbitrary moduli, i.e. $q < b^k$, proceeds in a rather different manner. It exploits the same matrix factorization $\mathbf{B}_q = \mathbf{TD}$ (Eq. (2)) as in [21]. Concretely, it performs a specialized Babai's nearest plane algorithm on $\mathbf{D}$ and applies a linear transformation of $\mathbf{T}$ to lift the solution to $\Lambda_u^{\perp}(\mathbf{g}^t)$. In the end, this algorithm runs in linear $O(k)$ time, requires $O(k \log q)$ random bits and achieves subgaussian parameter at most $(b+1)\sqrt{2\pi}$. Overall the subgaussian algorithm for arbitrary moduli is more complicated and randomness inefficient than the one for $q = b^k$.

4 Gadget Gaussian Sampling Without Floats

In contrast to the specialized gadget Gaussian sampler for $q = b^k$, the state-of-the-art sampler for arbitrary moduli is still complicated and heavily uses floating point arithmetic, despite the asymptotically same complexity (See Sect. 3.1). Floating point arithmetic has many drawbacks in practice in terms of security, numerical stability and efficiency. Particularly, once the gadget sampler relies on floating point operations, it would be inconvenient and inefficient to deploy the trapdoor cryptosystems [37] in constraint devices[1].

Here we present a new gadget Gaussian sampler for arbitrary moduli but without using floating point arithmetic. Our sampler achieves the complexity of $O(k)$ as the Genise-Micciancio sampler [21] and is even simpler. Moreover, the practical running time of our sampler is close to that of the Genise-Micciancio sampler; a large part of samplings in our algorithm are parallelizable.

4.1 The Algorithm

Let us recall that $\mathbf{g} = (1, b, \cdots, b^{k-1})$, the modulus $q < b^k$ and as shown in [21] the gadget lattice $\Lambda^{\perp}(\mathbf{g}^t) = \{\mathbf{z} \in \mathbb{Z}^k : \mathbf{g}^t\mathbf{z} = 0 \mod q\}$ has a basis

[1] Ideally, gadget sampling can be performed on a lightweight device while other costly computations are done on a powerful machine and in an offline phase.

$$\mathbf{B}_q = \begin{pmatrix} b & & & & q_0 \\ -1 & b & & & q_1 \\ & -1 & \ddots & & \vdots \\ & & \ddots & b & q_{k-2} \\ & & & -1 & q_{k-1} \end{pmatrix} = \begin{pmatrix} b & & & & \\ -1 & b & & & \\ & -1 & \ddots & & \\ & & \ddots & b & \\ & & & -1 & b \end{pmatrix} \begin{pmatrix} 1 & & & & d_0 \\ & 1 & & & d_1 \\ & & \ddots & & \vdots \\ & & & 1 & d_{k-2} \\ & & & & d_{k-1} \end{pmatrix} = \mathbf{TD}.$$

To sample $D_{\Lambda^\perp(\mathbf{g}^t),s,\mathbf{u}}$, our algorithm proceeds in two steps as per [39]. First, it generates a perturbation vector $\mathbf{p}$ of covariance $r^2\mathbf{\Sigma}_2 = s^2\mathbf{I}_k - r^2\mathbf{TT}^t$. Then it samples $\mathbf{v}'$ from $D_{\mathcal{L}(\mathbf{D}),r,\mathbf{T}^{-1}(\mathbf{u}-\mathbf{p})}$ and the final output is $\mathbf{v} = \mathbf{Tv}'$. The second step is easily implemented over integers. To avoid floating point operations in perturbation sampling, we use a similar technique in [18]. Specifically, we discover a simple binary matrix

$$\mathbf{A} = \begin{pmatrix} 1 & 1 & & & & 1 \\ & 1 & 1 & & & \\ & & \ddots & \ddots & & \\ & & & 1 & 1 & \end{pmatrix} \in \mathbb{Z}^{k\times(k+2)}$$

such that $\mathbf{A}\begin{pmatrix} b\cdot\mathbf{I}_{k+1} & \\ & 1 \end{pmatrix}\mathbf{A}^t = (b+1)^2\cdot\mathbf{I}_k - \mathbf{TT}^t = \mathbf{\Sigma}_2$ for $s=(b+1)r$ which coincides with [21]. According to Theorem 1, applying a linear transformation of $\mathbf{A}$ on some Gaussian of covariance $r^2\begin{pmatrix} b\cdot\mathbf{I}_{k+1} & \\ & 1 \end{pmatrix}$ gives the perturbation of covariance $r^2\mathbf{\Sigma}_2$. The matrix $\mathbf{A}$ has much less columns than the generic Gram decompositions in [18], which boosts the practical performance greatly. Additionally, the Gaussian transformed by $\mathbf{A}$ is non-spherical unlike the case in [18], which is crucial for non-square b. We formally describe our sampler in Algorithm 1 and prove its correctness in Lemma 4.

Algorithm 1: Gadget Gaussian sampler $\mathsf{GadgetGaussian}(b,k,q,l,s,u)$

Input: positive integers b,k,q,l such that $q < b^k$, $\mathbf{q} = [q]_b^k$ and $l \geq 4\sqrt{bk}$, $s = (b+1)r$ with $r \geq \overline{\eta_\epsilon}(\mathbb{Z}^k)$, $u \in \mathbb{Z}_q$ and $\mathbf{u} = [u]_b^k$.

Output: a sample $\mathbf{x}$ from a distribution within max-log distance $(2k+6)\hat{\epsilon}$ of $D_{\Lambda^\perp(\mathbf{g}^t),s,-\mathbf{u}}$

1: $d_0 = q_0/b$
2: **for** $i = 1,\cdots,k-1$ **do**
3: $\quad d_i = (d_{i-1}+q_i)/b$
4: **end for**
5: $\mathbf{p} \leftarrow \mathsf{Pert}(r,b,k,l)$ $\quad\{\mathbf{p} \sim D_{\mathbb{Z}^k/l,r\sqrt{(b+1)^2\mathbf{I}_k-\mathbf{TT}^t}}\}$
6: $\mathbf{c} \leftarrow \mathbf{T}^{-1}(\mathbf{p}-\mathbf{u})$
7: $\mathbf{z} \leftarrow \mathsf{SampleD}(r,\mathbf{c},\mathbf{d})$ $\quad\{\mathbf{Dz} \sim D_{\mathcal{L}(\mathbf{D}),r,\mathbf{c}}, \mathbf{D} = \begin{pmatrix} \mathbf{I}_{k-1} & \mathbf{d} \\ \mathbf{0} & \end{pmatrix}\}$
8: return $\mathbf{x} \leftarrow \mathbf{B}_q\mathbf{z}$

Algorithm 2: The subroutine $\mathsf{Pert}(r, b, k, l)$

Input: positive integers b, k, l such that $l \geq 4\sqrt{bk}$ and $r \geq \overline{\eta_\epsilon}(\mathbb{Z}^k)$.
Output: a sample $\mathbf{p}$ from a distribution within max-log distance $2\hat{\epsilon}$ of $D_{\mathbb{Z}^k/l, r\sqrt{(b+1)^2\mathbf{I}_k - \mathbf{T}\mathbf{T}^t}}$

$$\mathbf{A} = \begin{pmatrix} 1 & 1 & & & 1 \\ & 1 & 1 & & \\ & & \ddots & \ddots & \\ & & & 1 & 1 \end{pmatrix} \in \mathbb{Z}^{k \times (k+2)}$$

$\mathbf{y} \leftarrow (\bar{\mathbf{y}}, y_{k+1}) \in \mathbb{Z}^{k+2}$ where $\bar{\mathbf{y}} \leftarrow D_{\mathbb{Z}^{k+1}, lr\sqrt{b}}$, $y_{k+1} \leftarrow D_{\mathbb{Z}, lr}$
return $\mathbf{p} \leftarrow \frac{1}{l} \cdot \mathbf{A}\mathbf{y}$

Algorithm 3: The subroutine $\mathsf{SampleD}(r, \mathbf{c}, \mathbf{d})$

Input: vectors $\mathbf{c}, \mathbf{d}$ such that $\mathbf{D} = \begin{pmatrix} \mathbf{I}_{k-1} & \mathbf{d} \\ \mathbf{0} & \end{pmatrix}$, $r \geq \overline{\eta_\epsilon}(\mathbb{Z}^k)$.
Output: a sample $\mathbf{z}$ such that the distribution of $\mathbf{D}\mathbf{z}$ is within max-log distance $2k\hat{\epsilon}$ of $D_{\mathcal{L}(\mathbf{D}), r, \mathbf{c}}$

```
z_{k-1} ← D_{Z, r/d_{k-1}, c_{k-1}/d_{k-1}}
c ← c − z_{k-1} d
for i = 0, ··· , k − 2 do
    z_i ← D_{Z, r, c_i}
end for
return z
```

Lemma 4. *Let $b, k, q, l \in \mathbb{N}$ such that $q < b^k$ and $l \geq 4\sqrt{bk}$. Let $\epsilon \in (0, \frac{1}{2})$ and $s \geq (b+1) \cdot \overline{\eta_\epsilon}(\mathbb{Z}^k)$. For any $u \in \mathbb{Z}_q$ with $\mathbf{u} = [u]_b^k$, $\mathsf{GadgetGaussian}(b, k, q, l, s, u)$ returns a sample within a max-log distance $(2k+6)\hat{\epsilon}$ from $D_{\Lambda^\perp(\mathbf{g}^t), s, -\mathbf{u}}$.*

Remark 1. All involved base samplers are assumed to be perfect for simplicity. It is routine to adapt Lemma 4 to the setting of imperfect base samplers.

Proof. We first prove the correctness of $\mathsf{Pert}(r, b, k, l)$. Let $\mathbf{S} = \begin{pmatrix} \sqrt{b} \cdot \mathbf{I}_{k+1} & \\ & 1 \end{pmatrix}$ and $\mathbf{\Sigma}_2 = (b+1)^2\mathbf{I}_k - \mathbf{T}\mathbf{T}^t$. A routine computation shows $(\mathbf{AS})(\mathbf{AS})^t = \mathbf{\Sigma}_2$. Clearly, $\mathbf{y}$ follows $D_{\mathbb{Z}^{k+2}, rl\mathbf{S}}$ and $\mathbf{A}\mathbb{Z}^{k+2} = \mathbb{Z}^k$. Note that $\mathbb{Z}^{k+2} \cap \mathsf{ker}(\mathbf{A})$ is a lattice of rank 2 and contains two linearly independent vectors $\mathbf{v}_0 = (1, 0, \cdots, 0, -1), \mathbf{v}_1 = ((-1)^0, (-1)^1, \cdots, (-1)^k, 0)$ of norm $\leq \sqrt{k+1}$. According to Lemma 1, it holds that $\eta_\epsilon(\mathbb{Z}^{k+2} \cap \mathsf{ker}(\mathbf{A})) \leq \overline{\eta_\epsilon}(\mathbb{Z}^2)\sqrt{k+1} \leq rl$ and then $\eta_\epsilon(\mathbb{Z}^{k+2} \cap \mathsf{ker}(\mathbf{A})) \leq rl\mathbf{S}$ as $\mathbf{S} \geq \mathbf{I}$. By Theorem 1, we have

$$\Delta_{ML}(\mathbf{p}, D_{\mathbb{Z}^k/l, r\sqrt{\mathbf{\Sigma}_2}}) = \Delta_{ML}(l\mathbf{p}, D_{\mathbb{Z}^k, rl\mathbf{AS}}) = \Delta_{ML}(\mathbf{A}\mathbf{y}, D_{\mathbb{Z}^k, rl\mathbf{AS}}) \leq 2\hat{\epsilon}$$

and the correctness of $\mathsf{Pert}(r, b, k, l)$ follows.

Since $\|\tilde{\mathbf{D}}\|_{col} \leq 1$, Lemma 1 shows $s \geq (b+1)\eta_\epsilon(\mathbf{D})$. The algorithm $\mathsf{SampleD}(r, \mathbf{c}, \mathbf{d})$ is actually Klein algorithm [25] on $\mathbf{D}$, so $\Delta_{ML}(\mathbf{Dz}, D_{\mathcal{L}(\mathbf{D}),r,\mathbf{c}}) \leq 2k\hat{\epsilon}$ by Theorem 4.1 of [25] and $\|\tilde{\mathbf{D}}\|_{col} \leq 1$. It remains to show $r\sqrt{\mathbf{\Sigma}_3} \geq \eta_\epsilon(\mathbb{Z}^k/l)$ where $\mathbf{\Sigma}_3^{-1} = \mathbf{\Sigma}_1^{-1} + \mathbf{\Sigma}_2^{-1}$ and $\mathbf{\Sigma}_1 = \mathbf{TT}^t$ as per Theorem 2. Indeed [21] showed in Corollary 1 that $r'\sqrt{\mathbf{\Sigma}_3} \geq \eta_\epsilon(\mathcal{L}(\mathbf{\Sigma}_2))$ for $r' = \frac{\sqrt{2b}(2b+1)}{b+1}\overline{\eta_\epsilon}(\mathbb{Z}^k)$. From $\mathcal{L}(\mathbf{\Sigma}_2) \subset \mathbb{Z}^k$, it follows that $\eta_\epsilon(\mathbb{Z}^k) \leq \eta_\epsilon(\mathcal{L}(\mathbf{\Sigma}_2))$ and then

$$\eta_\epsilon(\mathbb{Z}^k/l) \leq \frac{\eta_\epsilon(\mathcal{L}(\mathbf{\Sigma}_2))}{l} \leq \frac{r'}{l}\sqrt{\mathbf{\Sigma}_3} \leq r\sqrt{\mathbf{\Sigma}_3}.$$

We now complete the proof. □

4.2 Comparison

The comparison between our gadget Gaussian sampler and the Genise-Micciancio one [21] is summarized as follows:

Gaussian Quality. Both two samplers are proposed to sample a spherical Gaussian over the gadget lattice. The quality of the sampler is measured by the minimal Gaussian width s it achieves. As shown in Lemma 4, the minimal s for our sampler is $(b+1) \cdot \overline{\eta_\epsilon}(\mathbb{Z}^k)$. While a lower bound of s given in [21] (Corollary 1) is $\sqrt{2b}(2b+1) \cdot \overline{\eta_\epsilon}(\mathbb{Z}^k)$, it is improved to $(b+1) \cdot \overline{\eta_\epsilon}(\mathbb{Z}^k)$ in [16] via replacing the integer perturbation sampling with a continuous version. Therefore, our sampler achieves the same quality with the Genise-Micciancio one.

Arithmetic. All intermediate numbers in Algorithm 1 are either integer or fraction with a simple bounded denominator, which supports a complete integer implementation. Indeed some base samplers (for $D_{\mathbb{Z},lr\sqrt{b}}$ and $D_{\mathbb{Z},r/d_{k-1},c_{k-1}/d_{k-1}}$) deal with irrational width or relatively complicated center. Nevertheless, they can still be implemented over integers by classic techniques [6,38]. In contrast, the Genise-Micciancio sampler needs floating point arithmetic in computing a square Gram root of $\mathbf{\Sigma}_2$, and to achieve higher quality, it also requires continuous Gaussian samplings.

Memory. As a direct result of integer arithmetic, our sampler requires less RAM and storage for precomputed values. In addition, the new-introduced matrix $\mathbf{A}$ is of regular structure and thus causes no storage overhead.

Time Complexity. Algorithm 1 consists of $(2k+2)$ integer samplings and other arithmetic computations, i.e. computing $\mathbf{d}, \mathbf{Ay}, \mathbf{c}$, need only $O(k)$ integer operations thanks to the nice structures of $\mathbf{A}, \mathbf{T}$. Therefore our sampler runs in

$O(k)$ assuming constant time for base samplings and scalar arithmetic, which is the same with the Genise-Micciancio sampler. Additionally, the subroutine Algorithm 2 is highly parallelizable.

Experimental Result. We implement our new sampler and compare with the implementations of the Genise-Micciancio sampler and its variant in [16] available in the PALISADE library[2]. For a fair comparison, we implement all base samplers with the open source code of Karney sampler. The experiments were run in C++ on a laptop with an Intel Core i7-10510U CPU with 4 cores @ 1.80 GHz, running Ubuntu 20.04.2 LTS.

Figure 1 shows the speed comparison among three algorithms under different moduli q and the same base $b = 2$ and width $s = 100$. Basically, our algorithm is as fast as the Genise-Micciancio sampler but about twice slower than the variant in [16]. Figure 2 shows the speed comparison under different bases b and a fixed modulus $q \approx 9 \cdot 10^{18}$. In the corresponding experiment, we work with $s = (b+1) \cdot \overline{\eta_\epsilon}(\mathbb{Z}^k) \approx 4.578(b+1)$ as used in practice [16]. Since the bound of s in [21] is greatly larger than that in the variant of [16], we omit the comparison with [21]. The samplers in [21] and [16] need floating-point arithmetic for Cholesky decomposition, and the one in [16] also uses continuous Gaussian sampling. In contrast, our algorithm avoids all floating-point operations. The efficiency advantage of the variant of [16] is due to the fact that the continuous Gaussian sampling in C++ header file "random" is significantly faster than the Karney sampling in the PALISADE library. With a faster base sampler, our algorithm hopefully outperforms the one of [16].

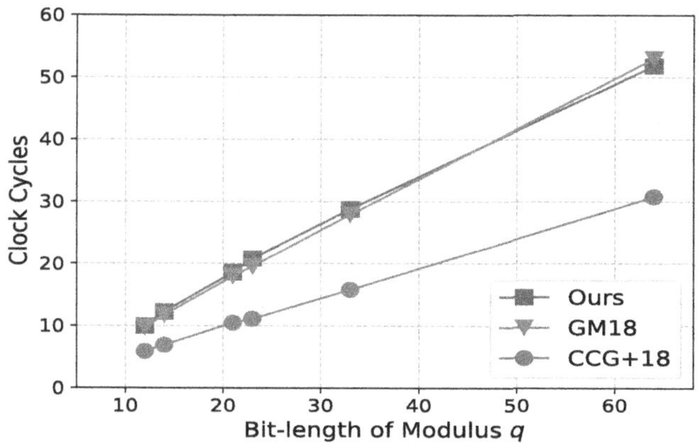

Fig. 1. Measured clock cycles with $q \in \{4093, 12289, 1676083, 8383498, 4295967357, \approx 9 \cdot 10^{18}\}$, $b = 2$ and $s = 100$ averaged over 1000,000 runs.

[2] https://palisade-crypto.org/.

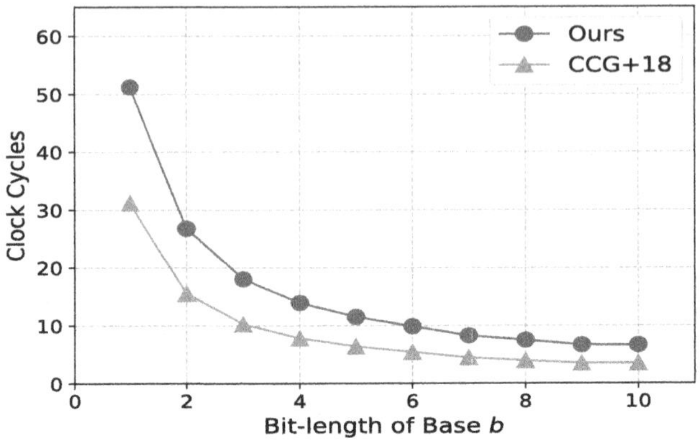

Fig. 2. Measured clock cycles with $b \in \{2^1, 2^2, \cdots, 2^{10}\}$, $q \approx 9 \cdot 10^{18}$ and $s = (b+1) \cdot \overline{\eta_\epsilon}(\mathbb{Z}^k)$ averaged over 1000,000 runs.

5 Improved Gadget Subgaussian Sampling

In this section, we present a new gadget subgaussian sampler for arbitrary moduli. Compared with the Genise-Micciancio-Polyakov algorithm [23] (See Sect. 3.2), our algorithm is simpler, faster and requires asymptotically less randomness. As for the quality, while the subgaussian parameter achieved by our sampler is $\sqrt{2}$ times as large as that by the Genise-Micciancio-Polyakov sampler for large b and in the worst case, the actual quality of our sampler is close to even better than that of the Genise-Micciancio-Polyakov sampler for practical parameters (q, b).

5.1 The Algorithm

Our algorithm distinguishes two cases of $q = b^k$ and $q < b^k$. For $q = b^k$, the sampling is identical to the existing algorithm (Algorithm 1, [23]) that is easy and efficient. But for $q < b^k$, our sampler proceeds very differently: it fully exploits the ease of the procedure for $q = b^k$ and does not use special linear transformation as the existing approach (Algorithm 2, [23]). The idea stems from a simple observation that for $q = b^k$ and $u \in \mathbb{Z}_q$, the output $\mathbf{x}$ satisfies $\langle \mathbf{x}, \mathbf{g} \rangle \in \{u, u-q\}$ (See Lemma 6). The values u and $u - q$ basically determine the most significant digit x_{k-1} and thus $\langle \mathbf{x}', \mathbf{g}' \rangle \bmod b^{k-1}$ where $\mathbf{x}' = (x_0, x_1 \cdots, x_{k-2})$ and $\mathbf{g}' = (1, b, \cdots, b^{k-2})$. Our sampler for $q < b^k$ is designed upon above facts; it consists of three steps: first, to choose $\langle \mathbf{x}', \mathbf{g}' \rangle \bmod b^{k-1}$ according to proper probability; then, to sample a subgaussian $\mathbf{x}'$ with the sampler for $q = b^{k-1}$ given $\langle \mathbf{x}', \mathbf{g}' \rangle \bmod b^{k-1}$; finally, to determine the last coefficient x_{k-1} as per $\mathbf{x}'$. The formal description is illustrated in Algorithm 4.

Lemma 5 shows the correctness and performance of Algorithm 4.

Lemma 5. *Let $b, k, q, u \in \mathbb{N}$ such that $q \leq b^k$ and $u \in \mathbb{Z}_q$. Then* $\mathsf{SubGaussian}(b, k, q, u)$ *outputs a subgaussian vector over $\Lambda_u^{\perp}(\mathbf{g}^t)$. More precisely,*

- *if $q = b^k$,* $\mathsf{SubGaussian}(b, k, q, u)$ *uses* $\log q$ *random bits, runs in $O(k)$ time and space and achieves subgaussian parameter at most $(b-1)\sqrt{2\pi}$;*
- *if $q < b^k$,* $\mathsf{SubGaussian}(b, k, q, u)$ *uses* $\log q + (k-1)\log b$ *random bits, runs in $O(k)$ time and space and achieves subgaussian parameter at most $\sqrt{(b-1)^2 + \alpha^2}\sqrt{2\pi}$ with $\alpha = \lfloor q/b^{k-1} \rfloor + 1$.*

Remark 2. As a by-product, a digit decomposition for an arbitrary modulus is obtained by de-randomizing Algorithm 4, that is replacing lines 8 and 17 with

---

Algorithm 4: Gaussian subgaussian sampler $\mathsf{SubGaussian}(b, k, q, u)$

Input: positive integers b, k, q, u such that $q \leq b^k$ and $u \in \mathbb{Z}_q$.
Output: subgaussian $\mathbf{x} \in \Lambda_u^{\perp}(\mathbf{g}^t)$ with parameter $(b-1)\sqrt{2\pi}$ when $q = b^k$;
with parameter $\sqrt{(b-1)^2 + \alpha^2}\sqrt{2\pi}$ with $\alpha = \lfloor q/b^{k-1} \rfloor + 1$ when $q < b^k$.

1: **if** $q = b^k$ **then**
2: $\quad \mathbf{x} \leftarrow \mathbf{0}$
3: $\quad$ **for** $i = 0, \cdots, k-1$ **do**
4: $\quad\quad y \leftarrow u \mod b \in \{0, \cdots, b-1\}$
5: $\quad\quad$ **if** $y = 0$ **then**
6: $\quad\quad\quad x_i \leftarrow 0$
7: $\quad\quad$ **else**
8: $\quad\quad\quad$ with probability y/b, $x_i \leftarrow y - b$, and $x_i \leftarrow y$ otherwise
9: $\quad\quad$ **end if**
10: $\quad\quad u \leftarrow (u - x_i)/b$
11: $\quad$ **end for**
12: $\quad$ return $\mathbf{x}$
13: **end if**
14: $u_0 \leftarrow u \bmod b^{k-1}$, $u_1 \leftarrow (u - q) \bmod b^{k-1}$
15: $a_0 \leftarrow \lfloor \frac{u}{b^{k-1}} \rfloor$, $a_1 \leftarrow \lfloor \frac{u-q}{b^{k-1}} \rfloor$
16: sample r uniformly over $[0, 1]$
17: **if** $r < \frac{q-u}{q}$ **then**
18: $\quad \mathbf{x}' \leftarrow \mathsf{SubGaussian}(b, k-1, b^{k-1}, u_0)$
19: $\quad$ **if** $\langle \mathbf{x}', \mathbf{g}' \rangle = u_0$ with $\mathbf{g}' = (1, b, \cdots, b^{k-2})$ **then**
20: $\quad\quad$ return $\mathbf{x} = (\mathbf{x}', a_0)$ $\quad \{\langle \mathbf{x}', \mathbf{g}' \rangle = u_0\}$
21: $\quad$ **else**
22: $\quad\quad$ return $\mathbf{x} = (\mathbf{x}', a_0 + 1)$ $\quad \{\langle \mathbf{x}', \mathbf{g}' \rangle = u_0 - b^{k-1}\}$
23: $\quad$ **end if**
24: **else**
25: $\quad \mathbf{x}' \leftarrow \mathsf{SubGaussian}(b, k-1, b^{k-1}, u_1)$
26: $\quad$ **if** $\langle \mathbf{x}', \mathbf{g}' \rangle = u_1$ **then**
27: $\quad\quad$ return $\mathbf{x} = (\mathbf{x}', a_1)$ $\quad \{\langle \mathbf{x}', \mathbf{g}' \rangle = u_1\}$
28: $\quad$ **else**
29: $\quad\quad$ return $\mathbf{x} = (\mathbf{x}', a_1 + 1)$ $\quad \{\langle \mathbf{x}', \mathbf{g}' \rangle = u_1 - b^{k-1}\}$
30: $\quad$ **end if**
31: **end if**

---

deterministically choosing the option of higher probability. It can be seen that the output of this digit decomposition is of infinity norm $\leq b/2$.

To prove Lemma 5, we need the following lemma.

Lemma 6. *Let $b, k, q, u \in \mathbb{N}$ such that $q = b^k$ and $u \in \mathbb{Z}_q$. Let $\mathbf{x}$ be the output of* SubGaussian$(b, k, q = b^k, u)$ *and $\mathbf{g} = (1, b, \cdots, b^{k-1})$. Then $\langle \mathbf{x}, \mathbf{g} \rangle = u$ with probability $(q-u)/q$; $\langle \mathbf{x}, \mathbf{g} \rangle = u - q$ with probability u/q.*

Proof. Since $|x_i| < b$, some simple computation yields that $\langle \mathbf{x}, \mathbf{g} \rangle \in (-b^k, b^k)$. Together with the fact that $\langle \mathbf{x}, \mathbf{g} \rangle = u \bmod q$, it follows that $\langle \mathbf{x}, \mathbf{g} \rangle \in \{u, u-q\}$. Let p denote the probability of $\langle \mathbf{x}, \mathbf{g} \rangle = u$, then

$$\mathbb{E}[\langle \mathbf{x}, \mathbf{g} \rangle] = p \cdot u + (1-p)(u-q).$$

At each step, x_i is chosen from $\{y, y-b\}$ with expectation 0. Therefore

$$p \cdot u + (1-p)(u-q) = \mathbb{E}[\langle \mathbf{x}, \mathbf{g} \rangle] = \sum_{i=0}^{k-1} b^i \cdot \mathbb{E}[x_i] = 0.$$

This shows $p = (q-u)/q$ and the proof is completed. □

Proof of Lemma 5. For the case $q = b^k$, Algorithm 4 is the same with Algorithm 1 in [23]. By Theorem 4 of [23], the statement for $q = b^k$ is proved. It remains to prove the statement for $q < b^k$.

To this end, we first prove that the output $\mathbf{x}$ satisfies $\langle \mathbf{x}, \mathbf{g} \rangle = u \bmod q$. Lemma 6 shows that $\langle \mathbf{x}', \mathbf{g}' \rangle \in \{u_{bit}, u_{bit} - b^{k-1}\}$ for $bit \in \{0, 1\}$. When $\langle \mathbf{x}', \mathbf{g}' \rangle = u_{bit}$, it holds that $x_{k-1} = a_{bit}$ and thus

$$\langle \mathbf{x}, \mathbf{g} \rangle = \langle \mathbf{x}', \mathbf{g}' \rangle + x_{k-1} \cdot b^{k-1} = u_{bit} + a_{bit} \cdot b^{k-1} = u - bit \cdot q.$$

When $\langle \mathbf{x}', \mathbf{g}' \rangle = u_{bit} - b^{k-1}$, it holds that $x_{k-1} = a_{bit} + 1$ and thus

$$\langle \mathbf{x}, \mathbf{g} \rangle = \langle \mathbf{x}', \mathbf{g}' \rangle + x_{k-1} \cdot b^{k-1} = u_{bit} - b^{k-1} + (a_{bit} + 1) \cdot b^{k-1} = u - bit \cdot q.$$

Therefore $\langle \mathbf{x}, \mathbf{g} \rangle = u \bmod q$ always holds.

Next, we show that $\mathbb{E}[x_{k-1}] = 0$ and $|x_{k-1}| \leq \alpha$, so that the random variable x_{k-1} is subgaussian with parameter $\alpha\sqrt{2\pi}$. Indeed as shown in Algorithm 4, x_{k-1} only has four possible values $\{a_0, a_0 + 1, a_1, a_1 + 1\}$. Since $u \in \mathbb{Z}_q$, we have that $a_0 = \lfloor \frac{u}{b^{k-1}} \rfloor \in [0, \lfloor \frac{q}{b^{k-1}} \rfloor] = [0, \alpha - 1]$ and $a_1 = \lfloor \frac{u-q}{b^{k-1}} \rfloor \in [\lfloor \frac{-q}{b^{k-1}} \rfloor, -1] = [-\alpha, -1]$. Immediately, $|x_{k-1}| \leq \alpha$. As for $\mathbb{E}[x_{k-1}]$, we note that $x_{k-1} = a_0$ occurs if and only if $r < \frac{q-u}{q}$ and $\langle \mathbf{x}', \mathbf{g}' \rangle = u_0$. By Lemma 6, it follows that

$$\Pr[x_{k-1} = a_0] = \frac{(q-u)(b^{k-1} - u_0)}{q \cdot b^{k-1}}.$$

Similarly,

$$\Pr[x_{k-1} = a_0 + 1] = \frac{(q-u) \cdot u_0}{q \cdot b^{k-1}}; \quad \Pr[x_{k-1} = a_1] = \frac{u \cdot (b^{k-1} - u_1)}{q \cdot b^{k-1}}; \quad \Pr[x_{k-1} = a_1 + 1] = \frac{u \cdot u_1}{q \cdot b^{k-1}}.$$

Thus we have

$$\begin{aligned}\mathbb{E}[x_{k-1}] &= a_0\frac{(q-u)(b^{k-1}-u_0)}{q\cdot b^{k-1}} + (a_0+1)\frac{(q-u)\cdot u_0}{q\cdot b^{k-1}} + a_1\frac{u\cdot(b^{k-1}-u_1)}{q\cdot b^{k-1}} + (a_1+1)\frac{u\cdot u_1}{q\cdot b^{k-1}}\\ &= \frac{(q-u)(a_0\cdot b^{k-1}+u_0)}{q\cdot b^{k-1}} + \frac{u\cdot(a_1\cdot b^{k-1}+u_1)}{q\cdot b^{k-1}}\\ &= \frac{(q-u)u}{q\cdot b^{k-1}} + \frac{u\cdot(u-q)}{q\cdot b^{k-1}} = 0\end{aligned}$$

Then we verify $\mathbf{x}$ is subgaussian with parameter $\sqrt{(b-1)^2+\alpha^2}\sqrt{2\pi}$. That is to show that $\langle\mathbf{x},\mathbf{v}\rangle$ is subgaussian with parameter $\sqrt{(b-1)^2+\alpha^2}\sqrt{2\pi}$ for all unit vectors $\mathbf{v}=(v_0,\cdots,v_{k-1})$. Let $\mathbf{v}'=(v_0,\cdots,v_{k-2})$. If $|v_{k-1}|=1$, then $\langle\mathbf{x},\mathbf{v}\rangle = x_{k-1}v_{k-1}$ is subgaussian with parameter $\alpha\sqrt{2\pi}$ as per above argument. If $v_{k-1}=0$, then $\langle\mathbf{x},\mathbf{v}\rangle=\langle\mathbf{x}',\mathbf{v}'\rangle$ and $\mathbf{v}'$ is a unit vector. As per Algorithm 4 and the statement for $q=b^k$, $\mathbf{x}'$ is subgaussian with parameter $(b-1)\sqrt{2\pi}$ and thus $\langle\mathbf{x},\mathbf{v}\rangle$ is subgaussian with parameter $(b-1)\sqrt{2\pi}$ if $v_{k-1}=0$. For the case $0<|v_{k-1}|<1$, let $p_0=\frac{1}{1-v_{k-1}^2}, p_1=\frac{1}{v_{k-1}^2}$, then $\frac{1}{p_0}+\frac{1}{p_1}=1$. By Hölder inequality, we have

$$\begin{aligned}\mathbb{E}[e^{2\pi t\langle\mathbf{x},\mathbf{v}\rangle}] &= \mathbb{E}[e^{2\pi t\langle\mathbf{x}',\mathbf{v}'\rangle+2\pi t x_{k-1}v_{k-1}}]\\ &\le \left[\mathbb{E}[e^{2\pi t\langle\mathbf{x}',\mathbf{v}'\rangle}]^{p_0}\right]^{1/p_0}\left[\mathbb{E}[e^{2\pi t x_{k-1}v_{k-1}}]^{p_1}\right]^{1/p_1}\\ &\le \exp\left(2\pi^2t^2[(b-1)^2(1-v_{k-1}^2)p_0+\alpha^2v_{k-1}^2p_1)]\right)\\ &= \exp\left(2\pi^2t^2((b-1)^2+\alpha^2)\right).\end{aligned}$$

In summary, we prove that $\mathbf{x}$ is subgaussian with parameter $\sqrt{(b-1)^2+\alpha^2}\sqrt{2\pi}$.

It is clear that the complexity of Algorithm 4 is $O(k)$. The random bits are used in two places: line 17 uses $\log q$ bits to determine $\langle\mathbf{x}',\mathbf{g}'\rangle \bmod b^{k-1}$ and the subroutine $\mathsf{SubGaussian}(b,k-1,b^{k-1},u_{bit})$ uses $(k-1)\log b$ bits to output $\mathbf{x}'$; thus $\log q+(k-1)\log b$ random bits are used in total. The proof is completed. □

5.2 Comparison

In this subsection, we compare our new gadget subgaussian algorithm with the Genise-Micciancio-Polyakov one [23]. The comparison is restricted to the case $q<b^k$.

Randomness. Less randomness is one of the main advantages of subgaussian sampling. The Genise-Micciancio-Polyakov algorithm uses $k\log q = O(k^2\log b)$ random bits, which was claimed to be "almost optimal" in [23]. In fact, our algorithm only needs $\log q+(k-1)\log b = O(k\log b)$ random bits. The reduced randomness is due to the fully use of the randomness-efficient subroutine for $q=b^{k-1}$ in which each coefficient consumes $\log b$ bits; in contrast, the i-th coefficient (before linear transformation) consumes $i\log b$ bits in Genise-Micciancio-Polyakov sampler. Notably, Algorithm 4 for $q<b^k$ needs an asymptotically same amount of randomness with the one for $q=b^k$. We therefore believe that it is essentially optimal in randomness requirement.

Complexity and Performance. Both the Genise-Micciancio-Polyakov algorithm and ours achieve $O(k)$ complexity in time and space. Nevertheless, our sampler proceeds in a direct and simple way, which actually saves the computation and storage with respect to the complicated linear transformation.

We implement Algorithm 4 fully over integers in C++. Since the implementation of the Genise-Micciancio-Polyakov sampler in the PALISADE library uses floating-point arithmetic, we also adapt it to a fully integer version for better comparison. The gadget base b is restricted to a power-of-2 in the experiment, which leads to faster and more convenient operations as verified in [23]. The experiment environment was a laptop with an Intel Core i7-10510U CPU with 4 cores @ 1.80 GHz, running Ubuntu 20.04.2 LTS. Figure 3 exhibits the practical performance of subgaussian samplers. It can be seen that our subgaussian sampler is faster than the Genise-Micciancio-Polyakov one whose the integer implementation outperforms the floating-point implementation in the PALISADE library. The speed of both algorithms mainly depends on the dimension $k = \lceil 60/\log b \rceil$. When $b = 2$ and $k = 60$, our algorithm is around 3.2 (resp. 2.3) times as fast as the PALISADE (resp. integer) implementation of the Genise-Micciancio-Polyakov algorithm. As k decreases, the speed advantage declines.

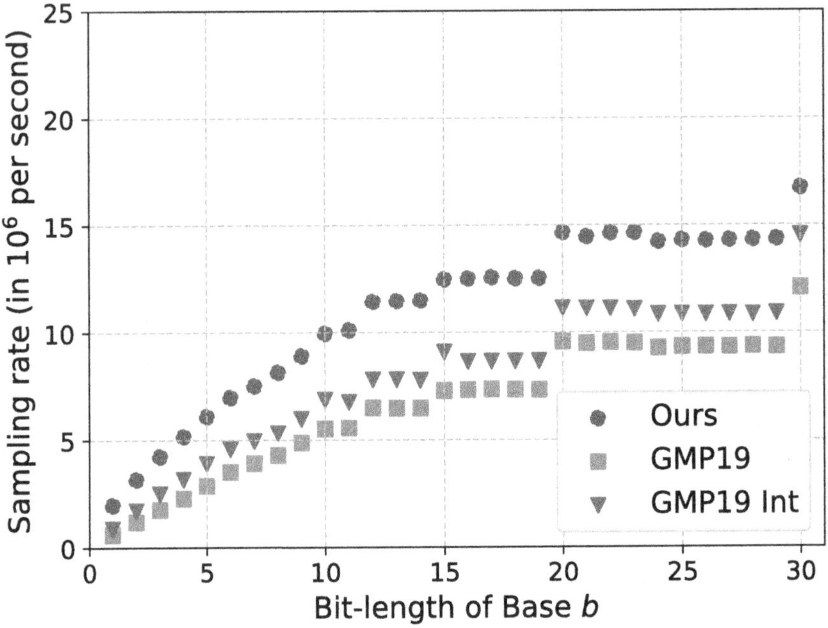

Fig. 3. Runtime of subgaussian sampling rate for native uniformly random integers (w.r.t a 60-bit modulus). Experimental values measure over 10^8 samplings.

Quality. The quality of the subgaussian sampler is measured by the subgaussian parameter it achieves. That is $Q_{our} = \sqrt{(b-1)^2 + \alpha^2\sqrt{2\pi}}$ for our sampler where

$\alpha = \lfloor q/b^{k-1} \rfloor + 1 \leq b$ and $Q_{GMP} = (b+1)\sqrt{2\pi}$ for the Genise-Micciancio-Polyakov one. While $Q_{our} \approx \sqrt{2} \cdot Q_{GMP}$ in the worst case ($\alpha = b$) for large b, our sampler can get close and even better quality in some typical situations:

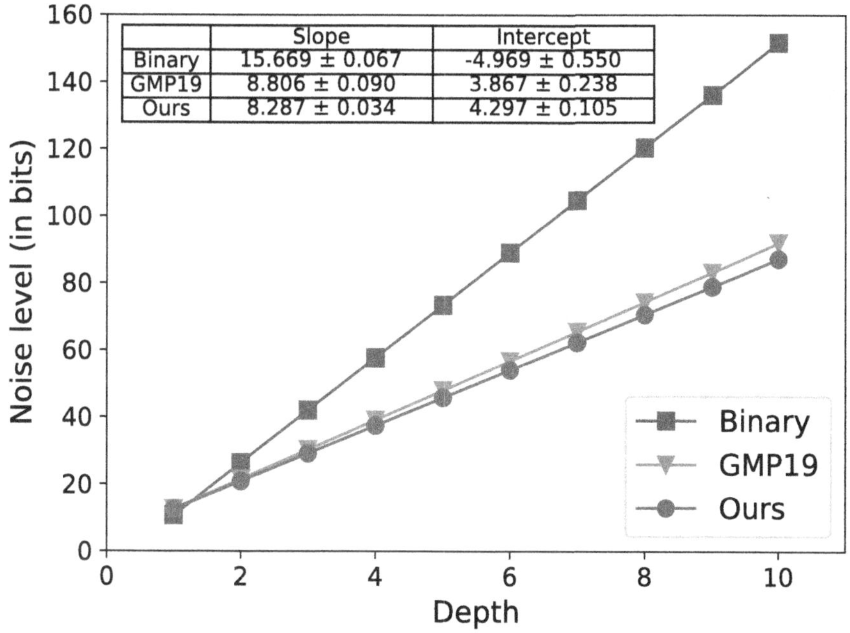

Fig. 4. Noise growth for GSW-type multiplication in the KP-ABE variant over $\mathbb{Z}[x]/(x^n + 1)$ ($n = 1024, b = 2, k = 180$). The slope of the linear interpolation is $\beta \log(mn)$ and β describes the rate of noise growth.

- for $b = 2$, the worst-case $Q_{our} = \sqrt{5}\sqrt{2\pi}$ is less than $Q_{GMP} = 3\sqrt{2\pi}$. For a visualized comparison, we examine the effect of our algorithm (with $b = 2$) on the noise growth in GSW-type products [26], which is a typical application of subgaussian sampling. In the experiment, we generate a random error vector in $\mathcal{R}_q^m$ where $\mathcal{R}_q = \mathbb{Z}_q[x]/(x^n+1)$ and $m = k+2$ and then iteratively multiply it by a matrix $(\mathbf{g}^{-1}(u_i)) \in \mathcal{R}^{m \times m}$ in which $\mathbf{g}^{-1}(u_i) \in \mathcal{R}^m$ denotes the output of either subgaussian or binary decomposition with input $u_i \in \mathcal{R}_q$. The noise level (in bits) grows almost linearly in the depth, and the noise growth rate is $(mn)^\beta$. As shown in Fig. 4, our algorithm achieves $\beta \approx 8.287/\log(mn) \approx 0.47$ less than 0.50 and 0.89 for the Genise-Micciancio-Polyakov one and the common binary decomposition, which means our subgaussian algorithm may lead to more compact parameters in some advanced applications.
- for a large base b, there exist a certain number of NTT moduli q such that $Q_{our} \leq 1.05 \cdot Q_{GMP}$. Moreover, some of these moduli can even achieve such a bounded Q_{our} for all possible b's. Table 1 shows five such NTT moduli and corresponding Q_{our}/Q_{GMP} with different b.

Overall, by choosing proper (q, b), it is convenient and flexible to make our sampler achieve a similar quality with the Genise-Micciancio-Polyakov one in practical use cases without efficiency and security loss.

Remark 3. The quality of the Genise-Micciancio-Polyakov sampler is determined by the maximal singular value of the used linear transformation $\mathbf{T}$ (Eq. (2)), and independent of the modulus q. As k grows, the maximal singular value of $\mathbf{T}$ converges to $(b+1)$ as shown in [33]. Therefore, we fix $Q_{GMP} = (b+1)\sqrt{2\pi}$ as a tight bound for the quality of the Genise-Micciancio-Polyakov sampler.

Remark 4. Despite the different subgaussian parameters, for both the Genise-Micciancio-Polyakov sampler and ours, the infinity norm of the output vector is bounded by b.

Table 1. The values of $\frac{Q_{our}}{Q_{GMP}}$ for some recommended NTT moduli.

b	q				
	$2^{22}+2^{13}+2^{12}+1$	$2^{30}+2^{13}+1$	$2^{40}+2^{15}+2^{14}+2^{11}+1$	$2^{52}+2^{16}+2^{13}+2^{11}+1$	$2^{60}+2^{15}-2^{11}+1$
2	0.745	0.745	0.745	0.745	0.745
2^2	0.721	0.721	0.721	0.721	0.721
2^3	0.846	0.808	0.846	0.846	0.808
2^4	0.930	0.930	0.890	0.890	0.890
2^5	0.951	0.941	0.941	0.951	0.941
2^6	1.004	0.969	1.003	1.003	0.969
2^7	0.984	0.985	1.017	0.986	0.993
2^8	1.023	1.023	0.992	0.994	0.994
2^9	0.996	0.996	0.996	1.027	1.004
2^{10}	0.998	0.998	0.998	0.998	0.998
2^{11}	0.999	1.006	1.001	1.006	0.999
2^{12}	1.030	0.999	1.030	0.999	0.999
2^{13}		0.999	0.999	0.999	1.000
2^{14}		0.999	1.030	1.001	0.999
2^{15}		0.999	1.000	0.999	0.999
2^{16}		1.030	0.999	0.999	1.001
2^{17}			0.999	0.999	0.999
2^{18}			0.999	1.030	0.999
2^{19}			0.999	1.000	0.999
2^{20}			0.999	1.000	0.999
2^{21}			1.030	0.999	1.007
2^{22}				0.999	1.000
2^{23}				0.999	1.000
2^{24}				0.999	0.999
2^{25}				0.999	0.999
2^{26}				0.999	0.999
2^{27}				1.030	0.999
2^{28}					0.999
2^{29}					0.999
2^{30}					0.999
2^{31}					1.030

6 Conclusion

To conclude, we develop new gadget Gaussian and subgaussian sampling algorithms. Our gadget Gaussian sampler for arbitrary moduli gets rid of the reliance on high-precision arithmetic while keeping a good efficiency and quality. It can be a potentially more efficient option for gadget sampling in the context of constrained environments and side-channel countermeasures. Additionally, our gadget subgaussian sampler is simpler, faster and needs asymptotically less randomness compared with the previous result. For practical parameters, it also achieves almost the same quality with the previous sampler. Hence it should be a refined alternative to the current subgaussian algorithm. Overall our results provide the current lattice gadget toolkit with some simpler and efficient algorithm candidates, and improve the practicality of the gadget toolkit.

6.1 Future Work

In this work, we focus on the gadget algorithms associated to the typical gadget $\mathbf{g} = (1, b, \cdots, b^{k-1})$. Some lattice applications [10,23,31] use the CRT gadget to improve the efficiency. The CRT gadget is a generalized gadget based on the Chinese Remainder Theorem, which is particularly effective for very large moduli. The algorithms for $\mathbf{g} = (1, b, \cdots, b^{k-1})$ can be directly adapted to the CRT form, thus we omit the related details. Nevertheless, it would be worthy to implement and evaluate our algorithms in the CRT setting.

The main interest of this work is the fundamental algorithms themselves, and we do not study deeply from an implementation aspect. With the post-quantum standardization underway, implementing more powerful lattice cryptosystems may gain increasingly attention. We leave the optimized implementation and the application of our results to practical implementations of lattice schemes as future works. Additionally, our subgaussian sampler and the Genise-Micciancio-Polyakov one seem susceptible to timing leakage. While this leakage is not an issue in most current applications, the side-channel protections of gadget algorithms require a future investigation.

While a general definition of gadget was proposed in [23], almost all known gadget algorithms are designed for the gadget $\mathbf{g} = (1, b, \cdots, b^{k-1})$ and its CRT generalization. To develop more practical gadgets and associated algorithms is an interesting problem.

Acknowledgements. We thank Léo Ducas for his helpful comments. This work is supported by the National Natural Science Foundation of China (No. 62102216), the National Key Research and Development Program of China (Grant No. 2018YFA0704701), the Major Program of Guangdong Basic and Applied Research (Grant No. 2019B030302008) and Major Scientific and Techological Innovation Project of Shandong Province, China (Grant No. 2019JZZY010133).

References

1. Agrawal, S., Boneh, D., Boyen, X.: Efficient lattice (H)IBE in the standard model. In: Gilbert, H. (ed.) EUROCRYPT 2010. LNCS, vol. 6110, pp. 553–572. Springer, Heidelberg (2010). https://doi.org/10.1007/978-3-642-13190-5_28
2. Agrawal, S., Boyen, X., Vaikuntanathan, V., Voulgaris, P., Wee, H.: Functional encryption for threshold functions (or Fuzzy IBE) from lattices. In: Fischlin, M., Buchmann, J., Manulis, M. (eds.) PKC 2012. LNCS, vol. 7293, pp. 280–297. Springer, Heidelberg (2012). https://doi.org/10.1007/978-3-642-30057-8_17
3. Agrawal, S., Freeman, D.M., Vaikuntanathan, V.: Functional encryption for inner product predicates from learning with errors. In: Lee, D.H., Wang, X. (eds.) ASIACRYPT 2011. LNCS, vol. 7073, pp. 21–40. Springer, Heidelberg (2011). https://doi.org/10.1007/978-3-642-25385-0_2
4. Alperin-Sheriff, J., Peikert, C.: Faster bootstrapping with polynomial error. In: Garay, J.A., Gennaro, R. (eds.) CRYPTO 2014. LNCS, vol. 8616, pp. 297–314. Springer, Heidelberg (2014). https://doi.org/10.1007/978-3-662-44371-2_17
5. Babai, L.: On Lovász' lattice reduction and the nearest lattice point problem. Combinatorica **6**(1), 1–13 (1986). https://doi.org/10.1007/BF02579403
6. Barthe, G., Belaïd, S., Espitau, T., Fouque, P.A., Rossi, M., Tibouchi, M.: GALACTICS: Gaussian sampling for lattice-based constant- time implementation of cryptographic signatures, revisited. In: ACM CCS 2019, pp. 2147–2164 (2019)
7. Bellare, M., Kiltz, E., Peikert, C., Waters, B.: Identity-based (Lossy) trapdoor functions and applications. In: Pointcheval, D., Johansson, T. (eds.) EUROCRYPT 2012. LNCS, vol. 7237, pp. 228–245. Springer, Heidelberg (2012). https://doi.org/10.1007/978-3-642-29011-4_15
8. Bert, P., Eberhart, G., Prabel, L., Roux-Langlois, A., Sabt, M.: Implementation of lattice trapdoors on modules and applications. In: Cheon, J.H., Tillich, J.-P. (eds.) PQCrypto 2021 2021. LNCS, vol. 12841, pp. 195–214. Springer, Cham (2021). https://doi.org/10.1007/978-3-030-81293-5_11
9. Bert, P., Fouque, P.-A., Roux-Langlois, A., Sabt, M.: Practical implementation of ring-SIS/LWE based signature and IBE. In: Lange, T., Steinwandt, R. (eds.) PQCrypto 2018. LNCS, vol. 10786, pp. 271–291. Springer, Cham (2018). https://doi.org/10.1007/978-3-319-79063-3_13
10. Bonnoron, G., Ducas, L., Fillinger, M.: Large FHE gates from tensored homomorphic accumulator. In: Joux, A., Nitaj, A., Rachidi, T. (eds.) AFRICACRYPT 2018. LNCS, vol. 10831, pp. 217–251. Springer, Cham (2018). https://doi.org/10.1007/978-3-319-89339-6_13
11. Brakerski, Z., Langlois, A., Peikert, C., Regev, O., Stehlé, D.: Classical hardness of learning with errors. In: STOC 2013, pp. 575–584 (2013)
12. Brakerski, Z., Vaikuntanathan, V.: Efficient fully homomorphic encryption from (standard) LWE. SIAM J. Comput. **43**(2), 831–871 (2014)
13. Cash, D., Hofheinz, D., Kiltz, E., Peikert, C.: Bonsai trees, or how to delegate a lattice basis. In: Gilbert, H. (ed.) EUROCRYPT 2010. LNCS, vol. 6110, pp. 523–552. Springer, Heidelberg (2010). https://doi.org/10.1007/978-3-642-13190-5_27
14. Chen, Y., Genise, N., Mukherjee, P.: Approximate trapdoors for lattices and smaller hash-and-sign signatures. In: ASIACRYPT 2019 (2019, to appear)
15. Chillotti, I., Gama, N., Georgieva, M., Izabachène, M.: TFHE: fast fully homomorphic encryption over the torus. J. Cryptol. **33**(1), 34–91 (2020)
16. Cousins, D.B., et al.: Implementing conjunction obfuscation under entropic ring LWE. In: 2018 IEEE Symposium on Security and Privacy (SP), pp. 354–371 (2018)

17. Dai, W., et al.: Implementation and evaluation of a lattice-based key-policy ABE scheme. IEEE Trans. Inf. Forensics Secur. **13**(5), 1169–1184 (2018)
18. Ducas, L., Galbraith, S., Prest, T., Yu, Y.: Integral matrix gram root and lattice Gaussian sampling without floats. In: Canteaut, A., Ishai, Y. (eds.) EUROCRYPT 2020. LNCS, vol. 12106, pp. 608–637. Springer, Cham (2020). https://doi.org/10.1007/978-3-030-45724-2_21
19. Ducas, L., Lyubashevsky, V., Prest, T.: Efficient identity-based encryption over NTRU lattices. In: Sarkar, P., Iwata, T. (eds.) ASIACRYPT 2014. LNCS, vol. 8874, pp. 22–41. Springer, Heidelberg (2014). https://doi.org/10.1007/978-3-662-45608-8_2
20. Ducas, L., Prest, T.: Fast Fourier orthogonalization. In: ISSAC 2016, pp. 191–198 (2016)
21. Genise, N., Micciancio, D.: Faster Gaussian sampling for trapdoor lattices with arbitrary modulus. In: Nielsen, J.B., Rijmen, V. (eds.) EUROCRYPT 2018. LNCS, vol. 10820, pp. 174–203. Springer, Cham (2018). https://doi.org/10.1007/978-3-319-78381-9_7
22. Genise, N., Micciancio, D., Peikert, C., Walter, M.: Improved discrete Gaussian and Subgaussian analysis for lattice cryptography. In: Kiayias, A., Kohlweiss, M., Wallden, P., Zikas, V. (eds.) PKC 2020. LNCS, vol. 12110, pp. 623–651. Springer, Cham (2020). https://doi.org/10.1007/978-3-030-45374-9_21
23. Genise, N., Micciancio, D., Polyakov, Y.: Building an efficient lattice gadget toolkit: subgaussian sampling and more. In: Ishai, Y., Rijmen, V. (eds.) EUROCRYPT 2019. LNCS, vol. 11477, pp. 655–684. Springer, Cham (2019). https://doi.org/10.1007/978-3-030-17656-3_23
24. Gentry, C.: Fully homomorphic encryption using ideal lattices. In: STOC 2009, pp. 169–178 (2009)
25. Gentry, C., Peikert, C., Vaikuntanathan, V.: Trapdoors for hard lattices and new cryptographic constructions. In: STOC 2008, pp. 197–206 (2008). https://doi.org/10.1145/1374376.1374407
26. Gentry, C., Sahai, A., Waters, B.: Homomorphic Encryption from learning with errors: conceptually-simpler, asymptotically-faster, attribute-based. In: Canetti, R., Garay, J.A. (eds.) CRYPTO 2013. LNCS, vol. 8042, pp. 75–92. Springer, Heidelberg (2013). https://doi.org/10.1007/978-3-642-40041-4_5
27. Gorbunov, S., Vaikuntanathan, V., Wee, H.: Attribute-based encryption for circuits. In: STOC 2013, pp. 545–554 (2013)
28. Gorbunov, S., Vaikuntanathan, V., Wee, H.: Predicate encryption for circuits from LWE. In: Gennaro, R., Robshaw, M. (eds.) CRYPTO 2015. LNCS, vol. 9216, pp. 503–523. Springer, Heidelberg (2015). https://doi.org/10.1007/978-3-662-48000-7_25
29. Gordon, S.D., Katz, J., Vaikuntanathan, V.: A group signature scheme from lattice assumptions. In: Abe, M. (ed.) ASIACRYPT 2010. LNCS, vol. 6477, pp. 395–412. Springer, Heidelberg (2010). https://doi.org/10.1007/978-3-642-17373-8_23
30. Gür, K.D., Polyakov, Y., Rohloff, K., Ryan, G.W., Sajjadpour, H., Savaş, E.: Practical applications of improved gaussian sampling for trapdoor lattices. IEEE Trans. Comput. **68**(4), 570–584 (2018)
31. Halevi, S., Halevi, T., Shoup, V., Stephens-Davidowitz, N.: Implementing BP-obfuscation using graph-induced encoding. In: ACM CCS 2017, pp. 783–798 (2017)
32. Hu, Y., Jia, H.: A new gaussian sampling for trapdoor lattices with arbitrary modulus. Des. Codes Crypt. **87**(11), 2553–2570 (2019)
33. Kulkarni, D., Schmidt, D., Tsui, S.K.: Eigenvalues of tridiagonal pseudo-Toeplitz matrices. Linear Algebra Appl. **297**, 63–80 (1999)

34. Laguillaumie, F., Langlois, A., Libert, B., Stehlé, D.: Lattice-based group signatures with logarithmic signature size. In: Sako, K., Sarkar, P. (eds.) ASIACRYPT 2013. LNCS, vol. 8270, pp. 41–61. Springer, Heidelberg (2013). https://doi.org/10.1007/978-3-642-42045-0_3
35. Lai, Q., Liu, F.-H., Wang, Z.: New lattice two-stage sampling technique and its applications to functional encryption – stronger security and smaller ciphertexts. In: Canteaut, A., Standaert, F.-X. (eds.) EUROCRYPT 2021. LNCS, vol. 12696, pp. 498–527. Springer, Cham (2021). https://doi.org/10.1007/978-3-030-77870-5_18
36. Langlois, A., Ling, S., Nguyen, K., Wang, H.: Lattice-based group signature scheme with verifier-local revocation. In: Krawczyk, H. (ed.) PKC 2014. LNCS, vol. 8383, pp. 345–361. Springer, Heidelberg (2014). https://doi.org/10.1007/978-3-642-54631-0_20
37. Micciancio, D., Peikert, C.: Trapdoors for lattices: simpler, tighter, faster, smaller. In: Pointcheval, D., Johansson, T. (eds.) EUROCRYPT 2012. LNCS, vol. 7237, pp. 700–718. Springer, Heidelberg (2012). https://doi.org/10.1007/978-3-642-29011-4_41
38. Micciancio, D., Walter, M.: Gaussian sampling over the integers: efficient, generic, constant-time. In: Katz, J., Shacham, H. (eds.) CRYPTO 2017. LNCS, vol. 10402, pp. 455–485. Springer, Cham (2017). https://doi.org/10.1007/978-3-319-63715-0_16
39. Peikert, C.: An efficient and parallel gaussian sampler for lattices. In: Rabin, T. (ed.) CRYPTO 2010. LNCS, vol. 6223, pp. 80–97. Springer, Heidelberg (2010). https://doi.org/10.1007/978-3-642-14623-7_5
40. Vershynin, R.: Introduction to the non-asymptotic analysis of random matrices. arXiv preprint arXiv:1011.3027 (2010)

SNARKs and NIZKs

Polynomial IOPs for Linear Algebra Relations

Alan Szepieniec[1(✉)] and Yuncong Zhang[2]

[1] Nervos Foundation, Panama City, Panama
alan@nervos.org
[2] Shanghai Jiao Tong University, Shanghai, China
shjdzhangyuncong@sjtu.edu.cn

Abstract. This paper proposes new Polynomial IOPs for arithmetic circuits. They rely on the monomial coefficient basis to represent the matrices and vectors arising from the arithmetic constraint satisfaction system, and build on new protocols for establishing the correct computation of linear algebra relations such as matrix-vector products and Hadamard products. Our protocols give rise to concrete proof systems with succinct verification when compiled down with a cryptographic compiler whose role is abstracted away in this paper. Depending only on the compiler, the resulting SNARKs are either transparent or rely on a trusted setup.

Keywords: SNARK · Polynomial IOP · Zero-Knowledge · Succinct Verification

1 Introduction

Succinct Non-Interactive Arguments of Knowledge (SNARKs) enable a resource-constrained verifier to cryptographically verify the authentic computations of an untrusted prover. The technology is particularly well-suited to the cryptocurrency setting, where participants are typically anonymous, untrusted, and where the success of the network depends on the capability of lightweight nodes to verify the network's consensus (however that is defined). In this setting, there is a large monetary incentive for malicious behavior.

Despite the flurry of rapid related and unrelated developments by diverse parties, two trends are emerging as good practices in this domain.

1. *Functional separation in the compilation pipeline.* The compilation process for general purpose zero-knowledge proofs is separated into multiple steps with clear boundaries. At the input of this pipeline is a computation, represented either as program source code or as a circuit. A technique called arithmetization turns this computation into a constraint system involving native operations over a finite field. The next step transforms this constraint system into an abstract proof system between two parties, prover P and verifier V, that are interactive Turing machines with access to unrealistic or unrealizable resources such as PCP oracles. These abstract proof systems in this

G. Hanaoka et al. (Eds.): PKC 2022, LNCS 13177, pp. 523–552, 2022.
https://doi.org/10.1007/978-3-030-97121-2_19

step are called *interactive oracle proofs (IOPs)* and typically achieve statistical or even perfect security. In the last step, the *cryptographic compilation*, the unrealistic resources are replaced by cryptographic approximations that achieve the same functionality at the expense of introducing computational hardness assumptions for security.
2. *Polynomial IOP formalism.* The abstract information-theoretical proof system in the step before cryptographic compilation could in principle rely on a variety of unrealistic resources, and build a sound proof system from their mathematical properties. However, for the purpose of establishing soundness, the Schwartz-Zippel lemma is an indispensable tool. The strategy is to reduce the satisfaction of arithmetic constraints arising from the constraint system to series of identities of *low-degree polynomials*. By evaluating these polynomials in random points, their equality is tested probabilistically. If the left and right hand sides of an equation represent identical polynomials, they are identical everywhere, but if they are unequal they are different *almost* everywhere. The Schwartz-Zippel lemma provides an exact concrete quantification of the security lost due to this probabilistic approximation. A *Polynomial IOP* is the abstract proof system tailored to this strategy. In this formalism, the prover sends low degree polynomials to the verifier, and rather than reading the entire list of coefficients, the verifier queries these polynomials in a given point through an oracle interface. The cryptographic compiler uses a *polynomial commitment scheme* to simulate this unrealistic resource.

These trends are visible in the rise of universal SNARKs with universal and updatable structured reference strings (SRS's) such as Sonic [11], PLONK [8], and Marlin [7]. The common idea here is to use the cryptographic pairing-based mathematics only to realize *polynomial commitment scheme*, typically the KZG scheme [10]. Since the SRS is used only for the KZG scheme, it is independent of the preceding abstract proof system and the circuit it encodes; this independence is precisely what enables updates to the SRS and its adaptation to any circuit. PLONK and Marlin independently formalize this abstraction and introduce the terms *Polynomial Protocol* and *Algebraic Holographic Proof (AHP)*, respectively. This paper adopts the terminology of Bünz *et al.* [6], who introduce a new polynomial commitment scheme (and hence a cryptographic compiler) based on groups of unknown order and in the process explore the landscape of protocols it can apply to.

These trends are *also* visible in the rise of IOPs based on Reed-Solomon codes [1,3,4]. The underlying abstract protocols here are not explicitly Polynomial IOPs. However, their common feature is the reliance on Reed-Solomon codewords as the proof oracles. Since Reed-Solomon codewords are obtained by evaluating polynomials in a domain of points whose cardinality is larger than the polynomials' degree, these proof oracles uniquely identify the originating low-degree polynomials. As a result, a Reed-Solomon IOP is a Polynomial IOP in disguise.

Despite the spontaneous convergence onto Polynomial IOPs as a useful formalism, there seems to be little agreement about the optimal interface between Polynomial IOPs and the arithmetic constraint systems that they realize. Arithmetic constraint systems typically express constraints using matrix algebra: in terms of vectors, and matrix multiplication, but also *Hadamard products*, which is a fancy word for the element-wise products of pairs of equal-length vectors. The set of operations that Polynomial IOPs natively offer are somewhat different. As a result, how the Polynomial IOP represents the objects in the arithmetic constraint system and how it simulates the equations that constrain them, are the key questions in the design process of Polynomial IOPs. The various answers to these questions are what set the various Polynomial IOPs for arithmetic circuits apart.

- Marlin and Aurora represent the objects of the arithmetic constraint system as the Reed-Solomon codewords of polynomials. Standard techniques establish the correct computation of a Hadamard product of such codewords. The computation of a linear transform applied to such a codeword is reduced to checking the sum of a related codeword.
- PLONK represents the vector of wire values as the values of a polynomial in a domain of points. A permutation argument establishes the assignment of wires to gates and the standard techniques for Reed-Solomon codewords establish the consistency of inputs and outputs to addition and multiplication gates.
- Sonic represents the vectors of left, right, and output wires of a series of multiplication gates as the coefficient vectors of three polynomials. The consistency of these multiplication gates, and of a linear transform, is established by checking several properties of bivariate polynomials. The paper furthermore explains under which conditions these bivariate polynomials can be simulated with univariate ones.

Contributions. In this paper we propose a new Polynomial IOP for arithmetic circuits, called Claymore.[1] Succinct verification is achieved with a trusted preprocessing phase. When compiled with any polynomial commitment scheme, the result is a concrete zk-SNARK with universal updatable structured reference string, or transparent setup, depending only on the nature of the polynomial commitment scheme.

The arithmetic constraint system chosen to represent the arithmetic circuit is the Hadamard Product Relation (HPR), in which the witness consists of three vectors representing the left, right, and output wires of a list of multiplication gates. We note that Sonic realizes a similar constraint satisfaction relation by reducing both the multiplication and linear constraints into one large equation. In Claymore, the multiplication gate consistency and linear consistency are achieved in two separate steps, both of which rely on a collection of subprotocols for linear algebra relations that we develop along the way. The separate steps are later merged as an explicit optimization.

Like Sonic but unlike Marlin and PLONK, Claymore opts for the *monomial coefficient basis* to represent the vectors of the arithmetic constraint system. DenseClaymore represents the linear transform as a dense matrix in the monomial coefficient basis and this choice results in the smallest number of polynomials in the transcript across all Polynomial IOPs. The price to pay for this brevity is the $O(n^2)$ scaling of the polynomials' degree, where n is the size of the circuit.

[1] A type of Scottish sword.

A question that naturally arises when using this basis, is whether it is also equipped to deal with the sparse linear transformations that typically come from long-winded computations. We answer this question positively by providing methods for dealing with sparse linear algebra relations, culminating in a sparse variant of Claymore. This variant concretely outperforms Marlin and Sonic in terms of the number of polynomials in the transcript. While this number is smaller still for PLONK, one notes that PLONK does not support arbitrary fan-in for linear constraints, whereas Marlin and Claymore (both variants) do.

Additionally, we compare the new and existing Polynomial IOPs both abstractly and concretely. In the abtract comparison we determine how the key performance-driving parameters of the Polynomial IOP evolve as a function of the circuit size. In the concrete comparison, we transform the various Polynomial IOPs with three different cryptographic compilers into concrete zk-SNARKs in order to compare the size of the resulting proofs. In this comparison, all proofs establish the integrity of the same benchmark computation.

Motivation and Applications. The motivation for this work is chiefly theoretical. We study the interface between arithmetic circuits and Polynomial IOPs in isolation of other constraints and demands. As a result of this focus, our protocol is arguably simpler than other protocols that achieve nominally the same thing. Complexity is the friend of mistakes, and our protocol may therefore be the preferred option for this reason even in circumstances where it is inferior in terms of performance.

The dense variant of Claymore performs extremely well for shallow arithmetic circuits, such as the verification circuits of lattice-based and MQ-based signature schemes, which typically involve operations on large matrices and vectors over a small finite field. As a result, a DenseClaymore-SNARK is an outstanding candidate for achieving post-quantum signature aggregation, or signature schemes with various fancy properties that zero-knowledge proofs enable.

Using SNARKs in combination with other cryptographic tools points to a useful property that SNARKs frequently lack—they typically require a finite field with a particular structure, such as a large multiplicative subgroup of smooth order. Marlin and PLONK have this property, while Sonic is defined for arbitrary fields. Using the SNARK in combination with a different cryptosystem that requires an incompatible field, requires the SNARK to simulate the cryptosystem's field operations using the arithmetic constraint system of the SNARK. In contrast, Claymore (like Sonic) induces no such costly simulation overhead as it works for any large enough finite field.

The protocols proposed here promote *simplicity through modularity.* However, we observe that once the basic protocol has been composed, there are available optimizations that improve its characteristics at the cost of violating the boundaries between modules. This observation highlights the utility of separating *design* from *optimization* considerations. Note that it is only the optimized SparseClaymore protocol that outperforms Marlin in the target metric, number of polynomials. The unoptimized version is inferior in all respects. Furthermore, the proof of zero-knowledge relies on a batching-related optimization that applies to both variants of Claymore; without this optimization the proof is tricky and complex. Lastly, the optimizations stand on their own, and can possibly improve other Polynomial IOPs beyond Claymore.

2 Preliminaries

2.1 Indexed Relations

Owing to their convenience, we use *indexed relations* [7]. An indexed relation is a set $\mathcal{R}$ of tuples $(\mathbb{i}, \mathbb{x}, \mathbb{w})$, whose three components are called the *index*, *instance*, and *witness*, respectively. The separation between index and instance captures the intuition that some properties of concrete proofs for $\mathcal{R}$ should be computable from $\mathbb{i}$ even before $\mathbb{x}$ is known. For instance, $\mathbb{i}$ can be the description of an arithmetic circuit, $\mathbb{x}$ the values of the output wires, and $\mathbb{w}$ an assignment of values to all wires that makes the all gates consistent. The projection $\{(\mathbb{i}, \mathbb{x}) \mid (\mathbb{i}, \mathbb{x}, \mathbb{w}) \in \mathcal{R}\}$ of triples in $\mathcal{R}$ onto the first two components is the *indexed language corresponding to* $\mathcal{R}$ and is denoted by $\mathcal{L}(\mathcal{R})$.

2.2 Constraint Systems

A constraint system is a representation of a computation in terms of equations with unknown variables. When there is an assignment to the unknown variables that satisfies all equations, we say the constraint system is *satisfiable*, and this assignment is the *witness*. The *index* determines all fixed constants in the equations, and the *instance* determines known variables that can vary independently of the index but are ultimately known by all parties involved.

The following constraint system is adapted from Bootle *et al.* [5].

Definition 1 (Hadamard Product Relation (HPR)). *Let* $\mathbb{F}$ *be a finite field. A triple* $(\mathbb{i}, \mathbb{x}, \mathbb{w})$ *where* $\mathbb{i} = (m, n, M)$ *with* $m, n \in \mathbb{N}$, *and* $M \in \mathbb{F}^{m \times (1+3n)}$, *where* $\mathbb{x} = \mathbf{x} \in \mathbb{F}^m$, *and where* $\mathbb{w} = (\mathbf{w_l}, \mathbf{w_r}, \mathbf{w_o}) \in \mathbb{F}^n \times \mathbb{F}^n \times \mathbb{F}^n$; *satisfies the* Hadamard Product Relation *iff both*

$$\mathbf{x} = M \begin{pmatrix} 1 \\ \hline \mathbf{w_l} \\ \hline \mathbf{w_r} \\ \hline \mathbf{w_o} \end{pmatrix} \tag{1}$$

and

$$\mathbf{w_l} \circ \mathbf{w_r} = \mathbf{w_o} \ , \tag{2}$$

where $\circ$ *denotes the Hadamard (i.e., entry-wise) product; and in this case we write* $(\mathbb{i}, \mathbb{x}, \mathbb{w}) \in \mathcal{R}_{\mathsf{HPR}}$.

2.3 Interactive Proof Systems

Definition 2 (Interactive Proof System). *Let $\mathcal{R}$ be an indexed relation with corresponding relation language $\mathcal{L}(\mathcal{R})$. An* interactive proof system *is a pair* (P, V) *of stateful interactive Turing machines such that: the input to* P *is* $(\mathbb{i}, \mathbb{x}, \mathbb{w})$*, the input to* V *is* $(\mathbb{i}, \mathbb{x})$*;* P *and* V *exchange* $\mathsf{r} = \mathsf{r}(|\mathbb{i}|)$ *messages in total; and in the last step of the protocol* V *outputs a single bit* $b \in \{\top, \bot\}$*. The system satisfies two more properties:*

- Completeness—V *accepts members of* $\mathcal{L}(\mathcal{R})$*:* $(\mathbb{i}, \mathbb{x}) \in \mathcal{L}(\mathcal{R}) \Rightarrow b = \top$.
- Soundness *(with* soundness error σ*)*—V *rejects non-members of* $\mathcal{L}(\mathcal{R})$ *except with probability at most* σ *taken over the all random coins involved:* $\Pr[(\mathbb{i}, \mathbb{x}) \notin \mathcal{L}(\mathcal{R}) \Rightarrow b = \bot] \geq 1 - \sigma$.

Soundness becomes a moot point when for the given index $\mathbb{i}$ every instance $\mathbb{x}$ has a matching witness $\mathbb{w}$ such that $(\mathbb{i}, \mathbb{x}, \mathbb{w}) \in \mathcal{R}$. In this case a stronger notion called *knowledge soundness* [2] is preferred, which informally requires that any adversary that successfully convinces the verifier can be made to leak a witness by an extractor machine that has the same interface as the verifier but can additionally reset the adversary to an earlier point in time without forgetting the observed transcripts. In our context, all witnesses are encoded into oracles, and the prover displays knowledge of them simply by providing the oracles to the verifier. As a result, at our level of abstraction, knowledge soundness follows automatically from soundness. When the oracles are simulated by a concrete cryptographic tool, knowledge soundness becomes an important consideration that is not automatically satisfied. However, this cryptographic instantiation is beyond the scope of this paper.

A proof system is zero-knowledge [9] if, informally, an authentic transcript could have been produced by an adversary who is ignorant of the witness. More formally, the distribution of authentic transcripts must be samplable with public information only.

Definition 3 (Honest-Verifier Zero-Knowledge). *Let $\mathcal{R}$ be an indexed relation and let* (P, V) *be a proof system for $\mathcal{R}$. Let* $tr \leftarrow \langle \mathsf{P}(\mathbb{i}, \mathbb{x}, \mathbb{w}), \mathsf{V}(\mathbb{i}, \mathbb{x}) \rangle$ *denote the assignment to the variable tr of the transcript arising from the interaction between* P *with input* $(\mathbb{i}, \mathbb{x}, \mathbb{w})$ *and* V *with input* $(\mathbb{i}, \mathbb{x})$*. The proof system* (P, V) *is* honest-verifier zero-knowledge *if there exists a polynomial-time Turing machine* S *such that the distribution* $\mathcal{D}_0$ *of authentic transcripts* $tr \leftarrow \langle \mathsf{P}(\mathbb{i}, \mathbb{x}, \mathbb{w}), \mathsf{V}(\mathbb{i}, \mathbb{x}) \rangle$*, is identical to the distribution* $\mathcal{D}_1$ *of simulated transcripts* $tr \leftarrow \mathsf{S}(\mathbb{i}, \mathbb{x})$*. When* $\mathcal{D}_0$ *and* $\mathcal{D}_1$ *are distinct, we consider the statistical distance and use the term* Statistical *Honest-Verifier Zero-Knowledge.*

2.4 Polynomial IOP

Informally, a Polynomial IOP is an abstract proof system, where the prover sends polynomials and the verifier, instead of reading the polynomials in their entirety, is allowed to query the polynomial as oracles in select points.

Definition 4 (Polynomial IOP). *Let $\mathcal{R}$ be an indexed relation with corresponding indexed language $\mathcal{L}(\mathcal{R})$, $\mathbb{F}$ some finite field, and $\mathsf{d} \in \mathbb{N}$ a degree bound. A* Polynomial IOP for $\mathcal{R}$ with degree bound d *is a pair of interactive machines* (P, V)*, satisfying the following description.*

- (P, V) *is an interactive proof for $\mathcal{L}(\mathcal{R})$ with r rounds, and with soundness error σ.*
- P *sends polynomials $f_i(X) \in \mathbb{F}[X]$ of degree at most d to* V.
- V *is an oracle machine with access to a list of oracles, which contains one oracle for each polynomial it has received from the prover.*
- *When an oracle associated with a polynomial $f_i(X)$ is queried on a point $z_j \in \mathbb{F}$, the oracle responds with the value $f_i(z_j)$.*
- V *sends challenges $\alpha_k \in \mathbb{F}$ to* P.
- V *is public coin.*

Definition 4 stipulates one global degree bound d for all polynomials. In Appendix A[2] we offer this alternative definition that stipulates individual degree bounds d_i for each polynomial $f_i(X)$. The same appendix presents a transformation between definitions to establish their equivalence. This transformation does lose some generality: queries in $z_j = 0$ are not allowed, the global-bound protocol has one polynomial more, and the soundness error increases by at most $\frac{2p+\mathsf{d}-1}{|\mathbb{F}|-1}$, where p is the original number of polynomials. However, these restrictions are not significant for typical applications of Polynomial IOPs, where the field $\mathbb{F}$ is large. Therefore, without too much loss of generality, we may assume for the sake of a simpler presentation that the polynomials come with individual degree bounds.

With a minor extension, Polynomial IOPs can appropriately capture preprocessing. This extension introduces third machine, the *indexer* I. As its name suggests, I reads only $\mathbb{i}$, and it outputs a list of polynomials to which V has oracle access.

Definition 5 (Polynomial IOP with Preprocessing). *Let $\mathcal{R}$ be an indexed relation with corresponding language $\mathcal{L}(\mathcal{R})$. A* Polynomial IOP with Preprocessing *is a tuple of interactive machines* $(\mathsf{I}, \mathsf{P}, \mathsf{V})$ *such that* (P, V) *is a Polynomial IOP for $\mathcal{L}(\mathcal{R})$ and such that*

- I *takes $\mathbb{i}$ for input and outputs a list of polynomials of degree at most* d*;*
- V *has oracle access to these polynomials in addition to the polynomials it receives from* P.

Some of the Polynomial IOPs in this paper are designed for modular composition. As a result, V does not begin with an empty list of polynomial oracles. In order to define the relations that these Polynomial IOPs realize, we denote by $[f_i(X)]$ a polynomial $f_i(X)$ that was sent to V by I or P at some earlier stage and to which V has oracle access.

---

[2] This and other appendices are available in the full version of this paper [13].

3 Dense Linear Algebra Relations

3.1 Inner Product

Bünz *et al.* [6] are the first to sketch a Polynomial IOP that realizes an inner product relation between two vectors. It relies on the fact that the inner product of the coefficient vectors of $f_{\boldsymbol{a}}(X)$ and $f_{\boldsymbol{b}}(X)$ is the middle coefficient of $f_{\boldsymbol{a}}(X) \cdot X^{\mathsf{d}} \cdot f_{\boldsymbol{b}}(X^{-1})$, assuming that both $f_{\boldsymbol{a}}(X)$ and $f_{\boldsymbol{b}}(X)$ are of degree d. To verify the middle coefficient is indeed the claimed inner product c, V needs two polynomials: the left half $l(X)$ and the right half $r(X)$, both of degree $\mathsf{d}-1$. Then the identity $f_{\boldsymbol{a}}(X) \cdot X^{\mathsf{d}} \cdot f_{\boldsymbol{b}}(X^{-1}) = l(X) + X^{\mathsf{d}} \cdot c + X^{\mathsf{d}+1} \cdot r(X)$ cannot hold in more than $2\mathsf{d}$ points unless c is the correct inner product.

Our variant of this protocol achieves the same result with the same number of queries but with one polynomial oracle less. This trade-off induces a doubling of the polynomial's degree and an increase-by-one in the number of distinct evaluation points. To see how this is achieved, observe that the coefficient on X^{d} of the polynomial $f_{\boldsymbol{a}}(X) \cdot X^{\mathsf{d}} \cdot f_{\boldsymbol{b}}(X^{-1}) - c \cdot X^{\mathsf{d}}$ is zero. The same is true for $h(X) = \bar{h}(X) \cdot \gamma^{\mathsf{d}} - \bar{h}(\gamma X)$ for *any* $\bar{h}(X)$ and any γ with a large enough multiplicative order. If $f_{\boldsymbol{a}}(X) \cdot X^{\mathsf{d}} \cdot f_{\boldsymbol{b}}(X^{-1}) = \sum_{i=0}^{2\mathsf{d}} c_i X^i$ (with $c_{\mathsf{d}} = c$), then P can obtain $\bar{h}(X)$ by setting its ith coefficient to $c_i/(\gamma^{\mathsf{d}} - \gamma^i)$ when $i \neq \mathsf{d}$, or uniformly at random when $i = \mathsf{d}$. The verifier V tests that the coefficient of X^{d} is indeed zero by sampling the left and right hand sides of the polynomial identity

$$\bar{h}(X) \cdot \gamma^{\mathsf{d}} - \bar{h}(\gamma \cdot X) = f_{\boldsymbol{a}}(X) \cdot X^{\mathsf{d}} \cdot f_{\boldsymbol{b}}(X^{-1}) - c \cdot X^{\mathsf{d}} \tag{3}$$

in a uniformly random point $z \xleftarrow{\$} \mathbb{F}\backslash\{0\}$. The multiplicative order of γ must be larger than $2\mathsf{d}$ for this $\bar{h}(X)$ to exist; for simplicity set γ to the smallest element that generates $\mathbb{F}\backslash\{0\}, \times$.

Formally, the relation realized by inner product protocols is

$$\mathcal{R}_{\mathrm{ip}} = \left\{ (\mathbb{i}, \mathbb{x}, \mathbb{w}) \left| \begin{array}{l} \mathbb{i} = \mathsf{d} \\ \mathbb{x} = ([f_{\boldsymbol{a}}(X)], [f_{\boldsymbol{b}}(X)], c) \\ \mathbb{w} = (f_{\boldsymbol{a}}(X), f_{\boldsymbol{b}}(X)) \\ f_{\boldsymbol{a}}(X) = \sum_{i=0}^{\mathsf{d}} a_i X^i \\ f_{\boldsymbol{b}}(X) = \sum_{i=0}^{\mathsf{d}} b_i X^i \\ c = \sum_{i=0}^{\mathsf{d}} a_i b_i \end{array} \right. \right\} . \tag{4}$$

Theorem 1 (Security of InnerProduct). *Protocol* InnerProduct *of Protocol 1 is a Polynomial IOP for* $\mathcal{L}(\mathcal{R}_{\mathrm{ip}})$ *with completeness and soundness with soundness error* $\sigma = \frac{2\mathsf{d}}{|\mathbb{F}|-1}$.

Proof. The protocol revolves around the polynomial identity of Eq. (3). The verifier tests this identity by sampling left and right hand sides in a random point z. Since this is an identity whenever $c = \boldsymbol{a}^{\mathsf{T}}\boldsymbol{b}$, completeness follows. For soundness, observe that when $c \neq \boldsymbol{a}^{\mathsf{T}}\boldsymbol{b}$ then the coefficient of X^{d} on the right hand side of (3) is nonzero whereas the matching coefficient of the left hand side

description: decides $\mathcal{L}(\mathcal{R}_{\text{ip}})$
inputs: $\mathbb{i} : \mathsf{d}$
$\mathbb{x} : ([f_a(X)], [f_b(X)], c)$
$\mathbb{w} : (f_a(X), f_b(X))$
begin
P computes $f_c(X) = \sum_{i=0}^{2\mathsf{d}} c_i X^i \leftarrow f_a(X) \cdot X^{\mathsf{d}} \cdot f_b(X^{-1})$
P computes $\bar{h}(X) = \sum_{i=0}^{2\mathsf{d}} \bar{h}_i X^i$ with $\bar{h}_i \leftarrow \frac{c_i}{\gamma^{\mathsf{d}} - \gamma^i}$ for all $i \neq \mathsf{d}$ and $\bar{h}_{\mathsf{d}} \xleftarrow{\$} \mathbb{F}$
P sends $\bar{h}(X)$ of degree at most $2\mathsf{d}$ to V
V samples $z \xleftarrow{\$} \mathbb{F}\backslash\{0\}$ and queries $([f_a(X)], [f_b(X)], [\bar{h}(X)], [\bar{h}(X)])$ in $(z, z^{-1}, z, \gamma \cdot z)$
V receives $y_a = f_a(z)$, $y_b = f_b(z^{-1})$, $y_h = \bar{h}(z)$, and $y_h^* = \bar{h}(\gamma \cdot z)$
V tests $y_h \cdot \gamma^{\mathsf{d}} - y_h^* \stackrel{?}{=} y_a \cdot y_b \cdot z^{\mathsf{d}} - c \cdot z^{\mathsf{d}}$

Protocol 1: InnerProduct

is zero. There are at most $2\mathsf{d}$ points z where left and right hand sides are equal, since both hands are bounded by this degree. By the Schwartz-Zippel lemma, the probability of a false accept is $\sigma = \frac{2\mathsf{d}}{|\mathbb{F}|-1}$. □

3.2 Batched Inner Product

We can batch multiple invocations of protocol InnerProduct into a single protocol that requires the prover to send only one polynomial oracle. Formally, the relation is given by

$$\mathcal{R}_{\text{bip}} = \left\{ (\mathbb{i}, \mathbb{x}, \mathbb{w}) \left| \begin{array}{l} \mathbb{i} = (m, \mathsf{d}) \\ \mathbb{x} = \{([f_{a_i}(X)], [f_{b_i}(X)], c_i)\}_{i=1}^m \\ \mathbb{w} = \{(f_{a_i}(X), f_{b_i}(X))\}_{i=1}^m \\ \forall i \in \{0, \ldots, m-1\} \,.\, f_{a_i}(X) = \sum_{j=0}^{\mathsf{d}} a_{ij} X^i \\ \forall i \in \{0, \ldots, m-1\} \,.\, f_{b_i}(X) = \sum_{j=0}^{\mathsf{d}} b_{ij} X^i \\ \forall i \in \{0, \ldots, m-1\} \,.\, c_i = \sum_{j=0}^{\mathsf{d}} a_{ij} b_{ij} \end{array} \right. \right\} . \quad (5)$$

Theorem 2 (Security of BatchedInnerProduct). *Protocol* BatchedInnerProduct *of Protocol 2 is a Polynomial IOP for $\mathcal{L}(\mathcal{R}_{\text{bip}})$ with completeness and soundness with soundness error $\sigma = \frac{2\mathsf{d}+m-1}{|\mathbb{F}|-1}$.*

Proof. Let $\sum_{j=0}^{2\mathsf{d}} c_{i,j} X^j = f_{a_i}(X) \cdot f_{b_i}(X^{-1}) \cdot X^{\mathsf{d}}$ for all $i \in \{1, \ldots, m\}$. Furthermore, let $\bar{H}(X, Y) = \sum_{i=1}^m \sum_{j=0}^{2\mathsf{d}} h_{i,j} X^j Y^{i-1}$ with $h_{i,j} = \frac{c_{i,j}}{\gamma^{\mathsf{d}} - \gamma^j}$ for $j \neq \mathsf{d}$, arbitrary $h_{i,\mathsf{d}}$ for $i > 0$, and $h_{0,\mathsf{d}}$ such that $\bar{h}(X) = \bar{H}(X, \alpha)$.

The protocol revolves around the bivariate polynomial identity

$$\bar{H}(X,Y) \cdot \gamma^{\mathsf{d}} - \bar{H}(\gamma \cdot X, Y) = X^{\mathsf{d}} \cdot \sum_{i=1}^{m} (f_{a_i}(X) \cdot f_{b_i}(X^{-1}) - c_i) \cdot Y^{i-1} . \quad (6)$$

description: decides $\mathcal{L}(\mathcal{R}_{\mathsf{bip}})$
inputs: $\mathbb{i} : (m, \mathsf{d})$
$\mathbb{x} : \{([f_{\boldsymbol{a}_i}(X)], [f_{\boldsymbol{b}_i}(X)], c_i)\}_{i=1}^m$
$\mathbb{w} : \{(f_{\boldsymbol{a}_i}(X), f_{\boldsymbol{b}_i}(X))\}_{i=1}^m$
begin
- P computes $f_{\boldsymbol{c}_i}(X) \leftarrow f_{\boldsymbol{a}_i}(X) \cdot f_{\boldsymbol{b}_i}(X^{-1}) \cdot X^{\mathsf{d}}$ for i from 1 to m
- V samples $\alpha \xleftarrow{\$} \mathbb{F}\backslash\{0\}$ and sends α to P
- P computes $f_{\boldsymbol{c}}(X) \leftarrow \sum_{i=1}^m f_{\boldsymbol{c}_i}(X) \cdot \alpha^{i-1}$
- P computes $\bar{h}(X) = \sum_{j=0}^{2\mathsf{d}} \bar{h}_j X^j$ with $\bar{h}_j \leftarrow \frac{c_j}{\gamma^{\mathsf{d}} - \gamma^j}$ for all $j \neq \mathsf{d}$ and $\bar{h}_{\mathsf{d}} \xleftarrow{\$} \mathbb{F}$
- P sends $\bar{h}(X)$ of degree at most 2d to V
- V samples $z \xleftarrow{\$} \mathbb{F}\backslash\{0\}$ and queries $(\{([f_{\boldsymbol{a}_i}(X)], [f_{\boldsymbol{b}_i}(X)])\}_{i=1}^m, [\bar{h}(X)], [\bar{h}(X)])$ in $(\{z, z^{-1}\}_{i=1}^m, z, \gamma \cdot z)$
- V receives $y_{a,i} = f_{\boldsymbol{a}_i}(z)$, $y_{b,i} = f_{\boldsymbol{b}_i}(z^{-1})$ for i from 1 to m, and $y_h = \bar{h}(z)$, $y_h^* = \bar{h}(\gamma \cdot z)$
- V tests $y_h \cdot \gamma^{\mathsf{d}} - y_h^* \stackrel{?}{=} z^{\mathsf{d}} \cdot \sum_{i=1}^m (y_{a,i} \cdot y_{b,i} - c_i) \cdot \alpha^{i-1}$

Protocol 2: BatchedInnerProduct

The verifier tests this identity by sampling left and right hand sides in a random point (z, α). Since this is an identity whenever $c_i = \boldsymbol{a}_i^\mathsf{T} \boldsymbol{b}_i$ for all i from 1 to m, completeness follows. For soundness, consider when for some i, $c_i \neq \boldsymbol{a}_i^\mathsf{T} \boldsymbol{b}_i$. Then left and right hand sides of (6) are unequal. There are at most $2\mathsf{d} + m - 1$ points (z, α) in which left and right hand sides are equal, since both hands are bounded by this total degree. By the (two-dimensional) Schwartz-Zippel lemma, the probability of a false accept is $\sigma = \frac{2\mathsf{d}+m-1}{|\mathbb{F}|-1}$. □

This inner product protocol and its batched version are convenient for zero-knowledge. The verifier V makes two queries to the polynomial $\bar{h}(X)$: one in z and one in $\gamma \cdot z$. Since $\bar{h}(X)$ has one uniformly random coefficient, one of the responses is uniformly random. The other one is such that the tested equality is true. So the honest verifier learns no new information from $\bar{h}(X)$.

3.3 Modular Reduction

We start with a protocol that will be used as a subprotocol in the sequel. This protocol establishes that one polynomial, $r(X)$, is the remainder after division of a second polynomial $f(X)$, by a third, $d(X)$. This third polynomial is assumed to be known, but the protocol can be naturally amended to allow V only oracle access to $[d(X)]$. Formally, the relation is given by

$$\mathcal{R}_{\text{reduce}} = \left\{ (\mathbb{i}, \mathbb{x}, \mathbb{w}) \;\middle|\; \begin{array}{l} \mathbb{i} = (\mathsf{d}_f, \mathsf{d}_r) \\ \mathbb{x} = ([f(X)], [r(X)], d(X)) \\ \mathbb{w} = (f(X), r(X)) \\ \exists q(X) \in \mathbb{F}[X] \,.\, f(X) = q(X) \cdot d(X) + r(X) \\ \mathsf{deg}(f) \leq \mathsf{d}_f \\ \mathsf{deg}(r) \leq \mathsf{d}_r \end{array} \right\} . \tag{7}$$

description: decides $\mathcal{L}(\mathcal{R}_{\text{reduce}})$
inputs: $\mathbb{i} : (\mathsf{d}_f, \mathsf{d}_r)$
$\mathbb{x} : ([f(X)], [r(X)], d(X))$
$\mathbb{w} : (f(X), r(X))$
begin
P computes q such that $f(X) = q(X) \cdot d(X) + r(X)$
P sends $q(X)$ of degree at most $\mathsf{d}_f - \mathsf{deg}(d)$ to V
V samples $z \xleftarrow{\$} \mathbb{F}\backslash\{0\}$ and queries $[f(X)]$, $[q(X)]$, and $[r(X)]$ in z
V receives $y_f = f(z)$, $y_q = q(z)$, and $y_r = r(z)$
V tests $y_f \stackrel{?}{=} y_q \cdot d(z) + y_r$

Protocol 3: ModReduce

Theorem 3 (Security of ModReduce). *Protocol* ModReduce *of Protocol 3 is a Polynomial IOP for* $\mathcal{L}(\mathcal{R}_{\text{reduce}})$ *with completeness and soundness with soundness error* $\sigma = \mathsf{d}_f/|\mathbb{F}|$.

Proof. Completeness follows from construction: dividing $f(X)$ by $d(X)$ gives quotient $q(X)$ and remainder $r(X)$. Therefore, $f(X) = q(X) \cdot d(X) + r(X)$ is an identity of polynomials and guaranteed to hold everywhere including in the point z.

For soundness, observe that when $r(X) \not\equiv f(X) \bmod d(X)$ then $d(X)$ does not divide $f(X) - r(X)$. As a result, $f(X) \neq q(X) \cdot d(X) + r(X)$ is an inequality of polynomials with degree $\mathsf{deg}(d) + \mathsf{deg}(q) = \mathsf{d}_f$. Due to the Schwartz-Zippel lemma, the left and right hand sides can evaluate to the same value in at most d_f choices for z. The probability of V accepting when $r(X) \not\equiv f(X) \bmod d(X)$ is therefore $\sigma = \mathsf{d}_f/|\mathbb{F}|$.

What is left to argue is that P fails to convince V when the congruence $r(X) \equiv f(X) \bmod d(X)$ holds, but $r(X)$ is not equal to the remainder after division of $f(X)$ by $d(X)$. The representatives of the congruence class of $r(X)$ are apart by polynomials of degree at least $\mathsf{deg}(d)$, there is only one representative of degree at most $\mathsf{d}_r < \mathsf{deg}(d)$. The index value d_r therefore already constrains $r(X)$ to a unique polynomial. □

3.4 Matrix-Vector Product

The next protocol involves two polynomials that represent vectors in the monomial coefficient basis. It establishes that the one vector is the result of applying a linear transformation to the other. This linear transformation itself can be known and computed explicitly by the verifier. However, for succinct verifiers it is more appealing to encode this matrix into a polynomial oracle. Depending on the context, either the protocol's preprocessing phase produces this oracle, or another external protocol does.

Specifically, let $\boldsymbol{a} \in \mathbb{F}^n$ and $\boldsymbol{b} \in \mathbb{F}^m$ and $M \in \mathbb{F}^{m \times n}$ with the element in row i and column j (both indices starting at zero) indexed as $M_{[i,j]}$. These objects are represented as polynomials with $a_{[i]}$ being ith element of $\boldsymbol{a}$ and simultaneously the coefficient of the monomial X^i in $f_{\boldsymbol{a}}(X)$, and similarly for $\boldsymbol{b}, b_{[i]}$, and $f_{\boldsymbol{b}}(X)$. When encoded into polynomial form, the matrix is encoded in row-first order, specifically $f_M(X) = \sum_{i=0}^{m-1} \sum_{j=0}^{n-1} M_{[i,j]} X^{in+j}$. The protocol establishes that $\boldsymbol{b} = M\boldsymbol{a}$. Formally, the relation is given by

$$\mathcal{R}_{\text{mvp}} = \left\{ (\mathbb{i}, \mathbb{x}, \mathbb{w}) \;\middle|\; \begin{array}{l} \mathbb{i} = (m, n, M) \\ \mathbb{x} = ([f_{\boldsymbol{a}}(X)], [f_{\boldsymbol{b}}(X)]) \\ \mathbb{w} = (f_{\boldsymbol{a}}(X), f_{\boldsymbol{b}}(X)) \\ f_{\boldsymbol{a}}(X) = \sum_{i=0}^{n-1} \boldsymbol{a}_{[i]} X^i \text{ for some } \boldsymbol{a} \in \mathbb{F}^n \\ f_{\boldsymbol{b}}(X) = \sum_{i=0}^{m-1} \boldsymbol{b}_{[i]} X^i \text{ for some } \boldsymbol{b} \in \mathbb{F}^m \\ \boldsymbol{b} = M\boldsymbol{a} \end{array} \right\} . \tag{8}$$

description: decides $\mathcal{L}(\mathcal{R}_{\text{mvp}})$
inputs: $\mathbb{i} : (m, n, M)$
$\mathbb{x} : ([f_{\boldsymbol{a}}(X)], [f_{\boldsymbol{b}}(X)])$
$\mathbb{w} : (f_{\boldsymbol{a}}(X), f_{\boldsymbol{b}}(X))$
// pre-processing
begin
I computes $f_M(X) \leftarrow \sum_{i=0}^{m-1} \sum_{j=0}^{n-1} M_{[i,j]} X^{in+j}$
I sends $f_M(X)$ of degree at most $mn - 1$ to P and V
begin
V samples $\alpha \xleftarrow{\$} \mathbb{F} \backslash \{0\}$ and sends α to P
P computes $r(X) \leftarrow f_M(X) \bmod X^n - \alpha$
P sends $r(X)$ of degree at most $n - 1$ to V
P and V run ModReduce with $\mathbb{i}^{(1)} = (mn - 1, n - 1)$, $\mathbb{x}^{(1)} = ([f_M(X)], [r(X)], X^n - \alpha)$, and $\mathbb{w}^{(1)} = (f_M(X), r(X))$
V queries $[f_{\boldsymbol{b}}(X)]$ in α and receives $y_{\boldsymbol{\alpha}^\intercal \boldsymbol{b}} = f_{\boldsymbol{b}}(\alpha)$
P and V run InnerProduct with $\mathbb{i}^{(2)} = n - 1$, $\mathbb{x}^{(2)} = ([r(X)], [f_{\boldsymbol{a}}(X)], y_{\boldsymbol{\alpha}^\intercal \boldsymbol{b}})$, and $\mathbb{w}^{(2)} = (r(X), f_{\boldsymbol{a}}(X))$

Protocol 4: DenseMVP

Theorem 4 (Security of DenseMVP). *Protocol* DenseMVP *of Protocol 4 is a Polynomial IOP for $\mathcal{L}(\mathcal{R}_{\text{mvp}})$ with completeness and soundness with soundness error $\sigma = \frac{mn+m+2n-4}{|\mathbb{F}|-1}$.*

Proof. Let $\boldsymbol{\alpha}^\top = (\alpha^0, \alpha^1, \cdots)$ and $\boldsymbol{r}^\top = \boldsymbol{\alpha}^\top M$, and consider the equations

$$\boldsymbol{b} = M\boldsymbol{a} \tag{9}$$

$$\boldsymbol{\alpha}^\top \boldsymbol{b} = \boldsymbol{\alpha}^\top M\boldsymbol{a} \tag{10}$$

$$\sum_{i=0}^{m-1} \alpha^i b_{[i]} = \boldsymbol{r}^\top \boldsymbol{a} \tag{11}$$

$$f_{\boldsymbol{b}}(\alpha) = \sum_{i=0}^{n-1} r_{[i]} a_{[i]} \tag{12}$$

$$y_{\boldsymbol{\alpha}^\top \boldsymbol{b}} = \mathsf{coeffs}(r(X)) \cdot \mathsf{coeffs}(f_{\boldsymbol{a}}(X)) \tag{13}$$

$$(\mathbb{i}^{(2)}, \mathbb{x}^{(2)}) = (n-1, ([r(X)], [f_{\boldsymbol{a}}(X)], y_{\boldsymbol{\alpha}^\top \boldsymbol{b}})) \in \mathcal{L}(\mathcal{R}_{\mathrm{ip}}) \ , \tag{14}$$

where $\mathsf{coeffs} : \mathbb{F}[X] \to \mathbb{F}^n$ is the function that returns the vector of coefficients of its argument. Observe that $\mathsf{coeffs}(r(X)) = \boldsymbol{r}$, by substituting X^n by α in the expression for $f_M(X)$:

$$\sum_{i=0}^{m-1}\sum_{j=0}^{n-1} M_{[i,j]} X^{in+j} \xrightarrow{X^n \mapsto \alpha} r(X) = \sum_{i=0}^{m-1}\sum_{j=0}^{n-1} M_{[i,j]} \alpha^i X^j \tag{15}$$

$$= \sum_{j=0}^{n-1} \left(\sum_{i=0}^{m-1} M_{[i,j]} \alpha^i \right) X^j \tag{16}$$

$$= \sum_{j=0}^{n-1} r_{[j]} X^j \ . \tag{17}$$

Completeness follows from the implications (9) $\Rightarrow$ (10) $\Leftrightarrow$ (11) $\Leftrightarrow$ (12) $\Rightarrow$ (13) $\Rightarrow$ (14).

For soundness, there are 3 events that can cause V to accept despite $\boldsymbol{b} \neq M\boldsymbol{a}$:

1. (9) $\not\Leftarrow$ (10). The probability of this event is at most $\frac{m-1}{|\mathbb{F}|-1}$ due to the Schwartz-Zippel lemma.
2. (12) $\not\Leftarrow$ (13) because $r(X)$ is not the remainder of $f_M(X)$ after division by $X^n - \alpha$. The probability of this event is at most $\frac{mn-1}{|\mathbb{F}|}$, the soundness error of $\mathsf{ModReduce}$.
3. (13) $\not\Leftarrow$ (14), because $y_{\boldsymbol{\alpha}^\top \boldsymbol{b}}$ is not the inner product of the coefficient vectors of $r(X)$ and $f_{\boldsymbol{a}}(X)$. The probability of this event is at most $\frac{2n-2}{|\mathbb{F}|}$, the soundness error of $\mathsf{InnerProduct}$.

By the union bound, the soundness error of $\mathsf{DenseMVP}$ is bounded by $\sigma = \frac{mn+m+2n-4}{|\mathbb{F}|-1}$. □

Note that after unrolling, the verifier the $\mathsf{DenseMVP}$ protocol tests two polynomial identities. One arises from expanding $\mathsf{ModReduce}$, and the other arises from $\mathsf{InnerProduct}$. Both polynomial identities involve the polynomial $r(X)$, and as a result it can be eliminated and the identities merged. We present the unrolled and optimized version in Appendix C.1.

To see that this merger has no effect on soundness, observe that the inequality $lhs_1 \neq lhs_2$ implies $r(X) \neq lhs_1$ or $r(X) \neq lhs_2$. The verifier therefore accepts this false instance with a probability bounded by the same soundness error as the unoptimized protocol. This optimization strategy translates more generally to (some) other Polynomial IOPs: to eliminate a polynomial that is common to two identities, move it to the right hand side and then equate both left hand sides.

3.5 Hadamard Product

The next protocol establishes that the Hadamard (or component-wise) product of two vectors is equal to a third. These vectors are represented as the coefficient vectors of polynomials $f_{\boldsymbol{a}}(X)$, $f_{\boldsymbol{b}}(X)$, and $f_{\boldsymbol{c}}(X)$ such that $\boldsymbol{c} = \boldsymbol{a} \circ \boldsymbol{b}$ and $\boldsymbol{a}, \boldsymbol{b}, \boldsymbol{c} \in \mathbb{F}^{\mathsf{d}+1}$. The protocol relies on the fact that $\boldsymbol{c} = \boldsymbol{a} \circ \boldsymbol{b}$ implies $\boldsymbol{\alpha}^\mathsf{T}(\boldsymbol{a} \circ \boldsymbol{b}) = \boldsymbol{\alpha}^\mathsf{T}\boldsymbol{c}$ for all vectors $\boldsymbol{\alpha}$. In other words, one can simply sample a random scalar $\alpha \xleftarrow{\$} \mathbb{F}\backslash\{0\}$, and check the inner product of $\boldsymbol{\alpha} \circ \boldsymbol{a}$ with $\boldsymbol{b}$ against the inner product $\boldsymbol{\alpha}^\mathsf{T}\boldsymbol{c}$. Note that the right hand side of this check amounts to $f_{\boldsymbol{c}}(\alpha)$ and the operands in the left hand side amount to the coefficient vectors of $f_{\boldsymbol{a}}(\alpha X)$ and $f_{\boldsymbol{b}}(X)$, respectively. Formally, the relation is given by

$$\mathcal{R}_{\text{hadamard}} = \left\{ (\mathbb{i}, \mathbb{x}, \mathbb{w}) \;\middle|\; \begin{array}{l} \mathbb{i} = \mathsf{d} \\ \mathbb{x} = ([f_{\boldsymbol{a}}(X)], [f_{\boldsymbol{b}}(X)], [f_{\boldsymbol{c}}(X)]) \\ \mathbb{w} = (f_{\boldsymbol{a}}(X), f_{\boldsymbol{b}}(X), f_{\boldsymbol{c}}(X)) \\ \forall i \in \{0, \ldots, \mathsf{d}\} \,.\, a_i b_i = c_i \end{array} \right\} . \tag{18}$$

description: decides $\mathcal{L}(\mathcal{R}_{\text{hadamard}})$
inputs: $\mathbb{i}$: d
$\mathbb{x}$: $[f_{\boldsymbol{a}}(X)], [f_{\boldsymbol{b}}(X)], [f_{\boldsymbol{c}}(X)]$
$\mathbb{w}$: $f_{\boldsymbol{a}}(X), f_{\boldsymbol{b}}(X), f_{\boldsymbol{c}}(X)$
begin
V samples $\alpha \xleftarrow{\$} \mathbb{F}\backslash\{0\}$ and sends α to P
P evaluates $y \leftarrow f_{\boldsymbol{c}}(\alpha)$
V queries $[f_{\boldsymbol{c}}(X)]$ in α and receives $y = f_{\boldsymbol{c}}(\alpha)$
P and V run InnerProduct with $\mathbb{i}^{(1)} = \mathsf{d}$, $\mathbb{x}^{(1)} = ([f_{\boldsymbol{a}}(\alpha X)], [f_{\boldsymbol{b}}(X)], y)$, $\mathbb{w}^{(1)} = (f_{\boldsymbol{a}}(\alpha X), f_{\boldsymbol{b}}(X))$, where V simulates $[f_{\boldsymbol{a}}(\alpha X)]$ using $[f_{\boldsymbol{a}}(X)]$ and the scalar α

Protocol 5: Hadamard

Theorem 5 (Security of Hadamard**).** *Protocol* Hadamard *of Protocol 5 is a Polynomial IOP for $\mathcal{L}(\mathcal{R}_{\text{hadamard}})$ with completeness and soundness with soundness error $\sigma = 3\mathsf{d}/(|\mathbb{F}| - 1)$.*

Proof. Consider the following sequence of equations.

$$\boldsymbol{a} \circ \boldsymbol{b} = \boldsymbol{c} \tag{19}$$

$$\boldsymbol{\alpha}^{\mathsf{T}} \cdot (\boldsymbol{a} \circ \boldsymbol{b}) = \boldsymbol{\alpha}^{\mathsf{T}} \cdot \boldsymbol{c} \tag{20}$$

$$\sum_{i=0}^{\mathsf{d}} (\alpha^i \boldsymbol{a}_{[i]}) \boldsymbol{b}_{[i]} = \sum_{i=0}^{\mathsf{d}} \alpha^i \boldsymbol{c}_{[i]} \tag{21}$$

$$\mathsf{coeffs}(f_{\boldsymbol{a}}(\alpha X)) \cdot \mathsf{coeffs}(f_{\boldsymbol{b}}(X)) = f_{\boldsymbol{c}}(\alpha) \tag{22}$$

$$\mathsf{coeffs}(f_{\boldsymbol{a}}(\alpha X)) \cdot \mathsf{coeffs}(f_{\boldsymbol{b}}(X)) = y \tag{23}$$

$$(\mathbb{i}, \mathbb{x}) = (\mathsf{d}, ([f_{\boldsymbol{a}}(\alpha X)], [f_{\boldsymbol{b}}(X)], y)) \in \mathcal{L}(\mathcal{R}_{\mathsf{InnerProduct}}) \tag{24}$$

Completeness follows from the sequence of implications (19) $\Rightarrow$ (20) $\Leftrightarrow$ (21) $\Leftrightarrow$ (22) $\Leftrightarrow$ (23) $\Rightarrow$ (24).

For soundness, consider when the reverse implications fail.

- (19) $\not\Leftarrow$ (20). This event happens with probability at most $\mathsf{d}/(|\mathbb{F}| - 1)$ due to the Schwartz-Zippel lemma.
- (23) $\not\Leftarrow$ (24). This event happens with probability at most $2\mathsf{d}/(|\mathbb{F}| - 1)$, the soundness error of InnerProduct.

Therefore, the probability that V accepts even though $\boldsymbol{a} \circ \boldsymbol{b} \neq \boldsymbol{c}$ is bounded by $\sigma = 3\mathsf{d}/(|\mathbb{F}| - 1)$. □

4 Sparse Linear Algebra Relations

The purpose of this section is to present an analogue of the DenseMVP Polynomial IOP but that works when the matrix M is represented sparsely, *i.e.*, as a list of nonzero coefficients and their coordinates. The full, formal presentation of this protocol is rather lengthy, and so we defer it to Appendix B. Here we present an intuitive, high-level overview with just enough detail so that the reader could reconstruct the deferred formal presentation.

4.1 High-Level Overview

Let $M \in \mathbb{F}^{m \times n}$ be a matrix with only K nonzero elements. It can be represented by a triple of functions $(\mathsf{col}, \mathsf{row}, \mathsf{val})$ via $M = \sum_{k=0}^{K-1} \mathbf{e}_{\mathsf{row}(k)} \mathbf{e}_{\mathsf{col}(k)}^{\mathsf{T}} \cdot \mathsf{val}(k)$, where $\mathbf{e}_i$ is the ith unit vector, where $\mathsf{row}, \mathsf{col} : \mathbb{N} \to \mathbb{N}$ indicate the column and row of the kth element, and where $\mathsf{val} : \mathbb{N} \to \mathbb{F}$ indicates its value. We detail a protocol to establish that $\mathbf{y} = M\mathbf{x}$. We first explain the steps from a high level point of view.

From MVP to *Bivariate Polynomial Evaluation*. A key component of the dense matrix-vector multiplication protocol is the evaluation of $(f_M(X) \bmod X^n - \alpha)$ at the point z, where $f_M(X)$ is the polynomial associated with the matrix M, *i.e.*, $f_M(X) = \sum_{i=0}^{m-1} \sum_{j=0}^{n-1} M_{[i,j]} X^{in+j}$. This step can equivalently be interpreted as the evaluation of the bivariate polynomial $f_M(X, Y) =$

$\sum_{i=0}^{m-1} \sum_{j=0}^{n-1} M_{[i,j]} X^i Y^j$ in the point (α, z). In other words, if we can achieve sparse bivariate polynomial evaluation, then we can achieve sparse matrix-vector products.

From *Bivariate Polynomials* to *Univariate Monomial vectors*. The reduction goes one step further: it is possible to achieve sparse bivariate polynomial evaluation given a procedure that establishes that the vector of coefficients of a dense polynomial is the same as the vector of monomials of a sparse univariate polynomial when evaluated in a given point. To see this, observe that a sparse bivariate polynomial $f(X,Y) = \sum_{k=0}^{K-1} c_k X^{a_k} Y^{b_k}$ can be evaluated in a point (x, y) using the polynomials $f_c(X) = \sum_{k=0}^{K-1} c_k X^k$, $f_x(X) = \sum_{k=0}^{K-1} x^{a_k} X^k$, and $f_y(X) = \sum_{k=0}^{K-1} y^{b_k} X^k$, simply by performing one Hadamard and one InnerProduct subprotocol. This reduction does introduce a problem, namely $f_x(X)$ and $f_y(X)$ cannot be known before V supplies x and y. So how does P commit to them, and how does V verify that the received oracles match with the commitment?

From *Univariate Monomial Vector* to *Bit Matrix*. Let's focus on $f_x(X)$, as $f_y(X)$ proceeds analogously. This polynomial can be represented by a bit matrix B, which takes the value 1 in cells (a_k, k) and 0 elsewhere. Let H denote the largest such a_k, *i.e.*, $H = \max_k a_k$. Let furthermore $\mathbf{x} = (x^0, x, x^2, \ldots, x^{H-1})^\mathsf{T}$, and $\mathbf{z} = (z^0, z, z^2, \ldots, z^{K-1})^\mathsf{T}$. Then B represents the polynomial $f_x(X)$ since $f_x(z) = \mathbf{x}B\mathbf{z}$.

From *bit matrix* to *Lagrange and Vandermonde* matrices. The idea is to decompose the matrix $B \in \mathbb{F}^{H \times K}$ as the product of two matrices, $L \in \mathbb{F}^{H \times H}$ and $R \in \mathbb{F}^{H \times K}$. Let $\mathcal{H} \subset \mathbb{F}$ be a set of H distinct elements of $\mathbb{F}$ and $\varphi : \mathbb{N} \rightarrow \mathcal{H}$ any mapping from $\{0, \ldots, H-1\}$ to $\mathcal{H}$. L is the Lagrange matrix, whose hth row is the coefficient vector of $\mathcal{L}_h(X)$, which is the Lagrange polynomial taking the value 1 in $\varphi(h)$ and 0 in all other points of $\mathcal{H}$. Symbolically:

$$\mathcal{L}_h(X) = \sum_{i=0}^{H-1} L_{[h,i]} X^i = \prod_{\substack{i=0 \\ i \neq h}}^{H-1} \frac{X - \varphi(i)}{\varphi(h) - \varphi(i)} \ . \tag{25}$$

R is the Vandermonde matrix, whose rows are the (Hadamard) powers of $(\varphi(a_k))_{k=0}^{K-1}$. Specifically:

$$R = \begin{pmatrix} 1 & 1 & \cdots & 1 \\ \varphi(a_0) & \varphi(a_1) & \cdots & \varphi(a_{K-1}) \\ \varphi(a_0)^2 & \varphi(a_1)^2 & \cdots & \varphi(a_{K-1})^2 \\ \vdots & \vdots & \cdots & \vdots \\ \varphi(a_0)^{H-1} & \varphi(a_1)^{H-1} & \cdots & \varphi(a_{K-1})^{H-1} \end{pmatrix} \ . \tag{26}$$

To verify that $LR = B$, observe that the inner product between $L_{[h,:]}$ and $R_{[:,k]}$ is equal to $\mathcal{L}_h(\varphi(a_k))$. When V provides (x, z) hoping to obtain $\mathbf{x}^\mathsf{T} B\mathbf{z}$, P will respond with $[\mathbf{x}^\mathsf{T} L]$ and $[R\mathbf{z}]$ (in polynomial form), and both proceed to an InnerProduct protocol. We will refer to these vectors as the Lagrange and Vandermonde vectors, respectively. The next question is, how and against what does V verify them?

Verifying the Lagrange Vector. After sending x and receiving the vector (encoded as a polynomial oracle) $[\mathbf{x}^\mathsf{T} L]$, V sends γ to P, who responds with the vector $[L\boldsymbol{\gamma}]$, where $\boldsymbol{\gamma} = (1, \gamma, \gamma^2, \ldots, \gamma^{H-1})^\mathsf{T}$. Let $Z_\mathcal{H}(X)$ be the unique monic polynomial of degree $H-1$ that vanishes on $\mathcal{H}$. By repeating the equation

$$\mathcal{L}_h(\gamma) \cdot (\gamma - \varphi(h)) = \frac{Z_\mathcal{H}(\gamma)}{\prod\limits_{\substack{i=0 \\ i \neq h}}^{H-1} (\varphi(h) - \varphi(i))} \tag{27}$$

for every h, V can check $L\boldsymbol{\gamma}$ using a Hadamard subprotocol, assuming that P or I previously committed to oracles for $f_\varphi(X) = \sum_{h=0}^{H-1} \varphi(h) X^h$ and $f_\mathcal{H}(X) = \sum_{h=0}^{H-1} \left(\prod_{i \in \{0 \ldots H-1\} \setminus \{h\}} (\varphi(h) - \varphi(i)) \right)^{-1} \cdot X^h$. The next step is to query the oracles $[\mathbf{x}L]$ and $[L\boldsymbol{\gamma}]$ in γ and x, respectively and verify that the responses match.

Verifying the Vandermonde Vector. A similar technique allows V to verify the Vandermonde vector. After sending z and receiving $[R\mathbf{z}]$ back, V sends δ, and P responds with $[\boldsymbol{\delta}^\mathsf{T} R]$. Next, V checks that for every $k \in \{0, \ldots, K-1\}$,

$$\left(\sum_{i=0}^{H-1} (\delta \cdot \varphi(a_k))^i \right) \cdot (\delta\varphi(a_k) - 1) = (\delta\varphi(a_k))^H - 1 \tag{28}$$

using another Hadamard protocol and the precommitted oracle $f_a(X) = \sum_{k=0}^{K-1} \varphi(a_k) X^k$. Lastly, V queries $[R\mathbf{z}]$ in δ to see if the response matches with $[\boldsymbol{\delta} R]$ when queried in z.

Batching Lagrange and Vandermonde Vectors. In order to establish the correct evaluation of the bivariate polynomial, the prover must establish the correct production of two univariate monomial vectors. A naïve implementation invokes the Lagrange vector and the Vandermonde vector procedure twice. However, it turns out to be possible to merge these two invocations, and save a total of 4 polynomials. We treat this optimization explicitly in Appendix C.

5 A Polynomial IOP for Arithmetic Circuits

5.1 The Protocol

The next protocol, Protocol 6 puts many of the previously developed tools together into a Polynomial IOP (with preprocessing) for arithmetic circuits as captured by the HPR. To differentiate our protocol from other similar ones, we name it Claymore.

description: realizes $\mathcal{R}_{\text{hpr}}$
inputs: $\mathbb{i}$: (m, n, M) with $M \in \mathbb{F}^{m\times(3n+1)}$
$\mathbb{x}$: $\mathbf{x} \in \mathbb{F}^n$
$\mathbb{w}$: $(\mathbf{w_l}, \mathbf{w_r}, \mathbf{w_o}) \in \mathbb{F}^n \times \mathbb{F}^n \times \mathbb{F}^n$
// preprocessing
begin
  I runs MVP.I on $\mathbb{i}^{(1)} = (m, 3n+1, M)$
// online
begin
  P computes $f_{wl} \leftarrow \sum_{j=0}^{n-1} \mathbf{w_l}_{[j]} X^j$, $f_{wr} \leftarrow \sum_{j=0}^{n-1} \mathbf{w_r}_{[j]} X^j$, and $f_{wo} \leftarrow \sum_{j=0}^{n-1} \mathbf{w_o}_{[j]} X^j$
  P sends $f_{wl}(X)$, $f_{wr}(X)$, and $f_{wo}(X)$, all of degrees at most $n-1$, to V
  P computes $f_{1w}(X) \leftarrow 1 + X f_{wl}(X) + X^{n+1} f_{wr}(X) + X^{2n+1} f_{wo}(X)$
  P computes $f_x(X)$, whose coefficient vectors correspond to $\mathbf{x} = M\,(1|\mathbf{w_l}^{\mathsf{T}}|\mathbf{w_r}^{\mathsf{T}}|\mathbf{w_o}^{\mathsf{T}})^{\mathsf{T}}$
  P and V run MVP with $\mathbb{i}^{(1)} = (m, 3n+1, M)$, $\mathbb{x}^{(1)} = ([f_{1w}(X)], [f_x(X)])$, $\mathbb{w}^{(1)} = (f_{1w}(X), f_x(X))$ where V simulates $[f_{1w}(X)]$ using $f_{1w}(X) = 1 + X f_{wl}(X) + X^{n+1} f_{wr}(X) + X^{2n+1} f_{wo}(X)$, $[f_{wl}(X)]$, $[f_{wr}(X)]$, and $[f_{wo}(X)]$; and where V computes $[f_x(X)]$ locally using $\mathbf{x} = \mathbb{x}$
  P and V run Hadamard with $\mathbb{i}^{(2)} = n-1$, $\mathbb{x}^{(2)} = ([f_{wl}(X)], [f_{wr}(X)], [f_{wo}(X)])$, $\mathbb{w}^{(2)} = (f_{wl}(X), f_{wr}(X), f_{wo}(X))$

Protocol 6: Claymore

Theorem 6 (Security of Claymore**).** *Protocol* Claymore *of Protocol 6 is a Polynomial IOP for $\mathcal{R}_{\text{HPR}}$ with completeness and soundness error $\sigma \leq \sigma_{\mathsf{Hadamard}} + \sigma_{\mathsf{MVP}}$.*

Proof. Completeness follows from construction. Since the arguments are computed honestly, the subprotocols succeed and guarantee equalities (1) and (2), respectively.

Soundness. If the HPR instance is a false instance, then $\mathbf{x} \neq M(1|\mathbf{w_l}^{\mathsf{T}}|\mathbf{w_r}^{\mathsf{T}}|\mathbf{w_o}^{\mathsf{T}})^{\mathsf{T}}$ or $\mathbf{w_l} \circ \mathbf{w_r} \neq \mathbf{w_o}$. As a result either the Hadamard protocol succeeds despite being run on a false instance, or the MVP protocol succeeds despite being run on a false instance. The probabilities of these events are respectively at most $\sigma_{\mathsf{Hadamard}}$ and at most σ_{MVP}. □

5.2 The Role of Preprocessing

The preprocessing phase can be omitted. In this case, V must compute $f_M(X)$ locally. This task requires $O(mn)$ work, or only $O(K)$ if the matrix M has only

K nonzero elements and is represented as such. When this phase is omitted, Claymore should be compared to the Polynomial IOP underlying Aurora [4].

When used with preprocessing, Claymore achieves fast verification. Specifically, the matrix M which determines the circuit being proved, is processed by the indexer. For long and drawn-out computations, this matrix is typically sparse and the SparseMVP is suitable. However, for short or shallow computations, DenseMVP is the better option. Depending on the choice of MVP protocol, the matching soundness error should be considered.

5.3 Optimizations

Reuse α Across Hadamard Protocols. DenseClaymore has only one invocation of the Hadamard subprotocol, but the (partially unrolled) SparseClaymore has many more. It is worth reusing the same α for all these invocations as this reduces the number of unique evaluation points.

First, observe that all invocations to Hadamard can be shuffled around until they can all be run simultaneously – none of the inputs to any of the Hadamard protocols depend on the outputs of any other. Second, we can concatenate all the Hadamard relations and prove one batched relation

$$\boldsymbol{a}_0 \| \boldsymbol{a}_1 \| \cdots \| \boldsymbol{a}_{k-1} \circ \boldsymbol{b}_0 \| \boldsymbol{b}_1 \| \cdots \| \boldsymbol{b}_{k-1} = \boldsymbol{c}_0 \| \boldsymbol{c}_1 \| \cdots \| \boldsymbol{c}_{k-1} \tag{29}$$

instead of k individual relations separately. This batching comes with no soundness degradation.

The batched equation can be verified with k separate InnerProduct protocols that prove the same inner product relations as would be proved without batching – except that α is now the same everywhere. So neither P nor any other observer can determine whether V is verifying Eq. 29 or k separate equations.

Batch the Inner Product Protocols. The unrolled SparseClaymore protocol consists of 10 invocations of InnerProduct protocol, and the unrolled DenseClaymore protocol consists of 2. We can replace these InnerProduct protocols with the Batched InnerProduct protocol presented in Protocol 2. To see that this replacement does not affect the soundness, note that the InnerProduct subprotocols do not involve any verifier randomness and we can safely postpone them to the end of the Claymore protocol. Next, we replace them with a BatchedInnerProduct, unifying the degrees by the maximal degree of these polynomials. The negligible soundness degradation of this modification is captured concretely by Lemma 2 of Appendix A.

Batch the Sparse Vector Protocols. We also present an alternative version of SparseBiEval by batching the two instances of VandermondeVector and the two LagrangeVector protocols. This optimization eliminates four polynomial oracles at the cost of doubling the polynomial degrees. We present the protocol details and security proofs in Appendix C.2.

Concatenate Left and Right Wire Vectors. Instead of sending three witness polynomials $(f_{wl}(X), f_{wr}(X), f_{wo}(X))$, the prover can get away with sending only two: $(f_{wi}(X), f_{wo}(X))$ where $f_{wi}(X) = f_{wl}(X) + X^n \cdot f_{wr}(X)$. This concatenation is already implicit in the matrix-vector product subprotocol. The input to the Hadamard subprotocol should be $\mathbb{x} = ([f_{wi}(X)], [X^n \cdot f_{wi}(X)], [X^n \cdot f_{wo}(X)])$. The subprotocol then establishes that

$$\begin{pmatrix} \mathbf{w_l} \\ \hline \mathbf{w_r} \\ \hline \mathbf{0}_n \end{pmatrix} \circ \begin{pmatrix} \mathbf{0}_n \\ \hline \mathbf{w_l} \\ \hline \mathbf{w_r} \end{pmatrix} = \begin{pmatrix} \mathbf{0}_n \\ \hline \mathbf{w_o} \\ \hline \mathbf{0}_n \end{pmatrix} , \tag{30}$$

which is clearly equivalent to the original Hadamard relation. With this technique, the polynomials are of degree $3n - 1$, and so the soundness error is $(9n - 3)/(|\mathbb{F}| - 1)$ instead of $(3n - 3)/(|\mathbb{F}| - 1)$.

This optimization also preserves zero knowledge. To see this, observe that any distinguisher D that uses $f_{wi}(X)$ can be simulated with a distinguisher D' that uses $f_{wl}(X)$ and $f_{wr}(X)$. As a result, the optimized protocol lacks zero knowledge only if the protocol before applying the optimization also lacks it.

6 Zero-Knowledge

The strategy for achieving zero-knowledge consists of appending $3q$ coefficients to the initial wire vectors $\mathbf{w_l}$, $\mathbf{w_r}$, and $\mathbf{w_o}$ such that each new vector has q uniformly random coefficients and such that their Hadamard relation remains. The randomizers will make the witness polynomials q-wise independent, meaning that no distinguisher restricted to at most q queries will obtain any information about the witness.

It is tricky to define zero-knowledge the context of Polynomial IOPs. The distinguisher D can always query the received oracles in enough points to interpolate and then extract the witness. The notion is only meaningful when the number of queries bounded by some parameter. We furthermore restrict the distinguisher's queries to be distributed identically to that of an honest verifier; this restriction therefore corresponds to *honest-verifier* zero knowledge. As a result, we are not concerned with finding a complete description of the polynomials that make up the transcript. Instead, we are only concerned with the verifier's view of the transcript. This view corresponds to the list of queries and responses to the various oracles.

description: realizes $\mathcal{R}_{\text{HPR}}$
inputs: $\mathbb{i}$: (m, n, M) with $M \in \mathbb{F}^{m \times n}$
$\mathbb{x}$: $\mathbf{x} \in \mathbb{F}^n$
$\mathbb{w}$: $(\mathbf{w_l}, \mathbf{w_r}, \mathbf{w_o}) \in \mathbb{F}^n \times \mathbb{F}^n \times \mathbb{F}^n$
additional parameters: q
offline preprocessing:
I runs Claymore.I on $\mathbb{i}^{(1)} = (m, n + 3q, M' = (M_{[:,0:(n+1)]}|0_{m\times 3q}|M_{[:,(n+1):(2n+1)]}|0_{m\times 3q}|M_{[:,(2n+1):(3n+1)]}|0_{m\times 3q}))$
online phase:
// *compute witness polynomial with randomizers*
P samples $\mathbf{r}^{(l)}_{[0:q]}, \mathbf{r}^{(r)}_{[q:2q]}, \mathbf{r}^{(o)}_{[2q:3q]} \xleftarrow{\$} \mathbb{F}^q$ and sets $\mathbf{r}^{(l)}_{[q:2q]} = \mathbf{r}^{(r)}_{[0:q]} = 0_{q\times 1}$, $\mathbf{r}^{(o)}_{[0:2q]} = 0_{2q\times 1}$, $\mathbf{r}^{(l)}_{[2q:3q]} = 1_{q\times 1}$, and $\mathbf{r}^{(r)}_{[2q:3q]} = \mathbf{r}^{(o)}_{[4:6]}$ // $\mathbf{r}^{(l)} \circ \mathbf{r}^{(r)} = \mathbf{r}^{(o)}$
P and V run Claymore with $\mathbb{i}^{(1)} = (m, n + 3q, M')$, $\mathbb{x}^{(1)} = \mathbf{x}$, $\mathbb{w}^{(1)} = ((\mathbf{w_l}^\mathsf{T}|\mathbf{r}^{(l)\mathsf{T}}), (\mathbf{w_r}^\mathsf{T}|\mathbf{r}^{(r)\mathsf{T}}), (\mathbf{w_o}^\mathsf{T}|\mathbf{r}^{(o)\mathsf{T}}))$

Protocol 7: ZKClaymore

Theorem 7. *When $q \geq 2$, the Polynomial IOP* ZKClaymore *of protocol 7 has statistical honest-verifier zero-knowledge if all the* InnerProduct *subprotocols are replaced by a single invocation of* BatchedInnerProduct. *Concretely, the statistical distance between the verifier's view of authentic transcript versus the verifier's view of simulated transcript is bounded by $\frac{3}{|\mathbb{F}|-1}$, which is negligible in the field size.*

Proof. We show how S produces the verifier view for $(\mathbb{i}, \mathbb{x})$ without knowledge of $\mathbb{w}$. In the process, we establish that this view is indistinguishable from that of an authentic protocol execution.

The protocol ZKClaymore consists of an invocation to Hadamard protocol and an invocation to either the dense or sparse variant of MVP. Note that both protocols DenseMVP and SparseMVP consists of:

1. a query to $f_x(X)$ at uniformly random $\alpha \xleftarrow{\$} \mathbb{F}\backslash\{0\}$;
2. a protocol invocation (ModReduce in DenseMVP, or SparseBiEval in SparseMVP) with inputs that are independent of $\mathbf{w_l}, \mathbf{w_r}, \mathbf{w_o}$;
3. an invocation of InnerProduct on input $f_{1w}(X)$ and another polynomial ($r(X)$ in DenseMVP or $f_{\boldsymbol{\alpha}^\mathsf{T} M}(X)$ in SparseMVP), denoted by $f_t(X)$ hereafter, that is also independent of $\mathbf{w_l}, \mathbf{w_r}, \mathbf{w_o}$.

Since S knows M and $\mathbf{x}$, S can compute all polynomials that do not depend on witnesses honestly, *i.e.*, as the honest P would. We therefore restrict attention to polynomials that depend on the witness.

What remains is to demonstrate how to sample the verifier view for InnerProduct on input $f_{1w}(X)$ and $f_t(X)$, and for Hadamard on input $f_{wl}(X)$, $f_{wr}(X)$ and $f_{wo}(X)$. These two subprotocols contribute two polynomial pairs each to the BatchedInnerProduct protocol. It suffices to sample the verifier view for the BatchedInnerProduct protocol just for these two polynomial pairs, because the remaining pairs are independent of the witness.

This verifier view consists of several elements, namely:

1. Uniformly random z, α^* (the symbol α^* is used for batching the various inner product relations into one)
2. $y_h = \bar{h}(z), y_h^* = \bar{h}(\gamma \cdot z)$
3. The verifier view contributed by the InnerProduct protocol in MVP:
   (a) $y_{l_1} = f_{wl}(z)$
   (b) $y_{r_1} = f_{wr}(z)$
   (c) $y_{o_1} = f_{wo}(z)$
   (d) $y_t = f_t(z^{-1})$ (S samples this one honestly)
4. The verifier view contributed by the top-level Hadamard protocol:
   (a) Uniformly random β
   (b) $y_{o_2} = f_{wo}(\beta)$
   (c) $y_{l_2} = f_{wl}(\beta z)$
   (d) $y_{r_2} = f_{wr}(z^{-1})$

In the verifier view of an honest run, the above values satisfy:

$$\begin{aligned} y_h \cdot \gamma^{3n+3q} - y_h^* = \quad & (y_{1w} \cdot y_t - f_x(\alpha)) \cdot z^{3n+3q} \\ & + \alpha^* \cdot \left((y_{l_2} \cdot y_{r_2} - y_{o_2}) \cdot z^{n+q-1}\right) \\ & + \alpha^{*2} \cdot (\cdots) \ , \end{aligned} \tag{31}$$

where the ellipses omit terms that are independent of the witness and thus already known to S, and where $y_{1w} = 1 + z^{-1} y_{l_1} + z^{-n-q-1} y_{r_1} + z^{-2n-2q-1} y_{o_1}$.

S samples uniformly random $\alpha^*, z, \beta \xleftarrow{\$} \mathbb{F}\backslash\{0\}$ and computes y_t honestly. Consider the matrices

$$Z_l = \begin{pmatrix} 1 & z & z^2 & \cdots & z^{n+3q-1} \\ 1 & \beta z & (\beta z)^2 & \cdots & (\beta z)^{n+3q-1} \end{pmatrix} \tag{32}$$

$$Z_r = \begin{pmatrix} 1 & z & z^2 & \cdots & z^{n+3q-1} \\ 1 & z^{-1} & z^{-2} & \cdots & z^{-n-3q+1} \end{pmatrix} \tag{33}$$

$$Z_o = \begin{pmatrix} 1 & z & z^2 & \cdots & z^{n+3q-1} \\ 1 & \beta & \beta^2 & \cdots & \beta^{n+3q-1} \end{pmatrix} \tag{34}$$

which satisfy $(y_{l_1}, y_{l_2})^\mathsf{T} = Z_l\,(\mathbf{w}_\mathbf{l}^\mathsf{T} | \mathbf{r}^{(l)\,\mathsf{T}})^\mathsf{T}$, $(y_{r_1}, y_{r_2})^\mathsf{T} = Z_r\,(\mathbf{w}_\mathbf{r}^\mathsf{T} | \mathbf{r}^{(r)\,\mathsf{T}})^\mathsf{T}$, and $(y_{o_1}, y_{o_2})^\mathsf{T} = Z_o\,(\mathbf{w}_\mathbf{o}^\mathsf{T} | \mathbf{r}^{(o)\,\mathsf{T}})^\mathsf{T}$. Capture the relation between polynomials' values and randomizers into a single equation:

$$\begin{pmatrix} y_{l_1} \\ y_{l_2} \\ y_{r_1} \\ y_{r_2} \\ y_{o_1} \\ y_{o_2} \end{pmatrix} = \begin{pmatrix} z^n & z^{n+1} & 0 & 0 & 0 & 0 \\ (\beta z)^n & (\beta z)^{n+1} & 0 & 0 & 0 & 0 \\ 0 & 0 & z^{n+q} & z^{n+q+1} & z^{n+2q} & z^{n+2q+1} \\ 0 & 0 & z^{-n-q} & z^{-n-q-1} & z^{-n-2q} & z^{-n-2q-1} \\ 0 & 0 & 0 & 0 & z^{n+2q} & z^{n+2q+1} \\ 0 & 0 & 0 & 0 & \beta^{n+2q} & \beta^{n+2q+1} \end{pmatrix} \begin{pmatrix} \mathbf{r}^{(l)}_{[0]} \\ \mathbf{r}^{(l)}_{[1]} \\ \mathbf{r}^{(r)}_{[q]} \\ \mathbf{r}^{(r)}_{[q+1]} \\ \mathbf{r}^{(o)}_{[2q]} \\ \mathbf{r}^{(o)}_{[2q+1]} \end{pmatrix} + \mathbf{c} \ , \tag{35}$$

where $\mathbf{c} \in \mathbb{F}^6$ is a constant vector independent of the randomizers.

Let $Z_l^\star, Z_r^\star, Z_o^\star$ be the 2×2 submatrices of Z_l, Z_r, Z_o whose columns are multiplied by $\mathbf{r}^{(l)}_{[0:2]}, \mathbf{r}^{(r)}_{[q:q+2]}$ and $\mathbf{r}^{(o)}_{[2q:2q+2]}$, respectively; or equivalently, the 2×2 submatrices on the diagonal of Eq. 35. If these 2×2 submatrices are all invertible, then $(y_{l_1}, y_{l_2}, y_{r_1}, y_{r_2}, y_{o_1}, y_{o_2})$ are uniform because the randomizers $\mathbf{r}^{(l)}_{[0:q]}$, $\mathbf{r}^{(r)}_{[q:2q]}$, $\mathbf{r}^{(o)}_{[2q:3q]}$ are. So S samples $(y_{l_1}, y_{l_2}, y_{r_1}, y_{r_2}, y_{o_1}, y_{o_2})$ uniformly at random from $\mathbb{F}^6$.

The 2×2 submatrices of $Z_l^\star, Z_r^\star, Z_o^\star$ are not all invertible if $z = 1$, if $\beta = 1$, or if $\beta = z$. The probability of this event is $3/(|\mathbb{F}| - 1)$.

Since we can solve for one of y_h, y_h^* given the other, we only need to show that y_h is uniformly random over $\mathbb{F}$. This is where the convenient arbitrary coefficient $\bar{h}_\mathsf{d}$ of $\bar{h}(X)$ comes into play. This coefficient is chosen uniformly at random, and so S samples $y_h \xleftarrow{\$} \mathbb{F}$. Lastly, S solves Eq. (31) for y_h^*.

To complete the argument, except with a negligible failure probability corresponding to the 2×2 submatrices $Z_l^\star$, $Z_r^\star$, $Z_o^\star$ being singular, S samples a verifier view from a distribution that is identical to the distribution of verifier views of an authentic protocol execution. The distinguishing advantage of any distinguisher D is bounded by the S's failure probability, which is $3/(|\mathbb{F}| - 1)$. This number also bounds the statistical distance in distributions of the view of the verifier of authentic transcripts versus simulated transcripts. □

7 Comparison

7.1 Abstract Comparison

We compare both variants of Claymore to some other Polynomial IOPs from the literature, namely Sonic, PLONK, Marlin, and Aurora. Of these Polynomial IOPs, the first three give rise to SNARKs after cryptographic compilation. In contrast, Aurora gives rise to a proof system generating short proofs but whose verifier complexity is linear in the size of the witness. Importantly, Claymore is comparable to both types of proof system: with preprocessing, it gives rise to a SNARK; when preprocessing is omitted, the proofs remain short at the expense of linear verifier complexity.

Table 1 contains an overview of the comparison. It considers the following key performance indicators for Polynomial IOPs.

- The number of polynomials sent by I during the offline preprocessing phase. This number determines the size of the universal or structured reference strings. While this number contributes to the complexity of I, this complexity is generally speaking not a make or break factor.
- The number of polynomials sent by P during the online proving phase. This number contributes to the size of the proof and to the complexity of both P and V.
- The number of evaluations. This number contributes to the size of the proof, as well as indirectly to the complexity of P and V.

- The number of distinct points for evaluation. Some cryptographic compilers (*e.g.*, [6]) enable the merger of two polynomial evaluations provided that they are being evaluated in the same point. This number limits the number of times this optimization can be applied.
- The maximum degree of all polynomials. This number contributes to indexer and prover complexity in two ways. First, before cryptographic compilation, I and P operate on polynomials of this degree and their complexity is affected accordingly. The exception is if the polynomials are sparse, or otherwise exhibit a structure that enables fast computation. Second, some cryptographic compilers induce overheads that are superlinear in this degree.

Table 1. Comparison between Claymore and other Polynomial IOPs from the literature, with respect to key performance indicators.

	# polynomials offline/online	# evaluations	# distinct points	max. degree
Sonic [11]	$12M/3M+7$	$11M+3$	$9M+2$	$O(n)$
PLONK [8]	8/6	7	2	$12(n+a)$
Marlin [7]	9/12	18	3	$6k+6$
Aurora [4]	–/7	8	2	$\max(m,n)$
DenseClaymore	1/4	10	6	$m(3n+1)-1$
SparseClaymore	8/10	30	10	$3K-1$

For Sonic, n refers to the number of multiplication gates and the degree of the largest polynomial is $7n$. However, due to their technique for simulating bivariate polynomials, the addition gates have fan-in bounded by a parameter M, corresponding to having at most M nonzero elements in every row of the linear transform matrix. The same bound applies to the number of nonzero elements in every column. As a result of converting the original circuit into one with this property, a number of multiplication gates may have to be added, thus explaining the Landau notation.

For PLONK, n refers to the number of multiplication gates and a refers to the number of addition gates, all of which have fan-in 2. We note that there is a variant of PLONK with larger proofs and smaller prover time, which is not shown in the table.

Aurora does not have a preprocessing phase and as a result the verifier's complexity is linear in the number of nonzero elements in the matrices A, B, C from the R1CS tuple. Marlin uses the same mechanics but uses preprocessing to shrink the verifier's workload for the matrix multiplication; this technique requires 9 polynomials in the uniform or structured reference string (3 per matrix) and a few more in the online protocol. The parameter k denotes the largest number of nonzero elements of $\{A, B, C\}$.

For Claymore the linear transform is either represented densely as an $m \times n$ matrix, or sparsely as a list of K nonzero coefficients in this matrix.

Marlin, PLONK, and Aurora work in the Reed-Solomon codeword basis and crucially rely on the structure of the field or of its multiplicative group. In contrast, Sonic and Claymore work for any field.

7.2 Concrete Comparison

To make the comparison more concrete, we compile the various Polynomial IOPs into concrete SNARKs with various compilers. In the following we use P to denote the number of polynomials, Q for the number of queries, U for the number of unique points, $|\mathbb{F}|$ for the size of a field element, and $|\mathbb{G}|$ for the size of a group element.

For the benchmark computation we choose the following: to prove the membership of an element in a set by verifying the Merkle tree authentication path in zero knowledge. The set holds 1024 elements and its Merkle root is known, as is the member element. The witness consists of the element's position in the tree, and the authentication path. The Merkle tree is constructed using the zero-knowledge-proof-friendly Rescue-Prime hash function [12] with $m = 3$ state elements, rate equal to $r = 2$, over a prime field with $p > 2^{256}$ elements, with $N = 18$ rounds, targeting a security level of $\lambda = 128$ bits against collisions.

After arithmetization, this computation can be cast into one of three constraint systems for arithmetic circuits.

- The computation can be represented as a PLONK-relation, in which case there are $a = 13021$ additions, $m = 17101$ multiplications, and 31234 distinct wires in total.
- The computation can be represented as a Hadamard Product Relation (HPR) with $n = 4631$ multiplications and $m = 7571$ linear relations with arbitrary fan-in. After coercing the constraint system to one whose matrix has at most $M = 3$ nonzero elements on every row and on every column, there are $n = 23850$ multiplications and $m = 26790$ linear relations.
- The computation can be represented as a Rank-1 Constraint Satisfaction System (R1CS) with 12202 rank-1 constraints and no more than $k = 38694$ nonzero elements in $\{A, B, C\}$.

The various cryptographic compilers differ in how they simulate evaluation queries. A polynomial oracle $[f(X)]$ is represented by a cryptographic commitment. When V queries it in z and obtains the response y, one option is to simply run the polynomial commitment's evaluation protocol to prove that $f(z) = y$. Another option is for V to use the commitment to $f(X)$ to derive the commitment to $\frac{f(X)-y}{X-z}$, and for P to prove that this polynomial has an appropriately bounded degree. The point is that degree bound checks might be simpler to combine than evaluation queries, depending on the nature of the polynomial commitment.

- KZG polynomial commitments. A commitment to a polynomial $f(X)$ is a single group element. When V queries its value in z, P responds with its value $y = f(z)$ along with another group element, a commitment to $\frac{f(X)-y}{X-z}$. Note that the zerofier $X - z$ must divide $f(X) - f(z)$. One pairing evaluation allows V to verify the correct relation between the received commitments. Evaluation queries in the same point z but to different polynomials can be batched using random weights supplied by V. However, the scheme does not support batching evaluations in distinct points, at least in terms of communication cost. To establish the proper degree bounds, P must supply a commitment to a *degree bound check polynomial* $F(X) = \sum_i \omega^{2i} \cdot f_i(X) + \omega^{2i+1} \cdot X^{\mathsf{d}-\delta(i)} \cdot f_i(X)$ where the sum ranges over all prior polynomials $f_i(X)$, where $\delta(i)$ is its degree bound, and where ω is a random challenge supplied by V. One more batch-evaluation is necessary to establish that the commitment to $F(X)$ is well formed. So the total size of a Polynomial IOP compiled with this KZG-based compiler is
$$(P+1) \times |\mathbb{G}| + (U+1) \times (|\mathbb{F}| + |\mathbb{G}|) \ . \qquad (36)$$
Using the BLS-384 pairing group, we can represent group elements with $|\mathbb{G}| = 385$ bits and scalar field elements with $|\mathbb{F}| = 256$ bits.
- DARK polynomial commitments. Evaluation queries to the same polynomial in distinct points can be batched, and evaluation queries to distinct polynomials in the same point can be batched. Evaluation queries to distinct polynomials in distinct points cannot be batched.[3] We choose to batch all queries into one evaluation proof for each polynomial, as opposed to batching all polynomials for each distinct point. Every evaluation protocol consists of at most $\lfloor \log_2 \mathsf{d} \rfloor$ rounds where d is the global degree bound. In every round except the last, P sends two group elements and at most U field elements, where U is the number of unique evaluation points. In the last round, P sends an integer of $\lfloor \log_2 \mathsf{d} \rfloor \times \lambda + |\mathbb{F}|$ bits. So the total size of a Polynomial IOP proof compiled with this DARK strategy is
$$P \times \lfloor \log_2 \mathsf{d} \rfloor \times (2|\mathbb{G}| + U|\mathbb{F}|) + \lfloor \log_2 \mathsf{d} \rfloor \times \lambda + |\mathbb{F}| \ . \qquad (37)$$
Concretely we use 2000 bit class group elements, so $|\mathbb{G}| = 2000$. The field elements are integers modulo p, a $2\lambda = 256$ bit prime, so $|\mathbb{F}| = \lfloor \log_2 p \rfloor = 256$.
- FRI polynomial commitments. A FRI commitment is a Merkle root of a Reed-Solomon codeword, obtained by evaluating the polynomial in a domain that is ρ times larger than its degree, where ρ is known as the expansion

[3] There is a natural method for this type of batching that relies on dividing out the zerofier. In response to queries z_1 to $[f(X)]$ and z_2 to $[g(X)]$, P supplies $y_1 = f(z_1), y_2 = g(z_2)$ and commitments to the polynomials $\frac{f(X)-y_1}{X-z_1}$ and $\frac{g(X)-y_2}{X-z_2}$. At this point, V can verify that the new commitments are correctly related to the old, and he can use all commitments to derive a new commitment to "zero" polynomial. Precisely speaking, this commitment is to an integer polynomial whose coefficients are multiples of p. Then *one* evaluation protocol suffices to establish that $y_1 = f(z_1)$ and $y_2 = g(z_2)$. This batching method has not been formally analyzed and such an analysis is out of the scope of this paper.

factor. The FRI protocol establishes the bounded degree by opening Merkle leafs. As a result, the technique for dividing out the zerofier applies even without supplying a new commitment. The Reed-Solomon codeword of the polynomial $\frac{f(X)-y}{X-z}$ can be computed given the Reed-Solomon codeword of the polynomial $f(X)$. So every query generates one field element. The FRI protocol is run on the degree bound check polynomial $F(X) = \sum_i \omega^{2i} \cdot f_i(X) + \omega^{2i+1} \cdot X^{\mathsf{d}-\delta(i)} \cdot f_i(X)$ where the sum ranges over all polynomials after dividing out the zerofiers. In this expression, $\delta(i)$ is its updated degree bound, *i.e.*, after dividing out the zerofiers, and ω is a random challenge supplied by V. The evaluations of this degree bound check polynomial on the codeword domain can be computed from evaluations of the constituent polynomials. The FRI protocol consists of $\lfloor \log_2 \mathsf{d} \rfloor$ rounds where d is the global degree bound. In every round, P supplies a new Merkle root along with s field elements and as many authentication paths of length at most $\lfloor \log_2 \rho \cdot \mathsf{d} \rfloor$. The protocol bounds the polynomial's degree with soundness error conjecturally approximately ρ^{-s} when $\mathbb{F}$ is large enough. So the total size of a Polynomial IOP compiled with FRI is less than

$$P \times 2 \cdot \lambda + Q \times |\mathbb{F}| + \lfloor \log_2 \mathsf{d} \rfloor \times s \times (\lfloor \log_2 \rho \cdot \mathsf{d} \rfloor \times 2 \cdot \lambda + |\mathbb{F}|) \ . \quad (38)$$

Concretely, we set $\rho = 16$, $s = 32$, and use $|\mathbb{F}| = 256$. Note that the hash function with which the FRI Merkle trees are built, must have at least $2 \cdot \lambda = 256$ bit outputs.

Table 2 summarizes the results. It shows the size of the SNARK in bytes obtained from the given Polynomial IOP and compiled with the given compiler. The computation whose integrity is proved, is the Merkle tree membership relation described above. The source code for reproducing these numbers is available at https://github.com/aszepieniec/claymore-benchmark.

Table 2. Comparison of concrete SNARK size.

	KZG	DARK	FRI
Sonic $P = 16$, $Q = 36$, $U = 20$, $M = 3$, $\mathsf{d} = 166950$	3 222	388 720	384 640
PLONK $P = 6$, $Q = 7$, $U = 2$, $\mathsf{d} = 361464$	578	61 232	424 352
Marlin $P = 12$, $Q = 18$, $U = 3$, $\mathsf{d} = 232170$	947	121 888	383 936
DenseClaymore $P = 4$, $Q = 10$, $U = 6$, $\mathsf{d} = 105327751$	802	72 416	825 792
SparseClaymore $P = 10$, $Q = 30$, $U = 10$, $\mathsf{d} = 158951$	1 411	139 704	384 256

8 Conclusion

The protocols proposed in this paper challenge the notion that the Reed-Solomon codeword basis is the appropriate basis for representing objects from the arithmetic constraint system in a Polynomial IOP. Instead, the monomial coefficient basis provides a natural and intuitive representation for these objects. In this basis, the native operations on polynomials are identifiable with the matrix operations in the arithmetic constraint system. Moreover, this basis does not impose any restrictions on the structure of the field. The resulting Polynomial IOP for arithmetic constraint systems outperforms similar constructions based on the Reed-Solomon codeword basis, at least as far as the number of polynomials in the transcript is concerned.

The modular approach followed in this paper admits a piece by piece presentation and analysis that benefits simplicity and accessibility. Nevertheless, some optimizations violate the boundaries implicit in this modular structure. These optimizations are of independent interest as they may also apply elsewhere; perhaps they have straightforward analogues in the Reed-Solomon codeword domain. Some of the more important optimizations are summarized as follows.

- In some cases it is possible to eliminate polynomials. In particular, when a polynomial is queried exactly twice and is involved in exactly two polynomial identities. By moving this polynomial to the left hand side, and equating the right hand sides, the polynomial identities are merged and the polynomial in question is eliminated, all without impacting soundness.
- After unrolling a Polynomial IOP, InnerProduct subprotocols appear in great numbers and many places. They can all be batched. In addition to saving polynomials, this batching facilitates a simpler and more direct proof of zero-knowledge that would not be possible otherwise.
- Batching may apply in more places still. For instance, the sparse MVP procedure benefits from two invocations of a subprotocol that establishes that a given vector is a Lagrange vector, and two more that another vector is a Vandermonde vector. The Lagrange and Vandermonde vector protocols can be merged in order to save polynomials. In fact, this merger extends to multivariate polynomials in more than two variables.
- Concatenating the vectors of left and right wires saves one polynomial, but only if the Hadamard subprotocol can be made to work with the concatenated vector. In particular, this adaptation requires shifting the protocol's second and third arguments. Performing this shift in either basis is possible, but this shift highlights an interesting difference. In the Reed-Solomon codeword basis, the query to the polynomial oracle is multiplied by a constant factor; in the monomial coefficient basis, however, it is the response that is multiplied by a factor that depends on the query.

One of the questions that led to the present line of research was to find the Polynomial IOP with the smallest possible number of polynomials in the transcript. In this respect, we report a mitigated success: DenseClaymore has only four polynomials, down 33% from runner-up PLONK; and when restricting to polynomials whose degrees grow linearly with the size of the circuit, then SparseClaymore achieves two polynomials less than Marlin, the only competitor that also admits arbitrary fan-in for linear gates.

However, the concrete comparison shows that we were optimizing the wrong metric. Contrary to our expectation, the number of polynomials in the transcript is *not* the dominant factor of proof size. Indeed, this comparison highlights the importance of balancing a Polynomial IOP's number of polynomials against its other parameters.

Acknowledgements. Both authors are supported by the Nervos Foundation. This work was supported in part by the National Key Research and Development Project 2020YFA0712300.

References

1. Ames, S., Hazay, C., Ishai, Y., Venkitasubramaniam, M.: Ligero: lightweight sublinear arguments without a trusted setup. In: Thuraisingham, B.M., Evans, D., Malkin, T., Xu, D. (eds.) ACM CCS 2017, pp. 2087–2104. ACM (2017). https://doi.org/10.1145/3133956.3134104
2. Bellare, M., Goldreich, O.: On defining proofs of knowledge. In: Brickell, E.F. (ed.) CRYPTO 1992. LNCS, vol. 740, pp. 390–420. Springer, Heidelberg (1993). https://doi.org/10.1007/3-540-48071-4_28
3. Ben-Sasson, E., Bentov, I., Horesh, Y., Riabzev, M.: Scalable zero knowledge with no trusted setup. In: Boldyreva, A., Micciancio, D. (eds.) CRYPTO 2019, Part III. LNCS, vol. 11694, pp. 701–732. Springer, Cham (2019). https://doi.org/10.1007/978-3-030-26954-8_23
4. Ben-Sasson, E., Chiesa, A., Riabzev, M., Spooner, N., Virza, M., Ward, N.P.: Aurora: transparent succinct arguments for R1CS. In: Ishai, Y., Rijmen, V. (eds.) EUROCRYPT 2019, Part I. LNCS, vol. 11476, pp. 103–128. Springer, Cham (2019). https://doi.org/10.1007/978-3-030-17653-2_4
5. Bootle, J., Cerulli, A., Chaidos, P., Groth, J., Petit, C.: Efficient zero-knowledge arguments for arithmetic circuits in the discrete log setting. In: Fischlin, M., Coron, J.-S. (eds.) EUROCRYPT 2016, Part II. LNCS, vol. 9666, pp. 327–357. Springer, Heidelberg (2016). https://doi.org/10.1007/978-3-662-49896-5_12
6. Bünz, B., Fisch, B., Szepieniec, A.: Transparent SNARKs from DARK compilers. In: Canteaut, A., Ishai, Y. (eds.) EUROCRYPT 2020. LNCS, vol. 12105, pp. 677–706. Springer, Cham (2020). https://doi.org/10.1007/978-3-030-45721-1_24
7. Chiesa, A., Hu, Y., Maller, M., Mishra, P., Vesely, N., Ward, N.: Marlin: preprocessing zkSNARKs with universal and updatable SRS. In: Canteaut, A., Ishai, Y. (eds.) EUROCRYPT 2020. LNCS, vol. 12105, pp. 738–768. Springer, Cham (2020). https://doi.org/10.1007/978-3-030-45721-1_26
8. Gabizon, A., Williamson, Z.J., Ciobotaru, O.: PLONK: Permutations over Lagrange-bases for Oecumenical Noninteractive arguments of Knowledge. IACR Cryptology ePrint Archive **2019**, 953 (2019). https://eprint.iacr.org/2019/953
9. Goldwasser, S., Micali, S., Rackoff, C.: The knowledge complexity of interactive proof-systems (extended abstract). In: Sedgewick, R. (ed.) ACM STOC, pp. 291–304. ACM (1985). https://doi.org/10.1145/22145.22178

10. Kate, A., Zaverucha, G.M., Goldberg, I.: Constant-size commitments to polynomials and their applications. In: Abe, M. (ed.) ASIACRYPT 2010. LNCS, vol. 6477, pp. 177–194. Springer, Heidelberg (2010). https://doi.org/10.1007/978-3-642-17373-8_11
11. Maller, M., Bowe, S., Kohlweiss, M., Meiklejohn, S.: Sonic: zero-knowledge SNARKs from linear-size universal and updatable structured reference strings. In: Cavallaro, L., Kinder, J., Wang, X., Katz, J. (eds.) ACM CCS 2019, pp. 2111–2128. ACM (2019). https://eprint.iacr.org/2019/099.pdf
12. Szepieniec, A., Ashur, T., Dhooghe, S.: Rescue-prime: a standard specification (sok). IACR Cryptology ePrint Archive **2020**, 1143 (2020). https://eprint.iacr.org/2020/1143
13. Szepieniec, A., Zhang, Y.: Polynomial IOPs for Linear Algebra Relations. IACR Cryptol. ePrint Arch., 1022 (2020). https://eprint.iacr.org/2020/1022

A Unified Framework for Non-universal SNARKs

Helger Lipmaa(✉)

Simula UiB, Bergen, Norway

Abstract. We propose a general framework for non-universal SNARKs. It contains (1) knowledge-sound and non-black-box any-simulation-extractable (ASE), (2) zero-knowledge and subversion-zero knowledge SNARKs for the well-known QAP, SAP, QSP, and QSP constraint languages that all by design have *relatively* simple security proofs. The knowledge-sound zero-knowledge SNARK is similar to Groth's SNARK from EUROCRYPT 2016, except having fewer trapdoors, while the ASE subversion-zero knowledge SNARK relies on few additional conditions. We prove security in a weaker, more realistic version of the algebraic group model. We characterize SAP, SSP, and QSP in terms of QAP; this allows one to use a SNARK for QAP directly for other languages. Our results allow us to construct a family of SNARKs for different languages and with different security properties following the same proof template. Some of the new SNARKs are more efficient than prior ones. In other cases, the new SNARKs cover gaps in the landscape, e.g., there was no previous ASE or Sub-ZK SNARK for SSP or QSP.

Keywords: NIZK · QAP · QSP · SNARK · SAP · SSP · simulation-extractability · subversion zero-knowledge

1 Introduction

There are many different SNARKs [21–23,30,31,36] that differ in the target language and the security objectives. Common target languages correspond to specific quadratic constraint satisfaction systems, and the choice of language depends on the application. The languages QAP [21] and SAP [23,25] are useful when arguing about arithmetic circuits, while QSP [21,31] and SSP [13] are handy when arguing about Boolean circuits.[1] While QAP, providing efficient reductions to arithmetic circuits, is the most useful language in general applications like cryptocurrencies [8], other languages have their applications. In particular, SSP is widely used in applications where Boolean circuits come naturally like in, say, shuffle arguments, [16].

[1] Within this paper, we *always* (though implicitly, without mentioning it) refer to the "strong" versions of these languages as defined in [21]. First, such versions are most useful and needed in applications. Second, modern SNARKs like [23] and the ones discussed in the current paper are for "strong' variants.' We omit further discussions.

G. Hanaoka et al. (Eds.): PKC 2022, LNCS 13177, pp. 553–583, 2022.
https://doi.org/10.1007/978-3-030-97121-2_20

The choice of security objectives depends on the application. Knowledge-soundness is often sufficient, but simulation-extractability (SE) is needed to get UC-security [12]. On the other hand, not having SE can be beneficial in applications that need malleability. Finally, security properties evolve. Both Sub-ZK (subversion zero-knowledge [1,3,7,17]; the argument stays zero-knowledge even if the CRS is not trusted) and non-black-box SE [25] for SNARKs were defined in 2017, after most of the mentioned zk-SNARKs were proposed. [1,3,17] showed that the most efficient known SNARK by Groth [23] is Sub-ZK.

This has resulted in an era of SNARK proliferation: there exist knowledge-sound SNARKs for the mentioned four languages, *some* of which are Sub-ZK or SE. Groth and Maller [25] proposed a non-black-box strong any-simulation-extractable (SASE) SNARK that is only slightly less efficient than Groth's SNARK [23]. Recall that knowledge-soundness means that a successful prover must know the witness, and SE means that the knowledge-soundness holds even if the prover had access to the simulation oracle, [37]. Dodis *et al.* [15] defined different variants of SE, see Sect. 2 for more information. Intuitively, in an ASE SNARK, one is allowed to maul an argument to a different argument for the same statement, while this is not allowed in a SASE SNARK. (Non-)black-box SE means that a (non-)black-box extractor extracts the witness. Black-box ASE is sufficient to obtain UC security.

However, the Groth-Maller SNARK is for the SAP language [23,25]. Since SAP has an efficient reduction from arithmetic circuits with squaring gates instead of general multiplication gates, the SNARK from [25] works with approximately two times larger circuits than SNARKs for the QAP language. While non-black-box SASE is insufficient to obtain UC security, it is a stronger security notion than knowledge-soundness. In particular, a much simpler transformation suffices to obtain UC security when one starts with non-black-box SE SNARKs [5]. Due to the use of SAP, this transformation is twice as costly as the ones starting from SE SNARKs for QAP. Other known simulation-extractable Sub-ZK SNARKs include [10], which works in the random oracle model, and [4], based on updatable signature schemes.

Recently, [6] showed that Groth's SNARK [23] satisfies the weaker non-black-box any-simulation-property ASE. As argued in [6,29], (black-box or non-black-box) ASE is sufficient in many applications. The only known SE SNARKs are for QAP and SAP, and no previous *efficient* SE or Sub-ZK SNARKs are known for SSP or QSP.

Finally, [1,3] proved the knowledge-soundness of Groth's SNARK in the generic group model (GGM) with hashing. The "with hashing" part means that one allows the adversaries to use (say) elliptic curve hashing to create random group elements without knowing their discrete logarithms. More modern knowledge-soundness (and ASE) proofs of SNARKs are given in the algebraic group model (AGM, [19]). Unfortunately, the AGM proof of Groth's SNARK in [19] does not allow the adversaries to hash. Proving the knowledge-soundness of Groth's SNARK in the AGM "with hashing" seems to be still an open problem.

We aim to consolidate SNARK research by investigating how the choice of security properties and target language influences an argument system's design.

This is important as only a few researchers have in-depth knowledge of *secure* SNARK design. It is easy for even well-established research groups to err in such an endeavor; see, for example, [11,18,20,35] for related cryptanalysis. The resulting complexity can be seen when following through the soundness proofs in say [23,25]. Each existing SNARK has a tailored construction with a tailored security proof in its specific security models, and even verifying all the security proofs for all mentioned SNARKs is probably well beyond the most talented cryptographer's capability.

This brings us to the main goal of this paper:

> *Construct a SNARK framework for a multitude of languages (e.g., QAP, SAP, QSP, and SSP) and satisfying a multitude of security objectives (knowledge-soundness vs. ASE, ZK vs. Sub-ZK) that allows for (1) a (relatively) simple security proof that can be easily modified to cover all the languages and security objectives, and (2) results in ASE and Sub-ZK SNARKs that are almost as efficient as the most efficient known knowledge-sound non-Sub-ZK SNARKs. Additionally, (3) prove their security in a realistic version of AGM "with hashing".*

Our Contributions. We propose a family of $2 \cdot 2 \cdot 4 = 16$ SNARKs that contains both knowledge-sound and ASE, and both ZK and Sub-ZK SNARKs, for all four mentioned languages (QAP, SAP, QSP, SSP). While the derivation of the first two SNARKs (namely, knowledge-sound no-Sub-ZK and its ASE version) is complicated, we obtain the other fourteen SNARKs with minor additional work. Thus, we obtain a framework for efficient random-oracle-less pairing-based SNARKs for both arithmetic and Boolean circuits. Previous knowledge-sound SNARKs for all four languages were each published in a separate paper, with corresponding ASE and Sub-ZK versions being proposed later, if at all.

The new knowledge-sound zk-SNARK $\mathsf{S}_{\mathsf{qap}}$ for QAP is similar to Groth's SNARK [23], except it has only two trapdoors instead of five. We replace 3 trapdoors with a well-chosen power of one trapdoor. After an even more careful choice of the powers, we also achieve CRS-verifiability [1,3] and thus Sub-ZK; otherwise, the Sub-ZK version is precisely the same and thus also as efficient. Unlike Groth, who proposed his SNARK without explaining how he arrived at the construction, we thoroughly motivate each step of it. This enables researchers aiming for a different goal to deviate from the construction at the appropriate point.Importantly, we provide a simpler knowledge-soundness proof.

To prove ASE, we observe that due to the structure of the new SNARKs, an ASE adversary can successfully use at most one simulation query answer in the forgery attempt. We show that if the adversary used one query answer, this was necessarily a SASE and not an ASE attack. The ASE of $\mathsf{S}_{\mathsf{qap}}$ follows. It is non-trivial that one-time ASE suffices. Moreover, unexpectedly, all powers of the trapdoor that result in $\mathsf{S}_{\mathsf{qap}}$ being knowledge-sound result in it also being ASE.

We prove knowledge-soundness and ASE in a more realistic version of the AGM. The knowledge-soundness proof in [23] was given in the generic group model, while [19] provided an AGM proof. However, [19] considers adversaries

Table 1. Efficiency comparison of QAP/SAP/SSP/QSP-based random-oracle-less SNARKs Ψ. m (or $\tilde{m}$) and n (or $\tilde{n}$) denote the number of wires and gates (or constraints) in the solutions. "✓" ("≈") means that the corresponding SNARK (its slight modification) is Sub-ZK, with a citation to the Sub-ZK construction if needed. "$\mathfrak{m}_\iota$" ("$\mathfrak{a}_\iota$") denotes scalar multiplication (addition) in group $\mathbb{G}_\iota$, "$\mathfrak{p}$" denotes pairing, and $\mathfrak{g}_\iota$ denotes the representation length of a $\mathbb{G}_\iota$ element in bits. In the case of $|\mathsf{crs}|$ and P's computation, we omit constant or m_0-dependent addends like $+(m_0+3)\mathfrak{g}_1$. We omit field operations and membership tests since they are dominated by significantly costlier group operations. $\mathsf{S}_{\mathsf{sap}}$, $\mathsf{S}_{\mathsf{ssp}}$, and $\mathsf{S}_{\mathsf{ssp}}$ are described in the full version, [33].

Ψ	security	$\|\mathsf{crs}\|$	P computation	$\|\pi\|$	V computation	Sub-ZK
		QAP-based (arithmetic circuit, with n gates), $\tilde{m}=m$				
[23]	KS/ASE [6]	$(m+2n)\mathfrak{g}_1+n\mathfrak{g}_2$	$(m+3n)\mathfrak{m}_1+n\mathfrak{m}_2$	$2\mathfrak{g}_1+1\mathfrak{g}_2$	$3\mathfrak{p}+m_0\mathfrak{m}_1$	✓ [1,3,17]
$\mathsf{S}_{\mathsf{qap}}$ Sect. 3	ASE	$(m+2n)\mathfrak{g}_1+n\mathfrak{g}_2$	$(m+3n)\mathfrak{m}_1+n\mathfrak{m}_2$	$2\mathfrak{g}_1+1\mathfrak{g}_2$	$3\mathfrak{p}+m_0\mathfrak{m}_1$	✓
	SAP-based (arithmetic circuit, with $\tilde{n}$ squaring gates): $u=v$, $\tilde{n}\approx 2n$, $\tilde{m}\approx 2m$					
[25]	SASE	$(\tilde{m}+2\tilde{n})\mathfrak{g}_1+\tilde{n}\mathfrak{g}_2$	$(\tilde{m}+2\tilde{n})\mathfrak{m}_1+\tilde{n}\mathfrak{m}_2$	$2\mathfrak{g}_1+1\mathfrak{g}_2$	$5\mathfrak{p}+m_0\mathfrak{m}_1$	≈ [26]
$\mathsf{S}_{\mathsf{sap}}$	ASE	$(\tilde{m}+2\tilde{n})\mathfrak{g}_1+\tilde{n}\mathfrak{g}_2$	$(\tilde{m}+2\tilde{n})\mathfrak{m}_1+\tilde{n}\mathfrak{m}_2$	$2\mathfrak{g}_1+1\mathfrak{g}_2$	$3\mathfrak{p}+m_0\mathfrak{m}_1$	✓
		SSP-based (Boolean circuit with n gates): $u=v=w$, $\tilde{n}=m+n$				
[13]	KS	$(m+\tilde{n})\mathfrak{g}_1+\tilde{n}\mathfrak{g}_2$	$2m\mathfrak{a}_1+\tilde{n}\mathfrak{m}_1+m\mathfrak{a}_2$	$3\mathfrak{g}_1+1\mathfrak{g}_2$	$6\mathfrak{p}+m_0\mathfrak{a}_1$	–
$\mathsf{S}_{\mathsf{ssp}}$	ASE	$(m+2\tilde{n})\mathfrak{g}_1+\tilde{n}\mathfrak{g}_2$	$2m\mathfrak{a}_1+\tilde{n}\mathfrak{m}_1+m\mathfrak{a}_2$	$2\mathfrak{g}_1+1\mathfrak{g}_2$	$3\mathfrak{p}+m_0\mathfrak{a}_1$	✓
		QSP-based (Boolean circuit with n gates): $w=0$, $\tilde{n}\approx 14n$ [31]				
[31]	KS	–	–	–	–	–
$\mathsf{S}_{\mathsf{qsp}}$	ASE	$(\tilde{m}+2\tilde{n})\mathfrak{g}_1+\tilde{n}\mathfrak{g}_2$	$4\tilde{m}\mathfrak{a}_1+\tilde{n}\mathfrak{m}_1+\tilde{m}\mathfrak{a}_2$	$2\mathfrak{g}_1+1\mathfrak{g}_2$	$3\mathfrak{p}+m_0\mathfrak{a}_1$	✓

that are purely algebraic and in particular do not have a capability to create random group elements without knowing their discrete logarithms. In our proofs, the adversary has such a capacity. We consider this proof (and the corresponding realistic version of the AGM) to be another major contribution of this paper.

Based on an observation about algebraic relations between the languages, we modify $\mathsf{S}_{\mathsf{qap}}$ to cover SAP, QSP, and SSP. Hence, almost automatically, we obtain a family of knowledge-sound (or ASE), and zero-knowledge (or Sub-ZK) SNARKs for four different languages.

Table 1 compares the efficiency of random-oracle-less SNARKs. It is fair to compare SNARKs for the same language; a comparison of SNARKs for different languages (for example, QAP vs. SAP) has to account for the complexity of the reduction from circuits to these languages. Note that [31] described a reduction from Boolean circuits to QSP and a linear PCP [9] for QSP but did not describe a SNARK. In all constructions, most of the prover's scalar multiplications in Table 1 are multi scalar-multiplications. As seen from the table, the new ASE SNARK for SAP is more efficient than the (SASE) SNARK for SAP by Groth and Maller. No previous SE or Sub-ZK SNARKs were known for SSP or QSP, and Groth's SNARK for QAP was only proven to be ASE in [6].

1.1 Technical Overview

In Sect. 3, we propose a knowledge-sound zk-SNARK $\mathsf{S}_{\mathsf{qap}}$ for QAP. The argument consists of evaluations[2] $[A(x,y)]_1, [B(x,y)]_2, [C_s(x,y)]_1$ of three bivariate polynomials $A(X,Y), B(X,Y), C_s(X,Y)$ at a random point (x,y). Here, $[A(x,y)]_1, [B(x,y)]_2$ commit to the vector of left and right inputs to all gates, while $[C_s(x,y)]_1$ combines a commitment to the vector of all output wires with the rest of the argument. The verifier checks that a bivariate polynomial $\mathcal{V}$, that depends in a known way on A, B, C_s, evaluates to 0 at the same point.

As in [23], we aim to make $[C_s(x,y)]_1$ to be computable only by the honest prover. The prover has access to the CRS that contains the evaluation of well-chosen polynomials at (x,y) in both $\mathbb{G}_1$ and $\mathbb{G}_2$. We optimize to get an efficient SNARK while not sacrificing (much) in the knowledge-soundness proof's simplicity. $\mathsf{S}_{\mathsf{qap}}$ is very similar to Groth's SNARK [23]; however, it uses only two trapdoors instead of five. This distinction is important: in [23], only two out of five trapdoors are used in simulation; thus, the other three trapdoors seem not to be needed. In general, it is important to minimize the number of components to the bare minimum so that the importance of each component is well understood. In $\mathsf{S}_{\mathsf{qap}}$, we use well-chosen powers of one trapdoor y as substitutes for four out of the five trapdoors of Groth's SNARK. (A similar technique to use one trapdoor to align "interesting" monomials together was used, e.g., in [24].)

Knowledge-Soundness Proof And A More Realistic Variant of The AGM. The knowledge-soundness proof is in the algebraic group model (AGM [19]). In the AGM, one considers algebraic adversaries that always know a linear relationship between their output and input group elements. As an important difference with the AGM of [19], we additionally allow the cheating prover to sample random elements of $\mathbb{G}_1$ and $\mathbb{G}_2$. Such an extension of the generic group model is well-known, [1,3,7], but not established in the case of the AGM. It is also well understood why this extension is needed since otherwise, one can prove the security of false knowledge assumptions. Really, without this extension, one can prove that if an adversary on input $[1]_1$ outputs $[y]_1$, it must know y. This assumption does not hold since it is easy to generate random group elements by using hash-then-increment or elliptic curve hashing.

Fuchsbauer *et al.* [19] give an adversary $\mathcal{A}$ access to a programmable random oracle [34] $\mathcal{O}$. $\mathcal{A}$ can create a random group element by querying $\mathcal{O}$ that returns a uniformly random group element. In the security proof, one allows the reduction to program $\mathcal{O}$ by creating random group elements together with their discrete logarithms. Unfortunately, since the reduction knows the discrete logarithms, also in this model, one can prove the security of the above false knowledge assumption. We overcome this issue by using a different oracle simulation strategy by defining two adversaries (one for each trapdoor x and y) and by using two different oracle programming strategies. This results in the first known

---

[2] We use the by now standard additive bracket notation for group elements, by fixing first a bilinear group $\mathsf{p} = (\mathbb{G}_1, \mathbb{G}_2, \mathbb{G}_T, \hat{e})$, and then denoting say $[a]_\iota = aP_\iota \in \mathbb{G}_\iota$ for a fixed generator $P_\iota \in \mathbb{G}_\iota$. See Sect. 2 for more information.

knowledge-soundness and ASE proof of (a version) of Groth's SNARK [23] in a variant of the AGM with hashing where false knowledge assumptions like the above cannot be proven. This result is of independent importance.

Choosing Powers of y. The way we choose the powers of y is interesting by itself. In the security proof, A, B, C_s are chosen maliciously and depend on additional indeterminates. Let Y be an indeterminate corresponding to y and $\boldsymbol{X}^*$ be the vector of all indeterminates, *except* Y, in the knowledge-soundness or ASE proof. $\boldsymbol{X}^*$ includes X (the indeterminate corresponding to x), indeterminates *created when the adversary samples* random group elements, and (in the case of ASE) indeterminates created by simulator queries. Since the adversary is algebraic, the polynomials $A(X)$, $B(X)$, and $C_s(X)$ belong to the span of the polynomials in the CRS, the random oracle answers, and (in the case of the ASE) the simulator answers. We use the AGM extractor to extract their maliciously chosen coefficients in this span, allowing us to recover the coefficients of the (Laurent) polynomial $\mathcal{V}$. The verification guarantees that $\mathcal{V}(\boldsymbol{x}^*, y) = 0$, where the trapdoor $\boldsymbol{x}^*$ instantiates the indeterminate $\boldsymbol{X}^*$.

The knowledge-soundness proof considers two cases, when $\mathcal{V}(\boldsymbol{X}^*, Y) = 0$ and $\mathcal{V}(\boldsymbol{X}^*, Y) \neq 0$ as a polynomial. Consider the first case. Then, $\mathcal{V}(\boldsymbol{X}^*, Y) = \sum \mathcal{V}_{Y^i}(\boldsymbol{X}^*)Y^i$ for known polynomials $\mathcal{V}_{Y^i}(\boldsymbol{X}^*)$, where i is a linear combination of the coefficients of a public but initially undetermined integer tuple $\boldsymbol{\Delta} = (\alpha, \beta, \gamma, \delta, \eta)$. We prove that an algebraic prover is honest iff $\mathcal{V}_{Y^i}(\boldsymbol{X}^*) = 0$ for six *critical values* i. (In Groth's security proof, the number of critical values is significantly larger.) We choose $\boldsymbol{\Delta}$ so that the corresponding six critical values i are distinct from each other and all other non-critical values j; in this case, we say that $\boldsymbol{\Delta}$ is *soundness-friendly*. Moreover, we choose $\boldsymbol{\Delta}$ so that the SNARK is relatively efficient. For example, we require that for all critical i, $|i|$ is as small as possible, and check if there is a way to make some non-critical values j to coincide (this can shorten the CRS).

Finding a suitable $\boldsymbol{\Delta}$, satisfying all the restrictions, is a moderately complex optimization problem. In particular, the number of non-zero coefficients of $\mathcal{V}_{Y^i}(\boldsymbol{X}^*)$ (even in the knowledge-soundness proof and without allowing the adversary to create new indeterminates) is at least 30, depending on the SNARK. Because of the complexity of the problem, we used an exhaustive computer search to find $\boldsymbol{\Delta}$. Due to the use of exhaustive search, exponents in the resulting SNARKs (see Eq. (11) for a recommended value of $\boldsymbol{\Delta}$ and Eq. (12) for the description of the CRS when using this value of $\boldsymbol{\Delta}$) may look somewhat obscure. However, the soundness-friendliness of the results of the exhaustive search are easy to verify manually (intuitively, this corresponds to checking that when $\boldsymbol{\Delta}$ is instantiated as in Eq. (11), then the critical six entries in Eq. (10) are different from each other and all other entries). It is easy to find suboptimal choices of the exponents; however, such choices will usually not be sufficient for Sub-ZK. We feel that using exhaustive search adds to the strength of this paper.

Other Results. In Sect. 4, we prove that $\mathsf{S}_{\mathsf{qap}}$ is ASE. We use the same proof strategy as in the case of knowledge-soundness. By analyzing the coefficients of

$\mathcal{V}$, we get that the ASE adversary can use the result of at most one simulation query in the forgery attempt. If she used none, ASE follows from the knowledge-soundness. If she used one, then, due to an easily satisfiable additional requirement on the QAP instance, she was performing a SASE attack that is not an attack in the sense of ASE. For this proof to work, one needs $\boldsymbol{\Delta}$ to satisfy additional restrictions on $\boldsymbol{\Delta}$; however, we will show that any soundness-friendly $\boldsymbol{\Delta}$ satisfies these requirements. Thus, *any* version of $\mathsf{S}_{\mathsf{qap}}$ that is knowledge-sound is ASE, modulo a small, easily satisfiable, technical restriction.

As we mentioned before, $\mathsf{S}_{\mathsf{qap}}$ is very similar to Groth's SNARK. Groth proved knowledge-soundness in the case of symmetric pairings, and this implies knowledge-soundness in the case of asymmetric pairing. Asymmetric pairings are much more efficient than symmetric pairings and thus strongly preferred in practice. We obtain a simpler direct knowledge-soundness proof by explicitly assuming that the pairing is asymmetric. One corollary of our knowledge-sound proof is the up to our knowledge novel observation that Groth's SNARK has a simple knowledge-soundness proof given that one uses asymmetric pairings. *Having simpler (or alternative) security proofs is important by itself due to the easier verifiability; simpler proofs can also result in the construction of other protocols.* We also use a more realistic variant of the AGM to prove knowledge-soundness. (The use of this variant of the AGM makes the security proof somewhat more complex again.) Moreover, we emphasize that the number of critical values i is much larger when one follows Groth's original proof.

Our goal was *not* to duplicate Groth's SNARK but to construct an efficient SNARK with a simple knowledge-soundness proof. Our exposition of the derivation of $\mathsf{S}_{\mathsf{qap}}$ can also be seen as an intuitive pedagogical re-derivation of (a slight variant of) the most efficient existing pairing-based SNARK.

We make $\mathsf{S}_{\mathsf{qap}}$ subversion-zero knowledge (Sub-ZK). According to the template of [1,3], we construct a public CRS verification algorithm that checks that the CRS corresponds to *some* trapdoor, and then use a knowledge assumption to recover the trapdoor and simulate the argument. For the CRS-verifiability, we restrict the choice of $\boldsymbol{\Delta}$ even more. This suffices: all new SNARKs are Sub-ZK when choosing $\boldsymbol{\Delta}$ carefully. We then use the standard BDH-KE [1,3] knowledge assumption to recover the trapdoor and simulate the argument.

	U	V	W
QAP			
SAP		$=U$	
SSP		$=U$	$=U$
QSP			$=0$

Fig. 1. Algebraic relations between languages.

In the full version [33], we consider the languages SAP [23,25], SSP [13], and QSP [21,31]. We explain their algebraic relation to QAP, and use it to lift $\mathsf{S}_{\mathsf{qap}}$ to the setting of the corresponding languages. In the case of SSP and QSP, the algebraic relation is not obvious; we explain it in detail in the full version [33]. See Fig. 1 for a brief summary. This summary becomes clear later (e.g., QAP states that $U\mathbb{z} \circ V\mathbb{z} = W\mathbb{z}$ for an input-witness vector $\mathbb{z}$, while SAP states that $U\mathbb{z} \circ U\mathbb{z} = W\mathbb{z}$ since $U = V$; here, U, V, and W are relation-dependent matrices that characterize the languages as constraint satisfaction problems), but we decided to have it here for an early reference.[3]

Our SNARK for SAP (and SSP) has a slightly different ASE proof compared to the SNARK for QAP. Previous research handled all four languages separately, and our (simple) relations seem to be novel in the case of SSP and QSP. We propose the first known either Sub-ZK or ASE SNARKs for SSP and QSP, and more generally, for Boolean circuits. Importantly, the new Sub-ZK ASE SNARK for SSP is more efficient than the knowledge-sound non-Sub-ZK SNARK of [13].

This work supersedes [32]. While the idea of using only two trapdoors is already present in [32], there are too many changes to enlist.

1.2 Further Work

Applications. We concentrate on the construction of the SNARKs themselves and leave possible applications for future work. The most evident efficiency benefit is in the case of the SSP, where the verifier computes only 3 pairings instead of 6 in [13]. This may result in more efficient shuffle arguments [16] that rely on SNARKs for SSP. The ASE and Sub-ZK properties of the new SNARKs, on the other hand, have the potential to guarantee the same properties in similar applications. For example, given the new ASE SNARK for SSP, it may be possible (but we leave it to future work) to construct an ASE shuffle argument.

Universal SNARKs. There is an even more significant SNARK proliferation when one also considers universal SNARKs. Within this paper, we only study SNARKs with circuit-dependent CRSs. Universal SNARKs deserve their own several papers, especially since much less is known in that scenario. (E.g., efficient SE universal SNARKs have only been proposed in a recent eprint [28].) However, some of the results of the current paper (like the relation between QAP, SAP, SSP, and QSP) are also interesting in the context of universal SNARKs. We are not aware, e.g., of any *efficient* universal SNARKs for SSP.

2 Preliminaries

For a matrix $\boldsymbol{A}$, $\boldsymbol{A}_i$ denotes its ith row and $\boldsymbol{A}^{(j)}$ denotes its jth column. Let $\mathrm{vect}(\boldsymbol{A})$ be the vectorization of matrix $\boldsymbol{A} \in \mathbb{Z}_p^{n \times m}$, $\mathrm{vect}(\boldsymbol{A}) = (A_{11}, A_{12}, \ldots, A_{1m}, A_{21}, \ldots, A_{nm})$. $\mathbb{Z}_p^{(\leq d)}[X]$ denotes the set of univariate polynomials of degree $\leq d$ over $\mathbb{Z}_p$. PPT denotes probabilistic polynomial-time; $\lambda \in \mathbb{N}$ is the security parameter. Let $\mathsf{negl}(\lambda)$ be an arbitrary negligible function, and $\mathsf{poly}(\lambda)$ be an arbitrary polynomial function. We write $i \approx_\lambda j$ if $|i - j| \leq \mathsf{negl}(\lambda)$. For an algorithm $\mathcal{A}$, $\mathrm{im}(\mathcal{A})$ is the image of $\mathcal{A}$, that is, the set of valid outputs of $\mathcal{A}$. $\mathsf{RND}_\lambda(\mathcal{A})$ denotes the random tape of $\mathcal{A}$ (for given λ), and $r \leftarrow\$ \mathsf{RND}_\lambda(\mathcal{A})$ denotes the uniformly random choice of r from $\mathsf{RND}_\lambda(\mathcal{A})$. By $y \leftarrow \mathcal{A}(\mathbb{x}; r)$ we denote the fact that $\mathcal{A}$, given an input $\mathbb{x}$ and a randomizer r, outputs y.

[3] Our definitions of SSP and QSP are very slight variations of the standard SSP and QSP. They are functionally equivalent but, to our mind, slightly more elegant. See the full version [33] for more discussion.

Assume n is a power of two. Let ω be the nth primitive root of unity modulo p. (ω exists, given that $n \mid (p-1)$.) Then, $Z(X) := \prod_{i=1}^{n}(X - \omega^{i-1})$ is the unique degree n monic polynomial such that $Z(\omega^{i-1}) = 0$ for all $i \in [1, n]$. For $i \in [1, n]$, let $\ell_i(X)$ be the *ith Lagrange polynomial*, the unique degree $n-1$ polynomial such that $\ell_i(\omega^{i-1}) = 1$ and $\ell_i(\omega^{j-1}) = 0$ for $i \neq j$. Given $\chi \in \mathbb{Z}_p$, $\ell_i(\chi)$ for $i \in [1, n]$ can be computed efficiently. Clearly, $L_{\boldsymbol{k}}(X) := \sum_{i=1}^{n} k_i \ell_i(X)$ is the interpolating polynomial of $\boldsymbol{k}$ at points ω^{i-1}, with $L_{\boldsymbol{k}}(\omega^{i-1}) = k_i$.

Bilinear Groups. Let $n \in \mathbb{N}_{>0}$ be an upper bound of the size of a circuit in the SNARKs. A bilinear group generator $\mathsf{Pgen}(1^\lambda, n)$ returns $(p, \mathbb{G}_1, \mathbb{G}_2, \mathbb{G}_T, \hat{e})$, where $\mathbb{G}_1$, $\mathbb{G}_2$, and $\mathbb{G}_T$ are three additive cyclic groups of prime order p, and $\hat{e} : \mathbb{G}_1 \times \mathbb{G}_2 \to \mathbb{G}_T$ is a non-degenerate efficiently computable bilinear pairing. Assume $n \mid (p-1)$. As in say [7], we assume that Pgen is deterministic and cannot be subverted. (In practice, one can use a standardized curve.) We require the bilinear pairing to be Type-3; that is, there is no efficient isomorphism between $\mathbb{G}_1$ and $\mathbb{G}_2$. We use the standard bracket notation, writing $[c]_\iota$ to denote cP_ι where P_ι is a fixed generator of $\mathbb{G}_\iota$. Note that P_ι is not given in p. We denote $\hat{e}([a]_1, [b]_2)$ by $[a]_1 \bullet [b]_2$. We use freely the bracket notation together with matrix notation, for example, $\boldsymbol{AB} = \boldsymbol{C}$ iff $[\boldsymbol{A}]_1 \bullet [\boldsymbol{B}]_2 = [\boldsymbol{C}]_T$.

Assumptions. Let $\mathcal{T}_1, \mathcal{T}_2$ be sets of small integers. Pgen is $(\mathcal{T}_1, \mathcal{T}_2)$-*PDL (Power Discrete Logarithm) secure* if for any non-uniform PPT adversary $\mathcal{A}$,

$$\Pr[\mathsf{p} \leftarrow \mathsf{Pgen}(1^\lambda, n), x \leftarrow\$ \mathbb{Z}_p^* : \mathcal{A}(\mathsf{p}; [x^i : i \in \mathcal{T}_1]_1, [x^i : i \in \mathcal{T}_2]_2) = x] \approx_\lambda 0 .$$

If $\mathcal{T}_1 = [0, n]$, then we talk about the $(n, \mathcal{T}_2)$-PDL assumption. The case $\mathcal{T}_2 = [0, n]$ is dual.

The BDH-KE assumption [1,3] holds for Pgen, if for every PPT adversary $\mathcal{A}$, there exists a PPT extractor $\mathsf{Ext}_{\mathcal{A}}$, such that

$$\Pr\left[\begin{matrix} \mathsf{p} \leftarrow \mathsf{Pgen}(1^\lambda); r \leftarrow \mathsf{RND}_\lambda(\mathcal{A}); ([y]_1, [z]_2) \leftarrow \mathcal{A}(\mathsf{p}; r); \\ y^* \leftarrow \mathsf{Ext}_{\mathcal{A}}(\mathsf{p}; r) : y = z \wedge y^* \neq y \end{matrix}\right] = \mathsf{negl}(\lambda) .$$

BDH-KE is one of the weakest known knowledge assumptions in the asymmetric pairing-based setting.

Algebraic Group Model (AGM). AGM is a new idealized model [19] used to prove the security of a cryptographic assumption, protocol, or a primitive. In addition, [19] proposed to combine the random oracle (RO) model with the AGM, allowing the adversary to create random group elements. Essentially, in the AGM with random oracles, one assumes that each PPT algorithm $\mathcal{A}$ is algebraic in the following sense. Assume $\mathcal{A}$'s input includes $[\boldsymbol{x}_\iota]_\iota$ and no other elements from the group $\mathbb{G}_\iota$. Moreover, $\mathcal{A}$ has an access to random oracles $\mathcal{O}_\iota$, $\iota \in \{1, 2\}$, such that $\mathcal{O}_\iota$ samples and outputs a random element $[q_{\iota k}]_\iota$ from $\mathbb{G}_\iota$. The oracle access models the ability of $\mathcal{A}$ to create random group elements without knowing their discrete logarithms $q_{\iota k}$. However, a reduction can program [34] the random oracle so that it knows $q_{\iota k}$. Intuitively, one assumes that if $\mathcal{A}$ outputs group elements $[\boldsymbol{y}_\iota]_\iota$, then $\mathcal{A}$ knows matrices $\boldsymbol{N}_\iota$ and $([\boldsymbol{q}_1, \boldsymbol{q}_2]_1)$, such that $\boldsymbol{y}_\iota = \boldsymbol{N}_\iota \binom{\boldsymbol{x}_\iota}{\boldsymbol{q}_\iota}$ while the reduction also knows $\boldsymbol{q}_\iota$.

Formally, a PPT algorithm $\mathcal{A}$ is *(*Pgen*-)algebraic* if there exists an efficient extractor $\mathsf{Ext}_\mathcal{A}$, such that for any PPT-sampleable distribution family $\mathcal{D} = (\mathcal{D}_\mathsf{p})_{\mathsf{p} \in \mathsf{Pgen}(1^\lambda)}$, $\mathsf{Adv}^{\mathrm{agm}}_{\mathsf{Pgen},\mathcal{D},\mathcal{A},\mathsf{Ext}_\mathcal{A}}(\lambda) :=$

$$\Pr\left[\begin{array}{l}\mathsf{p} \leftarrow\$\, \mathsf{Pgen}(1^\lambda); \mathbb{x} = ([\boldsymbol{x}_1]_1, [\boldsymbol{x}_2]_2) \leftarrow\$\, \mathcal{D}_\mathsf{p}; r \leftarrow\$\, \mathsf{RND}_\lambda(\mathcal{A});\\ ([\boldsymbol{y}_1]_1, [\boldsymbol{y}_2]_2) \leftarrow\$\, \mathcal{A}^{(\mathcal{O}_1, \mathcal{O}_2)}(\mathbb{x}; r); (\boldsymbol{N}_1, \boldsymbol{N}_2) \leftarrow \mathsf{Ext}_\mathcal{A}(\mathbb{x}; r) :\\ (\boldsymbol{y}_1 \neq \boldsymbol{N}_1 \binom{\boldsymbol{x}_1}{\boldsymbol{q}_1} \vee \boldsymbol{y}_2 \neq \boldsymbol{N}_2 \binom{\boldsymbol{x}_2}{\boldsymbol{q}_2})\end{array}\right] = \mathsf{negl}(\lambda) \ .$$

$\mathcal{O}_\iota$, $\iota \in \{1, 2\}$ is an oracle that samples and returns a random element from $\mathbb{G}_\iota$. $[\boldsymbol{q}_\iota]_\iota$ is the list of all elements output by $\mathcal{O}_\iota$. We denote the version of the AGM where the reduction can program $\mathcal{O}_\iota$, by first sampling a random element $q_{\iota k}$ from $\mathbb{Z}_p$ and then returning $\boldsymbol{q}_{\iota k}$, as $\mathrm{RO}_{\mathsf{fkl}}$-AGM. The $\mathrm{RO}_{\mathsf{fkl}}$-AGM states that, given such programmable random oracles, $\mathsf{Adv}^{\mathrm{agm}}_{\mathsf{Pgen},\mathcal{D},\mathcal{A},\mathsf{Ext}_\mathcal{A}}(\lambda) = \mathsf{negl}(\lambda)$ for any PPT-sampleable $\mathcal{D}$ and PPT algebraic $\mathcal{A}$.

SNARKs. Let RG be a relation generator, such that $\mathsf{RG}(1^\lambda)$ returns a polynomial-time decidable binary relation $\mathbf{R} = \{(\mathbb{x}, \mathbb{w})\}$ together with auxiliary information p. Here, $\mathbb{x}$ is a statement, and $\mathbb{w}$ is a witness. We assume that λ is explicitly deductible from the description of $\mathbf{R}$. Intuitively, $(\mathsf{p}, \mathbf{R})$ is the common auxiliary input to the honest parties, the adversary, and the corresponding extractor. We assume that $\mathsf{p} \leftarrow \mathsf{Pgen}(1^\lambda, n)$ for a well-defined n. (Recall that the choice of p and thus of the groups $\mathbb{G}_\iota$ depends on n and that p is not subvertible.) Let $\mathcal{L}_\mathbf{R} = \{\mathbb{x} : \exists \mathbb{w} \text{ such that } (\mathbb{x}, \mathbb{w}) \in \mathbf{R}\}$ be an NP-language.

A *non-interactive zero-knowledge (NIZK) argument system* Ψ for RG consists of five PPT algorithms: First, a probabilistic CRS generator G that, given $(\mathsf{p}, \mathbf{R}) \in \mathrm{im}(\mathsf{RG}(1^\lambda))$, outputs $(\mathsf{crs}, \mathsf{td})$ where crs is a CRS and td is a simulation trapdoor. Otherwise, it outputs a special symbol $\perp$. For the sake of efficiency and readability, we divide crs into crs_P (the part needed by the prover) and crs_V (the part needed by the verifier). Within this paper, crs explicitly encodes $\mathbf{R}$. We also implicitly assume that crs encodes p. Second, a probabilistic CRS verifier CV that, given crs, returns either 0 (the CRS is malformed) or 1 (the CRS is well-formed). CV is only required to exist in the case of Sub-ZK argument systems. Third, a probabilistic prover P that, given $(\mathsf{crs}_\mathsf{P}, \mathbb{x}, \mathbb{w})$ for $(\mathbb{x}, \mathbb{w}) \in \mathbf{R}$, outputs an argument π. Otherwise, it outputs $\perp$. Fourth, a probabilistic verifier V that, given $(\mathsf{crs}_\mathsf{V}, \mathbb{x}, \pi)$, returns either 0 (reject) or 1 (accept). Fifth, a probabilistic simulator Sim that, given $(\mathsf{crs}, \mathsf{td}, \mathbb{x})$, outputs an argument π.

A NIZK argument system must be complete (an honest verifier accepts an honest verifier), knowledge-sound (if a prover makes an honest verifier accept, then one can extract from the prover a witness $\mathbb{w}$), and zero-knowledge (there exists a simulator that, knowing the CRS trapdoor but not the witness, can produce accepting statements with the verifier's view being indistinguishable from the view when interacting with an honest prover). A Sub-ZK argument system [1,3] must additionally satisfy Sub-ZK (zero-knowledge holds even if the CRS is maliciously generated); for this, one requires CRS-verifiability (CV only accepts a CRS if there exists a trapdoor td corresponding to it).

We will now give the formal definitions. Let Ψ be a non-interactive argument. Ψ is *perfectly complete for* RG, if for all λ, $(\mathsf{p}, \mathbf{R}) \in \mathrm{im}(\mathsf{RG}(1^\lambda))$, and $(\mathbb{x}, \mathbb{w}) \in \mathbf{R}$,

$$\Pr\left[(\mathsf{crs}, \mathsf{td}) \leftarrow \mathsf{G}(\mathsf{p}, \mathbf{R}) : \mathsf{V}(\mathsf{crs}_\mathsf{V}, \mathbb{x}, \mathsf{P}(\mathsf{crs}_\mathsf{P}, \mathbb{x}, \mathbb{w})) = 1\right] = 1 \ .$$

Ψ is computationally (adaptively) *knowledge-sound for* RG, if for every PPT $\mathcal{A}$, there exists a PPT extractor $\mathsf{Ext}_\mathcal{A}$, such that for all λ,

$$\Pr\left[\begin{matrix}(\mathsf{p}, \mathbf{R}) \leftarrow \mathsf{RG}(1^\lambda); (\mathsf{crs}, \mathsf{td}) \leftarrow \mathsf{G}(\mathsf{p}, \mathbf{R}); r \leftarrow\$ \mathsf{RND}_\lambda(\mathcal{A}); \\ (\mathbb{x}, \pi) \leftarrow \mathcal{A}(\mathsf{crs}; r); \mathbb{w} \leftarrow \mathsf{Ext}_\mathcal{A}(\mathsf{crs}; r) : (\mathbb{x}, \mathbb{w}) \notin \mathbf{R} \wedge \mathsf{V}(\mathsf{crs}_\mathsf{V}, \mathbb{x}, \pi) = 1\end{matrix}\right] \approx_\lambda 0 \ .$$

A knowledge-sound argument system is called an *argument of knowledge.*

Ψ is *statistically composable zero-knowledge for* RG, if for all λ, $(\mathsf{p}, \mathbf{R}) \in \mathrm{im}(\mathsf{RG}(1^\lambda))$, and computationally unbounded $\mathcal{A}$, $\varepsilon_0^{zk} \approx_\lambda \varepsilon_1^{zk}$, where

$$\varepsilon_b^{zk} := \Pr\left[\begin{matrix}(\mathsf{crs}, \mathsf{td}) \leftarrow \mathsf{KGen}(\mathsf{p}, \mathbf{R}), (\mathbb{x}, \mathbb{w}) \leftarrow \mathcal{A}(\mathsf{crs}, \mathsf{td}); \pi_0 \leftarrow \mathsf{P}(\mathsf{crs}_\mathsf{P}, \mathbb{x}, \mathbb{w}); \\ \pi_1 \leftarrow \mathsf{Sim}(\mathsf{crs}, \mathsf{td}, \mathbb{x}) : (\mathbb{x}, \mathbb{w}) \in \mathbf{R} \wedge \mathcal{A}(\pi_b) = 1\end{matrix}\right] \ .$$

Ψ is *perfectly composable Sub-ZK for* RG if one requires that $\varepsilon_0^{zk} = \varepsilon_1^{zk}$.

Ψ is *statistically composable Sub-ZK for* RG, if for any PPT subverter $\mathcal{S}$ there exists a PPT $\mathsf{Ext}_\mathcal{S}$, such that for all λ, all $(\mathsf{p}, \mathbf{R}) \in \mathrm{im}(\mathsf{RG}(1^\lambda))$, and all computationally unbounded $\mathcal{A}$, $\varepsilon_0^{zk} \approx_\lambda \varepsilon_1^{zk}$, where

$$\varepsilon_b^{zk} := \Pr\left[\begin{matrix}r \leftarrow\$ \mathsf{RND}_\lambda(\mathcal{S}); (\mathsf{crs}, z_\mathcal{S}) \leftarrow \mathcal{S}(\mathsf{p}, \mathbf{R}; r); \mathsf{td} \leftarrow \mathsf{Ext}_\mathcal{S}(\mathsf{p}, \mathbf{R}; r); \\ (\mathbb{x}, \mathbb{w}) \leftarrow \mathcal{A}(\mathsf{crs}, z_\mathcal{S}); \pi_0 \leftarrow \mathsf{P}(\mathsf{crs}_\mathsf{P}, \mathbb{x}, \mathbb{w}); \pi_1 \leftarrow \mathsf{Sim}(\mathsf{crs}, \mathsf{td}, \mathbb{x}); \\ (\mathbb{x}, \mathbb{w}) \in \mathbf{R} \wedge \mathsf{CV}(\mathsf{crs}) = 1 \wedge \mathcal{A}(\pi_b) = 1\end{matrix}\right] \ .$$

Ψ is *perfectly composable Sub-ZK for* RG if one requires that $\varepsilon_0^{zk} = \varepsilon_1^{zk}$.

A *SNARK (succinct non-interactive argument of knowledge)* is a NIZK argument system where the argument is sublinear in the input size.

Simulation-Extractability (SE). An SE argument system [14,37] stays knowledge-sound even if the soundness adversary has access to the simulation oracle. SE is motivated by applications like non-malleability and UC security.

Dodis *et al.* [15] differentiated between several favors of SE. In the case of any-simulation-extractability (ASE), the simulator can be queried with any (potentially false) statements while in the case of true-simulation-extractability (TSE), the simulator can only be queried with true statements. The adversary wins if she can come up with a new argument for a statement she has not queried a simulation for. In the case of strong any-simulation-extractability (SASE), the adversary wins even if she can come up with a new argument for a statement she has queried a simulation for. ASE suffices for UC security.

$\text{MAIN } \mathbf{Exp}^{\boxed{\mathsf{s}}\mathsf{ase}}_{\Psi,\mathcal{A},\mathsf{Ext}_\mathcal{A}}(\lambda)$

$\mathcal{Q} \leftarrow \emptyset; (\mathsf{p}, \mathbf{R}) \leftarrow \mathsf{RG}(1^\lambda); (\mathsf{crs}, \mathsf{td}) \leftarrow \mathsf{G}(\mathsf{p}, \mathbf{R});$
$r \leftarrow \mathsf{RND}_\lambda(\mathcal{A}); (\mathbb{x}, \pi) \leftarrow \mathcal{A}^{\mathsf{Sim}^{\boxed{\mathsf{s}}\mathsf{ase}}_{\mathsf{crs},\mathsf{td}}}(\mathsf{crs}; r); \mathbb{w} \leftarrow \mathsf{Ext}_\mathcal{A}(\mathsf{crs}; r);$
if $\mathsf{V}(\mathsf{crs}_\mathsf{V}, \mathbb{x}, \pi) = 1 \wedge (\mathbb{x}\boxed{, \pi}) \notin \mathcal{Q} \wedge (\mathbb{x}, \mathbb{w}) \notin \mathbf{R}$
then return 1; **else return** 0; **fi**

$\mathsf{Sim}^{\boxed{\mathsf{s}}\mathsf{ase}}_{\mathsf{crs},\mathsf{td}}(\mathbb{x}_j)$

$\pi_j \leftarrow \mathsf{Sim}(\mathsf{crs}, \mathsf{td}, \mathbb{x}_j); \mathcal{Q} \leftarrow \mathcal{Q} \cup \{(\mathbb{x}_j\boxed{, \pi_j})\};$ **return** π_j;

Fig. 2. Any-simulation (ASE) and strong any-simulation (SASE) experiments. The $\boxed{\textit{boxed}}$ part is only present in the boxed (i.e., SASE) experiment.

Groth and Maller [25] define SE SNARKs, where one requires that for each PPT knowledge-soundness adversary $\mathcal{A}$ with oracle access to the simulator, there exists a non-black-box extractor $\mathsf{Ext}_\mathcal{A}$ that can extract the witness. [25]'s definition of SE corresponds to *non-black-box SASE*, [15]. We assume implicitly SE means non-black-box SE. [25] proved that the argument of any (non-black-box) SASE SNARK consists of at least three group elements and that there should be at least two verification equations. They proposed a SASE SNARK for the SAP (Square Arithmetic Program) language that meets the lower bounds.

The following definition of the SASE property corresponds to the definition of SE SNARKs in [25, Definition 2.10]. All definitions are inspired by the corresponding black-box definitions from [15].

Let Ψ be a SNARK for the relation $\mathbf{R}$. Let $\mathsf{x} \in \{\mathsf{ase}, \mathsf{sase}\}$. Define $\mathsf{Adv}^{\mathsf{x}}_{\Psi,\mathcal{A},\mathsf{Ext}_\mathcal{A}}(\lambda) := \Pr[\mathbf{Exp}^{\mathsf{x}}_{\Psi,\mathcal{A},\mathsf{Ext}_\mathcal{A}}(\lambda)]$, where the experiment $\mathbf{Exp}^{\mathsf{x}}_{\Psi,\mathcal{A},\mathsf{Ext}_\mathcal{A}}(\lambda)$ is depicted in Fig. 2. Then, (i) Ψ is *non-black-box any-simulation-extractable (ASE)* if for any PPT $\mathcal{A}$ there exists a PPT extractor $\mathsf{Ext}_\mathcal{A}$, such that $\mathsf{Adv}^{\mathsf{ase}}_{\Psi,\mathcal{A},\mathsf{Ext}_\mathcal{A}}(\lambda) \approx_\lambda 0$. (ii) Ψ is *non-black-box strong any-simulation-extractable (SASE)* if for any PPT $\mathcal{A}$ there exists a PPT extractor $\mathsf{Ext}_\mathcal{A}$, such that $\mathsf{Adv}^{\mathsf{sase}}_{\Psi,\mathcal{A},\mathsf{Ext}_\mathcal{A}}(\lambda) \approx_\lambda 0$.

3 Knowledge-Sound SNARK for QAP

Next, we will describe the new knowledge-sound SNARK $\mathsf{S}_{\mathsf{qap}}$. Its construction emphasizes two objectives: (i) simple soundness proof in the AGM and (ii) efficiency. $\mathsf{S}_{\mathsf{qap}}$ is similar to Groth's SNARK from EUROCRYPT 2016 [23] (shown to be Sub-ZK in [17]), with two major differences: (1) the use of only two trapdoors instead of five, and (2) an alternative, much more straightforward, knowledge-soundness proof in the case of asymmetric pairings. On the other hand, Groth provided a more complex knowledge-soundness proof that is valid for both asymmetric and symmetric pairings.

QAP. Quadratic Arithmetic Program (QAP) was introduced in [21] as a language where for an input $\mathbb{x}$ and witness $\mathbb{w}$, $(\mathbb{x}, \mathbb{w}) \in \mathbf{R}$ can be verified by using a parallel quadratic check. QAP has an efficient reduction from the (either Boolean or Arithmetic) CIRCUIT-SAT. Thus, an efficient zk-SNARK for QAP results in an efficient zk-SNARK for CIRCUIT-SAT.

We consider arithmetic circuits that consist only of fan-in-2 multiplication gates, but either input of each multiplication gate can be any weighted sum of wire values, [21]. Let $m_0 < m$ be a non-negative integer. For an arithmetic circuit, let n be the number of multiplication gates, m be the number of wires, and m_0 be the number of public inputs.

Let $\mathbb{F} = \mathbb{Z}_p$. For the sake of efficiency, we require the existence of the nth primitive root of unity modulo p, denoted by ω. Let U, V, and W be instance-dependent matrices and let $\mathbb{z}$ be a witness. A QAP is characterized by the constraint $U\mathbb{z} \circ V\mathbb{z} = W\mathbb{z}$. For $j \in [1, m]$, define $u_j(X) := L_{U^{(j)}}(X)$, $v_j(X) := L_{V^{(j)}}(X)$, and $w_j(X) := L_{W^{(j)}}(X)$ to be interpolating polynomials of the jth column of the corresponding matrix. Thus, $u_j, v_j, w_j \in \mathbb{Z}_p^{(\leq n-1)}[X]$. Let $u(X) = \sum \mathbb{z}_j u_j(X)$, $v(X) = \sum \mathbb{z}_j v_j(X)$, and $w(X) = \sum \mathbb{z}_j w_j(X)$. Then $U\mathbb{z} \circ V\mathbb{z} = W\mathbb{z}$ iff $Z(X) \mid u(X)v(X) - w(X)$ iff $u(X)v(X) \equiv w(X) \pmod{Z(X)}$ iff there exists a polynomial $h(X)$ such that $u(X)v(X) - w(X) = h(X)Z(X)$.

An QAP instance $\mathcal{I}_{\mathsf{qap}}$ is equal to $(\mathbb{Z}_p, m_0, \{u_j, v_j, w_j\}_{j=1}^m)$. This instance defines the following relation:

$$\mathbf{R}_{\mathcal{I}_{\mathsf{qap}}} = \left\{ \begin{array}{l} (\mathbb{x}, \mathbb{w}) \colon \mathbb{x} = (\mathbb{z}_1, \ldots, \mathbb{z}_{m_0})^\top \wedge \mathbb{w} = (\mathbb{z}_{m_0+1}, \ldots, \mathbb{z}_m)^\top \wedge \\ u(X)v(X) \equiv w(X) \pmod{Z(X)} \end{array} \right\} \tag{1}$$

where $u(X) = \sum_{j=1}^m \mathbb{z}_j u_j(X)$, $v(X) = \sum_{j=1}^m \mathbb{z}_j v_j(X)$, and $w(X) = \sum_{j=1}^m \mathbb{z}_j w_j(X)$ as above. That is, $(\mathbb{x}, \mathbb{w}) \in \mathbf{R} = \mathbf{R}_{\mathcal{I}_{\mathsf{qap}}}$ if there exists a (degree $\leq n - 2$) polynomial $h(X)$, such that the following key equation holds:

$$\chi(X) := u(X)v(X) - w(X) - h(X)Z(X) = 0 \ , \tag{2}$$

On top of checking Eq. (2), the verifier also needs to check that $u(X)$, $v(X)$, and $w(X)$ are correctly computed: that is, that (i) the first m_0 coefficients $\mathbb{z}_j$ in $u(X)$ are equal to the public inputs, and (ii) $u(X)$, $v(X)$, and $w(X)$ are all computed by using the same coefficients $\mathbb{z}_j$ for $j \leq m$.

SNARK Derivation. Let $u(X)$, $v(X)$, $w(X)$, and $\chi(X)$ be as in Sect. 2. Recall from Eq. (2) that the key equation of QAP states that the prover is honest iff $\chi(X) = 0$, that is, $h(X) := (u(X)v(X) - w(X))/Z(X)$ is a polynomial. We will use bivariate polynomials like $A(X, Y)$. The indeterminate X is related to the definition of QAP. The indeterminate Y groups together correct X-polynomials in the security proof; such a grouping approach was also used in say [24]. The argument in the new template consists of three elements, $\pi = ([\mathsf{a}, \mathsf{c}_s]_1, [\mathsf{b}]_2)$, where $\mathsf{a} = A(x, y)$, $\mathsf{b} = B(x, y)$, and $\mathsf{c}_s = C_s(x, y)$ for well-defined polynomials $A(X, Y)$, $B(X, Y)$, and $C_s(X, Y)$. Intuitively, $[\mathsf{a}]_1$ is a succinct commitment to $u(X)$, $[\mathsf{b}]_2$ is a succinct commitment to $v(X)$, and $[\mathsf{c}_s]_1$ is the "actual" argument that at the same time commits to $w(X)$.

As in all most efficient random-oracle-less zk-SNARKs [21,23,31,36], we aim to make $[\mathsf{c}_s]_1$ to be computable only by the honest prover. The prover has access to the CRS that contains the evaluation of well-chosen polynomials at (x, y) in both $\mathbb{G}_1$ and $\mathbb{G}_2$. The knowledge-soundness proof is in the AGM. There, we show that if the verification polynomial $\mathcal{V}(X, Y) = 0$, and $A(X, Y)$, $B(X, Y)$, and $C_s(X, Y)$ are in the span of the polynomials in the CRS, then it must hold that $\chi(X) = 0$ and thus the prover is honest.

More precisely, let $\boldsymbol{\Delta} := (\alpha, \beta, \gamma, \delta, \eta)$ be a tuple of small integers chosen later. We will give a complete derivation of the new SNARK. We will also derive the conditions $\boldsymbol{\Delta}$ has to satisfy for the SNARK to be knowledge-sound; in Sects. 5 and 4, we add more conditions to achieve both CRS-verifiability (and thus Sub-ZK) and ASE. We find it instructional to go first through the process with unfixed $\boldsymbol{\Delta}$. In Eq. (11), we propose a setting of $\boldsymbol{\Delta}$ that is sufficient to obtain all knowledge-soundness, ASE, and CRS-verifiability.

For randomizers r_a and r_b needed to make the commitment hiding, define

$$A(X, Y) := r_a Y^\alpha + u(X) Y^\beta \ , \quad B(X, Y) := r_b Y^\alpha + v(X) Y^\beta \tag{3}$$

to be "commitments" to $u(X)$ and $v(X)$. We use different powers of Y to separate the randomness from the committed values. Define also

$$\begin{aligned} C(X, Y) &:= (A(X, Y) + Y^\gamma)(B(X, Y) + Y^\delta) - Y^{\gamma+\delta} \\ &= u(X) Y^{\beta+\delta} + v(X) Y^{\beta+\gamma} + u(X) v(X) Y^{2\beta} + R(X, Y) Y^\alpha \\ &= P(X, Y) + (u(X) v(X) - w(X)) Y^{2\beta} + R(X, Y) Y^\alpha \end{aligned} \tag{4}$$

where $P(X, Y) := u(X) Y^{\beta+\delta} + v(X) Y^{\beta+\gamma} + w(X) Y^{2\beta}$ and $R(X, Y) := r_b(A(X, Y) + Y^\gamma) + r_a(v(X) Y^\beta + Y^\delta)$.

The inclusion of Y^γ and Y^δ in the definition of $C(X, Y)$ serves three goals. First, it introduces the addend $P(X, Y) = \sum_{j=1}^{m} \mathbb{z}_j P_j(X, Y)$, where

$$P_j(X, Y) := u_j(X) Y^{\beta+\delta} + v_j(X) Y^{\beta+\gamma} + w_j(X) Y^{2\beta} \ ; \tag{5}$$

this makes it easier to verify that P uses the same coefficients $\mathbb{z}_j$ when computing $[\mathsf{a}]_1$, $[\mathsf{b}]_2$, and $[\mathsf{c}_s]_1$. Second, it makes it possible to verify that P uses the correct public input. Third, the coefficient of $Y^{2\beta}$, $u(X)v(X) - w(X)$, divides by $Z(X)$ iff the prover is honest. That is, it is $h(X)Z(X)$ for some polynomial $h(X)$ iff the prover is honest and thus $\mathbb{x} \in \mathcal{L}_{\mathcal{I}_{\mathsf{qap}}}$.

On top of $\chi(X) = 0$, it must be possible to check that the public input $(\mathbb{z}_j)_{j=1}^{m_0}$ is correct. To this end, we define polynomials $C_s(X, Y)$ and $C_p(X, Y)$, s.t. $C(X, Y) = C_p(X, Y) Y^\eta + C_s(X, Y) Y^\alpha$. Here, $[\mathsf{c}_p]_1 = [C_p(x, y)]_1$ is recomputed by the verifier and thus $C_p(X, Y)$ must not depend on $\mathbb{z}_j$ for $j > m_0$ (i.e., on the secret information). To minimize the verifier's computation, $C_p(X, Y)$ has only m_0 addends. C_s depends both on public and secret inputs, and only an honest prover should be able to compute $[\mathsf{c}_s]_1 = [C_s(x, y)]_1$. Thus, we define

$$C_{\mathsf{p}}(X,Y) := \sum_{j=1}^{m_0} \mathbb{z}_j P_j(X,Y)Y^{-\eta}$$
$$C_s(X,Y) := \sum_{j=m_0+1}^{m} \mathbb{z}_j P_j(X,Y)Y^{-\alpha} + (u(X)v(X) - w(X))Y^{2\beta-\alpha} + R(X,Y) \ . \quad (6)$$

$\mathsf{G}(\mathsf{p},\mathbf{R})$: Sample $x, y \leftarrow_\$ \mathbb{Z}_p^*$ such that $x^n \neq 1$, let $\mathsf{td} \leftarrow (x,y)$. Let

$$\mathsf{crs_P} \leftarrow \begin{pmatrix} [\{P_j(x,y)y^{-\alpha}\}_{j=m_0+1}^{m}, y^\alpha, \{x^j y^\beta\}_{j=0}^{n-1}, \{x^i Z(x) y^{2\beta-\alpha}\}_{j=0}^{n-2}, y^\gamma, y^\delta]_1, \\ [y^\alpha, \{x^j y^\beta\}_{j=0}^{n-1}]_2 \end{pmatrix} ;$$

$$\mathsf{crs_V} \leftarrow ([\{P_j(x,y)y^{-\eta}\}_{j=1}^{m_0}, y^\gamma]_1, [y^\alpha, y^\delta, y^\eta]_2, [y^{\gamma+\delta}]_T) \ ;$$

$\mathsf{crs} \leftarrow (\mathsf{crs_P}, \mathsf{crs_V})$; return $(\mathsf{crs}, \mathsf{td})$;

$\mathsf{P}(\mathsf{crs_P}, (\mathbb{z}_j)_{j=1}^{m_0}, (\mathbb{z}_j)_{j=m_0+1}^{m})$:

$u(X) \leftarrow \sum_{j=1}^{m} \mathbb{z}_j u_j(X)$; $v(X) \leftarrow \sum_{j=1}^{m} \mathbb{z}_j v_j(X)$; $w(X) \leftarrow \sum_{j=1}^{m} \mathbb{z}_j w_j(X)$;
$h(X) \leftarrow (u(X)v(X) - w(X))/Z(X)$;
$(r_a, r_b) \leftarrow_\$ \mathbb{Z}_p^2$; $[\mathsf{a}]_1 \leftarrow r_a[y^\alpha]_1 + [u(x)y^\beta]_1$; $[\mathsf{b}]_2 \leftarrow r_b[y^\alpha]_2 + [v(x)y^\beta]_2$;
$[\mathsf{c}_s]_1 \leftarrow \sum_{j=m_0+1}^{m} \mathbb{z}_j[P_j(x,y)y^{-\alpha}]_1 + [h(x)Z(x)y^{2\beta-\alpha}]_1 + r_b([\mathsf{a}]_1 + [y^\gamma]_1) +$
$r_a([y^\delta]_1 + [v(x)y^\beta]_1)$;
return $\pi \leftarrow ([\mathsf{a}, \mathsf{c}_s]_1, [\mathsf{b}]_2)$;

$\mathsf{V}(\mathsf{crs_V}, (\mathbb{z}_j)_{j=1}^{m_0}, \pi = ([\mathsf{a}, \mathsf{c}_s]_1, [\mathsf{b}]_2))$:

$[\mathsf{c}_p]_1 \leftarrow \sum_{j=1}^{m_0} \mathbb{z}_j [P_j(x,y)y^{-\eta}]_1$; Check that

$$[\mathsf{c}_p]_1 \bullet [y^\eta]_2 + [\mathsf{c}_s]_1 \bullet [y^\alpha]_2 = [\mathsf{a} + y^\gamma]_1 \bullet [\mathsf{b} + y^\delta]_2 - [y^{\gamma+\delta}]_T \ . \quad (7)$$

$\mathsf{Sim}(\mathsf{crs}, \mathsf{td} = (x,y), \mathbb{x} = (\mathbb{z}_j)_{j=1}^{m_0})$: // x is not used by the simulator

$[\mathsf{c}_p]_1 \leftarrow \sum_{j=1}^{m_0} \mathbb{z}_j [P_j(x,y)y^{-\eta}]_1$; $d \leftarrow_\$ \mathbb{Z}_p$; $e \leftarrow_\$ \mathbb{Z}_p$; $[\mathsf{a}]_1 \leftarrow d[1]_1$; $[\mathsf{b}]_2 \leftarrow e[1]_2$;
$[\mathsf{c}_s]_1 \leftarrow y^{-\alpha}((de + y^\delta d + y^\gamma e)[1]_1 - y^\eta [\mathsf{c}_p]_1)$;
return $\pi \leftarrow ([\mathsf{a}, \mathsf{c}_s]_1, [\mathsf{b}]_2)$;

Fig. 3. The new SNARK $\mathsf{S_{qap}}$. Moreover, $\mathsf{S_{qsp}}$ is exactly like $\mathsf{S_{qap}}$, except $w_j(X) = 0$.

Here, we use the factors Y^η and Y^α to separate the public input and the witness in the security proof. For efficiency reasons, we use Y^α, instead of a new power of Y: now $C_s(X,Y)$ has an addend $r_b A(X,Y)$ that reuses the value $A(X,Y)$.

As mentioned before, the SNARK argument is $\pi = ([\mathsf{a}, \mathsf{c}_s]_1, [\mathsf{b}]_2)$. The verifier recomputes $[\mathsf{c}_p]_1 \leftarrow [C_p(x,y)]_1$ and $[C(x,y)]_T \leftarrow [\mathsf{c}_p]_1 \bullet [y^\eta]_2 + [\mathsf{c}_s]_1 \bullet [y^\alpha]_2$. Then, the verifier checks that $C(x,y)$ is computed correctly by checking that $C(x,y) = (A(x,y) + y^\gamma)(B(x,y) + y^\delta) - y^{\gamma+\delta}$.

We are now ready to describe the SNARK $\mathsf{S_{qap}}$, see Fig. 3. The CRS consists of elements needed by the honest prover, the honest verifier, and the simulator. We will explain the simulator in the proof of Theorem 1. The CRS has two trapdoors (x and y), but the simulator uses only one of them (y). ([1,3] formalized the difference by defining two different types of trapdoors, CRS trapdoors $\mathsf{td_{crs}}$ and simulation trapdoors $\mathsf{td_{sim}}$. In $\mathsf{S_{qap}}$, $\mathsf{td_{crs}} = (x,y)$ and $\mathsf{td_{sim}} = y$.)

Security Intuition. We prove knowledge-soundness in the AGM with random oracles. Recall that an algebraic adversary can use the oracle $\mathcal{O}_\iota$, $\iota \in \{1, 2\}$, to create new random group elements $[q_{1i}]_\iota$. Let $\boldsymbol{Q}_\iota$ be the vector of corresponding indeterminates in $\mathbb{G}_\iota$. Let $\boldsymbol{X} = (X, \boldsymbol{Q}_1, \boldsymbol{Q}_2, Y)$ (resp., $\boldsymbol{x} = (x, \boldsymbol{q}_1, \boldsymbol{q}_2, y)$) be the tuple of all indeterminates (resp., corresponding random integers).

Write the CRS in Fig. 3 as $\mathsf{crs} = (\mathsf{crs}_1, \mathsf{crs}_2)$, where $\mathsf{crs}_\iota = [(f(x, y))_{f \in \Gamma_\iota}]_\iota$ for a public set Γ_ι of polynomials. For example, $\Gamma_2 = \{Y^\alpha, Y^\delta, Y^\eta\} \cup \{X^j Y^\beta\}_{j=0}^{n-1}$. (As an optimization, the CRS of $\mathsf{S}_{\mathsf{qap}}$ also includes $[y^{\gamma+\delta}]_T$, but it can be recomputed from the available elements in $\mathbb{G}_1$ and $\mathbb{G}_2$.) Since we work in the AGM, the malicious prover is algebraic and thus we can extract matrices $\boldsymbol{N}_1$ and $\boldsymbol{N}_2$, such that $\binom{\mathsf{a}}{\mathsf{c}_s} = \boldsymbol{N}_1 \binom{\mathsf{crs}_1}{\boldsymbol{q}_1}$ and $\mathsf{b} = \boldsymbol{N}_2 \binom{\mathsf{crs}_2}{\boldsymbol{q}_2}$. This means, that we can write $\mathsf{a} = A^\dagger(\boldsymbol{x})$, $\mathsf{b} = B^\dagger(\boldsymbol{x})$, and $\mathsf{c}_s = C_s^\dagger(\boldsymbol{x})$, where $A^\dagger(\boldsymbol{X})$, $B^\dagger(\boldsymbol{X})$, and $C_s^\dagger(\boldsymbol{X})$ are maliciously computed polynomials with known coefficients. We can recover all coefficients of $A^\dagger(\boldsymbol{X})$, $B^\dagger(\boldsymbol{X})$, and $C_s^\dagger(\boldsymbol{X})$ from $\boldsymbol{N}_1$ and $\boldsymbol{N}_2$, as follows:

$$\begin{aligned} A^\dagger(\boldsymbol{X}) := & \textstyle\sum_{j=1}^{m_0} a_j^* P_j(X, Y) Y^{-\eta} + \sum_{j=m_0+1}^{m} a_j^* P_j(X, Y) Y^{-\alpha} + r_a Y^\alpha \\ & + u_a(X) Y^\beta + h_a(X) Z(X) Y^{2\beta-\alpha} + a_\gamma Y^\gamma + a_\delta Y^\delta + \textstyle\sum_k q_{ak} Q_{1k} , \\ C_s^\dagger(\boldsymbol{X}) := & \textstyle\sum_{j=1}^{m_0} c_j^* P_j(X, Y) Y^{-\eta} + \sum_{j=m_0+1}^{m} c_j^* P_j(X, Y) Y^{-\alpha} + r_c Y^\alpha \\ & + u_c(X) Y^\beta + h_c(X) Z(X) Y^{2\beta-\alpha} + c_\gamma Y^\gamma + c_\delta Y^\delta + \textstyle\sum_k q_{ck} Q_{1k} , \\ B^\dagger(\boldsymbol{X}) := & r_b Y^\alpha + v_b(X) Y^\beta + b_\delta Y^\delta + b_\eta Y^\eta + \textstyle\sum_k b_{qk} Q_{2k} , \end{aligned} \tag{8}$$

where, say $a_j^* \in \mathbb{Z}_p$, $u_a(X) \in \mathbb{Z}_p^{(\leq n-1)}[X]$, and $h_a(X) \in \mathbb{Z}_p^{(\leq n-2)}[X]$.

The verification equation Eq. (7) guarantees $\mathcal{V}(\boldsymbol{x}) = 0$, where

$$\mathcal{V}(\boldsymbol{X}) := (A^\dagger(\boldsymbol{X}) + Y^\gamma)(B^\dagger(\boldsymbol{X}) + Y^\delta) - Y^{\gamma+\delta} - C_p(X, Y) Y^\eta - C_s^\dagger(\boldsymbol{X}) Y^\alpha . \tag{9}$$

Note that C_p is honestly computed. Since we know all coefficients of polynomials like $A^\dagger(\boldsymbol{X})$, we also know all coefficients of $\mathcal{V}(\boldsymbol{X})$.

On the Use of AGM. In the knowledge-soundness proof, we assume that the knowledge-soundness adversary $\mathcal{A}$ is algebraic and then break the PDL assumption. More precisely, with use the AGM with random oracles. However, we note that $\mathrm{RO}_{\mathsf{fkl}}$-AGM is not realistic since it allows to prove the security of false knowledge assumptions.[4] Really, consider the assumption that any PPT adversary $\mathcal{A}$, that on input $[1]_1$ generates $[x]_1$, must know x. This assumption is false in the settings where $\mathcal{A}$ has access to an efficient method (e.g., hash-and-increment or elliptic curve hashing) of creating random group elements without knowing their discrete logarithms. However, in the $\mathrm{RO}_{\mathsf{fkl}}$-AGM, one can extract an integer vector $\boldsymbol{N}$ and group element vector $[\boldsymbol{q}]_1$, such that $[x]_1 = \boldsymbol{N}^\top \left[\begin{smallmatrix} 1 \\ \boldsymbol{q} \end{smallmatrix}\right]_1 = N_1[1]_1 + \sum_{i \geq 1} N_{1+i}[q_i]_1$. Moreover, the reduction can program the random oracle by first creating the discrete logarithms q_k of each coordinate

[4] This is probably one reason why [19] uses AGM with random oracles in the case where the analyzed protocol itself uses random oracles. [19] proves the knowledge-soundness of Groth's SNARK in the AGM *without* random oracles.

of $[\boldsymbol{q}]_1$. Then, $[x]_1 = (N_1 + \sum_{i>1} N_{1+i})[1]_1$ and thus the reduction can output its discrete logarithm $x \leftarrow N_1 + \sum_{i \geq 1} N_{1+i}$. One has exactly the same issue when using AGM without random oracles (in this case, $\boldsymbol{q}$ has length 0).

The problem is that the reduction knows $\boldsymbol{q}$ and can thus compute x. The knowledge of $\boldsymbol{q}$ should be impossible if $\mathcal{A}$ has created $[q_k]_1$ by using elliptic curve hashing. We modify the AGM with random oracles so that one can still prove the security of (thought to be) secure knowledge assumptions but not of assumptions of the above type. The first idea is to restrict the way the reduction is allowed to program the random oracle: given that the input of the reduction (who aims to break the PDL assumption) is $\mathbb{x}_{\mathcal{A}} = (\mathsf{p}; [x^i : i \in \mathcal{T}_1]_1, [x^i : i \in \mathcal{T}_2]_2)$, we require that the reduction programs the random oracle $\mathcal{O}_\iota$ by creating random integers $s, t \leftarrow\$ \mathbb{Z}_p$ and then outputting $s[x]_\iota + t$. Such "linear programming" was already used in [19] but in a different context. For example, it was used to implicitly create other CRS trapdoors from $\mathbb{x}_{\mathcal{A}}$ and in one case (the security proof of the RO-model BLS signature) also to program the random oracle. However, our usage of this strategy is in a novel context and for a novel goal.

We modify the strategy of AGM with random oracles of [19] even further. When using the described "linear programming" strategy to construct a PDL adversary $\mathcal{B}$ that obtains input, depending on one trapdoor (say, x), and then uses this to create a multivariate crs for the knowledge-soundness adversary $\mathcal{A}$. For the reduction to be successful, $\mathcal{B}$ creates other trapdoors (notably, including $q_{\iota k}$) implicitly as linear functions of x. E.g., $\mathcal{B}$ sets $[y]_1 \leftarrow s_y[x]_1 + t_y[1]_1$, for random s_y and t_y, and similarly $[y^i]_1 \leftarrow [(s_y x + t_y)^i]_1$; this assumes that $[1, x, \ldots, x^i]_1$ are given in the CRS. In the security proof, this means that one can write $\mathcal{V}$ as a univariate (Laurent) polynomial $\mathcal{V}_x(X) = \mathcal{V}(\boldsymbol{X})$ and then use a polynomial factorization algorithm to compute x in the case $\mathcal{V}(\boldsymbol{X}) \neq 0$ but $\mathcal{V}(\boldsymbol{x}) = 0$.

This strategy has some undesirable properties. First, for every monomial $[x^i y^j]_\iota$ in the CRS, we need to give $[x^{i+j}]_\iota$ as an input to the PDL adversary. Since $\max i, \max j < \max(i + j)$ and $(n + 1, n')$-PDL is stronger than (n, n')-PDL in the AGM, one uses a stronger PDL assumption. Second, this strategy is challenging to implement when, as in our case, the CRS depends on the negative powers of some trapdoors. Really, given $[1/x^i]_1$ for various i-s, it is presumably hard to compute $[1/(sx + t)^j]_1$ for $j > 1$ and random s and t; due to this reason, *the "linear programming" strategy cannot be used to prove the knowledge-soundness of* $\mathsf{S_{qap}}$ *(or Groth's SNARK since it also involves negative powers of trapdoors).*[5] Finally, the degree of $\mathcal{V}_x$ is related to the *total* degree of $\mathcal{V}$.

[5] In the case of the original Groth's SNARK, this holds true since there are two different trapdoors that are given in negative power in the CRS. One can solve this issue by modifying Groth's SNARK: for example, one can multiply all its CRS elements with a positive power of such trapdoors (but then one has to be carefully check that Sub-ZK still holds); [19] solved this issue by having an additional game inside the knowledge-soundness proof that modified the CRS correspondingly.

We use a different strategy. We define two different adversaries, one aiming to compute x (given a PDL input that depends on x) and another aiming to compute y (given a PDL input that depends on y). Both adversaries generate the second trapdoor randomly. The reduction programs the oracles differently, by using the "linear programming" strategy in one case and the $\mathrm{RO}_{\mathsf{fkl}}$ strategy in another case. (This is detailed in Fig. 4.) As a direct benefit, inside the reduction, we deal with polynomials of smaller degrees. Moreover, instead of giving $[x^{i+j}]_\iota$ to the adversary, we give $[x^i]_\iota$ as an input to one adversary and $[y^j]_\iota$ to another adversary. Hence, we can potentially rely on a weaker PDL assumption. Finally, since the second adversary ($\mathcal{B}^y$ in Fig. 4) uses the $\mathrm{RO}_{\mathsf{fkl}}$ strategy, it is easy to handle CRS elements of type $[y^{-1}]_1$ since one chooses y randomly. On the other hand, since the first adversary uses the "linear programming" strategy, one cannot prove the security of the false knowledge assumption described above.

On the Choice of Exponents. Another complicated part of the knowledge-soundness proof is the analysis of what happens if $\mathcal{V}(\boldsymbol{X}) \neq 0$ as a Laurent polynomial, but the verification succeeds, that is, $\mathcal{V}(\boldsymbol{x}) = 0$. Let $\boldsymbol{X}^* = (X, \boldsymbol{Q}_1, \boldsymbol{Q}_2)$ and $\boldsymbol{x}^* = (x, \boldsymbol{q}_1, \boldsymbol{q}_2)$. Writing $\mathcal{V}(\boldsymbol{X}) = \sum_i \mathcal{V}_{Y^i}(\boldsymbol{X}^*) Y^i$ for known Laurent polynomials $\mathcal{V}_{Y^i}(\boldsymbol{X}^*)$, we get $\mathcal{V}_{Y^i}(\boldsymbol{X}^*) = 0$ for each i. There are 29 non-trivial coefficients $\mathcal{V}_{Y^i}(\boldsymbol{X}^*)$, for $i \in$

$$\begin{aligned}&\{2\alpha, 2\beta, \alpha+\beta, 3\beta-\alpha, \alpha+\gamma, \beta+\gamma, -\alpha+2\beta+\gamma, 2\delta, \alpha+\delta, \beta+\delta,\\ &-\alpha+2\beta+\delta, \gamma+\delta, -\alpha+\beta+\gamma+\delta, -\alpha+\beta+2\delta, \alpha+2\beta-\eta, 3\beta-\eta,\\ &\alpha+\beta+\gamma-\eta, 2\beta+\gamma-\eta, \alpha+\beta+\delta-\eta, 2\beta+\delta-\eta, \beta+\gamma+\delta-\eta, \beta+2\delta-\eta,\\ &\alpha+\eta, \beta+\eta, -\alpha+2\beta+\eta, \gamma+\eta, -\alpha+\beta+\gamma+\eta, \delta+\eta, -\alpha+\beta+\delta+\eta\} \ .\end{aligned} \tag{10}$$

It is possible but very tedious to show that from $\mathcal{V}_{Y^i}(\boldsymbol{X}^*) = 0$ for each twenty nine i-s, we get that $\chi(X) = 0$ and thus, the prover is honest. To simplify the knowledge-soundness proof, we constructed $\mathsf{S}_{\mathsf{qap}}$ so that there exists a small set Crit of *six* elements, such that $\chi(X) = 0$ follows from $\mathcal{V}_{Y^i}(\boldsymbol{X}^*) = 0$ for $Y^i \in \mathsf{Crit}$.

For this idea to work, we need to restrict the choice of $\boldsymbol{\Delta}$: namely, $\boldsymbol{\Delta}$ has to be such that the exponents in Crit are different from each other and all other exponents of Y in $\mathcal{V}(\boldsymbol{X})$. More precisely, define $\mathsf{Coeff} := \{Y^i : \mathcal{V}_{Y^i}(\boldsymbol{X}^*) \neq 0\}$,

$$\mathsf{Crit} := \{Y^{2\beta}, Y^{\beta+\gamma}, Y^{\beta+\delta}, Y^{\gamma+\delta}, Y^{\gamma+\eta}, Y^{2\delta}\} \ ,$$

and let $\overline{\mathsf{Crit}} := \mathsf{Coeff} \setminus \mathsf{Crit}$ be the "symbolic" complement of Crit; that is, $Y^j \in \overline{\mathsf{Crit}}$ if j is *symbolically* not the same as one of the exponents in Crit, so $|\mathsf{Coeff}| = 29$ and $|\overline{\mathsf{Crit}}| = 29 - 6 = 23$. We highlighted the 6 critical coefficients in Eq. (10), not highlighted coefficients correspond to coefficients in $\overline{\mathsf{Crit}}$.

We say that $\boldsymbol{\Delta}$ is *soundness-friendly* if Crit consists of mutually different powers of Y ($|\mathsf{Crit}| = 6$) and $\mathsf{Crit} \cap \overline{\mathsf{Crit}} = \emptyset$. We will give a concrete soundness-friendly suggestion for $\boldsymbol{\Delta}$ in Eq. (11). We depict the critical coefficients $\mathcal{V}_{Y^i}(\boldsymbol{X}^*)$, $Y^i \in \mathsf{Crit}$, in Table 2. (The last rows in Table 2 are only relevant for the ASE proof in Sect. 4.) In the knowledge-soundness proof of Theorem 1, we show that if $\mathcal{V}_{Y^i}(\boldsymbol{X}^*) = 0$ for $Y^i \in \mathsf{Crit}$, then $\chi(X) = 0$ and thus the prover is honest.

Table 2. $\mathsf{S}_{\mathsf{qap}}$: the critical coefficients in the knowledge-soundness proof (up, left), addends to the same coefficients in the ASE proof (up, right), and coefficients that only occur in the ASE proof (bottom). Here, $\tilde{\mathbb{z}}_j = \mathbb{z}_j - b_\eta a_j^*$ for $j \le m_0$, $\tilde{\mathbb{z}}_j = c_j^* - r_b a_j^*$ for $j > m_0$, $u(X) = \sum_{j=1}^m \tilde{\mathbb{z}}_j u_j(X)$, $v(X) = \sum_{j=1}^m \tilde{\mathbb{z}}_j v_j(X)$, $w(X) = \sum_{j=1}^m \tilde{\mathbb{z}}_j w_j(X)$, and $h(X) = h_c(X) - r_b h_a(X)$.

$Y^i \dots$	$\mathcal{V}_{Y^i \dots}(\boldsymbol{X}^*)$ (KS and ASE)	$\hat{\mathcal{V}}_{Y^{i_1} \dots}(\boldsymbol{X}^*)$ (ASE only)
$Y^{\gamma+\delta}$	$(a_\gamma + 1)(b_\delta + 1) - 1$	
$Y^{\gamma+\eta}$	$(a_\gamma + 1)b_\eta$	
$Y^{2\delta}$	$(b_\delta + 1)a_\delta$	
$Y^{\beta+\delta}$	$(b_\delta + 1)u_a(X) + a_\delta v_b(X) - u(X)$	$\sum_k (s_{c2k} - r_b s_{a2k}) \sum_j \sigma_{kj} u_j(X)$
$Y^{\beta+\gamma}$	$(a_\gamma + 1)v_b(X) - v(X)$	$\sum_k (s_{c2k} - r_b s_{a2k}) \sum_j \sigma_{kj} v_j(X)$
$Y^{2\beta}$	$u_a(X)v_b(X) - w(X) - h(X)Z(X)$	$\sum_k (s_{c2k} - r_b s_{a2k}) \sum_j \sigma_{kj} w_j(X)$
	Used only in the ASE proof	
$Y^{-\alpha+2\delta} D_k$		$(b_\delta + 1)s_{a2k}$
$Y^\gamma E_k$		$r_b s_{a2k} + (a_\gamma + 1)s_{bk} - s_{c2k}$
$D_k E_k$		$r_b s_{a2k} + s_{a1k} s_{bk} - s_{c2k}$
$Y^\delta D_k$		$r_b s_{a2k} + (b_\delta + 1)s_{a1k} - s_{c2k}$
Used only in the case (ii) in the ASE proof, if $s_{a1k} = a_\gamma + 1$ and $s_{c2k} = (a_\gamma + 1)s_{bk}$		
$D_{k_1} E_{k_2}$, $k_1 \ne k_2$		$s_{a1k_1} s_{bk_2}$
$Y^\beta E_k$		$u_a(X)s_{bk}$

3.1 Security Theorem

Theorem 1. *Let* $\mathcal{I}_{\mathsf{qap}} = (\mathbb{Z}_p, m_0, \{u_j, v_j, w_j\}_{j=1}^m)$ *be a QAP instance. Let* $\mathsf{S}_{\mathsf{qap}}$ *be the SNARK in Fig. 3. Let* $\mathcal{T}_\iota^x$ *be the minimal set of exponents* i *such that the CRS of* $\mathsf{S}_{\mathsf{qap}}$ *in Fig. 3 can be computed by an algebraic adversary given* $[x^i : i \in \mathcal{T}_1^x]_1, [x^i : i \in \mathcal{T}_2^x]_2$ *and* y*. We define* $\mathcal{T}_\iota^y$ *dually.*
(1) Assume $\boldsymbol{\Delta}$ *is soundness-friendly. Then,* $\mathsf{S}_{\mathsf{qap}}$ *is knowledge-sound in the AGM under the* $(\mathcal{T}_1^x, \mathcal{T}_2^x)$*-PDL and the* $(\mathcal{T}_1^y, \mathcal{T}_2^y)$*-PDL assumptions.*
(2) $\mathsf{S}_{\mathsf{qap}}$ *is perfectly zero-knowledge.*

Here, $\mathcal{T}_1^x = [0, 2n-2]$, $\mathcal{T}_2^x = [0, n-1]$, $\mathcal{T}_1^y = \{\beta - \alpha + \delta, \beta - \alpha + \gamma, 2\beta - \alpha, \alpha, \beta, 2\beta - \alpha, \gamma, \delta, \beta - \eta + \delta, \beta - \eta + \gamma, 2\beta - \eta\}$, and $\mathcal{T}_2^y = \{\alpha, \beta, \delta, \eta\}$. This can be contrasted to [19] that provided an AGM knowledge-soundness proof under the stronger $([1, 2n-1], [1, 2n-1])$-PDL assumption.

We emphasize that the following knowledge-soundness proof depends minimally on the concrete SNARK: the only intrinsically $\mathsf{S}_{\mathsf{qap}}$-dependent part is the analysis of the abort probability. The rest of the proof can essentially be copied to the knowledge-soundness (*and ASE*) proofs of all following SNARKs.

$\boxed{\mathcal{B}^y(\mathsf{p}, \mathbf{R}, \mathbb{x}_y)}$ $\mathcal{B}^x(\mathsf{p}, \mathbf{R}, \mathbb{x}_x)$ // $\mathbb{x}_z = ([z^k : k \in \mathcal{T}_1^z]_1, [z^k : k \in \mathcal{T}_2^z]_2)$

$\boldsymbol{q}_1 \leftarrow \emptyset; \boldsymbol{q}_2 \leftarrow \emptyset; \xi_1 \leftarrow 0; \xi_2 \leftarrow 0;$
$\boxed{x \leftarrow_\$ \mathbb{Z}_p^*}$ $y \leftarrow_\$ \mathbb{Z}_p^*$; Create crs from $(\mathsf{p}, \mathbf{R}, \boxed{\mathbb{x}_y, x}\ \mathbb{x}_x, y)$;
$r_\mathcal{A} \leftarrow_\$ \mathsf{RND}_\lambda(\mathcal{A}); ([\mathsf{a}, \mathsf{c}_s]_1, [\mathsf{b}]_2) \leftarrow \mathcal{A}^{(\mathcal{O}_1, \mathcal{O}_2)}(\mathsf{p}, \mathbf{R}; \mathsf{crs}, r_\mathcal{A})$;
$(\boldsymbol{N}_1, \boldsymbol{N}_2) \leftarrow \mathsf{Ext}_\mathcal{A}(\mathsf{crs}; r_\mathcal{A})$;
if $\mathsf{Ext}_\mathcal{A}$ does not succeed **then** abort **fi** ; // Abort probability: $\varepsilon_{\mathsf{Ext}}$
Compute the coefficients of $\mathcal{V}(\boldsymbol{X}^*, Y)$ from $\boldsymbol{N}_\iota$;
(*)**if** $\mathcal{V}(\boldsymbol{X}^*, Y) = 0$ **then** abort **fi** ; // Abort prob.: 0
Let bad be the event $\mathcal{V}(\boldsymbol{x}^*, Y) = 0$;

$\mathcal{B}^y$ (full-boxed)	$\mathcal{B}^x$ (dash-boxed)
if bad **then** abort **fi** ;	**if** $\overline{\text{bad}}$ **then** abort **fi** ;
// Now, $\mathcal{V}(\boldsymbol{x}^*, Y) \neq 0$	// Now, $\mathcal{V}(\boldsymbol{x}^*, Y) = 0$
$\{y_j\} \leftarrow \mathit{roots}(\mathcal{V}(\boldsymbol{x}^*, Y), Y)$;	Write $\mathcal{V}(\boldsymbol{X}^*, Y) = \sum \mathcal{V}_i(\boldsymbol{X}^*) Y^i$;
$y \leftarrow y_j$ s.t. $[y_j^\delta]_1 = [y^\delta]_1$;	Let i be s.t. $\mathcal{V}_i(\boldsymbol{X}^*) \neq 0$ but $\mathcal{V}_i(\boldsymbol{x}^*) \neq 0$;
return y;	$\{x_j\} \leftarrow \mathit{roots}(\mathcal{V}_i(\boldsymbol{X}^*), X)$;
	return $x \leftarrow x_j$ s.t. $[x_j]_1 = [x]_1$;

$\mathcal{O}_\iota$ // $\iota \in \{1, 2\}$

$\xi_\iota \leftarrow \xi_\iota + 1; \boxed{q_{\iota\xi_\iota} \leftarrow_\$ \mathbb{Z}_p}; s_{\iota\xi_\iota}, t_{\iota\xi_\iota} \leftarrow_\$ \mathbb{Z}_p; [q_{\iota\xi_\iota}]_\iota \leftarrow s_{\iota\xi_\iota}[x]_\iota + t_{\iota\xi_\iota}[1]_1$; **return** $[q_{\iota\xi_\iota}]_\iota$;

Fig. 4. The adversaries $\mathcal{B}^z(\mathsf{p}, \mathbf{R}, \mathbb{x}_y)$, $z \in \{x, y\}$, and how they emulate $\mathcal{O}_\iota$ to $\mathcal{A}$ in the proof of Theorem 1. The parts where the two adversaries differ are boxed. Full-boxed entries are only in $\mathcal{B}^y$ and its emulation, and dash-boxed entries are only in $\mathcal{B}^x$ and its emulation. E.g., $\mathcal{B}^y$ samples a random x and $\mathcal{B}^y$ samples a random y.

Proof. **(1: knowledge-soundness)** Let $\mathcal{A}$ be an algebraic knowledge-soundness adversary. Assume that $\mathcal{A}^{(\mathcal{O}_1, \mathcal{O}_2)}(\mathsf{crs}; r_\mathcal{A})$ outputs $(\mathbb{x}, \pi)$, such that V accepts with a non-negligible probability $\varepsilon_\mathcal{A}$. Let $\mathsf{crs} = (\mathsf{crs}_1, \mathsf{crs}_2)$, with $\mathsf{crs}_\iota = [\{f(\boldsymbol{x})\}_{f \in \Gamma_\iota}]_\iota$, as before. Since $\mathcal{A}$ is algebraic and the distribution $\mathcal{D}_\mathsf{p}$ of crs is PPT-sampleable, there exists an extractor $\mathsf{Ext}_\mathcal{A}$, such that with probability $\varepsilon_\mathcal{A} - \varepsilon_{\mathsf{Ext}}$, where $\varepsilon_{\mathsf{Ext}} = \mathsf{Adv}^{\mathrm{agm}}_{\mathsf{Pgen}, \mathcal{D}, \mathcal{A}, \mathsf{Ext}_\mathcal{A}}(\lambda) = \mathsf{negl}(\lambda)$, $\mathsf{Ext}_\mathcal{A}(\mathsf{crs}; r_\mathcal{A})$ succeeds.

We construct two different PDL adversaries, $\mathcal{B}^x$ and $\mathcal{B}^y$, see Fig. 4. Intuitively, the main difference between them is that they use the knowledge-soundness adversary $\mathcal{A}$, whose input depends on either x or y, to break PDL with respect to x or y, correspondingly.

Let $z \in \{x, y\}$ and $Z \in \{X, Y\}$, correspondingly. $\mathcal{B}^z$ obtains an input $\mathbb{x}_z = ([z^k : k \in \mathcal{T}_1^z]_1, [z^k : k \in \mathcal{T}_2^z]_2)$. Intuitively, $\mathcal{B}^z$ reduces the actions of $\mathcal{A}$ to a univariate case by sampling the second trapdoor (y or x) uniformly at random. The verification equation states that $\mathcal{V}(\boldsymbol{x}^*, y) = 0$, where $\mathcal{V}(\boldsymbol{X}^*, Y)$ is a known Laurent polynomial due to the use of the AGM. The adversary aborts if $\mathcal{V}(\boldsymbol{X}^*, Y) = 0$ as a Laurent polynomial. The most complicated part of the proof is to show that if $\mathcal{A}$ is successful, then $\mathcal{V}(\boldsymbol{X}^*, Y) \neq 0$ and thus the abort on this step is never executed. (For this, we need to analyze the six critical coefficients of $\mathcal{V}$, and we will do it at the end of the proof.)

Otherwise, we choose a polynomial $f(Z)$, such that $f(Z) \neq 0$ but $f(z) = 0$. Note that $\mathcal{B}^y$ samples the oracle answers $q_{\iota k}$ uniformly at random, while $\mathcal{B}^x$ sets implicitly $q_{\iota k} \leftarrow s_{\iota k} x + t_{\iota k}$. (Differently from [19], we only use this technique in the case of $\mathcal{B}^x$.) Thus, $\boldsymbol{Q}_\iota = \boldsymbol{s}_\iota X + \boldsymbol{t}_\iota$. If $\mathcal{V}(\boldsymbol{X}^*, Y) \neq 0$ but $\mathcal{V}(\boldsymbol{x}^*, Y) = 0$, then $\mathcal{V}'(X, Y) := \mathcal{V}(X, \boldsymbol{s}_1 X + \boldsymbol{t}_1, \boldsymbol{s}_2 X + \boldsymbol{t}_2, Y)$ satisfies $\mathcal{V}'(x, Y) = 0$. We set $f(X)$ to be equal to some non-zero coefficient $\mathcal{V}'_i(X) \neq 0$ of $\mathcal{V}'(X, Y) = \sum \mathcal{V}'_i(X) Y^i$.

$\mathcal{B}^z$ finds all the roots of $f(Z)$ and then checks which of the roots is equal to z by using information given in her input. For this, we define event $\mathsf{bad} = 1$ if $\mathcal{V}(\boldsymbol{x}^*, Y) = 0$ as a Laurent polynomial, where x is either the value imminent in the input of $\mathcal{B}^x$ or sampled by $\mathcal{B}^y$. $\mathcal{B}^y$ aborts if $\mathsf{bad} = 1$ and otherwise finds y. $\mathcal{B}^x$ aborts if $\mathsf{bad} = 0$ and otherwise finds x. Clearly,

$$\begin{aligned}\Pr[\mathcal{A} \text{ succeeds}] \leq & \Pr[\mathsf{Ext}_\mathcal{A} \text{ failed}] + \Pr[\mathsf{Ext}_\mathcal{A} \text{ succeeds}|\mathsf{bad}] + \Pr[\mathsf{Ext}_\mathcal{A} \text{ succeeds}|\overline{\mathsf{bad}}] \\ \leq & \Pr[\mathsf{Ext}_\mathcal{A} \text{ failed}] + \Pr[\mathcal{B}^x \text{ succeeds}|\mathsf{bad}] + \Pr[\mathcal{B}^y \text{ succeeds}|\overline{\mathsf{bad}}] \enspace .\end{aligned}$$

Analysis of the abort probability in step (*). Both $\mathcal{B}^x$ and $\mathcal{B}^y$ abort if $\mathcal{V}(\boldsymbol{X}^*, Y) = 0$ as a Laurent polynomial. Assume now that $\mathcal{V}(\boldsymbol{X}) = 0$, thus $\mathcal{V}_{Y^i}(\boldsymbol{X}^*) = 0$ for $Y^i \in \mathsf{Crit}$. We must show that (a) the critical coefficients are as in Table 2 and (b) from "$\mathcal{V}_{Y^i}(\boldsymbol{X}^*) = 0$ for $Y^i \in \mathsf{Crit}$" it follows that $\chi(X) = 0$.

One can derive a by inspection (we verified it by using computer algebra), assuming that Crit satisfies the theorem conditions. For example, the coefficient of $Y^{\gamma+\delta}$ in $\mathcal{V}(\boldsymbol{X})$ is $(a_\gamma + 1)(b_\delta + 1) - 1$ since the coefficient of $Y^{\gamma+\delta}$ in $(A^\dagger(\boldsymbol{X}) + Y^\gamma)(B^\dagger(\boldsymbol{X}) + Y^\delta)$ is $(a_\gamma + 1)(b_\delta + 1)$. Other coefficients can be checked similarly.

Now, b follows. Really, since $\mathcal{V}_{Y^{\gamma+\delta}}(\boldsymbol{X}^*) = b_\delta + a_\gamma(b_\delta + 1) = 0$, we get $a_\gamma = -b_\delta/(b_\delta + 1)$. Thus, $a_\gamma, b_\delta \neq -1$ and $(a_\gamma + 1)(b_\delta + 1) = 1$. Since $\mathcal{V}_{Y^{\gamma+\eta}}(\boldsymbol{X}^*) = (a_\gamma + 1)b_\eta = 0$ and $a_\gamma \neq -1$, we get $b_\eta = 0$. Thus, $\tilde{\mathbb{z}}_j = \mathbb{z}_j - b_\eta a_j^* = \mathbb{z}_j$ for $j \leq m_0$. Since $\mathcal{V}_{Y^{2\delta}}(\boldsymbol{X}^*) = (b_\delta + 1)a_\delta = 0$ and $b_\delta \neq -1$, we get $a_\delta = 0$. From the remaining coefficients, we get $(b_\delta + 1)u_a(X) = u(X)$, $(a_\gamma + 1)v_b(X) = v(X)$, and $u(X)v(X) - w(X) = Z(X)h(X)$. Thus, $(\mathbb{x}, \mathbb{w}) \in \mathbf{R}_{\mathcal{I}_{\mathsf{qap}}}$.

(2: zero-knowledge) To see that V accepts, note that $(\mathsf{a} + y^\gamma)(\mathsf{b} + y^\delta) - \mathsf{c}_s y^\alpha - \mathsf{c}_p y^\eta - y^{\gamma+\delta} = de + dy^\delta + ey^\gamma - (de + dy^\delta + ey^\gamma - \mathsf{c}_p y^\eta) - \mathsf{c}_p y^\eta = 0$. Sim's output comes from the correct distribution since a and b are individually uniform in $\mathbb{Z}_p$, and c is chosen so that V accepts. □

Efficiency. Compared to [23], see Table 1, $\mathsf{S}_{\mathsf{qap}}$ has fewer trapdoors but otherwise the same complexity. For example, crs_P has $(m - m_0) + 1 + n + (n - 1) + 1 = m + 2n - m_0 + 1$ elements from $\mathbb{G}_1$ and $n + 2$ elements from $\mathbb{G}_2$. Moreover, crs_V has $m_0 + 1$ elements from $\mathbb{G}_1$, 3 elements from $\mathbb{G}_2$, and one element from $\mathbb{G}_T$. Since crs_P and crs_V have one common element in $\mathbb{G}_1$ then $|\mathsf{crs}| = (m + 2n + 2)\mathfrak{g}_1 + (n + 4)\mathfrak{g}_2 + \mathfrak{g}_T$. (Recall that $\mathfrak{g}_\iota$ denotes the representation length of an element of $\mathbb{G}_\iota$.) Clearly, $[\mathsf{a}]_1$ can be computed from $[y^\alpha]_1$ and $[x^i y^\beta]_1$ by using $n + 1$ scalar multiplications. It takes $\approx m + 2n$ additional scalar multiplications to compute $[\mathsf{c}]_1$.

A Soundness-Friendly Choice of $\boldsymbol{\Delta}$. Recall that we need to find values for $\boldsymbol{\Delta} = (\alpha, \ldots)$, such that $\mathsf{Crit} \cap \overline{\mathsf{Crit}} = \emptyset$ and $|\mathsf{Crit}| = 6$. We require that both sets Γ_1 and Γ_2 contain a non-zero monomial corresponding to $Y^0 = 1$ (then we can publish $[1]_1$ and $[1]_2$) and that the values i, for which $i \in \mathcal{T}_1^y \cup \mathcal{T}_2^y$, have as small absolute values as possible. The latter makes the PDL assumption somewhat

Table 3. Soundness-friendly values of $\boldsymbol{\Delta}$ with each parameter having absolute value ≤ 7. "✓" in the last column means that this choice of $\boldsymbol{\Delta}$ results in a Sub-ZK SNARK

α	β	γ	δ	η	Sub-ZK
−1	0	−7	3	−2	
0	−1	6	−4	1	
0	−1	7	−4	1	
0	−1	7	−5	1	
0	−2	−3	7	2	✓

α	β	γ	δ	η	Sub-ZK
0	−2	6	7	2	✓
0	−3	5	7	1	
0	1	−6	4	−1	
0	1	−7	4	−1	
0	1	−7	5	−1	

α	β	γ	δ	η	Sub-ZK
0	2	−6	−7	−2	✓
0	2	3	−7	−2	✓
0	3	−5	−7	−1	✓
1	0	7	−3	2	

more reasonable and additionally enables us to construct a CRS verification algorithm and thus prove Sub-ZK [1,3] in Sect. 5. We are also interested in minimizing the CRS length.

Since there are many coefficients to take into account, we have a moderately hard optimization problem. We used a computer search to find all possible values for $\alpha, \beta, \ldots$ under the restriction that each has an absolute value at most 7. See Table 3 for the full list of found tuples $\boldsymbol{\Delta}$. Note that for each $\boldsymbol{\Delta} = (\alpha, \beta, \ldots)$, this table contains also $-\boldsymbol{\Delta} = (-\alpha, -\beta, \ldots)$.

We recommend to use the following setting:

$$\alpha = 0, \quad \beta = -2, \quad \gamma = -3, \quad \delta = 7, \quad \eta = 2. \tag{11}$$

As we will see in Sects. 5 and 4, this is one of the settings that allow obtaining both ASE and Sub-ZK security. Assuming the setting of Eq. (11), $\mathsf{Crit} = \{Y^{-4}, Y^{-5}, Y^5, Y^4, Y^{-1}, Y^{14}\}$ and

$$\begin{aligned}
\mathsf{crs_P} &= \begin{pmatrix} [\{u_j(x)y^5 + v_j(x)y^{-5} + w_j(x)y^{-4}\}_{j=m_0+1}^{m}, y^0, \{x^j y^{-2}\}_{j=0}^{n-1}]_1, \\ [\{x^i Z(x) y^{-4}\}_{j=0}^{n-2}, y^{-3}, y^7]_1, [y^0, \{x^j y^{-2}\}_{j=0}^{n-1}]_2 \end{pmatrix}, \\
\mathsf{crs_V} &= ([\{u_j(x)y^3 + v_j(x)y^{-7} + w_j(x)y^{-6}\}_{j=1}^{m_0}, y^{-3}]_1, [y^0, y^7, y^2]_2, [y^4]_T) .
\end{aligned} \tag{12}$$

In addition, our computer search tries to minimize the CRS length, but none of the choices of $\boldsymbol{\Delta}$ in Table 3 results in a shorter CRS.

On 2-Phase Updatability. Each of $Y^\alpha, Y^\beta, \ldots$ can be changed to an independent indeterminant, $Y_\alpha, Y_\beta, \ldots$, without invalidating the knowledge-soundness (or ASE) proof. This offers us the flexibility of choosing the number of trapdoors. In particular, Kohlweiss *et al.* proved recently [27] that Groth's SNARK [23] is two-phase updatable. Similarly, $\mathsf{S_{qap}}$ is two-phase updatable, when one defines three trapdoors, x, y, z, and uses well-chosen powers of z instead of y^α and y^η throughout the construction of $\mathsf{S_{qap}}$. Then, one can update x and y in the first and z in the second phase. We will omit further discussion.

4 Any-Simulation Extractability of $\mathsf{S_{qap}}$

Next, we prove that $\mathsf{S_{qap}}$ is ASE. The ASE proof is similar to the knowledge-soundness proof Theorem 1. The main difference is the handling of the case when $\mathcal{V}(\boldsymbol{X}) = 0$ as a Laurent polynomial. We use some monomials of $\mathcal{V}(\boldsymbol{X})$ to simplify the formulas and then arrive at a crossroad: in one case, the adversary did not use simulation query results, and thus we are back to the knowledge-soundness proof. In the second case, the adversary used some of the query results; then, we use specific coefficients of $\mathcal{V}(\boldsymbol{X})$ to argue that she used the result of precisely one query. After that, we show that the adversary used the same input to the simulator in this query as in the forgery attempt. (This result relies on an additional assumption that each $u_j(X)$, for $j \le m_0$, is linearly independent of all other $u_i(X)$, $i \le m$. This assumption can be easily satisfied by adding to the QAP m_0 dummy constraints $u_j \cdot 1 = u_j$, similarly to [21].) Hence, this is not an ASE but a *SASE* attack, and thus not valid in our context. Thus, $\mathsf{S}_{\mathsf{qap}}$ is ASE.

In the ASE proof, the algebraic adversary $\mathcal{A}$ also sees the outputs of the simulator. Thus, $\mathcal{A}$ has more inputs than in the knowledge-soundness proof. Let $\boldsymbol{\sigma}_k = (\sigma_{kj})_{j=1}^{m_0}$ be the maliciously chosen simulator input that the adversary used, instead of $(\mathbb{z}_j)_{j=1}^{m_0}$, during the kth query. Let $\boldsymbol{X} = (X, \boldsymbol{Q}_1, \boldsymbol{Q}_2, \boldsymbol{D}, \boldsymbol{E}, Y)$ and $\boldsymbol{X}^* = (X, \boldsymbol{Q}_1, \boldsymbol{Q}_2)$, where D_k (resp., E_k) is the indeterminate corresponding to the trapdoor $d = d_k$ (resp., $e = e_k$) generated by the simulator during the kth query. Observing Fig. 3, Sim answers with $([d_k, y^{-\alpha}((d_k e_k + y^\delta d_k + y^\gamma e_k) - \sum_{j=1}^{m_0} \sigma_{kj} P_j(x,y))]_1, [e_k]_2)$. Thus, in the ASE proof, $A^\dagger(\boldsymbol{X})$, $B^\dagger(\boldsymbol{X})$, and $C_s^\dagger(\boldsymbol{X})$ have the following additional addends:

$$
\begin{aligned}
A^\dagger(\boldsymbol{X}) &= \ldots + \textstyle\sum_k s_{a1k} D_k + \sum_k s_{a2k} Y^{-\alpha}((D_k E_k + Y^\delta D_k + Y^\gamma E_k) - \sum_{j=1}^{m_0} \sigma_{kj} P_j(X,Y)) \ , \\
C_s^\dagger(\boldsymbol{X}) &= \ldots + \textstyle\sum_k s_{c1k} D_k + \sum_k s_{c2k} Y^{-\alpha}((D_k E_k + Y^\delta D_k + Y^\gamma E_k) - \sum_{j=1}^{m_0} \sigma_{kj} P_j(X,Y)) \ , \\
B^\dagger(\boldsymbol{X}) &= \ldots + \textstyle\sum_k s_{bk} E_k \ .
\end{aligned}
$$

Here, the coefficients like s_{a1k} are chosen by the adversary. Let $\mathcal{V}(\boldsymbol{X}) = \sum_{i_1,i_2,i_3,i_4,k_1,k_2,k_3} \mathcal{V}_{Y^{i_1} D_{k_1}^{i_2} E_{k_2}^{i_3} E_{k_3}^{i_4}}(\boldsymbol{X}^*) Y^{i_1} D_{k_1}^{i_2} E_{k_2}^{i_3} E_{k_3}^{i_4}$. The addition of new addends to polynomials like $A^\dagger(\boldsymbol{X})$ means that the existing critical coefficients of $\mathcal{V}_{Y^{i_1}\ldots}$ of $\mathcal{V}(\boldsymbol{X})$ change by extra addends; we have denoted these extras by $\hat{\mathcal{V}}_{Y^{i}\ldots}$ in Table 2. Moreover, there are a number of new critical coefficients, depicted in the bottom of Table 2. For example, $\mathcal{V}_{Y^{\beta+\delta}}(\boldsymbol{X}^*) = (b_\delta + 1) u_a(X) + a_\delta v_b(X) - u(X) + \sum_k (s_{c2k} - r_b s_{a2k}) \sum_j \sigma_{kj} u_j(X)$ and, for any k, $\mathcal{V}_{Y^\gamma E_k}(\boldsymbol{X}^*) = r_b s_{a2k} + (a_\gamma + 1) s_{bk} - s_{c2k}$. Since here, the index $Y^{i_1} D_{k_1}^{i_2} E_{k_2}^{i_3} E_{k_3}^{i_4}$ of $\mathcal{V}_{Y^{i_1}\ldots}$ depends on a non-constant number of indeterminates, here both $\mathsf{Coeff}_{se} := \{Y^{i_1} D_{k_1}^{i_2} E_{k_2}^{i_3} E_{k_3}^{i_4} : \mathcal{V}_{Y^{i_1} D_{k_1}^{i_2} E_{k_2}^{i_3} E_{k_3}^{i_4}}(\boldsymbol{X}^*) \neq 0\}$ and

$$
\begin{aligned}
\mathsf{Crit}_{se} =& \{Y^{2\beta}, Y^{\beta+\gamma}, Y^{\beta+\delta}, Y^{\gamma+\delta}, Y^{\gamma+\eta}, Y^{2\delta}\} \cup \{Y^{-\alpha+2\delta} D_k\}_k \cup \{Y^\gamma E_k\}_k \cup \\
& \{D_{k_1} E_{k_2}\}_{k_1,k_2} \cup \{Y^\delta D_k\}_k \cup \{Y^\beta E_k\}_k
\end{aligned}
$$

also contain a non-constant number of coefficients. For example, Crit_{se} contains $D_{k_1} E_{k_2}$ for any $k_1, k_2 \le q_s$, where q_s is the number of simulation queries. However, there are only 12 "families" of critical coefficients, and the members of the same family (say $D_1 E_2$ and $D_7 E_2$) can be analyzed similarly.

For Crit_{se} to consist of different monomials and for $\mathsf{Crit}_{se} \cap \overline{\mathsf{Crit}_{se}}$, the new critical monomials $Y^{i_1} D_k^{i_2} E_k^{i_3}$ (see Table 2, the last 6 monomials) must be different from all other monomials. We say that $\boldsymbol{\Delta}$ is *ASE-friendly* if these conditions are satisfied. While the number of additional monomials in Crit and Coeff

is huge, ascertaining that the new critical monomials are unique is relatively easy, even if tedious, since one needs to guarantee that for each fixed (i_2, i_3), if $Y^{i_1} D_k^{i_2} E_k^{i_3} \in \mathsf{Crit}_{se}$ and $Y^{i'_1} D_k^{i_2} E_k^{i_3} \in \mathsf{Coeff}_{se}$ then $i_1 \neq i'_1$. By inspection, one can establish that it means the following.

1. (a) When $i_2 = 1$ and $i_3 = 0$, we need $-\alpha + 2\delta \neq \delta$ (i.e., $\delta \neq \alpha$, which follows from the fact that $Y^{\beta+\delta} \in \mathsf{Crit}$ and $Y^{\alpha+\beta} \in \overline{\mathsf{Crit}}$) and $-\alpha + 2\delta, \delta \notin \{\alpha, \beta, -\alpha + \beta + \delta, \eta, -\alpha + \delta + \eta\}$.
   This guarantees, say, that $Y^{-\alpha+2\delta} D_k$ (which is a critical monomial) is not equal to $Y^{-\alpha+\delta+\eta} D_k$.
2. (b) When $i_2 = 0$ and $i_3 = 1$, we need $\gamma \neq \beta$ and $\gamma, \beta \notin \{\alpha, -\alpha + 2\beta, -\alpha + \beta + \gamma, \delta, -\alpha + \beta + \delta, -\alpha + \gamma + \delta, 2\beta - \eta, \beta + \gamma - \eta, \beta + \delta - \eta, -\alpha + \gamma + \eta\}$.
3. (c) When $i_2 = 1$ and $i_3 = 1$, we need $0 \notin \{-\alpha + \beta, -\alpha + \delta, -\alpha + \eta\}$.

By simple but tedious case analysis, one can prove the following lemma.

Lemma 1. *If $\boldsymbol{\Delta}$ is soundness-friendly, then it is also ASE-friendly.*

Proof. **(a)** Here, $-\alpha + 2\delta \neq \delta$ (i.e., $\delta \neq \alpha$) follows from the fact that $Y^{\beta+\delta} \in \mathsf{Crit}$ and $Y^{\alpha+\beta} \in \overline{\mathsf{Crit}}$. Moreover, $-\alpha + 2\delta \neq \alpha$ and $\delta \neq \alpha$ follow since $\alpha \neq \delta$, $-\alpha + 2\delta \neq \beta$ follows since $Y^{2\delta} \in \mathsf{Crit}$ and $Y^{\alpha+\beta} \in \overline{\mathsf{Crit}}$, $\delta \neq \beta$ follows since $Y^{2\beta}, Y^{2\delta} \in \mathsf{Crit}$, $-\alpha + 2\delta \neq -\alpha + \beta + \delta$ follows since $\beta \neq \delta$, $\delta \neq -\alpha + \beta + \delta$ follows since $\alpha \neq \delta$, $-\alpha + 2\delta \neq \eta$ follows from $Y^{2\delta} \in \mathsf{Crit}$ and $Y^{\alpha+\eta} \in \overline{\mathsf{Crit}}$, $\delta \neq \eta$ follows from $Y^{\gamma+\delta}, Y^{\gamma+\eta} \in \mathsf{Crit}$, $-\alpha + 2\delta \neq -\alpha + \delta + \eta$ follows from $\delta \neq \eta$, $\delta \neq -\alpha + \delta + \eta$ follows form $Y^{\gamma+\eta} \in \mathsf{Crit}$ and $Y^{\alpha+\gamma} \in \overline{\mathsf{Crit}}$.

(b) Next, $\gamma \neq \beta$ follows from $Y^{2\beta}, Y^{\beta+\gamma} \in \mathsf{Crit}$, $\gamma \neq \alpha$ follows from $Y^{\beta+\gamma} \in \mathsf{Crit}$ and $Y^{\alpha+\beta} \in \overline{\mathsf{Crit}}$, $\beta \neq \alpha$ follows from $Y^{2\beta} \in \mathsf{Crit}$ and $Y^{\alpha+\beta} \in \overline{\mathsf{Crit}}$, $\gamma \neq -\alpha + 2\beta$ follows from $Y^{2\beta} \in \mathsf{Crit}$ and $Y^{\alpha+\gamma} \in \overline{\mathsf{Crit}}$, $\beta \neq -\alpha + 2\beta$ follows from $\alpha \neq \beta$, $\gamma \neq -\alpha + \beta + \gamma$ follows from $\alpha \neq \beta$, $\beta \neq -\alpha + \beta + \gamma$ follows from $\alpha \neq \gamma$, $\gamma \neq \delta$ follows from $Y^{\beta+\gamma}, Y^{\beta+\delta} \in \mathsf{Crit}$, $\beta \neq \delta$ is already proven, $\gamma \neq -\alpha + \beta + \delta$ follows from $Y^{\beta+\gamma} \in \mathsf{Crit}$ and $Y^{-\alpha+2\beta+\delta} \in \overline{\mathsf{Crit}}$, $\beta \neq -\alpha + \beta + \delta$ follows from $\alpha \neq \delta$, $\gamma \neq -\alpha + \gamma + \delta$ follows from $\alpha \neq \delta$, $\beta \neq -\alpha + \gamma + \delta$ follows from $Y^{\gamma+\delta} \in \mathsf{Crit}$ and $Y^{\alpha+\beta} \in \overline{\mathsf{Crit}}$, $\gamma \neq 2\beta - \eta$ follows from $Y^{2\beta}, Y^{\gamma+\eta} \in \mathsf{Crit}$, $\beta \neq 2\beta - \eta$ (i.e., $\beta \neq \eta$) follows from $Y^{\beta+\gamma}, Y^{\gamma+\eta} \in \mathsf{Crit}$, $\gamma \neq \beta + \gamma - \eta$ follows from $\beta \neq \eta$, $\beta \neq \beta + \gamma - \eta$ (i.e., $\gamma \neq \eta$) follows from $Y^{\beta+\delta} \in \mathsf{Crit}$ and $Y^{\beta+\gamma+\delta-\eta} \in \overline{\mathsf{Crit}}$, $\gamma \neq \beta + \delta - \eta$ follows from $Y^{\beta+\delta}, Y^{\gamma+\eta} \in \mathsf{Crit}$, $\beta \neq \beta + \delta - \eta$ follows from $\delta \neq \eta$, $\gamma \neq -\alpha + \gamma + \eta$ follows from $Y^{\gamma+\eta} \in \mathsf{Crit}$ and $Y^{\alpha+\gamma} \in \overline{\mathsf{Crit}}$, $\beta \neq -\alpha + \gamma + \eta$ follows from $Y^{\gamma+\eta} \in \mathsf{Crit}$ and $Y^{\alpha+\beta} \in \overline{\mathsf{Crit}}$.

(c) Finally, $\alpha \neq \beta$ and $\alpha \neq \delta$ is already known, and $\alpha \neq \eta$ follows from $Y^{\gamma+\eta} \in \mathsf{Crit}$ and $Y^{\alpha+\gamma} \in \overline{\mathsf{Crit}}$. □

Theorem 2. *Let $\mathcal{T}_\iota^x$ and $\mathcal{T}_\iota^y$ be as in Theorem 1. Let $\mathcal{I}_{\mathsf{qap}} = (\mathbb{Z}_p, m_0, \{u_j, v_j, w_j\}_{j=1}^m)$ be a QAP instance. Let $\mathsf{S}_{\mathsf{qap}}$ be the SNARK in Fig. 3. Assume $\boldsymbol{\Delta}$ is soundness-friendly. Assume $u_j(X)$, $j \leq m_0$, are linearly independent from each other and from other polynomials u_i for $i > m_0$. $\mathsf{S}_{\mathsf{qap}}$ is non-black-box ASE in the AGM under the $(\mathcal{T}_1^x, \mathcal{T}_2^x)$-PDL and $(\mathcal{T}_1^y, \mathcal{T}_2^y)$-PDL assumptions.*

$\boxed{\mathcal{B}^y(\mathsf{p}, \mathbf{R}, \mathbb{x}_{\mathcal{B}})}$ $\mathcal{B}^x(\mathsf{p}, \mathbf{R}, \mathbb{x}_{\mathcal{B}})$

$[\boldsymbol{d}]_1 \leftarrow \emptyset; [\boldsymbol{e}]_2 \leftarrow \emptyset; \zeta \leftarrow 0;$
Run $\mathcal{B}^z(\mathsf{p}, \mathbf{R}, \mathbb{x}_{\mathcal{B}})$ in Fig. 4, except give $\mathcal{A}$ also access to $\mathcal{O}_{\mathsf{Sim}}$;

$\mathcal{O}_{\mathsf{Sim}}((\sigma_j)_{j=1}^{m_0})$

$[\mathsf{c}_p]_1 \leftarrow \sum_{j=1}^{m_0} \sigma_j [P_j(x, y) y^{-\eta}]_1;$
$\zeta \leftarrow \zeta + 1; \boxed{d_\zeta, e_\zeta \leftarrow_\$ \mathbb{Z}_p}; s'_\zeta, s''_\zeta, t'_\zeta, t''_\zeta \leftarrow_\$ \mathbb{Z}_p;$
$[d_\zeta]_1 \leftarrow s'_\zeta [x]_1 + t'_\zeta [1]_1; [e_\zeta]_2 \leftarrow s''_\zeta [x]_2 + t''_\zeta [1]_2; [\mathsf{a}]_1 \leftarrow [d_\zeta]_1; [\mathsf{b}]_2 \leftarrow [e_\zeta]_2;$
$[\mathsf{c}_s]_1 \leftarrow y^{-\alpha}([\mathsf{a}e_\zeta]_1 + y^\delta [\mathsf{a}]_1 + y^\gamma [e_\zeta]_1 - y^\eta [\mathsf{c}_p]_1);$ **return** $[q_{\iota \xi_\iota}]_\iota$;

Fig. 5. $\mathcal{B}(\mathsf{p}, \mathbf{R}, \mathbb{x}_{\mathcal{B}})$ in the proof of Theorem 2, and the emulation of $\mathcal{O}_{\mathsf{Sim}}$. Full-boxed and dashed-boxed are defined as in Fig. 4.

Proof. The ASE proof is similar to the knowledge-soundness proof. There are two main differences. First, $\mathcal{B}$ also has to emulate Sim to $\mathcal{A}$. Second, the analysis of the abort probability is different due to the larger number of critical monomials.

Hence, we refer to the proof of Theorem 1, except that the full description of $\mathcal{B}^z$ in Fig. 5 contains also the emulation of simulation queries. (Obviously, there is more going on behind the scene: for example, $\mathcal{V}$ is defined differently, and $\boldsymbol{X}^*$ includes $\boldsymbol{D}, \boldsymbol{E}$, but we already explained that part.)

The only thing left to do now is the different (more complicated) analysis of the abort probability.

Analysis of the abort probability in step (*). Assume that $\mathcal{V}(\boldsymbol{X}) = 0$, thus also $\mathcal{V}_{Y^{i_1} \dots}(\boldsymbol{X}^*) = 0$ for all critical monomials (see Theorem 2). From the coefficient of $Y^{\gamma+\delta}$ of $\mathcal{V}$, we get $b_\delta = -a_\gamma/(a_\gamma + 1)$ and thus $a_\gamma, b_\delta \neq -1$. From the coefficients of $Y^{\gamma+\eta}$ and $Y^{2\delta}$, and since $a_\gamma, b_\delta \neq -1$, we get $b_\eta = 0$ and $a_\delta = 0$. Up to now, the proof looks similar to that of Theorem 1. The rest of the coefficients have to be handled differently.

From the coefficients of $Y^{\beta+\delta}$ and $Y^{\beta+\gamma}$, we get

$$\begin{aligned} u_a(X) =& (a_\gamma + 1)(u(X) + \textstyle\sum_j (\sum_{k=1}^{m_0} \sigma_{kj}(r_b s_{a2k} - s_{c2k}))\, u_j(X)) \ , \\ v_b(X) =& (v(X) + \textstyle\sum_j (\sum_{k=1}^{m_0} \sigma_{kj}(r_b s_{a2k} - s_{c2k}))\, v_j(X))/(a_\gamma + 1) \ . \end{aligned}$$

From the coefficient of $Y^{-\alpha+2\delta} D_k$, we get $s_{a2k} = 0$. From the coefficients of $Y^\gamma E_k$ and $D_k E_k$, we get $s_{c2k} = (a_\gamma + 1) s_{bk} = s_{a1k} s_{bk}$. Thus, for all k, either (i) $s_{bk} = s_{c2k} = 0$ or (ii) $s_{a1k} = a_\gamma + 1 \neq 0$ and $s_{c2k} = (a_\gamma + 1) s_{bk} \neq 0$.

If the case (i) holds for all k, then the first three polynomials $\hat{V}_{Y^i}$ in Table 2 are 0 and we are back to the knowledge-soundness case. One can then follow the remaining proof of Theorem 1, and obtain knowledge-soundness and ASE. Note that then, from the coefficient of $Y^\delta D_k$, it follows that also $s_{a1k} = 0$ for all k. Thus, the adversary did not benefit from the simulation queries.

Consider the case when at least for one k, (ii) holds. From the coefficient of $Y^{\delta} D_k$ of this k, we get $0 = r_b s_{a2k} + (b_\delta + 1) s_{a1k} - s_{c2k} = 1 - (a_\gamma + 1) s_{bk}$ and thus $s_{bk} = 1/(a_\gamma + 1)$. From the coefficient of $D_{k_1} E_{k_2}$ for any $k_1 \neq k_2$, we get $s_{a1k_1} s_{bk_2} = 0$. Thus, if some $s_{a1k_2} \neq 0$, then (since we are in the case (ii)) also $s_{bk_2} \neq 0$, and thus $s_{a1k_1} = s_{bk_1} = s_{c2k_1} = 0$ for all $k_1 \neq k_2$. Hence, $r_b s_{a2k_1} - s_{c2k_1} = 0$, and thus making the k_1th simulation query, $k_1 \neq k_2$, does not help the adversary. Thus, we can assume that $\mathcal{A}$ makes only one query, say the k_2th one, with the simulator input $\boldsymbol{\sigma} = (\sigma_j)$.

From the coefficient of $Y^{\beta} E_{k_2}$, we get $s_{bk_2} u_a(X) = 0$. Since $s_{bk_2} \neq 0$ and $a_\gamma \neq -1$, $\sum_{j \leq m_0} (\sigma_j (r_b s_{a2k_2} - s_{c2k_2}) + \mathbb{z}_j)\, u_j(X) + \sum_{j > m_0} \tilde{\mathbb{z}}_j u_j(X) = 0$. Since $s_{a2k_2} = 0$ and $s_{c2k_2} = 1$, $\sum_{j \leq m_0} (\mathbb{z}_j - \sigma_j)\, u_j(X) + \sum_{j > m_0} \tilde{\mathbb{z}}_j u_j(X) = 0$. Since $u_j(X)$ are linearly independent for $j \leq m_0$, it means $\mathbb{z}_j = \sigma_j$ for all $j \leq m_0$. Thus, $\mathcal{A}$ made the only simulation query on the same input that she used to cheat on, and thus this corresponds to a SASE but not an ASE attack. Hence, $\mathcal{A}$ did not succeed in an ASE attack and thus $\chi(X) = 0$. □

On Lower-Bound of [25]**.** Groth and Maller proved that in any SASE SNARK, the verifier has to perform two verification equations. Our result does not contradict it since we achieve ASE, a weaker property. (Similarly, the ASE SNARK of [6] has only one verification equation.)

5 Subversion-Zero Knowledge

In a subversion zero-knowledge (Sub-ZK) SNARK [1,3,7,17], the goal is to obtain zero-knowledge even if the CRS creator cannot be trusted. As noted in [2], one has to use non-falsifiable assumptions to achieve Sub-ZK. Next, we show that $\mathsf{S}_{\mathsf{qap}}$ is Sub-ZK (under the BDH-KE assumption), assuming $\boldsymbol{\Delta}$ satisfies some additional requirements. The same argument applies in the case of all other new SNARKs. In particular, five different choices of $\boldsymbol{\Delta}$ in Table 3 result in a Sub-ZK SNARK; this includes the setting of Eq. (11).

According to the blueprint of [1,3,17], one can follow the next steps to make a SNARK subversion-resistant:

1. Construct a public CRS verification algorithm CV that checks that the CRS is correct (that is, it corresponds to *some* trapdoor td).
2. To facilitate public verification, this can mean adding new elements to the CRS. Let us denote the set of new elements by $\mathsf{crs}_{\mathsf{CV}}$. If $\mathsf{crs}_{\mathsf{CV}}$ is non-empty, then one must reprove knowledge-soundness and/or simulation-extractability, taking $\mathsf{crs}_{\mathsf{CV}}$ into account.
3. Under a reasonable knowledge assumption, extract td from the CRS.
4. Show how to simulate the argument by using the extracted trapdoor.

This blueprint is formalized in [3], and we refer the reader to it for a further discussion, including proof that trapdoor-extractability and ZK suffice to get Sub-ZK. Moreover, for trapdoor-extractability, it suffices to have CRS-verifiability and a strong enough extractability assumption.

Let us show that under the setting in Eq. (11) with CRS as in Eq. (12), the correctness (that is, that it corresponds to *some* choice of trapdoors) of the CRS of $\mathsf{S}_{\mathsf{qap}}$ can be verified by using a public CV algorithm. Modelling after [1,3], CV needs to check that (1) all trapdoors belong to correct domain (for example, it checks $y \in \mathbb{Z}_p^*$ by checking that $[y]_1 \neq [0]_1$), and that (2) all CRS elements $[f(\boldsymbol{x})]_\iota$, where f is a public rational function, are correctly computed from trapdoors $\boldsymbol{x}$. The last verification can be done step by step, starting from simpler (for example, lower-degree) functions and then using the already verified values as helpers to verify more complex functions.

We present the CRS verification algorithm CV for $\mathsf{S}_{\mathsf{qap}}$ in Fig. 6. Note that here we assume $u_j(X) = \sum u_{ji}X^i$, $v_j(X) = \sum v_{ji}X^i$, and $w_j(X) = \sum w_{ji}X^i$. It is easy (though tedious) to check that CV suffices to check that the CRS of $\mathsf{S}_{\mathsf{qap}}$ has been correctly generated but for the following two exceptions:

$\mathsf{CV}(\mathsf{crs}, \mathsf{crs}_{\mathsf{CV}})$:

Check that the following holds:
- // Trapdoors are not 0 and $x^n \neq 1$:
- $[xy^\beta]_1 \neq [0]_1; [Z(x)y^{2\beta-\alpha}]_1 \neq [0]_1;$
- // The bracketed elements $y^4 = y^\delta, z, x^j y^\beta = x^j y$ in $\mathbb{G}_1$ and $\mathbb{G}_2$ are consistent:
- $[y^\delta]_1 \bullet [1]_2 = [1]_1 \bullet [y^\delta]_2;$
- **for** $j = 0$ **to** $n-1$ **do** $[x^j y^\beta]_1 \bullet [1]_2 = [1]_1 \bullet [x^j y^\beta]_2;$ **endfor**
- // Degrees of y^i are consistent: depends on $\boldsymbol{\Delta}$; recall $\alpha = 0, \beta = -2, \gamma = -3, \delta = 7, \eta = 2$
- $\boxed{[1]_1 \bullet [y^\eta]_2 = [y]_1 \bullet [y]_2; [y^\beta]_1 \bullet [y^\eta]_2 = [1]_1 \bullet [1]_2; [y^\gamma]_1 \bullet [y]_2 = [y^\beta]_1 \bullet [1]_2;}$
- $\boxed{[y^\gamma]_1 \bullet [y^\delta]_2 = [y^\eta]_1 \bullet [y^\eta]_2;}$
- // Degrees of $x^j y^\beta = x^j y$ are consistent:
- **for** $j = 1$ **to** $n-2$ **do** $[x^{j+1}y^\beta]_1 \bullet [y^\beta]_2 = [x^j y^\beta]_1 \bullet [xy^\beta]_2;$ **endfor**
- // $x^j Z(x)y^{2\beta-\alpha} = x^j Z(x)y^2$ are consistent:
- $[Z(x)y^{2\beta-\alpha}]_1 \bullet [1]_2 = \boxed{xy^{\beta-\alpha}}_1 \bullet [x^{n-1}y^\beta]_2 - \boxed{y^{\beta-\alpha}}_1 \bullet [y^\beta]_2;$
- **for** $j = 0$ **to** $n-3$ **do** $[x^{j+1}Z(x)y^{2\beta-\alpha}]_1 \bullet [y^\beta]_2 = [x^j Z(x)y^{2\beta-\alpha}]_1 \bullet [xy^\beta]_2;$ **endfor**
- // Polynomials $P_j(x,y)y^{-\eta} = u_j(x)y^{\beta-\eta+\delta} + v_j(x)y^{\beta-\eta+\gamma} + w_j(x)y^{2\beta-\eta}$ are consistent:
- **for** $j = 1$ **to** m_0 **do**
  - $[P_j(x,y)y^{-\eta}]_1 \bullet [y^\eta]_2 =$
  - $\sum_{i=0}^{n-1} u_{ji}[x^i y^\beta]_1 \bullet [y^\delta]_2 + [y^\gamma]_1 \bullet \sum_{i=0}^{n-1} v_{ji}[x^i y^\beta]_2 + \sum_{i=0}^{n-1} w_{ji}[x^i y^\beta]_1 \bullet [y^\beta]_2;$
- **endfor**
- // Polynomials $P_j(x,y)y^{-\alpha} = u_j(x)y^{\beta-\alpha+\delta} + v_j(x)y^{\beta-\alpha+\gamma} + w_j(x)y^{2\beta-\alpha}$ are consistent:
- **for** $j = m_0+1$ **to** m **do**
  - $[P_j(x,y)y^{-\alpha}]_1 \bullet [1]_2 =$
  - $\sum_{i=0}^{n-1} u_{ji}[x^i y^\beta]_1 \bullet \boxed{y^{-\alpha+\delta}}_2 + \boxed{y^{-\alpha+\gamma}}_1 \bullet \sum_{i=0}^{n-1} v_{ji}[x^i y^\beta]_2 +$
  - $\sum_{i=0}^{n-1} w_{ji}[x^i y^\beta]_1 \bullet \boxed{y^{\beta-\alpha}}_2;$
- **endfor**

Fig. 6. The CRS verification algorithm CV in $\mathsf{S}_{\mathsf{qap}}$. dashed elements are guaranteed to be in the CRS if $\alpha = 0$. dotted equalities and the integer exponents in comments depend on the concrete of $\boldsymbol{\Delta}$ (namely, Eq. (11))

1. The dashed elements are not guaranteed to be in the CRS unless $\boldsymbol{\Delta}$ is well-chosen. A simple way of solving this problem is to set $\alpha \leftarrow 0$. This is not too restrictive, since 12 out of 14 $\boldsymbol{\Delta}$-s in Table 3 have $\alpha = 0$.

2. One must verify that, for some ι such that $[y^\kappa]_\iota$ is in the CRS, y^κ is correctly computed, where $\kappa \in \{\beta, \gamma, \delta, \eta\}$. (Recall that $\alpha = 0$.)
   This involves adding a small number of pairing equations of type $[y^i]_1 \bullet [y^j]_2 = [y^k]_2 \bullet [y^\ell]_2$, such that each equation introduces exactly one new degree (either i, j, k or ℓ) and reuses three degrees that are already "verified". For example, in the first equation $i, j, k \in \{0, 1\}$. In this case, one can use pairings to establish the correctness of y^ℓ for $\ell \in \{-1, 0, 1, 2\}$. This means we need to put additional restrictions on $\boldsymbol{\Delta}$.

Lemma 2. *From the* 14 *settings of* $\boldsymbol{\Delta}$ *in Table 2, the five ones marked with* ✓ *are CRS-verifiable.*

Proof. Intuitively, we just need to describe how we (manually) found which of the choices of $\boldsymbol{\Delta}$ from Table 3 satisfy both above restrictions. As already mentioned, the first restriction is straightforward to satisfy. Now, assuming that $\alpha = 0$, consider two cases of ℓ from the first pairing equation in the second restriction:

1. $\ell = -1$. In the second pairing equation, then (say) $i, j, k \in \{-1, 0, 1\}$. In this case, one can establish the correctness of y^ℓ for $\ell \in [-3, 3]$.
   To solve this, we look at the possible $\boldsymbol{\Delta}$-s in Table 3, such that $\alpha = 0$ and one of $\beta, \gamma, \delta, \eta$ is equal to either -1 or 2. This only weeds out one additional possibility (namely, $\boldsymbol{\Delta} = (0, -3, 5, 7, 1)$).
   In the case one of $\beta, \gamma, \delta, \eta$ is equal to -1, we will look at the cases when one of the three other values $\kappa \in \{\beta, \gamma, \delta, \eta\}$ belongs to $[-3, 3]$. This leaves still several possibilities, $\boldsymbol{\Delta} \in \{(0, -1, 6, -4, 1), (0, -1, 7, -4, 1), (0, -1, 7, -5, 1), \ldots\}$. However, in only one case, $\boldsymbol{\Delta} = (0, 3, -5, -7, -1)$, it is possible to verify all 5 values y^κ for $\kappa \in \{\alpha, \beta, \gamma, \delta, \eta\}$: namely, by checking that (say) $[y^\eta]_1 \bullet [y]_2 = [1]_1 \bullet [1]_1$, $[y^\eta]_1 \bullet [y^\beta]_2 = [y]_1 \bullet [y]_1$, $[y^\gamma]_2 \bullet [y^\beta]_1 = [y^\eta]_1 \bullet [y^\eta]_1$, and $[y^\delta]_2 \bullet [y]_1 = [y^\gamma]_1 \bullet [y^\eta]_1$.
2. $\ell = 2$. Then, in the second equation, one can establish the correctness of y^ℓ for $\ell \in [-2, 3]$. W.l.o.g., we assume that $\ell \neq -1$ (otherwise we are back to the previous case). Thus, after two verification equations, we have the following cases left: $\boldsymbol{\Delta} \in \{(0, -2, -3, 7, 2), (-2, 6, 7, 2), (2, -6, -7, 2), (2, 3, -7, -2)\}$.
   A simple inspection establishes that in all the three cases, where both -2 and 2 are present, one has an efficient CRS-verification algorithm. For example, one can take $\boldsymbol{\Delta} = (-2, -3, 7, 2)$, that is, the setting in Eq. (11). Then, one has to verify that $[1]_1 \bullet [y^\eta]_2 = [y]_1 \bullet [y]_2$, $[y^\beta]_1 \bullet [y^\eta]_2 = [1]_1 \bullet [1]_2$, $[y^\gamma]_1 \bullet [y]_2 = [y^\beta]_1 \bullet [1]_2$, and $[y^\gamma]_1 \bullet [y^\beta]_2 = [y^\eta]_1 \bullet [y^\eta]_2$. (Those are the dotted equations in Fig. 6.) □

For the sake of concreteness, we recommend to choose $\boldsymbol{\Delta}$ as in Eq. (11). However, one can use any of the five checkmarked choices in Table 3.

One can significantly speed up CV in Fig. 6 by using batching techniques, as explained in [1,3]. CV for other new SNARKs are essentially the same, modulo some simplifications due to say $w_i(X) = 0$ in the case of the QSP.

Trapdoor-Extractability and Sub-ZK. Trapdoor-extractability [3] means that if CV accepts the CRS, then one can extract the simulation trapdoor. In all new SNARKs, the simulation trapdoor is equal to $\mathsf{td} = y$ since Sim does not use x. Clearly, in all new SNARKs, if CV accepts crs, one can use the BDH-KE assumption to extract y. Thus, BDH-KE guarantees trapdoor-extractability, and the CRS-verifiability and the trapdoor-extractability together guarantee that one can extract td. Hence, by the general result of [3], all new SNARKs are Sub-ZK, assuming that their CRS is verifiable and that the BDH-KE holds.

Corollary 1. *Under the five* ✓*-ed settings of* $\boldsymbol{\Delta}$ *in Table 2,* $\mathsf{S}_{\mathsf{qap}}$ *is statistically composable Sub-ZK under the BDH-KE assumption.*

Acknowledgment. We thank Markulf Kohlweiss, Janno Siim, and Mikhail Volkhov for helpful comments. The author was partially supported by the Estonian Research Council grant (PRG49).

References

1. Abdolmaleki, B., Baghery, K., Lipmaa, H., Zając, M.: A subversion-resistant SNARK. In: Takagi, T., Peyrin, T. (eds.) ASIACRYPT 2017, Part III. LNCS, vol. 10626, pp. 3–33. Springer, Cham (2017). https://doi.org/10.1007/978-3-319-70700-6_1
2. Abdolmaleki, B., Lipmaa, H., Siim, J., Zając, M.: On QA-NIZK in the BPK model. In: Kiayias, A., Kohlweiss, M., Wallden, P., Zikas, V. (eds.) PKC 2020, Part I. LNCS, vol. 12110, pp. 590–620. Springer, Cham (2020). https://doi.org/10.1007/978-3-030-45374-9_20
3. Abdolmaleki, B., Lipmaa, H., Siim, J., Zając, M.: On subversion-resistant SNARKs. J. Cryptol. **34**(3), 1–42 (2021). https://doi.org/10.1007/s00145-021-09379-y
4. Abdolmaleki, B., Ramacher, S., Slamanig, D.: Lift-and-shift: obtaining simulation extractable subversion and updatable SNARKs generically. In: ACM CCS 2020, pp. 1987–2005 (2020)
5. Baghery, K.: On the efficiency of privacy-preserving smart contract systems. In: Buchmann, J., Nitaj, A., Rachidi, T. (eds.) AFRICACRYPT 2019. LNCS, vol. 11627, pp. 118–136. Springer, Cham (2019). https://doi.org/10.1007/978-3-030-23696-0_7
6. Baghery, K., Kohlweiss, M., Siim, J., Volkhov, M.: Another look at extraction and randomization of Groth's zk-SNARK. In: Borisov, N., Diaz, C. (eds.) FC 2021. LNCS, vol. 12674, pp. 457–475. Springer, Heidelberg (2021). https://doi.org/10.1007/978-3-662-64322-8_22
7. Bellare, M., Fuchsbauer, G., Scafuro, A.: NIZKs with an untrusted CRS: security in the face of parameter subversion. In: Cheon, J.H., Takagi, T. (eds.) ASIACRYPT 2016, Part II. LNCS, vol. 10032, pp. 777–804. Springer, Heidelberg (2016). https://doi.org/10.1007/978-3-662-53890-6_26
8. Ben-Sasson, E., et al.: Zerocash: decentralized anonymous payments from bitcoin. In: 2014 IEEE Symposium on Security and Privacy, pp. 459–474 (2014)
9. Bitansky, N., Chiesa, A., Ishai, Y., Paneth, O., Ostrovsky, R.: Succinct non-interactive arguments via linear interactive proofs. In: Sahai, A. (ed.) TCC 2013. LNCS, vol. 7785, pp. 315–333. Springer, Heidelberg (2013). https://doi.org/10.1007/978-3-642-36594-2_18

10. Bowe, S., Gabizon, A.: Making Groth's zk-SNARK simulation extractable in the random oracle model. Cryptology ePrint Archive, Report 2018/187 (2018). https://eprint.iacr.org/2018/187
11. Campanelli, M., Gennaro, R., Goldfeder, S., Nizzardo, L.: Zero-knowledge contingent payments revisited: attacks and payments for services. In: ACM CCS 2017, pp. 229–243 (2017)
12. Canetti, R.: Universally composable security: a new paradigm for cryptographic protocols. In: 42nd FOCS, pp. 136–145 (2001)
13. Danezis, G., Fournet, C., Groth, J., Kohlweiss, M.: Square span programs with applications to succinct NIZK arguments. In: Sarkar, P., Iwata, T. (eds.) ASIACRYPT 2014, Part I. LNCS, vol. 8873, pp. 532–550. Springer, Heidelberg (2014). https://doi.org/10.1007/978-3-662-45611-8_28
14. De Santis, A., Di Crescenzo, G., Ostrovsky, R., Persiano, G., Sahai, A.: Robust non-interactive zero knowledge. In: Kilian, J. (ed.) CRYPTO 2001. LNCS, vol. 2139, pp. 566–598. Springer, Heidelberg (2001). https://doi.org/10.1007/3-540-44647-8_33
15. Dodis, Y., Haralambiev, K., López-Alt, A., Wichs, D.: Efficient public-key cryptography in the presence of key leakage. In: Abe, M. (ed.) ASIACRYPT 2010. LNCS, vol. 6477, pp. 613–631. Springer, Heidelberg (2010). https://doi.org/10.1007/978-3-642-17373-8_35
16. Fauzi, P., Lipmaa, H., Siim, J., Zając, M.: An efficient pairing-based shuffle argument. In: Takagi, T., Peyrin, T. (eds.) ASIACRYPT 2017, Part II. LNCS, vol. 10625, pp. 97–127. Springer, Cham (2017). https://doi.org/10.1007/978-3-319-70697-9_4
17. Fuchsbauer, G.: Subversion-zero-knowledge SNARKs. In: Abdalla, M., Dahab, R. (eds.) PKC 2018, Part I. LNCS, vol. 10769, pp. 315–347. Springer, Cham (2018). https://doi.org/10.1007/978-3-319-76578-5_11
18. Fuchsbauer, G.: WI is not enough: zero-knowledge contingent (service) payments revisited. In: ACM CCS 2019, pp. 49–62 (2019)
19. Fuchsbauer, G., Kiltz, E., Loss, J.: The algebraic group model and its applications. In: Shacham, H., Boldyreva, A. (eds.) CRYPTO 2018, Part II. LNCS, vol. 10992, pp. 33–62. Springer, Cham (2018). https://doi.org/10.1007/978-3-319-96881-0_2
20. Gabizon, A.: On the security of the BCTV Pinocchio zk-SNARK variant. Cryptology ePrint Archive, Report 2019/119 (2019). https://eprint.iacr.org/2019/119
21. Gennaro, R., Gentry, C., Parno, B., Raykova, M.: Quadratic span programs and succinct NIZKs without PCPs. In: Johansson, T., Nguyen, P.Q. (eds.) EUROCRYPT 2013. LNCS, vol. 7881, pp. 626–645. Springer, Heidelberg (2013). https://doi.org/10.1007/978-3-642-38348-9_37
22. Groth, J.: Short pairing-based non-interactive zero-knowledge arguments. In: Abe, M. (ed.) ASIACRYPT 2010. LNCS, vol. 6477, pp. 321–340. Springer, Heidelberg (2010). https://doi.org/10.1007/978-3-642-17373-8_19
23. Groth, J.: On the size of pairing-based non-interactive arguments. In: Fischlin, M., Coron, J.-S. (eds.) EUROCRYPT 2016, Part II. LNCS, vol. 9666, pp. 305–326. Springer, Heidelberg (2016). https://doi.org/10.1007/978-3-662-49896-5_11
24. Groth, J., Kohlweiss, M., Maller, M., Meiklejohn, S., Miers, I.: Updatable and universal common reference strings with applications to zk-SNARKs. In: Shacham, H., Boldyreva, A. (eds.) CRYPTO 2018, Part III. LNCS, vol. 10993, pp. 698–728. Springer, Cham (2018). https://doi.org/10.1007/978-3-319-96878-0_24
25. Groth, J., Maller, M.: Snarky signatures: minimal signatures of knowledge from simulation-extractable SNARKs. In: Katz, J., Shacham, H. (eds.) CRYPTO 2017, Part II. LNCS, vol. 10402, pp. 581–612. Springer, Cham (2017). https://doi.org/10.1007/978-3-319-63715-0_20

26. Groth, J., Maller, M.: Snarky signatures: minimal signatures of knowledge from simulation-extractable SNARKs. Cryptology ePrint Archive, Report 2017/540 (2017). https://eprint.iacr.org/2017/540
27. Kohlweiss, M., Maller, M., Siim, J., Volkhov, M.: Snarky ceremonies. In: ASIACRYPT 2021 (3). LNCS, vol. 13092, pp. 98–127. Springer, Cham (2021). https://doi.org/10.1007/978-3-030-92078-4_4
28. Kohlweiss, M., Zajac, M.: On simulation-extractability of universal zkSNARKs. Technical Report 2021/511, IACR (2021). https://ia.cr/2021/511
29. Kosba, A.E., et al.: C∅C∅: a framework for building composable zero-knowledge proofs. Technical Report 2015/1093. International Association for Cryptologic Research (2015). https://ia.cr/2015/1093
30. Lipmaa, H.: Progression-free sets and sublinear pairing-based non-interactive zero-knowledge arguments. In: Cramer, R. (ed.) TCC 2012. LNCS, vol. 7194, pp. 169–189. Springer, Heidelberg (2012). https://doi.org/10.1007/978-3-642-28914-9_10
31. Lipmaa, H.: Succinct non-interactive zero knowledge arguments from span programs and linear error-correcting codes. In: Sako, K., Sarkar, P. (eds.) ASIACRYPT 2013, Part I. LNCS, vol. 8269, pp. 41–60. Springer, Heidelberg (2013). https://doi.org/10.1007/978-3-642-42033-7_3
32. Lipmaa, H.: Simulation-extractable ZK-SNARKs revisited. Technical Report 2019/612. IACR (2019). https://ia.cr/2019/612
33. Lipmaa, H.: A unified framework for non-universal SNARKs. Technical report. IACR (2021). https://ia.cr/2021
34. Nielsen, J.B.: Separating random oracle proofs from complexity theoretic proofs: the non-committing encryption case. In: Yung, M. (ed.) CRYPTO 2002. LNCS, vol. 2442, pp. 111–126. Springer, Heidelberg (2002). https://doi.org/10.1007/3-540-45708-9_8
35. Parno, B.: A note on the unsoundness of vnTinyRAM's SNARK. Cryptology ePrint Archive, Report 2015/437 (2015). https://eprint.iacr.org/2015/437
36. Parno, B., Howell, J., Gentry, C., Raykova, M.: Pinocchio: nearly practical verifiable computation. In: 2013 IEEE Symposium on Security and Privacy, pp. 238–252 (2013)
37. Sahai, A.: Non-malleable non-interactive zero knowledge and adaptive chosen-ciphertext security. In: 40th FOCS, pp. 543–553 (1999)

ECLIPSE: Enhanced Compiling Method for Pedersen-Committed zkSNARK Engines

Diego F. Aranha[1(✉)], Emil Madsen Bennedsen[2], Matteo Campanelli[1], Chaya Ganesh[3], Claudio Orlandi[1], and Akira Takahashi[1]

[1] Aarhus University, Aarhus, Denmark
{dfaranha,matteo,orlandi,takahashi}@cs.au.dk
[2] Concordium, Aarhus, Denmark
emil@bennedsen.eu
[3] Indian Institute of Science, Bangalore, India
chaya@iisc.ac.in

Abstract. We advance the state-of-the art for zero-knowledge commit-and-prove SNARKs (CP-SNARKs). CP-SNARKs are an important class of SNARKs which, using commitments as "glue", allow to efficiently combine proof systems—e.g., general-purpose SNARKs (an efficient way to prove statements about circuits) and Σ-protocols (an efficient way to prove statements about group operations). Thus, CP-SNARKs allow to efficiently provide zero-knowledge proofs for composite statements such as $h = H(g^x)$ for some hash-function H.

Our main contribution is providing the first construction of CP-SNARKs where the proof size is succinct in the number of commitments.

We achieve our result by providing a general technique to compile Algebraic Holographic Proofs (AHP) (an underlying abstraction used in many modern SNARKs) with special "decomposition" properties into an efficient CP-SNARK. We then show that some of the most efficient AHP constructions—Marlin, PLONK, and Sonic—satisfy our compilation requirements.

Our resulting SNARKs achieve universal and updatable reference strings, which are highly desirable features as they greatly reduce the trust needed in the SNARK setup phase.

1 Introduction

Zero-knowledge (ZK) proofs and argument systems (ZK) [35] are one of the most fascinating concepts in modern cryptography, as they allow proving that a statement is valid without revealing any additional information as to why said statement is true. Even further, *Succinct Non-interactive ARguments of Knowledge* (zk-SNARKs), allow to do so in such a way that the size of the proof and the work the verifier needs to perform in order to check the proof is

Full version available at [3].

G. Hanaoka et al. (Eds.): PKC 2022, LNCS 13177, pp. 584–614, 2022.
https://doi.org/10.1007/978-3-030-97121-2_21

sublinear in the size of the statement. Today, zk-SNARKs are a fundamental building block in complex cryptographic systems such as e.g., Zcash [9], where succinct zero-knowledge proofs are used to provide integrity while maintaining privacy. In such applications, it is crucial that the verification time is minimal (as every user in the system has to perform the verification) and that the proofs are short and non-interactive (as they need to be posted on the Blockchain).

In this work we focus on *commit-and-prove* SNARKs (CP-SNARKs) (introduced in [21]).

This is an important family of SNARKs in which the witness is committed using Pedersen commitments (the de-facto *lingua franca* of commitments). The presence of these commitments allow to "glue" together different proof systems. An important application of CP-SNARKs is proving composite statements using the most efficient tool for each part of the statement. Such modularity of the CP proof system enhances *interoperability* with other protocols specialized for efficiently proving certain *algebraic relations*: consider a composite computation that naturally presents different components, like an arithmetic circuit for a hash function, and algebraic representation for group exponentiation. A general-purpose zero-knowledge proof system for such a computation requires a single homogeneous representation, thus incurring a high cost in performance. Ideally, one would like to take advantage of the nuances of a computation and choose the best proof system for each component of the computation, e.g., SNARKs for an arithmetic circuit and Σ-protocol for an algebraic relation. One of the simplest examples of such a statement is proving knowledge of the secret key corresponding to a Bitcoin address e.g., proving knowledge of some x such that $y = H(g^x)$ (without revealing g^x).

There are many other practical scenarios where the CP extension is useful, including, but not limited to, anonymous credentials [2,24,29], verifiable encryption [44], proof stitching [26,47,52,53], and e-voting [44]. Given these various potential applications, a working group focused on CP-ZK has recently been launched as part of the ZKProof Standards [12].

Unfortunately, existing CP-SNARKs are not truly "succinct" since their proof size scales linearly with the number of commitments containing subvectors of the witness. In this work, we fill this gap in the literature and provide the first truly succinct CP-SNARK.

1.1 Applications

To further motivate the need for succinct CP-SNARKs, we now provide some example applications. In all these applications, the commitments to (subset of) the witness are part of the public statement and, in practice, often exist prior to the time we prove properties on them. Motivated by this, we do not count the commitments as part of the proof size in this work.

We denote by ℓ the number of individual commitments containing the partial witness vector.

1. *Anonymous and Delegated Credentials.* In the application of making digital certificates anonymous, one would like to prove knowledge of a message m

and a signature σ, where σ is a valid signature on message m with respect to some public verification key. The main challenge is that the statement being considered is a composite statement containing both Boolean (hash function) and algebraic (group operations) components, since either the message is hashed before being signed or one needs to prove properties on the signed message. Efficient NIZK for composite statements that use a zk-SNARK for the circuit part and Σ-protocols for the algebraic would yield a proof system that is more efficient for the prover.
Consider now the setting of "delegated credentials". Each citizen or member of an organization can have associated a bundle of properties (credentials), e.g., credit and employment history or digital certificates issued by governments. We assume these properties are fingerprinted through a (compressing) commitment and that each of these users delegates the storage of these properties to a service. Every time the user needs to prove a statement on these credentials with respect to the public commitment, it can issue an order to the service. Instead of providing a single proof per user, a service can wait to accumulate ℓ orders and provide a single proof for all of them. If the resulting proof is succinct in ℓ, then this batching technique results in important savings. Note here that in this application it would not be feasible to commit to the credentials of all users in a single (vector) commitment, because the ℓ commitments to the credentials already exist and each single user should be able to verify that on their own.[1]

2. *Blockchains.* CP-SNARKs are useful in many Blockchain applications like *confidential* transactions [49] where range proofs are required on committed values, and in systems balancing privacy and accountability [28] where credentials are proven on committed values.
An example Blockchain application where $\ell > 1$ and succinct CP-SNARKs are desirable is *proof of solvency.* In privacy-preserving proof of solvency [2], the number of commitments ℓ is typically large. This is because in proof of liabilities, each customer has to check that their own balance has been included in the total liabilities published by the exchange. This is done by having the exchange send the decommitment information to each customer privately. Thus, in this application too, using a single (vector) commitment is not a feasible solution. Since each customer's balance is private, there must be as many commitments as the number of customers instead of one vector commitment to all balances.
3. *Machine Learning.* Another example of an application that benefits from succinct CP-SNARKs is verifying integrity of Machine Learning (ML) models. A hospital owns sensitive patient data, and one wishes to construct a model by running a training algorithm on this sensitive data. The hospital does not wish to and/or legally cannot release the data; making it a challenge to check the integrity of the model. Such settings have been considered, for example,

[1] The service can afford to wait for ℓ orders depending on the application, and the expected throughput and time-to-service of the application. As an example, the ID-Layer in Concordium [28] orders may be even serviced each epoch.

in [54]. One way to do this is to have the hospital use a zkSNARK to prove that the model is the output obtained by training it on the sensitive data and that public commitments indeed open to the same sensitive data.
In practice, ML algorithms are run on data held by different entities (hospitals in the example above). Each of the ℓ entities publishes a commitment to their sensitive data. Now a single trusted party can perform training on the combined data, but has to prove integrity with respect to commitment of each individual entity. Succinct CP-SNARKs provide efficiency benefits also in this case.

1.2 Our Contributions

In this work we present the first CP-SNARKs whose proof size is succinct in the number of commitments to the partial witness vectors. To do so, we combine state-of-the-art SNARKs with state-of-the-art Σ-protocols, inheriting several important properties of the underlying tools which we use.

An important property of our resulting proof system is that it has *universal, updatable and linear-size reference string*: Since we are interested in practically efficient and succinct proof systems, our starting points are *preprocessing* SNARKs, in which some form of trusted setup (in the form of a *structured reference string* or SRS) is required. If the trusted setup is compromised, it becomes possible to break the soundness property of the proof system. However, using SNARKs with *universal and updatable setup* (as introduced in [38]) the trust in the setup phase can be reduced to a minimum, as this allows participants to dynamically update the SRS was proposed. Even though this does not completely remove the problem of trusted setup, the security now depends on at least one honest party deleting the contributed randomness. Moreover, the SRS is *universal* in the sense that it allows to prove statements about all circuits of some bounded size (as opposed to earlier systems in which a different SRS was needed for each circuit, thus increasing the need for trusted setups). Furthermore, the size of the setup will be linear in the size (or upper bound of) the circuit to be proven.

From a technical point of view, our contributions can be summarized as follows:

- *Compiler from AHP to CP-SNARK.* In Sec. 3 we present a compiler that takes an AHP (Algebraic Holographic Proof, the information-theoretic protocol underlying many existing zkSNARKs) and compiles it into a CP-SNARK. Our compiler is similar in spirit to compilers of [18,20,25] that convert information-theoretic protocols to succinct arguments, but it naturally allows efficient CP extensions because of our "decompose–and–link" paradigm outlined in Sect. 1.3. The main technical challenge in building this compiler is that existing SNARK constructions employ different ways to *encode* the witness into a polynomial, even though the underlying information-theoretic objects can be described in the language of AHP. This makes it hard to identify how to generically & succinctly link committed values to only a small fraction of the large witness vector used in SNARK. Yet, we are able to abstract out a set of basic properties that AHPs and commitment schemes should satisfy, in order to apply the same paradigm. Thanks to our abstract approach, one does not need to examine the entire machinery of the AHP protocol; instead, it is sufficient to look at a few *witness-carrying polynomials* present in the AHP, check if they satisfy the properties required by our compiler theorem, and then focus on designing a sub-protocol performing a minimum set of tasks for "linking". We believe that our techniques are general enough to extend to future AHPs and commitment schemes.

- *Concrete instantiations.* We then apply our compiler to the AHPs of Marlin, PLONK and Sonic to obtain concrete CP-SNARKs.[2] This immediately allows us to prove that the inputs (and/or outputs) used in the zk-SNARK for an arithmetic circuit/Rank 1 constraint system statement are the same as the values inside an algebraic (Pedersen) commitment. This helps to hide intermediate outputs of a composite statement by committing to it, thus allowing switching between the algebraic (Σ-protocols) and arithmetic (zk-SNARK) worlds. In order to make the argument for the composite statement succinct, we use recent advances in compressed Σ-protocol theory. We cast the statement about consistency with Pedersen commitments as statements about knowledge of pre-image of group homomorphisms. This allows us to apply the compression techniques of [4,15] that achieve logarithmic communication for the canonical Σ-protocol and the amortization technique that proves many statements efficiently. Thus, our linking protocol that needs to prove ℓ statements, where each statement is about equality of vectors of size d, achieves communication complexity $O(\log(\ell d))$, so the overall proof (the size of the SNARK together with the size of the linking proof) is still succinct.

1.3 Technical Overview

Most recent constructions of updatable SRS zkSNARKs [18,25,32] follow a modular approach where an information-theoretic protocol is constructed in an abstract model like Probabilistically Checkable Proof (PCP), linear PCP, Interactive Oracle Proof (IOP) etc., and then the information-theoretic protocol is compiled via a cryptographic compiler to obtain an argument system. While several abstractions for this information-theoretic parts exist, it is folklore among researchers in this community that these formalizations are to some extent equivalent. In this paper, we rely on the formalization of (public-coin) *Algebraic Holographic Proofs (AHP)* of [25] and we cast the other SNARKs (PLONK [32] and Sonic [48]) in the same language.

[2] The reason why we apply our compiler to all three proof systems is that Marlin, PLONK and Sonic are a sort of rock-paper-scissor for AHPs (the first can outperform the second, which can outperform the third, which can in turn outperform the first). This is because they use different models of computations, and therefore it may be possible to prove some statements more efficiently with one system rather than the others.

Plain AHP-to-SNARK Framework. In an AHP the prover P takes a statement x and a witness vector $\mathbf{w} = (w_1, \ldots, w_n)$ as inputs and sends some *oracle polynomials* to the verifier V in each round, who responds with a random challenge. In the query phase, V can query an oracle polynomial p with an *evaluation point* z to obtain $v = p(z)$. V can iterate this process for several different polynomials and evaluation points. Finally, V outputs a decision bit indicating "accept" or "reject", based on the result of the evaluation queries.

An AHP can be turned into an argument system by replacing the oracles and the query phase with a *polynomial commitment scheme (PCS)*. As proposed by [42], PCS can be succinctly instantiated by using the discrete log-based encoding of polynomial: $\mathsf{PC.Com}_{\mathsf{ck}}(p(X)) := g^{p_0 + p_1 \chi + \cdots p_{n-1} \chi^{n-1}}$ with a commitment key $\mathsf{ck} = (g, g^{\chi}, \ldots, g^{\chi^{n-1}})$. Then upon receiving an evaluation point z, the prover responds with an *evaluation proof* to convince the verifier that evaluation $v = p(z)$ is done correctly.

Witness-Carrying Polynomials and CP Extension. Typically, one or few oracles sent by an AHP prover are *witness-carrying polynomials (WCP)* [20], meaning that they encode the entire witness vector $\mathbf{w}$. For ease of exposition, we assume the AHP has a single WCP $w(X)$ here, but our abstract compiler works for AHP with multiple WCP as well. The encoding/decoding method differs depending on the protocol. For example, Sonic employs a simple *coefficient* encoding, therefore, decoding works by mapping the coefficients to a witness vector, i.e., $w(X) := \sum_i w_i X^i$; PLONK and Marlin use *interpolation*, and decoding works by evaluating WCP on some prescribed set, i.e., $w(X) := \sum_i w_i \cdot L_i(X)$, where $(L_i(X))_{i \in [n]}$ are the Lagrange polynomials associated with some set $\mathbb{H}$ of size n.

In our CP scenario, we additionally consider a commitment scheme AC for Auxiliary Commitments. They are "auxiliary" in the sense that they are used as auxiliary inputs to parts of the witness, and in some applications, these commitments already exist. For example, if a subvector of witness $(w_i)_{i \in I_{\mathsf{com}}}$ with $I_{\mathsf{com}} \subset [n]$ is committed in advance via vector Pedersen commitment, an argument system additionally takes $\hat{c} = \mathsf{AC.Com}_{\mathsf{ack}}((w_i)_{i \in I_{\mathsf{com}}}; r) := H^r \prod_{i \in I_{\mathsf{com}}} G_i^{w_i}$ as part of the statement, where $\mathsf{ack} := ((G_i)_{i \in I_{\mathsf{com}}}, H)$. The goal of CP extension is to guarantee consistency between what is committed to via PC and AC. To this end, it should suffice to provide a sub-protocol for relation

$$\mathcal{R} := \left\{ ((c, \hat{c}), (\mathbf{w}, r)) \;:\; c = \prod_{i=1}^{n} g_i^{w_i} \;\wedge\; \hat{c} = H^r \prod_{i \in I_{\mathsf{com}}} G_i^{w_i} \right\}.$$

where $g_i = g^{\chi^{i-1}}$ or $g_i = g^{L_i(\chi)}$, depending on how the AHP under consideration encodes the witness into WCP.

A naïve approach would be to describe an arithmetic circuit for $\mathcal{R}$ and invoke another instance of SNARK. However, if the committing function of AC involves certain algebraic operations, e.g., group exponentiation or elliptic curve scalar multiplications as required in the Pedersen commitment, it would be very costly for the prover to express them in a circuit[3]. This is where a Σ-protocol comes into play.

Decomposing WCP and Linking with Σ-Protocol. A simple Σ-protocol can be used for proving equality of Pedersen-committed messages. However, because naïve instantiation of such a protocol for $\mathcal{R}$ inevitably proves knowledge of the *entire vector* $\mathbf{w}$, it would incur $O(n)$ proof size and verification time, losing succinctness. Although it is possible to apply the compressed Σ-protocol theory [4,15] to achieve $O(\log(n))$ proof size, if logarithmic proof size is acceptable, one could instead use Bulletproofs, which supports CP extensions with the Pedersen commitment by construction and already achieves $O(\log(n))$ proof size.

In fact, proving $\mathcal{R}$ turns out to be quite wasteful, since at the end of the day we only care about a small fraction of $\mathbf{w}$ that are committed beforehand. We circumvent the issue by additively *decomposing* the WCP $w(X)$ into two parts $w_{\mathsf{com}}(X)$ and $w_{\mathsf{mid}}(X)$, such that $w(X) = w_{\mathsf{com}}(X) + w_{\mathsf{mid}}(X)$, $w_{\mathsf{com}}(X)$ encodes the committed part of the witness $(w_i)_{i \in I_{\mathsf{com}}}$, and $w_{\mathsf{mid}}(X)$ contains the rest. In Sect. 3.2 we formally define this intuition. Accordingly, assuming *additively homomorphic* PCS (satisfied by KZG), one can also decompose a polynomial commitment c into c_{com} and c_{mid} such that $c = c_{\mathsf{com}} + c_{\mathsf{mid}} = \mathsf{PC.Com}_{\mathsf{ck}}(w_{\mathsf{mid}}) + \mathsf{PC.Com}_{\mathsf{ck}}(w_{\mathsf{com}})$. Now we only need to *link* c_{com} and $\hat{c}$; it suffices to cast c_{com} to the Σ-protocol for relation

$$\mathcal{R}' := \left\{((c_{\mathsf{com}}, \hat{c}), (\mathbf{w}, r)\ :\ c = \prod\nolimits_{i \in I_{\mathsf{com}}} g_i^{w_i}\ \wedge\ \hat{c} = H^r \prod\nolimits_{i \in I_{\mathsf{com}}} G_i^{w_i}\right\}$$

which only incurs $O(\log(|I_{\mathsf{com}}|))$ proof size and verification time.

Proving "Non-overlapping" Decomposition. The above idea needs additional care in order to preserve knowledge soundness since it is not guaranteed that a cheating prover honestly decomposes WCP. For example, what if a prover crafted $\tilde{w}_{\mathsf{mid}}(X)$ such that it decodes to $\tilde{w}_{\mathsf{mid},i}$ for some $i \in I_{\mathsf{com}}$? In that case, the knowledge extractor for SNARK outputs $\tilde{w}_i = \tilde{w}_{\mathsf{com},i} + \tilde{w}_{\mathsf{mid},i}$ as one of the witness vector elements, whereas the Σ-protocol only proves that $\hat{c}$ contains $\tilde{w}_{\mathsf{com},i}$. This breaks consistency between the value in $\hat{c}$ and the actual witness used in SNARK. To fix this issue, we require a prover to show the decomposed WCPs are "non-overlapping", meaning that $w_{\mathsf{mid}}(X)$ *only* maps to $(w_i)_{i \notin I_{\mathsf{com}}}$.[4] In Sect. 5, 6, we present different ways to instantiate this additional check: for Sonic it amounts to perform a degree bound check for $w_{\mathsf{mid}}(X)$, while for PLONK and Marlin it suffices to verify $w_{\mathsf{mid}}(X)$ vanishes on certain evaluation points.

Compressing and Aggregating Many Equality Proofs. So far we have only considered a single auxiliary commitment $\hat{c}$. But clearly, as described earlier,

[3] While there are approaches that mitigate this problem [1,22,43], they are curve-dependent—hindering generality and interoperability—and still relatively expensive (at 4–6 constraints per curve operation).

[4] While it is also necessary to prove $w_{\mathsf{com}}(X)$ only maps to $(w_i)_{i \in I_{\mathsf{com}}}$, this is trivially achieved by knowledge soundness of the Σ-protocol.

we are interested in the case where the number ℓ of commitments is large and we want our proof to be succinct in ℓ. Naïvely, the above ideas can easily be generalized by invoking ℓ instances of the equality proof for $\mathcal{R}'$ with statement $(c_{\mathsf{com}}, \hat{c}_k)$ for $k \in [\ell]$. This in turn would incur in a multiplicative factor of $O(\ell)$ overhead in the proof size. In Sect. 4 we show how to amortize ℓ different protocol instances to achieve $O(\log(\ell d))$ proof size by adapting the amortization technique from [5], where d is a dimension of the vector committed to in each $\hat{c}_k$.

Table 1. Efficiency comparison among CP-SNARK constructions with universal and updatable SRS. Proving time expresses group operations. The first line refers to our compiler applied to AHPs with suitable decomposition properties (See Sect. 3). In the above we denote by n the number of constraints in an R1CS system, by ℓ the number of input commitments and by d the size of each committed vectors. (The same asymptotics apply also to other constraints systems with slight variations though. For example, they apply to the AHPs in PLONK if n above refers to the total number of gates).

	$\lvert\pi\rvert$	Prove (time)	Verify (time)
This work	$O(\log(\ell \cdot d))$	$O(n + \ell \cdot d)$	$O(\ell \cdot d)$
Lunar [20]	$O(\ell)$	$O(n + \ell \cdot d)$	$O(\ell)$
LegoUAC [21]	$O(\ell \log^2(n))$	$O(n) + \ell \cdot \tilde{O}(d)$	$O(\ell \log^2(n))$

1.4 Related Work

Σ-protocols are proof systems that are efficient for proving algebraic statements about discrete logarithms, roots, or polynomial relationships among values [19,27,39,51]. They yield short proof sizes, require a constant number of public-key operations, and do not impose trusted setup requirements. Moreover, they can be made non-interactive using the efficient Fiat-Shamir transformation [30]. A recursive argument for an inner product relation of committed values was presented in [15] and was subsequently improved in Bulletproofs [17]. These can be used to prove statements on algebraically committed inputs, and the proof can be made non-interactive using Fiat-Shamir. Even though proof sizes scale logarithmically, unfortunately, the verification time scales linearly with the size of the circuit. Recent work on compressed Σ-protocol theory [4] is a strengthening of Σ-protocols that compress the communication complexity from linear to logarithmic. The underlying pivot of the compressed protocol is a standard Σ-protocol for opening linear forms on Pedersen vector commitments, i.e., a Σ-protocol for proving that a committed vector $\mathbf{x}$ satisfies $L(\mathbf{x}) = y$ for a public scalar y and public linear form L.

The seminal paper of [33] proposed a pairing-based zk-SNARK for general NP statements based on the NP complete language of Quadratic Span Programs (QSP) for Boolean circuits and Quadratic Arithmetic Programs (QAP) for arithmetic circuits. This built on previous works of [36,40,45] and led to several follow ups [10,11,13,37,46,50] which have proofs that are very short and have fast verification time.

The first zk-SNARK with an updatable SRS was introduced by [38]. However, here the size of this universal updatable SRS is quadratic in the number of multiplication gates of the circuit representing the statement. In [48], the authors construct Sonic, the first zkSNARK that is universal and updatable with a linear-sized SRS. A different solution to SNARKs with universal and updatable SRS is to use a secure multi-party computation protocol (MPC) to conduct the setup [16], and as long as at least one party is honest, the setup remains secure.

Although several works on general-purpose CP-ZK exist in the literature, such as Geppetto [26], Cinderella [29], and [47], there are few examples of efficient zero-knowledge proof systems for *composite statements* like those we consider in this paper. The first paper in this important line of work [24] presents a zero-knowledge proof that can be used to prove that $F(x) = 1$ given a Pedersen commitment to x, where F is represented as a Boolean circuit. They provide an efficient way of combining the garbled-circuit based proof of [41] for circuit-based statements with Σ-protocols for algebraic parts. However, this is inherently interactive which is inherited from the interactivity of [41] where the verifier uses private coins. In [8], the authors show how to extend the MPC-in-the-head techniques of ZKBoo [34] and ZKB++ [23] to allow algebraic statements on Pedersen commitments. While allowing for non-interactive proofs via the Fiat-Shamir transform, this approach results in larger proof sizes. In [2], protocols combining zk-SNARKs with Σ-protocols are presented. This overcomes the disadvantage of interactivity, and also gives a system suitable for applications that require short proofs. Not only does their approach lead to more efficient anonymous credentials than Cinderella, but it also found new applications to the blockchain, such as proof-of-solvency. Our approach achieves better asymptotic efficiency as well as further generality compared to [2], which relies on naïve Σ-protocols and a specific QAP-based SNARK construction with non-updatable SRS.

The works most closely related to ours are LegoSNARK and Lunar. LegoSNARK [21] is a framework for CP-SNARKs that gives general composition tools to build new CP-SNARKs from proof gadgets in a modular way. The construction LegoUAC in [21] is a CP-SNARK with a universal and updatable SRS. Lunar [20] obtains CP-SNARKs with a universal and updatable SRS and presents proof systems for "linking" committed inputs to the polynomial commitments used in AHP-based arguments. Table 1 shows the efficiency comparison between our work, Lunar and LegoUAC. Note that Lunar constructions and ECLIPSE outperform each other in different settings. See also §1.2 of [20] for a technical comparison of Lunar and ECLIPSE.

2 Preliminaries

Notation. For positive integers a and b such that $a < b$ we use the integer interval notation $[a, b]$ to denote $\{a, a+1, \ldots, b\}$; we use $[b]$ as shorthand for

$[1, b]$. A finite field is denoted by $\mathbb{F}$. We denote by κ a security parameter. When we explicitly specify the random tape ρ for a randomized algorithm $\mathcal{A}$, then we write $a \leftarrow \mathcal{A}(\mathsf{srs}; \rho)$ to indicate that $\mathcal{A}$ outputs a given input srs and random tape ρ. For a pair of randomized algorithms $\mathcal{A}$ and $\mathcal{E}_{\mathcal{A}}$, we often use the handy notation $(a; x) \leftarrow (\mathcal{A}||\mathcal{E}_{\mathcal{A}})(\mathsf{srs})$ which denotes that $\mathcal{A}$ outputs a on input srs, and $\mathcal{E}_{\mathcal{A}}$ outputs x given the same input srs, and $\mathcal{A}$'s random tape. We denote by $\Pr\left[A : B\right]$ the conditional probability of an event A under the condition B. Throughout, $\mathbb{G}$ denotes an Abelian group of prime order q. For vectors of generators $\boldsymbol{g} = (g_1, \ldots, g_d) \in \mathbb{G}^d$ and exponents $\mathbf{x} = (x_1, \ldots, x_d) \in \mathbb{Z}_q^d$ we often write $\boldsymbol{g}^{\mathbf{x}} := \prod_{i=1}^{d} g_i^{x_i}$.

Definition 1 (Indexed relation [25]). *An indexed relation $\mathcal{R}$ is a set of triples $(\mathsf{i}, \mathsf{x}, \mathsf{w})$ where i is the index, x is the instance, and w is the witness; the corresponding indexed language $\mathcal{L}(\mathcal{R})$ is the set of pairs (i, x) for which there exists a witness w such that $(\mathsf{i}, \mathsf{x}, \mathsf{w}) \in \mathcal{R}$. Given a size bound $\mathsf{N} \in \mathbb{N}$, we denote by $\mathcal{R}_{\mathsf{N}}$ the restriction of $\mathcal{R}$ to triples $(\mathsf{i}, \mathsf{x}, \mathsf{w}) \in \mathcal{R}$ with $|\mathsf{i}| \leq \mathsf{N}$.*

A zero-knowledge proof (or argument)[5] for $\mathcal{L}$ allows a prover P to convince a verifier V that $x \in \mathcal{L}$ for a common input x without revealing w. A proof of knowledge captures not only the truth of a statement $x \in \mathcal{L}$, but also that the prover is in "possession" of a witness w.

Definition 2 (Preprocessing Argument with Universal SRS [25]). *A Preprocessing Argument with Universal SRS is a tuple $\mathsf{ARG} = (\mathcal{S}, \mathcal{I}, \mathcal{P}, \mathcal{V})$ of four algorithms. $\mathcal{S}$ is a probabilistic polynomial-time setup algorithm that given a bound $\mathsf{N} \in \mathbb{N}$ samples a structured reference string srs supporting indices of size up to N. The indexer algorithm $\mathcal{I}$ is deterministic and, given oracle access to srs produces a proving index key and a verifier index key, used respectively by $\mathcal{P}$ and $\mathcal{V}$. The latter two are probabilistic polynomial-time interactive algorithms.*
<u>**Completeness.**</u> *For all size bounds $\mathsf{N} \in \mathbb{N}$ and efficient $\mathcal{A}$,*

$$\Pr\left[\begin{array}{c} (\mathsf{i}, \mathsf{x}, \mathsf{w}) \notin \mathcal{R}_{\mathsf{N}} \vee \\ \langle \mathcal{P}(\mathsf{ipk}, \mathsf{x}, \mathsf{w}), \mathcal{V}(\mathsf{ivk}, \mathsf{x}) \rangle = 1 \end{array} : \begin{array}{c} \mathsf{srs} \leftarrow \mathcal{S}(1^{\kappa}, \mathsf{N}) \\ (\mathsf{i}, \mathsf{x}, \mathsf{w}) \leftarrow \mathcal{A}(\mathsf{srs}) \\ (\mathsf{ipk}, \mathsf{ivk}) \leftarrow \mathcal{I}^{\mathsf{srs}}(\mathsf{i}) \end{array}\right] = 1$$

<u>**Succinctness.**</u> *We call the argument succinct if the communication complexity between prover and verifier is bounded by $\mathsf{poly}(\kappa) \cdot \mathsf{polylog}(|x| + |w|)$.*

In [3] we recall the standard definitions of knowledge soundness and zero knowledge. We have the following two optional requirements on the arguments defined above. We say that an argument is *public-coin* if all the messages from the verifier are uniformly random strings of a bounded length. We say it is *updatable* if there exists an update algorithm that can be run by anyone at any time and to update the SRS. This algorithm guarantees security as long as at least one of the (sequential) updates have been carried out honestly.

[5] We use proof and argument as synonymous in this paper, as we are only interested in computational soundness.

2.1 Algebraic Holographic Proofs

Below we recall the definition of AHP from Marlin.

Definition 3 (AHP [25]). *An* Algebraic Holographic Proof (AHP) *over a field family $\mathcal{F}$ for an indexed relation $\mathcal{R}$ is specified by a tuple* $\mathsf{AHP} = (\mathsf{k}, \mathsf{s}, \mathsf{d}, \mathsf{I}, \mathsf{P}, \mathsf{V})$ *where* $\mathsf{k}, \mathsf{s}, \mathsf{d} : \{0,1\}^* \to \mathbb{N}$ *are polynomial-time computable functions and* $\mathsf{I}, \mathsf{P}, \mathsf{V}$ *are three algorithms known as the* indexer, prover, *and* verifier. *The parameter* k *specifies the number of interaction rounds,* s *specifies the number of polynomials in each round, and* d *specifies degree bounds on these polynomials. The protocol proceeds as follows:*

- ***Offline phase*** *The indexer* I *receives as input a field $\mathbb{F} \in \mathcal{F}$ and index* i *for $\mathcal{R}$, and outputs* $\mathsf{s}(0)$ *polynomials* $p_{0,1}, \ldots, p_{0,\mathsf{s}(0)} \in \mathbb{F}[X]$ *of degrees at most* $\mathsf{d}(|\mathsf{i}|, 0, 1), \ldots, \mathsf{d}(|\mathsf{i}|, 0, \mathsf{s}(0))$ *respectively. Note that the offline phase does not depend on any particular instance or witness, and merely considers the task of encoding the given index* i.
- ***Online phase*** *Given an instance* x *and witness* w *such that* $(\mathsf{i}, \mathsf{x}, \mathsf{w}) \in \mathcal{R}$, *the prover* P *receives* $(\mathbb{F}, \mathsf{i}, \mathsf{x}, \mathsf{w})$ *and the verifier* V *receives* $(\mathbb{F}, \mathsf{x})$ *and oracle access to the polynomials output by* $\mathsf{I}(\mathbb{F}, \mathsf{i})$. *The prover* P *and the verifier* V *interact over* $\mathsf{k} = \mathsf{k}(|\mathsf{i}|)$ *rounds. For* $i \in [\mathsf{k}]$, *in the* i*-th round of interaction, the verifier* V *sends a message* $\rho_i \in \mathbb{F}^*$ *to the prover* P; *then the prover* P *replies with* $\mathsf{s}(i)$ *oracle polynomials* $p_{i,1}, \ldots, p_{i,s(i)} \in \mathbb{F}[X]$. *After* k *interactions, the verifier outputs additional randomness* $\rho_{\mathsf{k}+1} \in \mathbb{F}^*$ *which serves as auxiliary input to* V *in subsequent phases. We note that* $\rho_1, \ldots, \rho_{\mathsf{k}}, \rho_{\mathsf{k}+1} \in \mathbb{F}^*$ *are public and uniformly random strings.*
- ***Query phase*** *Let* $\mathbf{p} = (p_{i,j})_{i \in [\mathsf{k}], j \in [\mathsf{s}(i)]}$ *be a vector consisting of all polynomials sent by the prover* P. *The verifier may query any of the polynomials it has received any number of times. Concretely,* V *executes a subroutine* Q_{V} *that receives* $(\mathbb{F}, \mathsf{x}; \rho_1, \ldots, \rho_{\mathsf{k}+1})$ *and outputs a query set Q consisting of tuples* $((i,j), z)$ *to be interpreted as "query* $p_{i,j}$ *at* $z \in \mathbb{F}$"*. We denote a vector consisting of query answers* $\mathbf{p}(Q)$.
- ***Decision phase*** *The verifier outputs "accept" or "reject" based on the answers to the queries (and the verifier's randomness). Concretely,* V *executes a subroutine* D_{V} *that receives* $(\mathbb{F}, \mathsf{x}, \mathbf{p}(Q); \rho_1, \ldots, \rho_{\mathsf{k}+1})$ *as input, and outputs the decision bit.*

  The function d *determines which provers to consider for the completeness and soundness properties of the proof system. In more detail, we say that a (possibly malicious) prover* $\tilde{\mathsf{P}}$ *is* admissible *for* AHP *if, on every interaction with the verifier* V, *it holds that for every round* $i \in [\mathsf{k}]$ *and oracle index* $j \in [s(i)]$ *we have* $\deg(p_{i,j}) \leq \mathsf{d}(|\mathsf{i}|, i, j)$. *The honest prover* P *is required to be admissible under this definition.*

We require an AHP *to satisfy completeness, (knowledge) soundness and zero-knowledge as defined below.*

Completeness. An AHP is complete if for all $\mathbb{F} \in \mathcal{F}$ and any $(\mathsf{i}, \mathsf{x}, \mathsf{w}) \in \mathcal{R}$, the checks returned by $\mathsf{V}^{\mathsf{I}(\mathbb{F},\mathsf{i})}(\mathbb{F}, \mathsf{x})$ after interacting with (honest) $\mathsf{P}(\mathbb{F}, \mathsf{i}, \mathsf{x}, \mathsf{w})$ are always satisfied.

Soundness. An AHP is ϵ-sound if for every field $\mathbb{F} \in \mathcal{F}$, relation-instance tuple $(\mathsf{i}, \mathsf{x}) \notin L_{\mathcal{R}}$ and prover P^* we have $\Pr[\langle \mathsf{P}^*, \mathsf{V}^{\mathsf{I}(\mathbb{F},\mathsf{i})}(\mathbb{F}, \mathsf{x})\rangle = 1] \leq \epsilon$.

Knowledge Soundness. An AHP is ϵ-knowledge-sound if there exists a polynomial-time knowledge extractor $\mathcal{E}$ such that for any prover P^*, field $\mathbb{F} \in \mathcal{F}$, relation i, instance x and auxiliary input z:

$$\Pr\left[(\mathsf{i}, \mathsf{x}, \mathsf{w}) \in \mathcal{R} : \mathsf{w} \leftarrow \mathcal{E}^{\mathsf{P}^*}(\mathbb{F}, \mathsf{i}, \mathsf{x}, z)\right] \geq \Pr[\langle \mathsf{P}^*(\mathbb{F}, \mathsf{i}, \mathsf{x}, z), \mathsf{V}^{\mathsf{I}(\mathbb{F},\mathsf{i})}(\mathbb{F}, \mathsf{x})\rangle = 1] - \epsilon$$

where $\mathcal{E}$ has oracle access to P^*, i.e., it can query the next message function of P^* (and rewind it) and obtain all the messages and polynomials returned by it.

Zero-Knowledge. The property of (b, C)−Zero-Knowledge for AHPs models the existence of a simulator that can interact with a malicious verifier and can effectively simulate under two conditions: there is a bound b on the number of evaluation queries asked by the verifier; these queries need to satisfy an admissible test modelled a a circuit C. We say an AHP is zero-knowledge for some bound $\mathsf{b} = \mathsf{poly}(\lambda)$ and some efficient checker circuit C. We refer the reader to Sect. 4 in [25] for formal details.

Public Coins and Non-adaptive Queries. In the remainder of this work, we only consider AHPs that are public coin and non-adaptive: the messages of the verifier are random elements and its checks are independent of the prover's messages.

Generalization to Multivariate Polynomials. Even though the above formalization is tailored to univariate polynomial oracles, it is straightforward to generalize it to support multivariate, Laurent polynomials $p_{i,j} \in \mathbb{F}[X_1, X_1^{-1}, \ldots, X_m, X_m^{-1}]$. In that case, a query set Q consists of $((i, j), (z_1, \ldots, z_m))$ and is to be interpreted as "query $p_{i,j}$ at $(z_1, \ldots, z_m) \in \mathbb{F}^m$". Likewise, the polynomial commitment scheme definition can also be adapted to support multivariate polynomials as inputs. Our Theorem 1 in the next section holds under this generalization because the proof does not rely on whether polynomials are univariate or not. This is analogous to the compiler theorem of [25]. However, the generalization is only required for Sonic and PLONK, and Marlin only deals with univariate polynomials. Therefore, we focus on the univariate version in the main body for ease of exposition.

2.2 Polynomial Commitment

Polynomial commitment schemes were introduced by Kate–Zaverucha–Goldberg [42]. Below we recall the definition of standard polynomial commitment scheme. The definition is taken verbatim from Sect. 6.1 of [25].

Definition 4 (Polynomial Commitment Scheme). *A polynomial commitment scheme (PCS) over a field family $\mathcal{F}$ is a tuple* $\mathsf{PC} = (\mathsf{Setup}, \mathsf{Trim}, \mathsf{Com}, \mathsf{Open}, \mathsf{Check})$ *such that*

- $\mathsf{Setup}(1^\kappa, D) \to \mathsf{pp}$. *On input a security parameter κ, and a maximum degree bound $D \in \mathbb{N}$,* Setup *samples public parameters* pp. *The parameters contain the description of a finite field $\mathbb{F} \in \mathcal{F}$.*
- $\mathsf{Trim}^{\mathsf{pp}}(1^\kappa, \mathbf{d}) \to (\mathsf{ck}, \mathsf{rk})$. *Given oracle access to public parameters* pp, *and on input a security parameter κ, and degree bounds $\mathbf{d}$,* Trim *deterministically computes a key pair* $(\mathsf{ck}, \mathsf{rk})$ *that is specialized to $\mathbf{d}$.*
- $\mathsf{Com}_{\mathsf{ck}}(\mathbf{p}, \mathbf{d}; \boldsymbol{\omega}) \to \mathbf{c}$. *On input* ck, *univariate polynomials $\mathbf{p} = (p_i)_{i=1}^n$ over the field $\mathbb{F}$ with $\deg(p_i) \leq d_i \leq D$,* Com *outputs commitments $\mathbf{c} = (c_i)_{i=1}^n$ to the polynomials $\mathbf{p}$. The randomness $\boldsymbol{\omega}$ is used if the commitments $\mathbf{c}$ are hiding.*
- $\mathsf{Open}_{\mathsf{ck}}(\mathbf{p}, \mathbf{d}, Q, \xi; \boldsymbol{\omega}) \to \pi$. *On input* ck, *univariate polynomials $\mathbf{p}$, degree bounds $\mathbf{d}$, a query set Q consisting of $(i, z) \in [n] \times \mathbb{F}$, and opening challenge ξ,* Open *outputs an evaluation proof π. The randomness must equal the one previously used in* Com.
- $\mathsf{Check}_{\mathsf{rk}}(\mathbf{c}, \mathbf{d}, Q, \mathbf{v}, \pi, \xi) \in \{0, 1\}$. *On input* rk, *commitments $\mathbf{c}$, degree bounds $\mathbf{d}$, query set Q, alleged evaluations $\mathbf{v} = (v_{(i,z)})_{(i,z) \in Q}$, evaluation proof π, and opening challenge ξ,* Check *outputs 1 iff π attests that, for every $(i, z) \in Q$, the polynomial p_i evaluates to $v_{(i,z)}$ at z.*

We recall a set of basic properties that the KZG scheme [42] and its variants described in Marlin and Sonic already satisfy.

Completeness. For every maximum degree bound $D \in \mathbb{N}$ and efficient adversary $\mathcal{A}$,

$$\Pr\left[\begin{array}{c} \deg(\mathbf{p}) \leq \mathbf{d} \leq D \\ \implies \mathsf{Check}_{\mathsf{rk}}(\mathbf{c}, \mathbf{d}, Q, \mathbf{v}, \pi, \xi) \end{array} : \begin{array}{c} \mathsf{pp} \leftarrow \mathsf{Setup}(1^\kappa, D) \\ (\mathbf{p}, \mathbf{d}, Q, \xi, \boldsymbol{\omega}) \leftarrow \mathcal{A}(\mathsf{pp}) \\ (\mathsf{ck}, \mathsf{rk}) \leftarrow \mathsf{Trim}^{\mathsf{pp}}(1^\kappa, \mathbf{d}) \\ \mathbf{c} \leftarrow \mathsf{Com}(\mathsf{ck}, \mathbf{p}, \mathbf{d}; \boldsymbol{\omega}) \\ \mathbf{v} \leftarrow \mathbf{p}(Q) \\ \pi \leftarrow \mathsf{Open}(\mathsf{ck}, \mathbf{p}, \mathbf{d}, Q, \xi; \boldsymbol{\omega}) \end{array}\right] = 1$$

Homomorphism. A PC is additively homomorphic if for every $D \in \mathbb{N}$, every $\mathbf{d}$ such that $d_i \leq D$, every query set Q, every opening challenge ξ, every $\mathbf{p}_1, \mathbf{p}_2, \boldsymbol{\omega}_1, \boldsymbol{\omega}_2$ that are consistent with the degree bound $\mathbf{d}$,

$$\Pr\left[\mathbf{c}_1 + \mathbf{c}_2 = \mathsf{Com}_{\mathsf{ck}}(\mathbf{p}_1 + \mathbf{p}_2, \mathbf{d}; \boldsymbol{\omega}_1 + \boldsymbol{\omega}_2) : \begin{array}{c} \mathsf{pp} \leftarrow \mathsf{Setup}(1^\kappa, D); \\ (\mathsf{ck}, \mathsf{rk}) = \mathsf{Trim}^{\mathsf{pp}}(1^\kappa, \mathbf{d}) \\ \mathbf{c}_1 = \mathsf{Com}_{\mathsf{ck}}(\mathbf{p}_1, \mathbf{d}; \boldsymbol{\omega}_1) \\ \mathbf{c}_2 = \mathsf{Com}_{\mathsf{ck}}(\mathbf{p}_2, \mathbf{d}; \boldsymbol{\omega}_2) \end{array}\right] = 1$$

In [3] we recall formal security requirements for PCS: *extractability*, *binding*, and *hiding*. On a high-level, the extractability property assures that the prover actually *knows* the polynomial p committed to c whenever the verifier accepts an evaluation proof π.

2.2.1 The KZG Scheme

Below we recall the polynomial commitment scheme due to Kate–Zaverucha–Goldberg [42], denoted by $\mathsf{PC}_{\mathsf{KZG}}$. The scheme is proven extractable under the strong Diffie–Hellman (SDH) assumption in the *algebraic group model (AGM)* [31], polynomial binding under the discrete-log assumption, and perfectly hiding [25,42]. For simplicity we omit challenge ξ used for batch opening as well as the Trim function, and set $\mathsf{ck} = \mathsf{rk} = \mathsf{pp}$. See Appendix B of [25] for details of such optimization techniques.

- $\mathsf{Setup}(1^\kappa, D) \to (g, g^\chi, \ldots, g^{\chi^D}, g, g^{\gamma\chi}, \ldots, g^{\gamma\chi^D}, h^\chi)$ where it determines a bilinear group public parameters $(q, \mathbb{G}_1, \mathbb{G}_2, \mathbb{G}_T, e, g, h)$, with $g \in \mathbb{G}_1$ and $\chi, \gamma \in \mathbb{F}$ are randomly chosen. We denote exponentiation in $\mathbb{G}_i$ by $[\cdot]_i$.
- $\mathsf{Com}_{\mathsf{ck}}(p, D; \omega) \to [p(\chi) + \gamma\omega(\chi)]_1$, where $\omega \in \mathbb{F}_{\leq D}[X]$ is a random masking polynomial.
- $\mathsf{Open}_{\mathsf{ck}}(p, D, z; \omega)$ computes $W(X) = \frac{p(X)-p(z)}{X-z}$, $\bar{W}(X) = \frac{\omega(X)-\omega(z)}{X-z}$, $\Pi := [W(\chi) + \gamma\bar{W}(\chi)]_1$, $\bar{v} := \bar{W}(z)$ and outputs $\pi := (\Pi, \bar{v})$.
- $\mathsf{Check}_{\mathsf{rk}}(c, D, z, v, \pi)$ checks $e(\Pi, [\chi]_2/[z]_2) \stackrel{?}{=} e(C/([v]_1 \cdot [\gamma\bar{v}]_1), h)$.

3 AHP-to-CP-SNARK Compiler

In this section, we present our general compiler that turns AHPs to commit-and-prove zkSNARKs.

3.1 Additional Preliminaries for Compiler

Auxiliary Commitment Scheme AC**.** We will assume a commitment scheme AC for Auxiliary Commitments. They are "auxiliary" in the sense that they are used as auxiliary inputs to parts of the witness. We assume AC to satisfy the standard properties of (computational) binding and (computational or otherwise) hiding. As we explicitly support a *vector* $\mathbf{x} \in \mathbb{F}^d$ as committed message, the definition is specialized for a vector commitment scheme. Specifically we assume $\mathsf{AC} = (\mathsf{Gen}, \mathsf{Com})$ such that $\mathsf{AC.Gen}(1^\lambda, d) \to \mathsf{ack}$ is a randomized algorithm returning a commitment key ack for messages of dimension $d \in \mathbb{N}$, where $d \in \mathsf{poly}(\lambda)$, and $\mathsf{AC.Com}_{\mathsf{ack}}(\mathbf{x}; r)$ is a committing algorithm returning a commitment $\hat{c}$ on input $\mathbf{x} \in \mathbb{F}^d$ for some randomness r. In our concrete instantiations, we use the Pedersen vector commitment scheme as AC.

Commit-and-Prove Relation. Our goal is to construct a general compiler that turns AHP for $\mathcal{R}$ into ARG for the relation over commitments $\mathcal{R}_{\mathsf{com}}$. Throughout we assume an indexed relation where the witness can be represented as a vector in $\mathbb{F}^n$.

Definition 5 (Commit-and-prove relation). *Let $\mathcal{R}$ be an indexed relation,* AC *a commitment scheme as defined above and* ack *an auxiliary commitment key in the range of* AC.Gen. *We define the corresponding* commit-and-prove relation

$$\mathcal{R}_{\mathsf{com}} = \left\{ \begin{matrix} ((\mathsf{i}, n, \ell, d, I_{\mathsf{com}}, (I_k)_{k\in[\ell]}, \mathsf{ack}), \\ (\mathsf{x}, (\hat{c}_k)_{k\in[\ell]}), ((\mathsf{w}_i)_{i\in[n]}, (r_k)_{k\in[\ell]})) \end{matrix} : \begin{matrix} (\mathsf{i}, \mathsf{x}, (\mathsf{w}_i)_{i\in[n]}) \in \mathcal{R} \ \wedge \\ I_{\mathsf{com}} \subset [n] \ \wedge \ |I_{\mathsf{com}}| = \ell d \ \wedge \\ I_{\mathsf{com}} = \bigcup_{k\in[\ell]} I_k \ \wedge \ |I_k| = d \ \wedge \\ \hat{c}_k = \mathsf{AC.Com}_{\mathsf{ack}}((\mathsf{w}_i)_{i\in I_k}; r_k) \end{matrix} \right\}$$

3.2 Additional Properties for AHP

We present basic properties that the underlying AHPs of PLONK, Marlin and Sonic already satisfy. First we describe our variant of Definition 3.3 from [20]: straight-line extractability for AHP. We note that our definition is in the AHP model, while that in [20] is for Polynomially Holographic Proofs. The reason why we explicitly define witness-carrying polynomials (WCPs) is that our compiler needs to identify a minimum set of polynomials containing enough information about the whole witness, with which auxiliary commitments are shown to be consistent. Note that we also restrict WitExt to be deterministic so that it can be essentially seen as a witness decoding algorithm that works for both honest and malicious provers once and for all.

Definition 6 (AHP with S-straight-line extractor). *Fix* AHP *for indexed relation $\mathcal{R}$ and index set $S \subseteq \{(i,j) : i \in [\mathsf{k}], j \in [\mathsf{s}(i)]\}$. An* AHP *is* ϵ-knowledge sound with S-straight-line extractor *if there exists an efficient deterministic extractor* WitExt *such that for any admissible* P^*, *every field* $\mathbb{F} \in \mathcal{F}$, *every index* i *and instance* x,

$$\Pr[(\mathsf{i}, \mathsf{x}, \mathsf{WitExt}(\{p_{i,j}(X)\}_{(i,j)\in S})) \in \mathcal{R}] \geq \Pr[\langle \mathsf{P}^*(\mathsf{i}), \mathsf{V}^{\mathsf{I}(\mathbb{F},\mathsf{i})}\rangle(\mathbb{F}, \mathsf{x}) = 1] - \epsilon$$

where $\{p_{i,j}(X)\}_{(i,j)\in S}$ is a subset of the polynomials output by P^* in an execution of $\langle \mathsf{P}^*, \mathsf{V}^{\mathsf{I}(\mathbb{F},\mathsf{i})}\rangle(\mathbb{F}, \mathsf{x})$. Let W be a smallest set such that there exists an efficient extractor satisfying the condition above. Then we say that $\{p_{i,j}(X)\}_{(i,j)\in W}$ are witness-carrying polynomials (WCPs) of AHP. *If all WCPs are sent during the same round $\mathsf{k}_{\mathsf{w}} \leq \mathsf{k}$, we call k_{w} a* witness-committing round.

Definition 7 (Disjoint witness-carrying polynomials). *We say that WCPs are* disjoint *if there exists some disjoint index sets $I_{i,j}$ such that $[n] = \bigcup_{(i,j)\in W} I_{i,j}$ and the corresponding* WitExt *independently invokes* $\mathsf{WitExt}_{i,j}$ *on $p_{i,j}$ to obtain $(\mathsf{w}_\iota)_{\iota\in I_{i,j}}$.*

Remark 1. Let $\mathsf{n}_{\mathsf{w}} = |W|$. For Marlin and Sonic we have $\mathsf{n}_{\mathsf{w}} = 1$ and $\mathsf{k}_{\mathsf{w}} = 1$; for PLONK we have $\mathsf{n}_{\mathsf{w}} = 3$ and $\mathsf{k}_{\mathsf{w}} = 1$ and disjoint WCPs. In our compiler formalization, we always assume that W is such that k_{w} is minimum, and that AHP has a witness-committing round.

The following two definitions are needed to guarantee completeness of our compiler.

Definition 8 (Unique extraction). *Consider an* AHP *for relation* $\mathcal{R}$ *with* S*-straight-line extractor* WitExt. *We say that* WitExt *performs* unique extraction, *if for any honest prover* P *and every* $(\mathsf{i}, \mathsf{x}, \mathsf{w}) \in \mathcal{R}$, $\mathsf{WitExt}(\{p_{i,j}(X)\}_{(i,j)\in S}) = \mathsf{w}$, *where* $\{p_{i,j}(X)\}_{(i,j)\in S}$ *is a subset of the polynomials output by* P *in an execution of* $\langle \mathsf{P}(\mathsf{i}, \mathsf{w}), \mathsf{V}^{\mathsf{I}(\mathbb{F},\mathsf{i})}\rangle(\mathbb{F}, \mathsf{x})$.

Definition 9 (Decomposable witness-carrying polynomials). *Consider an* AHP *for relation* $\mathcal{R}$ *with* W*-straight-line extractor* WitExt. *Let* $(p_{i,j}(X))_{(i,j)\in W}$ *be WCPs of* AHP. *We say that polynomials* $(p_{i,j}(X))_{(i,j)\in W}$ *are* decomposable *if there exists an efficient function* $\mathsf{Decomp}((p_{i,j}(X))_{(i,j)\in W}, I) \rightarrow (p^{(1)}_{i,j}(X), p^{(2)}_{i,j}(X))_{(i,j)\in W}$ *such that it satisfies the following properties for any* $I \subset [n]$.

- Additive decomposition: $p_{i,j}(X) = p^{(1)}_{i,j}(X) + p^{(2)}_{i,j}(X)$ *for* $(i,j) \in W$.
- Degree preserving: $\deg(p^{(1)}_{i,j}(X))$ *and* $\deg(p^{(2)}_{i,j}(X))$ *are at most* $\deg(p_{i,j}(X))$ *for* $(i,j) \in W$.
- Non-overlapping: *Let* $\mathsf{w} = \mathsf{WitExt}((p_{i,j}(X))_{(i,j)\in W})$, $\mathsf{w}^{(1)} = \mathsf{WitExt}((p^{(1)}_{i,j}(X))_{(i,j)\in W})$, *and* $\mathsf{w}^{(2)} = \mathsf{WitExt}((p^{(2)}_{i,j}(X))_{(i,j)\in W})$. *Then*

$$(\mathsf{w}_i)_{i\in I} = (\mathsf{w}^{(1)}_i)_{i\in I} \quad (\mathsf{w}_i)_{i\notin I} = (\mathsf{w}^{(2)}_i)_{i\notin I} \quad (\mathsf{w}^{(1)}_i)_{i\notin I} = (0) \quad (\mathsf{w}^{(2)}_i)_{i\in I} = (0)$$

Remark 2. If the above decomposition function is invoked on WCPs, one can observe that witness extraction/decoding is also additively homomorphic on such honest inputs, i.e.,

$$\mathsf{WitExt}((p_{i,j}(X))_{(i,j)\in W}) = \mathsf{WitExt}((p^{(1)}_{i,j}(X))_{(i,j)\in W} + (p^{(2)}_{i,j}(X))_{(i,j)\in W})$$
$$= \mathsf{WitExt}((p^{(1)}_{i,j}(X))_{(i,j)\in W}) + \mathsf{WitExt}((p^{(2)}_{i,j}(X))_{(i,j)\in W}).$$

3.3 Our Compiler

In order to prove the relation $\mathcal{R}_{\mathsf{com}}$ above, our compiler will use a commit-and-prove NIZKAoK subprotocol for following relation. Although the abstract relation $\mathcal{R}_{\mathtt{lnk}}$ looks cumbersome for the sake of generality, the actual instantiation of $\mathsf{CP}_{\mathtt{lnk}}$ will be rather simple: it can be achieved by "linking" committed witness sub-vectors and proving "non-overlapping" decomposition as outlined in 1.3. See Figs. 3 and 4 for concrete examples.

Definition 10 (Commitment-linking relation). *Fix an* AHP *for relation* $\mathcal{R}$ *with* W*-straight-line extractor* WitExt *and with witness carrying polynomials* $(p_{i,j}(X))_{(i,j)\in W}$, *a polynomial commitment scheme* PC, *and an auxiliary commitment scheme* AC. *We define the linking relation*

$$\mathcal{R}_{\mathtt{lnk}} = \left\{ \begin{array}{c} ((n, \ell, d, I_{\mathsf{com}}, (I_k)_{k\in[\ell]}, \mathsf{ck}, \mathsf{ack}), \\ ((\hat{c}_k)_{k\in[\ell]}, \mathbf{v}, Q, \\ (c^{\mathsf{com}}_{i,j}(X), c^{\mathsf{mid}}_{i,j}(X))_{(i,j)\in W}), \\ ((p^{\mathsf{com}}_{i,j}(X), p^{\mathsf{mid}}_{i,j}(X))_{(i,j)\in W}, \\ (\omega^{\mathsf{com}}_{i,j}(X), \omega^{\mathsf{mid}}_{i,j}(X))_{(i,j)\in W}, \\ (r_k)_{k\in[\ell]})) \end{array} : \begin{array}{c} I_{\mathsf{com}} \subset [n] \ \wedge \ |I_{\mathsf{com}}| = \ell d \ \wedge \\ I_{\mathsf{com}} = \bigcup_{k\in[\ell]} I_k \ \wedge \ |I_k| = d \ \wedge \\ c^{\mathsf{com}}_{i,j} = \mathsf{PC.Com}_{\mathsf{ck}}(p^{\mathsf{com}}_{i,j}(X), \mathsf{d}(|\mathsf{i}|, i, j); \omega^{\mathsf{com}}_{i,j}) \ \wedge \\ c^{\mathsf{mid}}_{i,j} = \mathsf{PC.Com}_{\mathsf{ck}}(p^{\mathsf{mid}}_{i,j}(X), \mathsf{d}(|\mathsf{i}|, i, j); \omega^{\mathsf{mid}}_{i,j}) \ \wedge \\ \hat{c}_k = \mathsf{AC.Com}_{\mathsf{ack}}((\mathsf{w}_i)_{i\in I_k}; r_k) \ \textit{where} \\ \mathsf{w} = \mathsf{WitExt}((p^{\mathsf{com}}_{i,j}(X) + p^{\mathsf{mid}}_{i,j}(X))_{(i,j)\in W}) \ \wedge \\ v_{((i,j),z)} = p^{\mathsf{com}}_{i,j}(z) + p^{\mathsf{com}}_{i,j}(z) \\ \textit{for all } ((i,j),z) \in Q \textit{ such that } (i,j) \in W \end{array} \right\}$$

Remark 3. On a high-level the relation guarantees "the prover knows polynomials committed via PC, such that their sum correctly decodes to the partial witnesses committed via AC". Although the correctness of polynomial evaluation (i.e., the condition "$v_{((i,j),z)} = p^{\mathsf{com}}_{i,j}(z) + p^{\mathsf{com}}_{i,j}(z)$") is also part of $\mathcal{R}_{\mathtt{lnk}}$, we remark that this is redundant since it is to be proven by the opening algorithm of PC outside $\mathsf{CP}_{\mathtt{lnk}}$ anyway. Looking ahead, security proof of our compiler indeed holds even without showing such a condition within $\mathsf{CP}_{\mathtt{lnk}}$. We rather include this for the ease of proving knowledge soundness of $\mathsf{CP}_{\mathtt{lnk}}$; in concrete instantiations, an extractor of $\mathsf{CP}_{\mathtt{lnk}}$ typically needs to extract what is committed to $c^{\mathsf{mid}}_{i,j}$ by internally invoking an extractor of PC, which however is only guaranteed to succeed if the evaluation proof is valid. Hence, by letting $\mathsf{CP}_{\mathtt{lnk}}$ take care of evaluation proof by default we can easily make such an argument go through. In later sections our $\mathsf{CP}_{\mathtt{lnk}}$ for Sonic takes advantage of this generalization, while the ones for PLONK and Marlin don't since they create a special evaluation proof independent of the AHP query phase.

Intuition About the Compiler. The compiler in Fig. 1 is close to those in Marlin [25], Lunar [20] and DARK [18]. One important difference is the use of polynomial decomposition where the prover will commit separately to each of the "parts" of the WCPs. This separate commitment will allow efficiently proving the commitment-linking relation.

Theorem 1. *Let $\mathcal{F}$ be a field family and $\mathcal{R}$ be an indexed relation. Consider the following components:*

- $\mathsf{AHP} = (\mathsf{k}, \mathsf{s}, \mathsf{d}, \mathsf{I}, \mathsf{P}, \mathsf{V})$ *is a knowledge sound AHP for $\mathcal{R}$ with W-straight-line unique extractor* WitExt, *and with a decomposition function* Decomp *for witness-carrying polynomials $(p_{i,j}(X))_{(i,j)\in W}$;*
- $\mathsf{PC} = (\mathsf{Setup}, \mathsf{Com}, \mathsf{Open}, \mathsf{Check})$ *is an additively homomorphic polynomial commitment over $\mathcal{F}$ with binding and extractability;*
- $\mathsf{CP}_{\mathtt{lnk}} = (\mathcal{I}_{\mathtt{lnk}}, \mathcal{P}_{\mathtt{lnk}}, \mathcal{V}_{\mathtt{lnk}})$ *is (preprocessing) non-interactive argument of knowledge for $\mathcal{R}_{\mathtt{lnk}}$ (Definition 10).*

Then the construction of $\mathsf{ARG} = (\mathcal{S}, \mathcal{I}, \mathcal{P}, \mathcal{V})$ *in Fig. 1 is a preprocessing argument system for the relation $\mathcal{R}_{\mathsf{com}}$. If* PC *is hiding,* $\mathsf{CP}_{\mathtt{lnk}}$ *is zero-knowledge, and* AHP *is zero-knowledge as defined in Definition 3, then* ARG *is also zero-knowledge.*

Moreover, if we additionally assume that the witness-carrying polynomials are disjoint and $I_{\mathsf{com}} \subset I_{i^*,j^*}$ *for some* $(i^*, j^*) \in W$*, then the above claim holds even if* $\mathsf{CP}_{\mathtt{lnk}}$ *shows a variant of* $\mathcal{R}_{\mathtt{lnk}}$ *such that all "*$(i,j) \in W$*" are replaced by* (i^*, j^*) *and* WitExt *is replaced by* $\mathsf{WitExt}_{i^*,j^*}$.

Remark 4. While in the description of our compiler we generically commit all polynomials with the same type of polynomial commitments, our instantiations use some ad-hoc tweaks. In particular, we commit to the witness carrying polynomials using a special version of KZG (see for example the input format of commitments in Fig. 3) different than the one we use for the rest of the oracle polynomials. Note that this is a standard optimization trick already used in previous works, e.g., [25],[32],[48], and we are still able to satisfy the security requirements of the general compiler this way.

Proof Sketch. Full proofs are deferred to [3]. Completeness follows from inspection. In particular, we benefit from a combination of homomorphism of PC and additive, non-overlapping decomposition of WCP. For zero-knowledge, we construct a simulator $\mathcal{S}$ by using the simulators $\mathsf{Sim}_{\mathsf{PC}}$ from the polynomial commitment (hiding property), the zero-knowledge simulator $\mathsf{Sim}_{\mathtt{lnk}}$ of $\mathsf{CP}_{\mathtt{lnk}}$ and the zero-knowledge simulator $\mathsf{Sim}_{\mathsf{AHP}}$ of AHP. For knowledge soundness, we construct the extractor $\mathcal{E}_{\mathsf{ARG}}$ that works as follows: (1) Extract the polynomials from the polynomial commitments sent at each round through the extractor $\mathcal{E}_{\mathsf{PC}}$ for the polynomial commitments; (2) From these, for each $(i,j) \in W$ reconstruct the WCP as $\tilde{p}_{i,j}(X)$; (3) On the other hand, extract auxiliary commitment randomness $(\tilde{r}_k)_{k\in[\ell]}$ as well as decomposed WCP $(p^{\mathsf{com}}_{i,j}(X), p^{\mathsf{mid}}_{i,j}(X))_{(i,j)\in W}$ such that $p_{i,j}(X) = p^{\mathsf{com}}_{i,j}(X) + p^{\mathsf{mid}}_{i,j}(X)$, by invoking the extractor $\mathcal{E}_{\mathtt{lnk}}$ for $\mathsf{CP}_{\mathtt{lnk}}$; (4) Extract witness $(\tilde{\mathsf{w}}_i)_{i\in[n]}$ from the W-straight-line extractor as $\mathsf{WitExt}(\tilde{p}_{i,j}(X))_{(i,j)\in W}$; (5) Return $((\tilde{\mathsf{w}}_i)_{i\in[n]}, (\tilde{r}_k)_{k\in[\ell]})$.

4 Compressed Σ-Protocol for Equality

We describe how to construct an efficient protocol proving equality of committed vectors, following the framework due to Attema and Cramer [4] and Attema, Cramer and Fehr [5]. This allows us to instantiate $\mathsf{CP}_{\mathtt{lnk}}$ with proof size of only $O(\log(\ell d))$ when ℓ Pedersen commitments are received as inputs.

4.1 AmComEq: Amortization of ℓ Commitment Equality Proofs

In our application, we would like to show equality of vectors within a single commitment containing vector of size ℓd (corresponding to a polynomial commitment) and ℓ chunks of vector of size d in multiple Pedersen commitments. Concretely, our goal is to give an efficient protocol for relation.

Protocol ECLIPSE compiler

Setup $\mathcal{S}(1^\kappa, \mathsf{N}, d)$. The setup $\mathcal{S}$ on input a security parameter $\kappa \in \mathbb{N}$ and size bound $\mathsf{N} \in \mathbb{N}$, uses N to compute a maximum degree bound D, samples $\mathsf{pp} \leftarrow \mathsf{PC.Setup}(1^\kappa, D)$, samples $\mathsf{ack} \leftarrow \mathsf{AC.Setup}(1^\kappa, d)$, and then outputs $\mathsf{srs} := (\mathsf{pp}, \mathsf{ack})$. The integer D is computed to be the maximum degree bound in AHP for indices of size N. In other words,

$$D := \max\{\mathsf{d}(\mathsf{N}, i, j) | i \in \{0, 1, \dots, \mathsf{k}(\mathsf{N})\}, j \in \{1, \dots, \mathsf{s}(i)\}\}$$

Indexer $\mathcal{I}^{\mathsf{srs}}(\mathsf{i}, I_{\mathsf{com}}, (I_k)_{k\in[\ell]})$. The indexer $\mathcal{I}$ upon input i, commitment index sets I_{com}, $(I_k)_{k\in[\ell]}$ and given oracle access to srs, deduces the field $\mathbb{F} \in \mathcal{F}$ contained in $\mathsf{srs} = (\mathsf{pp}, \mathsf{ack})$, runs the AHP indexer I on $(\mathbb{F}, \mathsf{i})$ to obtain s(0) polynomials $(p_{0,j})_{j=1}^{\mathsf{s}(0)} \in \mathbb{F}[X]$ of degrees at most $(\mathsf{d}(|\mathsf{i}|, 0, j))_{j=1}^{\mathsf{s}(0)}$. Then it proceeds by computing $(\mathsf{ck}, \mathsf{rk}) := \mathsf{PC.Trim}^{\mathsf{pp}}(\mathbf{d})$, where $\mathbf{d} = (\mathsf{d}(|\mathsf{i}|, i, j))_{i\in[\mathsf{k}], j\in[\mathsf{s}(i)]}$, and generating (de-randomized) commitments to index polynomials $(c_{0,j})_{j=1}^{\mathsf{s}(0)} = \mathsf{PC.Com}_{\mathsf{ck}}((p_{0,j})_{j=1}^{\mathsf{s}(0)})$. It also invokes the indexer of $\mathsf{CP}_{\mathsf{lnk}}$: $(\mathsf{ipk}_{\mathsf{lnk}}, \mathsf{ivk}_{\mathsf{lnk}}) \leftarrow \mathcal{I}_{\mathsf{lnk}}^{\mathsf{srs}}(I_{\mathsf{com}}, (I_k)_{k\in[\ell]})$. The indexer outputs $\mathsf{ipk} := (\mathsf{ck}, \mathsf{i}, (p_{0,j})_{j=1}^{\mathsf{s}(0)}, (c_{0,j})_{j=1}^{\mathsf{s}(0)}, \mathsf{ipk}_{\mathsf{lnk}})$ and $\mathsf{ivk} := (\mathsf{rk}, (c_{0,j})_{j=1}^{\mathsf{s}(0)}, \mathsf{ivk}_{\mathsf{lnk}})$.

Input. The ARG prover $\mathcal{P}$ receives $(\mathsf{ipk}, (\mathsf{x}, (\hat{c}_k)_{k\in[\ell]}), ((\mathsf{w}_i)_{i\in[n]}, (r_k)_{k\in[\ell]}))$ and the verifier $\mathcal{V}$ receives $(\mathsf{ivk}, (\mathsf{x}, (\hat{c}_k)_{k\in[\ell]}))$.

Online phase. For every round $i \in [\mathsf{k}]$, $\mathcal{P}$ and $\mathcal{V}$ run the i-th round of interaction between the AHP prover $\mathsf{P}(\mathbb{F}, \mathsf{i}, \mathsf{x}, \mathsf{w})$ and verifier $\mathsf{V}(\mathbb{F}, \mathsf{x})$.

1. $\mathcal{V}$ receives random challenge $\rho_i \in \mathbb{F}$ from V, and forwards it to $\mathcal{P}$.
2. $\mathcal{P}$ forwards ρ_i to P, which replies with polynomials $p_{i,1}, \dots, p_{i,\mathsf{s}(i)} \in \mathbb{F}[X]$ with $\deg(p_{i,j}) \le \mathsf{d}(|\mathsf{i}|, i, j)$.
3. $\mathcal{P}$ computes and outputs commitments as follows.
   - If $i = \mathsf{k}_{\mathsf{w}}$ (i.e. witness-committing round), then $\mathcal{P}$ first decomposes witness-carrying polynomials as
   $$(p_{i,j}^{\mathsf{com}}(X), p_{i,j}^{\mathsf{mid}}(X))_{(i,j)\in W} := \mathsf{Decomp}((p_{i,j}(X))_{(i,j)\in W}, I_{\mathsf{com}})$$
   such that $p_{i,j}(X) = p_{i,j}^{\mathsf{com}}(X) + p_{i,j}^{\mathsf{mid}}(X)$.
   - For every $(i, j) \in W$, $\mathcal{P}$ sends
   $$c_{i,j}^{\mathsf{com}} := \mathsf{PC.Com}_{\mathsf{ck}}(p_{i,j}^{\mathsf{com}}(X), \mathsf{d}(|\mathsf{i}|, i, j); \omega_{i,j}^{\mathsf{com}})$$
   $$c_{i,j}^{\mathsf{mid}} := \mathsf{PC.Com}_{\mathsf{ck}}(p_{i,j}^{\mathsf{mid}}(X), \mathsf{d}(|\mathsf{i}|, i, j); \omega_{i,j}^{\mathsf{mid}})$$
   to $\mathcal{V}$, where $\omega_{i,j}^{\mathsf{com}}$ and $\omega_{i,j}^{\mathsf{mid}}$ are uniformly sampled masking polynomials according the polynomial commitment scheme. $\mathcal{P}$ lets $\omega_{i,j} := \omega_{i,j}^{\mathsf{com}} + \omega_{i,j}^{\mathsf{mid}}$. $\mathcal{V}$ computes $c_{i,j} := c_{i,j}^{\mathsf{com}} + c_{i,j}^{\mathsf{mid}}$.
   - For every $(i, j) \notin W$, $\mathcal{P}$ sends
   $$c_{i,j} := \mathsf{PC.Com}_{\mathsf{ck}}(p_{i,j}(X), \mathsf{d}(|\mathsf{i}|, i, j); \omega_{i,j})$$
   to $\mathcal{V}$.

After k rounds of interaction, $\mathcal{V}$ obtains an additional challenge $\rho_{\mathsf{k}+1} \in \mathbb{F}^*$ from the AHP verifier V, used in the next phase. Let $\mathbf{c} := (c_{i,j})_{i\in[\mathsf{k}], j\in[\mathsf{s}(i)]}$, $\mathbf{p} := (p_{i,j})_{i\in[\mathsf{k}], j\in[\mathsf{s}(i)]}$, $\boldsymbol{\omega} := (\omega_{i,j})_{i\in[\mathsf{k}], j\in[\mathsf{s}(i)]}$ and $\mathbf{d} := (\mathsf{d}(|\mathsf{i}|, i, j))_{i\in[\mathsf{k}], j\in[\mathsf{s}(i)]}$.

Query phase.

1. $\mathcal{V}$ sends $\rho_{\mathsf{k}+1} \in \mathbb{F}^*$ that represents randomness for the query phase of $\mathsf{V}(\mathbb{F}, \mathsf{x})$ to $\mathcal{P}$.
2. $\mathcal{P}$ uses the query algorithm of V to compute the query set $Q := \mathsf{Q}_{\mathsf{V}}(\mathbb{F}, \mathsf{x}; \rho_1, \dots, \rho_{\mathsf{k}}, \rho_{\mathsf{k}+1})$.
3. $\mathcal{P}$ replies with answers $\mathbf{v} := \mathbf{p}(Q)$.
4. $\mathcal{V}$ samples and sends an opening challenge $\xi \in \mathbb{F}$ to $\mathcal{P}$.
5. $\mathcal{P}$ replies with an evaluation proof to demonstrate correctness of all claimed evaluations.
$$\pi_{\mathsf{Eval}} := \mathsf{PC.Open}_{\mathsf{ck}}(\mathbf{p}, \mathbf{d}, Q, \xi; \boldsymbol{\omega})$$

Linking phase. $\mathcal{P}$ invokes

$$\mathcal{P}_{\mathsf{lnk}}(\mathsf{ipk}_{\mathsf{lnk}}, ((\hat{c}_k)_{k\in[\ell]}, \mathbf{v}, Q, (c_{i,j}^{\mathsf{com}}(X), c_{i,j}^{\mathsf{mid}}(X))_{(i,j)\in W}), ((p_{i,j}^{\mathsf{com}}(X), p_{i,j}^{\mathsf{mid}}(X))_{(i,j)\in W}, (\omega_{i,j}^{\mathsf{com}}(X), \omega_{i,j}^{\mathsf{mid}}(X))_{(i,j)\in W}, (r_k)_{k\in[\ell]}))$$

to obtain and send linking proof π_{lnk}.

Decision phase. $\mathcal{V}$ accepts if and only if the following conditions hold:

- the decision algorithm of V accepts the answers, i.e., $\mathsf{D}_{\mathsf{V}}(\mathbb{F}, \mathsf{x}, \mathbf{v}, \rho_1, \dots, \rho_{\mathsf{k}}, \rho_{\mathsf{k}+1}) = 1$;
- the alleged answers pass the test, i.e., $\mathsf{PC.Check}_{\mathsf{rk}}(\mathbf{c}, \mathbf{d}, Q, \mathbf{v}, \pi_{\mathsf{Eval}}, \xi) = 1$;
- the alleged linking proof is verified, i.e., $\mathcal{V}_{\mathsf{lnk}}(\mathsf{ivk}_{\mathsf{lnk}}, ((\hat{c}_k)_{k\in[\ell]}, \mathbf{v}, Q, (c_{i,j}^{\mathsf{com}}(X), c_{i,j}^{\mathsf{mid}}(X))_{(i,j)\in W}), \pi_{\mathsf{lnk}}) = 1$;

Fig. 1. Compiler from AHP to Interactive AoK for $\mathcal{R}_{\mathsf{com}}$. The differences with the Marlin compiler are marked in red. (Color figure online)

$$\mathcal{R}_{\mathsf{AmComEq}} = \left\{ \begin{array}{c} ((g, \mathbf{h}, \mathbf{G}, \mathbf{H}, d, d', d'', \ell), \\ (C, \hat{C}_1, \dots, \hat{C}_\ell), \\ (\mathbf{w}, \boldsymbol{\alpha}, \boldsymbol{\beta}_1, \dots, \boldsymbol{\beta}_\ell)) \end{array} : \begin{array}{c} C = g^{\mathbf{w}} \mathbf{h}^{\boldsymbol{\alpha}}, \hat{C}_i = \mathbf{G}^{\mathbf{w}_i} \mathbf{H}^{\boldsymbol{\beta}_i}, \\ g \in \mathbb{G}^{\ell d}, \mathbf{G} \in \mathbb{G}^d, \mathbf{h} \in \mathbb{G}^{d'}, \mathbf{H} \in \mathbb{G}^{d''}, \\ \mathbf{w}_i \in \mathbb{Z}_q^d, \boldsymbol{\alpha} \in \mathbb{Z}_q^{d'}, \boldsymbol{\beta}_i \in \mathbb{Z}_q^{d''}, \mathbf{w} = [\mathbf{w}_1, \dots, \mathbf{w}_\ell] \end{array} \right\} \quad (1)$$

where we assume d' and d'' are small constants (for concrete instantiations in later sections, we only need $d' \le 4$ and $d'' = 1$). Our starting point is a naïve ComEq Σ-protocol proving equality of vectors committed in two Pedersen com-

Protocol AmComEq

1. $\mathcal{V}$ sends random challenge $x \in \mathbb{Z}_q$. Both parties compute $\tilde{\mathbf{G}} = [\mathbf{G}, \mathbf{G}^x, \dots, \mathbf{G}^{x^{\ell-1}}]$.
2. $\mathcal{P}$ samples random $\mathbf{r} \in \mathbb{Z}_q^{\ell d}$, $\boldsymbol{\delta} \in \mathbb{Z}_q^{d'}$, $\gamma \in \mathbb{Z}_q^{d''}$, and sends $A = \boldsymbol{g}^{\mathbf{r}}\mathbf{h}^{\boldsymbol{\delta}}$ and $\hat{A} = \tilde{\mathbf{G}}^{\mathbf{r}}\mathbf{H}^{\boldsymbol{\gamma}}$
3. $\mathcal{V}$ sends random challenge $e \in \mathbb{Z}_q$.
4. $\mathcal{P}$ sends $\mathbf{z} = \mathbf{r} + e\mathbf{w}$, $\boldsymbol{\omega} = \boldsymbol{\delta} + e\boldsymbol{\alpha}$, and $\boldsymbol{\Omega} = \gamma + e\sum_{i=1}^{\ell} \boldsymbol{\beta}_i x^{i-1}$.
5. $\mathcal{V}$ checks $\boldsymbol{g}^{\mathbf{z}}\mathbf{h}^{\boldsymbol{\omega}} \stackrel{?}{=} AC^e$ and $\tilde{\mathbf{G}}^{\mathbf{z}}\mathbf{H}^{\boldsymbol{\Omega}} \stackrel{?}{=} \hat{A}\prod_{i=1}^{\ell}(\hat{C}_i^{x^{i-1}})^e$.

Fig. 2. Four-move protocol for amortized equality of many vector Pedersen commitments.

mitments, with proof size of $O(d)$. To avoid invoking ComEq individually for many commitments we first amortize the statements. The main idea of amortization is to introduce additional challenge $x \in \mathbb{Z}_q$ and use it to take a random linear combination in the exponent. A similar idea has appeared in many contexts, e.g., amortization of many range proofs in Bulletproofs [17] and batch verification of EdDSA signatures. Note that the protocol below can be seen as a verifier-optimized version of the technique described by Attema–Cramer–Fehr [5, §3.4]. For completeness, in [3] we include a version derived by invoking their amortization of multiple group homomorphisms in a black-box way. The advantage of our AmComEq (Fig. 2) over AmComEq$'$ is that it allows to save ℓ group exponentiations on verifier's side (i.e., computation of $\tilde{\mathbf{H}}$), by letting the prover precompute amortization of commitment randomness $\boldsymbol{\beta}_i$. However, the proof sizes are identical.

Note also that the protocol is 4-round where the first message is a challenge, which does not really fit into the format of standard Fiat–Shamir transform [30]. However, one can easily make it applicable by either introducing additional round where the prover first sends a dummy randomness, or let them send A before receiving challenge x. Security proof is deferred to [3].

Theorem 2. AmComEq *is a four-move protocol for the relation* $\mathcal{R}_{\mathsf{AmComEq}}$. *It is perfectly complete, computationally* $(\ell, 2)$*-special sound if finding non-trivial discrete-log relation for the generators* $[\boldsymbol{g}, \mathbf{h}]$ *is hard, and special HVZK. Moreover, the communication costs are:*

- $\mathcal{P} \to \mathcal{V}$: *2 elements of* $\mathbb{G}$ *and* $\ell d + d' + d''$ *elements of* $\mathbb{Z}_q$.
- $\mathcal{V} \to \mathcal{P}$: *2 elements of* $\mathbb{Z}_q$.

4.2 CompAmComEq: Recursive Compression

The major drawback of AmComEq is that its proof size is still linear in the vector dimension ℓd, due to the response vector $\mathbf{z} \in \mathbb{Z}_q^{\ell d}$. Notice however that once the rest of transcript $x, A, \hat{A}, e, \boldsymbol{\omega}, \boldsymbol{\Omega}$ is fixed, it should be sufficient to prove knowledge of $\mathbf{z}$ such that $\boldsymbol{g}^{\mathbf{z}} = Y := AC^e\mathbf{h}^{-\boldsymbol{\omega}}$ and $\tilde{\mathbf{G}}^{\mathbf{z}} = \hat{Y} := \hat{A}\prod_{i=1}^{\ell}(\hat{C}_i^{x^{i-1}})^e\mathbf{H}^{-\boldsymbol{\Omega}}$, instead of sending $\mathbf{z}$. This is where the *compressed Σ-protocol theory* [4–7] comes into play. That is, the last move of AmComEq can invoke another protocol CompDLEq of proof size $O(\log(\ell d))$, for the relation

$$\mathcal{R}_{\mathsf{DLEq}} = \left\{((\boldsymbol{g}, \tilde{\mathbf{G}}, \ell d), (Y, \hat{Y}), \mathbf{z}) \,:\, Y = \boldsymbol{g}^{\mathbf{z}}, \hat{Y} = \tilde{\mathbf{G}}^{\mathbf{z}}\right\}. \tag{2}$$

The protocol CompDLEq for $\mathcal{R}_{\mathsf{DLEq}}$ is described in [3]. From [4, Theorem 2] we immediately get the following result.

Corollary 1. *Let* CompAmComEq *be a protocol identical to* AmComEq, *except that its last move is replaced by* CompDLEq. CompAmComEq *is a* $(2\mu + 4)$-*move protocol for the relation* $\mathcal{R}_{\mathsf{AmComEq}}$, *where* $\mu = \lceil \log_2(\ell d) \rceil - 1$. *It is perfectly complete and computationally* $(\ell, 2, k_1, \ldots, k_\mu)$-*special sound if finding nontrivial discrete-log relation for the generators* $[\boldsymbol{g}, \mathbf{h}]$ *is hard, where* $k_i = 3$ *for all* $i \in [1, \mu]$. *Moreover, the communication costs are:*

- $\mathcal{P} \to \mathcal{V}$: $4\lceil \log_2(\ell d) \rceil - 2$ *elements of* $\mathbb{G}$ *and* $2 + d' + d''$ *elements of* $\mathbb{Z}_q$.
- $\mathcal{V} \to \mathcal{P}$: $\lceil \log_2(\ell d) \rceil + 1$ *elements of* $\mathbb{Z}_q$.

5 Instantiation with PLONK

In this section we apply our ECLIPSE compiler to PLONK. We first go over the essential part of the PLONK protocol, using the language of AHP. More detailed preliminaries are provided in [3].

5.1 PLONK AHP

We consider an arithmetic circuit with fan-in two over $\mathbb{F}$, consisting of n gates. The PLONK AHP essentially proves knowledge of left, right and output wire values for every gate $i \in [n]$ in the circuit, such that they are also consistent with the constraints determined by the circuit topology. The per-gate constraints are specified by *selector vectors* $\mathbf{q}_L, \mathbf{q}_R, \mathbf{q}_O, \mathbf{q}_M, \mathbf{q}_C \in \mathbb{F}^n$. We call $\mathcal{C} = (n, m, \mathbf{L}, \mathbf{R}, \mathbf{O}, \mathbf{q}_L, \mathbf{q}_R, \mathbf{q}_O, \mathbf{q}_M, \mathbf{q}_C)$ *constraint systems.*

$\mathsf{AHP}_{\mathsf{PLONK}}$ relies on a multiplicative subgroup $\mathbb{H} = \{\zeta, \zeta^2, \ldots, \zeta^n\} \subset \mathbb{F}^*$ generated by an nth primitive root of unity $\zeta \in \mathbb{F}^*$. It follows that an associated vanishing polynomial $v_{\mathbb{H}}(X) = X^n - 1$ splits completely in $\mathbb{F}[X]$, i.e., $X^n - 1 = \prod_{i=1}^{n}(X - \zeta^i)$. Then we have the corresponding Lagrange basis $L_i(X) \in \mathbb{F}_{<n}[X]$ for $i \in [n]$ such that $L_i(\zeta^i) = 1$ and $L_i(\zeta^j) = 0$ for $j \neq i$.

During the first round of $\mathsf{AHP}_{\mathsf{PLONK}}$, the prover sends the following WCPs encoding both statement and witness $((\mathsf{w}_i)_{i \in [l]}, (\mathsf{w}_i)_{i \in [l+1, 3n]})$:

$$f_L(X) = \sum_{i \in [n]} \mathsf{w}_i L_i(X) \quad f_R(X) = \sum_{i \in [n]} \mathsf{w}_{n+i} L_i(X) \quad f_O(X) = \sum_{i \in [n]} \mathsf{w}_{2n+i} L_i(X) \tag{3}$$

To achieve zero-knowledge these polynomials are masked by polynomials $(\rho_{L,1}X + \rho_{L,2})v_{\mathbb{H}}(X)$, $(\rho_{R,1}X + \rho_{R,2})v_{\mathbb{H}}(X)$ and $(\rho_{O,1}X + \rho_{O,2})v_{\mathbb{H}}(X)$ where each coefficient is randomly sampled by the AHP prover.

5.2 CP-PLONK

Our goal is to turn $\mathsf{AHP}_{\mathsf{PLONK}}$ into CP-PLONK with our compiler. We first describe a commit-and-prove variant of relation $\mathcal{R}'_{\mathsf{PLONK}}$. The auxiliary commitment scheme AC is instantiated with vector Pedersen commitment and its key ack consists of randomly chosen generators of $\mathbb{G}$ with unknown relative discrete logarithms: $\mathbf{G} = (G_1, \ldots, G_d)$ and H.

We assume without loss of generality that every committed witness $(\mathsf{w}_i)_{i \in I_{\mathsf{com}}}$ is left input to gate i. Then we use the following disjoint witness index sets: $I_{\mathsf{pub}} = [l], I_{\mathsf{com}} = [l+1, l+\ell d], I_{\mathsf{mid}} = [l+\ell d+1, n]$, assuming that $\mathsf{w}_{l+1}, \ldots, \mathsf{w}_{l+\ell d}$ are ℓd witness values committed in advance. Moreover, every d values are batched into a single commitment, that is, every vector compound of d wires w_i, for $i \in I_k = [l+1+d(k-1), l+dk]$, is committed to in the kth auxiliary commitment $\hat{C}_k = \mathbf{G}^{(\mathsf{w}_i)_{i \in I_k}} H^{r_k}$ for $k \in [\ell]$. Then we have $I_{\mathsf{com}} = \bigcup_{k \in [\ell]} I_k$.

Definition 11 (CP-PLONK indexed relation). *The indexed relation $\mathcal{R}_{\mathsf{CP\text{-}PLONK}}$ is the set of all triples*

$$((\mathbb{F}, n, m, l, \mathbf{q}_L, \mathbf{q}_R, \mathbf{q}_O, \mathbf{q}_M, \mathbf{q}_C, \sigma, \mathcal{T}_C, I_{\mathsf{com}}, (I_k)_{k \in [\ell]}, \mathsf{ack}),$$
$$((\mathsf{w}_i)_{i \in [l]}, (\hat{C}_k)_{k \in [\ell]}), ((\mathsf{w}_i)_{i \in [l+1, 3n]}, (r_k)_{k \in [\ell]}))$$

such that

$$\begin{aligned}
\forall i \in [n]: \quad & \mathsf{w}_i = \mathsf{w}_{\sigma(i)} \\
\forall i \in [l]: \quad & (\mathbf{q}_L)_i \cdot \mathsf{w}_i + (\mathbf{q}_R)_i \cdot \mathsf{w}_{n+i} + (\mathbf{q}_O)_i \cdot \mathsf{w}_{2n+i} + (\mathbf{q}_M)_i \mathsf{w}_i \mathsf{w}_{n+i} \\
& + (\mathbf{q}_C)_i - \mathsf{w}_i = 0 \\
\forall i \in [l+1, n]: \quad & (\mathbf{q}_L)_i \cdot \mathsf{w}_i + (\mathbf{q}_R)_i \cdot \mathsf{w}_{n+i} + (\mathbf{q}_O)_i \cdot \mathsf{w}_{2n+i} + (\mathbf{q}_M)_i \mathsf{w}_i \mathsf{w}_{n+i} + (\mathbf{q}_C)_i = 0 \\
\forall k \in [\ell]: \quad & \hat{C}_k = \mathbf{G}^{(\mathsf{w}_i)_{i \in I_k}} H^{r_k}
\end{aligned}$$

5.2.1 Applying Our Compiler

We show that $\mathsf{AHP}_{\mathsf{PLONK}}$ as well as the polynomial commitment scheme meets the requirements of Theorem 1.

- Decomp takes $\mathsf{n_w} = 3$ masked WCPs (f_L, f_R, f_O) and $I_{\mathsf{com}} \subset [n]$, parses f_L as $\sum_{i \in [n]} \mathsf{w}_i L_i(X) + (\rho_1 X + \rho_2) v_{\mathbb{H}}(X)$, and decompose them as follows.

$$f_{L,\mathsf{com}}(X) := \sum_{i \in I_{\mathsf{com}}} \mathsf{w}_i L_i(X) + (\lambda_{\mathsf{com},1} X + \lambda_{\mathsf{com},2}) v_{\mathbb{H}}(X)$$
$$f_{R,\mathsf{com}}(X) := 0 \qquad f_{O,\mathsf{com}}(X) := 0$$
$$f_{L,\mathsf{mid}}(X) := \sum_{i \in [n] \setminus I_{\mathsf{com}}} \mathsf{w}_i L_i(X) + (\lambda_{\mathsf{mid},1} X + \lambda_{\mathsf{mid},2}) v_{\mathbb{H}}(X)$$
$$f_{R,\mathsf{mid}}(X) := f_R(X) \quad f_{O,\mathsf{mid}}(X) := f_O(X)$$

  where $\lambda_{\mathsf{com},i}$'s are randomly chosen and $\lambda_{\mathsf{mid},i} := \rho_i - \lambda_{\mathsf{com},i}$. Clearly, the decomposition is additive, degree-preserving, and non-overlapping.

- WitExt takes WCPs (f_L, f_R, f_O) and uniquely extracts witness vectors for every $i \in [n]$

$$\mathsf{w}_i = f_L(\zeta^i) \qquad \mathsf{w}_{n+i} = f_R(\zeta^i) \qquad \mathsf{w}_{2n+i} = f_O(\zeta^i)$$

  As it's independently extracting witness values within disjoint index sets $I_L = [n]$, $I_R = [n+1, 2n]$, and $I_O = [2n+1, 3n]$, respectively, we have that f_L, f_R and f_O are disjoint (see Definition 7).
- As PLONK retains zero-knowledge by masking WCPs, but without hiding commitment[6], we use de-randomized version of $\mathsf{PC_{KZG}.Com_{ck}}$ (see Sect. 2.2.1) that takes polynomial $f \in \mathbb{F}_{\leq D}[X]$ and outputs $[f(\chi)]_1$. Hence the polynomial commitment key is $\mathsf{ck} = \mathsf{pp} = (g, g^{\chi}, \ldots, g^{\chi^D})$. Clearly, this is an additively homomorphic commitment scheme. Its binding and extractability were formally shown in Appendix B-D of [25]. As mentioned in [32] and from how WitExt works, the knowledge soundness of PLONK holds only by enforcing degree bound to the maximum degree D for committed polynomials so the plain KZG construction should suffice for compiling $\mathsf{AHP_{PLONK}}$.

We now define a suitable commitment-linking protocol $\mathsf{CP_{lnk}}$ in Fig. 3. Since WCPs are disjoint it is enough to provide linking w.r.t. a polynomial f_L. The main idea is to (1) prove consistency between $f_{L,\mathsf{com}}$ and auxiliary commitments $\hat{C}_k$ with the AmComEq protocol from previous section, and (2) force the prover to show f_{mid} vanishes at all points in $\mathbb{H}_{\mathsf{com}} = \{\zeta^i\}_{i \in I_{\mathsf{com}}}$. The latter is in particular crucial for WitExt to successfully output a witness vector consistent with auxiliary commitments, even after taking the sum of $f_{L,\mathsf{com}}$ and $f_{L,\mathsf{mid}}$. This step only incurs constant overhead in the evaluation proof thanks to the batch evaluation technique proposed in [14]. On the other hand, the consistency between f_{com} and ℓ vector Pedersen commitments $\hat{C}_k = \mathbf{G}^{(\mathsf{w}_i)_{i \in I_k}} H^{r_k}$ for $k \in [\ell]$ are handled by CompAmComEq protocol (see Sect. 4).

Lemma 1. *Assuming extractability of* $\mathsf{PC_{KZG}}$ *and argument of knowledge of* CompAmComEq, *the protocol* $\mathsf{CP_{lnk}}$ *(Fig. 3) is an argument of knowledge. Assuming zero knowledge of Fiat–Shamir-transformed* CompAmComEq, *the protocol* $\mathsf{CP_{lnk}}$ *is zero-knowledge in the SRS model.*

Proof is deferred to [3].

[6] More formally, if the underlying AHP is $(\mathsf{b}+1, \mathsf{C})$-zero knowledge, where b is the maximum number of queries made by the verifier to polynomials, one can retain ZK of the resulting SNARK by compiling AHP via PCS with *somewhat hiding* security, a weaker notion of hiding [20]. Because the deterministic KZG is already somewhat hiding and every WCP in $\mathsf{AHP_{PLONK}}$ is queried once, it suffices to add $v_{\mathbb{H}}$ multiplied by a masking polynomial of degree 1 to tolerate 2 openings (i.e., one evaluation and one commitment).

Protocol $\mathsf{CP_{lnk}}$ **for PLONK**

Indexing $\mathcal{I}^{\mathsf{srs}}_{\mathsf{lnk}}(I_{\mathsf{com}}, (I_k)_{k\in[\ell]})$ precomputes $[v_{\mathbb{H}_{\mathsf{com}}}(\chi)]_2$ such that $v_{\mathbb{H}_{\mathsf{com}}}(X) = \prod_{a\in\mathbb{H}_{\mathsf{com}}}(X-a)$ and $\mathbb{H}_{\mathsf{com}} = \{\zeta^i : i \in I_{\mathsf{com}}\} \subset \mathbb{H}$, obtains generators $g_i := [L_i(\chi)]_1$ for $i \in I_{\mathsf{com}}$, $\boldsymbol{g} := (g_i)_{i\in I_{\mathsf{com}}}$, $h_1 = [\chi v_{\mathbb{H}}(\chi)]_1$, $h_2 = [v_{\mathbb{H}}(\chi)]_1$, $\mathbf{G}$ and H by accessing srs. It outputs $(\mathsf{ipk_{lnk}}, \mathsf{ivk_{lnk}})$ such that

$$\mathsf{ipk_{lnk}} = (\mathsf{pp}, v_{\mathbb{H}_{\mathsf{com}}}(X), \boldsymbol{g}, h_1, h_2, \mathbf{G}, H) \quad \text{and} \quad \mathsf{ivk_{lnk}} = ([v_{\mathbb{H}_{\mathsf{com}}}(\chi)]_2, \boldsymbol{g}, h_1, h_2, \mathbf{G}, H).$$

Input. $\mathcal{P}_{\mathsf{lnk}}$ (resp. $\mathcal{V}_{\mathsf{lnk}}$) receives $\mathsf{ipk_{lnk}}$ (resp. $\mathsf{ivk_{lnk}}$). The statement $((\hat{C}_k)_{k\in[\ell]}, (C_{L,\mathsf{com}}, C_{L,\mathsf{mid}}))$ is a common input. The $\mathcal{P}_{\mathsf{lnk}}$ has as input witness $(f_{L,\mathsf{com}}(X), f_{L,\mathsf{mid}}(X), (r_k)_{k\in[\ell]})$ such that $\hat{C}_k = \mathbf{G}^{(\mathsf{w}_i)_{i\in I_k}} H^{r_k}$, $C_{L,\mathsf{com}} = [f_{L,\mathsf{com}}(\chi)]_1$, $C_{L,\mathsf{mid}} = [f_{L,\mathsf{mid}}(\chi)]_1$, $f_{L,\mathsf{com}}(X) = \sum_{i\in I_{\mathsf{com}}} \mathsf{w}_i L_i(X) + (\lambda_{\mathsf{com},1}X + \lambda_{\mathsf{com},2})v_{\mathbb{H}}(X)$, and $f_{L,\mathsf{mid}}(X) = \sum_{i\in[n]\setminus I_{\mathsf{com}}} \mathsf{w}_i L_i(X) + (\lambda_{\mathsf{mid},1}X + \lambda_{\mathsf{mid},2})v_{\mathbb{H}}(X)$.

Prove.

- Compute a proof π_{ComEq} of the following statement.

$$\mathsf{CompAmComEq} : \mathsf{PK}\left\{ ((\mathsf{w}_i)_{i\in I_{\mathsf{com}}}, (r_k)_{k\in[\ell]}, \lambda_{\mathsf{com},1}, \lambda_{\mathsf{com},2}) : \begin{array}{c} \hat{C}_k = \mathbf{G}^{(\mathsf{w}_i)_{i\in I_k}} H^{r_k} \wedge \\ C_{L,\mathsf{com}} = \boldsymbol{g}^{(\mathsf{w}_i)_{i\in I_{\mathsf{com}}}} h_1^{\lambda_{\mathsf{com},1}} h_2^{\lambda_{\mathsf{com},2}} \end{array} \right\}$$

- Compute evaluation proof $W(X) = \frac{f_{L,\mathsf{mid}}(X)}{v_{\mathbb{H}_{\mathsf{com}}}(X)}$ and $\Pi := [W(\chi)]_1$. Output $\pi_{\mathsf{lnk}} = (\Pi, \pi_{\mathsf{ComEq}})$.

Verify. Given π_{lnk}, verify π_{ComEq} and check that $f_{L,\mathsf{mid}}$ vanishes on $\mathbb{H}_{\mathsf{com}}$: $e(C_{L,\mathsf{mid}}, h) \stackrel{?}{=} e(\Pi, [v_{\mathbb{H}_{\mathsf{com}}}(\chi)]_2)$.

Fig. 3. Commitment-linking protocol for PLONK

6 Instantiation with Marlin

In this section we apply our compiler to Marlin. As in the previous section, we first identify WCPs and how it encodes the witness vector in AHP. More detailed preliminaries are provided in [3].

6.1 Marlin AHP

Notations. For a finite field $\mathbb{F}$ and a subset $\mathbb{S} \subseteq \mathbb{F}$, we denote by $v_{\mathbb{S}}(X)$ the vanishing polynomial of $\mathbb{S}$ that is the unique non-zero monic polynomial of degree at most $|\mathbb{S}|$ that is zero everywhere on $\mathbb{S}$. We denote by $\mathbb{F}^{\mathbb{S}}$ the set of vectors indexed by elements in a finite set $\mathbb{S}$. For a function $f : \mathbb{S} \to \mathbb{F}$, we denote by $\hat{f}$, the univariate polynomial over $\mathbb{F}$ with degree less than $|\mathbb{S}|$ that agrees with f, that is, $\hat{f}(a) = f(a)$ for all $a \in \mathbb{S}$. In particular, the polynomial $\hat{f}$ can be expressed as a linear combination

$$\hat{f}(X) = \sum_{a\in\mathbb{S}} f(a) \cdot L_{a,\mathbb{S}}(X)$$

where $\{L_{a,\mathbb{S}}(X)\}_{a\in\mathbb{S}}$ are the *Lagrange basis polynomials* of degree less than $|\mathbb{S}|$ such that $L_{a,\mathbb{S}}(a) = 1$ and $L_{a,\mathbb{S}}(a') = 1$ for $a' \in \mathbb{S} \setminus \{a\}$.

Constraint Systems. Unlike PLONK, Marlin's AHP is for R1CS (Rank-1 constraint satisfiability) indexed relation defined by the set of tuples $(\mathsf{i}, \mathsf{x}, \mathsf{w}) =$

$((\mathbb{F}, \mathbb{H}, \mathbb{K}, A, B, C), x, w)$, where $\mathbb{F}$ is a finite field, $\mathbb{H}$ and $\mathbb{K}$ are subsets of $\mathbb{F}$, such that $n = |\mathbb{H}|$ and $m = |\mathbb{K}|$, A, B, C are $\mathbb{H} \times \mathbb{H}$ matrices over $\mathbb{F}$ with $|\mathbb{K}| \geq \max\{\|A\|, \|B\|, \|C\|\}$, and $z := (x, w)$ is a vector in $\mathbb{F}^{\mathbb{H}}$ such that $Az \circ Bz = Cz$.

Following [25], we assume efficiently computable bijections $\phi_{\mathbb{H}} : \mathbb{H} \to [n]$ and $\phi_{\mathbb{K}} : \mathbb{K} \to [m]$, and denote the first l elements in $\mathbb{H}$ and the remaining elements, via sets $\mathbb{H}[\leq l] := \{a \in \mathbb{H} : 1 \leq \phi_{\mathbb{H}}(a) \leq l\}$ and $\mathbb{H}[> l] := \{a \in \mathbb{H} : l < \phi_{\mathbb{H}}(a) \leq n\}$ respectively. We then denote the first part of the vector z as the public component $x \in \mathbb{F}^{\mathbb{H}[\leq l]}$ and the second part as witness component $w \in \mathbb{F}^{\mathbb{H}[>l]}$.

WCP. In $\mathsf{AHP}_{\mathsf{Marlin}}$, the prover P receives as input the instance $x \in \mathbb{F}^{\mathbb{H}[\leq l]}$, a witness $w \in \mathbb{F}^{\mathbb{H}[>l]}$. The verifier V receives as input x, and obtains oracle access to the nine polynomials output at the end of the preprocessing phase.

Let $\hat{x}(X) \in \mathbb{F}_{<l}[X]$ and $\hat{w}(X) \in \mathbb{F}_{\leq n-l}[X]$ be polynomials that agree with the instance x on $\mathbb{H}[\leq l]$, and with the shifted witness on $\mathbb{H}[> l]$ respectively. Concretely, these polynomials are defined as follows:

$$\hat{x}(X) := \sum_{a \in \mathbb{H}[\leq l]} x(a) \cdot L_{a,\mathbb{H}[\leq l]}(X)$$

$$\hat{w}(X) := \sum_{a \in \mathbb{H}[>l]} \left(\frac{w(a) - \hat{x}(a)}{v_{\mathbb{H}[\leq l]}(a)} \right) \cdot L_{a,\mathbb{H}[>l]}(X) + \rho \cdot v_{\mathbb{H}[>l]}(X)$$

where the second term of $\hat{w}$ is added to retain zero-knowledge when the number of evaluation queries to $\hat{w}$ is 1 (which is the case in Marlin AHP) and ρ is sampled uniformly at random from $\mathbb{F}$. Let $z := (x, w)$ denote the full assignment. Then the polynomial $\hat{z}(X) := \hat{w}(X) \cdot v_{\mathbb{H}[\leq l]}(X) + \hat{x}(X)$ agrees with z on $\mathbb{H}$.

6.2 CP-Marlin

We now turn $\mathsf{AHP}_{\mathsf{Marlin}}$ into CP-Marlin by applying our compiler. We begin by giving a commit-and-prove relation for R1CS.

Relation for CP-Marlin. We define an extended relation to accommodate consistency of partial witness wire values and commitment. For convenience we define the following subsets: $\mathbb{H}_{\mathsf{pub}} := \mathbb{H}[\leq l], \mathbb{H}_{\mathsf{com}} := \mathbb{H}[> l, \leq l + d\ell], \mathbb{H}_{\mathsf{mid}} := \mathbb{H}[> l + d\ell]$, assuming that $w(a)$ for $a \in \mathbb{H}_{\mathsf{com}}$ are $d\ell$ values committed to in advance. Moreover, every d values are batched into a single commitment, that is, every vector compound of d wires $w(a)$, for $a \in \mathbb{H}_{\mathsf{com},k} = \mathbb{H}[> l + d(k-1), \leq l + dk]$, is committed to in the kth auxiliary commitment $\hat{C}_k = \mathbf{G}^{(w(a))_{a \in \mathbb{H}_{\mathsf{com},k}}} H^{r_k}$ for $k \in [\ell]$. Then we have $\mathbb{H}_{\mathsf{com}} = \bigcup_{k \in [\ell]} \mathbb{H}_{\mathsf{com},k}$.

Definition 12 (CP-Marlin indexed relation). *The indexed relation $\mathcal{R}_{\mathsf{CP\text{-}Marlin}}$ is the set of all triples*

$$(\mathsf{i}, \mathsf{x}, \mathsf{w}) = ((\mathbb{F}, \mathbb{H}, \mathbb{K}, n, m, l, \ell, d, A, B, C), (x, (\hat{C}_k)_{k \in [\ell]}), (w, (r_k)_{k \in [\ell]}))$$

where $\mathbb{F}$ *is a finite field,* $\mathbb{H}$ *and* $\mathbb{K}$ *are subsets of* $\mathbb{F}$*, such that* $n = |\mathbb{H}|$ *and* $m = |\mathbb{K}|$*,* A, B, C *are* $\mathbb{H} \times \mathbb{H}$ *matrices over* $\mathbb{F}$ *with* $|\mathbb{K}| \geq \max\{\|A\|, \|B\|, \|C\|\}$*, and* $z := (x, w)$ *is a vector in* $\mathbb{F}^{\mathbb{H}}$ *such that*

$$Az \circ Bz = Cz \text{ and } \forall k \in [\ell], \hat{C}_k = \mathsf{AC.Commit}_{\mathsf{ack}}((w(a))_{a \in \mathbb{H}_{\mathsf{com},k}}; r_k)$$

Applying Our Compiler. We now show that $\mathsf{AHP}_{\mathsf{Marlin}}$ and the polynomial commitment scheme $\mathsf{PC}_{\mathsf{KZG}}$ [42] meet the requirements of Theorem 1.

- Unique witness extraction: WitExt takes $\hat{w}(X)$, evaluates $\hat{w}(X)$ on every $a \in \mathbb{H}[> l]$, multiplies the results by $v_{\mathbb{H}[\leq l]}(a)$, and add $\hat{x}(a)$ to constructs a vector of values $w \in \mathbb{F}^{\mathbb{H}[>l]}$. It is easy to see that WitExt satisfies unique extraction (Definition 8).
- Decomposable WCP: Decomp takes $\hat{w}(X)$ and $\mathbb{H}_{\mathsf{com}}$, and outputs $\hat{w}_{\mathsf{com}}$ and $\hat{w}_{\mathsf{mid}}$ of degree at most $n - l$ as follows:

$$\hat{w}_{\mathsf{com}}(X) := \sum_{a \in \mathbb{H}_{\mathsf{com}}} \left(\frac{w(a) - \hat{x}(a)}{v_{\mathbb{H}[\leq l]}(a)} \right) \cdot L_{a,\mathbb{H}[>l]}(X) + \lambda_{\mathsf{com}} \cdot v_{\mathbb{H}[>l]}(X)$$

$$\hat{w}_{\mathsf{mid}}(X) := \sum_{a \in \mathbb{H}_{\mathsf{mid}}} \left(\frac{w(a) - \hat{x}(a)}{v_{\mathbb{H}[\leq l]}(a)} \right) \cdot L_{a,\mathbb{H}[>l]}(X) + \lambda_{\mathsf{mid}} \cdot v_{\mathbb{H}[>l]}(X)$$

  where λ_{com} was sampled from $\mathbb{F}$ uniformly at random and $\lambda_{\mathsf{mid}} := \rho - \lambda_{\mathsf{com}}$. Clearly, the decomposition is additive, degree-preserving and non-overlapping.
- Marlin compiles $\mathsf{AHP}_{\mathsf{Marlin}}$ using the plain KZG polynomial commitment except that degrees of hiding polynomials are minimized. That is, to commit to the WCP $\mathsf{PC}_{\mathsf{KZG}}.\mathsf{Com}_{\mathsf{ck}}$ takes $\hat{w}(X)$ and $\omega(X) := \omega_0 + \omega_1 X$ as input and outputs $[\hat{w}(\chi) + \gamma\omega(\chi)]_1$, where $\omega_0, \omega_1 \in \mathbb{F}$ are randomly sampled masking coefficients. As mentioned in §9.2 of [25] and as it's clear from how WitExt works, the knowledge soundness of Marlin holds only by enforcing degree bound to the maximum degree D for committed polynomials. In order to construct our commitment-linking protocol for Marlin, we modify how hiding is achieved. Specifically, we now mask the two decomposed WCPs independently as follows: commitment to $\hat{w}_{\mathsf{com}}(X)$ is masked by a random polynomial $\omega_{\mathsf{com}}(X) := \omega_{\mathsf{com},0} + \omega_{\mathsf{com},1}X$ and $\hat{w}_{\mathsf{mid}}(X)$ is masked by a random polynomial $\omega_{\mathsf{mid}}(X)$ that vanishes on $\mathbb{H}_{\mathsf{com}}$; $\omega_{\mathsf{mid}}(X) := (\omega_{\mathsf{mid},0} + \omega_{\mathsf{mid},1}X)v_{\mathbb{H}_{\mathsf{com}}}(X)$. Note that, for $\hat{w}_{\mathsf{mid}}$, we do not apply Marlin's optimization of minimising the degree.

  Following PLONK and Lunar, one may alternatively compile $\mathsf{AHP}_{\mathsf{Marlin}}$ with the deterministic KZG by increasing the degree of masking factor to 1 (i.e., $\rho_1 X + \rho_2$) to hide one evaluation and the commitment. In this way, decomposition of WCPs as well as $\mathsf{CP}_{\mathtt{lnk}}$ can be done as in CP-PLONK and the number of SRS elements does not grow due to the CP extension.

In Fig. 4 we present a suitable commitment-linking protocol $\mathsf{CP}_{\mathtt{lnk}}$. The key idea is to have the prover commit to an encoding of the assignment in subsets $\mathbb{H}_{\mathsf{com}}$ and $\mathbb{H}_{\mathsf{mid}}$ into separate polynomials, and then show that $\hat{w}_{\mathsf{mid}}(X)$ vanishes at $\mathbb{H}_{\mathsf{com}}$, together with the consistency of $\hat{w}_{\mathsf{com}}(X)$ with vector Pedersen commitments $\hat{C}_k = \mathbf{G}^{(w(a))_{a\in\mathbb{H}_{\mathsf{com},k}}} H^{r_k}$ for $k \in [\ell]$ via $\mathsf{CompAmComEq}$ protocol (see Sect. 4). We assume that $\mathbb{H}_{\mathsf{com}} = \bigcup_{k\in[\ell]} \mathbb{H}_{\mathsf{com},k}$, $\mathbb{H}_{\mathsf{com},k}$'s are disjoint with each other and of same cardinality $d = |\mathbb{H}_{\mathsf{com},k}|$.

Protocol $\mathsf{CP}_{\mathtt{lnk}}$ **for Marlin**

Indexing $\mathcal{I}^{\mathsf{srs}}_{\mathtt{lnk}}(I_{\mathsf{com}}, (I_k)_{k\in[\ell]})$ precomputes $[v_{\mathbb{H}_{\mathsf{com}}}(\chi)]_2$ such that $v_{\mathbb{H}_{\mathsf{com}}}(X) = \prod_{a\in\mathbb{H}_{\mathsf{com}}}(X-a)$, obtains generators $g_a := [L_{a,\mathbb{H}[>l]}(\chi)/v_{\mathbb{H}[\leq l]}(a)]_1$ for $a \in \mathbb{H}_{\mathsf{com}}$, $\boldsymbol{g} := (g_a)_{a\in\mathbb{H}_{\mathsf{com}}}$, $h_1 := [v_{\mathbb{H}[>l]}(\chi)]_1, h_2 := [\gamma]_1, h_3 := [\gamma\chi]_1$, $\mathbf{G}$ and H by accessing srs. It outputs $(\mathsf{ipk}_{\mathtt{lnk}}, \mathsf{ivk}_{\mathtt{lnk}})$ such that

$$\mathsf{ipk}_{\mathtt{lnk}} = (\mathsf{pp}, v_{\mathbb{H}_{\mathsf{com}}}(X), \boldsymbol{g}, h_1, h_2, h_3, \mathbf{G}, H) \quad \text{and} \quad \mathsf{ivk}_{\mathtt{lnk}} = ([v_{\mathbb{H}_{\mathsf{com}}}(\chi)]_2, \boldsymbol{g}, h_1, h_2, h_3, \mathbf{G}, H).$$

Input. $\mathcal{P}_{\mathtt{lnk}}$ (resp. $\mathcal{V}_{\mathtt{lnk}}$) receives $\mathsf{ipk}_{\mathtt{lnk}}$ (resp. $\mathsf{ivk}_{\mathtt{lnk}}$). The statement $((\hat{C}_k)_{k\in[\ell]}, (C_{\mathsf{com}}, C_{\mathsf{mid}}))$ is a common input. The $\mathcal{P}_{\mathtt{lnk}}$ has as input witness $(\hat{w}_{\mathsf{com}}(X), \hat{w}_{\mathsf{mid}}(X), (r_k)_{k\in[\ell]})$ such that $\hat{C}_k = \mathbf{G}^{(w(a))_{a\in\mathbb{H}_{\mathsf{com},k}}} H^{r_k}$, $C_{\mathsf{com}} = [\hat{w}_{\mathsf{com}}(\chi) + \gamma\omega_{\mathsf{com}}(\chi)]_1$, $C_{\mathsf{mid}} = [\hat{w}_{\mathsf{mid}}(\chi) + \gamma\omega_{\mathsf{mid}}(\chi)]_1$, and

$$\hat{w}_{\mathsf{com}}(X) = \sum_{a\in\mathbb{H}_{\mathsf{com}}} \left(\frac{w(a) - \hat{x}(a)}{v_{\mathbb{H}[\leq l]}(a)}\right) \cdot L_{a,\mathbb{H}[>l]}(X) + \lambda_{\mathsf{com}} \cdot v_{\mathbb{H}[>l]}(X)$$

$$\hat{w}_{\mathsf{mid}}(X) = \sum_{a\in\mathbb{H}_{\mathsf{mid}}} \left(\frac{w(a) - \hat{x}(a)}{v_{\mathbb{H}[\leq l]}(a)}\right) \cdot L_{a,\mathbb{H}[>l]}(X) + \lambda_{\mathsf{mid}} \cdot v_{\mathbb{H}[>l]}(X)$$

Prove.

- Compute a proof π_{ComEq} of the following statement where $\bar{C}_{\mathsf{com}} := C_{\mathsf{com}} \cdot \boldsymbol{g}^{(\hat{x}(a))_{a\in\mathbb{H}_{\mathsf{com}}}}$.

$$\mathsf{PK}\left\{\begin{matrix}((w(a))_{a\in\mathbb{H}_{\mathsf{com}}}, (r_k)_{k\in[\ell]}, \\ \lambda_{\mathsf{com}}, \omega_{\mathsf{com},0}, \omega_{\mathsf{com},1})\end{matrix} : \begin{matrix}\hat{C}_k = \mathbf{G}^{(w(a))_{a\in\mathbb{H}_{\mathsf{com},k}}} H^{r_k} \\ \wedge\ \bar{C}_{\mathsf{com}} = \boldsymbol{g}^{(w(a))_{a\in\mathbb{H}_{\mathsf{com}}}} h_1^{\lambda_{\mathsf{com}}} h_2^{\omega_{\mathsf{com},0}} h_3^{\omega_{\mathsf{com},1}}\end{matrix}\right\}$$

- Compute evaluation proof $\Pi = [W_1 + \gamma W_2(\chi)]_1$, where $W_1(X) = \frac{\hat{w}_{\mathsf{mid}}(X)}{v_{\mathbb{H}_{\mathsf{com}}}(X)}$, $W_2(X) = \frac{\omega_{\mathsf{mid}}(X)}{v_{\mathbb{H}_{\mathsf{com}}}(X)}$. Set $\pi_{\mathtt{lnk}} = (\Pi, \pi_{\mathsf{ComEq}})$. Note that since $\omega_{\mathsf{mid}}(X)$ vanishes on $\mathbb{H}_{\mathsf{com}}$, is divisible by $v_{\mathbb{H}_{\mathsf{com}}}$, and therefore W_2 is a polynomial.

Verify. Given $\pi_{\mathtt{lnk}}$, verify π_{ComEq}, and check that $\hat{w}_{\mathsf{mid}}$ vanishes on $\mathbb{H}_{\mathsf{com}}$: $e(C_{\mathsf{mid}}, h) \stackrel{?}{=} e(\Pi, [v_{\mathbb{H}_{\mathsf{com}}}(\chi)]_2)$.

Fig. 4. Commitment-linking protocol for Marlin

Lemma 2. *Assuming extractability of* $\mathsf{PC}_{\mathsf{KZG}}$ *and argument of knowledge of* $\mathsf{CompAmComEq}$, *the protocol* $\mathsf{CP}_{\mathtt{lnk}}$ *(Fig. 4) is an argument of knowledge. Assuming zero knowledge of Fiat–Shamir-transformed* $\mathsf{CompAmComEq}$, *the protocol* $\mathsf{CP}_{\mathtt{lnk}}$ *is zero-knowledge in the SRS model.*

Proof is deferred to [3].

Acknowledgments. The authors are grateful for Sean Bowe, Ben Fisch, Ariel Gabizon, and Mary Maller for clarifying the details of their works. We thank the anonymous reviewers of PKC 2022 for helpful comments. This work has been supported by: the Concordium Blockchain Research Center, Aarhus University, Denmark; the Carlsberg

Foundation under the Semper Ardens Research Project CF18-112 (BCM); the European Research Council (ERC) under the European Unions's Horizon 2020 research and innovation programme under grant agreement No 803096 (SPEC).

References

1. What is Jubjub? https://z.cash/technology/jubjub
2. Agrawal, S., Ganesh, C., Mohassel, P.: Non-interactive zero-knowledge proofs for composite statements. In: Shacham, H., Boldyreva, A. (eds.) CRYPTO 2018, Part III. LNCS, vol. 10993, pp. 643–673. Springer, Cham (2018). https://doi.org/10.1007/978-3-319-96878-0_22
3. Aranha, D.F., Bennedsen, E.M., Campanelli, M., Ganesh, C., Orlandi, C., Takahashi, A.: ECLIPSE: enhanced compiling method for Pedersen-committed zkSNARK engines. Cryptology ePrint Archive, Report 2021/934
4. Attema, T., Cramer, R.: Compressed ς-protocol theory and practical application to plug & play secure algorithmics. In: Micciancio, D., Ristenpart, T. (eds.) CRYPTO 2020, Part III. LNCS, vol. 12172, pp. 513–543. Springer, Cham (2020). https://doi.org/10.1007/978-3-030-56877-1_18
5. Attema, T., Cramer, R., Fehr, S.: Compressing proofs of k-out-of-n partial knowledge. Cryptology ePrint Archive, Report 2020/753
6. Attema, T., Cramer, R., Kohl, L.: A compressed σ-protocol theory for lattices. Cryptology ePrint Archive, Report 2021/307
7. Attema, T., Cramer, R., Rambaud, M.: Compressed σ-protocols for bilinear group arithmetic circuits and applications. Cryptology ePrint Archive, Report 2020/1447
8. Backes, M., Hanzlik, L., Herzberg, A., Kate, A., Pryvalov, I.: Efficient non-interactive zero-knowledge proofs in cross-domains without trusted setup. In: Lin, D., Sako, K. (eds.) PKC 2019, Part I. LNCS, vol. 11442, pp. 286–313. Springer, Cham (2019). https://doi.org/10.1007/978-3-030-17253-4_10
9. Ben-Sasson, E., et al.: Zerocash: decentralized anonymous payments from bitcoin. In: 2014 IEEE Symposium on Security and Privacy, pp. 459–474. IEEE Computer Society Press (2014)
10. Ben-Sasson, E., Chiesa, A., Genkin, D., Tromer, E., Virza, M.: SNARKs for C: verifying program executions succinctly and in zero knowledge. In: Canetti, R., Garay, J.A. (eds.) CRYPTO 2013, Part II. LNCS, vol. 8043, pp. 90–108. Springer, Heidelberg (2013). https://doi.org/10.1007/978-3-642-40084-1_6
11. Ben-Sasson, E., Chiesa, A., Tromer, E., Virza, M.: Succinct non-interactive zero knowledge for a von Neumann architecture. In: USENIX Security 2014, pp. 781–796. USENIX Association (2014)
12. Benarroch, D., et al.: Proposal: commit-and-prove zero-knowledge proof systems and extensions. In: 4th ZKProof Workshop (2021)
13. Bitansky, N., Chiesa, A., Ishai, Y., Paneth, O., Ostrovsky, R.: Succinct non-interactive arguments via linear interactive proofs. In: Sahai, A. (ed.) TCC 2013. LNCS, vol. 7785, pp. 315–333. Springer, Heidelberg (2013). https://doi.org/10.1007/978-3-642-36594-2_18
14. Boneh, D., Drake, J., Fisch, B., Gabizon, A.: Efficient polynomial commitment schemes for multiple points and polynomials. Cryptology ePrint Archive, Report 2020/081

15. Bootle, J., Cerulli, A., Chaidos, P., Groth, J., Petit, C.: Efficient zero-knowledge arguments for arithmetic circuits in the discrete log setting. In: Fischlin, M., Coron, J.-S. (eds.) EUROCRYPT 2016, Part II. LNCS, vol. 9666, pp. 327–357. Springer, Heidelberg (2016). https://doi.org/10.1007/978-3-662-49896-5_12
16. Bowe, S., Gabizon, A., Miers, I.: Scalable multi-party computation for zk-SNARK parameters in the random beacon model. Cryptology ePrint Archive, Report 2017/1050
17. Bünz, B., Bootle, J., Boneh, D., Poelstra, A., Wuille, P., Maxwell, G.: Bulletproofs: short proofs for confidential transactions and more. In: 2018 IEEE Symposium on Security and Privacy, pp. 315–334. IEEE Computer Society Press (2014)
18. Bünz, B., Fisch, B., Szepieniec, A.: Transparent SNARKs from DARK compilers. In: Canteaut, A., Ishai, Y. (eds.) EUROCRYPT 2020, Part I. LNCS, vol. 12105, pp. 677–706. Springer, Cham (2020). https://doi.org/10.1007/978-3-030-45721-1_24
19. Camenisch, J., Stadler, M.: Efficient group signature schemes for large groups. In: Kaliski, B.S. (ed.) CRYPTO 1997. LNCS, vol. 1294, pp. 410–424. Springer, Heidelberg (1997). https://doi.org/10.1007/BFb0052252
20. Campanelli, M., Faonio, A., Fiore, D., Querol, A., Rodríguez, H.: Lunar: a toolbox for more efficient universal and updatable zkSNARKs and commit-and-prove extensions. Cryptology ePrint Archive, Report 2020/1069
21. Campanelli, M., Fiore, D., Querol, A.: LegoSNARK: modular design and composition of succinct zero-knowledge proofs. In: ACM CCS 2019, pp. 2075–2092. ACM Press (2019)
22. Campanelli, M., Hall-Andersen, M.: Veksel: simple, efficient, anonymous payments with large anonymity sets from well-studied assumptions. Cryptology ePrint Archive, Report 2020/1069
23. Chase, M., et al.: Post-quantum zero-knowledge and signatures from symmetric-key primitives. In: ACM CCS 2017, pp. 1825–1842. ACM Press (2017)
24. Chase, M., Ganesh, C., Mohassel, P.: Efficient zero-knowledge proof of algebraic and non-algebraic statements with applications to privacy preserving credentials. In: Robshaw, M., Katz, J. (eds.) CRYPTO 2016, Part III. LNCS, vol. 9816, pp. 499–530. Springer, Heidelberg (2016). https://doi.org/10.1007/978-3-662-53015-3_18
25. Chiesa, A., Hu, Y., Maller, M., Mishra, P., Vesely, N., Ward, N.: Marlin: preprocessing zkSNARKs with universal and updatable SRS. In: Canteaut, A., Ishai, Y. (eds.) EUROCRYPT 2020, Part I. LNCS, vol. 12105, pp. 738–768. Springer, Cham (2020). https://doi.org/10.1007/978-3-030-45721-1_26
26. Costello, C., et al.: Geppetto: versatile verifiable computation. In: 2015 IEEE Symposium on Security and Privacy, pp. 253–270. IEEE Computer Society Press (2015)
27. Cramer, R., Damgård, I., Schoenmakers, B.: Proofs of partial knowledge and simplified design of witness hiding protocols. In: Desmedt, Y.G. (ed.) CRYPTO 1994. LNCS, vol. 839, pp. 174–187. Springer, Heidelberg (1994). https://doi.org/10.1007/3-540-48658-5_19
28. Damgård, I., Ganesh, C., Khoshakhlagh, H., Orlandi, C., Siniscalchi, L.: Balancing privacy and accountability in blockchain identity management. In: Paterson, K.G. (ed.) CT-RSA 2021. LNCS, vol. 12704, pp. 552–576. Springer, Cham (2021). https://doi.org/10.1007/978-3-030-75539-3_23
29. Delignat-Lavaud, A., Fournet, C., Kohlweiss, M., Parno, B.: Cinderella: turning shabby X.509 certificates into elegant anonymous credentials with the magic of verifiable computation. In: 2016 IEEE Symposium on Security and Privacy, pp. 235–254. IEEE Computer Society Press (2016)

30. Fiat, A., Shamir, A.: How to prove yourself: practical solutions to identification and signature problems. In: Odlyzko, A.M. (ed.) CRYPTO 1986. LNCS, vol. 263, pp. 186–194. Springer, Heidelberg (1987). https://doi.org/10.1007/3-540-47721-7_12
31. Fuchsbauer, G., Kiltz, E., Loss, J.: The algebraic group model and its applications. In: Shacham, H., Boldyreva, A. (eds.) CRYPTO 2018, Part II. LNCS, vol. 10992, pp. 33–62. Springer, Cham (2018). https://doi.org/10.1007/978-3-319-96881-0_2
32. Gabizon, A., Williamson, Z.J., Ciobotaru, O.: PLONK: Permutations over Lagrange-bases for Oecumenical Noninteractive arguments of Knowledge. Cryptology ePrint Archive, Report 2019/953
33. Gennaro, R., Gentry, C., Parno, B., Raykova, M.: Quadratic span programs and succinct NIZKs without PCPs. In: Johansson, T., Nguyen, P.Q. (eds.) EUROCRYPT 2013. LNCS, vol. 7881, pp. 626–645. Springer, Heidelberg (2013). https://doi.org/10.1007/978-3-642-38348-9_37
34. Giacomelli, I., Madsen, J., Orlandi, C.: ZKBoo: faster zero-knowledge for Boolean circuits. In: USENIX Security 2016, pp. 1069–1083. USENIX Association (2016)
35. Goldwasser, S., Micali, S., Rackoff, C.: The knowledge complexity of interactive proof-systems (extended abstract). In: 17th ACM STOC, pp. 291–304. ACM Press (1985)
36. Groth, J.: Short pairing-based non-interactive zero-knowledge arguments. In: Abe, M. (ed.) ASIACRYPT 2010. LNCS, vol. 6477, pp. 321–340. Springer, Heidelberg (2010). https://doi.org/10.1007/978-3-642-17373-8_19
37. Groth, J.: On the size of pairing-based non-interactive arguments. In: Fischlin, M., Coron, J.-S. (eds.) EUROCRYPT 2016, Part II. LNCS, vol. 9666, pp. 305–326. Springer, Heidelberg (2016). https://doi.org/10.1007/978-3-662-49896-5_11
38. Groth, J., Kohlweiss, M., Maller, M., Meiklejohn, S., Miers, I.: Updatable and universal common reference strings with applications to zk-SNARKs. In: Shacham, H., Boldyreva, A. (eds.) CRYPTO 2018, Part III. LNCS, vol. 10993, pp. 698–728. Springer, Cham (2018). https://doi.org/10.1007/978-3-319-96878-0_24
39. Guillou, L.C., Quisquater, J.-J.: A practical zero-knowledge protocol fitted to security microprocessor minimizing both transmission and memory. In: Barstow, D., et al. (eds.) EUROCRYPT 1988. LNCS, vol. 330, pp. 123–128. Springer, Heidelberg (1988). https://doi.org/10.1007/3-540-45961-8_11
40. Ishai, Y., Kushilevitz, E., Ostrovsky, R.: Efficient arguments without short PCPs. In: Twenty-Second Annual IEEE Conference on Computational Complexity (CCC'07), pp. 278–291. IEEE (2007)
41. Jawurek, M., Kerschbaum, F., Orlandi, C.: Zero-knowledge using garbled circuits: how to prove non-algebraic statements efficiently. In: ACM CCS 2013, pp. 955–966. ACM Press (2013)
42. Kate, A., Zaverucha, G.M., Goldberg, I.: Constant-size commitments to polynomials and their applications. In: Abe, M. (ed.) ASIACRYPT 2010. LNCS, vol. 6477, pp. 177–194. Springer, Heidelberg (2010). https://doi.org/10.1007/978-3-642-17373-8_11
43. Kosba, A., et al.: How to use SNARKs in universally composable protocols. Cryptology ePrint Archive, Report 2015/1093
44. Lee, J., Choi, J., Kim, J., Oh, H.: SAVER: SNARK-friendly, additively-homomorphic, and verifiable encryption and decryption with rerandomization. Cryptology ePrint Archive, Report 2019/1270
45. Lipmaa, H.: Progression-free sets and sublinear pairing-based non-interactive zero-knowledge arguments. In: Cramer, R. (ed.) TCC 2012. LNCS, vol. 7194, pp. 169–189. Springer, Heidelberg (2012). https://doi.org/10.1007/978-3-642-28914-9_10

46. Lipmaa, H.: Succinct non-interactive zero knowledge arguments from span programs and linear error-correcting codes. In: Sako, K., Sarkar, P. (eds.) ASIACRYPT 2013, Part I. LNCS, vol. 8269, pp. 41–60. Springer, Heidelberg (2013). https://doi.org/10.1007/978-3-642-42033-7_3
47. Lipmaa, H.: Prover-efficient commit-and-prove zero-knowledge SNARKs. In: Pointcheval, D., Nitaj, A., Rachidi, T. (eds.) AFRICACRYPT 2016. LNCS, vol. 9646, pp. 185–206. Springer, Cham (2016). https://doi.org/10.1007/978-3-319-31517-1_10
48. Maller, M., Bowe, S., Kohlweiss, M., Meiklejohn, S.: Sonic: zero-knowledge SNARKs from linear-size universal and updatable structured reference strings. In: ACM CCS 2019, pp. 2111–2128. ACM Press (2019)
49. Maxwell, G.: Confidential transactions. https://people.xiph.org/greg/confidentialvalues.txt
50. Parno, B., Howell, J., Gentry, C., Raykova, M.: Pinocchio: nearly practical verifiable computation. In: 2013 IEEE Symposium on Security and Privacy, pp. 238–252. IEEE Computer Society Press (2013)
51. Schnorr, C.P.: Efficient identification and signatures for smart cards. In: Brassard, G. (ed.) CRYPTO 1989. LNCS, vol. 435, pp. 239–252. Springer, New York (1990). https://doi.org/10.1007/0-387-34805-0_22
52. Setty, S.: Spartan: efficient and general-purpose zkSNARKs without trusted setup. In: Micciancio, D., Ristenpart, T. (eds.) CRYPTO 2020, Part III. LNCS, vol. 12172, pp. 704–737. Springer, Cham (2020). https://doi.org/10.1007/978-3-030-56877-1_25
53. Wahby, R.S., Tzialla, I., Shelat, A., Thaler, J., Walfish, M.: Doubly-efficient zkSNARKs without trusted setup. In: 2018 IEEE Symposium on Security and Privacy, pp. 926–943. IEEE Computer Society Press (2018)
54. Wu, H., Zheng, W., Chiesa, A., Popa, R.A., Stoica, I.: DIZK: a distributed zero knowledge proof system. In: USENIX Security 2018, pp. 675–692. USENIX Association (20108)

Rational Modular Encoding in the DCR Setting: Non-interactive Range Proofs and Paillier-Based Naor-Yung in the Standard Model

Julien Devevey[1(✉)], Benoît Libert[1,2], and Thomas Peters[3]

[1] ENS de Lyon, Laboratoire LIP (U. Lyon, CNRS, ENSL, Inria, UCBL), Lyon, France
julien.devevey@ens-lyon.fr

[2] CNRS, Laboratoire LIP, Lyon, France

[3] FNRS and UCLouvain, ICTEAM, Louvain-la-Neuve, Belgium

Abstract. Range proofs allow a sender to convince a verifier that committed integers belong to an interval without revealing anything else. So far, all known non-interactive range proofs in the standard model rely on groups endowed with a bilinear map. Moreover, they either require the group order to be larger than the range of any proven statement or they suffer from a wasteful rate. Recently (Eurocrypt'21), Couteau *et al.* introduced a new approach to efficiently prove range membership by encoding integers as a modular ratio between small integers. We show that their technique can be transposed in the standard model under the Composite Residuosity (DCR) assumption. Interestingly, with this modification, the size of ranges is not a priori restricted by the common reference string. It also gives a constant ratio between the size of ranges and proofs. Moreover, we show that their technique of encoding messages as bounded rationals provides a secure standard model instantiation of the Naor-Yung CCA2 encryption paradigm under the DCR assumption.

Keywords: Range proofs · NIZK · standard model · Naor-Yung

1 Introduction

Zero-knowledge proofs [36] make it possible for a prover to convince a verifier about the truth of a statement while revealing nothing else. Since their introduction, they have been used in countless cryptographic protocols to protect users' privacy or to hedge against malicious adversaries. In many situations, it is desirable to have non-interactive zero-knowledge (NIZK) proofs comprised of a single message from the prover to the verifier. In the non-interactive setting, NIZK proofs necessarily rely on a common reference string generated by some trusted party. While the Fiat-Shamir paradigm [32] allows for non-interactive proofs without a trusted setup in the random oracle model, it is known to only provide heuristic arguments in terms of security.

G. Hanaoka et al. (Eds.): PKC 2022, LNCS 13177, pp. 615–646, 2022.
https://doi.org/10.1007/978-3-030-97121-2_22

In the standard model, NIZK proofs are known to exist for all NP languages under well-studied assumptions [6,7,40,56]. For specific languages, however, much more efficient constructions are often possible, by dispensing with the need for an expensive Karp reduction.

Efficient NIZK constructions exist in the context of range proofs [11], where a prover convinces a verifier that a committed value belongs to a specific interval. Range proofs served as a building block of a number of cryptographic protocols, including anonymous credentials or e-cash [15], auction protocols [51], e-voting [38], and many more. Recently, they also served as crucial components of cryptocurrencies [12,53], where transaction amounts are private and only appear in committed [53] or encrypted [12] form. Range proofs then come into play to ensure that the committed/encrypted value lives in the correct range instead of being, e.g., slightly larger than the order of the message space.

A widely used approach [10,38,49] proceeds by committing to integers [28,35], rather than finite field elements. By withholding the order $|\mathcal{M}|$ of the message space, it forces the prover argue over the integers in order to demonstrate that a committed integer fits in a range $[0, B]$, where $B \in \mathbb{Z}$ may be larger than $|\mathcal{M}|$.

Recently, Couteau *et al.* [24] suggested an elegant technique that surprisingly emulates the properties of integer commitments in the discrete logarithm setting over public-order groups. The core idea of their construction is to view each Pedersen commitment [55] $C = g^m \cdot h^r$ as committing to the rounded rational $\lfloor x/c \rceil \in \mathbb{Z}$, where x and c are small-magnitude integers $x, c \in \mathbb{Z}$ such that $m = x \cdot c^{-1} \bmod q$, where q is the group order. This approach yields instantiations in class groups and under lattice assumptions. In the discrete-log setting, it outperforms the BulletProof technique [13] for a wide range of parameters. It also enables either computational or statistical soundness (whereas integers commitments only offer computational soundness).

In this paper, we consider their approach in the Composite Residuosity setting [54], where we highlight several advantages when proving range membership of Paillier-encrypted values.

1.1 Our Contribution

Range Proofs. We provide the first *unbounded* non-interactive range proof with constant rate in the standard model. The rate is defined in the standard way, as the ratio between the length of the witness and the total length of commitments and proofs. By "unbounded", we mean that a fixed-size common reference string makes it possible to commit to arbitrarily large integers.[1] In the standard model, it is also the first non-interactive candidate that does not rely on pairing-friendly groups. Instead, we can prove security under the standard Composite Residuosity (DCR) and Learning-with-Errors (LWE) [57]

[1] It is tempting to believe that Groth-Sahai proofs achieve unboundedness. In the full version of this paper, we explain why it is not the case.

assumptions. While our construction provides statistical soundness (and computational zero-knowledge), it can be turned into a dual-mode NIZK system – where soundness/zero-knowledge can be either statistical or computational depending on the configuration of the CRS – at the cost of sacrificing unboundedness.

In either case, we obtain space-efficient proofs consisting of a constant number of Damgård-Jurik [29] ciphertexts. Asymptotically, the communication cost is dominated by $O(\lambda^{3-o(1)} + \log B)$ bits, where B is the range size, which is on par with constructions based on integer commitments [25,38,49] in the random oracle model. In comparison, standard-model solutions based on Groth-Sahai proofs [41] cost $O(\lambda \cdot \log B)$ per proof.

Our unbounded range proof makes it possible to prove that a Paillier ciphertext decrypts to a modular ratio $M = x \cdot c^{-1} \bmod N^{\zeta}$, for some $\zeta \in \mathbb{N}$ and bounded integers $x, c \in \mathbb{Z}$ such that $\lfloor x/c \rceil \in \mathbb{Z}$ belongs to a range $[0, B]$. As a second contribution, we show that this encoding technique can be used to instantiate the Naor-Yung CCA2-secure encryption paradigm [52].

DCR-BASED INSTANTIATION OF NAOR-YUNG IN THE STANDARD MODEL. We give a Σ-protocol proving plaintext equalities between Paillier ciphertexts encrypted under distinct moduli, which restores the soundness of a Σ-protocol used by Fouque and Pointcheval [33]. Recently, Devevey *et al.* [30, Appendix E] showed that the Σ-protocol of [33, Section 4.2] does not provide soundness as a cheating prover can exploit the distinct moduli to prove false statements. This invalidates the proof[2] that the DCR-based threshold cryptosystem of [33] provides IND-CCA2 security in the random oracle model. Devevey *et al.* [30] suggested to fix the problem by additionally proving that the plaintext is smaller than both Paillier moduli. While efficient range proofs (e.g., [13,25,38]) can solve this problem in the random oracle model, we do not know how to instantiate them in the standard model via the Fiat-Shamir paradigm. To achieve standard-model security by exploiting correlation-intractable hash functions as in [19,56], we show that no range proof is actually necessary if the decryption algorithm is modified and "undoes" the rational modular encoding of Couteau *et al.* [24].

We show that the modified decryption algorithm can be combined with the correlation-intractable hash functions of [19,56] so as to instantiate the scheme in the standard model. As a result, we obtain a new construction of a non-interactive threshold CCA2-secure cryptosystem without pairings. Devevey *et al.* [30] recently proposed such a construction under the DCR and LWE assumptions. Our scheme provides several advantages over their construction. It notably inherits a property of the Damgård-Jurik system [29], which makes it possible to encrypt very long messages[3] for a fixed size public key comprised of an RSA

[2] We are not aware of any effective attack. Only the proof of IND-CCA2 security in the ROM is affected.

[3] A common approach to encrypt long messages is to use hybrid encryption. However, it makes it harder to prove properties about encrypted data in zero-knowledge. It also destroys the additive homomorphic homomorphic properties that we retain when we discard ciphertext components that ensure chosen-ciphertext security. The latter property is useful in the context of voting protocols [5].

modulus N. Variable-length plaintexts can even be encrypted by flexibly choosing an integer $\zeta > 1$, depending on the message length, and working over $\mathbb{Z}_{N^{\zeta+1}}^*$. In the threshold setting, the key generation phase requires to set a bound on the maximal value of ζ. However, this constraint disappears in the centralized (i.e., non-threshold) case, where we can CCA2-encrypt variable-length messages using a fixed-size public key without using hybrid encryption. To our knowledge, this useful property of the Damgård-Jurik cryptosystem was never preserved in the chosen-ciphertext setting (at least in the standard model).

We believe that, even in the random oracle model, properly instantiating Naor-Yung under the DCR assumption is important. For example, it provides a convenient way to encrypt arbitrarily long messages with a fixed-size public key while preserving the possibility of efficiently proving properties (e.g., range membership) about encrypted data, which would be difficult using hybrid encryption. It also provides a "voting-friendly" encryption scheme – in the terminology of [5] – in the sense that the keys/ciphertexts of the threshold CCA2-secure system can be publicly mapped to the keys/ciphertexts of an embedded additively homomorphic encryption scheme.

1.2 Technical Overview

Our range proofs depart from all known standard-model candidates [14,58], which are based on Groth-Sahai proofs [41] and proceed by breaking the committed integers into bits. To our knowledge, this approach either restricts committed integers to be smaller than the group order, or they are inherently stuck with a somewhat wasteful rate $O(1/\lambda)$ caused by bit-by-bit comparisons (as discussed in the full version of this paper). In the discrete-log setting, the construction of Couteau *et al.* [24] also requires the group order to be sufficiently larger than the maximal magnitude of committed integers.

To avoid this a priori bound on the range of committed values, we leverage a property of the Damgård-Jurik cryptosystem in that the CRS only consists of an RSA modulus $N = pq$. The prover commits to an integer in a range $[0, B]$ by having the prover first choose a sufficiently large $\zeta \geq 1$ such that $B < N^\zeta$ exactly as in the Damgård-Jurik encryption scheme. Following the approach of Kiayias *et al.* [44], we can obtain a constant rate as the ratio between the size of the proof and that of witnesses becomes constant (actually, less than 20) for a large $\zeta \in \mathsf{poly}(\lambda)$. Unlike our main construction, our dual-mode variant requires a CRS that fixes an integer $\zeta \geq 1$ once-and-for-all.

In order to prove security in the standard model, we build on recent progress on instantiations of the Fiat-Shamir paradigm. Canetti *et al.* [16] and Peikert and Shiehian [56] showed that Fiat-Shamir can provide soundness in the standard model under the Learning-With-Errors (LWE) assumption [57], which yields *correlation intractable* (CI) hash functions [17] for efficiently searchable relations.

Correlation intractability for a relation R requires the infeasibility of finding x such that $(x, H_k(x)) \in R$ given a random hashing key k. It guarantees soundness by preventing a cheating prover's first message a from being hashed into a challenge $\mathsf{Chall} = H_k(a)$ admitting a valid response z. Canetti *et al.* [19] showed that CI hash functions for efficiently searchable relations suffice when Fiat-Shamir is applied to *trapdoor* Σ-protocols. These are Σ-protocols that assume a CRS and where an efficiently computable function $\mathsf{BadChallenge}$ can identify (on input of a trapdoor τ_Σ, the false statement x and the prover's first message a) the only challenge Chall such that an accepting transcript (a, Chall, z) exists for some z. Libert *et al.* [47] (based on earlier observations from [21,50]) showed that the group structure of Paillier allows $\mathsf{BadChallenge}$ to identify bad challenges within an exponentially large challenge space, thus eliminating the need for parallel repetitions to ensure soundness.

Here, we also achieve soundness without parallel repetitions by exploiting the group structure of $\mathbb{Z}_{N^{\zeta+1}}^*$. However, our $\mathsf{BadChallenge}$ functions additionally solve integer linear programming instances with a constant number of variables. They also apply the technique of Fouque, Stern and Wackers [34], which decodes Paillier-decrypted values into rational numbers. In our variant of Couteau *et al.*'s range proof [24], the prover first sends DCR-based commitments to integers $\{x_i\}_{i=0}^3$ such that $1+4x_0(B-x_0) = \sum_{i=1}^3 x_i^2$ over $\mathbb{Z}$ (recall that, for any positive integer y, there exist $\{x_i \in \mathbb{Z}\}_{i=1}^3$ such that $1 + 4y = \sum_{i=1}^3 x_i^2$, as observed in [38]). Our $\mathsf{BadChallenge}$ function first computes $\{\tilde{x}_i\}_{i=0}^3$ by decrypting Paillier ciphertexts. Following Fouque *et al.* [34], it then runs Gauss' algorithm to compute pairs $(x_i, c_i) \in [-B^*, B^*] \times [0, C]$ such that $\tilde{x}_i = x_i \cdot c_i^{-1} \bmod N^\zeta$ for each i. If no such decomposition exists for a given index $i \in [0, 3]$, the corresponding $\tilde{x}_i$ determines the only bad challenge that can admit a valid response element z_i. We show that this bad challenge is computable by solving an integer linear programming instance $\mathbf{A} \cdot \mathbf{t} \leq \mathbf{b}$ with 3 variables and 8 constraints. By the definition of the language, we know that the solution $\mathbf{t}$ is unique if the statement is false. Moreover, Lenstra's algorithm [45] allows computing it in polynomial time as the number of variables is fixed.

If all decrypted elements $\{\tilde{x}_i\}_{i=0}^3$ can be represented as pairs of integers $(x_i, c_i) \in [-B^*, B^*] \times [0, C]$ such that $\tilde{x}_i = x_i \cdot c_i^{-1} \bmod N^\zeta$, our $\mathsf{BadChallenge}$ function determines if such representations exist for a common denominator $c = c_i$ for each i. If not all $\tilde{x}_i$ have such a representation with $x_i \in [-B^*, B^*]$, then we know that no response elements $\{z_i\}_{i=0}^3$ will simultaneously satisfy all verification equations for the *same* challenge. In this case, the language definition implies that at most one challenge can satisfy all these verification equations and we can identify this bad challenge by solving an integer linear program with 9 variables. In the last case, the prover's first message commitments decrypt to elements $\{\tilde{x}_i \in \mathbb{Z}_{N^\zeta}\}_{i=0}^3$ that all admit a representation $(x_i', c) \in [-B^*, B^*] \times [0, C]$ such that $\tilde{x}_i = x_i' \cdot c^{-1} \bmod N^\zeta$. In this case, if the statement is false, the unique bad challenge is determined by the last verification equation and it is computable by solving a simple modular equation.

Our Paillier-based instantiation of Naor-Yung uses exactly the same Σ-protocol as in [33, Section 4.2]. We prove that its soundness is restored if we introduce a post-processing step in the (distributed) decryption mechanism. Each decryption server computes its partial decryption exactly as in the threshold variant of Damgård-Jurik [29] (as in [33], this is done without interaction among servers). When partial decryptions are combined together, we first compute a Paillier/Damgård-Jurik plaintext $M \in \mathbb{Z}_{N^\zeta}$. Using Gauss' algorithm as suggested by Fouque *et al.* [34], we then decode M as a modular ratio $M = x \cdot c^{-1} \bmod N^\zeta$ for small-magnitude $x, c \in \mathbb{Z}$ before outputting the rounded rational $\lfloor x/c \rceil \in \mathbb{Z}$ as a plaintext. We show that this modified decryption algorithm can be safely combined with the Σ-protocol in [33] as it ensures that both Paillier ciphertexts lead to the same plaintext $\lfloor x/c \rceil \in \mathbb{Z}$. In the case $\zeta = 1$, given two Paillier ciphertexts $\mathsf{ct}_1 = (1 + N_1)^{\mathsf{Msg}} \cdot r_1^{N_1} \bmod N_1^2$ and $\mathsf{ct}_2 = (1 + N_2)^{\mathsf{Msg}} \cdot r_2^{N_2} \bmod N_2^2$, the protocol of [33] guarantees the existence of $\bar{c} \in [0, C]$ and $\bar{m} \in [-R, R]$ such that $\mathsf{ct}_1^{\bar{c}} = (1 + N_1)^m \cdot w_1^{N_1} \bmod N_1^2$ and $\mathsf{ct}_2^{\bar{c}} = (1 + N_2)^m \cdot w_2^{N_2} \bmod N_2^2$, for some $w_1 \in \mathbb{Z}_{N_1}^*$, $w_2 \in \mathbb{Z}_{N_2}^*$. While there is no guarantee that $m \cdot \bar{c}^{-1} \bmod N_1$ equals $m \cdot \bar{c}^{-1} \bmod N_2$, we know from [34] that they both decode to the same pair $(m, \bar{c}) \in [-R, R] \times [0, C]$ as long as $2RC < N$ when we run Gauss' algorithm. This ensures plaintext equality when the decryption algorithm outputs $\lfloor m/\bar{c} \rceil$.

In order to obtain a trapdoor Σ-protocol, our $\mathsf{BadChallenge}$ function appeals again to Lenstra's algorithm and solves an integer linear programming instance with a constant number of variables/constraints. When it comes to proving CCA2-security in the standard model, we need to turn the Σ-protocol into a one-time simulation-sound[4] NIZK proof system [59]. For this purpose, we could use a construction put forth by Devevey *et al.* [30] but it would unfortunately ruin the length-flexible property of the scheme. If we were to combine it with our trapdoor Σ-protocol showing plaintext equalities, the public key would inherently bound the size of the message space. To avoid this problem, we build a new DCR-based construction that compiles any trapdoor Σ-protocol into a one-time simulation-sound NIZK argument. Unlike the solution of [30, Section 3], simulation-soundness is achieved by augmenting the CRS with a number of bits that does not depend on the underlying trapdoor Σ-protocol.

1.3 Related Work

Range proofs were introduced by Brickell *et al.* [11] and receive continuous attention [10,14,20,22,25,37,39,49] since then. So far, known solutions have been following two main approaches.

The first approach proceeds by breaking integers into bits or small digits [3, 11,13,14,29,37,39], which allows communicating a logarithmic (in the range size) number of group elements [13,14,37,39]. This technique is usually implemented using homomorphic commitment schemes over groups of public prime order,

[4] In short, one-time simulation-soundness means that seeing a simulated proof for a false statement of its choice does not help the adversary prove a new false statement.

while the optimized versions of [14,37,39] require pairings. Within this line of work, Bulletproof [13] obtains the best communication complexity via a clever recursive proof technique and can be realized over standard (i.e., non-pairing-friendly) discrete-logarithm-hard groups. Unfortunately, it is not known to be instantiable in the standard model without interaction.

The second approach [10,25,38,49] relies on integer commitments over groups of hidden order. This approach is often preferred for very large ranges (which arise in applications like anonymous credentials [15], where range elements may be comprised of thousands of bits) where it tends to be more efficient. Also, it does not require the maximal range length to be known ahead of time, when the commitment key is set up. Using homomorphic integer commitments, any range $[\alpha, \beta]$ can be proven by exploiting the homomorphic properties of the commitment scheme and demonstrating that $X - \alpha \in [0, \beta - \alpha]$. Indeed, working over the integers allows showing that $X - \alpha$ and $\beta - X$ are both positive by expressing them as a sum of squares. The idea to rely on square decompositions over the integers dates back to [11]. The square decomposition method was improved by Lipmaa [49] by relying on the Lagrange decomposition of any positive integer as a sum of four squares. Groth [38] observed any positive integer of the form $4Y + 1$, for some $Y \in \mathbb{Z}$, can be more efficiently expressed as a sum of three squares. Further efficiency and security improvements were given in [25]. In this second approach, the underlying integer commitment scheme builds on [28,35] and is usually instantiated using RSA groups. Couteau *et al.* [25] showed that its security relates to a slight variant of the RSA assumption rather than the less standard Strong RSA assumption.

Very recently, Couteau *et al.* [24] managed to reconcile the advantages of both approaches. Their core technique converts any (homomorphic) commitment scheme over groups of (public) prime order into a *bounded* integer commitment scheme. While the conversion does not completely preserve the homomorphic property, it allows committing to bounded-range integers by interpreting them as rounded rationals. It also allows reviving the square decomposition method so as to prove integer relations holding over public ranges. As a result, their range proof consists of a public-coin 3-move interactive protocol that only communicates a constant number of elements. It can be instantiated using standard Pedersen commitments [55] in prime-order groups as long as the group order is large enough to represent the bounded integers. Their technique also applies under lattice assumptions and in class groups. In the latter instantiation, it also inherits the unbounded property of solutions based on hidden-order groups.

We note that a generic transformation due to Ciampi *et al.* [23, Section 4.2] can be used to turn a slight modification (where the first-message group elements are not hashed) of Couteau *et al.*'s discrete-log-based range proof [24] into a trapdoor Σ-protocol, and thus obtain a non-interactive variant in the standard model. However, since the transformation of [23] only applies to Σ-protocols with small challenge space, it has to be repeated $O(\lambda)$ times in parallel to achieve negligible soundness error. In contrast, we achieve soundness without parallel repetitions as in [47]. Moreover, applying [23] to build a non-interactive variant of [24] would still require to fix the maximal cardinality of ranges ahead of time. As it turns out, none of the existing range proofs (even in the bounded case where the CRS depends on $\log(\beta - \alpha)$) in the standard model features proofs comprised of a constant number of element of the base ring/group.

The first non-interactive CCA-secure threshold cryptosystems date back to the work of Shoup and Gennaro [60] who gave DDH-based realizations in the random oracle model. Fouque and Pointcheval [33] gave a generic construction and a DDH-based instantiation using the Naor-Yung paradigm. Until the recent years, all non-interactive solutions in the standard model were pairing-based [8,48]. Boneh *et al.* gave a generic technique [9] to transform any IND-CCA secure encryption scheme into a non-interactive threshold system using fully homomorphic encryption. Using correlation-intractable hash functions, Devevey *et al.* [30] recently obtained constructions under the DCR and LWE assumptions in the adaptive corruption setting. Back in 1999, Canetti and Goldwasser [18] showed that chosen-ciphertext security was achievable in the standard model by allowing decryption servers to interact with one another. Their approach was subsequently extended to handle adaptive adversaries [1,43].

2 Background

Let S be a finite set. Then, $a \hookleftarrow U(S)$ means that a is sampled according to the uniform distribution over S. $|a|$ is the bit-length of a.

2.1 Hardness Assumptions

We first recall Paillier's Composite Residuosity assumption and its variant considered by Damgård and Jurik.

Definition 2.1 [29,54]. *Let integers $N = pq$ and $s > 1$ for primes p, q. The* **s-Decision Composite Residuosity** (s-DCR) *assumption states that the distributions $\{x = w^{N^s} \bmod N^{s+1} \mid w \hookleftarrow U(\mathbb{Z}_N^\star)\}$ and $\{x \mid x \hookleftarrow U(\mathbb{Z}_{N^{s+1}}^\star)\}$ are computationally indistinguishable.*

Lemma 2.2 (Adapted from [29]). *Let $s = \mathsf{poly}(\lambda)$. Then s-DCR is equivalent to $1-\mathsf{DCR}$, with a security loss $\leq s$. (The proof is straightforward.)*

2.2 Correlation Intractable Hash Functions

We consider unique-output efficiently searchable relations [16].

Definition 2.3. *A relation $R \subseteq \mathcal{X} \times \mathcal{Y}$ is* **searchable** *in time T if there exists a function $f : \mathcal{X} \to \mathcal{Y}$ which is computable in time T and such that, if there exists y such that $(x, y) \in R$, then $f(x) = y$.*

Let $\lambda \in \mathbb{N}$ a security parameter. A hash family with input length $n(\lambda)$ and output length $m(\lambda)$ is a collection $\mathcal{H} = \{h_\lambda : \{0,1\}^{s(\lambda)} \times \{0,1\}^{n(\lambda)} \to \{0,1\}^{m(\lambda)}\}$ of keyed functions induced by efficient algorithms $(\mathsf{Gen}, \mathsf{Hash})$, where $\mathsf{Gen}(1^\lambda)$ outputs a key $k \in \{0,1\}^{s(\lambda)}$ and $\mathsf{Hash}(k, x)$ computes $h_\lambda(k, x) \in \{0,1\}^{m(\lambda)}$.

Definition 2.4. *For a relation ensemble* $\{R_\lambda \subseteq \{0,1\}^{n(\lambda)} \times \{0,1\}^{m(\lambda)}\}$, *a hash function family* $\mathcal{H} = \{h_\lambda : \{0,1\}^{s(\lambda)} \times \{0,1\}^{n(\lambda)} \to \{0,1\}^{m(\lambda)}\}$ *is* R**-correlation intractable** *if, for any probabilistic polynomial time (PPT) adversary* $\mathbb{A}$, *we have* $\Pr\left[k \leftarrow \mathsf{Gen}(1^\lambda)),\ x \leftarrow \mathcal{A}(k) : (x, h_\lambda(k,x)) \in R\right] = \mathsf{negl}(\lambda)$.

Peikert and Shiehian [56] described a correlation-intractable hash family for any searchable relation (in the sense of Definition 2.3) defined by functions f of bounded depth.

2.3 Trapdoor Σ-Protocols

Canetti *et al.* [19] considered a definition of Σ-protocols that slightly differs from the usual formulation [26].

Definition 2.5 (Adapted from [2,19]**).** *Let a language* $\mathcal{L} = (\mathcal{L}_{\mathsf{zk}}, \mathcal{L}_{\mathsf{sound}})$ *associated with two NP relations* $\mathcal{R}_{\mathsf{zk}}, \mathcal{R}_{\mathsf{sound}}$. *A 3-move interactive proof system* $\Pi = (\mathsf{Gen}_{\mathsf{par}}, \mathsf{Gen}_{\mathcal{L}}, \mathsf{P}, \mathsf{V})$ *in the common reference string model is a Gap* Σ*-protocol for* $\mathcal{L}$ *if it satisfies the following conditions:*

- **3-Move Form:** P *and* V *both take as input* $\mathsf{crs} = (\mathsf{par}, \mathsf{crs}_{\mathcal{L}})$, *with* $\mathsf{par} \leftarrow \mathsf{Gen}_{\mathsf{par}}(1^\lambda)$ *and* $\mathsf{crs}_{\mathcal{L}} \leftarrow \mathsf{Gen}_{\mathcal{L}}(\mathsf{par}, \mathcal{L})$, *and a statement* x *and proceed as follows: (i)* P *takes in* $w \in \mathcal{R}_{\mathsf{zk}}(x)$, *computes* $(\mathbf{a}, st) \leftarrow \mathsf{P}(\mathsf{crs}, x, w)$ *and sends* $\mathbf{a}$ *to the verifier; (ii)* V *sends back a random challenge* Chall *from the challenge space* $\mathcal{C}$; *(iii)* P *finally sends a response* $\mathbf{z} = \mathsf{P}(\mathsf{crs}, x, w, \mathbf{a}, \mathsf{Chall}, st)$ *to* V; *(iv) On input of* $(\mathbf{a}, \mathsf{Chall}, \mathbf{z})$, V *outputs* 1 *or* 0.
- **Completeness:** *If* $(x, w) \in \mathcal{R}_{\mathsf{zk}}$ *and* P *honestly computes* $(\mathbf{a}, \mathbf{z})$ *for a challenge* Chall, $\mathsf{V}(\mathsf{crs}, x, (\mathbf{a}, \mathsf{Chall}, \mathbf{z}))$ *outputs* 1 *with probability* $1 - \mathsf{negl}(\lambda)$.
- **Special zero-knowledge:** *There is a PPT simulator* ZKSim *that inputs* crs, $x \in \mathcal{L}_{\mathsf{zk}}$ *and a challenge* $\mathsf{Chall} \in \mathcal{C}$. *It outputs* $(\mathbf{a}, \mathbf{z}) \leftarrow \mathsf{ZKSim}(\mathsf{crs}, x, \mathsf{Chall})$ *such that* $(\mathbf{a}, \mathsf{Chall}, \mathbf{z})$ *is computationally indistinguishable from a real transcript with challenge* Chall *(for* $w \in \mathcal{R}_{zk}(x)$*).*
- **Special soundness:** *For any CRS* $\mathsf{crs} = (\mathsf{par}, \mathsf{crs}_{\mathcal{L}})$ *obtained as* $\mathsf{par} \leftarrow \mathsf{Gen}_{\mathsf{par}}(1^\lambda)$, $\mathsf{crs}_{\mathcal{L}} \leftarrow \mathsf{Gen}_{\mathcal{L}}(\mathsf{par}, \mathcal{L})$, *any* $x \notin \mathcal{L}_{\mathsf{sound}}$, *and any first message* $\mathbf{a}$ *sent by* P, *there is at most one challenge* $\mathsf{Chall} = f(\mathsf{crs}, x, \mathbf{a})$ *for which an accepting transcript* $(\mathsf{crs}, x, \mathbf{a}, \mathsf{Chall}, \mathbf{z})$ *exists for some third message* $\mathbf{z}$. *The function* f *is called the "bad challenge function" of* Π. *That is, if* $x \notin \mathcal{L}_{\mathsf{sound}}$ *and the challenge differs from the bad challenge, the verifier never accepts.*

Definition 2.5 is taken from [19] and relaxes the standard special soundness property in that extractability is not required. Instead, it considers a bad challenge function f, which may not be efficiently computable. Canetti *et al.* [19] define *trapdoor* Σ-protocols as Σ-protocols where the bad challenge function is efficiently computable using a trapdoor. Here, we use a definition where the CRS and the trapdoor may depend on the language.

The common reference string $\mathsf{crs} = (\mathsf{par}, \mathsf{crs}_{\mathcal{L}})$ consists of a fixed part par and a language-dependent part $\mathsf{crs}_{\mathcal{L}}$ which is generated as a function of par and a language parameter $\mathcal{L} = (\mathcal{L}_{\mathsf{zk}}, \mathcal{L}_{\mathsf{sound}})$.

Definition 2.6 (Adapted from [19]). *A Σ-protocol* $\Pi = (\mathsf{Gen}_{\mathsf{par}}, \mathsf{Gen}_{\mathcal{L}}, \mathsf{P}, \mathsf{V})$ *with bad challenge function* f *for a trapdoor language* $\mathcal{L} = (\mathcal{L}_{\mathsf{zk}}, \mathcal{L}_{\mathsf{sound}})$ *is a* **trapdoor Σ-protocol** *if it satisfies the properties of Definition 2.5 and there exist PPT algorithms* $(\mathsf{TrapGen}, \mathsf{BadChallenge})$ *with the following properties.*

- $\mathsf{Gen}_{\mathsf{par}}$ *inputs* $\lambda \in \mathbb{N}$ *and outputs public parameters* $\mathsf{par} \leftarrow \mathsf{Gen}_{\mathsf{par}}(1^\lambda)$.
- $\mathsf{Gen}_{\mathcal{L}}$ *is a randomized algorithm that, on input of public parameters* par, *outputs the language-dependent part* $\mathsf{crs}_{\mathcal{L}} \leftarrow \mathsf{Gen}_{\mathcal{L}}(\mathsf{par}, \mathcal{L})$ *of* $\mathsf{crs} = (\mathsf{par}, \mathsf{crs}_{\mathcal{L}})$.
- $\mathsf{TrapGen}(\mathsf{par}, \mathcal{L}, \tau_{\mathcal{L}})$ *takes as input public parameters* par *and a membership-testing trapdoor* $\tau_{\mathcal{L}}$ *for the language* $\mathcal{L}_{\mathsf{sound}}$. *It outputs a common reference string* $\mathsf{crs}_{\mathcal{L}}$ *and a trapdoor* $\tau_{\Sigma} \in \{0,1\}^{\ell_\tau}$, *for some* $\ell_\tau(\lambda)$.
- $\mathsf{BadChallenge}(\tau_\Sigma, \mathsf{crs}, x, \mathbf{a})$ *takes in a trapdoor* τ_Σ, *a CRS* $\mathsf{crs} = (\mathsf{par}, \mathsf{crs}_{\mathcal{L}})$, *an instance* x, *and a first prover message* $\mathbf{a}$. *It outputs a challenge* Chall.

In addition, the following properties are required.

- **CRS indistinguishability:** *For any* $\mathsf{par} \leftarrow \mathsf{Gen}_{\mathsf{par}}(1^\lambda)$, *and any trapdoor* $\tau_{\mathcal{L}}$ *for the language* $\mathcal{L}$, *an honestly generated* $\mathsf{crs}_{\mathcal{L}}$ *is computationally indistinguishable from a CRS produced by* $\mathsf{TrapGen}(\mathsf{par}, \mathcal{L}, \tau_{\mathcal{L}})$. *Namely, for any* aux *and any PPT distinguisher* $\mathcal{A}$, *we have*

$$\begin{aligned}\mathbf{Adv}_{\mathcal{A}}^{\text{indist-}\Sigma}(\lambda) := |\Pr[\mathsf{crs}_{\mathcal{L}} \leftarrow \mathsf{Gen}_{\mathcal{L}}(\mathsf{par}, \mathcal{L}) : \mathcal{A}(\mathsf{par}, \mathsf{crs}_{\mathcal{L}}) = 1] \\ - \Pr[(\mathsf{crs}_{\mathcal{L}}, \tau_\Sigma) \leftarrow \mathsf{TrapGen}(\mathsf{par}, \mathcal{L}, \tau_{\mathcal{L}}) : \mathcal{A}(\mathsf{par}, \mathsf{crs}_{\mathcal{L}}) = 1]| \leq \mathsf{negl}(\lambda).\end{aligned}$$

- **Correctness:** *There exists a language-specific trapdoor* $\tau_{\mathcal{L}}$ *such that, for any instance* $x \notin \mathcal{L}_{\mathsf{sound}}$ *and all pairs* $(\mathsf{crs}_{\mathcal{L}}, \tau_\Sigma) \leftarrow \mathsf{TrapGen}(\mathsf{par}, \mathcal{L}, \tau_{\mathcal{L}})$, *we have* $\mathsf{BadChallenge}(\tau_\Sigma, \mathsf{crs}, x, \mathbf{a}) = f(\mathsf{crs}, x, \mathbf{a})$.

Note that the $\mathsf{TrapGen}$ algorithm does not take a specific statement x as input, but only a trapdoor $\tau_{\mathcal{L}}$ allowing to recognize elements of $\mathcal{L}_{\mathsf{sound}}$.

2.4 Trapdoor Σ-Protocol Showing Composite Residuosity

We recall a standard Σ-protocol that allows proving that an element of $\mathbb{Z}_{N^{\zeta+1}}^*$ is a N^ζ-th residue. In [47], it was shown that the latter protocol is a trapdoor Σ-protocol showing that an element of $\mathbb{Z}_{N^2}^*$ is a composite residue.

Namely, let $\mathcal{L}^{\mathsf{DCR}} := \{x \in \mathbb{Z}_{N^{\zeta+1}}^* \mid \exists w \in \mathbb{Z}_N^* : x = w^{N^\zeta} \bmod N^{\zeta+1}\}$, the language of N^ζ-th residues, for some integer $\zeta > 1$, where $N = pq$ is an RSA modulus. We assume that the challenge space is $\{0, \ldots, 2^\lambda - 1\}$ and that $p, q > 2^{l(\lambda)}$, for some polynomial $l : \mathbb{N} \to \mathbb{N}$ such that $l(\lambda) > \lambda$ for any sufficiently large $\lambda \in \mathbb{N}$. The condition $p, q > 2^\lambda$ will ensure that the difference between any two challenges be co-prime with N.

In order to obtain a $\mathsf{BadChallenge}$ function that identifies bad challenges for elements $x \notin \mathcal{L}^{\mathsf{DCR}}$, [47] uses an observation from Lipmaa [50], which shows that the factorization of N allows computing bad challenges even if $\gcd(x, N) > 1$.

$\mathsf{Gen}_{\mathsf{par}}(1^\lambda)$**:** Given the security parameter λ, define $\mathsf{par} = \{\lambda\}$.

$\mathsf{Gen}_{\mathcal{L}}(\mathsf{par}, \mathcal{L}^{\mathsf{DCR}})$: Given public parameters par and the description of a language $\mathcal{L}^{\mathsf{DCR}}$, consisting of an RSA modulus $N = pq$ with primes p and q such that $p, q > 2^{l(\lambda)}$, for some polynomial $l : \mathbb{N} \to \mathbb{N}$ such that $l(\lambda) > \lambda$, define the language-dependent $\mathsf{crs}_{\mathcal{L}} = \{N\}$. The global CRS is $\mathsf{crs} = (\{\lambda\}, \mathsf{crs}_{\mathcal{L}})$.

$\mathsf{TrapGen}(\mathsf{par}, \mathcal{L}^{\mathsf{DCR}}, \tau_{\mathcal{L}})$: Given par, the description of a language $\mathcal{L}^{\mathsf{DCR}}$ that specifies an RSA modulus N and a membership-testing trapdoor $\tau_{\mathcal{L}} = (p, q)$ consisting of the factorization of $N = pq$, output the language-dependent $\mathsf{crs}_{\mathcal{L}} = \{N\}$ which defines $\mathsf{crs} = (\{\lambda\}, \mathsf{crs}_{\mathcal{L}})$ and the trapdoor $\tau_{\Sigma} = (p, q)$.

$\mathsf{P}(\mathsf{crs}, x, w) \leftrightarrow \mathsf{V}(\mathsf{crs}, x)$: Given a crs, a statement $x = w^{N^\zeta} \bmod N^{\zeta+1}$, P (who has the witness $w \in \mathbb{Z}_N^\star$) and V interact as follows:

1. P chooses a random $r \hookleftarrow U(\mathbb{Z}_N^*)$ and sends $a = r^{N^\zeta} \bmod N^{\zeta+1}$ to V.
2. V sends a random challenge $\mathsf{Chall} \hookleftarrow U(\{0, \ldots, 2^\lambda - 1\})$ to P.
3. P computes the response $z = r \cdot w^{\mathsf{Chall}} \bmod N$ and sends it to V.
4. V checks if $a \cdot x^{\mathsf{Chall}} \equiv z^{N^\zeta} \pmod{N^{\zeta+1}}$ and returns 0 otherwise.

$\mathsf{BadChallenge}(\mathsf{par}, \tau_\Sigma, \mathsf{crs}, x, a)$: Given $\tau_\Sigma = (p, q)$, (Damgård-Jurik) decrypt x and a to obtain $\alpha_x = \mathcal{D}_{\tau_\Sigma}(x) \in \mathbb{Z}_{N^\zeta}$, $\alpha_a = \mathcal{D}_{\tau_\Sigma}(a) \in \mathbb{Z}_{N^\zeta}$.

1. If $\alpha_a = 0$, return $\mathsf{Chall} = 0$.
2. If $\alpha_a \neq 0$, let $d_x = \gcd(\alpha_x, N^\zeta)$, which lives in the set $\{p^i q^j \mid 0 \leq i < \zeta,\ 0 \leq j < \zeta\} \cup \{p^i q^\zeta \mid 0 \leq i < \zeta\} \cup \{p^\zeta q^j \mid 0 \leq j < \zeta\}$. Then,
   a. If $1 < d_x < N^\zeta$, return $\perp$ if d_x does not divide $N^\zeta - \alpha_a$.
   b. Otherwise, the congruence $\alpha_a + \mathsf{Chall} \cdot \alpha_x \equiv 0 \pmod{\frac{N^\zeta}{d_x}}$ has a unique solution $\mathsf{Chall}' = -\alpha_x^{-1} \cdot \alpha_a \in \mathbb{Z}_{N^\zeta/d_x}$ since $\gcd(\alpha_x, N^\zeta/d_x) = 1$. If $\mathsf{Chall}' \in \mathbb{Z}_{N^\zeta/d_x} \setminus \{0, \ldots, 2^\lambda - 1\}$, return $\perp$. Else, return $\mathsf{Chall} = \mathsf{Chall}'$.

In [47], it is shown that the above construction is a trapdoor Σ-protocol with large challenge space. By applying [56], this implies compact NIZK arguments (i.e., without using parallel repetitions to achieve negligible soundness error) for the language $\mathcal{L}^{\mathsf{DCR}}$ assuming that the LWE assumption holds.

Lemma 2.7 [47]. *The above protocol is a trapdoor Σ-protocol for $\mathcal{L}^{\mathsf{DCR}}$.*

2.5 Encoding and Decoding Bounded Rationals in $\mathbb{Z}_N$

In [34], Fouque *et al.* suggested a technique that allows computing over rational numbers when they are encrypted using Paillier. The idea is to encode a rational r/s, for co-prime integers $(r, s) \in [-R, R] \times [0, S]$, as the modular ratio $r \cdot s^{-1} \bmod N$. They showed that, as long as, $2RS < N$, it is possible to recover (r, s) from $t = r \cdot s^{-1} \bmod N$ using Gauss' lattice reduction algorithm in dimension 2.

Let an RSA modulus and bounds R, S. Let $r, s \in \mathbb{Z}$ such that $-R \leq r \leq R$, $0 < s \leq S$, $\gcd(r, s) = 1$ and $\gcd(s, N) = 1$. Let the rational $t = r/s \in \mathbb{Q}$

Define the encoding $\mathcal{E}(t) := t' = r \cdot s^{-1} \bmod N$. To decode it and recover $t \in \mathbb{Q}$ from t', consider the lattice

$$\Lambda := \{(x, y) \in \mathbb{Z}^2 : x = y \cdot t' \bmod N\} = \{(x, y) \in \mathbb{Z}^2 : s \cdot x = y \cdot r \bmod N\}.$$

A particular basis of Λ is formed by the vectors $(N, 0)$ and $(t', 1)$. Since s is invertible over $\mathbb{Z}_N$, the vector $(r, s) \in \mathbb{Z}^2$ also lives in Λ. To recover co-prime integers $(r, s) \in \mathbb{Z}^2$ such that $t' = r \cdot s^{-1} \bmod N$, one can run Gauss' algorithm on input of the initial basis $\vec{u} = (N, 0)$, $\vec{v} = (t', 1)$ to compute a minimal vector of Λ. A result of Vallée [61] ensures that the number of iterations is at most $3 + \log_{1+\sqrt{2}} \max(\|\vec{u}\|, \|\vec{v}\|)$ in the worst case.

Fouque *et al.* proved that the decoding procedure is correct and pointed out that it carries over when computations take place modulo N^ζ for $\zeta > 1$.

Lemma 2.8 ([34, Theorem 1]). *If $t' = r \cdot s^{-1} \bmod N$, $-R \leq r \leq R$, and $0 < s \leq S$, then Gauss' algorithm uniquely recovers r and s if $2RS < N$.*

2.6 Paillier Decryption of (Rounded) Rationals

We first describe a variant of Paillier's cryptosysem used by Fouque, Stern and Wackers [34] to perform homomorphic operations over rational numbers. While the encryption algorithm is identical to that of Paillier/Damgård-Jurik [29,54], the message space is restricted to a specific interval and the decryption algorithm runs Gauss' lattice reduction algorithm in dimension 2. In fact, we modify the decryption algorithm of [34] to make sure that it outputs an integer instead of a rational. In addition, we follow a suggestion of Damgård and Jurik [29] and assume that the message space is *not* a priori bounded by the public key. Instead, it can be flexibly adjusted by the encryption algorithm.

In the following, we let $\ell_M \in \mathsf{poly}(\lambda)$ denote the message length, which can be dynamically determined at encryption time. We also denote by $\mathrm{abs} : \mathbb{Z} \to \mathbb{N}$ the absolute value function defined as $\mathrm{abs}(x) = x \cdot (x \geq 0) + (-x) \cdot (x < 0)$. Letting $C = 2^\lambda - 1$, the encryptor will fix $R > 2^\lambda \cdot (M + 1)$, where $M = 2^{\ell_M} - 1$ is the largest possible message, and choose ζ in such a way that $2RC < N^\zeta$. After having obtained $\widetilde{\mathsf{Msg}} \in \mathbb{Z}_{N^\zeta}$ from the decryption algorithm of Damgård-Jurik, the receiver will be able to apply Lemma 2.8 so as to decode $\widetilde{\mathsf{Msg}}$ as the ratio $m \cdot c^{-1} \bmod N^\zeta$ between bounded rationals $-R \leq m \leq R$ and $1 \leq c \leq C$.

Keygen(1^λ): Given a security parameter, choose an RSA modulus $N = pq$ such that $p, q > 2^{l(\lambda)}$, for some polynomial $l : \mathbb{N} \to \mathbb{N}$ with $l(\lambda) \geq \lambda$, and an integer $\zeta \geq 1$. The public key is $\mathsf{pk} = N$ and the secret key is $\mathsf{sk} = (p, q)$.

Encrypt$(\mathsf{pk}, \mathsf{Msg})$: To encrypt $\mathsf{Msg} \in \{0,1\}^{\ell_M}$, interpret it as a positive integer in $[0, M]$, where $M = 2^{\ell_M} - 1$. Set $\zeta > 1$ as a small integer such that $N^\zeta \geq 2^{2\lambda+1} M$. Then, choose $r \hookleftarrow U(\mathbb{Z}_N^*)$ and compute

$$(\mathsf{ct}, \ell_M) = \left((1+N)^{\mathsf{Msg}} \cdot r^{N^\zeta} \bmod N^{\zeta+1}, \ell_M\right).$$

Decrypt$(\mathsf{sk}, (\mathsf{ct}, \ell_M))$: Given $(\mathsf{ct}, \ell_M) \in \mathbb{Z}_{N^{\zeta+1}}^* \times \mathbb{N}$ and $\mathsf{sk} = (p, q)$. Compute $\widetilde{\mathsf{Msg}} \in \mathbb{Z}_{N^\zeta}$ by running the Damgård-Jurik decryption algorithm, denoted $\mathcal{D}_{\mathsf{sk}}(\mathsf{ct})$. Then, using Gauss' algorithm, find the unique $(m, c) \in \mathbb{Z}^2$ such that $-R \leq m \leq R$, $1 \leq c \leq C$ and $\widetilde{\mathsf{Msg}} = m \cdot c^{-1} \bmod N^\zeta$. If no such pair exists, return $\perp$. Otherwise, return $\mathsf{Msg} = \mathrm{abs}(\lfloor m/c \rceil)$, where $m/c \in \mathbb{Q}$.

In the decryption algorithm, the absolute value is used to enforce positiveness. The scheme is identical to [34], except that it outputs a positive integer rather than a rational. This decoding method will be applied in our instantiation of Naor-Yung. In our non-interactive range proof of Sect. 3, we will also use the scheme as a perfectly binding extractable commitment with an extraction algorithm $\mathsf{Decrypt}'$ where $\mathsf{Msg}' = \lfloor m/c \rceil$, without absolute values.

3 Constant-Rate Unbounded Non-interactive Range Proofs in the Standard Model

This section presents a range proof where a fixed-size common reference string containing an RSA modulus $N = pq$ allows committing to arbitrarily large integers. We note that, after having committed to an integer, the committer is bound to a specific modulus $N^{\zeta+1}$ and all subsequent proofs related to this commitment are restricted to ranges smaller than a certain bound. Still, the CRS and the underlying algebraic structure do not have to be scaled with the size of the committed integers.

Let positive integers B, $C = 2^\lambda - 1$, $B^* = 2^\lambda BC$ and $\zeta \geq 1$ satisfying the conditions $2^{2\lambda+3}B^2C^2 < N^\zeta$. Let $\mathcal{L}_{\mathsf{range}}^{B,B^*,C} = (\mathcal{L}_{\mathsf{zk}}^{B}, \mathcal{L}_{\mathsf{sound}}^{B,B^*,C})$ be

$$\mathcal{L}_{\mathsf{zk}}^{B} := \left\{\mathsf{ct} \in \mathbb{Z}_{N^{\zeta+1}}^* \mid \exists x \in [0,B],\ w \in \mathbb{Z}_N^* \ :\ \mathsf{ct} = (1+N)^x \cdot w^{N^\zeta} \bmod N^{\zeta+1}\right\}$$

$$\begin{aligned}\mathcal{L}_{\mathsf{sound}}^{B,B^*,C} := \Big\{&\mathsf{ct} \in \mathbb{Z}_{N^{\zeta+1}}^* \mid \exists x \in [0,B^*],\ c \in [1,C],\ w \in \mathbb{Z}_N^* \ :\\ &\mathsf{ct} = (1+N)^{x \cdot c^{-1} \bmod N^\zeta} \cdot w^{N^\zeta} \bmod N^{\zeta+1} \ \wedge\ \lfloor x/c \rceil \in [0,B]\Big\}.\end{aligned}$$

To prove membership, we will have the prover generate auxiliary commitments $\{C_i\}_{i=1}^3$ and rely on $\bar{\mathcal{L}}_{\mathsf{range}}^{B,B^*,C} = (\bar{\mathcal{L}}_{\mathsf{zk}}^{B}, \bar{\mathcal{L}}_{\mathsf{sound}}^{B,B^*,C})$ such that

$$\begin{aligned}\bar{\mathcal{L}}_{\mathsf{zk}}^{B} := \Big\{&(\mathsf{ct}, \{C_i\}_{i=1}^3) \in (\mathbb{Z}_{N^{\zeta+1}}^*)^4 \ \mid\ \exists x_0, x_1, x_2, x_3 \in [0,B],\\ &\exists\ s_0, s_1, s_2, s_3 \in \mathbb{Z}_N^* \ :\ 1 + 4(B - x_0)x_0 = x_1^2 + x_2^2 + x_3^2\\ &\wedge\ (1+N)^B \cdot \mathsf{ct}^{-1} = (1+N)^{x_0} \cdot s_0^{N^\zeta} \bmod N^{\zeta+1}\\ &\wedge\ C_i = (1+N)^{x_i} \cdot s_i^{N^\zeta} \bmod N^{\zeta+1} \quad \forall i \in [3]\Big\},\end{aligned}$$

$$\begin{aligned}\bar{\mathcal{L}}_{\mathsf{sound}}^{B,B^*,C} := \Big\{&(\mathsf{ct}, \{C_i\}_{i=1}^3) \in (\mathbb{Z}_{N^{\zeta+1}}^*)^4 \ \mid\ \exists x_0, x_1, x_2, x_3 \in [-B^*, B^*],\\ &\exists\ s_0, s_1, s_2, s_3, \tau \in \mathbb{Z}_N^*,\ c \in [1,C] \ :\\ &\wedge\ \left((1+N)^B \cdot \mathsf{ct}^{-1}\right)^c = (1+N)^{x_0} \cdot s_0^{N^\zeta} \bmod N^{\zeta+1}\\ &\wedge\ C_i^c = (1+N)^{x_i} \cdot s_i^{N^\zeta} \bmod N^{\zeta+1} \quad \forall i \in [3]\\ &\wedge\ (1+N)^c = \prod_{i=1}^{3} C_i^{x_i} \cdot \mathsf{ct}^{-4x_0} \cdot \tau^{N^\zeta} \bmod N^{\zeta+1}\Big\},\end{aligned} \tag{1}$$

In Lemma 3.2, we show that $(\mathsf{ct}, \{C_i\}_{i=1}^3) \in \bar{\mathcal{L}}_{\mathsf{sound}}^{B,B^*,C}$ implies $\mathsf{ct} \in \mathcal{L}_{\mathsf{sound}}^{B,B^*,C}$, which in turn implies $\mathsf{Decrypt}'(\mathsf{sk}, (\mathsf{ct}, |B^*|)) \in [0, B]$, where $\mathsf{sk} = (p, q)$ and $N = pq$.

$\mathsf{Gen}_{\mathsf{par}}(1^\lambda)$: Given the security parameter λ, define $\mathsf{par} = \{\lambda\}$.

$\mathsf{Gen}_{\mathcal{L}}(\mathsf{par}, \mathcal{L}_{\mathsf{range}}^{B,B^*,C})$: Given public parameters par as well as a description of a language pair $\mathcal{L}_{\mathsf{range}}^{B,B^*,C}$, consisting of an RSA modulus $N = pq$ with primes $p, q > 2^{l(\lambda)}$, for some polynomial $l : \mathbb{N} \to \mathbb{N}$ such that $l(\lambda) > \lambda$, define the language-dependent CRS $\mathsf{crs}_{\mathcal{L}} = \{N\}$. The global CRS is $\mathsf{crs} = (\{\lambda\}, \mathsf{crs}_{\mathcal{L}})$.

$\mathsf{TrapGen}(\mathsf{par}, \mathcal{L}_{\mathsf{range}}^{B,B^*,C}, \tau_{\mathcal{L}})$: This algorithm is identical to $\mathsf{Gen}_{\mathcal{L}}(\mathsf{par}, \mathcal{L}_{\mathsf{range}}^{B,B^*,C})$, except that it also outputs the trapdoor $\tau_{\Sigma} = (p, q)$.

$\mathsf{P}(\mathsf{crs}, \vec{x}, \vec{w}) \leftrightarrow \mathsf{V}(\mathsf{crs}, \vec{x})$: On input of a CRS crs, a statement $\mathsf{ct} \in \mathcal{L}_{\mathsf{zk}}^{B}$, the prover P (who has $\vec{w} = (x, w) \in [0, B] \times \mathbb{Z}_N^*$) and V interact as follows:

1. P computes $x_1, x_2, x_3 \in [0, B+1]$ such that $1 + 4x(B - x) = \sum_{i=1}^3 x_i^2$ over $\mathbb{Z}$. Then, P sets $C_0 = (1+N)^B \cdot \mathsf{ct}^{-1} \bmod N^{\zeta+1}$, $x_0 = B - x$ and $s_0 = w^{-1} \bmod N$. It randomly picks $s_1, s_2, s_3 \hookleftarrow U(\mathbb{Z}_{N^\zeta}^*)$ and computes
$$C_i = (1+N)^{x_i} \cdot s_i^{N^\zeta} \qquad \forall i \in [3].$$
Next, to show that $(\mathsf{ct}, \{C_i\}_{i=1}^3) \in \bar{\mathcal{L}}_{\mathsf{zk}}^{B}$, it chooses $\sigma \hookleftarrow U(\mathbb{Z}_N^*)$, $r_i \hookleftarrow U([0, B^*])$ and $\alpha_i \hookleftarrow U(\mathbb{Z}_{N^\zeta}^*)$ for each $i \in [0,3]$, to compute
$$R_i = (1+N)^{r_i} \cdot \alpha_i^{N^\zeta} \bmod N^{\zeta+1} \qquad \forall i \in [0,3]$$
$$R = \sigma^{N^\zeta} \cdot C^{4 \cdot r_0} \cdot \prod_{i=1}^{3} C_i^{-r_i} \bmod N^{\zeta+1}.$$
and send $(R, \{R_i\}_{i=0}^3, \{C_i\}_{i=1}^3)$ to V.
2. V sends a random challenge $\mathsf{Chall} \hookleftarrow U(\{0, \dots, 2^\lambda - 1\})$ to P.
3. P computes the response
$$\tau = \sigma \cdot \big(s_0^{4 \cdot x_0} \cdot \prod_{i=1}^{3} s_i^{x_i}\big)^{\mathsf{Chall}} \bmod N$$
$$z_i = r_i + \mathsf{Chall} \cdot x_i, \qquad t_i = \alpha_i \cdot s_i^{\mathsf{Chall}} \bmod N \qquad \forall i \in [0,3]$$
and fails if there exists $i \in [0,3]$ such that $z_i \notin [0, B^*]$. Otherwise, it sends $(\tau, \{(z_i, t_i)\}_{i=0}^3)$ to V.
4. V sets $C_0 = (1+N)^B \cdot \mathsf{ct}^{-1} \bmod N^{\zeta+1}$. It accepts iff $z_i \in [0, B^*]$ for each $i \in [0,3]$ and the following equations hold:
$$R_i \equiv (1+N)^{z_i} \cdot t_i^{N^\zeta} \cdot C_i^{-\mathsf{Chall}} \pmod{N^{\zeta+1}} \qquad \forall i \in [0,3],$$
$$R \equiv \prod_{i=1}^{3} C_i^{-z_i} \cdot \mathsf{ct}^{4 \cdot z_0} \cdot \tau^{N^\zeta} \cdot (1+N)^{\mathsf{Chall}} \pmod{N^{\zeta+1}}. \qquad (2)$$

BadChallenge(par, τ_Σ, crs, $\mathbf{x}$, $\mathbf{a}$): Given the statement $\mathbf{x} = \mathsf{ct} \in \mathbb{Z}_{N^\zeta}$, the message $\mathbf{a} = (R, \{R_i\}_{i=0}^3, \{C_i\}_{i=1}^3)$ and the trapdoor $\tau_\Sigma = (p, q)$, return $\perp$ if $\mathsf{Decrypt}'_{\tau_\Sigma}(\mathsf{ct}) \in [0, B]$. Otherwise, do the following.

1. Let $C_0 = (1+N)^B \cdot \mathsf{ct}^{-1} \bmod N^{\zeta+1}$. For each index $i \in [0,3]$, compute $\tilde{x}_i = \mathcal{D}_{\tau_\Sigma}(C_i) \in \mathbb{Z}_{N^\zeta}$ using the Damgård-Jurik decryption algorithm. Also, compute $r = \mathcal{D}_{\tau_\Sigma}(R) \in \mathbb{Z}_{N^\zeta}$ and $r_i = \mathcal{D}_{\tau_\Sigma}(R_i) \in \mathbb{Z}_{N^\zeta}$ for each $i \in [0,3]$. Then, for each $i \in [0,3]$, run Gauss' algorithm to compute $x_i \in [-B^*, B^*]$ and $c_i \in [0, C]$ such that $\tilde{x}_i = x_i \cdot c_i^{-1} \bmod N^\zeta$.
2. If there exists $i \in [0,3]$ such that no pair $(x_i, c_i) \in [-B^*, B^*] \times [0, C]$ satisfies $\tilde{x}_i = x_i \cdot c_i^{-1} \bmod N^\zeta$, let $j \in [0,3]$ the smallest such index. Compute $(z_j, \mathsf{Chall}_j, k_j) \in \mathbb{Z}^3$ such that

$$\begin{aligned} &r_j = z_j - \tilde{x}_j \cdot \mathsf{Chall}_j + k_j \cdot N^\zeta \\ &0 \leq z_j \leq B^* \\ &0 \leq \mathsf{Chall}_j \leq 2^\lambda - 1 \\ &0 \leq k_j \leq 2^\lambda \end{aligned} \tag{3}$$

   This can be achieved by replacing the first equality by inequalities

$$z_j - \tilde{x}_j \cdot \mathsf{Chall}_j + k_j \cdot N^\zeta \leq r_j, \qquad -z_j + \tilde{x}_j \cdot \mathsf{Chall}_j - k_j \cdot N^\zeta \leq -r_j$$

   and solving an integer linear programming instance with 8 constraints and 3 variables $(z_j, \mathsf{Chall}_j, k_j) \in \mathbb{Z}^3$ using Lenstra's algorithm [45]. If a solution is found (in which case, it is unique), return $\mathsf{Chall} = \mathsf{Chall}_j$.
3. For each $i \in [0,3]$, let $(x_i, c_i) \in [-B^*, B^*] \times [0, C]$ such that $\{\tilde{x}_i\}_{i=0}^3$ satisfy $\tilde{x}_i = x_i \cdot c_i^{-1} \bmod N^\zeta$. Then, let $c \triangleq \mathrm{lcm}(c_0, c_1, c_2, c_3)$. Check if $c \in [0, C]$ and there exist integers $x'_0, x'_1, x'_2, x'_3 \in [-B^*, B^*]$ such that $\tilde{x}_i = x'_i \cdot c^{-1} \bmod N^\zeta$ for each $i \in [0,3]$. If no such $\{x'_i\}_{i=0}^3$ and c exist, find the (unique) integer vector $(z_0, z_1, z_2, z_3, \mathsf{Chall}, k_0, k_1, k_2, k_3) \in \mathbb{Z}^9$ such that $0 \leq \mathsf{Chall} \leq 2^\lambda - 1$ and

$$\forall j \in [0,3] : \begin{cases} r_j = z_j - \tilde{x}_j \cdot \mathsf{Chall} + k_j \cdot N^\zeta \\ 0 \ \leq z_j \leq B^* \\ 0 \ \leq k_j \leq 2^\lambda \end{cases}$$

   This is done by replacing equalities by pairs of inequalities and solving an integer linear programming instance with 9 variables and 26 constraints. If this vector exists, return the corresponding $\mathsf{Chall} \in [0, 2^\lambda - 1]$.
4. Let $c \in [0, C]$ and $\{x'_i \in [-B^*, B^*]\}_{i=0}^3$ such that $\tilde{x}_i = x'_i \cdot c^{-1} \bmod N^\zeta$. Let $d_x = \gcd(4\tilde{x}\tilde{x}_0 - \sum_{i=1}^3 \tilde{x}_i^2 + 1, N^\zeta)$, where $\tilde{x} = B - \tilde{x}_0 \bmod N^\zeta$, and compute

$$\mathsf{Chall}_0 \triangleq (r + \sum_{i=1}^{3} \tilde{x}_i \cdot r_i - 4\tilde{x} \cdot r_0) \cdot (4\tilde{x} \cdot \tilde{x}_0 - \sum_{i=1}^{3} \tilde{x}_i^2 + 1)^{-1} \bmod \frac{N^\zeta}{d_x}.$$

If $\mathsf{Chall}_0 \in \{0, \dots, 2^\lambda - 1\}$, return $\mathsf{Chall} = \mathsf{Chall}_0$. Otherwise, return $\mathsf{Chall} = \perp$.

The $\mathsf{BadChallenge}$ function computes the bad challenge (which is unique when the statement is false) using Lenstra's algorithm [45] that runs in polynomial time since the number of variables is fixed. For an instance with t constraints, each of binary encoding length $O(s)$, the algorithm requires $O(st+s^2)$ arithmetic operations on s-bit numbers.

COMPLETENESS. As long as $z_i \in [0, B^*]$ for all $i \in [0, 3]$ when P computes its response at step 3, i.e., P does not abort, we have

$$\prod_{i=1}^{3} C_i^{-z_i} \cdot \mathsf{ct}^{4 \cdot z_0} \cdot \tau^{N^\zeta} \cdot (1+N)^{\mathsf{Chall}}$$

$$= \prod_{i=1}^{3} C_i^{-r_i} \cdot \mathsf{ct}^{4 \cdot r_0} \cdot \Big(\prod_{i=1}^{3} (1+N)^{x_i} s_i^{N^\zeta}\Big)^{-x_i \mathsf{Chall}} \cdot \big((1+N)^x w^{N^\zeta}\big)^{4 x_0 \mathsf{Chall}}$$

$$\cdot \sigma^{N^\zeta} \cdot \Big(w^{-4 \cdot x_0} \cdot \prod_{i=1}^{3} s_i^{x_i}\Big)^{N^\zeta \cdot \mathsf{Chall}} \cdot (1+N)^{\mathsf{Chall}} \mod N^{\zeta+1}$$

$$= \prod_{i=1}^{3} C_i^{-r_i} \cdot \mathsf{ct}^{4 \cdot r_0} \cdot (1+N)^{-\mathsf{Chall} \cdot \sum_{i=1}^{3} x_i^2} \cdot (1+N)^{4 \cdot x_0 \cdot \mathsf{Chall} \cdot x}$$

$$\cdot \sigma^{N^\zeta} \cdot (1+N)^{\mathsf{Chall}} \mod N^{\zeta+1}$$

$$= \prod_{i=1}^{3} C_i^{-r_i} \cdot \mathsf{ct}^{4 \cdot r_0} \cdot \sigma^{N^\zeta} \mod N^{\zeta+1} = R$$

$$(1+N)^{z_i} \cdot t_i^{N^\zeta} \equiv (1+N)^{r_i + \mathsf{Chall} \cdot x_i} \cdot \alpha_i^{N^\zeta} \cdot s_i^{\mathsf{Chall} \cdot N^\zeta} \equiv R_i \cdot C_i^{\mathsf{Chall}} \pmod{N^{\zeta+1}},$$

Finally, P only aborts with probability at most $4 \cdot 2^{-\lambda}$.

SPECIAL ZERO-KNOWLEDGE. We first describe a simulator $\mathsf{ZKSim}_B^{\mathrm{range}}$ before showing that a simulated transcript produced by $\mathsf{ZKSim}_B^{\mathrm{range}}(\mathsf{crs}, \vec{x}, \mathsf{Chall})$ is *computationally* indistinguishable from a real transcript generated from a statement-witness pair $(\vec{x}, \vec{w}) \in \mathcal{R}_B^{\mathrm{range}}$ when the challenge is Chall.

Given $\mathsf{crs} = (\{\lambda\}, \mathsf{crs}_\mathcal{L})$, an element $\vec{x} = \mathsf{ct} \in \mathbb{Z}_{N^{\zeta+1}}^*$ of the language $\mathcal{L}^{B,B^*,C}$ and a challenge $\mathsf{Chall} \in [0, C]$, $\mathsf{ZKSim}_B^{\mathrm{range}}(\mathsf{crs}, \vec{x}, \mathsf{Chall})$ proceeds as follows: First, it sets $C_0 = (1+N)^B \cdot \mathsf{ct}^{-1} \mod N^{\zeta+1}$ and randomly picks $s_1, s_2, s_3 \hookleftarrow U(\mathbb{Z}_{N^\zeta}^*)$ in order to compute an encryption $C_i = s_i^{N^\zeta} \mod N^{\zeta+1}$ of 0 for each $i \in [3]$. Then, the simulator uniformly picks elements of the response $\mathbf{z}$ as $z_i \hookleftarrow [0, B^*]$, $t_i \hookleftarrow \mathbb{Z}_N^*$, for all $i \in [0, 3]$, and $\tau \hookleftarrow \mathbb{Z}_N^*$. Finally, it computes the remaining components $(R, \{R_i\}_{i=0}^3)$ of the first prover message $\mathbf{a}$ in such a way that satisfy the verification equations (2).

We now prove the computational indistinguishability between the transcripts generated by $\mathsf{ZKSim}_B^{\mathrm{range}}$ and real transcripts, which are faithfully computed from $\vec{w} \in \mathcal{R}_B^{\mathrm{range}}(\vec{x})$. We first observe that a simulated transcript $(\mathbf{a}, \mathsf{Chall}, \mathbf{z})$

is computationally indistinguishable from an hybrid transcript where, instead of encrypting 0 in the computation of $\{C_i\}_{i=1}^3$, we encrypt $\{x_i\}_{i=1}^3$ such that $1 + 4x(B - x) = \sum_{i=1}^3 x_i^2$ and $x_0 = B - x$ over $\mathbb{Z}$, as in the real protocol. In this hybrid transcript, however, we still compute $(R, \{R_i\}_{i=0}^3)$ and $\mathbf{z}$ as in the simulation. A simple reduction shows that the probability to distinguish between simulated transcripts and hybrid transcripts is at most 3 times the advantage of an adversary against the semantic security of Damgård-Jurik (and thus the ζ-DCR assumption). Finally, we show that the distributions of hybrid and real transcripts for $(\vec{x}, \vec{w}) \in \mathcal{R}_B^{\text{range}}$ and the challenge Chall are statistically close (assuming that we use a deterministic algorithm to compute the Lagrange decomposition of $1 + 4x(B - x) \geq 0$) into the sum of *3* squares). This follows from standard arguments. By relying on the generalized Paillier isomorphism we can and split the analysis. Over the "randomness" modulo N, the distributions are the same because each (t_i, α_i) are in one-to-one relation for $i \in [0, 3]$, as well as (τ, σ). Since the x_i's are constant, the distributions "over the plaintext" modulo N^ζ are statistically close because the statistical distance between the z_i-variables is negligible.

More precisely, the ciphertexts $\{C_i\}_{i=0}^3$ have exactly the same distribution in the hybrid and the real transcripts. Now, let $\psi\colon \mathbb{Z}_{N^\zeta} \times \mathbb{Z}_N^\star \mapsto \mathbb{Z}_{N^{\zeta+1}}^\star$ denote the generalized Paillier isomorphism. Let also $(r_i, \alpha_i) := \psi^{-1}(R_i)$, for all $i \in [0, 4]$, and $(r, \alpha) := \psi^{-1}(R)$ of an hybrid transcript. We thus have, for all $i \in [0, 3]$,

$$r_i \equiv z_i - \mathsf{Chall} \cdot x_i \pmod{N^\zeta} \qquad \alpha_i \equiv t_i \cdot s_i^{-\mathsf{Chall}} \pmod{N},$$

where $x_0 = B - x \bmod N^\zeta$ and $s_0 = w^{-1} \bmod N$, as well as

$$r \equiv 4z_0(B - x_0) - \textstyle\sum_{i\in[3]} z_i x_i + \mathsf{Chall} \pmod{N^\zeta},$$

and $\alpha \equiv w^{4z_0} \cdot \prod_{i\in[3]} s_i^{-z_i} \cdot \tau \pmod N$. For α and $\{\alpha_i\}_{i\in[0,3]}$, The congruences in the multiplicative group $\mathbb{Z}_N^*$ show that, given w and $\{(z_i, s_i)\}_{i\in[0,3]}$, there is a one-to-one relation between α and τ, and between α_i and t_i, for all $i \in [0, 3]$. Then, their distributions are the same as those of the real distributions. (Note that α in the real distribution is also random due to σ.) We are thus left with analyzing the distributions over the additive group $\mathbb{Z}_{N^\zeta}$. For all $i \in [0, 3]$, the congruences on the r_i ensure that, unless $z_i \in [0, CB]$ (which occurs with negligible probability $2^{-\lambda}$), we have $0 \leq r_i = z_i - \mathsf{Chall} \cdot x_i \leq B^*$. That means that, over the integers, we have to show that the statistical distance between $U([0, B^*])$ (which is the distribution of the hybrid z_i) and $\mathsf{Chall} \cdot x_i + U([0, B^*])$ (which is the distribution of the real z) is negligible. Since $x_i \cdot \mathsf{Chall} \leq BC \leq 2^{-\lambda} B^*$, it is actually bounded by $2^{-\lambda}$. Finally, since $1 + 4x(B - x) = \sum_{i=1}^3 x_i^2$ and $x_0 = B - x$ in both transcripts, we can rewrite the hybrid r as $r = 4r_0(B - x_0) - \sum_{i\in[3]} r_i x_i \bmod N^\zeta$, which, given the x_i, is a deterministic function evaluated on independent statistically-closed distributions.

Lemma 3.1 [24]. *Let integers $n, d \in \mathbb{Z}$, $B \geq 2$ and $x = \lfloor \frac{n}{d} \rceil$. If there exist $x_1, x_2, x_3 \in \mathbb{Q}$ such that $1 + 4 \cdot \frac{n}{d} \cdot \left(B - \frac{n}{d}\right) = \sum_{i=1}^3 x_i^2$, then we have $x \in [0, B]$.*

Lemma 3.2. *The above construction is a trapdoor Σ-protocol for $\bar{\mathcal{L}}^{B,B^*,C}$ assuming that $2^{2\lambda+3}B^2C^2 < N^\zeta$, for any $\lambda \geq 1$.*

Proof. We first prove that $(\mathsf{ct}, \{C_i\}_{i=1}^3) \in \bar{\mathcal{L}}^{B,B^*,C}$ ensures that $\mathsf{ct} \in \mathcal{L}^{B,B^*,C}$.

Indeed, letting $\gamma = c^{-1} \bmod N^\zeta$ and $k \in \mathbb{Z}$ such that $\gamma \cdot c + k \cdot N^\zeta = 1$, the first four equations of (1) imply

$$
\begin{aligned}
C_i &= (1+N)^{x_i \cdot \gamma} \cdot (s_i^\gamma \cdot C_i^k)^{N^\zeta} \bmod N^{\zeta+1}, \qquad\qquad \forall i \in [0,3] \\
&= (1+N)^{x_i \cdot (c^{-1} \bmod N^\zeta)} \cdot \tilde{s}_i^{N^\zeta} \bmod N^{\zeta+1}
\end{aligned}
$$

for some $\tilde{s}_i \in \mathbb{Z}_N^*$, and thus $\mathsf{ct} = (1+N)^{B - x_0 \cdot (c^{-1} \bmod N^\zeta)} \cdot \tilde{s}_0^{-N^\zeta} \bmod N^{\zeta+1}$. Hence, the ciphertexts $(\mathsf{ct}, \{C_i\}_{i=1}^3)$ decrypt to $\tilde{x} = B - x_0 \cdot c^{-1} \bmod N^\zeta$ and $\{\tilde{x}_i = x_i \cdot c^{-1} \bmod N^\zeta\}_{i=1}^3$. Then, decrypting the last equation of (1) implies

$$c = \sum_{i=1}^{3} \left(\frac{x_i}{c}\right) \cdot x_i - 4x_0 \cdot \left(B - \frac{x_0}{c}\right) \bmod N^\zeta.$$

If we multiply both members of the latter equation by c, we obtain

$$c^2 + 4(Bc - x_0)x_0 = \sum_{i=1}^{3} x_i^2 \bmod N^\zeta. \tag{4}$$

The latter equality holds over $\mathbb{Z}$ if we represent it over $[-N^\zeta/2, N^\zeta/2]$. Indeed, the absolute value the left-hand-side member is bounded by $C^2 + 4(BC + B^*)B^* = C^2 + 4(BC)^2(1+2^\lambda)2^\lambda \leq 2^{\lambda+3}B^2C^2 < N^\zeta/2$ and the right-hand-side member is bounded by $3B^{*2} = 3 \cdot 2^{2\lambda}B^2C^2 < N^\zeta/2$. If we divide both members by c^2 over the rationals, we obtain

$$1 + 4\left(B - \frac{x_0}{c}\right) \cdot \frac{x_0}{c} = \sum_{i=1}^{3} \left(\frac{x_i}{c}\right)^2 \quad \text{over } \mathbb{Q}.$$

By Lemma 3.1, this in turn implies $\lfloor x_0/c \rceil \in [0, B]$ and thus $B - \lfloor x_0/c \rceil \in [0, B]$.

We now prove that $\mathsf{BadChallenge}$ output the correct result when the prover sends commitments $\{C_i\}_{i=1}^3$ such that $(\mathsf{ct}, \{C_i\}_{i=1}^3) \notin \bar{\mathcal{L}}^{B,B^*,C}$. For a given first message $\mathbf{a} = (R, \{R_i\}_{i=0}^3, \{C_i\}_{i=1}^3)$ sent by the prover, $\mathsf{BadChallenge}$ obtains $r, \{r_i\}_{i=0}^3 \in \mathbb{Z}_{N^\zeta}$ and $\{x_i\}_{i=0}^3 \in \mathbb{Z}_{N^\zeta}$ at step 1. It only stops at step 2 if there exists $i \in [0,3]$ such that C_i decrypts to a value $\tilde{x}_i \in \mathbb{Z}_{N^\zeta}$ which has no representation $\tilde{x}_i = x_i \cdot c_i^{-1} \bmod N^\zeta$ with $(x_i, c_i) \in [-B^*, B^*] \times [0, C]$. In this case, only one pair $(\mathsf{Chall}_i, z_i) \in [0, C] \times [0, B^*]$ can satisfy the first verification equation of (2). Indeed, if we had distinct such pairs $(\mathsf{Chall}_i, z_i), (\mathsf{Chall}_i, z_i') \in [0, C] \times [0, B^*]$ with $\mathsf{Chall}_i' \neq \mathsf{Chall}_i$, we would have $C_i^{\mathsf{Chall}_i - \mathsf{Chall}_i'} = (1+N)^{z_i - z_i'} \cdot (t_i/t_i')^{N^\zeta} \bmod N^{\zeta+1}$ and thus $\tilde{x}_i = (z_i - z_i') \cdot (\mathsf{Chall}_i - \mathsf{Chall}_i')^{-1} \bmod N^\zeta$. Hence, the unique valid pair $(\mathsf{Chall}_i, z_i) \in [0, C] \times [0, B^*]$ that can satisfy the first equation (2) can be found by applying Gauss' algorithm. Note that $\mathsf{BadChallenge}$ might output

$\mathsf{Chall} \neq \perp$ when no bad challenge exists at all.[5] However, $\mathsf{BadChallenge}$ only needs to find the bad challenge when it exists. When there is no bad challenge, the Fiat-Shamir hash function can output arbitrary values without hurting soundness.

If step 3 is reached, each plaintext in $\{\tilde{x}_i \in \mathbb{Z}_{N^\zeta}^*\}_{i=0}^3$ is decoded as a pair $(x_i, c_i) \in [-B^*, B^*] \times [0, C]$ such that $\tilde{x}_i = x_i \cdot c_i^{-1} \bmod N^\zeta$. We then define $c \triangleq \mathrm{lcm}(c_0, c_1, c_2, c_3)$ and distinguish two cases:

(a) $c \notin [0, C]$ or $c \in [0, C]$ but there exist no integers $x_0', x_1', x_2', x_3' \in [-B^*, B^*]$ such that $\tilde{x}_i = x_i' \cdot c^{-1} \bmod N^\zeta$ for each $i \in [0, 3]$.
(b) $c \in [0, C]$ and there exist integers $x_0', x_1', x_2', x_3' \in [-B^*, B^*]$ such that we have $\tilde{x}_i = x_i' \cdot c^{-1} \bmod N^\zeta$ for each $i \in [0, 3]$.

In case (a), we observe from the first four verification equations (2) that a valid response $(\tau, \{(z_i, t_i)\}_{i=0}^3)$ can exist for at most one $\mathsf{Chall} \in [0, 2^\lambda - 1]$. This unique challenge value can be determined by solving an integer linear program and finding $(z_0, z_1, z_2, z_3, \mathsf{Chall}, k_0, k_1, k_2, k_3) \in \mathbb{Z}^9$ satisfying (4).

We are left with case (b). In order to satisfy the verification equations (2), the challenge-response pair $(\mathsf{Chall}, (\tau, \{(z_i, t_i)\}_{i=0}^3))$ must satisfy

$$z_i = r_i + \tilde{x}_i \cdot \mathsf{Chall} \mod N^\zeta \qquad r = -\sum_{i=1}^{3} \tilde{x}_i \cdot z_i + 4\tilde{x} z_0 + \mathsf{Chall} \mod N^\zeta.$$

Letting $\tilde{x} = B - \tilde{x}_0 \bmod N$, the above implies

$$\mathsf{Chall} \cdot (4\tilde{x} \cdot \tilde{x}_0 - \sum_{i=1}^{3} \tilde{x}_i^2 + 1) = r + \sum_{i=1}^{3} \tilde{x}_i \cdot r_i - 4\tilde{x} \cdot r_0 \mod N^\zeta, \tag{5}$$

Observe that we cannot have $4\tilde{x} \cdot \tilde{x}_0 - \sum_{i=1}^3 \tilde{x}_i^2 + 1 = 0 \bmod N^\zeta$ as this would imply $4\tilde{x} \cdot x_0' - \sum_{i=1}^3 \tilde{x}_i \cdot x_i' + c = 0 \bmod N^\zeta$, which would mean that

$$(1+N)^c \cdot \prod_{i=1}^{3} C_i^{-x_i'} \cdot \mathsf{ct}^{4x_0'} \mod N^{\zeta+1}$$

is an N^ζ-th residue in $\mathbb{Z}_{N^{\zeta+1}}^*$. Since we are in case (b), this would contradict the hypothesis $(\mathsf{ct}, \{C_i\}_{i=1}^3) \notin \bar{\mathcal{L}}^{B,B^*,C}$.

From the inequality $4\tilde{x} \cdot \tilde{x}_0 - \sum_{i=1}^3 \tilde{x}_i^2 + 1 \neq 0 \bmod N^\zeta$, we are guaranteed that $d_x = \gcd(4\tilde{x}\tilde{x}_0 - \sum_{i=1}^3 \tilde{x}_i^2 + 1, N^\zeta) < N^\zeta$ and (5) then yields

$$\mathsf{Chall} \cdot (4\tilde{x} \cdot \tilde{x}_0 - \sum_{i=1}^{3} \tilde{x}_i^2 + 1) = r + \sum_{i=1}^{3} \tilde{x}_i \cdot r_i - 4\tilde{x} \cdot r_0 \mod \frac{N^\zeta}{d_x}. \tag{6}$$

---

[5] This can happen when more than one $\{\tilde{x}_i\}_{i=0}^3$ has no valid representation $(x_i, c_i) \in [-B^*, B^*] \times [0, C]$, in which case they can possibly determine incompatible bad challenges.

Since $\gcd(4\tilde{x}\cdot\tilde{x}_0 - \sum_{i=1}^{3}\tilde{x}_i^2+1, N^\zeta/d_x) = 1$, Eq. (6) has a unique solution $\mathsf{Chall}_0 \in \mathbb{Z}_{N^\zeta/d_x}$. Since $N^\zeta/d_x > \min(p,q) > 2^\lambda$, we have $\mathsf{Chall} = \mathsf{Chall} \bmod N^\zeta/d_x$ for any $\mathsf{Chall} \in \{0,1,\ldots,2^\lambda-1\}$, meaning that $\mathsf{BadChallenge}$ returns the correct result by outputting Chall_0 whenever $\mathsf{Chall}_0 \in \{0,\ldots,2^\lambda-1\}$. □

COMPILING THE Σ-PROTOCOL INTO MULTI-THEOREM NIZK. The trapdoor Σ-protocol immediately implies a single-theorem NIZK construction via the Fiat-Shamir transform when we apply the CI hash function of [56]. In order to obtain NIZK proofs in the multi-theorem setting, we could apply the compiler of [46, Appendix B]. One issue is that the latter proceeds by encrypting the Σ-protocol's first prover message using an equivocable lossy encryption system [4]. Unfortunately, while Paillier can serve as an equivocable lossy encryption scheme (as observed in [42]), we would lose the unbounded property of the range proof if we were to use it. The reason is that the CRS should contain a lossy/injective Paillier public key component that should be longer than messages to be encrypted.

Fortunately, multi-theorem NIZK proofs can be achieved (with computational zero-knowledge and statistical soundness) by adapting the Feige-Lapidot-Shamir compiler using correlation intractable hash functions. The OR trick of [31] builds multi-theorem NIZK proofs by showing OR statements of the form "either the statement is true OR some component of the CRS is in the image of a pseudorandom generator." Here, we can instantiate their approach using a DCR-based PRG. Recall that the DCR assumption immediately implies a length-doubling PRG that maps a seed $s \in \mathbb{Z}_N^*$ to $y = s^N \bmod N^2$. Here, we can apply the trapdoor Σ-protocol of [47] (which is recalled in Sect. 2.4) together with the OR Σ-protocols of [26] to prove that "either the range statement is true OR the CRS component $y \in \mathbb{Z}_{N^2}^*$ is an N-th residue." In the real construction, the CRS contains a uniformly random $y \sim U(\mathbb{Z}_{N^2}^*)$ so as to obtain statistical soundness. In the simulation, y is sampled as a composite residue and its N-th root allows simulating proofs. Using this approach, since the zero-knowledge property is only computational, we can obtain adaptive soundness by hashing the statement together with the prover's first message when the Fiat-Shamir transform is applied (as observed in [23, Theorem 4]).

In Sect. 4.2, we will apply a similar instantiation of the FLS paradigm to obtain one-time simulation-soundness in our DCR-based variant of Naor-Yung.

DUAL-MODE RANGE PROOFS/ARGUMENTS. If we give up unboundedness, we can obtain statistically zero-knowledge or even dual-mode range arguments as follows. The CRS initially chooses $\zeta > 1$ and a modulus N such that committed integers always live in a range $[0,B]$ for which $2^{3\lambda+1}B < N^\zeta$. The CRS is augmented with an element $g \in \mathbb{Z}_{N^{\zeta+1}}^*$ that is chosen as an N^ζ-th residue in the zero-knowledge setting (and uniformly over $\mathbb{Z}_{N^{\zeta+1}}^*$ in the soundness setting).

Then, each occurrence of $1+N$ is replaced by g in the Σ-protocol. The DCR assumption immediately implies the indistinguishability of CRS distributions for the soundness and zero-knowledge settings. Moreover, our simulator $\mathsf{ZKSim}_B^{\mathrm{range}}$ produces statistically indistinguishable transcripts as it computes $\{C_i\}_{i=1}^3$ as dual-mode (or lossy) encryption of 0 instead of random elements modulo $N^{\zeta+1}$.

ACHIEVING CONSTANT RATE. Let $x \in [0, B]$ and $N^{\zeta'-1} \leq B \leq N^{\zeta'}$, for some integer ζ', and where only N is fixed by the CRS. We now assess the ratio between the input size and the proof size assuming that $n := |N|$. We see the witness x as a $|B|$-bit string since the zero-knowledge property requires a commitment whose message space contains $[0, B]$. For simplicity we assume that $\zeta = 2\zeta' + 1$ since our proof system requires $2^{2\lambda+3}B^2C^2 < N^\zeta$.

Since the commitment ct to x is a ciphertext over $\mathbb{Z}^*_{N^{\zeta+1}}$, we have

$$\frac{|\mathsf{ct}|}{|B|} \leq \frac{(\zeta+1)n}{m} \leq \frac{(2\zeta'+2)n}{(\zeta'-1)n} = 2 + \frac{4}{(\zeta'-1)} \downarrow 2.$$

The range proof π for x consists of $\{C_i\}_{i=1}^3, \{R_i\}_{i=0}^3, R$, each of size $(\zeta+1)n$, and of $\tau, \{(z_i, t_i)\}_{i=0}^3$, where $|\tau| = n$ and $|(z_i, t_i)| = (m + 3\lambda + 1) + n \leq (\zeta+1)n$, for each $i = 0$ to 3. The total proof size amounts to $12(\zeta+1)n + n$ and

$$\frac{|\pi|}{|\mathsf{ct}|} \leq \frac{12(\zeta+1)n + n}{(\zeta+1)n} = 12 + \frac{1}{2\zeta'+2} \downarrow 12,$$

leading to a total rate of $|\pi|/|B| \leq (24(\zeta'+1)+1)/(\zeta'-1) \leq 73$ for $\zeta' > 1$, which goes down to 24 when ζ grows. If the OR trick is used in the multi-theorem case, it is easy to see that the asymptotic rate remains unchanged as the OR-branch involving the N-th residue only adds a component of size at most $4n$.

4 Instantiating Naor-Yung Under the DCR Assumption

In this section, we show that decoding Paillier plaintexts as rounded rationals provides a secure instantiation of Naor-Yung under the DCR assumption. We first give a trapdoor Σ-protocol showing plaintext equalities before upgrading it into a one-time simulation-sound NIZK argument.

4.1 A Trapdoor Σ-Protocol Showing Plaintext Equalities Between Paillier Ciphertexts for Distinct Moduli

We now give a trapdoor Σ-protocol showing that two ciphertexts decrypt to the same plaintext in the encryption scheme of Sect. 2.6. Let $N_1 = p_1q_1$ and $N_2 = p_2q_2$ be RSA moduli. Let $C = 2^\lambda - 1$ and let also the languages

$$\begin{aligned}\mathcal{L}_{\mathsf{zk}}^{\text{eq-dcr}} := \{(\mathsf{ct}_1, \mathsf{ct}_2, \ell_M) \in \mathbb{Z}^*_{N_1^\zeta} \times \mathbb{Z}^*_{N_2^\zeta} \times \mathbb{N} \mid \exists m \in [0, M],\\ w_1 \in \mathbb{Z}^\star_{N_1},\ w_2 \in \mathbb{Z}^\star_{N_2} \ :\ \mathsf{ct}_1 = (1+N_1)^m \cdot w_1^{N_1^\zeta} \bmod N_1^{\zeta+1}\\ \wedge\ \mathsf{ct}_2 = (1+N_2)^m \cdot w_2^{N_2^\zeta} \bmod N_2^{\zeta+1}\},\end{aligned}$$

$$\begin{aligned}\mathcal{L}_{\mathsf{sound}}^{\text{eq-dcr}} := \{(\mathsf{ct}_1, \mathsf{ct}_2, \ell_M) \in \mathbb{Z}^*_{N_1^{\zeta+1}} \times \mathbb{Z}^*_{N_2^{\zeta+1}} \times \mathbb{N} \mid \exists m \in [-R, R],\ \bar{c} \in [0, C],\\ w_1 \in \mathbb{Z}^\star_{N_1},\ w_2 \in \mathbb{Z}^\star_{N_2} \ :\ \mathsf{ct}_1^{\bar{c}} = (1+N_1)^m \cdot w_1^{N_1^\zeta} \bmod N_1^{\zeta+1}\\ \wedge\ \mathsf{ct}_2^{\bar{c}} = (1+N_2)^m \cdot w_2^{N_2^\zeta} \bmod N_2^{\zeta+1}\},\end{aligned}$$

where $M = 2^{\ell_M} - 1$ and $\zeta \geq 1$ is the smallest integer such that

$$2RC < 2^{\lambda+1}R < \min(N_1^\zeta, N_2^\zeta)$$

with $R > 2^\lambda(C+1)(M+1)$. Note that $\mathcal{L}_{\mathsf{zk}}^{\text{eq-dcr}} \subset \mathcal{L}_{\mathsf{sound}}^{\text{eq-dcr}}$ since $M < R$.

We note that, for any pair of ciphertexts $((\mathsf{ct}_1, \ell_M), (\mathsf{ct}_2, \ell_M))$ such that $(\mathsf{ct}_1, \mathsf{ct}_2, \ell_M) \in \mathcal{L}_{\mathsf{sound}}^{\text{eq-dcr}}$, the decryption algorithms of Sect. 2.6 for N_1 and N_2 output the same $\mathsf{Msg} = \mathrm{abs}(\lfloor m/\bar{c} \rceil)$. Indeed, there exist $u_1, v_2, u_2, v_2 \in \mathbb{Z}$ with $|u_1| < N_1^\zeta$ and $|u_2| < N_2^\zeta$ such that $u_1 \cdot \bar{c} + v_1 \cdot N_1^\zeta = 1$ and $u_2 \cdot \bar{c} + v_2 \cdot N_2^\zeta = 1$, which implies

$$\mathsf{ct}_1 = (1+N_1)^{u_1 \cdot m} \cdot (w_1^{u_1} \cdot \mathsf{ct}_1^{v_1})^{N_1^\zeta} \bmod N_1^{\zeta+1},$$
$$\mathsf{ct}_2 = (1+N_2)^{u_2 \cdot m} \cdot (w_2^{u_2} \cdot \mathsf{ct}_2^{v_2})^{N_2^\zeta} \bmod N_2^{\zeta+1}.$$

Since $u_1 = \bar{c}^{-1} \bmod N_1^\zeta$ and $u_2 = \bar{c}^{-1} \bmod N_2^\zeta$, the decryption algorithm necessarily outputs $\mathsf{Msg} = \lfloor m/\bar{c} \rceil$ in both cases.

We assume that the challenge space is $\{0, \ldots, C\}$, where $C = 2^\lambda - 1$, and that $p, q > 2^{l(\lambda)}$, for some polynomial $l : \mathbb{N} \to \mathbb{N}$ such that $l(\lambda) > \lambda$ for any sufficiently large $\lambda \in \mathbb{N}$. We now give a trapdoor Σ-protocol proving membership of $\mathcal{L}_{\mathsf{sound}}^{\text{eq-dcr}}$.

$\mathsf{Gen}_{\mathsf{par}}(1^\lambda)$: Given the security parameter λ, define $\mathsf{par} = \{\lambda\}$.

$\mathsf{Gen}_{\mathcal{L}}(\mathsf{par}, \mathcal{L}^{\text{eq-dcr}})$: Given public parameters par and a language description $\mathcal{L}^{\text{eq-dcr}}$, consisting of RSA moduli $N_1 = p_1 q_1$ and $N_2 = p_2, q_2$ with primes $p_1, q_1, p_2, q_2 > 2^{l(\lambda)}$, for some polynomial $l : \mathbb{N} \to \mathbb{N}$ such that $l(\lambda) > \lambda$, define the language-dependent CRS $\mathsf{crs}_{\mathcal{L}} = \{N_1, N_2\}$.

The global CRS is $\mathsf{crs} = (\{\lambda\}, \mathsf{crs}_{\mathcal{L}})$.

$\mathsf{TrapGen}(\mathsf{par}, \mathcal{L}^{\text{eq-dcr}}, \tau_{\mathcal{L}})$: This algorithm is identical to $\mathsf{Gen}_{\mathcal{L}}(\mathsf{par}, \mathcal{L}^{\text{eq-dcr}})$, except that it also outputs the trapdoor $\tau_\Sigma = (p_1, q_1, p_2, q_2)$.

$\mathsf{P}(\mathsf{crs}, \vec{x}, \vec{w}) \leftrightarrow \mathsf{V}(\mathsf{crs}, \vec{x})$: On input of a common reference string crs, a statement $\vec{x} = (\mathsf{ct}_1, \mathsf{ct}_2, \ell_M) \in \mathbb{Z}_{N_1^{\zeta+1}}^* \times \mathbb{Z}_{N_2^{\zeta+1}}^* \times \mathbb{N}$, the prover P (who has $\vec{w} = (m, w_1, w_2) \in [0, M] \times \mathbb{Z}_{N_1}^\star \times \mathbb{Z}_{N_2}^\star$) and the verifier V interact as follows:

1. P chooses $a \hookleftarrow U([0, R])$, $r_1 \hookleftarrow U(\mathbb{Z}_{N_1}^*)$, $r_2 \hookleftarrow U(\mathbb{Z}_{N_2}^*)$ and sends

$$A_1 = (1+N_1)^a \cdot r_1^{N_1^\zeta} \bmod N_1^{\zeta+1}, \qquad A_2 = (1+N_2)^a \cdot r_2^{N_2^\zeta} \bmod N_2^{\zeta+1}.$$

2. V sends back a random challenge $\mathsf{Chall} \hookleftarrow U(\{0, \ldots, 2^\lambda - 1\})$.
3. P aborts if $a + \mathsf{Chall} \cdot m \notin [0, R]$. Otherwise, it sends V the response

$$z = a + \mathsf{Chall} \cdot m, \quad z_1 = r_1 \cdot w_1^{\mathsf{Chall}} \bmod N_1^\zeta, \quad z_2 = r_2 \cdot w_2^{\mathsf{Chall}} \bmod N_2^\zeta$$

4. V checks if $z \in [0, R]$ and accepts iff the following conditions hold:

$$A_1 \cdot \mathsf{ct}_1^{\mathsf{Chall}} \equiv z_1^{N_1^\zeta} \cdot (1+N_1)^z \pmod{N_1^{\zeta+1}},$$
$$A_2 \cdot \mathsf{ct}_2^{\mathsf{Chall}} \equiv z_2^{N_2^\zeta} \cdot (1+N_2)^z \pmod{N_2^{\zeta+1}}$$

$\mathsf{BadChallenge}(\mathsf{par}, \tau_\Sigma, \mathsf{crs}, \mathbf{x}, \mathbf{a})$: Given $\mathbf{x} = (\mathsf{ct}_1, \mathsf{ct}_2, \ell_M) \in \left(\mathbb{Z}^*_{N_1^{\zeta+1}}\right)^2 \times \mathbb{N}$, the message $\mathbf{a} = (A_1, A_2) \in \left(\mathbb{Z}^*_{N_1^{\zeta+1}}\right)^2$ and the trapdoor $\tau_\Sigma = (p_1, q_1, p_2, q_2)$,

1. Using $\mathsf{sk}_1 = (p_1, q_1)$, decrypt ct_1 and A_1 using Paillier's decryption algorithm to obtain $m_1 \in \mathbb{Z}_{N_1^\zeta}$ and $a_1 \in \mathbb{Z}_{N_1^\zeta}$. Likewise, use $\mathsf{sk}_2 = (p_2, q_2)$ to compute $m_2 \in \mathbb{Z}_{N_2^\zeta}$ and $a_2 \in \mathbb{Z}_{N_2^\zeta}$ by decrypting ct_2 and A_2.
2. Find an integer vector $(z, \mathsf{Chall}, k_1, k_2) \in \mathbb{Z}^4$ satisfying

$$\begin{aligned} a_1 &= z - m_1 \cdot \mathsf{Chall} + k_1 \cdot N_1^\zeta \\ a_2 &= z - m_2 \cdot \mathsf{Chall} + k_2 \cdot N_2^\zeta, \\ 0 &\le \mathsf{Chall} \le 2^\lambda - 1 \\ 0 &\le k_1 \le 2^\lambda \\ 0 &\le k_2 \le 2^\lambda \end{aligned} \tag{7}$$

This can be achieved by replacing the equalities by inequality pairs

$$\forall b \in \{1, 2\} : \begin{cases} z - m_b \cdot \mathsf{Chall} + k_b \cdot N_b^\zeta \le a_b, \\ -z + m_b \cdot \mathsf{Chall} - k_b \cdot N_b^\zeta \le -a_b \end{cases}$$

and running Lenstra's algorithm [45] to solve an integer linear programming instance with 10 constraints and 4 variables.

If a suitable $(z, \mathsf{Chall}, k_1, k_2) \in \mathbb{Z}^4$ is found (in which case, Chall is uniquely determined), output the corresponding Chall. Otherwise, return $\perp$.

Again, Lenstra's algorithm [45] allows computing the unique bad challenge (when it exists) in polynomial time since the number of variables is fixed.

Lemma 4.1. *The construction is a trapdoor Σ-protocol for $(\mathcal{L}_{\mathsf{zk}}^{\text{eq-dcr}}, \mathcal{L}_{\mathsf{sound}}^{\text{eq-dcr}})$.*

Proof. We first show the completeness and special zero-knowledge properties.

Completeness. Given $\vec{w} \in \mathcal{R}_{zk}^{\text{eq-dcr}}(\vec{x})$, P computes $(\mathbf{a}, \mathbf{z})$ for a challenge Chall such that $\mathsf{V}(\mathsf{crs}, \vec{x}, (\mathbf{a}, \mathsf{Chall}, \mathbf{z})) = 1$ as long as P does not abort at step 3 of the interactive protocol. Therefore, an honest run of the protocol always leads to a valid transcript except if $a + \mathsf{Chall} \cdot m \notin [0, R]$ which occurs with probability at most $2^{-\lambda}$ since $\mathsf{Chall} \cdot m \le CM < 2^{\lambda + \ell_M}$ and $R > 2^{2\lambda + \ell_M}$.

Special Zero-Knowledge. The simulator ZKSim proceeds in a standard way. It that inputs $\mathsf{crs} = (\{\lambda\}, \mathsf{crs}_\mathcal{L})$, a statement $\vec{x} = (\mathsf{ct}_1, \mathsf{ct}_2, \ell_M) \in \mathcal{L}_{\mathsf{zk}}^{\text{eq-dcr}}$ and a challenge $\mathsf{Chall} \in \{0, \ldots, 2^\lambda - 1\}$. First, the simulator $\mathsf{ZKSim}(\mathsf{crs}, \vec{x}, \mathsf{Chall})$ picks $z \hookleftarrow U([0, R])$ as well as $z_1 \hookleftarrow U(\mathbb{Z}^*_{N_1})$ and $z_2 \hookleftarrow U(\mathbb{Z}^*_{N_2})$. Then, it computes $A_1 = z_1^{N_1^\zeta} \cdot (1 + N_1)^z \cdot \mathsf{ct}_1^{-\mathsf{Chall}} \bmod N_1^{\zeta+1}$, as well as

$$A_2 = z_2^{N_2^\zeta} \cdot (1 + N_2)^z \cdot \mathsf{ct}_2^{-\mathsf{Chall}} \bmod N_2^{\zeta+1},$$

and outputs $(\mathbf{a}, \mathbf{z})$, where $\mathbf{a} = (A_1, A_2)$ and $\mathbf{z} = (z, z_1, z_2)$. We turn to showing that $(\mathbf{a}, \mathsf{Chall}, \mathbf{z})$ is statistically indistinguishable from a real transcript computed using the witness $\vec{w} = (m, w_1, w_2) \in [0, M] \times \mathbb{Z}_{N_1}^\star \times \mathbb{Z}_{N_2}^\star$ (i.e., $\vec{w} \in \mathcal{R}_{zk}^{\text{eq-dcr}}(\vec{x})$) and with challenge Chall. For each $i \in \{1, 2\}$, let $\psi_i \colon \mathbb{Z}_{N_i^\zeta} \times \mathbb{Z}_{N_i}^\star \mapsto \mathbb{Z}_{N_i^{\zeta+1}}^\star$ denote the generalized Paillier isomorphism. By applying $\{\psi_i^{-1}\}_{i=1}^2$ to compute $(a_1, r_1) := \psi_1^{-1}(A_1)$ and $(a_2, r_2) := \psi_2^{-1}(A_2)$ for a simulated transcript $((A_1, A_2), \mathsf{Chall}, (z, z_1, z_2))$, we find

$$a_1 \equiv z - \mathsf{Chall} \cdot m \pmod{N_1^\zeta} \qquad r_1 \equiv z_1 \cdot w_1^{-\mathsf{Chall}} \pmod{N_1},$$
$$a_2 \equiv z - \mathsf{Chall} \cdot m \pmod{N_2^\zeta} \qquad r_2 \equiv z_2 \cdot w_2^{-\mathsf{Chall}} \pmod{N_2}.$$

The congruences on the left ensure that, unless $z \in [0, CM]$ (which occurs with negligible probability $2^{-\lambda}$), we have $0 \le a_1 = z - \mathsf{Chall} \cdot m = a_2 \le R$. Given Chall, the distributions of $\{(z_i, r_i)\}_{i=1}^2$ over the multiplicative rings are exactly the same between the real and the simulated transcripts. Finally, we show that, over the integers, the statistical distance between $U([0, R])$ (which is the distribution of the simulated z) and $\mathsf{Chall} \cdot m + U([0, R])$ (in the real z) is negligible. Since $m \cdot \mathsf{Chall} \le MC < 2^{\lambda + \ell_M} < 2^{-\lambda} R$, it is actually bounded by $2^{-\lambda}$.

Special Soundness. Let us assume two transcripts $((A_1, A_2), \mathsf{Chall}, (z, z_1, z_2))$ and $((A_1, A_2), \mathsf{Chall}', (z', z_1', z_2'))$ that both satisfy the verification equations with $z, z' \in [0, R]$ and $\mathsf{Chall} \neq \mathsf{Chall}'$ for a given first message (A_1, A_2) sent by the prover. We assume w.l.o.g. that $0 \le \mathsf{Chall}' < \mathsf{Chall} \le 2^\lambda - 1$. This implies that $\bar{c} = \mathsf{Chall} - \mathsf{Chall}' \in [0, 2^\lambda - 1]$ and $\bar{z} = z - z' \in [-R, R]$ satisfy the congruences $\mathsf{ct}_1^{\bar{c}} \equiv (z_1/z_1')^{N_1^\zeta} (1 + N_1)^{\bar{z}} \pmod{N_1^{\zeta+1}}$ and

$$\mathsf{ct}_2^{\bar{c}} \equiv (z_2/z_2')^{N_2^\zeta} (1 + N_2)^{\bar{z}} \pmod{N_2^{\zeta+1}},$$

which implies $(\mathsf{ct}_1, \mathsf{ct}_2) \in \mathcal{L}_{\mathsf{sound}}^{\text{eq-dcr}}$. This shows that, for any first message (A_1, A_2) sent by the prover, only one bad challenge can exist if $(\mathsf{ct}_1, \mathsf{ct}_2) \notin \mathcal{L}_{\mathsf{sound}}^{\text{eq-dcr}}$.

CRS Indistinguishability. The distribution of the CRS output by $\mathsf{TrapGen}$ is exactly the same as the distribution of the CRS output by $\mathsf{Gen}_{\mathcal{L}}$.

BadChallenge Correctness. Let a false statement $\vec{x} \notin \mathcal{L}_{\mathsf{sound}}^{\text{eq-dcr}}$. Special soundness ensures the existence of at most one bad challenge for any given $\mathbf{a}$. Lenstra's algorithm can efficiently determine if the bad challenge exists since it can solve the integer feasibility problem in polynomial time when the number of variables is fixed. Moreover, whenever an admissible integer solution $(z, \mathsf{Chall}, k_1, k_2) \in \mathbb{Z}^4$ exists (in which case it is unique), it is efficiently computable from the decrypted values (m_1, m_1, a_1, a_2). □

4.2 New Construction of One-Time Simulation-Sound NIZK Arguments from Trapdoor Σ-Protocols

In this section, we aim at one-time simulation soundness without imposing a bound on the plaintext space in the centralized version our scheme of Sect. 4.3.

To this end, we cannot use the constructions of [30,47] because they follow an idea from [27] and encrypt the prover's first message using a DCR-based lossy encryption scheme [4]. Unfortunately, the latter's public key should be larger than the first prover message in the underlying trapdoor Σ-protocol.

We describe a new one-time simulation-sound argument which departs from [30,46,47] in that it does not proceed by encrypting the first prover message of the trapdoor Σ-protocol. Instead, it uses an OR proof [26] inspired by the FLS technique [31]. In order to achieve one-time simulation-soundness, we introduce a twist and program the CRS $(u,v) \in (\mathbb{Z}_{N^2}^*)^2$ in such a way that $u^{\mathsf{VK}} \cdot v$ is a composite residue for exactly one VK.

- A trapdoor Σ-protocol $\Pi^{(1)} = (\mathsf{Gen}_{\mathsf{par}}^{(1)}, \mathsf{Gen}_{\mathcal{L}}^{(1)}, \mathsf{P}^{(1)}, \mathsf{V}^{(1)})$ for an NP language $\mathcal{L}$. This protocol should satisfy the properties of Definition 2.6. We assume that $\Pi^{(1)}$ has challenge space $\mathcal{C} = \{0,1\}^\lambda$, where λ is the security parameter. In addition, the function $\mathsf{BadChallenge}^{(1)}$ should be computable within time $T_1 \in \mathsf{poly}(\lambda)$ for any input $(\tau, \mathsf{crs}^{(1)}, x, a_1)$.
- A strongly unforgeable one-time signature scheme $\mathsf{OTS} = (\mathcal{G}, \mathcal{S}, \mathcal{V})$ with verification keys in $\{0,1\}^L$, where $L \in \mathsf{poly}(\lambda)$.
- An RSA modulus $N = pq$, for large primes $p, q > 2^L$.
- A trapdoor Σ-protocol $\Pi^{(0)} = (\mathsf{Gen}_{\mathsf{par}}^{(0)}, \mathsf{Gen}_{\mathcal{L}}^{(0)}, \mathsf{P}^{(0)}, \mathsf{V}^{(0)})$ for the language $\mathcal{L}^{\mathsf{DCR}} := \{x \in \mathbb{Z}_{N^2}^* \mid \exists w \in \mathbb{Z}_N^* : x = w^N \bmod N^2\}$. We assume that the function $\mathsf{BadChallenge}^{(0)}$ is computable within time $T_0 \in \mathsf{poly}(\lambda)$ for any input $(\tau, \mathsf{crs}^{(0)}, x, a_0)$. This protocol can be instantiated as in Sect. 2.4
- A correlation intractable hash family $\mathcal{H} = (\mathsf{Gen}, \mathsf{Hash})$ for the class $\mathcal{R}_{\mathsf{CI}}$ of relations that are efficiently searchable within time T.

$\mathsf{Gen}_{\mathsf{par}}(1^\lambda)$: Run $\mathsf{par} \leftarrow \mathsf{Gen}_{\mathsf{par}}^{(1)}(1^\lambda)$ and output par.

$\mathsf{Gen}_{\mathcal{L}}(\mathsf{par}, \mathcal{L})$: Given public parameters par and a language $\mathcal{L}$, the CRS is generated as follows.

1. Generate a CRS $\mathsf{crs}_{\mathcal{L}}^{(1)} \leftarrow \mathsf{Gen}_{\mathcal{L}}^{(1)}(\mathsf{par}, \mathcal{L})$ for the trapdoor Σ-protocol $\Pi^{(1)}$.
2. Choose the description of a one-time signature scheme $\mathsf{OTS} = (\mathcal{G}, \mathcal{S}, \mathcal{V})$ with verification keys in $\{0,1\}^L$, where $L \in \mathsf{poly}(\lambda)$.
3. Choose an RSA modulus $N = pq$, for primes $p, q > 2^L$, where $L \in \mathsf{poly}(\lambda)$ is the verification key length of OTS. Then, choose $u_0, v_0 \hookleftarrow \mathbb{Z}_N^*$ and compute $u = u_0^N \bmod N^2$, $v = v_0^N \bmod N^2$.
4. Generate a CRS $\mathsf{crs}^{(0)} \leftarrow \mathsf{Gen}_{\mathcal{L}}^{(0)}(\mathsf{par}, \mathcal{L}^{\mathsf{DCR}})$ for $\Pi^{(0)}$, where $\mathcal{L}^{\mathsf{DCR}}$ is associated with $N = pq$.
5. Generate a key $k \leftarrow \mathsf{Gen}(1^\lambda)$ for a correlation intractable hash function with output length λ.

Output the language-dependent CRS $\mathsf{crs}_{\mathcal{L}} := \big(N, u, v, \mathsf{crs}^{(0)}, \mathsf{crs}_{\mathcal{L}}^{(1)}, k\big)$ and the simulation trapdoor $\tau_{\mathsf{zk}} := (u_0, v_0)$. The global common reference string consists of $\mathsf{crs} = (\mathsf{par}, \mathsf{crs}_{\mathcal{L}}, \mathsf{OTS})$.

$\mathsf{P}(\mathsf{crs}, x, w, \mathsf{lbl})$: To prove a statement $x \in \mathcal{L}$ for a label $\mathsf{lbl} \in \{0,1\}^*$ using the witness w, generate a one-time signature key pair $(\mathsf{VK}, \mathsf{SK}) \leftarrow \mathcal{G}(1^\lambda)$. Then,

1. Compute $(a_1, st) \leftarrow \mathsf{P}^{(1)}(\mathsf{crs}_{\mathcal{L}}^{(1)}, x, w)$. Then, generate a simulated proof $(a_0, \mathsf{Chall}_0, z_0) \in \mathbb{Z}_{N^2}^* \times \{0,1\}^\lambda \times \mathbb{Z}_N^*$ that $(u^{\mathsf{VK}} \cdot v) \in \mathcal{L}^{\mathsf{DCR}}$. Namely, choose random elements $z_0 \hookleftarrow U(\mathbb{Z}_N^*)$, $\mathsf{Chall}_0 \hookleftarrow U(\{0,1\}^\lambda)$ and compute $a_0 = z_0^N \cdot (u^{\mathsf{VK}} \cdot v)^{-\mathsf{Chall}_0} \bmod N^2$.
2. Compute $\mathsf{Chall} = \mathsf{Hash}\big(k, (x, a, \mathsf{VK})\big) \in \{0,1\}^\lambda$, where $a = (a_0, a_1)$, and set $\mathsf{Chall}_1 = \mathsf{Chall} \oplus \mathsf{Chall}_0$.
3. Compute $z_1 = \mathsf{P}^{(1)}(\mathsf{crs}_{\mathcal{L}}^{(1)}, x, w, a_1, \mathsf{Chall}_1, st)$ by executing the prover of $\Pi^{(1)}$. Define $z = (z_0, z_1, \mathsf{Chall}_0, \mathsf{Chall}_1)$.
4. Generate $sig \leftarrow \mathcal{S}(\mathsf{SK}, (x, a, z, \mathsf{lbl}))$ and output $\vec{\pi} = \big(\mathsf{VK}, (a, z), sig\big)$.

$\mathbf{V}(\mathsf{crs}, x, \vec{\pi}, \mathsf{lbl})$: Given a statement x, a label lbl as well as a purported proof $\vec{\pi} = \big(\mathsf{VK}, (a, z), sig\big)$, return 0 if $\mathcal{V}(\mathsf{VK}, (x, a, z, \mathsf{lbl}), sig) = 0$. Otherwise,

1. Write $z = (z_0, z_1, \mathsf{Chall}_0, \mathsf{Chall}_1)$ and return 0 if any of these does not parse properly or if $\mathsf{Hash}\big(k, (x, a, \mathsf{VK})\big) \neq \mathsf{Chall}_0 \oplus \mathsf{Chall}_1$.
2. If $\mathsf{V}^{(1)}(\mathsf{crs}_{\mathcal{L}}^{(1)}, x, a_1, \mathsf{Chall}_1, z_1)) = 1$ and $a_0 \cdot (u^{\mathsf{VK}} \cdot v)^{\mathsf{Chall}_0} = z_0^N \bmod N^2$, return 1. Otherwise, return 0.

Theorem 4.2. *The above construction is a one-time simulation-sound NIZK argument if: (i)* OTS *is a strongly unforgeable one-time signature; (ii) The* DCR *assumption holds; (iii) The hash function is correlation-intractable for efficiently searchable relations. (The proof is given in the full version of this paper.)*

4.3 A DCR-Based CCA2-Secure Threshold Cryptosystem from the Naor-Yung Paradigm

The syntax and the security definitions of threshold PKE schemes are recalled in the full version of this paper. Using the tools of Sect. 4.1 and Sect. 4.2, we obtain the following variant of the threshold encryption scheme in [33].

We assume that the key generation step chooses a value ζ' that determines a maximal length of encrypted messages (note that this is only necessary in the threshold setting and not in the centralized version of the scheme). However, the encryptor can still choose $\zeta \leq \zeta'$ in a flexible way at encryption time.

For simplicity, we first describe the non-robust version of the scheme, where decryption servers do not provide a proof that partial decryptions are correctly generated. However, robustness can be achieved in a modular way as in [30].

$\mathbf{Keygen}(1^\lambda, 1^B, 1^t, 1^n)$: On input of a security parameter λ, a maximal bitlength $B \in \mathsf{poly}(\lambda)$ of encrypted messages, a number of servers $n \in \mathsf{poly}(\lambda)$, and a threshold $t \in \mathsf{poly}(\lambda)$, conduct the following steps.

1. Generate two safe prime products $N_1 = p_1 q_1$ and $N_2 = p_2 q_2$ such that $p_i, q_i > 2^{l(\lambda)}$, for some polynomial $l : \mathbb{N} \to \mathbb{N}$, and primes $p_i = 2p_i' + 1$, $q_i = 2q_i' + 1$ for which p_i', q_i' are also prime for each $i \in \{1, 2\}$.
2. Choose an integer $\zeta' > 0$ such that $2^{B+2\lambda+1} < \min(N_1^{\zeta'}, N_2^{\zeta'})$.
3. Choose an integer d such that $d = 1 \bmod N_1^{\zeta'}$ and $d = 0 \bmod \lambda(N_1)$.

4. Choose a random polynomial $f[X] = \sum_{i=0}^{t-1} a_i X^i \in \mathbb{Z}_{N_1^{\zeta'} p_1' q_1'}[X]$ such that $a_0 = d \bmod N_1^{\zeta'} p_1' q_1'$.
5. Generate the CRS $\mathsf{crs}_{\mathcal{L}} := \left(N, u, v, \mathsf{crs}^{(0)}, \mathsf{crs}_{\mathcal{L}}^{(1)}, k\right)$ of a simulation-sound NIZK argument for the language $(\mathcal{L}_{\mathsf{zk}}^{\text{eq-dcr}}, \mathcal{L}_{\mathsf{sound}}^{\text{eq-dcr}})$ of Sect. 4.1, which is induced by the moduli N_1 and N_2.

The public key is $\mathsf{pk} = (N_1, N_2, \mathsf{crs}_{\mathcal{L}})$ and the secret key shares $\{\mathsf{sk}_i\}_{i=1}^n$ are defined as $\mathsf{sk}_i = f(i) \bmod N_1^{\zeta'} p_1' q_1'$ for each $i \in [n]$.

Encrypt$(\mathsf{pk}, \mathsf{Msg})$: To encrypt $\mathsf{Msg} \in \{0,1\}^{\ell_M}$, return $\perp$ if $\ell_M > B$. Otherwise, interpret Msg as a positive integer in $[0, M]$, where $M = 2^{\ell_M} - 1$. Set $\zeta > 1$ as the smallest integer such that $\min(N_1^{\zeta}, N_2^{\zeta}) \geq 2^{2\lambda+1} M$. Then, choose $(r_1, r_2) \hookleftarrow U(\mathbb{Z}_{N_1}^* \times \mathbb{Z}_{N_2}^*)$ and compute

$$\mathsf{ct}_1 = (1 + N_1)^{\mathsf{Msg}} \cdot r_1^{N_1^{\zeta}} \bmod N_1^{\zeta+1}, \quad \mathsf{ct}_2 = (1 + N_2)^{\mathsf{Msg}} \cdot r_2^{N_2^{\zeta}} \bmod N_2^{\zeta+1}.$$

Then, using the empty label $\mathsf{lbl} = \varepsilon$, generate a simulation-sound NIZK argument $\vec{\pi} \leftarrow \mathsf{P}\big(\mathsf{crs}, (\mathsf{ct}_1, \mathsf{ct}_2, \ell_M), (\mathsf{Msg}, r_1, r_2), \mathsf{lbl}\big)$ that $(\mathsf{ct}_1, \mathsf{ct}_2, \ell_M) \in \mathcal{L}_{\mathsf{zk}}^{\text{eq-dcr}}$. Finally, output $\mathsf{ct} = (\mathsf{ct}_1, \mathsf{ct}_2, \ell_M, \vec{\pi})$.

PartDec$(\mathsf{sk}_i, \mathsf{ct})$: Given a ciphertext $\mathsf{ct} = (\mathsf{ct}_1, \mathsf{ct}_2, \ell_M, \vec{\pi})$ and $\mathsf{sk}_i \in \mathbb{Z}_{N_1^{\zeta'} p_1' q_1'}$, the i-th server proceeds as follows.

1. If $\mathsf{V}(\mathsf{crs}, (\mathsf{ct}_1, \mathsf{ct}_2, \ell_M), \vec{\pi}, \mathsf{lbl}) = 0$, return $\perp$.
2. Compute $\mu_i = \mathsf{ct}_1^{2\Delta \cdot \mathsf{sk}_i} \bmod N_1^{\zeta+1}$, where $\Delta = n!$, and return (i, μ_i).

Combine$(\mathsf{pk}, \mathcal{S}, \{\mu_i\}_{i \in \mathcal{S}}, \mathsf{ct})$: Let $R = 2^{\lambda} \cdot (M+1)$ and $C = 2^{\lambda} - 1$. If $\mathcal{S}$ contains less than t shares in $\mathbb{Z}_{N_1^{\zeta+1}}^*$, return $\perp$. Otherwise, do the following.

1. Define scaled Lagrange coefficients $\lambda_{0,i}^{\mathcal{S}} = \Delta \cdot \prod_{i' \in \mathcal{S} \setminus \{i\}} \frac{-i}{i-i'} \in \mathbb{Z}$ for each $i \in \mathcal{S}$ and compute $\mu_0 = \prod_{i \in \mathcal{S}} \mu_i^{2 \cdot \lambda_{0,i}^{\mathcal{S}}} \bmod N_1^{\zeta+1}$, which should be of the form $\mu_0 = \mathsf{ct}_1^{4\Delta^2 f(0)} = \mathsf{ct}_1^{4\Delta^2 d} \bmod N_1^{\zeta+1}$.
2. Compute $\tilde{\mu} = L(\mu_0, N_1^{\zeta}) \cdot 4^{-1} \cdot (\Delta)^{-2} \bmod N_1^{\zeta}$, where $L(\cdot, N_1^{\zeta})$ extracts the discrete logarithm w.r.t. base $(1 + N_1)$ of the elements modulo $N_1^{\zeta+1}$ that are congruent to 1 modulo N_1 as in [29]. Then, using Gauss' algorithm, find the unique $(m, c) \in \mathbb{Z}^2$ such that $-R \leq m \leq R$, $0 \leq c \leq C$ and $\tilde{\mu} = m \cdot c^{-1} \bmod N^{\zeta}$. If no such pair exists, return $\perp$. Otherwise, return $\mathsf{Msg} = \text{abs}(\lfloor m/c \rceil)$, where the division is computed over $\mathbb{Q}$.

Theorem 4.3. *The scheme provides IND-CCA security under static corruptions if: (i) The* DCR *assumption holds; (ii)* Π^{OTSS} *is a one-time simulation-sound argument. (The proof is given in the full version of this paper.)*

COMPARISONS. Devevey *et al.* [30, Section 4] gave a non-interactive threshold CCA2-secure scheme based on DCR and LWE in the standard model. While they can prove security under adaptive corruptions, our scheme provides several advantages over [30] although we only prove static security.[6] In the robust version of the scheme, if we do not consider commitments to the secret key shares as being part of the public key (which is reasonable as the encryptor does not need them), the public key size grows with $|N|$ instead of $|N^\zeta|$. Also, the scheme of [30] requires larger secret key shares, which grow super-linearly with the number of servers. Finally, our scheme allows the sender to adjust the block length by choosing ζ according to the message length.

The full version of this paper provides more comparisons.

Acknowledgements. Part of this research was funded by the French ANR ALAMBIC project (ANR-16-CE39-0006). This work is also partially supported by Indo French Center for the Promotion of Advanced Research (IFCPAR, project number: 6002-1). Thomas Peters is a research associate of the Belgian Fund for Scientific Research (F.R.S.-FNRS).

References

1. Abe, M., Fehr, S.: Adaptively secure Feldman VSS and applications to universally-composable threshold cryptography. In: Franklin, M. (ed.) CRYPTO 2004. LNCS, vol. 3152, pp. 317–334. Springer, Heidelberg (2004). https://doi.org/10.1007/978-3-540-28628-8_20
2. Asharov, G., Jain, A., Wichs, D.: Multiparty computation with low communication, computation and interaction via threshold FHE. Cryptology ePrint Archive: Report 2011/613 (2012)
3. Bellare, M., Goldwasser, S.: Verifiable partial key escrow. In: ACM-CCS (1997)
4. Bellare, M., Hofheinz, D., Yilek, S.: Possibility and impossibility results for encryption and commitment secure under selective opening. In: Joux, A. (ed.) EUROCRYPT 2009. LNCS, vol. 5479, pp. 1–35. Springer, Heidelberg (2009). https://doi.org/10.1007/978-3-642-01001-9_1
5. Bernhard, D., Cortier, V., Pereira, O., Smyth, B., Warinschi, B.: Adapting Helios for provable ballot privacy. In: Atluri, V., Diaz, C. (eds.) ESORICS 2011. LNCS, vol. 6879, pp. 335–354. Springer, Heidelberg (2011). https://doi.org/10.1007/978-3-642-23822-2_19
6. Blum, M., De Santis, A., Micali, S., Persiano, G.: Non-interactive zero-knowledge. SIAM J. Comput. **20**, 1084–1118 (1991)
7. Blum, M., Feldman, P., Micali, S.: Non-interactive zero-knowledge and its applications. In: STOC (1988)
8. Boneh, D., Boyen, X., Halevi, S.: Chosen ciphertext secure public key threshold encryption without random oracles. In: Pointcheval, D. (ed.) CT-RSA 2006. LNCS, vol. 3860, pp. 226–243. Springer, Heidelberg (2006). https://doi.org/10.1007/11605805_15
9. Boneh, D., et al.: Threshold cryptosystems from threshold fully homomorphic encryption. In: Shacham, H., Boldyreva, A. (eds.) CRYPTO 2018. LNCS, vol. 10991, pp. 565–596. Springer, Cham (2018). https://doi.org/10.1007/978-3-319-96884-1_19

[6] Adaptive security is non-trivial to achieve when $t, n \in \mathsf{poly}(\lambda)$. In many applications like e-voting, one can expect the number of servers to be small (e.g., logarithmic in λ), in which case adaptive security can be achieved via complexity leveraging.

10. Boudot, F.: Efficient proofs that a committed number lies in an interval. In: Preneel, B. (ed.) EUROCRYPT 2000. LNCS, vol. 1807, pp. 431–444. Springer, Heidelberg (2000). https://doi.org/10.1007/3-540-45539-6_31
11. Brickell, E.F., Chaum, D., Damgård, I.B., van de Graaf, J.: Gradual and verifiable release of a secret (extended abstract). In: Pomerance, C. (ed.) CRYPTO 1987. LNCS, vol. 293, pp. 156–166. Springer, Heidelberg (1988). https://doi.org/10.1007/3-540-48184-2_11
12. Bünz, B., Agrawal, S., Zamani, M., Boneh, D.: Zether: towards privacy in a smart contract world. In: Bonneau, J., Heninger, N. (eds.) FC 2020. LNCS, vol. 12059, pp. 423–443. Springer, Cham (2020). https://doi.org/10.1007/978-3-030-51280-4_23
13. Bünz, B., Bootle, J., Boneh, D., Poelstra, A., Wuille, P., Maxwell, G.: Bulletproofs: short proofs for confidential transactions and more. In: IEEE S&P (2018)
14. Camenisch, J., Chaabouni, R., Shelat, A.: Efficient protocols for set membership and range proofs. In: Pieprzyk, J. (ed.) ASIACRYPT 2008. LNCS, vol. 5350, pp. 234–252. Springer, Heidelberg (2008). https://doi.org/10.1007/978-3-540-89255-7_15
15. Camenisch, J., Lysyanskaya, A.: An efficient system for non-transferable anonymous credentials with optional anonymity revocation. In: Pfitzmann, B. (ed.) EUROCRYPT 2001. LNCS, vol. 2045, pp. 93–118. Springer, Heidelberg (2001). https://doi.org/10.1007/3-540-44987-6_7
16. Canetti, R., et al.: Fiat-Shamir: from practice to theory. In: STOC (2019)
17. Canetti, R., Goldreich, O., Halevi, S.: The random oracle methodology, revisted. J. ACM **51**(4), 557–594 (2004)
18. Canetti, R., Goldwasser, S.: An efficient *threshold* public key cryptosystem secure against adaptive chosen ciphertext attack (extended abstract). In: Stern, J. (ed.) EUROCRYPT 1999. LNCS, vol. 1592, pp. 90–106. Springer, Heidelberg (1999). https://doi.org/10.1007/3-540-48910-X_7
19. Canetti, R., Lombardi, A., Wichs, D.: Fiat-Shamir: from practice to theory, part II (NIZK and correlation intractability from circular-secure FHE). Cryptology ePrint Archive: Report 2018/1248
20. Chaabouni, R., Lipmaa, H., Zhang, B.: A non-interactive range proof with constant communication. In: Keromytis, A.D. (ed.) FC 2012. LNCS, vol. 7397, pp. 179–199. Springer, Heidelberg (2012). https://doi.org/10.1007/978-3-642-32946-3_14
21. Chaidos, P., Groth, J.: Making sigma-protocols non-interactive without random oracles. In: Katz, J. (ed.) PKC 2015. LNCS, vol. 9020, pp. 650–670. Springer, Heidelberg (2015). https://doi.org/10.1007/978-3-662-46447-2_29
22. Chan, A., Frankel, Y., Tsiounis, Y.: Easy come — easy go divisible cash. In: Nyberg, K. (ed.) EUROCRYPT 1998. LNCS, vol. 1403, pp. 561–575. Springer, Heidelberg (1998). https://doi.org/10.1007/BFb0054154
23. Ciampi, M., Parisella, R., Venturi, D.: On adaptive security of delayed-input sigma protocols and Fiat-Shamir NIZKs. In: Galdi, C., Kolesnikov, V. (eds.) SCN 2020. LNCS, vol. 12238, pp. 670–690. Springer, Cham (2020). https://doi.org/10.1007/978-3-030-57990-6_33
24. Couteau, G., Kloß, M., Lin, H., Reichle, M.: Efficient range proofs with transparent setup from bounded integer commitments. In: Canteaut, A., Standaert, F.-X. (eds.) EUROCRYPT 2021. LNCS, vol. 12698, pp. 247–277. Springer, Cham (2021). https://doi.org/10.1007/978-3-030-77883-5_9
25. Couteau, G., Peters, T., Pointcheval, D.: Removing the strong RSA assumption from arguments over the integers. In: Coron, J.-S., Nielsen, J.B. (eds.) EUROCRYPT 2017. LNCS, vol. 10211, pp. 321–350. Springer, Cham (2017). https://doi.org/10.1007/978-3-319-56614-6_11

26. Cramer, R., Damgård, I., Schoenmakers, B.: Proofs of partial knowledge and simplified design of witness hiding protocols. In: Desmedt, Y.G. (ed.) CRYPTO 1994. LNCS, vol. 839, pp. 174–187. Springer, Heidelberg (1994). https://doi.org/10.1007/3-540-48658-5_19
27. Damgård, I.: Efficient concurrent zero-knowledge in the auxiliary string model. In: Preneel, B. (ed.) EUROCRYPT 2000. LNCS, vol. 1807, pp. 418–430. Springer, Heidelberg (2000). https://doi.org/10.1007/3-540-45539-6_30
28. Damgård, I., Fujisaki, E.: A statistically-hiding integer commitment scheme based on groups with hidden order. In: Zheng, Y. (ed.) ASIACRYPT 2002. LNCS, vol. 2501, pp. 125–142. Springer, Heidelberg (2002). https://doi.org/10.1007/3-540-36178-2_8
29. Damgård, I., Jurik, M.: A generalisation, a simplification and some applications of Paillier's probabilistic public-key system. In: Kim, K. (ed.) PKC 2001. LNCS, vol. 1992, pp. 119–136. Springer, Heidelberg (2001). https://doi.org/10.1007/3-540-44586-2_9
30. Devevey, J., Libert, B., Nguyen, K., Peters, T., Yung, M.: Non-interactive CCA2-secure threshold cryptosystems: achieving adaptive security in the standard model without pairings. In: Garay, J.A. (ed.) PKC 2021. LNCS, vol. 12710, pp. 659–690. Springer, Cham (2021). https://doi.org/10.1007/978-3-030-75245-3_24
31. Feige, U., Lapidot, D., Shamir, A.: Multiple non-interactive zero knowledge proofs based on a single random string (extended abstract). In: FOCS (1990)
32. Fiat, A., Shamir, A.: How to prove yourself: practical solutions to identification and signature problems. In: Odlyzko, A.M. (ed.) CRYPTO 1986. LNCS, vol. 263, pp. 186–194. Springer, Heidelberg (1987). https://doi.org/10.1007/3-540-47721-7_12
33. Fouque, P.-A., Pointcheval, D.: Threshold cryptosystems secure against chosen-ciphertext attacks. In: Boyd, C. (ed.) ASIACRYPT 2001. LNCS, vol. 2248, pp. 351–368. Springer, Heidelberg (2001). https://doi.org/10.1007/3-540-45682-1_21
34. Fouque, P.-A., Stern, J., Wackers, G.-J.: CryptoComputing with rationals. In: Blaze, M. (ed.) FC 2002. LNCS, vol. 2357, pp. 136–146. Springer, Heidelberg (2003). https://doi.org/10.1007/3-540-36504-4_10
35. Fujisaki, E., Okamoto, T.: Statistical zero knowledge protocols to prove modular polynomial relations. In: Kaliski, B.S. (ed.) CRYPTO 1997. LNCS, vol. 1294, pp. 16–30. Springer, Heidelberg (1997). https://doi.org/10.1007/BFb0052225
36. Goldwasser, S., Micali, S., Rackoff, C.: The knowledge complexity of interactive proof systems. SIAM J. Comput. **18**, 186–208 (1989)
37. González, A., Ráfols, C.: New techniques for non-interactive shuffle and range arguments. In: Manulis, M., Sadeghi, A.-R., Schneider, S. (eds.) ACNS 2016. LNCS, vol. 9696, pp. 427–444. Springer, Cham (2016). https://doi.org/10.1007/978-3-319-39555-5_23
38. Groth, J.: Non-interactive zero-knowledge arguments for voting. In: Ioannidis, J., Keromytis, A., Yung, M. (eds.) ACNS 2005. LNCS, vol. 3531, pp. 467–482. Springer, Heidelberg (2005). https://doi.org/10.1007/11496137_32
39. Groth, J.: Efficient zero-knowledge arguments from two-tiered homomorphic commitments. In: Lee, D.H., Wang, X. (eds.) ASIACRYPT 2011. LNCS, vol. 7073, pp. 431–448. Springer, Heidelberg (2011). https://doi.org/10.1007/978-3-642-25385-0_23
40. Groth, J., Ostrovsky, R., Sahai, A.: New techniques for noninteractive zero-knowledge. J. ACM **59**, 1–35 (2012)
41. Groth, J., Sahai, A.: Efficient non-interactive proof systems for bilinear groups. In: Smart, N. (ed.) EUROCRYPT 2008. LNCS, vol. 4965, pp. 415–432. Springer, Heidelberg (2008). https://doi.org/10.1007/978-3-540-78967-3_24

42. Hemenway, B., Libert, B., Ostrovsky, R., Vergnaud, D.: Lossy encryption: constructions from general assumptions and efficient selective opening chosen ciphertext security. In: Lee, D.H., Wang, X. (eds.) ASIACRYPT 2011. LNCS, vol. 7073, pp. 70–88. Springer, Heidelberg (2011). https://doi.org/10.1007/978-3-642-25385-0_4
43. Jarecki, S., Lysyanskaya, A.: Adaptively secure threshold cryptography: introducing concurrency, removing erasures. In: Preneel, B. (ed.) EUROCRYPT 2000. LNCS, vol. 1807, pp. 221–242. Springer, Heidelberg (2000). https://doi.org/10.1007/3-540-45539-6_16
44. Kiayias, A., Leonardos, N., Lipmaa, H., Pavlyk, K., Tang, Q.: Near optimal rate homomorphic encryption for branching programs. Priv. Enhancing Technol. (2015)
45. Lenstra, H.: Integer programming with a fixed number of variables. Math. Oper. Res. **8**(4), 538–548 (1983)
46. Libert, B., Nguyen, K., Passelègue, A., Titiu, R.: Simulation-sound arguments for LWE and applications to KDM-CCA2 security. In: Moriai, S., Wang, H. (eds.) ASIACRYPT 2020. LNCS, vol. 12491, pp. 128–158. Springer, Cham (2020). https://doi.org/10.1007/978-3-030-64837-4_5
47. Libert, B., Nguyen, K., Peters, T., Yung, M.: One-shot Fiat-Shamir-based NIZK arguments of composite residuosity in the standard model. Cryptology ePrint Archive: Report 2020/1334 (2020)
48. Libert, B., Yung, M.: Non-interactive CCA-secure threshold cryptosystems with adaptive security: new framework and constructions. In: Cramer, R. (ed.) TCC 2012. LNCS, vol. 7194, pp. 75–93. Springer, Heidelberg (2012). https://doi.org/10.1007/978-3-642-28914-9_5
49. Lipmaa, H.: On diophantine complexity and statistical zero-knowledge arguments. In: Laih, C.-S. (ed.) ASIACRYPT 2003. LNCS, vol. 2894, pp. 398–415. Springer, Heidelberg (2003). https://doi.org/10.1007/978-3-540-40061-5_26
50. Lipmaa, H.: Optimally sound sigma protocols under DCRA. In: Kiayias, A. (ed.) FC 2017. LNCS, vol. 10322, pp. 182–203. Springer, Cham (2017). https://doi.org/10.1007/978-3-319-70972-7_10
51. Lipmaa, H., Asokan, N., Niemi, V.: Secure vickrey auctions without threshold trust. In: Blaze, M. (ed.) FC 2002. LNCS, vol. 2357, pp. 87–101. Springer, Heidelberg (2003). https://doi.org/10.1007/3-540-36504-4_7
52. Naor, M., Yung, M.: Public-key cryptosystems provably secure against chosen ciphertext attacks. In: STOC (1990)
53. Noether, S.: Ring signature confidential transactions for monero. Cryptology ePrint Archive Report 2015/1098 (2015)
54. Paillier, P.: Public-key cryptosystems based on composite degree residuosity classes. In: Stern, J. (ed.) EUROCRYPT 1999. LNCS, vol. 1592, pp. 223–238. Springer, Heidelberg (1999). https://doi.org/10.1007/3-540-48910-X_16
55. Pedersen, T.P.: Non-interactive and information-theoretic secure verifiable secret sharing. In: Feigenbaum, J. (ed.) CRYPTO 1991. LNCS, vol. 576, pp. 129–140. Springer, Heidelberg (1992). https://doi.org/10.1007/3-540-46766-1_9
56. Peikert, C., Shiehian, S.: Noninteractive zero knowledge for NP from (plain) learning with errors. In: Boldyreva, A., Micciancio, D. (eds.) CRYPTO 2019. LNCS, vol. 11692, pp. 89–114. Springer, Cham (2019). https://doi.org/10.1007/978-3-030-26948-7_4
57. Regev, O.: On lattices, learning with errors, random linear codes, and cryptography. In: STOC (2005)

58. Rial, A., Kohlweiss, M., Preneel, B.: Universally composable adaptive priced oblivious transfer. In: Shacham, H., Waters, B. (eds.) Pairing 2009. LNCS, vol. 5671, pp. 231–247. Springer, Heidelberg (2009). https://doi.org/10.1007/978-3-642-03298-1_15
59. Sahai, A.: Non-malleable non-interactive zero knowledge and adaptive chosen-ciphertext security. In: FOCS (1999)
60. Shoup, V., Gennaro, R.: Securing threshold cryptosystems against chosen ciphertext attack. In: Nyberg, K. (ed.) EUROCRYPT 1998. LNCS, vol. 1403, pp. 1–16. Springer, Heidelberg (1998). https://doi.org/10.1007/BFb0054113
61. Vallée, B.: Gauss' algorithm, revisited. J. Algorithms **12**(4), 556–572 (1991)

Author Index

Author Index

Printed in the United States
by Baker & Taylor Publisher Services